Methods of Regional Analysis:
an Introduction to Regional Science

THE REGIONAL SCIENCE STUDIES SERIES

edited by Walter Isard

Methods of Regional Analysis: an Introduction to Regional Science

by
WALTER ISARD

in association with:
DAVID F. BRAMHALL
GERALD A. P. CARROTHERS
JOHN H. CUMBERLAND
LEON N. MOSES
DANIEL O. PRICE
EUGENE W. SCHOOLER

THE M.I.T. PRESS
Massachusetts Institute of Technology
Cambridge, Massachusetts, and London, England

To C. I.

Preface

This book is the second of what threatens to be at least a trilogy. The first volume is entitled *Location and Space-Economy: A General Theory Relating to Industrial Location, Market Areas, Land Use, Trade, and Urban Structure.* It purports "to improve the spatial and regional frameworks of the social science disciplines, especially economics, through the development of a more adequate general theory of location and space-economy" (p. viii). It derives a general location principle through reducing to common simple terms the basic elements of the diverse location theories embodied in the works of von Thünen, Launhardt, Weber, Predöhl, Ohlin, Palander, Hoover, Lösch, Dunn, and others. Thereby it seeks to synthesize the separate location theories into one general doctrine, and, where possible, to fuse the resulting doctrine with existing production, price, and trade theory.

But it is fully recognized that a general theory of location and space-economy is of little direct use in treating concrete problems of reality. Such a theory must be supplemented by techniques of regional analysis which are operational—techniques which yield estimates of basic magnitudes for the space-economy and for each region of a system. These magnitudes are requisite for both the proper understanding of social problems and policy formulation. Hence, the imperative need for this second volume.

For example, several location theories assume that the market is specified beforehand. A firm chooses a plant location with respect to that market. But, theoretically, the size of the relevant market may vary from zero to a large magnitude. Hence, given scale economies and other forces, it becomes impossible to make a rational location decision until that size is at least approximately estimated. This necessitates, then, techniques for estimating the size of a market at any point, or, from a practical standpoint, for a continuum of points which form the meaningful area for the given firm.

In the determination of the size of markets, obviously population is a key factor. Since the future as well as the current market is pertinent to a location decision, population projections are vital. Hence, the relevance to practical location analysis of Chapter 2 of this book, which treats direct techniques for population projection.

Clear also is the fact that forecast population numbers of a market do not conform to expectations based on birth and death rates alone. Social, political, and economic forces compel both in-migration and out-migration. A significant number of these forces are tied to economic opportunities for gainful employment, and thus migration analysis cannot be fully performed without simultaneous economic location analysis which determines the spatial spread of these economic opportunities. But to some extent at least future migration is justifiably estimated through direct techniques discussed in Chapter 3.

Yet, to determine market size, it is not enough to estimate population after correction for migration. The dollar or other money sign, after all, is in an industrialized society the most relevant unit by which to measure market. Consequently, we must estimate income by regions—in terms not only of wages and salaries but also of dividends, interest, profits, rent, etc. Chapter 4 discusses this topic with respect to both the residents of a region and the nonresidents who purchase in the market places of the region. Moreover, balance of payments and credit restrictions can limit growth of markets; and the cyclical sensitivity and the industrial structure and diversification of a region may influence a businessman's appraisal of its markets. Thus materials discussed in Chapters 5 through 7 are pertinent. Finally, many markets (1) reflect indirect demands (the requirements of industries for each other's products), and (2) alter with change in the propensity of people to interact spatially; hence the relevance of Chapters 8 through 10, and Chapter 11, respectively—and, also of Chapter 12 which is perhaps most pertinent of all since it synthesizes the diverse techniques and develops the most rigorous frameworks for market estimation.

Beyond the establishment of market magnitudes, the various chapters of this volume implement in numerous ways the general theory given in *Location and Space-Economy*. If an industry tends to be labor-oriented à la Volume I, a firm within it must investigate labor cost differentials in selecting a plant location. But to approximate such differentials the firm must have on hand for the region of each potential location estimates of total labor force and total employment, which in turn are related to estimates of population numbers (corrected for migration) and total output by industry. These estimates are derivable through the use of techniques discussed in Volume II. Or if an industry tends to be power-oriented à la Volume I, a firm within it must investigate power cost differentials among locations. This means that for the region of each potential location the firm must make estimates of power consumption both by households (based on disposable income) and by industry in order to contrast them with energy supplies and facilities available for the generation of power at different average (and marginal) costs. Or, a firm contemplating a location decision may wish to consider the substitution of, say, transport outlays for production outlays, when savings in the latter can be made at sites where significant localization and urbanization economies are obtainable. (Scale economies may be assumed to be treated in connection with the estimation of market magnitudes.) Again, the techniques of Volume II are useful in estimating numbers and outputs of other firms producing like output and size of relevant population and industrial agglomerations within the hierarchy of urban-metro-politan regions.

The actual determination of market and supply (purchasing) areas in accordance with the theoretical principles of Volume I is also dependent on the derivation of diverse magnitudes by the frameworks of Volume II. This is so whether we consider two or more firms competing for consumers spread over an area or for raw materials available from a supply area or several deposits, or whether we probe into the service regions and tributary agricultural supply areas of existing cities. Furthermore, the theoretical agricultural land use pattern—that is, the width of Thünen-type rings and the intensity of cultivation within each—and other resource use patterns are functions of the size and spatial pattern of urban masses as well. And even were we able to iron out the inconsistencies of the Lösch-type abstractions discussed in Volume I, these abstractions alone cannot suggest specific intrametropolitan patterns of population, shopping centers, and satellite towns, industrial-commercial-residential land use configurations, networks of transport routes, and even transport rates (which are so basic in the establishment of transport cost differentials for plant location decisions). Required as well is the estimation of magnitudes such as population, employment, Gross Product, income and government expenditures, all by region, and interregional commodity and population flows—magnitudes which can be derived through the use of the techniques of Volume II.

The preceding remarks portray some of the many close bonds between the two books in terms of the contributions which the second makes to the empirical implementation of the theoretical structures

of the first. However, it is equally important not to lose sight of the
basic contributions which Volume I has made to the development of
the models and operational techniques of Volume II. To illustrate,
location theory for the firm has clearly laid the base for the systematic
industry-by-industry comparative cost approach developed in Chapter 7 of Volume II. This theory has also provided a classification of
types of firms and industries—market-oriented, raw-material-oriented,
labor-oriented, power-oriented. This classification, together with
concepts of other locational theories discussed in Volume I, greatly
reduces the data collection costs and computational requirements of
interregional and regional input-output schemes, and facilitates the
synthesis of these schemes with comparative cost analysis (see Chapter 8). Further, these theories help isolate the more important structural processes to be empirically implemented. In particular, their
emphasis on agglomeration economies has paved the way for the
development of the industrial complex approach of Chapter 9 of
Volume II and has stimulated explorations with the relative income
potential models of Chapter 11 of this volume. Further, through
their supposedly full coverage of locational forces and their logical
structures, these theories assist in the formulation of meaningful objective functions and constraints for interregional linear programs, such
as those outlined in Chapter 10 of this volume. In sum, the theories
of Volume I have led to the development of techniques and assisted
the construction of others which, either individually or in combination
via the channels of synthesis of Chapter 12 of Volume II, can lead to
superior projections of magnitudes relevant for business and government planning and for social policy formulation. A number of these
magnitudes are discussed in the early chapters as well as in the later
chapters of Volume II.

Volume I contributes to Volume II in other ways. As indicated in
the preface of the first volume, the first and third chapters of that
volume present materials which relate to Volume II as well. In particular, the first fifteen pages of Volume I should be reread in connection with the second volume in order to achieve a proper historical
perspective on spatial and regional development. For the most part
the techniques of Volume II are of the "comparative statics" variety.
They may yield snapshot pictures of spatial systems at each of several
points of time, but they all fail to catch or satisfactorily approximate
the dynamic processes of reality. It is therefore recommended that
the reader constantly refer to the materials of the first fifteen pages of
Volume I, or other writings of an historical nature which relate to the
evolution of society in its spatial aspects. These materials can serve

as an antidote to zealous and overenthusiastic attempts to apply the techniques of Volume II in ways that are unwarranted in terms of some of their sweeping assumptions.

Although the two volumes cover considerable ground, a tremendous amount remains to be done. Still to be achieved are more adequate syntheses of location and production theories [1] and of location and trade theories, as well as much more explicit statements of these syntheses. Better agglomeration and locational decision-making analyses are needed to supplement the relevant concepts and techniques developed in the first two volumes. The pursuit of a host of fruitful research projects (outlined in Chapter 13) is required in connection with the further development and fusion of the techniques of this second volume. And so forth. But perhaps even more basic is the need for a much more comprehensive general theory which not only covers equilibrium with respect to location, trade, price, and production for a system of regions whose boundaries and transport network are themselves variables, but also treats the fundamental interactions of political, social, and economic forces as these interactions affect the values of a society, condition its behavior patterns and goal-setting processes, and lead to concrete decisions and policies relating to interregional structure and function. We hope to explore this area in another volume.[2]

It is appropriate to make a few remarks about certain objectives of this volume, the manner in which it was written, and ways it can be used in both teaching and research.

One purpose of this volume is to make available in a relatively simple and clear-cut form the several techniques of regional analysis which have been proved to have at least some validity. An attempt is made to set forth the virtues and limitations of each of these techniques so that the research worker and policy maker may be able to judge its applicability for a particular regional situation and problem. In general, we do not seek a complete presentation of any given tech-

---

[1] Since the publication of Volume I, steps have been taken to obtain a better integration of location and production theories. For example, see the brief article by L. N. Moses, "Location and Theory of Production," *Quarterly Journal of Economics*, Vol. 73 (May 1958).

[2] Some of my thinking in this general theory direction may be gleaned from the following articles: "General Interregional Equilibrium," *Papers and Proceedings of the Regional Science Association*, Vol. 3, 1957; "Existence of a Competitive Interregional Equilibrium," *Papers and Proceedings of the Regional Science Association*, Vol. 4, 1958; and "General Interregional Equilibrium," *Journal of Regional Science*, Vol. 2, No. 1 (1960).

nique; rather we seek to investigate its major elements at a depth sufficient to permit its sound appraisal.

In addition, this volume presents, particularly in Chapters 10 through 12, some more recently developed techniques and synthesized frameworks which appear very promising but which have not yet had a chance to be tested. Necessarily any evaluation at this time of these techniques and frameworks can only be tentative. Still other techniques and frameworks—such as dynamic input-output models and quadratic programming [3]—which are less developed or less amenable to empirical implementation, or both, are not discussed in this second volume.

Because economics tends to be the most highly developed of the social sciences, and because in recent years regional economists have been especially active in developing new ideas, in part reflecting the new possibilities of utilizing high-speed computing machines in processing large masses of data, this volume tends to emphasize economic approaches. With further research, particularly on general political and sociological theory for a system of regions, it is hoped that this imbalance in regional science can be rectified in part.

This volume was conceived and first outlined in 1954. Since then the progress in regional science has been so great that without doubt the structure of the manuscript would be quite different were it to be reconceived today. Thus this volume is already partially obsolete. Also, although it was possible to incorporate new materials published after 1954 into the final draft, in general it was not possible to extend this updating beyond the summer of 1958.

Partly because of its length and partly because of the need to start from scratch in developing the techniques and frameworks for regional analysis, this volume can be used in several different ways for teaching and research purposes. Generally speaking, the first chapters are the most elementary ones, and the last chapters are the most advanced, although difficult materials may crop up occasionally in the earlier chapters and easy materials in the last. Therefore, Chapters 1 through 7, except sections D and E of Chapter 6 and the appendices to Chapter 7, may be used as basic text assignments for elementary courses in regional science, economic geography, regional economics, and city planning. Sections of these chapters may also be used as a text for certain parts of elementary courses in urban and regional sociology, human ecology, marketing, and real estate. For inter-

---

[3] These, as well as materials on the concepts of region, regional structure, and regional function, may be presented in a later volume treating general theories and general interregional equilibrium models.

mediate-level courses, Chapters 5 through 9, and sections A through D of Chapter 10, and sections A through F of Chapter 11 may constitute the basic text. For advanced courses, Chapters 8 through 13 and the appendices of Chapter 7 may serve as text. Or if this book is to be used as a text for two-term courses which are in sequence, a convenient cutting point between the materials of the two courses may occur at the end of Chapter 8, with perhaps the appendices of Chapters 7 and 8 discussed at relevant places in the second-term course. Obviously, many other arrangements of the materials of this volume are possible; their use should be a function of the interests of the students and the instructor. For example, in elementary courses in regional economics, sections A through F of Chapter 8 may substitute for Chapters 2 and 3 whose subject matter may be of less interest to the students and instructor. Or in an intermediate course in economic geography, sections D and E of Chapter 6 and the appendices of Chapter 7 may be omitted in order to cover some materials of section B of Chapter 12.

For research purposes, the same general principles are applicable in the use of this volume. The analyst who has both limited training and research resources will not be interested in techniques presented in Chapters 8 through 13, except perhaps those discussed in the early sections of Chapter 11. In contrast, the analyst who has advanced training and abundant research resources is likely to want to concentrate his attention on the frameworks discussed in Chapters 8 through 13, although he may find it useful to scan the contents of Chapters 1 through 7.

The writing of this volume testifies to the fact that I have been abundantly blessed with a group of outstanding students, whose cooperation and efforts made possible the development of this volume. Most of the chapters were written jointly, with persons who, except Daniel O. Price, are or were students of mine. In the writing of these chapters first drafts were typically prepared jointly. Revisions and later drafts were largely mine; hence I must assume full responsibility for all erroneous statements and other shortcomings. I am particularly indebted to David F. Bramhall who as a graduate student worked with me during the last two years of the writing of this book. His constant inquisitiveness and dissatisfaction with statements forced me, particularly in Chapters 11 and 12, to set down systematically and comprehensively various ideas which had been haphazardly roaming through my lecture notes and seminar discussions.

In addition to those persons listed on the title page, other students who to my great profit have jointly worked with me on studies that have contributed significantly to this volume include Joseph Airov, Edgar S. Dunn, Guy E. Freutel (deceased), Robert A. Kavesh, Robert E. Kuenne, J. Robert Lindsay, Benjamin H. Stevens, and Thomas Vietorisz.

As in Volume I, I must express deep gratitude to my former teachers for past guidance and stimulation—especially to John F. Bell, Alvin H. Hansen, and Abbott P. Usher. I am indebted to former associates in the Department of City Planning at the Massachusetts Institute of Technology—Frederick J. Adams, Roland B. Greeley, John T. Howard, Burnham Kelly, Kevin A. Lynch, and especially Lloyd Rodwin—for spurring me on in the development of ideas. Edward A. Ackerman, Harold J. Barnett, Roy F. Bessey, Irving Fox, Maynard Hufschmidt, Henry Jarrett, Harvey S. Perloff, and especially Morris E. Garnsey and Joseph L. Fisher were helpful in one connection or other when I was associated with Resources for the Future, Inc. At the University of Pennsylvania, Britton Harris, Robert B. Mitchell, and William L. C. Wheaton have provided both constructive criticism and encouragement, and Irving B. Kravis and Willis J. Winn have generously made possible the conditions for productive work. At the risk of failing to list all those former teachers and associates whom I should mention, I acknowledge the helpful criticisms and comments of Robert Dorfman, James S. Duesenberry, Gottfried Haberler, Chauncy Harris, Seymour E. Harris, Edgar M. Hoover, Wassily W. Leontief, Arthus A. Maass, Robert S. Platt, Stefan Robock, and Edward L. Ullman.

Permission to quote and to reproduce maps, tables, and materials has been kindly granted by the Addison-Wesley Press, the Agricultural Experiment Station of Purdue University, the Association of American Geographers, the Board of Governors of the Federal Reserve System, the Cambridge University Press, J. Dewey Daane, the Federal Reserve Bank of Kansas City, the Federal Reserve Bank of St. Louis, the Free Press, the International Cooperation Administration, Charles L. Leven, the National Bureau of Economic Research, the Regional Science Association, Richard D. Irwin, Inc., the U. S. Department of Commerce, the University of Washington Press, and the editors of the *American Economic Review, American Sociological Review, Econometrica, Economic Geography, Journal of Regional Science, Review of Economics and Statistics*, and *Social Forces*.

I am grateful to Resources for the Future, Inc., for financial support in the development of this book. The careful, detailed index was prepared by Eugene W. Schooler. The set of excellent figures and maps was constructed by my student Michael B. Teitz.

For many reasons, besides those that are self-evident, I am the most indebted to my wife to whom this book is dedicated.

WALTER ISARD

Philadelphia
July 1960

Contents

List of Tables

List of Figures

List of Maps

Chapter 1

The Setting

A birth occurs. The need for an additional hospital worker becomes urgent. A Southern field hand and his family migrate to New York. Income of the New York region rises. Gross Regional Product as well as household expenditures and government outlays in New York edge up. Personal savings increase slightly, as do private investment and the deficit of New York's account with the Rest of the World.

Impulses are transmitted to other regions. Citrus shipments from California register some gain. In part payment, money flows in the opposite direction. Too, California's balance of payments position improves. Income generated by new exports has a multiplier effect on California's economy. California's service and nonbasic trades expand. So do her imports from other regions, which in turn generate multiplier effects in these other regions. Regional and interregional expansionary forces operate through an interregional interindustry linkage system. Thus they influence industrial composition of regions. They also affect both national and regional investment behavior. Hence, they color the cyclical sensitivities of regions.

Concomitant with the phenomenon of impulse transmission through time and space is virtually a continuous succession of births. Each birth in its turn generates small-order repercussions. But in the aggregate, effects are major. Major migratory movements occur. Major changes in

1

regional income, Gross Regional Product, household expenditures, government outlays, personal savings, and investment obtain. Major realignments of interregional commodity and money flows develop. Major shifts in regional balance of payments positions, credit, tax, and other monetary and fiscal policy are evoked. Major impacts upon regional industrial structures are experienced. These in association with major shifts in consumption and investment behavior propagate significant though differential cyclical fluctuations for the regions of a system. Moreover, in addition to output adjustments of the diverse industries of regions, major market change provokes significant locational rearrangements. Cost minimization and profit maximization motives repattern cost-sensitive activities, individually or in groups as meaningful complexes. They even reallocate activities whose costs are insensitive to location but whose sales are attuned to the factor of market accessibility. Trip volumes, land use patterns, and urban-metropolitan structures and hierarchies adapt accordingly and in line with changed probabilities for social interactions over space. Even beyond this array of repercussions, as they operate through an interregional interindustry linkage system, an interregional money flow system, and an interregional communications and other systems, cultural values and social goals change. Such change, whether reflected in citizens' voting behavior, or in political platforms proffered, or in administrative practices, or in business decisions and rate of capital formation, or merely in consumers tastes, leads to new social welfare policy.

But the causal matrix underlying the spatial panorama of events of reality is not as simple as this. Intricate and complex interdependencies course through all facets of a culture. A region's births are not detached from economic and social forces. They are closely tied to the region's culture and goals, to its resource endowment, to major industrial shifts in or out, and to its levels of income, savings, exports, and imports. A region's births are indirectly interwoven with phenomena in, and structure and material welfare of, other regions. They are influenced as well by the features of the system of regions as a whole—by the system's state of technological advance, pace of investment and rate of consumption, research and development and educational policies, level of health and welfare services and social security programs, and other governmental activities reflecting the ojectives of a culture. In fact, *all* the characteristics of a region and its very development path are thus intertwined in a maze of interdependencies. This maze interlaces *interregional systems* of population, resource patterns, industrial locations, local economies, social accounts, balance of payments positions, markets, central places and urban-metropolitan areas, administrative and political structures and institutions, and even values, motives, and social goals. It interlaces all these systems via *interregional systems* of interindustry (interactivity) linkage, of commodity flows and money flows, of population movements, and of communications, and, in general, of sociocultural interaction inclusive of decision-making processes.

The maze of interdependencies in reality is indeed formidable. It becomes more and more awesome as we probe it. Its tale is unending, its circularity unquestionable. Yet its dissection is imperative if analysis is to lead to social progress. At some point we must cut into its circumference. We choose to do so at *population*.

The chapters of this book parallel the sequence of events recorded in the first paragraphs. Chapter 2 begins with population numbers and its projection. In this chapter, as in several succeeding ones, the approach must necessarily be narrow, direct, and somewhat elementary. Only after the contents of a number of chapters have been digested can the problems of the early chapters be broadly attacked.

Techniques for population projection for open regions require migration estimates. Methods for the derivation of such estimates are the subject of Chapter 3. But sound social and regional policy requires more than knowledge of population numbers and migration. Measures of economic welfare are essential. Regional income is one such measure, and it is discussed along with other regional social accounts in Chapter 4.

Chapter 5 digs into interregional connections. It examines the potential of commodity flow and money flow studies, and of balance of payments statements. It also evaluates the location quotient as a tool. The close bonds between a region's internal structure and an interregional system are more fully exposed in Chapter 6, where analytical studies of regional cycles and of regional and interregional multiplier effects are appraised. Chapter 7 continues the careful probing into regional and interregional structure, its subject being industrial location analyses and measures. It, together with the previous chapters, paves the way for the presentation of more general techniques which aim to encompass a significant amount of the interdependence of reality.

Chapter 8 takes a first major stab at general interdependence. It develops the basic elements of regional and interregional input-output frameworks, particularly in their proven forms. Chapter 9 continues this attack. It presents the industrial complex approach, an approach not as comprehensive as input-output but one which is more searching and capable of greater depth in the restricted areas it does dissect. Still another thrust at general interdependence is attempted in Chapter 10. This chapter spells out the rudiments of interregional linear programming, an analytical method involving optimizing behavior and a broader concept of social and economic efficiency than input-output. And in Chapter 11, an array of gravity, potential, and spatial interaction models are evaluated. These models aim to capture to some extent both the spatial regularity of social behavior in the aggregate and the pervasive effects of agglomeration economies.

Finally, Chapter 12 attempts several types of synthesis. Each synthesis purports to fuse into a superior framework for analysis the stronger elements of the several techniques discussed in the previous chapters. Each synthesis aims thereby to permit the investigator to probe more productively and effectively into the complex phenomena of reality. Each synthesis permits a broader attack on the regional and interregional problems posed in preceding discussion. Viewed from a methodological standpoint, Chapter 12 develops basic principles and approaches of regional science, the emphasis being on analytical frameworks which can penetrate interdependence not only within systems but among systems. The book closes with a few words of evaluation and a forward look.

Chapter 2

Population Projection*

A. PRELIMINARY REMARKS

As indicated in the introductory chapter, one of the most useful sets of data in regional analysis relates to population numbers, past, current, and future. This is reflected in the fact that past and current materials on population are generally available for political units and regions where only relatively little attention is given by official agencies to the collection and processing of statistics. However, *future* population numbers must necessarily be estimated. Because of the importance of such estimates, many techniques of population projection have been proposed and subjected to experimentation and verification.[1] In general, these techniques can be roughly classified as either *direct* or *indirect*. The *direct* techniques are usually based on current and past data on population

---

* This chapter has been written with Gerald A. P. Carrothers and draws heavily upon his doctoral dissertation, *Forecasting the Population of Open Areas*, M.I.T. Library, Cambridge, Massachusetts, June 1959.

[1] Recent general discussions of population projection techniques are to be found, among others, in American Society of Planning Officials [5], M. J. Hagood and J. S. Siegel [98], J. Hajnal [100], A. J. Jaffe [124], H. K. Menhinick [155], R. C. Schmitt [222, 233], J. S. Siegel [252], J. J. Spengler [260, 261], V. B. Stanbery [266], United Nations Population Division [302], and H. H. Wolfenden [345]. For an extensive bibliography see I. Taeuber [286].

numbers. The *indirect* techniques usually relate numbers to other economic, social, and political indices. In this chapter we shall discuss primarily *direct* techniques. In later chapters, especially Chapter 12, which treat the projection of other facets of the regional economy, we shall refer to the way in which population numbers can be associated with these projections. Such association leads to more sophisticated techniques in population projection which we shall explicitly identify. Hence this chapter covers only the less sophisticated techniques.

B. COMPARATIVE FORECASTING

The comparative method of forecasting the population of open areas[2] is relatively simple in practice but has complex implications. Briefly, the future growth of the study area is assumed to follow the pattern of another older area whose earlier growth has exhibited characteristics similar to those anticipated for the study area. By selecting a pattern area whose growth is substantially completed, the entire course of growth of the study area is defined. Once such a pattern area has been selected, the desired forecast is obtained by extending into the future the growth curve of the study area according to the past growth curve of the pattern area.

However, serious problems arise in the prior selection of the pattern area. First, it is necessary to find an older area for whose initial growth the social, economic, and political determinants are comparable to those currently shaping the development of the study area. This necessitates a highly complex analysis, usually impractical or impossible, if such comparability is to be more than intuitively demonstrated. In practice this question is usually begged through a selection of a pattern area whose initial *rates* of growth were similar to those currently associated with the study area, with only a superficial acknowledgment of the underlying causes of growth.

Second, suppose there is identified a pattern area whose initial growth characteristics do compare with the present stage of development of the study area. How can we be sure that the future growth of the study area will parallel what is, in reality, *past* growth of the pattern area, not only in general character but also over the same span of time? Again, comparability of social, economic, and political conditions must be established. Such comparability implies not only that forces of population growth which operated in the past in the pattern area will operate in the future in

---

[2] An "open" area is defined as one in which migratory movements of population are not controlled or directly counted, for example, a city, state, or region. In general, a "closed" area is one in which control is exercised or migration enumerated, for example, a nation.

the study area, but also that they will do so with the same intensity and timing.

The comparative method is of limited application. It is, perhaps, most useful in the forecasting of the population of new growth components of an expanding metropolitan area. As population pushes outward, successive areas might conceivably be expected to follow a similar pattern of growth as did areas closer to the center at an earlier date. At least, this expectation is relevant for certain spatial sectors of a Greater Metropolitan Region, which are equidistant from the core in terms of effective distance, and which are unlike only in position and direction of growth. Because such sectors are so similar and so closely related environmentally and socially, they may develop in much the same manner though at different periods of time.[3]

C. PROJECTION BY EXTRAPOLATION

1. GRAPHIC TECHNIQUES

Forecasting population by means of graphic extrapolation consists of (1) plotting the population of past census years against time; (2) sketching a line which, in the judgment of the forecaster, appears to fit the past data; and (3) extending this line into the future to obtain population numbers in future years.

The method falls into two general classifications depending on the type of coordinate paper used for the process. In both cases population is usually plotted as the dependent variable and time as the independent variable.[4]

[3] An early example of this method is T. H. C. Stevenson [277]: rates of population growth and densities in two London (England) suburbs, whose development had been substantially completed, were used to obtain twenty-year forecasts of the population of other London suburbs. H. W. Taylor [289] refers to a study done in 1915 where seven pattern cities were used to project the population of Norwich, New York, to 1940. In that year the forecast was 61 per cent higher than the actual population. For other early examples see N. L. Engelhardt and F. Engelhardt [77], pp. 55, 77. Later studies include H. Bartholomew [9], in which the population of South Bend, Indiana, was forecast by using five other cities for comparison, each having in 1900 the same population as South Bend in 1920. The forecast for 1950 was 21 per cent high.

Although popular during the first three decades of the century, the technique is at the present time normally used, if used at all, only as a check on projections by other methods. For example, see L. Segoe [241, 242], Bucks County Planning Commission [30], J. E. McLean [147], and W. A. Wachter [321], and Phoenix City Planning Commission [198].

[4] On occasion it may be desirable to designate time as the dependent variable and forecast the period (or a range) of time necessary to attain a given population, rather than to forecast a range of possible populations at a given time.

When plain coordinate paper is used, a linear curve, that is, a straight line, indicates constant absolute increments of growth over time. Such a line can be applied to the given data in a number of ways. The last two points of the historical data may be joined and extended; this implies that the character of the most recent period of development is expected to continue into the future. The first and last points of the given data (or, for that matter, any two points) may be joined and extended; this hypothesizes that future growth will exhibit some kind of combination of the characteristics of recent and previous growth. Finally, as a refinement of this latter process, a straight line may be selected which appears visually to approximate a least-squares regression line for the historic data. The resulting forecasts will vary widely, depending on the particular line selected and the interval between dates for which past population is known.

A nonlinear curve on plain coordinate paper indicates other than constant incremental growth. One such nonlinear curve indicates a constant rate of population increase and yields a straight-line relationship when plotted on semi-logarithmic paper. Use of such a curve for projection recognizes that a growing population tends to produce a continually larger absolute natural increase (assuming no migration). On the other hand a constant *rate* of growth does imply mounting numerical gains during successive periods which frequently exceed those that can be realistically anticipated. Hence, a nonlinear curve on semi-logarithmic paper exhibiting a falling rate of increase together with increasing absolute increments may be desirable.[5]

Since other than linear curves are difficult to apply graphically, the graphic method is usually used only for the projection of arithmetic rates of growth (linear extrapolation on plain coordinate paper) and of geometric rates of growth (linear extrapolation on semi-logarithmic paper).

Graphic extrapolation has serious limitations, especially when linear curves are applied uncritically. The procedure assumes that relationships which have existed in the past will continue to exist in the future and with the same intensity. Only where it is possible to demonstrate the continuing relationships of the social, economic, and political determinants of population growth is the method valid. Clearly populations of areas that have

[5] For example, in 1922 Nelson P. Lewis used a freehand extension of a nonlinear curve on semi-logarithmic paper to forecast the population of the New York Region up to the year 2000. In 1950 his estimate was running 23 per cent high. See H. James [125], p. 110. Earlier, in 1909, C. E. Woodruff [349], p. 175, utilized a graphical extrapolation of declining percentage decennial increases of the population of the United States, projecting to the year 2000. A recent example, for Dixon, Illinois, is in J. E. McLean [147].

been subject to rapid or erratic fluctuations in growth are not readily susceptible to graphic extrapolation.

The chief advantage of graphic extrapolation for population forecasting lies in the simplicity of the method. It is undoubtedly the simplest (mechanically) of all forecasting techniques. Since it relies on the use of good judgment, arbitrariness is always involved. Where past growth has been relatively stable, it is at least useful as a check on other methods of forecasting.[6]

2. EXTRAPOLATION BY MATHEMATICAL FUNCTION

For each of the curves that may be derived by graphical extrapolation there exists a formal mathematical equation. When this is explicitly acknowledged, and the equation identified, extrapolation by mathematical function becomes possible.

The use of a mathematical function for forecasting assumes that past population growth has followed some law of growth in which population is explicitly a function of time, and that future growth will follow a pattern predictable from this past relationship. Thus we have the equation

$$P_{t+\theta} = P_t + f(\theta)$$

where $P_{t+\theta}$ = population of the study area at any year $t + \theta$;

P_t = population of the study area at base year t;

θ = number of years from base year t to the forecast year $t + \theta$

and where the nature of the function f (its constants, exponents, etc.) reflect the biological, social, economic, and political determinants of population growth.

Extrapolation by mathematical function is subject to the same basic criticism as graphical extrapolation: that is, past relationships are assumed to determine future growth. However, by being specified in mathematical terms, the relationships may be subjected to statistical analysis and testing, which is not possible in graphical methods. Moreover, it is possible to introduce modifications and refinements into the equations to take into account expected future variations in the determinants of growth. To this extent the mathematical methods represent an improvement over graphical extrapolation.

a. Polynomial curves. The simplest of the mathematical functions is the straight-line, or first-degree, polynomial, which derives from an arithmetic progression (i.e., constant absolute increments per unit of time).

[6] See, for example, J. C. Riley [215].

This function produces the same projection as a linear graphic extrapolation on plain coordinate paper.[7]   It takes the form

$$P_{t+\theta} = a + b\theta$$

where a = actual or theoretical population P_t at base year t; and
         b = the average annual absolute increment derived from past data over a period considered relevant.

In a crude form this curve is derivable from the actual populations at an initial base year and a terminal base year.   In a more refined aspect this curve is a linear regression fitted to the past data by the method of least squares.[8]

When three or more observations of past population are available, it is possible to utilize higher-degree polynomials (i.e., nonlinear curves) which may also be fitted by the method of least squares.   The simplest of such curves is the second-degree polynomial (parabola) which takes the form

$$P_{t+\theta} = a + b\theta + c\theta^2$$

where a, b, and c are constants.   When the constant c is positive, the curve is concave from above, and the pattern of population growth assumed has a smooth and continuous rate of change with growth increments increasing in size.[9]

Any number of polynomials may be applied to past population data, each yielding a satisfactory fit but varying widely from one another with respect to future populations.   That is, the future pattern of population growth clearly is *not* inherent in any given polynomial curve which describes past growth, no matter how adequately the curve describes that growth.   Moreover, many of these curves have no upper limit.   They imply that growth, even though it may gradually taper off, will continue indefinitely into the future, and that population will approach an infinite size.   Although it is conceivable that growth may continue for an indefinite time into the future, it is inconceivable that population size could reach infinity, especially within a politically subordinate area of limited physical size.[10]

---

[7] See R. Pfister [195] and Phoenix City Planning Commission [198], respectively, for recent examples of straight-line extrapolation of the trend of growth of total population in a closed area and in an open area.

[8] For a simple exposition of the least-squares method see F. E. Croxton and D. J. Cowden [61], pp. 399–400.

[9] When the constant c is negative, the parabolic curve is convex from above.   The rate of change of population is again smooth and continuous, but the increments of growth decrease.

[10] Polynomials of the second degree or higher have been used mainly for the projection of the population of closed areas.   For example, in 1891 H. S. Pritchett [201] used a

b. Exponential curves. Much use has been made in population fore-casting of a variety of curves derived from the ordinary exponential form

$$P_{t+\theta} = ab^\theta$$

in which a and b are constants.[11] The characteristics of these curves vary according to the behavior of the parameters a and b and may be fitted to the recorded data of past growth in a number of ways, one of the more refined being the method of least squares. Of the family of exponential curves, the compound interest curve, which yields a constant rate of population growth over time, is one of the more familiar.[12] As already indicated in the discussion of graphical methods, the compound interest

third-degree polynomial, fitted to data from 1790 to 1890, to project the population of the United States to the year 2000. For 1950 the estimate was 27 per cent too large. A. L. Bowley [22] used a second-degree parabola to describe the population of England and Wales from 1801 to 1911 and a third-degree polynomial to describe the population of the United States from 1790 to 1910.

Examples of the application of higher-degree polynomials to the population of open areas include the 1938 Massachusetts State Planning Board study [153] which utilized a parabolic equation as one of ten methods to project the state population. The estimates by this equation were 3 per cent above the census figure for 1940 and 5 per cent below the figure for 1950. In 1949 H. Bartholomew [10] used a second-degree polynomial, fitted by the method of least squares, as a check on forecasts of the population of New Orleans made by four other methods.

[11] The best-known example of the early application of geometric projection is to be found in Malthus' theory of population growth, which is described mathematically by the equation

$$P_{t+\theta} = ae^{r\theta}$$

where $e = 2.71828$ (the base of the Naperian logarithm system). In 1815 Elkanah Watson used a geometric equation to project the population of the United States up to the year 1900, at which date his forecast was 33 per cent high. See R. Hunter [118], pp. 358–359.

The geometric method was popular in the early years of the present century, and A. B. Wolfe [344] cites eleven such studies between 1915 and 1923, most of which were concerned with closed areas. Since that time the curve has been used quite regularly to project the population of open areas. For example, see the 1929 report of the Denver, Colorado, Planning Commission [68], the 1947 Phoenix, Arizona report [198], studies by H. Bartholomew for New Orleans, Louisiana [10], and for Utica, New York [6], and the 1953 projections of the population of Duval County, Florida, by R. P. Wolff [348]. More typically, the method is used as a check on forecasts made by other methods, such as in the 1938 study by the Massachusetts State Planning Board [153] and the 1949 study of California's population by W. A. Spurr [264].

[12] The compound interest curve is derived from the general exponential, when b is a positive number greater than unity. In this case the amount of change in the curve increases by a constant percentage. A frequent form of the curve is

$$P_{t+\theta} = P_t(1 + r)^\theta$$

where r is the average annual rate of change, derived from past data over a period considered relevant.

curve (straight line on semi-logarithmic paper) overcomes some of the difficulties that arise when the first-degree polynomials are used: that is, it recognizes the tendency of population to compound itself. But it does not account for the frequent empirical observation that over long periods of time the relative growth rate tends to decline.[13] Nor does it take into account the impossibility of growth to an infinite size.[14]

A modified exponential curve of the form

$$P_{t+\theta} = k + ab^\theta$$

in which b is a positive number less than unity and a is negative allows for a constant percentage decrease in the absolute growth increments.[15] Here total population approaches k as an upper asymptote. Since the growth increment approaches zero as a limit, it also acknowledges the impossibility of infinite growth.[16] However, it still cannot cope with objections to the postulate that future growth is a function only of past relationships.[17]

c. Gompertz and logistic curves. A refinement of the modified exponential curve, and one which is more widely used, is the Gompertz curve.[18]

[13] For example, it is reported in the Compendium of the 1850 Census of the United States [306], pp. 95–96, 130–131, that between 1790 and 1840 there was a regular diminution in the per cent increase of population per decade. In that study eight varieties of the geometric curve were used to project the population of the United States to 1950. Three of these forecasts attempted to account for decreasing rates of growth by arbitrarily reducing the rate of increase midway in the forecast period. The forecasts for 1950 ranged from 48,760,043 to 479,246,365. The census count for 1950 was 150,697,361.

[14] A. J. Jaffe [124], p. 213, cites the case in which the population of Corpus Christi, Texas, and the population of the entire state of Texas would be equal in number in the year 2015 if each is projected geometrically.

[15] That is, the curve is convex from above when plotted on plain coordinate paper.

[16] A second-degree parabola may also be derived whose rate of growth is decreasing, and a third-degree polynomial was used by H. S. Pritchett [201] to introduce this factor, but such curves are not asymptotic.

[17] A modified exponential curve was used by Tucker in the Compendium of the 1850 Census of the United States [306], p. 130, in conjunction with different assumptions regarding immigration, to make two projections of the population of the United States to 1900. The projections for that year, of 80 million and 74 million, straddled the census count of 76 million.

In projecting the population of the New York Region in 1929, E. P. Goodrich utilized a modified exponential to obtain estimates of the future population of the United States. See H. James [125], pp. 113–114. A decline of slightly less than $1\frac{1}{2}$ per cent each decade from 1930 to 1980 in the percentage population increase of the Philadelphia Tri-State District is postulated in the 1932 Regional Plan [196]. In 1952 J. E. McLean [147] used a modified exponential as one of six methods of projecting the population of Dixon, Illinois.

[18] This curve describes a series in which the growth increments of the logarithms are declining by a constant per cent. The natural values of the series grow by a rate which

Although the modified exponential has only an upper limit, the Gompertz curve is asymptotic at both ends. It is an S-shaped curve on plain coordinate paper. In the initial period of growth, the absolute increments are increasing in size, and, in the subsequent period of growth, the absolute increments are decreasing. The general shape of this curve is believed by many to describe realistically the actual growth of population in a physically delimited area. Such growth proceeds through an initial period of relatively slow increase as the population becomes established, followed by a period of relatively rapid growth; after a point (corresponding to the point of inflection on the curve) the rate of growth declines and continues to as population numbers and density approach a maximum. In particular, by the establishment of upper and lower limits to possible population, the curve overcomes the defect of forecasting obviously impossible populations (i.e., infinite and/or negative numbers).[19]

The logistic curve, a curve which is more widely used in population forecasting than either the modified exponential or the Gompertz, is a further modification of the exponential form.[20] It is S-shaped and has the

is declining, but by neither a constant amount nor a constant per cent. The mathematical formula is

$$P_{t+\theta} = ka^{b^{\theta}}$$

or

$$\log P_{t+\theta} = \log k + (\log a)b^{\theta}$$

If the rate of growth is declining, b will always be less than unity. The curve approaches zero as a lower limit and k as an upper limit. See F. E. Croxton and D. J. Cowden [61], pp. 447–452.

[19] In 1922 R. D. Prescott [200] used a Gompertz curve to describe his "law" of population growth. G. R. Davies [63] applied the same formula in 1927 to population data for the United States from 1810 to 1920. He did not make specific forecasts, other than to predict an upper population limit k of 1,382,000,000 persons. For later examples see A. Bocaz S. [14–16].

[20] The general mathematical form is

$$\frac{1}{P_{t+\theta}} = k + ab^{\theta};$$

or, alternatively,

$$P_{t+\theta} = \frac{k}{1 + e^{a+b\theta}}$$

where k is the upper limit and b a negative constant. In this curve the growth increments of the reciprocal decline by a constant percentage. The first differences of the logistic form a symmetrical curve when graphed, whereas those of the Gompertz yield a skewed curve.

The logistic curve is usually fitted through three points, selected subjectively from past data, which are equidistant in time from one another. See F. E. Croxton and D. J. Cowden [61], pp. 452–456. In 1940 C. J. Velz and H. F. Eich [316] reported a technique of converting the curve to a straight-line form by deriving the essential measures graphically from a "logistic population grid." By this method the curve is fitted to all the past

same general characteristics as the Gompertz curve. Since its parameters are based on past data, its use implies that the determinants of past population growth will continue to act in the future. As with the Gompertz curve, this implication constitutes a basic weakness. No matter how well a curve may fit past data, this does not ensure that it will adequately describe future growth, particularly of open areas.[21]

data rather than to just three points. In 1948 W. A. Spurr and D. R. Arnold [265] added, to this logistic grid, the use of a nomograph for determining the upper limit of the curve from three selected points of past data. See also E. A. Rasor [206].

[21] The logistic curve was first propounded and named in 1838 by P. F. Verhulst [317], who subsequently applied it to early census counts of various European countries and of the United States [318]. In 1920 R. Pearl and L. J. Reed [189] reintroduced the curve as a result of experiments concerning the growth in numbers of fruit flies under controlled conditions of food consumption.

In applying the curve to human populations, Pearl and Reed [184, 187, 188, 207], later modified the equation to account for the hypothesis that growth may occur in waves or cycles as a result of expansion of available subsistence. Each wave is spliced onto the previous one, a two-wave system being defined mathematically by the equation

$$P_{t+\theta} = k_1 + \frac{k_2}{1 + e^{a+b\theta}}$$

where k_1 is the lower limit of the second wave and $k_1 + k_2$ is the upper limit. Pearl and Reed further postulated that the growth curve need not be symmetrical and therefore developed a skewed logistic curve of the form

$$P_{t+\theta} = k_1 + \frac{k_2}{1 + e^{a+b\theta+c\theta^2}}$$

Subsequently, in 1936, Reed [208] stated that he did not consider these elaborations of the equation justified in applying the curve to the population growth of the United States.

In 1923 Pearl and Reed [190] utilized their skewed logistic form to forecast the population of the New York Region and some of its component areas up to the year 2100. They used an upper asymptote of 34.9 million and obtained a forecast for 1950 of a population of 16,840,000 which was 25 per cent higher than the census figure for that year. E. B. Wilson and W. J. Luyten[341] objected to the method used by Pearl and Reed to fit their curve to the past data. Pearl and Reed fitted the curve by the method of least squares utilizing *absolute* differences between the observed points and the corresponding values, whereas Wilson and Luyten fitted the same form of curve utilizing *percentage* differences. The Pearl-Reed curve appears to be a better fit when plotted on plain coordinate paper, but the Wilson-Luyten curve appears to be a better fit when plotted on semi-logarithmic paper. See H. James [125], pp. 112–113. The Wilson-Luyten curve for New York has an upper asymptote of 16,667,000 and forecast a regional population for New York of 13,110,000 in 1950, which was 3 per cent below the actual. This emphasizes the fact that the use of the logistic curve, as of any mathematical curve, is a highly subjective process, in spite of its superficial appearance of rational elegance.

Modification of the logistic curve to take into account absolute declines in population numbers was suggested by V. Volterra [320] and by E. C. Rhodes [213] in 1938. This

In spite of their fundamental defects, exponential curves are useful as rough checks on forecasts of population growth obtained by other methods, as is true for the previously described methods.

D. RATIO AND CORRELATION METHODS

1. RATIO METHODS

Population growth in any given area may exhibit a relationship to population or other growth in another area if there are interconnections among the social, economic, political, and biological factors governing growth in the two areas. Such interconnections have provided the foundation for ratio methods of population forecasting. For example, given a projection of the population of a pattern area, these methods forecast the population of a study area through a projection into the future of the ratio which this population has formed with the population of a pattern

problem is also raised in the 1946 study of New York by Consolidated Edison [56], but the logistic curve utilized for projection does not show a decline.

Since Pearl and Reed rediscovered the logistic curve extensive use has been made of the technique for projecting the population of closed areas. For example, see V. G. Valaoras [315] for Greece in 1936; S. Vianelli [319] for Italy and the United States in 1936; M. C. MacLean and A. W. Turner [149] for Canada in 1937; S. Swaroop and R. B. Lal [282] for India in 1938; R. Pearl and others [191] for the United States in 1940; B. Narain [165] for India in 1942; A. P. León and C. A. Aldama [142] for Central and Caribbean America in 1945; and J. D. Keller [131] for various countries in 1946. However, in recent years the method appears not to have been as popular as formerly and seems to have been largely displaced by other methods, in particular by techniques of growth composition analysis. (See section E, following.)

The logistic curve has also been extensively applied to open areas, although not to the same extent as for closed areas. In their study, Velz and Eich [316] applied the graphical "logistic grid" technique to all cities and metropolitan areas in the United States with a population in 1930 of over 25,000 persons. In 1945 J. L. Janer [126] fitted a two-cycle logistic curve to population data for Puerto Rico for the period 1760 to 1940. In the same year W. S. Thompson [294] used a logistic curve as one of three basic methods of projecting the population of Cincinnati to the year 1970. In 1950 the forecast from this curve was 6 per cent below the census figure. In 1946 T. Casanova [42] applied such a curve to the population of Puerto Rico. In 1947 R. C. Schmitt [221] used a logistic curve as one of two methods of projecting the population of the metropolitan area of Flint, Michigan. In 1949 W. A. Spurr [264] used the technique, along with four other methods, to project the population of California up to 1960. In 1950 W. I. Johnson [128] used a logistic curve as a check on a separate forecast of the population of Cuyahoga County, Ohio. In 1952 J. E. McLean [147] applied the Velz and Eich graphical method as one of six methods of forecasting the population of Dixon, Illinois.

Further general discussion of the use of the logistic curve for projecting population numbers is to be found, among other items, in R. Pearl [183], [185], ch. 18, [186], ch. 24; G. U. Yule [353]; G. R. Davies [63]; E. B. Wilson and R. R. Puffer [342]; H. Hart [102]; and United Nations, Department of Social Affairs [301], pp. 41–44.

area.[22]   These methods are used almost exclusively with respect to open areas.

The particular technique by which the ratio is projected into the future critically affects the accuracy of the method. In the crudest form the method employs a constant ratio, where the ratio is calculated from the most recently available data.[23] In more refined forms, these methods allow for changing ratios, where the changing ratios may be derived through extrapolation of past trends by any of the graphical and mathematical methods previously discussed, or may be determined from a subjective analysis of the trend and of other relevant information.[24]

There are two basic ways in which the ratio technique may be applied: (1) through the use of total population numbers of another area (or areas) as the denominator of the ratio; and (2) through the use of some component of the population of the study area or a pattern area as the denominator.

a. Ratio to total populations. This method is somewhat similar in concept to "comparative forecasting." It utilizes population growth experience of other areas to derive ratios by which to forecast the population of a study area. But in one sense, at least, it represents an improvement over the comparative method. It does not arbitrarily assume that

---

[22] The general mathematical form for projecting a ratio as a function of current and past ratios is

$$\frac{P_{t+\theta}}{\pi_{t+\theta}} = f\left(\frac{P_t}{\pi_t}, \frac{P_{t-1}}{\pi_{t-1}}, \frac{P_{t-2}}{\pi_{t-2}}, \ldots, \frac{P_{t-n}}{\pi_{t-n}}\right)$$

where P is the population of the study area, π the population or other base magnitude of the pattern area, and n the number of years before base year t. Ratio techniques seem to have been used only infrequently before World War II but have since come into extensive use. Early examples include E. P. Goodrich's 1925 study [90] for the New York Region (see also H. James [125]) and the 1932 Philadelphia Tri-State District study [196]. As early as 1917 N. L. Engelhardt and F. Engelhardt [77], p. 76, suggested use of the ratio method for obtaining forecasts of school enrollment.

[23] For example, see H. Bartholomew [7, 10, 11], the 1945 Omaha, Nebraska, study [192], and the 1945 study of Peoria, Illinois, reported by the National Housing Agency [309].

[24] W. I. Johnson [128] apparently extrapolated his ratios graphically. The 1945 Peoria study [309], W. S. Thomson's Cincinnati report [294], and the California estimates by G. B. Johnson and D. Driver [127] extrapolate ratios linearly by means of the method of least squares. The Phoenix, Arizona, study [198] and W. A. Spurr [264] extrapolate geometrically. The 1951 Philadelphia study [197] utilizes logistic curves. The 1932 Philadelphia Tri-State District report [196], the San Bernadino Valley study [121], and the Greenwich, Connecticut, report [321] utilize subjective projections. M. J. Hagood and J. S. Siegel [99] use a geometric extrapolation wherein the average annual rate of change is subjectively reduced to zero over a period of twenty-five years. This last technique has been applied in a number of subsequent studies: see, for example, [38, 55, 96, 168, 312, 338].

the study area will grow in the future precisely as the pattern area grew in the past.

In its more usual form this method postulates that the factors governing the growth of the study area are a reflection of the factors governing the growth of a larger area, of which the study area forms a part. If projections of the population of the pattern area do not exist, it is necessary for the forecaster to prepare such projections. Frequently, the nation is taken as the pattern area because carefully prepared projections may exist. Also, at this level, the elusive item of migration can be more easily controlled, and, as a consequence, it may be maintained that national projections tend to be more accurate.[25] However, as the study area decreases in size, there may often be a closer relationship between the study area and a pattern area smaller than the nation. Thus, although the nation may be a suitable base for projection of the population of large regions of the country or of states, it may frequently be justifiable to use the regional and state projections in turn, to forecast the populations of smaller areas and communities.[26]

The ratio method may also be used in reverse. Future population of a study area may be determined from independent projections of the population of constituent areas within the study area.[27] The necessary ratios may be based on one key area or may use several such areas. In the latter case, areas constituting the whole of the study area are usually

[25] Examples of studies which use national projections directly for forecasting city or metropolitan area populations include: U.S. National Housing Agency [309], W. S. Thompson [294], Philadelphia Tri-State District [196], E. P. Goodrich [90], Omaha, Nebraska, City Planning Commission [177], H. Bartholomew [7, 8, 11], and Consolidated Edison Company of New York [56]. Studies that utilize national projections primarily to forecast populations of states or larger regions include: G. B. Johnson and D. Driver [127], W. I. Johnson [128], M. J. Hagood and J. S. Siegel [99], H. L. White and J. S. Siegel [338], A. H. Hawley [107], Columbia Basin Inter-Agency Committee [55], and W. A. Spurr [264].

[26] For instance, in 1950 W. I. Johnson [128] utilized the following set of ratios, as one of ten sets, to obtain projections of the population of Cuyahoga county: U. S. urban to U. S. total, "eastern industrial states" urban to U. S. urban, "tri-city region" urban to "eastern industrial states" urban, "fourteen-counties" urban to "tri-city region" urban, county urban to "fourteen-counties" urban, county urban to county total. Earlier, in 1939, L. Segoe [241] used a similar technique for Charleston, West Virginia. In 1950 his forecast was approximately 19 per cent too large. Other studies where independent subnational forecasts are used to project populations of smaller areas include: Detroit City Plan Commission [69], D. S. Campbell and D. Brown [38], Phoenix City Planning Commission [198], New Jersey Department of Conservation and Economic Development [168], Philadelphia City Planning Commission [197] and W. A Wachter [322].

[27] See, for example, the 1944 California study by V. B. Stanbery and others [271].

utilized, in which event so-called "apportionment" or "capacity" methods are often applied.

In the apportionment method, independent population forecasts are made for each of the constituent areas and for the whole area. The sum of the projected populations of the constituent areas is then compared with the independent forecast of the entire area and modifications made in the projections, either through adjustment of the projection of the whole study area or through apportionment of the discrepancy among the various constituent areas, or both.[28]

In the capacity method, each of the constituent areas is analyzed to determine the amount of residential land, or water supply, or other limited resource available for future development. Their populations may then be projected on the basis of permissible land densities, potential water consumption patterns, and the like in each area. The resulting total can be taken to be the forecast for the whole study area; or the total may be modified as in the apportionment method.[29]

b. Ratio to population components. This modification of the ratio method assumes that there are relationships between the growth of total population numbers in an area and of some element of that population, or of the population of a larger (or smaller) area. School enrollment and employment are elements internal to a region which are commonly used as the denominator.[30] The former may also be disaggregated into elementary school and high school enrollment, and the latter into different categories of employment. It is also possible to use numbers in a specific age group to determine the denominator.[31]

When population components external to the area are used as a base, they are generally employed to forecast the equivalent component within

[28] For typical examples for open areas see Buffalo City Planning Commission [31], M. M. Carroll and S. Weber [40], and V. B. Stanbery and J. C. Riley [272]. F. J. Eberle [74] reports using this technique for Los Angeles as early as 1923, and E. P. Goodrich [89] used a similar technique for New York in 1925. An example for a closed area is in E. Charles, N. Keyfitz, and H. Roseborough [49].

[29] An early example is contained in the 1929 Denver, Colorado, Plan [68] which forecast a population of 520,000 in 1950. This "conservative" forecast was 25 per cent too high. More recent examples include R. C. Schmitt [232], A. H. Crosetti and J. Moehring [59], P. M. Reid [209], Bucks County Planning Commission [30], R. P. Wolff [347], and Homer Hoyt [114]. See also H. W. Stevens [276].

[30] For example, see R. Pfister [195] and P. M. Reid [210] for the use of employment data in this way. F. L. R. Kidner and P. Neff [133] use such a ratio, in reverse, to obtain employment estimates. For the use of school enrollment data in this way, see A. J. Jaffe [124], pp. 225–226; B. L. Weiner [327]; and U. S. Bureau of the Census [306].

[31] See F. Lorimer [143] and M. J. Hagood and J. S. Siegel [99]. W. I. Johnson [128] uses size and numbers of families in the denominator. V. B. Stanbery and M. Roher [273] use a ratio of numbers of families to total population.

the study area. For instance, the future population of an urban area may be projected through the use of total national urban population numbers as the base.[32] Or again, employment in general, or of a particular kind, within the area may be linked in terms of a ratio to the respective total national figure.[33]

To the extent that ratio methods utilize the graphical and mathematical extrapolation techniques to determine relevant future ratios, they are subject to the same disadvantages and criticisms as these techniques. However, they do represent an improvement over the previous methods in so far as greater insight into the future growth of an area or sector may be derived from an analysis of its constituent parts or of the growth of another area of which it forms a part.

2. REGRESSION AND COVARIANCE ANALYSIS

The relationship between the growth of population in a study area and the growth of population in a pattern area or sector suggested by the ratio method can be attacked in statistical form more satisfactorily by means of regression and correlation analysis.[34] In addition, and more usually, population growth in the study area is associated statistically with such factors as employment, investment, income, exports, school enrollment, population density, persons per household, rents, telephone installations, and automobile registrations.[35] In such statistical analysis, population growth in the study area is usually designated in a noncausal sense as the dependent variable and the other factors as the independent variables.

There are several approaches of a statistical nature that have been employed to explain and occasionally project population growth. We shall

[32] For example, see Oklahoma City Planning Commission [176], P. M. Reid [210], and H. Bartholomew [8, 11].

[33] For example, see Cincinnati City Planning Commission [51]. In addition to these techniques, D. J. Bogue [19] has developed a projection method which makes use of ratios of vital rates within the study area to those of a larger area.

[34] Correlation analysis has been used mainly for intercensal population estimates. See, for example, F. J. Eberle [74], R. Kubek [136], and R. C. Schmitt [223]. Postcensal projections by this method were made as early as 1911 by E. C. Snow [259]. Subsequently, until the late 1940's the method seems not to have been in general use. For an example of its use during this period see E. F. Young [352]. In recent years interest in the method has been restimulated in particular by R. C. Schmitt. See V. Roterus and R. C. Schmitt [218], R. C. Schmitt and A. H. Crosetti [234], and R. C. Schmitt [221, 225, 228, 229, 232].

[35] For instance, R. C. Schmitt [225, 228, 229] makes use of the following symptomatic data: population density, distance to the Central Business District, per cent population growth, proportion of owner-occupied dwellings, national income, and employment in the automotive industry. W. A. Spurr [264] and V. B. Stanbery and M. Roher [273] use national income data. The Consolidated Edison Company of New York [56] uses numbers of electricity accounts. See also F. S. Chapin [47].

discuss some of these later. However, these approaches are *statistical* and have been used widely in various sciences. They are not peculiar to regional study. We therefore present them in only a sketchy fashion. The reader is referred to standard statistical treatises for their full development.[36]

a. Simple regression. One of the statistical approaches widely used is simple regression analysis. Population growth is taken as the dependent variable. Another factor is taken as the independent variable. For a given set of observations the association between the values which these two variables take is examined. The simplest form of association is described by a linear regression fitted to the data, whether they be current or past.[37] The equation of the resulting line is

$$P = a + bX$$

where P is population of the study area and X is the value taken by the independent (symptomatic) variable. Usually each observation (point on the graph) refers to a value of both P and X at the same given point of time, such that when $X_{t+\theta}$ is given for projection purposes, we have

$$P_{t+\theta} = a + bX_{t+\theta}$$

Occasionally, however, each observation may refer to values for P and X at different points of time. For example, the value for P for any given year may be paired with a value for X for the previous year. In such a case, we have a lagged model, and the projection of population for any future year, $t + \theta$, is based on the value of X in year $t + \theta - 1$.

In these equations, when b is positive the correlation is direct; when it is negative, the correlation is inverse. Also in this approach, a correlation coefficient is typically computed. The correlation coefficient is used to indicate the degree to which the regression line explains the deviations of the individual values of the dependent variable from their mean value.

To illustrate the simple regression technique, the hypothesis may be advanced that the population growth of a state in the South, say Virginia, is associated with increase in per capita income. Based on data for the period 1947–1953, the equation of the regression line would be

$$P = 2,095,000 + 1062X$$

[36] For example, on simple and multiple regression see F. E. Croxton and D. J. Cowden [61], chs. 22–25; M. Ezekiel [78]; H. Walker and J. Lev [322], chs. 10, 13; G. U. Yule and M. G. Kendall [354], chs. 9–13 and other standard texts. For treatment of covariance analysis see particularly D. J. Bogue and D. L. Harris [20], and H. Walker and J. Lev [322], ch. 15.

[37] Examples of projections by means of simple correlation include R. C. Schmitt [225] and F. L. R. Kidner and P. Neff [133].

where P and X represent respectively population and per capita income of the state of Virginia. The coefficient of correlation is 0.96; the proportion of total variation which is statistically explained is 0.93.

If now a per capita income of \$1500 is independently estimated for year 1960, the value of X becomes 1500 and the 1960 population based on the use of the equation as an estimating equation is 3,688,000.

However, an examination of the data when plotted often suggests that the association is nonlinear. For example, the association may be of an exponential form (straight line on double-log paper). There may also be a theoretical basis for a nonlinear association. In this case, the equation of the regression line is

$$P = a + f(X)$$

where $f(X)$ indicates any function of the independent variable (such as, for example, a parabolic or exponential curve). Typically, a nonlinear regression involves added computation and is not pursued unless its superiority to a linear regression is indicated by empirical and theoretical materials.

b. Multiple regression. Frequently in regional study it is judged that population growth is simultaneously associated with more than one independent variable. Here, a multiple regression (correlation) analysis is pursued.[38] When the regression is taken to be linear, the form of the equation is

$$P_{t+\theta} = a + b_1 X_1 + b_2 X_2 + \cdots + b_n X_n$$

where $X_1, X_2, \cdots, X_n$ represent the values taken by the several independent variables, and $b_1, b_2, \cdots, b_n$ are constant coefficients, either positive or negative. Any coefficient, say b_2, indicates the change in $P_{t+\theta}$ to be associated with a unit change in the corresponding variable X_2 when allowance has been made for the other independent variables.[39]

For example, Bogue and Harris have performed a multiple regression correlating 1940–1950 population growth rates of 125 standard metropolitan areas in the United States with six independent variables: (1) density of central city, 1950 (X_1); (2) age of standard metropolitan area (X_2); (3) degree of industrialization, 1940 (X_3); (4) change in industrialization,

[38] Examples of projections by means of multiple correlation are to be found in R. C. Schmitt [228, 229].

[39] When the regression is judged to be of a nonlinear nature, one general form of the equation is
$$P_{t+\theta} = a + f_1(X_1) + f_2(X_2) + \cdots + f_n(X_n)$$
If it is desired to separate the effect of each independent variable by eliminating the effects of the other independent variables, the technique of partial correlation may be used. See M. Ezekiel [78], pp. 213–219.

1939–1947 (X_4); (5) logarithm of distance to nearest standard metropolitan area (X_5); and (6) growth rate of standard metropolitan area, 1930–1940 (X_6). Their regression (estimating) equation where year 1950 represents $t + \theta$ is

$$P_{1950} = P_{1940} + \frac{P_{1940}}{100}(1.543 - 0.007X_1 - 0.137X_2 - 0.081X_3$$
$$+ 0.111X_4 + 5.676X_5 + 0.952X_6)$$

where P_{1940} is actual 1940 population and where P_{1950} is the 1950 population as *estimated* by the regression.[40] The coefficient of multiple correlation obtained is 0.75 which, when squared, equals 0.53 and signifies the proportion of total variation that is "explained."[41]

Bogue and Harris carry through a number of other multiple regressions to explain such phenomena as the per cent of the population of standard metropolitan areas living in the urban fringe in 1950; per cent of population of standard metropolitan areas residing more than 5 miles from the central city in 1950; the density of the urban fringe in 1950; and per cent change in population of central city, 1940–1950. Significantly, Bogue and Harris refrain from projection into the future. Aside from the fact that several independent variables such as density of central city and change in industrialization would themselves need to be projected, involving another source of possible error, there are serious doubts about the validity of the estimating equation for projection purposes. These doubts are common to all multiple and, for the most part, simple regression analyses; and some may now be briefly mentioned.

First, it must be assumed that causal relationships existing in the past or present will continue to operate in the future with the same relative intensity. Such an assumption which characterizes most if not all projection techniques is seldom if ever justified. Second, and more peculiar to regression methods, a high degree of correlation implies no necessary causal relation between the dependent and independent variables. In fact, the variation of a dependent variable may be statistically linked with the variation of an independent variable, when in fact no causal bond at all exists, even though on the surface such a bond seems reasonable; for the dependent variable may be causally linked with a second independent variable unrelated to the first. More typically, variation in the dependent variable may be statistically associated with variation in an independent variable when both variables are related to some unidentified third variable

---

[40] The form of this estimating equation differs somewhat from the general linear form of the regression equation cited because Bogue and Harris use *growth rates* as the dependent variable, rather than *population size*.

[41] However, for a discussion of the standard error of this estimate see D. J. Bogue and D. L. Harris [20], p. 24.

which is omitted from the regression analysis but is causally the significant factor. In still other cases important independent variables are defined so broadly that they contain (and conceal) a host of specific factors which are linked in different ways with the dependent variable. When one or more actual causal links are submerged in such fashion, a firm theoretical basis for establishing the stability of relationships is difficult to achieve.

Third, certain conditions are necessary if the derived statistical inferences are to be valid. Deviations of the dependent variable from the regression must be normally distributed with constant variance about the regression. Observations must be independent. Multivariate normality must exist for establishing the significance of coefficients. And so forth.

c. Covariance analysis. Even though there are many serious limitations to multiple regression analysis, still the technique has value. Bogue and Harris, for example, express the hope that additional research will more clearly identify the relevant variables, establish significant and stable values for the appropriate parameters, and thereby lay a foundation for more complete scientific explanation of the basic forces that determine population growth and distribution. Such superior explanation would in turn lead to improved projections.

If with further study the applicability of multiple regression analysis is more fully established, another avenue for population projection becomes promising. This avenue is covariance analysis. At the present time no projection has been made on the basis of this technique. Yet the promise of fruitful results seems to warrant a brief, nontechnical exposition.

It has been indicated that regression analysis is useful to "explain" some of the deviations of population increments at different points of time (or for different areas) from the grand mean of these increments. The more the regression line (curve) explains these deviations, the greater the correlation coefficient—and very loosely speaking, the more reliable a population projection, if any projection is justified. But typically, a large part of the total variation remains unexplained, and an attempt may be made to reduce this "unexplained" portion by introducing nonquantifiable factors. Such an attempt can employ *covariance analysis.*

To sketch the fundamentals and illustrate the utility of covariance analysis, we present Figures 1a–d. Figure 1a measures, say, population (dependent variable) along the vertical axis and magnitude of factor X (independent variable) along the horizontal axis. For a given point of time we plot for each metropolitan area both its population and its magnitude for factor X. We also compute the grand mean of population for all metropolitan areas and indicate this simple average by a bold horizontal line. Also depicted on Figure 1*a* is a dashed vertical line for each observation which measures the deviation of the population of the corresponding metropolitan area from the average, that is, the grand mean.

In this example it is not the purpose of covariance analysis to explain the

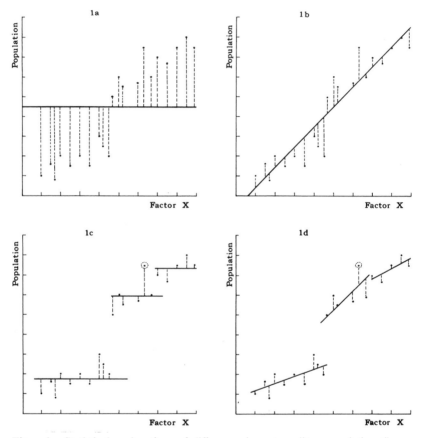

Figure 1.   Statistical explanations of differences in metropolitan populations (hypothetical).

average population of metropolitan areas.   But it is the purpose of this analysis to explain the deviation from the average.[42]

In Figure 1*b* a first attempt is made at such an explanation.   Factor *X* is advanced as an explanatory (independent) variable.   To the data of

---

[42] Technically speaking, we wish to explain the total variation which is measured by the sum of the squares of the vertical deviations of each observation from the grand mean.

Figure 1*a*, which are reproduced in Figure 1*b*, a regression line is fitted by the method of least squares.[43] The dashed vertical line for each observation measures for the corresponding metropolitan area the deviation of its actual population from the theoretical population given by the regression line (the regression line is an explanatory line in a statistical sense; it explains variation in population in terms of variation in factor X). It is to be noted that on the average the deviations in Figure 1*b* are noticeably smaller than the deviations in Figure 1*a*. The deviations over all cases are suggestive of total unexplained variation. Thus, the use of a regression diminishes the amount of total unexplained variation.[44]

An alternative approach can sometimes be pursued in order to reduce the total unexplained variation, whose existence is depicted in Figure 1*a*. The data, when classified by some meaningful nonquantifiable factor, may tend to fall into separate clusters. For example, in Figure 1*a* the observations at the lower half and to the left may represent metropolitan areas in the South; those toward the center in the upper half (including an extreme item which is circled in Figure 1*c*) may represent metropolitan areas in the North; and the five observations at the upper right may represent metropolitan areas of the West. For the metropolitan areas of each region, an average (a subgroup mean) may be taken and represented as a bold horizontal line, as is done in Figure 1*c*. The deviation of the population of each metropolitan area from the average for its region may then be indicated by a dashed vertical line. Comparison of such deviations in Figure 1*a* with the deviations in Figure 1*c* demonstrates clearly that total unexplained variation has been reduced by the introduction of subgroup means. Or, put otherwise, a fraction of the total variation exhibited in Figure 1*a* is now explained by the variation of the subgroup means indicated in Figure 1*c*, that is, by the regional factor. However, this analysis of *variance* furnishes no explanation of why the region (subgroup) means differ and why they assume the particular values depicted in Figure 1*c*. Thus this variance analysis furnishes no theoretical or causal explanation, merely a statistical explanation.

If two steps, each taken independently, lead to a reduction in the amount of total variation which is unexplained, it would seem logical that the same two steps taken concomitantly might permit still greater reduction in this amount. Pursuing both these steps concomitantly is logically

[43] The method of least squares fits a line which minimizes the sum of the squared deviations of values of the dependent variable when these deviations are measured vertically from the line. Total unexplained variation is then measured by the sum of these squared deviations.

[44] The difference between the sum of the squared vertical deviations of Figure 1*a* and the sum of the squared deviations of Figure 1*b* represents the amount of total variation which has been "explained" by the regression line.

termed *covariance* analysis. Figure 1*d* presents the results graphically.
As in Figure 1*c* the data are classified by region. But now, for each
subgroup, the mean is not calculated; rather a simple regression line is
fitted separately to the data of each subgroup. (When in addition to
factor X other independent variables are involved, the lines would be
multiple regression lines). In Figure 1*d* the deviation of the actual population of a metropolitan area from the theoretical population given by the
regression line of its region is indicated by a dashed vertical line. It
can be seen that the deviations of Figure 1*d* are smaller than the deviations
in any of the other figures, and therefore that the unexplained part of total
variation has been still further reduced. Thus, this procedure recognizes
that both the regional factor and other quantifiable factors may offer
better statistical explanation in conjunction with each other than when
taken alone.[45] Further, within each region allowance may be made for
different intensities of the association of the dependent variable with each
of the independent variables.[46]

This statement represents the essence of covariance analysis. As
already indicated this approach has not yet been used for population projection. One major study, that by Bogue and Harris, employs this
approach to explain statistically population growth of metropolitan areas
during the period 1940–1950. After performing the multiple regression
analysis outlined in the preceding section, Bogue and Harris introduce
via covariance analysis the regional factor. They find that a five-region
classification of the data raises the per cent of the total explained variation
in growth rates from 53 to 69.

Bogue and Harris do not proceed to any projections and are careful to
avoid any inference that their statistical explanation has validity for
forecasting. In addition to the several major weaknesses of simple and
multiple regression analysis (which are indicated at the end of the preceding
sections), there are other limitations to covariance analysis. The chief
new weakness is associated with the significance to be attached to the one
or more bases of classification employed. That metropolitan areas grow

[45] It must be recognized, of course, that every time a new independent variable or
basis of classification is introduced, the degrees of freedom are simultaneously reduced.
Consequently, the confidence that can be attributed to the results is correspondingly
diminished. In the extreme, when large numbers of independent variables and classification bases are introduced, the findings lose all statistical significance. For example,
it may no longer be possible to prove that a correlation coefficient is significantly different
from zero. Note also that when more than one basis of classification is employed the
cell frequencies (clusters) which result will frequently be too small for reliable analysis.

[46] Such different intensities may be reflected in the different slopes and intercepts of
the regression lines of the several regions, that is, in the different values which a and b
may assume in the respective regression equations.

less rapidly in the South than in the West does not explain anything in a meaningful way, although the improvement in statistical explanation resulting from the introduction of a regional classification may lead to causal insights. On the other hand, such improvement in statistical explanation may be spurious and may lead the investigator to both fruitless paths and misleading conclusions. Stated in another way, covariance analysis may throw light on certain important relations; on the other hand, by attributing statistical significance to seemingly meaningful variables, it can easily obscure deep underlying causal bonds.

Again we do not expand upon the limitations associated with covariance analysis, since they as well as the full presentation of this technique rightfully belong to treatises on statistics. Nor do we discuss the problem of computation which can readily become cumbersome for many purposes of population projection, particularly in multiple regressions where nonlinear functions are indicated.

E. Growth Composition Analysis

A number of methods of forecasting population of open areas are based on the analysis of the following major elements of population growth: natural increase (or decrease), in-migration (or out-migration), and annexation (or abandonment). The last element is of significance only when dealing with a political entity, such as a city, and may be considered to be a special case of the migration element. The relationship may be written in general form:

$$P_{t+\theta} = P_t + N_\theta + M_\theta$$

where N_θ = net natural increase during period θ, and
  M_θ = net migration during period θ.

Table 1 presents some selected forecasts by growth composition analysis.[47]

---

[47] Extensive use has been made of methods of growth composition analysis in projecting the population of closed areas, for which data on the elements involved has been more readily available than for open areas. Early development of these methods in the United States, especially of the more refined techniques, is associated chiefly with the names of P. K. Whelpton [331, 333, 336] and W. S. Thompson [295]. Starting in the late 1920's, they have prepared, individually or in association, a series of projections of the population of the United States by these methods; see [296–300, 334, 337]. The later Whelpton and Thompson projections were prepared for the United States government and form part of a series, published by various government agencies, which also includes forecasts made by the U. S. Bureau of the Census in 1949 [305], by J. S. Siegel and H. L. White in 1950 [255], by R. J. Myers and E. A. Rasor in 1952 [161], and by R. A. Hornseth in 1953 [110]. Table 1 is a summary of some of these estimates. See

TABLE 1. SELECTED UNITED STATES POPULATION FORECASTS BY GROWTH COMPOSITION ANALYSIS

(000 omitted)

Year	Census Count	Whelpton 1928 [336]	1933 [299]	Thompson and Whelpton 1938 [300] Low	1938 [300] High	1943 [297] Low	1943 [297] High	Whelpton 1947 [337] Low	1947 [337] High	Siegel and White 1950 [255] Low	1950 [255] High	Myers and Rasor 1952 [161] Low	1952 [161] High
1920	105,711	—	—	—	—	—	—	—	—	—	—	—	—
1930	122,755	123,600	—	—	—	—	—	—	—	—	—	—	—
1940	131,669	138,250	133,100	131,157	132,496	—	—	—	—	—	—	—	—
1950	150,697	151,620	142,900	136,177	144,247	142,989	145,206	144,922	147,986	150,944	151,618	154,900	154,900
1955	165,248ᵃ	—	—	137,172	149,786	145,912	151,272	147,990	155,126	157,738	165,741	165,555	165,624
1960	—	162,670	149,800	137,089	154,941	147,653	156,841	149,827	162,011	161,241	179,839	172,855	174,403
1970	—	171,460	153,800	134,049	164,672	148,729	167,967	151,627	177,118	—	—	182,727	190,851
1980	—	—	155,200	127,571	173,541	145,820	179,001	—	—	—	—	194,730	211,483
1990	—	—	—	—	—	138,851	188,902	—	—	—	—	203,610	232,117
2000	—	—	—	—	—	129,071	198,561	—	—	—	—	210,197	254,456

ᵃ Census estimate.

1. NATURAL INCREASE METHODS

The natural increase methods are the least refined of the techniques of composition analysis. Migration is completely ignored, by either of two assumptions concerning in-migration and out-migration: (1) that neither takes place, or (2) that they balance each other. Thus, these methods are concerned only with the biological determinants of population growth.

In their crudest form, the forecast population is obtained as follows:

$$P_{t+\theta} = P_t + \alpha P_t - \beta P_t$$

where α = the expected crude birth rate for the period θ, and
         β = the expected crude death rate for the period θ.

These expected crude birth and death rates may be determined by a subjective analysis of the past trend or by any of the methods of extrapolation previously described. In any event, they are subject to the limitations already discussed.[48]

An improvement in the projections might be expected if: (1) year-by-year changes in the total population to which the rates apply are recognized; (2) birth rates are derived from fertility or net reproduction rates; and (3) different rates are applied to the several ethnic, age, sex, and other components of the population.

One of the more precise variations of the technique is the "cohort-survival" method.[49]   Here account is taken of differences in birth and death rates for various age and sex groups and, commonly, for racial origin. The initial population is disaggregated, customarily into five-year age groups, according to sex and racial origin. The number of survivors of each of these groups is calculated from age-specific mortality tables or life tables, for time intervals of usually one or five years. For each time interval, the natural increase of population is projected by: (1) obtaining the expected number of births through multiplying age-specific birth rates

also L. Dublin [71] for a similar series of projections made at about the same time as the earliest of the Whelpton and Thompson projections.

For discussions of the development and use of these methods in Europe and elsewhere, see D. V. Glass [85], E. C. Rhodes [214], and F. W. Notestein [173]. Examples of the early use of these techniques in projecting the population of open areas, as developed originally by the Bell Telephone Company in the 1920's, are to be found in F. H. Sterns [275] and N. L. Engelhardt and F. Engelhardt [77]. See also F. Lorimer and F. Osborn [144] and F. Lorimer [143].

[48] Early in the development of these methods it was recognized that migration could not properly be ignored. Thus, estimates from only net natural increase are to be found, usually, as but one of a number of projections by variations of the composition analysis methods. See, for example, Tacoma City Planning Commission [284], Detroit City Planning Commission [69], and U. S. National Housing Agency [309].

[49] For a technical discussion of this method see A. J. Jaffe [124], ch. 7.

by the average number of women in each of the age groups of child-bearing age; and (2) calculating the number of survivors of these births via infant mortality rates. The number of survivors in this lowest age group is then added to the number of survivors in the other categories, already calculated. This procedure is repeated for each time interval up to the forecast date.

Results obtained from cohort-survival techniques can be expected to be only as accurate as the mortality and birth rates assumed for the forecast period. These may be based subjectively on past trends or may be extrapolated by the previous methods. Precision of calculation and further disaggregation, based on such characteristics as occupation and income, cannot compensate for limitations in the validity of the vital rates. Where vital rates are fairly reliable and *where in-migration and out-migration have on balance a negligible influence on both number and composition*, this method can be very useful, especially when information about the future composition of the population is desired.

2. INFLOW-OUTFLOW ANALYSIS

The previous natural increase methods can be extended to incorporate the influence of in-migration and out-migration. Inflow of population is defined as the sum of births and in-migration and outflow as the sum of deaths and out-migration. In general form the relationship is

$$P_{t+\theta} = P_t + (\alpha P_t + \gamma) - (\beta P_t + \delta)$$

where α = birth rate during period θ;
        β = death rate during period θ;
        γ = in-migration during period θ; and
        δ = out-migration during period θ.

Regardless of which of the natural increase methods is extended, it is necessary first to project migration, in order to apply to the migrant population appropriate birth and death rates.

Future migration, either in terms of numbers or rates, may be projected (1) subjectively, (2) from analysis of the regional economy and society by methods to be described in subsequent chapters, (3) by extrapolation from past data, to be discussed in the following chapter, or (4) by some combination of these procedures.

In the inflow-outflow method where birth and death rates are applied to *total* population numbers, as in the simplest of the natural increase methods, only figures on total net migration are needed. Where net reproduction or fertility rates are applied to the female population, migrants need to be identified as to sex. Where cohort-survival techniques are utilized, figures for net migration need to be disaggregated by age, sex, etc., in the same fashion as for resident population. In fact, strict rigor would require disaggregation for both in-migration and out-migration, and not merely for net migration.[50]

Clearly, where statistics on migration of such a detailed character are not obtainable, or where, at most, crude migration estimates are possible, the use of the more precise inflow-outflow methods cannot be justified.[51] The precision and refinement in the projection of certain growth elements do not significantly reduce the range of error in total and component population estimates stemming from the crudity of migration estimates. These precise inflow-outflow methods therefore find their greatest usefulness and validity when other methods of analysis can yield reliable information on the number, composition, and timing of migration to be anticipated.

On the other hand, excellent projections on the number, composition, and timing of in- and out-migration do not necessarily guarantee equally fine total population projections. Despite complete census and other data,

[50] Examples of the projection of the population of open areas from net natural increase plus net migration include studies for Broome County, New York [23]; New York City [56]; Metropolitan Detroit [210]; Westchester County, New York [329]; Tulare County, California [127]; California State [79, 264, 272, 328]; Providence, Rhode Island [203]; Mobile, Alabama [157]; and Lethbridge, Alberta [41]. N. Lawrence and B. Greenberg [140] describe a technique whereby age-specific migration figures are added to total net natural increase figures. Examples of projection by cohort-survival techniques, with no migration allowance, include Seattle City Planning Commission [239] and A. Mallach [151].

In 1937 the Wisconsin State Planning Board [343] published population forecasts for the state, based on cohort-survival techniques, with an allowance for total net migration. The estimate of 3,344,938 for 1950 was 3 per cent above the census figure. This study also contains similar estimates for all the principal cities of the state. In 1943 the Los Angeles Planning Commission [145] published similar forecasts for the city. The 1950 estimate of 2 million was $1\frac{1}{2}$ per cent too high. Other examples of the projection of the population of open areas by cohort-survival techniques, with allowance only for total net migration, include studies for Madison, Wisconsin [242]; Kalamazoo, Michigan [129]; Greensboro, North Carolina [92]; the state of Massachusetts [153]; Cleveland, Ohio [113]; Seattle, Washington [240]; and various parts of the United States [193].

Examples of the projection of the population of open areas by the more refined inflow-outflow techniques include L. Worley [351], R. Clapp [52], A. A. Heath [108], California Teachers Association [36], D. J. Bogue [20], and C. M. Frisén [80]. For examples containing particularly complete discussion, see the 1945 Cincinnati study by W. S. Thompson [294] and the 1946 Philadelphia study by S. Kuznets [137]. Thompson's estimates for Cincinnati in 1950 ranged from 455,415 to 485,525; the census count was 503,988. Kuznets' estimate for the city of Philadelphia of 2,023,000 in 1950 was 2 per cent below the census count, and his estimate for the Philadelphia region of 3,445,000 was 6 per cent too low.

[51] See A. J. Jaffe [124] chs. 5 and 6, respectively, for discussion of the problems of enumerating vital statistics and of measuring migration. See also D. J. Bogue [18].

birth and death rates may be subject to considerable unpredictable change during the period of projection (as the United States birth rates during 1940–1950). However, it is argued by some that, generally speaking, over the years migration tends to be more volatile and less predictable than both birth rates and death rates, and that in highly industrialized nations birth rates tend to be less stable and predictable than death rates; thus migration estimates tend to be the source of greatest error for projections for *open* areas.

F. CONCLUSIONS

This cursory examination of population projection techniques indicates the wide range of error possible in the use of any one method. Each must be employed with considerable caution. None per se can be recommended for general use. On balance, no one can be identified as the "best."[52] The problem at hand and the region under study are two of the most influential factors determining the choice of the most appropriate population projection method to be used in a given situation. Only in this sense can one technique be judged superior to another.[53]

[52] For discussion of the accuracy of various methods of population projection see, among others, J. S. Davis [64–66], H. F. Dorn [70], F. Engelhardt [76], H. Hotelling [111], G. C. Houser [112], R. J. Myers and E. A. Rasor [161], R. C. Schmitt and A. H. Crosetti [234–236], J. R. L. Schneider [237], H. Schultz [238], H. S. Shryock [244, 247], J. S. Siegel, H. S. Shryock, and B. Greenberg [254], H. Silcock [256], United Nations Department of Social Affairs [303], and H. R. White [339].

[53] In addition to the various techniques described in this chapter, a number of methods have been derived as the result of empirical observation. In forecasting the population of New York City, E. P. Goodrich [90] developed a method in the 1920's, based on the theory of probability. See also H. James [125]. Goodrich found that by dividing all municipalities in the United States of over 2500 population into groups such that the upper limit of each group was twice the lower limit, the series of numbers consisting of the totals for each group was essentially the same as that produced by counting the sequences in the fair toss of a fair coin. At the same time it was found that the total number of such municipalities had been increasing at a uniform rate during the previous four decades. It was assumed that this rate would continue into the future and a formula, based on probability, was then derived which gave the size of the largest single community at any given time in the future. Because the method was designed specifically to forecast the population of the largest city in the United States, it is doubtful whether it could be applied equally well to other areas.

A second empirical "law" which is of pertinence is the "rank size" rule which is claimed to have widespread validity. See W. Isard [123], pp. 55–60, and B. J. L. Berry and W. L. Garrison [13] for discussion and citation of the more important theoretical and empirical studies on this rule. This rule is given by the equation

$$r \cdot P^q = K; \qquad \text{or } P^q = K/r$$

where q and K are predetermined constants for a given meaningful set of cities, r indicates the rank of a given city in terms of population, and P is its population. If

It is clear that population projection techniques must be supplemented with other methods of analysis to attain a validity and certainty of the order usually desirable in social science research. In the following chapters some of the existing techniques which are logical concomitants of population projections will be discussed. We indicate, especially in Chapter 12, their linkage to population projections and how they permit valid and fruitful "indirect" population projections.

References

1. Alabama State Planning Board, *Health and Medical Care in Alabama*, Birmingham, Alabama, May 1945.
2. Alexander, J. W., *Economic Base Study of Madison, Wisconsin*, University of Wisconsin, School of Commerce, Madison, Wisconsin, 1953.
3. Ali, M. Ahmed, *Modesto Looks Ahead*, City Planning Commission, Modesto, California, Dec. 1949.
4. Alves Martins, C. M., "A Sociometric Approach of Human Ecology," Lisbon, 1955, paper submitted to the U.N. World Population Conference, Rome, Sept. 1954.
5. American Society of Planning Officials, "Population Forecasting," *Planning Advisory Service*, Information Report No. 17, Chicago, Aug. 1950.
6. Bartholomew, Harland, *Comprehensive City Plan*, City Planning Board, Utica, New York, March 1950.
7. ———, *Comprehensive City Plan, St. Louis, Missouri*, City Planning Commission, St. Louis, Missouri, 1947.
8. ———, *The Comprehensive City Plan for Schenectady, New York*, City Planning Commission, Schenectady, New York, Sept. 1948.
9. ———, *Major Street Report for South Bend, Indiana*, St. Louis, Missouri, 1924.
10. ———, *The Master Plan for New Orleans: Population*, City Planning and Zoning Commission, New Orleans, Louisiana, June 1949.
11. ———, *A Preliminary Report on Past, Present, and Probable Future Population*, Report No. 3, City Planning Commission, Richmond, Virginia, Aug. 1941.
12. ———, *Wichita's Population, its Background, Growth, and Future Pattern: the Basis of the Master Plan*, City Planning Commission, Wichita, Kansas, Oct. 1943.

---

the United States is considered a meaningful entity, and if for the United States q is unity, as G. K. Zipf [355, 356] contends, then K represents the population of the largest city or metropolitan area (New York). And the rule states that to derive the population of any given city (or metropolitan area), divide the population of New York City (or metropolitan region) by the rank of the given city (or metropolitan area). According to the rule, as applied to the United States, the largest city is twice the size of the second, three times the size of the third, etc. Hence, if K (or total population residing in cities of 2500 or more, or some other magnitude from which K can be derived) can be projected, and also if the rank (r) of a given city (or metropolitan area) can be projected, the population of that city (or metropolitan area) may also be projected by this rule. When possible, such *indirect* projection may at times yield firmer estimates than direct projection of the type discussed in this chapter.

13. Berry, B. J. L,, and W. L. Garrison, "Alternate Explanations of Urban Rank-Size Relationships," *Annals of the Association of American Geographers*, Vol. 48 (March 1958).

14. Bocaz S., Albino, "The Gompertz Curve Applied to the City of Santiago," *Estadistica Chilena*, Vols. 10, 11 (Oct.–Nov. 1953).

15. ———, "The Gompertz Curve Applied to the Growth of the Chilean Population," *Estadistica Chilena*, Vol. 7 (July 1953).

16. ———, "The Population Curve of Chile," *Estadistica Chilena*, Vol. 9 (Sept. 1953).

17. Bogue D. J., *An Estimate of Metropolitan Chicago's Future Population: 1955 to 1965*, a report to the Chicago Plan Commission and the Office of the Housing and Redevelopment Coordinator, published jointly by the Chicago Community Inventory, University of Chicago, and the Scripps Foundation, Miami University, Oxford, Ohio, Feb. 2, 1955.

18. ———, *A Methodological Study of Migration and Labor Mobility in Michigan and Ohio in 1947*, Scripps Foundation Studies in Population Distribution No. 4, Miami University, Oxford, Ohio, June 1952.

19. ———, "A Technique for Making Extensive Population Estimates," *Journal of the American Statistical Association*, Vol. 45 (June 1950).

20. ———, and D. L. Harris, *Comparative Population and Urban Research via Multiple Regression and Covariance Analysis*, Scripps Foundation, Miami University, Oxford, Ohio, and Population Research and Training Center, University of Chicago, Studies in Population Distribution No. 8, 1954.

21. Bowley, A. L., "Births and Population of Great Britain," *Journal of the Royal Economic Society*, Vol. 34 (1934).

22. ———, "discussion on 'The Laws Governing Population,' paper by T. H. C. Stevenson," *Journal of the Royal Statistical Society*, Vol. 88 (Jan. 1925).

23. Broome County Planning Board, *Population Predictions for Broome County*, Binghamton, New York, April 1950.

24. Brown, Hugh H., "Intercensal Estimates of Population, January 1, for Years Between 1940 and 1950 Censuses," *Tax Digest*, Vol. 32 (Jan. 1954).

25. ———, "People Come—and People Go," *Tax Digest*, Vol. 32 (March 1954).

26. ———, "Population of California Counties—Estimates as of January 1st," *Tax Digest*, Vol. 32 (Dec. 1954).

27. ———, "A Technique for Estimating the Population of Counties," *Journal of the American Statistical Association*, Vol. 50 (June 1955).

28. ———, "What About 1960? And A.D. 2000?" *Tax Digest*, California Taxpayers' Association, Vol. 28 (Oct. 1950).

29. Bryant, W. D., *Housing Market Analysis of Greater Kansas City*, Department of Research and Information, Report No. 6, Kansas City, Missouri, Dec. 1945.

30. Bucks County Planning Commission, *Population and Housing, Lower Bucks County*, Doylestown, Pennsylvania, March 1954.

31. Buffalo City Planning Commission, *Looking at Buffalo's Population in 1975*, Buffalo, New York, April 1949.

32. California, State Department of Finance, *Estimated Population of California's Areas and Counties, 1950–1955*, Sacramento, California, 1955.

33. ———, *Projected Population of California by Broad Age Groups, 1956–1966*, Sacramento, California, 1955.

34. California Population Commission, *California by 1950*, Sacramento, California, 1943.

35. California State Reconstruction and Reemployment Commission, *Second Report on Postwar Employment in California*, prepared under direction of V. B. Stanbery, Sacramento, California, Sept. 1945.

36. California Teachers Association, *California's Future School Population: 1948–1960*, Research Bulletin No. 3, San Francisco, Oct. 1948.

37. Calvert, G. N., *The Future Population of New Zealand: A Statistical Analysis*, The King's Printer, Wellington, New Zealand, 1946.

38. Campbell, D. S., and D. Brown, "Population Forecasts of the New England–New York Area," *Business Information Service*, U. S. Department of Commerce, Area Development Division, Office of Industry and Commerce, Washington, D.C., Oct. 1952.

39. Canada, Dominion Bureau of Statistics, *Memorandum on the Projection of Population Statistics, 1954*, The Queen's Printer, Ottawa, 1954.

40. Carroll, M. M., and S. Weber, *School and Preschool Population*, Department of Planning, Greensboro, North Carolina, 1950.

41. Carrothers, Gerald A. P., *Survey for Planning—1951: A Study of Factors Affecting the Growth of Lethbridge, Alberta*, School of Architecture, University of Manitoba, Winnipeg, 1951.

42. Casanova, T., "The Growth of the Population of Puerto Rico," *Social Forces*, Vol. 24 (March 1946).

43. Case, R. A. M., "Cohort Analysis of Mortality Rates as an Historical or Narrative Technique," *British Journal of Preventive and Social Medicine*, Vol. 10 (Oct. 1956).

44. Casey, Harry J., "The Law of Retail Gravitation Applied to Traffic Engineering," *Traffic Quarterly*, Vol. 9 (July 1955).

45. Chamberlain, Leo M., and A. B. Crawford, *The Prediction of Population and School Enrollment in the School Survey*, University of Kentucky, Lexington, Kentucky, 1932.

46. Chapel Hill Town Planning Board, *Population and Economy*, Chapel Hill, North Carolina, April 1949.

47. Chapin, F. S., "Employment Forecasts for City Planning," *Journal of the American Institute of Planners*, Vol. 20 (Spring 1954).

48. Chapman, W. D., and C. F. Riley, *Granite City: A Plan for Aberdeen*, for the Corporation of the City and Royal Burgh of Aberdeen, Batsford, London, 1952.

49. Charles, Enid, N. Keyfitz, and H. Roseborough, *The Future Population of Canada*, Dominion Bureau of Statistics, Bulletin No. F-4, Ottawa, 1946.

50. Chicago Plan Commission, *Population Facts for Planning Chicago*, Chicago, Feb. 1942.

51. Cincinnati City Planning Commission, "The Economy of the Cincinnati Metropolitan Area," *Cincinnati Metropolitan Master Plan Study*, Cincinnati, Ohio, Dec. 1946.

52. Clapp, Raymond, *Population Change and Governmental Planning in the District of Columbia*, Budget Office, Washington, D.C., May 1952.

53. Cleveland, Regional Association of, *Population Forecasts for Suburban Areas of Greater Cleveland*, Plan Bulletin No. 8, Cleveland, Ohio, Jan. 1942.

54. Cleveland City Planning Commission, *The General Plan of Cleveland*, Cleveland, Ohio, Dec. 1950.

55. Columbia Basin Inter-Agency Committee, Subcommittee on Comprehensive Program, *Population Projections for the Pacific Northwest States and Region, 1960 and 1975*, July 21, 1952.

56. Consolidated Edison Company of New York, *New York City's Population Growth, 1790–1970*, Consolidated Edison Co., Economic Research Department, New York, Dec. 1946.

57. Cox, P. R., "Population Projections: Notes on the Choice of Bases," *Journal of the Actuaries Students' Society*, Part 2, Vol. 11 (1952).

58. Crampon, L. J., and others, *Report on the Economic Potential of Western Colorado*, report to the Colorado Water Conservation Board, Bureau of Business Research, University of Colorado, Boulder, Colorado, 1953.

59. Crosetti, A. H., and Jean Moehring, "Population Trends and Projections, Seattle Standard Metropolitan Area by Major Divisions: 1920–1970," *Current Planning Research*, No. 14, City Planning Commission, Seattle, Washington, April 1, 1954.

60. ———, and Robert C. Schmitt, "A Method of Estimating the Intercensal Population of Counties," *Journal of the American Statistical Association*, Vol. 51 (Dec. 1956).

61. Croxton, F. E., and D. J. Cowden, *Applied General Statistics*, Prentice-Hall, New York, 1939.

62. Curtis Publishing Company, Research Department, *Projections of the United States Population by Age and Sex, 1954–1975*, Release 213, Curtis Publishing Co., Philadelphia, 1954.

63. Davies, G. R., "The Growth Curve," *Journal of the American Statistical Association*, Vol. 22 (Sept. 1927).

64. Davis, Joseph S., "Our Changed Population Outlook and Its Significance," *American Economic Review*, Vol. 17 (June 1952).

65. ———, "The Population Upsurge and the American Economy, 1945–80," *Journal of Political Economy*, Vol. 61 (Oct. 1953).

66. ———, *The Population Upsurge in the United States*, Food Research Institute, War-Peace Pamphlets No. 12, Stanford University, Standford, California, Dec. 1949.

67. Davis K., "Demographic Fact and Policy in India," *Milbank Memorial Fund Quarterly*, Vol. 22 (July 1944).

68. Denver Planning Commission, *The Denver Plan, Volume I*, Denver, Colorado, Dec. 27, 1929.

69. Detroit City Plan Commission, *The People of Detroit*, City Planning Commission, Master Plan Reports, Detroit, 1946.

70. Dorn, H. F., "Pitfalls in Population Forecasts and Projections," *Journal of the American Statistical Association*, Vol. 45 (Sept. 1950).

71. Dublin, L. I., "The Outlook for the American Birth Rate," in *Problems of Population*, Proceedings of the International Union for Scientific Investigation of Population Problems, George Allen and Unwin, London, 1932, pp. 115–123.

72. ———, ed., *Population Problems in the United States and Canada*, Houghton Mifflin, Boston, 1926.

73. Duncan, O. D., and R. W. Redick, "Illustrative Projections of College Enrollment in Illinois and the Chicago Standard Metropolitan Area to 1990," *Journal of General Education*, Vol. 8 (Jan. 1955).

74. Eberle, F. J., "Population Estimates of Local Communities and Economic Planning," *Journal of the American Statistical Association*, Vol. 33 (Dec. 1938).

75. Eldridge, Hope T., "Suggested Procedures for Estimating the Current Population of Counties," *Population—Special Reports*, Series P-47, No. 4. U. S. Bureau of the Census, Washington, D.C., 1947.

76. Engelhardt, Fred, *Forecasting School Population*, Columbia University Teachers College, New York, 1925.

77. Engelhardt, N. L., and Fred Engelhardt, *Planning School Building Programs*, Columbia University Teachers College, New York, 1930.

78. Ezekiel, Mordecai, *Methods of Correlation Analysis*, 2nd ed., John Wiley, New York, 1941.

79. Frisén, C. M., *Estimated Population of California, 1950–1954 with Projections to 1965*, California State Department of Finance, Division of Budgets and Accounts, Financial Research Section, Sacramento, California, July 1954.

80. ———, *Projections of Public School Enrollment in California to 1960 and 1965*, California State Department of Finance, Division of Budgets and Accounts, Financial Research Section, Sacramento, California, April 1954.

81. Garnsey, Morris E., and R. E. Pelz, *A Projection of the Population of Colorado*, University of Colorado Studies, Series in Economics, No. 2, Boulder, Colorado, 1955.

82. Gibbs, J. B., and W. T. Martin, "The Components of Population Growth and The Process of Change in Counties of the Pacific Northwest, 1940–50," *State College of Washington Research Studies*, Pullman, Washington, Vol. 22 (June 1954).

83. Gini, Corrado, "A Coordination of the Different Population Theories," *Revue de l'institut international de statistique*, Vol. 11 (1943).

84. Glass, D. V., "Estimates of Future Populations of Various Countries," *Eugenics Review*, Vol. 35 (Oct. 1943, Jan. 1944).

85. ———, *Population Policies and Movements in Europe*, Clarendon Press, Oxford, England, 1940.

86. Glick, P. C., "Estimates of the Future Number of Families," *American Journal of Sociology*, Vol. 52 (Nov. 1946).

87. ———, "Estimates of Number of Families in the United States: 1940 to 1960," *Population—Special Reports*, Series P-46, No. 4, U. S. Bureau of the Census, Washington, D.C., June 1, 1946.

88. ———, Elizabeth A. Larmon, and E. Landau, "Projections of the Number of Households and Families 1955 and 1960," *Current Population Reports, Population Characteristics*, Series P-20, No. 42, U. S. Bureau of the Census, Washington, D.C., Dec. 28, 1952.

89. Goodrich, E. P., reported in notes on "Meeting on the Problem of Forecasting City Population with Special Reference to New York City," October 30, 1925, *Journal of the American Statistical Association*, Vol. 20 (Dec. 1925).

90. ———, "The Statistical Relationship Between Population and the City Plan," *Papers and Proceedings of the American Sociological Society*, Vol. 20 (1925).

91. Greenberg, Benjamin, "Illustrative Example of a Method of Estimating the Current Population of Subdivisions of the United States," *Current Population Reports, Population Estimates*, Series P-25, No. 133, U. S. Bureau of the Census, Washington, D.C., March 1956.

92. Greensboro, N. C., Department of Planning, *Future Employment and Population in the Greensboro Metropolitan Area*, Technical Report No. 1, Greensboro, North Carolina, June 1948.

93. Hagood, Margaret J., *Prospects for Regional Distribution of the Population of the United States*, U. S. Bureau of Agricultural Economics, Washington, D.C., Nov. 1949.

94. ———, *Statistics for Sociologists*, Holt, New York, 1941.

95. Hagood, Margaret J., and L. Persh, *Population Projections by Age and Sex for the Mountain and Pacific Divisions, 1975*, U. S. Bureau of Agricultural Economics, Washington, D.C., Dec. 2, 1947.

96. ———, and E. F. Sharp, *Rural–Urban Migration in Wisconsin, 1940–1950*, Research Bulletin 176, University of Wisconsin, Madison, Wisconsin, Aug. 1951.

97. ———, and ———, "Wisconsin's Population, 1940–1950," *Economic Information for Wisconsin Farmers*, University of Wisconsin, Vol. 22 (Sept.–Oct. 1951).

98. ———, and J. S. Siegel, "Population Projections for Sales Forecasting," *Journal of the American Statistical Association*, Vol. 47 (Sep. 1952).

99. ———, and ———, "Projections of the Regional Distribution of the Population of the United States to 1975," *Agricultural Economics Research*, U. S. Department of Agriculture, Vol. 3 (April 1951).

100. Hajnal, John, "The Prospects for Population Forecasts," *Journal of the American Statistical Association*, Vol. 50 (June 1955).

101. Hamilton, C. H., and F. M. Henderson, "Use of the Survival Rate Method in Measuring Net Migration," *Journal of the American Statistical Association*, Vol. 39 (June 1944).

102. Hart, H., "Logistic Social Trends," *American Journal of Sociology*, Vol. 50 (March 1945).

103. Hauser, Philip M., "How Declining Urban Growth Affects City Activities," *Public Management*, Vol. 22 (Dec. 1940).

104. ———, "Population Shifts and Income Changes," *Marketing Series*, No. 52. American Management Association, New York, Jan. 1943.

105. ———, "Wartime Population Changes and Postwar Prospects," *Journal of Marketing*, Vol. 8 (Jan. 1944).

106. ———, and Hope T. Eldridge, "Projection of Urban Growth and Migration to Cities in the United States," *Milbank Memorial Fund Quarterly*, Vol. 25 (July 1947).

107. Hawley, A. H., *The Population of Michigan, 1840 to 1960: an Analysis of Growth, Distribution, and Composition*, University of Michigan Governmental Studies No. 19, Ann Arbor, Michigan, 1949.

108. Heath, A. A., "Population Forecasting for Planning Purposes," *Journal of the Town Planning Institute*, Vol. 34 (Jan.–Feb. 1948).

109. Held, Harry, "New York City in the Postwar World," *Harvard Business Review*, Vol. 21 (Summer 1943).

110. Hornseth, R. A., "Illustrative Projections of the Population of the United States, By Age and Sex: 1955 to 1975," *Current Population Reports—Population Estimates*, Series P-25, No. 78, U. S. Bureau of the Census, Washington, D.C., Aug. 21, 1953.

111. Hotelling, Harold, "Differential Equations Subject to Error and Population Estimates," *Journal of the American Statistical Association*, Vol. 22 (Sept. 1927).

112. Houser, G. C., "How Accurately Can Engineers Predict Future Population Growth of Cities?" *The American City*, Vol. 39 (Sept. 1928).

113. Howard, J. T., *Preliminary Estimates of Future Population*, Regional Association of Cleveland, Publication No. 6, Cleveland, Ohio, Sept. 1939.

114. Hoyt, Homer, *Economic Survey of Montgomery and Prince George Counties, Maryland*, Homer Hoyt Associates, Washington, D.C., Jan. 1955.

115. ———, *Economic Survey of the Land Uses of Arlington County, Virginia*, Department of Public Service, Arlington County, Virginia, 1951.

116. ———, "Homer Hoyt on Development of Economic Base Concept," *Land Economics*, Vol. 30 (May 1954).

117. Hoyt, Homer, "Is City Growth Controlled by Mathematics or Physical Laws?" *Land Economics*, Vol. 27 (Aug. 1951).

118. Hunter, R., *Poverty*, Macmillan, New York, 1917.

119. Hutchinson, E. P., "The Use of Routine Census and Vital Statistics Data for the Determination of Migration by Age and Sex," Appendix C2 in Dorothy S. Thomas, *Research Memorandum on Migration Differentials*, Social Science Research Council, New York, 1938.

120. Iklé, F. C., "Sociological Relationship of Traffic to Population and Distance," *Traffic Quarterly*, Vol. 8 (April 1954).

121. Industrial Survey Associates, *The Future of Industry in the San Bernardino Valley*, prepared for the San Bernardino Valley Industrial Committee, San Francisco, April 23, 1951.

122. ———, *Mendocino County, Its Economic Assets, Needs and Prospects*, prepared for the Mendocino County Chamber of Commerce, San Francisco, Feb. 1951.

123. Isard, Walter, *Location and Space–Economy*, John Wiley, New York, 1956.

124. Jaffe, A. J., *Handbook of Statistical Methods for Demographers*, preliminary ed., 2nd printing, U. S. Bureau of the Census, Washington, D.C., 1951.

125. James, H., "Estimates of Future Population," in *Population, Land Values and Government*, Vol. 2, Regional Survey of New York and its Environs, Regional Plan of New York and Its Environs, New York, 1929.

126. Janer, J. L., "Population Growth in Puerto Rico and Its Relation to Time Changes in Vital Statistics," *Human Biology*, Vol. 17 (Dec. 1945).

127. Johnson, G. B., and D. Driver, *Preliminary Population Estimates for Tulare County, California 1950–1980*, Planning Commission, Tulare County, California, Nov. 1952.

128. Johnson, W. I., *Report of Future Population of Cuyahoga County*, Regional Planning Commission, Division of Regional Planning, Cleveland, Ohio, June 6, 1950, preliminary draft.

129. Kalamazoo City Planning Commission, *The Population of Kalamazoo, Michigan*, City Plan Report No. 3, Kalamazoo, Michigan, Nov. 1950.

130. Karpinos, B. D., "Stabilized Method of Forecasting Population," *Public Health Reports*, United States Public Health Service, Vol. 54 (Oct. 1939).

131. Keller, J. D., "Growth Curves of Nations," *Human Biology*, Vol. 18 (Dec. 1946).

132. Kelley, S. C., Jr., and others, *The Population, Labor Force, and Income of North Dakota, 1900–1975*, University of North Dakota, Bureau of Economic and Business Research (in cooperation with the U. S. Bureau of Reclamation), North Dakota Economic Studies No. 1, Grand Forks, North Dakota, 1954.

133. Kidner, F. L. R., and P. Neff, *An Economic Survey of the Los Angeles Area*, Haynes Foundation, Monograph No. 7, Los Angeles, 1945.

134. Kirk, Dudley, "Population Trends in Postwar Europe," *The Annals of the American Academy of Political and Social Science*, Vol. 237 (Jan. 1945).

135. Kiser, C. V., "The Demographic Position of Egypt," *Milbank Memorial Fund Quarterly*, Vol. 22 (Oct. 1944).

136. Kubek, R., *Inter–Census Estimation of Population Trends*, City Planning Commission, Grand Rapids, Michigan, May 27, 1948.

137. Kuznets, Simon S., *The Population of Philadelphia and Environs in 1950*. Institute of Local and State Government, University of Pennsylvania, Philadelphia, 1946.

138. Landau, Emanuel, "Projections of the Number of Households and Families: 1960 to 1975," *Current Population Reports, Population Characteristics*, Series P-20, No. 69, U. S. Bureau of the Census, Washington, D.C., Aug. 31, 1956.

139. Landis, P. H., *Population Problems*, American Book, New York, 1943.
140. Lawrence, N., and B. Greenberg, "Illustrative Examples of Two Methods of Estimating the Current Population of Small Areas," *Current Population Reports, Population Estimates*, Series P-25, No. 20, U. S. Bureau of the Census, Washington, D.C., May 6, 1949.
141. Lehman, Leland C., *Population Trends in the Ninth District*, Research Department, Federal Reserve Bank of Minneapolis, Minneapolis, Minnesota, April 15, 1956.
142. León, A. P., and C. A. Aldama, "Population Problems in Central and Caribbean America," *Annals of the American Academy of Political and Social Science*, Vol. 237 (Jan. 1945).
143. Lorimer, Frank, *Suggestions on Population Studies for State Planning Boards*, revised ed., U. S. National Resources Committee, Washington, D.C., 1938.
144. ——, and F. Osborn, *Dynamics of Population*, Macmillan, New York, 1934.
145. Los Angeles City Planning Commission, *Accomplishments 1943*, Los Angeles, 1944.
146. Lotka, 'A. J., "Some Recent Results in Population Analysis," *Journal of the American Statistical Association*, Vol. 33 (March 1938).
147. McLean, J. E., "More Accurate Population Estimates by Means of Logistic Curves," *Civil Engineering*, Vol. 22 (Feb. 1952).
148. MacLean, M. C., "Projection of Canada's Population on the Basis of Current Birth and Death Rates, 1931–1971," *Canadian Papers*, 6th Conference of the Institute of Pacific Relations, Yosemite National Park, California, 1936.
149. ——, and A. W. Turner, "The Logistic Curve Applied to Canada's Population," *Canadian Journal of Economics and Political Science*, Vol. 3 (May 1937).
150. McNamara, K., "Bibliography on the Economic Base," *Land Economics*, Vol. 30 (May 1954).
151. Mallach, A., *Population Trends in Southwestern Pennsylvania*, prepared for Allegheny Conference on Community Development, Pittsburgh, Pennsylvania, Feb. 1947.
152. Maryland State Planning Commission, *A Functional Plan for the Baltimore Metropolitan District*, Annapolis, Maryland, April 15, 1948.
153. Massachusetts State Planning Board, "Population Study of Massachusetts," *A Planning Forum*, Vol. 2 (March 1938).
154. Mayer, H. M., "Current and Prospective Population Trends," *Appraisal Journal*, Vol. 23 (April 1955).
155. Menhinick, H. K., ed., *Local Planning Administration* (see also earlier edition ed. by L. Segoe), International City Managers Association, Chicago, 1948.
156. Milwaukee County Regional Planning Department, *Population: Milwaukee County, Wisconsin; Facts and Forecasts*, Milwaukee County, Wisconsin, 1945.
157. Mobile City Planning Commission, *Housing Market Analysis*, Mobile, Alabama, Aug. 1945.
158. Moore, E., and J. F. Staehle, "Estimates of Population of Oregon for 1948–1960," in *People, Jobs, and Income on the Pacific Coast, 1949–1960*, Pacific Coast Board of Inter-Governmental Relations, San Francisco, 1949.
159. Muhsam, Helmut V., "The Utilization of Alternative Population Forecasts in Planning," *Bulletin of the Research Council of Israel*, Vol. 5 (March–June 1956).
160. Myers, Robert J., "Comparison of Demographic Rates Assumed by the National Resources Committee with Actual Experience," *Journal of the American Statistical Association*, Vol. 38 (June 1943).
161. ——, and E. A. Rasor, *Illustrative United States Population Projections, 1952*, U. S. Federal Security Agency, Social Security Administration, Actuarial Study No. 33, Washington, D.C., Nov. 1952.

162. Myers, Robert J., and E. A. Rasor, *Long–Range Cost Estimates for Old–Age and Survivors' Insurance 1954*, U. S. Social Security Administration, Actuarial Study No. 39, Washington, D.C., 1954.

163. Myklebost, H., "Population Forecasts by Simple Methodology, "*Land Economics*, Vol. 26 (Aug. 1950).

164. Nader, A., *The Bio-Economic Problem of India : India's Population Problem from a New Angle of View*, Vidya Mandir Ltd., New Delhi, 1940.

165. Narain, B., *The Curve of Population*, Ripon Press, Lahore, Pakistan, 1942.

166. Nash, Peter H., "Techniques for Calculating Demographic Changes and Density Standards," in *Planning, 1950*, American Society of Planning Officials, Chicago, 1951.

167. National Capital Park and Planning Commission, *Washington, Present and Future*, Monograph No. 1, Washington, D.C., April 1950.

168. New Jersey Department of Conservation and Economic Development, *Projection of Population in New Jersey by Counties, 1960*, Trenton, New Jersey, May 1952.

169. New York Regional Plan Association, *Population, 1954–1975, in the New Jersey–New York–Connecticut Metropolitan Region*, Regional Plan Bulletin 85, New York, Nov. 1954.

170. Newark Central Planning Board, *A Preliminary Report on Past, Present, and Probable Future Population for Newark, N.J.*, Report No. 3, Newark, New Jersey, 1944.

171. Nielson, Howard C., *Population Trends in the United States through 1975*, Stanford Research Institute, Menlo Park, California, 1955.

172. Notestein, F. W., "Population—the Long View," in *Food for the World*, ed. by T. W. Schultz, University of Chicago Press, Chicago, 1945.

173. ———, and others, *The Future Population of Europe and the Soviet Union*, League of Nations, Geneva, 1944.

174. Ogburn, W. F., *War, Babies, and the Future*, Public Affairs Committee, Inc., Public Affairs Pamphlets No. 83, New York, 1943.

175. Ohio State Planning Board, *Future Population of the State of Ohio*, Columbus, Ohio, 1937.

176. Oklahoma City Planning Commission, *The Comprehensive City Plan*, Harland Bartholomew, consultant, Oklahoma City, Oklahoma, July 1949.

177. Omaha City Planning Commission, *Omaha, Nebraska—Chapter One : Population*, Omaha, Nebraska, March 1945.

178. Oshkosh, Wisconsin, Planning Commission, *A Complete Population Survey*, Oshkosh, Wisconsin, 1950.

179. Pacific Coast Board of Intergovernmental Relations, *Basic Assumptions and Factors Considered in Estimating Increases of Population; Labor Force and Employment in the Pacific Coast States, 1948–60*, San Francisco, Jan. 1949.

180. ———, *Economic Outlook for the Pacific Coast, 1950–1960*, San Francisco, Jan. 1950.

181. ———, *People, Jobs, and Income on the Pacific Coast, 1949–60*, San Francisco, 1949.

182. Palmer, G. L., and A. Ratner, *Labor Force and Employment Estimates for Philadelphia and Environs with a Projection for 1950*, Institute of Local and State Government, University of Pennsylvania, Philadelphia, 1946.

183. Pearl, Raymond, *The Biology of Population Growth*, 2nd ed., Alfred A. Knopf, New York, 1930.

184. Pearl, Raymond, "The Curve of Population Growth," *Proceedings of the American Philosophical Society*, Vol. 63 (1924).

185. ———, *Introduction to Medical Biometry and Statistics*, 3rd ed., W. B. Saunders, Philadelphia, 1940.

186. ———, *Studies in Human Biology*, Williams and Wilkins, Baltimore, Maryland, 1924.

187. ———, and L. J. Reed, "A Further Note on the Mathematical Theory of Population Growth," *Proceedings of the National Academy of Science*, Vol. 8 (1922).

188. ———, and ———, "On the Mathematical Theory of Population Growth," *Metron*, Vol. 3 (1923).

189. ———, and ———, "On the Rate of Growth of the Population of the United States Since 1790 and its Mathematical Representation," *Proceedings of the National Academy of Science*, Vol. 6 (1920).

190. ———, and ———, *Predicted Growth of Population of New York and Its Environs*, Plan of New York and Its Environs, New York, 1923.

191. ———, ———, and J. F. Kish, "The Logistic Curve and the Census Count of 1940," *Science*, Vol. 92 (New Series, Dec. 1940).

192. Pearlman, L. M., "Prospective Labor Supply on the West Coast," U. S. Bureau of Labor Statistics, *Monthly Labor Review*, Vol. 64 (April 1947).

193. ———, and L. Eskin, *State and Regional Variations in Prospective Labor Supply*, U. S. Bureau of Labor Statistics, Bulletin No. 893, Washington, D.C., 1947.

194. Pennsylvania State Planning Board, "The Population of Pennsylvania," *Pennsylvania Planning*, Vol. 8 (1942).

195. Pfister, Richard, *Water Requirements Survey in the Wichita–Hutchinson Trading Area*, School of Business, University of Kansas, Lawrence, Kansas, Nov. 1952.

196. Philadelphia, Regional Planning Federation of the Tri-State District, *The Regional Plan of the Philadelphia Tri-State District*, Philadelphia, 1932.

197. Philadelphia City Planning Commission, *Estimates of Future Long-Term Trend of Population Growth in the Philadelphia–Camden Industrial Area 1950–2000*, 2nd ed., Planning Study No. 1, Philadelphia, March 1951.

198. Phoenix City Planning Commission, *Population Study and Forecast*, Phoenix, Arizona, 1947.

199. Pickard, Jerome P., *Population Growth in the Washington Metropolitan Area*, Washington Board of Trade, Economic Development Committee, Washington, D.C., 1956.

200. Prescott, R. D., "Law of Growth in Forecasting Demand," *Journal of the American Statistical Association*, Vol. 18 (Dec. 1922).

201. Pritchett, H. S., "A Formula for Predicting the Population of the United States," *Quarterly Publications of the American Statistical Association*, Predecessor of the *Journal*, Vol. 2 (New Series, June 1891).

202. ———, "The Population of the United States During the Next Ten Centuries," *Popular Science Monthly*, Vol. 58 (Nov. 1900).

203. Providence City Plan Commission, *The Future Population of Providence, 1940–1980*, Publication No. 1, Providence, Rhode Island, Oct. 1945.

204. ———, *Master Plan for Public School Sites*, Publication No. 7, Providence, Rhode Island, March 1950.

205. Rapkin, Chester, L. Winnick, and D. M. Blank, *Housing Market Analysis, A Study of Theory and Methods*, U. S. Housing and Home Finance Agency, Division of Housing Research, Washington, D.C., 1953.

206. Rasor, E. A., "The Fitting of Logistic Curves by Means of a Nomograph," *Journal of the American Statistical Association*, Vol. 44 (Dec. 1949).

207. Reed, L. J., "A Form of Saturation Curve," *Journal of the American Statistical Association*, Vol. 20 (Sept. 1925).

208. ———, "Population Growth and Forecasts," *The Annals of the American Academy of Political and Social Science*, Vol. 188 (Nov. 1936).

209. Reid, P. M., *Industrial Decentralization, Detroit Region 1940–1950 (Projection to 1970)*, Metropolitan Area Regional Planning Commission, Detroit, June 1951.

210. ———, *Population Prospectus for the Detroit Region 1960 and 1970*, Metropolitan Area Regional Planning Commission, Detroit, Oct. 1950.

211. ———, *Projected Population, Detroit Region Development Areas, 1960 and 1970*, Metropolitan Area Regional Planning Commission, Detroit, Dec. 1950.

212. Reilly, William J., *The Law of Retail Gravitation*, Pilsbury Publishers, New York, 1953.

213. Rhodes, E. C., "A Population Growth Curve for England and Wales," *Congres international de la population* (Paris, 1937), Vol. 1, Hermann et Cie., Paris, 1938.

214. ———, "Population Mathematics, " *Journal of the Royal Statistical Association*, Vol. 103 (1940).

215. Riley, J. C., "Forecasts of Population of Sacramento County for 1960 and 1970," in *The Economy of the Sacramento Area*, prepared for the Sacramento Chamber of Commerce, Industrial Survey Associates, San Francisco, Feb. 16, 1951.

216. Rochester City Planning Commission, *A Study of Population Growth of Rochester and Monroe County*, Rochester, New York, Dec. 1947.

217. Roterus, V., and R. C. Schmitt, "Short-Range Economic Forecasting for Cities," *Management Information Service*, Report No. 84, International City Managers' Association, Chicago, Jan. 1951.

218. ———, and ———, "Short-Range Forecasting for Municipal Purposes," *Business Information Service*, U. S. Department of Commerce, Area Development Division of the Bureau of Foreign and Domestic Commerce, Washington, D.C., April 1951.

219. Russell Sage Foundation, *The Estimation of Population Changes for New York City*, recommendations to the Mayor by the Committee on Statistical Program for the City of New York, New York, 1955.

220. Schmid, C. F., V. A. Miller, and H. W. Mooney, "A Century of Population Growth, State of Washington, 1860 to 1960," in *People, Jobs, and Income on the Pacific Coast, 1949–60*, Pacific Coast Board of Intergovenmental Relations, San Francisco, 1949.

221. Schmitt, R. C., "An Application of Multiple Correlation to Population Forecasting," *Land Economics*, Vol. 30 (Aug. 1954).

222. ———, "Demography and City Planning," *Social Forces*, Vol. 30 (March, 1952).

223. ———, "Estimates of Intercensal Population for the Seattle Metropolitan Area: 1860–1950," *Current Planning Research*, No. 4, City Planning Commission, Seattle, Washington, Aug. 15, 1951.

224. ———, "Forecasting City Population by the Ratio Method," *Journal of the American Water Works Association*, Vol. 46 (Oct. 1954).

225. ———, *The Future Population of Metropolitan Flint*, Horace R. Rackham School for Graduate Studies, Institute for Human Adjustment, University of Michigan, Ann Arbor, Michigan, July 1947.

226. ———, "A Method of Estimating the Population of Cities," *American Journal of Public Health*, Vol. 44 (Nov. 1954).

227. Schmitt, R. C., "Methods of Estimating the Postcensal Population of Census Tracts," *Land Economics*, Vol. 32 (Nov. 1956).

228. ———, "A Method of Projecting the Population of Census Tracts," *Journal of the American Institute of Planners*, Vol. 20 (Spring 1954).

229. ———, "A New Method of Forecasting City Population," *Journal of the American Institute of Planners*, Vol. 19 (Winter 1953).

230. ———, "Population Forecast for the City of Seattle by Census Tracts: 1970," *Current Planning Research*, No. 10, City Planning Commission, Seattle, Washington, Sept. 25, 1952.

231. ———, "Population Forecast King County: 1960–1970," *Current Planning Research*, No. 8, City Planning Commission, Seattle, Washington, May 15, 1952.

232. ———, "Short-Cut Methods of Estimating County Population," *Journal of the American Statistical Association*, Vol. 47 (June 1952).

233. ———, "Short-Cut Methods of Forecasting the Population of Census Tracts," *The Journal of Marketing*, Vol. 18 (Jan. 1954).

234. ———, and A. H. Crosetti, "Accuracy of the Ratio-Correlation Method for Estimating Postcensal Population," *Land Economics*, Vol. 30 (Aug. 1954).

235. ———, and ———, "Accuracy of the Ratio Method for Forecasting City Population," *Land Economics*, Vol. 27 (Nov. 1951).

236. ———, and ———, "Short-Cut Methods of Forecasting City Population," *The Journal of Marketing*, Vol. 17 (April 1953).

237. Schneider, J. R. L., "Note on the Accuracy of Local Population Estimates," *Population Studies*, Vol. 8 (Nov. 1954).

238. Schultz, Henry, "The Standard Error of a Forecast from a Curve," *Journal of the American Statistical Association*, Vol. 25 (June 1930).

239. Seattle City Planning Commission, *The Population of Metropolitan Seattle: an Interim Report*, prepared under the direction of R. C. Schmitt, Seattle, Washington, Dec. 1950.

240. ———, "Population Trends and Projections, Seattle Standard Metropolitan Area, 1900–1970," *Current Planning Research*, No. 13, Seattle, Washington, Nov. 1, 1953.

241. Segoe, L., *The Population of Charleston and its Environs*, Municipal Planning Commission, Charleston, Virginia, Feb. 1939.

242. ———, "The Population of Madison, Its Composition and Characteristics," *Comprehensive Plan of Madison, Wisconsin and Environs*, Vol. 1, Book III, Trustees of Madison Planning Trust, Madison, Wisconsin, Oct. 1938.

243. Shannon, H. A., and E. Grebenik, *The Population of Bristol*, Macmillan, New York, 1942.

244. Shryock, H. S., "Accuracy of Population Projections for the United States," *Estadistica*, Vol. 12 (Dec. 1954).

245. ———, "Forecasts of Population in the United States," *Population Studies*, Vol. 3 (March 1950).

246. ———, "Methods of Estimating Postcensal Populations," *The American Journal of Public Health*, Vol. 28 (Sept. 1938).

247. ———, "Population Estimates in Postcensal Years," *The Annals of the American Academy of Political and Social Science*, Vol. 188 (Nov. 1936).

248. ———, "Postcensal Population Data for Cities," *American Journal of Public Health*, Vol. 37 (Nov. 1947).

249. ———, and N. Lawrence, "The Current Status of State and Local Population Estimates in the Census Bureau," *Journal of the American Statistical Association*, Vol. 44 (June 1949).

250. Shryock, H. S., and J. S. Siegel, "The Outlook for Population Increase in Texas," *Southwestern Social Science Quarterly*, Vol. 17 (Sept. 1947).
251. Sibley, E., "Problems in Population Estimation," *American Journal of Public Health*, Vol. 34 (Feb. 1944).
252. Siegel, J. S., "Forecasting the Population of Small Areas," *Land Economics*, Vol. 29 (Feb. 1953).
253. ———, and C. H. Hamilton, "Some Considerations in the Use of the Residual Method of Estimating Net Migration," *Journal of the American Statistical Association*, Vol. 47 (Sept. 1952).
254. ———, H. S. Shryock, and B. Greenberg, "Accuracy of Postcensal Estimates of Population for States and Cities," *American Sociological Review*, Vol. 19 (Aug. 1954).
255. ———, and Helen L. White, "Illustrative Projections of the United States 1950 to 1960," *Current Population Reports, Population Estimates*, Series P-25, No. 43, U. S. Bureau of the Census, Washington, D.C., Aug. 10, 1950.
256. Silcock, H., "Precision in Population Estimates," *Population Studies*, Vol. 8 (Nov. 1954).
257. Slayton, W. L., *Population Estimates for Milwaukee County*, County Board of Public Land Commissioners, Milwaukee, Wisconsin, 1945.
258. Smith, T. L., *Population Analysis*, McGraw-Hill, New York, 1948.
259. Snow, E. C., "The Application of the Method of Multiple Correlation to the Estimation of Post-Censal Populations," *Journal of the Royal Statistical Society*, Vol. 74 (May 1911).
260. Spengler, J. J., "Population Prospects in Areas of Advanced Industrialization," in *World Population and Future Resources*, ed. by P. K. Hatt, American Book, New York, 1952.
261. ———, "Population Theory," in *A Survey of Contemporary Economics*, Vol. II, ed. by B. F. Haley, Richard D. Irwin, Inc., Homewood, Illinois, 1952.
262. ———, and O. D. Duncan, eds., *Population Theory and Policy*, The Free Press, Glencoe, Illinois, 1956.
263. Spiegelman, Mortimer, *Introduction to Demography*, The Society of Actuaries, Chicago, 1955.
264. Spurr, W. A., *Forecasts of California's Population and Production, 1950–1960*, Graduate School of Business, Business Research Series No. 4, Stanford University, Stanford, California, 1949.
265. ———, and D. R. Arnold, "A Short-Cut Method of Fitting a Logistic Curve," *Journal of the American Statistical Association*, Vol. 43 (March 1948).
266. Stanbery, V. B., *Better Population Forecasting for Areas and Communities*, U. S. Department of Commerce, Domestic Commerce Series, No. 32, Washington, D.C., 1952.
267. ———, *More Income and Buying Power for the Pacific Northwest*, prepared for the Columbia Basin Inter-Agency Committee, U.S. Department of Commerce Field Service, Washington, D.C., Dec. 1950.
268. ———, *Population Analysis and Projections 1960 and 1970 County and City of San Diego, California*, part of a report on Transportation Needs, Industrial Survey Associates, San Francisco, May 1953.
269. ———, *A Production and Employment Estimate for California*, California State Reconstruction and Reemployment Commission, Sacramento, California, Oct. 16, 1945.

270. Stanbery, V. B., *Projections of Rural Farm Population and Agricultural Employment in Washington, Oregon, and Idaho, 1960 and 1975*, prepared for the Columbia Basin Inter-Agency Committee, U. S. Department of Commerce, Washington, D.C., May 13, 1953.

271. ———, Ross Miller, and George Sabagh, *Estimates of Population Growth in California, 1940–1950*, California State Reconstruction and Reemployment Commission, Sacramento, California, June 1944.

272. ———, and J. C. Riley, *Estimated Range for Population Growth in California to 1960*, California State Reconstruction and Reemployment Commission, Sacramento, California, Nov. 1946.

273. ———, and M. Roher, *Forecasting a City's Future—Sacramento, California*, California State Reconstruction and Reemployment Commission, Pamphlet No. 12, Sacramento, California, 1946.

274. ———, M. Roher, and G. Sabagh, *Estimates of Population Growth in California 1940–1950*, California State Reconstruction and Reemployment Commission, Sacramento, California, July 1944.

275. Sterns, F. H., "Methods of Forecasting Future Population," *Public Management*, Vol. 12 (Nov. 1930).

276. Stevens, H. W., "Forecasting Urban Population Distribution," *Journal of the American Institute of Planners*, Vol. 13 (Summer-Fall 1947).

277. Stevenson, T. H. C., "A Method of Estimating Future Populations," *Journal of Hygiene*, Vol. 4 (April 1904).

278. Stewart, J. Q., "A Basis for Social Physics," *Impact of Science on Society*, Vol. 3 (Summer 1952).

279. ———, "The Development of Social Physics," *American Journal of Physics*, Vol. 18 (May 1950).

280. ———, "Empirical Mathematical Rules Concerning the Distribution and Equilibrium of Population," *Geographical Review*, Vol. 37 (July 1947).

281. Strand, William H., *Forecasting the Enrollment in Public Schools*, University Microfilms Publication No. 10393, Ann Arbor, 1954.

282. Swaroop, S., and R. B. Lal, "Logistic Law of Growth and Structure of Indian Population," *Population*, Vol. 2 (July 1938).

283. Syracuse–Onondaga Post-War Planning Council, *Preliminary Report on Population Characteristics, Trends and Prospects*, Syracuse, New York, 1943.

284. Tacoma City Planning Commission, *Site—History—Population, A Preliminary Report*, Tacoma, Washingtom, May 1948.

285. Taeuber, Irene B., "The Development of Population Predictions in Europe and the Americas," *Estadistica*, Vol. 2 (Sept. 1944).

286. ———, "Literature on Future Populations, 1943–48," *Population Index*, Vol. 15 (Jan. 1949).

287. ———, "Population Studies in the U. S.," *Population Index*, Vol. 12 (Oct. 1946).

288. Taylor, Griffith, "Future Population in Canada; A Study in Technique," *Economic Geography*, Vol. 22 (Jan. 1946).

289. Taylor, H. W., "Graph Estimates of Future Population," *Public Works*, Vol. 77 (Jan. 1946).

290. Texas Research League, *Projection of the Population of Texas, 1950–1975*, Austin, Texas, 1954.

291. Thaden, J. F., "Forecasts of Future Public School Enrollments, by Grades, in Michigan," *Michigan Agricultural Experiment Station Quarterly Bulletin*, Vol. 31, No. 4.

292. Thompson, W. S., *Growth and Changes in California's Population*, Haynes Foundation, Los Angeles, 1955.

293. ——, "Population Growth and Housing Demand," *The Annals of the American Academy of Political and Social Science*, Vol. 190 (March 1937).

294. ——, *The Population of the Cincinnati Metropolitan Area*, City Planning Commission, Cincinnati, Ohio, Dec. 1945.

295. ——, *Population Problems*, 4th ed., McGraw-Hill, New York, 1953.

296. ——, and P. K. Whelpton, *Estimates of Future Population by States*, U. S. National Resources Board, Washington, D.C., Dec. 1934.

297. ——, and ——, *Estimates of Future Population of the United States 1940–2000*, U. S. National Resources Planning Board, Washington, D.C., 1943.

298. ——, and ——, *Population Statistics, 1. National Data*, U. S. National Resources Committee, Washington, D.C., Oct. 1937.

299. ——, and ——, *Population Trends in the United States*, McGraw-Hill, New York, 1933.

300. ——, and ——, "The Trend of Total Population," in *The Problems of a Changing Population*, U. S. National Resources Committee, Washington D.C., May. 1938.

301. United Nations, Department of Social Affairs, Population Division, *The Determinants and Consequences of Population Trends*, United Nations, Population Studies No. 17, New York, 1953. (ST/SOA/Series A/17. Sales No.: 1953. XIII. 3.)

302. ——, *Methods for Population Projections by Sex and Age*, Methods of Estimating Population, Manual III, United Nations, Population Studies No. 25, New York, Aug., 1956. (ST/SOA/Series A/25. Sales No.: 1956. XIII. 3.)

303. ——, *Methods of Estimating Total Population for Current Dates*, Methods of Estimating Population, Manual I, United Nations, Population Studies No. 10, New York, 1952. (ST/SOA/Series A/10. Sales No.: 1952. XIII. 5.)

304. U. S. Bureau of Agricultural Economics, *1952 Agricultural Outlook Charts*, U. S. Government Printing Office, Washington, D.C., 1951.

305. ——, "Forecasts of Population and School Enrollment in the United States: 1948 to 1960," *Current Population Reports, Population Estimates*, Series P-25, No. 18, U. S. Department of Commerce, Washington, D.C., Feb. 14, 1949.

306. U. S. Bureau of the Census, *Statistical View of the United States, Being a Compendium of the Seventh Census (1850)*, U. S. Senate Printer, Washington, D.C., 1854.

307. U. S. Congress (79th, 2nd Session), *Adequate Future Water Supply for the District of Columbia and Metropolitan Area*, U. S. Government Printing Office, House Doc. 480, Washington, D.C., 1946.

308. U. S. Federal Power Commission, "Population," in *Power Market Survey, Power Requirements in New Hampshire, Vermont, Massachusetts, Connecticut, and Rhode Island*, Regional Office of the Bureau of Power, New York (See, also, similar F.P.C. reports for other regions of the United States), Aug. 1949.

309. U. S. National Housing Agency, *The Population Factor in Housing Market Analysis*, Housing Market Analysis Bulletin No. 5, Washington, D.C., July 1945.

310. U. S. National Resources Committee, *The Problems of a Changing Population*, U. S. Government Printing Office, Washington, D.C., 1938.

311. U. S. Office of Industry and Commerce, *Population Report Arkansas–White–Red River Basins, Section 3, Population Forecasts*, an interim report by the Economic Base Survey Work Group of the Arkansas–White–Red Basins Inter-Agency Committee, Area Development Division of the Office of Industry and Commerce, Washington, D.C., Aug. 1951.

312. U. S. Office of Industry and Commerce, *Population Report Arkansas–White–Red River Basins, Section 3A, Part I, Population Forecasts Supplement*, prepared by David Brown, Area Development Division of the Office of Industry and Commerce, Washington, D.C., Feb. 1952.

313. U. S. Public Health Service, "United States Abridged Life Tables 1930–1939 (Preliminary) by Geographic Divisions, Color, and Sex," *Vital Statistics— Special Reports, Selected Studies*, U. S. Federal Security Agency, National Office of Vital Statistics, Vol. 23 (June 1947).

314. ———, "United States Abridged Life Tables, 1939, Urban and Rural by Regions, Color, and Sex, "*Vital Statistics—Special Reports, Selected Studies*, U. S. Federal Security Agency, National Office of Vital Statistics, Vol. 23 (June 1947).

315. Valaoras, V. G., "The Growth of the Population of Greece as Described by the Logistic Curve," *Extrait des Praktika de l'Academie d'Athenes* (Seance du 23 Janvier, 1936), Vol. 11 (1936).

316. Velz, C. J., and H. F. Eich, "How Old Are Our Cities?" *Civil Engineering*, Vol 10 (Oct. 1940).

317. Verhulst, P. F., "Notice sur la loi que la population suit dans son accroisement," *Correspondence Mathematique et Physique Publieé par A. Quetelet*, Tome X, 1838.

318. ———, "Recherches mathematiques sur la loi d'accrossement de la population," *Nouveaux Memoires de l'Academie Royale des Sciences et Belles-Lettres de Bruxelles*, Tome XVIII, 1845.

319. Vianelli, Silvio, "A General Dynamic Demographic Scheme and Its Application to Italy and the United States," *Econometrica*, Vol. 4 (July 1936).

320. Volterra, Vito, "Population Growth, Equilibria, and Extinction under Specified Breeding Conditions : A Development and Extension of the Theory of the Logistic Curve," *Human Biology*, Vol. 10 (Feb. 1938).

321. Wachter, W. A., *Study of Population Growth, Characteristics, Composition and Distribution, Greenwich, Connecticut*, Town Plan Commission, Greenwich, Connecticut, May 1944.

322. Walker, Helen and Joseph Lev, *Statistical Inference*, Henry Holt, New York, 1953.

323. Walter, P., and R. Calvin, *The Population of New Mexico*, Department of Government, Division of Research, University of New Mexico, Albuquerque, New Mexico, 1947.

324. Washington Board of Trade, Postwar Planning Committee, in cooperation with the Committee for Economic Development, *Population and Business Prospects for Metropolitan Washington*, Washington, D.C., 1944.

325. ———, *Postwar Plans of Metropolitan Washington Employers*, Opinion Research Corp., Princeton, New Jersey, 1945.

326. Weimer, A. M., and H. Hoyt, *Principles of Urban Real Estate*, 3rd ed., Ronald Press, New York, 1954.

327. Weiner, Betty L., *Projection of Public School Enrollments in the Detroit Region by Grade, 1950 through 1970*, Metropolitan Area Regional Planning Commission, Detroit, June 1951.

328. Wendt, Paul F., "Estimating California's Housing Demand," *The Appraisal Journal*, Vol. 22 (Oct. 1954).

329. Werthamer, S. K., *Westchester Population 1920–2000*, Westchester County, Department of Planning, Population Report No. 1, New York, July 1952.

330. Wheeler, B. O., *An Economic Analysis of Vancouver, Washington, and its Environs*, Part I of the Vancouver Plan, City Planning Commission and Housing Authority, Vancouver, Washington, 1947.

331. Whelpton, P. K., "Cohort Analysis of Fertility," *American Sociological Review*, Vol. 14 (Dec. 1949).

332. ———, *Cohort Fertility—Native White Women in the United States*, Princeton University Press, Princeton, New Jersey, 1954.

333. ———, "An Empirical Method of Calculating Future Population," *Journal of the American Statistical Association*, Vol. 31 (Sept. 1936).

334. ———, "The Future Growth of the Population of the United States," in *Problems of Population*, Proceedings of the International Union for Scientific Investigation of Population Problems, George Allen and Unwin, London, 1932.

335. ———, *Needed Population Research*, for the Population Association of America, Committee on Research, The Science Press Printing Co., Lancaster, Pennsylvania, 1938.

336. ———, "Population in the United States, 1925–1975," *American Journal of Sociology*, Vol. 34 (Sept. 1928).

337. ———, with H. T. Eldridge and J. S. Siegel, *Forecasts of the Population of the United States 1945–1975*, U. S. Bureau of the Census, Washington, D.C., 1947.

338. White, Helen L., and J. S. Siegel, "Projections of the Population by States: 1955 and 1965," *Current Population Reports, Population Estimates*, Series P-25, No. 56, U. S. Bureau of the Census, Washington, D.C., Jan. 27, 1952.

339. White, Helen R., "Empirical Study of the Accuracy of Selected Methods of Projecting State Populations," *Journal of the American Statistical Association*, Vol. 49 (Sept. 1954).

340. Whitney, V. H., "The Estimation of Population for Unincorporated Places," *American Sociological Review*, Vol. 11 (Feb. 1946).

341. Wilson, E. B., and W. J. Luyten, "The Population of New York and its Environs," *Proceedings of the National Academy of Sciences*, Vol. 2 (Feb. 1925).

342. ———, and Ruth R. Puffer, "Least Squares and Laws of Population Growth," *Proceedings of the American Academy of Arts and Sciences*, Vol. 68 (1933).

343. Wisconsin State Planning Board, *An Analysis of Population Growth in Wisconsin*, Bulletin 4, Madison, Wisconsin, 1937.

344. Wolfe, A. B., "The Optimum Size of Population," in *Population Problems in the United States and Canada*, ed. by L. I. Dublin, Houghton Mifflin, Boston, 1926.

345. Wolfenden, H. H., *Population Statistics and their Compilation*, University of Chicago Press, Chicago, 1954.

346. ———, *Transactions of the Actuarial Society of America*, Vol. 35 (1934).

347. Wolff, R. P., "The Forecasting of Population by Census Tracts in an Urban Area," *Land Economics*, Vol. 28 (Nov. 1952).

348. ———, *A Short-Term Forecast of the Housing Market, Jacksonville, Florida*, U. S. Housing and Home Finance Agency, Division of Housing Research, Washington, D.C., June 1953.

349. Woodruff, C. E., *Expansion of Races*, Rebman, New York, 1909.

350. Wool, Harold, "Long-Term Projections of the Labor Force," in *Long-Range Economic Projection*, National Bureau of Economic Research, Studies in Income and Wealth, Vol. 6, Princeton University Press, Princeton, New Jersey, 1954.

351. Worley, L., *Alabama's People*, Bureau of Public Administration, University of Alabama, Tuscaloosa, Alabama, 1945.

352. Young, E. F., "Estimating Population for Dynamic Communities: A Short Method of Computing Inter-Censal and Post-Censal Population," *American Journal of Sociology*, Vol. 38 (Jan. 1933).

353. Yule, G. U., "The Growth of Population and the Factors which Control It," *Journal of the Royal Statistical Society*, Vol. 88 (Jan. 1925).

354. ———, and M. G. Kendall, *An Introduction to the Theory of Statistics*, Charles Griffin, London, 1950.

355. Zipf, G. K., *Human Relations and the Principle of Least Effort*, Addison-Wesley Press, Cambridge, Massachusetts, 1949.

356. ———, *National Unity and Disunity*, Principia Press, Bloomington, Indiana, 1941.

357. Zitter, Meyer, "Illustrative Projections of the College-Age Population, by States: 1958 to 1973," *Current Population Reports*, *Population Estimates*, Series P-25, No. 132, U. S. Bureau of the Census, Washington, D.C., Feb. 20, 1956.

358. ———, "Illustrative Projections of the Population, by States, 1960 and 1965," *Current Population Reports*, *Population Estimates*, Series P-25, No. 110, U. S. Bureau of the Census, Washington, D.C., Feb. 20, 1955.

359. ———, "Projections of School Enrollment in the United States 1953–1965," *Current Population Reports*, *Population Estimates*, Series P-25, No. 85, U. S. Bureau of the Census, Washington, D.C., Dec. 7, 1953.

360. ———, "Revised Projections of the Population of the United States by Age and Sex: 1960 to 1975," *Current Population Reports*, *Population Estimates*, Series P-25, No. 123, U. S. Bureau of the Census, Washington, D.C., Oct. 20, 1955.

Chapter **3**

Migration Estimation*

A. INTRODUCTORY REMARKS[1]

As already indicated, the derivation of reliable population projections may also require the construction of migration estimates. For a closed economy where both in-migration and out-migration are restricted, migration estimation is not a severe problem. For such an economy migration flows are a direct result of government policy, and data are readily obtained. For open areas, however, such as the regions of the United States and many other countries, where population flows are not directly determined by government policy, the need for estimating migration is basic. For these economies people are relatively free to move in and out. Especially when the in and out movements are not of equal magnitude (as is typically the case with the regions of the United States), "direct" population projections of the type discussed in the previous chapter have limited value. Such projections must be supplemented with in- and out-migration

* This chapter has been written with Gerald A. P. Carrothers and draws heavily upon his doctoral dissertation, *Forecasting the Population of Open Areas*, M.I.T. Library, Cambridge, Massachusetts, June 1959.
[1] General discussions concerning migration estimation may be found in D. S. Thomas [141], A. J. Jaffe [79], ch. 6, and United Nations, Department of Social Affairs [152], pp. 106–111, 123–128, 300–305. In addition to these, see W. S. Thompson [146] and U. S. Congress [165] for extensive bibliographies.

estimates, or, at a minimum, with net migration estimates in order to be useful in systematic planning for a region.

In a comprehensive river basin development program, how much water should be furnished to diverse users by key years in the future? What magnitude of resources should be allocated to hydroelectric power installation by these years? How much land should be irrigated and how many recreation facilities constructed? What pattern of inter- and intraregional highways should evolve? Within a metropolitan complex how much land should be zoned for residential, commercial, industrial, and other uses? How much housing development may be expected or needed? For what size population and for what area should regional cities be planned? These are but some of the many important questions whose answers depend on reliable estimation of population numbers, and, for open economies, such estimation involves migration forecasts when the projection techniques described in the previous chapter are utilized.

Knowledge concerning the movement of population is important in itself, quite apart from its relation to the forecasting of total population. Resolution of the important questions posed depends not only on knowledge of population totals but also on the spatial characteristics of this population. The movement of population varies tremendously in character: from the continual shifting of the itinerant transient to the once-in-a-lifetime move of the established homeowner; from a change of residence within a city block to a transcontinental removal; from the movement of an occasional individual or family to the mass migrations of entire populations. Insight into these movements can be essential for attacking basic regional problems.

Like the population forecasting techniques already discussed, methods for estimating migration are not nearly as good as we might like them to be. Nevertheless, these methods are useful and yield estimates that are worth the effort involved *provided the results are used with discretion.*

In the following discussion we distinguish among methods designed to answer different needs. First are methods aimed at estimating past and current migration. Unlike data on population totals, the census provides only a limited amount of direct data on migration. Therefore, in understanding the historical development of regions and their current structure it is often essential to make estimates of past migration. These estimates concern interregional migration as well as rural-urban migration, where the latter may be both interregional and intraregional.

Migration estimation becomes important, too, in the forward look. A second group of methods to be discussed are those designed to forecast migration. Once again, these forecasts may be for interregional movement only, or for rural-urban movement (whether inter- or intraregional).

Before a discussion of these methods is undertaken, a few general comments are in order. Estimates of interregional migration are significantly affected by both (1) the size and shape of spatial units chosen for study and (2) the time period considered. Lee states that "in general, the greater the size of the spatial unit by which migration is defined the smaller the number of migrants."[2] Census figures for 1940, for example, record, between 1935 and 1940, 15.7 million intercounty migrants, 6.5 million interstate migrants, and 3.0 million migrants between census regions.[3]

Even when a given type of political or administrative unit has been selected for migration study, frequently the area varies greatly among units of the given type. As of 1957, the largest state in the United States was over 200 times the size of the smallest. Hence, migration rates based on the state as the relevant political unit are not comparable; they are biased toward high values in the very small states and toward low values in the very large states. Further, even among regions (states) of equal size, disparity of shape may introduce another bias. Ohio and Tennessee have approximately the same area; yet because of Tennessee's elongated shape many more short migrations cross the state line than they do for Ohio.

Distribution of population within the spatial units is yet another factor conditioning the volume of migration. Concentrations of population, such as Chicago, which are near the boundaries of a state (or region) lead to greater interstate (interregional) migration than would be the case if the same population were centrally located or evenly distributed within states (regions).

Finally, as the time period considered increases, total migration increases; but migration per unit of time, as estimated by a number of methods, declines. The first result is due to greater chance of migration in a longer span of time. The second result is due to (1) failure to record migrations of persons who have died previous to census count, or who have crossed a boundary and returned during the interval between census counts, and (2) failure to count as more than one the migrations of persons who have shifted two or more times between census counts. Thus, a relatively accurate estimate of net migration patterns over a long period such as a decade may mask significant differences among the short-run patterns which arise in response to changing economic and social conditions.

[2] See E. S. Lee et al., [89], p. 10.
[3] *Ibid.*

B. Estimation of Past Interregional Migration

1. gross and net migration totals

Methods of estimating past migration totals may be classed into two general types according to the kind of information obtained. The first derives figures for net migration only, normally by means of the so-called *residual* methods, which include the *survival* technique. The second type, utilizing more direct data, yields gross figures both for in-migration and for out-migration, and, by subtraction, for net migration. This type includes the *nativity* and *residence* methods and the use of special procedures such as continuous population registration.

The latter methods using more direct data are to be preferred for most purposes of regional analysis, since they yield more detail on directional flows of population. Unfortunately, in most instances, direct data on migration are not available, and recourse must be had to the more roundabout residual methods.

a. Residual methods. The residual methods assume that, in the absence of population migrations, the growth of the population of a given area over a given period of time will be equal to the difference between births and deaths in the area. Any discrepancy between this theoretical change and the actual change, which is obtained from census or other enumerations, is defined as net migration during the period. In mathematical symbols,

$$M_\theta = (P_{t+\theta} - P_t) - N_\theta$$

where M_θ = net migration during time period θ;
     $P_{t+\theta}$ = total population of area under study in year $t + \theta$;
     P_t = total population of area under study in year t; and
     N_θ = net natural increase during time period θ.

The validity of this procedure depends on the accuracy with which natural increase during the period is obtained. If statistics are available for births and deaths occurring among the original population during the period, a direct subtraction of deaths from births may be made to obtain net natural increase.[4] Normally, however, vital statistics for any given period of time do not differentiate between the original and the migrant populations of an area, between the births and deaths of the original

---

[4] In this case, the equation becomes

$$M_\theta = (P_{t+\theta} - P_t) - (B_\theta - D_\theta)$$

where B_θ = births to original population during the period θ and
     D_θ = deaths of original population during the period θ.

population and the births and deaths of the migrant population.   Hence, without such a distinction, the investigator is often forced to use a crude form of the residual technique to obtain a migration estimate.   From increase in total population over a period he subtracts natural increase of total (including migrant) population.[5]   The resulting figure on net migration over the period (either in or out) tends to be an underestimate.   Where migration is small, the error involved may justifiably be ignored; but where migration is significant, this error becomes more serious, since the balance of births and deaths for the total population over the period is no longer likely to be a close approximation of that for the original population.[6]

For cases of in-migration this defect may be overcome to some extent by applying to the original population birth and death *rates* obtained from previous experience of the area or of a larger area, in order to obtain the natural increase over the period under study.[7]   (For out-migration, relevant rates should be applied in reverse to actual population at year $t + \theta$).   The use of vital rates is less desirable than the use of direct vital statistics in view of the multitude of objections against applying the experience of one period (or area) to a different period (or area).[8]

Where vital statistics are inadequate, a refinement of the residual method may be attempted with the use of survival rates, obtained from either life tables or census data.   First, by the application of these rates

[5] The method was used in this way by V. B. Stanbery and J. C. Riley [129] in their 1946 California study and by C. W. Thornthwaite [149] in his 1934 study of the United States.

[6] C. H. Hamilton and F. M. Henderson [57] have described a method of crudely approximating the number of those who migrated and subsequently died during the period.   This number is determined by (1) subtracting from the number of persons alive at year t the number of theoretical survivors of this population at year $t + \theta$; and (2) applying to half the resulting difference (which measures theoretical deaths) the net migration rate for the total population during the period θ.   (Taking half the resulting difference assumes an even flow of migration and mortality throughout the period.)

[7] The equation becomes
$$M_\theta = (P_{t+\theta} - P_t) - (\alpha P_t - \beta P_t)$$
where α = crude birth rate for the period θ and
        β = crude death rate for the period θ.

[8] During the 1930's C. Goodrich and others [48–50] used a modified residual method for determining migration in the United States by counties.   Net population change in each county was compared with the national average.   Where the county change was higher than the national average, net in-migration was assumed; and where it was lower, net out-migration was assumed.   This procedure is warranted, however, only if rates of natural increase are uniform throughout the nation.   C. E. Lively and C. Taeuber [92] have used a residual-type migration analysis, working both forward from year t to year $t + \theta$ and, as a check, backward from year $t + \theta$ to year t.   A similar technique is discussed at some length in J. S. Siegel and C. H. Hamilton [124].

the expected number of survivors of P_t at year $t + \theta$ is obtained.[9] Second, the actual population $(P_{t+\theta})$ at year $t + \theta$ is recorded, and from it is subtracted the component of $P_{t+\theta}$ which is under θ years of age. The figure thus obtained, in the absence of migration during the period θ, will be the same as the expected number of survivors of P_t obtained in the first step. Therefore, any difference between these two figures can be considered to be a rough estimate of total net migration during period θ.[10]

A basic defect common to all residual techniques of estimating net migration lies in the failure to provide knowledge concerning spatial patterns of population movement. Since only migration *numbers* are derived, the origins of the in-migrants and the destination of the out-migrants are wholly unknown. Indeed, no insight can be expected concerning the spatial character of the net movements, let alone of the gross movements; it can only be said that a certain number of people have, on balance, come or gone.[11]

b. Census population data. Less roundabout methods of estimating past migration totals generally provide more complete knowledge on population movements since they depend on more complete and accurate statistical information, such as place of birth and place of residence, typically employing census population data.[12] They use either *nativity* data to compare place of birth with current place of residence, or *residence* data to compare previous place of residence with current place of residence. In both cases either gross or net migration may be determined. The

[9] The survival rate for P_t during period θ is the complement of the mortality rate for the period, normally represented as a decimal fraction per unit of population. E. S. Lee et al. [89] presents extensive comparisons of survival rates for individual states and the United States.

[10] For specific discussion of the survival-rate method of migration estimation see, among others, F. Lorimer [93], J. S. Siegel and C. H. Hamilton [124], and D. O. Price [111]. Also see Simon Kuznets [84] for a use of a survival-rate technique in estimating migration for Philadelphia.

[11] For general discussion of the problems and limitations of the residual methods see J. S. Siegel and C. H. Hamilton [124] and L. E. Truesdell [151]. Examples of the use of residual methods in the United States include D. J. Bogue's forecast of Chicago's population from 1955 to 1965 [12]; the 1947 study of migration to cities in the United States by P. M. Hauser and H. T. Eldridge [62]; L. Segoe's study of Madison in 1938 [120]; W. S. Thompson's study of Michigan of 1937 [143]; and E. S. Lee et al. [89] For a discussion of the use of residual methods of migration estimation in Germany, see R. Heberle [65] and F. Meyer [99]. For the use of Swedish data in residual analysis see E. P. Hutchinson [74].

[12] In the United States, data on state of birth have been collected in censuses since 1850 and data on place of residence at a previous date since 1940. In addition, the U. S. Bureau of the Census periodically publishes reports on internal migration based on sample surveys. See, for example [154–164].

degree of detail on population flows which is obtained depends partly on the size of census unit for which the data are reported. In the United States the unit is customarily the state, which thus defines the smallest area that may be studied on the basis of this data.[13]

The *nativity* method requires, for each person, data on state in which he was born and on state in which he resides at year $t + \theta$. Therefore, the number of persons who were born in any given state and who were surviving at year $t + \theta$ can be disaggregated into those who were living in that state at $t + \theta$ and those who were living in each of the other states at $t + \theta$. From such disaggregation can be determined the gross in- and out-migrations for any given state, the origins of the in-migration, and the destinations of the out-migration. No information is obtained concerning the time of movement, except that the movement must have occurred during the life of the surviving individuals. However, some estimate of movement during period θ may be obtained by a comparison of migration up to year $t + \theta$ with migration up to year t. Care must be taken, in this comparison, to account for differential mortality and fertility rates and similar factors which may also have a bearing on the migration totals for the two periods.[14] A disadvantage inherent in comparing place of birth data with place of residence data is that in applying differential rates and other refinements, often only native-born population can be effectively

[13] E. S. Lee et al. [89] has prepared extensive estimates of interstate migration from census data on state of birth for census periods from 1870 to 1950. Use of the 1940 census nativity and residence data was made by W. S. Thompson [143] in analyzing Ohio migration and by C. F. Schmid and M. J. Griswold [117] in studying Washington migration. Thompson's 1937 study of depression migration in Michigan [146] deals with the survival-rate method as well as with the nativity and residence methods. C. N. Reynolds and S. Miles [116] used census nativity and residence data in their 1944 statistical study of California migration. Similar data are used in the 1938 report of the U. S. National Resources Committee [167], pp. 91–103. A recent example of the use of such data may be found in Homer L. Hitt [69].

For German experience in the use of nativity methods see R. Heberle [65]; and for the German use of both nativity and residence methods see F. Meyer [99]. For the use of Swedish census data for migration estimation see E. P. Hutchinson [74]; and for the use of Korean nativity data, see G. T. Trewartha and W. Zelinsky [150].

[14] In this connection, see A. J. Jaffe [79]. From census nativity data, C. W. Thornthwaite [149] developed his "birth-residence" index which measures, for a given state, the difference between its residents who were born in other states and those who were born in that state but now reside in other states. He used this index in analyzing internal migration in the United States, by state and by county. C. D. Clark and R. L. Roberts [25] used nativity data in their 1936 study of Kansas. N. Clark and G. W. Hill [26] used nativity data in estimating in-migration for Wisconsin. H. J. Burt [20] used the same data to calculate internal migration in the United States for each census period from 1850 to 1930. C. J. Galpin and T. B. Manny [43] mapped interstate migration of the native white population in the United States for census periods between 1870 and 1930, using census nativity data.

considered.   In areas containing large numbers of foreign-born persons
this defect may be significant.

In the *residence* method, data on current place of residence at year
$t + \theta$ are compared with data on place of residence as of year t, to determine the movements during any given period θ.   In this technique the time
period during which migration took place is more readily identified,
although only in terms of census periods.   Migration figures obtained by
this method do not include either persons less than θ years of age at year
$t + \theta$ or persons alive at year t but deceased at year $t + \theta$, since only
persons alive on both dates can be counted.[15]

Neither the nativity method nor the residence method can take into
account the number of intermediate moves made by the population, from
time of birth to year $t + \theta$ in the former case and during period θ in the
latter case.

   c. Population registers.   The most straightforward of the more direct
methods of calculating past net migration, and the one which provides the
most refined data, uses continuous population registers.   These registers
can record any or all movements of any or all individuals in an area.
Such registers are most effectively maintained by a national authority
since, among other reasons, a subordinate local authority within a nation
is not as able to impose the necessary requirement that the individual report
each of his moves, and since a national authority is better able to achieve
uniform standards of data collection whereby comparable data may be
obtained.   The advantages of a system of con-
tinuous population registration for measuring migration are self-evident.
Data can be cross-classified in a great variety of ways, with the result that
relatively complete knowledge of spatial characteristics of migration may
be obtained.   The problem of measuring migration-by-stages does not
arise, since all moves of an individual or a group within any given period
may be determined; and temporary moves may be distinguished from
permanent ones.

Population registers have been maintained in some European countries,[16]
but have not been used as extensively elsewhere, partly because of the
necessary expense and complexity of administration and the overtones of

[15] Extensive use of the 1940 census data on place of residence was made by the Scripps
Foundation [119] in its study of United States migration.   Glenn Hutchinson [75] has
used residence data from the 1940 and 1950 United States censuses in estimating
migration in the Philadelphia metropolitan area.

[16] See D. S. Thomas [139–142] for discussion of the use of population registers in
Sweden, Belgium, and The Netherlands; S. Reimer [115] for use by Gunnar Myrdal and
Svend Reimer of the Swedish register data; and E. W. Hofstee [71] for use of The
Netherlands' population register data.

regimentation. Registers have never been used in the United States. In the absence of continuous population registration, some limited data of a similar character may be available from such sources as special local censuses,[17] school enrollment data,[18] social security and unemployment insurance data,[19] city directories,[20] wartime rationing registrations, draft registrations, and the like.[21]

2. DIFFERENTIAL MIGRATION

For most purposes of regional analysis it is important to know more about population movements than may be described by total numbers.[22] Some of the characteristics of the migrant population about which it may be highly desirable to obtain information are age and sex composition, economic status, ethnic origins, level of educational achievement, occupational patterns, and the like.[23]

All the methods used for measuring gross and net migration totals

---

[17] A special census of unemployment in Michigan conducted during the 1930's was made use of by W. S. Thompson [146] and A. Westefeld [173].

[18] N. Lawrence and B. Greenberg [86] have described a technique evolved by the U. S. Bureau of the Census for estimating net migration for small areas by using school enrollment data. P. V. Lane [85] has used school enrollment data in his 1933 study of California migration; C. W. Thornthwaite [149] has used school census material in his 1934 study of United States migration.

[19] D. J. Bogue [12] has used "Old-Age and Survivors Insurance" data in studying migration in Michigan and Ohio, in 1947. The U. S. Congress study [165] has also used this source of data. H. Makower, J. Marschak, and H. W. Robinson [97] have used British unemployment insurance statistics. F. Meyer [99] has discussed the use of German social insurance statistics.

[20] Sydney Goldstein [45–47] has used data from city directories in conjunction with local school records and vital statistics in his studies of migration for Norristown, Pennsylvania.

[21] R. Heberle [65] and F. Meyer [99] have discussed the use of police registration statistics to estimate German internal migration.

[22] One of the most extensive studies on the measurement of differentials in internal migration was conducted by D. S. Thomas [141]. The specific differentials with which the study was concerned are age, sex, family status, physical and mental health, intelligence, occupation, and motivation and assimilation.

[23] For example, in the pioneer studies of British migration made by E. G. Ravenstein [113] in the 1880's, differentials of sex and of origins (urban and rural) are treated. Some mention of age and sex differentials in migration is made in the 1938 report of the U. S. National Resources Committee [167]. In C. W. Thornthwaite [149], age, sex, and race migration differentials in the United States are measured. In P. F. Coe [27] racial origins are treated. In Margaret S. Gordon [51] differentials of age, sex, occupation, race, and origins of migrants to California are discussed. In H. L. Hitt [70] migration of older population in the United States is examined. Also, a number of studies have been made of selective aspects of intelligence of migrants, such as C. T. Pihlblad and C. L. Gregory [106].

described in the previous paragraphs may be modified and developed for measuring various differential components of migration, provided the basic data are sufficiently detailed.

The assumptions behind the residual methods of obtaining net migration figures remain unaltered when they are utilized for measuring differential components of net migration.[24] If totals are obtainable for the particular differential component breakdown of the population under study at both the beginning and the end of the period, and if the necessary data are available on the natural increase (or decrease) of these components, all the residual methods may be applied on a component basis. For any given differential component x of the population of the area, net migration during the period is

$$_xM_\theta = (_xP_{t+\theta} - _xP_t) - _xN_\theta$$

where $_xM_\theta$ = net migration during period θ of differential component x of the total population under study $(x = 1, 2, \cdots, n)$;

  $_xP_{t+\theta}$ = total number of persons contained in component x at year $t + \theta$;

  $_xP_t$ = total number of persons contained in component x at year t; and

  $_xN_\theta$ = net natural increase of component x during period θ.

Therefore the total net migration is:[25]

$$M_\theta = [(_1P_{t+\theta} - _1P_t) + (_2P_{t+\theta} - _2P_t) + \cdots + (_nP_{t+\theta} - _nP_t)]$$
$$- [_1N_\theta + _2N_\theta + \cdots + _nN_\theta]$$
$$= \sum_{x=1}^{n} [(_xP_{t+\theta} - _xP_t) - _xN_\theta]$$

The most commonly utilized of the residual methods for measuring differential migration is the survival-rate technique, and the most commonly

---

[24] An early example (1921) of the use of the residual method is contained in H. N. Hart [58].

[25] When birth and death totals are available, the equation becomes

$$M_\theta = \sum_{x=1}^{n} (_xP_{t+\theta} - _xP_t) - \sum_{x=1}^{n} (_xB_\theta - _xD_\theta)$$

where $_xB_\theta$ = births to component x during period θ, and
  $_xD_\theta$ = deaths in component x during period θ.

When vital rates are utilized, the equation becomes

$$M_\theta = \sum_{x=1}^{n} (_xP_{t+\theta} - _xP_t) - \sum_{x=1}^{n} (_x\alpha \cdot _xP_t - _x\beta \cdot _xP_t)$$

where $_x\alpha$ = birth rate of component x during period θ, and
  $_x\beta$ = death rate of component x during period θ.

measured differential components are based on age and sex. These components are usually defined in terms of five-year age groups, at ten-year intervals, since census data are characteristically gathered in this form.

The method is generally as follows. The enumerated population at year t is obtained by age-sex-specific cohort groups. The survival rates for the several cohorts are calculated from appropriate life tables or census age distribution tables for the period θ.[26] These rates are then applied to the appropriate cohorts to obtain the number of survivors at year $t + \theta$. These numbers of theoretical survivors are then compared with the enumerated population by age-sex cohorts at year $t + \theta$ to obtain an estimate of net migration for each cohort. The estimates thus obtained for the various component parts of the population may then be assembled in any desired combination. In mathematical terms,

$$M_\theta = \sum_{x=1}^{n} [(_x P_{t+\theta} - _{\hat{x}} P_{t+\theta}) - _x\pi \cdot _x P_t]$$

where $_{\hat{x}} P_{t+\theta}$ = the numbers in the x component of population who are less than θ years of age at $t + \theta$; and

$_x\pi$ = survival rate for differential population component x.

The accuracy of this method depends on the existence of complete and accurate enumerations of the differential population components for both years t and $t + \theta$ and on the accuracy of the survival rates employed.[27]

The survival-rate technique just described utilizes what may be termed "forward" survival rates. That is, for any given cohort at year t, the survival rate relates to the number of persons expected to survive to year $t + \theta$. This technique does not allow either for persons who migrated in or out of the area and then died or for migration of the cohort unborn at time t. A "reverse" survival-rate technique may be utilized which makes such allowances.[28] The numbers in any given cohort at year t may be estimated by dividing the numbers in that cohort at year $t + \theta$ by the

[26] For discussion of the calculation of survival rates for age-sex cohorts see A. J. Jaffe [79], pp. 5–7, and C. H. Hamilton and F. M. Henderson [57]. For the advantages and disadvantages of using life tables versus census age distribution tables to determine the survival rates, see C. H. Hamilton and F. M. Henderson [57], and C. H. Hamilton [55, 56]. P. G. Beck [9] has used life tables to obtain survival rates for estimating age and sex selectivity in migration. In his 1955 estimate of Chicago's future population, D. J. Bogue [11] has analyzed the survival-rate technique based on both census data and life tables to study differential migration by sex, age, and color. E. P. Hutchinson [74] has dealt with age-sex cohorts in Stockholm between 1920 and 1930 by the survival-rate method, using census data.

[27] For a discussion concerning problems of evaluating census returns see A. J. Jaffe [79], ch. 4.

[28] For a general discussion of the "reverse" technique and the subsequent "average" technique, see J. S. Siegel and C. Horace Hamilton [124].

survival rate. If this theoretical number in the cohort at year t is greater than the enumerated number, net in-migration for that cohort during the period θ is suggested. This reverse technique may also be applied to the cohort from zero to θ years of age at year $t + \theta$ to obtain an estimate of migration during θ of the cohort unborn at year t.

Although the forward method implies that *no* persons who died during period θ have migrated, the reverse method implies that *all* those in the estimated migrating cohort who died during period θ are migrants. To avoid either of these extreme errors, an "average" technique may be used, which implies an even flow of migration during period θ.

As with the other residual methods, the various survival-rate techniques, as portrayed to measure migration differentials, are concerned only with net movements and provide no insight into the spatial characteristics of migration.

The residence[29] and nativity[30] methods of estimating migration from population census data, as previously described, may be readily utilized to measure migration differentials, provided it is possible to disaggregate the necessary data into the particular population component categories desired.[31]

Once again, since the information contained in continuous population registers is likely to be relatively complete, these registers are by far the most satisfactory source of data from which measures of differentials in migration may be made.[32]

[29] In using the "place of residence" data of the 1940 U. S. Census for studying differential migration, D. J. Bogue and M. J. Hagood [15] have distinguished between differential proportions and differential rates, and between origin differentials and destination differentials. The differential characteristics with which they were concerned include age, household status, marital status, educational attainment, employment status, type of occupation, income, and unemployment.

[30] H. J. Burt [20] has utilized the nativity method of estimating race differentials in migration.

[31] H. F. Dorn and F. Lorimer [36] have computed an "index of migration" of the native white population in the United States, based on census data which consists of the ratio of the number of persons in a given age-sex group in 1930 to the number of persons in the same group ten years younger in 1920. They have expressed the ratio for each community as a percentage above or below corresponding ratio for total native white population in the United States in order to eliminate the effect of mortality. See also F. Lorimer and F. Osborn [94]. E. H. Johnson [82] has developed a technique for using data from the 1940 U. S. Census to measure migration differentials, based on the specific reported characteristic of educational attainment. L. Purdy [112] has treated race differentials in migration and has inferred migratory movement from data contained in the 1920 and 1950 censuses relating to the nine censal divisions of the United States. C. D. Clark and R. L. Roberts [25] have inferred age selection in migration from differences in population pyramids for Kansas.

[32] In his study of migration in Michigan and Ohio in 1947, in which social security

C. Estimation of Rural-Urban Migration

The process of urbanization of the population of many areas of the world, particularly in the United States, has been occurring at a significant rate for the past century. This phenomenon has focused attention on rural-urban migration, a movement for the most part distinct from interregional migration. Discussion of urbanization processes, as such, lies for the most part outside the scope of this book, but a few comments on the estimation of rural-urban migration are appropriate here.

As with interregional migration, studies of rural-urban migration have been more concerned with the measurement of past movements than with estimation of future movements. The methods used to estimate these past movements are essentially the same as those used for estimating past interregional movements. They are the residual methods,[33] the methods based on census data,[34] and the methods involving the use of population registers.[35]

In the analysis of rural-urban movements, less emphasis has been placed on identifying directional flows than has been true in the analysis of interregional movements. This could be expected since, in general, the directional variable in rural-urban movement is associated with social and economic problems only when such movements are also interregional.

Historically, considerable effort has been given to the measurement of selective differentials in rural-urban migration. Such effort has been associated with testing hypotheses about the "quality" and characteristics of the migrant population. For example, do the more educated, more intelligent, and more productive segments of the rural population leave the country for the city, or do they remain? Unfortunately many early studies have not had adequate data on which to base analysis and conclusions. They are frequently burdened with value judgments regarding the quality of the migrant population and are of little use to the impartial analyst.[36] More recently, however, better data have become available.

data were used, D. J. Bogue [12] has dealt with such differentials as sex, race, age, type of industrial employment, seasonal employment, and income. E. W. Hofstee [71] has examined differentials of distance, sex, and marital status as indicated by data from population registers in The Netherlands. Otto Klineberg [83] has used school enrollment data in studying intelligence selectivity in Negro migration in the United States. For a later application of this technique in Philadelphia, see E. S. Lee [87].

[33] See, among others, O. E. Baker [6–7], P. G. Beck [9], M. J. Hagood and E. F. Sharp [54], H. Hart [58, 59], P. M. Hauser and H. T. Eldridge [62], and C. E. Lively and C. Taeuber [92].

[34] See, for example, O. E. Baker [6, 7], and D. J. Bogue and M. J. Hagood [15].

[35] See D. S. Thomas [141].

[36] See T. Lynn Smith [125], p. 355, for a typical quotation from such a study.

More objective research is now possible on selective differentials in rural-urban migration,[37] and more light can be thrown on such questions as the loss of wealth from rural areas to cities through the loss of population in which a heavy investment has been made.[38]

D. Forecasting Future Migration

1. projection of historical trends

a. Extrapolation. The simplest (but in many situations probably the least satisfactory) method of obtaining a forecast of migration into and out of an open area is by extrapolation of past trends.

The procedure is to (1) determine migration totals or rates for some desired sequence of periods in the past, by means of one or another of the methods discussed in the previous sections; (2) fit a trend line or curve to the data by use of freehand, graphic, or mathematical methods; and (3) extrapolate to obtain total migration for desired periods in the future or to obtain future rates of movement. This process may be applied to the migratory population as a whole or to any one or more of its components.

The greater the number of past periods utilized, the better a given curve may be said to describe the past data and, superficially at least, the better the resulting forecast.[39]

The various types of mathematical curves which may be applied to past data and the various ways in which these curves may be fitted have been discussed at some length in the previous chapter on population projection, to which the reader is referred.

The fundamental postulate of the extrapolation techniques, namely, that future trends can be identified solely on the basis of past relationships, was pointed out to be a weakness when forecasting total population numbers. This defect is even more glaring when these techniques are used to forecast migration. Certain of the determinants of population growth, such as births and deaths, may be considered relatively stable phenomena. In the absence of physical calamity, these determinants usually change character slowly, reflecting the net effect of change in a complex matrix of social, economic, and political forces. They may

[37] D. J. Bogue and M. J. Hagood [15] made extensive use of the 1940 U. S. Census data on migration to measure differentials in migration and made generalizations with respect to selectivity.

[38] See, for example, O. E. Baker [6, 7], and P. G. Beck [9].

[39] For examples of the use of a relatively short period (one decade) to determine a trend, see R. Clapp [24] and William Blakey [10]; for an example of the use of a longer period (three decades) see L. Segoe [120]; and for an example of the use of a relatively long period (eight decades), see W. A. Spurr [127].

therefore be described reasonably safely by extrapolation of past trends.[40]
In contrast, the migration element of population growth in an open area
is much more volatile and marginal. It tends to be linked more directly,
and to respond much more quickly, to a few dominant economic and other
forces. Therefore future migration cannot be forecast as firmly with the
use of extrapolation techniques as may population numbers. Hence,
forecasts of future migration by trend extrapolation must be used with
considerable caution and preferably only as a check on forecasts made by
other methods.[41]

b. Ratio and other similar methods. Ratio methods, when judiciously
employed, represent an improvement over simple extrapolation. They
recognize that migration is not an isolated phenomenon, and they obtain
forecasts which are not wholly dependent on the mere facts of previous
migration.

The general procedure is to relate migration, via a constant or changing
ratio, to some aspect of population growth. The reader will recognize that
in many respects the ways in which the ratio techniques may be applied to
forecast migration are similar to the ways (already discussed in the previous
chapter) in which these techniques can be used to forecast total population.

In the least-refined form, the ratio methods assume that migration for a
given area is a simple function (e.g. a percentage) of total population
growth of the area, and that this relationship over the past will continue
in the future.[42] An alternative form relates migration in the area to total
population growth of some other (larger) area, such as the nation, whose
numbers may be considered to have a bearing on that migration and for
which there exists a population forecast.[43] Various components of total
population may also be used as the base to which the ratio is applied.

Other variants of the ratio method involve relating migration in a given
area (1) to forecasts of migration in a different area,[44] or (2) to forecasts
of migration in a component group of the population of the given area.[45]

Better estimates of future migration may be expected from ratio methods
where an attempt is made to identify possible determinants of migration.
One such determinant is economic opportunity. For example, migration
might be estimated in terms of a percentage (or some similar ratio) of

[40] However, see Joseph S. Davis [31–33], for example, for critical comment on the
deficiencies in such projections in practice.

[41] For instance, see W. A. Spurr [127].

[42] See, for example, P. M. Reid [114], V. B. Stanbery [128], and F. Lorimer [93].

[43] V. B. Stanbery [128] has used ratios based on total national population and on
total national population less that of the area under study. See also F. Lorimer [93].

[44] W. D. Bryant [19] has used national migration figures in this way.

[45] P. V. Lane [85] has related migration in a given area to migration in the school age
component of the population of the area as determined from school enrollment data.

projected new employment opportunities. A more refined type of ratio analysis might relate migration to projections of new employment opportunities as measured by occupational structure, by skill and educational requirements, or by other significant characteristics.[46] A number of the succeeding chapters will treat and evaluate the projection of new employment opportunities by alternative procedures. They will thereby furnish to the migration analyst pertinent information on type of base to which a ratio may be applied, as well as knowledge on appropriate techniques for projecting the size of a selected base.

Where adequate data exist, the more refined methods of regression and covariance analysis may be applied to the relationships suggested in the foregoing ratio techniques.[47]

The degree of accuracy obtained in forecasts of migration made by the ratio and similar methods will depend on the correctness of the particular relationship selected to establish the ratio. The basic weakness of the methods as typically used lies in the dependence on past trends to determine future ratios (as is the case with similar methods applied to future population forecasting). This is particularly true where cruder graphic and mathematical techniques of extrapolation are employed to obtain future ratios. Where an attempt is made to obtain independent estimates, by more refined forecasting techniques, of the future interplay of forces which forms the basis of the ratios, better forecasts of migration flows may be expected.

  c. Subjective projection. The great majority of forecasts of migration in open areas are made subjectively. This procedure is undoubtedly the consequence of the rapid and erratic fashion in which population movements respond to the various changes in the social, economic, and physical conditions which determine migration. These determinants are themselves extremely difficult to identify and to measure, since they do not necessarily operate in the same combinations or with the same relative importance in different circumstances of time and location. It is therefore impossible to generalize concerning subjective methods of migration forecasting—the particular method used will depend on the knowledge and understanding which the forecaster has of the area under study and his skill in applying this knowledge. The most that can be said is that the forecaster should examine past migration trends to attempt to identify the factors that have determined migration in the past, make a selection of

___

[46] Analysis by means of a ratio of migration to future employment opportunities is implicit in P. M. Reid [114] and Greensboro Department of Planning [53].

[47] W. A. Spurr [127] has correlated net migration figures with past data on national income and with an independent forecast of national income. For further discussion of correlation analysis see previous chapter on population projections and references.

the factors likely to be the determinants of future migration, make some estimate of the future significance of these factors, and thus arrive at an estimate of future migration,[48] This procedure may, of course, be carried out for net migration, for both in-migration and out-migration, for total migration, or for any desired component breakdown.[49]

2. THEORETICAL MODELS

Up to this point we have discussed techniques which have been used to estimate past or future migration with little or insufficient explanation of the forces at play.   Clearly, if we can understand the underlying forces that govern migration, we are in a stronger position to take the next step and project into the future.

Several authors have attempted to explain migration via models of one sort or another.   Although they have not made forecasts, it is worthwhile to record their contribution.   Their theoretical formulations do furnish additional insights to the regional analyst who is compelled to make projections.   However, their theoretical formulations are also closely related to gravity models, which will be discussed fully in Chapter 11. Therefore, in this chapter, we sketch only some of the earlier thinking. The reader is referred to Chapter 11 for presentation of other formulations and their evaluation.

Most of the hypotheses to be discussed here are either modifications or elaborations of the "laws" of migration postulated by E. G. Ravenstein [113] in the latter part of the nineteenth century.   Working with British migration data, Ravenstein developed the following classification of migrants: (1) the local migrant, (2) the short-journey migrant, (3) the long-journey migrant, (4) the migrant-by-stages.   He then distinguished between temporary and permanent migrants and between areas of "absorption" and of "dispersion."   The "laws" which he derived are as follows.

> (1) . . . the great body of . . . migrants only proceed a short distance, and . . . there takes place . . . shifting or displacement of the population . . . in the direction of the great centres of commerce and industry . . .

[48] Well-documented examples of subjective estimates are to be found in V. B. Stanbery [128], V. B. Stanbery and J. C. Riley [129], Columbia Basin Inter-Agency Committee [28], W. S. Thompson [144], and C. M. Frisén [41].

[49] For example, D. J. Bogue [11], in his Chicago study, determined migration rates from past data and applied these rates by cohorts in the same proportions as in the immediate past.   The California Teachers Association [21] distributed migration in California by age, in proportion to figures for national migration, and adjusted the resulting forecasts to agree with independent "target" estimates for total population. S. Kuznets [84] accepted the 1920–1930 trends of migration in Philadelphia as "typical" and projected them by age and sex cohorts.

(2) . . . the process of absorption . . . [goes] on in the following manner:—
The inhabitants . . . immediately surrounding a town of rapid growth flock
into it; the gaps thus left . . . are filled up by migrants from more remote
districts, until the attractive force . . . makes its influence felt, step by step,
to the most remote corner of the kingdom. Migrants enumerated in a
certain centre of absorption will consequently grow less with the distance
[from, and proportionately to,] the native population which furnishes
them. . .

(3) The process of dispersion is the inverse of that of absorption. . .

(4) Each main current of migration produces a compensating counter-
current.

(5) Migrants proceeding long distances generally go . . . to one of the
great centres of commerce or industry.

(6) The natives of towns are less migratory than those of the rural parts
of the country.

(7) Females are more migratory than males.

Among other ways, the first five of these laws may be formulated with the
use of mathematical symbols, as follows:

$$M_{ij} = \frac{P_j}{d_{ij}} \cdot f(z_i)$$

where M_{ij} = migration to destination i from source j;

  $f(z_i)$ = some function of Z_i where Z_i measures the attractive force
    of destination i;

  P_j = population of source j; and

  d_{ij} = distance between source j and destination i.

It is implicit in Ravenstein's investigations that the "attractive force" of
the destination is somehow related to economic opportunity. If the particular function of this force were known, then according to this interpretation migration between any two locations could be predicted, since
the size of the source and the distance between the source and the destination would also be known.[50]

In recent years much attention has been paid to the interrelationship of
the three elements (population size, distance, and forces of attraction and
repulsion) which Ravenstein identified in his pioneer study as having a
major bearing on migration. Various explanations of migration are based
on the reasoning that (1) social and/or economic imbalances between
localities generate attractive influences in the more "prosperous" locality
and dispersive influences in the less "prosperous" locality, which result in
migration from the less prosperous to the more prosperous locality;[51]

[50] For further discussion of Ravenstein's contribution, see, among others, D. O.
Price [107], F. Strodtbeck [136], and D. S. Thomas [141].

[51] For examples of attempts to determine economic and social variables in migration
see Carter Goodrich et al. [50], J. Isaac [77], D. O. Price [111], and E. L. Thorndike [148].

(2) migration is affected by the economic and/or social costs of traversing the intervening space between any pair of localities;[52] and (3) migration from a given area is affected by the number of persons able to move.[53]

Among analysts there seems to be fairly general agreement that the relationship of distance to migration is inverse and that the relationship of force of attraction (and repulsion) and of population size to migration is direct. But there is little agreement regarding the specific functions of distance and population size that are relevant, and regarding the way in which force of attraction should be measured. As examples, an early hypothesis advanced by E. C. Young [177] contended that movement varies inversely with the square of the distance between the source and terminal areas. C. E. Lively [91] found that movement "falls away from the polar center after the manner of a hyperbolic surface."[54] S. A. Stouffer [134] maintained that there is no necessary relationship between distance and mobility, but that the number of persons going a given distance is directly proportional to the number of opportunities *at* that distance and inversely proportional to the number of *intervening* opportunities between the origin and destination. Finally, R. Vining [170] has recognized that the migrant's conception of distance may also play an important role and has suggested that intervening space may result in discounting on the part of the migrant similar in character to that resulting from intervening time.

As already indicated, these hypotheses are intimately associated with the gravity model to be fully discussed in Chapter 11. We therefore must postpone an evalution of these and later hypotheses until the materials of that chapter are treated.

E. CONCLUSIONS

In conclusion we can only reiterate that methods for estimating migration are not nearly as good as we might like them to be. For fairly obvious reasons more reliable estimates can be made for past migration than for future migration.

Aside from the use of population registers and direct census enumeration of migration, the best methods of calculating past migration would

[52] For examples of attempts to measure the impact of distance on migration, see D. J. Bogue and W. S. Thompson [16], D. O. Price [107], A. Westefeld [172], and C. E. Lively [91].

[53] T. R. Anderson [3] and others distinguish between two types of theory embraced in this reasoning: (*a*) the "socio-economic push-pull theory" represented by (1); and (*b*) the "gravitational theory" represented by (2) and (3). See Chapter 11 for full citation of references on gravitational theory.

[54] See C. E. Lively [91], p. 101.

seem to involve the residence and nativity techniques. Such methods are linked to the use of more direct data. They yield more detail on direction of flows of population. Residual methods, which include the survival techniques, are in general less satisfactory, although their data requirements in many situations are less demanding.[55] Each of these techniques can yield differential migration (which is generally desirable) when the necessary additional basic data are available.

In estimating future migration less firm results than those for past migration can be expected from considerations of data availability alone. The simple extrapolation techniques are very unsatisfactory and should, at the minimum, be supplemented by a subjective projection in which the significance of various relevant factors is weighed. When the future interplay of economic and social forces can be anticipated and causal relationships identified with some degree of reliability, superior estimates of future migration can frequently be obtained in an indirect manner. The ways in which such estimates may be derived are discussed in later chapters, particularly Chapters 8 and 12. But it is also clear that much more theoretical analysis and understanding of migration are required before we can achieve the degree of reliability in estimating future migration that is to be desired. One promising avenue of theoretical investigation is examined in Chapter 11 where gravity, potential, and spatial interaction models are discussed.

REFERENCES

1. Anderson, Theodore R., *Characteristics of Metropolitan Subregions Associated with Intermetropolitan Migration, 1935 to 1940*, unpublished Ph.D. dissertation, University of Wisconsin, Madison, Wisconsin, 1953.
2. ———, "Intermetropolitan Migration: A Comparison of the Hypotheses of Zipf and Stouffer," *American Sociological Review*, Vol. 20 (June 1955).
3. ———, "Intermetropolitan Migration: A Correlation Analysis," *American Journal of Sociology*, Vol. 61 (March 1956).
4. ———, "Potential Models and Spatial Distribution of Population," *Papers and Proceedings of the Regional Science Association*, Vol. 2, 1956.
5. Ashley, E. Everett, 3rd, "Mobility and Migration as Factors in Housing Demand," *Housing Research*, No. 6, U. S. Housing and Home Finance Administration, Washington, D.C., Oct. 1953.
6. Baker, O. E., "Rural and Urban Distribution of the Population in the United States," *The Annals of the American Academy of Political and Social Science*, Vol. 188 (Nov. 1936).
7. ———, "Rural-Urban Migration in the National Welfare," *Annals of the Association of American Geographers*, Vol. 23 (June 1933).
8. Bassett, Raymond E., "Stouffer's Law as a Measure of Intergroup Contacts," *Sociometry*, Vol. 9 (1946).

[55] However, see Lee et al. [89].

9. Beck, P. G., *Recent Trends in the Rural Population of Ohio*, Ohio Agricultural Experiment Station, Bulletin 533, Wooster, Ohio, May 1934.

10. Blakey, William, and others, *The Future Population of Providence, 1940–80*, City Plan Commission, Publication No. 1, Providence, Rhode Island, Oct. 1945.

11. Bogue, D. J., *An Estimate of Metropolitan Chicago's Future Population: 1955 to 1965*, a report to the Chicago Plan Commission and Office of the Housing and Redevelopment Coordinator, published jointly by The Chicago Community Inventory, University of Chicago, and the Scripps Foundation, Miami University, Oxford, Ohio, Feb. 2, 1955.

12. ———, *A Methodological Study of Migration and Labor Mobility in Michigan and Ohio in 1947*, Scripps Foundation Studies in Population Distribution No. 4, Miami University, Oxford, Ohio, June 1952.

13. ———, *Methods of Studying Internal Migration*, technical paper prepared for a regional seminar on population in Central and South America, held in Rio de Janeiro, Dec. 1955.

14. ———, "Residential Mobility and the Migration of Workers," in *Manpower in the United States: Problems and Policies*, Industrial Relations Research Association Publication No. 11, Harper and Brothers, New York, 1954.

15. ———, and M. J. Hagood, *Subregional Migration in the United States, 1935–40, Vol. II, Differential Migration in the Corn and Cotton Belts*, Scripps Foundation Studies in Population Distribution No. 6, Miami University, Oxford, Ohio, 1953.

16. ———, and W. S. Thompson, "Migration and Distance," *American Sociological Review*, Vol. 14 (April 1949).

17. Bowles, Gladys K., *Farm Population: Net Migration from the Rural-Farm Population 1940–50*, U. S. Agricultural Marketing Service, Statistical Bulletin No. 176, Washington, D.C., 1956.

18. Bright, Margaret, and Dorothy S. Thomas, "Interstate Migration and Intervening Opportunities, *American Sociological Review*, Vol. 6 (Dec. 1941).

19. Bryant, W. D., *Housing Market Analysis of Greater Kansas City*, Department of Research and Information, Report No. 6, Kansas City, Missouri, Dec. 1945.

20. Burt, Henry J., *The Population of Missouri: A General Survey of its Sources, Changes, and Present Composition*, Missouri Agricultural Experiment Station Research Bulletin 188, Columbia, Missouri, May 1933.

21. California Teachers Association, *California's Future School Population: 1948–1960*, Research Bulletin No. 3, San Francisco, Oct. 1948.

22. Carrothers, Gerald A. P., "An Historical Review of the Gravity and Potential Concepts of Human Interaction," *Journal of the American Institute of Planners*, Vol. 22 (Winter 1956).

23. Cavanaugh, Joseph A., "Formulation, Analysis, and Testing of the Interactance Hypothesis," *American Sociological Review*, Vol. 15 (Dec. 1950).

24. Clapp, Raymond, *Population Change and Governmental Planning in the District of Columbia*, Budget Office, Washington, D.C., May 1952.

25. Clark, C. D., and R. L. Roberts, *People of Kansas: A Demographic and Sociological Study*, Kansas State Planning Board, Topeka, Kansas, 1936.

26. Clark, Noble and G. W. Hill, *Wisconsin's Changing Population*, Science Inquiry Publication IX, University of Wisconsin, Madison, Wisconsin, Oct. 1942.

27. Coe, Paul E., "Nonwhite Population Increases in Metropolitan Areas," *Journal of the American Statistical Association*, Vol. 50 (June 1955).

28. Columbia Basin Inter-Agency Committee, Subcommittee on Comprehensive Programs, *Population Projections for the Pacific Northwest States and Region 1960 and 1975*, July 21, 1952.

29. Consolidated Edison Company of New York, *New York City's Population Growth 1790–1970*, Consolidated Edison Company, Economic Research Department, New York, Dec. 1946.

30. Cox, Peter R., "Demographic Developments in Great Britain Since the Royal Commission on Population," *Eugenics Review*, Vol. 47 (April 1955).

31. Davis, Joseph S., "Our Changed Population Outlook and Its Significance," *American Economic Review*, Vol. 17 (June 1952).

32. ———, "The Population Upsurge and the American Economy, 1945–80," *The Journal of Political Economy*, Vol. 61 (Oct. 1953).

33. ———, *The Population Upsurge in the United States*, Food Research Institute, War-Peace Pamphlets No. 12, Stanford University, Stanford, California, Dec. 1949. .

34. Dodd, Stuart C., "All-or-None Elements and Mathematical Models for Sociologists," *American Sociological Review*, Vol. 17 (April 1952).

35. ———, "The Interactance Hypothesis: A Gravity Model Fitting Physical Masses and Human Groups," *American Sociological Review*, Vol. 15 (April 1950).

36. Dorn, H. F., and Frank Lorimer, "Migration, Reproduction, and Population Adjustment," *The Annals of the American Academy of Political and Social Science*, Vol 188 (Nov. 1936).

37. Edsall, R. L., "This Changing Canada: How Canadians Move Around Canada (Migration and Population Gains 1946–54)," *Canadian Business*, Jan. 1955.

38. Figá-Talamanca, Mario, "Forms of Population Gravitation on Spatial Units," *Bulletin of the International Statistical Institute*, Vol. 34, No. 3 (1954).

39. Folger, John, "Some Aspects of Migration in the Tennessee Valley," *American Sociological Review*, Vol. 18 (June 1953).

40. Freedman, Ronald, *Recent Migration to Chicago*, University of Chicago Press, Chicago, 1950.

41. Frisén, C. M., *Estimated Population of California, 1950–1954 with Projections to 1965*, California State Department of Finance, Division of Budgets and Accounts, Financial Research Section, Sacramento, California, July 1954.

42. Froomkin, Joseph N., "The Migration of Capital, People, and Technology," in *Economic Development: Principles and Patterns*, ed. by Harold F. Williamson and John A. Buttrick, Prentice-Hall, Englewood Cliffs, New Jersey, 1954.

43. Galpin, C. J., and T. B. Manny, *Interstate Migrations among the Native White Population as Indicated by Differences between State of Birth and State of Residence: A Series of Maps Based on the Census 1870–1930*, U. S. Bureau of Agricultural Economics, Washington, D.C., Oct. 1934.

44. Goldner, William, "Spatial and Locational Aspects of Metropolitan Labor Markets," *American Economic Review*, Vol. 45 (March 1955).

45. Goldstein, Sydney, "City Directories as Sources of Migration Data," *American Journal of Sociology*, Vol. 60 (Sept. 1954).

46. ———, "Migration and Occupational Mobility in Norristown, Pennsylvania," *American Sociological Review*, Vol. 20 (Aug. 1955).

47. ———, "Repeated Migration as a Factor in High Mobility Rates," *American Sociological Review*, Vol. 19 (Oct. 1954).

48. Goodrich, Carter, "Internal Migration and Economic Opportunity," *The Annals of the American Academy of Political and Social Science*, Vol. 188 (Nov. 1936).

49. Goodrich, Carter, B. W. Allin, and M. Hayes, *Migration and Planes of Living 1920–1934*, University of Pennsylvania Press, Philadelphia, 1935.

50. ———, and others, *Migration and Economic Opportunity*, The Report of the Study of Population Redistribution, University of Pennsylvania Press, Philadelphia, 1936.

51. Gordon, Margaret S., *Employment Expansion and Population Growth, the California Experience: 1900–1950*, Institute of Industrial Relations, University of California, Los Angeles, 1954.

52. Great Britain, *Report of the Royal Commission on the Distribution of the Industrial Population*, His Majesty's Stationery Office, London, 1940.

53. Greensboro, N. C., Department of Planning, *Future Employment and Population in the Greensboro Metropolitan Area*, Technical Report No. 1, Greensboro, North Carolina, June 1948.

54. Hagood, Margaret J., and E. F. Sharp, *Rural-Urban Migration in Wisconsin, 1940–50*, University of Wisconsin, Research Bulletin 176, Madison, Wisconsin, Aug. 1951.

55. Hamilton, C. Horace, *Rural-Urban Migration in North Carolina, 1920 to 1930*, Agricultural Experiment Station Bulletin No. 295, North Carolina State College, Raleigh, North Carolina, Feb. 1934.

56. ———, "Rural-Urban Migration in the Tennessee Valley Between 1920 and 1930," *Social Forces*, Vol. 13 (Oct. 1934).

57. ———, and F. M. Henderson, "Use of the Survival Rate Method in Measuring Net Migration," *Journal of the American Statistical Association*, Vol. 39 (June 1944).

58. Hart, Hornell, N., *Selective Migration as a Factor in Child Welfare in the U. S.*, Studies in Child Welfare, Vol. 1, No. 7, University of Iowa, Iowa City, Iowa, 1921.

59. ———, "Urbanization of Population," in *Population Problems in the United States and Canada*, ed. by L. I. Dublin, Houghton Mifflin, Boston, 1926.

60. Hauser, P. M., "Population Shifts and Income Changes," *Marketing Series*, No. 52, American Management Association, New York, Jan. 1943.

61. ———, "Wartime Population Changes and Postwar Prospects," *Journal of Marketing*, Vol. 8 (Jan. 1944).

62. ———, and Hope T. Eldridge, "Projection of Urban Growth and Migration to Cities in the United States," *Milbank Memorial Fund Quarterly*, Vol. 25 (July 1947).

63. Hawley, Amos H., *Intrastate Migration in Michigan: 1935–40*, University of Michigan Press, Ann Arbor, Michigan, 1953.

64. Heath, A. A., "Population Forecasting for Planning Purposes," *Journal of the Town Planning Institute*, Vol. 34 (Jan.–Feb. 1948).

65. Heberle, Rudolf, "German Approaches to Internal Migrations," Appendix B1 in Dorothy S. Thomas, *Research Memorandum on Migration Differentials*, Social Science Research Council, New York, 1938.

66. ———, "Types of Migration," *Southwestern Social Science Quarterly*, Vol. 36 (June 1955).

67. Henderson, Sidney, *Labor Force Potentials: Farm Migration Available for Urban Growth, Eight Nebraska Cities, 1940–50*, Business Research Bulletin No. 60, College of Business Administration, University of Nebraska, Lincoln, Nebraska, 1956.

68. Hitt, Homer L., "Migration and Southern Cities," in *The Sociology of Urban Life*, ed. by T. Lynn Smith and C. A. McMahon, The Dryden Press, New York, 1951.

69. ———, "Peopling the City: Migration," in *The Urban South*, ed. by Rupert B. Vance and N. J. Demerath, University of North Carolina Press, Chapel Hill, North Carolina, 1954.

70. Hitt, Homer L., "The Role of Migration in Population Change Among the Aged," *American Sociological Review*, Vol. 19 (April 1954).

71. Hofstee, E. W., "Some Preliminary Conclusions Concerning Internal Migration of Families and Individual Males and Individual Females in The Netherlands, Based on New Statistical Data," *Research Group for European Migration Problems, Bulletin*, Vol. 2 (July–Sept. 1954).

72. Holloway, Robert J., *A City is More than People: A Study of Fifteen Minnesota Communities*, Studies in Economics and Business No. 17, University of Minnesota Press, Minneapolis, Minnesota, 1954.

73. Hopper, Mabel L., and Marjorie Cantor, *Migrant Farm Workers in New York State*, Consumers League of New York, New York, 1953.

74. Hutchinson, E. P., "The Use of Routine Census and Vital Statistics Data for the Determination of Migration by Age and Sex," Appendix C2 in Dorothy S. Thomas, *Research Memorandum on Migration Differentials*, Social Science Research Council, New York, 1938.

75. Hutchinson, Glenn, *Population Movement in the Philadelphia Standard Metropolitan Area 1940–1950*, Southeastern Pennsylvania Regional Planning Commission, Bridgeport, Pennsylvania, May 1955.

76. Iklé, F. C., "Sociological Relationship of Traffic to Population and Distance," *Traffic Quarterly*, Vol. 8 (April 1954).

77. Isaac, Julius, *Economics of Migration*, Kegan Paul, London, 1947.

78. Isbell, E. C., "Internal Migration in Sweden and Intervening Opportunities," *American Sociological Review*, Vol. 9 (Dec. 1944).

79. Jaffe, A. J., *Handbook of Statistical Methods for Demographers*, preliminary edition, 2nd printing, U. S. Bureau of the Census, Washington, D.C., 1951.

80. ———, and R. O. Carleton, *Occupational Mobility in the United States 1930–1960*. Columbia University, King's Crown Press, New York, 1954.

81. Jerome, Harry, *Migration and Business Cycles*, Publications of the National Bureau of Economic Research No. 9, New York, 1926.

82. Johnson, Elmer H., "Methodological Note on Measuring Selection in Differential Migration," *Social Forces*, Vol. 33 (March 1955).

83. Klineberg, Otto, *Negro Intelligence and Selective Migration*, Columbia University Press, New York, 1935.

84. Kuznets, Simon S., *The Population of Philadelphia and Environs in 1950*, Institute of Local and State Government, University of Pennsylvania, Philadelphia, 1946.

85. Lane, Paul V., *The Estimation of Migration in the Progression of Population*, California Taxpayers' Association, Report No. 266, Los Angeles, Oct. 1933.

86. Lawrence, N., and B. Greenberg, "Illustrative Examples of Two Methods of Estimating the Current Population of Small Areas," *Current Population Reports, Population Estimates*, Series P-25, No. 20, U. S. Bureau of the Census, Washington, D.C., May 6, 1949.

87. Lee, Everett S., "Negro Intelligence and Selective Migration: A Philadelphia Test of the Klineberg Hypothesis," *American Sociological Review*, Vol. 16 (April 1951).

88. ———, and G. K. Bowles, "Selection and Use of Survival Ratios in Population Studies," *Agricultural Economics Research*, Vol. 6 (Oct. 1954), U. S. Department of Agriculture, Washington, D.C.

89. ———, A. R. Miller, C. P. Brainerd, and R. A. Easterlin, *Population Redistribution and Economic Growth, United States, 1870 to 1950, Vol. I, Methodological Considerations and Reference Tables*, American Philosophical Society, Philadelphia, 1957.

90. Lively, C. E., "The Development of Research in Rural Migration in the United States," *Démographie Statistique: études spéciales*, Congrès international de la population, Paris 1937, Vol. IV, Paris, 1938.

91. ———, "Spatial Mobility of the Rural Population with Respect to Local Areas," *American Journal of Sociology*, Vol. 43 (July 1937).

92. ———, and C. Taeuber, *Rural Migration in the United States*, U. S. Works Progress Administration, Research Monograph 19, Washington D.C., 1939.

93. Lorimer, Frank, *Suggestions on Population Studies for State Planning Boards*, revised edition, U. S. National Resources Committee, Washington, D.C., 1938.

94. ———, and F. Osborn, *Dynamics of Population*, Macmillan, New York, 1934.

95. Maclaurin, W. R., and C. A. Myers, "Wages and the Movement of Factory Labor," *The Quarterly Journal of Economics*, Vol. 57 (Feb. 1943).

96. McNamara, R. L., and others, *Rural-Urban Population Changes and Migration in Missouri 1940–1950*, Missouri Agricultural Experiment Station, Bulletin No. 620, Columbia, Missouri, April 1954.

97. Makower, H., J. Marschak, and H. W. Robinson, "Studies in Mobility of Labour: A Tentative Statistical Measure," and "Studies in Mobility of Labour: Analysis for Great Britain," *Oxford Economic Papers*, Vol. 1 (Oct. 1938), Vol. 2 (April 1939), and Vol. 4 (Sept. 1940).

98. Mayer, Kurt B., *The Population of Switzerland*, Columbia University Press, New York, 1952.

99. Meyer, Fritz, "German Internal Migration Statistics: Methods, Sources, and Data," Appendix C1 in Dorothy S. Thomas, *Research Memorandum on Migration Differentials*, Social Science Research Council, New York, 1938.

100. Moreno, J. L., "Contributions of Sociometry to Research Methodology in Sociology," *American Sociological Review*, Vol. 12 (June 1947).

101. ———, *Who Shall Survive?* Beacon House, Beacon, New York, 1953.

102. Myers, Charles A., "Patterns of Labor Mobility," in *Manpower in the United States: Problems and Policies*, Industrial Relations Research Association, Publication No. 11, Harper and Brothers, New York, 1954.

103. Pearlman, L. M., "Prospective Labor Supply on the West Coast," *Monthly Labor Review*, U. S. Bureau of Labor Statistics, Vol. 64 (April 1947).

104. ———, and L. Eskin, *State and Regional Variations in Prospective Labor Supply*, U. S. Bureau of Labor Statistics, Bulletin No. 893, Washington, D.C., 1947.

105. Pearson, Karl, "A Mathematical Theory of Random Migration," *Drapers' Company Research Memoirs*, Biometric Series III, Mathematical Contributions to the Theory of Evolution, No. XV, Cambridge University Press, 1906.

106. Pihlblad, C. T., and C. L. Gregory, "Selective Aspects of Migration Among Missouri High School Graduates," *American Sociological Review*, Vol. 19 (June 1954).

107. Price, D. O., "Distance and Direction as Vectors of Internal Migration, 1935–40," *Social Forces*, Vol. 27 (Oct. 1948).

108. ———, "Estimates of Net Migration in the United States, 1870–1940," *American Sociological Review*, Vol. 18 (Feb. 1953).

109. ———, "Examination of Two Sources of Error in the Estimation of Net Internal Migration," *Journal of the American Statistical Association*, Vol. 50 (Sept. 1955).

110. ———, "Nonwhite Migrants to and from Selected Cities," *American Journal of Sociology*, Vol. 54 (Nov. 1948).

111. ———, "Some Socio-Economic Factors in Internal Migration," *Social Forces*, Vol. 29 (April 1951).

112. Purdy, Lawson, "Negro Migration in the United States," *American Journal of Economics and Sociology*, Vol. 13 (July 1954).

113. Ravenstein, E. G., "The Laws of Migration," *Journal of the Royal Statistical Society*, Vol. 48 (June 1885) and Vol. 52 (June 1889).

114. Reid, P. M., *Population Prospectus for the Detroit Region 1960 and 1970*, Detroit Metropolitan Area Regional Planning Commission, Oct. 1950.

115. Reimer, Svend, "Notes on Method of Analysis of Swedish Migration Data," Appendix C3 in *Research Memorandum on Migration Differentials*, ed. by Dorothy S. Thomas, Social Science Research Council, New York, 1938.

116. Reynolds, C. N., and Sara Miles, *Statistical Memorandum No. 6, Growth of Population Series No. 3, Migration*, Bureau of Agricultural Economics, for Population Committee for The Central Valley Project Studies, Berkeley, California, July 5, 1944.

117. Schmid, C. F., and M. J. Griswold, "Migration within the State of Washington, 1935–40," *American Sociological Review*, Vol. 17 (June 1952).

118. Schneider, J. R. L., "Local Population Projections in England and Wales," *Population Studies*, Vol. 10 (July 1956).

119. Scripps Foundation, *Subregional Migration in the United States, 1935–40: Volume I, Streams of Migration*, Scripps Foundation Studies in Population Distribution, No. 5, published jointly with the U. S. Bureau of the Census, Oxford, Ohio, 1953.

120. Segoe, L., "The Population of Madison, Its Composition and Characteristics," Vol. 1, Book III, *Comprehensive Plan of Madison, Wisconsin and Environs*, Trustees of Madison Planning Trust, Madison, Wisconsin, Oct. 1938.

121. Shevky, E., and Marilyn Williams, *The Social Areas of Los Angeles*, University of California Press, Berkeley, California, 1949.

122. Shryock, H. S., "Population Estimates in Postcensal Years," *The Annals of the American Academy of Political and Social Science*, Vol. 188 (Nov. 1936).

123. ———, "Population Redistribution Within Metropolitan Areas: Evaluation of Research," *Social Forces*, Vol. 35 (Dec. 1956).

124. Siegel, J. S., and C. H. Hamilton, "Some Considerations in the Use of the Residual Method of Estimating Net Migration," *Journal of the American Statistical Association*, Vol. 47 (Sept. 1952).

125. Smith, T. L., *Population Analysis*, McGraw-Hill, New York, 1948.

126. Spengler, J. J., "Population Theory," in *A Survey of Contemporary Economics*, Vol. II, ed. by B. F. Haley, Richard D. Irwin, Homewood, Illinois, 1952.

127. Spurr, W. A., *Forecasts of California's Population and Production, 1950–1960*, Graduate School of Business, Business Research Series No. 4, Stanford University, Stanford, California, 1949.

128. Stanbery, V. B., *Better Population Forecasting for Areas and Communities*, U. S. Department of Commerce, Domestic Commerce Series No. 32, Washington, D.C., 1952.

129. ———, and J. C. Riley, *Estimated Range for Population Growth in California to 1960*, California State Reconstruction and Reemployment Commission, Sacramento, California, Nov. 1946.

130. Stewart, J. Q., "A Basis for Social Physics," *Impact of Science on Society*, Vol. 3 (Summer 1952).

131. ———, "Demographic Gravitation: Evidence and Applications," *Sociometry*, Vol. 11 (Feb.–May 1948).

132. ———, "Empirical Mathematical Rules Concerning The Distribution and Equilibrium of Population," *Geographical Review*, Vol. 37 (July 1947).

133. Stewart, J.Q., "Potential of Population and its Relationship to Marketing," in *Theory in Marketing*, ed. by Reavis Cox and Wroe Alderson, Richard D. Irwin, Homewood, Illinois, 1950.

134. Stouffer, Samuel A., "Intervening Opportunities: A Theory Relating Mobility and Distance," *American Sociological Review*, Vol. 5 (Dec. 1940).

135. Strodtbeck, Fred, "Equal Opportunity Intervals: A Contribution to the Method of Intervening Opportunity Analysis," *American Sociological Review*, Vol. 14 (Aug. 1949).

136. ———, "Population, Distance and Migration from Kentucky," *Sociometry*, Vol. 13 (May 1950).

137. Taeuber, Irene B., "Family, Migration, and Industrialization in Japan," *American Sociological Review*, Vol. 16 (April 1951).

138. Thomas, Brinley, *Migration and Economic Growth*, Cambridge University Press, Cambridge, England, 1954.

139. Thomas, D. S., "The Continuous Register System of Population Accounting," in *The Problems of a Changing Population*, U. S. National Resources Committee, Washington, D.C., 1938.

140. ———, "Economic and Social Aspects of Internal Migrations: An Exploratory Study of Selected Swedish Communities," in *Economic Essays in Honor of Wesley Clair Mitchell*, Columbia University Press, New York, 1935.

141. ———, *Research Memorandum on Migration Differentials*, Social Science Research Council, New York, 1938.

142. ———, "Streams of Internal Migration: A Further Exploration with Swedish Data," *Rural Sociology*, Vol. 2 (June 1937).

143. Thompson, W. S., *Migration within Ohio, 1935–1940: a Study in the Redistribution of Population*, Scripps Foundation, Oxford, Ohio, 1951.

144. ———, *The Population of the Cincinnati Metropolitan Area*, City Planning Commission, Cincinnati, Ohio, Dec. 1945.

145. ———, *Population Problems*, 4th edition, McGraw-Hill, New York, 1953.

146. ———, *Research Memorandum on Internal Migration in the Depression*, Social Science Research Council Bulletin 30, New York, 1937.

147. ———, and D. J. Bogue, "Subregional Migration as an Area of Research," *Social Forces*, Vol. 27 (May 1949).

148. Thorndike, E. L., "The Causes of Interstate Migration," *Sociometry*, Vol. 5 (Dec. 1942).

149. Thornthwaite, C. W., *Internal Migration in the United States*, University of Pennsylvania Press, Study of Population Distribution, Bulletin No. 1, Philadelphia, 1934.

150. Trewartha, Glenn T., and W. Zelinsky, "Population Distribution and Change in Korea, 1925–1949," *Geographical Review*, Vol. 45 (Jan. 1955).

151. Truesdell, Leon E., "Residual Relationships and Velocity of Change as Pitfalls in the Field of Statistical Forecasting," *Journal of the American Statistical Association*, Vol. 33 (June 1938).

152. United Nations, Department of Social Affairs, Population Division, *The Determinants and Consequences of Population Trends*, United Nations, Population Studies No. 17, New York, 1953. (ST/SOA/Series A/17. Sales No.: 1953. XIII. 3.)

153. ———, *Problems of Migration Statistics*, United Nations, Population Studies No. 5, New York, 1949. (ST/SOA/Series A/5. Sales No.: 1950. XIII. 1.)

154. U. S. Bureau of the Census, "Civilian Migration in the United States: December 1941 to March 1945," *Population*, Series P–S, No. 5, Department of Commerce, Washington, D.C., 1945.

155. ———, "Internal Migration in the United States: 1935 to 1940," *Population— Special Reports*, Series P–44, No. 10, Department of Commerce, Washington, D.C., April 7, 1944.

156. ———, "Internal Migration in the United States: April 1940 to February 1946," *Population*, Series P–S, No. 11, Department of Commerce, Washington, D.C., 1946.

157. ———, "Interstate Migration and Other Population Changes: 1940 to 1943," *Population—Special Reports*, Series P–44, No. 17, Department of Commerce, Washington, D.C., Aug. 28, 1944.

158. ———, "Migration in the United States: August 1945 to August 1946," *Population*, Series P–S, No. 24, Department of Commerce, Washington, D.C., 1947.

159. ———, "Mobility of the Population, for the United States: April 1950 to April 1951," *Current Population Reports, Population Characteristics*, Series P-20, No. 39, Department of Commerce, Washington, D.C., July 14, 1952.

160. ———, "Mobility of the Population of the United States: April 1952," *Current Population Reports, Population Characteristics*, Series P-20, No. 47, Department of Commerce, Washington, D.C., Sept. 27, 1953.

161. ———, "Mobility of the Population of the United States: April 1952 to April 1953," *Current Population Reports, Population Characteristics*, Series P-20, No. 49, Department of Commerce, Washington, D.C., Dec. 1, 1953.

162. ———, "Mobility of the Population of the United States: April 1953, to April 1954," *Current Population Reports, Population Characteristics*, Series P-20, No. 57 Department of Commerce, Washington, D.C., April 25, 1955.

163. ———, "Mobility of the Population of the United States: April 1954 to April 1955," *Current Population Reports, Population Characteristics*, Series P-20, No. 61, Department of Commerce, Washington, D.C., Oct. 28, 1955.

164. ———, "Postwar Migration and its Causes in the United States: August 1945 to October 1946," *Current Population Reports, Population Characteristics*, Series P-20, No. 4, Department of Commerce, Washington, D.C., Oct. 7, 1947.

165. U. S. Congress (77th, 1st Session), *Interstate Migration*, Report of the Select Committee to Investigate the Interstate Migration of Destitute Citizens, U. S. Government Printing Office, House Report No. 369, Washington, D.C., 1941.

166. U. S. National Housing Agency, *The Population Factor in Housing Market Analysis*, Housing Market Analysis Bulletin No. 5, Washington, D.C., July 1945.

167. U. S. National Resources Committee, *The Problems of a Changing Population*, U. S. Government Printing Office, Washington, D.C., 1938.

168. U. S. President's Commission on Migratory Labor, *Migratory Labor in American Agriculture*, U. S. Government Printing Office, Washington, D.C., 1951.

169. Vining, Rutledge, "A Description of Certain Spatial Aspects of an Economic System," *Economic Development and Cultural Change*, Vol. 3 (Jan. 1955).

170. ———, "The Region as an Economic Entity and Certain Variations to be Observed in the Study of Systems of Regions," *American Economic Review*, Vol. 39 (May 1949).

171. Webb, J. N., and Malcolm Brown, *Migrant Families*, U. S. Works Progress Administration, Research Monograph 18, Washington D.C., 1938.

172. Westefeld, A., "The Distance Factor in Migration," *Social Forces*, Vol. 19 (Dec. 1940).

173. Westefeld, A., *Michigan Migrants*, U. S. Works Progress Administration, Washington, D.C., March 1939.
174. Whelpton, P. K., *Iowa's Population Prospect*, Agricultural Experiment Station, Research Bulletin No. 177, Iowa State College of Agriculture and Mechanic Arts, Ames, Iowa, Oct. 1934.
175. Whetten, Nathan L., and Robert G., Burnight, "Internal Migration in Mexico," *Rural Sociology*, Vol. 21 (June 1956).
176. Wisconsin State Planning Board, *An Analysis of Population Growth in Wisconsin*, Bulletin No. 4, Madison, Wisconsin, 1937.
177. Young, E. C., *The Movement of Farm Population*, Cornell Agricultural Experiment Station, Bulletin 426, Ithaca, New York, 1924.

Chapter 4

Regional Income Estimation
and Social Accounting*

A. INTRODUCTION

Population numbers are a variable with which any regional analyst must be concerned. Equally important is the income associated with these numbers. What is average per capita income? What is the distribution of the total regional income among the several social, ethnic, and occupational groups? How can such income distribution and per capita income be projected into the future? These are basic questions which relate to welfare of people and which lie at the heart of much regional analysis and development work. In fact, the desire to increase per capita real income is one of the fundamental reasons for undertaking a development program. The ability to measure income accurately is therefore basic.

A number of techniques have been developed for estimating regional income. Much less progress has been made in the analysis of distribution of income within any meaningful set of population classes. And, unfortunately, the major problem of projecting future per capita income and its distribution is largely untouched. It should be noted that this last problem is closely linked with, and requires just as penetrating an analysis as, the associated problem of projecting industrial growth and economic

* Sections A–D of this chapter were written with John H. Cumberland, and section E with David F. Bramhall.

80

development. Because of this interrelation the discussion of the projection problem will be presented in later chapters, especially Chapter 12, after more materials have been covered.

Beyond the concept of income are other concepts which are intertwined and which also relate to social and economic welfare. There are a group of concepts, such as Gross Regional Product, net regional expenditures, balance of payments with other areas, which along with income help indicate how well an economic and social system is performing. They, and their constituent parts, such as household consumption expenditures, government purchases of goods and services, net private investment, personal savings, describe the manner in which a system has and continues to function. They also furnish greater insight into the interrelation of economic and social processes.

When the size of the accounts to which these concepts refer is measured, a social accounting system emerges.[1] As we shall see, the particular type of social accounting system which is of greatest significance for a particular study will vary not only with the region but with the purpose and policy orientation of the study. The social accounting system which an investigator selects has basic interrelations with other systems—population systems (as discussed in Chapters 2 and 3), interindustry systems, money flows systems, social-cultural interaction systems, and others. But these interrelations will be fully developed in subsequent chapters after more ground is covered.

We shall broadly view procedures for the estimation of income and other major social accounts. We shall consider (1) regions greater than states where they may consist of whole states or parts of states; (2) regions identical with states; and (3) regions smaller than states. We shall therefore consider ways of constructing social accounts based on national accounts and state income statistics as well as a variety of local materials such as data on income taxes, sales taxes by commodities, power consumption by industries, wage earners and occupation breakdown by industry, industrial production, retail and wholesale sales, monetary and financial operations, and social security payments.

In the first section to follow we shall outline briefly *National Income Accounts*, particularly as they have developed in the United States. This outline will furnish the reader with background and perspective which will facilitate his understanding of regional income and other social accounting

---

[1] It should be noted that the distinction between an income accounting system and a social accounting system is not clear-cut. Although it is not necessary to retain such a distinction, for purposes of exposition we shall generally do so. (The materials to be presented will not require that we retain the distinction at all times.) Many analysts regard the two systems as synonymous.

concepts. In the following two sections we shall treat in turn *conceptual problems* of regional income measurement in developed areas and *procedures* used in regional income measurement in the United States. Although these two sections will emphasize income measurement, much of the material will relate as well to the measurement of other social accounts for regions. The discussion of *social accounting systems for both underdeveloped and developed open regions* will then follow at some length in still another section, and the chapter will be brought to a close with some evaluative remarks in a concluding section.

B. NATIONAL INCOME ACCOUNTS

As a preface to a discussion of regional income estimation, it is helpful to review briefly the essential elements of national income accounting as they have been developed in advanced areas. There are two reasons for this. First, the concepts of regional income now generally in use are adaptations of concepts developed for national income measurement, even though in practice the unsatisfactory results of applying national income concepts to regions have suggested the importance of developing income accounts tailored to the dimensions of the regional problem. Secondly, regional income estimates have frequently taken the form of percentage breakdowns of national income estimates.

The concept of national income as a flow of goods and services was developed as early as 1767 by Graslin.[2] Quesnay's famous *Tableau Économique* represents a later effort to work out the process of income creation in terms of production and distribution.[3] However, only since the development of effective interest in measuring national income during the 1930's has the U. S. Department of Commerce, building on the conceptual work of Simon Kuznets[4] and earlier investigators,[5]

[2] J. J. L. Graslin, *Essai Analytique sur la Richesse et sur l'Impôt*, cited in J. A. Schumpeter [64], p. 175. Schumpeter also mentions the publication of *National Income in 1868* by Robert D. Baxter, p. 522, and an earlier attempt in 1696 by Gregory King to estimate English income and expenditure in 1688 (pp. 212–213, fn).

[3] J. A. Schumpeter [64], p. 241.

[4] S. Kuznets [43].

[5] Other names associated with the earliest attempts at national income estimation in the United States are Charles B. Spahr, Frank H. Streightoff, Willford I. King, and Oswald W. Knauth. For descriptions of their work, see J. L. Lancaster [45], pp. 7–9, and W. M. Adamson [1], pp. 1–2. Other outstanding contributions have originated largely within the British Empire and are associated with the names of Bowley, Stamp, Colin Clark, J. E. Meade, and J. R. N. Stone, to mention only a few. The Reprint Series of the Department of Applied Economics, University of Cambridge, directed by Stone, is a particularly rich source of contributions to the theory and practice of social accounting.

pioneered in the large-scale, detailed accounts of income in the United States.[6]

National income is a set of theories as well as magnitudes, and there are thus as many definitions of income as there are conceptual schemes. Kuznets summarizes and orders the concepts as follows:

> National income is the net product of or net return on the economic activity of individuals, business firms, and the social and political institutions that make up a nation. Because product or income yielding activities can be gauged at several stages of the economic process, national income can be measured in various ways, each permitting different groupings of components. At its origin in the productive system, it can be estimated as the sum of returns to the several factors of production—labor, capital, enterprise—each allocated by industrial origin. At this stage, the total can also be obtained by subtracting from the gross value-product of each industry the value of materials, semifabricates, durable capital, and services of other industries consumed in the production process. The corresponding allocation would be that of net income (and of gross value of product) by industrial origin. At the stage of the distribution of money compensation for economic activity, national income is the sum of income receipts of individuals and undistributed net profits of enterprises, the former possibly classified by type (wages, salaries, dividends, etc.), by size among groups of recipients, and by industrial origin, and the latter by industrial affiliation and type of enterprise. Finally, at the stage of use, national product or its monetary equivalent, national income, is the sum of either the flow of goods to consumers and net capital formation, allocated to whatever divisions of these two major categories are significant; or of expenditures and savings of consumers plus outlays of enterprises financed from their undistributed profits, also allocated to divisions of these three major categories.
>
> National income can, therefore, be described in various ways, corresponding to the several stages in the flow-process of economic activity at which it can be measured. However measured, the totals should be identical. Likewise, they can be subdivided into various categories, of which those mentioned above are a few. Indeed, the interest and usefulness of national income estimates lies in their distribution, so that the level of and changes in the total can be understood and interpreted in terms of its origin in the industrial system and of types of ultimate use. As problems in the solution of which national income estimates may be helpful shift, the emphasis in the measurement and analysis of national income shifts from one grouping of components to another.[7]

To illustrate the various income concepts, their composition, and relationships to each other we present in Table 1 several estimates for the United States in 1953.

The most comprehensive measure of income, Gross National Product (GNP), which summarizes the total value of output at market prices, is

[6] See the monthly *Survey of Current Business* [75], and its supplement [73].

[7] S. Kuznets [42], pp. 1–2. Further descriptions of the concepts of income categories are given in [73].

TABLE 1. INCOME CONCEPTS AND RELATIONSHIPS

(Millions of dollars)

1953

Gross National Product		$364,857
Less:	Capital consumption allowances	27,226
Equals:	*Net National Product*	337,631
Plus:	Subsidies minus current surplus of Government enterprises	− 529
Less:	Indirect business tax and nontax liability	30,037
	Business transfer payments	1,016
	Statistical discrepancy	1,047
Equals:	*National Income*	305,002
Less:	Undistributed corporate profits	8,921
	Corporate profits tax liability	21,141
	Corporate inventory valuation adjustment	− 964
	Contributions for social insurance	8,752
	Excess of wage accruals over disbursements	− 76
Plus:	Net interest paid by government	5,040
	Government transfer payments	12,785
	Business transfer payments	1,016
Equals:	*Personal Income*	286,066
Less:	[a]Noncorporate depletion charges	
	Net imputed rent of owner-occupied dwellings	
	Changes in farm inventories not held for sale	
	Employer contributions to private pension and welfare funds	
	Income in kind to armed forces	
	Government military life insurance benefits	
	Business transfer payments	
	Inventory valuation adjustment (noncorporate)	
Plus:	Premiums to military life insurance funds	
	Private pension payments	
Equals:	*Income Payments to Individuals* including:	270,577
	Wages and salaries	188,383
	Proprietors' income	38,086
	Property income	28,360
	Other income	15,748

[a] These components not reported since they are not estimated as such. They represent the uncomputed differences reflecting the disparity between the two concepts, Personal Income and Income Payments to Individuals.

Sources: U.S. Department of Commerce, [75] July 1947, pp. 14, 51, and Aug. 1954, p. 16; and [73], 1954, p. 164.

useful in evaluating the total performance of an economy. It may be obtained *either* by summing the market value of all goods and services produced *or* by totaling all the costs incurred in producing these goods and services.[8]   Gross National Product for the United States in 1953 is · estimated at $365 billion.   This includes both the private and public sectors of an economy and hence might be a particularly valuable measurement over time in areas in which the central government looms large in development programs.

Net national product is identical with Gross National Product, except that capital consumption allowances are deducted from the gross measure in order to obtain the net.   In 1953 it amounted to $338 billion in the United States, or 92 per cent of GNP.   However, the most widely used income account is not net national product but national income.   Unlike GNP, which measures the value of production at market prices, national income measures the value of output at factor prices.   Therefore, as shown in Table 1, in order to derive national income from GNP, income statisticians subtract not only capital consumption allowances but also other charges, notably indirect business taxes, which are not considered to constitute income to factors of production.   In 1953, national income in the United States was $305 billion or 83 per cent of GNP.

National income may be obtained by adding *either* the factor incomes paid out by sectors of the economy *or* factor payments received by all sectors.   The totals should be identical.

Personal income is defined as payments received by individuals, both as payment for factor services, including labor, and as transfer payments from government and business, but not from other individuals.   This account in the United States in 1953 totaled $286 billion or 78 per cent of GNP.   Personal income is more inclusive than income payments to individuals because of two major factors.   Personal income includes an estimate of the imputed value of rents on owner-occupied dwellings.   It also classifies as persons such institutions as nonprofit organizations and private trust, pension, health, and welfare funds.   Therefore, personal income includes all income accruing to these groups.   It may be measured *either* at the point at which income payments are made *or* by totaling personal expenditures plus savings.

The more comprehensive income accounts, GNP and national income, are particularly useful on the national level in that they can be constructed on a double-entry basis.   The fact that the two sides of the account should balance helps in filling in gaps in the data and in assessing their accuracy.

---

[8] The reader unfamiliar with income accounting may gain a better understanding of the alternative ways of deriving certain magnitudes by referring to Table 2 which is a triple-entry table and to Table 7 which is a double-entry table.

For example, GNP may be measured *either* by summing the total costs incurred in producing GNP *or* by summing all the expenditures incurred by private and public sectors in purchasing this total output. National income may be measured *either* as the gross output of all industries minus the value of materials, services, and durable capital consumed, *or* as net returns to factors of production.

These are the national accounts which have formed the basis for most of the regional income estimates discussed below. This system of accounts has formed the outline for national income accounts in the United States, which are also broken down into the institutional sectors of business, government, and private consumers together with consolidated accounts for savings, investments, and foreign transactions.[9]

C. CONCEPTUAL PROBLEMS OF REGIONAL INCOME MEASUREMENT IN DEVELOPED AREAS[10]

In regional income estimation, a number of basic conceptual problems arise which are not encountered in as serious a form in national income estimation. These problems emerge on a much larger scale because regions within a nation are generally speaking open economies. There are few if any barriers to their trade and social-cultural interaction, and they have in common many political institutions. In contrast a nation such as the United States is a relatively closed economy. Its international trade is significant but is not nearly as important for its economy as interregional trade is for a regional economy. Hence, both parties to any given transaction are much more likely to be found within a nation than within the same region of a nation. For example, the steel producers of a nation sell a much higher proportion of their output to customers within the nation than the steel producers of a given region sell to customers within their region (provided the region is an open area within the nation). Thus, a much greater percentage of the transactions of a nation are identifiable in several different ways and are subject to double-entry bookkeeping, given the types and forms of data collection prevalent in the United States.[11]

Further, because the nation is a cultural-political unit, which for policy considerations is distinct from the rest of the world, domestic transactors

---

[9] U. S. Department of Commerce [72].

[10] This section draws very heavily on the studies of Werner Hochwald, a leading investigator in this field, especially [32], pp. 9–26. Also see discussion papers by Richard Easterlin, F. H. Leacy, and D. J. Daly [56], pp. 26–34.

[11] The difficulty of identifying transactions in several different ways as well as several other difficulties discussed below tend to increase as the size of the region decreases, *ceteris paribus*.

tend to distinguish in their accounting system between home and foreign business and operations. However, even if their facilities and organization are entirely contained within a given region, these same transactors typically do not distinguish between transactions with parties in the same region and those with parties in other regions.[12] Moreover, many important transactors—such as large corporations and the federal government, who customarily do not maintain an accounting system on a regional basis—cannot be said to be located wholly within a given region. They are spread over many, if not all, regions, and it is exceedingly difficult to determine what fraction of a supraregional transactor is internal to a given region. In fact it can be said that, as in balance of payments and money-flow studies to be discussed in the next chapter, the fraction of a supraregional transactor which is assigned to a given region varies with the purpose of a study.[13] Hence, even when we contrast a region in the United States with a nation outside the United States equally dependent on interregional trade, the problems of regional income estimation are much greater.[14] As Hochwald has neatly put it, regional income estimates as developed in the United States "form essentially a single-entry subcategory of the national accounts, rather than a self-contained double-entry bookkeeping system."[15]

Some of these difficulties can be illustrated with reference to Table 1. Suppose we were to build up a similar table for a region. Starting with the last major category, *Income Payments to Individuals*, we would first attempt to estimate Wages and Salaries. Immediately a situs problem

[12] This is not unexpected since so many monetary, financial, tax, and other policies within the nation have little if any regional differentiation.

[13] See Chapter 5, pp. 169–170.

[14] It should be pointed out that *sizable* errors are present even in national income accounts which are among the most accurate of social statistics. These errors arise because of (1) the necessity to use data which have been collected for purposes other than income estimation, (2) the estimating procedures involved, particularly when the available data must be reconciled with income concepts and components which are most significant in terms of the policy objectives lying behind a national accounts study, and (3) the inherent problems of measurement which are especially troublesome in the social sciences. Kuznets, for example, has estimated that although the size of error in the various industrial components of national income may vary from 9.5 to 27.3 per cent, the over-all average error in national income estimates are of the order of 10 per cent. (O. Morgenstern [53], p. 84; and S. Kuznets [43], pp. 501–537. For an analysis of the possible types of errors involved, see O. Morgenstern [53], pp. 73–85.)

[15] W. Hochwald [32], p. 14. More specifically, in a closed economy "changes in net product, in aggregate incomes, and in total expenditures, are all closely interrelated and refer to the same set of institutions. Consequently, each account or system of measurement aids in the interpretation or evaluation of changes in the other two measures, and the welfare implications of the total are relatively clear" (*ibid.*). All this is not true for the open economy where each system of measurement refers to a different universe of institutions, albeit with considerable and undeterminable overlap.

arises for many regions where a sizable commuting population crosses boundary lines in the journey to work. Different results are obtained, depending on whether wages and salaries are measured by an examination of the payroll records of the employers in the state or by an examination of the income records of residents. If the investigator were dependent on payroll data and desired to obtain income received by residents, he would need to subtract from his data an estimate of wages and salaries paid to nonresidents and add an estimate of wages and salaries paid to residents for work in other regions. However, for the national economy which is relatively closed, the two ways of measurement yield approximately the same results, and one result can be used as a check on the other[16] or to fill in the gaps in the data derived from a second way of measurement.

Or take the item property income, which consists of dividends, interest, and net rents and royalties. If we attempt to break down by regions the available national data on corporate payments of interest and dividends, we find that a sizable part of these payments are made through financial intermediaries such as commercial banks, from whom pertinent data are not generally available. We may be forced to use data from records of individuals, which we may consider inadequate but which we cannot check independently.

Additionally, suppose the investigator, after having obtained a fair estimate of Income Payments to Individuals,[17] desires an estimate of *Regional Income* comparable to the concept of National Income. To Income Payments to Individuals he would need to add or subtract estimates of various items, one of which would be *Undistributed Corporate Profits*. In one type of study any undivided profit of a corporation may be viewed as income of those holding stock in the corporation. But with the use of what available data can these undistributed corporate profits be assigned to various regions?

The investigator may insist on going further up the ladder of Table 1, even though this may strain the validity of the resulting magnitudes. He may desire to derive a *Gross Regional Product* comparable to Gross National Product. One of the items that would need to be added to Regional Income is regional capital consumption allowances. Again,

---

[16] In a double-entry bookkeeping system wages and salaries paid out locally by industry would represent a debit entry against gross product; and wages and salaries received by households of a region, a credit entry on consumer account.

For a discussion of problems in the estimation of wages and salaries, see such writings as W. Hochwald [32], pp. 15–16, and others cited later.

[17] As already indicated, consumer expenditures data may be useful, too, in the estimation of income. But where consumers cross regional boundary lines in their shopping trips, expenditures data may be of help only after major adjustments have been made.

little if any data are available on the basis of which he could reliably proceed from national capital consumption allowances to regional capital consumption allowances.[18]

Returning to the main thread of our discussion, we can note other difficulties. Income estimates are useful for the information they convey not only on total income but also on the various major and minor categories which contribute to or comprise total income. Since a region is not a small-scale replica of the nation, and in industrial and social structure may be strikingly different from the nation, the set of sectors most useful in regional income studies is not the same as that in national studies. Hence, the available data for income estimation within a nation such as the United States which has traditionally placed much greater importance on national income estimation than on regional income estimation are much more suited for the former than the latter.

Further, regional income estimates are frequently designed to permit comparisons among regions, an objective which is more common in the study of regions of a nation than of the nation as a whole (vis-à-vis other nations). This objective forces on the regional income investigator a standard set of accounts. He may not be able to use in the estimation of a given region's income the best set of industry definitions and available data on the region, since this best set varies from region to region. More important, in striving for comparative analysis, he may not be able to develop a set of income accounts for a given region that will be most useful for policy determination within that region. This point follows since the selection of income components for any region should emphasize the critical sectors of that region. In one region a critical sector may be a declining industry—such as coal mining—which in the past has dominated the region's development. In a second region, coal mining may be trivial and logically lumped together with many other industries. For the second region, another special-resource industry—say electronics—with tremendous growth potential should be segregated from others. Yet, by the use of standard sectors, comparative income work tends to suppress important differences among regions with respect to their critical sectors.[19]

---

[18] For fuller discussion of the data problems mentioned in this and the preceding paragraphs, see S. L. Booth [5]. For discussion of many similar data problems, see Chapter 5, pp. 167–172. However, where there is an abundance of required statistics—as for Hawaii—and where these statistics are ingeniously processed to make full use of their potentialities—as in the case of C. F. Schwartz [65]—most of these problems can be handled adequately. Schwartz has been very successful in developing for Hawaii a reliable set of estimates of Personal Income, Territorial Income, and Gross Product.

[19] A closely related problem is that of determining the extent of nonmarket transactions within a region, for which data are not normally recorded. The magnitude of these transactions varies from region to region and hence the importance of identifying

In addition, a set of general data problems may be mentioned. Where national data are derived from sample surveys, a sampling procedure which yields results valid for the nation may not yield reliable data for a region. In certain cases, regional samples must be much larger in order to reduce errors of estimate to tolerable dimensions and may require a generally different sample design. Another factor intensifying the data problem are disclosure rules, which tend to reduce the data available for a region by more than for a nation. Finally, the use of benchmark data for interpolation, especially for intercensal years, is generally much less justifiable for the region than for the nation, since some of the basic stability assumptions for interpolation tend to lose validity as the size of the pertinent area decreases.[20]

D. Procedures in Regional Income Measurement in the United States

For the reasons given and others, the development of regional income measures has lagged behind national income accounting. Until very recently little progress occurred in the construction of regional (including state and county) counterparts of Gross National Product and national income.[21] As long as these accounts were oriented toward closed economies, little advance could have been anticipated. The 1958 income and product accounts study by Leven,[22] however, surmounts a number of the obstacles to the needed development of new income concepts more applicable to a live, dynamic regional organism and tailored to regional data availability. The advances stemming from this study will be treated in a later section. We discuss in this section past and current practices.

1. state income estimates

As noted, regional income measurements in the United States have been limited in scope and concept and relate to those accounts for which data

them. As a consequence, techniques suitable for approximating them in one region may not be suitable for a second region. Further complications arise from differentials in regional prices. Where the price-cost and industrial structures of a region correspond to those of the nation, the use of national prices may be justified. Where they do not, regional prices and costs must be pieced together and approximated from diverse sources in order to avoid considerable error.

[20] See W. Hochwald [32].

[21] However, see S. L. Booth [5], C. F. Schwartz [65], and G. Freutel [19]. It should also be mentioned that Schwartz has constructed for Hawaii not only accounts such as gross product and territorial income comparable to the United States accounts but also accounts such as Territorial Income Produced and Gross Geographical Product which are of additional use in a study of the Hawaiian economy.

[22] C. L. Leven [46]. Also see his article [47].

are available and which are useful and meaningful on a single-entry basis. Notable among these measurements are the state income estimates of Easterlin for the historical period 1840–1950,[23] and of the U. S. Department of Commerce since 1929. Up to September 1955 the U. S. Department of Commerce state estimates, which for current purposes are the basic source, are in terms of income payments to individuals. They include four categories: wages and salaries, proprietors' income, property income, and other income.[24] Estimates of certain components are very reliable, such as those on wages and salaries by industries which are largely based on wages actually paid out by establishments located in each state as compiled by the Bureau of Employment Security. Estimates of other components, such as net income of proprietors in nonagricultural industries, are based on sampling or the use of allocators or both, and as a consequence are not as firm.[25]

Since September 1955 the state income estimates from 1929 on have been converted to a personal income basis. (See Table 1 for the difference between the concepts of personal income and income payments on a national basis.) Aside from providing state income estimates consistent with national estimates,[26] such conversion makes possible more precise estimates of state income, places state income work in a more comprehensive framework, furnishes additional detail, and yields estimates more relevant for certain purposes of regional analysis.[27]

2. COUNTY INCOME ESTIMATES

Other notable regional income work in the United States has been associated with county income estimates. The resulting data furnish one

[23] R. A. Easterlin [15, 16].

[24] For details on the construction of estimates on these four categories, see U. S. Department of Commerce [75], Aug. 1950, pp. 22–24, and Sept. 1955, pp. 19–22, and 32. Of interest, too, are the definitions and details in C. F. Schwartz [65], Parts 2 and 3. Also, see [55], pp. 200–206.

[25] The Department of Commerce increases the flexibility and value of its income estimates by providing a situs adjustment figure for the income of interstate commuters, thereby permitting the data to be put at least in part on a "where received" basis. This also makes possible for certain studies more meaningful per capita income estimates for each state.

[26] In 1947 the concept of income payments to individuals was dropped by the Department of Commerce in favor of the concept of personal income in the construction of national accounts for the United States.

The corresponding modifications in the state accounts are associated with the work of Charles F. Schwartz and Robert E. Graham, Jr., of the Department of Commerce. For a full discussion of concepts, sources, and methodology, see [74].

[27] When it is desirable to have state income estimates on a monthly basis, a short-cut construction is obviously required. For a study using bank debits as one of several series upon which to base monthly income, see J. H. Cumberland [10].

of the most valuable types of objective economic criteria available to state and federal officials as well as to businessmen in matters such as assessing relative need for grants-in-aid, measuring relative tax and debt load, defining sales territories, and determining sales quotas and performance. They are also of assistance in planning programs of health, education, welfare, agriculture and resource development, highways, forestry, as well as of industrial development.[28]

In the estimation of county income either of two approaches, or some combination of the two, may be adopted. One approach involves thorough investigation of a particular county somewhat independently of studies on other counties. Census-type enumerations can be performed, although the cost of such data collection is usually too prohibitive except for special use. Detailed statistics available on the county's industry, population, power consumption, bank debts, commercial and retail activities; detailed tabulations based on income tax returns; and data from sample surveys and direct inquiries may be utilized as scaffolding for income estimates by component sectors.

The second approach involves (1) the determination as accurately as possible of total state income and of its components (disaggregated into as fine sectors as is feasible); and (2) the apportionment of these amounts among counties of the state by means of the best set of indicators available. This approach avoids the limitations imposed by the inadequacy of certain types of county data, permits more valid comparisons among counties, and has the advantage of forcing the investigator to recognize more fully and state more explicitly his underlying assumptions. On the other hand, it may yield estimates of components for a given county, such as imputed rents, which could have been more reliably determined by the first approach.

In practice, the sophisticated analyst adopts neither of the two approaches alone but uses some combination of the two, the exact combination depending on the available data and purpose of his income study.[29] Since the Department of Commerce has done outstanding work on state income and has developed a relatively reliable set of state income estimates, the county income work in the United States has in general placed greater emphasis on the second approach.

[28] For discussion of the different purposes which county income studies serve, see W. M. Adamson [2], pp. 479–492, and J. W. Martin [48]. In addition to others to be noted in subsequent footnotes, some of the county income studies are: California State Chamber of Commerce [6], J. A. Guthrie and S. E. Boyle [26], R. H. Johnson [40], L. A. Thompson [70–71], and the University of Maryland [77]. As with state estimates, the work on county income has been greatly facilitated by the coincidence of data collection areas and administrative regions.

[29] For much fuller discussion, see J. W. Martin [50], W. M. Adamson [2], W. Hochwald [32], and L. R. Salkever [61].

For example, the Southeastern Conference, whose studies and recommended procedures have had by far the greatest influence on county income work in the United States, decided more or less in favor of the second approach.[30] Using as controls the data available by states on the various detailed components of state income—these state totals in turn are controlled by the corresponding totals on a national basis—the Conference established three major steps in the county estimates:

1. County allocators are established for each of the industrial and functional subtotals of state income (e.g., for the state total of income from retailing, the number employed in retailing in each county is a typical allocator).

2. The allocator for each county associated with a particular type of income is expressed as a percentage of that county's share of the state total.

3. The Commerce state total for that income item is multiplied by each of the county allocators in order to divide that type of income among the counties.

For a given county, income is then estimated by a summation of the county's dollar share of each component of state income.[31]

In breaking down the Commerce estimates of state income among the counties, a *single* set of percentages can be used to apportion *total* state income payments among the counties (or a single set for each of the major categories of total state income). However, the use of as much industrial detail as possible, if reliable county allocators are available, usually yields more accurate results than does the use of a single allocator applied to total state income.[32] This is more often true for states and counties in which income is from a variety of industrial and agricultural sources than

[30] The conference was composed of the state universities of Alabama, Georgia, Kentucky, Mississippi, North Carolina, Tennessee, Virginia, and T.V.A. Under the auspices of the state universities, T.V.A., the Federal Reserve Bank of St. Louis, and the U. S. Department of Commerce, estimates of county income in 1939 and 1947 were made for these seven states. See J. L. Lancaster [45], and the technical supplement, L. C. Copeland [8]. Some of the income studies made in connection with or stimulated by this Conference are: W. S. Myers, J. L. Johnson, and J. W. Martin [54], W. H. Baughn and G. M. Jones [4], L. D. Ashby and E. P. Truex [3], O. C. Corry [9], University of Florida [76], and D. McKinney [52].

[31] For full details see J. L. Lancaster [45] and L. C. Copeland [8]. Also see W. M. Adamson [2] and L. R. Salkever [61] for other relevant discussion particularly on allocators. It should be mentioned that the situs problem becomes exceedingly difficult in income estimation for certain counties, especially for a year distant from a census benchmark year.

[32] Yet in certain situations short-cut methods involving the use of a general allocator for estimating several of the major components of income can be effectively employed within limits without an undue sacrifice of accuracy. For interesting discussion, see L. A. Thompson [69].

it is for states and counties where income is more homogeneous as to source, such as in a primarily agricultural state.[33]

Although the apportionment method of income estimation in the United States has the considerable advantage of providing rather consistent individual regional income estimates obtained through a common methodology and governed by a single official control total, it also has certain limitations. One is that the accuracy of all the regional estimates is contingent on the accuracy of the single Commerce estimate of United States personal income or income payments to individuals. A second is that the accuracy of regional estimates is further dependent on the accuracy and relevance of a set of particular allocators. This second limitation suggests that it is at least as desirable, if not more so, to use relevant data directly available if they are of the same order of accuracy as allocators, or to collect data directly rather than to develop allocating indexes if no greater expense is incurred. A third is that the use of national data to a major degree straitjackets regional income work by the imposition on such work of a standard system of concepts and accounts. As already indicated, the use of a standard system denies the unique characteristics of regions, infers that regions are identical except for industrial-agricultural mix, and in a sense implies that regional policy should be the same as national policy after adjustment of the latter for each region's industrial-agricultural mix and economic resource features. Such denial of folk culture and local character is a weakness which must be balanced against the powerful advantage of comparative analysis. In any event, in the United States the careful regional investigator will utilize the excellent state income data which are available, but at the same time he will increasingly supplement these data and the apportionment method by a reliance on materials of a more local character which are adapted to a superior set of local accounts.[34] The development of a superior set of local accounts which would measure more meaningfully the welfare of a community or region represents one of the most challenging areas for future research.[35] Current progress in this area will be discussed in a

[33] It should be observed that at least in the past the detailed-type approach has benefited from offsetting statistical errors in state income work. As C. F. Schwartz notes: "In our national and state income work it has been found that errors in individual income components invariably tend to compensate in the total" ([65], p. 35).

[34] Actually, the very excellence of the state income data has tended to discourage experimentation with the use of new accounts, concepts, methods, and data which might result in a cross check of the official figure.

[35] Obviously such research will require unorthodox approaches as well as syntheses of materials from the various social sciences. Local attitudes, integration and stability of local social and political groups and institutions, and many other factors interweave with the economic to yield the level of welfare which may be said to be associated with any community, large or small.

following section. However, it is pertinent to indicate here some of the more promising sources of new local materials which at least can supplement and upgrade regional income estimates based on the apportionment of state income data and which may also facilitate the construction of a new set of local accounts.[36]

One such source are the Federal and state tax returns. If all persons were compelled to report accurately income by a detailed classification which would cover completely all forms of income, an ideal source of local data would exist. Unfortunately, such reporting does not occur in practice. A number of administrative, statistical, and conceptual problems must yet be unraveled in the use of this source of data. Of these problems a major one is that of coverage. Many persons simply do not file tax returns. This group includes those with low incomes, those with higher incomes and correspondingly high exemptions, those not covered by the withholding system, as well as others who simply have not fallen into the habit of filing tax forms. One study estimates that in 1947 only 81 per cent of United States income payments to individuals was reported as covered by income tax returns and that this coverage was only 76 per cent in Virginia.[37] This disparity results both from underreporting and from the fact that not all categories of income are taxable.[38] Additional problems with respect to data comparability from year to year result from frequent changes in income tax definitions, coverages, and rates, and as a consequence in the amount of avoidance and evasion which takes place from year to year.

The Internal Revenue Service has begun to recognize the potential value of tax statistics for purposes of income measurement and other economic analyses. However, much remains to be done to improve the usefulness of the tax statistics.[39] In addition to more complete coverage,[40] the time lag between the reporting and publication of the data should be cut

[36] For supplementary discussion, see J. H. Cumberland [9].

[37] S. K. Gilliam [25], p. 8. Also see [7].

[38] Nontaxable income includes a wide range of personal exemptions, deductions, and various types of income in kind. In view of the J-shaped Pareto curve of income distribution with its heavy concentration of recipients in the lower brackets, the total amount of income not reported because of exemptions, deductions, and low total income may become a source of considerable distortion in income accounting.

[39] It should be noted that the question on the federal tax form relating to county residence has the great advantage of automatically putting the data on a "where received" basis, except insofar as persons maintain fictitious residence because of differential tax treatment as between states.

[40] The fact that some states have income taxes makes possible an intercomparison and hence a more effective use of federal tax data, e.g., see S. K. Gilliam [25].

considerably,[41] capital gains currently reported on a partial basis as income for tax purposes should be isolated, and so forth. Should these improvements be effected, the data will be of considerable additional value in the analysis of distribution of income by size of incomes within both large and small regions. Little is currently known about such distribution.

Another potential source of regional income data which has been neglected, and which would be of particular value for benchmark years, is the decennial Census of Population. In 1940 the Bureau of the Census included on a sample basis a question on income which, however, was limited to income from wages and salaries only. In 1950 the question was enlarged to include income from all sources.

The Census information in its published form has failed to be as useful as it could be to regional income statisticians for a number of reasons. First, the results are given in terms of median incomes. This makes it impossible to multiply by population in order to obtain totals. Although there are good statistical reasons for the use of the median, the means should also be published.

Second, the Census reports income for "families and unrelated individuals" and for "families." Although these categories are useful, the value of the data would have been considerably enhanced had materials on average per capita income by types of income been presented. Such materials could have permitted the establishment of valuable benchmarks for the estimation of regional income for intercensal years, in addition to the construction of badly needed cross comparisons with national and state income data.

As with materials from tax forms, the Census data have a tremendous potential for the stimulation of income distribution studies within regions. This follows since the data are not by source of income but by persons and family. Already, the 1950 median data for states, cities, and counties by income groups have provided some insight into comparative income distributions. If an improved set of Census data were made available for benchmark years, and if materials for Federal and state tax forms could be effectively gathered, not only to check and improve the benchmark year

---

[41] The preliminary Statistics of Income currently appear one and a half years after the close of the year to which they apply. As high-speed electronic computing machinery and advanced sampling techniques become adopted, it would seem that in the release of preliminary estimates this time lag might be cut to six months. Fairly reliable estimates based on samples for regions as small as counties might be constructed and released within a few months after the due date for tax returns. Of course, final estimates would have to await decisions with respect to forms under litigation. In some cases these involve large sums, which, however, are a rather small, and perhaps predictable, fraction of the total regional income.

data but also to furnish a basis for estimating income distributions for intercensal years, reliable income distribution studies could be made. Such studies would be of considerable value to Federal, state, and local governments and to businessmen in planning and executing the type of programs mentioned.

Still another promising source of data, albeit indirect, for local income estimation are the results of regression, covariance, and similar studies.[42] The promise is particularly significant for the estimation of farm income, one of the most troublesome sectors in regional income work.   Local income from agriculture is difficult to estimate by standard apportionment techniques because records are inadequate; because much farm income is in "kind" and does not pass through the market; because farm incomes are low and from place to place are subject to wide annual fluctuations at different times and with different intensities owing to weather, etc.; and because of other factors.[43]   A supplemental approach has therefore been explored which relates the local flow of farm income via a multiple regression approach to such supposedly independent variables as value of crops sold by the locality, value of livestock sold, average farm wage rates, farm wage rates of the subsequent year as a percentage of those in the given year, and the ratio of labor input to the imputed costs of other factors of production.   For example, Johnson and Nordquist, using state data, have correlated the Commerce estimates of net income from agriculture with the two assumed independent variables, value of all farm crops sold and value of all farm livestock sold.   With the equation thus derived they estimated county income from agriculture on the basis of county data on the two assumed independent variables.   They fully recognized the many limitations of this procedure, such as the implicit assumption that any variations among Colorado counties in soil, climate, topography, etc., are represented by similar variations among the several states.[44]

Despite its promise, the multiple regression approach must be used with considerable caution not only because relationships among the states of a nation—which generally form the basis for an estimating equation—

[42] For a brief sketch of regression and covariance analyses, see Chapter 2, pp. 19–27.

[43] For a typical application of the apportionment technique to estimate farm income see W. M. Adamson [1, 2].

[44] B. L. Johnson and C. G. Nordquist [39].   In similar fashion, John L. Fulmer has correlated agricultural income by states with the state data on the variables: (1) average farm wage rates; (2) farm wage rates of the subsequent year as a percentage of those in the given year; and (3) the ratio of labor input to the imputed costs of other factors of production.   From the constants of the resulting equation, corresponding county estimates were made.   Fulmer, too, recognizes limitations of this procedure [21], pp. 343–358.   Also see [21].

cannot be assumed to be always valid for counties within a state, but also because difficult problems of multicollinearity and serial correlation arise in connection with the use of a set of "independent" variables.[45]

3. INCOME ESTIMATES FOR REGIONS OF OTHER TYPES

The excellence of the Department of Commerce state income estimates has led to their use for most regional income estimates in the United States. This has been the consequence whether we consider regions composed of integral states, of several counties within one or several states, or of integral states and some counties of other states. As one example, various government agencies very frequently define a region as a set of integral states and obtain regional income by summing the incomes of the relevant states. As a second example, the Tennessee Valley Authority constructs income estimates for any of its subregions by summing the incomes of the counties contained by that subregion.[46] As a third example, the Federal Reserve Bank of St. Louis (which is an observer of county boundaries, but not of state) constructs an income estimate for its region by adding to the income of Arkansas the incomes of counties in each of six other states.[47] Even when a region cuts across county boundaries, the tendency has been to allocate the county income derived previously from state income to the parts of the county.[48]

In short, there has not been any large-scale effort in the United States to construct regional income estimates, entirely independent of national, state, and county income estimates.[49] In view of the expensiveness of making independent income estimates, in view of the failure to develop a more fruitful conceptual framework, and in view of the available data collected by traditional political administrative units, this is understand-

---

[45] For further discussion of these latter problems, see standard advanced texts on statistics, such as those cited on p. 20.

[46] Some consider this income estimation procedure suitable for metropolitan regions as well.

[47] See W. Hochwald [33, 34]; also see [17].

[48] It should be added that for such an apportionment reliable allocators are difficult to obtain; and in urban areas the situs problem is formidable when dealing with parts of counties. (L. R. Salkever [61].)

[49] This has been generally true of work in other developed nations. For example, see P. Deane [14], F. R. E. Mauldon and A. M. Kerr [51], W. E. G. Salter [62], W. E. G. Salter and R. W. Peters [63], and R. W. Peters [60]. The papers by Mauldon and Kerr, Salter and Peters, and Peters throw considerable light from a different angle on the conceptual and procedural problems in regional income estimation. Their studies also illustrate how excellent local data on the output of farm commodities and their costs of production can be combined with allocation procedures with respect to nonagricultural sectors to derive local income.

able. At the present time most regional income analysts continue to concentrate efforts at improvement of estimates at the national level, state level, and county (or small groups of counties) level, and to determine income for other types of regions by a summation process.[50]

[50] Associated with regional income estimates have been studies which attempt to explain differences among the per capita incomes of counties, of states, and of regions. Notable among these have been the investigations of Frank A. Hanna. Hanna interprets his initial results as indicating that 80 per cent of the observed differences in average earnings between states can be explained statistically by differences in occupational composition with the remainder caused by or associated with wage rates, age composition of population, degree of urbanization, participation of women in the labor force, etc. See F. A. Hanna [27–31] and E. Mansfield [48]. However, see the discussion of Hanna's approach by E. F. Denison and R. M. Williams in [56]. Also see other types of explanatory studies, such as R. H. Johnson [40], D. H. Fisher [18], E. M. Hoover and J. L. Fisher [36], J. L. Fulmer [23], P. B. Simpson [66], R. J. Wolfson [79], and H. S. Perloff [59]. Perloff pushes beyond the conventional primary, secondary, and tertiary classification of industries in explaining statistically the income differences among states and in establishing valid criteria in the formulation of economic development programs. His tentative conclusions suggest the fruitfulness of industrial disaggregation which at the same time recombines Census industrial classes.

It should be noted that even if income differences among regional units can be associated with, or statistically explained by, differences in occupational and industrial structure, the regional analyst is interested in taking still another step, namely, in explaining why differences in occupational and industrial structure and in other factors have developed. This takes him into the realm of location theory, of optimum programming of resource use and industrial output and other areas to be discussed in subsequent chapters. It also compels him to examine the general process of economic growth *over the long run*. In this latter connection the works by R. A. Easterlin [15, 16] and a report by S. Kuznets [44] on research in progress are particularly promising.

Examining the experience of each of the 48 states (against the background of a similar study for nations of the world), Kuznets reports a number of interesting results. As in his international comparative studies, he finds that among regions (states) per capita income is: (1) negatively associated with the shares of *agriculture and related industries* in income and labor force; (2) positively associated with the shares of *mining, manufacturing, and construction* in income and labor force; (3) positively, but weakly, associated with the shares of *all service activities* in income and labor force. *Over time*, in the majority of states, there has been: (1) a decline in the share of *agriculture and related industries* in income and labor force; (2) an appreciable increase in the share of *mining, manufacturing, and construction* in income and a slight increase in the share of this sector in labor force; and (3) a slight increase in the share of *all service activities* in income but a fairly substantial increase in the share of this sector in labor force. Also, over time, the faster this change in the industrial structure of a state, the faster the rate of growth of its per capita income.

Such inquiry into growth paths, particularly when pursued in terms of both meaningful aggregates (industrial sectors) and particular activities (which is possible with the excellent detail on the industrial composition of states and regions composed of states) affords another set of basic insights for projection purposes. This is especially so when experiences of regions in a national system can be contrasted with those of regions in an international system.

E. Approaches to Regional Social Accounting

At the beginning of the section on National Income accounts several conceptual schemes for national income accounting were sketched in the quotation from Kuznets. It was indicated that national income can be measured at several stages in the flow process of economic activity. Several types of social accounting schemes were also implied, each associated with a particular way of measuring national income. In this section we wish to develop more fully frameworks for regional social accounting.[51] Such frameworks tend to broaden the perspective obtainable from income accounting alone and thus facilitate the understanding and the consistent projection of regional processes and magnitudes. But still more important, such frameworks are crucial for regions, particularly underdeveloped regions, for which few data are available; for these regions all feasible alternative accounting schemes must be exploited in order to utilize fully the few figures available.

1. ACCOUNTING FOR UNDERDEVELOPED REGIONS

To motivate the discussion, consider an underdeveloped region for which few data exist. Population figures for such a region may be little more than guesses. The census of the chief economic activity—agriculture—may be unsatisfactory. Few, if any, records may exist on the volume of internal trade. How develop a useful system of accounts and income measures? The pioneering work of Phyllis Deane in evolving a triple-entry system of accounts for the two regions, Northern Rhodesia and Nyasaland, furnishes one answer.

In her study, from which we largely draw the following discussion, Deane aims at the development of a meaningful triple-column *income–output–expenditure table*. This table would show "in the first column by what groups of individuals or institutions the incomes are earned, in the second column in what industries they are earned and in the third column how they are consumed or invested."[52] In this table "each transaction would appear three times, once as it became part of income received, once as it represented the value of a particular kind of good or service produced, and once as it entered into some form of consumption or investment."[53] With this triple-entry system of balancing accounts Deane attempts to organize the *miscellaneous* data on her two regions. Her system "permits the effective utilization of every scrap of economic information by provid-

---

[51] The reader who views income measurement and social accounting as synonomous may consider this section as an extension of income measurement techniques.

[52] P. Deane [12], p. 3.

[53] [12], pp. 3–4.

ing a considerable number of cross checks. It thereby reduces the area of unconfirmed estimate to the smallest possible range and presents . . . the sum of the available data and of the deductions that can be drawn from that material."[54]

Deane's basic *conceptual* table is reproduced as Table 2. Clearly, the data on wages, salaries, profits, interest, and rent (the first column) which represent earnings of factors of production can be conceptually rearranged to indicate the *net output* (value added) or *factor earnings* by *industrial sector* (the second column). Further, the third column is simply another

TABLE 2.   A BASIC SYSTEM OF TRIPLE-ENTRY SOCIAL ACCOUNTS

Net Regional Income	Net Regional Output	Net Regional Expenditure
	Net Output of:	
1. Wages and Salaries	6. Agriculture	13. Expenditures on
2. Profits	7. Mining	Goods and Services
3. Interest	8. Manufacture	for Current Con-
4. Rent	9. Distribution and	sumption
	Transport	14. Net Investment
	10. Government	
	11. Other Goods and	
	Services	
5. Total Regional Income	12. Total Regional Output	15. Total Regional Expenditure

Source: Adapted from P. Deane [12], p. 13.

way of organizing the data of the second column, that is, it organizes the sales data of industrial sectors according to whether the purchaser uses (or intends to use) the output for current consumption or investment. Hence, all three columns add to the same figure.

Actually, the specific form of the table may significantly vary from study to study, not only because of variation among basic characteristics of regions and available data but also because of differences in study objectives and meaningful conceptual frameworks. This point can be fruitfully elaborated.

Already we have recorded how the relative paucity of data affects the number of required cross checks and thus the form of multiple-entry accounting to be employed. The characteristics of a region are also

[54] [12], p. 8.

influential. Where for a region a considerable proportion of economic activity is concentrated on subsistence agriculture and handicraft, basic new accounts are required. What should these accounts be? Moreover, the problem of how to measure the volume of subsistence output that is produced arises. Even if some crude measure of this output can be obtained, how assign a money value to it (particularly when quality is a variable)? Once a money value is approximated, this value represents income generated. This leads into another thorny question: how allocate income generated to the appropriate factors of production, that is, how disaggregate into wages and salaries, profits, interest, and rent? But are the classical economic categories of factors of production appropriate for an underdeveloped region? Deane has found them to be inappropriate for her studies of Northern Rhodesia and Nyasaland. She overlays the distinction between income earned as wages and salaries, profits, interest, and rent with the more significant distinction between income earned by (1) European individuals and local companies, (2) other Non-Africans, (3) Africans, and (4) government. Consequently, in the first column of Table 3 (p. 104) this latter classification for income earned replaces the former (first column, Table 2). Deane's study, as well as others, thus suggests that the standard Western World functional classification (wages, rent, interest, and profit) be replaced in many cases by a more meaningful classification. This more meaningful classification might involve a set of categories based on color, race, social class, or some other feature more significant for a primitive subsistence economy, or some combination of the latter set of categories and the standard Western World set of categories. Such combination may be desirable when an underdeveloped region has an important export sector tied to the industrialized world.

Still more, how account for the significant volume of barter transactions which do not pass through a formal market? This question raises problems of valuation somewhat similar to subsistence activity. But to pursue the point still further, how set a value on the contributions of those women and children (not normally included in a Western World definition of labor force) who manage the agricultural and craft functions while the men are primarily engaged in military, symbolic, and ceremonial functions? Are ceremonial pursuits, such as the crafting of a family totem and the preparation of beer for a festival, properly considered as production of economic goods; or do these pursuits represent the consumption of leisure time? Further, in those societies in which marriageable girls are sold to their husbands at prices involving a sizable transfer of real wealth, is marriage a form of investment and the procreation of daughters an economic activity?

It is clear that social accounting for underdeveloped regions raises not only most of the conventional questions encountered in income accounting for developed regions (as discussed in the preceding sections of this chapter) but also many more. Whatever the answers to these latter questions— and these answers can only be partial and dated—and whatever the preliminary estimates obtained, these estimates cannot be statistically removed from their cultural context without losing significance. It is all too easy (1) to impose on an underdeveloped region (nation) a set of social accounts appropriate for industrialized regions; (2) to overstate the importance of money transactions and the accounts measurable in currency (partly because of availability of data on these transactions and accounts); and, as a consequence, (3) to derive distorted measures of welfare.[55]

To illustrate an actual set of social accounts for underdeveloped regions we present both Tables 3 and 4. Table 3 depicts social accounts for *residents* of Northern Rhodesia. Each item in Table 3 is derived from a separate subtable, the items in the subtable for any one sector being used as a cross check on items of other subtables. For example, the account for the mining industry estimates salaries, wages, and bonuses paid to Europeans at 2,597,800 pounds for 1945. This figure which is part of item 6 (Mining) in column 2 must be consistent with the figure on earnings from the mining industry in the subtable on incomes of European individuals which constitutes part of item 1 (European individuals and local companies) of column 1 of Table 3. Moreover, this figure, when added to other figures on incomes of European individuals, must give a sum which is consistent with the subtable estimates on Personal Consumption Expenditure by Europeans and Savings by Europeans. These latter estimates in turn are combined with other estimates to obtain item 20 (Total Personal Consumption) and item 22 (Investment and Saving), both of column 3 in Table 3.

As a comprehensive set of social accounts derived *in actuality*, Table 3 contrasts with the hypothetical set of accounts in Table 2. We have already commented on the use of a different classification of income for column 1. In column 2 of Table 3 an item on *Income from Abroad* (*including income tax*) has been added since residents (including government) do receive income from abroad and do spend it; therefore this item must be added to net regional output. In column 3 of Table 3 a detailed breakdown is recorded which for all major items except one is in keeping with the two aggregate accounts in column 3 of Table 2. The one major

---

[55] For fuller discussion of these problems and points, the reader is referred among others to R. Stone and K. Hansen [67], M. Gilbert and R. Stone [24], and in particular to references 119 to 149 cited therein; to W. O. Jones [41]; and in particular to P. Deane [12, 13]. For an interesting discussion of existing income data for underdeveloped countries, see H. T. Oshima [58].

TABLE 3. RESIDENTS' INCOME, OUTPUT, AND OUTLAY : NORTHERN RHODESIA, 1945

(In thousands of pounds)

Residents' Income		Residents' Output		Residents' Outlay	
Incomes of:		Net Output of:		Personal Consumption:	
1. European Individuals and Local Companies	5,916	6. Mining	3,908	14. Cash Expenditure at Market Price	9,109
2. Other Non-Africans	325	7. Agriculture and Live-stock	5,590	15. Less Indirect Taxes	−799
3. Africans	10,270	8. Manufacture, Building, Forestry	1,400	16. Plus Subsidies	136
4. Government (including receipts from foreign taxpayers)	1,989	9. Distribution and Transport	1,659	17. Domestic Cash Expenditure at Factor Cost	8,446
		10. Government	1,645	18. Subsistence Consumption	4,734
		11. Income from Abroad (including income tax)	2,397	19. Expenditure Abroad by Individuals	1,482
		12. Other Goods and Services	1,901	20. Total Personal Consumption	14,662
				21. Government Current Expenditure at Home and Abroad	2,080
				22. Investment and Saving	1,758
5. Total Residents' Income	18,500	13. Total Residents' Output	18,500	23. Total Resident's Outlay	18,500

Source: P. Deane [12], p. 63.

item, subsistence consumption, is added to column 3, Table 2, for reasons already cited.[56]

Table 3 presents only one broad perspective on welfare. As most national and regional income accounts, it points up the economic activity and related welfare of *residents* of a region. However, another perspective on welfare is possible and particularly relevant for open regions such as dependent colonies and the regions of the United States. This second perspective views the region on a geographical basis and accounts for all economic activity within the borders of the region. It points up the net productivity of a *meaningfully defined region*, irrespective of the relative degrees to which residents and nonresidents are responsible for this productivity. It seeks measures of how efficiently the resource complex of a region is being utilized and how well the *regional economy* is performing.[57] In the case of Northern Rhodesia, such a point of view leads to a set of social accounts as presented in Table 4, which refers to Territorial Income, Output, and Outlay. The total of each column of Table 4 exceeds the corresponding total of Table 3. This result is largely due to the inclusion in Table 4 of the undistributed profits, dividends, and royalties of non-resident mining and other companies which have made heavy investments in Northern Rhodesia.[58]

In addition to tables, such as Tables 3 and 4, and to the subtables from which are derived the items of these tables, it is customary to complete the social accounting framework with a *balance of payments* table. Such a table records the transactions of the region with the rest of the world.

[56] The value of subsistence consumption also represents real output which is included in the appropriate items of column 2, and residents' income in kind which is included in the appropriate items of column 1.

[57] Viewing an open region in both these ways may be particularly important when the development of a region has largely relied on outside capital. Also, for planning purposes, for evaluating tax potentialities, etc., a double perspective can be extremely valuable.

For a discussion of the several uses of each perspective for an industrialized nation, see G. Stuvel [68].

[58] It may be instructive to make a column-by-column comparison of Tables 3 and 4. Column 1, Table 4, includes the income of nonresident companies which largely accounts for the amount by which its total exceeds the total of column 1, Table 3. Note, however, that income of the government sector is smaller in Table 4 than in Table 3. This reduction is due to the fact that in Table 3 a considerable part of government income is taxes drawn from the income of nonresident companies. To include this latter income in the government sector of Table 4 would constitute double counting.

The total of column 2, Table 4, exceeds the total of the same column, Table 3, primarily because it includes that output in mining, distribution, and transport which is assigned to outside capital. The total of column 3, Table 4, exceeds the total of the same column in Table 3 by the amount of remittances abroad by nonresident companies.

TABLE 4.   TERRITORIAL INCOME, OUTPUT, AND OUTLAY : NORTHERN RHODESIA, 1945

(In thousands of pounds)

Territorial Income		Territorial Output		Territorial Outlay	
Income of:		Net Output of:		Personal Cash Expenditure on:	
1. European Individuals	5,666	7. Mining	7,417	18. Food, Drink, Tobacco	3,781
2. Other Non-Africans	325	8. Agriculture and Livestock		19. Clothing, Footwear, etc.	2,835
3. Africans	10,270	a. European	600	20. Other Local Produce	2,493
4. Companies	5,400	b. African	4,990	21. Total at Market Price	9,109
5. Government	339	9. Forestry and Sawmilling	970	22. Less Indirect Taxes	−799
		10. Manufacture and Building	450	23. Plus Subsidies	136
		11. African Village Industry and Miscellaneous Independent Works	896	24. Total at Factor Cost	8,446
		12. Distribution	2,072	25. Subsistence Consumption	4,734
		13. Transport	1,148	26. Government Current Expenditure	1,689
		14. Government	1,645	27. Expenditure Abroad by	
		15. Miscellaneous Services	1,060	a. Individuals	1,482
		16. Income from Abroad	752	b. Government	391
				28. Investment, Savings, Remittances Abroad by Non-resident Companies	5,258
6. Total Territorial Income	22,000	17. Total Territorial Output	22,000	29. Total Territorial Outlay	22,000

Source: P. Deane [12], p. 64.

Again, the contents of such a table depend on the purpose of a study, the region, and in particular the measure of welfare to be highlighted by the study. For her study of Northern Rhodesia, Deane has constructed two balance of payments tables, one for the region when it is viewed in terms of human population and activity, another for the region when it is viewed on a geographical basis as a resource complex under productive utilization. We present the latter table as Table 5, which therefore serves as the complement to Table 4.

TABLE 5. TERRITORIAL BALANCE OF PAYMENTS: NORTHERN RHODESIA,
1945

(In thousands of pounds)

Receipts from Abroad		Payments Abroad	
1. Value of Domestic Merchandise at Border	12,285	5. Value of Retained Imports at Border	9,000
2. Expenditures by Tourists and Missions	140	6. Expenditure Abroad	1,873
3. Income from Abroad	752	7. Net Commercial Remittances and Expenditure Abroad	2,304
4. Total Receipts from Abroad	13,177	8. Total Payments Abroad	13,177

Source: P. Deane [12], p. 64.

There are many problems, both conceptual and empirical, in the construction of a balance of payments table. Many of these problems are associated with money flow phenomena which will be discussed in the next chapter.[59] Therefore, we defer the discussion of these problems, and of balance of payments in general, to the subsequent chapter after we have evaluated money flow studies.

2. ACCOUNTING FOR DEVELOPED OPEN REGIONS

As indicated earlier there are several ways of devising social accounting frameworks for regions. Deane's framework has been presented not only

[59] For an extremely interesting and useful set of *financial accounts* for Rhodesia and Nyasaland, which relate to the sources and uses of funds by the following four sectors—government, persons and enterprises, banks, and the Rest of the World—and which supplement Deane's social accounts, see A. G. Irvine [37].

as one which is implemented but also as one which pioneers social accounting for underdeveloped regions. Although this framework breaks ground in one direction, it does not make the major strides required in a second direction. It follows the standard social accounting practice of placing greater emphasis on domestic accounts than on the *Rest of the World* (Import-Export) accounts.[60] Yet it is essential for open regions, particularly within a nation, that major change in emphasis be made. Typically, the import-export relations of an open region are quantitatively more significant than for a closed region. Further, many analysts claim that these relations afford the *raison d'être* for a regional economy and at least theoretically are the prime movers of an economy. Regardless of the point of view, it is certainly clear that these relations must not be treated as residuals, as they too frequently are.

Again, there are several conceptual ways of adequately developing the Rest of the World account for an open region. Each way, however, should at least be consistent with an import-export classification which explicitly cuts across all, or practically all, accounts.[61] In fact, in the minds of some analysts, the export sector is the sector that primarily determines the level of income and economic welfare of a region, much as in Keynesian doctrine the investment sector is the determining sector in closed regions. In contrast, the nonexport sector is passive, being dependent on the level of the export sector and local welfare. Hence, for these analysts, an across-the-board import-export classification is a *sine qua non*.

Whatever the causal significance attributed to the export sector, clearly production for export is a sector that should be neatly identified. Although production of an activity in a region could be measured by total value of final goods produced, as in the national accounts in the United States, for open regions it seems more meaningful to use the alternative measure of value added at all production stages. This alternative is desirable since it separates from the total value of final goods produced for export the part that consists of imports of raw materials and intermediates. Thus, it permits a more explicit identification of the impact of export activity on the region. Additionally, it keeps neatly identified the production of intermediates for export,[62] which may be of critical importance.

[60] For another interesting presentation of a set of regional social accounts using national procedures, see E. Nevin [57].

[61] Thus, Deane's classification of net output by each industry as a whole (e.g. mining, agriculture, etc.) and each category of income as a whole (e.g. European, African, etc. or by more standard categories of wages, profits, etc.) does not meet this criterion.

[62] Included in production of intermediates are those raw materials of a region which are necessarily processed locally when they are exported. Such processed raw materials could be kept distinct from industrial production in the following conceptual framework; but this only adds to the number of categories specified.

Accordingly, we set up as a first sector in Table 6 [63] on the Rest of the World account a category *Value added in the production of goods for export*.[64] (This sector will also be the first item in Table 7 on Gross Regional Product). The counterpart of exports are obviously imports. In the Rest of the World account the value of these imports are to be subtracted from exports. But in the sector, *Value added in the production of goods for export*, we have already netted out those imports of intermediates required for this production. Thus, from item 1 in Table 6 we need subtract only *Imports of final and intermediate goods for local consumption* (item 2*a*) and *for local capital formation* (item 2*b*).[65]

Beyond these items, still others are desirably incorporated, especially for study of the welfare of residents of a region. When summed, the first two items of Table 6 yield a region's standing with the Rest of the World on *commodity* account. But residents receive income from the Rest of the World, that is (1) wages and salaries, if they commute to work places outside the region, and (2) interest, rent, dividends, and profit if they own property or equity or operate activities, etc., outside the region. Residents of a region may also receive gifts. Concomitantly, similar income and gifts may flow from the given region to residents in other regions. Thus to the first two items of Table 6 we add a set of accounts to record the *net* flow of gifts and of each of these incomes. Finally, in regions within nations we must add an item to account for the difference between payment to and receipts from nonlocal government.[66] Summing all items yields, as noted in the left-hand column of Table 6, Net Current Payments Due to Residents of Region. Automatically, there corresponds to this last total

[63] For the moment the reader should ignore the numerical data of Table 6, which will be discussed subsequently. In the following paragraphs we draw heavily on the work of C. L. Leven [46].

[64] Following the census definition, value added ". . . is derived by subtracting the cost of raw materials, semimanufactured parts and components, supplies, fuels, purchased electric energy and contract work, from the value of shipments . . . ," U. S. Bureau of the Census [72], p. xxi. Since all imports which enter production are one of the items subtracted from value of shipments, value added in production in any region necessarily is net of the imports required for production.

For any given region value added in the production of goods *for export* is obviously only a part of value added in the production of goods. It is determined by splitting each production activity into two fractions, one geared directly or indirectly to export trade, the other to local needs. This classification, which involves a thorny conceptual problem, also arises in *economic base* studies. The logic of such a classification is discussed at length in connection with the presentation of economic base studies in Chapter 6, pp. 195–198, to which the reader is referred.

[65] For discussion relating to the use of commodity flow data and to the estimation of imports see Chapter 5, pp. 166–168, and Chapter 12, section B.2.d.

[66] Where nonlocal government is not distinguished from nonlocal production, this item is covered by the account for the production sectors.

TABLE 6.   REST OF THE WORLD ACCOUNT: ELGIN–DUNDEE REGION,
ILLINOIS, 1956
(In thousands of dollars)

1. Value Added in the Pro- duction of Goods for Ex- port Less:	92,555	7. Net Investment in the Private Sector Abroad by Residents	49,059
2. Imports of Final and Intermediate Goods for (a) Local Consumption (b) Local Capital For- mation	64,454 20,458 ―――― 7,643		
3. Excess of Out-commuters Wages over In-commuters Wages	24,735		
4. Net Receipts of Interest, Rent, Dividends, and Pro- fits from Abroad	17,516		
5. Net Receipts of Gifts from Abroad Less:	−835	Less:	
6. Excess of Payment to over Receipts from Nonlocal Government	39,160	8. Net Transfers to Nonlocal Govern- ment	39,160
Net Current Payments Due to Residents of Region	9,899	Net Investment Abroad by Residents of Region	9,899

Source: Adapted from C. L. Leven [46], p. 216.

account a balancing account, namely, net investment abroad by the residents of the region.   Conveniently, this latter account may be disaggregated into net investment in the private sector abroad and net transfers to
(or receipts from) nonlocal government.   If the total of the left-hand
column is positive, the claims of residents on the Rest of the World have
increased, and therefore net investment is positive.   If negative, the claims
of residents have decreased, and therefore disinvestment occurs.

Table 6 represents a meaningful *Rest of the World account*.   However,
it does not present the complete picture; it fails to cover gold and currency
movements, changes in capital account from purchase and sale of securities,

and other money flows which are included in a complete balance of payments statement.   This type of statement will be fully discussed in Chapter 5.

Also, Table 6 yields neither a measure of Gross Regional Product nor of Regional Income.   To the first item of Table 6, namely, value added in the production of goods for export, we must add value added in the production of goods for both local consumption and local capital formation in order to obtain Gross Regional Product.   This we do in the left-hand column of Table 7.   The resulting Gross Regional Product may be viewed as representing the contributions made in the region by the employed factors of

TABLE 7.   GROSS REGIONAL PRODUCT: ELGIN–DUNDEE REGION, ILLINOIS,
1956

(In thousands of dollars)

1. Value Added in the Production of Goods for Export	92,555	3. Sales of Goods to the Rest of the World	220,282
2. Value Added in the Production of Goods for		Less:	
(a) Local Consumption	38,319	4. Imports of Final and Intermediate Goods for:	
(b) Local Capital Formation	5,722	(a) Production of Goods for Export	127,727
		(b) Local Consumption	64,454
		(c) Local Capital Formation	20,458
			7,643
		5. Purchases of Goods by Local Consumers	102,773
		6. Purchases of Capital Goods by Local Businesses	26,180
Gross Regional Product (Charges Against)	136,596	Gross Regional Product (Sales Value)	136,596

Source: Adapted from C. L. Leven [46], p. 219.

production and represents factor costs or charges against sales value. Too, Gross Regional Product may be viewed from another standpoint, as in the right-hand column of Table 7. It may be considered as the total value of sales of goods to the Rest of the World (Exports) *less* total value of purchases from the Rest of the World (Imports) *plus* purchases of final goods by local consumers *plus* purchases of capital goods by local businesses. This view emphasizes the value of final and capital goods made available for local consumers and businesses after adjustment for change in the account with the Rest of the World resulting from trade (Exports less Imports).

From Gross Regional Product, the analyst may proceed to various other welfare measures. In Table 8 we list at the top Gross Regional Product.

TABLE 8. REGIONAL PRODUCT AND INCOME MEASURES: ELGIN–DUNDEE
REGION, ILLINOIS, 1956
(In thousands of dollars)

Gross Regional Product			136,596
Less: Capital Consumption Allowances (and statistical discrepancies)			19,459
Net Regional Product			117,137
Plus: Excess of Out-commuters Wages over In-commuters Wages	24,735		
Net Receipts of Interest, Rent, Dividends, and Profits from Abroad	17,516		
Net Receipts of Gifts from Abroad	−835	41,416	
Less: Indirect Business Taxes to Nonlocal Government		6,737	34,679
Regional Income (Residents)			151,816
Plus: Transfer Payments from Nonlocal Government		7,533	
Less: Corporate Income Tax Liability	21,197		
Undistributed Corporate Profits	9,346		
Employment Taxes	2,918	33,461	−25,928
Personal Income (Residents)			125,888
Less: Personal Income Tax Liability			15,841
Disposable Personal Income (Residents)			110,047

Source: Adapted from C. L. Leven [46], p. 220.

Subtracting capital consumption allowances we obtain Net Regional Product. Net Regional Product refers to the region on a geographical basis, that is, accounts for all economic activity within its borders. It corresponds to Deane's Territorial Output (Income or Outlay). But it is also pertinent to determine the welfare of the region's residents. To Net Regional Product we add net receipts from abroad of wages and salaries, interest, rent, dividends, profits, and gifts.[67] Also, we must deduct indirect business taxes to nonlocal government, since these taxes are not considered factor income and since they flow out of the region.[68] We obtain Regional Income (Residents).

Regional Income (Residents) is still not Personal Income (Residents). For one thing, residents may receive payments from nonlocal government which are not returns for services rendered. These must be added. Further, the residents of a region may have a considerable amount of their earned income subject to corporate income and employment taxes and tied up in undistributed corporate profits.[69] These items must be deducted. The result is Personal Income (Residents).[70]

Finally, we may wish to distinguish between personal income received and disposable personal income. We obtain Disposable Personal Income of Residents by subtracting from their personal income their income tax liabilities.

With this set of social accounts, we can briefly survey the set of data developed by Leven for the Elgin–Dundee region, 1956. From Table 6 it is to be noted that this region increased its claims on the Rest of the World via Export and Import by $7.6 million.[71] Further, the wages which its residents received from the Rest of the World (largely from

[67] See the relevant discussion on pp. 103–105 and pp. 109–110.

[68] For additional conceptual discussion relating to these taxes, see [73] for year 1954, p. 33.

[69] Following Leven, we employ the fiction that corporations with head offices in the region are residents of the region, and thus their undistributed profits are profits accruing to residents. (Dividend payments of such corporations to nonresidents are treated as flows out of the region.) For further discussion of the very difficult conceptual problem see C. L. Leven [46], pp. 53–55, W. Hochwald [32], and Chapter 5, pp. 169–170.

[70] Because of different sectoring and data procedures, neither Regional Income (Residents) nor Personal Income (Residents) is exactly equivalent to Residents' Income as developed by Deane (Table 3).

[71] Specifically, Leven defines exports as the sum of (1) goods shipped out of the region; (2) intermediate goods which enter into the production of goods which are shipped from the region (see footnote 64, p. 109); (3) goods sold to nonresidents who come to the region to make purchases; (4) goods sold to establishments of nonlocal government located within the region; and (5) goods sold to persons residing within institutions (including military personnel and students) within the region. Leven derives data on these categories from surveys of business establishments in the region.

Imports include goods shipped into the region, plus purchases made outside the region by residents. Because of data problems Leven derives import figures as residuals from other direct estimates of Table 7. For further discussion of problems and procedures, see C. L. Leven [46], pp. 29–37, 58, and Parts II and III.

Chicago) exceeded the wages paid to in-commuters by $24.7 million. And other income payments to residents from the Rest of the World in the form of interest, rent, dividends, and profits exceeded corresponding out-payments by $17.5 million.[72] But the payments of residents to non-local government (state and federal) exceeded receipts by $39.2 million.[73] All in all, the region increased its account with (investment in) the Rest of the World by $9.9 million.

In Table 7 value added in production of goods for export accounts for roughly two-thirds of the total Gross Regional Product of $136.6 million. For the Elgin–Dundee region, a few industries such as watch manufacture, which have higher than average value-added per employee, dominate the export trade. This partly explains the relatively high proportion of Gross Regional Product assignable to export activity. As can be expected, the right-hand side of Table 7 shows that total value of exports is balanced to a large degree by imports ; and that purchase of goods by local consumers accounts for most of the region's Gross Regional Product (from the sales standpoint).

Finally, in Table 8, we note that capital consumption allowances (and statistical discrepancies)[74] account for roughly 14 per cent of Gross Regional Product and when subtracted yield a Net Regional Product of $117.1 million. To Net Regional Product are added the large *net* inflows on commuter wage account and on interest, rent, dividends, and profits account, which have already been noted. After adjustment for indirect business taxes, a Regional Income (Residents) of $151.8 million is obtained. Note that in contrast with National Income Accounts where National Income tends to be less than Net National Product (see the United States data for 1953 reported in Table 1), the Regional Income for the Elgin–Dundee region well exceeds its Net Regional Product. Part of this excess is undoubtedly due to the particular way in which arbitrary decisions had to be made during the course of the study. But clearly part of this excess reflects the fact that the Elgin–Dundee region is an *open* region (in contrast

---

[72] Flows of wages, salaries, interest, and rent are estimated by Leven from business and household surveys and offer little conceptual difficulty. For treatment of dividends and undistributed profits of locally headquartered multiplant corporations, see footnote 69, p. 113.

[73] The outpayments to nonlocal government as recorded in Table 6 exaggerate the actual outpayments. There are certain functions of nonlocal government such as the post office service of federal government which are essentially local functions involving little net inflow or outflow from the region. However, the separation of nonlocal government functions into those basically local and those interregional was not possible for the study. See C. L. Leven [46], pp. 34–36.

[74] In the Elgin–Dundee study, statistical discrepancies are estimated at 5 to 6 per cent of Gross Regional Product; see C. L. Leven [46], pp. 232–233.

with the United States which is relatively closed). And for open regions, there is no necessary relationship between Net Regional Product (as defined above) and Regional Income as received by residents.[75]

From Regional Income (Residents) for Elgin–Dundee, a Personal Income (Residents) of $125.9 million and a Disposable Personal Income (Residents) of $110.0 million are obtained in the manner prescribed.

Tables 6, 7, and 8 summarize one effective approach to social accounting for regions. As contrasted with Deane's approach summarized in Tables 2, 3, and 4, they place greater emphasis on export relations. For example, they present a set of more detailed accounts with the Rest of the World. Yet, each approach confronts both conceptual and data problems; and it is to be expected that with time and further research effort still more effective social accounting frameworks can be designed and empirically implemented.[76]

F. Concluding Remarks

As with population and its components, it is very desirable to have a knowledge of the income of a region, of its distribution among families, of income inflows and outflows by type income, of Gross Regional Product and various other items in a social accounting system, and, more specifically, of the receipts of factors of production by type factor, of the value of output and investment of industries by type industry, of the value of imports and exports by industry and by households, of the expenditures and savings of consumers by class of consumers, of the activities of governments by type of government, etc. All this information is extremely valuable for economic planning as well as for the measurement of the achievements of development programs. Even though there are many conceptual and data problems in the construction of these estimates, and

[75] Leven discusses several other conceptual and technical differences between national income accounts for the United States and his system of regional accounts ([46], pp. 70–71, 234–235). Among others, these include the omission in the regional accounts of imputed rents and inventory adjustments.

[76] For an excellent study of local accounts which, as the Leven and Deane investigations, explores new concepts, see P. de Wolff and P. E. Venekamp [78].

This study is particularly interesting in the hierarchy of regions which it employs, namely Amsterdam, the Netherlands, and the World. Its classifications may prove of considerable value when a social accounting framework is required to supplement other studies based on a regional hierarchy, such as the balanced regional input-output model to be discussed below. Also this study develops in a balanced fashion, the important local government sector.

In addition, see A. G. Irvine [37] for new directions in developing finance accounts and P. B. Simpson [66], pp. 106–107, for an illuminating way of presenting basic sets of data in one over-all table.

even though these estimates may be shaky and somewhat fragmentary, they are usually worth the effort involved. Yet it cannot be too frequently stated that the resulting magnitudes of income and other social accounts are not good welfare measures, particularly where the volume of non-monetary transactions is understated often unconsciously because of the greater availability of data on market transactions. Welfare involves far more considerations, at least some of which are equally important as income.

Much income and social accounting work has been oriented to the needs of national economies, and thus, too, the collection and processing of relevant data. As a consequence, our current endowment of concepts, accounts, and data is much less relevant for the purposes of regional studies. Clearly one fruitful channel of research is to continue to reconceive for the region the problem of measuring income, gross product, and output. Better systems of accounts are required to facilitate double-entry and triple-entry procedures and to reduce the size of the situs problem. New kinds and sources of data and new data-processing techniques need to be explored and to be more effectively utilized for income distribution studies. These concepts, techniques, and data should emphasize much more than hitherto : (1) the interregional setting of any region and the mutual dependence of regions in order to derive a set of regional accounts and estimates more meaningful for policy decisions for the given region, other regions, and the nation ; and (2) the folk culture and unique character of each region, and hence ways of allowing for different types of accounts, categories of activities, and pricing and valuation procedures for different regions. The individualities of regions as well as their similarities must be captured. This also suggests that to obtain estimates of regional income and product, several different sets of building blocks must be designed, and conversely that major aggregates must be so conceived and constructed as to permit several different schemes for disaggregation. All this implies that there is relevance and validity to income and social accounting work which is based on both allocation methods and the collection and processing of local materials. Each approach must be more fully developed and both utilized for any given study, the particular blend finally selected depending on the purpose and region of study.

As such, income materials and social accounts are descriptive tools (although frequently they have been interwoven with Keynesian type of economic analysis to establish meaningful social and economic goals). In themselves, they cannot indicate desirable paths of economic and industrial development. However, they take on added depth and value for regional analysis and for the planning of the resource development of regions when they are combined with studies relating to other types of systems. Among such are industry location studies, population migration and projection studies, interregional and intraregional money flow studies, consumer expenditures and savings studies, regional multiplier and economic base studies, interregional and regional input-output studies and spatial interreaction studies.[77]   At the same time these studies furnish a basis for double-entry and triple-entry frameworks in regional income estimation and thus permit the attainment of more reliable regional estimates.   Additionally, coupling these types of investigations with regional income and social accounts for the several regions of the United States promises to lead, by summation procedures, to improved state and national income estimates.   Finally, as already indicated in the introduction, by this same coupling process a fruitful attack can be made on the problem of income projection, which is discussed later.[78]

REFERENCES

1. Adamson, W. M., *Income in Counties of Alabama, 1929 and 1935*, multilithed series No. 1, Bureau of Business Research, University of Alabama, University, Alabama, 1939.

2. ———, "Measurement of Income in Small Geographic Areas," *Southern Economic Journal*, Vol. 8 (April 1942).

3. Ashby, Lowell D., and Everett P. Truex, *The Estimation of Income Payments to Individuals in North Carolina Counties*, School of Business Administration, University of North Carolina, Chapel Hill, North Carolina, 1952.

4. Baughn, William H., and Gardner M. Jones, *Income Payments in Louisiana; Estimates by Parishes, 1947–48*, Division of Research, Louisiana State University, Baton Rouge, Louisiana, March 1952.

5. Booth, S. Lees, *Application of National Aggregates to a State Level*, The Graduate Economics Seminar of Syracuse University, Syracuse, New York, 1950.

6. California State Chamber of Commerce, *Income Payments to Residents of California by Counties, 1935–1941*, April 1942, mimeographed.

7. Commonwealth of Kentucky, Department of Revenue, *Kentucky Income: A Statistical Study of the Tax Returns, 1941 and 1942*, Special Report No. 5, 1944.

8. Copeland, Lewis C., *Methods for Estimating Income Payments in Counties*, Bureau of Population and Economic Research, University of Virginia, Charlottesville Virginia, 1952.

9. Corry, Ormond C., *Income Payments to Individuals in Tennessee Counties, 1939, 1947, and 1949–51*, Bureau of Business and Economic Research, University of Tennessee, Knoxville, Tennessee, May 1953.

---

[77] Some of these studies will be described in later chapters. Notable progress in the use of several types of studies in conjunction with income accounting has been scored in the study of the Eighth Federal Reserve District. See W. Hochwald [33–35], G. Freutel [19, 20], and various industry and other studies published in the *Monthly Review*, Federal Reserve Bank of St. Louis.

[78] See Chapter 12 and Chapter 8, section H. Also, W. Isard and G. Freutel [38].

10. Cumberland, John H., *Monthly Income Estimates for Maryland*, The Chesapeake and Potomac Telephone Companies, Washington, D.C., July 1955.

11. ———, "Suggested Improvements in Regional Income Accounting," *Papers and Proceedings of the Regional Science Association*, Vol. 2 (1956).

12. Deane, Phyllis, *Colonial Social Accounting*, Cambridge University Press, Cambridge, England, 1953.

13. ———, *The Measurement of Colonial National Incomes, an Experiment*, National Institute of Economic and Social Research, Occasional Paper No. 12, Cambridge University Press, Cambridge, England, 1948.

14. ———, "Regional Variations in United Kingdom Incomes from Employment, 1948," *Journal of the Royal Statistical Society*, Series A (General), Vol. 116, Part II (1953).

15. Easterlin, Richard A., "Growth of Income in United States Regions: 1880–1950," in *Population Redistribution and Economic Growth: United States, 1870–1950*, ed. by Everett S. Lee, et al., Vol. 1, American Philosophical Society, Philadelphia. 1957.

16. ———, "Interregional Differences in Per Capita Income, Population and Total Income, United States, 1840–1950," in Conference on Research in Income and Wealth, *Studies in Income and Wealth*, Vol. 24, National Bureau of Economic Research, Princeton University Press, Princeton, New Jersey, forthcoming.

17. Federal Reserve Bank of St. Louis, Research Department, *Eighth District Income and Expenditure, 1948: Technical Notes*, St. Louis, Jan. 1950.

18. Fisher, Dorothy H., *Income Trends in Virginia for Selected Years, 1939–1951, by Source*, Bureau of Population and Economic Research, University of Virginia, Charlottesville, Virginia, 1953.

19. Freutel, Guy, "The Eighth District Balance of Trade," *Monthly Review*, Federal Reserve Bank of St. Louis, Vol. 34 (June 1952).

20. ———, "Regional Interdependence and District Development," *Monthly Review*, Federal Reserve Bank of St. Louis, Vol. 33 (Aug. 1951).

21. Fulmer, John L., "Measurement of Agricultural Income by Counties," in *Regional Income*, National Bureau of Economic Research, Studies in Income and Wealth, Vol. 21, Princeton University Press, Princeton, New Jersey, 1957.

22. ———, "Regression Methods of Estimating Agricultural Income of Counties," *Review of Economics and Statistics*, Vol. 38 (Feb. 1956).

23. ———, "State Per Capita Income Differentials: 1940 and 1950," *Southern Economic Journal*, Vol. 22 (July 1955).

24. Gilbert, Milton, and Richard Stone, "Recent Developments in National Income and Social Accounting," *Accounting Research*, Vol. 5 (Jan. 1954).

25. Gilliam, Sara K., *Distribution of Income in Virginia in 1947*, Bureau of Population and Economic Research, University of Virginia, Charlottesville, Virginia, 1950.

26. Guthrie, John A., and Stanley E. Boyle, *County Income Payments in Washington, 1950–1952*, Bureau of Economic and Business Research, State College of Washington, Pullman, Washington, Aug. 1954.

27. Hanna, Frank A., "Age, Labor Force, and State Per Capita Incomes, 1930, 1940, and 1950," *Review of Economics and Statistics*, Vol. 37 (Feb. 1955).

28. Hanna, Frank A., "Analysis of Interstate Income Differentials: Theory and Practice," in *Regional Income*, National Bureau of Economic Research, Studies in Income and Wealth, Vol. 21, Princeton University Press, Princeton, New Jersey, 1957.

29. Hanna, Frank A., "Contribution of Manufacturing Wages to Regional Differences in Per Capita Income," *Review of Economics and Statistics*, Vol. 33 (Feb. 1951).

30. ———, "Cyclical and Secular Changes in State Per Capita Incomes, 1929–50," *Review of Economics and Statistics*, Vol. 36 (Aug. 1954).

31. ———, "State Per Capita Income Components, 1919–1951," *Review of Economics and Statistics*, Vol. 38 (Nov. 1956).

32. Hochwald, Werner, "Conceptual Issues of Regional Income Estimation," in *Regional Income*, National Bureau of Economic Research, Studies in Income and Wealth, Vol. 21, Princeton University Press, Princeton, New Jersey, 1957.

33. ———, "District Income Through a Generation of Change," *Monthly Review*, Federal Reserve Bank of St. Louis, Vol. 35 (Oct. 1953).

34. ———, "Eighth District Income in 1951," *Monthly Review*, Federal Reserve Bank of St. Louis, Vol. 34 (Oct. 1952).

35. ———, "Sources and Uses of District Funds in 1952," *Monthly Review*, Federal Reserve Bank of St. Louis, Vol. 35 (May 1953).

36. Hoover, Edgar M. and Joseph L. Fisher, "Research in Regional Economic Growth," in *Problems in the Study of Economic Growth*, National Bureau of Economic Research, July 1949, mimeographed.

37. Irvine, A. G., "The Preparation of National Finance Accounts in Under-Developed Economies (with Special Reference to Rhodesia and Nyasaland)," *Economic Journal*, Vol. 65 (June 1955).

38. Isard, W., and G. Freutel, "Regional and National Product Projections and their Interrelations," in *Long-Range Economic Projection*, Studies in Income and Wealth, Vol. 16, National Bureau of Economic Research, Princeton University Press, Princeton, New Jersey, 1954.

39. Johnson, Byron L., and Carl C. Nordquist, *An Estimation of Personal Income Payments by Colorado County, 1948*, Studies in Social Sciences, No. 2, University of Denver Press, Denver, Colorado, 1951.

40. Johnson, Robert H., *An Analysis of Iowa Income Payments by Counties*, Bureau of Business and Economic Research, State University of Iowa, Iowa City, Iowa, March 1950.

41. Jones, William O., "Colonial Social Accounting," *Journal of the American Statistical Association*, Vol. 50 (Sept. 1955).

42. Kuznets, Simon, *National Income: A Summary of Findings*, National Bureau of Economic Research, New York, 1946.

43. ———, *National Income and its Composition, 1919–1938*, National Bureau of Economic Research, New York, 1941.

44. ———, "Quantitative Aspects of the Economic Growth of Nations: III, Industrial Distribution of Income and Labor Force by States, United States, 1919–1921 to 1955," *Economic Development and Cultural Change*, Vol. 6, Part II (July 1958).

45. Lancaster, John Littlepage, *County Income Estimates for Seven Southeastern States*, Bureau of Population and Economic Research, University of Virginia, Charlottesville, Virginia, 1952.

46. Leven, Charles L., *Theory and Method of Income and Product Accounts For Metropolitan Areas, Including the Elgin–Dundee Area as a Case Study*, Iowa State College, Ames, Iowa, 1958, mimeographed.

47. ———, "A Theory of Regional Social Accounting," *Papers and Proceedings of the Regional Science Association*, Vol. 4 (1958).

48. Mansfield, Edwin, "City Size and Income, 1949," in *Regional Income*, National Bureau of Economic Research, Studies in Income and Wealth, Vol. 21, Princeton University Press, Princeton, New Jersey, 1957.
49. Martin, James W., *Conference on the Measurement of County Income: A Report of Three Years of Work*, Bureau of Business Research, University of Kentucky, Lexington, Kentucky, June 1952, mimeographed.
50. ———, *Methods of Estimating Income Payments by Counties Employed by Members of the Conference on the Measurement of County Income*, Bureau of Business Research, University of Kentucky, Lexington, Kentucky, mimeographed.
51. Mauldon, F. R. E., and A. M. Kerr, "The Estimation of Regional Income," paper presented at the 29th meeting of the Australian and New Zealand Association for the Advancement of Science, Sydney, Australia, Aug. 20–27, 1952, mimeographed.
52. McKinney, David, *Income Payments to Mississippians*, Bureau of Business Research, University of Mississippi, University, Mississippi, 1952.
53. Morgenstern, Oskar, *On the Accuracy of Economic Observations*, Princeton University Press, Princeton, New Jersey, 1950.
54. Myers, Will S., John L. Johnson, and James W. Martin, *Kentucky Income Payments by Counties 1939, 1947, 1950, and 1951*, Bureau of Business Research, University of Kentucky, Lexington, Kentucky, Feb. 1953.
55. National Bureau of Economic Research, *The National Economic Accounts of the United States*, General Series No. 64, U. S. Government Printing Office, Washington, D.C., 1958.
56. ——, *Regional Income*, Studies in Income and Wealth, Vol. 21, Princeton University Press, Princeton, New Jersey, 1957.
57. Nevin, E., "The Gross National Product of Wales, 1950," *Bulletin of the Oxford Institute of Statistics*, Vol. 18 (Feb. 1956).
58. Oshima, H. T., "National Income Statistics of Underdeveloped Countries," *Journal of the American Statistical Association*, Vol. 52 (June 1957).
59. Perloff, Harvey S., "Interrelations of State Income and Industrial Structure," *Papers and Proceedings of the Regional Science Association*, Vol. 2 (1956).
60. Peters, R. W., "The Measurement of Regional Incomes in Western Australia, 1947–48 to 1950–51," *Research Studies in Community Income*, The University of Western Australia, Perth, Australia, 1954, mimeographed.
61. Salkever, Louis R., *Personal Income in Philadelphia*, Department of Commerce, City of Philadelphia, Dec. 1955.
62. Salter, W. E. G., "The Measurement of Factor Income Generated by Productive Sectors in Western Australia, 1947–48 to 1950–51," *Research Studies in Community Income*, The University of Western Australia, Perth, Australia, 1953, mimeographed.
63. ——, and R. W. Peters, "A Preliminary Investigation into the Possibility of Estimating Regional Incomes for Western Australia," *Research Studies in Community Income*, The University of Western Australia, Perth, Australia, 1953, mimeographed.
64. Schumpeter, Joseph A., *History of Economic Analysis*, Oxford University Press, New York, 1954.
65. Schwartz, Charles F., *Income of Hawaii*, Office of Business Economics, United States Department of Commerce, Washington, D.C., 1953.
66. Simpson, Paul B., *Regional Aspects of Business Cycles and Special Studies of the Pacific Northwest*, Bonneville Administration and the University of Oregon, June 1953.

67. Stone, Richard, and Kurt Hansen, "Inter-Country Comparisons of National Accounts," in *Income and Wealth*, Series III, Bowes and Bowes, Ltd., Cambridge, England, 1953.

68. Stuvel, G., "A System of National and Domestic Accounts," *Economica*, Vol. 22, Part I (1955).

69. Thompson, Lorin A., "Appraisal of Alternative Methods of Estimating Local Area Income," in *Regional Income*, National Bureau of Economic Research, Studies in Income and Wealth, Vol. 21, Princeton University Press, Princeton, New Jersey, 1957.

70. ———, *Income Payments by Cities and Counties of Virginia*, Bureau of Population and Economic Research, University of Virginia, Charlottesville, Virginia.

71. ———, *Patterns of Income Payments by Areas, 1949*, Bureau of Population and Economic Research, University of Virginia, Charlottesville, Virginia.

72. U. S. Bureau of the Census, *United States Census of Manufactures, 1954*, Vol. 1, Summary Statistics, U. S. Government Printing Office, Washington, D.C., 1957.

73. U. S. Department of Commerce, *National Income*, supplement to *Survey of Current Business*, U. S. Government Printing Office, Washington, D.C., annual.

74. ———, *Personal Income by States*, supplement to the *Survey of Current Business*, U. S. Government Printing Office, Washington, D.C., 1956.

75. ———, *Survey of Current Business*, Washington, D.C., monthly.

76. University of Florida, Bureau of Economic and Business Research, *Income Payments to Individuals in Florida Counties, 1952*, Gainesville, Florida, June 1955.

77. University of Maryland, Bureau of Business Research, *Personal Income in Maryland Counties 1951–55*, College Park, Maryland, March 1957.

78. Wolff, P. de, and P. E. Venekamp, "On a System of Regional Social Accounts for the City of Amsterdam," *International Statistical Institute Bulletin*, Vol. 35, Part 4, 1957.

79. Wolfson, Robert J., "An Econometric Investigation of Regional Differentials in American Agricultural Wages," *Econometrica*, Vol. 26 (April 1958).

Chapter 5

Interregional Flow Analysis and Balance of Payments Statements*

A. INTRODUCTION

The World, each of its major meaningful Divisions, and each of its larger nations may be viewed as a system of regions. Within the limits imposed by transportation cost, political and cultural barriers, etc., individual regions of a system can draw freely on the resources, products, and skills of other regions in their efforts to develop their industries and raise their own incomes. The goods and services a region imports must be paid for in the long run by exports or by the transfer of assets, including bank reserves. Or, viewed from the other side of the coin, a region's exports provide the wherewithal for its imports and accumulation of assets.

Regional analysis therefore must look outward as well as inward. We have already probed the export-import relations of regions from an accounting standpoint. But the analysis of flows of goods, money, and wealth among regions requires broader and much deeper scrutiny than is involved in a regional accounting framework. The analysis of these flows frequently requires special study.

Commodity flow studies seek to point up in concrete terms the manner and extent to which any region (1) does and can avail itself of the natural advantages of other regions through imports, and (2) does and can compete

* This chapter has been written with Leon N. Moses.

with these other regions in the disposal of its products in the several regional and subregional markets.

Money flow studies are also of value, partly because each import and export is tagged with a dollar sign, thereby to provide a common denominator for the exchange of goods and transfer of assets. They can lead to the formulation of more effective credit, tax, and other monetary and fiscal policies both within a region and a nation.

Balance of payments studies are called for in order to assess the current financial position of a region's economy and its general economic health. In the long run the region, like an individual person, must bring into balance its income and expenditures to remain economically solvent or avoid loss of assets. If a region's industries are not efficient enough to compete in the markets of an interregional system, if it cannot provide on current account the basis to pay for its imports, it tends to lose bank reserves and may suffer financial stringency. This in turn may generate conditions that curtail economic growth and even exert downward pressure on existing levels of income and employment.

Ideally, in the study of a given region we should be able to develop in considerable detail and over time its financial and commodity and service trading relationships with other regions. This detail would depict commodity and money flow systems. Such systems could then be related to the several systems portraying other basic interconnections within and among regions. In turn the mutual dependence and linkage between the determinants of the several pertinent systems could be studied to understand the internal structure of the region as well as the interregional system in its totality.

Unhappily, our current stock of tools and methods of analysis together with the available data do not allow us to depict commodity and money flow systems in a comprehensive ideal fashion. Nonetheless, these tools and methods, imperfect as they are, do give us considerable insight into the functioning and growth process of regions. In this chapter we shall discuss in order: (1) the location quotient, as an indicator of the extent to which a region's industries are in balance; (2) commodity flow studies; (3) money flow studies; and (4) the construction and analysis of regional balances of payments.

B. The Location Quotient[1]

Frequently, a study of a region's export-import relations begins at least on a preliminary basis with a simple analysis employing the location

---

[1] Logically, this section on the location quotient belongs to Chapter 7 where similar quotients and coefficients are discussed. However, this quotient is treated here since it

quotient. This quotient does not require extensive data collection and processing. It is a device for comparing a region's percentage share of a particular activity with its percentage share of some basic aggregate. If Region A, for instance, accounts for 10 per cent of the national total of, say, hat manufacture and the region's total income is 5 per cent of the nation's total, the region's location quotient (with income as base) for hat making would be 2.

In the early 1940's the U. S. National Resources Planning Board computed for every state its location quotient with respect to each manufacturing activity.[2] The N.R.P.B. used as a base total wage earners in all manufacturing. For any given manufacturing activity, it therefore presented for each state a coefficient which was computed by dividing (1) the state's share of the national total of wage earners for a given manufacturing industry by (2) the state's share of all manufacturing.[3] Such location quotients have been used extensively by Florence[4] and other location analysts.[5]

In computing the location quotient, a quantity named in various ways,[6] an investigator can use any base he considers significant for the problem and region under study. If he is interested in the location (or the region's share) of an industry relative to the geographic distribution of the household market for the industry's product, he may find *income* to be a significant base.[7] If he is interested in a region's share of an industry relative to its labor productivity in manufacture as a whole, he may find *valued added* by manufacture to be a more sensitive base. If he is interested in welfare conditions and criteria and with balanced per capita distributions, *population* may be the most relevant base. If he is interested in the problem of reducing vulnerability, *area* would be a pertinent base. If he wishes to test a hypothesis relating to the orientation of an industry, or if he wishes to

is related to export-import study, and since its discussion will facilitate the exposition of materials in this chapter and is required for the development of materials in Chapter 6.

[2] [63], pp. 107–119.

[3] Let S_i = number of wage earners in manufacturing industry i in a given state,

S = number of wage earners in all manufacturing industry in the same state,

N_i = number of wage earners in manufacturing industry i in the nation,

N = number of wage earners in all manufacturing industry in the nation.

The location quotient for industry i in the given state is

$$\frac{S_i/N_i}{S/N}; \quad \text{or} \quad \frac{S_i/S}{N_i/N}$$

[4] P. S. Florence [20].

[5] P. Neff and R. M. Williams [43]; Federal Reserve Bank of Kansas City [17], pp. 1–7; and G. Hildebrand and A. Mace [27].

[6] For example, P. Neff and R. M. Williams [43] call it a self-sufficiency ratio.

[7] In this connection the location quotient may be used to test whether or not a particular operation is oriented to household markets.

judge whether or not other factors in his region have operated to give it a greater or lesser share of industry than could be expected from an analysis of orientation, or if he wishes to study geographic linkages between the given industry and a second industry, he might use as a base *employment in a second industry* where the latter will furnish either an input to, or consume a product of, the first industry. In addition, he may order by size the location quotient for a given industry for all regions of a nation and so obtain a localization curve which yields a picture of the geographic concentration of that industry.[8]

As already noted, the advantages of the location quotient method are its simplicity and the fact that it can be based on readily available data. These probably account for its wide use, for it has many limitations. As will be seen, the fact that a region has more or less than its "proportionate" share of an activity does not, of itself, tell us much.

Because of its simplicity, the location quotient is useful in the early exploratory stages of research. One of the more fruitful ways of employing it is as a rough benchmark in the analysis of a region's exports and imports, although there is a temptation to read too much into the results of such an analysis.

Suppose, for example, we compute for a region under study the location quotient for each activity relative to total manufacturing. On the surface it would appear that the industries whose location quotients exceed unity are export industries, and those whose location quotients are below unity are import industries. We find in the regional literature suggestions that those industries with location quotients greater than unity represent the areas of strength within a region and ought therefore to be further developed; and, in somewhat contradictory fashion, that those industries with location quotients less than unity ought to be encouraged in order to reduce the drain of imports.[9]

Such statements must be seriously qualified, if not totally rejected. Consider the use of the location quotient to identify the export and import industries of a region.

First, tastes and expenditure patterns (propensities to consume) of households of the same type and income differ among regions. In the South little fuel is required by households; in the North, significant amounts. *Ceteris paribus*, this means that in the fuel-manufacturing industry a location quotient of unity for the South could be consistent with major exports of fuel oil; and for the North it could be consistent with major imports of fuel oil.

[8] E. M. Hoover, Jr. [30], pp. 182–184. Further discussion of the localization curve appears in Chapter 7, section D.3.

[9] A. Gosfield [22].

Second, income levels of households differ among regions. The Northeast consumes per household many more men's suits than does the Southeast. Thus, a location quotient well in excess of unity in the Northeast for the men's suits manufacturing industry can be consistent with major net imports of men's suits; and a location quotient below unity in the Southeast can be consistent with major net exports.

Third, production practices (including labor productivity) differ among regions. In its production of steel ingots, the Pacific Northwest utilizes on the average much more scrap per ton steel than the Great Lakes region. Therefore, the location quotient for the steel scrap industry for the Pacific Northwest can exceed unity and yet be theoretically consistent with major scrap imports.

Finally, and perhaps most important, industrial "mixes" vary considerably among regions. The location quotient for the power industry in the Pacific Northwest exceeds unity because of the relatively high concentration there of intensive power-consuming activities. Yet the region as a whole does not export major blocks of power as the location quotient would imply.

In sum, the location quotient when used alone can be a meaningless coefficient.[10] It is of some use in exploratory work and can be of considerable use in conjunction with other tools and techniques of analysis which fully recognize and incorporate in their framework nonlinear production and consumption functions and regional differences in tastes, income levels and distributions, production practices, and industrial mixes.

C. COMMODITY FLOW ANALYSIS

The physical aspects of the flow of individual commodities and groups of commodities are of great significance. Their analysis requires much finer tools than the location quotient. Such data as those published by the U. S. Interstate Commerce Commission on commodities shipped by Class I steam railways[11] and by the U. S. Army Engineers Corps on receipts and shipments of commodities by ports[12] are basic to this type of study.

Commodity flow studies have an obvious descriptive value. Just as regional data on industrial production, income, employment, and popula-

---

[10] This is apparent not only from the discussion given but also from the discussion in subsequent chapters, especially Chapter 7 which evaluates other types of coefficients and indices.

[11] U. S. Interstate Commerce Commission, Bureau of Transport Economics and Statistics [60, 62], and related publications.

[12] U. S. Army, Board of Engineers for Rivers and Harbors [58].

tion provide useful information on the levels at which a regional economy is operating, point-to-point data on internal as well as external movements of commodities provide useful information on the strategic connections of a region. The former data may be said to relate to basic vertical dimensions, the latter to horizontal. Both sets are essential.

One striking conclusion of most flow studies, early perceived by the investigator, is the kaleidoscopic variety of connections which most regions have. These connections take place over a variety of distances. Their importance by weight and by dollar value also evidence marked variation. These facts immediately dispel any unsophisticated mercantilist notions which are too frequently propounded by many groups within regions. These facts usually point up the importance of imports as well as exports in a regional economy. For example, in a study of the Iowa economy,[13] the flow data clearly indicate that "a major portion of Iowa's imports are for use in the production of finished products which dominate the state's export movement."[14] Large quantities of grain and other constituents for the production of feed enter the state and are basic inputs for the animal-raising and grain-processing industries which ship their products all over the United States. The Iowa economy is not only an integral part of the corn-animal-producing region but also of the national economy. It achieves "its high scale of living and its high individual income from a large-scale program of specialization of production and exchange of surplus products."[15] To cut down its imports, as a doctrinaire mercantilist might urge, would undermine the entire Iowa economy.

Another illusion which flow studies usually dispel is the belief that the economy of any large nation or Division of the World represents one large open market. The very fact that a large volume of traffic terminates over short distances testifies to the omnipresent "friction of distance," to the realization of economies of scale at several locations, and to other location forces. Thus the flow data clearly point up the hierarchy of markets existing within any nation (or World Division)—local, subregional, regional, supraregional, and national (Divisional), to use one kind of classification—entrance into any of which can be restricted by economic as well as political and social factors.

Geographers have done outstanding work in mapping commodity flows. For example, Ullman has developed an excellent set of maps for a number of states based on the 1 per cent waybill sample data of the U. S. Interstate Commerce Commission.[16] These maps present the tonnage

---

[13] L. W. Sweeney [52].
[14] [52], p. 1.
[15] [52], p. 1.
[16] E. L. Ullman [54], [56], pp. 320–322, and [57].

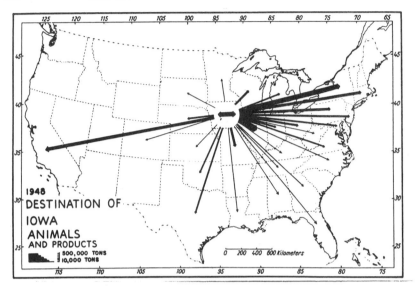

Map 1.   Destination of Iowa animals and products, 1948.   Source: E. L. Ullman [57], p. 144.

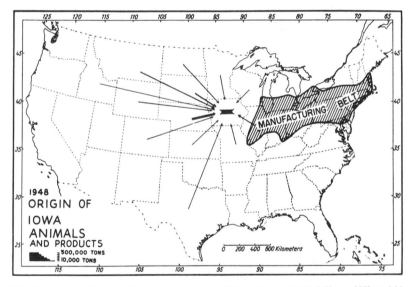

Map 2.   Origin of Iowa animals and products, 1948.   Source: E. L. Ullman [57], p. 144.

inflows and outflows of all commodities, of major groups of commodities, and of individual commodities. The way in which these maps can be used to illuminate the operation of a regional economy is illustrated by the following statement by Ullman. This statement was made in connection with the interpretation of the two maps (Maps 1, 2) which are taken from Ullman and which depict the shipment of animals and products to and from the state of Iowa. It supplements the previous comments on the economy of Iowa.

> Briefly, these two representative maps show for the first time graphically and quantitatively: (1) the generally greater volume of shipments to nearby points than to more distant points, a reflection of the friction of distance; (2) the greater volume of outbound over inbound traffic, reflecting Iowa's role as the leading animal producer, chiefly hogs and hog products, in the United States; (3) the heavy movement to the markets of the industrial northeast, which is sufficient to counteract the friction of distance (note especially the shipments to the deficit meat areas of New York and New England); (4) the small but distinctive flow to the rising California market, a new feature of American economic geography; and (5) the general west-to-east movement in the United States, a fundamental feature of American economic geography, reflecting heavy raw materials moving to eastern industrial areas, generally outweighing the backflow of lighter-weight industrial products.[17]

The significance of this type of analysis becomes more pointed when additional maps relating to the regional economy of Iowa are presented. Maps 3 and 4 depict for Iowa the origin and destination respectively of products of agriculture. Note the outflow not only to the rising California market but also to the rising Gulf Coast markets in Texas and Louisiana. Maps 5 and 6 depict respectively the origin and destination of products of forests. The heavy dependence of the Iowa economy on the timber resources of the Pacific Northwest is manifest. Maps 7 and 8 depict respectively the origin and destination of petroleum products ; the major inflows from Oklahoma and Texas reflect the effect of scale economies and relative transport costs via different media in orienting to the raw material sites that production designed to serve the Iowa market. Maps 9 and 10 depict respectively the origin and destination of products of mines ; they clearly indicate that because such products typically have high weight and bulk relative to value of product, they tend to move over shorter distances than other products in general. Maps 11 and 12 respectively portray origin and destination of manufactures and miscellaneous products ; these typify the general tendency for inflows and outflows to fall with distance in a somewhat skew-symmetric fashion, although not as sharply as products of mines. Finally, Maps 13 and 14 respectively portray the origin and

[17] See [56], pp. 317, 319.

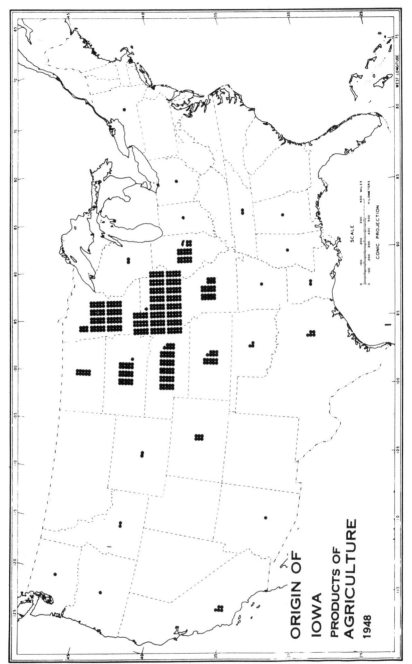

Map 3.   Origin of products of agriculture to Iowa, 1948.   Source: E. L. Ullman [54], p. 33.

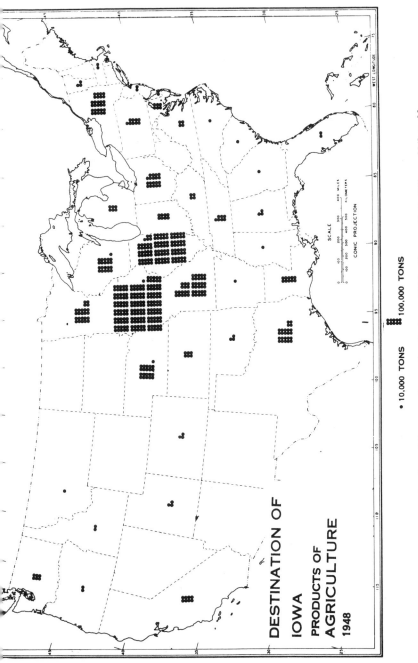

Map. 4. Destination of Iowa products of agriculture, 1948. Source: E. L. Ullman [54], p. 33.

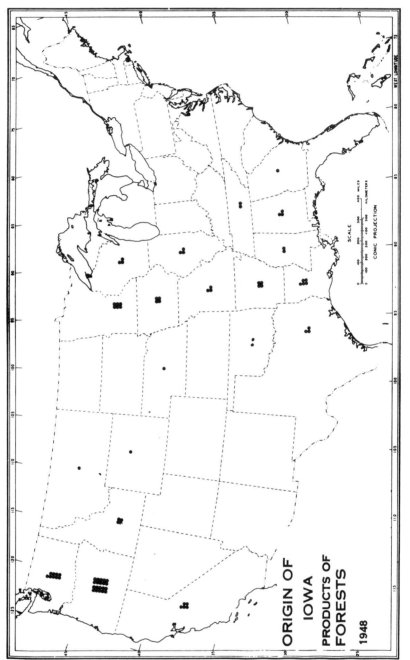

Map 5. Origin of products of forests to Iowa, 1948. Source: E. L. Ullman [54], p. 35.

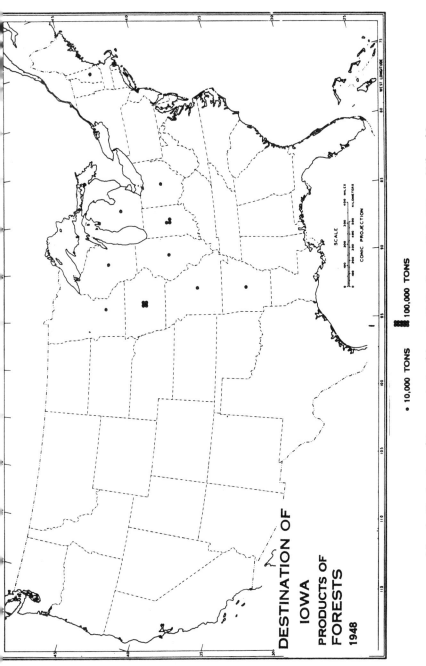

Map 6. Destination of Iowa products of forests, 1948. Source: E. L. Ullman [54], p. 35.

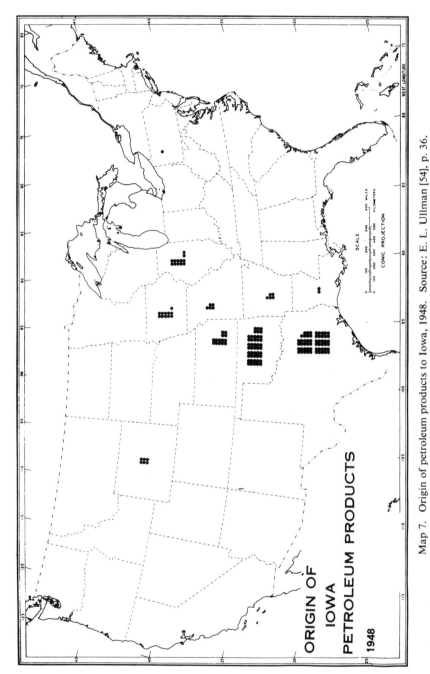

ORIGIN OF
IOWA
PETROLEUM PRODUCTS
1948

Map 7. Origin of petroleum products to Iowa, 1948. Source: E. L. Ullman [54], p. 36.

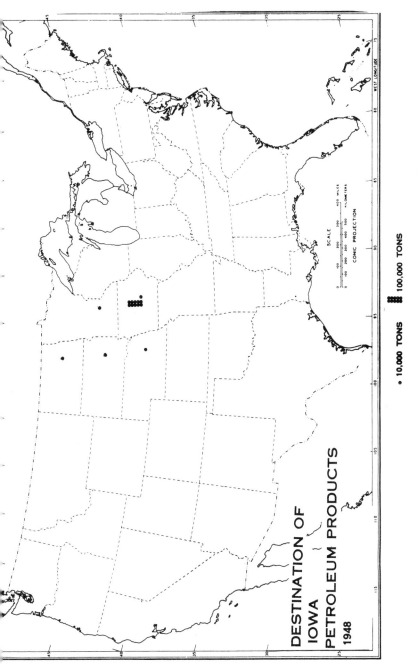

Map. 8.   Destination of Iowa petroleum products, 1948.   Source: E. L. Ullman [

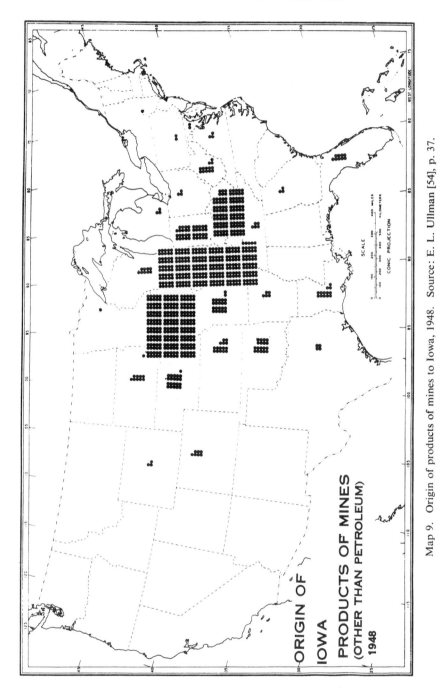

Map 9. Origin of products of mines to Iowa, 1948. Source: E. L. Ullman [54], p. 37.

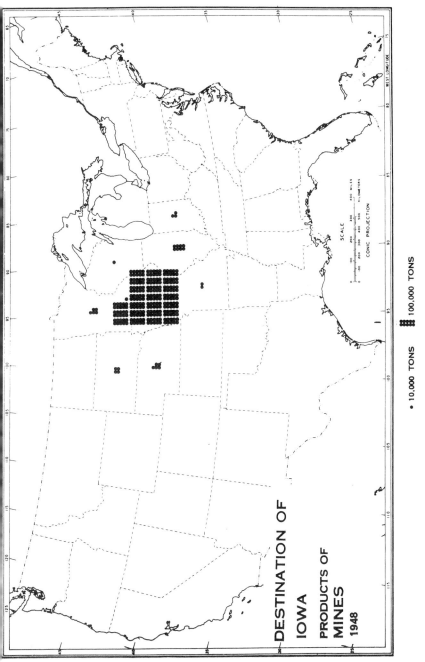

Map 10. Destination of Iowa products of mines, 1948.   Source: E. L. Ullman [54], p. 37.

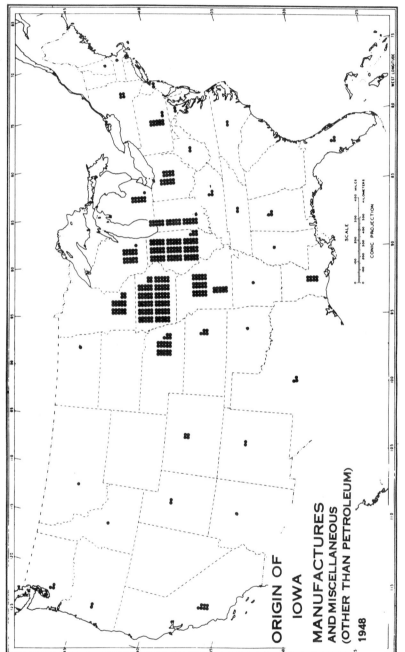

Map 11. Origin of manufactures and miscellaneous to Iowa, 1948. Source: E. L. Ullman [54], p. 38.

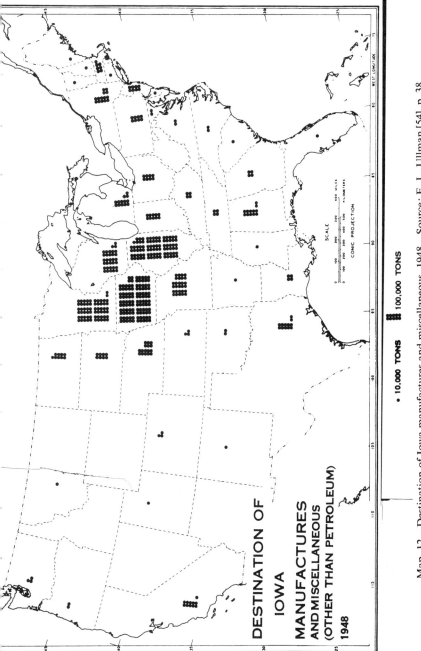

Map. 12.   Destination of Iowa manufactures and miscellaneous, 1948.   Source: E. L. Ullman [54], p. 38.

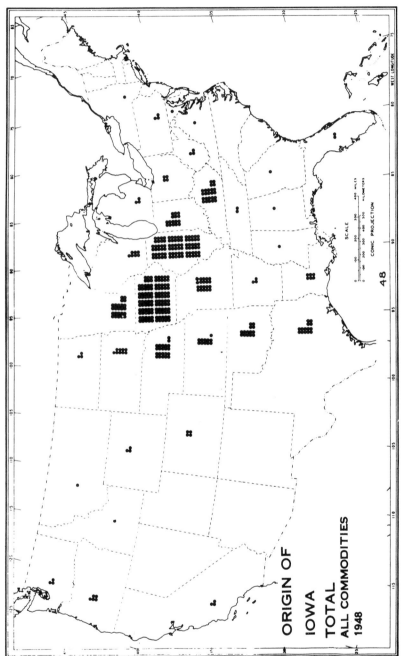

Map 13.   Origin of all commodities to Iowa, 1948.   Source: E. L. Ullman [54], p. 39.

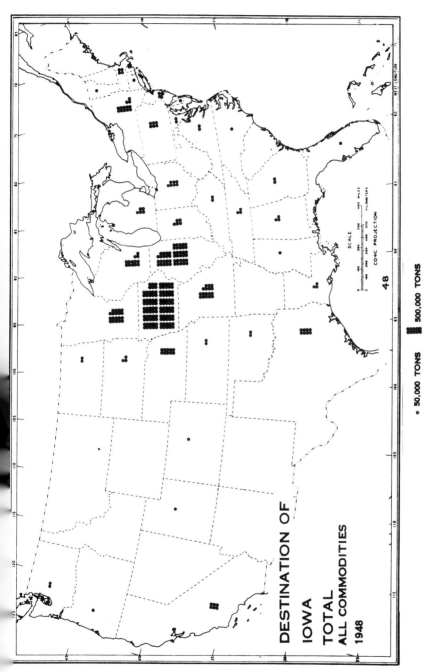

Map 14.   Destination of all Iowa commodities, 1948.   Source: E. L. Ullman [54], p. 39.

destination of all commodities; they summarize the tonnage volume linkages between Iowa and other regions. In one sense, total maps such as
Maps 13 and 14 are valuable when only highly aggregative state analysis
can be pursued. In another sense, such summation is undesirable since it
conceals the fascinating and highly suggestive detail of individual commodity flows.

This set of maps constitute only one cut of the kaleidoscopic interregional flow pattern within an interregional system such as the United
States. Another revealing cut presents the pattern over all pairs of regions
by single commodity. To illustrate only briefly, we present Maps 15 and

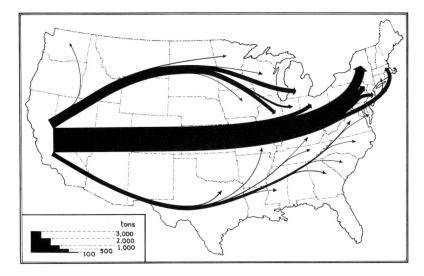

Map 15. Citrus fruit shipments, United States, 1956, Part I (shipments of 25 tons or
more, 1 per cent waybill sample). Source: U. S. Interstate Commerce Commission [62],
Statement S.S.–2, Feb. 1958.

16. These indicate annual shipments of citrus fruits which exceed 25 tons
in the 1 per cent waybill sample of the Interstate Commerce Commission.
The concentration of such production in the subtropic areas of Florida and
California is neatly pointed up, and the pull of the major metropolitan
markets is manifest, distance notwithstanding.

Typically, a complete pattern of the interregional flows of a single
commodity is much more difficult to map than that of citrus fruit flows.
Yet systematic and comprehensive analysis of flows of this sort is not only
possible but exceedingly fruitful.

Additional insight into the operation of a regional economy, especially of its dynamic characteristics, can be obtained when commodity flows are analyzed over an historical period. The U. S. Bureau of Economics and Statistics of the Interstate Commerce Commission has done some investigation of shifts of commodity flows in projecting volume of interregional traffic.[18] Careful study of such shifts adds valuable historical perspective to any regional analysis. More studies of this sort are needed and will be possible with the accumulation of higher quality and larger quantities of data.

As many scholars have noted, the value of flow studies are circumscribed

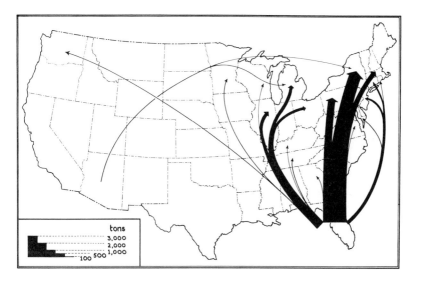

Map 16. Citrus fruit shipments, United States, 1956, Part II (shipment of 25 tons or more, 1 per cent waybill sample). Source: U.S. Interstate Commerce Commission [62], Statement S.S. –2, Feb. 1958.

by inadequate data. In the United States, for example, studies are handicapped by the almost complete absence of data on truck movement, by gaps in, and inadequate reporting and processing of, port-to-port water shipments over different routes, external and internal, and by insufficient data on rail and air traffic.[19] As these data obstacles are overcome, flow

[18] See [61].
[19] A good discussion of the virtues and limitations of the I.C.C. rail data is contained in R. T. Smith [49], pp. 227–239. A general discussion on all flow data is contained in E. L. Ullman [56], pp. 317–324.

studies, especially if developed with historical depth, can better illumine current regional structure and recent changes experienced and can better measure interregional linkages.[20]

Flow studies as such are for the most part descriptive. They are not explanatory, even though they can be extremely useful for generating and testing hypotheses and models. They can record historical changes, but they cannot probe into causes. More important, they do not by themselves provide a basis for anticipating future changes in a regional economy. As with population and migration, we can project historical trends into the future. But it is clear that projecting historical trends in regional structure as revealed by flow studies has limitations as severe as, if not more severe than, those discussed earlier in connection with population and migration projections. There is no reason to expect that certain changes will continue to occur just because they have taken place in the past.

In short, commodity flow studies must be supplemented with analysis, hypotheses, and models to be useful in estimating future markets and other aggregates and in identifying resource and industrial development potentials.[21] In the chapters to follow, we indicate how commodity flow studies may be linked with the conceptual frameworks of regional and interregional input-output techniques, multiplier and location analysis, and interregional linear programming. With such linkage descriptive commodity flow studies take on added meaning. Additionally, the area in common between commodity flow studies and gravity models and central place theory will be noted. In this frontier area, Vining's search for regularities in the spatial flows of commodities and population represents one of the foremost research studies.[22]

D. Money Flow Studies

The physical flows of commodities and of population are among several types of bonds which link regions. Others, such as money flows and communication flows, although for the most part invisible, relate to equally important connections. These connections are not always unrelated to those that are visible. For example, the shipment of a product from one

[20] Among other flow studies of note are K. E. Carlson [11]; E. H. Lewis [39]; W. Beckerman [3]; T. Ouren and A. Sømme [44]; E. L. Ullman [55], pp. 242–256; H. L. Buma and H. S. Schwartz [10]; and N. Wollman [67].

An interesting study of motor vehicle traffic within the United States is U. S. House of Representatives [59].

[21] An interesting move in this direction is contained in N. Wollman [67], especially with relation to regional welfare considerations.

[22] R. Vining [64, 65]. In this connection also see W. Isard and G. Freutel [34], pp. 434–449; W. Isard and M. J. Peck [35], pp. 98–104; and W. Isard [32], pp. 307–309.

region to a second region may have as its counterpart the flow of money from the second region to the first.

Money flows are in large part financial counterparts of the flows of commodities and services. They also cover the transfer of wealth and titles to wealth from individuals or organizations in one region to the same or different individuals or organizations in a second. These transfers of wealth may involve direct gifts, shift of funds, or purchases and sales of securities, property, and other assets.

To the extent that money flows are merely the counterpart of the movement of goods and services among regions, it might be claimed that money flow studies are repetitious—that they do not cast additional light on the problems of projecting the magnitude of basic aggregates of regions, of identifying industrial potentials of regions, and of formulating appropriate regional policies. This, however, is not so. As already indicated, we do not have complete data on the physical flows of commodities and services. Where money flows depict, in reverse, the movement of commodities for which the shipment data are lacking, or where they permit the estimation of such data through reconciliation of totals and subtotals and similar procedures, money flow studies can fruitfully supplement commodity flow studies.

Even if we had complete data on commodity movements, it would still be highly desirable to conduct money flow studies. Usually, connected with each region is a banking system. This system either independently or jointly with governmental agencies and perhaps other organizations exerts diverse controls over credit facilities, and in general determines monetary and fiscal policies. Money flow studies can be extremely valuable in determining when and by how much various operations should be performed—such as raising and lowering interest rates, buying and selling bonds and securities, and expanding and contracting the volume of loans.

The monetary and financial structure of any region of the world reflects the region's cultural, political, and resource patterns. Hence, among regions different monetary and financial institutions emerge. Different kinds of money flow data become available. Therefore, what can be done with money flow studies varies from region to region.

In the United States, the Federal Reserve System provides, among many other benefits, an efficient method of clearing payments between its twelve districts, each of which has a definite regional orientation. This is accomplished through the Interdistrict Settlement Fund, known formerly as the Gold Settlement Fund. Each Federal Reserve bank must maintain a certain volume of reserves in the form of gold certificates in this fund. Daily the district banks wire to Washington the total of their claims against each other. These claims arise because an individual in one district purchases goods produced in a second, or because a corporation shifts its revenue from sales in one district to another in order to be able to meet its payroll, or, to take one final example, because the Federal Reserve notes issued by one district bank have been carried or sent out of the district and spent elsewhere.[23] Clearing is accomplished by shifting reserves on the books of the Interdistrict Settlement Fund.

The available data from the Interdistrict Settlement Fund and the Federal Reserve banks make possible several types of valuable studies. One type of study has concentrated on the money flows in and out of a single Federal Reserve region without reference to interregional relations. For example, a study of the Boston Federal Reserve Bank has analyzed the annual gain or loss of gold reserves in its district over the period 1934–1951.[24] One set of data available are on Treasury transactions. They depict the difference between (1) Federal government receipts in this district from taxes, securities sales, and all other sources, and (2) Federal government expenditures and redemption of debt in the district. Another set of data available relate to interreserve bank transactions. They indicate separately: (1) the district bank's participation in the Federal Reserve System's open-market operations and in the System's foreign transactions (conducted through the New York Federal Reserve Bank); and (2) the difference between the notes of other Federal Reserve banks which the Boston district bank wishes to exchange for gold certificates and the amount of its notes which other Federal Reserve banks wish to redeem.

From these sets of data the Federal Reserve Bank of Boston was able to compute, as a residual, the net gold inflow or outflow arising from private commercial and financial transactions. With this breakdown, it becomes possible to understand better the operations of the regional economy served by the Federal Reserve Bank of Boston.

The accompanying chart (Figure 1), which on a cumulative basis records the factors causing gain or loss in gold reserves for the Boston Federal Reserve District, is helpful in diagnosing the region's ills. Over the period covered, knowledge of the cumulating loss of reserves on account of Treasury transactions, of the cumulating gains from private commercial and financial transactions, of the falling off of the rates of accumulation, etc., suggests various hypotheses, forces revision of others, and provides a useful perspective in the analysis of the New England economy.

Money flow studies can be more than descriptive. They can point up critical relations which other types of studies can easily miss. For New

[23] For a thorough discussion of the variety of such claims, see B. H. Beckhart and J. G. Smith [4], Vol. II, pp. 295–308.

[24] See [16], pp. 1–4.

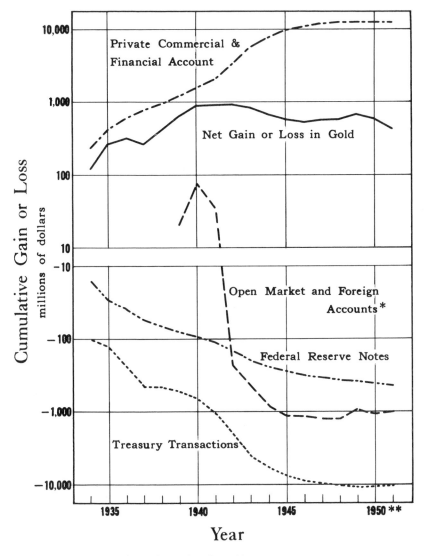

Figure 1. Factors causing gain or loss in gold reserves. Boston Federal Reserve District (cumulative from Jan. 1, 1934). *Prior to 1939, less than $10 million. ** 1951, through Aug. 31. Source: Federal Reserve Bank of Boston [16].

England, we note the important role which the federal government plays. More than any other factor, Treasury transactions have balanced the tendency for increase in gold reserves. How has this been possible? Has it affected the New England economy adversely? These are important questions which a money flow study generates, and to which, in the case of New England, many persons have addressed themselves in a fruitful way.[25]

Although money flow studies can point up critical relations, they must be pursued with care. Frequently, the data are inadequate or are available in a form that may conceal many transactions. The Interdistrict Settlement Fund data refer to net clearings. They do not catch clearings effected when a bank in one district clears directly with a correspondent bank in a second district. Furthermore, data on Treasury transfers must be adjusted if they are to reflect true burdens and gains by regions. Not all Federal tax revenues collected in a district can be said to be borne by individuals in that district. Many taxes are shifted in various ways to consumers and producers in other districts. Interest on government securities is not always paid by the Treasury (and thus listed as expenditure) in the district in which the owner resides. These and similar considerations make it necessary to use money flow data and interpret them with considerable caution.[26]

It has been recognized among Federal Reserve economists that the type of money flow study just outlined is only a starting point for the detailed analysis of interregional payments required for full comprehension of economic interdependence. One further step, however, can be and has been taken in order to increase the fruitfulness of money flow studies. This step involves the disaggregation to different extents of gold inflows by originating region and subregion and of outflows by terminating region and subregion. The available data make this step possible. For example, on Map 17 are indicated the net inflows through the Interdistrict Settlement Fund to the New York Federal Reserve Office June–July 1954. As with Map 13 on the origins of *all* commodities flowing into the regional economy of Iowa, this type of map plays up basic interconnections.[27]

[25] Among others, see Federal Reserve Bank of Boston [15], pp. 1–7; P. Hartland [26], especially pp. 400–407; S. E. Harris [23], 174–192; [24], ch. 10; A. A. Bright, Jr. and G. H. Ellis (eds.) [9], ch. 16; and R. A. Kavesh and J. B. Jones [36], pp. 152–167.

[26] For fuller discussion of these points, see J. D. Daane [13], G. J. Hile [28], and other literature cited.

[27] Note that these interconnections are on a *net* basis in contrast to the gross basis of commodity flow interconnections. The net outflows from the New York Federal Reserve Office are not depicted on Map 17. They are, however, indicated on Maps 19–20 (pp. 155–156).

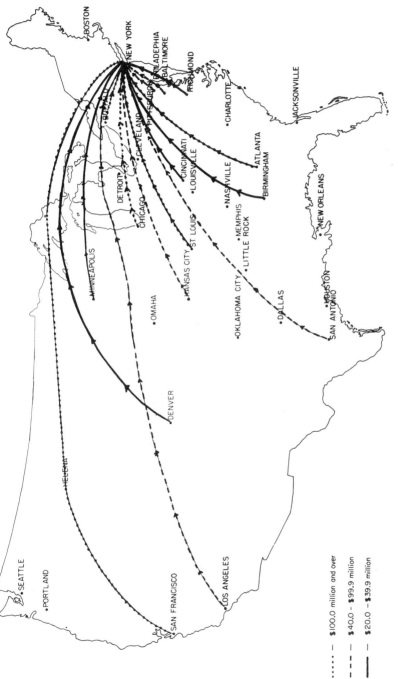

Map 17. Net inflows through Interdistrict Settlement Fund to the New York Federal Reserve Office, June–July 1954. Source: N. N. Bowsher, J. D. Daane, R. Einzig [8], p. 142.

······· — $100.0 million and over

– – – — $40.0 - $99.9 million

——— — $20.0 - $39.9 million

Beckhart and Smith appear to have been the first to add an inter-regional dimension to the flow of funds.[28] In their study of the New York money market they estimated the net change of its reserve funds. This net change was based partly on the net movement of funds between New York and the rest of the country due to all operations reflected in the Interdistrict Settlement Fund data. However, in order to better understand this movement, they considered over the period 1919–1930 the cumulated balance of the New York District with respect to each of the other Federal Reserve districts.

The approach can be made still more fruitful, as Daane demonstrates,[29] when not only *net* transit clearings between any pair of regions is presented and interpreted, but also *total* receipts and *total* payments via the Interdistrict Settlement Fund. The latter set of data catches both secular and cyclical expansions and contractions of trade between the pair of regions, which net data do not. In this and other ways the more gross data used in conjunction with the net data permit more penetrating analysis.

No region is uniform throughout. Its various parts do not have connections of like character and intensity with the outside world, whether taken as a whole or disaggregated into a set of regions. This fact suggests still another fruitful breakdown of the data, particularly for the Federal Reserve districts, the logic of whose boundary lines and constituent areas has been the subject of much criticism. As Bowsher has demonstrated,[30] the data for a given district and its branches can be presented with respect to each of the eleven other districts and each of their branches. This disaggregation is not justifiable for all types of regional studies, but for many, for example, those that may be concerned with local sore spots (distressed areas), it can be exceedingly fruitful.

In their several studies, Beckhart and Smith, Daane, and Bowsher have clearly demonstrated the potentialities of money flow studies in gaining a better understanding of a regional economy, in diagnosing its monetary and even industrial ills, and in suggesting some solution to problems when the analysis is combined with other types of regional studies to be outlined later. They have played up the close interrelations between interregional flows of money and regional credit availability. In the analysis of the factors affecting the reserve positions of the member banks of a district, greater insight can be gained when the interdistrict flow of funds disaggregated by districts is considered concomitantly with currency move-

[28] B. H. Beckhart and J. G. Smith [4], Vol. II, ch. XVII. Other related studies of interest are: J. W. Angell [1], ch. III; R. P. Terrill [53]; and I. O. Scott, Jr. [45], pp. 269–284.

[29] J. D. Daane [13], ch. 4.

[30] N. N. Bowsher [5, 6]. Also see Federal Reserve Bank of Richmond [18], pp. 3–6.

ments within the district, district Treasury operations, internal Federal Reserve float, borrowings within the district, and miscellaneous factors.

Yet the most promising type of money flow study, although already alluded to and feasible in the light of the available data and our high-speed computing equipment, is still to be executed. This study would be based on the weekly tabulation furnished by the Board of Governors of the Federal Reserve System of a 36 × 36 grid of Interdistrict Settlement Fund data on district clearings excluding Treasury transfers. Such a grid is presented as Table 1.[31] Each row and column of the grid refers to one of the 36 Federal Reserve head offices and branches. Study of this grid over time would reveal as a whole the patterns of financial relationships among the 36 Federal Reserve areas of the United States.

Helpful in such study would be maps which depict flows in diverse ways. If we add to Map 17, Maps 18, 19, and 20, a simple comprehensive picture is possible. Map 18 portrays net inflows to the Federal Reserve offices of Chicago and Philadelphia. Map 19 portrays net inflows to Detroit, Pittsburgh, and Atlanta. And Map 20 portrays all other inflows of $20 million or over. (An inflow into an office is by definition an outflow from the office of origin.)

Tables and maps such as Table 1 and Maps 17–20 reveal certain patterns. After closely studying the data of such tables and maps, Bowsher, Daane, and Einzig state:

> "Overall it appears from these data that what may be identified as 'rural' areas normally lose funds on balance year in and year out to what may be termed 'local financial centers' (i.e., the major financial Reserve Bank or branch areas outside of New York and Chicago). Most of these local financial centers in turn are drained of funds by the money market centers (New York and Chicago). Completing the circle, the money market centers have an 'unfavorable' balance of transactions with certain rural areas. In general, there is a circular geographic pattern of net movements of funds which may be illustrated by superimposing on a map of the United States the larger net flows between districts and zones.
>
> Superimposed on this circular geographic movement of funds are other clearly recognizable patterns, both in terms of seasonal and trend relationships between districts. For example, both in the Fifth and Eighth Districts banks tend to lose funds through commercial and financial transactions in the spring and gain funds in the fall. . . .
>
> Trend relationships in these commercial and financial flows between districts are also readily identifiable from the present data. Banks in some of the Reserve districts or zones persistently gain funds from, or lose funds to, other areas via clearings. For example, the Fifth District apparently

---

[31] This grid is taken from N. N. Bowsher, J. D. Daane, and R. Einzig [7], pp. 150–151. For further details see the Task Force report by the same authors presented at the Federal Reserve System Conference on the Interregional Flow of Funds, Washington, D.C., 1955 [8].

TABLE 1.   NET COMMERCIAL AND FINANCIAL FLOWS BETWEEN FEDERAL RESERVE ZONES, WEEK ENDED OCTOBER 13, 1954

(Millions of dollars; plus sign indicates net inflow to area at top of column)

	Boston	New York	Buffalo	Philadelphia	Cleveland	Cincinnati	Pittsburgh	Richmond	Baltimore	Charlotte	Atlanta	Birmingham	Jacksonville	Nashville	New Orleans	Chicago	Detroit	St. Louis
Boston	—	+26	+1	+3	+1	+1	+4	+1	+1	+3	0	0	+1	+1	0	+8	+6	-1
New York	-26	—	+3	-25	+33	-3	+27	+4	+6	+24	-36	-19	+10	-9	+19	+70	+77	-66
Buffalo	-3	-3	—	0	+2	0	+1	0	-3	-4	0	-1	0	-1	0	+6	-3	0
Philadelphia	-1	+25	0	—	+3	+3	+6	+4	+1	-1	-5	-1	-2	-1	-1	+7	-5	-1
Cleveland	-1	-33	-2	+3	—	-3	+5	+2	+5	0	-1	0	+1	-1	0	+10	-5	+3
Cincinnati	-1	+3	0	+3	-1	—	-1	-1	+8	0	0	0	0	+1	0	+8	-3	0
Pittsburgh	-4	-27	-1	+6	-5	+1	—	-5	+1	-15	-5	-1	0	-1	-1	+7	+1	-1
Richmond	-1	+4	0	+4	-2	+1	+5	—	0	-1	+6		+2	+1	0	+7	+3	+2
Baltimore	-1	+6	0	+3	-1	0	0	-8	—	-9	0	0	-1	0	0	+3	-1	0
Charlotte	-3	-24	0	+4	+1	0	+5	+15	0	—	+9	0	0	0	0	-4	0	-1
Atlanta	0	+36	-1	+5	+1	0	-1	+6	+3	+1	—	-1	-1	-4	-12	+5	+3	+2
Birmingham	-1	+19	0	+1		0	-1	0	-1	0	+6	—	-1	-1	-1	+1	0	+1
Jacksonville	-1	-10	-1	+2		+1	-1	+2	0	0	+11	+2	—	+1	+1	-3	0	+2
Nashville	-1	+9	0	-1		+1	-1	0	+1	0	+4	+1	0	—	-1	-1	0	+1
New Orleans	0	-19	+	-1	0		+1	0	+1	0	+12	-1	-1	-1	—	+5	-1	+2
Chicago	-8	-70	-6	-7	-10		0	-7	-3	0	-5		+3	-2	-5	—	+9	+3
Detroit	-6	-77	+3	+5	+5		0	-3	-1	0	-2		0	0	-1	+9	—	+9
St. Louis	+1	+66	0	+5	-3	0	0	-2	0	0	-1		+1	0	-3	-1	0	—
Little Rock	0	-1		0	0	+1	-2							-1	-1	+3	0	+4
Louisville	-1	-30		0	-2	0	+1				-2	+2	-1	0	0	-1	0	+9
Memphis	+2	-11	-4	0	0	+1	0				+1	-1		-1	-1	-15	+2	+15
Minneapolis	0	+34		0	-4	+2	-4	0	0	0	-3				+1	+10	+3	+4
Helena	0	-1		0	0		0	-1	0	0					-4	-2	0	0
Kansas City	0	+21		+2	+3	0	0	0	0	0	0	0		+2	0	-21	+1	+5
Denver	-1	+5	+2	0	+1	+1	+4	+1	0	0	0			0	-3	-1	+	+2
Oklahoma City	0	+12		+1	0	+1		-1	0	0	+3			0	0	-7	0	+5
Omaha	-3	+3		0	+	+1	0				0			0	+4	+7	+2	+1
Dallas	-1	-46	0	0	0		-1	+1	+1	+1	+2			0	-1	+3	0	+10
El Paso	-1	-1		0	0		0							0	+5	+6	0	+1
Houston	0	-31		-3	0	+1	0	-5	0	0	-1			0	+0	+22	/	+1
San Antonio	+14	+6		+1	0	+1	0	+1	-1	0	-1			+2	-1	+15	+11	+1
San Francisco	+3	-23	+2	+1	-1	+1	-4	+1	0	+1	0			0	0	+1	+1	+2
Los Angeles	-1	+56	+1	+2	+2	0	+1		0		-1			0		-2	+0	+3
Portland	-	+5	0	-3	0	0	0	-1	-1		-1			-1	-1	-2	+2	-1
Salt Lake City	0	-2		-1	0	0	0	+1	0		-1			0	0			+1
Seattle	0	+7	0	+1	0	0	0	0	0		0						+2	+1

	Little Rock	Louisville	Memphis	Minneapolis	Helena	Kansas City	Denver	Oklahoma City	Omaha	Dallas	El Paso	Houston	San Antonio	San Francisco	Los Angeles	Portland	Salt Lake City	Seattle	Total
Boston	0	+1	-2	0	0	0	+1	0	0	+3	-1	-1	0	-14	-3	+1	0	0	+45
New York	+1	+30	+11	-34	+1	-21	-5	-12	-3	+46	+1	+31	-6	+23	-56	-5	+2	-7	+66
Buffalo	0	0		+4		-2	0	-1	0	0		0		-2	-1	0	-1	0	-2
Philadelphia	0	+2	0	+4		-3		0	0	-1	0	+3		-1	-2	+3		-1	-12
Cleveland	0	+3	0	-1		-2		-1	0	-2		0		-1	-2	0	0	0	-14
Cincinnati	0	0	0	0		+1	0	0	0	0	+1	+4		+1	-1	0	0	0	-8
Pittsburgh	0	0	0	-1		+2	0	-1	-1	0	0	0		+4	-1	0	0	0	-16
Richmond	0	-1	0	0		-1	0	0	0	0	0	0	0	+5	0	-1	0	0	+25
Baltimore	0	+1	+7	-1		0	0	0	+1	+2	-1	0	0	-1	+1	-1	-1	0	-5
Charlotte	0	+1	+2	0		0	0	-3	0	+2	0	+1	0	0	0	0	0	0	+9
Atlanta	-1	+1	+1	0		0	0	0	+1	-1	0	+2	0	0	+1	+2	+2	+1	+8
Birmingham	0	+1	+1	0		-1	-1	-1	0	+3	-1	+4	0	0	0	-1	-1	-1	+25
Jacksonville	0	0	+1	0		+1	+2	-1	+1	-1	0	-3	0	0	0	0	0	0	+8
Nashville	+1	0	+1	-1		+1	-1	0	-1	+7	+1	-1	0	0	0	0	0	0	+20
New Orleans	+1	-3	+2	+15	-1	-10	+2	+4	0	+2	0	0	0	+5	-1	0	0	0	0
Chicago	+1	0	-1	+15	+1	-1	+1	+21	+16	-10	-1	-1	-6	-22	-15	-1	+1	+2	-160
Detroit	-4	-1	-3	-3		-5	-2	-5	-1	-1	0	0	0	-2	-11	+2	0	+2	-96
St. Louis	0	0	+1	-4	0	0	+1	0	+1	+3	+1	+1	0	0	0	-1	-1	-1	-3
Little Rock		0	-1	0		+3	-1	-5	0	-10	0	0	0	0	-1	-1	0	0	+3
Louisville	0		-1	0	0	+1	-2	0	0	+3	0	-2	0	0	-3	0	0	0	-26
Memphis	-2	+2		-1	0	0	0	0	0	0	0	0	0	0	0	+1	0	+1	-1
Minneapolis	0	0	0			+3	+1	-1	+5	+3	+1	0	0	+3	0	+2	-1	0	+21
Helena	0	0	0	+3		+1	+1	-1	-1	0	0	-1	0	-1	0	+2	0	+2	+3
Kansas City	0	0	0	+3	-1		-9	-19	-16	0	0	+1	0	-3	0	+1	0	+1	-2
Denver	0	0	0	-2	+1	+9		+1	+5	+3	+1	+5	-1	-10	-3	-1	-1	0	+15
Oklahoma City	+1	0	0	+1	+1	+19	-1		-1	+14	0	-1	0	0	-1	0	0	+12	+48
Omaha	-1	0	0	+1	+1	+16	+1	+5		-1	0	+1	+1	0	-3	0	0	0	+11
Dallas	+1	0	-3	-1	-1	-3	0	-5	0		+1	+5	+1	+5	-3	+3	0	0	-42
El Paso	0	0	-1	0	0	-1	0	-1	0	0		+1	0	-1	0	-1	0	0	+1
Houston	0	0	+1	-1	0	0	0	+1	0	+1	+1		+1	+3	-1	-1	0	0	-21
San Antonio	0	0	+2	+2	-1	-1	0	+5	+1	+5	-1	+1		+3	-3	+1	0	0	+12
San Francisco	0	0	-1	+1	0	-1	0	-1	0	-1	0	+1	0		0	+1	0	0	-3
Los Angeles	0	+1	0	0	0	0	0	0	+3	0	0	0	0	+5		0	0	+1	+104
Portland		0	-1	0	-1	-1	-1	+1	-1	-1	0	0	0	0	+1		0	-1	-4
Salt Lake City			-1	+1	-1	0	+1	0	0	0	0	0	0	-1	-1	0		-1	-3
Seattle		0		0		-1	0	-12	0	-1		-1							-6

Source: N. N. Bowsher, J. D. Daane, and R. Einzig [7], pp. 150, 151.

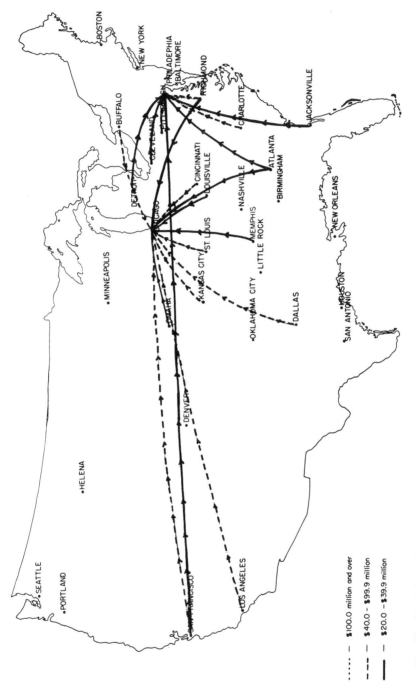

Map 18. Net inflows through Interdistrict Settlement Fund to the Federal Reserve Offices of Chicago and Philadelphia, June–July 1954.
Source: N. N. Bowsher, J. D. Daane, R. Einzig [7], p. 143.

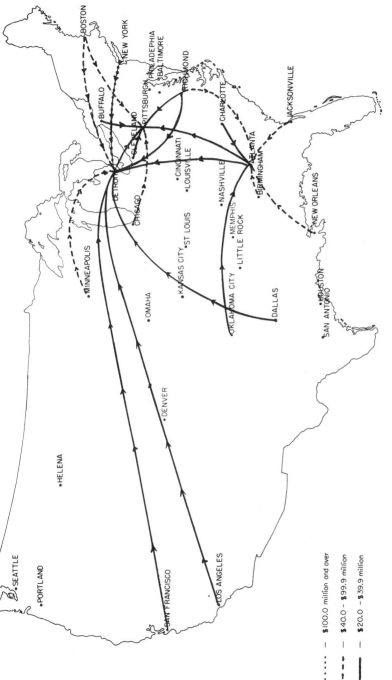

Map 19. Net inflows through Interdistrict Settlement Fund to the Federal Reserve Offices of Detroit, Pittsburgh, and Atlanta, June-July 1954. Source: N. N. Bowsher, J. D. Daane, R. Einzig [7], p. 144.

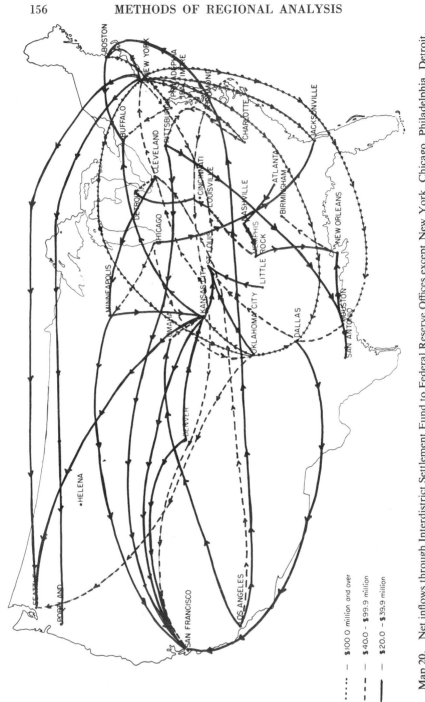

Map 20. Net inflows through Interdistrict Settlement Fund to Federal Reserve Offices except New York, Chicago, Philadelphia, Detroit, Pittsburgh, and Atlanta, June-July 1954. Source: N. N. Bowsher, J. D. Daane, R. Einzig [7], p. 144.

consistently loses funds on commercial and financial account to the Philadelphia, Chicago, St. Louis, Atlanta, and San Francisco Districts and normally draws funds from the New York, Boston, Cleveland, and Minneapolis Districts, and increasingly, from the Dallas District."[32]

This type of interregional money flow study, if executed on a regular and systematic basis, would constitute an important advance over existing money flow studies which single out a region and its relations with all other regions.   However, still more significant advance is possible, advance which would go beyond the presentation of the data on a *gross* basis (i.e., on both inflows and outflows) and beyond the presentation of the data by a larger number of smaller subregions.[33]   As with total commodity flows, the data can be disaggregated (at least conceptually) into types of money flows.   Just as Maps 1–12 depict flows by category of commodities (more specifically: animals and products, products of agriculture, products of forests, petroleum products, products of mines, and manufactures and miscellaneous), so comparable maps may also depict flows by category of money transaction (say, payroll payments, interest,. rent and dividend payments and receipts, securities sales and purchases, currency and deposit changes, etc.).

To facilitate the discussion of the previous point, we present Table 2. This table summarizes the flow of funds accounts for the United States as a whole, 1955.[34]   Listed at the extreme left are types of transactions, both nonfinancial and financial.   Across the top are transactors classified by sector.   For each sector (type of transactors) there are two columns, one designated by the letter S which indicates sources of funds (i.e., inflows of funds to the corresponding sector), and the other designated by the letter U which indicates uses of funds (i.e., outflow of funds from the corresponding sector).   Thus the figure of 208.4 at the top of the first column of Table 2 signifies that the consumer sector. *received* $208.4 billion in the form of payrolls (an inflow).   This amount represents the sum of outflows from each sector (on payroll account) as shown in the U column of each sector. For example, corporate business *used* $124.9 billion of its funds for payroll payments (outflows).   In short, each column of Table 2 represents either

[32] N. N. Bowsher, J. D. Daane, and R. Einzig [8], pp. 55–58.

[33] The materials covered in the rest of this section are purely conceptual and are likely to remain so for a number of years.   They are presented for the theoretical researcher. Readers concerned with applied analysis may skip to the next section.   Logically, the materials to follow belong to the last chapters where unproven as well as proven methods are discussed.   They are, however, presented at this point for expository reasons.

[34] Federal Reserve Board [19] and earlier articles in the same *Bulletin*.   The reader is also referred to the set of accounts in the major pioneering work, M. A. Copeland [12]. For an excellent summary of this work, see M. Mendelson [40].

TABLE 2. SUMMARY OF FLOW OF FUNDS ACCOUNTS FOR 1955

(S = sources of funds, U = uses of funds; annual flows, in billions of dollars)

Transaction Category	Consumer S	Consumer U	Corporate S	Corporate U	Non-corporate S	Non-corporate U	Farm S	Farm U	Federal S	Federal U	State and Local S	State and Local U	Banking S	Banking U	Insurance S	Insurance U	Other Investors S	Other Investors U	Rest of the World S	Rest of the World U	All Sectors S	All Sectors U
Nonfinancial																						
A. Payroll	208.4	3.0	—	124.9	—	32.4	—	2.3	—	19.6	—	15.9	—	2.2	—	3.0	—	5.1	—	*	208.4	208.4
B. Receipts from and payments on investment	65.6	18.8	10.7	22.8	18.7	42.7	1.1	13.3	1.1	5.7	0.9	1.3	6.9	2.4	4.4	0.6	2.2	2.1	0.5	2.5	112.1	112.1
C. Insurance and grants	28.9	25.7	1.7	12.9	1.3	4.5	0.4	0.4	9.5	18.2	13.4	13.1	*	0.3	31.6	19.2	6.6	1.4	2.7	0.3	96.0	96.0
D. Taxes and tax refunds	3.1	41.2	0.5	35.8	—	7.2	1.1	1.1	63.2	3.6	24.1	*	—	1.2	—	0.9	—	*	—	*	90.8	91.1
E. Capital acquisitions	29.2	81.5	0.3	27.9	2.8	8.3	0.4	3.4	*	2.8	0.1	10.6	—	0.2	—	0.4	—	2.7	—	—	32.7	137.9
F. Net change in inventory	—	—	—	2.9	—	1.0	—	*	—	—	—	—	—	—	—	—	—	—	—	—	—	3.8
G. New fixed capital[a]	—	49.3	—	25.0	—	7.4	0.4	3.4	—	2.8	0.1	9.6	—	—	—	0.1	—	—	—	—	—	100.5
H. Other capital acquisitions	29.2	32.2	0.3	0.1	2.8	—	0.4	—	*	*	0.1	0.9	—	0.2	—	0.3	—	2.7	—	—	32.7	33.6
I. Other purchases and sales	—	168.0	573.0	363.1	212.8	142.7	29.6	12.0	7.0	29.6	6.8	6.6	0.9	1.1	0.2	4.0	5.4	3.8	17.2	17.1	852.9	747.9
J. Total	335.2	338.2	586.1	587.4	235.5	237.8	31.5	32.5	80.7	79.6	45.2	47.4	7.8	7.4	36.2	28.1	14.2	15.1	20.4	19.9	1393.0	1393.4
Financial[b]																						
K. Currency and demand deposits	0.1	3.0	—	0.5	—	-0.1	—	-0.2	*	*	—	0.4	3.1	—	—	0.1	—	*	0.2	-0.1	3.1	0.5
L. Time deposits	—	3.0	—	—	—	0.2	—	—	*	*	—	-0.1	3.0	—	—	—	—	—	—	-0.1	3.0	3.0
M. Federal obligations	—	1.8	—	4.3	—	0.1	—	—	1.2	—	—	1.0	—	-7.6	—	-0.4	—	0.4	—	1.2	1.2	0.9
N. State and local obligations	—	1.8	—	0.2	—	—	—	—	—	—	3.6	0.4	—	0.1	—	1.0	—	*	—	—	3.6	3.6
O. Corporate securities	—	2.3	6.3	—	—	0.2	—	—	—	—	—	*	0.1	-0.5	—	3.8	0.8	0.5	*	0.2	7.2	7.2
P. Mortgages	11.2	1.4	1.4	—	2.8	0.3	0.6	—	—	0.5	—	—	—	4.8	—	3.5	0.1	5.3	—	—	16.2	16.2
Q. Consumer credit	6.4	—	3.3	0.5	1.1	0.3	0.1	—	-0.2	—	—	—	—	2.4	—	—	0.1	0.4	—	—	6.4	6.4
R. Other trade credit	—	—	6.1	3.3	0.8	0.8	0.4	—	-1.2	—	—	—	—	—	—	0.1	0.4	—	0.5	—	4.4	7.5
S. Bank loans n.e.c.	0.3	—	—	6.6	—	—	—	—	*	—	—	—	7.2	7.2	—	—	—	—	—	0.1	7.3	7.2
T. Gold and Treasury currency	—	—	—	—	—	—	—	—	*	0.4	—	—	—	*	—	—	—	—	—	—	*	0.1
U. Savings and loan and credit union shares	—	5.3	—	—	—	—	—	—	—	—	—	—	—	—	—	—	5.4	0.1	—	—	5.4	5.4
V. Other	0.7	0.4	*	—	—	—	-0.4	*	—	—	—	—	-0.5	—	—	—	0.9	0.2	0.8	0.3	2.0	2.0
W. Total	18.6	16.2	17.1	15.5	4.8	2.0	0.8	-0.2	-0.2	0.9	3.6	2.4	5.7	6.5	0.4	8.3	7.7	6.9	1.5	1.5	59.8	60.1
X. Valuation adjustment and discrepancy	0.5	-0.1	*	0.3	—	0.4	—	—	—	—	—	-1.0	—	-0.4	—	0.2	—	-0.2	0.5	—	0.5	-0.3
Y. Grand total	354.3	354.3	603.3	603.3	240.3	240.3	32.3	32.3	80.5	80.5	48.8	48.8	13.4	13.4	36.5	36.5	21.9	21.9	21.8	21.8	1453.2	1453.2

* Less than $50 million.

[a] For the consumer sector, acquisitions of new fixed capital consist of purchases of new durable goods of $34.9 billion and purchases of new houses of $14.4 billion.

[b] Financial sources of funds represent net changes in liabilities; financial uses of funds, net changes in financial assets.

Source: Federal Reserve Board [19], p. 381.

the sources of funds or uses of funds for a given sector, broken down by type of source or use. Each row indicates for a given type of transaction the amount of funds which each sector both receives (inflows) and disburses (outflows) on account of that type of transaction.

With this table, it becomes possible to suggest meaningful categories of interregional money flows. The first set of categories might disaggregate *gross* interregional money flows by type of transaction category as listed at the left of Table 2. This step would yield interregional *payroll* flows, interregional flows from *receipts and payments on investments*, interregional flows from *insurance and grants*, etc. Such a disaggregation of gross interregional money flows would be comparable to a disaggregation of gross commodity flows into types of commodities. Maps comparable to Map 17–20 would in effect be cut (horizontally sliced) into as many parts as the number of transactions categories employed. For each category of transactions a separate map on *net inflows* (by region, from every other region) would result. And corresponding to each category of transactions there would be a table of the order of Table 1. For example, for the transactions category *mortgages* there would be both a map and table indicating the net money inflows to each region from every other region. Here the net money inflow (on account of mortgage transactions) from any region j to any region i is equal to (1) the amount of mortgages held by sectors of region i and paid off by sectors in region j; *plus* (2) the amount of mortgages extended by sectors in region j to sectors in region i; *less* (3) the amount of mortgages held by sectors of region j and paid off by sectors of region i; *less* (4) the amount of mortgages extended by sectors in region i to sectors in region j.

Thus, if interregional money flows are classified by n different categories of transactions (in Table 2, $n = 18$), we obtain n different maps and tables, which when aggregated yield maps such as Maps 17–20 and a table such as Table 1.

Conceptually, further disaggregation is possible. In the case of mortgage transactions, the net money inflows may be presented in greater detail. Instead of summing the four items just noted to yield a net money inflow, the difference between items (1) and (4) might be mapped as well as tabulated to indicate for region i money inflows from change in the amount of mortgages which it has outstanding with respect to region j; and the difference between items (2) and (3) might be mapped as well as tabulated to indicate for region i money inflows from change in the amount of mortgages which region j has outstanding with respect to region i. A still grosser picture of money inflows could be obtained if each of these four items were mapped and tabulated for all possible pairs of originating and terminating regions.

The presentation of each money flow on as gross a basis as possible would of course multiply the number of possible maps and tables. As is true with mortgages, for each category of *financial* transactions there tend to be four parts into which a net money inflow figure can be sliced. For each category of *nonfinancial* transactions, however, there may be only two corresponding parts into which a net money inflow figure can be sliced. For example, take net money inflows from payroll transactions. At the present level of disaggregation this money figure can be divided into (1) payroll payments by sectors of region j to residents of region i; and (2) payroll payments by sectors of region i to residents of region j. (On the physical level, however, there are two corresponding commodity flows which would exist if both items (1) and (2) were positive, namely, labor services exported by region i to region j and labor services exported by region j to region i.)

For many types of studies, this kind of detailed classification of inter-regional money flows would be exceedingly useful. It would provide a set of data comparable in comprehensiveness to the 1 per cent I.C.C. waybill sample on Class I rail shipments. It would make possible maps on individual or refined categories of money flows such as Maps 15 and 16 on the shipments of citrus fruits. Further, the *money flow* bonds of any given region with all other regions could be seen on both an aggregative and disaggregative basis. Corresponding to Maps 1–14 and other individual commodity maps which could be constructed and which altogether would portray the physical linkages the Iowa economy has with other regions, a set of money flow maps would be possible for any given region. These latter maps would present a comprehensive picture of the money (financial) linkages of that region with other regions.

Still more disaggregation may be desirable, at least for certain categories of transactions. Such disaggregation would be in terms of originating sector, or receiving sector, or both of each region. For example, it may be fruitful in several types of studies to know how payrolls received by residents of region i from region j are broken down by originating sector of region j, that is, by corporations, noncorporate businesses, farm enterprises, state and local government agencies, etc. of region j. This would yield money flows such as payroll payments to residents of region i by corporations of region j, payroll payments to residents of region i by noncorporate businesses of region j, and payroll payments to residents of region i by local government agencies of region j. Or it may be valuable to know how the amount of new mortgages extended by region j to region i is shared by the financing sectors in region j—banks, insurance companies, and other investors. This would yield money flows such as one reflecting the extension of new mortgages to region i by banks of region j, and another reflecting the extension of new mortgages to region i by insurance companies of region j.

Each of these money flows associated with a breakdown by sector of the originating region j may be subdivided by sector of receiving region i to yield an even finer disaggregation. For example, take the money flow corresponding to extension of new mortgages to region i by banks of region j. This flow may be subdivided into (1) a flow of money (on new mortgage account) from banks of region j to consumers (households) in region i; (2) another flow of money (on new mortgage account) from banks of region j to corporations of region i; (3) a third flow of money (on new mortgage account) from banks of region j to noncorporate businesses of region i; (4) a fourth flow of money (on new mortgage account) from banks of region j to farm enterprises of region i, etc.[35]

In many ways, such fine-grained disaggregation—by category of transaction, by sector of originating region, and by sector of receiving region—for every possible pair of originating and terminating regions[36] is similar to the disaggregation sought in national income and social accounting systems and in interregional input-output and linear programming techniques, to be discussed in subsequent chapters. Obviously, where similar or consistent definitions, concepts, and classifications are pursued in input-output, social accounting, money flow, and other interregional studies, each can contribute to the other in filling gaps in the data and providing essential cross checks.[37]

To recapitulate, the limited number of current money flow studies relating to regions are subject to considerable improvement. For example, in the United States, at the minimum an interregional money flow grid based on Interdistrict Settlement Fund data for the 36 Federal Reserve zones ought to be regularly developed, studied, and made available *on a gross basis*. Beyond this, the flow between each pair of areas might be subdivided into category of transaction, preferably on as gross a basis as possible. Still more, many of the resulting flows may be profitably disaggregated by sector of originating region, by sector of receiving region, or

[35] As another example of disaggregation by sector of receiving region, consider the money flow to region j resulting from the retirement of bonds (obligations) of local government units of region i. This flow can be subdivided into a flow of money (on bond account) from local government units of region i to consumers in region j; another flow of money (on bond account) from local government units of region i to corporations of region j; etc.

[36] This disaggregation also implies a tabulation for each region which records on the same fine-grained basis the internal money flows between sectors. Each such tabulation in broad outline would resemble the national table developed by M. A. Copeland [12] and the Federal Reserve Board [19].

[37] For example, see S. J. Sigel [46], pp. 253–285; and National Bureau of Economic Research [42], especially pp. 234–242.

by both. It is recognized that a complete system of disaggregated money flows as previously sketched is probably infeasible and moreover may not yield results commensurable with the expense entailed. We have sketched this system primarily to suggest some of the many types of disaggregation which may prove fruitful in research.

As in input-output analysis and other systems discussed in this book, there is implicit in an interregional money flow approach a conception of a general equilibrium system in which changes in money supply and financial conditions of any area are dependent on what is happening in all other areas. This approach, if implemented and if combined with regional elements analysis,[38] would provide a more dynamic perspective of banking operations. It would permit the formulation of more effective monetary and fiscal policies, for both regions and for the nation as a whole.[39] Yet it must constantly be borne in mind that such a study per se would yield only one system representing the interregional structure of the United States. It would need to be combined with studies of other types of systems already mentioned and others to be discussed later in order to

[38] For discussion of regional elements analysis, see N. N. Bowsher, J. D. Daane, and R. Einzig [7], and other individual works by these authors which have been cited in this, chapter.

[39] To be specific, it is generally assumed that open-market operations, which are pursued at the national level and are considered a major tool for credit control, have pervasive effects throughout the entire economy. "Reserves put into or drawn from the central money market are postulated to flow out to or away from every Reserve area both automatically and uniformly. Yet experience suggests that this assumption is invalid, that lags of different magnitudes exist, and that regional effects are not of the same intensity. These findings imply that open market operations are offset by other factors to different degrees in the several Reserve districts. Hence, one must study these factors as they operate in each region and reflect the particular attributes and endowment of each region in order to achieve a more effective use of this credit instrument on a national level" (W. Isard [33], p. 76). Such study of these factors would be facilitated if interregional money flow analyses were regularly conducted.

"Furthermore, in view of the imperfect mechanism by which funds flow from one district to another, and in view of the unique characteristics of each regional organism, it would seem that a more effective national discount rate policy ought to embody differentials in discount rates among districts. This hypothesis finds support in empirical materials. For example, the existence of excess reserves nationally is not typically associated with the existence of the same amount of excess reserves in each district. Rather, at any given time the extent to which excess reserves are present in each district varies considerably; and in some instances a district's reserves may be under pressure when substantial excess reserves persist nationally. This suggests that a policy based on national aggregates alone is an inferior one" ([33], pp. 76–77). A policy oriented to regional as well as to national conditions and credit needs is required. Once again, policy implementation would be greatly facilitated if interregional money flow analyses were regularly conducted. Such flow analyses would be of great value too in other types of study such as the interregional equilibrium study by N. Wollman [66].

yield results which would go much beyond description and which would permit penetrating analysis of the basic forces at play.

E. Balance of Payments Statements

Closely related to commodity flow and money flow investigations are balance of payments studies.[40] Such studies must utilize commodity flow and money flow data. In certain respects they integrate these data and thereby permit a more complete view of a regional economy. In other respects, however, balance of payments studies proceed within a narrower framework than commodity or money flow investigations. The former, at least traditionally, consider a single region vis-à-vis the rest of the world and thus preclude the general interregional perspective captured by the latter through identifying the interconnections between every pair of regions.[41]

All the transactions which result in inflows and outflows and which occur during the course of the year may be accounted for in a balance of payments statement. Such a statement can indicate any number of different categories of transactions. The specific set of categories chosen depends on the exact purpose to be served by the statement. However, regardless of the purpose to be served, a balance of payments statement by definition must equate total inflows and total outflows, however they may be recorded. This equality must obtain since a transaction is an exchange of equal values. For example, if we record an export of $1000 of wheat (an outflow), we must also record somewhere in the balance of payments statement an import (inflow) of (1) $1000 in cash (gold), (2) $1000 worth of one or several commodities and services, (3) $1000 worth of certificates of indebtedness (where the seller extends credit or a loan to the nonresident purchaser), or (4) some combination of these.

[40] The following are among the more important regional balance of payments studies: R. P. Terrill [53]; J. D. Daane [13], ch. 3; P. C. Hartland [25]; G. Freutel [21], pp. 70–78; P. B. Simpson and S. Burr [48]; P. B. Simpson [47], ch. VI and Appendix C; G. J. Hile [28, 29]; W. F. Stolper and C. M. Tiebout [51]. Abbreviated balance of payments statements associated with sets of social accounts are to be found in P. Deane [14], pp. 63–64, 107, 215, and in Table 5 of Chapter 4.

For discussion of balance of payments studies in an international framework the reader is referred to such standard literature as International Monetary Fund [31], Part I, and C. P. Kindleberger [37].

[41] However, a balance of payments can theoretically be disaggregated to show for any given region its "partial" balance of payments position with respect to each other region. Such disaggregation represents a new direction in research which can and should be fully explored. Daane moves somewhat in this direction when he segregates for the Fifth Federal Reserve District *interregional* (with United States regions only) and *international* commodity trade.

In Table 3 we present a typical breakdown of transactions.[42]　The first major category (*Current Account*) comprises that part of both parts of any transaction completed in the current period.　As an instance, the export of wheat is recorded in this category.　If it is balanced by an import of ore during the same year, this import and thus both sides of the transaction are recorded under current account.　If the export of wheat is balanced by

TABLE 3.　BALANCE OF PAYMENTS IN REGION X, 196Y

Item	Exports	Imports	Net
A. Current Account			
1. Commodity Trade			
a. Wheat	+ $5,000,000	− $50,000	+ $4,950,000
b. Ore	0	− 160,000	− 160,000
c. Other	+ 20,000,000	− 22,000,000	− 2,000,000
2. Service Trade			
a. Freight and Shipping	+ 100,000	− 500,000	− 400,000
b. Education	+ 50,000	− 150,000	− 100,000
c. Recreation	+ 200,000	− 20,000	+ 180,000
d. Property Income	+ 300,000	− 70,000	+ 230,000
e. Insurance and Other	+ 100,000	− 20,000	+ 80,000
3. Gifts and Unilateral Transfers	+ 25,000	− 15,000	+ 10,000
Totals	+ $25,775,000	− $22,985,000	+ $2,790,000
B. Gold and Currency Movement			+ 100,000
C. Capital Account			
1. U. S. Treasury Transfers			− 1,000,000
2. Private Savings			− 2,000,000
Net Capital Movement			− 3,000,000
D. Errors and Omissions			+ 110,000

a $1000 loan (import of certificates of indebtedness), the second side of the transaction is not *current* and is excluded from current account.

The second major category (*Gold and Currency Movement*) indicates the gold flows during the current period.　Logically, this second category should fall under current account, but because gold flows tend to represent the final balancing of all other payments and receipts, they are typically

[42] A breakdown more relevant for a city region or small area is presented in W. F. Stolper and C. M. Tiebout [51], pp. 27–30.

included in a separate category. It is usually important to separate this flow since it directly affects the credit base of a region, which is customarily of primary concern.

The third major category (*Capital Account*) includes transactions which require time to complete and which relate to the creditor-debtor position of a region. For example, the $1000 loan to balance the $1000 export of wheat would be recorded under capital account. Sometimes this account is subdivided into short-term and long-term capital movements, if such a breakdown is meaningful for a study and if the data are available.

A fourth major category, which may be set up separately or combined with either the second or third, is *Errors and Omissions*. Because of many data limitations and conceptual difficulties, which will be discussed later, it is almost impossible to avoid omissions and errors in estimating flows. Even recorded data, census or other, contain many and sizable errors.[43] Therefore, the errors and omissions category is necessary to reconcile total inflow and total outflow, as well as appropriate subtotals.

A balance of payments statement should contain three columns. One refers to exports, another to imports, and a third to the difference (net). Thus Region X in 196Y exports $5,000,000 of wheat, imports $50,000 of wheat, and thus on net ships out $4,950,000 of wheat. Exports of commodities are customarily given a positive (+) sign since they correspond to an *inflow* of funds and thus an *increase* of the region's gold stock (or the equivalent). Imports of commodities are then designated by a negative (−) sign.

Ore may be a second commodity whose inflows and outflows are important to identify. These may be listed, along with those of wheat and still other commodities, under the subheading *Commodity Trade*.

Region X may perform services for persons, businesses, and organizations outside its boundaries. Its railroads may carry the freight of various nonresident manufacturers, in which case it would be selling to outsiders or exporting freight service. In contrast, if manufacturers in Region X use nonresident trucking firms to transport their goods within the region, Region X will be buying from outsiders or importing freight service. Likewise, when nonresidents vacation in Region X, Region X is in effect exporting recreation services. When inhabitants of Region X vacation outside the region, Region X imports recreation services. Somewhat similar remarks hold true for education, insurance, and other services.

Finally, where the stock of gold or assets of a region rises because a nonresident has donated funds, say $25,000, to an educational institution, or where similar *unilateral* transfers are made, there is a "giving" but no "taking" of an equal value. There is only an inflow of gold or assets,

43 See O. Morgenstern [41].

which is represented by a negative ($-$) figure.   In order not to disrupt the balance, a current account entitled *Gifts and Unilateral Transfers* is set up to provide a second side to any such transfer.   The $25,000 donation would be recorded in the gifts and unilateral transfers row as a positive amount, since, like the export of wheat, it corresponds to an *inflow* of gold (or the equivalent).

If there were no capital accounts (i.e., no borrowing and lending) and no errors and omissions, the net gold flow into or out of a region would balance the net surplus or deficit on current account.   Thus, to maintain balance, a net surplus ($+$) on current account must be matched by a net gold inflow ($-$) or, in other words, a net import of gold ; and a net deficit ($-$) on current account by a net gold outflow ($+$), that is, by an export of gold.   When data are available on types of gold inflows and outflows, it is often desirable to maintain the breakdown in a balance of payments statement.[44]

Depending on the available data and the purpose of the investigation, the analyst may disaggregate the capital account in several ways.   In Table 3 this account is subdivided into *U. S. Treasury Transfers* and *Private Savings* (comprising the *net* savings of individuals, businesses, and state and local governments within the region).[45]   When the Federal government collects more within a region than it disburses, it will customarily shift the surplus funds out of the region.   Such an outflow of funds is designated by a ($-$) sign, its counterpart being an export of gold ($+$) or the equivalent.   When Federal disbursements exceed collections, the resulting *inflow* of funds is accordingly designated by a ($+$) sign, since this inflow corresponds to an import of gold ($-$).   Finally, when *all* resident units of a region *on balance* save, this corresponds to a net increase of their assets (as will be discussed briefly below) and therefore a capital outflow ($-$) to other regions.   Dis-saving is associated with a net decrease in assets (or increase in liabilities) within the region, and thus with a capital inflow ($+$).[46]

In Table 3 gross as well as net items are recorded for current accounts but not for gold and currency movement and capital accounts.   Ideally, all the data are to be desired, gross as well as net.   Such a complete set of accounts would help to eliminate errors in the data and would provide a better comprehension of the total transactions of Region X.   For example,

[44] For example, see P. Hartland [25], Table 1.

[45] In contrast, Hartland combines the two major categories, capital account and errors and omissions, and subdivides the resulting category into (1) interbank deposits, (2) Federal Reserve foreign account, (3) Treasury transfers, and (4) gross capital movement and residual [25], p. 6).

[46] For a fuller discussion, see G. J. Hile [28], pp. 151–156.

the $2 million net on other commodities, if presented alone, will not reveal the magnitude and significance to Region X of trade in other commodities. Unfortunately, the gross data are frequently not available, especially for capital accounts.

Before we can appraise a balance of payments study, we must be cognizant of the quality of the data employed and of the postulates and conceptual frameworks underlying their use in the study. Since the type and quality of the available data vary considerably among the several regions of the world, so must the conceptual frameworks designed to utilize them, and so must our appraisals of the resulting balance of payments studies. The following discussion relates to the available data and conceptual frameworks for studies with respect to regions of the United States.

As already indicated, the Interstate Commerce Commission and the Army Engineers Corps furnish considerable data on Class I rail shipments and receipts and shipments by ports, respectively.[47] However, the use of these data for estimating a region's commodity exports and imports involves many limitations. The I.C.C. data are based on a 1 per cent sample and therefore are subject to sampling errors, especially with respect to commodities whose volume of shipment is small.[48] The Army Engineers Corps data are generally not broken down on an origin-destination basis (i.e., do not indicate the destination of a shipment from a given port, and vice versa) and therefore are less useful than the I.C.C. data.[49] More important, the commodity classifications of the I.C.C. and Army Engineers Corps are not comparable. Errors unavoidably crop up in the process of reconciling these classifications.

There are no comprehensive data concerning truck shipments. This constitutes the most serious problem in estimating a region's commodity exports and imports. Only spotty information is available; consequently attempts at accounting for such shipments introduce large possibilities for errors.[50] Because of this major gap in the data, indirect methods, in

---

[47] See [58, 60, 62].

[48] Minor errors occur from railway billing practices which sometimes differ from I.C.C. reporting rules and the necessity of withholding data that would disclose operations of individual firms.

[49] In the case of I.C.C. data the state of origin and destination are given, and therefore intraregional trade can be estimated and subtracted from total trade to obtain movement of commodities into and out of a region by rail. For Army Engineers Corps data, we must take the difference between total receipts and shipments of each commodity at each port, and sum for the ports of a region to obtain either net surplus (exports) or net deficit (imports). By this procedure the commodity flows that both originate and terminate at the ports of a region tend to cancel out.

[50] See G. J. Hile [28], pp. 66–71 for a discussion of the available data on truck shipments and of attempts to approximate them. See also P. Hartland [25], pp. 69–75, and W. L. Smith [50].

particular those utilizing input-output techniques (which will be discussed in Chapter 8), are used increasingly in estimating commodity trade.[51]

Even if all the physical data were available on commodity flows, still another important problem must be dealt with. Tonnage flows of commodities must be multiplied by relevant prices to obtain the dollar value of these flows. Unfortunately, data on prices—even average yearly wholesale prices, at the point of production of each commodity in each region[52]—are largely nonexistent. As a substitute for regional prices, national average prices are typically used. Moreover, additional errors are introduced because, among many other reasons: (1) a variety of sources of national price data must be used, which are not always consistent; (2) price data are available in units other than tons, and these units are frequently not easily converted into tons; (3) many commodities for which prices are available are combined into commodity classes when shipment data are presented—hence a "weighted" price representative of the commodity class must be "manufactured"; and (4) a single price is typically used for each commodity (or commodity group) which is thus inconsistent with important qualitative differences (and therefore price differences) among units of a given commodity, especially between the units that are imported and those that are exported.[53] Consideration of all these gaps and shortcomings in the physical and value data compels us to use whatever results we obtain with considerable caution.[54]

[51] If indirect methods are used to estimate total net trade in each commodity, truck shipments can be obtained as a residual from subtracting trade in the commodity via rail and water. (See G. J. Hile [28], pp. 64–104.) Such a residual procedure, which must encounter all the sources of error already listed in the text and others to be listed later in the valuation process, is subject to serious question, especially since the errors involved are not small and random.

[52] F.O.B. prices are desired since transportation costs represent the value of freight and shipping service and since freight and shipping service is a subcategory in its own right in the balance of payments statement.

[53] For a fuller discussion of these and other sources of errors, see G. J. Hile [28], pp. 90–104; P. Hartland [25], pp. 76–91; P. B. Simpson [47], pp. 102–105; P. B. Simpson and S. Burr [48], pp. 5–10; J. D. Daane [13], pp. 78–158; and W. L. Smith [50]. An example may be helpful. Suppose ten units of commodity A are imported by a region and four units of commodity B are exported. If their prices are $2.00 and $6.00, respectively, the region's net balance with respect to these two commodities is plus $4.00. However, if these commodities are alike (or different grades of the same general product, such as women's wear) and fall in the same commodity classification (which occurs frequently in the published data), then on balance the region is depicted as importing six units which when multiplied by an average unweighted price of $4.00 (this type of price must frequently be used when data on component shipments are unavailable) yields for the region a net balance of minus $24.00.

[54] Not all the data limitations and conceptual difficulties are noted in this discussion. The reader is referred to the literature already cited for a much more complete presenta-

The next two subdivisions in the current account of the balance of payments statement relate to various *Service Trade* items and to *Gifts and Unilateral Transfers*. So far as freight and shipping, education, recreation, insurance and other, and gifts and unilateral transfers are concerned, the problems of obtaining reliable data and the sources of error in general resemble those confronted in estimating commodity trade. In estimating the freight and shipping item, we encounter the difficulty of determining whether a resident or a nonresident is purchasing a given shipping service and to what extent the service is performed by an internal transportation agency. In deriving net imports or exports on education account, we must develop appropriate assumptions about differences in expenditure patterns between nonresidents studying within the region and students from the region who attend institutions elsewhere. In arriving at the export and import of recreational services, we are generally compelled to work with sparse data, which are frequently unreliable. And in accounting for in-flows and outflows due to insurance services, on which the data are generally considered adequate, we must still use crude methods for estimating an item such as fire and marine insurance.[55]

When we attempt to estimate the category *property income* (interest, dividends, rent, and royalties), we must explicitly handle certain difficult conceptual questions, to which we have alluded in the previous chapter. For example, what is a resident? Individuals who live in the region are clearly residents. For the most part, too, the activities of unincorporated businesses and of internal local and state governments can be considered the activities of residents. Not so for the Federal government and for incorporated firms. In the case of the Federal government, the term "federal" implies an agency which is neither internal nor external to a region. Accordingly, a fraction of the Federal government might be assigned to each region. On the other hand, the Federal government may be considered to exist completely outside the region, since its basic decisions are for the most part made externally.

As for a major corporation which has one or more of many plants located in the region, it, too, may be considered as neither wholly included nor wholly excluded from the region. The particular fraction of it to be

tion. It should be noted that the derivation of the trade account for a metropolitan-type region or for a town or other small area involves somewhat different types of data pro-blems, e.g., the determination of that part of retail sales, wholesale sales, and service transactions associated with nonresidents (i.e., exports). For further discussion, see W. F. Stolper and C. M. Tiebout [51], pp. 20–22; and Chapter 4, pp. 86–90, and references cited therein.

[55] For a full discussion of the difficulties in estimating these accounts, the reader is referred to G. J. Hile [28], pp. 104–126, 142–144; P. Hartland [25], pp. 95–110; J. D. Daane [13], pp. 158–168; P. B. Simpson [47], p. 53; and W. L. Smith [50].

treated as located within the region might be determined by relative importance of branch plant activity internal to the region. Yet, in another sense, the home offices of the corporation may lie outside the region, and in terms of basic decisions the corporation is external to the region. However, from still another standpoint, even a corporation which engages in no activities within a region may be considered as partly located within the region because residents of the region own equity stock in the corporation.

Clearly, the way in which we define a resident, or, put otherwise, the extent to which incorporated business, Federal government, and other units are considered residents of a region, is determined by the objectives of a balance of payments study. (For example, if we were to place heavy emphasis on insights into per capita income and other welfare considerations which might be gained from a balance of payments study, we might distribute a corporation among regions according to wages and salaries paid out by the corporation in the several regions.) Thus, before rent, interest, and other property income accruing to incorporated business, Federal government, and like units can be determined, these conceptual questions must be answered. Then problems of obtaining data arise; and, as can be expected, they resemble those already discussed.[56]

The second major category of Table 3 concerns gold and currency movements. Where a region corresponds to a Federal Reserve district, the data of the Interdistrict Settlement Fund can be directly utilized. For example, in her study pertaining to New England, Hartland was able to present a breakdown of gold and currency movements due to (1) commercial and financial transactions ;[57] (2) Federal Reserve note clearings arising from the return of Federal Reserve notes to the bank of issue ; and (3) the transfer of Federal government funds among the several Federal Reserve banks. In contrast, because her region of study did not closely correspond to a Federal Reserve district, Hile was not able to use the data of the Interdistrict Settlement Fund. She was compelled to estimate the sum of gold and currency movement and errors and omissions (the fourth major category of Table 3) as a residual balancing item. This was done after the net balances on current account and capital account were determined.[58]

[56] For a full discussion, see G. J. Hile [28], pp. 126–136; P. Hartland [25], pp. 110–115; P. B. Simpson [47], pp. 47–53; and C. L. Leven [38], ch. 2, 3.

[57] However, because the firms of one region may hold checking accounts in the banks of a second region and make payments to residents of the second region through such an account (which corresponds to a real gold flow not reported in transit clearings), and for other reasons, the use of the transit clearings data of the Interdistrict Settlement Fund to represent gold flows due to commercial and financial transactions involves a certain amount of inaccuracy. See P. Hartland [25], pp. 116–118.

[58] Needless to say, the accuracy of any item determined residually is influenced by the accuracy of the estimate of other items, qualified by the extent to which errors in the estimates of other items are compensatory or cancel out.

The third major category of Table 3 pertains to the capital account. Although Federal government activities are to a large extent current in nature, the transfer of Treasury funds from one region to the next (via Federal Reserve banks) is typically viewed as a capital movement.[59] When regions correspond to Federal Reserve districts, such transfers are reported by the Interdistrict Settlement Fund. When regions cut across Federal Reserve districts in a major way, the investigator must estimate on current account Federal receipts and expenditures in dealings with both individuals and businesses of the region under study. Apart from the customary problems associated with gaps in data, allocating procedures, etc., once again the problem of determining the extent to which the Federal government is part of the region must be faced. This is typically assumed away by explicitly positing the Federal government as wholly nonresident.[60]

The second major subdivision of the capital account of Table 3 relates to private savings which in turn may be broken down into savings of individuals, businesses, and state and local governments within the region. As already indicated, the capital account should include all transactions which result in changes in the creditor-debtor position of the region or in its assets-liabilities standing. The difficulties in obtaining for all types of resident units data on loans, investments, borrowings, sales of securities, bank deposits, and like items preclude direct estimation of changes in the capital account (aside from Treasury transfers). However, on the assumption that positive savings refer to a net increase in assets (or decrease in liabilities, or both)—such as the purchase of real estate and securities, the repayment of debt, the deposit of funds in banks, the granting of loans, and similar activities—and that negative savings refer to the opposite types of activities, we can indirectly estimate the net change in a region's assets-liabilities standing. We can do this by summing savings of all individuals, businesses, and local and state governments in the region. This summing procedure tends to cancel out the intraregional transactions and yields a net figure which, if positive, refers to capital outflow (or export), and, if negative, to capital inflow (or import).[61]

---

[59] Actually, such transfer may either in part or whole reflect an adjustment of over-estimated and underestimated "real" receipts and payments accounts among regions. For example, when a region receives credit for excise taxes paid by nonresidents on goods which it produces (because the price charged includes the Federal excise), the transfer out of the region by the Federal government of an amount equal to that credit is in effect simply a "real" adjustment and not a capital flow. In other respects, too, it is questionable whether Treasury transfers represent capital movements.

[60] For a full discussion, see G. J. Hile [28], pp. 144–151, and P. B. Simpson [47], pp. 51–53.

[61] Refer to G. J. Hile [28], pp 151–156. In estimating the various items for the

As is true of other items, the data problems in estimating private savings are major.[62] For example, even after we determine how much of a particular corporation is resident in a region and therefore what per cent of its retained earnings should be reported as savings for the region, we must still identify the capital inflow when a corporation constructs a branch plant in the region. From what sources—and sources which must be classified by regions—do the investment funds come?

In summing up the discussion and appraising the value of balance of payments statements, we cannot avoid a sense of discouragement when confronted with the multitude of data and conceptual problems. Yet the results of a careful investigation can well repay the effort involved. A balance of payments study permits a type of comprehensive view of a regional economy which is otherwise very difficult to obtain. When such a study is well presented, it can greatly increase the understanding of a region's problems by its citizens, businessmen, and civic and political leaders. This is neatly illustrated by the following statement in Table 4 on Puerto Rico's account with the Mainland and other areas.[63]

Notwithstanding the values already noted, a balance of payments statement is still primarily a descriptive device. In a sense it merely reflects the entire network of economic relations of a region with the rest of the world. Hence, by itself it cannot be very useful for analysis. However, as a statistical framework against which the investigator orders his thinking, it can be of considerable value. It facilitates analyses of terms of trade,[64] studies of the implications of Federal policies and internal development programs, inquiries into the potential for the growth of a region's income and industries, studies of the transmission of cyclical impulses and of

---

breakdown of the capital account as reported in footnote 45, Hartland was able to approximate (1) short-term capital movements via bank deposits (interbank deposits), (2) Treasury transfers (from Interdistrict Settlement Fund data), and (3) Federal Reserve foreign account. However, she was unsuccessful in estimating other capital items and was compelled to combine her errors and omissions category with the remaining capital items to yield the subcategory *gross capital movement and residual*. Because Hartland's study was of a region which corresponded to a Federal Reserve district, she was able to estimate this item residually, since data on gold and currency movement were available from the Interdistrict Settlement Fund (P. Hartland [25], pp. 21–29, 123–125). In contrast, Hile was not able to obtain data on gold and currency movement from the Interdistrict Settlement Fund and had to estimate this movement residually. As a consequence, Hile could not residually determine any part of the capital account category. In this connection, however, see a refinement of Hile's method suggested by W. L. Smith [50].

[62] See G. J. Hile [28], pp. 156–169.

[63] The basic form of this statement is taken from an excellent set of accounts for Hawaii prepared by J. H. Shoemaker in Bank of Hawaii [2].

[64] For example, see P. Hartland [25], ch. VII.

expansionary as well as deflationary effects flowing from developments in other regions. The value of balance of payments studies are enhanced when they are performed for the same regional unit over a period of years so as to provide an historical perspective.[65] When additional and higher-quality data are made available for their construction, particularly regarding capital inflows and outflows by type and source, and when regional income and social accounting, interregional commodity and money flow, and interregional input-output and other studies are utilized to provide both estimates and checks of original sources of data, these statements can be of still greater value. Further, when they are coupled with projection techniques and other tools of regional analysis, they can yield to an analyst well seasoned in the limitations of data and models valuable guideposts for the formulation of sound regional policy as well as national policy.

F. CONCLUSIONS

In this chapter we have examined the location quotient, commodity flow investigations, regional and interregional money flow studies, and balance of payments statements. When the limitations of the available data are adequately recognized and conclusions properly qualified, each of these tools and studies can be of value. However, the key to the most fruitful use of each lies in integration with other types of regional analysis.

The location quotient is particularly useless in and of itself. It takes on meaning when built into comparative cost-location analysis, industrial complex analysis, and input-output studies to be presented later.

Commodity flow investigations, per se, may possess somewhat more than descriptive value; but when such investigations are pursued within a conceptual framework embodying mutually dependent systems governing the interrelations of regions, their value is considerably enhanced. To be specific, when commodity flows, viewed as a system of interregional flows, are tied with interregional money flows, again viewed as a system, *and in particular* with the spatial system of industrial locations implied by comparative cost and industrial complex analysis, *and* with the technical interindustry linkage system of interregional input-output, *and* with the

---

[65] Hartland's study of New England's balance of payments over the period 1929–1939 has provoked a considerable amount of enlightening debate on the New England economy. Why during this period were New England's receipts for interregional commercial and financial transactions consistently greater than its payments? Why did the gold reserves of the Federal Reserve Bank of Boston keep on rising? To what extent are these questions related to the difficulties experienced by industrial sectors of New England? For interesting discussion see, among others, S. E. Harris [23] and A. A. Bright and G. E. Ellis (eds.) [9].

METHODS OF REGIONAL ANALYSIS

TABLE 4. BALANCE OF

Dollar Inflows

		(1)
A. On Current Account		
In 1955, we received dollars from the outside world as follows:		
1. *We exported Puerto Rican products* amounting to		$372 million
(a) Income from our export of sugar and related products was	$133 million	
(b) Income from our export of textiles was	90 million	
(c) Income from our export of leaf tobacco, cigars, and related products was	22 million	
(d) Income from our export of rum, footwear, leather manufactures, and all other products was	127 million	
2. *The Federal government bought goods and services in Puerto Rico* in operating agencies in Puerto Rico amounting to		109 million
(a) Expenditures of defense agencies were	98 million	
(b) Expenditures of civilian agencies were, after deductions for collected revenues,	10 million	
3. *Mainland and foreign firms and individuals purchased goods and services in Puerto Rico* amounting to		50 million
(a) To tourists and transients including crews of commercial carriers, we sold goods and services amounting to	25 million	
(b) To shipping and air lines, and to other Mainland and foreign businesses, we sold goods and services amounting to	25 million	
4. *We earned dividends, interest and profits from overseas investments* amounting to		6 million
5. *We provided seasonal labor, insurance services, and other miscellaneous services* amounting to		27 million
6. *We received gifts and transfer payments* amounting to		125 million
(a) Remittances from institutions and persons were	26 million	
(b) Federal contributions to Puerto Rico governmental agencies were	22 million	
(c) Federal benefit payments to veterans, social security payments to the aged, subsidy payments to farm operators and other transfers were	78 million	
Total dollar inflow on Current Account		$689 million
Net outflow on Current Account		

(continued on p. 176)

PAYMENTS: PUERTO RICO, 1955

Dollar Outflows		Net
	(2)	(Col. 1–Col. 2)

A. On Current Account

In 1955, we paid out dollars to the outside world as follows:

	(2)	(Col. 1–Col. 2)
1. *We bought goods* amounting to	$583 million	− $211 million
(a) From the Mainland we purchased food, raw materials, construction materials, clothing, household appliances, cars and trucks, machinery and equipment, drugs, and a host of other items amounting to, after adjustment, $533 million		
(b) From foreign countries we purchased fish, drugs, lumber, newsprint, bags and sacks, fuel oil, steel bars, fertilizers, and other products amounting to 50 million		
2. *Tax payments to the Federal government* amounted to	3 million	+ $106 million
3. *We purchased services from Mainland and foreign concerns* amounting to	86 million	− $36 million
(a) Travel and transportation expenses of Puerto Rican residents overseas were 41 million		
(a) For ocean and air freight and insurance we paid 45 million		
4. *We paid interest, dividends, and profits to overseas investors* amounting to	42 million	− $36 million
5. *We purchased insurance and other miscellaneous services* amounting to	24 million	+ $ 3 million
6. *We made gifts and transfer payments* amounting to	24 million	+ $101 million
(a) Remittances from Puerto Rico to institutions and residents overseas were 12 million		
(b) Contributions of Puerto Rican residents for social security, retirement and similar programs of the Federal government were 12 million		
Total dollar outflow on Current Account	$762 million	
		− $ 73 million

(continued on p. 177)

TABLE 4—

Dollar Inflows

	(1)
Net Outflow on Current Account (from pp. 174–175)	

B. On Gold and Currency Account

C. On Capital Account

1. *Long-term investments in Puerto Rico by Mainland and other nonresident groups and persons* rose by .... **$72 million**

   (*a*) The increase of Mainland and foreign holdings of bonds of Puerto Rico governmental agencies was .... $12 million

   (*b*) The net amount of new mortgages and loans extended was .... 10 million

   (*c*) Direct investments were .... 50 million

2. *Short-term capital made available to Puerto Rico by overseas groups and persons* rose by .... **32 million**

   (*a*) The increase of such funds extended to Puerto Rican public housing authorities and governmental agencies was .... 16 million

   (*b*) The net increase in nonresident deposits in Puerto Rico banks was .... 5 million

   (*c*) The increase in other short-term loans and funds made available to Puerto Rico was .... 10 million

Total increase in investment in Puerto Rico by nonresidents .... **$104 million**

Net inflow on Capital Account

D. Errors and Omissions .... —

Discrepancies in the data are due to rounding to the nearest million.
a Balancing United States currency inflow are hidden gold (dollar) outflows.
Source: *Balance of Payments, Puerto Rico, 1955*, and *External Trade Statistics, 1955* Puerto Rico Planning Board, Bureau of Economics and Statistics, 1955.

continued

Dollar Outflows		Net
	(2)	(Col. 1–Col 2)
		− $ 73 million

B. On Gold and Currency Account

1. *We increased our net holdings of United States currency[a] by* — $ 1 million — — $ 1 million

C. On Capital Account

1. *Long-term investments overseas by Puerto Rican governmental agencies and residents rose by* — $ 18 million — + $ 54 million
   (a) The net increase in our holdings of United States government securities was — $ 3 million
   (b) The net increase in our holdings of miscellaneous investments was — 15 million

2. *Short-term assets of Puerto Rico abroad remained approximately unchanged* — – — + $ 32 million
   (a) The increase in these assets held by Puerto Rican governmental agencies was — 1 million
   (b) The decrease in these assets held by Puerto Rico banks was — − 4 million
   (c) The increase in these assets held by Puerto Rican residents was — 4 million

Total increase in investment abroad by Puerto Rico — $ 18 million

| | | + $ 86 million |

D. Errors and Omissions — $ 12 million — − $ 12 million

efficiency system of interregional linear programming, then commodity flow studies attain maximum value.

In like manner, interregional money flows, viewed as a system, and balance of payments statements, when consistently constructed for a system of regions, may be fruitfully tied not only to each other but also to the income and social accounts for a system of regions, to the system of interregional commodity flows, to the spatial system of industrial locations, and to the interregional interindustry system of input-output. Thereby, the value of money flow studies and balance of payments statements are increased manyfold.

REFERENCES

1. Angell, James W., *The Behavior of Money*, McGraw-Hill, New York, 1936.
2. Bank of Hawaii, Department of Business Research, *Hawaii: Patterns of Island Growth*, Honolulu, 1958.
3. Beckerman, W., "Distance and the Pattern of Intra-European Trade," *Review of Economics and Statistics*, Vol. 38 (Feb. 1956).
4. Beckhart, Benjamin H., and James G. Smith, *The New York Money Market*, Columbia University Press, New York, 1932.
5. Bowsher, Norman N., "Bank Reserves and the Flow of Funds," *Monthly Review*, Federal Reserve Bank of St. Louis, Vol. 34 (Nov. 1952).
6. ———, "The Money Market and District Banking," *Monthly Review*, Federal Reserve Bank of St. Louis, Vol. 35 (Nov. 1953).
7. ———, J. Dewey Daane, and Robert Einzig, "The Flows of Funds Between Regions of the United States, "*Papers and Proceedings of the Regional Science Association*, Vol. 3 (1957).
8. ———, ———, and ———, "Task Force Report on Interregional Flow of Funds and District Member Bank Reserves," in the *Record of the Federal Reserve System Conference on the Interregional Flow of Funds*, Washington, D.C. April 1955, mimeographed.
9. Bright, Arthur A., and George H. Ellis, eds., *The Economic State of New England*, Yale University Press, New Haven, Connecticut, 1954.
10. Buma, Harold L., and Harry S. Schwartz, "An Analysis of Commodity Trade of the Twelfth District Federal Reserve Bank, 1950," in *Interregional Linkages*, Western Committee on Regional Economic Analysis, Berkeley, California, 1954.
11. Carlson, Knute E., *Interregional and Intraregional Traffic of the Mountain-Pacific Area in 1939*, United States Department of Commerce, Washington, D.C. (no date).
12. Copeland, Morris A., *A Study of Moneyflows in the United States*, National Bureau of Economic Research, New York, 1952.
13. Daane, J. ·Dewey, *The Fifth Federal Reserve District: A Study in Regional Economics*, doctoral dissertation, Harvard University, 1948.
14. Deane, Phyllis, *Colonial Social Accounting*, Cambridge University Press, Cambridge, England, 1953.
15. Federal Reserve Bank of Boston, "Federal Receipts and Expenditures," *Monthly Review*, Vol. 32 (Aug. 1950).

16. Federal Reserve Bank of Boston, "New England's Gold Reserves and Inter-district Payments," *Monthly Review*, Vol. 33 (Oct. 1951).

17. Federal Reserve Bank of Kansas City, "The Employment Multiplier in Wichita," *Monthly Review*, Vol. 37 (Sept. 1952).

18. Federal Reserve Bank of Richmond, "The Balance of Payments of the Fifth Federal Reserve District," *Monthly Review* (July 1949).

19. Federal Reserve Board, "Summary Flow-of-Funds Accounts, 1950–55," *Federal Reserve Bulletin*, Vol. 43 (April 1957).

20. Florence, P. Sargant, *Investment, Location, and Size of Plant*, Cambridge University Press, Cambridge, England, 1948.

21. Freutel, Guy, "The Eighth District Balance of Trade," *Monthly Review*, Federal Reserve Bank of St. Louis, Vol. 34 (June 1952).

22. Gosfield, Amor, "Input-Output Analysis of the Puerto Rican Economy," in *Input-Output Analysis: An Appraisal*, National Bureau of Economic Research, Studies in Income and Wealth, Vol. 18, Princeton University Press, Princeton, New Jersey, 1955.

23. Harris, Seymour, E., *The Economics of New England*, Harvard University Press, Cambridge, Massachusetts, 1952.

24. ———, *International and Interregional Economics*, McGraw-Hill, New York, 1957.

25. Hartland, Penelope C., *Balance of Interregional Payments of New England*, Brown University Studies, Vol. 14, Providence, Rhode Island, 1950.

26. ———, "Interregional Payments Compared with International Payments," *Quarterly Journal of Economics*, Vol. 63 (Aug. 1949).

27 Hildebrand, G., and A. Mace, "The Employment Multiplier in an Expanding Industrial Market: Los Angeles County, 1940–47," *Review of Economics and Statistics*, Vol. 32 (Aug. 1950).

28. Hile, Gloria J., *The Balance of Payments of the Southeast in 1950*, doctoral dissertation, University of Michigan, Ann Arbor, Michigan, 1954.

29. ———, "The Balance of Payments of the Southeast in 1950," *Papers and Proceedings of the Regional Science Association*, Vol. 1 (1955).

30. Hoover, Edgar M. Jr., *Location Theory and the Shoe and Leather Industries*, Harvard University Press, Cambridge, Massachusetts, 1937.

31. International Monetary Fund, *Balance of Payments Yearbook, 1938–1946–1947*, Washington D.C., 1949.

32. Isard, W., "Location Theory and Trade Theory: Short-Run Analysis," *Quarterly Journal of Economics*, Vol. 68 (May 1954).

33. ———, "The Value of the Regional Approach in Economic Analysis," in *Regional Income*, National Bureau of Economic Research, Studies in Income and Wealth, Vol. 21, Princeton University Press, Princeton, New Jersey, 1957.

34. ———, and G. Freutel, "Regional and National Product Projections and their Interrelations," in *Long-Range Economic Projection*, National Bureau of Economic Research, Studies in Income and Wealth, Vol. 16, Princeton University Press, Princeton, New Jersey, 1954.

35. ———, and M. J. Peck, "Location Theory and International and Interregional Trade Theory," *Quarterly Journal of Economics*, Vol. 68 (Feb. 1954).

36. Kavesh, Robert A., and James B. Jones, "Differential Regional Impacts of Federal Expenditures," *Papers and Proceedings of the Regional Science Association*, Vol. 2 (1956).

37. Kindleberger, Charles P., *International Economics*, Richard D. Irwin, Inc., Homewood, Illinois, 1953.

38. Leven, Charles L., *Theory and Method of Income and Product Accounts for Metropolitan Areas, Including the Elgin–Dundee Area as a Case Study*, Iowa State College, Ames, Iowa, 1958, mimeographed.

39. Lewis, Edwin H., *Minnesota's Interstate Trade*, Studies in Economics and Business, No. 16, University of Minnesota, Minneapolis, Minnesota, March 1953.

40. Mendelson, M., "A Structure of Moneyflows," *Journal of the American Statistical Association*, Vol. 50 (March 1955).

41. Morgenstern, Oskar, *On the Accuracy of Economic Observations*, Princeton University Press, Princeton, New Jersey, 1950.

42. National Bureau of Economic Research, *The National Economic Accounts of the United States*, General Series No. 64, U. S. Government Printing Office, Washington, D.C., 1958.

43. Neff, Phillip, and Robert M. Williams, "Identification and Measurement of an Industrial Area's Export Employment in Manufacturing," *Proceedings of the Western Committee on Regional Economic Analysis*, 1952.

44. Ouren, T., and A. Sømme, *Trends in Inter-War Trade and Shipping*, Norwegian University School of Business, Geographical Series, No. 5, Bergen, Norway, 1949.

45. Scott, Ira O. Jr., "The Regional Impact of Monetary Policy," *Quarterly Journal of Economics*, Vol. 69 (May 1955).

46. Sigel, S. J., "A Comparison of the Structures of Three Social Accounting Systems," in *Input–Output Analysis: An Appraisal*, National Bureau of Economic Research, Studies in Income and Wealth, Vol. 18, Princeton University Press, Princeton, New Jersey, 1955.

47. Simpson, Paul B., *Regional Aspects of Business Cycles and Special Studies of the Pacific Northwest*, Bonneville Administration and the University of Oregon, June 1953.

48. ———, and Shirley Burr, "Estimating Regional Balance of Payments in the Pacific Northwest," mimeographed paper presented to the Western Committee on Regional Economic Analysis of the Social Science Research Council, June 1953.

49. Smith, R. Tynes, "Technical Aspects of Transportation Flow Data," *Journal of the American Statistical Association*, Vol. 49 (June 1954).

50. Smith, Warren L., "Areas of Regional Research," in the *Record of the Federal Reserve System Conference on the Interregional Flow of Funds*, Washington, D.C., April 1955, mimeographed.

51. Stolper, Wolfgang F., and Charles M. Tiebout, "The Balance of Payments of a Small Area as an Analytic Tool," 1950, mimeographed paper.

52. Sweeney, Leo W., "The Iowa Economy as Portrayed by Rail Freight Traffic Movement," *Iowa Business Digest*, University of Iowa, Vol. 22 (Dec. 1951).

53. Terrill, Robert P., *The Interregional Balance of Payments of Southern California, 1920–1934*, thesis, Stanford University, Stanford, California, 1941.

54. Ullman, Edward L., *American Commodity Flow*, University of Washington Press, Seattle, Washington, 1957.

55. ———, "The Railroad Pattern of the United States," *Geographical Review*, Vol. 39 (April 1949).

56. ———, "Transport Geography," in *American Geography: Inventory and Prospect*, ed. by Preston E. James and Clarence F. Jones, Syracuse University Press, Syracuse, New York, 1954.

57. Ullman, Edward L., "Die wirtschaftliche Verflechtung verschiedener Regionen der U.S.A. betrachtet am Güteraustausch Connecticuts, Iowas, und Washingtons mit den anderen Staaten," *Die Erde*, Heft 2 (1955).

58. U. S. Army, Board of Engineers for Rivers and Harbors, *Commercial Statistics: Water-borne Commerce*, Washington, D.C., annually.

59. U. S. House of Representatives, *Interregional Highways*, House Document No. 379, 78th Congress, 2d Session, Washington, D.C., 1944.

60. U. S. Interstate Commerce Commission, Bureau of Transport Economics and Statistics, *Carload Waybill Analyses, State to State Distribution of Tonnage by Commodity Groups*, Washington, D.C., quarterly.

61. U. S. Interstate Commerce Commission, Bureau of Transport Economics and Statistics, *Regional Shifts in the Postwar Traffic of Class I Railways*, Vols. I and II, Washington, D.C., Sept. 1946, mimeographed.

62. U. S. Interstate Commerce Commission, Bureau of Transport Economics and Statistics, *Tons of Revenue Freight Originated and Tons Terminated in Carloads by Groups of Commodities and by Geographic Areas—Class I Steam Railways*, Washington, D.C., annually.

63. U. S. National Resources Planning Board, *Industrial Location and National Resources*, U. S. Government Printing Office, Washington, D.C., 1943.

64. Vining, Rutledge, "Delimitation of Economic Areas: Statistical Conceptions in the Study of the Spatial Structure of an Economic System, *Journal of the American Statistical Association*, Vol. 48 (March 1953).

65. ———, "A Description of Certain Spatial Aspects of an Economic System," *Economic Development and Cultural Change*, Vol. 3 (Jan. 1955).

66. Wollman, Nathaniel, "Regional Variations in Money, Credit and Interest Rates," *Papers and Proceedings of the Regional Science Association*, Vol. 2 (1956).

67. ———, "The Southwest in the Nation: Some Interregional Relations," in *Interregional Linkages*, Western Committee on Regional Economic Analysis, Berkeley, California, 1954.

Chapter 6

Regional Cycle and Multiplier Analysis*

A. INTRODUCTION

In planning the utilization of the resources of a region and its economic development, we cannot be satisfied with data on (1) population, current and future, and migration estimates; (2) Gross Regional Product, regional income, income per capita, income distribution by class of family, commodity trade balance, and Rest of the World account; (3) current money and commodity flows, capital movements, reserve ratios, balance of payments position, and similar items. We must probe more deeply and consider other basic factors. Of these, one is the cyclical sensitivity of the mix of industrial activities which may be incorporated in a development plan, and beyond this of the region itself.

Historically, many regions of the world and of the United States and other nations have experienced severe ups and downs in their growth. A part of these fluctuations are undoubtedly associated with the dynamics of capitalistic development and probably are unavoidable in a free or partly controlled enterprise system. However, it is the belief of many that another part of these fluctuations are avoidable and that a study of strategic factors generating such fluctuations is of great value. For example, in area development studies we frequently encounter the view,

* Section B of this chapter was written with Leon N. Moses, sections C and D with Eugene W. Schooler, and the Appendix with David F. Bramhall.

sometimes only implicitly, that it is desirable to proceed with a program of development at a slower pace, or to set goals for development which are not as high as can be obtained, if in the process of transition the severe ups and downs of the regional economy can be avoided.

Whatever the view expressed, clearly a development policy for a region should consider the cyclical implications of such a policy. Other things being equal, it is generally more desirable to develop an industrial mix whose cyclical tendencies tend to balance out or at least do not intensify each other. Thus, one valuable avenue of inquiry has been concerned with the *industrial composition* of regions and the cyclical fluctuations of different types of industries, especially as they may offset each other. This type of investigation has particular bearing on policy with respect to "soft spots" and "depressed areas" within the national economy.

As we dig into the materials on the oscillations of different types of industry, we become aware of their different impacts on regional cycles. We discover that in the short run at least certain industries are basic, particularly those that serve national markets. Their fluctuations lead to fluctuations in local income, which in turn induce fluctuations in retail sales and various service trades, which lead to still more indirect fluctuations. In short, the fluctuations of basic industry have a multiplier effect. Recognition of this multiplier effect has led to a second type of study, the *economic base* study, or the study for cities and regions of basic-service ratios, that is, of the ratio of employment (total or change in total) in basic activities to employment in nonbasic activities, or in short, of *regional multipliers*.

A far-sighted resources development analyst, although he may be concerned with a particular region, investigates further. Regions are not isolated entities. They are interrelated. To any given region are transmitted the ups and downs of regions which are its neighbors. Therefore, the analyst wants to employ an interregional framework. He wants to know something about the cyclical sensitivities of other regions and the ways in which their cycles may be spread to his own region. He recognizes the fact that the *next* region's imports are *his* region's exports, that in effect a system of regions exists. Hence a third type of study which is of value concerns the sensitivity of different kinds and types of regions, with particular emphasis on fluctuations in exports and imports, that is, on the contractions and expansions of the economic bonds which link regions. This type of study leads to a more precise, but at the same time more theoretical, formulation of multiplier effects and of the mechanisms by which cycles are spatially transmitted within the system of regions. It centers around the *interregional trade multiplier*, a concept closely akin to Keynesian doctrine.

Beyond these areas, the regional investigator probes into the relationship of regional cycles to national cycles. He is fully aware that national conditions bear heavily on regional developments. Many of the forces which interplay to determine national conditions are outside the scope of regional analysis and lie in the traditional realm of business cycle theory. These shall not be discussed in this book. Yet he is also aware that because nations are composed of regions, regional development programs and conditions can influence in part national fluctuations. After all, statistically speaking, national cycles are weighted averages of regional cycles. Therefore, the regional analyst may be interested in a fourth type of study, one less theoretical than the third, which collects, processes, and interprets data on a multiregional as well as a national basis, or which digs deeply into the historical framework in order to unearth the several strategic sets of regional and national factors, and the important sequences of repercussions which they have generated within and between the several regions of the national economy. He thereby gains deeper insights into the *interrelations of regional and national cycles* and thus greater understanding of both.

B. INDUSTRIAL COMPOSITION AND REGIONAL CYCLES

In the United States, research into the regional aspects of business cycles began when there was already a good deal known about the responsiveness of individual industries, such as steel, and groups of industries, such as durables and nondurables. Therefore one of the first types of study, which is still being fruitfully pursued, is to examine the extent to which the different cyclical patterns of areas can be attributed to the industrial composition variable.[1] The over-all procedure is to compare by regions the timing, duration, and amplitude of cycles in each of a number of key sectors—such as retail sales, employment, bank debits, and power sales.

For example, Neff and Weifenbach[2] investigate the cyclical experience of several major cities which are different in industrial composition and which exhibit different degrees of industrial diversity. Major cities are considered relevant regions for analysis, since they exemplify functional specialization and contain large-scale cyclically vulnerable businesses. Furthermore, they are frequently breeding grounds of major innovation

---

[1] The part of the pattern that cannot be attributed to the industrial composition variable may be ascribed to within-industry differences among regions, differences which are presumably due to differences in other regional characteristics.

[2] P. Neff and A. Weifenbach [52]. Also see P. Neff [51].

and changes in the rate of investment. Even if they do not play a major role in originating cyclical impulses, they are certainly sensitive barometers of the cyclical forces transmitted through their intricate financial and industrial structures.

Neff and Weifenbach reach several conclusions which they are obliged to qualify in many respects.[3] When fluctuations are severe they find no major differences among the several areas in *timing* of cycles during the period 1919–1945. Only when fluctuations are small do they find wide differences in peak and trough dates, but even then the distribution of the areas from earliest to latest differs from one minor cycle to another. There is a faint suggestion, however, that Cleveland and Detroit, areas with heavy concentration of durable goods production, do tend to lead the others. This finding, although tenuous, does lend a bit of support to the thesis that, because durable production industries are most sensitive to the cycle,[4] regions possessing heavy concentrations of such industries tend to respond first to changes in stimuli.

Although the several areas exhibit variations in the *duration* of their fluctuations, these variations do not follow any regular pattern. No area can be singled out as having cyclical phases of the longest or shortest duration.· As for cycle *amplitude*, again the experiences of the areas suggest that there is little if any direct and simple association of industrial pattern with relative amplitude.[5]

Other studies seem to support the view that regional variations in cycles cannot be attributed solely or even largely to differences in industrial composition.[6] One of these, for example, investigated unemployment

[3] [52], ch. 8.

[4] According to this thesis durable-goods production tends to be more sensitive because, among other reasons, the income elasticity of demand for durables tends to be much higher than for nondurables, a point to be discussed more fully below.

[5] As Neff and Weifenbach state: "Pittsburgh, relatively constant in size and in concentration in producers' durable goods, does not generally have abnormally severe cyclical swings. Los Angeles, growing rapidly, and like Chicago in its diversity, failed to show evidence of comparative stability and resembled Pittsburgh in its response to cycles more than any other area. Cleveland likewise differs from Los Angeles in nearly every respect except the intensity of its business cycles. Only in Detroit did industrial pattern invariably reflect itself in measurably different cycles, and here the influence of its one great industry, automobiles, is sufficient to affect noticeably not only the real series but also debits and store sales" ([52], p. 193).

[6] It should be mentioned that there is some disagreement about the nature of the differences that exist among regional cycles. For example, Williams claims that existing studies have not clearly demonstrated, as some interpreters believe they have, that significant differences do exist between regions at the turning points of major cycles. Williams suggests that differences which are noted result from the use of imperfect statistical techniques. He questions whether important differences can exist in turning points of regional cycles in the United States in view of the extremely close ties of these

rates during the recession period 1949–1950 for a sample of eleven important manufacturing industries chosen for their homogeneity and presence among all census regions.[7] It found that, in general, regional differences in these unemployment rates for a given industry were greater than differences in these rates among the industries of a given region. Put another way, the limited data of this study suggest that if we wish to estimate the unemployment rate for an industry in a region, we would on the whole obtain a better approximation by using the average unemployment rate in the region than by using the average unemployment rate for the industry in the nation as a whole.

Another type of classification considered meaningful for regional cycle analysis distinguishes between growth and nongrowth regional situations. A typical argument claims that during a depression investment opportunities in areas of high-growth potential pile up so that, when a change in the national climate of anticipations occurs, it is quickly followed by a flood of new investment in these areas. The rapid rise in their incomes and outputs often attract migrants. These migrants represent an increase in the labor supply which keeps wages from increasing as quickly as they might otherwise and which may forestall bottlenecks. Further, new population will encourage expansions in residentiary industries, particularly construction. And so forth.

In examining arguments such as that advanced in the previous paragraph, Neff and Weifenbach found that for their urban areas, each taken as a whole, "high rates of growth do not guarantee either unusually long or unusually short cycles . . . nor does a decline in growth seem to affect the length of cycles."[8] Also, Kidner found a high degree of similarity in regions made possible by modern means of communications and transportation and of the rapidity with which impulses spread.

However, Williams does recognize major differences in the amplitude of regional cycles. Contrary to Neff, he finds that these differences are related to industrial composition, in particular to the per cent of manufacturing wage earners in nondurables production (R. M. Williams [76]).

Supporting Williams' position are recent findings by George H. Borts. In examining manufacturing employment in 33 states, 1914–1953, Borts observes significant differences in the amplitudes of the cycles experienced by states. He notes that these differences can be explained to a significant degree by industrial composition, the states subject to most cyclical variation being characterized by a high proportion of durable-goods manufactures (G. H. Borts [9]).

A somewhat different point of view is taken by Simpson. He finds that the direction and amplitude of income changes are different among regions. He also finds some support for his hypothesis that "On the upturns, the expanding regions usually lead and the contracting ones lag, while on downturns, the contracting ones lead and the expanding ones lag" (P. B. Simpson [62], p. 45).

[7] J. W. Garbarino [21].

[8] [52], p. 192.

the cyclical fluctuations of California (an area of high growth) and of the United States.[9] However, Kidner did observe one important difference. Although experiences of the United States and California are very much alike in the contraction phase, "there is an apparent tendency for economic activity in California to recover from business depression more rapidly and more fully than is true for the United States as a whole."[10] This latter phenomenon occurs even though, according to Kidner, there is similarity throughout the entire cycle between United States and California in business anticipations and in the *direction* of change in general business activity. One explanation of the contrasting comparative behavior in the contraction and expansion phases, which is consistent with the argument stated earlier, is the following. During periods of contraction no significant investment is undertaken anywhere in the economy. Therefore a high-growth regional economy is hit as hard as others. However, during revival, when new investments are initiated, relatively greater expansions tend to take place in areas of rapid secular growth (such as California), for then the existence among regions of differential profitabilities in investment opportunities can lead to differential recovery experiences.[11]

Hence, we are led to conclude from the limited materials which are statistically valid [12] that cyclical responsiveness of any given region cannot

[9] In general, the greatest dissimilarity is found in comparisons of minor cycles, a finding consistent with Neff's and Weifenbach's conclusions. Minor fluctuations of a region, Kidner feels, may be largely determined by the composition of its economy. "In a major cycle, however, the effect of national policy, and the consequences of sharp expansions or contractions in employment and investment resulting therefrom for the nation, may be sufficiently powerful to overcome the influences of regional differences in structure and to impose a high degree of similarity on the cyclical behavior of the whole country" ([41], p. 113).

In examining unemployment rates in the United States and California, Gordon found there, too, similarity of short-run cyclical experience ([28], ch. VII, IX).

[10] F. L. Kidner [41], p. 114.

[11] Another related point made by Kidner is worthy of note. In discussing the hypothesis that diversification leads to less intense cyclical fluctuations, he notes that "mere diversification, in any case, is no guarantee of stability. The relevant question has to do not with the existence of highly specialized industrial development and the consequent dependence upon one or a few principal industries, but rather it has to do with the particular composition of industrial activity in the region covered. Particular types of specialization might yield better promise of stability than a random diversification" ([41], pp. 111–112). He illustrates with California materials.

[12] Numerous questions may be raised regarding the validity of the statistical materials developed and the research methodologies adopted in the several studies on regional cycles. For example, with regard to amplitude what statistics should be studied? Most authors have concentrated on the absolute changes, but there is much to be said for Vining's contention that for a group of regions closely knit together by a system of

be divorced entirely from its industrial composition and from its secular trend position. The per cent of a region's activities in durables, the presence of growth industries in its industrial mix, the diversity of its industrial structure, the sensitivities of each of its individual production lines, the direction and rate of change of its underlying secular position are all factors to be considered in the formulation of policy for the region and in the programming of its development. Yet, until considerably more research is conducted to clear up the clouded picture thus far presented, we must rely heavily on intuition and sound judgment in evaluating the cyclical implications of the industrial composition and growth variables.[13]

modern communication and transportation facilities differences in rates of change are the more significant.

If absolute changes are to be used, the difficult question arises whether it is meaningful to decompose time series into seasonal, cyclical, and trend movements. If so, still another basic question regards the procedure for isolating cyclical movements. As is well known, injudicious (and even at times judicious) trend removal can alter the timing, duration, and amplitude of cycles; it can make cycles appear where there were only changes in the rate of increase or decrease in the original data, and it can also suppress actual cycles in the processing of the data. Very often the use of linear trends is particularly questionable.

Even the use of the meticulously developed procedures of the National Bureau of Economic Research whereby trend removal is generally avoided is open to serious question, especially in the measurement, identification, and comparison of regional cycles where the several regions are subject to significantly different secular rates of growth. There is also the additional basic question of what specific series to employ to reflect the cyclical experiences of a region.

Recognition of these and many other problems regarding statistical procedures and data point up the important need for further research in this area.

[13] Of interest here is the forthcoming study by G. H. Borts [9]. Observing that industrial composition fails to explain entirely cyclical behavior for states, Borts standardizes states. Specifically he constructs a series showing the cycle the United States as a nation would have experienced if each national industry were given the weight it has in a particular state. That is, for each state he produces a hypothetical nation which in industrial structure is a replica of the state. Comparison for each state of the derived cyclical behavior of the hypothetical nation with the actual cyclical behavior of the state yields fruitful hypotheses. Borts finds that almost always the states whose *actual* growth rates increased over a relevant sequence of time periods had less amplitude than industrial composition (i.e., their standardization as hypothetical nations) would suggest; whereas the states retarded in growth had more amplitude than industrial composition would suggest. Borts claims that "retardation may be regarded as a discontinuity in the growth trend. States which retard have lower relative growth rates than previously. This may be indicative of the appearance of unprogressive firms, high-cost production facilities and local cost characteristics which inhibit growth at the old relative rate. These conditions will cause industries in the region to have sharper cyclical amplitudes than their national counterparts. Conversely, acceleration may indicate the appearance of cost characteristics which stimulate growth. Under this

C. Regional Multipliers : The Economic Base Type

Another type of regional analysis which is closely linked to regional cycle studies concerns regional multipliers. This analysis stresses the inter-relations of sectors *within* a regional economy and the spread of impulses originating in any one sector to all other sectors either directly or indirectly. Such spreading in essence has a multiplying result. Through the continuous back and forth play of forces (or round-by-round process of inter-action), such spreading leads to a series of effects on each sector, including the original one, although these effects need not always be in the same direction and of significant magnitude. The relevance of multiplier studies for programming regional development is obvious. It neatly points up how growth in one sector induces growth in another. The relevance of such studies for understanding regional cycles is also obvious as soon as we recognize that some impulses may be positive, others negative ; some expansionary, others deflationary.

Regional multiplier analysis can be designed to handle any number of variables. Yet, the more variables a design encompasses, the more difficult it is to leave the conceptual stage and derive results of direct usefulness. The most comprehensive regional multiplier analysis to yield quantitative results of some value is that associated with the use of the interregional input-output technique to be discussed at length in Chapters 8 and 12. In contrast, the most simple and straightforward type of regional multiplier analysis is associated with economic base studies. These latter studies for the most part avoid the interregional variable and employ a very gross industrial classification.[14]

argument the characteristics which change the growth ranking will also change the cyclical behavior of the affected states."

A related study, which does not differentiate between secular and cyclical position of regions, attempts to explain shifts in regional income in terms of changes in four factors: (1) value added by manufacture, (2) value of agricultural crops and government payments, (3) value of mineral production, and (4) property income. For any given region two aspects of change are considered in each of these categories. One is the change in the relative position of the region within a category. The other is the change in the relative importance of the category in accounting for total national income. Hence if a region has obtained an increasing share of the total value added by the nation's manufactures, and if value added by manufactures has represented an increasing per cent of national income, the region's income can be expected to have increased on both scores. See P. Simpson [62], pp. 26–38.

It should be kept in mind that frequently in studies which attempt to "explain" regional cycles and shifts, it is as important to investigate "residuals" as it is to identify the effects of "explanatory" variables.

[14] Among some of the better writings on the economic base are R. B. Andrews [4, 5]; J. W. Alexander [1, 2]; H. Blumenfeld [8]; Federal Reserve Bank of Kansas City [18]; B. Barford [6]; M. C. Daly [16]; University of New Mexico [70]; Cincinnati City

The economic base type of analysis distinguishes between basic (primary) industry and service (nonbasic or residential) industry. This distinction is in keeping with a premise that has been increasingly taken as a point of departure for regional study. This premise states that the reason for the existence and growth of a region—whether it is a community or a small resource area at one extreme or a huge metropolitan or resource region at the other extreme—lies in the goods and services it produces locally but sells beyond its borders. These "basic" activities not only provide the means of payment for raw materials, food, and manufactured products which the region cannot produce itself but also support the "service" activities, which are principally local in productive scope and market areas.[15]

It was not until the late 1930's that attempts were made to measure quantitatively the basic and service components of individual urban or regional economies. Homer Hoyt developed the idea of a "basic-service ratio." This ratio purports to describe either (1) the proportion between *total* employment in a city's basic or export activities and *total* employment in its service or local activities; or (2) the proportion between the *increase* in employment in a city's basic or export activities and the *increase* in its service or local activities.[16] From the data required to compute this basic-service ratio, a regional multiplier is easily calculated. This multiplier is equal to total (or increase in) employment in both basic and service activities divided by total (or increase in) basic employment.

For example we present in Table 1 a relevant classification of the data required for the calculation of basic-service ratios and regional multipliers for the city of Wichita, Kansas. The unit of measurement is employment.

Planning Commission [15]; G. Hildebrand and A. Mace, Jr. [31]; H. Hoyt [33]; A. M. Weimer and H. Hoyt [75], ch. 18; C. L. Leven [45, 46]; J. M. Mattila and W. R. Thompson [48]; H. M. Mayer [49]; R. L. Steiner [63]; W. F. Stolper and C. M. Tiebout [65]; C. M. Tiebout [67, 68]; E. L. Ullman [69]; A. W. Wilson [77]; R. W. Pfouts [55]; M. D. Thomas [66]; R. W. Pfouts and E. T. Curtis [57]; and V. Roterus and W. Calef [60].

[15] This conception of the economic primacy of a city's exports has existed for many years. (For a synopsis of the historical development of the concept, see J. W. Alexander [1], pp. 247–250.) Depending on the approach taken by the analyst, the concept may appear to be neomercantilistic, stressing the need for exports (export balances) to support local service activities; or it may seem to support the free trader, emphasizing the inability of a community to be self-sufficient and thus its need for specialized exports to pay for all its required imports. (See H. Blumenfeld [8], pp. 118–119.)

[16] Hoyt's initial hurried studies led him to conclude that the ratio in all cities would ordinarily be one to one. Later he discovered through more thorough and comprehensive studies that the basic-service ratio varies markedly among cities. For a resumé of the experiences and circumstances which influenced Hoyt in this development, see R. B. Andrews [5], May 1953, pp. 163–165.

TABLE 1. WICHITA EMPLOYMENT, 1940 AND 1950, CLASSIFIED BY
THE TYPE OF MARKET SERVED

	Employment		Local (Service)		Regional, National, and World (Basic)	
	1940	1950	1940	1950	1940	1950
Total	52,091	88,575	37,148	59,325	14,943	29,250
Agriculture	4,074	3,276	1,109	1,442	2,965	1,834
Total non-agricultural	48,017	85,299	36,039	57,883	11,978	27,416
Mining	925	971	50	71	875	900
Construction	2,837	7,297	2,837	7,297	–	–
Manufacturing	8,692	23,931	2,705	4,605	5,987	19,326
Food and kindred products	2,624	3.243	1,232	1,193	1,392	2,050
Textile mill products	16	53	16	53	–	–
Apparel	146	205	–	–	146	205
Furniture	135	459	135	459	–	–
Printing	1,208	1,714	686	1,200	522	514
Chemicals	172	242	–	–	172	242
Petroleum	572	548	–	–	572	548
Metals	985	1,973	–	–	985	1,973
Machinery	637	1,857	–	–	637	1,857
Transportation equipment	1,561	11,937	–	–	1,561	11,937
Other manufacturing	636	1,700	636	1,700	–	–
Transportation, communications, public utilities	4,473	6,833	3,752	5,576	721	1,257
Wholesale trade	3,003	4,616	1,498	2,774	1,505	1,842
Retail trade	10,216	16,542	8,617	14,509	1,599	2,033
Finance, insurance, and real estate	3,115	4,118	2,729	3,447	386	671
Service	12,105	16,711	11,200	15,324	905	1,387
Public administration	1,765	3,437	1,765	3,437	–	–
Industry not reported	886	843	886	843	–	–

Source: Federal Reserve Bank of Kansas City [18], p. 4. Data based on Census of Population, 1940 and 1950.

Total employment for years 1940 and 1950 is listed in the first two columns, by industry. For each industry the total figure is broken into two parts. That part which produces for and caters to the local market is classified as *service* activity and is noted in the middle two columns of Table 1. That part which produces for (is oriented to) the regional, national, and world markets is classified as *basic* and is noted in the last two columns.

From the materials of Table 1 we may calculate both basic-service ratios and regional employment multipliers. In Table 2 the basic-service ratios are calculated on the basis of total employment in 1940, total employment in 1950, and change in employment in 1940–1950. The corresponding regional employment multipliers are simply the ratio of the total employment to basic employment (or change in total employment to change in

TABLE 2. BASIC-SERVICE RATIOS AND MULTIPLIERS, WICHITA

	Basic-Service Ratio	Regional Employment Multiplier
1. Based on total employment: 1940	$\dfrac{14,943}{37,148} = 1:2.5$	3.5
2. Based on total employment: 1950	$\dfrac{29,250}{59,325} = 1:2.0$	3.0
3. Based on change in employment: 1940–1950	$\dfrac{14,307}{22,177} = 1:1.6$	2.6

basic employment), that is, unity plus the basic-service ratio. It is to be noted that different ratios and multipliers obtain, depending on both the selected key year and the method of computation. That method based on *change* in employment is generally considered to yield the more relevant results, although it is generally recognized that the type of computation employed should depend on the nature and purpose of a particular study.

Some analysts have made extensive use of the employment multiplier concept for projection purposes. By evaluating future prospects of expansion in the *basic* activities of the cities and regions they study, and then applying the employment multipliers derived from the basic-service ratios relating to existing industrial composition, they have forecast future expansions in *total* employment. By the use of employment-to-population ratios, these forecasts are often extended to include the future population that could be supported by the total future employment opportunities.[17]

17 R. B. Andrews [5], May 1953, p. 163.

(Thus this procedure represents one of the many *indirect* methods of projecting population and migration after allowance for other factors, which may be used to supplement the *direct* techniques discussed in Chapters 2 and 3.)

Other analysts have been more cautious about employing the multiplier concept. Many urban and regional economic base studies have had the more limited objective of an improved understanding of the economic composition of the city or region and of its relations with other cities and regions.[18]

Whether the basic-service ratio (already designated in the literature by several different terms) and the associated "simple" regional multiplier are employed for description alone, or are adapted for projection and prediction purposes, numerous limitations are involved in their use. These limitations are both technical and conceptual. We now turn to a discussion of them.[19]

[18] For example, Alexander asserts that the division of a city's economic activities into export and local categories illustrates a "space-relationship" and is thus of more interest to geographers than traditional urban livelihood structure studies. He points out several ways in which the basic-service concept can aid in an understanding of cities:

  1. The concept brings into sharper focus the economic ties of a city or region to other areas. Further, the composition of a city's or region's basic activities may be quite different from that of its total economic structure. Since it is the basic activity which is important to the economic existence and growth of the city or region, the explicit identification of such activity is significant for analysis and for distinguishing between types of regions.

  2. The concept makes possible a more satisfactory classification of cities in terms of regional function. Certain basic activities express a city's service to its surrounding region; by reference to these activities a city can be better classified as commercial, industrial, or governmental.

  3. The concept provides a new and important method of classifying individual businesses. For example, two firms might be engaged in manufacturing, but because of the location of their markets, one could be basic and the other service (J. W. Alexander [1]).

In a recent study, Alexandersson employs the dichotomy of *city-forming* and *city-serving* production. The former produces for markets outside the city's boundaries, whereas the latter produces for the city's own inhabitants. He estimates the per cent of total employment of a city which must be engaged in the *city-serving* portion of any industry as that per cent engaged in the given industry in *that* city which is at the 5 percentile mark *when all cities are ranked according to the percentage of their employment occurring in the given industry*. The amount by which a city's percentage of employment in the given industry exceeds this benchmark measures the extent to which the industry is *city-forming* for the given city (G. Alexandersson [3]). In this manner, Alexandersson derives a basis for classifying cities by several criteria. However, the significance of this basis of classification is to be seriously questioned in view of the discussion of this and succeeding chapters.

[19] A rather complete discussion of these limitations may be found in R. B. Andrews [5] upon whose work we draw heavily. It is significant to note that Andrews after completing an extensive survey and evaluation of economic base theory concludes that "the

1. TECHNICAL DIFFICULTIES

One of the chief technical problems the analyst must face in constructing basic-service ratios concerns the selection of a unit of measurement. Up to now, almost all actual economic base studies have used employment (number of jobs) as such a unit. This partly reflects the fact that employment figures are easier to obtain than are data relating to any other possible unit of measurement. Also, total employment and its breakdown by occupation and industry are generally considered significant economic magnitudes with which planners and policymakers must be concerned. Nevertheless, employment as a unit of measure of a community's basic and service components has drawbacks. First, data on number of jobs do not catch the significance for total expansion of different wage levels in different industries or activities. For example, the same increases in employment for two industries paying significantly different wages lead to different secondary (multiplier) effects.[20] Second, employment data do not reflect the expansionary effects which result over a period of years from changes in physical productivity. Associated with little or no change in employment in basic industry can be considerable expansionary effects resulting from the increase in productivity in these industries.[21]

These difficulties can be overcome to some extent by the use of total payrolls as a unit of measurement. In fact, some studies have employed payrolls as a weighting factor, or at least as a check on conclusions reached from employment data. The use of payrolls as a sole unit of measure, however, is limited by the fact that payrolls give no direct evidence of the actual number of jobholders in any given industry, and that changes in the general price level may vitiate any period-by-period comparison.

A significant drawback of both employment and payrolls as units of measurement is their failure to indicate either precisely or crudely the influence of "unearned" income (primarily property income and income payments from governmental agencies) on a community's basic-service ratio. At least one study has attempted to remedy this defect by computing a basic-service ratio based on estimates of income payments to individuals in the Tucson, Arizona, metropolitan area.[22] Admittedly, the

deepest meaning and utility of the ratio theory lies in its dynamics. For it is from an understanding of dynamics that the city planner can not only predict the action of his economy in differing circumstances but can also take steps toward more effective guidance and control," ([5], Feb. 1955, p 52).

Another balanced discussion of the basic-service ratio as a tool for description and analysis may be found in M. D. Thomas [66].

[20] R. B. Andrews [5], Feb. 1954, p. 53.

[21] *Idem.*

[22] A. W. Wilson [77]. Still another unit of measure which can be used is "value added." For a discussion of the virtues of this unit, see C. L. Leven [45, 46].

estimates were subject to considerable error. The fact, however, that the "unearned" income made up nearly 20 per cent of total estimated income payments is significant because of the very magnitude of the figure.[23] Clearly, deeper insight into the character of an area's economic support can be obtained when employment data are supplemented by income data.[24]

Another bothersome technical problem is that of identifying basic and service components.[25] In most of the actual economic base studies which have been made, the practice with respect to commercial or industrial firms has been first to divide them into those that are wholly basic, those that are wholly service, and those that are "mixed." For example, in the Wichita study, the aircraft firms were considered wholly basic, the construction industry wholly service, and wholesale and retail trading firms mixed.[26] Once the decision is made to consider a firm entirely basic or service, there is no further problem involved in allocating its employment, payroll, or whatever the measurement unit may be, to the basic or service category. It is in connection with the "mixed" class of firms that the serious allocation problems arise.

In many studies of large metropolitan regions the ultimate basis for determining the basic and service components of *mixed* industries is some form of location quotient (or concentration ratio). This is true of the Wichita study, in which for each industry the per capita employment in Wichita is divided by the per capita employment in the United States.[27] Ratios greater than unity were taken to indicate an export or basic industry and the amount by which the ratio exceeded unity to indicate the extent to which total employment or payroll is basic.[28] As indicated in Chapter 5, the unqualified use of location quotients (or concentration ratios), whether for allocation or other purposes, makes implicit assumptions. It assumes that, with reference to the mixed industry, local patterns of use and habits of consumption are the same as average national ones, and that all local demands are served by local production. Clearly there are many instances in which either or both of these assumptions are erroneous. The author

[23] A. W. Wilson [77], pp. 3–4.

[24] It should perhaps be pointed out that in the Tucson case the actual numerical values of the basic-service ratio (and therefore the derived multiplier) were not much different when calculated on the basis of employment, of earned income payments, or of all income payments. However, it does not follow that these values will not differ significantly for other regions or cities.

[25] See R. B. Andrews [5], May 1954, pp. 164–172.

[26] Federal Reserve Bank of Kansas City [18], p. 3.

[27] Also, the location quotient used involved the comparison of Wichita's percentage share of each industry with its percentage share of United States population. For definition of location quotient, see Chapter 5, section B.

[28] For an excellent detailed discussion of the construction and implications of concentration and similar ratios, see J. M. Mattila and W. R. Thompson [48].

of the Wichita study examined each mixed industry to determine whether there were local deviations from average national consumption patterns and, if so, modified accordingly the allocation of an industry's employment.[29] However, the resulting modifications are not without question. Further, there are situations where adjustment of the location quotient is extremely difficult, if at all possible. For example, how treat a situation where the entire output of a firm or industry is "exported," although a substantial quantity of the same or similar product is "imported" and consumed locally? Use of an unmodified location quotient in such an instance would lead to an overestimate of local or service employment.[30]

It is possible to utilize an alternative approach to the problem of identifying basic and service components. Instead of allocation on the basis of concentration ratios, empirical information with respect to the location of each firm's market may be used. For example, if it is known that 70 per cent of a firm's sales are to customers outside the community and 30 per cent to local customers, at first flush it appears logical to allocate 70 per cent of the firm's employment or payroll to the basic category and 30 per cent to the service category. This approach is often used in combination with the concentration ratio method. For example, in the Wichita study, the allocation of certain mixed industries as well as the determination of industries wholly basic and wholly service was partly based on available empirical data on sales, markets, etc. However, some economic base studies employ the empirical firm-by-firm approach exclusively.[31] Information regarding each firm's proportions of export and local sales is obtained, usually by personal interview or questionnaire, and these proportions are applied to the firm's total employment or payroll to determine the basic and service components. There are a number of limitations to this method.[32] For anything but small communities, the firm-by-firm canvass (which has also been suggested in connection with social accounting studies) becomes tedious and time consuming as well as expensive.[33]

[29] Federal Reserve Bank of Kansas City [18], p. 3.

[30] A related technical difficulty is associated with the choice of a relevant industrial classification. If a very fine breakdown of industry is used, many activities (such as transistor production and uranium mining) will be highly localized and among areas exhibit a wide range of location quotients. If a rather gross breakdown of industry is employed, general activities (such as manufacturing and trade) will be less localized and among areas exhibit a much narrower range of location quotients.

[31] For example, see J. W. Alexander [2].

[32] See J. W. Alexander [1], p. 259; R. B. Andrews [5], May 1954, pp. 168–170; and H. Blumenfeld [8], pp. 120–121.

[33] However, when in addition to an economic base study a team of investigators contemplates several other types of studies (such as regional income, social accounting, commodity flow, input-output, and industrial complex), most of the expense of a firm-by-firm canvass can be shared.

Furthermore, the method is necessarily dependent on the estimates of firm officials or on firm sales records, both of which may often be inaccurate with respect to the destination of the firm's sales. If the questionnaire method is used, the problem of inadequate number or quality of returns often arises. A problem that applies particularly to retail stores is the inability to distinguish accurately on-the-spot sales to residents and nonresidents of the community. This difficulty may assume major proportions if the community attracts large numbers of tourists, to whom sales logically constitute exports and thus reflect basic activity.

A more fundamental difficulty inherent in the firm-by-firm approach—one that should be considered as much a conceptual as a technical defect—exists because of the *indirect* and linked nature of modern production. In any large city or region there are likely to be independent, specialized firms whose products are sold almost exclusively to other firms in the same city to be incorporated into finished products for export. Strict application of the firm-by-firm approach would result in the employment of the specialized firm being assigned to the local or service category. On the other hand, if the manufacture of the specialized intermediate product occurs in a division or subsidiary of the final producer, the associated employment will be classified as basic, since it contributes to the final product which is sold outside the community. Clearly, some adjustment must be made to take account of such "linked" activities.[34] It seems apparent that if most of the specialized firm's product becomes an integral part of a final product which is almost entirely exported, the firm's employment should be considered basic, regardless of the fact that its sales are all local. However, there are cases which are not so clearcut. Andrews cites the example of coal mined locally and sold for fuel to a local steel producer exporting finished steel. Is the coal mine a basic or a service activity?[35] And what of the electric power company and the telephone company that serve the steel mill and the coal mine? Ullman points out that "It might of course be argued that if foundries serving local export industries are classified as basic . . . then drug store clerks or lawyers serving the same industry should also be considered basic and that even the drug store clerks serving lawyers who serve basic industry should be basic, etc."[36]

It should be noted that the location quotient method of identification avoids some of the questions which emerge because of linked activities. If a high ratio of concentration is associated with the steel industry in a community and if this steel industry is the chief customer of the local coal

[34] In the Wichita study an industry is considered basic if it serves in the area another industry principally of the export category.

[35] R. B. Andrews [5], Aug. 1954, pp. 267–268.

[36] E. L. Ullman [69].

mining industry, coal mining will probably be associated with a quotient greater than unity, although its entire sales may be local. On the other hand, unless steel making and coal mining specifically require in large quantity the services of lawyers and drugstore clerks, those activities will tend to reflect average population needs and be associated with quotients not too much greater than unity.

It is evident that differences in methods of basic and service component identification and in methods of dealing with such questions as linked activities can cause significant variation in the computed basic-service ratio, and thus in any derived multiplier value.[37] This question of methods is also tied to the conceptual problem of determining the appropriate type of multiplier, which will be discussed later.

Still another issue turns around the delineation of the geographic area for which a base study is to be made. This is a complex problem which has been extensively discussed elsewhere.[38] It is apparent, however, that the area chosen should form a region meaningful in terms of the study. Hence, the choice of the area depends on the purpose of an investigation and the character of regional ties as well as on practical considerations of data availability, of the possibility of delimiting labor market areas, and similar matters. It should be fully appreciated that the analytical procedures, the resulting numerical values of the various ratios, and the conclusions of a study may certainly be greatly affected by the base area boundaries chosen.[39]

[37] In addition to the more or less general technical problems already discussed, any specific study is likely to run into a number of special or particular problems. Examples are how to treat schools and universities and local and nonlocal government activities. The "products" of universities and government activities are not sold on the market; hence there can be no ratio of export to local sales. However, it is possible to identify the source of support for such nonmarketed activities, for example, taxes in the case of government work and state-supported schools, and to determine how much of that support comes from inside and how much from outside the community.

Another specific problem relates to the commuter. This problem arises because basic data may be available only for communities or regions defined by arbitrary or economically artificial boundaries, or because the community or region being studied is itself economically artificial. The principal difficulty involved is that of obtaining an accurate estimate of commutation into and out of the area. For further discussion see R. B. Andrews [5], Aug. 1954, pp. 261–269 and H. Blumenfeld [8], p. 125.

[38] R. B. Andrews [5], Nov. 1954, pp. 309–319.

[39] V. Roterus and W. Calef [60] neatly indicate how the definitions of both basic and service employment, and hence the basic-service ratio, change as an analyst proceeds from one extreme of a crossroads hamlet to the other extreme of the nation. Taking the hamlet as an area for analysis, the investigator must classify employment in the hamlet's tavern, filling station, and grocery store as primarily basic (export). These activities, however, must be classified as service as soon as the relevant area of analysis is expanded to embrace the township within which this hamlet is located. And

2. CONCEPTUAL DIFFICULTIES

Attention is now turned to difficulties of a more fundamental nature—difficulties inherent in the economic base and regional multiplier concepts themselves and in their use for projection purposes. It can perhaps be generally agreed that a careful economic base study contributes to an understanding of the functions of the various economic components of a city or region. In particular, it identifies and highlights the export activities, which to a greater or lesser extent are necessary for the existence of the city or region. This also helps to point up the city's or region's economic connections with and services to other cities and regions.[40] However, the present discussion is concerned not with these static or descriptive aspects but with the use of the economic base and regional multiplier concepts in a dynamic setting for projection. (Supplementary discussion of the implications for an economic base study of a city's position within an evolving hierarchy of central places is presented in the Appendix to the chapter.)

The use of a multiplier to estimate the results of future changes in basic activities of a city or region is an attempt at prediction. This prediction

in turn, the basic (export) employment of the township becomes primarily service activity as successively larger areas of analysis are defined. . . . Finally, practically all activity becomes service activity when the nation is viewed as the relevant area for analysis.

[40] It must be emphasized that even in a static sense an economic base study falls far short of the goal of *complete* economic understanding of a city or region. Blumenfeld points out that the preoccupation with export activities leads to virtually complete disregard of the other side of the trade coin—imports. Thus the picture of the city's or region's ties with outside areas is really only half a picture. See H. Blumenfeld [8], pp. 121–123.

With reference to planning or policy measures, the economic base study probably tends to direct attention to the prospects of growth or decline in specific export industries. A better procedure would be to analyze the general locational and other advantages which the area possesses and all the possible industries which could benefit from these advantages. Furthermore, imports should be scrutinized in order to determine the conditions or circumstances which would allow an advantageous shift from imports to local production.

Blumenfeld criticizes the fundamental nature attributed to exports by the terms "base" and "basic." He contends that although export industries and activities are to some degree necessary to the community's existence, it is wrong to consider each specific export industry as basic, because there is always the possibility that in time any industry may decline and disappear and its place be taken by a new industry. Furthermore, any export industry is dependent on the existence of the organized community with its labor pool, its transport and communications network, and the whole complex of local income-generating activities. Thus the city or community itself and its local activities are "basic" and the export industries "serve" the community by furnishing means of payment for needed imports. See H. Blumenfeld [8], pp. 130–132. Also, refer to C. M. Tiebout [67], R. L. Steiner [63], R. W. Pfouts and E. T. Curtis [57], and R. B. Andrews [7] for relevant discussion.

is based on past or present data and is subject to error because of future qualitative changes in social, technological, and economic conditions, the influences of many of which cannot be crudely, let alone precisely, estimated. One of the least troublesome changes to identify is the general increase in productivity which makes possible the support of more and more service-type activities.[41] This will apply to a growing national economy generally and therefore to a greater or lesser extent to regions within it.

Along with the broad productivity increase associated with national economic growth, there will be changes in locational factors affecting any particular region. These changes may tend to make it either more self-sufficient or more specialized. For example, as the population of a community grows, it provides a constantly growing local market. This tends to encourage the local development of a succession of industries which are significantly affected by economies of scale, and whose products must be imported until the community's effective demand reaches a size large enough to absorb the output of an economic-size unit of production. On the other hand, improvements in transport technology and, in general, in production technology will in some industries tend to expand the market of producers having access to superior sources of raw materials or other productive factors. From location analysis, increasing geographic specialization and interdependence may be anticipated. As a consequence, some regions will gain, others lose. In any event, the basic-service ratio for any region will tend to change over time in a manner reflecting the operation of these and many other location forces.

Aside from the fact that in the future a region may not experience modifications of its economic framework similar in type and character to what occurred in the past, there is yet another reason why the region's over-all basic-service ratio *at any one time* is quite likely to be inaccurate as a basis for computing a multiplier value. This is a result of the fact that the change in volume of service activity associated with a change in basic activity is typically not an instantaneous but a delayed reaction. At any given time, the over-all ratio may well be influenced (distorted) by recent changes in basic activity whose multiplier effects have not yet appeared. This difficulty can be resolved in some measure by calculating the basic-service ratio from data showing changes in basic and service activity totals over a period of time. From an ideal standpoint, this period of time over which past changes are computed should be chosen so as to include as few of the complicating influences mentioned earlier as possible. Some analysts might argue that since many such complicating influences are

41 R. B. Andrews [5], May 1955, pp. 149–150.

long-run in character, it would seem that relatively short "undisturbed" periods are best. However, in the Wichita study, multiplier values computed for periods less than ten years in length show a range of variations wide enough to render them virtually useless for purposes of prediction.[42] In short, the difficulty of this argument may be summarized as follows : in order to be conceptually valid, a multiplier derived from a basic-service ratio must be considered as a short-run phenomenon, yet evidence shows that it needs a comparatively long time to work out.[43]

But let us ignore these general equilibrium difficulties. Postulate a community in which all long-run influences are unchanging and in which the effects of increases in basic components are fully worked out. Assume that the unit of measurement to be used is employment, and that adequate data are available to show changes in employment in each industry or activity during recent years. There are still difficulties facing the analyst, whether he uses the firm-by-firm approach or the location quotient (concentration ratio) method.

An economic base multiplier derived by a strict application of the firm-by-firm method can be claimed to be a combination of two types of multipliers, which at times are rather difficult to unravel. The *first* type of multiplier is determined by the extent to which the *final* export products contain or utilize intermediate products locally manufactured ; for example, in the case cited of a local steel producer exporting finished steel, it would take into account the coal mined locally which was used to produce this steel *plus* the electric power required both to mine the needed coal as well as to produce the steel *plus* lawyer services required in connection with the production of these outputs, *plus* . . . etc. The *second* type of multiplier is the Keynesian-type multiplier dependent on changes in local income flows and determined by the consumption habits of employees of the export industry, of the intermediate industry, and of the service industry ; for example, it takes into account that part of coal production, steel production, lawyer services, and other products and services demanded by consumers as a result of the new income generated by the export of steel and by the production of goods and services *technically* required to produce that steel.

Although an economic base multiplier derived by the strict application

---

[42] For the period 1940–1950 the regional employment multiplier was 2.55. For the periods 1939–1944 and 1939–1948, the same multiplier was approximately 1.2 and 3.0, respectively. These different values for the multiplier reflect the highly fluctuating character of employment in aircraft and the relatively stable character of employment in service activities (Federal Reserve Bank of Kansas City, [18], pp. 4–7).

[43] In this connection, also see J. Gillies and W. Grigsby [26] and the discussion in the Appendix to this chapter.

of the firm-by-firm method may be claimed to be a combination of two types of multipliers, the economic base multiplier associated with the location quotient method embraces only one type of multiplier, namely the Keynesian-type multiplier. But this statement is true only if we assume that accurate adjustment is made for all local deviations from national averages and that, if products are produced locally, local demands for such products will be supplied from local production.[44]

The analyst using the firm-by-firm method can eliminate the first of its two multiplier components by determining the extent of linked activities and considering local intermediate linked components as basic to the same extent that the final products represent basic activity. This procedure in effect provides one logical basis for attacking the problem discussed earlier of identifying the basic (export) and service (local) components of any given activity. The part of any activity that is linked technologically or productionwise to export trade is classified as export. The part of an activity that can be linked to export trade only via household income and demand and local capital formation is classified as local.[45] (As will be evident when we discuss the interregional and regional input-output techniques in Chapter 8, the former part, that is, the technologically linked part, can be determined via a round-by-round iteration with a structural matrix from which the household and capital formation sectors have been excluded.[46]) Thus, that part of the lawyer's activity required to service that part of the electric power activity required to mine that part of the

[44] However the multiplier is calculated, its value will partially reflect over the observed period any increases or decreases in local investment activity. For the multiplier to be what it is represented to be in economic base studies, one more additional assumption must be made, namely, that the rate of local investment remains constant over the period.

[45] This basis of classification is consistent with a theoretical framework which considers household demand *and* local investment as determined to a large extent endogenously and export trade as determined to a large extent exogenously. There are, of course, other possible procedures for classifying local investment activity and those parts of other activities linked with local investment. Each procedure tends to yield a different value for the Keynesian-type multiplier. For some further relevant discussion see the following section.

Note that this basis of classification cuts through the inconsistency posed by the following two statements: (1) all of any given activity may be classified as *oriented to export trade*, since all activities are mutually dependent, and any one in its entirety may be linked with export activity; and (2) all of any given activity may be classified as *oriented to local trade*, since again all the given activity may be linked with others which directly serve local needs.

[46] In practice, a complete round-by-round iteration is seldom required. Frequently, an interation of a relatively few rounds plus approximation of subsequent rounds will suffice.

The parts of activities not linked through production to export activity can readily be determined residually.

coal required by that fraction of steel activity producing for export trade is to be classified as export activity. In contrast that part of the lawyer's activity required to service that part of a drugstore operation, or for that matter of any activity directly oriented to local household demand and local capital investment, must be classified as local (service). Thus, those parts of activities directly serving the demands of householders employed in exporting activity are still designated as local (service).[47]

Although it is possible for the analyst using the firm-by-firm method to eliminate the first of its two multiplier components by considering local intermediate-linked components as basic (export) activity, it does not follow that this step is desirable. Aside from the difficulties of determining intermediate linkage, the analyst who uses the firm-by-firm approach does so partly because he is convinced of the primacy of export activities. He would doubtless consider linked intermediate activities as *results* of the production and exports of the final products and thus may not wish to allocate linked activities to the basic category. He may consider the double multiplier as the more relevant.

It is quite likely that one important use of this "double" multiplier or any other regional multiplier is to apply it to proposed or potential employment increases in specific export industries in order to estimate the effect on total employment. (We assume that the major difficulties involved in making reliable projections of specific basic activities have been met, partly through the use of techniques to be described in subsequent chapters.) For example, if a firm which exports automobile accessories triples its plant size and employment, what will be the resulting total increase in employment?

The multiplier presumably provides a basis for such an estimate. The difficulty is that the multiplier value is an *average* and does not necessarily apply to any specific export activity. Industry A may import all its intermediate products, whereas industry B may purchase all its intermediates locally. Thus the appropriate multiplier to apply to an increase in B's employment would be considerably larger than the one to apply to an identical increase in A's employment. This illustrates the limitation of applying an essentially averaging technique to situations involving only one or a few individual components of the average.[48]

---

[47] For an actual determination of the export and local parts of activities of a region, see C. L. Leven [46], Part II.

[48] The misleading effects of averaging also crop up in comparative analysis. Evidence indicates that multiplier effects of an industrial expansion vary not only by type of industry but for any given industry by type and size of region in which expansion takes place. Among others, see H. Blumenfeld [8] and E. L. Ullman [69]. Also see the discussion in the Appendix to this chapter.

A similar difficulty arises if an attempt is made to apply an economic base multiplier derived by the location quotient method to specific industry employment increases. In this method the problem of the nature of individual linkages is bypassed. But by so doing there is no way of determining the linked basic employment increase associated with an increase in employment in a particular final export activity. Using the same illustration as before, although the multiplier value would be the same for A as for B, the *multiplicand* (the magnitude that is to be multiplied) should be considerably larger for B than it is for A since it should include the increase in employment to produce the intermediate goods for B.

One way to approach this troublesome problem of individual linkages would be by use of the concept of value added locally. In the illustration, the sales value of B's extra output less the value of any extra imported intermediates could be compared to the same thing for A's extra output. Industry B, involving more linkages, would show a higher amount than A. If it were, say, twice as much, the multiplier or multiplicand, depending on the method, could be estimated at twice as much for B as for A. Of course, the problem remains of estimating the actual numerical values. Possibly this could be accomplished by comparing the value added per worker in A and B with an average or over-all value added per worker which would be associated with the average or over-all computed multiplier or multiplicand.[49] Admittedly, this approach to the problem encounters additional difficulties. For one thing, value-added figures are affected by many more factors than volume of employment. Furthermore, this approach requires considerably more empirical data on product interconnections, commodity flows, and trade balances than are ordinarily available in an economic base study. It could very well be argued that if such data were available, a better and more direct way to approach the whole problem would be to set up interregional input-output tables to be discussed later. These tables would greatly facilitate tracing the effects of individual changes, whether in basic or service activities.

It is quite evident from this discussion (which covers only some of the more important shortcomings and problems in economic base study and its associated regional multiplier analysis) and from the supplementary discussion in the Appendix to this chapter that a regional multiplier derived from the basic-service ratio of an economic base study has a strictly limited degree of usefulness and validity.[50] As an instrument for projection, it can be used only under certain ideal conditions. Even then, it can

[49] In this connection see C. L. Leven [44], pp. 369–371, [45].

[50] It is not surprising that statistical tests applied to economic base hypotheses fail to support such hypotheses, particularly when these hypotheses are narrowly construed. For example, see R. W. Pfouts [56] and R. W. Pfouts and E. T. Curtis [57].

give no more than an average or approximate value. This is not to deny that the economic base study itself is useful. Its value, particularly in a static, descriptive sense, has already been pointed out. The analyst, however, should realize its limitations and should be especially cautious about extending its application to include the computation of regional multipliers for projection purposes. Above all, he should supplement its use with other forms and types of regional analysis. And without question he will have to consider at least implicitly a framework to account for interregional relations in order to catch interregional "feedback" effects.

D. The Interregional Trade Multiplier

Economic base studies have not been quite as circumscribed in conception as depicted in the previous section. Many of them have adequately recognized the close connection between the forces governing interregional trade and those affecting the expansion and contraction of a given region. However, it must be said that economic base studies, almost by definition, have placed chief emphasis on the local area.

In contrast stand the interregional trade multiplier studies. They have focused on interregional factors, frequently to the neglect of forces internal to a region. In their treatment of regions which are "open" economies they have given primary attention to the transmission to other regions of impulses emitted at any local level via changes in imports, exports, investment, consumption, and income. Direction and intensity of transmission, the nature of carrier industries and interregional interindustrial relationships, the cyclical and secular sensitivities of different types of import and export mixes have been topics of particular concern. When compared with studies of the regional multiplier derived via the economic base concept, investigations into the interregional trade multiplier can be said to be theoretically more precise and to involve a much greater use of mathematical functions. Unfortunately, empirical work on interregional trade multipliers, although promising considerable fruit, has been scanty.

The basic elements of an interregional trade multiplier are certain Keynesian-type relations.[51] A region's income, Y, is typically defined as

(1) $$Y = I + E + C - M$$

where I is the region's investment expenditures, C is its consumption expenditures, and E and M are its exports and imports respectively.[52] If

---

[51] For some account of the development of the foreign trade multiplier, with which our interregional trade multiplier is almost identical, see J. S. Chipman [14], pp. 13–15.

[52] In this and the following two paragraphs we draw heavily upon R. Vining [72], pp. 212–218.

we now distinguish between imports of consumption goods (M_c) and imports of investment goods (M_i) where $M = M_c + M_i$, and if we consider the *average propensity to consume local goods*, namely, the ratio of consumption expenditure on local goods to local income, that is, $(C - M_c)/Y$, we note

(2) $$\frac{C - M_c}{Y} = \frac{C}{Y} - \frac{M_c}{Y} = \frac{C}{Y}\left(1 - \frac{M_c}{C}\right) = p(1 - q)$$

where p is the average propensity to consume, and q is the proportion of local consumption expenditures accounted for by imports of consumer goods.

If we now posit that only consumer goods are imported so that by definition $M = M_c$ (and $M_i = 0$), and if we divide equation 1 through by Y, and as given by equation 2 substitute $p(1 - q)$ for $(C - M)/Y$, we obtain

(3) $$1 = \frac{I + E}{Y} + p(1 - q)$$

If we transpose to the left the second term on the right, and let $1 - p(1 - q) = 1/k$, we find

(4) $$\frac{1}{k} = \frac{I + E}{Y}; \text{ or}$$
$$Y = k(I + E)$$

In this oversimplified formulation k is the interregional trade multiplier. It is an "average" multiplier. It indicates the multiple regional income is of the sum of regional investment and exports.[53]

A similar procedure can be followed to derive the "marginal" multiplier. It can be shown that

(5) $$\Delta Y = k'\Delta(I + E)$$

where $k' = 1/[1 - p'(1 - q')]$. Here k' is the "marginal" multiplier, p' is the marginal propensity to consume (dC/dY), and q' is the marginal rate of change of imports of consumer goods with change in total consumption (dM_c/dC).[54]   Equation 5 purports to indicate the change in regional income resulting from (and as a multiple of) a change in regional investment, exports, or both.

A more rigorous statement of the interregional trade multiplier relation explicitly recognizes and allows for imports of investment goods, desig-

---

[53] Generally involved in this formulation are the equilibrium equality of savings plus imports to investment plus exports, and the assumptions that consumption is a well-behaved function of income and that consumption goods import is a well-behaved function of total consumption.

[54] The marginal propensity to consume local goods is therefore $p'(1 - q')$.

nated as M_i. Since the import of an investment good substitutes for the regional production of such a good, such an import must be subtracted from regional investment if the expansionary effect of regional investment on regional output and income is to be identified. Hence, in these equations $I - M_i$ should be substituted for I.

Further, the reciprocal relations of regional imports and exports must be introduced. In a world of many regions, region A's imports serve to stimulate the expansion of other regions since these imports are the exports of these other regions. As the incomes of these other regions rise, so do their imports from A which, being exports from the standpoint of A, serve to stimulate A's economy, and so forth. This modification necessitates a distinction between exports of investment goods E_i and exports of consumption goods E_c where $E = E_i + E_c$, since these two types of exports when considered as imports into other economies have differential implications for these other economies. Unlike the first approximative formulation given in equations 1–5, in which the exports of a region are considered an independent or autonomous magnitude, this more rigorous formulation postulates that a region's exports are a function of the incomes of other regions, and that these incomes are influenced by the imports of the region under consideration, which in turn are a function of its own income. Thus, the multiplier effect of, say, an autonomous increase in a region's home investment will be influenced not only by its own savings (consumption) and import functions but also, via indirect effects on its own exports, by the savings and import functions of other regions.[55]

[55] For an example, see L. Metzler [50]. Also see the discussion of sector multipliers (although without reference to regions per se) in R. Goodwin [27], J. S. Chipman [13], and W. Beckerman [7].

An interesting two-region model of this sort has been developed by Fouraker. Distinguishing between *autonomous* and *induced* investment, and assuming that a region's imports of consumption goods, imports of investment goods, savings, taxes, and induced investment are each a simple linear function of the region's Gross Product, Fouraker derives the following multipliers:

$$k_{1.1} = \frac{s_2}{s_1 s_2 - m_1 m_2}$$

$$k_{1.2} = \frac{m_1}{s_1 s_2 - m_1 m_2}$$

The first multiplier refers to the effect on its Gross Product of a change in autonomous investment in the first region; the second multiplier refers to the effect of the same change on the second region's Gross Product. (If the two regions constitute the nation, the sum of the two multipliers refers to the effect of the same change on Gross National Product). In these equations, where subscripts refer to the relevant region, s is equal to the sum of the marginal propensity to save, to import consumer goods, to import investment goods, plus the effective tax rate and minus the marginal propensity to invest (induced); and m is equal to the sum of the marginal propensities to import consumer goods and to import investment goods. See L. Fouraker [19], pp. H-1 to H-3.

There are many types of interregional trade multiplier formulations which are possible. Each involves its own particular emphasis on the several variables, parameters, and types of functions already alluded to and others not mentioned.[56] Clearly, the choice of any specific formulation depends very much on the nature of the region or regions under investigation, the character of the problems on hand, and the specific objectives of the inquiry. But whatever the region(s), the problems, and the objectives, it is well to recognize that many of the functional relationships involved are extremely difficult to estimate empirically.[57] Hence, the chief use of the interregional trade multiplier, at least in its more rigorous formulations, is as an aid in reaching certain qualitative conclusions about the long- or short-term behavior of different types of regions. For example, "under given conditions, an increase in region A's home investment would tend to stimulate local industry more than would be the case for a similar increase in region B's home investment," or "because of the character of region C's exports and imports, region C is likely to be more affected by national economic fluctuations than region D."

In exploring this qualitative phase of interregional trade multiplier analysis, Vining has found the ratio of the marginal to the average multiplier useful as a *measure of the relative stability* of a region, that is,

$$\frac{k'}{k}, \quad \text{or} \quad \frac{1 - p(1 - q)}{1 - p'(1 - q')}$$

[56] For example, Chipman has developed a set of biregional multipliers which apply to the effect of not only a change in autonomous investment (as Fouraker's do), but also a change in the savings function, or in the induced investment function, or in the import function. Further, Chipman has formulated generalized multisector multipliers (J. S. Chipman [14], chs. 4–6).

Another construction of considerable interest is Simpson's. His construction implicitly assumes that changes in a particular region's imports will have a negligible effect on the incomes of other regions, and that the given region's exports are thus an autonomous magnitude. Further, it sets the value of imports of consumer goods in fixed proportion to the value of consumer goods consumed and produced at home, and the value of imports of investment goods in fixed proportion to the value of investment goods produced and used at home. For full details, see P. B. Simpson [62], pp. 78–80.

Also see R. M. Williams [76], pp. 47–48; R. W. Pfouts [56]; J. Gilbert [25]; and J. V. Krutilla [42], pp. 126–132.

[57] Vining states that he originally hoped to utilize regional multipliers to predict short-run regional business changes but became much less hopeful after encountering the measurement problems involved. As he put it, "even though the functions involved could be so formulated as to provide the requisite short-run stability in time, it is difficult to conceive of the range of statistical error being narrowed to useful dimensions" ([72], p. 212).

This measure indicates the relative change in income for a given relative change in *net* investment plus exports,[58] that is, in $I - M_i + E$, which we shall henceforth designate as R. Accordingly, the more of its consumer goods a region imports, that is, the greater is q, the larger will be $1 - p(1 - q)$, and thus the greater will be the relative change in income in response to a given relative change in R (that is, in net investment plus exports). Also, the less a region's short-run income demand elasticity for its *imported* consumption goods, the less will be q', the smaller will be $1 - p'(1 - q')$, and thus the greater will be the relative change in income per given relative change in R. Finally, of direct bearing on these two relations is a third, namely, the greater the income demand elasticities of other regions for a given region's export commodities, the greater the relative change in the given region's R in response to a given relative change in national income.[59]

The full implications of this type of qualitative analysis can be best illustrated by Figure 1 which has been developed by Vining. This figure portrays fluctuations in income for an hypothetical national economy and for each of its four constituent regions. Two of these regions, namely regions I and III, were given structural features which lead to relative instability of income as the regions react to changes in investment; the other two, namely regions II and IV, were given a structure which contributes to relative stability of income.[60] The critical significance of regional structure and the obvious value to a regional analyst of knowing the particular structure of his region are evident.

In another connection, Fouraker has examined general economic instability among regions which may result from the growth of an underdeveloped region. With a biregion model, he suggests that the tendency of underdeveloped regions to place chief emphasis on the growth of home industry as their incomes expand may lead to their having negatively sloped import functions. Where these regions have as neighbors more

---

[58] Such a measure for an interregional system is comparable to Keynes's measure of relative stability, namely,

$$\frac{\dfrac{dY}{Y}}{\dfrac{dI}{I}}, \quad \text{or} \quad \frac{1 - \dfrac{C}{Y}}{1 - \dfrac{dC}{dY}},$$

for a closed economy.

[59] R. Vining [72], pp. 213–215. Also for the use of this measure in interpreting actual experience of regions, see R. Vining [72], pp. 217–218, and [71], especially pp. 66–68.

Generalizations similar to Vining's are contained in Williams [76], p. 48.

[60] For full details on this model, see R. Vining [73], pp. 93–97.

mature regions (with positive import functions), it is possible for an increase in the incomes of underdeveloped regions to set off a cyclical process of income expansion and contraction in all regions.[61]

Despite the recognition that the primary use of interregional trade multiplier studies is to arrive at general, qualitative conclusions, some

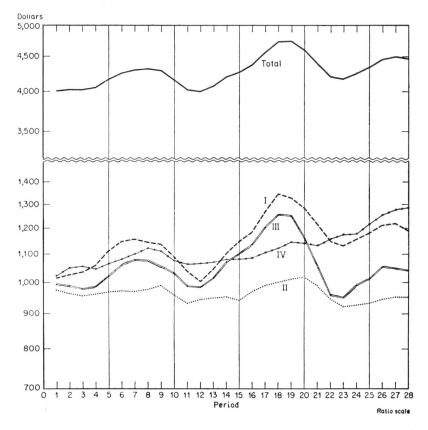

Figure 1. Income payments received in each of the four regions and the "total economy" for a four-region hypothetical model. Source: R. Vining [73], p. 95.

empirical estimation has been attempted. For a few agricultural regions in Arkansas, for which it was rather legitimate to use models in which exports are considered an autonomous variable, Vining was able to collect (and estimate) sufficient data to arrive at multipliers of approximately 2.

---

[61] Of course, the possibility of such cycles, as well as their behavior patterns, depends on the various average and marginal propensities discussed. For fuller discussion, see L. Fouraker [19].

In making such a computation for the Pine Bluff region, Vining had to subtract from the census data on the per cent of total employment engaged in agriculture that part (an estimate) producing output consumed on the farm, and that part (another rough estimate) producing for the local market. To the remainder had to be added the per cent of total employment engaged in lumbering from which had to be subtracted that part producing for the local lumber market. Next, an allowance had to be made for those engaged in miscellaneous export activities, in order to arrive at the over-all per cent engaged in export activities. Additionally, an estimate had to be made of those engaged in home investment. Finally, employment estimates had to be converted into value of output estimates.[62]

The procedure just described illustrates the point that because the relevant functional relationships are extremely difficult to estimate, the analyst must use an indirect approach; he must compare, *ex post*, magnitudes of total employment or product value with employment or product value associated with exports and home investment. But this is essentially the same procedure as is used in economic base studies. It leads to an estimate of the numerical multiplier value but furnishes the analyst little additional understanding of the many complex economic relationships behind that value. The method itself is subject to most of the practical and conceptual difficulties discussed in the previous section on regional multipliers derived from economic base studies; these difficulties we need not repeat here. Furthermore, the analyst must explicitly face the problem of estimating both autonomous and induced home investment. In the terminology of economic base study, he must include in "basic activity" autonomous home investment production or employment as well as production or employment in the export industries. In this sense the interregional trade multiplier as derived à la Vining is superior to the regional multiplier derived by an orthodox economic base study.[63] This superiority becomes especially marked when it is appreciated that for some, if not many, regions a significant and perhaps major portion of local investment may be considered autonomous. Indeed, it is logical to expect that under

---

[62] Vining emphasizes that his estimate of a multiplier value of 2 is of the roughest nature and is intended merely to illustrate the possible order of magnitude of the multiplier for a rural region. P. B. Simpson ([62], pp. 79–80) estimates the multiplier value for a "fairly small region" in an even rougher fashion. He states that the propensity to save, q_s, for such a region can be taken as 0.25, and that 0.5 may be considered a typical value for the propensity to import, q_c. These values substituted into his multiplier expression give it a numerical value of 2.

[63] If an economic base study employs the firm-by-firm method of analysis, typically all local investment activity is assigned to the "service" category. If it employs the location quotient method, only that portion of the region's home investment above the national average is assigned to the "basic" category.

certain conditions exports themselves depend partially and indirectly on local investment.[64]

Presumably some method could be developed to identify and measure the employment or production representing both autonomous and induced local investment.[65]   Once developed, it might be considered as merely a modification or adjustment of the procedure of the economic base study. Ultimately, the analyst might combine the export and autonomous local investment figures and compare the sum with the remaining amount (covering local or service and induced local investment employment) to secure the basic-service ratio, from which the multiplier value could be derived.

However, this modification cannot be achieved without considerable difficulty; and the hazards of applying an over-all multiplier value to estimate the effects of a change in a particular export industry or activity mount in number.   In addition to the hazards due to different degrees of economic linkage associated with different activities, there are hazards arising because other types of linkage must be considered.   As an instance, an expansion in the output of an export industry may directly stimulate investment expenditure by one or more of its local suppliers.   Concomitantly, investment expenditures by these same suppliers may be indirectly induced (via either effective or anticipated demand or both) by the rising level of income caused by the increased exports.   But how determine the amount of home investment which is induced?   This problem becomes particularly perplexing when we recognize that the behavior of induced investment generally, to say nothing of its variation in individual cases, is one of the complex relationships which help determine but are not explained by an empirically derived over-all multiplier value.

One final point.   The calculation of the ratio of the sum of export and autonomous local investment employment to total employment yields an average multiplier only.   A marginal multiplier would of course be more useful for predicting short-run changes and cyclical movements, but such a multiplier cannot be inferred from average data.   As already intimated, the average and marginal propensities to import are likely to be quite different.[66]

[64] See the interesting discussion by C. M. Tiebout [67], and D. C. North [53].

[65] Vining's method for the Pine Bluff region case was merely to assume that local investment would not exceed roughly triple the value of local construction.   Since construction in the region accounted for 3 per cent of total employment, it was estimated that total local investment would amount to 10 per cent of total employment and Gross Regional Product (R. Vining [72], p. 216).

[66] For example, although Vining estimated the average multiplier to be approximately two for both his Pine Bluff and Fayetteville regions, his analysis of the character of economic activity in each region and application of the generalizations cited in the text

We may summarize the foregoing discussion as follows :

1. The interregional trade multiplier concept performs a valuable service by drawing attention to the number and complexity of economic functional relationships, especially of an interregional character, which lie behind a region's pattern of income growth and change.

2. Most of the functions utilized by the interregional trade multiplier formulations are very difficult to estimate empirically. For that reason, the principal use of such multiplier concepts will probably be to aid in the deduction of qualitative statements regarding regional economic behavior under given sets of characteristics and circumstances.

3. Estimates of numerical multiplier values per se must rely mainly on economic base study methods. The predictive value of such multipliers is quite limited, especially in view of the additional linkage problems encountered when autonomous home investment is included in the basic category. However, when linked with interregional input-output techniques, industrial complex analysis, and other location and regional techniques to be discussed later, multiplier estimates can take on added meaning.

E. Interrelations of Regional and National Cycles

The previous section considers a region in its interregional setting, particularly its export-import relationships with each of many regions. The cyclical reaction paths of the region are found to be dependent on certain structural characteristics of itself and other regions. In particular, the type of features considered strategic are those customarily associated with Keynesian doctrine. However, a regional analyst may not be willing to accept wholeheartedly or even in large part the Keynesian doctrine. He may be inclined to favor another form of theoretical reasoning. Or the regional analyst may find of value more empirical types of multiregion studies. Or, in addition to the more empirical materials, he may wish to identify concretely specific impulses, for example, new investment opportunities, technological changes, migration, etc., which have been significant in the past or are likely to be in the future, or both. Moreover, he may wish to perceive on a more concrete and empirical level the inter-connections of national cycles and of the cycles of the several regions constituting the national system, especially since he may be sensitive to the interplay of

led to the conclusion that the Fayetteville region would have considerably more short-run income stability than the Pine Bluff region. This illustrates the fact that regional marginal multipliers differ in value from the corresponding regional average multipliers, but, of course, it does not help in estimating the value of the marginal multipliers.

cyclical forces from region to region, from region to nation, and from nation to region.

There are several studies which have probed in these directions and which involve a type of framework of general value to regional analysis. Some of these studies have explored that direction (already noted) which tends to view the nation as the sum of a set of regions, and at least partially to explain the behavior of the national economy in terms of the behavior of its component regional economies.[67] Noteworthy in this connection is certain work by Vining which is closely linked to his theoretical and empirical work already reported in the previous section.[68]

As an instance, Vining has put forward the hypothesis that for a given year the national rate of change of income (a magnitude significant from both a secular and cyclical standpoint) may be validly conceived as a mean (weighted or, for approximative purposes, unweighted) of the rates of change of income of the several regions which comprise the nation. These latter rates of change form a frequency distribution which "appear to have a characteristic shape suggestive of a logarithmic normal curve."[69] Further, such a frequency distribution of regional rates of change behaves at least somewhat systematically over the business cycle. This point tends to be illustrated by Figure 2 (taken from Vining) where states are considered to be regions.[70] Along the horizontal axis is measured percentage gain or loss of income over the preceding year; and along the vertical axis is measured number of states. Hence the height of any bar indicates the number of states experiencing the corresponding percentage change for the specified year. As Vining observes these frequency distributions over the years, which by themselves are enlightening, he finds evidence in support of an hypothesis, namely that

> . . . so long as income is decreasing at an increasing rate (for example, as was the case from 1929 through 1932) we should expect the distribution of income by regions expressed as percentages of the preceding period to have a negative skew. As the rate at which income is declining itself begins to decline, the skew of these link-relatives should become positive. This positive skew should prevail throughout the phase during which the rate of decline is diminishing and should continue, as the diminishing rate of decline merges into an increasing rate of increase, throughout the period of this expanding rate of increase. As the rate of increase begins to decline, the

---

[67] If we pushed this approach to the extreme, we would consider the behavior of the ultimate components of an economy, namely the individual firms and households.

[68] Also see P. B. Simpson [62], ch. 5; W. Isard and G. Freutel [40]; and P. Neff and A. Weifenbach [52].

[69] R. Vining [74], p. 212.

[70] R. Vining [74], p. 199. See also other statistical materials contained in this article.

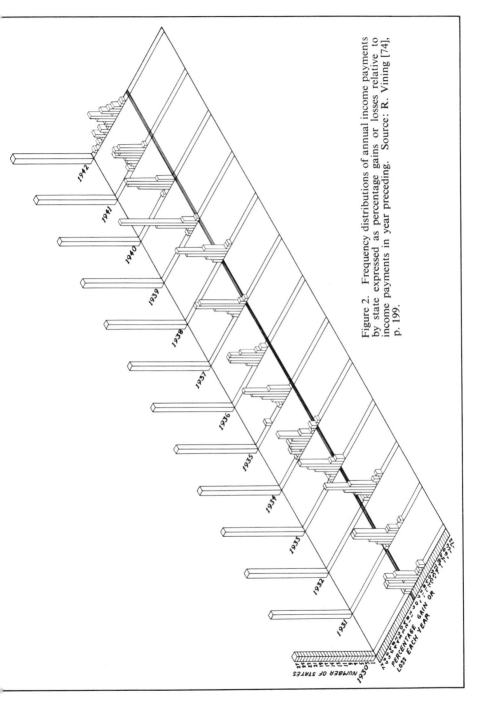

Figure 2. Frequency distributions of annual income payments by state expressed as percentage gains or losses relative to income payments in year preceding. Source: R. Vining [74], p. 199.

skew of the link-relatives should again become negative, continuing so through the period of the increasing rate of decline . . . .[71]

Vining has pushed his inquiry much farther. Recognizing the inadequacy of employing states as regional units, he has, after observing the cyclical behavior of each state, attempted to consolidate states to form more meaningful regional units than states alone constitute.[72] He finds that certain groups of geographically contiguous states can be found where the states within any group behave cyclically in a fairly uniform fashion, which fashion differs from group to group. For example, one group may respond more violently to cyclical impulses than another; a third group may consistently be sensitive on the downswing but insensitive on the upswing, etc.

Further investigation uncovers interesting connections with materials discussed in the preceding sections. The group of states consisting of Arkansas, Mississippi, and Alabama, states which show greater rates of increase in income in years of rising national income and larger percentage declines in years of falling income—and which therefore fall in the tails of the frequency distributions depicted in Figure 2—tend to produce commodities for export, for example, cotton and lumber, which have high income elasticities of demand. The relatively violent fluctuations of the incomes of these states are therefore consistent with the reasoning behind the interregional trade multiplier, and also with the logic of the economic base approach since these export industries would be considered basic. A second group of states consisting of New York, Massachusetts, Rhode Island, and New Jersey[73] are economically relatively diversified. They tend to be self-sufficient and tend to export products with relatively low income elasticities of demand. Their fluctuations of income tend to be mild, as interregional trade multiplier analysis and industrial composition analysis would suggest. Still a third group of states consisting of Indiana, Ohio, Michigan, Illinois, and Pennsylvania possess economies which concentrate much more on a few dominant industries, particularly in-

[71] R. Vining [74], pp. 197–200. In addition his statistical findings suggest "that secular changes may take place that alter the extent of the variation of the regional rates of change around the national rate of change, but that, given an economic structure, a functional relationship exists between the magnitude of the dispersion and the magnitude of the rate of change" (p. 212).

Also in this connection see F. A. Hanna [30].

[72] As Vining well recognizes, the most meaningful regions will have boundary lines which need not, and typically will not, coincide with political boundary lines. Also the size of these regions may range from exceedingly small areas to multistate groupings, depending on, among other factors, the objectives of an inquiry.

[73] Connecticut's behavior conforms partly to the pattern of this group and partly to the pattern of a third group mentioned later.

dustries that are heavy and put out durable producers goods such as industrial equipment. The amplitude of the income fluctuations of this group of states tends to be greater than that for the preceding group, as our several types of analyses would suggest.[74]

Such findings, which Vining would insist are only tentative, strongly point up the fruitfulness of a combined national and multiregion approach to the collection, processing, and interpretation of various sets of data significant for the study of cyclical behavior.[75] Further, they suggest the desirability of applying more formal variance analyses to such sets of data. Aside from the increased understanding of one's region which comes when a regional analyst views and interprets its cyclical behavior in the light of the behavior of other regions of the nation, knowledge and insight into the behavior of the national economy can be greatly enhanced through observing and interrelating the behavior of its parts.

Another type of study which has an empirical bent and which is of general value to the regional analyst attempts to trace out in a much less formal and more historical manner the repercussions of an impulse or set of impulses. These repercussions spelled out in terms of specific incidents and decisions may be studied intensively and in great detail with reference to the cyclical behavior of a given region and perhaps by comparison with the nation.[76] Or these repercussions may be investigated in a multiregional framework wherein the transmission of impulses from one region to another may be emphasized. In the latter connection such concrete events as the settlement of the West, the construction of the Erie Canal, the discovery of gold, railroadization, etc., may be studied. Often the analysis is presented in Schumpeterian terms.[77]

---

[74] See R. Vining [71], pp. 62–66.

[75] Vining has also systematically examined data on bank debits. See [73].

[76] Among others, excellent illustrations of this type of study are M. S. Gordon [28]; F. L. Kidner [41]; and P. B. Simpson [62].

[77] Closely related to this type of study are hypotheses which might attach *causal* significance to space itself or to certain regional factors in generating both regional and national cycles.

From investigations that have been undertaken, it would appear that for the most part space per se is a passive factor in generating cycles. However, because movement in space does involve overcoming physical resistance as well as a time cost, the space factor does condition in a major way and sets important restraints on the operation of various causal factors, and thus can theoretically have a significant influence on the timing, severity, and length of cycles among regions.

Of interest, too, are hypotheses which suggest that certain types of regions tend to generate cyclical disturbances. As already noted, P. Neff and A. Weifenbach [52] stress the significant role played by major urban regions. As Neff states: "Only with the modern city and attendant high specialization and large size of business units did the inherent instability which we call business cycles appear. In view of the coincident

For example, transport development as it has affected the cyclical behavior of the several regions of the United States and of the nation has on several occasions been studied. Empirical materials on outbursts of construction of transport facilities have been assembled.[78] The national data on such construction have been broken down regionally in some instances. Doing so points up (1) the interrelations of the development of a new region (i.e., penetration into new space) and the growth of already settled areas ; and (2) certain necessary sequences in the development of each region and the nation.

In the United States, outbursts of construction of transport facilities have typically been vast in magnitude. This has been the result of, among other factors, the relatively large size of a minimum unit of transport construction, in particular of a railway, and the financial character and the speculative practices of the United States economy.[79] But whatever the causal matrix of such outbursts, these outbursts have in turn led to severe ups and downs of the regional and national economies and of interregional trade. Such consequences could have been anticipated. Major railroad development implies marked reductions in transport costs. Such reductions lead to the reallocation of market areas, the revaluation of existing resources, and redistribution of industrial production to the benefit of the most efficient and best-located firms. Greater industrial concentrations emerge in the favored regions, which in turn generate mass production economies and still greater extension of the market areas of the best locations, and hence still further selection between superior and inferior sites, trade centers, and nodes. When transport facilities penetrate new space, new resource deposits become economic to exploit, which may lead

development of cycles and of large urban masses, it may well be that impulses originating in cities and transmitted to other parts of the nation sometimes constitute the causes of cycles" ([51], p. 105).

Such an hypothesis is not inconsistent with the regional multiplier and interregional trade multiplier analysis already discussed, since with the growth of urban economies has come marked increase in the absolute and relative magnitude of regional exports and interregional trade within the United States. This hypothesis is also consistent with the reasoning of some who put great emphasis on the role played by very sensitive centers of reaction. These centers, responding strongly to impulses affecting the level of operation of their industries, in turn radiate to both neighboring and distant regions with whom they have import-export ties a set of impulses which are in turn transmitted (although constantly dampened by the friction of distance) back and forth among all regions, at times being magnified by these sensitive centers of reaction.

Unfortunately, Neff and Weifenbach were not able to process in an appropriate fashion the time series data for cities (classified by sizes) and their hinterland areas, and to conduct other inquiries to test their hypothesis, although some of their findings such as those on the Detroit area are suggestive.

[78] Among others, see N. J. Silberling [61], ch. 10, and W. Isard [39].

[79] See N. J. Silberling [61].

to revolutionary changes in the world supply of primary goods. Such opening up of new regions and capitalizing opportunities for profitable local operations sets off a process of expansion for the whole economy wherein all regions may gain and be stimulated into expansion, although to different extents. In the new region opportunities for export cause an influx of new labor from other regions. The settlement and urbanization phenomena in the new region entail the creation of a host of other economic activities, both residentiary and import. Social overhead investment is required in huge amounts and is largely imported. All this in turn affects other regions, their patterns of export, their industrial structures, their rates of growth, etc., the particular manner in which any one region is affected depending on the ways in which its resources both directly and indirectly complement the resources of the new region.[80]

The study, through data collection, processing, and interpretation, of the ways in which these forces pervade the multiregion economy can be very illuminating, both in the expansionary phase and later in the contractionary phase. Unfortunately, relatively little empirical study tracing these effects through the interregional matrix of the United States economy has been undertaken. Facts on transport development have been linked to facts on migration, on residential and industrial building, on population numbers and urban growth, on iron and steel production, and on output of other major industries. But such linkage has been done mostly on a national level.[81] Much more should be done on the multiregional level.[82]

Similarly with major developmental factors other than transport. They, too, should be investigated in a multiregional framework if we are better to understand the regional and national fluctuations of the past and anticipate those of the future. Such studies, with a heavy historical bent, could fruitfully complement the more formal, multiregional empirical studies employing variance analyses and other advanced statistical techniques. They could complement, too, those studies discussed in other chapters as well as the studies that center around the *industrial composition* of regions and the different cyclical sensitivities of industries;

---

[80] For a more complete description of types of effects, see D. C. North [54, 55], and N. J. Silberling [61]. More theoretical discussion of the implications of transport cost reduction are contained in W. H. Dean, Jr. [17], E. M. Hoover [32], and W. Isard [39].

[81] For example, see N. J. Silberling [61], W. Isard [35], C. and W. Isard [34], and H. Hoyt [32].

[82] As an instance, it has been suggested that the 18 to 20-year cycle which New England experienced in the last quarter of the nineteenth century in her physical development (building, urban expansion, population growth, etc.) was in large part due to impulses stemming from the railroad development of the rest of the country, particularly of the West. New England's manufactured exports and employment opportunities mounted and lapsed with expanding and contracting markets elsewhere. (See W. Isard [38].)

and they could provide firmer groundwork for estimating *regional multipliers* when projections are required, and for anticipating interregional impacts of concrete developments and specific programs of regions via the *interregional trade multiplier*.

F. Some Remarks in Evaluation

The seemingly diverse slants at regional cycle and multiplier analysis presented in this chapter—the industrial composition, the economic base, the interregional trade multiplier, and the statistical-historical slants— are more basically interrelated than has been made explicit. Each after all constitutes a look at one or more facets of the functioning and structure of a systems complex. This complex of systems may be viewed either horizontally as an intricate network of regions, each in itself a system, or vertically as a nonadditive overlay of interregional systems of money flows, commodity flows, population flows, industrial locations, etc., reflecting the spatial configuration of resources, technological development, etc., and such motives as efficiency and welfare. However conceived, each slant evaluated in this chapter yields a very imperfect look.

The industrial composition slant primarily focuses on a single region; it fails to recognize the interregional system, viewing as an undifferentiated mass the regions external to the one being studied. Further, this slant treats the industries of a region as independent units, or at least without setting forth in quantitative terms their interrelations. Hence, it is not surprising that a look at a region without consideration of its bonds to the several regions of a system and without explicit consideration of its internal interindustry linkages is not too satisfying. Certainly if we are to understand (and explain) better the timing, duration, and amplitude of a region's cycles, our analysis must come to grips with interindustry linkages within both an industrial and interregional system—as interregional and regional input-output, industrial complex and location analysis, interregional linear programming, and other techniques would have us do. Progress in the direction of integrating the industrial composition approach with one or more of these techniques is to be desired.

The industrial composition approach suppresses interindustry linkages. The economic base–regional multiplier approach does not. But the gains scored by the latter approach are in large part nullified by the loss of detail stemming from the high degree of aggregation in this approach. True, the twofold classification of industries in terms of those whose output and employment are exogenously determined[83] and those whose output and

---

[83] That is, by forces outside the framework of the region being studied.

employment are endogenously determined[84] is useful.   It does point up an important causal relation (process).   But it is questionable whether this procedure does so in the proper fashion, as is evidenced by the debate on the definition of the dichotomy : " basic " and " service." And although the identification and estimation of the impact of exogenously determined sectors on endogenously determined sectors is valuable, nonetheless the level of aggregation at which this estimation is performed in economic base analysis suppresses the intricate structure and fabric by which decision-making units and groups of units are linked within a region.   At most, only when crude, hurried research is required can the use of the economic base–regional multiplier approach be justified as more than a descriptive device.   As with the industrial composition slant, movement in the direction of integrating with other techniques is to be desired.

The economic base–regional multiplier approach is deficient not only because it embodies a high degree of industrial aggregation but also because it fails to recognize explicitly the interregional system and the non-homogeneous character of the outside world.   This existence of nonhomogeneous regions within a system is, however, clearly appreciated by the interregional trade multiplier concept.   In this sense, such a concept adds another dimension to analysis and is much more intellectually satisfying than the simple economic base multiplier.   But intellectually satisfying as it may be, to date it has yielded few morsels of empirical food.   The Keynesian-type functions are not easily approximated.   And like the economic base approach it manipulates large aggregates of decision-making units and conceals vital detail.   It lacks the fine knit of inter-regional input-output, industrial complex, interregional linear programming, commodity flow investigations, and of potential interregional money flow and social accounting studies.   Yet the conceptual framework of the interregional trade multiplier does uncover a basic structure of motives— motives governing decisions by consumers, businesses, governments, and other units.   Further, these motives are regionally differentiated within the system examined.   Synthesis of this conceptual framework with the portions of the interregional fabric that can be encompassed by the type of studies already alluded to in this paragraph provides a major challenge to regional scientists and other analysts.   Some of the dimensions of this challenge will be indicated in later chapters.

Finally, there is the rich and relatively untapped potential for significant regional analysis oriented to the broad sweeping historical process. Whether this analysis involves either statistical or nonstatistical study of regions as an evolutionary system, it is able to probe into the interplay of

---

[84] That is, by forces within the framework (model) of the region being studied.

forces on a time scale denied the more careful, detailed quantitative approaches and the more theoretically precise conceptual frameworks. In the historical dimension, these latter approaches are severely circumscribed and cannot achieve that kind of fruitful weighing and evaluation of forces possible from the careful, thorough, yet selective long-run study of the diverse factors affecting the dynamic path of the system. Studies such as interregional input-output, interregional linear programming, etc., cannot attain the insight into the future provided by the long-run associations and cause-and-effect hypotheses unearthed by sophisticated historical analysis. The desirability of synthesis is once more obvious.

APPENDIX

ECONOMIC BASE AND CENTRAL PLACE THEORY

It was pointed out in the concluding section that one of the major shortcomings of economic base studies is their failure to look outside the city or region and consider the city or region as occupying a position in an existing hierarchy of cities and regions. The development over the last two decades of central place theory highlights this deficiency.

As noted in *Location and Space-Economy*, a meaningful system of regions, such as comprises the United States, or a large homogeneous territory such as Southern Germany, may be conceived as patterned and structured. Within the system, there is a definite and regular ordering of cities (or regions). Such an ordering may range from hamlets (cities of the first order) through villages, towns, . . ., and regional cities up to primate cities (cities of the *n*th order) such as New York and London. Each order has associated with it a specific spatial spread of hinterland (tributary area). The hinterland of a city in any given order fully contains the hinterlands of a finite number of cities of the next lower order (which have smaller size hinterlands). Moreover, corresponding to each order there is both a definite number of functions which each city of that order performs and a population size typical for each city of that order.

The theoretical underpinnings for such a system were first developed by Lösch. These and additional theoretical materials together with empirical findings of Lösch, Christaller, and others have been covered in *Location and Space-Economy*.[85] Since the publication of this book, further empirical materials and perceptive schema have been developed. Carruthers has developed empirical materials for service centers in England and Wales.[86] Garrison and Berry have statistically verified the existence of a three-order hierarchy of central places in Snohomish County, Washington.[87] Their findings lend additional statistical refinement to certain of the central place hypotheses advanced by Brush [88] and

[85] W. Isard [37], pp. 11–12, 17–19, 42–50, 58–60, 68–70, 143–144, 152–154, 239–242, 270–280. These pages cite the relevant works of Lösch, Christaller, Bogue, Hawley, Hoover, Ullman, Vining, and Zipf. Also see W. L. Garrison and B. J. L. Berry [24].

[86] I. Carruthers [12].

[87] W. L. Garrison and B. J. L. Berry [22, 23].

[88] J. E. Brush [10].

Brush and Bracey,[89] based on data for cities in southwestern Wisconsin and Southern England.

Among the perceptive materials which best indicate the relation of economic base to central place ordering are those developed by Philbrick.[90] First, Philbrick distinguishes between seven broad categories (orders) of functions. These are graphically depicted in Figure A-1. The first-order category covers consumption which is conducted in the household establishment (residential

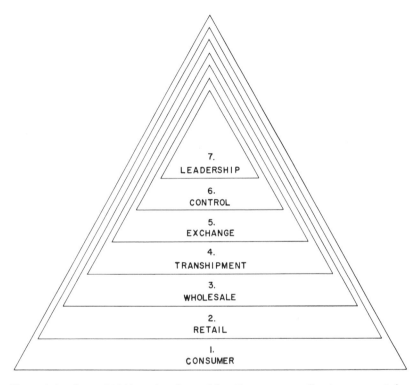

Figure A-1.   Seven-fold hierarchy of nested functions corresponding to seven nested orders of areal units of organization.   Source: A. K. Philbrick [58], p. 92.

unit).   The second-order category covers retail trade, the third-order wholesale trade, etc.   Finally, the seventh-order category covers leadership.   Corresponding to each order of function is an order in the hierarchy of nodal points (regions).   As already indicated the household establishment, the first-order central place, performs the first and only the first category of functions (i.e., consumption).   The second-order central places are clusters of retail (including service) activities, such as primarily characterize villages and hamlets.   Within the hinterland of each second-order central place are a finite number of first-order establishments.   The third-order central places are clusters of not only retail activities

[89] J. E. Brush and H. E. Bracey [11].   Also see F. H. W. Green [29].
[90] A. K. Philbrick [58, 59].

but also wholesale activities; they embrace a finite number of second-order places as well as a finite number of first-order places. And so forth. Finally, the seventh-order central place, of which there is only one, is a cluster of leadership activities as well as all other (lower-order) functions. Its hinterland covers the entire system of cities (regions) and thus includes a finite number of each of the lower-order central places.

An idealized conception of this sevenfold nested areal hierarchy of economic

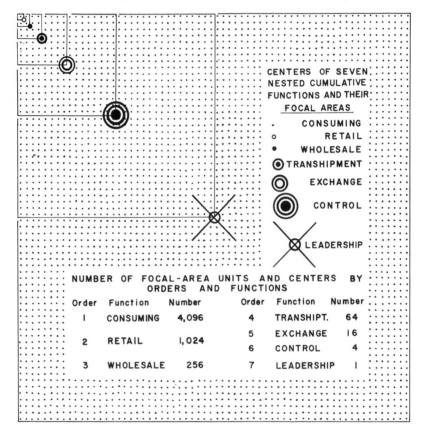

Figure A-2. An idealized seven-fold nested areal hierarchy of economic functions. Source: A. K. Philbrick [58], p. 93.

functions and central places is presented in Figure A-2. In this figure, each central place of a given order is defined to contain four central places of the next lower order. The figure is self-explanatory.

Although an idealized framework facilitates understanding, the real test of the value of a conceptual framework is its empirical significance. Philbrick has studied carefully available data on the number and types of functions performed by various cities of the United States. Some of his empirical findings are neatly summarized in Maps A-1 and A-2. Map A-1 covers part of the system of central

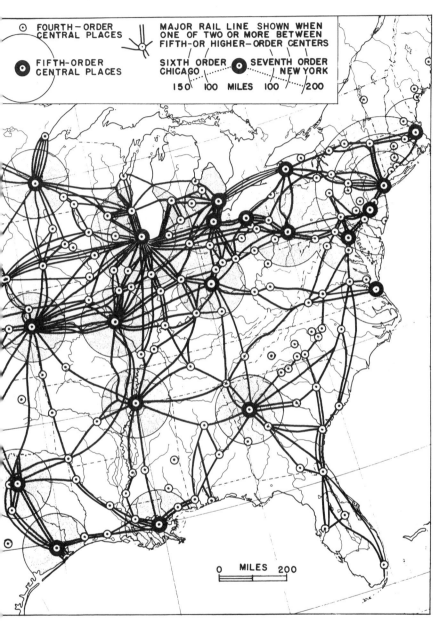

Map A-1. Areal functional organization in the eastern United States. Source: A. K. Philbrick [59], p. 330.

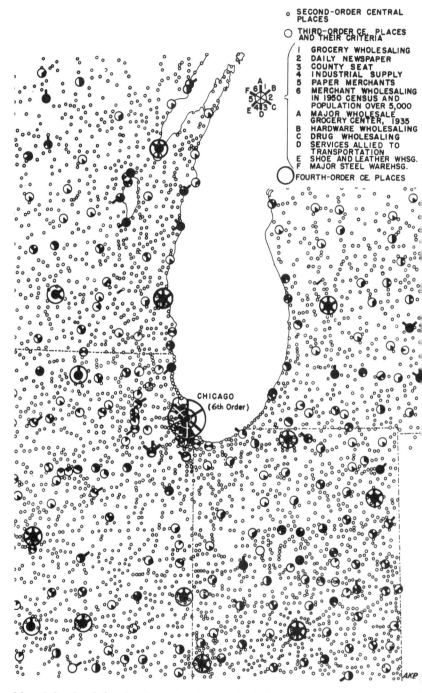

CHICAGO
(6th Order)

Map A-2. Areal functional organization in the Chicago region. Source: A. K. Philbrick [59], p. 321.

places in the United States, namely the eastern United States. The seventh-order central place (New York City) is indicated. The sixth-order central place, Chicago, is also noted. (New York City performs the sixth-order function for the East as well as seventh-order functions for the entire system; Los Angeles, the third of the sixth-order central places for the United States, is not shown on this map.) The several fifth-order central places, fourth-order central places, and the basic rail interconnections between higher-order central places are also depicted in Map A-1.

Map A-2 presents for a selected portion of the United States system the pattern of second-order, third-order, and fourth-order central places. In addition, the third-order and fourth-order central places are classified by types of third-order functions.

In light of the theoretical, perceptual, and empirical materials developed here and elsewhere, the simple outlook of economic base studies is to be seriously questioned. For one thing it is clear, as noted in *Location and Space-Economy*, that associated with a statistically regular hierarchy of cities must be a statistically regular hierarchy of commodity flows as characterized by both average length and volume of flow. The export-import relations of cities in the different orders of the hierarchy must therefore differ both in volume and average length of commodity flow. Therefore it is to be expected that the structure of the internal economy of cities will differ according to order in hierarchy. To each order of city will correspond a different set of activities producing for export. These activities will require different inputs from other activities and generate different amounts of value added and income; that is, they will have different "double" multipliers or Keynesian-type multipliers. Such different multipliers may be expected to obtain, even when it is recognized that there are many resource-oriented functions (such as mining, electroprocess activities, recreation, and textiles) and other activities whose location central place theory cannot explain. When the locations of such functions and activities are superimposed on the areal pattern of central-place-type functions,[91] there exists little, if any, theoretical or empirical basis for anticipating that these differences in multipliers will be eliminated. Among some central places, differences in multipliers may be narrowed or even eliminated; but among other central places differences in multipliers may be expected to be intensified.

When it is also recognized that at any given point of time a city or region occupies a position within a dynamic system whose spatial structure is undergoing constant change, the economic base multiplier may also be expected to be subject to constant change. Simply put, growth of an hierarchy of regions implies changing economic base and basic-service ratios for these regions.[92]

REFERENCES

1. Alexander, John W., "The Basic-Nonbasic Concept of Urban Economic Functions," *Economic Geography*, Vol. 30 (July 1954).
2. ———, *An Economic Base Study of Madison, Wisconsin*, University of Wisconsin Press, Madison, Wisconsin, 1953.

[91] For example, refer to W. Isard [37], pp. 57–60, ch. 11.

[92] Particularly illuminating on this point is J. R. P. Friedman [20]. See also E. E. Lampard [43], the comment on Lampard's paper by W. Stolper [64], and C. H. Madden [47].

3. Alexandersson, Gunnar, *The Industrial Structure of American Cities*, University of Nebraska Press, Lincoln, Nebraska, 1956.

4. Andrews, Richard B., "Comment re : Criticisms of the Economic Base Theory," *Journal of the American Institute of Planners*, Vol. 24 (1958).

5. ———, "Mechanics of the Urban Economic Base," series of articles in *Land Economics*, Vols. 29 to 31 (May 1953 to Feb. 1956).

6. Barford, Børge, *Local Economic Effects of a Large-Scale Industrial Undertaking*, Copenhagen, 1938.

7. Beckerman, W., "The World Trade Multiplier and the Stability of World Trade, 1938 to 1953," *Econometrica*, Vol. 24 (July 1956).

8. Blumenfeld, Hans, "The Economic Base of the Metropolis," *Journal of the American Institute of Planners*, Vol. 21 (Fall 1955).

9. Borts, George H., *Regional Cycles of Manufacturing Employment in the United States, 1914–1953*, National Bureau of Economic Research, forthcoming.

10. Brush, J. E., "The Hierarchy of Central Places in Southwestern Wisconsin," *Geographical Review*, Vol. 43 (July 1953).

11. ———, and H. E. Bracey, "Rural Service Centers in Southwestern Wisconsin and Southern England," *Geographical Review*, Vol. 45 (Oct. 1955).

12. Carruthers, Ian, "A Classification of Service Centers in England and Wales," *The Geographical Journal*, Vol. 123 (Sept. 1957).

13. Chipman, John S., "Professor Goodwin's Matrix Multiplier," *Economic Journal*, Vol. 60 (Dec. 1950).

14. ———, *The Theory of Intersectoral Money Flows and Income Formation*, The Johns Hopkins Press, Baltimore, Maryland, 1950.

15. Cincinnati City Planning Commission, *Economy of the Area*, Cincinnati, Ohio, 1946.

16. Daly, M. C., "An Approximation to a Geographical Multiplier," *Economic Journal*, Vol. 50 (June–Sept. 1940).

17. Dean, William H., Jr., *The Theory of the Geographic Location of Economic Activities*, selections from the doctoral dissertation (Harvard University), Edward Brothers, Ann Arbor, Michigan, 1938.

18. Federal Reserve Bank of Kansas City, "The Employment Multiplier in Wichita," *Monthly Review*, Vol 37 (Sept. 1952).

19. Fouraker, L., "A Note on Regional Multipliers," *Papers and Proceedings of the Regional Science Association*, Vol. 1 (1955).

20. Friedmann, John R. P., "Locational Aspects of Economic Development," *Land Economics*, Vol. 32 (Aug. 1956).

21. Garbarino, Joseph W., "Some Implications of Regional and Industrial Differences in Unemployment," *Proceedings of the Twenty-ninth Annual Conference of the Western Economics Association, 1954.*

22. Garrison, W. L., and B. J. L. Berry, "Central Place Theory and the Range of a Good," *Economic Geography*, Vol. 34 (Oct. 1958).

23. ———, and ———, "The Functional Bases of the Central Place Hierarchy," *Economic Geography*, Vol. 34 (April 1958).

24. ———, and ———, "Recent Developments of Central Place Theory," *Papers and Proceedings of the Regional Science Association*, Vol. 4 (1958).

25. Gilbert, Jerome, *Explorations in the Development of Measuring Regional Income Analysis*, Port of New York Authority, New York (no date), mimeographed.

26. Gillies, J., and W. Grigsby, "Classification Errors in Base-Ratio Analysis," *Journal of the American Institute of Planners*, Vol. 22 (Winter 1956).

27. Goodwin, R., The Multiplier as Matrix," *Economic Journal*, Vol. 59 (Dec. 1949).

28. Gordon, Margaret S., *Employment Expansion and Population Growth: The California Experience, 1900–1950*, University of California Press, Berkeley, California, 1954.

29. Green, F. H. W., "Community of Interest Areas," *Economic Geography*, Vol. 34 (July 1958).

30. Hanna, F. A., "Cyclical and Secular Changes in State Per Capita Incomes, 1929–50," *Review of Economics and Statistics*, Vol. 36 (Aug. 1954).

31. Hildebrand, George, and Arthur Mace, Jr., "The Employment Multiplier in an Expanding Industrial Market : Los Angeles County, 1940–47," *Review of Economics and Statistics*, Vol. 32 (Aug. 1950).

32. Hoover, Edgar M., Jr., *Location Theory and the Shoe and Leather Industries*, Harvard University Press, Cambridge, Massachusetts, 1937.

33. Hoyt, Homer, *The Economic Base of the Brockton, Massachusetts Area*, Brockton, Massachusetts, 1949.

34. ———, *One Hundred Years of Land Values in Chicago*, University of Chicago Press, Chicago, 1933.

35. Isard, C., and W. Isard, "The Transport-Building Cycle in Urban Development : Chicago," *Review of Economics and Statistics*, Vol 25 (Nov. 1943).

36. Isard, Walter, "Discussion on Interregional Variations in Economic Fluctuations," *Papers and Proceedings of the American Economic Association*, Vol. 39 (May 1949).

37. ———, *Location and Space-Economy*, John Wiley, New York, 1956.

38. ———, "A Neglected Cycle : The Transport-Building Cycle," *Review of Economics and Statistics*, Vol. 24 (Nov. 1942).

39. ———, "Transport Development and Building Cycles," *Quarterly Journal of Economics*, Vol. 57 (Nov. 1942).

40. ———, and G. Freutel, "Regional and National Product Projections and their Interrelations," in *Long Range Economic Projection*, National Bureau of Economic Research, Studies in Income and Wealth, Vol. 16, Princeton University Press, Princeton, New Jersey, 1954.

41. Kidner, Frank L., *California Business Cycles*, University of California Press, Berkeley and Los Angeles, 1946.

42. Krutilla, J. V., "Criteria for Evaluating Regional Development Programs," *American Economic Review*, Vol. 45 (May 1955).

43. Lampard, E. E., "The History of Cities in the Economically Advanced Areas," *Economic Development and Cultural Change*, Vol. 3 (Jan. 1955).

44. Leven, Charles L., "An Appropriate Unit for Measuring the Economic Base," *Land Economics*, Vol. 30 (Nov. 1954).

45. ———, "Measuring the Economic Base," *Papers and Proceedings of the Regional Science Association*, Vol. 2 (1956).

46. ———, *Theory and Method of Income and Product Accounts for Metropolitan Areas, Including the Elgin–Dundee Area as a Case Study*, Iowa State College, Ames, Iowa, 1958, mimeographed.

47. Madden, C. H., "Some Spatial Aspects of Urban Growth in the United States," *Economic Development and Cultural Change*, Vol. 4 (July 1956).

48. Mattila, J. M., and W. R. Thompson, "Measurement of the Economic Base of the Metropolitan Area," *Land Economics*, Vol. 31 (Aug. 1955).

49. Mayer, Harold M., "Urban Nodality and the Economic Base," *Journal of the American Institute of Planners*, Vol. 20 (Summer 1954).

50. Metzler, L., "A Multiple-Region Theory of Income and Trade," *Econometrica*, Vol. 18 (Oct. 1950).
51. Neff, Phillip, "Interregional Cyclical Differentials: Causes, Measurement, and Significance," *Papers and Proceedings of the American Economic Association*, Vol. 39 (May 1949).
52. ———, and Annette Weifenbach, *Business Cycles in Selected Industrial Areas*, University of California Press, Berkeley, California, 1949.
53. North, Douglass C., "Exports and Regional Economic Growth, A Reply," *Journal of Political Economy*, Vol. 64 (April 1956).
54. ———, "Location Theory and Regional Economic Growth," *Journal of Political Economy*, Vol. 63 (June 1955).
55. ———, "The Spatial and Interregional Framework of the United States Economy: An Historical Perspective," *Papers and Proceedings of the Regional Science Association*, Vol. 2 (1956).
56. Pfouts, R. W., "An Empirical Testing of the Economic Base Theory," *Journal of the American Institute of Planners*, Vol. 23, No. 2 (1957).
57. ———, and E. T. Curtis, "Limitations of the Economic Base Analysis," *Social Forces*, Vol. 36 (May 1958).
58. Philbrick, A. K., "Areal Functional Organization in Regional Geography," *Papers and Proceedings of the Regional Science Association*, Vol. 3 (1957).
59. ———, "Principles of Areal Functional Organization in Regional Human Geography," *Economic Geography*, Vol. 33 (Oct. 1957).
60. Roterus, V., and W. Calef, "Notes on the Basic-Nonbasic Employment Ratio," *Economic Geography*, Vol. 31 (1955).
61. Silberling, Norman J., *The Dynamics of Business*, McGraw-Hill, New York, 1942.
62. Simpson, Paul B., *Regional Aspects of Business Cycles and Special Studies of the Pacific Northwest*, Bonneville Administration and the University of Oregon, June 1953.
63. Steiner, Robert L., "Urban and Inter-Urban Economic Equilibrium," *Papers and Proceedings of the Regional Science Association*, Vol. 1 (1955).
64. Stolper, W. F., "Spatial Order and the Economic Growth of Cities," *Economic Development and Cultural Change*, Vol. 3 (Jan. 1955).
65. ———, and Charles M. Tiebout, "The Balance of Payments of a Small Area as an Analytical Tool," 1950, mimeographed.
66. Thomas, Morgan D., "The Economic Base and a Region's Economy," *Journal of the American Institute of Planners*, Vol. 23, No. 2 (1957).
67. Tiebout, Charles M., "Exports and Regional Economic Growth," *Journal of Political Economy*, Vol. 64 (April 1956).
68. ———, "A Method of Determining Incomes and their Variation in Small Regions," *Papers and Proceedings of the Regional Science Association*, Vol. 1 (1955).
69. Ullman, Edward L., "The Basic-Service Ratio and the Areal Support of Cities," 1953, mimeographed.
70. University of New Mexico, Bureau of Business Research, and Federal Reserve Bank of Kansas City, *The Economy of Albuquerque, New Mexico*, Albuquerque, 1949.
71. Vining, R., "Location of Industry and Regional Patterns of Business-Cycle Behavior," *Econometrica*, Vol. 14 (Jan. 1946).
72. ———, "The Region as a Concept in Business Cycle Analysis," *Econometrica*, Vol. 14 (July 1946).

73. Vining, R., "The Region as an Economic Entity and Certain Variations to be Observed in the Study of Systems of Regions," *Papers and Proceedings of the American Economic Association*, Vol. 39 (May 1949).

74. ———, "Regional Variation in Cyclical Fluctuation Viewed as a Frequency Distribution," *Econometrica*, Vol. 13 (July 1945).

75. Weimer, Arthur M., and Homer Hoyt, *Principles of Urban Real Estate*, Ronald Press, 3rd edition, 1954.

76. Williams, Robert M., "The Timing and Amplitude of Regional Business Cycles," *Proceedings of the Twenty-Fifth Annual Conference of the Pacific Coast Economic Association*, 1950.

77. Wilson, Andrew W., "The Supporting-Dependent Analysis of Income Payments to Individuals," *Arizona Business and Economic Review*, University of Arizona, Aug. 1955.

Chapter 7

Industrial Location Analysis and Related Measures*

A. INTRODUCTION

In the previous chapters we have, more or less, assumed that an economic base, usually composed to a large extent of industry, exists in each region. We have touched on reasons for the existence of such industry. We have related population numbers, migration, Gross Regional Product and income, commodity and money flows, balance of payments, etc., to existing industrial bases and their characteristics. We have in addition considered cyclical effects and multipliers associated with change in the economic (industrial) base. However, nowhere have we probed with depth and with as much analysis as we can into the questions of what industries and how much of each can be expected to exist or develop in a region.

These questions of what industries and how much of each are basic to all forms of regional economic analysis. Fortunately, we can attack these questions with sharper tools than some of the questions we have already treated. We can go beyond mere description, which for example characterizes much work on regional income, population, migration, commodity and money flows, and balances of payments. We can get at more of the

* Sections B–E of this chapter were written with Eugene W. Schooler, and Appendices A and B with David F. Bramhall and Daniel O. Price.

relations governing decisions by business firms and government units. This consequence partly reflects the development of a considerable and rather sophisticated literature on location theory.[1] Although this literature is abstract and for the most part does not bear directly on the problems with which regional analysts and planners are concerned, it has led to at least one basic, general procedure which is exceedingly useful. This is the comparative cost technique, which also has roots in international trade theory. We shall discuss the comparative cost approach in the following section, an approach that casts considerable light on the "why" of systems of industrial locations. Then in succeeding sections we shall present materials on diverse types of coefficients and related concepts—the labor coefficient, the coefficients of localization and specialization, the localization curve, the index of diversification. These coefficients and related concepts are generally associated with location analysis. However, because they largely portray the "what" of systems of industrial locations, that is, are descriptive, they are not as useful as the comparative cost approach.

Finally, in Appendices A and B, we outline scaling and latent structure techniques and factor analysis, respectively. Scaling and latent structure techniques bear on community attitudes and other important subjective factors which must supplement a cost calculus for understanding systems of industrial location ; in addition, these and related techniques promise to illumine several facets of regional behavior. Factor analysis, as discussed in Appendix B, pertains particularly to the proper delineation of regions within a system, a problem of major concern when coefficients of localization and related concepts are comprehensively employed to depict industrial location systems ; too, factor analysis has potential applications in several forms of regional study.

B. COMPARATIVE COST APPROACH

A comparative cost study typically proceeds for any given industry on the basis of an established or anticipated pattern of markets and a given geographic distribution of raw materials and other productive factors used in the industry. The objective of the study is to determine in what region or regions the industry could achieve the lowest total cost of producing and delivering its product to market. If the analyst is concerned with the industrial growth prospects of a particular region, a series of such comparative cost studies is rather essential.

[1] Among other literature on location theory, the reader is referred to J. H. von Thünen [65] ; W. Launhardt [46, 47] ; A. Weber [68] ; T. Palander [53] ; A. Lösch [52] ; W. H. Dean, Jr. [11] ; E. M. Hoover [34] ; E. S. Dunn [16] ; M. L. Greenhut [24] ; W. Isard [38].   There is an elementary statement on location analysis in E. M. Hoover [33].

Frequently the initial justification for one or more comparative cost studies arises because of changes in general technology, or in the technology of a particular industry, or in the production of an individual raw material or intermediate good. For example, general improvement in a region's internal and external transport situation—the completion of a system of superhighways, the erection of more modern and efficient railroad terminal facilities, the construction of deep-water river channels, etc.—can have a significant effect on the relative advantages of the given region for industrial location. If the region is lightly populated with a plentiful variety and supply of natural resources, the transport improvement could tip the scales of regional advantage in its favor. Such improvement might give the region an advantage over locations using inferior or high-cost raw materials which had nevertheless *been* best because of nearness to markets. On the other hand, if the region itself is a densely populated market area, the transport improvement might drastically cut costs of assembling raw materials there. Thus, in certain heavy raw-material-using activities, such improvement would allow a shift in advantage from raw material regions to the region under consideration.[2] In any case, because the transport improvement affects all industry in general, the regional analyst should pursue comparative cost studies for a number of industries.

Another situation that could be usefully analyzed by means of one or more individual-industry comparative cost studies might arise because of a change in market conditions. For example, as a region grows and develops, its population expands. Its local market becomes capable of absorbing the outputs of economic-size plants in a growing number of industries. Comparative cost studies can indicate for which of these industries local production can be justified.

Still another situation might be associated with a changing raw material supply pattern, for example, from the gradual depletion of a locationally dominant ore source. Or it might be associated with a prospective new industry, such as nucleonics or electronics, or with a new productive process, such as irradiation or continuous casting. In each of these situations a regional comparative cost study, taking these changes into account, can help to indicate whether there is a basis for a relocation or new growth of industry and, if so, the nature of the location patterns to be expected.

With these comments illustrating some of the many possible situations in which individual-industry comparative cost studies are useful, we turn

2 As an instance, the relatively recent construction of large-diameter, long-distance natural gas pipelines has provided a practical possibility for the production of ammonia and other natural-gas-based petrochemicals in regions far from the natural gas fields.

to procedures for conducting such studies. The most direct way to pursue a comparative cost study for an industry would be to secure enough information to calculate the total production costs the industry would incur in each of the regions to be compared. The region or regions with the lowest production costs (including transport cost) would be the most desirable location, in an economic sense. Since the difference in total cost from region to region is the important magnitude, it becomes clear with further reflection that the regional comparative cost study need consider only the production and transport cost elements which actually differ from region to region. The components of production and transport cost that do not vary regionally in amount may be ignored ; they give rise to no regional advantage or disadvantage. In practice, this consideration of cost differentials only can lead to considerable saving of research time, since many items of production cost for most industries do not exhibit systematic or significant regional variation.[3]

It should also be observed that in considering an element of production cost which does vary regionally, it is often possible to estimate the amount of its difference between regions without knowing its absolute regional levels. For example, take two similar plants, one in New York City, the other in a coal town near Pittsburgh. Each consumes ten tons of coal a day, the cost of coal in New York City tending to exceed the cost of coal in the coal town by the cost of transporting coal from the coal town to New York City. If it is known that the transport rate is $3 per ton, the daily coal cost of the New York plant would exceed by $30 the daily coal cost of the other plant. However, this method of computing a regional cost differential can be used only if the relevant productive factor input is the same in each region, both in type and quantity. Thus, if the New York plant used only eight tons of coal a day as compared to ten in the other plant, the analyst would have to know the price or cost of coal in at least one of the sites as well as its transport cost in order to compute the daily coal cost differential. Also, if one of the plants adopted a productive process that used electricity rather than coal, the analyst would need to know the absolute cost of both electricity and coal in order to calculate the energy (fuel and power) cost differential between the two plants.

1. PETROCHEMICAL LOCATION

To illustrate the comparative cost technique, which in essence involves

---

[3] Also of practical importance is the fact that industrial companies are often willing to furnish information regarding a few individual production cost items but refuse to divulge a complete itemized summary of unit production costs.

a systematic listing of regional cost differentials,[4] we summarize a recent analysis of factors affecting the future location pattern of the natural gas-based petrochemical industry.[5]

The first task of the analysis was to determine which components of petrochemical production cost could be expected to vary regionally. Generally, these components are fuel and raw material gas, steam, electric power, labor, and transportation. Additionally, major cost differentials result if feasible sizes of productive units differ regionally. (Large units achieve "economies of scale" which are denied to small units.)

The second step of the analysis was to choose and define the regions to be compared. Consideration of various geographic and technological factors led to the conclusion that feasible locations for the production of petrochemicals are limited to (1) sites in the Gulf Coast and adjoining interior area (in which are concentrated most of the country's reserves of natural gas) and (2) several sites within the country's major petrochemical market area generally extending from the industrial Northeast through the Great Lakes region.[6] This over-all market area was divided into several smaller market regions, each constituting the natural hinterland or distribution area of a city strategically located with respect to interregional transport connections. The relevant regional cost comparisons were thus between (1) a site in the Gulf Southwest raw material region and (2) the focal or distributional point site in each of the several market regions.

The following tables summarize the results of the calculation of regional cost differentials in the production of a typical petrochemical, *ethylene glycol* (the basic component of permanent-type antifreeze).[7] Table 1 lists the raw material, utilities, and labor inputs which may lead to regional cost differentials. The cost comparisons are between a Mississippi River location in the raw materials region near Monroe, Louisiana, and a market region location at Cincinnati, Ohio.

It is demonstrated in the study that regional differentials in the cost of ethane (a raw material gas contained in natural gas) may be viewed as approximately equal to regional differentials in the cost of the equivalent volume of natural gas. Similarly, since the gas used for fuel is natural gas, regional differentials in the cost of process fuel gas are regional differentials in the cost of natural gas. Further, differences in steam costs

---

[4] For the formal, theoretical approach see W. Isard [38]. A brief, step-by-step exposition of a modern Weberian comparative cost approach as applied in industrial complex analysis is found in Chapter 9.

[5] W. Isard and E. W. Schooler [42].

[6] Other possible sites for the production of certain petrochemicals are within the Pacific Southwest region.

[7] These tables are based on figures appearing in similar tables in W. Isard and E. W. Schooler [42], pp. 19, 22–24.

depend mainly on fuel cost differences. This means that regional steam cost differentials can be expressed as equal to the regional differentials in the cost of the required fuel gas (natural gas). Thus raw material gas, fuel gas, and steam cost differentials can be combined into a net cost differential on the equivalent volume of natural gas. This net cost differential will in the long-run tend to equal the interregional pipeline transport cost on that volume of natural gas.

A market site location incurs transport inputs (costs) on raw material gas, process fuel gas, and fuel gas for steam; practically speaking, it avoids transport inputs (costs) on finished product. A raw material site location avoids transport inputs (costs) on raw material gas, process fuel gas, and fuel gas for steam; it incurs transport inputs (costs) on finished product.

TABLE 1. PRODUCTION OF ETHYLENE GLYCOL FROM ETHANE
(Via oxidation process)

Selected Inputs	Requirements per 100 Pounds of Ethylene Glycol
Ethane	108 lb.
Utilities	
Fuel gas	377 cu. ft.
Steam	1248 lb.
Electric power	10 kw-hr.
Labor	0.19 man-hours

Because of their different requirements of transport inputs, a comparison must be made in order to calculate the transport cost differential which may exist between these two locations. This comparison is presented in Table 2.[8] Monroe has a net transport cost advantage of 13 cents if large-volume barge shipment is possible. Cincinnati has a net transport cost advantage of 60 cents if the finished product must move by rail.

Another major cost differential in petrochemical production is associated with differences in plant size. Table 3 presents the results of a calculation of such scale economies. These economies may amount to as much as $4.00 per 100 pounds of ethylene glycol.

[8] Transport cost on fuel and raw material gas was calculated on the basis of the ethane, steam, and fuel gas requirements shown in Table 2 converted to their natural gas equivalents as follows:

1 pound ethane—12.7 cubic feet
1 pound steam—1.5 cubic feet
1 cubic foot fuel gas—1 cubic foot

The interregional pipeline transport rate on natural gas was taken to be 1.3¢ per thousand cubic feet per hundred miles.

TABLE 2. TRANSPORT COST DIFFERENTIALS PER 100 POUNDS

Case A. Shipment of Product by Barge

| Location | Transport Cost on: | | Total Transport Cost | Net Advantage of Monroe |
	Equivalent Natural Gas	Finished Product		
Monroe	0	16 ¢	16¢	13¢
Cincinnati	29¢	0	29¢	

Case B. Shipment of Product by Rail

| Location | Transport Cost on : | | Total Transport Cost | Net Advantage of Cincinnati |
	Equivalent Natural Gas	Finished Product		
Monroe	0	89¢	89¢	
Cincinnati	29¢	0	29¢	60¢

Other possible cost differentials which may be significant are those in direct labor and electric power. With respect to these two items, the estimated maximum possible cost differentials between any two regions in the United States are presented in Table 4. For the two regions actually being compared, analysis indicates that differentials in power cost and labor costs will be so small as to be virtually insignificant. This leaves transport cost differentials and economies of scale as the important factors in this comparative cost study. How can we interpret the materials on these factors?

TABLE 3. ECONOMIES OF SCALE PER 100 POUNDS ETHYLENE GLYCOL ASSOCIATED WITH DIFFERENT SIZES OF ETHYLENE-ETHYLENE GLYCOL PRODUCTION UNITS

Scale economies of medium plant
over small plant $2.45

Scale economies of large plant
over medium plant $1.53

Scale economies of large plant
over small plant $3.98

Initially it should be noted that feasible plant size at a natural gas site location will generally be as large or larger than the feasible plant size at a market site because a natural gas site can serve various markets whereas a market site can serve efficiently only its own market area.   Therefore, any regional cost differential due to economies of scale will always tend to favor a natural gas site location.

If the market demand were large enough to justify the shipment of ethylene glycol to market by river barge, it would be large enough to absorb the output of at least one large optimum-size market site plant. Hence, the ethylene glycol production serving this market would come from a large-size plant, whether the plant was at the market site or the natural gas site.   This would mean little or no regional cost differential due to economies of scale.   The net transport cost differential would constitute the entire regional cost differential.   In the case depicted by Table 2 it would amount to 13 cents per hundred pounds of ethylene glycol, favoring a natural gas site location.

If the market demand were small, that is, if it were insufficient to justify shipment of product by barge, a potential natural gas site plant would

TABLE 4.   MAXIMUM LABOR AND POWER COST DIFFERENTIALS
PER 100 POUNDS

Maximum labor cost differential	12¢
Maximum power cost differential	6¢

have to ship by railroad tank car.   Under such conditions, a potential market site plant would possess a decided transport cost advantage, but at the same time the smallness of the market demand would indicate that the market could absorb the output of only a small-size market site plant. There would exist regional cost differentials stemming from economies of scale, since the potential natural gas site plant could be of large or at least medium size because of its possibility of serving multiple markets.   A comparison of the figures in Table 4 and Table 3 shows that the scale advantage of even a medium-size plant at Monroe (which advantage is $2.45) will much more than offset the transport advantage of a small plant at Cincinnati (which advantage is $0.60).   The resulting net regional cost differential in favor of the Monroe location is $1.85 per hundred pounds of ethylene glycol.

The general conclusion supported by this regional comparative cost study is that a natural gas raw materials region site on the Mississippi River near Monroe, Louisiana, is the better location for producing ethylene glycol for the Cincinnati market area.

It is evident from these materials and other extensive sets of data that in a regional comparative cost study of the production of petrochemicals from natural gas, regional differences in total transport costs and possible regional differences in feasible plant sizes are the only major considerations. In one sense, regional differences in plant sizes, owing to limited individual market demand, are of overriding importance. When these differences exist the resulting scale economies of the large plants in the raw-materials region will in virtually every case completely overshadow any other individual or combined regional cost differential. However, for all the principal volume petrochemicals there are individual market regions, each of which encompasses a demand sufficient to absorb the output of at least one optimum-size plant. In such cases there can be no appreciable regional cost differentials from economies of scale, and total transport cost differentials become the only significant regional location factor.[9]

2. IRON AND STEEL LOCATION

An essentially similar picture is presented by analysis of the iron and steel industry. A study of the feasibility of a New England location for an integrated iron and steel works may be used as an illustration.[10] Considering first the obviously important factor of transport cost differentials, the study presents tables showing total transport costs on major raw materials and finished steel products incurred by various actual and hypothetical

[9] The theoretical schema which formalizes the methodology of the comparative cost study is substitution analysis as developed in the first volume on *Location and Space-Economy*. Essentially this analysis considers alternative locations in terms of substitution between transport inputs, between diverse outlays, between diverse revenues, between outlays and revenues, and between combinations of these substitutions. The best location, in an economic sense, is one where no move elsewhere could result in further favorable substitution, that is, in reduction in total production and delivery cost. Each of the regional cost differentials of a comparative cost study measures the effect of either a single or combined substitution involved in the decision to locate in one region rather than another. In the petrochemical industry case, the only relevant regional substitution possibilities were between transport inputs (if market demand is large and concentrated), or between transport inputs and between outlays on transport inputs and outlays on production in general (if market demand is small and scattered). Because of various technological and economic reasons, the analysis of the petrochemical industry was limited to a comparison of location at a raw material site versus location at a market site. The formal substitution analysis encompasses the general case of multiple location possibilities, including intermediate sites, and variable factor proportions.

A graphic presentation of the substitution analysis can be accomplished by means of the isodapane technique. Isodapanes are essentially contour lines showing loci of points of equal production and delivery cost, equal additional transport cost, equal percentages of some base amount, etc. See T. Palander [53] and E. M. Hoover [34].

[10] W. Isard and J. Cumberland [41].

production locations in serving various New England market centers. Table 5 is the transport cost table applying to the Boston market.[11]

The figures show that for serving the Boston market either of the two New England locations considered, Fall River or New London, has a net transport cost advantage over other locations. For example, Pittsburgh incurs a total transport cost of $22.31, and Fall River and New London incur costs of $13.91 and $15.90, respectively (when Labrador ore is smelted). Similar results appear in the tabulations for other New England

TABLE 5. TRANSPORTATION COSTS ON ORE AND COAL REQUIRED PER NET TON
OF STEEL AND ON FINISHED PRODUCTS FOR SELECTED ACTUAL AND
HYPOTHETICAL PRODUCING LOCATIONS SERVING BOSTON

Location		Transportation Costs on :			
		Ore	Coal	Finished Product	Total
Fall River {	Labrador ore	$4.56	$6.01	$4.60	$15.17
	Venezuela ore	3.68	5.63	4.60	13.91
New London {	Labrador ore	4.56	5.79	6.80	17.15
	Venezuela ore	3.68	5.42	6.80	15.90
Pittsburgh		5.55	1.56	15.20	22.31
Cleveland		3.16	3.85	15.20	22.21
Sparrows Point		3.68	4.26	12.40	20.34
Buffalo		3.16	4.27	12.60	20.03
Bethlehem		5.56	5.06	10.60	21.22
Trenton		3.68	4.65	10.40	18.73

market centers, with the exception that for those in southern and western New England the transport cost advantages of Fall River and New London over Trenton are sharply reduced and under some conditions disappear.

The study proceeds by analyzing other production costs. Most of these are shown to be subject to no significant regional variation. Labor costs in the highly unionized iron and steel industry are effectively equalized among regions. It is stated that taxes may vary significantly from state to state and from locality to locality, but that there is no basis for estimating

[11] This is Table II in W. Isard and J. Cumberland [41], p. 249. A detailed explanation of the sources of the estimates and the assumptions under which they were derived appears as a note to Table I, p. 248.

the amount and direction of such variation. It is also pointed out that a New England location would enjoy an initial advantage because of lower prices on scrap iron and steel, but that this would tend to disappear when a New England steel mill became a major scrap user. And so forth.

Finally, account is taken of the influence exerted by the size of the New England market demand. In order to achieve economieȿ of scale and juxtaposition, each productive unit of an integrated steel works must be of at least minimum economic size. The demand and capacity estimates used in the study indicate that, although the total New England steel demand would well exceed the total tonnage output of an efficient integrated steel works, it is uncertain that the demand for each of the specialized components of total output would be sufficient to absorb the output of an economic-size unit. Because of the uncertainty of market demand magnitudes and in view of other intangibles, the study concludes that the net regional advantage of a New England location is not proved, even though it does enjoy a significant transport cost advantage.

3. ALUMINUM AND OTHER INDUSTRY LOCATION

The regional location patterns of the petrochemicals industry and the iron and steel industry are influenced primarily by transport costs, given the existence of large-scale individual market demands. They are essentially transport-oriented industries. A somewhat different situation exists with respect to the aluminum industry. From the standpoint of transport costs alone, the best locations within the United States for serving several of its major industrial aluminum markets are generally market locations.[12] Yet there is little aluminum production capacity at major market centers. Clearly there is some locational influence at work which is stronger than that exerted by regional transport cost differentials. It proves to be the influence of regional differences in the cost of electric power. For illustration, a location in the New York City area, a major market center, may be compared with a location in the Pacific Northwest, a region possessing major aluminum reduction capacity. Table 6 compares regional transport costs alone.[13]

Now consider the influence of the power cost differential. The production of 1 pound of pig aluminum requires approximately 9 kilowatt-hours of electric power. This means that a difference of 1.91 mills (which equals 1.714 cents divided by 9) per kilowatt-hour in the cost of electric power would be enough to offset completely the net transport cost advantage of the New York location. Actually, power rates in the Pacific Northwest

---

[12] W. Isard and V. H. Whitney [43].

[13] These transport cost figures are taken from W. Isard and V. H. Whitney [43], Tables XXII, XXIII, pp. 125, 127.

range from 2.5 to 3.5 mills per kilowatt-hour whereas in the New York area rates are approximately 8 mills per kilowatt-hour.[14] Thus, any advantage that New York possesses on transport cost account is clearly overshadowed by its disadvantage on power cost account.

Other regional cost differentials in the production of aluminum are relatively slight. As a result, the aluminum industry can be expected to be located and grow in a cheap-power region. It is a power-oriented industry.

With respect to other industries, analysis may show that some other production cost component gives rise to a major regional cost differential.[15] For example, the dominating locational influence in the textile industry is exerted by regional differentials in labor costs. But whatever the relative

TABLE 6.   REGIONAL TRANSPORTATION COSTS : ALUMINUM PRODUCTION FOR NEW YORK MARKET

	Location at :	
Item	New York	Pacific Northwest
Transport costs per pound pig aluminum		
a. On raw materials	0.548¢	1.312¢
b. On pig aluminum	0.000	0.950
Total	0.548¢	2.262¢

Net transport cost advantage of New York : 1.714¢

importance of the various types of regional cost differentials, the general approach to the regional comparative cost study is the same. The analyst must identify the components of production cost which vary regionally and then estimate the amount of each resulting cost differential. Finally, calculation of net differentials will identify the region or regions in which the industry would enjoy minimum production costs, given the set of simplifying assumptions which must underlie such a study.

[14] These rates are characteristic of 1955 conditions.

[15] In addition to the references cited in connection with the illustrations in the text, particular industry studies which illustrate the comparative cost approach are J. V. Krutilla [44], J. R. Lindsay [50, 51], J. Airov [2, 3], E. W. Schooler [58], W. Isard and W. M. Capron [40] and J. Cumberland [9].

Summaries of comparative cost studies and discussion of comparative cost factors in various industries are found in, among others, S. H. Schurr and J. Marschak [59], W. Isard [39], and T. R. Smith [62].

4. SOME LIMITATIONS

In this manner a researcher may systematically pursue comparative cost analysis for each industry considered relevant for a region. In doing so, it may be said that in at least one sense he is effectively studying the internal industrial structure of a region. Further, if he extends his analysis for each industry to embrace all regions in a system, it may be said that he is effectively studying the internal structure of the system (and as a necessary consequence the internal structure of each region).

Upon reflection, however, it is seen that this statement of possible achievement is misleading. It is to be recalled that in a comparative cost study for a given industry with reference to a specific region, both the price-cost structure and the magnitude of the market existing in each region are assumed given. Where the given industry is small and has little influence on income, demand, prices, and costs in any region, these assumptions may be justifiable. But such assumptions are clearly not warranted when the geographic pattern of the industry does have a marked influence on income, demand, prices, and costs in one or more regions. And certainly these assumptions are untenable when the researcher purports to analyze locationally each industry relevant for a region, since the estimated income and markets of the region and much of its price-cost structure is largely contingent upon the amount of industry to be located in a region.

These remarks point up the need to supplement comparative cost analysis, *when it is pursued on a systematic basis*, with other techniques which are aimed at uncovering interrelations of industry and the mutual dependence of their markets. These techniques, such as interregional input-output, industrial complex analysis, and interregional linear programming will be discussed in subsequent chapters. When coupled with comparative cost analysis, it will be seen that they can provide greater insight into the interindustry structure and other interrelations of a system of regions.

Despite the promise of comparative cost analysis when combined with the techniques mentioned, results which may be obtained must be qualified with respect to at least another major factor. It frequently happens that a comparative cost study points up a particular area as an ideal location for a given industry. Yet because of the resistance of the business units, social groups, and household residents of the area—which resistance may be formal (e.g. zoning restrictions), informal, or both—the industry does not locate in the area. More broadly speaking, from a cost standpoint a region may be ripe for industrial development. Yet because of native attitudes, cultural patterns and institutions, and other noneconomic factors, attempts at industrial development are aborted. Ideally, regional analysis should incorporate the play of such noneconomic factors which are largely nonquantitative in character. Unfortunately, only little can be done in this direction at the present time. What can be achieved, drawing upon scaling, latent structure, and similar techniques developed by psychologists and sociologists, is sketched in Appendix A to this chapter.

C. The Labor and Similar Coefficients

It was indicated in the preceding discussion that a series of regional comparative cost studies is an effective analytical tool. The researcher can use this tool to appraise the locational attractiveness of a region which possesses an abundance or cheap source of some particular mineral, commodity or service input, or other factor or market advantage. In a "cheap labor" region, for example, each individual industry comparative cost study would not only indicate in quantitative terms the pulling power of cheap labor for that industry but would also indicate whether or not the region's cheap labor advantage is sufficient to outweigh any locational disadvantages it might suffer compared to other regions. The analyst could, from an examination of the series of comparative cost studies, compare the net locational effect, industry by industry, of the region's cheap labor.

It is quite possible, however, that the analyst would have neither the time nor the resources to carry out a thorough series of regional comparative cost studies. He might desire to short-cut the extensive computations by using various coefficients. He might consider, as a first step, an industry-by-industry calculation of average labor costs per dollar of output.[16] The larger this value, the larger would be the absolute labor cost differential per dollar of output associated with a given regional wage rate differential. Thus, it would appear that industries most likely to locate in the cheap-labor region are those with the highest average labor cost per dollar of output. However, a few moments' reflection can usually bring to mind a number of instances in which industries with comparatively high labor costs per unit or per dollar output have not established production in possible cheap-labor areas but have continued to expand operations in regions of relatively dear labor. At the same time it may be quite possible to point out cases of industries which have lower labor costs per dollar output but which have actually been attracted by the cheap-labor regions. The logical explanation for such situations is that there are costs other than labor costs which vary regionally, and that these other cost variations

[16] Variants would be labor cost per unit of output and labor cost as a percentage of total unit cost.

are of different magnitudes for different industries and thus exercise varying degrees of locational influence. The problem in assessing the relative strength of a cheap-labor region's attraction for various industries lies in devising some method to take account of differences not only in labor costs among industries but also in other cost items.

One quite universal element of cost which varies significantly among industries and which, for any given industry, is generally subject to persistent regional variation is that of transport cost. To indicate the relative attractiveness of a cheap-labor location for different industries, with due regard to interindustry transport cost differences, Weber developed his "labor coefficient." It is the ratio of the labor cost per unit of product (at existing locations) to the "locational weight" of that unit. The locational weight is the sum of the required weights of localized raw materials plus product.[17] Other things being equal, the higher an industry's labor coefficient, the more likely it is that the labor cost savings it could achieve in a cheap-labor area will exceed the additional transport costs incurred by not locating at a minimum transport cost site. Generally speaking, the locational attraction of cheap-labor areas is greater for industries with high labor coefficients than for those with low.

Although the method of ranking industries by their labor coefficients affords a useful priority list of industries from the standpoint of their attraction to cheap-labor areas in general, it has definite limitations. First, more information than the labor coefficient is required to determine whether a given industry should actually be established in a given region, even if labor costs and transport costs are the only significant locational variables. The numerator of the labor coefficient must be multiplied by the "percentage of compression" of wage rates achieved by the cheap-labor region relative to the rate used in computing the labor coefficient.[18] This yields the labor cost saving per unit of product. Then the denominator (locational weight per unit product) must be multiplied by the transport rate and the net additional distance involved in location away from a minimum transport site. This yields the additional transport cost incurred

[17] Ubiquitous raw materials (ubiquities) are not included in locational weight, since in their unprocessed state they never need be transported.

All weights are expressed as "ideal weights," that is, actual weight adjusted so as to have the effect of equalizing transport rates on all materials and product. (E.g., a ton of a commodity which incurs a rate twice as great as a standard commodity is considered to have an ideal weight of two tons.) In the use of this coefficient, transport costs are generally assumed to be proportional to distance.

For supplementary discussion, see *Location and Space-Economy*, pp. 126–142.

[18] The percentage of compression thus represents the per cent by which the wage rate at a cheap-labor location is lower than the wage rate at existing locations (after adjustment to an equivalent efficiency basis).

by locating in the cheap-labor region. Only if the labor cost saving is greater in amount than the additional transport cost would it be to the industry's advantage to locate in the cheap-labor region, *ceteris paribus*.

Second, consider the relative attraction held by a specific cheap-labor area for two industries with identical labor coefficients but with geographically different minimum transport cost production sites. Except for special cases, the relative pull of the cheap-labor area would be different for the two industries; it is quite possible that location there would represent a net advantage for one but a net disadvantage for the other, depending on the net additional distance involved in location away from the respective minimum transport cost sites.[19]

It is even possible that the distance factor could be so different for two industries with reference to a specific cheap-labor site that one could have a relatively low labor coefficient and yet be attracted to the site, and the other could have a relatively high labor coefficient and yet tend to locate away from the site. It becomes evident that even when labor costs and transport costs are the only significant locational influences, a ranking of industries by their labor coefficients is a valid indicator of the relative degree to which they are attracted to a specific cheap-labor site only when the net additional distance involved in a location away from the minimum transport cost site is the same for each industry.[20] Such a ranking can be definitely misleading if the distances involved vary among industries, as they commonly do. The ranking can be still more misleading if we consider too the possibility of transport savings at a cheap-labor site from the use of substitute sources of raw materials, since this possibility may vary greatly from industry to industry and from region to region.[21] The relative degree of the cheap-labor site's attraction for different industries can be assessed under such conditions only by individual calculation for each industry of the labor cost saving per unit compared with the additional transport cost per unit.

[19] For example, a cheap-labor area in, say, South Carolina might attract an industry utilizing lower Mississippi Valley raw materials and serving a Middle Atlantic industrial market; yet for an industry having an identical labor coefficient but using raw materials from the Central Plains states and serving a Chicago-Detroit market, the labor cost savings attainable at the South Carolina location could very well be entirely inadequate to offset the additional transport cost incurred on the shipment of raw materials and product.

[20] Also, in Weberian terminology, the location figures must be identical (or, practically speaking, approximately equal).

[21] Additionally, the possibility of cost savings from substituting cheap labor for other factor inputs may exist, and to a different extent from industry to industry. Such cost savings must be allowed for in the final cost comparisons.

The reader will perceive that this sort of calculation is actually an industry comparative cost study in an abridged form. That is, cost differentials are calculated between two regions, the region of the minimum transport cost site and the region of the cheap-labor site, with respect to only two cost elements, transportation and labor. This illustrates the basic limitation of the labor coefficient and of any comparative cost calculation derived from it. At the end, the analyst finds himself with a set of incomplete regional comparative cost studies. A better method would be to proceed from the outset with a more complete and systematic set of industry-by-industry comparative cost studies (embracing, if possible, recognition of community attitudes and other similar subjective factors discussed in Appendix A to this Chapter).

Of what use then is the labor coefficient? It has already been noted that a ranking of industries by their labor coefficients furnishes an indication of the extent of their attraction to cheap-labor regions *generally*. To the analyst concerned with the growth prospects of a specific cheap-labor region, such a ranking is an aid in deciding for which industries to carry out comparative cost studies. Certainly those with high labor coefficients would be included at the start. The ones with lower coefficients should not be summarily rejected, but the analyst would realize that their growth in his region, in all likelihood, depends on other factors in addition to possible labor cost savings.

Although the labor coefficient has been discussed to illustrate a device useful to a limited extent in the analysis of a region possessing a particular resource, similar coefficients can be developed in connection with other specific regional resource advantages. Thus, a power coefficient, a fuel coefficient, a steam coefficient, among others, could be developed to indicate the relative extent to which various industries are attracted to regions of cheap power, fuel, steam, etc. These coefficients would, as in the case of the labor coefficient, have as a numerator the average cost of the specific resource input per unit output of product, and as a denominator the locational weight associated with the unit output of product.[22] Their

___

[22] In the computation of these as well as labor coefficients, it is sometimes possible and desirable to take account, in the *denominator*, of the effects of using such resources as power, fuel, and steam. Often regional differences in power and steam costs are attributable almost wholly to regional differences in the cost of the fuel required; these fuel differences, in turn, may simply reflect the cost of transporting fuel such as coal or gas from one region to another. If the process power, steam, and fuel requirements are expressed in terms of their required fuel equivalents, the latter can then be considered as part of the locational weight. For a more complete discussion of this point, see W. Isard and E. W. Schooler [42], pp. 15–16.

If regional differences in power or steam costs are wholly due to differences in transport cost between regions of required fuel, a set of power coefficients or steam co-use would likewise be principally as general indicators rather than as specific measuring devices.

If a region possessed more than one resource advantage, for example, cheap labor *and* cheap power, a combined coefficient might perhaps prove useful in certain situations. The numerator in this case would consist of the combined labor and power cost per unit output, and the denominator would again be the locational weight of the unit output of product. However, the two elements of the numerator would have to be weighted, the weights for any region being the respective percentage compressions achievable in the region for these elements. Since the weights would differ from region to region, the usefulness of a combined coefficient is greatly curtailed.

D. COEFFICIENT OF LOCALIZATION, LOCALIZATION CURVES AND RATIOS, AND RELATED CONCEPTS

The coefficients discussed so far are primarily applicable to the analysis of a region with an abundant and cheap endowment of one or more particular resource. However, the regional analyst may be concerned not so much with finding which industries can best use an abundant resource as with finding industries to diversify the economic base of the community. Or he may be concerned with possible lines of development in a region committed to a specific policy of small industries or small plants or both. Or he may be concerned with the change over time of the spatial pattern of population and total employment, or with the change over time in the degree to which one or more industries are material- or market-oriented.

1. PRELIMINARY ORGANIZATION OF DATA

To help deal with such concerns and problems and many similar ones, a number of coefficients, ratios, and indexes have been developed. Many of these pertain to the same sets of data. It therefore is desirable to discuss them in a rather systematic manner. To facilitate this discussion, we sketch the outlines of a table containing certain basic data.

Table 7 relates to 1954 manufacturing employment by industry for the United States viewed as a system of regions. (The problem of selecting appropriate sets of regions and industries will be discussed later and in Appendix B.) Each column refers to a particular state (region) of the United States ; the total manufacturing employment in each state (region)

efficients indicate, in effect, the relative importance, among the different industries, of transport inputs associated with power and steam requirements, compared with other transport inputs, in establishing the minimum transport cost site.

TABLE 7.   LOCATION QUOTIENTS AND EQUIVALENT EMPLOYMENT PERCENTAGE RATIOS BY REGION AND INDUSTRY, 1954

	Employment: United States	Maine	New Hampshire	Indiana	Michigan	California
Employment (total)	16,125,550	104,507	77,332	587,782	1,056,564	1,052,785
Meat products	311,336	$\frac{0.36}{0.65}=0.55=\frac{1.06}{1.93}$	$\frac{0.15}{0.48}=0.31=\frac{0.59}{1.93}$	$\frac{3.54}{3.65}=0.97=\frac{1.88}{1.93}$	$\frac{2.00}{6.55}=0.31=\frac{0.59}{1.93}$	$\frac{5.76}{6.53}=0.88=\frac{1.70}{1.93}$
Dairy products	283,431	$\frac{0.49}{0.65}=0.76=\frac{1.33}{1.76}$	$\frac{0.36}{0.48}=0.74=\frac{1.30}{1.76}$	$\frac{3.37}{3.65}=0.93=\frac{1.63}{1.76}$	$\frac{4.26}{6.55}=0.65=\frac{1.14}{1.76}$	d
Heating and plumbing equipment	105,888	d	$\frac{0.17}{0.48}=0.35=\frac{0.23}{0.66}$	$\frac{4.54}{3.65}=1.25=\frac{0.82}{0.66}$	$\frac{5.01}{6.55}=0.76=\frac{0.50}{0.66}$	$\frac{9.38}{6.53}=1.44=\frac{0.94}{0.66}$
Structural metal products	284,121	$\frac{0.50}{0.65}=0.77=\frac{1.35}{1.76}$	$\frac{0.10}{0.48}=0.22=\frac{0.38}{1.76}$	$\frac{3.95}{3.65}=1.09=\frac{1.91}{1.76}$	$\frac{6.02}{6.55}=0.92=\frac{1.62}{1.76}$	$\frac{7.80}{6.53}=1.19=\frac{2.10}{1.76}$
Miscellaneous Manufactures	357,153	d	$\frac{0.57}{0.48}=1.20=\frac{2.64}{2.22}$	$\frac{5.64}{3.65}=1.55=\frac{3.43}{2.22}$	$\frac{6.67}{6.55}=1.02=\frac{2.26}{2.22}$	$\frac{12.62}{6.53}=1.93=\frac{4.28}{2.22}$

d indicates the unavailability of census data for computation.

is listed directly below the name of the state. Each row refers to an industry in the three-digit classification of the United States census ; the total United States employment in each industry is listed in the corresponding cell of the first column. Each of the other cells of the table contains a pure number and two employment percentage ratios. The first ratio of percentages has as its *numerator* the given region's percentage share of total system employment in the given industry. (For example, the numerator of the first ratio in the second cell of the second row records the per cent of total United States employment in the meat products industry which is in Maine.) The first ratio of percentages has as its *denominator* the given region's percentage share of *all* manufacturing employment in the system. (For example, the denominator of the first ratio in the second cell of the second row records Maine's percentage share of total manufacturing employment in the United States.)[23]

When the first ratio of each cell in the body of the table is expressed as a pure number, we have the location quotient, as defined in section B, Chapter 5. Where the location quotient is less than unity, the given region has less than its "fair" share of the industry in question. Where the location quotient exceeds unity, the given region has more than a proportionate share of the industry in question.

But as has also been indicated in section B of Chapter 5, the location quotient is equal to a second ratio of employment percentages. The numerator of this second ratio indicates the per cent of the given region's total manufacturing employment accounted for by the given industry. (For example, employment in meat products manufacture accounts for 1.06 per cent of total manufacturing employment in Maine.) The denominator of this second ratio indicates the per cent of the over-all system's total manufacturing employment accounted for by the given industry. (For example, employment in meat products manufacture accounts for 1.93 per cent of total United States manufacturing employment.)[24]

2. THE COEFFICIENTS OF LOCALIZATION AND REDISTRIBUTION

With the systematic recording of data such as outlined in Table 7, the analyst is in a position to derive a number of useful descriptive coefficients and indexes. One that has been used extensively is the coefficient of localization.[25] This is a measure of relative regional concentration of

[23] It is to be noted that the denominator of the first ratio remains the same for any given column and only differs from column to column.

[24] Note that in any given row the denominator of the second ratio remains a constant; it varies only from row to row.

[25] See P. S. Florence [19], pp. 34ff; or P. S. Florence, W. G. Fritz, and R. C. Gilles [20], ch. 5.

a given industry compared to some total national magnitude such as population, land area, manufacturing employment, or income. It is essentially a comparison of the percentage distribution by region of employment in the given industry with the regional percentage distribution of the base magnitude, for example total national manufacturing employment. The actual computation of the coefficient typically consists of (1) subtracting for each region its percentage share of total system employment in the given industry (as recorded in the numerators of the first ratio in the cells of the given row of Table 7) from its percentage share of total manufacturing employment in the system (as recorded in the denominators

TABLE 8. DATA FOR COMPUTATION OF COEFFICIENT OF LOCALIZATION

Item	Regions			
	A	B	C	D
1. Per cent of employment of industry i	20	30	35	15
2. Per cent of total United States manufacturing employment	15	20	30	35
Difference (row 1 − row 2)	+5	+10	+5	−20
(Location Quotient)	(1.33	1.5	1.17	0.43)

of the first ratio in the cells of the same row of Table 7); (2) adding all positive differences, or all negative differences; and (3) dividing the sum of the positive (or negative) differences by 100. For example, if the data for a four-region system are as shown in Table 8, the coefficient of localization is

$$+20/100 = 0.2 \text{ (footnote 26)}$$

The limits to the value of the coefficient are 0 and 1. If the given industry is distributed exactly the same as is the base magnitude, the value will be 0. In contrast, if the entire industry is concentrated in one (small) region, the value will approach unity.

For the regional analyst seeking to implement a policy of diversification, a series of localization coefficients, each derived from the data of a relevant row in Table 7, could be useful. It could provide the basis for a preliminary and tentative judgment about which industries to seek and encourage or at least to investigate further. Industries with low coefficients are relatively

[26] The summation could just as well be of the minus deviations, since the percentage distributions are such that the sum of total plus and minus deviations is zero.

nonconcentrated regionally and are thus presumably amenable to location in a region seeking industrial diversification.

The basic feature of the localization coefficient—the comparison of two percentage distributions applicable to a given set of regions—can, of course, be extended to the comparison of any two meaningful percentage distributions. As already suggested, instead of using total manufacturing employment as the base, an analyst can use other magnitudes such as employment in another related industry or industrial complex, population, land area, Gross Product, and income. (The data may again be organized along the lines of Table 7.) If employment in another related industry is used as the base, the coefficient of localization is essentially the coefficient of geographic association, as defined by Florence.[27] It compares the geographic distribution of a given industry to the geographic distribution of the base industry. If population is used as base, the coefficient of localization may again be alternatively stated as a coefficient of geographic association whereby the geographic distribution of a given industry is associated with the geographic distribution of population.[28]

Not only are there many possible base magnitudes but also there are many magnitudes relevant for comparison with a base. That is, not only may tables like Table 7 be constructed in order to relate regional employment by industry to such base magnitudes as population, land area, and income, but they may also be constructed to relate to a pertinent base many other variables: for example, population by age group, color, or native stock; value added by industry; and urbanization by size class of city. Each such table then provides the data in the basic form for the

[27] When the value of the coefficient is zero, complete geographic association exists; when the value is unity, no geographic association exists.

[28] When in Table 7 a new base is substituted for total manufacturing employment, the row of numbers representing totals for the United States and its regions, which comes at the top of the columns, must be changed. And as a consequence the denominator of the first ratio, the pure number, and both the numerator and denominator of the second ratio must be changed.

For example, if population substitutes for total manufacturing employment as base, the population of the United States, and of each of its states, must be listed at the head of the respective columns. The numerator of the first ratio remains unchanged, since it represents a region's percentage share of employment in a given industry. The denominator of the first ratio changes; it now represents the region's percentage share of United States population. The numerator of the second ratio changes; it is the fraction formed by dividing a region's employment in a given industry by that region's population (which equals the region's per capita employment in the given industry). The denominator of the second ratio also changes; it is the fraction formed by dividing United States employment in a given industry by United States population (which equals United States per capita employment in the given industry). Also, as a consequence the pure number (location quotient) in each cell changes.

computation of the relevant set of coefficients of localization (or geographic association).[29]

One variant of the coefficient of localization which is of general value is the coefficient of redistribution. This coefficient is essentially a measure of the deviation between two distributions of the same phenomenon taken at different key points of time. For example, for two successive census years the percentage distribution of population by region could be compared. Taking one percentage distribution as the base, the deviations of the other percentage distribution can be computed. Summing all positive (or negative) deviations yields a figure which when divided by 100 can be designated a coefficient of redistribution. The value of such a coefficient will range from 0 (no redistribution) to unity (complete redistribution).

A number of other related coefficients may be constructed for various purposes. Some of these, together with the coefficient of geographic association and coefficient of redistribution, are listed in Table 9.[30] The relationships expressed by these coefficients and their possible uses are for the most part self-evident.[31]

[29] When in Table 7 a new nonbase magnitude is substituted for employment by industry, the first column of numbers representing totals for the several classes of industries must be changed. They must represent relevant totals for the new set of sectors (item classes or groups). And as a consequence the numerator of the first ratio, the pure number, and both the numerator and denominator of the second ratio must be changed.

For example, if the base magnitude is population (as in the previous footnote) and if number of families by income group substitutes for employment by industry as the nonbase magnitude, the number of families in each income group must be recorded in the first column. The numerator of the first ratio changes; it comes to represent a region's percentage share of the total number of families in a given-size income group in the United States. The denominator of the first ratio remains unchanged; it still represents the region's percentage share of total United States population. The numerator of the second ratio changes; it is the fraction formed by dividing the number of families of a given-size income group in a region by that region's population. The denominator of the second ratio also changes; it is the fraction formed by dividing the total number of families of the given-size income group in the United States by the population of the United States. Also, as a consequence, the pure number (location quotient) in each cell changes; it now reflects the extent to which the total population of each region has a proportionate share of United States families in a given-size income group.

[30] Also see P. M. Hauser, O. D. Duncan, and B. Duncan [30].

[31] As with the coefficient of localization, the coefficients of Table 9 are based on ratios of two percentages or fractions which in turn may yield the location quotient or one of its many possible variants. In connection with the use of the 1954 *Census of Manufactures* data, Alexander lists the following fractions (or percentages) of possible value for geographic analysis: number employed in manufacturing divided by total employed labor force, by total population, by total number of factories, or by employment in activity i; value added divided by total population or by number employed in

3. THE LOCALIZATION CURVE

A tool superior in several ways to the coefficient of localization and related coefficients listed in Table 9 is the *localization curve*.[32]   The localiza-

TABLE 9.   COEFFICIENTS: TYPE *A*

Name of Coefficient	Author	Distributions Compared
Coefficient of geographic association	Florence et al. [20].	Shares of manufacturing employment by states : industry *i* versus industry *j*.
Coefficient of concentration of population	Hoover [36]	Shares by states : population versus area
Coefficient of redistribution	Hoover [36] Florence, et al. [20]	Shares of population (or total wage earners, or employment in selected manufacturing industries) by states : year α versus year β
Coefficient of deviation	Hoover [36]	Shares of population by states : white versus Negro
Index of dissimilarity	Duncan [14, 15]	Shares of workers by areas : occupation group *A* versus occupation group *B*
Index of segregation	Duncan [14, 15]	Shares of workers by areas : specific occupation group versus all other occupation groups

tion curve is constructed from a set of regional percentage figures by plotting on the vertical axis a cumulative percentage figure for the given industry's employment and on the horizontal axis the corresponding

manufacturing; value of payroll divided by value added ; number of small factories divided by total number of factories (J. W. Alexander [4], pp. 20–26).

A series, by areas, of any one of these fractions when compared with the relevant fractions for the total system (say United States) could form the basis for a coefficient similar to those listed in Table 9.   For example, the quotients of the per cent of a county's factories which are small factories to the per cent of United States factories which are small factories may be computed.   The resulting series, by county, can be transformed into a series of ratios indicating a county's percentage share of all small factories in the United States to that county's share of all factories in the United States.   By a summation of positive (or negative) deviations, a coefficient of geographic association of small factories relative to all factories can be computed.

[32] This curve is developed and discussed in E. M. Hoover [35].   Also see E. M. Hoover [34], pp. 182–184.

cumulative percentage figure for the base magnitude. Typically, the required regional percentages can be obtained from the data included in a row of such tables as Table 7. [For every row (industry) of Table 7, a localization curve can be constructed.] The procedure involves (1) ranking regions by location quotients along the relevant row; and (2) plotting regions by rank on a cumulative percentage basis. For example, we may

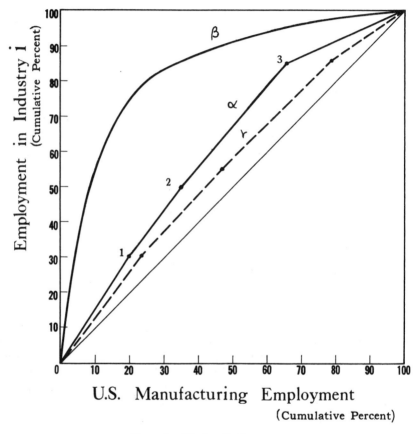

Figure 1. The localization curve.

take the data given in Table 8. Region B has the highest location quotient. As the first step, we therefore plot its percentages in Figure 1 (point 1 on curve α). Region A has the next highest location quotient. We therefore add region B's percentages to the corresponding percentages of region A and plot the two sums (point 2 on curve α). Region C ranks third in size of location quotient for industry i. Its percentages are added to the corresponding sums already obtained and the resulting two new sums are plotted (point 3 on curve α). Finally, region D's percentages are added to yield 100 per cent for both magnitudes. Joining the successive points by straight-line segments yields localization curve α.

Localization curves are essentially a device to depict and rank regions by location quotient since the slopes of their straight-line segments are identical with the location quotients of the several regions. If it turns out that a given industry is distributed regionally exactly the same as the base magnitude, the location quotients will all be unity and the localization curve will be a $45°$ diagonal from the origin. However, any divergence in the two distributions will be reflected in a deviation of the localization curve above and to the left of the diagonal. The extent of this deviation is a measure of the regional concentration of the industry, compared to the base magnitude. In this connection, we may compute the ratio of (1) the area between the localization curve and the diagonal to (2) the total area of the right triangle formed by the diagonal, the vertical axis, and the top of the graph. The limiting values of the ratio would be zero and one, as they were for the coefficient of localization computed from the plus or minus deviations of the percentage distributions.

In addition to using a localization curve to summarize the geographic pattern of an industry at a given point of time, an analyst may wish to proceed further with this tool. He may wish to contrast the geographic patterns of several industries at a given point of time. On a figure such as Figure 1 he may wish to construct another localization curve representing a second industry, still another localization curve representing a third industry, etc. For example, in Figure 1 a second localization curve β is constructed.[33] The advantage that a graphic presentation of two or more localization curves has over a presentation of two coefficients is clear-cut. This advantage exists whether or not the same set of regions is used in constructing the localization curve (and calculating the coefficient of localization) for each of the two or more industries under study.[34]

Moreover, an analyst may wish to compare the geographic pattern of an industry at a key point of time with its pattern for one or more other key points in time. On a figure such as Figure 1 he may wish to construct a localization curve for each time point to be considered. For example, on

---

[33] The β curve is taken from E. M. Hoover [34], p. 183, and represents shoe manufacture in the United States. States are taken as regions. The base magnitude is population. The nonbase magnitude is employment in shoe manufacturing.

‾ [34] When different sets of regions are justifiably used from one industry to the next, considerable care must be exercised in reaching conclusions, whatever the tool used for descriptive comparison. See later remarks on the variation of the coefficient of localization with change in regional classification.

Figure 1 we have constructed localization curve γ which represents the same industry i as does curve α but is applicable to a different point of time. A comparison of curves α and γ, particularly when the ranking of regions is the same for both, has clear advantage over a mere presentation of two coefficients.

Thus, it may be concluded that the localization curve is a useful supplement (if not substitute) of the coefficient of localization. It retains regional detail in that the slopes of its line segments register the relevant regional location quotients, that is, show the regional components of a geographic

TABLE 10.   CURVES AND COEFFICIENTS: TYPE B

Name of Coefficient	Author	Cumulative Distributions Compared	Order of Cumulation
Urbanization curve and coefficient	Hoover [36]	Shares by cities: employment in individual industry versus total population	By city size (small to large)
Urbanization curve and coefficient	Duncan [12]	Shares by city-size groups: retail sales in a given business versus total retail sales	By size of group (small to large)
Index of centralization	Duncan [15]	Shares by census tracts: specific occupation group versus all occupation groups (alternatively, employment in a given industry versus all industry)	By distance from city center

pattern. And it permits a visual comparison which for many studies may effectively complement (or replace) the presentation of one or more coefficients. Yet, for systematic studies which are based on a comprehensive set of tables, such as Table 7, and in which a fine industrial classification is employed, a complete set of localization curves may be an unwieldy tool for analysis. It may be much less efficient than the summary presentation of a set of coefficients, such as those listed in Table 9, particularly when supplemented by one or more sets of other coefficients, such as those listed in Table 10.[35]

[35] Hoover and others have attempted to extend the graphic technique of the localization curve to compare distributions ordered in accordance with other external criteria. For example, Hoover's urbanization curve is obtained by the same method as the

4. THE SHIFT RATIO AND RELATIVE GROWTH CHART

In section 2 we have already commented on the coefficient of redistribution. Another measure of regional shift in industry which is very similar to this coefficient is a *shift ratio*.[36] The rate of growth of employment in a given industry is first calculated over an intercensal period on an over-all or national basis. Then there is computed for each region the difference between the actual employment in the industry and the employment that would have resulted had the region's rate of growth in the industry been the same as the national rate. A positive difference signifies a shift of the industry into the region; a negative difference indicates a shift out of the region. The shift ratio for the industry is calculated by summing all the positive (or negative) shifts in employment and expressing the result as a proportion of total industry employment.[37]

It is apparent that an important defect of both shift ratios and coefficients of redistribution as measures of interregional industrial shifts is the fact that they take no account of changes in other major variables. Regional realignments in population, total income payments, value added by manufacture, private investment expenditure, public spending on waterways and highways, etc., may significantly influence or modify the possible implications of an industry's shift ratio or redistribution coefficient.[38]

localization curve, except that the units of the distributions are cities of various sizes rather than regions or states, and the order of the graphic cumulations is according to city size. Unlike the localization curve, the urbanization curve may be quite irregular or erratic. In fact, it may be above the diagonal in some places and below it in others. A numerical coefficient of urbanization can be computed as an area ratio, similar to the Hoover derivation of the coefficient of localization. Table 10 contains a summary list of a few such "externally ordered" curves and coefficients which are designated type *B*.

[36] See D. Creamer [8], ch. 4. For a more recent application of this general type of thinking, see V. R. Fuchs [22].

[37] In addition to his use of shift ratios to measure regional redistribution of industrial employment, Creamer developed a rough measure of regional concentration of industry —the coefficient of scatter ([8], p. 90). It is expressed as the least number of states necessary to account for 75 per cent of total industry employment. Clearly, this can offer only a very general indication of the extent of industry concentration. More accurate comparisons are possible via the localization curve or coefficient of localization.

[38] For example, the fact that an industry has had a high shift ratio or coefficient of redistribution over a period of time may be considerably less striking if it is found that the coefficient of population redistribution was correspondingly high during the same period, particularly if there was a high coincidence in the individual components of the two types of ratios. Conversely, an industry with a low shift ratio or redistribution coefficient may be thought to have few implications of regional change—until it is found that the coefficient of population redistribution was high for the period. One possible way to attack the type of difficulty illustrated would be to compute a supplementary

One approach to this problem which can take account of one variable in addition to the industry change is the *relative growth chart*.[39]   This is a graphic presentation of the scatter diagram type and can be adapted to the problem of industry redistribution using a figure such as Figure 2.   In Figure 2, the vertical axis measures for a given industry employment at the

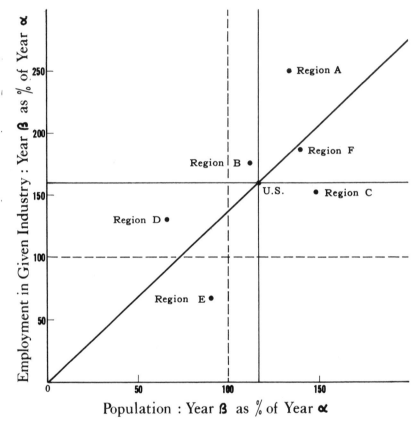

Figure 2.   Relative growth chart, by region.

end of the period of analysis as a percentage of the employment at the beginning of the period.   The horizontal axis measures a similar percentage for the other variable, say population.   Each region of a system, here taken to be the United States, is represented by a point on the graph with coordinates determined by its percentage changes in industry employment and in population.   The system's average percentage changes in coefficient measuring the deviation between the regional percentage distributions of growth in population and growth in the given industry.

[39] See E. M. Hoover and J. L. Fisher [37], pp. 195–203.

these magnitudes are also indicated by a point, here indicating the average changes for the United States.   A diagonal drawn from the origin through the United States point has a slope equal to the ratio of the two relevant percentages for the United States as measured on the two axes.   This slope is also equivalent to the percentage change in United States per capita employment in the given industry.[40]   The diagonal permits easy visual comparison of the several regional per capita changes with the United States per capita change.   If a region is represented by a point lying above and to the left of the diagonal, its per capita change in the given industry employment is greater than that for the nation (system) as a whole.   In addition to the diagonal, a vertical and a horizontal line may be extended from the axes through the point representing United States experience, as is done in Figure 2.   These permit visual comparison of regional rates of both population change and employment change in the given industry with the corresponding United States rates.[41, 42]

[40] That is, if E represents employment, P population, and α and β the beginning and end of the period respectively, then

$$\frac{E_\beta/E_\alpha}{P_\beta/P_\alpha} = \frac{E_\beta/P_\beta}{E_\alpha/P_\alpha} = \frac{\text{per capita employment in year } \beta}{\text{per capita employment in year } \alpha}$$

[41] To illustrate the use of such a graph, a few of many possible situations may be hypothesized.   An industry growing at somewhat the same rate as national population might show a wide scatter of points clustered along the diagonal.   This would indicate that, although the industry had a high coefficient of redistribution, it had little change in *per capita* importance by regions.   On the other hand, a wide scatter of points along the horizontal line would indicate considerable divergence among the regions in *per capita* changes in the given industry, in spite of a low coefficient of redistribution.   If, however, there had been a situation of major regional redistribution of the industry combined with little relative regional change in population, the result would be a wide scatter of points all close to the vertical line.   Not only would the industry show a high redistribution coefficient; it would also show a wide extent of change in its regional per capita importance.

[42] For regional analysis, the relative growth chart is useful in ways other than indicated in the text.   To cite two such ways, it can compare by regions (1) per cent changes in income, in per capita income, and in population; or (2) per cent changes in Gross Product, in productivity per worker, and in total employment.

Also, in line with certain suggestions of Zelinsky, the influence of population change could be accounted for directly in computing the individual ratios of the redistribution coefficient (W. Zelinsky [69]).   In measuring change in United States manufacturing activity between 1939 and 1947, Zelinsky develops certain "factors" or expressions which take account of the interrelations between areal changes in amount of manufacturing, population, and number of production workers.   For example, he writes the $V:P$ factor for an area as

$$V_{1947} - \frac{V_{1939} \cdot P_{1947} \cdot K}{P_{1939}}$$

where V is value added by manufacture, P is area population, and K is a constant such

5. TECHNICAL LIMITATIONS

Thus far, we have suggested some possible uses for the various co-efficients and related concepts which have been discussed. However, like most techniques, they are subject to major limitations. One of the most evident shortcomings of any coefficient or graphic representation which is based on the deviation between, or ratio of, two percentage distributions is that the results obtained will differ, depending on the degree of areal subdivision. For example, the coefficient of localization of an industry compared to total manufacturing workers would almost certainly be higher if the nation were broken down by counties rather than by states.[43] Furthermore, the degree of variation in the value of the coefficient under such conditions would differ for different industries. Thus, two industries might have virtually the same coefficient of localization if states were the unit of subdivision but substantially different ones if counties were. This reduces the usefulness of interindustry comparison based on the coefficient of localization and similar devices.

This shortcoming is neatly portrayed by Figure 3, taken from Duncan, Cuzzort, and Duncan.[44] This figure indicates indexes of population concentration, for five alternative systems of areal subdivision of the United States, 1900–1950. These indexes are essentially coefficients of localization of population, where land area is the base magnitude. That these coefficients decrease as the size of region increases is clear from this figure. For any one year, the smaller the areal subdivision the greater the coefficient proves to be. More striking, however, is the fact that over the time period examined the coefficients based on large areal subdivisions

that the sum of the $V:P$ factors for all areas is zero (i.e., $\sum V:P = 0$). (K thus approximates the ratio for the nation of per capita value added by manufacture for 1947 to the same magnitude for 1939.) Thus, if the ratio of per capita value added had increased at a uniform rate in all areas between 1939 and 1947, the $V:P$ factor for each area would be zero.

Although Zelinsky presents his findings as a set of positive and absolute differences (see Map 2), they can be expressed in terms of percentile differences. Such percentile differences in turn could form the basis for the calculation of a redistribution coefficient as already discussed. Use of magnitudes other than value added and population would also lead to other relevant redistribution coefficients.

[43] Thompson points out that virtually any industry exhibits a high coefficient of localization if the areal subdivision scheme is fine enough. However, in his view, of more significance may be the rate at which the value of the coefficient decreases as larger subdivisions are considered. A rapid rate of decrease suggests that the industry is in reality rather dispersed, with the several sites (or areas) of production contiguous with areas of nonproduction. A slower rate of decrease indicates that the production sites are "clustered" within a smaller number of separate producing areas. See W. R. Thompson [64].

[44] O. D. Duncan, R. P. Cuzzort, B. Duncan [13].

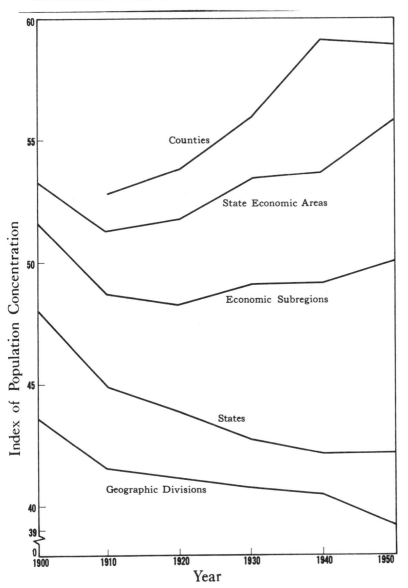

Figure 3.   Indexes of population concentration, for various systems of areal subdivision of the United States: 1900 to 1950.   Source: O. D. Duncan, R. P. Cuzzort, and B. Duncan [13].

tend to become smaller, whereas the same coefficients based on small areal subdivisions tend to become larger. This fact corroborates the point that as a descriptive device any given coefficient can be meaningful *only* with reference to the set of areal subdivisions adopted. Furthermore, this fact suggests that a series of coefficients based on different areal subdivisions is necessary to indicate the complex pattern of population changes over time.[45]

A second major difficulty of the coefficient of localization and related concepts reflects the tendency of any such measure to vary considerably, depending on the choice of base. Localization, centralization, redistribution, etc., are necessarily expressed relative to a base magnitude—there is no absolute measure. Thus, if a large portion of a country's total industry is concentrated in a relatively few metropolitan areas, a specific industry also heavily concentrated in these same areas will quite likely show a low coefficient of localization when the coefficient is computed with total industry employment or output as a base. If the coefficient were computed with geographic area as a base, the value would be considerably higher.[46]

[45] For further discussion, see O. D. Duncan, R. P. Cuzzort, and B. Duncan [13].

In view of this limitation, an analyst may seek measures of geographic distribution which are essentially independent of the scheme of subdivision used. One such measure is a centrographic technique which has been developed by Bachi for summarizing the extent of population dispersion. (See R. Bachi [5], as reported by O. D. Duncan, R. P. Cuzzort, and B. Duncan [13]). In a population distribution each areal unit, with a population of P_i, can be approximated as a point with a horizontal coordinate x_i and a vertical coordinate y_i. Then the "mean center" of population is at $(\bar{x}, \bar{y})$ where

$$\bar{x} = \sum_i P_i \cdot x_i \Big/ \sum_i x_i \text{ and } \bar{y} = \sum_i P_i \cdot y_i \Big/ \sum_i y_i.$$

Dispersion around the mean center can be measured by the "standard distance,"

$$d = \sqrt{\frac{\sum_i P_i \cdot (x_i - \bar{x})^2 + \sum_i P_i \cdot (y_i - \bar{y})^2}{\sum_i P_i}}$$

Similarly, the dispersion of population can be measured in terms of distances separating the centers of the individual areas. There is a constant relationship between these two measures of dispersion, and their values are affected only incidentally by the type of subdivision employed. (Generally speaking, the measures are more precise the smaller the subdivisions.)

Clearly, such measures could be of considerable help in evaluating the degree of concentration or dispersion of given industries, number of manufacturing workers, etc. However, as Duncan, Cuzzort, and Duncan point out, when one is concerned with changes in a distribution pattern (e.g. over time), it is hardly likely that any single centrographic technique could furnish a complete or adequate description. A series of coefficients based on different sets of areal subdivisions might well be preferable.

[46] W. R. Thompson [64] has pointed out this problem of the implicit weighting of the individual regions by their respective shares of the base magnitude. In order to weight

As already noted, a defect which applies particularly to the numerical coefficients and shift ratios is that they express a combined or net value and give no indication of the behavior of the individual components making up that value.[47]   In this connection, preserving the detail on the behavior pattern of the individual regions via the use of a localization curve would be highly desirable, although perhaps cumbersome.

As already pointed out in a previous footnote, the graphic approach has been extended to the construction of curves and the calculation of ratios and coefficients in which the distributions are ordered, not according to the magnitude of the individual deviations but according to some external standard, such as size of city, distance from city center, etc.   Coefficients and curves of this type (type B) can be of only limited use.   The curves are not typically smooth or symmetric and can give only a very rough idea of what they purport to describe.   They can be badly distorted by major deviations anywhere in the ranking.   The corresponding coefficients based on ratios of graphic areas are noncomparable.[48]

A final major difficulty of the coefficient of localization and related concepts is the problem of designing a proper set of industrial categories, income classes, occupational groups, population sectors, etc.   Thus far we have assumed that a set of categories is predetermined, for example, that the most desirable industrial classification has been determined.   Or

regions equally (when such is desirable), he suggests that a coefficient of spatial variation be substituted for the coefficient of localization.   If we let E_j^L be employment in the given industry j in region L (where regions are numbered from 1 to U), E^L be total manufacturing employment (or population) in region L; h_j^L equal E_j^L/E^L, and U be the number of regions, then the coefficient of spatial variation equals σ/h_j where

$$\sigma = \sqrt{\frac{\sum_L \left(h_j^L - h_j\right)^2}{U}}$$

and

$$h_j = \frac{\sum_L h_j^L}{U}$$

[47] For example, a specific value for the coefficient of redistribution of employment in a given industry may have resulted from a major exodus from one region and minor increases in most of the others; or from a major expansion in one region coupled with small losses in the others.   The knowledge of which situation (if either) actually existed would certainly be helpful to a regional analyst concerned with future prospects of the industry, but the coefficient itself would not furnish this information.

[48] For example, suppose that the urbanization curves of industry i and industry j enclose equal areas between the curve and the diagonal, giving the two industries equal coefficients of urbanization.   However, if the curve for i has a bulge near one end of the ranking, and the curve for j has a similar bulge toward the other end, we could not state that industries i and j are equally "urbanized."

we have been concerned with a given industry (already defined), or manufacturing industry as a whole, etc., and have probed into its geographic pattern. But suppose our concerns center around broad issues such as resource development policy and industrial diversification within a system of regions. Suppose we wish to select, out of the whole array of industries, a few that *initially* appear suitable for development for' each of a number of areas. Suppose, too, for this task we judge that there ought to be constructed a complete set of coefficients of localization, ratios, etc. based on systematic sets of data such as those contained in Table 7. Unfortunately, the values of the coefficients, ratios, etc., obtained will be very much dependent on the fineness of the industrial classification employed. A gross industrial classification, such as a two-digit one, for example, would tend to yield low coefficients of localization, etc., just as large geographic divisions do. In contrast, a fine industrial classification, such as a four- or five-digit one, would tend to yield high coefficients just as small areal subdivisions do. And, as will be evident in the next section, the ranking of regions by degree of specialization may be greatly influenced by the nature of industrial classification. Further, the pattern of change in these coefficients over time may be very much a function of the degree of industrial disaggregation.

6. CONCEPTUAL LIMITATIONS AND SUMMARY REMARKS

The limitations and defects discussed to this point are technical. They are direct consequences of the method by which the coefficients, ratios, and curves are defined or derived and data and regions classified. A more serious and fundamental limitation to their use is that they are of little help in identifying cause and effect relationships. They are essentially mechanical devices with which empirical facts can be processed to reveal certain statistical tendencies or regularities.

For example, consider Map 1. This map effectively presents basic data which might be used to develop a shift ratio, or a coefficient of redistribution. It portrays by State Economic Areas (S.E.A.'s) differences between value added by manufacture in 1947 and the amounts required to retain 1939 shares of national total value added by manufacture. (This is defined by Zelinsky as the V factor.) It shows, for example, that over the period 1939–1947, the shares of S.E.A.'s in the Middle Atlantic states and New England generally declined, whereas those of the S.E.A.'s in the Ohio–Indiana–Michigan region generally increased.

Since during this same period population growth of the S.E.A.'s has also varied considerably, another type of map such as Map 2 may be considered more relevant. Map 2 presents the value added changes of Map 1 after they have been adjusted by the population changes. (This set of

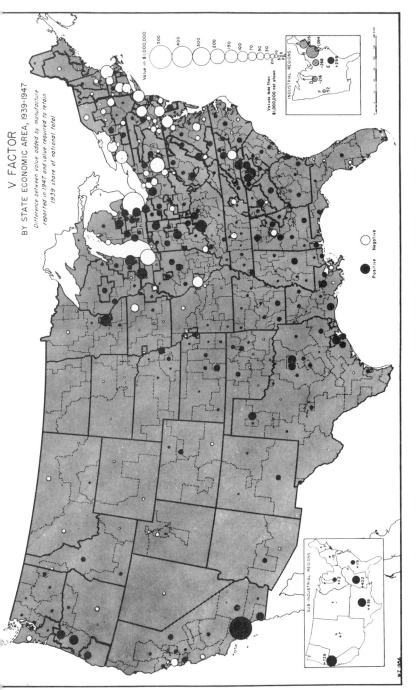

Map 1. *V* factor, by state economic area, 1939–1947. Source: W. Zelinsky [69], p. 110.

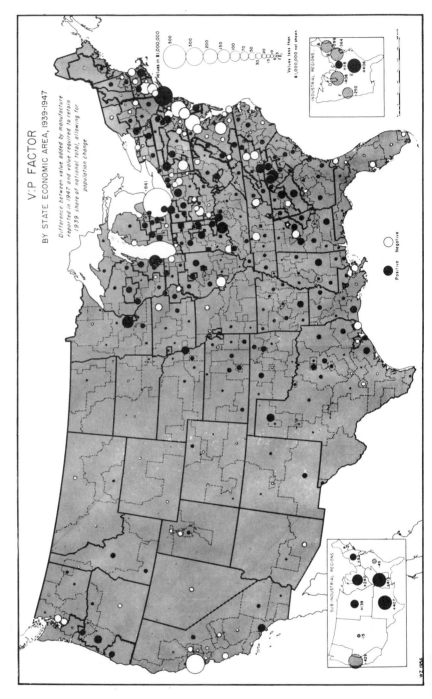

V.P FACTOR

BY STATE ECONOMIC AREA, 1939-1947

Difference between value added by manufacture
reported in 1947 and value required to retain
1939 share of national total, allowing for
population change

adjusted changes, which is defined by Zelinsky as the $V:P$ factor,[49] is closely related to the localization curve, location quotients, and the coefficient of localization.) Map 2 indicates the same general pattern of change as does Map 1, but certain significant modifications can be noted. There are significant exceptions to the generally declining shares experienced by S.E.A.'s along the northern Atlantic Seaboard. Certain strategic areas in western New York State and in western Pennsylvania are associated with only *slightly* decreased shares.[50]

Clearly, maps such as these are extremely effective in establishing trends and patterns of change. Yet, it must be remembered that neither maps nor the corresponding coefficients explain or identify the economic and other forces which interact to produce these tendencies and regularities.[51] As a consequence, the current general trends and patterns revealed by the various curves and coefficients cannot be assumed to apply automatically to future development or, by analogy, to individual regional situations. This is not to deny that the various coefficients are valuable to the regional analyst as an aid in ordering and classifying his empirical data and in deciding which avenues of further research are likely to be fruitful. However, the definite limitations of the measures should be understood, and they should not be considered as "short cuts" to conclusions that can only result from more basic analysis.

The discussion of the general type of statistical measure exemplified by the localization curve, the shift ratio, and the coefficient of localization can be briefly summarized:

1. The coefficient, curve, or ratio is derived essentially from a comparison of two percentage distributions which have common units of classification, for example, states, counties, cities, census tracts, etc.[52] This formulation results in three important technical limitations. First, a change in the degree of fineness of area classification will generally cause a change in the coefficient, curve, or ratio. Second, the value of the coefficient, or ratio, or the shape of the curve is relative; it describes a

---

[49] This factor is defined in footnote 42.

[50] A relative growth chart could be constructed as an alternative method of presenting the data of Map 2. On the vertical axis would be measured value added in 1947 as a percentage of value added in 1939. On the horizontal axis would be measured population in 1947 as a percentage of population in 1939. Thus each region, and the United States as a whole, could be represented by a point on the relative growth chart with coordinates determined by the relevant percentages. Comparative analysis could then proceed as sketched in the text.

[51] For a detailed explanation of this basic limitation as it applies to one particular measure, the coefficient of geographic association, see Robert E. Kuenne [45], ch. 2.

[52] The relative-growth (Hoover-Fisher) chart is more flexible and permits comparison of per cent changes of three magnitudes, although one of the three is not independent.

given distribution in terms of a base distribution and is only as good as the base is relevant. Third, the value of the coefficient, or ratio, or the shape of the curve will tend to vary, depending on how broadly the non-base magnitude (e.g., industry sector, income class, and occupation group) is defined.

2. As is true of virtually all statistical measures, the devices and concepts discussed are of little value in identifying or evaluating cause and effect relationships. They can assist the analyst to perceive certain general empirical associations but can be considered only as rough guideposts for basic regional analysis and planning.

E. COEFFICIENT OF SPECIALIZATION, INDEX OF DIVERSIFICATION AND RELATED CONCEPTS

Closely associated with the concepts discussed in the previous section are the coefficient of specialization, index of diversification, and related concepts.[53] Objectives similar to those mentioned at the start of the previous section have motivated the development of these latter tools and concepts. Also, these tools and concepts are based on data similar to those discussed in the preceding section.

To point up these interconnections, we re-examine Table 7. There we noted that each cell was made up of two ratios, each equivalent to the location quotient (the pure number) recorded. These two ratios are obtainable from one another simply by carrying through the algebraic operation of substituting for one another the denominator and numerator of the nonbase and base precentages, respectively.[54] We have already discussed how the set of the first ratios in a given *row* and the location quotients along a given *row* can be used to develop coefficients of localization and redistribution, localization curves, etc. If we now concentrate on the ratios (in particular the second ratio of each cell) and the location quotients *by columns* (i.e., by regions), we can derive the several tools and concepts to be discussed in this section.

As already noted, the numerator of the second ratio of a cell in Table 7 indicates for the given region (at the head of the column) the per cent of the employment of a region accounted for by the industry in the row of the cell, whereas the denominator of the same ratio indicates for the entire system (the United States) the per cent of its total manufacturing employment accounted for by the same industry. Paralleling the discussion of

[53] Because of such association, we shall not treat in this section certain fine points which have already been treated in the previous section. The reader interested in such points should read this section in parallel with the previous section.

[54] See footnote 3, Chapter 5.

previous sections, we may compute a coefficient comparable to the coefficient of localization. We call this new coefficient, which pertains to a given region, *the coefficient of specialization* of that region. This coefficient is computed for the given region by : (1) subtracting the numerator from the denominator of each of the second ratios in the region's column ; (2) adding all positive (or negative) differences ; and (3) dividing the sum (without regard for sign) by 100. The limits to the value of this coefficient are 0 and 1. If the region has a proportional mix of industry identical with the system (United States), the coefficient will be 0. In contrast, if all the employment of the region is concentrated in a single industry, the coefficient will approach unity. This coefficient thus measures the extent to which the distribution of employment by industry classes in the given region deviates from such distribution for the United States. As with the coefficient of localization, this coefficient is helpful to the regional analyst seeking to implement a policy of diversification.

The basic feature of the specialization coefficient—the comparison of two percentage distributions applicable to a given set of classification units (e.g. industries, in Table 7)—can be extended to the comparison of any two meaningful percentage distributions for a given region versus the United States. For example, the percentage shares of total regional income accounted for by the members of each of the several income groups in a region can be contrasted with the corresponding percentage shares of national income accounted for by these same income groups. Or the percentage share of total regional employment accounted for by members of each occupational group in a region can be contrasted with the corresponding percentage shares for the nation. And so forth.[55]

When coefficients of specialization have been obtained for a number of regions, it is often helpful to map the coefficient values in order to point up contrasts among the regions. Such a map would resemble Map 3, which has been developed by Rodgers and which refers to values along an index of industrial diversification, a concept similar to the coefficient of specialization.[56]

[55] Comparisons such as the ones noted may involve changes (with respect to the data of Table 7) not only in the base magnitude and the nonbase magnitude, but also in the classification units to which the distributions of base and nonbase magnitudes apply. Consequently, any given comparison may involve changes in any of or all the percentages and ratios which appear in Table 7. See the discussion in footnotes 28 and 29.

[56] A. Rodgers [56, 57]. Rodgers' map depicts what he terms the refined index of diversification for each of a large number of metropolitan industrial areas. The refined index of diversification for an area is derived from the area's crude index of diversification, which crude index is computed as follows. Percentages of total area employment in each of 22 manufacturing groups are calculated. These percentages are ranked in order from highest to lowest. Then the percentages are cumulated, one at a time, to

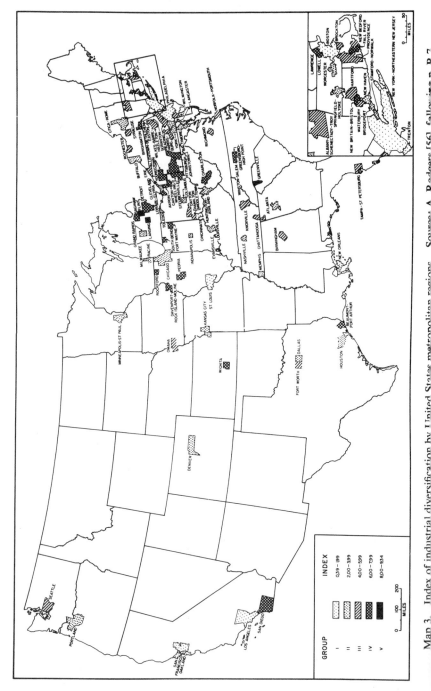

Map 3. Index of industrial diversification by United States metropolitan regions. Source: A. Rodgers [56], following p. B-7.

Corresponding to the coefficient of specialization for a region is a *specialization (or diversification) curve*. Such a curve is constructed in essentially the same manner as the localization curve. The vertical coordinates of successive points on the curve measure cumulative percentages, industry by industry, of the region's total manufacturing employment. The corresponding horizontal coordinates measure cumulative percentages, industry by industry, of total United States manufacturing employment. The industries are ordered according to the value of the given region's location quotients for the industries, as recorded in a column of such tables as Table 7. The ordering is from largest to smallest. For any given region, the deviation of the curve from a diagonal from the origin will measure the degree to which the distribution among industries of the region's manufacturing employment differs from the corresponding distribution of United States manufacturing employment. A variant of the coefficient of specialization could be derived from the specialization curve by computing the ratio of (1) the area between the specialization curve and the diagonal, to (2) the total area of the right triangle formed by the diagonal, the vertical axis, and the top of the graph. The limiting values of this ratio will be zero and one, as they are for the coefficient of specialization computed from the plus or minus deviations of the percentage distributions.[57]

yield a set of cumulative subtotals, that is, the largest is set down first, then the sum of the largest and the next largest, then the sum of the largest and the next two largest, etc. Summing these cumulative subtotals yields the area's crude diversification index. If all the employment of an area were concentrated in one manufacturing group, the area's crude index of diversification would be 2200. This figure would represent the crude index value for least diversity. In contrast, if employment were equally distributed among the 22 manufacturing groups, the area's index value would be approximately 1150, a value representing greatest diversity.

The refined index of diversification for an area, as defined by Rodgers, is equal to (1) the area's crude index minus the crude index for all industrial areas taken together, divided by (2) the crude index for least diversity minus the crude index for all industrial areas taken together. Thus, a refined index of zero for an area would indicate the same degree of diversification for that area as for all areas taken together. A value of $+1.0$, on the other hand, would indicate complete nondiversification.

The similarity of the refined index of diversification to the coefficient of specialization is apparent. An advantage of the index, however, is that it would take a negative value for areas which had a more even or equal distribution of employment among manufacturing industries than the over-all system of areas. The coefficient, on the other hand, measures only the degree of *deviation* of an area from the diversification pattern of the over-all system, whether that deviation is in the direction of more or less even distribution.

[57] A curve could be constructed based on an industry (or other) distribution ordered in accordance with some criterion other than size of location quotient. For example, the order could be based on the number of employees in each industry. The resulting curve would be irregular in shape, and ordinarily its usefulness would be greatly circumscribed.

In addition to utilizing a specialization curve to summarize the industrial diversification of a given region, the analyst may wish to achieve an inter-regional comparison by means of a set of these curves. For a given point of time he may plot on the same graph a specialization curve for each of

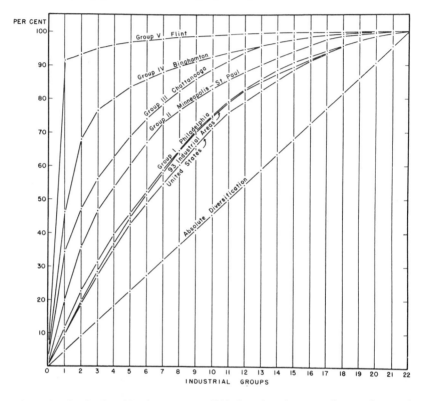

Figure 4. Crude diversification patterns, 1950; by selected metropolitan regions and the United States. Source: A. Rodgers, [56], following p. B-6.

several regions. Such a group of curves may resemble those of Figure 4. [58] Considerable insight into the comparative industrial structures of the regions of a system can be gained by a careful study of such a figure.

[58] It is evident from Figure 4 that Rodgers' curves are constructed in a fashion slightly different from the way specialization curves (as defined) would be derived. Instead of comparing a region's distribution of manufacturing employment by industry with the corresponding total system distribution, Rodgers compares the individual region's distribution with an hypothetical equal distribution of employment among all industries. The latter is considered by Rodgers as "absolute diversification." The use of this latter curve has the advantage of providing an absolute point of reference with which to compare not only individual regions but also the system taken as a whole.

Moreover, a group of specialization curves can be plotted, each representing the pattern of specialization for a given region at a different point of time. Such curves can helpfully guide and facilitate the analysis of historical changes in regional diversification patterns.

In many instances the specialization curve (or group of such curves) has clear-cut advantages over the corresponding coefficient(s) of specialization. Perhaps of principal importance is the fact that the curves give some indication of the relative contribution of the individual industries or industry groups to over-all diversification. This distinction may be particularly useful when several regions or several time periods are being compared.

As already indicated, we can compute for a given region a series of specialization coefficients over time as well as plot a series of specialization curves over time. In addition we may wish to summarize such analysis for the whole system of regions in order to observe the over-all change in specialization over time within the system. This problem can be attacked by (1) computing for each region the difference between its coefficients of specialization at two successive points of time; (2) summing over all regions; and (3) dividing by the number of regions. However, in view of the technical shortcomings of the coefficient of specialization, such a summarization will possess only a limited degree of validity and usefulness. Of much more use in this connection is a map that records changes in coefficients. Although such a map is not available, a similar map, constructed by Rodgers, on changes in the crude diversification index, 1940–1950, illustrates this point well.[59] This map is reproduced here as Map 4.

Corresponding to the coefficient of redistribution discussed in the preceding section, which coefficient summarizes the change over time of the regional distribution of some magnitude (e.g., population, industry employment, total manufacturing employment, etc.), *a coefficient of redistribution* within a region over time can be computed. This latter coefficient may relate to employment by industry, employment by occupation group, income shares by income group, etc. For example, the percentage distribution in a region of employment by industry group can be compared for any two successive census years. The resulting coefficient of redistribution based on differences of corresponding percentages will indicate the extent to which on a relative basis interindustry shifts of employment have taken place in the region during the intercensal period.

Similar results can be obtained by calculating an interindustry *shift ratio* for the region. The over-all rate of growth of the region's industrial employment can be calculated for the intercensal period. Then for each

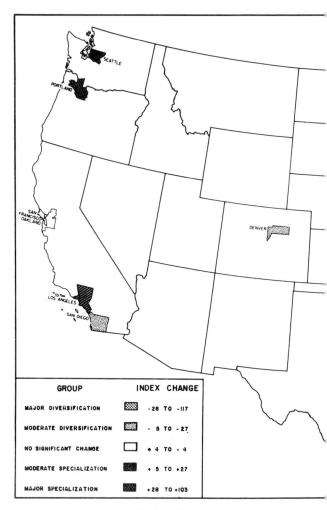

Map 4.   Changes in crude diversification index 1940–1950 by

industry in the region there can be computed the difference between the
actual employment in the latter census year and the employment that
would have resulted had the industry's employment grown at the same
rate as the region's total industrial employment.   A positive difference will
indicate a relative shift of employment into the industry, a negative
difference a relative shift out of the industry.   The actual shift ratio will
be calculated by summing all the positive (or negative) interindustry shifts

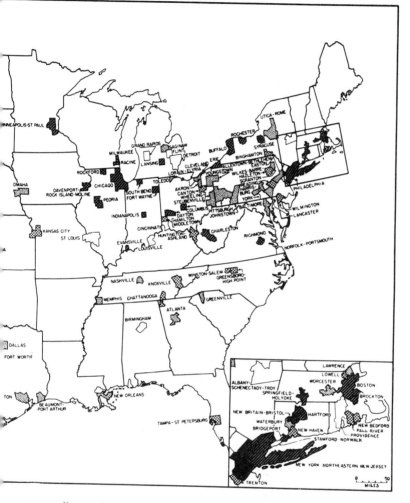

metropolitan regions. Source: A. Rodgers [56], following p. B-10.

in employment for the region and expressing the result as a proportion of the region's total industrial employment.

It is evident that for some purposes a measure which can compare interindustry shifts of employment over time in a given region to the corresponding shifts for all regions will be more useful than just the coefficient of redistribution or shift ratio for the given region. One such device is a type of *relative growth chart*, illustrated by Figure 5. The vertical axis of this figure measures, for region A, employment in year β as a per cent of employment in year α, either for a single industry or for industry as a whole. The horizontal axis measures for the system (United States) the same percentage. Along the vertical axis point M represents this percentage for industry as a whole in region A. Along the horizontal axis point R represents the same percentage for industry as a whole for the

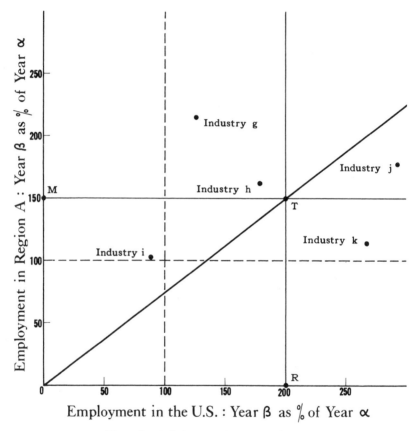

Figure 5.   Relative growth chart, by industry.

United States. Therefore, the slope of the diagonal from the origin through point T (whose coordinates are OM and OR) measures the ratio of these two percentages. This slope is also equivalent to the ratio of region A's percentage share of total system (United States) employment in year β to region A's percentage share of total system employment in year α. The steeper the diagonal, the faster has been the growth in the region's total industrial employment compared to the United States rate of growth.

The diagonal of Figure 5 permits interesting comparisons for any particular industry of its growth in a given region relative to its growth in the total system. For example, the position of industry i in Figure 5 indicates that this industry is slow-growing. Additionally, although this industry's growth in region A was slower than average industrial growth in both this region and the United States, its relative decline in region A was less severe than in the system as a whole. Thus the industry fared better in region A than could have been expected on the basis of its performance in the United States. Or, to take another example, we may examine industry j. Its position on Figure 5 indicates that it is a fast growing industry. Its growth over the period exceeded average industrial growth in both region A and the United States. However, its growth performance in region A was less than could have been expected on the basis of performance in the total system. Hence, region A's share of this industry declined relative to region A's share of total industry.

This discussion of the relative growth chart completes the summary presentation in this section of concepts relating to specialization and diversification which parallel the concepts relating to localization covered in the preceding section. Because of this parallel, virtually the same general technical and conceptual limitations apply to the concepts presented in this section as apply to those in the previous section. Hence, it would be only repetitious to undertake a critical evaluation at this point. Suffice it to say that the values of the specialization coefficients and the shapes of the related curves are dependent on the degree of fineness of the units of classification as well as on the size of regions. More important, the coefficients, curves, and other devices discussed in this section are essentially descriptive and cannot identify cause-effect relationships. They, too, take on meaning only when embraced by a valid conceptual and theoretical framework.

F. GENERAL CONCLUSIONS

In earlier chapters we have not explicitly injected into regional analysis the major factor of optimizing behavior. This factor underlies the comparative cost approach. It lends to this approach a causative significance, of considerable validity for predictive purposes. In the orthodox single-industry framework, the comparative cost approach has had a widespread and fruitful application. And because of its optimizing rationale, in the future it promises to be one of the most powerful tools in the kit of the regional scientist. Yet it is recognized that this approach in its traditional framework pertains to partial equilibrium only; that is, comparative cost analysis looks at behavior within a single industry, the structure of all other industries as well as demand, prices, and costs being assumed as given. Therefore, as already noted, sound regional analysis requires that the traditional comparative cost approach be supplemented with more general techniques capable of cutting through the restrictive bounds of single-industry analysis. This supplementation will be pursued in the subsequent chapters dealing with interregional and regional input-output techniques, industrial complex analysis, interregional linear programming, and gravity models. Additionally, factors outside the economic sphere must be weighed in forming locational decisions, and some developing techniques which attempt to appraise such factors are sketched in Appendices A and B.

Surrounding the comparative cost approach are a number of measures relating to industrial location and regional distribution of phenomena. Some of these measures—the labor coefficient and others discussed in section C—are very useful in preliminary stages of research. They represent incomplete comparative cost ratios, which in a general way short-cut analysis. Full analysis, however, requires that they be converted into comparative cost ratios. Other measures—coefficients of localization, localization curves, shift ratios, indexes of specialization, and the several other measures discussed in sections D and E—are essentially designed to describe and summarize systems of industrial locations, population and subpopulation locations, and locations of other relevant items and phenomena. They are valuable for portraying the "what" of systems as they are or have been. They permit a view of the internal structure of regions along several dimensions. They permit the comparison of a given region's structure with the structure of other regions and, where justifiable, with the system as a whole or other fictitious norms. Moreover, they permit identification of changes over time in the structure of both the region and the system. Thus, in a very important way they supplement approaches such as comparative cost analysis which requires, both for implementation and testing, structural knowledge in the form of factual materials on the outcome of the interplay of underlying forces, both currently and in the past.

It is to be noted, however, that such supplementation is not of an analytical nature. For example, although comparative cost analysis can suggest changes to be expected in coefficients of localization, shift ratios, specialization curves, etc., the converse cannot be stated. True, a high coefficient of localization for a particular industry may reflect a major cost differential or scale economy factor, but of itself it tells nothing of what the factor is, how important it is in relation to others, and to what extent this factor is expected to persist. Likewise, when the coefficient of localization and other related measures are used in conjunction with population and migration estimation, income and balance of payments statements, and commodity and money flow studies, they add little to the understanding of basic interrelations and to the framework for projection, although they perform the major functions of testing hypotheses and of motivating their reformulation.

In contrast, comparative cost analysis does add a firm analytical scaffolding to many of the types of studies discussed in previous chapters. Although this point will be fully developed in the final chapters, we may briefly touch upon it here. For the derivation of population projections, industry-by-industry comparative cost studies provide a first approximation[60] to the regional pattern of new job opportunities. These opportunities in turn suggest a regional pattern for that large segment of population whose location is tied to economic opportunities. Moreover, comparison with natural rates of increase by region leads to first approximations of interregional migration of persons within this segment of population. The major fraction of changes in regional income can be anticipated directly from the regional pattern of new job opportunities and of projected industrial output. In like manner, implications for commodity flows, money flows, balance of payments, and cyclical sensitivity can be drawn with a fair amount of confidence, as we shall detail in Chapter 12.

APPENDIX A

SCALING AND LATENT STRUCTURE TECHNIQUES

In section B of this chapter, the promise of a systematic industry-by-industry comparative cost study for a region was indicated. Comcomitantly it was recognized that other important noneconomic factors—for example, political organization, community attitudes, cultural patterns, and business confidence— are at play in locational decisions. They are largely subjective in character and, accordingly have usually been treated in an intuitive manner. Recently, however, new quantitative techniques, which pertain particularly to attitude measurement and pattern identification, have been emerging in the fields of psychology and sociology. Although they have found little application in regional studies, their current promise for advancing the state of regional analysis is sufficient to justify a brief discussion in this Appendix.

1. SCALING TECHNIQUES

To begin, suppose we consider a region, say New England. Suppose, too, it has been possible to pursue a systematic industry-by-industry comparative cost

---

[60] This approximation is, of course, subject to improvement through the use of techniques to be discussed in subsequent chapters. As noted, these techniques cut through certain important postulates which restrict comparative cost study.

study for this region. (Perhaps, too, it has been possible to supplement the comparative cost study with industrial complex and interregional input-output studies to be discussed in subsequent chapters.) After appropriate check on available resources—for example, port facilities, water of appropriate quality, road and rail transportation, labor skills, and power supplies—for each industry, a set of conclusions is reached with respect to the feasibility of locating a new plant in New England.

Such analysis is frequently insufficient, as the historical record testifies. New industrial development can be precluded not only by unfavorable cost conditions but also by unfavorable community attitudes and cultural patterns (even when cost conditions are very favorable). Further, not only must attitudes and patterns be generally favorable or at least neutral in the region (New England) as a whole; they must also be generally favorable, or at least not too hostile, in the particular community possessing the specific resources (such as a port facility) to which potential new industrial plants must be oriented. Put otherwise, there must be at least some spatial association of favorable community attitude and specific potential plant sites for industrial development to ensue even when other necessary conditions are met.

Measurement of attitude—favorable, neutral, unfavorable—is a problem which presents major difficulties, both conceptually and technically. One significant approach—the Guttman scaling or scalogram technique—attempts to identify a single scale along which effective measurement of attitude in a given situation can be attained.[61] Typically a set of questions are asked, each of which requires a "yes" or "no" answer. Ideally, these questions (items) are to be so phrased and arranged that a positive answer by a respondent to any given question implies or requires for consistency a positive answer by the respondent on all questions of lower position. As an obvious example, if the following questions are asked:

1. Do you weigh over 150 pounds?
2. Do you weigh over 125 pounds?
3. Do you weigh over 100 pounds?

a respondent who answers positively to question 1 must answer positively to questions 2 and 3 to be consistent.

As a second example, consider the general attitude (past and current) toward the Negro as reflected in institutional practices in four representative states, Virginia, Maryland, West Virginia, and Pennsylvania.[62] Such attitude may be scaled according to the presence or absence of certain characteristics: white primary (1); Jim Crow railways (2); and school segregation laws (3). In 1944, these four states ranked as indicated in Table A-1. Presence of characteristic (1) (corresponding to a positive response) thus implies presence of lower charac-

[61] For full discussion of this technique, the reader is referred to, among others, S. A. Stouffer et. al. [63], ch. 1–9; L. Guttman and E. A. Suchman [25]; M. W. Riley, J. W. Riley, J. Toby, et. al. [55]; L. Festinger and D. Katz [18], pp. 260–269, 525–528; M. J. Hagood and D. O. Price [29], pp. 144–152; G. Shapiro [60], pp. 619–621; N. E. Green [23], pp. 8–13; P. L. Lazarsfeld et. al. [49], pp. 216–257; J. A. Davis [10], pp. 371–380; and J. S. Coleman [7].

[62] The materials presented are selected, for pedagogical purposes only, from G. Shapiro [60], pp. 619–621.

teristics (2) and (3); and presence of characteristic (2) implies presence of lower characteristic (3).

Note that the Guttman scale is a cumulative-type scale. To repeat, it involves ranking respondents so that in a perfect scale each respondent will agree with or react positively to all items up to the point that represents his own attitude and disagree with all items beyond that point. (That is, respondents are arranged in order from those with the most positive attitude to those with the most negative attitude.) Or it involves ranking regions so that in a perfect scale each region possesses all characteristics up to the item representing its own position on the scale and lacks all characteristics beyond that item. But not only does the technique rank respondents or regions; it also arranges the items (questions, or characteristics) in order according to the relative position they represent along the scale of measurement. To be specific, in scaling the general attitude toward the Negro in the four states given, it is not apparent at the start which of the three characteristics (white primary, Jim Crow railways, or school segregation laws) represents the highest point on the scale measuring discrimination against the Negro. Once the data are compiled, it is evident that item (1) (white primary)

TABLE A-1.   SCALOGRAM 1

State	Presence of			Absence of		
	(1)	(2)	(3)	(1)	(2)	(3)
Virginia	×	×	×			
Maryland		×	×	×		
West Virginia			×	×	×	
Pennsylvania				×	×	×

must represent the highest point along the assumed unidimensional scale. This statement follows since a state with three discriminatory characteristics must be ranked higher than a state with only two of these three characteristics. On a cumulative-type scale such can only be true if that characteristic not common to both states represents a higher point on the scale than any characteristic common to the two states. Thus, characteristic (1) must represent a higher point than either (2) or (3).

It is also evident that characteristic (2) must represent a higher point on the scale than (3). For, from the data given, one state (West Virginia) possesses characteristic (3) alone, whereas a second state (Maryland) possesses both characteristics (2) and (3). [Neither state possesses characteristic (1).] Since Maryland possesses both characteristics, it must be ranked higher than West Virginia. But this can only be if (2) represents a higher point on the cumulative, unidimensional scale.

Thus, on the assumption that characteristics (1), (2), and (3) measure the same attitude, we obtain a rank of states by intensity of discrimination.

Unfortunately, perfect unidimensional scales of the type illustrated are atypical. Usually, there is one or more deviations from the ideal pattern of Scalogram 1 (Table A-1). This situation obtains even though in the application of the technique the analyst tends to exclude items that cannot be arranged along a single scale. When there are many deviations from a perfect pattern, the analyst may search for scalable subareas or sectors; or, if such are not found, he may forgo the use of the technique.

These points can be more lucidly developed if we return to the discussion of the industrial development problem of New England. On the basis of past and current studies it would not appear fruitful to use the limited research resources available to scale the *general New England attitude* toward new industry. There is overwhelming evidence that a significant fraction of the area and its population favors industrial growth. A more relevant investigation would attempt to classify communities by attitude toward industrial development, and thereby to determine the extent to which advantageous potential plant sites exist in or around communities with favorable attitudes.

Although we could conduct a thorough and extensive attitude survey for each New England community, such a study would be costly and time consuming; and in view of the limitations of survey techniques, such an attack may not be justifiable. An alternative procedure, much less direct and perhaps inferior but much less costly and time consuming, is to (1) advance a reasonable hypothesis such as "a community's resistance to industrial development varies directly with its socio-economic status", and (2) attempt to classify New England communities according to their position along a unidimensional Guttman scale of socio-economic status. Such a scale would be based on existing sets of information, typically of a census variety such as per capita income, residential density, educational level, and home ownership.

As far as the authors are aware, no such scale study of socio-economic status of communities within a large region has been conducted. However, a scale study of census tracts, ranked by socio-economic status, has been undertaken for the metropolitan region of Birmingham, Alabama. Since a scale study for the communities of a region would likely parallel in the most important respects the completed study for Birmingham, we sketch it in order to illustrate the virtues and limitations of scaling techniques in general for regional analysis.

In the Birmingham study, 28 of the 58 census tracts in the city area were chosen as a representative sample. Five social-data items were selected for the development of a socio-economic status scale. These items are recorded in Table A-2. Note that these items are trichotomous rather than dichotomous. Three responses *A(negative)*, *B(neutral)*, and *C(positive)*, are possible for each item. When the response on each of the five items is recorded for each of the 28 census tracts, 140 responses are obtained. Scale analysis of these 140 responses shows that the five items may be taken to represent a single-dimension scale applicable to these census tracts. The scalogram developed in this study is reproduced as Scalogram 2 (Table A-3).

In Scalogram 2 (Table A-3), the 28 census tracts are identified by number in column 2. The letters *C*, *B*, and *A* at the top of the table indicate positive, neutral, and negative responses, respectively. The numbers 1, 2, 3, 4 and 5 refer respectively to *income, crowding within dwellings, home ownership, social disorganization*, and *education*, as detailed in Table A-2. The response pattern for each census tract is noted, the particular arrangement presented being the one which the author of the study found to conform most closely to the ideal (perfect-scale) parallelogram depicted in Scalogram 1 (Table A-1). This particular arrangement, as already discussed, then determines the ranking of the census tracts as well as the point on the scale represented by each type response to each item.   For example, tract 21 ranks in the highest group (scale type I) ; and a positive response to item 1 (i.e., a position within the highest levels of median annual income) represents the highest point on the cumulative scale of socio-economic status.

Note that there are eleven responses which are not in place, that is, are deviations from the perfect parallelogram.   The ratio of this number of deviations to 140, which is the total number of responses, measures in one sense the extent

TABLE A-2.   ITEM AND CATEGORY DEFINITIONS FOR SCALE OF SOCIO-ECONOMIC STATUS

Item	Subject	A(Negative)	B(Neutral)	C(Positive)
1.	Median annual income of all employed persons	Lowest 7 ranks	Middle 14 ranks	Highest 7 ranks
2.	Prevalence of crowding within dwellings (1.01 or more persons per room)	Highest 7 ranks	Middle 14 ranks	Lowest 7 ranks
3.	Prevalence of home ownership (percentage of dwellings owner-occupied)	Lowest 7 ranks	Middle 14 ranks	Highest 7 ranks
4.	Prevalence of social disorganization (percentage of families involved in crime, delinquency, divorce, etc.)	Highest 7 ranks	Middle 14 ranks	Lowest 7 ranks
5.	Educational achievement (median years of school completed by persons 25 and over)	Lowest 7 ranks	Second lowest 7 ranks	Highest 14 ranks

Source : N. E. Green [23], p. 11.

to which the scalogram in and of itself fails to reproduce exactly the pattern of responses.   Or, if this ratio is subtracted from unity, we obtain a coefficient which has been designated the *coefficient of reproducibility*, and which measures the extent to which the scalogram can reproduce the pattern of responses. Conventionally, a coefficient of reproducibility of at least 0.90 has been viewed as a necessary condition for a scalogram to have content.   Other criteria should also be met, for example, criteria with respect to randomness of deviations.   The reader is referred to the literature already cited for their discussion.

Note on Scalogram 2 that at the extreme left is a column indicating *scale type*. This column simply differentiates and ranks the different possible response

TABLE A-3.　SCALOGRAM 2: SCALE OF SOCIO-ECONOMIC STATUS FOR TWENTY-EIGHT CENSUS TRACTS IN BIRMINGHAM, ALABAMA

(Coefficient of reproducibility = 0.92)

Item Number and Response Category

Scale Type	Tract Number	C					B					A					Scale Score
		1	3	4	2	5	1	3	4	2	5	1	3	4	2	5	
I	21	×	×	×	×	×											20
I	38	×	×	×	×	×											20
I	1	×	×	×	×	×											20
I	23	×	×		×	×			×								20
II	19		×	×	×	×	×										18
II	22		×		×	×	×	×									18
II	4		×		×	×	×	×									18
III	31	×		×	×	×			×								16
III	30			×	×	×	×	×									16
III	47	×		×	×	×			×								16
IV	3				×	×	×	×	×								14
IV	50				×	×	×	×	×								14
IV	40	×			×	×		×	×								14
V	34					×	×	×	×	×							12
VI	33						×	×	×	×					×		10
VI	42						×	×	×	×	×						10
VI	18						×	×	×	×	×						10
VI	9						×	×	×						×	×	10
VI	8						×	×	×	×	×						10
VI	5						×	×	×	×	×						10
VI	13						×	×	×	×	×						10
IX	27				×						×	×	×	×			4
IX	45										×	×	×	×		×	4
XI	26											×	×	×	×	×	0
XI	44											×	×	×	×	×	0
XI	43											×	×	×	×	×	0
XI	28											×	×	×	×	×	0
XI	46											×	×	×	×	×	0
Frequency		7	7	7	14	14	14	14	14	7	7	7	7	7	7	7	(140)
Errors		3	0	0	1	0	0	0	3	0	0	0	0	0	2	2	(11)

Source : N. E. Green [23], p. 12.

patterns for the perfect parallelogram which serves as the model for the scalogram; and tracts are assigned to a particular type as if they had no deviant responses. At the extreme right of Scalogram 2 is another column indicating the score of the corresponding scale type. It is based on arbitrary weights but can be useful for certain comparative purposes.

Now we return to the problem of industrial development in New England. Suppose a scalogram such as Scalogram 2 were developed for all communities above a specified size in New England. (For the moment we set aside the evaluation of such a scalogram.) According to our hypothesis, this scalogram would rank communities by degree of resistance to new industry. A check on this hypothesis would be obtained by ranking communities that have recently responded to the possibility of new industry. Those communities that have most successfully resisted the introduction of new industry should be among the highest (first) scale types in the socio-economic status continuum; those that have most actively encouraged new industry should be among the lowest scale types; and so forth. If there is not sufficient correspondence between rank by experience and rank on the Guttman scale, then clearly the hypothesis, the particular Guttman scale, or both are inappropriate.

If there is a reasonable correspondence between rank by experience and rank on the Guttman scale, the analyst can proceed to identify certain scale types (the lower ones) that are likely to be receptive to new industry as well as certain scale types (the higher ones) that are likely to be resistant to new industry.[63] He also would note the rank of *the communities that possess the specific plant sites potentially advantageous from a cost standpoint for new industry*. If most or all these communities are of the scale types classed as receptive to new industry, he might proceed to use his projections of industrial development based on comparative cost study with little if any modification. In contrast, if most or all these communities are of the scale types classed as resistant to new industry, he would be compelled to qualify seriously his projections of new industrial development. Such qualification would be particularly necessary if there were no indications that attitudes in these communities could be changed through educational efforts, economic pressures and other forces.

Finally, if a large number of these communities are of the scale types classed as neither receptive nor resistant, the analyst would need to qualify his comparative cost projections to some extent at least. The extent of qualification would be conditioned, say, by intensive survey analysis of perhaps a sample of these communities in order to appraise better the internal forces at play,[64] or by

[63] In effect, the analyst chooses "cutoff points" based on the historical record of community reactions. The two cutoff points implied in the text lead to a three-way classification of communities.

In other cases such cutoff points might be chosen arbitrarily at levels which would include a specific proportion of communities studied. This procedure is somewhat analogous to the choice of confidence limits in statistical research.

[64] It should be noted that when we construct a scalogram relating to an attitude where the response ranges from positive to negative, we may also construct an intensity function or curve. Such a function or curve reflects the strength of the attitude held by a respondent and is determined by asking a set of questions such as : "How strongly do you feel . . .? Very Strongly, Fairly Strongly, Not So Strongly, or Not At All Strongly." A generally accepted hypothesis is that respondents in the extreme class types of a scalogram react much more intensively than respondents in the middle class types such

an estimation of promotion efforts which may be concentrated on these communities by business, governmental, and other groups, etc.[65]

The relevance of this application of scaling techniques in conjunction with comparative cost and other analysis obviously depends on the validity of the several techniques and hypotheses employed. Apropos the scaling technique, a number of major limitations should be recognized. First, the analyst may be forced at several steps in the scaling procedure to make arbitrary decisions on subjective grounds. The original choice of items thought relevant to the scale being sought depends frequently on the judgment of the researcher. Further, the subsequent arrangement of both items and respondents in the scalogram requires a subjective balancing of criteria, which criteria often have conflicting requirements. Consequently, on many occasions, when the coefficient of reproducibility is relatively low, different patterns may result from the same data as studied by different analysts.[66]

Beyond these considerations are certain basic problems of interpretation of results. Once a relevant scalogram has been constructed, how should we determine whether a pattern of deviation is random (quasi-scale) or nonrandom (i.e., indicative of the presence of other dimensions)? Moreover, what significance should be attached to a coefficient of reproducibility when the coefficient itself varies with the fineness of the steps between items? Still more, the scalogram procedure tends to eliminate from the study items (or characteristics) significant for the problem being attacked but yielding patterns too deviant (unique) to satisfy the scaling criteria.[67]

Despite these and other limitations—the reader is referred to the literature cited for their full discussion—the scaling technique has considerable potential and has in fact been extensively applied by psychologists and sociologists. As already noted, its value in the social sciences for measuring attitudes and identifying dimensions of social structure lies in its transformation of qualitative and noncomparable quantitative information into numerical rankings (ordinal values). Such rankings, moreover, permit the subsequent use of rank correlation, index construction, and other quantitative techniques.

that a U- or J-shaped intensity function results when intensity is plotted along the vertical axis and class types are plotted in order along the horizontal axis. The minimum point (designated the zero point) of such a function is held to divide a population into two sectors such as "for" and "against"; or "receptive" and "hostile." To the extent that these hypotheses are valid in a given situation, to that same extent they permit less intensive study of respondents in certain class types, in some cases those types clustered around the zero point as a cutoff point, in other cases those types clustered at the extreme. Generally speaking, such hypotheses allow economy in more extensive attitude investigations.

[65] Obviously if this type of analysis is valid, it yields as a by-product vital information on the need for educational and similar efforts, if such are desirable, and the particular communities at which such efforts should be aimed.

[66] For example, in Scalogram 2, census tracts 31 and 47 (both scale type III) have identical response patterns; yet they are separated in the ranking by tract 30 with a different response pattern. A similar situation exists in scale type IV.

[67] For example, an item basic to the general attitudes toward industrial development in New England, say ethnic stock, may be eliminated from a scalogram on socio-economic status because of a unique pattern. This would reflect a limitation of both the scaling technique and the hypothesis relating attitude to socio-economic status.

More specifically, in regional analysis the scaling technique can be used for such a variety of purposes as (1) to estimate effectiveness of birth control and public health practices and other factors as they relate to key parameters of regional population projections; (2) to contrast attitudes of various groups of migrants, or of migrants versus nonmigrants, the better to estimate interregional and intraregional population movements; (3) to construct meaningful (unidimensional) categories of welfare and social accounts in nonmarket activities, especially in underdeveloped regions; (4) to determine more efficiently and accurately whether or not a regional population favors a particular resource development proposal or policy; (5) to judge whether governmental units in the several regions have sufficient authority and power to implement different regional programs (in a manner analogous to that suggested in the hypothetical case of community attitudes about industrial development in New England); (6) to identify groups of individuals who might be more receptive to soil conservation and similar resource development programs; and to plan an effective chronological sequence of administrative steps; and finally, (7) to uncover with more objectivity bonds (interrelations) among regions and subareas within any given region which are of an attitudinal-cultural nature.

2. LATENT STRUCTURE METHODS

Conceptually more satisfying, but operationally much more lean, are latent structure methods. These methods have conceptual appeal because they can successfully attack "nonscale" situations. As indicated earlier, nonscale situations are those involving response patterns (or patterns of characteristics) which are not satisfactorily scalable along a single dimension. However, these situations and their response patterns may be consistent with a meaningful underlying set of classes of respondents, where these classes are identifiable with respect to one or more dimensions. The latent structure framework aims at such identification and therefore represents a generalization of scaling techniques.[68]

Basic to latent structure methods is a reasoning process which starts with data obtained from relevant questionnaires and other empirical study and which may conveniently be termed *manifest data*. Given such data, a model is constructed which assumes the existence of a system of classes of respondents. Such classes are termed *latent* classes. Each of these classes is defined in terms of a set of probabilities. That is, for a given class each possible response pattern (such as those in Scalogram 2) is associated with a probability factor. More specifically, in Table A-4 are listed in column 1 all possible types of response patterns relating to four items (the sign + indictates a positive response and the sign − a negative response). Also, in column 3 are listed the probabilities associated with latent class I. Each figure in column 3 indicates the probability that the respondent who checks the corresponding response pattern belongs to class I. Thus, the figure of 0.995 at the top of column 3 indicates that anyone who checks off a + + + + response pattern has 995 chances out of a thousand of being in class I.

Behind the probabilities recorded for each latent class (e.g., those in columns

---

[68] For full discussion of this technique, see especially S. A. Stouffer et al. [63], pp. 19–33, chs. 10, 11; P. F. Lazarsfeld et al. [49], pp. 349–387; P. F. Lazarsfeld [48], pp. 391–403; and L. Festinger and D. Katz [18], pp. 524–532.

3, 4, and 5 of Table A-4) is the basic mechanism which generates hypothetical frequencies for each response pattern listed in column 1. (This mechanism is too complex to develop in the brief scope of this Appendix.) This basic mechanism essentially determines another set of probabilities, namely the probabilities that any member of a *given class* will check off the several possible response patterns. Thus, if we wish to determine the total number of times a particular response pattern (say + − − +) will be found from (generated by) the operation of the

TABLE A-4. GENERATED DATA OF A HYPOTHETICAL LATENT STRUCTURE MODEL

(1)				(2)	(3)	(4)	(5)	(6)	(7)
					Probabilities by Latent Class			Sum of Cols.	Generated Frequency
Response Pattern Item				Observed Frequency					
1	2	3	4		I	II	III	3–5	
+	+	+	+	147	0.995	0.004	0.001	1.0	148.4
+	+	−	+	11	0.978	0.004	0.018	1.0	13.4
−	+	+	+	128	0.856	0.123	0.021	1.0	133.9
+	+	+	−	1	0.852	0.004	0.144	1.0	0.8
+	−	+	+	58	0.807	0.164	0.029	1.0	60.0
−	+	−	+	27	0.573	0.083	0.344	1.0	17.8
+	−	−	+	9	0.487	0.099	0.414	1.0	8.9
−	−	+	+	341	0.113	0.756	0.131	1.0	331.9
−	−	−	+	112	0.028	0.188	0.784	1.0	118.9
+	+	−	−	4	0.196	0.001	0.803	1.0	0.3
−	+	+	−	2	0.149	0.021	0.830	1.0	3.7
+	−	+	−	5	0.110	0.022	0.868	1.0	2.1
−	−	+	−	47	0.004	0.025	0.971	1.0	48.2
−	+	−	−	5	0.007	0.001	0.992	1.0	6.7
+	−	−	−	3	0.005	0.001	0.994	1.0	4.0
−	−	−	−	100	0.000	0.001	0.999	1.0	101.0
Totals in each class				1000	381.0	304.2	314.8	−	1000.0

Source: Data fictitious. Numerical figures identical with data in Table 11, Stouffer [63], p. 440.

model, we (1) take each class and multiply the number of respondents within it by the probability that its respondents will check off the particular response pattern (+ − − +), and (2) sum over all classes.

The last statement provides the basis for testing a model. An analyst simply compares for each response pattern the hypothetical frequency generated by the model (say column 7 of Table A-4) with the actual frequency as recorded in the manifest data (say column 2 of Table A-4). To the extent that there is a close correspondence, a correspondence closer than yielded by any other meaningful model, he may infer that the classes of respondents postulated by the model exist and form a latent, underlying structure. Note that such a structure need not be ordered along any dimension.[69]

We have merely sketched the basic approach of the latent structure method.[70] Unfortunately, this method still requires extensive development before the major computational (as well as conceptual) problems associated with most of its potential applications can be overcome. (These computational problems stem from the need to solve complex systems of simultaneous equations in order to derive the parameters of the generating mechanism.) Therefore, we shall not go into further details in this Appendix. The reader is referred to the literature cited for full treatment. In the remaining paragraphs, however, we wish to indicate some directions for its potential use in regional analysis.

One direction of possible future use might, for example, be indicated by a study of industrial development in New England which has already been alluded to. Suppose the analyst finds it impossible to scale along the socio-economic dimension examined. At best, suppose he obtains a coefficient of reproducibility of 0.7, an unacceptable level. Such a finding does not preclude a more sophisticated analysis. It simply signifies that the response patterns are nonscalable. The analyst may still investigate a latent structure model to unearth the system of classes of respondents which may underlie the response patterns.

To illustrate let Table A-4 depict data on the response patterns (or patterns of characteristics) of communities of New England. Four basic questions (characteristics), represented by items 1, 2, 3 and 4 in column 1,[71] are considered relevant. A response indicating resistance (or the presence of an unfavorable characteristic, e.g. high median income) is indicated by a plus sign. A response indicating a receptive attitude (or the absence of an unfavorable characteristic) is indicated by a minus sign. All possible response patterns are listed; they number 16 (i.e., 2^n where n = the number of items). In column 2 are listed the number of communities having each pattern.

In line with this discussion, a model is constructed. According to Table A-4 this model is found consistent with three latent classes, I, II, and III. As noted before, the probability data generated by the model are presented in columns 3, 4, and 5. Again, each column refers to a particular latent class and shows for

[69] A system of classes is simply identified as a set of points in the positive quadrant of n-dimensional space, where the components of any point (each a probability) sum to unity, and where n is the number of possible response patterns. If the classes do lie along a unidimensional continuum, a latent structure analysis should give the same results as a scale analysis.

It should also be noted that the identification of a set of latent classes does not prove any causal hypothesis. However, it may be used to test hypotheses in the statistical sense, and in conjunction with other materials to suggest possibly significant causal hypotheses.

[70] It is also to be observed that latent structure analysis is somewhat analogous to factor analysis, which will be touched upon in Appendix B to this chapter. Factor analysis assumes that the variables with which an analyst deals are continuous and have normal joint distributions. Latent structure analysis utilizes items which are noncontinuous (typically dichotomous or trichotomous) and does for such items a job similar to what factor analysis does for quantitative variables.

[71] These questions or characteristics may be similar to the items of Scalogram 2 or may relate to a host of other pertinent traits and features.

each response pattern the probability that a respondent (community) with that response pattern will be found in that latent class. And each row indicates for the relevant response pattern the probabilities that a respondent (community) with that response pattern will be found in the several latent classes. Therefore, the three probabilities along any row must add to unity as indicated in column 6. Finally, the frequency data generated by the model are recorded in column 7. Note that the generated data correspond well with the actual data ; hence the model may be said to be a relatively good fit (the reader is referred to the literature for relevant tests of fit).

At this point it must be reiterated that the model does not furnish a basis for ordering classes. It merely tests the existence of classes. Therefore, it becomes necessary, at least in a number of instances, to introduce additional information in order to acquire further insight. In the particular problem of the industrial development of New England, the analyst may have worded his questions in such a manner, or have selected such characteristics, that the two response patterns, $+ + + +$ and $- - - -$, can be taken to represent only the two extreme positions along the single dimension of community resistance. Scrutiny of the generated data on probabilities (columns 3 to 5) does suggest that the model is consistent with the initial choice of questions or characteristics. The data do show that of all response patterns the extreme pattern $+ + + +$ has the greatest probability of being found in one class of communities. Accordingly this class, latent class I, can be considered as tending to be resistant to industrial development, especially when the probability that response pattern $+ + + +$ will be checked off by members of that class is comparatively high. (In the model behind Table A-4, this probability is approximately 0.37.) Simultaneously, the generated data do show that of all response patterns the extreme pattern $- - - -$ has the greatest probability of being found in another class of communities. Accordingly, this class, latent class III, can be considered as tending to be receptive to industrial development, especially when the probability that response pattern $- - - -$ will be checked off by members of that class is comparatively high. (This probability is approximately 0.32.)

From these assumptions and the derived partial order of response patterns, the analyst can proceed to certain conclusions. As before, he may determine cutoff points of significance. He may judge that, in addition to response pattern $+ + + +$, the response patterns $+ + - +$, $- + + +$, and $+ + + -$ are also suitably classified as resistant. For each respondent indicating one of these patterns the probability of belonging to latent class I (already designated as tending to be resistant) is 0.850 or more. Likewise, he may judge that, in addition to response pattern $- - - -$, the response patterns $+ - - -$, $- + - -$, $- - + -$, and $+ - + -$ are also suitably classified as receptive. For each respondent indicating one of these patterns, the probability of belonging to latent class III (already designated as tending to be receptive) is 0.850 or more.[72]

The researcher may now examine the response patterns (characteristics) of those communities possessing specific potential plant sites based on resource availability, etc. If most of or all these communities have response patterns which he has classified as receptive, he may leave unqualified his conclusions based on comparative cost analysis. In contrast, if most of or all these communities have response patterns which he has classified as resistant, his com-

---

[72] In determining cutoff points the analyst may pay attention to the distribution of probabilities among all classes, as well as the concentration in any one class.

parative cost conclusions must be seriously qualified. Lastly, if most of or all these communities have response patterns which do not lend themselves to neat classification (as the central response patterns of Table A-4), he will need to qualify his conclusions. The extent of qualification will be influenced by the findings of other studies and by the anticipated effectiveness of any promotional or educational efforts by business or governmental units.[73]

We have illustrated one potential use of latent structure models. When the potential uses of scaling techniques which were listed at the end of the previous section involve situations that turn out to be non-scalable or not meaningfully depicted along a single dimension, the latent structure approach may be investigated. For example, migration phenomena might turn out to be non-analyzable in terms of a single dimension, and the analyst may judge it worthwhile to search for latent classes of migrants. If such classes of migrants are found, the motivating forces of each class can be studied in turn and can lead to firmer interregional and intraregional projection of flows of migrants.

There are other potential uses for the latent structure approach, such as to identify latent classes in a population from which representative individuals can be drawn to estimate, say, a community participation potential function which will be discussed in Chapter 11. But it would be premature at this time to detail any such potential application of latent structure approach; the conceptual and computation difficulties confronting the widespread use of this approach are both many and severe. Their enumeration and discussion are beyond the limited objective of this Appendix, which has been merely to sketch the promise of latent structure methods.

Appendix B

Factor Analysis, with Particular Reference to Regional Delineation

At a number of points in this book, the problem of selecting appropriate sets of regions for analysis has been alluded to. This problem is particularly acute in connection with the last section of this chapter concerned with coefficients of localization, specialization, redistribution, localization curves, shift ratios, etc. This problem is present in most regional investigations and is rarely fully resolved. This situation obtains not only because of different philosophical approaches and welfare values connected with regional studies, topics beyond the scope of this volume, but also because an analyst typically finds reasonable alternative interpretations of the same objective data for delineating regions. Nonetheless, certain techniques are available for objective treatment of the data so as to reduce the possibility of error (or inconsistency) in the areas where subjective judgment must be made. One of these techniques is factor analysis, a technique which has found some useful application in the delineation of meaningful regions, and which can profitably find greater use in other facets of regional analysis. As with scaling and latent structure techniques, we shall

---

[73] As with the scalogram, if this type of analysis has validity, it yields as a by-product valuable information on key points in particular communities to which educational and similar efforts might be directed, if such are desirable.

attempt only to sketch the basic elements of factor analysis and some of its potential applications. The reader is referred to the cited literature for fuller discussion.[74]

Like many other research methods, factor analysis is designed to develop a simple framework of factors whose interplay can adequately represent the inter-

TABLE B-1.   HYPOTHETICAL INTERCORRELATIONS

Item	1	2	3	4	......	50	......	100
1. Per capita income ($)	*	0.36	0.42	0.24	......	−0.12	......	0.06
2. Industrial Employment (% of total)	0.36	*	0.42	0.24	......	−0.12	......	0.06
3. Years of schooling, average	0.42	0.42	*	0.28	......	−0.14	......	0.07
4. Divorce rate	0.24	0 24	0.28	*	......	−0.08	......	0.04
.	.	.	.	.	.	.	.	.
.	.	.	.	.	.	.	.	.
.	.	.	.	.	.	.	.	.
.	.	.	.	.	.	.	.	.
.	.	.	.	.	.	.	.	.
.	.	.	.	.	.	.	.	.
.	.	.	.	.	.	.	.	.
50. Miles of highway per capita	−0.12	−0.12	−0.14	−0.08	......	*	......	−0.02
.	.	.	.	.	.	.	.	.
.	.	.	.	.	.	.	.	.
.	.	.	.	.	.	.	.	.
.	.	.	.	.	.	.	.	.
.	.	.	.	.	.	.	.	.
.	.	.	.	.	.	.	.	.
.	.	.	.	.	.	.	.	.
100. Household accidents per capita	0.06	0.06	0.07	0.04	......	−0.02	......	*

* Data for intercorrelation of any one characteristic are not included since they are meaningless.

action of the complex set of forces in actuality. It has much in common with scalogram and latent structure analysis in that it attempts to combine or reduce variables which are linked to each other into indexes describing particular basic dimensions, or reflecting basic structural features of the total situation being studied ; no dependent variable as such need be specified. It has less in common

[74] Among others, the following are useful general references : L. L. Thurstone [66] ; K. J. Holzinger and H. H. Harman [32] ; R. B. Cattell [6] ; S. Stouffer et al. [63] ; L. Festinger and D. Katz [18], especially pp. 274–278 ; B. Fruchter [21] ; C. J. Adcock [1] ; and M. J. Hagood and D. O. Price [29], ch. 26.

with regression and variance analysis for it does not attempt to explain statistically variation in a dependent variable by variation in a set of key independent variables, the discarded independent variables being judged as relatively insignificant. Rather it retains the many variables relevant in a study by attempting to account for their behavior in terms of relatively few basic dimensions.

To motivate the discussion, let us consider a simple case. Let the United States comprise the area corresponding to a system of regions. The problem is to divide the United States into a specific set of meaningful regions. For the problem to be studied, let us assume that an abundance of data is available, but only by state units. Hence for operational purposes, each region must be composed of whole states.

As a first step, a number of characteristics are to be selected, where the variation in each characteristic is hypothesized to reflect significantly the differentiation among underlying regions. Suppose that 100 characteristics are identified, as listed in the left-hand tab of Table B-1. Suppose, too, the intercorrelations of the 48 state scores on each pair of these characteristics are computed and recorded in the same table. If these intercorrelations take the specific "pure" form shown in the table, certain generalizations can be readily made. Since we may hypothesize at the start a single basic factor—namely a single basic set of meaningful regions—we may schematically represent this factor by the circle in Figure B-1. This circle cuts across a series of rectangles, each rectangle representing a particular characteristic. The amount of overlap with each rectangle indicates the extent to which the general factor accounts for (statistically explains) the variation among states in the corresponding characteristic. By each area of overlap is placed a decimal figure, which is customarily designated a factor loading. Squaring this factor loading and multiplying by 100 yields the per cent of the area of the corresponding rectangle which overlaps the circle; that is, for the characteristic represented by that rectangle it yields the per cent of the variation among states which is associated with regional differentiation. (In this respect as well as many others, the factor loading behaves like a correlation coefficient.) For example, the factor loading on characteristic 1 (per capita income) is 0.6. Squaring and multiplying by 100, we obtain the percentage figure of 36; hence 36 per cent of the variation among states in per capita income is to be explained, according to our hypothesis, by the basic factor of regions. Similarly, this basic factor statistically explains 36 per cent of the variation among states in characteristic 2 (industrial employment as a per cent of total employment), 49 per cent of variation in characteristic 3 (average number of years of schooling), etc.[75]

Given the hypothetical data of Figure B-1, and on the very important assumption that there is no other factor which relates any pair of characteristics, we may calculate expected intercorrelation between any two characteristics. (For the moment, the dashed ellipse coursing through rectangles 3 and 4 is to be ignored.) We simply compute the product of the two decimal factor loadings. For example, the expected intercorrelation between characteristics 2 and 3 is the product of 0.6 and 0.7, which product (0.42) is found in both the cell of row 2 and column 3 and the cell of row 3 and column 2 in Table B-1.

Thus the relationships depicted in Figure B-1 (when the dashed ellipse is nonexistent) afford in a pure statistical sense an explanation of all the intercorrelations which have been recorded in Table B-1. Or conversely the set of intercorrelations

[75] Note that the basic factor statistically explains 4 per cent of the variation in characteristic 50 which varies *inversely* relative to the other characteristics.

of Table B-1 implies one and only one basic factor and the specific factor loadings of Figure B-1. This strong implication results because the inter-correlations were deliberately constructed to be pure or, in other words, to be 100 per cent predictable by a single basic factor. That is, all columns (excluding

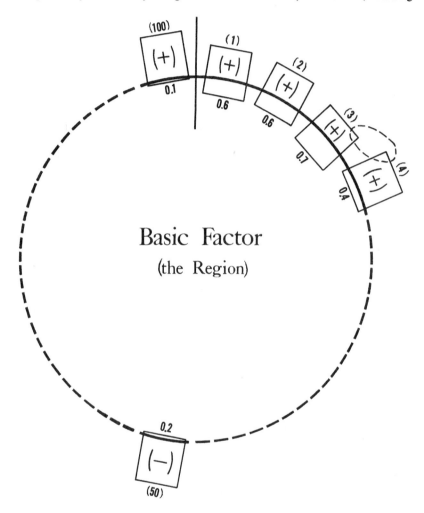

Figure B-1. Hypothetical factor-loading diagram.

items along the principal diagonal) are proportional to each other.[76] (For example, the 100th column is one-sixth of the first column.) Therefore the intercorrelations can reflect the play of only one general factor, even though this factor has a different impact on each characteristic. However, exactly what this

[76] In matrix algebra parlance, the rank of the intercorrelation matrix is one.

factor is, or how the result is to be interpreted, must rest solely on the analyst's conceptual and theoretical frameworks. (Recall that the choice of the characteristics is also largely determined by these frameworks.) In this simple example, we have hypothesized a system of regions which can be differentiated and whose diverse influences pervade the national system. We may then say that factor analysis has shown that the data are consistent with this hypothesis, and that only one basic factor exists. We interpret this factor as signifying that regions are present and do have differential impact. Yet, many other interpretations are possible, as the reader may discover from his own explorations with diverse hypotheses.

Once a single basic factor is found and interpreted as verifying the presence of a set of regions, the specific arrangement of states into regions can proceed via the construction of an index number and determination of cutoff points. Procedure for this step will be presented later when we report on some of Hagood's work.

Unfortunately, pure cases of this sort are rarely, if ever, found. A typical situation involves the interplay of a host of nonrandom factors as well as chance, as the reader by now fully appreciates. The intercorrelation data are then exceedingly complex. Yet this situation does not preclude a fruitful search for a single general factor in cases where strong theoretical support for such an hypothesis can be mustered. For example, in the delineation of single-purpose regions or of regions to be distinguished by a relatively narrow set of related characteristics, a single-factor approach may have considerable justification. However, when multiple-purpose regions are sought, or regions classifiable by the totality of characteristics, the single-factor approach, when intercorrelations are highly impure, is not readily accepted. Some of the pertinent reservations can be illustrated with reference to the pioneering and stimulating effort of Odum, Hagood, and others to demarcate a best set of major regions for the United States.

Hagood, who has perhaps developed most thoughtfully and carefully the single-factor approach in the delineation of regions, begins, as the factor analyst must, with a selection of relevant characteristics of states from which regions are to be fashioned. (It must be borne in mind that the limited availability of data on both state and other areal units may at the outset significantly restrict the extent to which valid results and tests are achievable.) Seeking a set of regions to be distinguished primarily by agricultural and demographic characteristics, she selects 104 characteristics, 52 agricultural and 52 demographic. The 52 agricultural characteristics are grouped into 6 classes, and the demographic into 8 classes. For each of the resulting 14 classes, a single-factor analysis is pursued. For example, one of the 6 agricultural classes is designated land use and covers the items listed in Table B-2.[77] The state values for each pair of these characteristics are correlated ; the coefficients are listed in bold type in Table B-3. Application of standard computational procedures for single-factor analysis yields the factor loadings in column 1 of Table B-2. Thus the square of the factor loading of 0.540 at the head of the column indicates that the single factor (however interpreted) accounts for 29 per cent of the variation among states in the per cent farmland is of all land.

---

[77] The other agricultural classes relate to crops, livestock, tenure, farm values and farm finance.

TABLE B-2. SINGLE-FACTOR LOADINGS FOR LAND USE INDEX

Item	Factor Loading
	(1)
1. Per cent farmland is of all land	0.540
2. Per cent cropland (harvested and failure) is of all farmland	0.789
3. Per cent woodland is of all farmland not used for crops	0.479
4. Mean size of farm (acres)	−0.760

Source: Computed from data in M. J. Hagood [27].

As already noted, once factor loadings are obtained, "expected" intercorrelations when no other common factor is at play can be computed by multiplying the relevant pair of loadings. These expected intercorrelations are recorded in parentheses in Table B-3. Comparison of the "expected" with the "actual" data yields one test of the adequacy of the single-factor hypothesis. The considerable discrepancies of the data of Table B-3 do suggest the operation of one or more additional factors which are common to two or more of the four items (characteristics).

However, if the investigator does judge that the empirical results do not invalidate his single-factor hypothesis, he can proceed to construct an index, as Hagood does. For each state the index value is computed from the following equation:

$$I^J = 0.540Z_1^J + 0.789Z_2^J + 0.479Z_3^J - 0.760Z_4^J$$

where Z_1^J, Z_2^J, Z_3^J, and Z_4^J are the ratings of state J ($J = 1, \ldots, 48$) on each of the

TABLE B-3. INTERCORRELATIONS: ACTUAL AND IDEAL

Item	1	2	3	4
1		0.624 (0.426)	−0.091 (0.259)	−0.189 (−0.410)
2	0.624 (0.426)		0.169 (0.378)	−0.590 (−0.600)
3	−0.091 (0.259)	0.169 (0.378)		−0.597 (−0.364)
4	−0.189 (−0.410)	−0.590 (−0.600)	−0.597 (−0.364)	

Source: Derived from M. J. Hagood [27].

four characteristics of Table B-2.   Each rating is in standard form (i.e., $Z_i^J = (X_i^J - M_i)/\sigma_i$ where $i = 1, \ldots, 4$; and where X_i^J is the actual value for characteristic i in state J, M_i is the mean value of the characteristic i over all states, and σ_i is the standard deviation of the state values).   The coefficients which respectively multiply $Z_1^J, \ldots, Z_4^J$ are the factor loadings of Table B-2.

Once a set of index values for states is obtained, these values can be examined for cutoff points.   If cutoff points can be located to set apart groups of states which are contiguous and on other counts can be expected to be homogeneous with respect to the phenomena being studied, it may be said that a single-factor analysis has helped in the objective determination of regions.   For example, Map B-1 reproduces in a modified form the land use index map developed by Hagood.   There is at least some indication of regional structure in this map.

Hagood proceeds further.   Once she obtains a land use index and an index for each of the other thirteen classes, she condenses these indices into two major group indices.   One major group index is obtained from a single-factor analysis for the six indices representing the six agricultural classes.   The second major group index is derived from another single-factor analysis for the eight indices representing the eight agricultural classes.   This operation can lead to the determination of two additional sets of regions, a set of agricultural regions and a set of demographic regions.

Finally, Hagood performs a single-factor analysis on all fourteen indices, representing the fourteen classes of characteristics.   Before actually combining states to form regions on the basis of significant cutoff points on her derived composite agriculture-population index, she takes another essential step.   States may have the same index value because they have identical patterns (profiles) with respect to the 104 characteristics initially selected for study.   They also may have the same value because differences in their patterns (which differences may be sharp) have compensatory effects on the index scale when weighted by factor loadings.   (For example, in constructing an index based on the six classes of agricultural characteristics, Hagood finds that the states of Arizona and Iowa, which are highly dissimilar with respect to agricultural profiles, score 59 and 62 respectively.)   Therefore another criterion for combining two or more states into one region is that they have similar patterns, to be evidenced for any pair of these states by positive and fairly high correlations between the values for the 104 selected characteristics.[78]

With the resulting index values and correlation coefficients, it becomes possible to organize states into regions, although a number of subjective elements still remain, as Hagood well recognizes.   One set of possible regions is indicated in Map B-2 which is reproduced from Hagood's study.   On this map the composite agriculture-population index value for each state is in bold type and is encircled.   The correlation coefficients between the profiles (based on 104 characteristics) for selected pairs of adjacent and nearby states are indicated in light type.

Close scrutiny of Map B-2 does reveal that a number of sets of regions are possible.   On the other hand, it does uncover certain clusters of states which, in a sense, tend to form the nuclei of regions (e.g., Mississippi, Alabama, Georgia,

[78] States within a region should also be contiguous.   In another connection, Hagood has introduced latitudinal and longitudinal positions as relevant characteristics in factor analysis so that index values will to some extent reflect contiguity.   See M. J. Hagood [26].

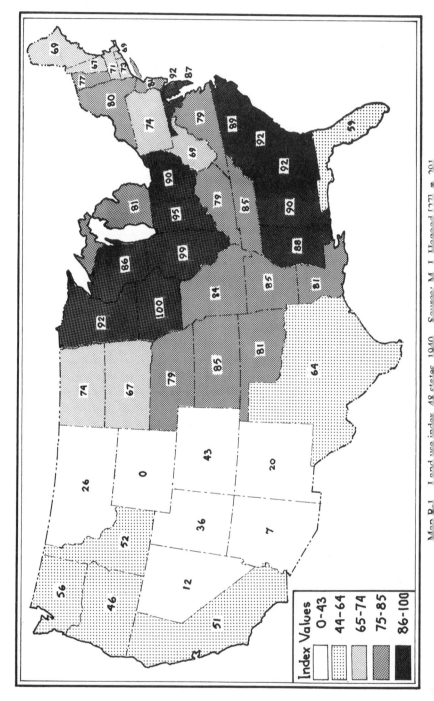

Map P-1. Land use index, 48 states, 1940. Source: M. J. Hagood [27], p. 301.

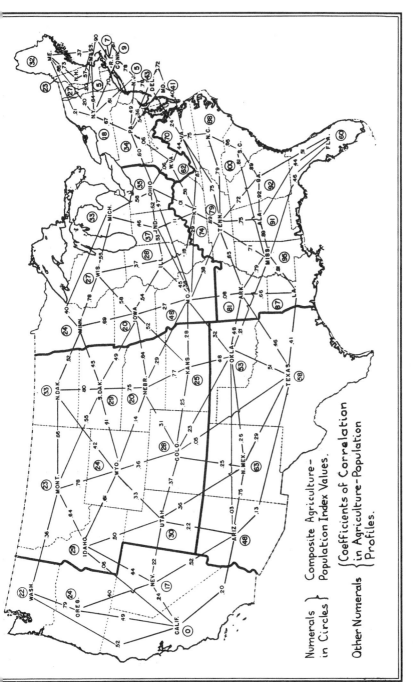

Map B-2.   Composite agriculture-population index values and coefficients of correlation in agriculture-population profiles, 48 states, 1940.
Source: M. J. Hagood [27], p. 296.

and South Carolina; Maine, New Hampshire, and Vermont; and Idaho, Montana, and Wyoming). Since state political units are poor units for the construction of regions, and since in a highly urbanized society the peripheral areas of regions are transitional, that is, are the zones where phenomena reflect mixed orientation, it is not unexpected that several alternative sets of regions are possible. In particular, it is not unexpected that alternative sets of regions may be formed by different assignments of such states as Missouri and West Virginia which contain or comprise transition areas.

In brief, it may be concluded that single-factor analysis of the type depicted can be of considerable value as an objective tool to complement theory and other analysis in the delineation of regions.[79] Yet we must recognize certain severe limitations in the use of this tool. As already noted, the single-factor approach finds its greatest validity when in fact all intercorrelations of characteristics are pure, that is, 100 per cent predictable from the single-factor loadings. But when these intercorrelations are not pure, difficult problems of interpretation arise.

We can illustrate this last point with reference to Table B-3. There the actual intercorrelations (boldface type) contrast rather sharply in a number of the cells with the expected intercorrelations (lightface type) based on the single-factor loadings of Table B-2. Hence many analysts would conclude that other common factors are at play. Such factors may account for part of or, at the extreme, all the discrepancy between the actual and expected intercorrelations for one or more pairs of characteristics. For example, in Figure B-1 the dashed ellipse coursing through rectangles 3 and 4 may be taken to represent a second factor common to characteristics 3 and 4, and therefore to explain an amount of correlation (if positive) over and above that explained by the first basic factor (the large circle). If other common factors are at play, then how interpret the findings from single-factor analysis?

One possible interpretation, which is implied by the work of Odum and Hagood and which would seem reasonable if the discrepancies are smallish, is that the findings from single-factor analysis are the really significant findings. An analyst might argue that although there are many factors in operation, a single one is dominant, and that in view of other limitations of the study, the presence of any secondary factors may be safely ignored. This line of reasoning might be particularly valid for the time being if the most relevant theoretical construct were oriented to a single cause-effect relationship.

But other lines of reasoning may also be plausible, in particular when the discrepancies are not small. An analyst's hypothesis may suggest two basic factors at play, or three, or four, etc. Factor analysis would then be required to unearth these several factors, for which task computation procedures have been developed. But, aside from the thorny theoretical problem of determining how many basic factors are at play, there is the major difficulty of interpreting results of multiple-factor analysis, even when the analytical framework unambiguously denotes the number of relevant factors.

To illustrate, set up a simple two-factor hypothesis relating to only four relevant characteristics, say any four listed in Table B-1. Let the actual inter-

---

[79] A somewhat similar tool for the delineation of meaningful spatial units, but one less sophisticated from a statistical standpoint, is developed in E. Shevky and W. Bell [61]. For relevant evaluation see A. H. Hawley and O. D. Duncan [31]; and M. D. Van Arsdol, Jr., S. F. Camilleri, and C. F. Schmid [67].

correlations be as recorded in Table B-4. Factor analysis operations, by one of the several standard techniques, yield loadings for factors I and II as indicated in Table B-5. Now, if we square 0.6, the first factor loading for characteristic 1, and add the result to the square of 0.4, the second factor loading for characteristic 1, we obtain 0.52. This number multiplied by 100 yields the per cent of variation in characteristic 1 which can be explained by the two factors. Also note

TABLE B-4. HYPOTHETICAL INTERCORRELATIONS

Item	1	2	3	4
1		0.60	0.30	0.04
2	0.60		0.24	−0.06
3	0.30	0.24		0.43
4	0.04	−0.06	0.43	

that the intercorrelations of Table B-4 are pure, that is, fully explainable by the two factors. For example, on the basis of factor I alone we can expect intercorrelation between characteristics 2 and 3 of 0.6 × 0.7 = 0.42. On the basis of factor II alone we can expect intercorrelation between the same two characteristics of 0.6 × − 0.3 = −0.18. Summing over both factors, we can expect intercorrelation of 0.42 − 0.18 = 0.24 which is identical with the "actual"

TABLE B-5. HYPOTHETICAL FACTOR LOADINGS

Characteristic (Variable)	Factor I	II
1	0.6	0.4
2	0.6	0.6
3	0.7	−0.3
4	0.4	−0.5

intercorrelation recorded in both the cell of row 3, column 2, and the cell of row 2, column 3.

Despite the appearance of objectivity in the determination of the loadings for factors I and II, such objectivity does not in fact exist. For it can easily be demonstrated that many other sets of loadings for only two factors will explain just as well the intercorrelations of Table B-4. In fact, there is an infinity of such sets. The loadings of Table B-6 illustrate one of this infinity, as the reader may verify.[80]   It thus becomes clear that, even for an hypothesis based on the operation of two and only two basic factors and even when all intercorrelations are fully explainable, multiple interpretations are possible.   These different interpretations revolve around the diverse sets of factor loadings which can be considered pertinent to the problem studied.

From this discussion it is also clear that two-factor hypotheses where intercorrelations are only partially explainable require still more subjective judgment and intuition on the part of the analyst.   Likewise with hypotheses involving three or more factors, whether or not intercorrelations are fully explainable in the statistical sense.

Although we have only touched on some of the basic features of factor analysis —the reader is referred to the cited literature for full discussion—some of its chief virtues and limitations are clear.   It does offer a fruitful approach to condensing voluminous sets of data into relatively few useful indices or dimensions.   As already illustrated, it can be an effective tool for delineating regions within a system which has firm theoretical foundations.   It is a useful tool in constructing level-of-living indices[81] which along with correlation analysis of

TABLE B-6.   ALTERNATIVE FACTOR LOADINGS

Characteristic (Variable)	Factor	
	I	II
1	0.08	0.72
2	−0.07	0.85
3	0.68	0.34
4	0.64	−0.02

profiles may aid comparative regional analysis.   In certain connections it can furnish a useful basis for stratification in sampling.[82]   As many statistical tools, it can serve as a partial test of an hypothesis or reflect on the adequacy of the characteristics initially selected as relevant, etc.[83]

Moreover, whether or not factor analysis is employed to test an hypothesis, it may suggest workable typologies and classification schemes and fruitful models or conceptual frameworks on the interrelations of variables.   As one illustration, Price has employed factor analysis in searching for fundamental dimensions of metropolitan centers.   He is able to explain statistically the intercorrelations in the variation of 15 characteristics among 93 cities in terms of 4 factors.   The

[80] For example, multiplying −0.07 by 0.68 (factor I loadings on characteristics 2 and 3) yields −0.0476 which when added to 0.2890 (the product of 0.85 and 0.34, the respective factor II loadings) gives 0.2414, which is within rounding error of the value of 0.24 of Table B-4.

In factor analysis parlance, the loadings of Table B-6 are obtained by rotating the reference axes clockwise 50 degrees.

[81] For example, see A. L. Ferriss [17].

[82] For example, see M. J. Hagood and E. H. Bernert [28].

[83] For example, see M. D. Van Arsdol, S. F. Camilleri, and C. F. Schmid [67].

factor loadings obtained combined with his accumulated knowledge and judgment on forces at play in metropolitan centers leads him to identify tentatively these factors as (1) degree of maturity of city; (2) the extent to which a city is a service center; (3) the level of living within a city; and (4) the per capita trade volume of a city.[84] Finally, factor analysis (perhaps in conjunction with scalogram and latent structure methods) may be helpful in research on attitudes, political participation, and related topics which have an important bearing on resource development and planning for a region or system of regions. It may make possible the narrowing down of the range of alternative interpretations of complex sets of data, often incomplete, where such data might relate to voting patterns, use of government facilities (e.g., health centers, libraries, adult education programs, extension services), contacts among different social groups and institutions, etc. It may even suggest alternative hypotheses not apparent from scrutiny of raw data.

In considering the virtues of factor analysis, the analyst must also bear in mind the extent to which factor analysis cannot eliminate his responsibility for sound reasoning and judgment, and in many cases cannot eliminate the need to resort to arbitrary procedures. Briefly put, factor analysis is not nearly as objective as appears to the unsophisticated analyst. At the very start, the choice of relevant characteristics must depend on an investigator's intuition and previous knowledge, as well as the availability of data. Next, the number of factors deemed appropriate involves a judgment factor despite certain procedures designed to furnish objective criteria. Most important of all, many alternative sets of factor loadings are possible for a given set of data on intercorrelations, the particular one chosen and its interpretation (if any can be put forth) being largely determined by the theoretical or conceptual construct deemed most significant. In addition, there are a number of shortcomings both conceptual and technical, such as those relating to the assumptions involved in the initial correlation procedures, the additive or multiplicative nature of factors, and measures of error variance. The discussion of these shortcomings is beyond the scope of this Appendix.

REFERENCES

1. Adcock, C. J., *Factorial Analysis for Non-Mathematicians*, Melbourne University Press, Melbourne, Australia, 1954.
2. Airov, Joseph, "Location Factors in Synthetic Fiber Production," *Papers and Proceedings of the Regional Science Association*, Vol. 2 (1956).
3. ———, *The Location of the Synthetic Fiber Industry: A Study in Regional Analysis*, John Wiley, New York, 1959.
4. Alexander, J. W., "Location of Manufacturing: Methods of Measurement," *Annals of the Association of American Geographers*, Vol. 48 (March 1958).
5. Bachi, Roberto, *Statistical Analysis of Geographical Series*, Kaplan School, Hebrew University and Israel Central Bureau of Statistics, Jerusalem, 1957.
6. Cattell, R. B., *Factor Analysis: An Introduction and Manual for the Psychologist and Social Scientist*, Harper, New York, 1952.
7. Coleman, J. S., "Multi-dimensional Scale Analysis," *American Journal of Sociology*, Vol. 63 (Nov. 1957).

---

84 D. O. Price [54], pp. 449–455.

8. Creamer, Daniel, "Shifts of Manufacturing Industries," in *Industrial Location and National Resources*, U. S. National Resources Planning Board, Washington, D.C., 1943.

9. Cumberland, John, *The Locational Structure of the East Coast Steel Industry with Emphasis on the Feasibility of an Integrated New England Steel Mill*, doctoral dissertation, Harvard University, Cambridge, Massachusetts, 1951.

10. Davis, J. A., "On Criteria for Scale Relationships," *American Journal of Sociology*, Vol. 63 (Jan. 1958).

11. Dean, William H., Jr., *The Theory of the Geographic Location of Economic Activities*, doctoral dissertation, Harvard University, selections published by Edward Brothers, Inc., Ann Arbor, Michigan, 1938.

12. Duncan, Otis D., "Urbanization and Retail Specialization," *Social Forces*, Vol. 30 (March 1952).

13. ———, R. P. Cuzzort, and Beverly Duncan, *Statistical Geography*, The Free Press, Glencoe, Illinois, 1960.

14. ———, and Beverly Duncan, "A Methodological Analysis of Segregation Indexes," *American Sociological Review*, Vol. 20 (April 1955).

15. ———, and ———, "Residential Distribution and Occupational Stratification," *American Journal of Sociology*, Vol. 60 (March 1955).

16. Dunn, Edgar S., *The Location of Agricultural Production*, University of Florida Press, Gainesville, Florida, 1954.

17. Ferris A. L., "Rural-Farm Level of Living Indexes for Two Southeastern States," *Social Forces*, Vol. 26 (May 1948).

18. Festinger, Leon, and D. Katz, *Research Methods in the Behavioral Sciences*, Dryden Press, New York, 1953.

19. Florence, P. Sargant, *Investment, Location, and Size of Plant*, University Press, Cambridge, England, 1948.

20. ———, W. G. Fritz, and R. C. Gilles, "Measures of Industrial Distribution," in *Industrial Location and National Resources*, U. S. National Resources Planning Board, Washington, D.C., 1943, ch. 5.

21. Fruchter, B., *Introduction to Factor Analysis*, Van Nostrand, New York, 1954.

22. Fuchs, Victor R., "Changes in the Location of U. S. Manufacturing Since 1929," *Journal of Regional Science*, Vol. 1 (Spring 1959).

23. Green, N. E., "Scale Analysis of Urban Structures," *American Sociological Review*, Vol. 21 (Feb. 1956).

24. Greenhut, Melvin L., *Plant Location in Theory and Practice*, University of North Carolina Press, Chapel Hill, North Carolina, 1956.

25. Guttman, L., and E. A. Suchman, "Intensity and Zero Point for Attitude Analysis," *American Sociological Review*, Vol. 12 (Feb. 1947).

26. Hagood, M. J., "An Examination of the Use of Factor Analysis in the Problem of Subregional Delineation," *Rural Sociology*, Vol. 6 (Sept. 1941).

27. ———, "Statistical Methods for Delineation of Regions Applied to Data on Agriculture and Population," *Social Forces*, Vol. 21 (March 1943).

28. ———, and E. H. Bernert, "Component Indexes as a Basis for Stratification in Sampling," *Journal of the American Statistical Association*, Vol. 40 (Sept. 1945).

29. ———, and Daniel O. Price, *Statistics for Sociologists*, Henry Holt, New York, 1952.

30. Hauser, Phillip, M., Otis D. Duncan, and Beverly Duncan, *Methods of Urban Analysis: A Summary Report*, Research Report, U. S. Air Force Personnel and Training Research Center, San Antonio, Texas, 1956.

31. Hawley, A. H., and O. D. Duncan, "Social Area Analysis : A Critical Appraisal," *Land Economics*, Vol. 33 (Nov. 1957).

32. Holzinger, K. J., and H. H. Harman, *Factor Anlaysis: A Synthesis of Factorial Methods*, University of Chicago Press, Chicago, 1941.

33. Hoover, Edgar M., *Location of Economic Activity*, McGraw-Hill, New York 1948.

34. ———, *Location Theory and the Shoe and Leather Industries*, Harvard University Press, Cambridge, Massachusetts, 1937.

35. ———, "The Measurement of Industrial Localization," *Review of Economics and Statistics*, Vol. 18 (Nov. 1936).

36. ———, "Redistribution of Population, 1850–1940," *The Journal of Economic History*, Vol. 1 (Nov. 1941).

37. ———, and Joseph L. Fisher, "Research in Regional Economic Growth," *Problems in the Study of Economic Growth*, Universities-National Bureau Committee on Economic Research, National Bureau of Economic Research, New York, 1949.

38. Isard, Walter, *Location and Space-Economy*, John Wiley, New York, 1956.

39. ———, "Some Locational Factors in the Iron and Steel Industry Since the Early Nineteenth Century," *Journal of Political Economy*, Vol. 56 (June 1948).

40. ———, and William M. Capron, "The Future Locational Pattern of Iron and Steel Production in the United States," *Journal of Political Economy*, Vol. 57 (April 1949).

41. ———, and John Cumberland, "New England as a Possible Location for an Integrated Iron and Steel Works," *Economic Geography*, Vol. 26 (Oct. 1950).

42. ———, and Eugene W. Schooler, *Location Factors in the Petrochemical Industry*, Office of Technical Services, U. S. Department of Commerce, Washington, D.C., 1955.

43. ———, and Vincent H. Whitney, *Atomic Power, an Economic and Social Analysis*, McGraw-Hill, New York, 1952.

44. Krutilla, John V., *The Structure of Costs and Regional Advantage in Primary Aluminum Production*, doctoral dissertation, Harvard University, Cambridge, Massachusetts, 1952.

45. Kuenne, Robert E., *The Use of Input-Output Techniques for the Estimation of Employment in the Delaware Valley*, doctoral dissertation, Harvard University, 1953.

46. Launhardt, Wilhelm, "Die Bestimmung des Zweckmässigsten Standortes einer gewerblichen Anlage," *Zeitschrift des Vereins deutschen Ingenieure*, Vol. 26, No. 3 (1882).

47. ———, *Mathematische Begründung der Volkswirtschaftslehre*, Leipzig, 1885.

48. Lazarsfeld, Paul F., "Recent Developments in Latent Structure Analysis," *Sociometry*, Vol. 18 (1955).

49. ——— et al., *Mathematical Thinking in the Social Sciences*, Free Press, Glencoe, Illinois, 1954.

50. Lindsay, John Robert, *The Location of Oil Refining in the United States*, doctoral dissertation, Harvard University, Cambridge, Massachusetts, 1954.

51. ———, "Regional Advantage in Oil Refining," *Papers and Proceedings of the Regional Science Association*, Vol. 2 (1956).

52. Lösch, August, *The Economics of Location*, Yale University Press, New Haven, Connecticut, 1954.

53. Palander, Tord, *Beitrage zur Standortstheorie*, Almqvist & Wiksells Boktryckeri-A.-B., Uppsala, Sweden, 1935.

54. Price, Daniel O., "Factor Analysis in the Study of Metropolitan Centers," *Social Forces*, Vol 20 (May 1942).
55. Riley, M. W., J. W. Riley, J. Toby, et al., *Sociological Studies in Scale Analysis*, Rutgers University Press, New Brunswick, New Jersey, 1954.
56. Rodgers, Allan, "Some Aspects of Industrial Diversification in the United States," *Papers and Proceedings of the Regional Science Association*, Vol. 1 (1955).
57. ———, "Some Aspects of Industrial Diversification in the United States," *Economic Geography*, Vol. 33 (Jan. 1957).
58. Schooler, Eugene W., *Regional Advantage in the Production of Chemicals from Petroleum and Natural Gas*, doctoral dissertation, Harvard University, Cambridge, Massachusetts, 1954.
59. Schurr, Sam H., and Jacob Marschak, *Economic Aspects of Atomic Power*, Princeton University Press, Princeton, New Jersey, 1950.
60. Shapiro, G., "Myrdal's Definition of the South: A Methodological Note," *American Sociological Review*, Vol. 13 (Oct. 1948).
61. Shevky, Eshref, and Wendell Bell, *Social Area Analysis*, Stanford University Press, Stanford, California, 1955.
62. Smith, Thomas R., *The Cotton Textile Industry of Fall River, Massachusetts*, King's Crown Press, New York, 1944.
63. Stouffer, Samuel A. et al., *Measurement and Prediction*, Princeton University Press, Princeton, New Jersey, 1950.
64. Thompson, Wilbur R., "The Coefficient of Localization: An Appraisal," *Southern Economic Journal*, Vol. 23 (Jan. 1957).
65. Thünen, Johann Heinrich von, *Der isolierte Staat in Beziehung auf Landwirtschaft und Nationalökonomie*, Hamburg, 1826.
66. Thurstone, L. L., *Multiple Factor Analysis: A Development and Expansion of the Vectors of Mind*, University of Chicago Press, Chicago, 1947.
67. Van Arsdol, M. D., Jr., S. F. Camilleri, and C. F. Schmid, "An Application of the Shevky Social Area Indexes to a Model of Urban Society," *Social Forces*, Vol. 37 (Oct. 1958).
68. Weber, Alfred, *Theory of the Location of Industry*, translated by C. Friedrich, University of Chicago Press, Chicago, 1929.
69. Zelinsky, W., "A Method for Measuring Change in the Distribution of Manufacturing Industry: The United States, 1939–47," *Economic Geography*, Vol. 34 (April 1958).

Chapter 8

Interregional and Regional

Input-Output Techniques*

A. Introduction

It is commonplace among those who wish to embark upon regional studies to ask what kind of study would be most fruitful, given their set of objectives and terms of reference. As they scan the list of possible types of studies, such as regional income studies, commodity flow studies, balance of payments studies, economic base studies, multiplier studies, industrial location studies, etc., they are perplexed as to which one to attempt. They see the virtues and limitations of each. Often they clearly perceive the partial character of each and are dissatisfied. They want to study more of the whole of the region or of the system of regions. Or if they have the resources to do more than one partial study, they seek ways by which these studies may be interrelated and may be conceived and formulated to contribute to one another.

It is in this connection that the general interdependence techniques are of value. These techniques have many limitations: they involve sweeping assumptions; they abstract from many important realities of folk, regional, national, and international life. Yet, after all their limitations are set down, the fact remains that they provide essential mortar for cementing various partial studies.

* This chapter was written with John H. Cumberland.

Of the general interdependence approaches which have been investigated, the *interregional input-output* approach is most prominent, both in terms of accomplishment and recognition. It represents a fruitful approach for depicting and investigating the underlying processes which bind together the regions of a system and all the separate facets of their economies. Its strength lies in its detailed presentation of (1) the production and distribution characteristics of individual industries of different regions, and (2) the nature of the interrelationships among these industries themselves and among these industries and other economic sectors. In essence, it expresses the basic fabric of an interindustry system as it exists not only within each region but also among regions.

As an approach we shall find that interregional input-output analysis is not unimpeachable. For certain problems it cannot be utilized or does not furnish the most useful and relevant general framework. Hence, we need other general interdependence approaches. A second, which we shall discuss in Chapter 9 but which has only recently been developed, is the *industrial complex* approach. Still another which has considerable promise but as yet relatively little application is the *interregional linear programming* or, more broadly, the *interregional activity analysis* approach, to be discussed in Chapter 10.

In the discussion of this chapter, we shall begin at a very elementary level. Although the large number of relationships to be handled in input-output models leads to the use of matrix algebra to describe the system and electronic computers to solve the set of equations, the underlying concepts are relatively easy to grasp. To facilitate the presentation, we shall describe the system in a highly simplified framework, and add realities and complexities one by one. (This presentation will be supplemented by a brief and simple mathematical exposition to be developed in the Appendix to this chapter.) Finally, we shall develop the materials to a point where the interindustry system is synthesized with the industrial location system of a comparative cost framework.

It is of historical interest to note that input-output analysis has antecedents in the *Tableau Économique* of Francoise Quesnay, and is a direct outgrowth of the general equilibrium analysis of Walras.[1] It was pioneered by Leontief, and most of its development is attributable to Leontief and his associates.[2] In its most advanced form it pertains to national economies. However, considerable progress has also been scored in applying input-output techniques to regions within nations,[3] and promising

[1] See A. Phillips [44] and L. Walras [55].

[2] See W. W. Leontief [36], W. W. Leontief et al. [37], and Harvard Economic Research Project [14]. For general reference to the literature, see V. Riley and R. L. Allen [45].

[3] Relevant citations on this type of application are noted in Chapter 12 as well as in this chapter,

explorations are being conducted on an international system composed of several national economies.

One further remark. In a discussion of the use of input-output analysis for interregional and regional studies, it is desirable to view regions broadly, and to define nations as those types of regions bounded by political, cultural, and similar institutional barriers and lines. Hence, by definition, national input-output analysis becomes a special form of regional input-output analysis, which in turn is a special form of interregional input-output analysis. By this convention, international input-output analysis becomes a special form of interregional input-output analysis, the most general form.

It cannot be too strongly emphasized that this set of definitions, which we shall employ in this chapter, is only one of several valid types. A more typical set of definitions views regional input-output analysis as a variation of national input-output analysis. Clearly the conventions utilized depend on the purpose of a study and the inclinations of the investigator.

B. The Statistical Framework

1. an isolated region

To begin, assume a region having no trade relations with the rest of the world. This isolated, self-sufficient region functions at a stationary level; it experiences no growth, changes in inventory, or changes in its plant, equipment, and other elements of capital stock. The economy of this region consists of a number of industries, or more broadly, sectors.

If a traditional census were taken of the economy of such a region, the value of total output in each of these industries or sectors would be reported. The census might also record for certain industries some of their major purchases, such as power, labor, and raw materials.

For many regional studies we generally desire a more comprehensive census than the traditional type. Suppose we wish to know for each industry its purchases from every other industry. Or suppose we wish to know how the output of each industry is distributed to every other industry. If either of these more comprehensive censuses were conducted, we would wish to present the materials in orderly fashion. We might construct a table such as Table 1. In Table 1, a twelve-industry classification is employed (at a later point we shall consider the problems associated with the number of industries and type of industrial classification to be used). Industries are arrayed in the same order horizontally (at the top) and vertically (at the left); households are treated as an industry (row 11 and

TABLE 1. INPUT-OUTPUT FLOW TABLE: REGION A, 19xx[a]

(In thousands of dollars)

Industry Producing \ Industry Purchasing	1. Agriculture and extraction	2. Light manufacturing	3. Heavy manufacturing	4. Power and communications	5. Transportation	6. Trade	7. Finance, insurance, and rental	8. Business and personal services	9. Educational and other basic services	10. Construction	11. Households	12. All others	Total Gross Output
1. Agriculture and extraction	21,014	21,327	4,497	558	887	265	930	83	1,126	5,095	12,649	6,735	75,166
2. Light manufacturing	4,241	28,257	3,285	118	395	917	340	2,686	4,344	1,110	43,114	12,574	101,381
3. Heavy manufacturing	1,046	1,928	24,414	173	749	492	16	1,759	346	5,235	7,365	30,642	74,165
4. Power and communications	992	905	737	1,366	600	819	3,226	864	524	74	1,402	869	12,378
5. Transportation	2,590	2,434	1,499	194	1,172	386	557	99	596	1,278	6,023	5,271	22,099
6. Trade	1,631	1,605	1,104	47	459	202	790	521	1,360	2,506	27,107	4,325	41,657
7. Finance, insurance, and rental	2,951	662	470	151	620	1,963	2,825	908	1,159	484	27,282	2,194	41,669
8. Business and personal services	542	1,596	477	127	337	3,121	318	812	493	953	7,512	3,110	19,398
9. Educational and other basic services	–	–	–	–	–	–	16	–	244	–	22,334	7,005	29,599
10. Construction	291	294	282	443	1,233	182	4,116	59	440	– 7	154	21,203	28,704
11. Households	30,411	25,801	25,543	7,231	12,794	26,240	22,018	8,995	14,909	11,492	2,116	32,924	220,474
12. All others	9,457	16,572	11,857	1,970	2,853	7,070	6,517	2,612	4,058	470	63,418	5,000	131,852
Total Inputs	75,166	101,381	74,165	12,378	22,099	41,657	41,669	19,398	29,599	28,704	220,474	131,852	798,542

[a] The industrial classification and data are for the most part those developed in R. A. Kavesh [32], ch. 3. In most cells of this hypothetical table the data relate to conditions in the United States, 1947.

column 11); they purchase products from, and sell labor and other services to, other industries.[4]

If the more comprehensive census were of purchases made by each industry from every other industry, we would fill in the cells of Table 1 by columns. For example, if the census reports that the agriculture and extraction industry received as inputs $21,014,000 of products from itself, $4,241,000 of products from the light manufacturing sector, $1,046,000 of products from the heavy manufacturing sector, etc., these figures would be placed in the appropriate cells of column 1, as we have done. At the bottom of Table 1 is a totals row. The entry in the first column of this row indicates the sum total of purchases (inputs) of the agricultural and extraction industry from all industries including itself and households. After all columns of Table 1 are completed in this manner, we have a complete set of input purchases, total and by type (where the input purchases by the households industry represent consumption expenditures).

On the other hand, if the more comprehensive census were of sales made by each industry to itself (i.e., its retention and use of its own products) and to every other industry (including households), we would fill in the cells of Table 1 by rows. For example, if the census reports that the agricultural and extraction industry retained for its own use $21,014,000 of product; and sold to the light manufacturing sector $21,327,000 of its product; to the heavy manufacturing sector $4,497,000 of its product, etc., these figures would be placed in the appropriate cells of row 1, as we have done. At the extreme right of Table 1 is a totals column. The entry in the first cell of this column records the gross output (gross total of sales) of the agricultural and fisheries industry.

After all rows of Table 1 are completed in this manner, we have for the region a comprehensive and systematically organized set of data on the total outputs of its industries and the distribution of these outputs to all industries.

Whether the census reports purchases by each industry from every industry, or sales by each industry to every industry, Table 1 turns out to be the same (assuming the data are 100 per cent accurate). This identity must follow since every *sale* is at the same time a *purchase*. For example, the *sale* of $4,497,000 of products of the agricultural and extraction industry to the heavy manufacturing sector (as recorded in row 1, column 3) represents a *purchase* by the heavy manufacturing industry of $4,497,000 of products of the agriculture and extraction industry. Thus Table 1 is both a table of input purchases and output sales and has been conveniently termed an *input-output* table.

A table such as Table 1, which may also be called a flow or transactions

[4] At a later point we shall examine this convention at some length.

table, can be extremely valuable. Its utility as a descriptive device is immediately apparent when a fine industrial classification is used—such as the 450 industry classification employed by the Bureau of Labor Statistics in the 1947 input-output study for the United States. Such a table presents in an internally consistent fashion a comprehensive set of basic data for a regional economy. It helps measure important dimensions of an economy, whether they be the size of small, but perhaps strategic, sectors, or (through aggregation and consolidation of sectors) the level of such significant magnitudes as national income and national product.

Also, such a table is frequently of value from the standpoint of data collection. Apart from indicating data that are available, it suggests ways for obtaining or inferring figures when there are gaps in statistical information. For example, because farmers may not keep sufficient records, a census of business of agricultural firms might not be able to indicate sales of the agricultural industry to certain industries. However, it may be possible to obtain these sales by examining records of purchases by these industries from agriculture. Or, it may be possible to obtain from engineering manuals on these industries the kinds and amounts of agricultural products that are technologically required to support the recorded total output of each of these industries. Or, because for an industry the totals of dollar inputs and outputs must be equal,[5] it may be possible to infer the sales of agricultural products to an industry if we have a record of the total output of that industry and of all its other inputs.[6]

Another merit of arranging economic data in an input-output table lies in the statistical discipline and common set of definitions, concepts, and terms it tends to impose on data collection agencies. This helps to avoid costly duplication and overlapping of efforts and to increase the comparability and usefulness of the resulting statistics.

2. A GROWING REGION

We now consider a region that is not stationary but is growing and encountering diverse problems associated with economic development. For such a region we could still use the statistical framework of Table 1. We could collect for each industry data on purchases from every industry or sales to every industry. However, when we are studying the dynamic problems of growth, it is frequently very desirable, or even essential, to have knowledge of the resources devoted to or required for building up the

---

[5] It is to be noted that profits, rents, wages, interest, dividends, etc., are treated as payment for services of (inputs from) households. This convention will be discussed later.

[6] Or if we have a record of the total output of the agriculture industry and of the total purchases of agricultural products by all industries except the one under consideration.

productive potential or capital stock of an economy, that is, its factories, equipment, social plant, know-how, and quality of labor and management. We therefore want to keep separate the sales (or purchases) on *current* account (i.e., to produce current output) and those on *capital* account (i.e., to build up capital stock). One convenient way to do this is to add another column and row to Table 1. The column might be headed *Gross Capital Formation* (or *Gross Investment*). Figures in this column would indicate the outputs from each industry devoted during a year to the building up of the capital stock of an economy. The corresponding row might be entitled *Depreciation and Other Capital Consumption Allowance*. This row would indicate for each industry the value of inputs from the capital goods sector, or its consumption during the year of capital goods; it therefore would represent the depreciation reserves which each industry should set aside because of its depletion of capital stock. The sum of the items in this row represents capital goods formation required for replacement purposes alone and when subtracted from the sum of the Gross Capital Formation column yields net capital formation, or that part of capital formation which represents a pure addition to capital stock.[7]

Another way to present the data relative to growth and capital formation would be to construct a *capital flow* table. This would in form resemble Table 1. It would contain a row and column for each industry and would indicate for each industry its sales to and purchases from every industry in connection with replacing and increasing the capital stock of the region (gross capital formation). However, the difficulties in obtaining data for such a table must be recognized. Hence still another approach might be followed. From both census and technical and engineering literature a table might be constructed, any column of which indicates for the corresponding industry required inputs (on capital goods account) from every other industry per unit of new capacity of this industry.[8] The elements of such a table (matrix) are termed *capital coefficients*.[9]

Clearly, a comprehensive capital flow or capital coefficient table would be of great value for understanding the investment process and the functioning of an economy. Together with a table on current transactions (such as Table 1) it would help furnish a sound statistical base (1) for

[7] It is not very meaningful to substitute for both the Gross Capital Formation column and the Depreciation row a single column headed Net Capital Formation. This point follows since every industry tends to subtract diverse items regularly (through use) from the pool of capital goods while it contributes to the pool one or a few products, frequently irregularly.

[8] The industry headings of the columns and rows of this table would be arranged in the same order as those for Table 1.

[9] See R. N. Grosse [12, 13]. Also see the various capital and capacity studies listed in V. Riley and R. L. Allen [45], pp. 156–173.

studying problems of growth and (2) for programming development, about which more will be said later.[10]

3. AN INTERREGIONAL NETWORK

Let our region (region *A*) not only grow but also trade with a second region (region *B*). Together these two regions form an entity isolated from the rest of the world (or conceivably comprising the world). Into Table 1 for region *A* we could introduce another column (headed *Exports*) and row (headed *Imports*). The column would show for each industry of region *A* its total exports to region *B*; it would thus recognize that outputs may be sold abroad as well as to home industries. The row would indicate for each industry of region *A* the total value of its imports from all industries of region *B*; it would thus recognize that inputs may come from other regions as well as from domestic industry.

A superior way of treating exports and imports, although one that may incur much more costly data collection, would be to disaggregate both the export and import data. If there were available for region *B* an input-output table similar in character to that for region *A*, we might break down or disaggregate (1) the exports of any given industry of region *A* by type of receiving industry in region *B*, and (2) the imports of any given industry of region *A* by type of originating industry in region *B*. If such disaggregation were complete for both the exports and imports of region *A*, we would also have for each industry of region *B* the breakdown of its exports by type of receiving industry in region *A*, and a breakdown of its imports by type of originating industry in region *A*.[11]

---

[10] It should be noted that if we conducted a census which recorded sales or purchases without reference to whether they were on current or capital account, we could still construct a useful transactions table, one which would record in each cell the sum of the pair of figures in the corresponding cells in a current flow table (such as Table 1) and a capital flow table. However, this transactions table would not present as much and as meaningful detail as the combination of a current flow table and a capital flow table, and would not be as useful for projection purposes as will be indicated later.

[11] Still other ways of treating imports and exports are possible. One of special interest, employed in the 1947 Bureau of Labor Statistics study, is to distinguish between competitive and noncompetitive imports. (Noncompetitive imports do not have a domestically produced counterpart.) The value of competitive imports is recorded as an input into the domestic counterpart industry; and at the same time competitive imports are considered to increase the output of the domestic counterpart industry by the amount of their value. This increased (fictitious) total output of the domestic counterpart industry is then considered available for distribution to all industries. In contrast, noncompetitive imports are simply shown as additional inputs into the industry where they are first consumed; thus no statistical additions need be made to the outputs of these consuming industries. For further details, see W. D. Evans and M. Hoffenberg [10], pp. 108–109; University of Maryland [51], pp. 20–21; and M. Weitzman and P. M. Ritz [56].

Let us now consider a still more general setting, one in which there are many regions. Imagine we have input-output tables for each regional economy. In addition, we have a complete set of data on exports and imports of each region. This set permits us to disaggregate the exports of each industry of each region, that is, to obtain exports from any industry of any region to each industry in each region. This set would also yield the imports of any industry of any region from each industry in each region. To illustrate, let us construct an interregional input-output table for *three* regions, of the order of Table 2.

In addition to a total output column and a total inputs row, there are nine major sets of cells in Table 2,[12] each outlined by heavy rules. The major set at the upper left-hand corner is an input-output table for the East of the order of Table 1. (For the moment ignore the number of sectors and industrial classification employed.) The major set at the lower right-hand corner is an input-output table for the West. And the major set in the center is an input-output table for the South. Now consider any row, let us say the first row. In its first major set of cells, this first row indicates the sales of the agricultural and extraction industry of the East to every industry in the East. In its second and then third major set of cells, the first row records the sales of the agriculture and extraction industry of the East to every industry in the South and West, respectively.[13] In similar fashion, any other row indicates for the corresponding industry of the corresponding region its sales to every industry in every region. Viewed in this way, Table 2 presents a complete set of sales transactions, intra- and interregionally.

Additionally, consider any column of Table 2, let us say the first column. In its first major set of cells this column indicates the inputs into (purchases of) the agriculture and extraction industry of the East from every industry in the East. In its second and third major set of cells the first column records the inputs into the agriculture and extraction industry of the East from every industry in the South and West, respectively.[14] In similar fashion, any other column indicates for the corresponding industry of the corresponding region its purchases from every industry in every region. From this standpoint, Table 2 presents a complete set of purchase transactions, intra- and interregionally.

[12] In an *n*-region setup, there would be n^2 major cells.

[13] Of course, if the respective data in the second and third major sets of cells are aggregated, we would obtain the total exports of the agriculture and extraction industry of the East to the South and West.

[14] When the respective data in the second and third major sets of cells of the first column are aggregated, we obtain the total imports of the agriculture and extraction industry of the East from the South and West.

TABLE 2. INTERREGIONAL INPUT-OUTPUT FLOW TABLE, 19XX

Industry Purchasing → Industry Producing ↓	East: 1. Agriculture and extraction	2. Food Processing	⋯	9. Chemicals	⋯	21. Government	South: 1. Agriculture	2. Extraction	3. Food Processing	⋯	9. Iron and Steel	⋯	23. Government	West: 1. Agriculture and food processing	2. Extraction	⋯	9. Chemicals	⋯	21. Government	Total Gross Output
East 1. Agriculture and extraction																				
2. Food processing																				
⋯																				
9. Chemicals																				
⋯																				
21. Government																				
South 1. Agriculture																				
2. Extraction																				
3. Food processing																				
⋯																				
9. Iron and steel																				
⋯																				
23. Government																				
West 1. Agriculture and food processing																				
2. Extraction																				
⋯																				
9. Chemicals																				
⋯																				
21. Government																				

Further, consider for the interregional network the dynamic aspects of reality. Ideally, we would desire the purchase (input) and sales (output distribution) data to be available on both current account and capital account. In such an ideal situation, Table 2 might record the data on current account; and a table of similar form might contain the data on capital account.[15] Thus exports and imports would be detailed in terms of industry and region of origin, industry and region of destination, and current and capital account.

Needless to say, such a set of data, when made available for a meaningful set of regions—say the nine census regions of the United States, or a workable set of major world regions—would be invaluable for analysis. It would greatly facilitate that extension of regional methods and techniques to embrace the interregional framework, which we have already noted several times as being essential. Although we recognize that such an ideal set of data has not thus far been assembled,[16] we present the outlines of this ideal set because these outlines enable us better to appreciate and evaluate the potentials, problems, and limitations of the interregional input-output approach.[17] To some of these potentialities, problems, and limitations we now turn.

C. Some Basic Problems

1. the choice of a set of industries (sectors)

One of the chief problems in input-output work concerns the choice of the particular set of industries to be employed. Among other factors this choice is dependent on costs of, and resources available for, data collection and processing, amount and kind of existing data, type of regional and interregional situation, objectives of a study, and the inclinations of the researcher. In Table 1 a twelve-industry classification is used. Clearly, a larger and more detailed classification of industries would be desirable if no additional costs are involved. But costs of a census and its processing do rise with increase in number of industries in a classification; and

[15] Or, alternatively, this second table might contain capital coefficient data.

[16] Nor does it follow that such a set of data should be collected for the study of every region. Since the costs of collecting and processing certain of these data are high, their collection may be justified only where the external trade of a region is large or critical. For a region with relatively little external trade, such collection may not be warranted.

[17] As implied above, we may carry through a major consolidation of the interregional input-output table to yield for any region its internal interindustry sales and purchases, and an exports and imports column with the Rest of the World, which may be conveniently termed a second region. On occasion this quasi-interregional framework may be justified.

the benefit from greater detail must be balanced against additional costs.[18]

The type of industrial classification which is efficient also depends on the type of regional and interregional situation being studied. The industrial classification of Table 1 might pertain to a relatively underdeveloped region. In a much more industrialized situation, such as we find in the United States or the regions of the United States, it would be almost essential to adopt another twelve-industry classification (assuming we are limited to the use of only twelve sectors). It would be almost essential to tear government activities out of the service industry and to recognize government explicitly as a sector in its own right.[19] The government column (which is explicit in Table 2) would record the purchases of (inputs into) government from every sector. The government row (explicit in Table 2) would record the inputs of government services into every sector, or the (sales) distribution of government services to every sector, which from another angle represent the tax and nontax payments of these sectors to government.[20]

Moreover, the industrial classification used may justifiably vary from region to region in any given interregional scheme or system. In Table 2, where it is postulated that an industrial classification consisting of approximately twenty sectors is feasible and desirable for each region, the classification scheme does vary from region to region. In the South, agriculture, extraction, and food processing are each retained as a distinct sector, whereas in the East agriculture is combined with extraction to form a single sector, and in the West agriculture is combined with food processing to form a single sector. Among other reasons, such differences in industrial classification (including differences in the number of sectors for each region) may be explained in terms of the different relative importance

[18] It should be borne in mind that when the industrial classification is judged to be too fine for a particular study, it is always possible (1) to consolidate industries in an input-output classification to obtain a lesser degree of disaggregation (a more aggregative framework), and (2) to collapse the input-output table accordingly to secure the relevant interindustry transactions. On the other hand, it is not possible to start with the data of an input-output table for a given industrial classification and secure the data for an expanded input-output table pertaining to a finer industrial classification.

[19] Since it would probably be considered desirable to retain service activities as a second major sector, it would be necessary to consolidate two other sectors into one sector, or to rearrange the parts of other sectors in order to reduce their number by one.

It should be noted that for a much larger industry classification it might be desirable to distinguish between the several levels of government (such as the Federal, state and local in the United States) and treat each as a separate sector.

[20] These payments can be for services which are rendered only indirectly. For fuller details on the government sector, see W. D. Evans and M. Hoffenberg [10], p. 110, and I. H. Licht [38].

of these activities in the several regions,[21] or of the different degrees of technical linkage between these sectors in the several regions,[22] or of the different degrees of interlocking corporate and management structures,[23] or of the different extents to which available data are disaggregated, or of several of these factors.

The type of industrial classification efficient for a given situation also depends on the purposes of a study. For example, if we are interested in using an input-output table in connection with a short-run cyclical study for an industrialized region, we might wish to have data on inventory change pointed up. We might wish to add both a column and a row to the input-output table. The column might be headed *Inventory Change* (*Additions*). Its elements would indicate the output of each sector that was added to inventories during the year, whether or not such output is held by producing or consuming sectors. The row might be headed *Inventory Change* (*Depletions*). Any one of its elements would indicate the amount of the inventory of finished product of the corresponding sector that was used up by all consuming sectors during the course of the year.[24]

The industrial classification problem involves still other considerations. One concerns the definition of an industry (or sector) and the exact meaning of the figures on total outputs and inputs associated with an industry (or sector). For example, in the 50-order Bureau of Labor Statistics classification there is industry 17, Plumbing and heating supplies, and industry 26, Motor vehicles. We know that in practice the automobile producers also produce plumbing and heating fixtures. How is a study to deal with this problem? There are several ways. All the products and activities of a multiproduct firm can be lumped together as the output of that particular firm, and the firm can be assigned to the industry corresponding to its chief (primary) product. This procedure, however, has the disadvantage of including a heterogeneous product mix in the output figures for a particular industry. An alternative procedure is to separate the output of all firms by various types of product, and to assign to each industry that corresponding fraction of the firm. This procedure has the

---

[21] If two of these sectors are relatively unimportant in a region, and not too unlike, an efficient use of financial resources for research might suggest their consolidation into one.

[22] If the products of agriculture of a region were almost entirely consumed by its food-processing industry, a consolidation of these two sectors into one might be desirable in the light of limited research resources.

[23] If the same financial groups control two sectors, which are somewhat related technically, a consolidation of these two sectors might be warranted, especially if the input-output table were used in connection with development and investment research.

[24] For further discussion, see W. D. Evans and M. Hoffenberg [10], pp. 108, 118–119; and S. A. Jaffe [29].

advantage of including only homogeneous products in industry totals. However, it has the disadvantage of requiring a great deal of product information and ignores the corporate business structure of industry.[25]

In other respects there are problems in defining industries and attributing meaning to them. These problems become increasingly acute as interindustry tables grow in size and require more detail.[26] For the largest input-output tables, a complex system of definitions and conventions must be set up and followed. And as with regions, the best specific set of definitions employed will often vary with the purpose of the study.[27]

2. THE CHOICE OF REGIONS AND THE INTERREGIONAL NETWORK

As with the choice of industries, the selection of a set of regions is a perplexing one.[28] Among other factors the fund of existing data, collection and processing costs, available resources, regional and interregional setting, research objectives, and inclinations of the researcher influence this selection. For example, in Table 2 we present a three-region framework. However, if adequate resources were not available for the collection and processing of those data required but currently unavailable, it would not be possible to complete the table for this system. Of course, if the region under study, say the East, were largely self-sufficient and had few, if any, critical bonds with other regions, the inability to detail interregional flows would not be a major shortcoming. On the other hand, if a region does have many significant ties to other regions, as say the Great Lakes area has with other areas of the United States, the lack of a comprehensive

---

[25] Other systems of industrial (sector) classification might be based on activities (such as construction) or processes (such as stamping metal) or on establishments similar with respect to use of raw materials or equipment. Depending on the sources of data, it may be necessary in any one study to use more than one of these classification systems. For example, the 1947 BLS study used an establishment classification for manufacturing industries, a product classification in agriculture, an activity basis for construction, and a process basis for wholesale and retail trade.

[26] As an instance, the problem of differentiating between primary and secondary products in general increases with the amount of detail in the table (that is, with the degree of industrial disaggregation).

[27] For a system of industrial classification widely used in most United States input-output studies, see the U. S. Bureau of the Budget [49].

For further discussion on industrial classification, see W. D. Evans and M. Hoffenberg [10], pp. 105–107, 113–114; W. W. Leontief et al. [37], ch. 9; T. Barna [1]; and items pertaining to classification systems and problems cited in V. Riley and R. L. Allen [45], pp. 79–84.

[28] For relevant discussion on the concepts of region, regional core, regional boundaries, and similar matters, see materials contained in Appendix B of Chapter 7 and in P. E. James and C. F. Jones [31], pp. 19–68; W. Isard [20], pp. 13–26; M. E. Garnsey [11], pp. 27–39; P. E. James [30]; R. Vance [52]; H. W. Odum [43]; and R. Vining [53, 54].

set of interregional data would constitute a serious handicap for study of the region.

As is to be expected, the extent of this handicap would be related to research objectives.   If we were engaged solely in a study of the market structure of the service trades and industry in the large region for which Minneapolis–St. Paul is the focal point, we might not be seriously concerned with the absence of interregional data.   In contrast, if we were engaged in a study of the region's basic industries, many of which export significant fractions of their outputs, the lack of interregional data would be a critical deficiency.

The regional setting, too, affects the selection of an appropriate regional-interregional framework for study.   For example, the analyst studying the market structure of service trades in the large region oriented to Minneapolis–St. Paul may justifiably consider a single-region model.   Service exports from the region are relatively minor.   On the other hand, the analyst studying the market structure of service trades in the Greater New York Metropolitan Region would wish to consider a system or framework of several regions, and in particular one that would point up most efficiently the region's service exports to other regions.[29]

There are still more complex considerations than these.   Certain types of study desirably require an hierarchy of regions, for example, sub-regions within regions (as New England within the United States, when the United States is considered a region).[30]   To determine appropriate hierarchies of regions is still more difficult; and the associated data requirements place still greater strain on financial resources available for study. Another complication lies in the mutual dependence of the choice of an industrial classification and of a set of regions.   Among other things, a given *industrial* classification, by affecting the usefulness of existing data (i.e., the existing data which can be used to fill in the cells of the input-output table), affects the value of any given *interregional* classification; and vice versa.[31]

Finally, and even more so than the choice of an industrial classification, the choice of a particular interregional framework depends upon the stock of existing data, and the manner in which existing data collecting and

[29] To take another example, the analyst studying the base of the New England region would want to select an interregional framework different both in number, size, and regional content from that chosen by the analyst studying the Pacific Northwest.   This would be so because not only are the positions and resource endowments of these two regions different but also their stages of development and maturity contrast sharply.

[30] Or the Los Angeles and the San Francisco metropolitan regions within the Pacific Southwest.

[31] For a fuller discussion of this point, see W. Isard [22].

processing agencies are organized and their procedures subject to change. To these data considerations we now turn.

3. DATA DIFFICULTIES

There are many difficulties encountered in obtaining the voluminous data for an input-output table. In this section we have space to discuss briefly only a few major ones. Let us first consider a region for which either justifiably or by necessity interregional flows are aggregated to yield a single export column and a single import row.

As already mentioned it would be ideal to obtain data both by rows (i.e., on sales) and by columns (i.e., on purchases). Since statistical observations are not infallible, this double approach would permit cross-checking. Unfortunately, even in the most advanced industrial regions (nations) neither the sales nor purchase information is available in the detail desired. Indeed for many cells the researcher will find he is unable to obtain the information from standard sources on either sales or purchases. For example, the U. S. Census of Manufactures for 1947, which formed the major statistical source for the 1947 Bureau of Labor Statistics input-output table, contains little or no information on output distribution or sales from industries to other industries and only very meager information on inputs in terms of materials consumed. In this situation the researcher has to rely on auxiliary and secondary sources of information, such as engineering manuals and trade associations and journals.

Even after all available information has been assembled and checked and the new data gathered as far as resources permit, the researcher may be left with a large amount of unallocated output for a given industry. This is output which he is unable to assign as sales to (or purchases by) other industries. Such unallocated output must then be assumed to be sold to an *undistributed* sector (a fictitious industry) in order that the researcher can account for the sales of the total output of the industry. He then must add a column headed *Undistributed*, the items of which represent the unallocated outputs of the respective industries. Likewise, after adding up for a given industry the inputs for which he has statistical evidence, technical justification, or both, he may find that this sum (total purchases accounted for) falls considerably short of the value of gross output. Since total purchases (including wages, salaries, interest, dividends, rents, and profits which represent the purchase value of various household services) should equal the value of gross output, he must then assume that the difference between total purchases accounted for and gross output represents purchases from a fictitious industry, which again may be termed *undistributed*. He thus adds to the table an undistributed row, each item representing for the respective industry its inputs which are un-accounted for.[32]

Another major difficulty is associated with the very desirable objective of identifying and distinguishing between flows (or sales and purchases) on current account and those on capital account.[33] Unfortunately, statistics are generally not organized to make possible the separation of these two sets of flows; and such separation is obtained, if at all, only with considerable effort.[34] Other aspects of the data problem concern the use of purchasers' values or producers' values,[35] the inclusion of invisible as well as visible items in imports and exports, the choice of foreign or domestic prices in valuing imports and exports, the derivation of control totals, the reconciliation of row and column totals, etc.[36]

The data problem, already formidable for a regional input-output table (in which exports and imports are aggregated into a single column and a single row respectively), is still more massive for a truly interregional input-output table, such as Table 2.   In addition to the data required by a table such as Table 1, Table 2 requires (1) a breakdown of each item in the *Export* column in terms of receipts by each industry of each region, and (2) a breakdown of each item in the *Import* row in terms of receipts from each industry of each region.   In many situations interregional flow data for such breakdowns are sparse or seriously incomplete.   For example, if we were to construct an interregional model for the regions of the United States, an area for which we have relatively abundant regional and inter-regional data, we would find the following situation.   Rather excellent sample data are regularly published by the Interstate Commerce Com-

---

[32] It should be noted that in later stages of input-output analysis it is often possible to reduce the amounts assigned to both the Undistributed column and row.   For further discussion relating to the undistributed sector, see W. D. Evans and M. Hoffen-berg [10], pp. 107–108.

[33] The reader is reminded that the latter represent transactions that are required both to maintain and to increase the capital stock (plant, equipment, etc.) of the economy. These should be separated from the former not only to understand better the interplay of forces within the region but also to make it possible to use input-output information for projection purposes which will be discussed later.

[34] For further discussion see W. D. Evans and M. Hoffenberg [10], pp. 104–105, 116–117.

[35] When values are producers' values, spread items on the finished product (such as transportation costs, warehousing, and storage charges, wholesale and retail trade margins, and Federal, state, and local excise taxes) are assigned as direct costs to the industry consuming the finished product.   When values are purchasers' values, spread items on the finished product are assigned as costs to the industry producing the finished product.   See W. D. Evans and M. Hoffenberg [10], pp. 102–104.

[36] For extensive discussion, see W. D. Evans and M. Hoffenberg [10], and National Bureau of Economic Research [41], Technical Supplement.

mission on state-to-state shipments of individual commodities and groups of commodities by Class I steam railways; unfortunately these data do not break down any state's receipts of a particular commodity by consuming industry within the region, and they do not cover shipments of other (although less important) classes of railways.[37] Less satisfactory data are published by the Army Engineers Corps on water shipments by commodities into and out of each port; unfortunately they do not specify the respective ports of origin or destination.[38] And grossly inadequate data, if any at all, exist on truck shipments, which are rapidly growing in importance. Because of these data shortcomings[39] for the regions of the United States, we find that no interregional input-output table has yet been completed which has enough detail within it to be of use for studying a region's economy.[40] Input-output tables that have been profitably employed in regional analysis have been of a noninterregional character (such as Table 1 is), in which exports have been aggregated into a single column and imports into a single row. Moreover, the data problem often compels the investigator to select as regions those areas for which data have already been collected (such as census regions and states) and as sectors those industries for which interregional shipment and output data are available. Furthermore, he will tend to delineate regions which exhibit self-sufficiency with respect to a maximum number of like goods and services, thereby to reduce as much as possible the cost of collecting and processing interregional shipment data.

As can be expected, the data problem varies from region to region, from interregional network to interregional network, and from system to system. In a real sense it is inextricably bound up with the industrial classification problem and the choice of appropriate regions, all of which are related to the specific characteristics of the region and the objectives of a study. It can be generally stated that until new types of data are collected, an interregional input-output table can be pieced together in most situations only with difficulty and expense.

[37] Also nondisclosure rules, rebilling, and other railroad practices qualify somewhat the usefulness of the I.C.C. 1 per cent sample. See U. S. Interstate Commerce Commission [50].

[38] U. S. Army [48]. There is, however, promise of better water shipment data. See U. S. Army [47].

[39] For further discussion, see W. Isard [16], pp. 326–328; W. Isard [19], pp. 175–180; Harvard Economic Research Project [14], 1954 Report, pp. 173–182.

[40] The nearest approaches to useful interregional input-output tables are in L. N. Moses [40]; R. A. Kavesh [32]; and W. Isard and R. A. Kavesh [27]. However, see a recent study published in Japanese by the Kansai Economic Federation, 1957, Osaka, Japan.

D. Use for Projection

Thus far we have discussed input-output tables as descriptive devices which are extremely useful because (1) they record rather concisely, in an internally consistent manner, a large amount of information about a regional economy and the interrelations of its sectors; (2) they impose a desirable statistical discipline on data collection agencies and empirical investigations; (3) they reveal gaps in our data and may help in filling them; and (4) they present an economy in perspective and facilitate comparison of the magnitudes of its major sectors and bonds with other economies.[41]   To some, however, the input-output approach has a still more valuable use.   Namely, it offers a technique to project into the future the magnitude of important sectors and linkages of the economy.[42]

The use of the input-output approach for projection, rather than for description alone, involves a number of basic assumptions and additional procedures.   To some analysts these assumptions are much too unrealistic, and hence these analysts discard input-output analysis for projection purposes.   To others, these assumptions are acceptable for a sufficient number of important real situations so as to warrant an extensive use of input-output analysis for projection purposes when supplemented by other forms of analysis and when proper qualifications are made.

Perhaps the most basic and at the same time the most questionable assumption is that of *constant production coefficients* in the noninterregional (national or single regional) model, and of *constant interareal input coefficients* (involving constant supply channels) in the interregional model. To understand this assumption, and its implications, let us return to Table 1 (where Table 1 pertains to an isolated region).   Consider its fifth column. The column lists in order the inputs of each sector of the region into the transportation industry during year 19xx.   At the bottom of the column is recorded the total value of output of the transportation industry during 19xx.   If we now divide this total into the inputs listed above it, we obtain the cents' worth of each input used per dollar output of the transportation industry during year 19xx.   These cents' worth of inputs are listed in the fifth column of Table 3.   Similarly for every other column of Table 1, we

[41] Viewed from still another standpoint, the type of double-entry social accounting which input-output tables represent is a convenient way of depicting both the circular flow of income and the corresponding (but opposite in direction) circular flow of goods and services.   This relation to social accounting systems as developed in Chapter 4 will be examined in some detail in Chapter 12.

[42] Still a third use, namely, for a determination of optimum production and transportation patterns, is more appropriately associated with activity analysis (linear programming) to be discussed in Chapter 10.

TABLE 3. DIRECT INPUTS PER DOLLAR OF OUTPUT^a: REGION A, 19xx

Industry Producing	1. Agriculture and extraction	2. Light manufacturing	3. Heavy manufacturing	4. Power and communications	5. Transportation	6. Trade	7. Finance, insurance, and rental	8. Business and personal services	9. Educational and other basic services	10. Construction	11. Households	12. All others
1. Agriculture and extraction	$0.28	$0.21	$0.06	$0.05	$0.04	$0.01	$0.02	$ —	$0.04	$0.18	$0.06	$0.09
2. Light manufacturing	0.06	0.28	0.04	0.01	0.02	0.02	0.01	0.14	0.15	0.04	0.20	0.13
3. Heavy manufacturing	0.01	0.02	0.33	0.01	0.03	0.01	—	0.09	0.01	0.18	0.03	0.09
4. Power and communication	0.01	0.01	0.01	0.11	0.03	0.02	0.08	0.04	0.02	—	0.01	0.02
5. Transportation	0.03	0.02	0.02	0.02	0.05	0.01	0.01	0.01	0.02	0.04	0.03	0.03
6. Trade	0.02	0.02	0.01	—	0.02	—	0.02	0.03	0.05	0.09	0.12	0.05
7. Finance, insurance, and rentals	0.04	0.01	0.01	0.01	0.03	0.05	0.07	0.05	0.04	0.02	0.12	0.05
8. Business and personal services	0.01	0.02	0.01	0.01	0.02	0.07	0.01	0.04	0.02	0.03	0.03	0.02
9. Educational and other basic services	—	—	—	—	—	—	—	—	0.01	—	0.10	0.04
10. Construction	—	—	—	0.04	0.06	—	0.10	—	0.01	—	—	0.04
11. Households	0.40	0.25	0.34	0.58	0.58	0.63	0.53	0.46	0.50	0.40	0.01	0.28
12. All others	0.14	0.16	0.17	0.16	0.12	0.18	0.15	0.14	0.13	0.02	0.29	0.17
Total	1.00	1.00	1.00	1.00	1.00	1.00	1.00	1.00	1.00	1.00	1.00	1.00

^{a} Rounded to nearest cent. Dashes indicate inputs less than one-half cent per dollar output.

Source: Based on data in R. A. Kavesh [32].

can divide the total of each column into the input items listed in the same column to derive for the respective industry its relevant set of cents' worth of each input per dollar of its output. We thus obtain Table 3, which records for year 19xx the cents' worth of each input per dollar output of every industry.

If we now postulate that for any industry these cents' worth of inputs hold regardless of the size of output of the given industry, we have the essence of the assumption of constant production coefficients. Immediately, we can appreciate that there are situations for which such an assumption is valid, and that there are others for which it is invalid. For example, take the production of aluminum ingot. It is fairly realistic to assume (for the United States economy in 1956) that as the output of aluminum ingot rises, inputs of alumina and power will rise *pari passu*, that is, that the amounts of alumina and power used per pound of aluminum ingot will not change by any significant amount, if at all. Contrasted with aluminum ingot production is steel ingot production. As the output of steel ingot changes, we can in general expect definite changes in the steel input structure, such as in the use of scrap per ton ingot and of pig iron per ton ingot (which changes would also be associated with changes in the prices of scrap, pig iron, and steel ingot).

For the moment, however, let us accept the assumption of constant production coefficients. We shall examine its validity after spelling out the projection procedure for the isolated region to whose economy Tables 1 and 3 relate.

Suppose our isolated region is confronted with the problem of planning internal development and physical facilities for a population expected to double in size by 1975. Suppose, too, a team of expert sociologists, economists, and other scientists has advanced its best judgment on the consumption patterns of this population in 1975, and has developed a set of estimates on household consumer expenditures by type (which may be considered final demand in this situation).[43] The first estimate is on household consumption of agriculture and extraction products and is $18.1 million, an increase of 50 per cent over year 19xx. (Compare with row 1, column 11 of Table 1.) The second estimate relates to household purchases of light manufactures and is $75.4 million, an increase of 75 per cent over year 19xx. The third estimate refers to consumer expenditures on heavy manufactures and is $11.8 million, an increase of 60 per cent over 19xx. And so forth. Finally, the estimate of household purchases of products from the "All other" sector (the last category) is $126.8 million. Given these estimates, how project the corresponding (or required) total

---

[43] For the moment, we postulate that no new products will appear in the consumer basket of goods.

outputs of all industries and the pattern of interindustry shipments (or sales)?

Consider first the $18.1 million of agriculture and extraction products which households are expected to consume in 1975. If we go down column 1 of Table 3, we can see how much input from every industry or sector is required to produce one dollar of agriculture and extraction products. Therefore, if we multiply down this column by 18.1 million, we obtain the inputs from every industry which are required to produce the $18.1 million of agriculture and extraction products.[44] Next, we consider the $75.4 million of light manufactures which households are expected to purchase in 1975. If we go down column 2 of Table 3, we can see the cents' worth of inputs from each industry required to produce one dollar of light manufactures. If we multiply down this column by 75.4 million, we obtain the inputs from every industry which are required to produce the $75.4 million of light manufactures. We add these required inputs by type to those required to produce the $18.1 million of agriculture and extraction products. Likewise, by multiplying down column 3 of Table 3 by 11.8 million, we derive the inputs required to produce the $11.8 million of heavy manufactures which households are expected to purchase in 1975. And so forth. Finally, by multiplying down column 12 by 126.8 million, we obtain inputs from each industry required to produce the $126.8 million of products from the "All other" sector which households are estimated to consume in 1975. If we now sum these inputs by type of input, we obtain the *first round of input requirements*.[45] These first-round requirements are the inputs directly required to produce the final demand items that households are estimated to consume in 1975. However, the first round of input requirements must be produced, too. They require a whole set of inputs, too. For example, the first-round transportation requirement (the sum of the transportation services required to produce the final demand items) might be $4.5 million. To be able to provide this $4.5 million of transportation, we would require various inputs—more specifically, that set of inputs obtained by multiplying down column 5 of

[44] For reasons to be discussed later, we delete both the households row and column before beginning computation.

[45] For example, if we add to the transportation inputs required to produce $18.1 million of agriculture and extraction products the transportation inputs required to produce $75.4 million of light manufactures, the transportation inputs required to produce $11.8 of heavy manufactures, etc., and finally the transportation inputs required to produce $126.8 million of "All other" products, we obtain first-round requirements of transportation inputs. In similar manner, we obtain the first-round requirements of trade services, of finance, insurance, and rental services, and of every other sector including agriculture and extraction, light manufacturing, and heavy manufacturing.

Table 3 by 4.5 million. Likewise, to be able to provide the first-round requirement for agriculture and extraction products, we would need a set of inputs; and similarly for the first-round requirements of light manufactures, of heavy manufactures, of power and communications, etc. If we obtain the set of inputs needed to furnish each of the items in the first round of input requirements, and sum these sets by type of input (product), we obtain the *second round of input requirements*. In essence the second round of input requirements are those necessary to produce the first round.

In turn, a third round of inputs is required to support the production of the second round, and a fourth round to support the production of the third round, and a fifth round to support the fourth, etc. Theoretically, we continue this round-by-round computation, which is termed an *iterative* approach, until an infinite number of rounds has been computed. By summing the input requirements of all rounds by type input, we obtain the output of each sector required both directly and indirectly to yield the set of household purchases estimated by 1975.[46] By adding to each of these outputs the household purchases (final demand), we obtain the 1975 projections of industrial activity which we seek.[47]

In practice, however, the round-by-round computation need not be performed *ad infinitum*. The rounds of input requirements become smaller and smaller so that after the fourth, fifth, sixth, or seventh round (depending on the problem and the refinement required) the sum of successive rounds of input requirements can be approximated with a sufficient degree of accuracy.[48] This *convergence* of rounds results from an operation

[46] For example, if we add to the amount of transportation directly consumed by households in 1975, the $4.5 million first-round requirement of transportation, the second-round requirement of transportation, the third-round requirement, etc., and finally the nth-round requirement, we obtain the grand total of transportation services required (both directly and indirectly) to meet the household demand for all items. This grand total must also be the grand total output of the transportation industry, for we have accounted for the transportation associated with the movement of all people and goods in an isolated region.

[47] These projected industrial outputs via the coefficients on labor inputs per dollar output can be translated into employment estimates by industry, as well as income payments by industry, etc. Thus, these outputs may be related to regional income projection and population and migration estimation as discussed in previous chapters. It is very important at this point to apply a consistency check, that is, to observe the size of the discrepancy, if any, between the sum of employment estimates by sectors and the total labor force associated with the 1975 population, income, and consumption patterns. Major discrepancies would suggest unrealistic assumptions on household income, average productivity per worker, consumption patterns, population participation in the labor force, etc., and would have to be eliminated through reformulation of the problem and revision of the assumptions.

[48] In fact, in view of errors in the basic data provided by the census and other agencies (e.g. see O. Morgenstern [39], p. 84), carrying the round-by-round computations any

which it would be necessary to perform before computing the round-by-round requirements. It would be necessary to eliminate from Table 3 both the households column and households row. We would want to eliminate the households row since, by specifying at the start the level of each type of household expenditure in 1975, we have implied the magnitude of disposable household income in 1975 and accordingly the total of inputs (services) provided by households to earn this income. Not to remove the households row would lead to double counting, that is, to requirements for household services which we have already postulated as having been provided in order to earn the income to support the 1975 levels of household expenditures. Similarly, we would want to eliminate the households column. For we have already specified the total of each type of household expenditure in 1975, and therefore we do not need to derive these totals via input-output coefficients and the summation of round-by-round consumer purchases.

It is also important to bear in mind that these *n* round-by-round computations can be in effect performed through the use of an *inverse* matrix derived from the cents' worth of inputs (coefficients of Table 3). Such a matrix yields both the direct and indirect (through an infinite number of rounds) requirements of each type of input per dollar output of each industry. Since the matrix can be constructed by high-speed computing machines, its use when appropriate can result in considerable savings of research time and resources. In the Appendix to this chapter we shall discuss in elementary terms the construction and use of the inverse matrix.

Now let us leave the isolated region framework and consider an inter-regional situation, let us say that one depicted by Table 2. Any column of Table 2 indicates for the corresponding industry of the indicated region the inputs from each industry of each region. If we divide these inputs by the total output (or total purchases) of the given industry of the indicated region, we obtain by type of input the cents' worth of inputs per dollar output. Obtaining these cents' worth of inputs for every industry of every region, and recording them in an arrangement similar to that of Table 2, yields a table of direct inputs per dollar of output. This table would bear the same relation to Table 2 in our interregional situation as Table 3 does to Table 1 in the isolated region case.

If we now postulate that these direct inputs from every industry in every region to each industry in each region remain constant regardless of the level of output of these latter industries, we are in essence assuming constant interareal input coefficients. For example, if we find that in

farther would imply a false accuracy; in general such a degree of refinement cannot be justified.

19xx steel fabricators in the West used, per dollar of output, three cents of steel sheet produced in the East, two cents of steel sheet produced in the South, and one cent of steel sheet produced in the West, we are assuming that this interareal supply pattern of steel sheet per dollar output persists as well as the per dollar input patterns of Western labor, Western power, Western chemicals, etc.[49]   Or, if in 19xx Eastern households on the average consumed per dollar income one cent of Eastern textiles, one cent of Southern textiles, one-quarter cent of Western textiles, one-third cent Eastern fuels, one-half cent of Western fuels, one-third cent of Eastern steel-fabricated products, one-tenth cent of Southern steel-fabricated products, etc., we are assuming that this interareal pattern of purchases (of supply of inputs) remains invariant.

At a later point we shall question the validity of the postulate of constant interareal input coefficients.   If we accept it, we can proceed to projections of various sorts.   (The basic steps for making projections via round-by-round computations—the iterative approach—have already been outlined.)   As an instance, we might inquire into the impact of interregional migration of population—say of one million population from the East to the West.[50]   Such migration might be sparked by non-economic factors such as climate but would include within it the necessary labor force directly and indirectly required to provide services and otherwise support those foot-loose migrants initially attracted by climate.

The first step in such an inquiry would be to alter the household columns of the East and West in Table 2 (which reflect consumption patterns of 19xx) to take into account the new population of the East and West. (Since no explicit statement regarding population numbers in the South is made, it is assumed that these numbers are hypothesized to remain unchanged.)   Such alteration would reflect differences in consumption patterns between the households sectors of the two regions,[51] as well as

---

[49] Of course, we are also assuming that, per dollar output of steel fabricators in the West, inputs of any item (such as steel sheet) from all producers irrespective of region is constant.

[50] We assume that attention would be focused on how the interregional system might operate on current account after the period of transition during which necessary plant, equipment, and social facilities would have been constructed, and other necessary adjustments effected.

[51] These differences would recognize that for the migrant population the sources of supply of each item consumed would change as well as the relative expenditures on the several items, as they changed their habitat.   Hence, there would not be a set of expansions in household purchases in the West that would match the contractions in the East.

It might be observed that the investigator could also incorporate at this point expected changes in the typical household consumption pattern for each region, if he is inclined to do so.

change in numbers. Adding the new households columns for the East and West with the unchanged households column for the South would yield the *final demands* placed by all households on the interregional system in terms of the output of each industry of each region.

The next step would be to delete the three households columns and the three households rows in that table on direct inputs per dollar of output that would pertain to our interregional system. Then by (1) multiplying down each of the columns of this adjusted table by the appropriate item in the set of final demands, and (2) summing horizontally by type input and region of origin, we would obtain the first round of inputs required to produce these final demands. In turn, by (1) multiplying down each of the columns of the same adjusted table by the appropriate item in the set of first-round input requirements, and (2) summing horizontally by type input and region of origin, we would obtain the second round of inputs needed to produce the first-round input requirements. Similarly, we would obtain the third round of inputs needed to produce the second-round input requirements, the fourth round needed to produce the third-round requirements and so forth. When the computations reached the point where, in the light of the convergence of the rounds, it becomes permissible to approximate the successive rounds of inputs, we would sum all the round requirements by type input and region of origin to obtain the set of inputs required both directly and indirectly to meet the final demands placed on the interregional system by all households. If we add this set of inputs to the final demands, item by item, we obtain the projected output of each industry in each region.[52] This projected output can then be translated into an employment estimate via the relevant labor coefficient for the same industry of the same region.[53]

[52] For example, if the final demand for the products of the agriculture and extraction industry of the East were $1 million, and for the products of the food-processing industry of the East were $2 million, etc., . . . , and finally for the services of the government sector of the West were $3 million, we would multiply down the first column of the adjusted table by 1 million, the second column by 2 million, etc., . . . , and finally the last column by 3 million. After multiplying down the columns we would add horizontally to derive each item in the list of first-round input requirements. As an instance, by adding horizontally along the ninth row we would be adding to the Eastern chemical inputs required to produce $1 million of agriculture and extraction output in the East, the Eastern chemical inputs required to produce $2 million of food-processing output in the East, etc., . . . , and finally the Eastern chemical inputs required to produce $3 million of government output in the West. The resulting sum would be the total first-round inputs from the Eastern chemical industries required to produce the entire set of final demands of all households.

[53] By adding the employment changes by industry in the West and by converting the resulting increase in employment into an increase in population, we would obtain the part of the one-million migration that was secondary, that is, tied directly and indirectly

In this manner it becomes possible to trace out the interregional impact of any basic force, such as a change in the geographic distribution of population, in consumer tastes, in industrial location, in resource availabilities, or in federal development activities. This impact may be studied, as will be noted later, with reference to such matters as interregional commodity movement, regional balances of payments, interregional money flows, regional income and employment, and regional resource requirements. And as already indicated, the cumbersome round-by-round computation can be avoided by the careful and properly qualified use of an inverse matrix.

All these observations are predicated, however, on the validity of our assumption of constant interareal input coefficients and on the formulation of a meaningful problem and set of initial hypotheses. To a discussion of these and related matters we now turn.

E. The Final Demand Sectors

We have suggested that the assumption of constant coefficients may be a relatively poor one for explaining the output (or level of operations) of certain sectors of the economy, such as inventory accumulations. Further we may be able to explain the level of certain sectors, and thus their requirements for produced goods and services, in terms of noneconomic factors only, such as military operations. Clearly then it is sensible not to attempt to explain these sectors with an input-output analysis. It becomes sensible to distinguish between (1) these sectors which may be termed the *final demand*, or *bill of goods*, or *exogenous* sectors, and (2) other sectors which may be termed *endogenous* or *processing* sectors whose outputs we judge can be reliably approximated by a set of coefficients. The endogenous or processing sectors constitute the structural matrix, from which are excluded the columns and rows referring to the final-demand sectors.[54]

to the support of the footloose migrants. The remaining part would represent the migration which was sparked by the noneconomic factor, namely climate.

Once again, a consistency check is to be applied. Not only must the two parts of this migration bear a reasonable relation to each other, but also the decrease in total employment in the East should correspond to the increase in total employment in the West (after suitable adjustments for those migrants leaving the labor force), and the net change in total employment in the South should be minor, if not zero. Existence of major deviations from these "control" relations would necessitate reformulation of the problem and revision of assumptions.

[54] In a typical input-output table the final demand sectors come last in the array of sectors, their columns being at the extreme right of a table and their rows at the bottom. These sectors are separated from the structural matrix by heavy rules. Such an arrangement is shown in Table 1 of Chapter 12, although this table is more than an input-output table, as will be explained in Chapter 12.

The set of sectors which should be considered as final demand sectors will frequently vary with the problem on hand, the region under study, its stage of development, the interregional setting, the availability of different types of industry studies, the cost of gathering and processing new forms of data, and many other factors. Almost without exception government activities are considered a final demand sector. This partly reflects the fact that many of the factors controlling its level of operations are political and sociological—such as the size of its military program and the extent of its resource development activities (river valley development, highway construction, etc.). This also reflects the fact that we do not have adequate data and studies on certain government operations, such as postal services, garbage collection, fire and police protection, etc., whose levels might be reliably approximated by the use of a set of coefficients.

Foreign exports (i.e., exports from a nation) have also been typically treated as a final demand sector, especially if foreign exports are not of major significance to an economy, as is true of the United States. United States exports are better explained in terms of political factors than in terms of economic relations with the other regions of the world, at least until better economic relations studies are available.[55]

Inventory change (additions) is another typical final demand sector. The size of the stock of a commodity held by producers and consumers of a good is not easily explainable in terms of a set of constant coefficients. This size is much more explainable in terms of expectations, entrepreneurial decisions, and other socio-economic and psychological factors which are of a nonengineering character.[56]

---

[55] In a less self-sufficient economy, like that of Great Britain which is more dependent on foreign trade, it is much more imperative that such studies be made and that some form of interregional framework be constructed to relate meaningfully the foreign exports of Great Britain to other regional economies. At least parts of her foreign exports (and imports) should be included within the structural matrix.

[56] As with the row on Foreign Trade (Imports), the row on Inventory Change (Depletions), which is usually placed at the bottom of the input-output table and is separated from the structural matrix by a heavy rule, makes it possible to account fully for the total quantity of a commodity (industry output) available for current distribution to (and consumption by) both industry and households. Current distribution of a commodity can exceed current industrial output by the sum of current inventory depletions and imports from foreign countries.

It should also be noted that the inclusion of the Inventory Change (Additions) column as a final demand sector permits us to distinguish between total industrial output and total consumption. Finally, by providing a column and row for both Inventory Change and Foreign Trade, we are able to relate input requirements of an industry to its current production, and to dissociate these input requirements from total consumption of its products. By such a step, we strengthen the basis for the use of constant coefficients.

Households is another sector which is more often than not placed in the final demand category. A primary reason for this procedure is the inability to establish meaningful technological or engineering relations between the level of household output (i.e., the provision of labor and other services which yield household income) to household expenditures as inputs. Such relations are assumed to underly for the most part the constant coefficients employed in input-output analysis. On the other hand, there are clear grounds for relating via constant coefficients a large fraction of household output (income) to the levels of output of other sectors; and in many situations there are grounds for relating household expenditures by type to household income via constant coefficients.[57] This is particularly true in interregional analysis when relative shifts and growth of population are involved. As a consequence, in regional-interregional models the households sector, at least in part, may be left within the structural matrix; the change of this sector is assumed to be meaningfully related to changes in other industrial sectors included in the structural matrix.[58]

Finally, input-output models, except the dynamic type, include a capital formation sector (which includes the activities involved in the building of industrial plant, equipment, housing, and social facilities in general). Such a convention explicitly recognizes that an operational input-output model at the present time can only be a *static* one. It cannot explain (1) the processes by which investment decisions are made by firms, households, government, and other decision-making units, and hence (2) the level of capital formation and the corresponding input requirements. Therefore it becomes essential to segregate out of the sales and purchases recorded in a transactions table (such as Table 1) those sales and purchases on capital account, and to list these by type of producing industry in a separate column (headed Capital Formation) in the final demand sector. Doing so not only throws light on the requirements placed currently on an economy to enable it to grow and accumulate productive facilities but also leaves in the transactions table the sales and purchases which are directly related to current production, and from which meaningful coefficients can be computed. These coefficients would not be distorted by capital transactions which have no immediate relationship to current

---

[57] For reports on current research which aims to close at least in part the input-output system along these lines, see Harvard Economic Research Project [14], 1955 Report, Section C, and 1956–1957 Report, Section F.

[58] As we have noted in previous chapters, a prime objective of many regional and interregional studies would be to determine changes in regional incomes and population numbers. For such studies, it is essential that at least part of the households sector remains in the structural matrix.

production and which are indivisible and too frequently fortuitous.[59] Rather they would reflect the more stable input-output relations which generally have roots in slowly changing and economically meaningful technological and marketing structures.

Thus we find that the typical input-output model contains a set of final demand sectors whose levels of operations and requirements are not to be explained by the model. They are to be explained by non-economic factors, or by other means than the technological and marketing relations which constant interareal input coefficients can be employed to reflect. This convention removes considerable strain from the assumption of constant coefficients. At the same time it requires that reliable estimates be made of the size and final demands of the exogeneous sectors, which must be specified beforehand.[60] Projected results can be no better than the quality of final demand estimates. For this reason projections are frequently made for alternative estimates of the size and requirements of the final demand sectors.[61]

F. Validity of Constant Coefficients

Having more clearly identified what input-output analysis can help to explain, and what it cannot explain, we ask how valid are constant production coefficients and constant interareal input coefficients. We ask this question, bearing in mind that much of traditional economic analysis is devoted to the study of factors affecting variation in inputs per unit of output.

Consider first the factors which in our isolated regional economy lead to changing cents' worth of inputs per dollar output as output varies. One is economies of scale, which is present in most industries.[62] A second is

[59] It should be kept in mind that meaningful coefficients can also be derived for the production of capital items, coefficients which are termed capital coefficients and which are the basis for dynamic models. (We do not discuss these dynamic models, since as yet they have not yielded significant results.) However, these coefficients are in general quite different from the coefficients associated with current production. See the discussion in section 2.

[60] The critical importance of final demand estimates in interindustry analysis has been emphasized in H. J. Barnett [3], pp. 214–215.

[61] For example, projections may be made for high-fertility, medium-fertility, and low-fertility populations, or for high-investment or low-investment economic atmospheres.

Put somewhat differently, both the size and distribution of the exogenous sectors may be viewed as variables, so far as the input-output system is concerned, whose values are subject to decision and policy. For further discussion, see J. DeW. Norton [42]; E. B. Berman [4]; and Chapter 12.

[62] For further discussion, see W. W. Leontief [35], pp. 18–19, and various references cited in V. Riley and R. L. Allen [45].

localization economies—external economies which accrue when like plants agglomerate at one place.   A third is urbanization economies—external economies which derive when unlike plants agglomerate at one locality. These economies tend to deny the use of a set of constant production coefficients largely reflecting technological relations.

Another major factor is price change.   In the real world prices do change relative to each other; and to some extent at least (and often to a major extent) relative price changes induce substitutions among inputs, such as scrap for pig iron in the production of steel ingot.[63]

Still another factor militating against the use of constant coefficients is associated with the limitations of the data which can be feasibly processed. Statistics are not always organized so that it is possible to differentiate purchases on current and capital account.   Thus production coefficients computed from transactions tables may be distorted by capital transactions inextricably mixed with current transactions.   Moreover, there is the product-mix difficulty.   This difficulty arises from the fact that most transactions tables are constructed on an establishment or industry basis rather than on a product basis.   If for a multiproduct firm the input patterns of the several commodities produced vary significantly, and if the percentages these commodities comprise of the total output of the firm varies over time, the pattern of input requirements within this firm must also change (except in an unusual situation), even when constant production coefficients truly obtain in the manufacture of each commodity. Presumably it is possible to solve this problem by constructing transactions tables on a process or product basis rather than on an industry or establishment basis.   However, the number of individual commodities produced by the economy is very large.   It is improbable that any input-output table could identify them all.[64]

Technological advance is a further factor limiting the validity of a set of constant coefficients for projection purposes, particularly when these coefficients are derived from transactions of a base year which must reflect technological structure of that year.   Where technological advance leads to a rather regular pattern of change in the amount of an input required— as has been true of coal required per kilowatt-hour of electricity generated by the thermal process—coefficients can be altered justifiably by means of reasonable extrapolations to reflect future conditions of production.   But where technological advance (including the introduction of new products)

[63] For further discussion, see R. Dorfman [9].
[64] For further discussion, see W. W. Leontief et al. [37], ch. 9; W. W. Leontief [35], pp. 21–22; and various items on classification systems and problems cited in V. Riley and R. L. Allen [45], pp. 79–84.

is unpredictable, this limitation of the input-output model for projection purposes cannot be circumvented.[65]

Lastly, a general objection to projection based on constant coefficients is that such projection leaves little role, if any, for choice and decision making by firms, consumers, and governmental units in the future. Expectations, consumer and business psychology, political forces, and other important variables are de-emphasized. Attention is centered on a rather mechanical concept of regional economy, on engineering-type relationships which are assumed to be dominant in the future.[66] Resource limitations, time lags, and frictions and obstacles of all sorts which restrict and place limits on rates of expansion and contraction are generally ignored or given insufficient emphasis.

When we leave the isolated regional economy and consider an interregional system, the objections to the use of constant coefficients mount. (Of course, the increase in objections must be balanced against the extended potentialities for analysis.) Why should the relative supply prices of any commodity in the several regions be expected to show stability, as is in general implied by the assumption of constant interareal input coefficients? Or, put still more rigorously, why should the pattern of supply channels remain constant when any input of an industry is considered?[67] In reality, relative supply prices frequently do change as regional requirements change; and so do the relative magnitudes of the geographic flows of any input associated with a given industry—say, because of capacity limitations, or different marginal costs at the several regional mineral deposits, or limited labor supplies, or agglomeration economies and diseconomies, to cite only several factors.[68]

When these and other limitations to interregional input-output analysis are listed together with the restrictions imposed by inadequate data, we may question whether there is any merit at all in the use of this analysis for projection. Upon further reflection, however, it becomes apparent to many that there is room for the input-output technique in the regional scientist's kit of tools, provided this technique is used in a flexible manner[69] and complemented with other techniques of analysis. Many of the objections to its use can be met.

[65] For further discussion, see H. J. Barnett [2], J. H. Cumberland [8], and Harvard Economic Research Project [14].

[66] E.g. see R. E. Kuenne [34].

[67] Or, in still other terms, why should an individual industry of a region have associated with it a constant region-by-region pattern of resource use?

[68] For further discussion, see W. Isard [16], pp. 322–324; and L. N. Moses [40], pp. 810–815.

[69] For example, see W. Isard and R. A. Kavesh [27], and R. A. Kavesh [32].

We may grant that the input-output technique cannot incorporate into its framework unforeseeable technological change (and new products). But neither can any other existing social science technique. Of necessity, any projection must be imperfect in such a dynamic society as ours. At the same time, projections, however imperfect, must be made. When combined with intuition and hunch, input-output projections yield results at least as good as those based on intuition and hunch alone. Further, it can be argued that we are less likely to overlook important possibilities for technological change when we construct the projection within the detailed, systematic, and consistent framework of an input-output table. We are likely to emerge with a more thorough and balanced appraisal of likely technological change. Such an appraisal of change is incorporated in an input-output table by changing the coefficients and perhaps by adding new columns and rows for new industries. In this connection, it should be kept in mind that the coefficients in Table 3 which are derived from the transactions of Table 1 (or the coefficients which might be derived from a table of the order of Table 2) refer only to the base year. They serve as benchmarks for the year of projection. Whenever we have additional information—such as changes in technology or household expenditures—we can incorporate this information in the input-output analysis by substituting coefficients based on the additional knowledge for the old coefficients derived from the transactions of a base year. For example, if information from a consumers' survey leads us to believe that, per dollar income, expenditures on educational and other basic services will rise by 10 per cent by the year of projection, we will substitute a coefficient of 0.11 for the coefficient of 0.10 in the eleventh column, ninth row of Table 3, *ceteris paribus*.[70] Ideally, the investigator uses a minimum of coefficients derived from the base year. He obtains from surveys and from engineers, location and marketing experts, industry specialists and other social scientists a maximum amount of information on input structures and expenditure patterns likely to characterize each sector in the year of projection. Yet because of the difficulty and expense of gathering such information, considerable recourse must still be had to base year data, despite their limited validity and shortcomings.

We may also grant the existence of major economies of scale. Such a position does not preclude a qualified use of input-output projections. Suppose we anticipate efficient industrial operations in the future, an assumption which characterizes many projections whether by intuition, hunch, or scientific technique. The output of a commodity is assumed to be produced in plants whose size and use of diverse inputs roughly

---

[70] At the same time, we would need to change one or more other coefficients in the eleventh column so that the sum of the coefficients in the column would be 1.00.

correspond to best practice. The use of constant coefficients corresponding to the scale and inputs of best practice would seem to be justifiable, even though the full economies of scale might not be realized in all plants.[71] Or, as a more realistic step, we might visualize in the year of projection a state of inefficiency (and of economic irrationality) of the same order as that existing in the base year. It does not seem unreasonable to use base year coefficients adjusted for estimated technological change and perhaps for some scale effects, particularly in the light of the many uncertainties of the future.[72] Somewhat similar remarks may be made with respect to the problem of allowing for localization and urbanization economies.[73]

We may moreover grant relative price changes. At times these changes can be anticipated as the increase in the price of coal as wages rise, or of Lake Superior ore as deposits are depleted, or of steel as wholly new capacity must be constructed. We may estimate as best we can the substitutions among inputs and trade channels which might result from such changes and alter the coefficients accordingly.[74] Of course, the interregional input-output system is more applicable the greater the stability of relative prices. Thus, in general, it is more applicable to a set of regions within a nation or currency bloc than to a set of regions having different currency and monetary systems interconnected by a set of variable

[71] For example, if the required output of an industry was not an exact multiple of the scale of a best-practice plant, one or more plants would have to operate at less than full capacity, and hence would not realize the full economies of scale. In such a situation, however, use of constant production coefficients would not generally involve a major error.

[72] Or other alternative assumptions might be used and appropriate adjustments made in the coefficients. (For example, different coefficients may be used for different ranges of output, with or without the use of an intercept.) But whatever the alternative, it is not at all certain that other projection techniques can handle the problem of economies of scale any better.

[73] Moreover, the investigator may wish to apply a set of base year "average" coefficients to the current levels of output and final demand, and a set of different coefficients (which reflect such factors as more advanced technology or additional agglomeration economies) to the expansions (or contractions) in outputs and final demand. The latter set of coefficients may be termed "marginal" coefficients. See W. Isard [18], pp. 314–317; and W. Isard and R. A. Kavesh [27], pp. 157–159, 161–162.

[74] We must not, however, overlook the fact that cultural and institutional factors (including custom, habit, and inertia) frequently operate to fix supply channels, production techniques, and consumption patterns despite price changes.

Also, it should be borne in mind that for commodities which incur significant transport costs, e.g. brick, cement, glass, the pattern of supply channels to a given industry of a region does not evidence much relative change with small-to-modest changes in the demand at that region. Moreover, different attributes of a product may effectively distinguish the output of one region from another.

foreign exchange rates. It is still more applicable to situations where prices must be specified beforehand, however poor the prediction is. Such would be the case in the planning of the development of a new region. In a new region where prices must be postulated, at least for certain commodities, in order to determine interregional advantage, the use of an interregional input-output system for projection purposes can be extremely fruitful.[75]

Hence, despite its limitations, it seems reasonable to view the use of the interregional input-output technique for projection purposes as an approximative procedure. The more we can foresee changes in the structure of the interregional interindustry system and alter the coefficients accordingly, the firmer the resulting projections. It likewise follows that the accuracy of the projections will tend to be greater the closer the projection year is to the base year, in time as well as in size and composition of the variables to be measured.[76] As a consequence, the more frequently an input-output table is revised and brought up to date, the greater the applicability of the technique.[77]

[75] For example, suppose an area possessing an excellent hydro site is to be developed, its chief export to be aluminum ingot. Prior to the decision to produce aluminum in this area, a calculation would have been made regarding the profitability of such a venture. If such a calculation were a sound one, it would have involved estimates of power costs, transport costs of various sorts, delivered prices of various raw materials, delivered prices of food and other items entering the laborer's bread basket, etc. Once the background of price-cost estimates has been sketched and the decision made to proceed with development, an interregional input-output framework becomes valuable for projecting such magnitudes as employment, population numbers, requirements of housing and community facilities, total power output, levels of local industry, and other possible export industries, regional income, commodity flows into and out of the area, etc. In the construction of the interregional framework, it would of course be necessary to estimate for each sector of the given area the relevant set of input coefficients, since there would be for this area no base year period. Such estimation would be geared to engineering estimates, experience and data in comparable areas, market and industrial location analyses, and other sources of information and studies which the investigator would be able to utilize to a large extent if he construes the interregional input-output framework as a flexible technique and so designs his model.

[76] Also existing capacities and their utilization must be considered. In general, the projections of an interregional input-output model will be more accurate the more adequate the existing regional capacities are for yielding the projected regional outputs, or the more accurately we can designate the input requirements needed for expansion of regional capacities.

[77] As already noted, the interregional input-output approach has potentialities for extensive use in world trade and development analysis, provided appropriate data are made available by agencies in diverse regions of the world and provided satisfactory procedures are devised to preserve the behavioral aspects of a problem, particularly the political and cultural. Thus far, only a few simple models have been sketched. For example, see H. B. Chenery [5] and W. Isard [18].

G. ALTERNATIVE INTERREGIONAL AND REGIONAL INPUT-OUTPUT
MODELS

As has been indicated several times, a chief limitation of the inter-regional input-output model as thus far described is the dearth of relevant data. This weakness has led to the design of models requiring considerably less data. One such design has already been examined, namely, that design in which all the commodity outflows and inflows of a region are consolidated in an export column and an import row respectively. This restricted design is in general most applicable to those politically bounded regions whose foreign trade sector is not major and whose boundaries are national boundaries. The greater the importance of a region's foreign trade sector, and the greater the factor mobility among regions, in general, the less applicable is this design. However, this design has been used most extensively in regional input-output analysis, and we shall have further reference to it in a subsequent chapter in which we discuss applications of interregional and regional input-output models in combination with other techniques.

A second design retains for all commodity flows the detail on region of termination but eliminates the need for disaggregation by industry of termination.[78] This design can thus utilize directly the I.C.C. flow data and other data on commodity imports which are published, once an appropriate industrial classification has been constructed and the data thereby ordered. This design postulates that all industries of a region obtain any particular commodity input from other regions in the same manner. For example, if in the base year (or year of projection) regions A and B provide region C with 60 per cent and 40 per cent respectively of the commodity i required by region C, every industry in region C which uses commodity i as an input must be assumed to derive 60 per cent and 40 per cent of its requirement from industry i of region A and B, respectively.[79] Not only are trading patterns by type input assumed constant

---

[78] See H. B. Chenery [6], ch. 5, and L. N. Moses [40]. In his study Moses presents a thorough and comprehensive statement on this design and its empirical implementation.

[79] Regions A, B, and C would in general obtain commodity i in different proportions from the supplying regions. Also, in such a model, we might distinguish between types of commodities, as is done in the balanced regional model to be discussed later. Inputs of purely local commodities which are furnished to the industries of a region would come from the industry of production in that region alone. Inputs of national commodities might come from producing industries of all regions. Inputs of regional or "intermediate" commodities might come from producing industries of all regions too but would tend to come in greater proportion from the producing industry of the region of consumption and of neighboring regions. E.g. see H. B. Chenery [6].

on an aggregate regional level, but they are also constant and identical for each receiving industry of a region.   This more restrictive postulate eliminates from analysis the reality, among industries of a region, of significant differences in their individual supply patterns of an input because of vertical integration,[80] because of different locations in the given region,[81] or because of persisting historical, financial, and other institutional ties.[82]   Thus the considerable advantage of such a design in the use of existing data and in the collection of new data must be weighed against the loss of flexibility and the additional unreality which it imposes on the analysis.[83]

A third design, one which rigorously speaking is not *interregional* but rather *intranational*, is the balanced regional model.[84]   The balanced regional model explicitly recognizes for a given nation an hierarchy of regions and commodities.   Some commodities (e.g. motor vehicles) are able to stand transportation over great distances, because of a low weight-to-value ratio, because of economies of scale in production, because of large weight losses in the processing of certain localized raw materials, or because of a number of other factors.   Others (e.g. cement) may have more restricted market areas—such as a large region, a cluster of states, or a metropolitan region and its hinterland.   Still others (e.g. shoe repair service) may have severely restricted market areas, such as a community

[80] This might be particularly true of the use of a raw material such as oil or coal, whose geographic pattern of supply to any industry of a region may be greatly affected by the degree of vertical integration within that industry.

[81] In a large region, the geographic supply patterns of an input may differ greatly, and for sound economic reasons, for industries concentrated in the different parts of the given region.   Such difference would be explicit in the model of this paragraph if it were feasible, as typically it is not, to subdivide regions into meaningful subregions.

[82] In particular, the geographic supply pattern of an input may differ considerably between old industries (sectors) and new industries (sectors), despite the profit (utility)-maximizing premises of economics.

[83] In this connection it should be observed that in the pure interregional model, where for each commodity outflow both industry and region of termination are specified, it is possible to allow each industry of a receiving region to obtain its input of each commodity i in the same proportions from the supplying regions.   Where location and marketing analysis suggests this step, we can thereby automatically proceed from a pure interregional model to the model of this paragraph.   In contrast, where location and marketing analysis suggests that this step would be inappropriate for some major sectors—among others, for reasons already enumerated—it is not possible to proceed automatically from the model of this paragraph to a purer interregional model encompassing different patterns of regional supply for certain inputs and identical patterns for other inputs.

[84] This model was developed by W. Leontief and implemented by W. Isard in W. Leontief et al. [37], chs. 4, 5, respectively.   For a non-technical presentation of this model, see W. Isard and G. Freutel [26], pp. 460–468; and W. Isard [21], pp. 243–250.

within a city or, at the extreme, a small neighborhood or nucleus of dwelling units.

Associated with this continuum of market areas is a continuum of commodities where each commodity is classified by the size of market within which it is sold, or by the size of region within which the production and consumption of the commodity balance. National commodities are those commodities whose production and consumption balance only within the nation as a whole. Regional commodities of the first order are those whose production and consumption balance within the nation as well as within each first-order region. Regional commodities of the second order, whose market areas are smaller than those of the first order, are those whose production and consumption balance not only within the nation and each region of the first order but also within each region of the second order. Finally, local commodities (regional commodities of the nth order) are those whose production and consumption balance not only within the nation, each region of the first order, each region of the second order, . . ., and each region of the $(n - 1)$ order but also within each local area (region of the nth order).[85] In practice, however, only a limited number of commodity classes can be feasibly treated, and hence only a highly restricted hierarchy of regions can be considered.[86]

To illustrate the workings of a balanced regional model, imagine a three-order hierarchy of regions—nation, census region, and local area—and a corresponding classification of commodities—national, regional, and local. Given the final demand items for the nation as a whole, the outputs of national industries (industries producing national commodities) are determined in typical input-output manner by the use of an inverse matrix or a round-by-round iteration.[87] Once the national outputs of those national industries are determined, a set of coefficients must be derived by which to allocate these national outputs among the several regions. These coefficients may be based on the geographic distribution of current production, on location studies, or on some other analysis. These coefficients remain constant throughout the operation. They are multiplied by the national outputs of national industries to yield for each census region the

[85] In this model each region of any order is completely subdivided into a finite number of whole regions of any higher order. There can be no intersection of any regional boundary lines. No region of any given order can be situated in more than one region of any lower order.

[86] For further discussion relating to the concepts of this paragraph, see the Appendix to Chapter 6; *Location and Space-Economy*, pp. 57–60; and references cited in these places.

[87] Where an iterative procedure is used, there will of course be some discrepancies in the results obtained owing to errors of estimation.

part of the output of each national industry to be produced in that census region.

To produce these outputs of national industries in each census region, inputs of both regional and local commodities are required. Utilizing national input coefficients, the inputs of regional and local commodities necessary to support the production of national industries in any given census region can be determined. All these inputs must be furnished by that census region, since by definition no regional or local commodity may cross a regional boundary, that is, be provided to one region by another region. In addition to these inputs of regional and local commodities, any given census region must furnish the part of the national final demand for regional and local commodities that is to be consumed in that region, since again regional and local commodities cannot be shipped from one region to another.[88] But to furnish the region's share of final demand for regional and local commodities and the first-round requirement of national industries for regional and local commodities, the producers in the given census region will require a second round of inputs of regional and local commodities,[89] which round will lead to a third round, etc. The sum of these round-by-round and final demand requirements for regional and local commodities in the given census region can be determined either by the use of an inverted matrix or by iteration. This yields the required output of regional and local commodities for the given census region. Likewise for every other census region.

The next step is to subdivide each census region into a set of local areas. Then for each local area we determine:

1. Required outputs of *national* industries (through use of a set of constant coefficients based on the geographic distribution of current production, on location studies, or on some other analysis).[90]

2. Required outputs of *regional* industries (through use of other sets of constant coefficients to allocate any given census region's outputs of regional commodities among its constituent local areas).

3. Required outputs of *local* industries (calculated in a manner similar

[88] That share of national commodities in the national bill of goods, for which the given region is responsible, has already been accounted for in the determination of the output of national industries to be produced in the region.

[89] Inputs of national commodities will also be required, but the share of these inputs for which producers in the region are responsible has already been accounted for in the determination of the output of national industries to be produced in the region.

[90] These coefficients, when aggregated by each census region, must by definition yield the coefficients used to allocate output of national industries among census regions. That is, within any given census region, the sum of the coefficients for the several local areas which pertain to a given national industry must equal that coefficient previously used to allocate the national output of that industry to the given census region.

to the way in which regional outputs of regional industries are determined for census regions).[91]

This is a brief sketch of the workings of the balanced regional model, a model which can be expanded to embrace more than three orders of regions and classes of commodities. In addition to the shortcomings which generally characterize input-output models, there are others peculiar to the model. There is no reason to anticipate that as final demand changes all regions will expand or contract outputs of any national industry in fixed proportion. (This is implied by the use of invariant allocating coefficients.) Nor is there any sound reason to expect all local areas in a census region to change their outputs of regional commodities by identical per cents.[92]

Moreover, there are both conceptual and statistical difficulties in classifying commodities and in ranking them by size of market area. In one part of the nation commodities may tend to balance on a local level, in another part only on a census region level. Such contrast may have sound economic justification. Also, balances of production and consumption based on existing data can at best be merely approximated for most commodities, and for some only crudely established.

Similarly, it is difficult to select a meaningful and useful hierarchy of regions. In practice, regions of any given order do not break down into regions of higher order in the precise way required by the model. Regional boundaries do intersect. A meaningful region may lie in two or more regions of a lower order. Forcing the data into the neat regional mold of the model frequently introduces unrealities into the situation. The investigator must therefore explore different classifications and systems of both commodities and regions in order to minimize inconsistencies and the artificiality of the model and to achieve the best compromise for model operation.[93]

Aside from an inability to indicate the region of origin of any national commodity, the model generally precludes different production practices among regions. The national input coefficients must characterize production in each region; and if the household sector is contained in the

[91] For any given local area we first determine (1) the inputs of local commodities required *directly* to produce the outputs of regional and national commodities in that local area, and (2) the part of the national final demand for local commodities to be consumed in that local area. Then the *indirect* requirements for local commodities are computed by use of an inverse matrix or a round-by-round iteration. Summing the direct requirement, the local final demand, and the indirect requirements yields the required outputs of local industries in the given local area.

[92] They could be expected to alter outputs in the same degree only if certain generally unrealistic assumptions were made regarding transport cost and marginal costs in the several local areas (regions).

[93] For full discussion, see W. Isard [22].

structural matrix, regional consumption patterns must resemble the national pattern and thus be identical. This intensifies the discrepancies between the operation and character of a regional price structure in an input-output model and in reality.[94]

Despite these additional limitations the balanced regional model has considerable promise. It is particularly useful for examining the regional implications of national projections or policies, or of alternative levels of international trade, or of different domestic investment programs, etc., when there is no advance knowledge of the geographic pattern of new capacity. Put in another way, it can be extremely helpful in identifying for programs such as national ones relating to river valley and nuclear developments significant capacity limitations and bottlenecks for producing regional and local commodities, such as power, housing and urban services, and local transportation. Additionally, this model promises to be of value for the study of metropolitan regions, where assumptions on the balance of production and consumption of regional commodities may be workable in connection with a number of private and public functions and services performed on the metropolitan level. More will be said on this point in Chapter 12. Thus far, however, no real application of this model has been attempted, although there has been considerable exploration with its operation.

H. Applications and Synthesis with Location Analysis

We have now presented the basic structural elements of diverse regional and interregional input-output models. We have discussed their limitations and the data problems associated with their use. Before bringing this chapter to a close, we wish to illustrate how interregional and regional input-output techniques have been fruitfully applied to specific regional problems. As can be expected, the most extensive applications have occurred in connection with regions which are at the same time nations and which can to a large extent be treated as isolated regions. Models for such regions raise considerably less difficult problems and require considerably less new data for implementation than interregional models or models for regions within nations, or for regions comprising more than one nation. However, we shall not discuss such national applications at this point, since a nation is a specialized type of region and does not well illustrate regional situations.

In view of the many limitations of input-output for projection purposes,

---

[94] In an interesting input-output study for the St. Louis Metropolitan region, Hirsch finds significant differences between national input coefficients and input coefficients for this region obtained directly from local sources (W. Z. Hirsch [15]).

it is not surprising to find greatest returns when input-output models are used in conjunction with other regional and national techniques. We shall not discuss the two regional input-output studies that have involved the most extensive *empirical* investigation and analysis,[95] for these studies were designed to test the feasibility of particular input-output models; for the most part they were not combined with other regional techniques, were abstract, and were not focused on particular regional problems and situations.

Rather we choose to discuss in detail a regional model whose interindustry system has been partially fused with the industrial location system of a comparative cost framework. We also map the outlines of a full synthesis of these two systems. Later, in Chapter 12, we cover other applications, both actual and potential, of interregional and regional input-output models in conjunction with one or more other regional techniques. That is, we broadly paint the synthesis of the interindustry system with the several systems implied by these techniques.

Our case study involves a partial projection of the economic base, population, and related aspects of the Greater New York–Philadelphia Industrial Region.[96] As implied in the previous chapter on location analysis, one sound approach to regional development has been to undertake comparative cost study to determine efficient location patterns for a number of basic industries, each independently of the others. One such industry whose comparative cost situation was briefly sketched is the iron and steel industry. Both theoretical and empirical analysis in general suggest location at major markets, provided the market is capable of absorbing the total output of each of the set of semi-finishing mills comprising a modern integrated works.[97] Such a market is the Greater New York–Philadelphia Industrial Region. Given transport rates and the pattern of ore, coal, and scrap sources for efficient production points both within and outside the region, location theory suggests that a market location would minimize transport inputs (where weights are "ideal" weights). Empirical materials, such as those in Table 4, suggest a Trenton location as the minimum transport cost point for serving the market in this region.[98] In assembling coal and ore and shipping products to that

[95] W. Isard [22] and L. N. Moses [40].

[96] W. Isard and R. E. Kuenne [28]. Also see R. E. Kuenne [33].

[97] After allowing for sales of competitors from outside the region, for purchasing practices of steel fabricators who may find it desirable to obtain their steel from several companies and plants in order to insure a steady supply of steel, for local tax rates, and for many other factors. See W. Isard [23], W. Isard and W. M. Capron [24], W. Isard and J..Cumberland [25], A. Rodgers [46], and P. G. Craig [7].

[98] Trenton lies in the heart of this region and is very close to the site at Morristown where the United States Steel Corporation has erected major facilities.

part of the market at New York City, Trenton incurs a cost of $13.13, an advantage of more than $3.00 per ton steel over the next best production point.   Thus, the rationale for location of an integrated iron and steel works in this region is clear-cut.[99]

Once the feasibility of a major industrial development is established, it becomes necessary to define its magnitude before we can appraise the potential impact on both the region of location and other regions.   On the basis of steel consumption data by geographic regions, of market growth estimates for the region and for other regions which might be served, of

TABLE 4. TRANSPORTATION COSTS ON ORE, COAL, AND FINISHED PRODUCTS
FOR SELECTED PRODUCING LOCATIONS SERVING NEW YORK CITY

(In dollars)[a]

	Transportation Costs on:			
Location	Ore	Coal	Finished Products	Total
New London (hypothetical)	3.68	5.42	8.80	17.90
Pittsburgh	5.55	1.56	12.40	19.51
Cleveland	3.16	3.85	14.00	21.01
Sparrows Point	3.68	4.26	8.40	16.34
Buffalo	3.16	4.27	11.60	19.03
Bethlehem	5.56	5.06	5.80	16.42
Trenton	3.68	4.65	4.80	13.13

[a] The costs on iron ore and coal are calculated per net ton of steel.

Source: W. Isard and J. H. Cumberland [25], p. 257.

actual and potential competition from producers in neighboring regions, of capacity expansion practices and policies in the steel industry, and of many other considerations, the study concluded that a *firm minimum*[100] estimate of three million tons of new capacity by 1962 was justified.

Before a regional input-output analysis can be attempted, one additional

[99] As a matter of interest, the rationale for such expansion on the Eastern Seaboard had been established well before the actual decision of the United States Steel Corporation to locate at Morristown.

[100] For various reasons the study was designed to yield firm estimates of minimum expansion effects rather than infirm estimates of most likely effects.   Thus its results definitely err in the direction of understatement.

step is necessary. We must estimate the size of new (including expansion in existing) steel-fabricating and other activities technically or production-wise geographically linked *directly* to basic iron and steel activity. Such might be termed the *direct* agglomeration effect. Because of limitations of research resources, examination of this effect was confined to the steel-fabricating activities. Through the use of location theory, materials on historical trends, and empirical measures such as the location quotient and the coefficient of geographical association, and through interviews with informed persons in the region, minimum estimates of new production employment in the region by steel-fabricating activity were made. They are recorded in Table 5. For example, industry 341 (Tin cans and other tinware) is expected to grow by 10 per cent, or to employ 923 more production workers.

As the next step the study had to design an appropriate input-output model for use. It was decided to employ a model of an "incremental" type which would examine the impact of the new steel and steel-fabricating industry as if for the most part this impact were a pure addition (or subtraction) to the existing regional structure. Further, it was felt that the national input coefficients developed for the 50-sector classification of the 1947 Bureau of Labor Statistics interindustry study[101] would be relevant. The households sector was removed from the final demand items, and placed within the structural matrix in order to catch the local income multiplier effect. The sector construction and maintenance was removed from the structural matrix. Other steps were taken, perhaps the most important of which was to ignore interregional feedback effects (effects on the region of study because of changes in industrial structure and output of other regions directly and indirectly supplying imports to the region of study).[102]

Once these decisions were made, it was possible to proceed with the calculations. The first calculation involved the determination of the first round of input requirements, that is, the inputs required by the operation at full capacity of the new steel and steel-fabricating plants. These inputs are calculated from the input coefficient matrix, and they are recorded in column 1 of Table 6.[103] Because an "incremental" model is used, these

---

[101] W. D. Evans and M. Hoffenberg [10]. However, see W. Z. Hirsch [15] for a different judgment with respect to the St. Louis Metropolitan region.

[102] For full details, see W. Isard and R. E. Kuenne [28] and R. E. Kuenne [33].

[103] They are obtained (1) by multiplying the cents' worth of every input required per dollar output of steel by the estimated dollar value of 3 million tons of steel; (2) by multiplying the cents' worth of every input per dollar output of a given steel-fabricating activity by the dollar volume of that activity corresponding to the new employment estimate of Table 5; and (3) by summing horizontally for each of the 45 different types of inputs the requirements by steel and each fabricating activity.

TABLE 5. ESTIMATES OF NEW PRODUCTION EMPLOYEES IN THE REGION BY
STEEL-FABRICATING ACTIVITY

Industry Number	Title	Per Cent Rate of Growth	New Production Employees
341	Tin cans and other tinware	10.0	923
342	Cutlery, hand tools, and general hardware	0.0	0
343	Heating apparatus (except electric) and plumbers' supplies	20.0	2,593
344	Fabricated structural metal products	4.6	1,132
346	Metal stamping, coating, and engraving	10.0	2,408
347	Lighting fixtures	2.5	1,911
348	Fabricated wire products	10.0	670
349	Miscellaneous fabricated metal products	17.5	2,695
351	Engines and turbines	8.0	723
352	Agricultural machinery and tractors	10.0	294
353	Construction and mining machinery and equipment	10.0	252
354	Metal-working machinery	13.5	2,137
355	Special-industry machinery (except metal-working machinery)	16.0	5,204
356	General industrial machinery and equipment	25.0	5,566
357	Office and store machines and devices	10.0	1,225
358	Service industry and household machines	20.0	4,512
359	Miscellaneous machinery parts	25.0	5,666
36	Electrical machinery, equipment, and supplies	5.0	8,025
371	Motor vehicles and motor vehicle equipment	20.0	7,331
372	Aircraft and parts	3.0	871
373	Ship and boat building and repairing	5.0	1,989
374	Railroad equipment	3.0	364
375	Motorcycles, bicycles, and parts	0.0	0
379	Transportation equipment (n.e.c.)	·7.0	32
38	Professional, scientific, and controlling instruments; photographic, etc.	0.0	0
39	Miscellaneous manufacturing industries	10.5	4,803
	Total		61,326

Source: W. Isard and R. E. Kuenne [28], p. 295.

TABLE 6.   DIRECT AND INDIRECT REPER

Industry	Input Requirements of initial Steel and Steel-Fabricating Activities (in $ thousand) (1)	Minimum Percentage of Input Requirements to be Produced in Area (2)	First-Round Expansions in Area (in $ thousand) (3)
1. Agriculture and fisheries	50.0	0	0.0
2. Food and kindred products	294.6	60	176.8
3. Tobacco manufactures	0.0	0	0.0
4. Textile mill products	3,864.7	10	386.5
5. Apparel	1,285.6	75	964.2
6. Lumber and wood products	5,610.7	5	280.5
7. Furniture and fixtures	1,753.4	33	578.6
8. Paper and allied products	4,818.7	40	1,927.5
9. Printing and publishing	425.5	90	383.0
10. Chemicals	10,626.4	45	4,781.9
11. Products of petroleum and coal	10,936.6	25	2,734.2
12. Rubber products	8,381.5	15	1,257.2
13. Leather and leather products	647.7	20	129.5
14. Stone, clay, and glass products	9,031.7	15	1,354.8
15. Iron and steel	121,170.5	50	60,585.3
16. Nonferrous metals	33,997.4	20	6,799.5
17. Plumbing and heating supplies	3,192.4	25	798.1
18. Fabricated structural metal products	3,480.7	40	1,392.3
19. Other fabricated metal products	31,770.9	40	12,708.4
20. Agricultural, mining, and construction machinery	3,651.3	5	182.6
21. Metal-working machinery	7,389.1	25	1,847.3
22. Other machinery (except electric)	28,463.6	40	11,385.4
23. Motors and generators	11,265.9	20	2,253.2
24. Radios	4,562.2	30	1,368.7
25. Other electrical machinery	21,773.9	50	10,887.0
26. Motor vehicles	50,530.8	10	5,053.1
27. Other transportation equipment	2,605.5	20	521.1
28. Professional and scientific equipment	3,221.4	50	1,610.7
29. Miscellaneous manufacturing	5,116.8	60	3,070.1
30. Coal, gas, and electric power	7,767.0	50	3,883.5
31. Railroad transportation	13,575.8	75	10,181.9
32. Ocean transportation	457.3	75	343.0
33. Other transportation	4,179.4	95	3,970.4
34. Trade	13,969.8	95	13,271.3
35. Communications	1,790.7	90	1,611.6
36. Finance and insurance	3,086.2	90	2,777.6
37. Rental	3,018.8	95	2,867.9
38. Business services	5,338.5	95	5,071.6
39. Personal and repair services	396.9	95	377.1
40. Medical, educational and nonprofit organizations	0.0	90	0.0
41. Amusements	0.0	90	0.0
42. Scrap and miscellaneous industries	8,388.2	50	4,194.1
43. Undistributed	103,638.6	50	51,819.3
44. Eating and drinking places	0.0	95	0.0
45. Households	348,281.0	82	285,590.4
Totals	903,807.7		521,377.2

Source : W. Isard and R. E. Kuenne [28], p. 297.

CUSSIONS OF NEW BASIC STEEL CAPACITY

Second-Round Expansions in Area (in $ thousand) (4)	Third-Round Expansions in Area (in $ thousand) (5)	Sum of Round Expansions in Area (in $ thousand) (6)	Total New Employees Corresponding to Round Expansions (7)	Total New Employees in Initial Steel and Steel-Fabricating Activities (8)	Over-all Total of New Employees (9)
0	0	0	0		0
17,660	8,249	42,492	1,833		1,833
0	0	0	0		0
406	39	1,280	142		142
10,124	3,461	21,155	2,302		2,302
93	36	450	64		64
802	198	2,000	234		234
1,674	1,297	6,574	426		426
5,929	3,014	14,617	1,667		1,667
3,599	1,630	12,077	601		601
2,547	1,118	7,634	228		228
355	102	1,879	169		169
679	194	1,371	150		150
441	139	2,083	268		268
13,566	2,965	78,335	6,093	11,666	17,759
1,667	381	9,063	505		505
248	50	1,189	118	3,640	3,758
312	33	1,809	151	1,420	1,571
2,146	561	16,121	1,537	10,060	11,597
46	11	251	22	707	729
270	43	2,210	289	2,705	2,994
2,675	551	15,384	1,486	28,607	30,093
226	42	2,560	301	⎫	⎫
428	101	2,026	192	⎬10,392	⎬12,312
2,011	432	13,903	1,427	⎭	⎭
742	260	6,421	389	8,770	9,159
276	69	958	117	4,605	4,722
801	287	3,123	416		416
2,888	982	8,418	845	6,108	6,953
1,843	2,693	11,079	1,100		1,100
6,010	2,390	21,532	3,308		3,308
331	170	1,021	110		110
8,422	2,836	19,694	2,394		2,394
36,585	11,855	83,642	13,874		13,874
2,409	1,283	7,305	1,191		1,191
9,472	5,062	25,252	2,329		2,329
26,222	9,603	55,680	909		909
2,385	2,406	13,384	1,305		1,305
14,399	5,088	24,212	4,443		4,443
9,811	2,160	17,271	4,370		4,370
3,677	1,066	6,591	1,100		1,100
2,054	727	7,411	771		771
5,875	6,019	69,236	7,208		7,208
16,916	3,903	29,551	3,705		3,705
63,002	80,894	509,578			
282,024	164,400	1,177,822	70,089	88,680	158,769

first-round input requirements may be viewed as the incremental bill of goods (final demand) to be furnished to the region.[104]

But it is immediately clear that not all these first-round requirements can be expected to be furnished by the producers within the region. Coal, for example, would be furnished by producers outside the region. To determine the amount of each input which would be produced internally necessitates, for most inputs, extensive and sound marketing, comparative cost and other location analysis, which was beyond the scope of the study. As a consequence, with the available resources the best possible estimates were made of the minimum per cent of each first-round input which might be forthcoming from producers in this region. These per cents are listed in column 2 of Table 6. For example, it is anticipated that 60 per cent of the first-round requirements for food and kindred products will be furnished by producers in this region. Multiplying these per cents by the corresponding first-round input requirements yields the first round of output expansions required of producers in the region. These are listed in column 3 of Table 6.

To produce the first round of output expansions in turn requires inputs, namely, a second round of input requirements. This second round was calculated from the input coefficient table.. Of this second round of input requirements, only part will be furnished by the producers of the region. Again it is necessary to apply extensive and sound marketing and location analysis to determine the per cent of each input which will be. Because of the restricted scope of the study, it was assumed that the per cents listed in column 2 would apply as well to the second (and also later) rounds of input requirements. Multiplying this second round by the corresponding per cents in column 2 yields the second round of output expansions required of producers in the region.

Second-round output expansions require a third round of input requirements, which lead to a third round of output expansions, and in turn to a fourth round of input requirements and a fourth round of output expansions, etc. In view of the convergence of these round-by-round expansions,[105] computations were pursued through the sixth round of expansions, and rough extrapolations were made to account for expansions in the infinite number of succeeding rounds. The round expansions were summed to yield total output expansions required in dollar terms. They

[104] Alternatively, the incremental bill of goods may be viewed as the outputs corresponding to the full use of the new steel and steel-fabricating capacity to be furnished by the region. In either case, the same results are obtained.

[105] The reader may refer to the totals of columns 3, 4, and 5 in Table 6. It should also be noted that the individual input requirements converge in later rounds in a more regular fashion than is indicated in the first three rounds in the table.

are listed in column 6.   These dollar expansions were then translated into total new employees which are recorded in column 7.   To these total new employees were added the employees engaged in the initial steel and steel-fabricating activities, which are listed in column 8, in order to obtain the over-all total of new employees by industry which is listed in column 9. When there is added to column 9 employment in the excluded sectors of government (estimated at 12,884) and construction (estimated at 8574), we obtain one way of summarizing the expected impact of the new steel development.[106]   Alternative methods may be used, as will be indicated in later discussion.

In the study many qualifications had to be made.   A general one concerns the removal of the households sector from the final bill of goods to the structural matrix.   As pointed out previously, an input-output model as such contains no restrictions on rates of expansion and contraction and on multiplier effects.   The sophisticated analyst usually allows for such restrictions; typically he establishes the final demand sectors at such magnitudes that, being fixed, they automatically set reasonable restraints on rates of change and multiplier effects.   When, however, the important households sector is removed from the final demand sectors, unrealistic rates of change and multiplier effects do result[107] unless other modifications of the model are made which introduce compensating restrictions or leakages.

Associated with this basic shortcoming of the model is a second basic inadequacy which, however, does tend to have compensatory effects.   As noted, the study ignores the interregional feedback effect.   It assumes negligible the expansion of output of producers in the region because of increase of demand from consumers and producers in other regions; this increase in demand exists because of increase in incomes and outputs of these other regions which are directly and indirectly linked to the study region's increased need for imports resulting from the study region's expansion.   The study concludes that its failure to encompass this interregional feedback effect tends to balance the exaggeration of the expansionary effect resulting from placing the households sector in the structural matrix.

Clearly sounder analysis would result if both these shortcomings could

[106] For further details, see W. Isard and R. E. Kuenne [28].

[107] When households are a final demand sector, level of household consumption expenditure for each commodity is fixed and remains unchanged in the round-by-round computations.   When, however, households are in the structural matrix, the level of household consumption expenditure for each commodity does expand or contract *pari passu* with household income; and such expansion or contraction of effective demand leads to considerably greater industrial output expansions or contractions than in the previous case.

be corrected simultaneously.   Part of the households sector could and logically should be left in the final demand sectors.   Part of the other sectors in the structural matrix might also be removed to the final demand sectors, or other leakages or limiting factors might be injected into the model.   A consistent interregional structure, even if only of the "Region A and All Other Regions" variety, should be constructed.

One major development in this latter direction is an interregional input-output study for Italy by Chenery.   Italy is meaningfully decomposed into two regions, Northern Italy and Southern Italy.   Including in the structural matrix for each region 22 industrial sectors and the households sector, utilizing national production coefficients to characterize production practices in each region, and allowing regionally different household consumption patterns, Chenery examines the impact upon the two regions (and on imports) of a specific investment program in Southern Italy.[108] He uses an "incremental" type of interregional model, where coefficients tend to be marginal coefficients, and employs, because of data limitations, a set of regional supply coefficients.   These regional supply coefficients are presented in Table 7.   They are employed to avoid the need to dis-aggregate flows by industry of termination.   Their use involves the assumption that any individual input absorbed by the several industries of a region is furnished to each of these industries in identical fashion. Thus, according to Table 7 each industry in the South using chemicals as an input receives 85 per cent of its requirements from the North, 8.4 per cent from the South, and 6.6 per cent from imports.[109]

Given this design, Chenery computes the impact of an investment program in Southern Italy of 150 billion lire.[110]   This program is set up as a bill of goods sector, disaggregated into a set of final demands for

[108] This program is of the type which was then being undertaken by the *Cassa per il Mezzogiorno*, which was authorized to spend over a period of twelve years 110 billion lire per year on investment in Southern Italy.   See H. B. Chenery [6], ch. 5.

[109] The coefficients of Table 7 are related to a three-category commodity classifica-tion.   Local commodities (such as transportation and services) are furnished to the industries and households of a given region by producers in that region.   Their supply coefficients are 1.000 from the given region and 0.0 from other regions and foreign countries (imports).   National commodities (such as chemicals and ferrous metals) are those that may be, and generally are, furnished to industrial and household consumers from several sources of supply and in *identical* fashion, irrespective of location of con-sumer.   Intermediate commodities (such as the products of agriculture and fuel extraction) are furnished to individual and household consumers from several sources of supply, but in a fashion which *differs* according to the location of the consumer.   For further discussion, see H. B. Chenery [6], ch. 5.

[110] This program was based upon 100 billion lire of investment by *Cassa per il Mezzogiorno*, and 50 billion lire of private investment which it was assumed would be induced by the public investment.

specific commodities (e.g. 1.065 billion lire of chemicals), which when summed by region of supply involves final demand for 95.486 billion lire of commodities to be produced in the South, 52.497 billion lire of commodities to be produced in the North, and 2.017 billion lire of imported commodities.[111]   After the round-by-round computations are made, it is

TABLE 7.   REGIONAL SUPPLY COEFFICIENTS

Demand in:	North			South		
Supply from:	Imports	North	South	Imports	North	South
A. Agriculture	0.082	0.844	0.074	0.082	–	0.918
B. Fuel extraction	0.615	0.345	0.040	0.800	–	0.200
C. Mining	0.076	0.591	0.333	0.076	0.591	0.333
D. Food	0.031	0.862	0.107	0.031	–	0.969
E. Textiles	0.020	0.931	0.049	0.020	0.931	0.049
F. Artificial fibers	0.132	0.859	0.009	0.132	0.859	0.009
G. Clothing	0.005	0.995	–	0.005	–	0.995
H. Lumber	0.009	0.991	–	0.009	–	0.991
I. Paper	0.042	0.920	0.038	0.042	0.920	0.038
J. Rubber	0.108	0.847	0.045	0.108	0.847	0.045
K. Other industries	0.010	0.822	0.168	0.010	0.822	0.168
L. Chemicals	0.066	0.850	0.084	0.066	0.850	0.084
M. Ferrous metals	0.091	0.818	0.091	0.091	0.818	0.091
N. Nonferrous metals	0.239	0.548	0.213	0.239	0.548	0.213
O. Mechanical	0.075	0.879	0.046	0.075	0.879	0.046
P. Nonmetallic minerals	0.041	0.959	–	0.041	–	0.959
Q. Construction	–	1.000	–	–	–	1.000
R. Petroleum refining	0.070	0.750	0.180	0.070	–	0.930
S. Gas and coke	0.019	0.981	–	0.019	–	0.981
T. Electric power	0.008	0.992	–	–	–	1.000
U. Services	–	1.000	–	–	–	1.000
V. Transportation	–	1.000	–	–	–	1.000
W. Households	–	1.000	–	–	–	1.000

Source: H. B. Chenery [6], p. 111.

estimated, for example, that the agriculture sector of the South would have furnished 57.645 billion lire of inputs, of the North 60.283 billion lire; and that all industries of the South together would have furnished 430.654 billion lire of inputs, of the North 523.693 billion lire.   New income of

[111] For example, of the 1.065 billion lire final demand for chemicals, 0.090 is furnished by the South, 0.905 by the North, and 0.070 from imports.

194 billion lire would have been generated in the South, 160 billion in the North.

This two-region model represents an important step in catching the interregional feedback effect. Although the model was designed to examine the impact of a planned investment program, it can be readily adapted to investigate the impact of a major steel development, such as the one already commented upon in connection with the Greater New York–Philadelphia Industrial Region. The impact of major steel development could have been examined within a two-region model, the two regions consisting of the Greater New York–Philadelphia Industrial Region and the rest of the United States. It would have been still more desirable if the impact could have been examined within a three- or four-region model. As a consequence, interregional input-output analysis can be integrated in part with comparative cost location analysis, where location analysis is employed to determine meaningful incremental final demands.

The synthesis of location and interregional input-output analysis can be still more extensive. Imagine that in addition to the location study of the iron and steel industry there had been location studies of the oil refinery industry, the chemicals industry, the nucleonics industry, the aluminum industry, the aircraft industry, and other basic sectors. Imagine that these studies had led to a set of best estimates for 1962 of new oil refinery production in the region, of new chemical activity, of new nucleonics output, of new aluminum production, of new aircraft construction, and of new production in other basic sectors. All these expansions in production might have been considered together with the new steel and steel-fabricating production to derive the first round of input requirements. This first round of input requirements would have been the sum, by type input, of direct inputs required to support the expansion in each basic sector and could have been set down as column 1 is in Table 6. By following the steps already outlined, the impact of the entire set of basic activities could have been investigated. As a result, we would have acquired a more comprehensive projection of the regional economy in 1962.

However, important modifications of the input-output design are necessary if we are to attempt such a comprehensive projection. For example, it is essential to avoid double counting. If the expected expansion in chemicals includes chemicals that are to be fed to the new steel and other new capacity, we must remove from the structural matrix the part of the chemical industry that supplies these chemicals, a task which is very difficult. However, if the expected expansion in chemicals includes only those chemicals that can be profitably sold in export markets, the chemicals sector can be left in the structural matrix for the region of study; but care must be taken to allow for contraction of chemical output in other regions if this expansion substitutes for chemical output elsewhere, or for eliminating any interregional feedback effect on chemical output in the region of study if this expansion is based on new demand for chemicals resulting from growth of other regions.[112]

The use of a combined locational-interregional input-output type of study (or, for that matter, a simple interregional or regional input-output study) can be extended in connection with market analysis and location studies requiring market estimation. For example, take an area like Puerto Rico or the Pennsylvania anthracite coal fields. Both these areas have excellent access to the Greater New York–Philadelphia Industrial Region. Both these areas are concerned with expanding their industrial base and thus with possibilities for new exports to outside markets.

TABLE 8. REQUIREMENTS OF THE PRODUCTS OF SELECTED CHEAP-LABOR-ORIENTED INDUSTRIES

Industry Number	Name	Induced Demand (in $ thousand)
30	Spinning, weaving, and dyeing	9731
31	Special textile products	1471
69	Footwear (excluding rubber)	4560
139	Radio and related products	2448
140	Tubes	163

Source: W. Isard and R. E. Kuenne [28], p. 301.

Sound location analysis for these areas requires estimates of the size and growth of the outside markets. The Greater New York–Philadelphia Region is one of these outside markets. Hence, if we were to sum the round-by-round input requirements (not the round-by-round expansions) associated with Table 6, we would obtain an estimate by type input of the market growth in this region resulting from steel development alone. We record in Table 8 some of these estimates of growth for certain commodities whose production might profitably be located in Puerto Rico.[113] Such derived demand estimates are clearly of value. Of still

[112] Or if expansion of chemicals output in the study region substitutes for imports of chemicals from other regions, appropriate contraction of the chemical sector (and indirectly of all other sectors) in these other regions must be introduced into the model.

[113] The activities listed in Table 8 are chosen because they tend to be locationally sensitive to labor cost differentials, especially where the source of cheap labor possesses the requisite skills. For further details, see W. Isard and R. E. Kuenne [28], pp. 300–301.

greater value would be estimates for those commodities of derived demand in the Greater New York–Philadelphia Industrial Region resulting from growth not only in steel but also in chemicals, nucleonics, and other basic activities.

These cases illustrate how a regional or interregional input-output study, when combined with locational techniques, can lead in turn to superior analysis. Numerous other illustrations of fruitful synthesis are possible, as will be suggested in Chapter 12.

I. Concluding Remarks

This chapter and the Appendix to follow cover a step-by-step development of interregional and regional input-output analysis. An over-all appraisal of this technique must yield a positive result. Without question, of operational techniques this is the most powerful one yet devised to express the interdependence of the economy of a region and of a system of regions in their interindustry aspects. This technique is of critical importance, too, because more than any other operational technique thus far developed and extensively applied, this technique does furnish a skeletal framework to which the less general structures of a number of other techniques can be functionally connected. We have, for example, demonstrated how the industrial location system of the comparative cost approach can be fused with the interindustry system of interregional and regional input-output analysis. To the resulting schema other basic elements and dimensions covering other organic phenomena can be grafted.

Counter to these virtues and advantages of input-output run its many limitations. We need not repeat these here. Most of them are not likely to be overcome by improved input-output models per se which are under construction. For example, though the dynamic input-output model promises to imbed a process of growth (and contraction?) within the interindustry system, it must still labor under such basic shortcomings as constant production coefficients. (Except for an oversimplified version outlined in Chapter 12—the Moore model—we do not sketch this dynamic model in this book since it has yet to be proved operational to a significant degree.) Hence, major progress in interregional and regional analysis is likely to come via the development of new techniques, together with their fusion with input-output.

In the two chapters to follow we discuss techniques which are capable of partially overcoming two basic weaknesses of input-output. In the chapter on industrial complex analysis, to which we now turn, we attempt to incorporate into an interindustry or interactivity system the flexibility that can allow for changes in factor proportions, particularly those relating to scale, localization, and urbanization economies. In the second chapter to follow, which treats interregional linear programming, we attempt to introduce into an interindustry, or interactivity system, a part of optimizing behavior characterizing reality.

APPENDIX

SOME NOTES ON THE DERIVATION AND USE OF THE INVERSE MATRIX

As already stated several times, the use of an inverse matrix can in many input-output problems permit considerable savings in the time and cost of computations. In this Appendix we wish therefore to discuss some of the basic procedures and aspects in the construction and use of an inverse matrix. We shall attempt to present the necessary mathematics in as elementary a manner as possible.

Suppose we consider the stationary isolated region depicted in section B of this chapter. Further, in order to ease our presentation, let the structural matrix of this region's economy be comprised of three sectors (1) agriculture, (2) manufacturing, and (3) trade and services, and let the households sector be entirely exogenous to the structural matrix and account entirely for *all final demand*. Hence, if we were to take a census for a base year, we would find that:

1. The gross output of the agricultural sector (designated by X_1) less sales to itself (designated by x_{11}) less sales to manufacturing (designated by x_{12}) less sales to trade and services (designated by x_{13}) equals final or household demand (designated by Y_1) for agricultural products, there being no inventory accumulation or depletion, and no capital formation and consumption in this isolated region.

2. The gross output of the manufacturing sector (X_2) less sales to agriculture (x_{21}) less sales to itself (x_{22}) less sales to trade and services (x_{23}) equals final demand (Y_2) for manufactured products.

3. The gross output of the trade and services sector (X_3) less sales to agriculture (x_{31}) less sales to manufacturing (x_{32}) and less sales to itself (x_{33}) equals final demand (Y_3) for trade and services. Thus we have the following set of three equations:

$$
\begin{aligned}
X_1 - x_{11} - x_{12} - x_{13} &= Y_1 \\
X_2 - x_{21} - x_{22} - x_{23} &= Y_2 \\
X_3 - x_{31} - x_{32} - x_{33} &= Y_3
\end{aligned}
$$

(1)

When a complete census is obtained for a base year, we have the data of Table A-1.

Equations 1 therefore become:

$$
\begin{aligned}
12 - 1 - 3 - 2 &= 6 \\
24 - 4 - 6 - 4 &= 10 \\
18 - 2 - 3 - 5 &= 8
\end{aligned}
$$

However, for a future year we cannot have such data; they do not exist. In

TABLE A-1. INPUT-OUTPUT FLOW TABLE

(In billions of dollars)

Industry Producing \ Industry Purchasing	1. Agriculture	2. Manufacturing	3. Trade and services	4. Final (household) demand	Total Gross Output
1. Agriculture	1	3	2	6	12
2. Manufacturing	4	6	4	10	24
3. Trade and services	2	3	5	8	18

using the input-output approach we typically begin analysis with estimates of final demands (bill of goods) for the future year. These final demands (Y_1, Y_2, and Y_3) may be based on demographic analysis and best judgment concerning the consumption pattern of the projected·population in the future year. Given our best projections of Y_1, Y_2, and Y_3, the problem is to determine values for

$$X_1, X_2, \text{ and } X_3; \quad \text{and} \quad \begin{matrix} x_{11}, x_{12}, x_{13} \\ x_{21}, x_{22}, x_{23} \\ x_{31}, x_{32}, x_{33} \end{matrix}$$

of equations 1.

We have twelve unknowns and only three equations for their determination. Provided these equations are consistent and independent, we must reduce the number of unknowns to *three* if we are to hope for a solution.[114] Input-output achieves this step through its assumption of constant production coefficients. From Table A-1 we observe that in the base year for which complete information was obtained the agricultural sector required:

1. $1 billion of agricultural product as inputs in order to produce $12 billion of output, or $0.083 of inputs of agricultural products per dollar output.

2. $4 billion of manufactured products as inputs in order to produce $12 billion of output, or $0.333 of inputs of manufactured products per dollar output.

3. $2 billion of trade and services as inputs in order to produce $12 billion of output, or $0.167 of inputs of trade and services per dollar output.

[114] The reader may recall from his high school algebra that the equation $x + y = 2$ does not yield a unique set of values for x and y. We have two unknowns and only one equation. If we add a second equation which is consistent with and independent of the first, such as $x - y = 0$, we have two equations in two unknowns and hence can determine a unique set of values for x and y.

In general, we must have as many independent and consistent equations as there are unknowns in a system if we are to determine the values of the unknowns.

If we assume that these cents' worth of inputs ($0.083, $0.333, and $0.167) per dollar output also obtain for all future years, we can estimate:

1. Purchases of agricultural products by the agricultural sector (the x_{11} of our equations) as equal to $0.083 times X_1, where X_1 is the unknown dollar output of the agricultural sector in the future year, that is, $x_{11} = a_{11}X_1$ where $a_{11} = \$0.083$.

2. Purchases of manufactured products by the agricultural sector (the x_{21} of our equations) as equal to $0.333 times X_1, that is, $x_{21} = a_{21}X_1$ where $a_{21} = \$0.333$.

3. Purchases of trade and services by the agricultural sector (the x_{31} of our equations) as equal to $0.167 times X_1, that is, $x_{31} = a_{31}X_1$ where $a_{31} = \$0.167$.

Similarly, where X_2 represents total output of the manufacturing sector in the future year, we have

$$x_{12} = a_{12}X_2$$
$$x_{22} = a_{22}X_2$$
$$x_{32} = a_{32}X_2$$

where, from Table A-1,

$$a_{12} = \tfrac{3}{24} = \$0.125$$
$$a_{22} = \tfrac{6}{24} = \$0.250$$
$$a_{33} = \tfrac{3}{24} = \$0.125$$

Finally, where X_3 represents total output of the trade and service sector in the future year, we have

$$x_{13} = a_{13}X_3$$
$$x_{23} = a_{23}X_3$$
$$x_{33} = a_{33}X_3$$

where from Table A-1,

$$a_{13} = \tfrac{2}{18} = \$0.111$$
$$a_{23} = \tfrac{4}{18} = \$0.222$$
$$a_{33} = \tfrac{5}{18} = \$0.278$$

By substitution of $a_{11}X_1$ for x_{11}, $a_{12}X_2$ for x_{12}, etc., equations 1 become

(2)
$$X_1 - a_{11}X_1 - a_{12}X_2 - a_{13}X_3 = Y_1$$
$$X_2 - a_{21}X_1 - a_{22}X_2 - a_{23}X_3 = Y_2$$
$$X_3 - a_{31}X_1 - a_{32}X_2 - a_{33}X_3 = Y_3$$

Thus by the assumption of constant production coefficients, input-output reduces the number of unknowns from twelve to three, namely X_1, X_2, and X_3. The set of constant production coefficients of equations 2 can be conveniently set down in matrix form as follows:

$$\begin{bmatrix} a_{11}, & a_{12}, & a_{13} \\ a_{21}, & a_{22}, & a_{23} \\ a_{31}, & a_{32}, & a_{33} \end{bmatrix}$$

which in our example equals

$$\begin{bmatrix} 0.083, & 0.125, & 0.111 \\ 0.333, & 0.250, & 0.222 \\ 0.167, & 0.125, & 0.278 \end{bmatrix}$$

Having reduced the number of unknowns so that there are only as many unknowns as equations, we must now solve for the values of the unknowns Here we may follow standard algebraic procedures. For example, we may multiply each term of the first of the set of equations 2 by a_{23} and of the second by a_{13}. Subtracting the resulting second equation from the first, we obtain

(3) $\quad (a_{23} - a_{23}a_{11} + a_{13}a_{21})X_1 + (a_{13}a_{22} - a_{13} - a_{23}a_{12})X_2 = a_{23}Y_1 - a_{13}Y_2$

from which equation the unknown variable X_3 has been eliminated.

In similar fashion we can multiply the second of equations 2 by $1 - a_{33}$ and the third by $- a_{23}$; and by subtracting one of the resulting equations from the other, we derive a second equation in two unknowns (X_1 and X_2), from which the unknown variable X_3 has been eliminated. We have now derived two equations in two unknowns. Following the same procedure, we can multiply through each of these two equations by an appropriate term, subtract, and obtain an equation which yields X_1 in terms of the constant a's of the equations. Likewise, we can derive X_2 in this manner; and, by repeating the entire set of steps, except that we multiply through by different constants, we obtain X_3. We find that

$$\begin{aligned} X_1 &= A_{11}Y_1 + A_{12}Y_2 + A_{13}Y_3 \\ (4) \qquad X_2 &= A_{21}Y_1 + A_{22}Y_2 + A_{23}Y_3 \\ X_3 &= A_{31}Y_1 + A_{32}Y_2 + A_{33}Y_3 \end{aligned}$$

where A_{11} equals

$$\frac{(1 - a_{22})(1 - a_{33}) - a_{23}a_{32}}{\begin{aligned}(1 - a_{11})(1 - a_{22})(1 - a_{33}) &- a_{12}a_{23}a_{31} - a_{13}a_{21}a_{32} - a_{13}a_{31}(1 - a_{22}) \\ &- a_{12}a_{21}(1 - a_{33}) - a_{23}a_{32}(1 - a_{11})\end{aligned}}$$

and where every other A coefficient in equations 4 is a *constant* which is derived from the a coefficients of equations 2 and which involves as many terms as A_{11}.

It is important to emphasize that these A coefficients are constants. They are derived from standard operations with constant production coefficients (the a's) which are given at the start. The A coefficients are independent of the magnitude and composition of final demand (bill of goods), that is, of Y_1, Y_2, and Y_3. No matter how the Y_1, Y_2, and Y_3 vary, we multiply them respectively by the same A's to derive the unknown sector outputs, namely, X_1, X_2, and X_3. The A's in essence register both direct and indirect requirements. For example, in the second of equations 4, A_{21} represents the cents' worth of the output of industry 2 required both directly and indirectly to produce one dollar of commodity 1 for final demand, and $A_{21}Y_1$ represents *total* direct and indirect requirements of the output of industry 2 in order that the system be able to deliver Y_1 quantity of the first commodity to the final demand sector; A_{22} represents direct and indirect requirements by industry 2 of its own product to produce one dollar of its output for final demand, and $A_{22}Y_2$ represents total direct and indirect requirements of such product in order that the system be able to deliver Y_2 quantity of its product to the final demand sector, etc. Thus $A_{21}Y_1 + A_{22}Y_2 + A_{23}Y_3$ equals total direct and indirect requirements of the product of industry 2 to produce the set of outputs to be delivered to the final demand sectors and which must, in the input-output framework, equal total output of industry 2 (i.e., X_2).

It should be noted that these A's provide a general solution to the problem. When they are arranged in the following way

$$\begin{bmatrix} A_{11}, & A_{12}, & A_{13} \\ A_{21}, & A_{22}, & A_{23} \\ A_{31}, & A_{32}, & A_{33} \end{bmatrix}$$

they form a matrix, and in particular a matrix which is the inverse of a second matrix:

$$\begin{bmatrix} (1 - a_{11}), & -a_{12}, & -a_{13} \\ -a_{21}, & (1 - a_{22}), & -a_{23} \\ -a_{31}, & -a_{32}, & (1 - a_{33}) \end{bmatrix}$$

where the a's are the constant production coefficients already set down in matrix form and where each A is defined in terms of the a's as was A_{11}. If we take values for the a's as they have been computed, the values of the A's are found to be:

$$A_{11} = 1.2264 \quad A_{21} = 0.6570 \quad A_{31} = 0.4003$$
$$A_{12} = 0.2493 \quad A_{22} = 1.5398 \quad A_{32} = 0.3412$$
$$A_{13} = 0.2623 \quad A_{23} = 0.5677 \quad A_{33} = 1.5465$$

These values can be set down in corresponding matrix form:

$$\begin{bmatrix} 1.2264, & 0.6570, & 0.4003 \\ 0.2493, & 1.5398, & 0.3412 \\ 0.2623, & 0.5677, & 1.5465 \end{bmatrix}$$

and they represent the constants by which Y_1, Y_2, and Y_3 are to be multiplied in order to derive estimates of X_1, X_2, and X_3. Hence we quickly estimate the implications of diverse hypotheses and assumptions, such as high, medium, and low levels of consumption, and high, medium, and low fertility of a population. Corresponding to each hypothesis or assumption is a set of values of Y_1, Y_2, and Y_3 which can be quickly multiplied by the appropriate constants (the A's) to obtain estimates of X_1, X_2, and X_3.

Thus far we have thought in terms of 3 sectors within the structural matrix of our isolated region. We may now generalize. There are n sectors. The matrix of constant production coefficients becomes

$$\begin{bmatrix} a_{11}, & a_{12}, & a_{13}, & \cdots, & a_{1n} \\ a_{21}, & a_{22}, & a_{23}, & \cdots, & a_{2n} \\ a_{31}, & a_{32}, & a_{33}, & \cdots, & a_{3n} \\ \cdots & \cdots & \cdots & \cdots & \cdots \\ a_{n1}, & a_{n2}, & a_{n3}, & \cdots, & a_{nn} \end{bmatrix}$$

Once again, as we go down any column, the a's tell us the cents' worth of diverse inputs (as produced by the industries indicated by the first subscript) required to produce one dollar of output in the industry indicated by the second subscript. With these a's, we reformulate equations 2 as follows:

$$\begin{aligned} X_1 - a_{11}X_1 - a_{12}X_2 - a_{13}X_3 - \cdots - a_{1n}X_n &= Y_1 \\ X_2 - a_{21}X_1 - a_{22}X_2 - a_{23}X_3 - \cdots - a_{2n}X_n &= Y_2 \\ X_3 - a_{31}X_1 - a_{32}X_2 - a_{33}X_3 - \cdots - a_{3n}X_3 &= Y_3 \\ \cdots \cdots \cdots \cdots \cdots \cdots \cdots \cdots \cdots \cdots \\ X_n - a_{n1}X_1 - a_{n2}X_2 - a_{n3}X_3 - \cdots - a_{nn}X_n &= Y_n \end{aligned}$$

(5)

Again each equation indicates how the total gross output of any industrial sector is allocated to each industrial sector (including itself) and to final demand.

The set of equations 5 which are in n unknowns, and which are n in number, may be solved. We find that:

$$
\begin{aligned}
X_1 &= A_{11}Y_1 + A_{12}Y_2 + A_{13}Y_3 + \cdots + A_{1n}Y_n \\
X_2 &= A_{21}Y_1 + A_{22}Y_2 + A_{23}Y_3 + \cdots + A_{2n}Y_n \\
X_3 &= A_{31}Y_1 + A_{32}Y_2 + A_{33}Y_3 + \cdots + A_{3n}Y_n \\
&\cdots \cdots \cdots \cdots \cdots \cdots \cdots \cdots \cdots \cdots \cdots \\
X_n &= A_{n1}Y_1 + A_{n2}Y_2 + A_{n3}Y_3 + \cdots + A_{nn}Y_n
\end{aligned}
$$

(6)

Each of the A's in equations 6 is related to all the n^2 constant production coefficients (the a's) in much the same way as A_{11} in equation 4 is related to each of the nine constant production coefficients of equations 2 that relate to a three-sector structural matrix. If, for example, we were to consider a 500-sector breakdown of an isolated regional economy, the denominator of each A in equations 6 would contain 1000 terms ($= 2n$), each term being the product of 500 constants [a's and $(1 - a_{ii})$]; and the numerator of each A would contain 998 ($= 2n - 2$) terms, each term being the product of 499 constants [a's and $(1 - a_{ii})$]. These A's can be arranged once again in matrix form:

$$
\begin{bmatrix}
A_{11}, & A_{12}, & \cdots, & A_{1n} \\
A_{21}, & A_{22}, & \cdots, & A_{2n} \\
\cdot & \cdot & \cdots & \cdot \\
A_{n1}, & A_{n2}, & \cdots, & A_{nn}
\end{bmatrix}
$$

which is the inverse of

$$
\begin{bmatrix}
(1 - a_{11}), & -a_{12}, & \cdots, & -a_{1n} \\
-a_{21}, & (1 - a_{22}), & \cdots, & -a_{2n} \\
\cdot & \cdot & \cdots & \cdot \\
-a_{n1}, & -a_{n2}, & \cdots, & (1 - a_{nn})
\end{bmatrix}
$$

and which provides the constants by which the final demands (the $Y_1, Y_2, \cdots, Y_n$) of any given problem are to be multiplied in order to yield estimates of sector outputs ($X_1, X_2, \cdots, X_n$).

Immediately apparent is the tremendous saving in time and effort which a general solution entailing the calculation of the set of A's provides. In the text we described the cumbersome round-by-round (iterative) procedure for evaluating the impact of a change in the bill of goods. When there are many industrial sectors, this procedure can be extremely unwieldy, time consuming, and expensive. This is so even if, because of the convergence of the rounds, it is only necessary to compute the first five or six rounds. In sharp contrast, the computation is direct, quick, and simple once the inverse has been calculated.[115]

[115] Inverses for systems of equations which number below ten have been successfully computed on desk calculators. However, as the number of equations increases, the number of computations to be performed on a desk calculator mounts very rapidly. Therefore, in large systems it is essential that electronic computing equipment be used. Codes are now generally available which permit the solution of systems of equations numbering in the hundreds by suitable machines within a relatively short time.

It then becomes feasible to examine the impact of many different types of changes in the government, households, capital formation, and other final demand sectors.   We simply multiply any relevant set of estimates of $Y_1, \cdots, Y_n$ by the A's as indicated in equations 6.

As already observed, the A coefficients register direct and indirect requirements For example, the coefficient A_{ij} reflects the sum of direct and indirect input requirements of the commodity i in order for the system to deliver one dollar of output of industry j to the final demand sector.   In essence, the use of the inverse composed of these A's permits us to calculate at one blow the n rounds of requirements.   Notwithstanding these major computational advantages of an inverse, we must use such an inverse with caution.   Full reliance on an inverse tends to lead to an overmechanical approach to the analysis of economic problems.   Because an investigator feeds into a computing machine a set of constant production coefficients (about many of which he may have qualms) and receives in return a set of constant coefficients (the A's) by which to multiply the final demands, he has a minimum of control, if any, over the operation.   He cannot apply that kind of check on his assumptions regarding the set of constant production coefficients to be used, on his judgment regarding the number and kinds of industries and regions, on his implicit postulates concerning the price system and resource limitations, etc., which is possible when he calculates each round of requirements.   He does not have an opportunity to obtain that "feel" for magnitudes which he acquires in a round-by-round computation, nor does he gain those insights into the structure of a regional economy and that understanding of its functioning which stem from such a computation.

At this point it may be helpful to state the problem in matrix form.   Let $\mathbf{a}$ represent the matrix of given production coefficients

$$
\mathbf{a} = \begin{bmatrix}
a_{11}, & a_{12}, & \cdots, & a_{1n} \\
a_{21}, & a_{22}, & \cdots, & a_{2n} \\
\cdot & \cdot & \cdots & \cdot \\
a_{n1}, & a_{n2}, & \cdots, & a_{nn}
\end{bmatrix}
$$

Let $\mathbf{I}$ represent the identity or unit matrix of n columns and n rows, all of whose elements have zero value, except the ones along the principal diagonal and these have values of unity, that is,

$$
\mathbf{I} = \begin{bmatrix}
1, & 0, & \cdots, & 0 \\
0, & 1, & \cdots, & 0 \\
\cdot & \cdot & \cdots & \cdot \\
0, & 0, & \cdots, & 1
\end{bmatrix}
$$

If we subtract the matrix $\mathbf{a}$ from $\mathbf{I}$ (which in matrix algebra involves subtracting each element of $\mathbf{a}$ from the corresponding element in $\mathbf{I}$), we obtain a third matrix which may be designated $(\mathbf{I} - \mathbf{a})$ where

$$
\mathbf{I} - \mathbf{a} = \begin{bmatrix}
(1 - a_{11}), & - a_{12}, & \cdots, & - a_{1n} \\
- a_{21}, & (1 - a_{22}), & \cdots, & - a_{2n} \\
\cdot & \cdot & \cdots & \cdot \\
- a_{n1}, & - a_{n2}, & \cdots, & (1 - a_{nn})
\end{bmatrix}
$$

We now let $\mathbf{Y}$ stand for the column sequence of final demands ordered by industry number, namely $\begin{bmatrix} Y_1 \\ Y_2 \\ \cdot \\ \cdot \\ \cdot \\ Y_n \end{bmatrix}$, which ordered sequence may be termed a *vector*.

Also let $\mathbf{X}$ stand for the column sequence of sector outputs ordered by industry number, namely $\begin{bmatrix} X_1 \\ X_2 \\ \cdot \\ \cdot \\ \cdot \\ X_n \end{bmatrix}$, which also may be considered a vector. Then, bearing

in mind the process of multiplying a matrix by a column vector, which involves multiplying each element of a matrix row by the corresponding element of the column vector and summing,[116] and which yields as the product a column vector, we may state equations 5 as

(7) $\qquad\qquad\qquad (\mathbf{I} - \mathbf{a})\mathbf{X} = \mathbf{Y}$ (footnote 117)

Further if we let $\mathbf{A}$ represent the matrix of A's, that is,

$$\mathbf{A} = \begin{bmatrix} A_{11}, & A_{12}, & \cdots, & A_{1n} \\ A_{21}, & A_{22}, & \cdots, & A_{2n} \\ \multicolumn{4}{c}{\cdot\ \cdot\ \cdot\ \cdot\ \cdot\ \cdot\ \cdot\ \cdot} \\ A_{n1}, & A_{n2}, & \cdots, & A_{nn} \end{bmatrix}$$

we can state equations 6 as

(8) $\qquad\qquad\qquad\qquad \mathbf{X} = \mathbf{A}\mathbf{Y}$

where $\mathbf{A}$ is termed the inverse of the matrix $(\mathbf{I} - \mathbf{a})$, that is, $\mathbf{A} = (\mathbf{I} - \mathbf{a})^{-1}$ (footnote 118).

[116] Thus by (1) multiplying the first element in row i of the $(\mathbf{I} - \mathbf{a})$ matrix by the first element in the column vector, the second element in the same matrix row by the second element in the column vector, etc., $\ldots$, and finally the nth element in matrix row i by the nth element in the column vector, and (2) summing the resulting n products, we have the value of the ith element (namely Y_i) in the column vector resulting from the multiplication, that is,

$$- a_{i1}X_1 - a_{i2}X_2 - a_{i3}X_3, \cdots, (1 - a_{ii})X_i, \cdots, - a_{in}X_n = Y_i$$

which is the ith equation (with some terms rearranged) of the set of equations 5. Obviously, for such multiplication to be performed, the column vector must be conformable to the matrix, that is, have as many elements in its column as the matrix has in each of its rows.

[117] Or, $\mathbf{I}\mathbf{X} - \mathbf{a}\mathbf{X} = \mathbf{Y}$ which, since $\mathbf{I}\mathbf{X} = \mathbf{X}$, can be stated $\mathbf{X} = \mathbf{a}\mathbf{X} + \mathbf{Y}$. This last equation simply states that total output of any sector is composed of that part absorbed by industrial operations of an economy plus that part required to satisfy final demand.

[118] Thus, the inverse $\mathbf{A}$ may be thought of as a complex reciprocal of $(\mathbf{I} - \mathbf{a})$, which can be multiplied by any size and composition of final demand in order to determine the size of total output from each industry.

If we relax the assumption of an isolated region, and consider a closed system of several regions, that is, an interregional input-output model of the Isard variety, which has been discussed previously, the same equations 7 and 8 pertain, except that if there are U regions:

1. The **a** matrix contains U^2n^2 elements, the elements along any row being Un in number and running from $a_{i1}^{K1}, a_{i2}^{K1}, \cdots, a_{ij}^{KL}, \cdots, a_{in}^{KU}$ where the row refers to the ith industry of region K. Each element a_{ij}^{KL} is a constant and indicates the cents' worth of the product of industry i in region K required per dollar output of industry j in region L.

2. The **I** and $(\mathbf{I} - \mathbf{a})$ matrices have Un, instead of n rows and columns.

3. The final demand vector **Y** consists of Un elements, $\{Y_1^1, Y_2^1, \cdots, Y_i^K, \cdots, Y_n^U\}$.

4. The sector output vector **X** consists of Un elements, $\{X_1^1, X_1^2, \cdots, X_i^K, \cdots, X_n^U\}$.

5. The **A** matrix contains U^2n^2 elements, the element A_{ij}^{KL} being a constant and indicating the direct and indirect requirements for the output of industry i in region K in order for the system to deliver to the final demand sectors one dollar of output of industry j of region L.

Alternatively, for an isolated region we could present equations 5 as

$$(9) \qquad X_i - \sum_{j=1}^{n} a_{ij} X_j = Y_i \quad \text{(footnote 119)} \qquad i = 1, \cdots, n$$

And equations 6 as

$$(10) \qquad X_i = \sum_{j=1}^{n} A_{ij} Y_j \qquad i = 1, \cdots, n$$

For an interregional framework, we would have as the counterpart to equations 9

$$(11) \qquad X_i^K - \sum_{L=1}^{U} \sum_{j=1}^{n} a_{ij}^{KL} X_j^L = Y_i^K \quad \text{(footnote 120)} \qquad \begin{matrix} i = 1, \cdots, n \\ K = 1, \cdots, U \end{matrix}$$

and as a counterpart to equations 10

$$X_i^K = \sum_{L=1}^{U} \sum_{j=1}^{n} A_{ij}^{KL} Y_j^L \qquad \begin{matrix} i = 1, \cdots, n \\ K = 1, \cdots, U \end{matrix}$$

---

[119] Equations 1 when extended to encompass n endogenous sectors could be presented as

$$X_i - \sum_{j=1}^{n} x_{ij} = Y_i \qquad i = 1, \cdots, n$$

[120] Equations 1 when extended to encompass U regions and n endogenous sectors in each could be presented as

$$X_i^K - \sum_{L=1}^{U} \sum_{j=1}^{n} x_{ij}^{KL} = Y_i^K \qquad \begin{matrix} i = 1, \cdots, n \\ K = 1, \cdots, U. \end{matrix}$$

References

1. Barna, Tibor, "Input-Output Analysis in the United Kingdom," in *Input-Output Relations*, Netherlands Economic Institute, Leiden, 1953.

2. Barnett, Harold J., *Energy Coefficients and Autonomous Demands for the Emergency Model*, U. S. Bureau of Mines, Interindustry Research Item No. 4, Washington, D.C., April 1952.

3. ———, "Specific Industry Output Projections," in *Long-Range Economic Projections*, Studies in Income and Wealth, Vol. 16, National Bureau of Economic Research, Princeton University Press, Princeton, New Jersey, 1954.

4. Berman, Edward B., *The 1955 and 1975 Interindustry Final Bills of Goods and Generated Activity*, U. S. Bureau of Mines, Interindustry Analysis Branch, Item No. 16, Washington, D.C., Feb. 1953.

5. Chenery, Hollis B., "Interregional and International Input-Output Analysis," in *Structural Interdependence of the Economy*, ed. by Tibor Barna, John Wiley, New York, 1954.

6. ———, "Regional Analysis," in *The Structure and Growth of the Italian Economy*, U. S. Mutual Security Agency, Rome, 1953.

7. Craig, Paul G., "Location Factors in the Development of Steel Centers," *Papers and Proceedings of the Regional Science Association*, Vol. 3 (1957).

8. Cumberland, John H., *Examples of Variations in the Behavior of Critical Material Input Coefficients*, U. S. Bureau of Mines, Interindustry Research Item No. 17, Washington, D.C., Nov. 1952.

9. Dorfman, Robert, "The Nature and Significance of Input-Output," *Review of Economics and Statistics*, Vol. 36 (May 1954).

10. Evans, W. Duane, and Marvin Hoffenberg, "The Interindustry Relations Study for 1947," *Review of Economics and Statistics*, Vol. 34 (May 1952).

11. Garnsey, Morris E., "The Dimensions of Regional Science," *Papers and Proceedings of the Regional Science Association*, Vol. 2 (1956).

12. Grosse, Robert N., *Capital Requirements for the Expansion of Industrial Capacity*, Vols. I and II, U. S. Bureau of the Budget, Washington, D.C., Nov. 1953.

13. ———, "The Structure of Capital," in *Studies in the Structure of the American Economy*, ed. by W. W. Leontief et al., Oxford University Press, New York, 1953.

14. Harvard Economic Research Project, *Report on Research*, Cambridge, Massachusetts, annual.

15. Hirsch, Werner Z., "An Application of Area Input-Output Analysis," *Papers and Proceedings of the Regional Science Association*, Vol. 5 (1959).

16. Isard, Walter, "Interregional and Regional Input-Output Analysis: A Model of a Space-Economy," *Review of Economics and Statistics*, Vol. 33 (Nov. 1951).

17. ———, *Location and Space-Economy*, John Wiley, New York, 1956.

18. ———, "Location Theory and Trade Theory: Short-Run Analysis," *Quarterly Journal of Economics*, Vol. 68 (May 1954).

19. ———, "Regional Commodity Balances and Interregional Commodity Flows," *American Economic Review*, Vol. 43 (May 1953).

20. ———, "Regional Science, the Concept of Region and Regional Structure," *Papers and Proceedings of the Regional Science Association*, Vol. 2 (1956).

21. ———, "Some Emerging Concepts and Techniques for Regional Analysis," *Zeitschrift für die Gesamte Staatswissenschaft*, Vol. 109 (1953).

22. Isard, Walter, "Some Empirical Results and Problems of Regional Input-Output Analysis," in *Studies in the Structure of the American Economy*, ed. by W. W. Leontief et al., Oxford University Press, New York, 1953.

23. ———, "Some Locational Factors in the Iron and Steel Industry Since the Early Nineteenth Century," *Journal of Political Economy*, Vol. 56 (June 1948).

24. ———, and William M. Capron, "The Future Locational Pattern of Iron and Steel Production in the United States," *Journal of Political Economy*, Vol. 57 (April 1949).

25. ———, and John Cumberland, "New England as a Possible Location for an Integrated Iron and Steel Works," *Economic Geography*, Vol. 26 (Oct. 1950).

26. ———, and Guy Freutel, "Regional and National Product Projections and Their Interrelations," in *Long-Range Economic Projection*, National Bureau of Economic Research, Studies in Income and Wealth, Vol. 16, Princeton University Press, Princeton, New Jersey, 1954.

27. ———, and Robert A. Kavesh, "Economic Structural Interrelations of Metropolitan Regions," *American Journal of Sociology*, Vol. 60 (Sept. 1954).

28. ———, and Robert E. Kuenne, "The Impact of Steel Upon the Greater New York–Philadelphia Industrial Region: A Study in Agglomeration Projection," *Review of Economics and Statistics*, Vol. 35 (Nov. 1953).

29. Jaffe, S. A., "Final Demand Sectors," in Technical Supplement to National Bureau of Economic Research [41].

30. James, Preston E., "Toward a Further Understanding of the Regional Concept," *Annals of the Association of American Geographers*, Vol. 42 (Sept. 1952).

31. ———, and Clarence F. Jones, eds., *American Geography: Inventory and Prospect*, Syracuse University Press, Syracuse, New York, 1954.

32. Kavesh, Robert A., *Interdependence and the Metropolitan Region*, doctoral dissertation, Harvard University, Cambridge, Massachusetts, 1953.

33. Kuenne, Robert E., *The Use of Input-Output Techniques for the Estimation of Employment in the Delaware Valley*, doctoral dissertation, Harvard University, Cambridge, Massachusetts, 1953.

34. ———, "Walras, Leontief, and the Interdependence of Economic Activity," *Quarterly Journal of Economics*, Vol. 67 (Aug. 1954).

35. Leontief, Wassily W., "Some Basic Problems of Empirical Input-Output Analysis," in National Bureau of Economic Research [41].

36. ———, *The Structure of American Economy 1919–1939*, Oxford University Press, New York, 1951.

37. ——— et al., *Studies in the Structure of the American Economy*, Oxford University Press, New York, 1953.

38. Licht, I. H., "Government," in Technical Supplement to National Bureau of Economic Research [41].

39. Morgenstern, Oskar, *On the Accuracy of Economic Observations*, Princeton University Press, Princeton, New Jersey, 1950.

40. Moses, Leon N., "The Stability of Interregional Trading Patterns and Input-Output Analysis," *American Economic Review*, Vol. 45 (Dec. 1955).

41. National Bureau of Economic Research, *Input-Output Analysis: An Appraisal*, Studies in Income and Wealth, Vol. 18, Princeton University Press, Princeton, New Jersey, 1955.

42. Norton, J. DeW., "Research Required in the Application of Interindustry Economics," in National Bureau of Economic Research [41].

43. Odum, Howard W., "The Promise of Regionalism," in *Regionalism in America*, ed. by M. Jensen, University of Wisconsin Press, Madison, Wisconsin, 1952.

44. Phillips, A., "The Tableau Économique as a Simple Leontief Model," *Quarterly Journal of Economics*, Vol. 69 (Feb. 1955).

45. Riley, Vera, and Robert L. Allen, *Interindustry Economic Studies: A Comprehensive Bibliography on Interindustry Research*, Operations Research Office, Johns Hopkins University Press, Baltimore, Maryland, 1955.

46. Rodgers, Allan, "Industrial Inertia—A Major Factor in the Location of the Steel Industry in the United States," *Geographical Review*, Vol. 42 (Jan. 1952).

47. U. S. Army, Board of Engineers for Rivers and Harbors, *Water-Borne Commerce of the United States, Domestic Deep-Sea and Lakewise Traffic, 1950*, Washington, D.C., June 1952.

48. U. S. Army, Office of the Chief of Engineers, *Commercial Statistics: Water-Borne Commerce of the United States*, Washington, D.C., annually.

49. U. S. Bureau of the Budget, *Standard Industrial Classification Manual*, Washington, D.C., 1949.

50. U. S. Interstate Commerce Commission, Bureau of Transport Economics and Statistics, *Carload Waybill Analyses, State-to-State Shipments of Commodities*, Washington, D.C., annually.

51. University of Maryland, Bureau of Business and Economic Research, *Some Relationships Between U. S. Consumption and Natural Resources, 1899, 1947, 1954*, College Park, Maryland, June 1958.

52. Vance, Rupert, "The Regional Concept as a Tool for Social Research," in *Regionalism in America*, ed. by M. Jensen, University of Wisconsin Press, Madison, Wisconsin, 1952.

53. Vining, Rutledge, "Delimitation of Economic Areas: Statistical Conceptions in the Study of the Spatial Structure of an Economic System," *Journal of the American Statistical Association*, Vol. 48 (March 1943).

54. ———, "A Description of Certain Spatial Aspects of an Economic System," *Economic Development and Cultural Change*, Vol. 3 (Jan. 1955).

55. Walras, Léon, *Elements of Pure Economics*, translated by W. Jaffé, Richard Irwin Inc., Homewood, Illinois, 1954.

56. Weitzman, M., and P. M. Ritz, "Foreign Trade," in the Technical Supplement to National Bureau of Economic Research [41].

Chapter 9

Industrial Complex Analysis*

A. INTRODUCTION

Crystal-clear is the fact that the location of many activities is directly linked with the location of one or more other activities. Examples range from fish canning and the fishing industry to the intricate network of activities found in the garment center of New York City, or in the metal trades complex of Birmingham, England. If an industry-by-industry comparative cost approach can deal satisfactorily with such relation, frequently it can do so only by extensive comparison and cumbersome reworking. Hence, the analyst seeks an approach which cuts across several industries, treating at one time the interrelated factors as they affect the location of each.

Input-output, as developed in the previous chapter, is one such approach. It is a general technique which points up well the complex interdependence among diverse business, consumer, political, and other cultural units of society. It effectively uncovers a significant amount of the intricate structure of an economy and thus has had much appeal to regional scientists dissatisfied with the more partial studies characteristic of the past. Unfortunately, the use of such a general technique as interregional input-output is not without opportunity cost. The gains scored by being able to cut into more of the interrelatedness of society must be

* This chapter was written with Eugene W. Schooler.

375

weighed against the sacrifice of certain elements of reality, that is, the need to work with such unrealistic postulates as constant cost production and unchanging supply channels. As a consequence, on a number of occasions the analyst, after he has completed an elaborate general interdependence study, comes to question whether the returns from such a broad framework justified its cost. And after considerable thought he asks whether it would not have been more profitable to have sought less generality, to have attempted to cut across less of the interrelatedness of society in order not to have been compelled to make *all* the unrealistic assumptions required by interregional or regional input-output. It is at this point that he is led to scrutiny of the industrial complex technique.

Put in more specific terms, the regional scientist is particularly sensitive to the inability of interregional input-output to handle adequately economies of scale, localization economies, urbanization economies, and regional price variations resulting in or associated with the use of different factor proportions. At the same time, he is fully aware that the industry-by-industry comparative cost approach misses the heart of interindustry relations. Cannot a hybrid interdependence technique be evolved which might retain the more important inter-industry relations, yet not lose the strength of the comparative cost approach and its treatment of such forces as economies of scale? This is the basic question to which we address ourselves in this chapter in presenting and evaluating the industrial complex approach.[1]

In what follows, we first define the concept and structure of an industrial complex, with the liberal use of the concept of an interindustry matrix as developed in the previous chapter. We then proceed in a rather orthodox but extended comparative cost fashion. We examine in order transport cost differentials, labor cost differentials, and other processing cost differentials, scale economies, and localization and urbanization economies. All this inquiry, however, will be conducted in a framework which permits changing factor proportions and changing activity mix (process substitution). The particular set of steps in this comparative cost approach follows the modern Weberian framework as developed in *Location and Space-Economy*.

In contrast with previous chapters, we shall illustrate the approach with extensive empirical materials from a single case study, since only in this manner can a balanced appraisal of this approach be achieved.

[1] Detailed materials and procedures and further discussion of industrial complex analysis are contained in W. Isard and T. Vietorisz [6], W. Isard and E. W. Schooler [3], and W. Isard, E. W. Schooler, and T. Vietorisz [5].

B. The Industrial Complex: Definition and Identification

1. definition

An industrial complex may be defined as a set of activities occurring at a given location and belonging to a group (subsystem) of activities which are subject to important production, marketing, or other interrelations. (In the extreme, the set of activities may reduce to a single activity, which for convenience of exposition is still defined as a complex.[2])

For example, one reference group of activities may comprise the successive stages in the manufacture of an end product or class of end products— such as coal and ore mining through pig iron and steel ingot production to the final fabricated steel products. From this group of activities, any number of complexes may develop at different locations. Starting from the mining of the raw materials ore and coal, each successive stage or activity constitutes at least part of the market for the immediately preceding stage; conversely each stage looks to the preceding stage for its basic inputs. The locational interdependence of activities within any particular complex stands in bold relief. The location pattern of steel ingot production cannot be ascertained without a knowledge of the location of pig iron production. But the location pattern for pig iron production cannot be established unless the location of its market, that is, the production of ingot steel, is known. Furthermore, these activities are also influenced by the location of ore and coal deposits as well as steel-rolling and finishing operations and the markets for fabricated steel products. Hence, to repeat, an adequate regional analysis must consider the whole combination of activities in their various interrelations.

Another type of complex may derive from the joint production of two or more commodities from a single class of raw materials—such as diverse food, fertilizer, and industrial products derived from livestock. Still another type of complex might be based on a single but fairly broad industrial process, such as a nucleonics complex oriented to either fission, fusion, or both. Or a complex might evolve from a reference group of

[2] For example, in considering what set of steel–steel-fabricating activities may be profitably located at a coal site, that is, the nature of a steel–steel-fabricating complex which may evolve at that site, it may turn out that only coal mining is justified. Then the steel–steel-fabricating complex at the coal site reduces down to a single activity only, and the term complex can be discarded when reference is made to the coal site. However, before the completion of an empirical study we cannot know whether or not a single activity is justified at the coal site. Therefore, in order to avoid constant use of the phrase "industrial complex or single activity" when speaking of possible industrial development at the coal site, or any other site, we simply define industrial complex to include the single-activity case as a limit. The analysis remains unaffected by this broadening of the definition.

activities centered around a single end product or service, broadly defined, such as shelter or clothing, including all the activities directly related and antecedent to the end product.

Finally, a complex might involve two or more basic raw materials and processes, two or more intermediate products which may or may not enter into the production of intermediates, all of which may combine to form two or more end products. As will be developed in greater detail below, acetylene and hydrogen cyanide can be produced from alternative sources of hydrocarbons, such as oil, natural gas, and coal. In turn these intermediates can be used to manufacture other intermediates, for example acrylonitrile, which can be transformed into final-stage intermediates such as orlon fiber, and ultimately into end products such as textile fabrics. In this group of activities three industries are represented, petroleum refining, chemicals, and textiles. Furthermore, most of the intermediate commodities have alternative uses and thus alternative markets. But with regard to this particular production sequence, none of the activities could be considered a priori as having an independent production location pattern. And from the required joint locational evaluation, multiple locations may be indicated for some of the activities as a consequence of the multiple uses for the commodities.

At this juncture, it is wise to recognize a possible objection to this definition. It may be contended that since *all* economic activities are interrelated—since everything depends on everything else—the analyst can, strictly speaking, justify nothing less than the evaluation of a general spatial equilibrium in each locational study. Actually, the very selection of the group of activities to be evaluated involves, in one sense, a consideration of all economic activities, with the decision that the interrelations of most of them with the activity or activities under investigation are of such a small order that they can justifiably be ignored (particularly when research resources are limited).

2. SELECTION OF MEANINGFUL COMPLEXES

As with the precise delimitation of specific industries and regions meaningful for a given study, the selection of specific industrial complexes to be analyzed is relative. It is relative to the purpose of the study, availability of data, research resources at hand, and inclinations of the researcher. This point is well illustrated by an industrial complex study undertaken with reference to potential industrial development in Puerto Rico.

In a study of Puerto Rico, the investigator may be inclined to begin analysis in a rather traditional fashion, namely to make a reconnaisance of resources. (This was in fact the approach adopted in the study from which the empirical materials of this chapter are taken.) He notes that Puerto Rico has an abundance of labor possessing certain types of skills (frequently associated with the textiles trades) and available at relatively low cost. He also bears in mind Puerto Rico's excellent access to Venezuelan oil, which in a broad sense constitutes its second-best resource. To him the problem may then be to study the ways in which the use of these two resources can be linked in order to identify desirable industrial development in this region. (Note that already the range of meaningful complexes for Puerto Rico is narrowed to those based on oil as the primary hydrocarbon source.) But this is not a simple problem. There are a large number of products which can be produced from oil, and there are many ways of producing each. Figure 1 sketches some of the technological possibilities. The basic raw material, crude oil, yields the familiar products: gasoline, kerosene, fuel oil, and lubricating oil. In addition, it yields less familiar gases and liquid fractions such as hydrogen, methane, ethane, ethylene, propane, propylene, butanes, butylenes, and benzene. Moreover, various products such as gasoline, kerosene, fuel oil, and lubricating oil can be subjected to pressure and temperature and cracked to yield more of these refinery gases and liquid fractions.

Given the current and likely future state of technology, we may judge on the basis of engineering studies that these various gases and liquid fractions will find increasing use in the production of various end products. A glance at the top of Figure 1 indicates that methane can be converted into hydrogen, and this in successive stages into nitric acid, ammonium nitrate, urea, and ultimately fertilizer. Methane also yields methanol which, via formaldehyde, yields plastics. Or methane can be converted into HCN and acetylene and ultimately the synthetic fibers, Orlon, Dynel, and Acrilan. Or acrylonitrile can be produced from acetylene, which in turn may be produced from ethane, ethylene, propane, or propylene. Acetylene, however, may be used to produce acetic acid which leads to rayon or to vinyl chloride which can be processed into polyvinyl chloride and plastics. Or the ethylene can be converted into any number of products and ultimately into plastics, synthetic rubber, antiknock fluid, synthetic fibers, antifreeze, detergents, and explosives. Propane converted into propylene can also be used for the production of many of these end products or can enter into LPG (liquid petroleum gases), a high-grade fuel. The naphthenes yield an interesting group of products, of which the most familiar are nylon, synthetic rubber, plastics, paints, insecticides, and synthetic fibers.

In short, there is a tremendous number of possibilities for the utilization of crude oil and refinery gases and liquid fractions. Which of these production possibilities or combination of these possibilities (or of other

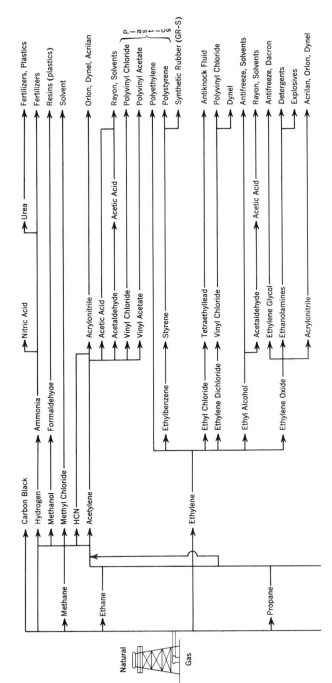

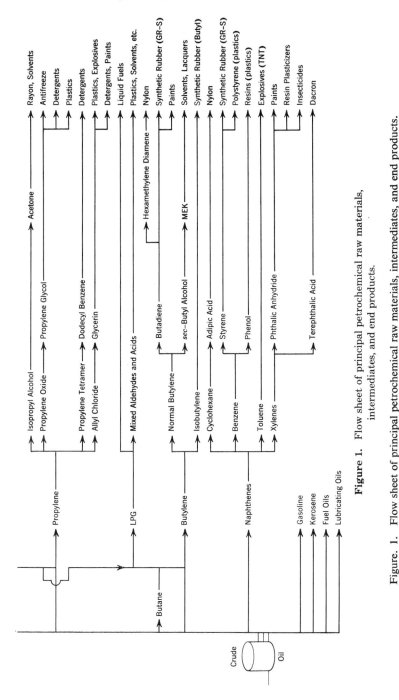

Figure 1. Flow sheet of principal petrochemical raw materials, intermediates, and end products.

Figure. 1.   Flow sheet of principal petrochemical raw materials, intermediates, and end products.

possibilities not listed in Figure 1) is optimal for Puerto Rico? From a knowledge of Puerto Rico which can readily be accumulated by an investigator, it becomes fairly evident that there are certain types of products in whose production Puerto Rico has a good chance for comparative advantage. For example, consider the various end products, listed at the extreme right of Figure 1, which stem from ethylene. Since Puerto Rico's chief economic resource tends to lie in its labor force and is associated with low labor cost per efficiency unit of labor, it is clear that of the several products which might use a million pounds of ethylene, those requiring the greatest amount of labor of the type available in Puerto Rico are likely to show greatest advantage for a Puerto Rico location, *ceteris paribus*. Of these, synthetic fibers require the greatest amounts of labor. On this account they are of interest. However, this is only one of many considerations. The investigator must view the entire economy of Puerto Rico to isolate the several important considerations which should govern the type of industrial complex to be recommended. If the commodity balance of trade of Puerto Rico is examined, he finds a very heavy import of fertilizer. In fact, practically all commercial fertilizers which Puerto Rico consumes are imported. This suggests that fertilizers might also be examined as a possibility for production in Puerto Rico, since this would involve a substantial saving on transportation cost, *ceteris paribus*.

Other considerations permit a narrowing down of products and combinations to be considered. For example, antifreeze production does not make sense for Puerto Rico, since no market for antifreeze exists in Puerto Rico and only small amounts of labor are required in the production and packaging of the final product. Synthetic rubber and rubber tires are excluded from serious consideration because studies have indicated that significant economies of scale persist up to very large outputs beyond the realm of achievement for Puerto Rico, which thereby suggests the Gulf Coast area with its huge oil-refining capacity as the best location. Considering these and other factors, the investigator may narrow down the possibilities to a few sets of end products, namely, gasoline, fuel oil, and related refinery products, fertilizer, and synthetic fibers. (At a later stage he may reintroduce into the analysis certain products excluded at this point.)

Even with this narrowing down of the problem, the investigator faces literally thousands of possible combinations of activities in the production of these commodities. Here again it is possible to delimit. One of the basic considerations influencing development is economies of scale. From engineering sources information may be accumulated on minimum feasible plant sizes for different intermediate and end products. With this knowledge the investigator may eliminate as a possibility the production of any product whose required output would be well below the minimum feasible plant size.[3] He still confronts many meaningful industrial complexes from which he seeks to find an optimal one, but his problem is reduced to manageable proportions.

The preceding paragraphs illustrate well how the purpose of a study and the particular region under examination condition the selection of meaningful industrial complexes for analysis. They also reflect how the inclinations of the investigator and his accumulated stock of knowledge influence in a subtle manner this selection. For example, in the Puerto Rico study the narrowing-down process was constrained so that *full* sets of activities, starting with the raw material and ending with at least one finished product, would remain for subsequent analysis; this reflects the interests of the authors in facilitating empirical analysis within a general interdependence framework. As noted, the availability of data also affects the nature of industrial complexes to be investigated; this will be obvious from the discussion in the next section.

3. DETERMINATION OF STRUCTURES OF SPECIFIC COMPLEXES

Once meaningful complexes are broadly sketched in a very general way, it is necessary to detail these structures. Just as a comparative cost study of a single activity requires knowledge of the precise weights and quantities of raw materials and intermediates, of power, labor and capital inputs, of the several outputs, etc., so does study of an industrial complex. But an industrial complex is, generally speaking, composed of more than one activity. Therefore the internal interrelations, that is, the interactivity linkages, must be explicitly expressed in quantitative terms. It is at this point that the concept of the interindustry matrix of input-output is called into play and in essence becomes basic to the analysis. However, as will be demonstrated at a later point, this concept of an interindustry matrix will be extended into a concept of an interactivity matrix. The latter concept will permit at least some important variations in production coefficients (i.e., nonlinearities) and will introduce at least a limited number of alternative processes in order to allow for process substitution in the linear programming sense (to be discussed fully in Chapter 10).

The procedure may now be illustrated, again with reference to the Puerto Rico study. First a table is constructed showing the amounts of

---

[3] This procedure involves some preliminary cost analysis relating to scale economies. This is appropriate here in the elimination of activities which are obviously infeasible. The refined scale economy analysis is systematically injected at a much later point in the analysis.

TABLE 1.   ANNUAL INPUTS AND OUTPUTS FOR SELECTED OIL

	Oil Refinery, Prototype 1 (1) ⋯	Oil Refinery, Prototype 4 (4) ⋯	Ethylene Separation Prototype 4 (10) ⋯	Ethylene Glycol (oxidation) (22) ⋯	Ammonia from Hydrogen (31)	Ammonia from Methane (32)
1. Crude Oil MM bbl.	−9.428	−9.428				
2. Gasoline, straight-run MM bbl.	+2.074	+1.300				
3. Gasoline, cracked MM bbl.	+1.484	+2.226				
4. Gasoline, reformed MM bbl.		+1.486				
5. Gasoline, polymerized MM bbl.	+0.219	+0.415	+0.029			
6. Naphtha, MM bbl.	+0.660					
7. Kerosene, MM bbl.	+0.943	+0.707				
8. Diesel oil MM bbl.	+1.414	+0.896				
9. Gas oil MM bbl.						
10. Cycle oil MM bbl.	+1.320	+1.980				
11. Heavy residual MM bbl.	+0.943					
12. Coke and carbon 10XMM lb.		+4.033				
13. L.P.G. 10XMM lb.	+6.860	+15.050	+0.508			
14. Hydrogen MM lb.	+0.950	+8.900			−2.000	
15. Methane MM lb.	+12.780	+34.860				−5.500
16. Ethylene (mixed) MM lb.	+6.510	+17.410	−16.100			
17. Ethane (mixed) MM lb.	+9.930	+32.250	−30.190			
18. Propylene MM lb.	+3.630	+7.580	−7.580			
19. Propane MM lb.	+2.150	+5.080	−5.080			
20. Butylenes MM lb.						
21. Butanes MM lb.						
22. Pure ethylene MM lb.			+16.100	−8.300		
23. Pure ethane MM lb.			+30.190			
24. Steam MMM lb.	−0.801	−1.402	−0.148	−0.103		−0.023
25. Power MM kw. hr.	−2.511	−3.999	−0.194	−0.800	−4.640	−5.600
26. Fuel 10XMMM Btu.	−139.000	−242.000		−2.010		−0.450
. . . .						
34. Nitrogen MM lb.				+68.000		
35. Ethylene Glycol MM lb.				+10.000		
. . . .						
39. Ammonia MM lb.					+10.000	+10.000
40. HCN MM lb.						
41. Acrylonitrile MM lb.						
42. Methanol MM lb.						
43. Sulphur MM lb.						
44. Sulphuric acid MM lb.						
45. Nitric acid MM lb.						
46. Paraxylene MM lb.						
47. Dimethyl terephthalate MM lb.						
48. Dacron polymer MMlb.						
49. Dacron Staple MM lb.						
. . . .						
59. Ammonium nitrate MM lb.						
60. Urea MM lb.						
61. Carbon dioxide MM lb.						
. . . .						
74. Nylon salt MM lb.						
. . . .						
76. Nylon filament MM lb.						

REFINERY, PETROCHEMICAL, AND SYNTHETIC FIBER ACTIVITIES

Ammonia from Ethylene (33)	Ammonia from Ethane (34)	...	Nitric Acid from Ammonia (43)	Dimethyl Terephthalate (air oxidation) (44)	...	Dacron Polymer (46)	Dacron Staple (47)	...	Ammonium Nitrate from Ammonia (55)	Urea from Ammonia (56)	...	Nylon Filament (73)
− 6.290												
	− 5.780											
− 0.023	− 0.023			− 0.030		− 0.060	− 0.500		− 0.007	− 0.028		− 0.555
− 5.600	− 5.600		− 1.200	− 5.200		− 2.500	− 12.000		− 0.170	− 0.340		− 16.000
− 0.450	− 0.450			− 2.800		− 1.000				− 2.250		
												− 2.200
				− 3.230								
+ 10.000	+ 10.000		− 2.860						− 2.380	− 5.800		
				− 4.000		+ 3.350						
			+ 10.000						− 7.630			
				− 6.800								
				+ 10.000		− 10.100						
						+ 10.000	− 10.000					
							+ 10.000					
									+ 10.000			
										+ 10.000		
										− 7.500		
												− 10.000
												+ 10.000

various inputs and outputs associated with operating at a "unit" level[4] each individual or combined productive process (activity) that may be encountered in a specific selected complex.[5] Part of such a table is reproduced here as Table 1. (Processes technically infeasible or economically unreasonable for Puerto Rico are not included.) It is to be noted that unlike the input-output tables of the previous chapter, which are typically in dollar terms and are based on census data, this table is based on physical data obtained from engineering sources.

The columns of Table 1 are numbered, and each represents one activity. The rows of the table are also numbered, and here each represents a commodity. When the commodity is used in a process as an input, this is so indicated by a minus sign; when it is yielded as an output, this is so indicated by a plus sign.[6] For example, column 1 records the annual inputs and outputs associated with operating at unit level a given hypothetical oil-refining setup (designated prototype 1).[7] The annual *inputs* include 9.428 million barrels (MM bbl.) of crude oil (row 1), 0.801 billion pounds (MMM lb.) of steam (row 24), 2.511 million kilowatt-hours (MM kw.-hr.) of electric power (row 25), and 1390 MMM Btu of fuel (row 26). The annual *outputs* of the activity include 2.074 MM bbl. of straight-run gasoline (row 2), 1.484 MM bbl. of cracked gasoline (row 3), etc. The cells in column 1 in which no figures appear refer to inputs or outputs not associated with the operation of oil-refining prototype 1.

Many of the columns of Table 1 deal with activities which produce just one output. For example, column 47 shows the annual inputs necessary to produce a unit amount (in this case 10 MM lb.) of dacron staple (row 49). These inputs include 0.500 MMM lb. of steam (row 24), 12 MM kw.-hr. of electric power (row 25), and 10 MM lb. of Dacron polymer (row 48).

Table 1 does not list all inputs and outputs encountered in all activities noted. A complete list would be necessary if full cost and profit estimates had to be constructed. In the situation studied, however, such estimates are not required. The basic question is whether expected expansions

---

[4] The determination of the unit level for any activity is arbitrary. The investigator usually defines it at a scale so as to facilitate computation and understanding of the problem. Thus, in Table 1, the unit level of most petrochemical activities is set at 10 MM lb. per year of the primary product.

[5] The required data on inputs and outputs of the various activities are fully reported in W. Isard and E. W. Schooler [4], J. Airov [1], and J. R. Lindsay [7].

[6] Unlike input-output tables, this interactivity table reports on both the several outputs as well as inputs involved in a given activity; hence, inputs and outputs must be differentiated by sign.

[7] This refinery includes a topping and vacuum flash unit, a fluid catalytic cracking unit, a catalytic polymerization unit, and a simple gas separation plant.

should occur at locations on the Mainland or on both the Mainland and Puerto Rico. Hence the only inputs and outputs that need to be considered are those leading to systematic variations in cost or revenue between Puerto Rico and Mainland locations.[8] Furthermore, Table 1 lists only those inputs and outputs whose amounts vary in direct proportion with the scale of the productive activity, for example, those that double when output doubles. Such inputs as labor and capital services are thus excluded. These inputs are part of an interactivity matrix but must be individually considered at a later stage, since they generally vary nonlinearly with scale of operation.

Finally, note that in Table 1 alternative processes are included. There are many refinery prototypes that could be considered, although only two are explicitly noted in the condensed table. Several ammonia production processes are noted (columns 31–34). This is consistent with our extended notion of an interactivity matrix.

The next step is to proceed from a table of inputs and outputs to the detailed structure of each of a number of complexes hypothesized to be meaningful. That is, it is necessary to put together in a logical way and at specific quantitative levels several types of activities which in combination might prove to be desirable for the regional situation under investigation. For Puerto Rico a number of technical considerations as well as marketing and other economic factors influence the specifics of a complex and the scales of its activities. For example, the choice of refinery activities and the over-all refinery size selected are largely geared to the possibility of marketing gasoline on the Mainland along the Atlantic Coast. However, it is considered unlikely that a Puerto Rican operation could profitably produce, at least initially, basic tonnage chemical intermediates (e.g. ethylene glycol) for Mainland markets. For this reason the production level scheduled for any chemical intermediate is limited to the internal requirements of the complex. In the initial group of complexes selected, these internal requirements for chemicals stem from the scheduling of production activities for synthetic fibers and for fertilizer components. Synthetic fiber activities can effectively utilize Puerto Rico's abundant labor resources; fertilizer produced locally in Puerto Rico can replace at least some types of high-cost imported fertilizer. The scales of the fiber and fertilizer activities are based largely on levels of demand conservatively assumed for their products—Mainland demand for fibers and Puerto Rican demand for fertilizer.

The next step is to compute the *total* inputs and outputs associated with each of the selected production complexes. As an example, consider the

---

[8] This point has been developed in the discussion of comparative cost studies in section B of Chapter 7.

complex designated "Dacron A". This complex is depicted in Figure 2. Each box of Figure 2 contains the name and number of an activity in Table 1 required in the complex. The number atop each box is the multiple of "unit level" at which that activity must be operated to meet the requirements of the complex. To explain Figure 2 more fully, it is convenient to begin with the Dacron staple box at the upper left. A plant producing annually 36.5 MM lb. of Dacron staple is considered, a priori, reasonable for Puerto Rico. Since Dacron staple corresponds to activity 47 in Table 1, and since a unit level of activity 47 yields 10 MM lb. annually of Dacron staple, all the items in column 47 must be multiplied by 3.650 to obtain the inputs and outputs corresponding to an annual production of 36.5 MM lb. of Dacron staple. Note that above the Dacron staple box in Figure 2 is placed the figure 3.650, which indicates the level of operations at which activity 47 must be pursued.

One of the chemical intermediates required is Dacron polymer and specifically 36.5 MM lb. of Dacron polymer annually. Since Dacron polymer is activity 46, and since the unit level of activity 46 is 10 MM lb. of Dacron polymer, all the items of column 46 must be multiplied by 3.650. This number has been put in Figure 2 above the box designated Dacron polymer.

To produce 36.5 MM lb. of Dacron polymer requires 36.87 MM lb. of dimethyl terephthalate. Since a unit level of activity 45 yields 10 MM lb. of dimethyl terephthalate annually, all the items of column 45 must be multiplied by 3.687 to obtain the required dimethyl terephthalate. The number 3.687 is put on top of the dimethyl terephthalate box in Figure 2. The paraxylene required to produce dimethyl terephthalate is to be imported for various reasons not to be discussed here.

To produce 36.5 MM lb. of Dacron polymer also requires 11.79 MM lb. of ethylene glycol. Therefore activity 22, whose unit level of operations yields 10 MM lb. of ethylene glycol, must be carried on at level 1.179. Accordingly, all items of column 22 of Table 1 must be multiplied by 1.179; this number is put on top of the ethylene glycol box in Figure 2.

The production of 11.79 MM lb. of ethylene glycol via the oxidation process requires 9.79 MM lb. of ethylene. Since a unit level of operations of activity 10, an ethylene separation process, yields 16.10 MM lb. of ethylene, this activity must be operated at a level of only 0.608. Hence all the items of column 10 must be multiplied by 0.608; and this number is put on top of the ethylene box in Figure 2.

The gas stream containing ethylene comes directly from an oil refinery which is taken to be prototype 4 and which for various reasons is operated at unit level. Accordingly all items of column 4 are multiplied by 1.000; and this number is put on top of the oil refinery box in Figure 2.

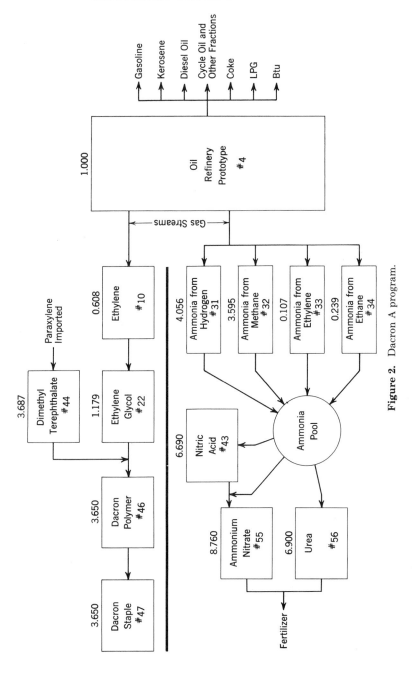

Figure 2. Dacron A program.

TABLE 2. TOTAL REQUIREMENTS AND YIELDS OF SELECTED INDUSTRIAL COMPLEXES

	Dacron A (1)	Dacron B (2)	Dacron C (3)	Dacron D (4)	Orlon B (5)	Orlon J (6)	Dynel A (7)	Dynel F (8)
1. Crude oil MM bbl.	−9.428	−9.428	−9.428	−9.428	−9.428	−9.428	−9.428	−9.428
2. Gasoline, straight-run MM bbl.	+1.300	+1.300	+1.300	+1.300	+1.300	+1.300	+1.300	+1.300
3. Gasoline, cracked MM bbl.	+2.226	+2.226	+2.226	+2.226	+2.226	+2.226	+2.226	+2.226
4. Gasoline, reformed MM bbl.	+1.486	+1.486	+1.486	+1.486	+1.486	+1.486	+1.486	+1.486
5. Gasoline, polymerized MM bbl.	+0.433	+0.428	+0.433	+0.428	+0.444	+0.415	+0.444	+0.415
6. Naphtha, MM bbl.	−	−	−	−	−	−	−	−
7. Kerosene, MM bbl.	+0.707	+0.707	+0.707	+0.707	+0.707	+0.707	+0.707	+0.707
8. Diesel oil MM bbl.	+0.896	+0.896	+0.896	+0.896	+0.896	+0.896	+0.896	+0.896
9. Gas oil MM bbl.	−	−	−	−	−	−	−	−
10. Cycle oil MM bbl.	+1.980	+1.980	+1.980	+1.980	+1.906	+1.887	+1.980	+1.980
11. Heavy residual MM bbl.	−	−	−	−	−	−	−	−
12. Coke and carbon 10 × MM lb.	+4.033	+4.033	+4.033	+4.033	+4.033	+4.033	+4.033	+4.033
13. LPG 10 × MM lb.	+15.359	+15.270	+15.359	+15.270	+14.006	+15.050	+15.558	+15.050
14. Hydrogen MM lb.	+0.788	+0.845	+0.470	+0.524	+3.553	+1.640	+2.793	+0.610
15. Methane MM lb.	+15.088	+16.083	+9.549	+10.545	+9.658	−0.006	+3.536	+0.038
16. Ethylene (mixed) MM lb.	+6.948	+9.794	+6.715	+9.561	+3.359	+0.950	+1.106	+5.451
17. Ethane (mixed) MM lb.	+12.513	+17.812	+12.264	+17.564	+2.373	+1.528	+1.059	+9.805
18. Propylene MM lb.	+2.971	+4.290	+2.971	+4.290	+3.542	−0.066	−	+2.331
19. Propane MM lb.	+1.991	+2.875	+1.991	+2.875	−	+0.001	−	+1.562
20. Butylenes MM lb.	−	−	−	−	−	−	−	−
21. Butanes MM lb.	+0.003	+0.007	+0.003	+0.007	−0.012	−	+0.003	−
22. Pure ethylene MM lb.	+18.356	+13.102	+18.356	+13.102	+0.004	−	+20.721	−
23. Pure ethane MM lb.	−4.113	−4.192	−4.547	−4.342	−4.885	−5.021	−4.233	−4.401
24. Steam MMM lb.	−127.799	−128.750	−132.386	−163.048	−140.933	−142.383	−219.177	−148.253
25. Power MM kw-hr.	−275.642	−277.528	−270.971	−272.855	−313.006	−277.014	−281.806	−272.244
26. Fuel 10 × MMM Btu	−	−	−	−	−	−	−	−
27. Salt MM lb.	−	−26.435	−	−26.435	−	−	−93.075	−26.469
28. Caustic Soda MM lb.	−	+17.494	−	+17.494	−	−	+61.594	+17.516

33. Ethylene oxide MM lb.	–	–	–	–	+0.013	–	+0.003	–
34. Nitrogen MM lb.	+80.172	–	+80.172	–	+265.948	–	–	–
35. Ethylene glycol MM lb.	+0.001	+0.001	+0.001	+0.001	–	–	–	–
36. Ethylene dichloride MM lb.	–	–	–	–	–	–	−0.003	–
37. Acetylene MM lb.	–	–	–	–	–	+0.002	–	+0.002
38. Vinyl Chloride MM lb.	–	–	–	–	–	–	+0.005	+0.005
39. Ammonia MM lb.	−0.032	−0.024	−0.018	+0.004	−0.003	−0.020	+0.001	+0.017
40. HCN MM lb.	–	–	–	–	+0.002	+0.002	+0.002	+0.002
41. Acrylonitrile MM lb.	–	–	–	–	+0.005	+0.005	–	–
42. Methanol MM lb.	−2.522	−2.522	−2.522	−2.522	–	–	–	–
43. Sulphur MM lb.	–	–	−1.777	−1.777	–	–	–	–
44. Sulphuric acid MM lb.	–	–	−0.002	−0.002	–	–	–	–
45. Nitric acid MM lb.	+0.061	+0.061	+0.065	+0.065	+0.060	+0.060	+0.061	−0.020
46. Paraxylene MM lb.	−25.072	−25.072	−21.753	−21.754	–	–	–	–
47. Dimethyl terephthalate MM lb.	+0.005	+0.005	+0.005	+0.005	–	–	–	–
48. Dacron polymer MM lb.	–	–	–	–	–	–	–	–
49. Dacron staple MM lb.	+36.500	+36.500	+36.500	+36.500	–	–	–	–
50. Dacron filament MM lb.	–	–	–	–	–	–	–	–
51. Dynel polymer MM lb.	–	–	–	–	–	–	–	–
52. Acetone MM lb.	–	–	–	–	–	–	−10.950	−10.950
53. Dynel staple MM lb.	–	–	–	–	–	–	+36.500	+36.500
54. Dynel filament MM lb.	–	–	–	–	–	–	–	–
55. Orlon polymer MM lb.	–	–	–	–	–	–	–	–
56. Dimethyl formamide MM lb.	–	–	–	–	−8.395	−8.395	–	–
57. Orlon staple MM lb.	–	–	–	–	+36.500	+36.500	–	–
58. Orlon filament MM lb.	–	–	–	–	–	–	–	–
59. Ammonium nitrate MM lb.	+87.600	+87.600	+87.600	+87.600	+87.680	+87.680	+87.600	+87.680
60. Urea MM lb.	+69.000	+69.000	+69.000	+69.000	+68.960	+68.960	+69 000	+68.960
61. Carbon dioxide MM lb.	−51.750	−51.750	−51.750	−51.750	−51.720	−51.720	−51.750	−51.720
Textile labor MM m-hr.	−5.284	−5.359	−5.283	−5.358	−5.315	−5.280	−5.396	−5.334
Chemical petroleum labor MM m-hr.	−2.229	−2.473	−2.226	−2.469	−2.329	−2.217	−2.590	−2.390

In similar manner, the computation proceeds with the end product fertilizer and leads back, via various activities, to gas streams from the oil refinery.

Figure 2 concisely depicts the complex Dacron A. If the investigator multiplies down each column of Table 1 whose number appears in a box in Figure 2 by the figure on top of the corresponding box in Figure 2, and if he sums for each type of input and output, he obtains all but the last two items of column 1 of Table 2. This column indicates the total requirements of each input and yields of each output for the Dacron A complex. The first item in column 1 of Table 2 is − 9.428 which indicates an annual input of 9.428 MM bbl. of crude oil. The second figure is + 1.300. It signifies an annual output of 1.3 MM bbl. of straight-run gasoline. The twenty-fifth item is − 127.799 and indicates an annual input of 128 MM kw-hr. And so on for each figure listed in column 1 which refers to the Dacron A complex. In many cells these figures are zero or insignificant in amount. Either no inputs or outputs of the corresponding items are associated with this complex, or the corresponding item is an *intermediate* commodity (such as ethylene glycol), whose output from one or more activities matches its use as an input in one or more other activities.

At this point it is also necessary to estimate total labor and total capital requirements of the Dacron A complex. For unit level of each activity in this complex, the requirements of both labor and capital are noted. To each of these unit requirements is applied an engineering-type factor, which summarizes the nonlinear relation of that input requirement with scale. (This factor is typically based on empirical information and accumulated experience.) For example, in the production of ethylene glycol from plants with annual capacity of 10 MM lb. or more, the labor factor is typically set at 0.22. This factor signifies that as output changes from unit level O_1 to a level O_k, the required labor at level O_k is equal to the required labor at unit level O_1 times the ratio of the two outputs O_k/O_1 raised to the 0.22 power. Once there is computed for each activity its requirements of labor and capital at the scale designated in the Dacron A complex, summation yields total labor and capital inputs for this same complex.[9] Labor requirements, both textile and chemical-petroleum, are listed as the last two items in the first column of Table 2.[10]

Similarly, total inputs and outputs for each of a host of other complexes can be obtained. For several complexes such inputs and outputs are listed in Table 2.

[9] For full details, see W. Isard, E. W. Schooler, and T. Vietorisz [5], ch. 3.

[10] In the particular study from which these materials were drawn, it was not necessary to develop capital requirements. Hence they are not reported here.

In this manner, the investigator determines the structure of specific complexes, each detailed in terms of precise weights and quantities of raw materials and intermediates, of labor, power, and capital inputs, and of the several outputs.

Having employed an interactivity matrix (i.e., an extended interindustry matrix which encompasses data on both relevant factors for nonlinear inputs as well as their unit requirements), the investigator is in a position to proceed with a comparative cost framework. He, of course, constantly bears in mind that the specific structure of a complex may vary from location to location, just as do factor proportions and other production characteristics of a single firm.

C. Comparative Cost Procedures: A Modern Weberian Framework

Although several variants of a comparative cost analysis may be pursued, we choose to develop a variant which follows traditional Weberian dogma. We first examine transportation as a basic location factor in industrial complexes. Next, labor, power, and other production cost differentials will each in turn be injected as elements which distort the optimal transport pattern. Finally, scale, localization, and urbanization economies will be introduced as additional distorting elements.[11]

1. TRANSPORT COST ORIENTATION

Following Weber, the analyst assumes a fixed pattern of markets for the products of a specific industrial complex. (Later, he checks his "first-run" results against the assumed pattern of markets, changes his postulates if there are major inconsistencies, and proceeds in an iterative fashion.) Also, he assumes as given the geographic positions of the sources of each of the raw materials. (At the start he assumes a utilization of the single source or combination of sources of each raw material that seems best; after the first-run results are obtained, he considers à la standard market analysis whether or not a second, third, etc. source, or some other combination of sources is still more desirable.)

With the weights and quantities of raw materials and other inputs and outputs designated and with the geographic position of each set, the minimum transport cost location may be determined. This determination may be accomplished via a dollar and cents calculation, or through use of geometry and a Weberian locational polygon, or through a Varignon

---

[11] This variant of the comparative cost approach parallels the general framework developed in *Location and Space-Economy*, to which the reader is referred for elaboration.

physical model, or through construction of isodapanes à la Palander and Hoover, or by some other means.[12]

To illustrate this step, we once again turn to empirical materials derived in the study of full oil refinery–petrochemical–synthetic fiber industrial complexes. For the given pattern of markets initially set—Eastern Seaboard for refinery products, the textile South for fiber, and Puerto Rico for fertilizer—a comprehensive dollar and cents cost computation indicates the Texas–Louisiana Gulf Coast as generally the point of minimum transport cost. (An alternative minimum transport cost pattern for some complexes involves location in the textile South of the activity producing the fiber from the chemical intermediates and the location at the Gulf Coast of all other activities.)[13]   Generally speaking, any other location encounters an over-all transport cost disadvantage. For example, for a Puerto Rico location the transport cost *disadvantage* of each of several full industrial complexes is indicated in column 1 of Table 3. (The derivation of this disadvantage will be discussed later.)

2. LABOR AND OTHER PRODUCTION COST DIFFERENTIALS

Once the point of minimum transport cost is determined, the analyst, using a modern Weberian approach, searches for possible deviation to other locations on the basis of cheap labor, power, etc., at the latter.   For example, if he investigates possible deviation to a cheap-labor point, he must compute transport cost differentials with which to determine the transport cost disadvantage of the cheap-labor site as well as labor cost differential with which to determine the labor cost advantage of the cheap-labor site. (In more technical terms, he may construct a critical

---

[12] For further materials on these several technical procedures, see *Location and Space-Economy*, especially ch. 5 and its Appendix.

[13] For full details see J. R. Lindsay [7], W. Isard and E. W. Schooler [4], and J. Airov [1].   Although this problem is too complex to be handled by simple geometry and a Weberian locational polygon, an isodapane technique could be employed to determine a minimum transport cost location.   In this technique, which would be very cumbersome in this type of problem, the analyst would construct several sets of iso-vectors.   For example, in studying the Dacron A complex (as detailed in column 1, Table 2), he would construct his several sets of isovectors using as focal points the following locations: (1) for the crude oil input (the first item of column 1), a major oil source on the Gulf Coast (later an alternative source, say one in Venezuela, would be considered); (2) for gasoline, straight-run, cracked, reformed, and polymerized, a major market location, say Philadelphia, on the Atlantic Seaboard; (3) for fuel input, a major oil or natural gas source on the Gulf Coast; (4) for Dacron staple, a central location in the textile South; (5) for urea and ammonium nitrate (fertilizer), a location in Puerto Rico; etc.

Once his several sets of isovectors were constructed, the analyst would combine them in standard fashion into a set of isodapanes and therewith identify the point of minimum transport cost.

TABLE 3. OVER-ALL NET ADVANTAGE OR DISADVANTAGE OF A PUERTO RICO LOCATION IN DOLLARS PER YEAR BY COMPLEX

(data rounded to nearest thousand)

Complex	Transport Cost Disadvantage (1)	Relative to Full Complex at Gulf Coast		Relative to Split Complex at Gulf Coast and Textile South			Final Net Over-all Advantages (+) or Disadvantages (−) [(1) + (4) + (5) + (6)] (7)
		Advantage on Textile Labor (2)	Disadvantage on Chemical-Petroleum Labor (3)	Advantage on Textile Labor (4)	Disadvantage on Chemical-Petroleum Labor (5)	Scale (Moderate)[a] and/or Process Disadvantage (6)	
Dacron A	− 263,000	+ 4,861,000	− 2,229,000	+ 3,963,000	− 2,229,000	− 1,160,000	+ 311,000
Dacron C	− 339,000	+ 4,860,000	− 2,226,000	+ 3,962,000	− 2,226,000	− 1,909,000	− 512,000
Orlon B	− 608,000	+ 4,890,000	− 2,329,000	+ 3,986,000	− 2,329,000	− 2,017,000	− 968,000
Orlon J	− 565,000	+ 4,858,000	− 2,217,000	+ 3,960,000	− 2,217,000	− 708,000	+ 470,000
Dynel A	− 760,000	+ 4,963,000	− 2,590,000	+ 4,046,000	− 2,590,000	− 2,916,000	− 2,220,000
Dynel F	− 437,000	+ 4,907,000	− 2,390,000	+ 4,000,000	− 2,390,000	− 1,445,000	− 272,000
Nylon A	− 457,000	+ 4,974,000	− 2,624,000	+ 4,055,000	− 2,624,000	− 2,543,000	− 1,569,000
Nylon G	− 772,000	+ 4,875,000	− 2,275,000	+ 3,974,000	− 2,275,000	− 335,000	+ 592,000

[a] Based on the operation of all Mainland activities except refinery and fiber production at scales moderately larger than in Puerto Rico.

Source: W. Isard, E. W. Schooler, and T. Vietorisz [5].

isodapane corresponding to the labor cost advantage of the site, etc.) He also considers alternative sources of one or more materials for serving the complex at a cheap-labor site, as well as other possible cost differentials (both positive and negative) and potential savings from changes in factor proportions and process substitution, which can be logically examined at a later point.

By way of illustration, it is clear that the location of a *full* refinery–petrochemical–synthetic fiber complex at a point of minimum transport cost on the Gulf Coast (Texas–Louisiana area) suffers a labor cost disadvantage. On the basis of transport and labor cost differentials alone, it is easily established that the activity producing the staple fiber from the chemical intermediates should be deviated. It should be deviated from a Gulf Coast site to a cheap-labor site in the textile South, whereas all other activities of a full complex should remain at the Gulf Coast. This conclusion is reached since the additional cost of shipping the chemical polymer or salt to a Southern textile fiber plant is approximately matched by savings which such a plant realizes in shipping the finished product to the market, and since such a plant does experience major labor cost savings.

To illustrate the procedure further, other cheap-labor locations may be considered, particularly Puerto Rico. A consideration of Puerto Rico as a cheap-labor location, for both full and partial complexes, involves, first of all, the use of what Weber would designate a replacement deposit. That is, Venezuela would substitute for the Gulf Coast as the source of the raw material crude oil, for reasons noted earlier. Second, the consideration of Puerto Rico necessitates the use of a more refined set of transport cost differentials. Specifically, for each item listed in the left-hand tab of Table 2 which may involve shipment for either or both locations, it is necessary to develop a relevant transport cost differential. For example, a transport cost differential must be estimated for crude oil, the first item in Table 2. Since a Gulf Coast location at an oil source incurs zero transport cost on oil, and since a Puerto Rico location incurs an estimated 13.2¢ per barrel of transport cost on Venezuelan oil, an unfavorable transport cost differential of 13.2¢ per barrel of oil exists for Puerto Rico.[14]

14 Additionally, at this or a later point, the analyst must introduce differences in F.O.B. prices at raw material sources if a substitute source is considered. In the case of Puerto Rico he must expressly examine the difference in price between Venezuelan and Gulf Coast oil. Since the New York area is a market location served by both Venezuela and Gulf Coast producers, the F.O.B. price at Venezuela may be estimated as New York price less transport cost from Venezuela to New York, and simultaneously the F.O.B. price at the Gulf may be estimated as New York price less transport cost from the Gulf to New York. On this basis, the F.O.B. price per barrel at Venezuela (which is the closer source) is 1.1¢ greater than that at the Gulf. Hence, a Puerto Rico location labors at an additional disadvantage of 1.1¢ per barrel in relation to a Gulf Coast location.

Likewise, a transport cost differential must be estimated for straight-run gasoline, the second item in Table 2. Since both the Gulf Coast and Puerto Rico locations are to serve the given market, namely, the Atlantic Seaboard (say New York), the Puerto Rico location has an advantage because it is closer. This advantage amounts to a favorable transport cost differential of 7.3¢ per barrel.

In similar manner a transport cost differential may be estimated for each item subject to shipment. The analyst can then take any one complex, say Dacron A, column 1, Table 2. He multiplies each item of column 1 by the relevant transport cost differential (e.g., 9.428 MM bbl. of crude oil × 14.3¢ per barrel, and 1.300 MM bbl. of straight-run gasoline × 7.3¢ per barrel, etc.). He nets these individual transport cost disadvantages and advantages. For the Dacron A complex he obtains an over-all transport cost disadvantage of $263,000 annually, *assuming at this point that the specific structure of this complex will be identical for both locations.*[15] This figure and corresponding figures for other selected complexes are listed in column 1 of Table 3.[16]

Against this over-all transport cost disadvantage of the cheap-labor location, Puerto Rico, must be balanced the labor cost saving achievable at this site. From the interactivity matrix the total requirements of both chemical-petroleum labor and textile labor have already been calculated for each complex and recorded in Table 2. On the assumption that textile labor would be relatively cheap and abundant in Puerto Rico, and more specifically that on an equivalent efficiency basis the wage rate per hour for such labor would be $0.92 less than on the Gulf Coast, the annual labor cost savings achievable for each complex at a Puerto Rico location can be calculated. They are recorded in column 2 of Table 3. For example, Dacron A would have an annual textile labor cost savings of $4,861,000.

[15] As indicated in Chapter 7, one approach in a location study is to calculate both total costs for all inputs and total revenues from all outputs at two alternative sites. However, if the specific structure of a production operation or industrial complex is identical for both sites, as is assumed in the text, it is no longer necessary to estimate total cost of each input or price of each output. For location analysis, it is only necessary to infer, in one way or another, the differences between the two sites in the cost of each input and price of each output. Essentially, this inference has been performed in the illustration of the text for those inputs and outputs whose cost and price differences between the Gulf and Puerto Rico can be traced back to transport cost differentials.

[16] Actually, there is included as part of this transport cost disadvantage the net additional cost which a Puerto Rico location incurs in being oriented to the higher-price Venezuela crude. (See footnote 14 and W. Isard, E. W. Schooler, and T. Vietorisz [5].) The analyst, however, may wish to keep separate in two columns the pure transport cost disadvantages and other price-cost advantages and disadvantages stemming from the use of substitute raw material (input) sources.

Partly counterbalancing this advantage of Puerto Rico is a second disadvantage. Skilled chemical-petroleum labor is relatively scarce in Puerto Rico, and it is reasonable to assume that on an equivalent efficiency basis the wage rate per hour of such labor would be $1.00 greater in Puerto Rico than on the Gulf Coast. The resulting disadvantage for each complex is recorded in column 3 of Table 3.

Thus in this illustration the investigator concludes, after comparing the advantages and disadvantages of each complex as recorded in the first three columns of Table 3, that the labor cost savings achieved at the cheap-labor point, Puerto Rico, would be sufficient to deviate the full complex from the minimum transport cost point at the Gulf Coast, *ceteris paribus*. (Puerto Rico lies within Weber's critical isodapane.) But this comparative cost procedure must be carried farther. For a complex to be deviated to a specific cheap-labor point, it must be demonstrated that such a point involves lower cost production than not only the transport cost minimum point but also any other competitive cheap-labor point. As already noted, a better Mainland location pattern (actually the best for the given market) involves a split pattern with the synthetic fiber operation in the textile South and all other activities of a full complex on the Gulf Coast. Thus, Puerto Rico must be contrasted with such a Mainland pattern, as can be done with the data of columns 1, 4, and 5 of Table 3.[17] Scrutiny of the data in these columns indicates that Puerto Rico is still the best location, on the basis of transport costs and labor costs alone.

These materials illustrate the general procedure for considering possible deviation of a full industrial complex from its minimum transport cost location to another site which has one or more processing advantages. One processing advantage, a labor cost one, has been well outlined. Other cases involving a processing advantage other than a labor cost advantage can be treated following the same general procedure. However, as in single-industry analysis, variation among locations in *more than one* processing cost are to be considered, that is, the *ceteris paribus* clause is to be relaxed. In addition to transport cost and labor cost differentials, the analyst evaluates possible power cost differentials, capital cost differentials, tax differentials, water and land cost differentials, etc. He can then reach a more complete appraisal,[18] although other critical factors must still be examined.

[17] The textile labor advantage of Puerto Rico relative to the South is assumed to be $0.75 per man-hour. Her disadvantage on chemical-petroleum labor is still assumed at $1.00 per man-hour.

[18] In the Puerto Rico study, power, steam, and fuel cost differentials were translatable into transport cost differentials on fuel oil of equivalent British thermal unit value and consequently are encompassed in the materials already reported. Capital cost and tax

3. VARIABLE FACTOR PROPORTIONS AND PRODUCT MIXES, AND PROCESS SUBSTITUTION

Hitherto we have pictured the analyst for the most part as considering identical complexes only, when comparing the pros and cons of two locations. But this picture is purely pedagogical; from the start the analyst has in mind changes in factor proportions and product mixes and substitution among processes. Suppose, for example, he is considering for an industrial complex alternative locations at a resource site or at a market site. It is wrong, at least theoretically, for him to postulate that the internal structure of the complex will be identical at both sites. For at the resource site the delivered price of the resource will be lower than the delivered price of the resource when location is at the market. Therefore he can expect that, relative to the most appropriate internal structure at the market, location at the resource site will tend to involve substitution of the resource for other inputs. Or if a complex either in whole or in part deviates to a cheap-labor point, he anticipates the general substitution of the cheap factor, labor, for other factors, as well as a host of subsidiary substitutions.

In certain industrial complexes some factor substitutions may proceed continuously and involve little or no process change for a given product output, such as the substitution of scrap for pig iron in the open hearth of a steel–steel-fabricating complex. In other industrial complexes, some factor substitutions can occur only when process change is permitted, as is frequently true with refinery–petrochemical–synthetic fiber complexes. For example, at locations where natural gas is in excess supply and obtainable at a low cost relative to fuel oil, we can expect for given product outputs the greater use of this raw material than at other locations where its price is high relative to fuel oil; this factor substitution entails the simultaneous substitution of processes using natural gas for processes using fuel oil (for example, in the production of ammonia and fertilizer when all by-product refinery gases have been exploited).

Paralleling the possibility of different factor proportions at different locations is the possibility of different product mixes. This possibility exists because the set of relative prices may be expected to vary at least to some extent from location to location. For example, the products of a Mainland refinery might not be yielded in the same proportions as those of a Puerto Rico refinery; because of a much lower local price for fuel oil, the Mainland refinery might produce more gasoline and less fuel oil. Or the basic raw material ethylene derived from the waste gas of a Mainland

differentials, although extremely important, are very much a result of political policy in Puerto Rico; their consideration rightly belongs to other phases of the study. Water and other cost differentials were not found to be generally significant.

refinery might be used to make polyethylene, a plastic, rather than being used in the production of Dacron.

Obviously, if factor proportions and product mixes do vary from location to location, the analyst must adjust his cost advantage and disadvantage calculations accordingly. For example, if for the chlorhydrin processes of a given complex are substituted oxidation processes when the location of a complex on the Gulf Coast is envisaged, the cost saving on the Gulf Coast by such substitution (for a given output) must be calculated and subtracted from Puerto Rico's over-all advantage figure for the given original complex. (The resulting complex on the Gulf Coast may be identified as another type of complex, say Dacron Z instead of Dacron Y, since it would involve a different mix of processes.) Thus in the Puerto Rico study, which covered complexes in which significant change in factor proportions for given product outputs usually involved simultaneous process substitution, it was necessary to estimate Mainland production costs for each chemical intermediate product by each feasible alternative process. These calculations provided the basis for downward adjustment of the Puerto Rico advantage figures where different relative factor prices on the Gulf Coast justified process substitution.[19] Such downward adjustment combined with scale economy adjustments (to be discussed in the next section) is recorded in column 6 of Table 3.

It is also to be noted that variable factor proportions and product mixes as well as process substitution are closely interrelated with scale of operation of any individual activity, of a set of activities, and of the community and regional economy itself. (Up to now we have assumed that for the most part the scale factor has no effect.) This interrelation will become manifest in the following paragraphs.

4. SCALE ECONOMIES

Having treated transport cost differentials, labor, power, water, and other production cost differentials (within a framework permitting factor, product, and process substitution), modern Weberian doctrine would next

---

[19] However, it is to be noted that in this study no attempt was made to compute adjustments where different relative product prices on the Gulf Coast justified a different product mix. It was broadly argued that Mainland competition would tend to equalize on the Gulf Coast the profitabilities among the various uses to which the basic hydrocarbon sources, oil, and natural gas could be put. Therefore it was reasoned (perhaps with insufficient basis) that comparison of a Puerto Rico complex of a given product mix with a Gulf Coast complex of a different product mix would yield the same results as a comparison of that Puerto Rico complex with a Gulf Coast complex of identical product mix, the general scale of operation of the two Gulf Coast complexes being roughly the same. Hence, no adjustment was attempted for the product mix variable. For further details, see W. Isard, E. W. Schooler, and T. Vietorisz [5].

turn to agglomeration economies (and diseconomies). These economies are traditionally and usefully disaggregated into economies of (1) scale, (2) localization, and (3) urbanization (regionalization). We now discuss scale economies which have reference to those economies (diseconomies) achieved only through the change in the level of a given activity, the level of all other activities and other external variables being held constant.

The relevance of scale economies for location analysis of a single activity has been discussed in Chapter 7. It is obvious that these same scale economies are relevant for the location analysis of industrial complexes. This point is clearly demonstrated in the Puerto Rico study. The Gulf Coast is a major industrial area. Puerto Rico is at best a minor industrial area. Therefore, practically all petrochemical activities can be operated at scales and achieve scale economies in the Gulf Coast not possible for Puerto Rico.[20] And paralleling factor and product substitution (based on different relative prices), changes in scale may also involve process change and thus influence in a significant way factor proportions and the internal structure of an industrial complex at any site. As a case in point, because the market for nylon salt is relatively small in Puerto Rico, an *all-adipic acid process* which achieves relatively low unit costs at relatively small outputs is employed in a complex for Puerto Rico. In contrast, because the market for nylon salt is relatively large at the Gulf Coast, an *adipic acid–adiponitrile process*, which does not achieve low unit costs at small outputs but is best for achieving low unit costs at high outputs, is used at the Gulf Coast.

As with factor substitution, the actual estimate of change in advantage due to scale economies requires extensive cost-revenue computation for each of the possible activities involved. First, the scale of each activity in a standard reference complex at a given location is noted. For each new scale considered for any given activity, the change (if any) in revenue to the reference complex needs to be calculated. This requires knowledge of product prices. Next the change in total input cost to the reference complex needs to be determined. This step requires estimates of the unit cost of production of the given activity at the scale in the reference complex and at every other scale to be considered. Such estimates require knowledge of the unit cost, at the location designated, of all the inputs that enter

---

[20] For example the Dacron A complex for Puerto Rico calls for the production of 11.79 MM lb. per year of ethylene glycol. On the Mainland, however, new glycol plants are typically being built to produce 75–100 MM lb. per year or even more. Even if the Dacron output of the Mainland plant were the same as that for the Puerto Rico plant, it might be profitable because of scale economies to produce ethylene glycol at the larger scale and sell the excess glycol to users outside the complex. Once again, the assumption of identical complexes becomes untenable.

into the activity. The excess of increase (or decrease) in total revenue over the increase (or decrease) in total input costs equals the amount by which the profitability of the reference complex at the given location is increased by the specific scale change for the given activity. This amount also indicates the adjustment required in dollar-advantage estimates for the altered reference complex at its given location, when compared with complexes elsewhere whose scales have not been changed.

Concrete illustrations of this general step are afforded by the Puerto Rican study. For example a Dacron C complex which has most of its activities at the specific scales noted in Figure 2 and is located on the Gulf Coast was taken as one of a number of reference complexes.[21] For most of its activities several scales were considered and changes in profitability noted.[22] As an instance, production of ethylene glycol at scales of both 50 MM and 100 MM lb. annually were examined, as compared to the scale of 11.79 MM lb. annually noted in Figure 2 and specified in the reference complex. On the assumption that the ethylene glycol in excess of the requirements of the complex would be marketed at a break-even price—an assumption reasonable for the Gulf Coast at the time of the study—production at these two scales resulted in annual economies of $505,000 and $674,000, respectively. (These economies of scale were influenced by the previous calculation of economies of scale in the production of the prior intermediate, ethylene.)

In such a manner economies at pertinent scales for most of the activities included in the Dacron C complex were estimated. However, since, as has been noted, these scale economies are inextricably bound with process substitution and changes in factor proportion and product mixes, it was necessary to estimate the combined effect of scale economies and process substitution.[23]

One particular process substitution which cost calculations proved to be warranted was the substitution of dimethyl terephthalate production via air oxidation for dimethyl terephthalate production via nitric acid oxidation (a substitution of power, fuel, and some paraxylene and labor for nitric acid and some sulphuric acid). The resulting complex on the Gulf Coast based on the use of most efficient processes had the pattern of activities of a

[21] In a Dacron C complex on the Gulf Coast, several boxes relating to paraxylene production must be added to those of Figure 2, and the box on dimethyl terephthalate production must be changed to refer to the alternative dimethyl terephthalate process 45 run at the same level of 3.687.

[22] Change in the scales of the refinery activity (4) and of the fiber production activity (47) was not considered, since it was hypothesized that further economies of scale in these activities would not be appreciable.

[23] Again, differences in profitability from differences in product mix alone were assumed to be eliminated by competitive forces.

Dacron A complex of Figure 2, but with local production of paraxylene included. The improvement in profitability of operating such a Gulf Coast complex *at moderate scales* rather than a Gulf Coast Dacron C complex at *minimum scales* (of the order of those indicated in Figure 2) amounts to $1,909,000 annually. This is noted in row 2, column 6, of Table 3. This profitability represents a decrease in the Gulf Coast's disadvantage (i.e., a decrease in Puerto Rico's advantage) when contrasted with a Dacron C complex in Puerto Rico operating with the processes at minimum scales of the order of those indicated in Figure 2. (Recall that the previous calculations recorded in the Dacron C row of Table 3 refer to minimum-scale operations of identical Dacron C complexes in Puerto Rico and the Mainland.) Since no scale economies are envisaged for larger-size fiber operations than encompassed in the Dacron C complex, and since no new significant factor substitutions are anticipated with change in location of the fiber operation, the adjustment of $1,909,000 annually is also relevant for the more economic Mainland complex which involves the location of the fiber process in the textile South and all other activities at the Gulf Coast.

In similar fashion, the Puerto Rico study calculated for each of the complexes listed in the left tab of Table 3 (and many others) the required profitability adjustment for Mainland operation.[24] This profitability adjustment represents the scale and/or process disadvantage at which each of these complexes at minimum scales would labor in Puerto Rico vis-à-vis the best Gulf Coast–textile South complex at moderate scales, for the specific fiber indicated. As an illustration, the Dynel A complex in Puerto Rico labors not only at a scale disadvantage relative to the best Gulf Coast–textile South Dynel complex but also utilizes in Puerto Rico a set of processes which are not as efficient on the Gulf Coast as those embodied in the Dynel F complex.

Once the profitability adjustments of column 6 of Table 3 were calculated for each complex considered for Puerto Rico, a final net over-all advantage or disadvantage figure for each complex in Puerto Rico could be obtained.[25] These are listed in column 7 of Table 3. Note that these

[24] For certain short-cut computation procedures, see W. Isard, E. W. Schooler, and T. Vietorisz [5], ch. 6.

[25] Just as there are scale and process substitutions which are meaningful for a Gulf Coast location, so are there scale and process substitutions meaningful for a Puerto Rico location. For example, it does develop that it is meaningful to substitute dimethyl terephthalate production via air oxidation for dimethyl terephthalate production via nitric acid oxidation when Dacron is produced in Puerto Rico. It does develop, as suggested by Gulf Coast calculations, that in Puerto Rico a Dacron A complex is superior to a Dacron C complex. However, from other comparisons it does not follow that the process mix which is the best for the Gulf Coast turns out to be best for Puerto Rico, too.

refer to *moderate-scale* operations on the Mainland. In a similar manner additional calculations were made for *maximum-scale* operations on the Mainland and can be made for a host of other scale assumptions. In this way the scale factor may be encompassed in industrial complex analysis.

5. ECONOMIES OF LOCALIZATION, URBANIZATION, AND SPATIAL JUXTAPOSITION

The next step in a modern Weberian framework is to consider localization economies (diseconomies). These economies obtain when plants of like character (generally within a given industry) congregate at one site. For example, in the garment trades complex of New York City such economies stem from more effective exploitation of a common labor pool, from a high level of accessibility to buyers, and from fuller utilization of diverse specialized facilities. In refinery–petrochemical–synthetic fiber complexes, however, localization economies are not frequently encountered, since scale economies are so major that one rather than two or more plants of the same type tends to evolve.

Closely associated with localization economies, and in certain cases indistinguishable from them, are urbanization economies (diseconomies). These are usually defined as economies which emerge when unlike plants congregate around one site, that is, are spatially juxtaposed rather than geographically separated. Frequently these economies are closely linked with regional development processes and may be properly termed urbanization-regionalization economies. To be more concrete we may enumerate some of these economies. In an integrated steel works, heat economies achieved in the transferal of molten pig iron to open-hearth furnaces are such economies. Or in refining–petrochemical–synthetic fiber complexes, the economy in the use of optimum-size power and steam plants is such an economy. This latter economy would not be realized if we were to separate geographically two or more activities, where each had to produce its own power but did not require the output of an optimum steam plant.

These examples of urbanization-regionalization economies are relatively easy to identify. Others are much more difficult to estimate. Among these are (1) administrative economies and other savings in indirect production costs; (2) finer articulation of production among the several stages; (3) more effective quality control; and (4) social welfare gains, including improved attitude toward work and higher labor productivity resulting from more adequate incomes.

Such urbanization-regionalization economies when combined with localization economies (including those aspects of scale economies which stem from optimum size of auxiliary and ancillary facilities—e.g. steam and power plants) are extremely important in industrial complex analysis. *As a whole,* they represent *spatial-juxtaposition economies.*

Conceptually speaking, spatial-juxtaposition economies may be incorporated into an analysis of industrial complexes in a way somewhat resembling that previously outlined for scale economies. The over-all revenues and costs for a full reference complex at a given location may be calculated (such as Dacron A plus paraxylene production, all at one site on the Gulf Coast). Then for every meaningful combination of two groups of activities into which this reference complex might be split (where the two groups are locationally separated), over-all revenues and costs may be calculated. Likewise for every meaningful combination of three groups, four groups, etc., until the complex is sliced into as many "groups" as there are activities, that is, is completely geographically split. By this procedure, variation in the spread between over-all revenues and costs may be noted for the several degrees of spatial juxtaposition and may be broadly interpreted as economies (diseconomies) of spatial juxtaposition. As an instance, an increase (decrease) in this spread when a full complex is located at one site rather than being split among two separated locations may be broadly interpreted as economies (diseconomies) of spatial juxtaposition possible at this degree of juxtaposition.

It is fully recognized that spatial-juxtaposition economies are a function of innumerable variables and are closely interrelated with the scales of the activities in the reference complex, the factor proportions for each of these activities, the existing pattern of cost differentials of all sorts, the pattern of geographic distribution of population, and the spread of industry in general, etc. Frankly speaking, their adequate, let alone complete, identification is impossible with our given stock of social science methods and tools. Yet, in many situations some insight on important policy questions can be gleaned when the problem of their identification is explicitly posed. For illustration, we may once more draw upon the Puerto Rico study.

In the Puerto Rico study, the objective was to identify feasible lines of industrial development in the refinery–petrochemical–synthetic fiber area by means of industrial complex analysis. This objective conditioned the scope and emphasis of the study. Spatial-juxtaposition economies were attacked not in a full comprehensive manner but in a very limited framework, in particular as they related to Puerto Rico vis-à-vis any other competitive location. Hence, the spatial-juxtaposition analysis was reduced to the study of diverse economies at both Puerto Rico and the Gulf Coast when there are juxtaposed at each location two rather than one activity; three rather than two activities; four rather than three; etc. For this purpose Table 4 is constructed.

TABLE 4. OVER-ALL NET ADVANTAGE OF A PUERTO RICO LOCATION FOR
SELECTED FULL AND PARTIAL COMPLEXES, IN THOUSANDS OF DOLLARS
PER YEAR

Complex in Puerto Rico	Assumed Wage Rate Differentials					
	Textile Labor: + 75¢/m-hr. Chemical Labor: − 100¢/m-hr.			Textile Labor: + 37 1/2¢/m-hr. Chemical Labor: − 50¢/m-hr.		
	Mainland Scale Economies			Mainland Scale Economies		
	Max. (1)	Mod. (2)	Min. (3)	Max. (4)	Mod. (5)	Min. (6)
1. Nylon G	− 2841	592	927	− 3691	− 258	77
2. Dynel F	− 1122	− 272	681	− 1927	− 1077	− 124
3. Orlon J	− 569	383	1093	− 1441	− 489	221
4. Dacron A: DMT plus Dacron polymer plus Fiber plus Refinery plus Petrochem-Fertilizer	− 790	311	1471	− 1657	− 556	604
5. Dacron polymer plus Fiber plus Refinery plus Petrochem-Fertilizer	73	633	1426	− 794	− 234	559
6. Dacron fiber plus Refinery plus Petrochem-Fertilizer	983	1373	1662	− 99	291	580
7. Refinery plus Petrochem-Fertilizer	− 612	− 222	67	− 498	− 108	181
8. Dacron fiber plus Petrochem-Fertilizer	1395	1785	2074	248	638	927
9. Petrochem-Fertilizer only	− 168	222	511	− 119	271	560
10. Refinery only	− 704	− 704	− 704	− 639	− 639	− 639
11. Dacron fiber only	1563	1563	1563	367	367	367

Source: W. Isard, E. W. Schooler, and T. Vietorisz [5].

In the left-hand tab of Table 4 are listed various full and incomplete complexes which were among those examined for Puerto Rico. The first four rows relate to full programs, the composition of the fourth one, Dacron A, being somewhat detailed. The fifth row relates to a *reduced* Dacron A complex, that is, a Dacron A complex which imports rather than produces DMT (dimethyl terephthalate); the DMT activity is therefore split off from the Dacron A complex. The sixth row refers to a complex which is still further reduced, that is, which imports rather than produces Dacron polymer; the DMT and Dacron polymer activities are therefore split off from the Dacron A complex. The seventh row refers to a complex of still smaller size, namely one in which the refinery and only the petrochemical activities leading to fertilizer production are included (as depicted in the lower half of Figure 2). The eighth refers to the spatial juxtaposition in Puerto Rico of fiber and fertilizer activities only. Finally, rows nine, ten, and eleven refer to the juxtaposition of still fewer activities.

The columns of the table are designed to reflect the implications of several assumptions on wage rates and scale of operations. The first three columns refer to a situation, already discussed, in which Puerto Rico has an advantage of 75¢ per equivalent man-hour in textile labor and a disadvantage of $1.00 per equivalent man-hour in chemical-petroleum labor. The last three columns pertain to a situation where each of these labor cost differentials has been cut in half. (Other reasonable assumptions can easily be introduced).

Also, a set of scale assumptions are examined in Table 4. Columns 3 and 6 refer to a situation in which Mainland operations would be in plants similar in size to those envisaged for Puerto Rico, a situation representing a minimum of scale advantage for the Mainland. Columns 2 and 5 refer to a situation in which Mainland operations would be in plants (except fiber and refinery) of moderately larger size. Columns 1 and 4 refer to a situation in which Mainland operations would be in plants (except fiber and refinery) of maximum economic size, thereby realizing maximum scale economies.

The data of Table 4 summarize for each complex noted the materials previously collected on cost advantages (positive) and disadvantages (negative) of Puerto Rico vis-à-vis the most efficient competitive Mainland production pattern for the markets already designated. They do not depict spatial-juxtaposition economies as such but constitute a framework for policy decisions on regional development which take into account the possibility of spatial-juxtaposition economies. For example, observe column 2, the column reflecting perhaps the most realistic set of assumptions. Of the four full complexes listed (and of all complexes scrutinized in the study), Nylon G has the greatest advantage, namely $592,000 annually. But of all possible complexes for Puerto Rico, varying from full- to single-activity complexes, Nylon G is not the best. Of those listed in Table 4, the complex (row 8) involving a Dacron fiber plant and the petrochemical activities producing fertilizer (from imported fuel oil) has the greatest advantage. Its annual savings over Mainland operations is $1,785,000. The next best complex under the set of assumptions of column 2 is the single activity producing Dacron fiber.

It is at this point that valuable insight is acquired. The analyst is subjectively aware of the many spatial-juxtaposition economies associated with a location in Puerto Rico, juxtaposition economies common to many underdeveloped regions. In Puerto Rico a full industrial complex would tend to have important advantages over a smaller industrial complex— advantages in developing a pool of engineering labor; in changing entre- preneurial attitudes, savings, and investment habits; in accelerating the pace of industrialization and basic development processes. These spatial- juxtaposition economies ought rightly to be added to the data of Table 4, but because they can be only subjectively noted, this required final step cannot be taken. Yet, policy decision is facilitated by this explicit posing of the problem. In the context of Table 4, are the spatial-juxta- position economies (including welfare effects) which a full Nylon G com- plex can expect to achieve in Puerto Rico relative to a Dacron fiber plus petrochemical-fertilizer complex greater than $1,193,000 annually— the amount by which the latter's cost advantages exceed those of the former? An economic development agency may well reply positively to this question and judge that a subsidy of at least $1,193,000 annually for a Nylon G operation is justified.

We have illustrated only one of many situations in which the explicit posing of the problem of spatial-juxtaposition economies does not cast light on the magnitude of these economies—which are exceedingly difficult to estimate[26]—but does facilitate decision making. It should also be

[26] Some of the spatial-juxtaposition economies are of course much more amenable to calculation than others. For example, the heat and power economies mentioned in the examples given in the text are rather easily identified or estimated. Also, savings in clerical labor and other indirect costs as well as scale advantages in steam and power production, all resulting from spatial juxtaposition, can in certain cases be fairly accu- rately estimated. And even such advantages as better organization of production and more effective quality control can conceivably be estimated quantitatively. The principal problem in this connection—one that it may optimistically be hoped is not insuperable—is in persuading interested parties who possess the required data to make the relevant calculations, or at least to make the data available.

The most difficult economies to estimate are of course the positive welfare effects. However, it is possible that certain indirect effects of alternative-size complexes on community or regional growth can be compared by some sort of regional multiplier approach, perhaps utilizing input-output concepts and other tools already discussed, in

noted that in other situations the subjective character of spatial-juxta-position economies may not constitute a serious obstacle to analysis. For example, in certain cases the interrelations of activities might be such that spatial juxtaposition of all the activities leads to substantial economies which could be achieved only in full combination. If so, a realistic locational or regional analysis need only evaluate for each potential location a complex containing the full group of activities and need not consider split-location patterns. Furthermore, in such a situation it can often be further postulated that the economies of spatial juxtaposition are approximately equal in magnitude at all feasible locations. Thus it is sufficient for the analyst to pursue a locational comparison of the full complex, using only the relatively objective data on regional differences in production and transport costs; such data are more easily obtainable.[27] And even when spatial-juxtaposition economies are not so large and pressing as to require full complexes at each possible location, these economies nonetheless may permit the analyst to consider only a small number of possible split-location patterns, and to some extent to narrow down the alternatives for policy consideration.

D. GENERAL EVALUATION

To sum up, industrial complex analysis is concerned with regional patterns of incidence and growth of groups of industrial activities subject to important technological (production), marketing, and other interrela-tions. These interrelations can be attacked by a modern Weberian framework. In such a framework we look at locational interdependence via an interactivity matrix (i.e., an interindustry matrix with alternative processes and with added data which permit adjustments for certain nonlinearities and scale economies). By so doing, we attack several forms of locational interdependence, where one activity constitutes the market for the product of another activity, where the scale of operation of one activity affects factor proportions and costs in another, etc. We follow

ways to be indicated in Chapter 12. If such an analysis could be carried out success-fully, the results could be used as a partial basis for decisions by regional governments concerning a variable tax subsidy program applicable to a full complex on the one hand and to various possible smaller subcomplexes on the other.

[27] It might be objected in this connection that such a procedure disregards possible differences in the magnitude of external economies, for example urbanization economies, available to the industrial complex in question at different locations. This objection is valid to some extent. Yet on the other hand some of these advantages which are largely a function of the existing configuration of economic and social activities at each possible location tend to be reflected in the set of regional prices and costs used in the initial locational comparison.

typical comparative cost procedures. We evaluate differences among regions in transport, labor, power, and fuel costs, etc., and in production cost arising from scale of operation. From such evaluation any one of a number of possible efficient location patterns can emerge. We may find that for one configuration of markets all the activities might best be included in one giant complex concentrated at a single location; for another configuration of markets the activities might best be geographically split in three parts, giving rise to several types of smaller complexes at three locations; and for yet another configuration of markets a still greater number of still smaller complexes might be indicated, etc. In short, many diverse patterns are possible, depending on the geographic spread of markets as well as on other major factors such as the geographic spread of basic raw material sources.

   However, industrial complex analysis, just as single-industry location analysis, must attack spatial-juxtaposition economies; and in attacking these economies, industrial complex analysis may permit more meaningful industrial projections or greater understanding of industrial location patterns. If economies of spatial juxtaposition are known to be of major significance in *full* complexes and roughly of the same magnitude from location to location, comparative analysis may safely proceed with an evaluation of only objective locational factors of transport cost differentials and production cost differentials (including the scale factor for each individual activity) affecting the full complex at each potential location. If spatial-juxtaposition economies are modest, they must be calculated in order to compare full complexes with split-location patterns of smaller complexes. Because of the intangible nature of many spatial-juxtaposition advantages, they are not subject to accurate calculation. Any comparative cost conclusions in which these subjective factors enter must accordingly be interpreted with caution.

   In developing the conceptual framework and procedures we have drawn empirical materials almost exclusively from a study of hydrocarbon complexes for the region of Puerto Rico. But as with most regional techniques, the industrial complex approach has relevance and can yield valid empirical materials for many regions of the world. In the analysis of complexes based on hydrocarbons, oil is not the only major source; coal and natural gas are among other major sources. Each region of the world is unique in its relations to these sources. Each region is unique with reference to potential markets. Each region is unique in its labor resources, capital stock, mineral endowment, and so forth. Nonetheless, this does not raise obstacles in the use of a common industrial complex approach. The unique characteristics of each region show up in the cost and revenue differentials which are relevant for its situation, in the choice of end products to be produced, in the specific chemical intermediate stages which are selected. For example, if the region is New England, we would, because of the labor factor, consider producing plastics rather than synthetic fibers. Or if it is Venezuela, we would consider starting with natural gas rather than oil as the basic raw material. Or if it is a state in India, we would give considerable weight to capital requirements in designing meaningful programs. And so forth. Briefly put, the industrial complex approach with respect to the use of hydrocarbons is relevant for many regions of the world and has at least some general validity, although the data employed in each matrix and the considerations governing the selection of relevant processes and products are different from region to region.

Generalizing further, the industrial complex approach can be applied to a wide variety of interrelated groups (subsystems) of activities, some of which have been noted earlier in this chapter. Whatever the group (subsystem) considered, the specific procedures and structure of study will tend to vary from complex to complex, as well as from region to region.

In conclusion, it may be stated that for many problems of resource use, industrial location, and regional development, industrial complex analysis is a useful technique. It can identify and evaluate profitable situations and activity combinations which cannot be accurately assessed, either by industry-by-industry comparative cost studies or by strictly linear inter-industry techniques. In one sense, the industrial complex approach is a hybrid approach; it can effectively isolate and evaluate the interplay of key variables among groups (subsystems) of highly interrelated activities.

Yet there are limits to the use of the industrial complex approach in understanding and projecting an interregional system of industrial locations. Obviously it should not be employed where the production and marketing interrelations among activities of a reference group are relatively insignificant. Further, its effectiveness may be severely restricted in situations in which some of the activity interrelations result in economies of spatial juxtaposition which are largely nonquantifiable. More important, it fails to penetrate as deeply into a specific industry as an individual comparative cost study does. Nor in attacking systems of activity does it achieve the breadth of the typical regional and interregional input-output technique and other promising techniques of a general equilibrium orientation. However, the real merit of the industrial complex approach is not as a substitute for any one or more of the regional techniques already discussed. Rather its merit is as a complement to these techniques. For example, in the study of an interregional system the analyst may employ the industrial complex approach in handling variation in the level of certain sectors (industries or activities) which are highly interrelated (such as the refinery, petrochemical, synthetic materials in each region), while he permits variation in the level of other sectors (such as power and retailing in each region) via input-output procedures, and even variation in the level of still other sectors (such as coal mining in each region) via the optimization procedures of a linear programming approach to be discussed in the next chapter.

But discussion of such complementary use and synthesis is the province of Chapter 12 and should await the full exposition of (1) *interregional linear programming* as another optimizing approach which in breadth of activity and industry coverage promises to push beyond the limits confining the industrial complex approach and (2) *gravity models* which may cast greater light on spatial-juxtaposition phenomena present in the several systems of society.

REFERENCES

1. Airov, Joseph, *The Location of the Synthetic-Fiber Industry: A Study in Regional Analysis*, John Wiley, New York, 1959.
2. Isard, Walter, *Location and Space-Economy*, John Wiley, New York, 1956.
3. ———, and Eugene W. Schooler, "Industrial Complex Analysis, Agglomeration Economies and Regional Development," *Journal of Regional Science*, Vol. 1 (Spring 1959).
4. ———, and ———, *Location Factors in the Petrochemical Industry*, Office of Technical Services, U. S. Department of Commerce, Washington, D.C., 1955.
5. ———, ———, and Thomas Vietorisz, *Industrial Complex Analysis and Regional Development*, John Wiley, New York, 1959.
6. ———, and Thomas Vietorisz, "Industrial Complex Analysis and Regional Development, with Particular Reference to Puerto Rico," *Papers and Proceedings of the Regional Science Association*, Vol. 1 (1955).
7. Lindsay, J. Robert, *The Location of Oil Refining in the United States*, doctoral dissertation, Harvard University, Cambridge, Massachusetts, 1954.

Chapter 10

Interregional Linear
Programming

A. INTRODUCTION

An analyst is perplexed with many problems when he looks at a region. One problem may be to identify specific industries which can individually or in groups operate efficiently and with profit in the region. Another related problem may be to improve the welfare of the people of the region, that is, to raise per capita incomes and perhaps achieve a more equitable distribution of income; the auxiliary problem of measurement of income and of the performance of a society is also present. Still another problem may be to avoid an industrial mix which is too sensitive to the ups and downs of national and world business, and which is composed too heavily of old, slow-growing, or declining industries; this is the problem of diversification. Finally, a fourth problem which can be mentioned is to plan industrial development for a region, as part of a system of regions, in an internally consistent manner.

Techniques geared to these problems have been discussed at some length in previous chapters. One pressing problem, however, which up to now has been largely skirted, and which for many regions is the most critical, is the problem of how to put to best use a limited, if not a niggardly, endowment of resources. For example, a region may have limited water available for industrial development. How best employ that water in terms of a predetermined goal? Or a region may be short on both capital and skilled labor, as is true of many underdeveloped regions. How exploit these resources most efficiently to attain certain income, employment, or other objectives? Or a metropolitan area may confront a land shortage. How plan an industrial expansion program to maximize revenue or to achieve any other goal, subject to certain capital budget restrictions?

To some extent, the techniques already discussed have bearing on this resource scarcity problem, but none do so as forcefully and directly as interregional linear programming.[1]

Like interregional input-output and industrial complex techniques, interregional linear programming emphasizes general interdependence. Unlike interregional input-output, it is an optimizing technique. And compared to the industrial complex technique, it can treat a much broader framework in the analysis of an interindustry system.

Generally speaking, interregional linear programming pertains to problems in which the objective is to maximize or minimize some linear function, subject to certain linear inequalities. In such situations it purports to answer this kind of question: given a set of limited resources (which may include plant capacities, transportation, and urban facilities, as well as mineral, labor, and other natural and human endowments), given a technology in the form of a set of constant production coefficients, given a set of prices (except on the factors in limited supply), how program diverse production activities in order to maximize profits, social gains, total income, per capita income, employment, gross social product, or some other magnitude? Or how program diverse production activities in order to minimize transportation volumes, man-hours of work, or some other magnitude, subject to the achievement of certain levels of output and consumption? In an interregional setting the question can be still broader. For each of the several regions of a system, there is given a set of limited resources, a technology (which may be the same from region to region but which may lead to different production practices among regions because of different resource endowments), a set of prices on factors and commodities not in limited supply (where prices in the region

---

[1] Some general references on linear programming are R. G. D. Allen [1], chs. 16–19; A. Charnes, W. W. Cooper, and A. Henderson [4]; J. Chipman [5, 6]; R. Dorfman, P. A. Samuelson, and R. M. Solow [7]; and T. C. Koopmans [20]. Among others, the following papers deal in one way or another with regional and locational aspects of linear programming; M. Beckman and T. Marschak [2]; E. B. Berman [3]; W. L. Garrison and D. F. Marble [8]; T. A. Goldman [9]; J. M. Henderson [11–14]; A. R. Koch and M. M. Snodgrass [19]; T. C. Koopmans [20], chs. 14, 23; L. Lefeber [21, 22]; F. T. Moore [23]; L. N. Moses [24]; E. W. Orr [25]; P. A. Samuelson [26]; B. H. Stevens [28, 29]; and T. Vietorisz [30], Part 1.

are interrelated with prices in other regions through the existence or possibility of trade). How program the diverse production and shipping activities of any given region in order to maximize income, employment, or some other magnitude relating to the region? Or, more broadly, how program the diverse production and shipping activities of the several regions in order to maximize income, employment, or some other magnitude of the interregional system (or nation, if the several regions do comprise a nation)?

As yet, there has not been a general linear programming model which has been both designed and profitably applied to a regional or interregional question of such broad scope as those posed in these paragraphs. Yet there is considerable promise in this direction.[2] Some of the major difficulties encountered along the way will become evident in the discussion of the following sections.

In the next section we begin at the most elementary level. We look at a regional problem involving two activities and four resources only. Step by step, reality (and complexity) is added to this framework, until a rather pure, general interregional model is developed. It is not intended that the model as such be implemented. Rather the model is constructed to furnish a framework for the design of more specific interregional linear programs aimed at application to regional problems. Finally, in the next to last section some applications of rather simple interregional linear programs are examined.[3]

B. A Simple Linear Programming Problem: A Graphic Solution

To illustrate the use of the technique on a specific, oversimplified level, consider a hypothetical isolated region desiring to realize a maximum of new income from productive activities but having available for such purposes only a limited quantity of each of four resources: water, land, labor, and capital, the last being free for investment. Two economic activities have been identified as "profitable." To generate one dollar of new income, each activity requires a set of inputs of each of these resources as listed in Table 1. (In linear programming we must generally assume, as we

[2] A series of significant steps have been taken and have already culminated in several important, although restricted, studies. For example, see J. M. Henderson [11–14].

[3] The reader unversed in mathematics and advanced social science analysis may choose to read the first sections of this chapter and then skip to the last two sections on applications and conclusions, respectively. Also the reader is reminded that this chapter aims at exposition rather than evaluation. Interregional linear programming is a very recent development, and as yet there is insufficient experience by which to attempt to enumerate and discuss its virtues and limitations and reach a balanced judgment on its general applicability.

do in this problem, constant production coefficients and fixed prices on all commodities but resources in limited supply.)

If we define the unit level of operation of each activity as that level which generates one dollar of new income, the data of Table 1 refer to unit levels of operations. We now desire to find the most desirable combination of levels (i.e., multiples of these unit levels) at which to operate these activities. Since these levels are unknowns, they may be designated X_1 and X_2, respectively. To work with, the region has only 6 MM units of water, 1.8 MM units of land, 3 MM units of labor, and 24 MM units of capital.

The problem can be solved rather easily with the use of a graph. Along the vertical axis of Figure 1 we measure level of activity 1; along the horizontal axis that of activity 2. Next we construct resource limitation lines. The water limitation line NU indicates the various combinations of levels of activities 1 and 2, whose water requirements do not exceed the

TABLE 1.   RESOURCE REQUIREMENTS PER DOLLAR NEW INCOME

Required Units of:	Activities	
	1	2
Water	0.5	0.6
Land	0.2	0.15
Labor	0.4	0.2
Capital	3.0	2.0

6 MM units available for consumption. At one extreme (given by point N) operation of activity 1 at a level of 12 MM units could be achieved provided activity 2 were carried on at zero level. At the other extreme (given by point U) operation of activity 2 at a level of 10 MM units could be achieved, provided activity 1 were carried on at zero level. Along the line and in between points N and U are the various combinations of levels of the two activities which just exhaust the available 6 MM units of water. Below and to the left of line NU are an infinite number of points, each of which, however, represents combinations of levels which require less than 6 MM units of water. Since for any given point below and to the left of NU there can always be found a point on line NU which corresponds to greater levels of both activities, all points in the positive quadrant bounded by NU (but not including NU) may be said to represent *inefficient* combinations *so far as the water limitation is pertinent.*

However, if we move up along the vertical axis (corresponding to zero level of activity 2), we find that well before the water limitation on the level of activity 1 takes effect, the limitations on labor, capital, and land have become effective. At point R, for example, the labor limitation becomes operative. At this extreme point, given only 3 MM units of labor and the requirement of 0.4 units of labor at unit level, the maximum level at which activity 1 can be operated is 7.5 MM units. Thus it becomes necessary to consider other resource limitations. To do so we

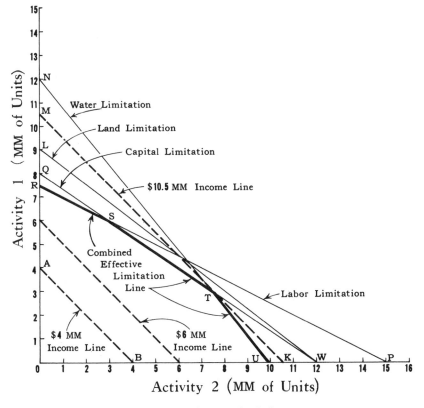

Figure 1. Graphic solution to a simple linear program.

have constructed the labor limitation line RP, the capital limitation line QW, and the land limitation line LW. These lines are constructed on the same basis as the water limitation line. For example, point P at the other extreme of the labor limitation line indicates that activity 2 can be carried on at a maximum level of 15 MM units, provided activity 1 is pursued at zero level. And points along line RP indicate all combinations of levels of the two activities whose requirements of labor just equal the available

3 MM units.   Points below and to the left of the labor limitation line *RP* are inefficient, *so far as the labor limitation is pertinent.*

In this problem the implications of *all* resource limitations must be considered.   It is clear that any combination of levels represented by a point in the area above the stretch *RS* (e.g., the combination of 7.7 MM units of activity 1 and 0.1 MM units of activity 2) is unattainable.   Although such a combination may consume amounts of capital, land, and water which do not exceed the available quantities of these resources, it does require labor in excess of available supply.   Hence the labor limitation line, in particular stretch *RS*, is binding in this area of the positive quadrant.   Passing to the right of point *S*—or more strictly to the right of a line drawn from the origin through *S*—another resource limitation line, namely that representing capital, becomes binding.   In this area, any point representing a combination of activity levels that is feasible from the standpoint of available capital is also feasible, from the standpoint of other available resources.   On the other hand, any point representing a combination that is feasible from the standpoint of these other resources is not necessarily feasible from the standpoint of capital.   For example, combinations represented by points directly above the stretch *ST* require a capital supply in excess of that available, although these combinations do not exceed other resource limitations.   Hence, the capital limitation line, in particular stretch *ST*, is effective in this area.

Going still further to the right beyond *T*—more strictly to the area to the right of the ray from the origin through *T*—another resource limitation becomes binding, namely water.   Water is the first resource whose available supply is fully utilized by combinations of levels of activities 1 and 2 which can be represented by points in this area.   In particular, the stretch *TU* of the water limitation line becomes effective.

In brief, then, the segmented line *RSTU* delineates a closed set of points in the positive quadrant which represent all combinations of activity levels feasible from the standpoint of each and every resource limitation.   These are attainable points.   Combinations represented by points in the positive quadrant but outside this closed set require at least one resource in excess of available supply.   These combinations are not feasible; the corresponding points are *unattainable*.   Further, since it can be demonstrated that any point in this closed area not on *RSTU* is inferior to some point on the line, in the sense that the latter point corresponds to greater achievable levels for both activities, we can state that all *efficient* points of the feasible set of points lie on the segmented line *RSTU*.[4]

<hr>

[4] In linear programming parlance, the segmented line *RSTU* is designated the "efficiency frontier," or in mathematical parlance the "convex hull" of attainable points.

Having eliminated "inefficient" combinations of activity levels, we now seek to determine what efficient combination will maximize new income, that is, the optimal combination. To do this is relatively simple since for each activity we have already defined the unit level as the level that generates $1.00 of new income. Following standard procedures in economic analysis, we may construct "iso-income" lines. For example, point A in Figure 1 represents a combination of a 4 MM-unit level of activity 1 and a zero-unit level of activity 2; therefore, it corresponds to $4 MM of new income. Point B represents a combination of a zero-unit level of activity 1 and a 4 MM-unit level of activity 2; it also corresponds to $4 MM of new income. Likewise, combinations of levels represented by all points lying along a straight line from A to B yield $4 MM of income. Thus we have a $4 MM-income line (dashed in Figure 1). Similarly, we can obtain a $6 MM-income line (dashed in Figure 1) and other lines, each representing a locus of points which represent combinations yielding the same total income, and each with a slope of -1 when the scales along the vertical and horizontal axes are identical. Since the "iso-income" lines increase in value as we move farther and farther from the origin, we wish to identify the highest "iso-income" line on which any of our "efficient" points (i.e., points on $RSTU$) lie. Such a line is the $10.5 MM-income line upon which point T lies. Thus point T represents the combination of activity levels (namely, 3 MM units for 1 and 7.5 MM units for 2) which maximizes new income. It is the optimal solution, which is therefore the solution to our simple problem.

C. A SIMPLEX-TYPE COMPUTATION

This type of graphic solution is simple and effective when only two activities are considered. Unfortunately, the graphic solution becomes complex when a third activity is introduced into the problem. Three dimensions must then be used, the level of the third activity being measured along the third dimension. And when we introduce a fourth activity, a fifth, a sixth, ..., and finally an nth activity into the problem, a direct graphic solution is not possible. It is at this point that other types of solutions must be sought to the linear programming problem. It also becomes desirable at this point to state the problem in more formal, mathematical terms.

To begin, suppose $n = 3$, that is, that there are three activities to be considered. Associated with each activity is a set of data indicating inputs of each resource required in order for that activity to operate at unit level and thus generate one dollar of new income.   We represent these data by a set of coefficients as follows:

$$\begin{bmatrix} a_{11}, & a_{12}, & a_{13} \\ a_{21}, & a_{22}, & a_{23} \\ a_{31}, & a_{32}, & a_{33} \\ a_{41}, & a_{42}, & a_{43} \end{bmatrix}$$

If the data of Table 1 are still relevant for the first two activities, then a_{21} which represents the requirement of *resource 2* (namely land) per unit level of *activity 1* is 0.2; a_{12} which represents the requirement of *resource 1* (namely water) per unit level of *activity 2* is 0.6; a_{32} which represents the requirement of *resource 3* (namely labor) per unit level of *activity 2* is 0.2, etc.   Letting X_1, X_2, and X_3 represent the levels of activities 1, 2, and 3, respectively, which are to be determined and which are restricted to nonnegative values, we wish to maximize income which is equal to $1.00 \times Z$ where

(1) $Z = X_1 + X_2 + X_3;$

or more specifically, to maximize Z (i.e., the number of dollar-generating units) subject to the conditions that the sum of the requirement of any one resource by all activities not exceed the supply of that resource.   If we denote R_1, R_2, R_3, and R_4 as the available supplies of water, land, labor, and capital, respectively (which in our problem are 6 MM, 1.8 MM, 3 MM, and 24 MM units, respectively), and if we note, for example, that $a_{12}X_2$ represents the requirement of the first resource by the second activity [since this involves multiplying the requirements of resource 1 per unit level of activity 2 (i.e., a_{12}) by the level of activity 2 (i.e., X_2)], the conditions can be written

(2)
$$a_{11}X_1 + a_{12}X_2 + a_{13}X_3 \leq R_1$$
$$a_{21}X_1 + a_{22}X_2 + a_{23}X_3 \leq R_2$$
$$a_{31}X_1 + a_{32}X_2 + a_{33}X_3 \leq R_3$$
$$a_{41}X_1 + a_{42}X_2 + a_{43}X_3 \leq R_4$$

The first of these inequalities, for example, states that the requirement of resource 1 by activity 1 *plus* the requirement of resource 1 by activity 2 *plus* the requirement of resource 1 by activity 3 is less than or equal to the available supply of resource 1.

Note that our problem conforms to the general framework of linear programming.   We are maximizing Z, which is a *linear* function of nonnegative variables (X_1, X_2, and X_3) subject to four restraints, each one of which is a *linear* inequality.

Once the problem has been appropriately formulated, a computational procedure must be adopted. There are several which are possible,[5] the one in most general use being the simplex method. The simplex method is one of iteration and typically involves in a many resource–many activity problem an extensive set of computations for which a high-speed computing machine is utilized.

In order to illustrate the simplex method in a manageable way, we shall confine our problem to only two limited resources (say water and land) and three activities. We therefore wish to maximize income, that is, $\$1.00 \times Z$ where

$$(3) \qquad Z = X_1 + X_2 + X_3$$

subject to

$$(4) \qquad \begin{aligned} a_{11}X_1 + a_{12}X_2 + a_{13}X_3 &\le R_1 \\ a_{21}X_1 + a_{22}X_2 + a_{23}X_3 &\le R_2 \end{aligned}$$

and where $X_1 \ge 0$; $X_2 \ge 0$; $X_3 \ge 0$. The first step is to change the inequalities 4 into a set of equations by introducing *slack* variables. Each slack variable refers to the level at which we operate a corresponding *disposal* activity, where a disposal activity can dispose of a resource at zero cost and does not give rise to any additional income. For the sake of convenience, the unit level of a disposal activity may be defined as that level which disposes of a unit of the relevant resource. In our problem we may therefore inject two new activities: a fourth activity which disposes of water and whose level is X_4, and a fifth activity which disposes of idle land and whose level is X_5. Thus, for nonnegative values of X_1, X_2, X_3, X_4, and X_5 we wish to maximize income, namely Y, where

$$(5) \qquad Y = c_1 X_1 + c_2 X_2 + c_3 X_3 + c_4 X_4 + c_5 X_5$$

in which c_1, c_2, and c_3 represent the new income from operating at unit level activities 1, 2, and 3, respectively, and which in our problem have the value of $\$1.00$; and c_4 and c_5 represent new income from operating at unit level the disposal activities 4 and 5, respectively, and which by definition have the value of $\$0.00$. [Equation 5 states the objective; it therefore is called the *objective function*.] In maximizing Y, we are subject to the constraints

$$(6) \qquad \begin{aligned} a_{11}X_1 + a_{12}X_2 + a_{13}X_3 + a_{14}X_4 + a_{15}X_5 &= R_1 \\ a_{21}X_1 + a_{22}X_2 + a_{23}X_3 + a_{24}X_4 + a_{25}X_5 &= R_2 \end{aligned}$$

The first three coefficients in each of equations 6 are the corresponding coefficients of the resource input matrix represented previously. The coefficient a_{14} is unity, indicating the using up of one unit of water per

[5] See T. C. Koopmans [20] and R. Dorfman, P. A. Samuelson, and R. M. Solow [7].

unit level of operation of the water disposal activity, and the coefficient a_{24} is zero, indicating that no land inputs are required by the water disposal activity. For analogous reasons, a_{15} is zero and a_{25} is unity. Thus, for example, the first of equations 6 states that the requirement of water by the first activity plus the requirement of water by the second activity plus the requirement of water by the third activity plus the requirement of water by the water disposal activity plus the requirement of water by the land disposal activity (which requirement is zero) equals the total supply of water available.[6]

Next we select a set of values for the X's which satisfy equations 6. Note that we have only two such equations. If we so desired, we could consider any two of the five variables involved by setting the other three

TABLE 2.   RESOURCE REQUIREMENTS PER UNIT LEVEL OF ACTIVITY

Resource	Activities				
	1	2	3	4	5
1. Water	0.5	0.6	0.7	1.0	0.0
2. Land	0.2	0.15	0.1	0.0	1.0

variables equal to zero, in essence eliminating their corresponding activities from the problem. We would then have two equations in two unknowns. Provided these equations (the initial constraints) are independent and are not inconsistent, we could solve for these two unknowns; their values would represent the levels at which corresponding activities are to be operated. For example, if we take as the relevant coefficients those indicated in Table 2,[7] and if we retain the values of 6 MM and 1.8 MM units for R_1 and R_2 respectively, we have the following two equations:

$$(7) \qquad \begin{aligned} 0.5X_1 + 0.6X_2 + 0.7X_3 + 1.0X_4 + 0.0X_5 &= 6 \text{ MM} \\ 0.2X_1 + 0.15X_2 + 0.1X_3 + 0.0X_4 + 1.0X_5 &= 1.8 \text{ MM} \end{aligned}$$

[6] If we refer to the graphic solution of the problem which involved two activities and four resources, we observe that the available supply both of water and capital were fully employed, but that the requirements of land fell short of available supply by 1.275 MM units. If we were to introduce into that problem a land disposal activity which used up one unit of land per unit level of operations, and which operated at a level of 1.275 MM units, the total requirements of land would equal total supply available, that is, $a_{21}X_1 + a_{22}X_2 + a_{25}X_5$ would equal R_2.

[7] In this table of coefficients a_{11}, a_{12}, a_{21}, and a_{22} (0.5, 0.6, 0.2, and 0.15) are taken from Table 1. The coefficients a_{13} and a_{23} (0.7 and 0.1) are new and indicate respectively the requirements of water and land per unit level of the third activity. The coefficients a_{14}, a_{15}, a_{24}, and a_{25} (1.0, 0.0, 0.0, and 1.0) are in keeping with the statements already made in the text.

If we now set $X_1 = X_2 = X_3 = 0$, we obtain

(8)
$$1.0X_4 + 0.0X_5 = 6 \text{ MM}$$
$$0.0X_4 + 1.0X_5 = 1.8 \text{ MM}$$

Immediately apparent is the solution to equations 8, which gives $X_4 = 6$ MM and $X_5 = 1.8$ MM.

In the same manner, we could obtain solutions for every other pair of variables, provided we confront consistent and independent equations.[8] Further, there are still many other solutions possible. There are many with positive values for three variables and zero for the other two (e.g., $X_1 = 1$ MM, $X_2 = X_3 = 0$, $X_4 = 5.5$ MM, and $X_5 = 1.6$ MM). There are also many with positive values for four variables and zero for the other (e.g., $X_1 = 2$ MM, $X_2 = 3$ MM, $X_3 = 0$, $X_4 = 3.2$ MM, and $X_5 = 0.95$ MM). Finally, there are many with positive values for all five variables.

In our problem, however, we are interested in finding that solution which yields maximum income (or that set of solutions, each of which is associated with the same maximum income). Since we are dealing with linear equations, we can use a simple logical process to reduce by many-fold the number of necessary computations. Take a solution which involves more than two variables, say the one where $X_1 = 4.5$ MM, $X_2 = X_3 = 0$, $X_4 = 3.75$ MM, and $X_5 = 0.9$ MM. This solution may be termed a three-variable solution since only three variables have values greater than zero, the others being zero. Further, this three-variable solution can be viewed as a weighted average of two other solutions, each involving only two variables, where the weights add to unity. In this specific case the first of these other two-variable solutions is

$$X_1 = 9 \text{ MM} \quad \text{and} \quad X_4 = 1.5 \text{ MM}$$

and the second is

$$X_4 = 6 \text{ MM} \quad \text{and} \quad X_5 = 1.8 \text{ MM}$$

a two-variable solution which we already noted. If we multiply the first solution by 0.5 and the second solution by 0.5 and add, we obtain the solution in three variables.

Now suppose we calculate according to equation 5 the income generated by each of these two two-variable solutions. Suppose the first has a higher income than the second. Then, since the solution in three variables is an average of the two two-variable solutions, it must follow that the

---

[8] Some of these might involve a negative value for one of the variables and hence would be discarded since we are limiting solutions to those that involve nonnegative values for all variables. For example, the solution for equations 7 where $X_2 = X_3 = X_4 = 0$ is $X_1 = 12$ MM and $X_5 = -0.6$ MM; this solution is excluded.

income associated with the three-variable solution must be less than the income associated with the better of the two-variable solutions. Thus, the better of the two-variable solutions is to be preferred to the three-variable solution.

However, it might develop that both of the two-variable solutions are equally good, that is, yield the same income. Then the three-variable solution being an average of these two solutions yields the identical income. We therefore conclude that no three-variable solution can have an income associated with it which is greater than the income associated with the best of two-variable solutions, where the best may refer to a *single* solution or to *several* solutions if more than one yield the same maximum income.

In the same manner, it can be shown that any four-variable solution can be considered a weighted average of a set of two-variable solutions, where the weights add to unity. Since such a solution is an average, the income associated with it cannot be any higher than the income associated with the best (one or several) of the two-variable solutions. At most it can only be equal to the income associated with the best of the two-variable solutions. Similarly, any five-variable solution can be expressed as a weighted average of two-variable solutions and hence cannot have an income associated with it which is any greater than the income of the best (one or several) two-variable solutions.

As a result of this simple logic we can say that if from among the two-variable solutions we find that one (or the several) which yields the highest income, we know that no other solution involving more than two variables can yield a higher income. We therefore short-cut the computation procedure for our problem by paying attention solely to two-variable solutions. The simplex method is one of several methods which aims at identifying the best (one or several) of these two-variable solutions.

For our problem the procedure of the simplex method is as follows. We pick a two-variable solution which is usually called a *basic* solution.[9] For example, take our solution where $X_4 = 6$ MM and $X_5 = 1.8$ MM. Associated with this solution is an income which is calculated by substituting these values into equation 6. The resulting income is zero. Since we suspect that we can find a higher income solution, let us consider another two-variable solution. But which one? Several are possible.

[9] A basic solution is a solution which involves no more variables than there are constraints. When the values of these variables are nonnegative, the basic solution is also feasible. A nonbasic solution is a solution which involves more variables than there are constraints. It is also feasible when the values of these variables are nonnegative. Since one of the possible optimal solutions will be a basic solution, we can always obtain an optimal solution which involves no more positive-level activities than there are constraints.

In the simplex method—which aims to examine systematically the various two-variable solutions in a relatively efficient manner—the next step is to substitute for one of the activities in the first basic solution another activity which was formerly excluded (i.e., operated at zero level). To determine which activity should be excluded and which one should take its place, we may develop a table such as Table 3.   In Table 3 the first

TABLE 3.   TEST FOR SOLUTION SUPERIOR TO FIRST BASIC SOLUTION

1st Basic Solution: Activities at Positive Levels (1)	Level at Which Operated (2)	Income per Unit Level (3)	Combination of Activities at Positive Levels in Basic Solution Technically Equivalent to (for which can be substituted) a Unit Level of:		
			Activity 1 (4)	Activity 2 (5)	Activity 3 (6)
4	6 MM	$0.00	0.5	0.6	0.7
5	1.8 MM	0.00	0.2	0.15	0.1
A. Income generated by above combinations of activities 4 and 5			$0.00	$0.00	$0.00
B. New income generated by unit level of			1.00	1.00	1.00
C. Difference $(B - A)$ = Net gain from substituting for above combination a unit level of			1.00	1.00	1.00

An excluded activity associated with the maximum difference: activity 1.
Number of units of activity 1 which can be substituted into the problem until the
level of $\begin{cases} \text{activity 4 falls to zero: 6 MM/0.5} = \text{12 MM,} \\ \text{activity 5 falls to zero: 1.8 MM/0.2} = \text{9 MM.} \end{cases}$

column indicates the activities at positive levels in the initial basic solution. The second column indicates the levels at which each of these is operated. The third column indicates income per unit level of each of these activities.

Thus far we have recorded data already noted.   In columns 4 through 6 we present new data.   These new data indicate the *combination* of activities at positive levels in the initial basic solution, namely activities 4 and 5, which are technically equivalent to a unit level of each one of the three "excluded" activities, that is, activities which are not included in the first basic solution.   For example, the technical requirements of activity 1 at unit level are 0.5 units of water and 0.2 units of land, as given by the coefficients of Table 2.   If we reduce activity 4 by 0.5 units, we will save

0.5 units of water and none of land (since by Table 2 a unit level of activity 4 requires 1.0 units of water and 0.0 units of land). If we reduce activity 5 by 0.2 units, we will reduce requirements of water by 0.0 units and of land by 0.2 units (since by Table 2 a unit level of activity 5 requires 0.0 units of water and 1.0 units of land). Thus, our total requirements of water and land remain the same if we increase activity 1 by 1.0 units and decrease activity 4 by 0.5 units and activity 5 by 0.2 units. Thus, a unit level of activity 1 is technically equivalent to the combination of 0.5 units of activity 4 plus 0.2 units of activity 5. This combination is recorded in column 4 of Table 3.

In like manner we obtain the data for columns 5 and 6. As indicated in column 5, a unit level of activity 2 requires the same quantities of water and land as the combination of 0.6 units of activity 4 and 0.15 units of activity 5; it is therefore technically equivalent (substitutable) for this combination. Similarly, as column 6 notes, a unit level of activity 3 is technically equivalent to the combination of 0.7 units of activity 4 and 0.1 units of activity 5.

The next step is to determine whether it is profitable to substitute in our solution a unit of any "excluded" activity for its technically equivalent combination of activities 4 and 5. We therefore ask (1) what will be the direct gain in income from operating an excluded activity at unit level? (2) What will be the corresponding loss in income by curtailing the operation of activities 4 and 5 in order to release the necessary resources? (3) Is the gain greater or smaller than the loss? The answers to these questions are given in rows A, B, and C of Table 3. To illustrate, take activity 1. To increase it from zero to unit level necessitates first the curtailment of activity 4 by 0.5 units which results in a zero loss of income since income from a unit level of operation of activity 4 (the water disposal activity) is zero; and second the reduction of activity 5 by 0.2 units which also results in a zero loss of income, since income from a unit level of operation of activity 5 (the land disposal activity) is zero. All told the loss of income, that is, the income generated by this combination of activities 4 and 5, is zero. This figure is given in row A, column 4, Table 3. The new income generated by increasing activity 1 from zero level to unit level is $1.00, as defined in connection with equation 5. This figure is noted in row B, column 4. The difference between the figures in rows B and A of column 4 is $1.00 and represents the net gain in income from increasing activity 1 by a unit level while necessarily decreasing activities 4 and 5 by that combination of levels technically equivalent to a unit level of activity 1 in the use of resources. This difference is given in row C, column 4. Since this difference is positive, it is profitable to substitute activity 1 for its technically equivalent combination of activities 4 and 5.

But perhaps it is still more profitable to substitute still another "excluded" activity, say activity 2 or 3, for its equivalent combination of activities 4 and 5. To determine whether or not this is true, we perform the same computation for each of these activities, the resulting data being recorded in Table 3. Looking at Table 3, in particular row C, we note that it is as equally profitable to substitute a unit level of activity 2 (or 3) for its equivalent combination of activities 4 and 5 as it is to substitute a unit level of activity 1 for its corresponding equivalent combination. To break the deadlock, we choose to substitute activity 1 for activities 4 and 5; that is, our procedure is to choose to substitute for a combination of the included activities an "excluded" activity associated with the maximum difference (recorded in row C).

Since in our framework each activity operates at constant unit cost, if it is profitable to substitute one unit of activity 1 for an equivalent combination of activities 4 and 5, it is profitable to substitute many units for a like multiple of this combination. But the terms of reference in our problem state that no activity can be operated at a negative level. Therefore, all we can do is to continue to substitute unit levels of activity 1 for equivalent combinations of 0.5 units of activity 4 and 0.2 units of activity 5 until the over-all level of one of these activities is reduced to zero. From the calculations at the bottom of Table 3, we note that activity 4 will not reach the zero level until we have substituted in 6 MM/0.5 or 12 MM units of activity 1; whereas activity 5 will not reach the zero level until we have substituted in 1.8 MM/0.2 or 9 MM units of activity 1. We therefore are allowed to substitute only 9 MM units of activity 1 into the problem. When this occurs, the operation of activity 5 has been reduced to zero; the level of activity 5 has been eliminated as a variable.

Our next step is to consider the superior solution in which activities 1 and 4 are operated at positive levels. (We have demonstrated that a solution with activities 1, 4, and 5, as well as one with just activities 4 and 5, is inferior.) We return to equations 7. We set $X_2 = X_3 = X_5 = 0$. We solve and find that $X_1 = 9$ MM units and $X_4 = 1.5$ MM.[10] We call this the second basic solution. We are now ready to set up a second table, Table 4, which evaluates the second basic solution.

In Table 4 the first column indicates the activities to be operated at positive levels. The second column indicates the levels at which they are operated. The third column indicates income per unit level of each of the included activities (as given in equation 5). The fourth and fifth columns pertain to activities 2 and 3 which are "excluded" from this second basic

[10] We could have derived this solution directly from Table 3 since we have already established the fact that X_1 should be 9 MM units (the level at which one of the previously included activities first becomes zero.)

solution. (Note that there is no column for the excluded activity 5. This is so because it can be demonstrated—as intuitively seems logical—that once an activity has been eliminated in proceeding from one basic solution to a second, superior basic solution, it will not be one of the included activities in the one or more basic solutions which will be associated with *maximum* income. Therefore, we need not consider reintroducing activity 5 by substitution for an equivalent combination of "included" activities.)

We now investigate the profitability of substituting one of the excluded

TABLE 4. TEST FOR SOLUTION SUPERIOR TO SECOND BASIC SOLUTION

Second Basic Solution: Activities at Positive Levels (1)	Level at which Operated (2)	Income per Unit Level (3)	Combination of Activities at Positive Levels in Basic Solution Technically Equivalent to (for which can be substituted) a Unit level of:	
			Activity 2 (4)	Activity 3 (5)
1	9 MM	$1.00	0.75	0.5
4	1.5 MM	0.00	0.225	0.45
A. Income generated by above combination of activities 1 and 4			$0.75	$0.50
B. New income generated by unit level of:			1.00	1.00
C. Difference $(B - A)$ = Net gain from substituting for above combination a unit level of:			0.25	0.50

Activity associated with maximum positive difference: activity 3.

Number of units of activity 3 which can be substituted into the problem until the level of $\begin{cases} \text{activity 1 falls to zero: } 9 \text{ MM}/0.5 = 18 \text{ MM,} \\ \text{activity 4 falls to zero: } 1.5 \text{ MM}/0.45 = 3.33 \text{ MM.} \end{cases}$

activities (2 or 3) for one of the included ones (1 or 4). The first two items in columns 4 and 5 indicate the combinations of activities 1 and 4 to which a unit level of activity 2 and 3 is respectively technically equivalent. Thus, for example, activity 2 is technically equivalent to a combination of 0.75 units of activity 1 and 0.225 units of activity 4. That is, if we reduce activity 1 by 0.75 units and activity 4 by 0.225 units, we will release just enough water and land to make possible a unit level of activity 2. If we do reduce activity 1 by 0.75 units, we lose $0.75 of income since activity 1 generates $1.00 income per unit level, and if we do reduce activity 4 by

0.225 units, we lose zero income since activity 4 generates zero income per unit level. All told, if we reduce activity 1 by 0.75 units and activity 4 by 0.225 units, we lose $0.75 income, which is recorded in row A, column 4, Table 4. But as we reduce these activities by these amounts, we can increase activity 2 by one unit. This increase generates $1.00 of new income, since income per unit level of activity 2 is $1.00. This $1.00 is recorded in row B, column 4. The difference between the gain and the loss, namely $0.25, is recorded in row C, column 4. Thus our total income would rise by $0.25 every time we substitute one unit of activity 2 for 0.75 units of activity 1 and 0.225 units of activity 4.

In similar manner we perform the same computations for activity 3 (and in the general case for any other "excluded" activity which has not previously been eliminated). The results of this computation are recorded in column 5 of Table 4.

As we look over row C of Table 4 we note that the maximum gain per unit level of any excluded activity is associated with activity 3. We therefore wish to substitute units of activity 3 for technically equivalent combinations of activities 1 and 4. We can proceed with this substitution until the level of either activity 1 or 4 falls to zero. There we must stop, since no activity is permitted to be operated at negative levels. From the bottom of Table 4 we note that the level of activity 1 falls to zero when 9 MM/ 0.5 = 18 MM units of activity 3 are substituted into the solution, and that the level of activity 4 falls to zero when 1.5 MM/0.45 = 3.33 MM units of activity 3 are substituted in. Thus, we substitute 3.33 MM units of activity 3 into the solution at which point activity 4 falls to a level of zero. At that point we have a third basic solution consisting of the two activities 1 and 3. In equations 5 we let $X_2 = X_4 = X_5 = 0$ and solve. We find that $X_1 = 7.33$ MM units and $X_3 = 3.33$ MM units. This basic solution is superior to either of the first two basic solutions, or to any three- or four-variable solution consisting of activities 1 and 3 (which are included in this third basic solution) and activities 4 and 5 (which have been eliminated).

We still must ask: Is there any other basic solution which is superior to the best one we have found thus far, namely the third basic solution? To answer this question we once again carry through a set of computations. The results are presented in Table 5 which is constructed in the same manner as Tables 3 and 4. Since two of the three variables excluded from this third basic solution, namely activities 4 and 5, have already been eliminated, we need a column for only one activity, namely activity 2 which is the only activity to be considered for substitution into this third basic solution. However, we have added a column for activity 5, which was the first activity to be eliminated. We have done so in order to illustrate the unprofitability of considering excluded activities which have already been eliminated from previous basic solutions. If we consider the data pertaining to activity 5 in column 5, we note that for every unit of activity 5 which might be substituted for its technically equivalent combination of activities 1 and 3, there is a loss of $2.22.

Observing the data in column 4 which pertains to activity 2, we note that the increase in income resulting from a unit increase in the level of activity 2 is just matched by the loss of income from the necessary reduction of 0.5 units in the levels of both activities 1 and 3. The net gain as recorded in row C of column 4 is zero. Therefore, it is not possible to

TABLE 5. TEST FOR SOLUTION SUPERIOR TO THIRD BASIC SOLUTION

Third Basic Solution: Activities at Positive Levels (1)	Level at which Operated (2)	Income per Unit Level (3)	Combination of Activities at Positive Levels in Basic Solution Technically Equivalent to (for which can be substituted) a Unit Level of:	
			Activity 2 (4)	Activity 5 (5)
1	7.33 MM	$1.00	0.5	7.77
3	3.33 MM	1.00	0.5	−5.55
A. New income generated by above combination of activities 1 and 3			$1.00	$2.22
B. New income generated by unit level of:			1.00	0.00
C. Difference $(B − A)$ = Net gain from substituting for above combination a unit level of:			0.00	−2.22

Activity associated with maximum positive difference: none.

increase total income by substituting into the third basic solution a unit of activity 2 (or any other activity) for its technically equivalent combination of activities 1 and 3. We have come to the end of our journey. We have found a two-variable solution which is as good or better than any other two-variable solution, and hence as good or better than any three-variable solution, or four-variable solution, or five-variable solution. We must, however, reiterate that the third basic solution may be, and in fact is, only one of many solutions which yield the maximum attainable income. This is readily seen from Table 5. There we note that a unit level of activity 2 can be substituted for its technically equivalent combination of activities 1 and 3 without either gain or loss in total income. (Again note the data of column 4.) Hence, we can substitute into the third basic solution any number of units of activity 2 for a like multiple of activity 2's technically equivalent combination of activities 1 and 3 (provided the level of either of the latter two activities is not forced below zero). Any such substitution yields a solution which provides the same maximum income. The reader may test this for himself.

We have sketched the basic procedures in the solution of a linear programming problem via the iterative process of the simplex method. Actually, a high-speed computing machine does not carry through the operations in the exact manner we have described. Essentially, however, the machine performs the same steps based on the same logic. At times difficulties crop up in the solution, such as the problem of degeneracy. We do not look into these difficulties here since they involve rather technical discussion and since they have been fully discussed in the literature cited.

D. The Dual: A Graphic Analysis

Having presented the essence of linear programming by graphic analysis, and having illustrated the use of the simplex method in solving a linear programming problem, we have one remaining important aspect to discuss. This aspect concerns the dual of a linear program.

Mathematically speaking, every linear program expressed as a minimum has a dual problem expressed in terms of a maximum, and every linear program expressed as a maximum has a dual problem expressed in terms of a minimum. Generally in social science and regional analysis the dual problem is artificial, but it does when solved yield meaningful results. Often its significance is not direct and immediately apparent, as will be seen in the following discussion. Nonetheless, it can still be extremely useful to examine the dual. New insights can be gained on the structure and interrelation of regional forces. A check on the formulation of the original linear program can be had. Finally, as will be demonstrated later, an easier and quicker way of arriving at the solution to the linear program may be possible.

To develop the notion of the dual, we may reconsider the problem of the preceding section. The region possesses the given quantities of the two resources, water and land, which are to be priced in such a manner as to lead to a wise program of utilization. Assume that among firms conditions of perfect competition prevail, that is, that there are many firms, and that each firm is free to engage in, or abandon, any productive activity and has unrestricted opportunity to bid for resources. (For any given activity, each firm faces the same set of input requirements, as given by Table 2.)   In such a situation it is clear that no activity will be operated by any firm at a profit (where profit per unit level is defined as the difference between income and costs per unit level).[11]   For if a firm were operating an activity at a profit, new firms could begin to engage in this activity and would bid for the scarce water and land and thereby drive up the prices of these resources until all profits were eliminated.   Hence, we may conclude that costs per unit level of an activity will be at least as great as income per unit level.

But what are costs?   In this problem they are simply the costs of water and land.   (To be more realistic, the reader may suppose that there are other costs—such as costs for raw materials, labor, capital services, and management ability—which are constant and fixed per unit level of activity and which have already been deducted from gross sales value per unit level of activity to yield the income per unit level of activity.)[12]   Since a_{11} units of water are required per unit level of activity 1, this amount multiplied by the price of water, namely P_1, yields water costs $(a_{11}P_1)$ per unit level of activity 1.   Also, since a_{21} units of land are required per unit level of activity 1, this amount multiplied by the price of land, namely P_2, yields land costs $(a_{21}P_2)$ per unit level of activity 1.   The sum of these two cost items, namely $a_{11}P_1 + a_{21}P_2$, represents costs per unit level of activity 1, which by the assumption of perfect competition must not be less than c_1, the income per unit level of activity 1.   That is,

$$(9) \qquad a_{11}P_1 + a_{21}P_2 \geq c_1$$

Similarly, we derive that $a_{12}P_1 + a_{22}P_2$ (the cost per unit level of activity 2) must not be less than c_2 (the income per unit level of activity 2), and that $a_{13}P_1 + a_{23}P_2$ (the cost per unit level of activity 3) must not be less than c_3 (the income per unit level of activity 3).   That is,

$$(10) \qquad \begin{aligned} a_{12}P_1 + a_{22}P_2 &\geq c_2 \\ a_{13}P_1 + a_{23}P_2 &\geq c_3 \end{aligned}$$

[11] The term profit is used here in the sense of "excess" returns to management, over and above what is considered normal payment for capital, managerial ability, and other factors which the owner of the firm may supply.   See the following footnote for further clarification.

[12] As noted earlier, we must assume that prices are fixed not only for any commodity produced by an activity but also for any of its inputs *excluding* scarce resources, but including such items as capital services, management services, raw materials, and labor (when labor is not considered a *scarce* resource in the problem).   Since a set of co-efficients is also posited which indicates constant outputs and inputs per unit level of any activity, the supposition suggested in the text is in keeping with the nature of a customary linear program.

Thus, for any activity (whether engaged in or not) unit-level costs must equal or exceed unit-level income.[13]

In Table 2 are given the values for the a coefficients. We put these values into inequalities 9 and 10 as well as the values for c_1, c_2, and c_3. We obtain

(11)
$$0.5P_1 + 0.2P_2 \geq \$1.00$$
$$0.6P_1 + 0.15P_2 \geq \$1.00$$
$$0.7P_1 + 0.1P_2 \geq \$1.00$$

We now wish to graph what these relations would be if only the equality held, that is, if the sum of terms on the left-hand side of each equation exactly equaled $1.00. On Figure 2 lines AB, CD, and EF represent these relations in their equality form, referring respectively to activities 1, 2, and 3. [The prices of water and land (P_1 and P_2) are measured along the horizontal and vertical axes, respectively. For the moment we ignore the dashed lines.] Thus we can say that all points representing combinations of values for the prices of land and water which satisfy the first constraint (i.e., yields unit-level cost at least as great as unit-level income for activity 1) lie either on line AB or above and/or to the right. Likewise, only points on or above and/or to the right of line CD represent values for the prices which satisfy the second constraint (i.e., yields unit-level cost equal or greater than unit-level income for activity 2). Finally, only points on or above and/or to the right of line EF represent values for the prices of land and water which satisfy the third constraint. All together, therefore, only points lying on or above and/or to the right of the segmented line EMB represent combinations of prices which satisfy *all three* constraints; by the assumption of perfect competition they are the only combinations from which we are allowed to choose.[14]

Now consider the choice of a set of prices for the resources, water and land. Let us select any one from the set represented by points above

---

[13] Thus, in the typical situation when the equality holds for one or more of these constraints (i.e., unit-level costs = unit-level income), the inequality will hold for one or more other constraints (i.e., unit-level costs will exceed unit-level income). The activities corresponding to these latter constraints will not be operated.

[14] Suppose we were to consider a combination of prices which is not represented by one of these points. Suppose that this combination is given by point J in Figure 2. The combination satisfies the first two constraints but not the third constraint. Consequently, if prices as given by J had been in effect, unit-level costs of activity 3 would have been less than unit-level income, that is, there would have been a profit from engaging in activity 3. This would have led to expansion of the level of activity 3 by both new and old firms, such that resource prices would have been bid up and the profit in activity 3 would have been reduced to zero. Thus point J represents a set of prices inconsistent with an equilibrium state under assumptions of perfect competition. We are not permitted to consider this combination.

and/or to the right of the segmented line *EMB*. For ease of exposition, let us select the price of $2.00 for water and $10.00 for land, as given by point *K*. If all the stock of water and land were employed, total returns to the owners of these resources, represented by *W* where

(12) $$W = R_1 P_1 + R_2 P_2$$

would be $30 MM since from above $R_1 = 6$ MM units of water and $R_2 =$

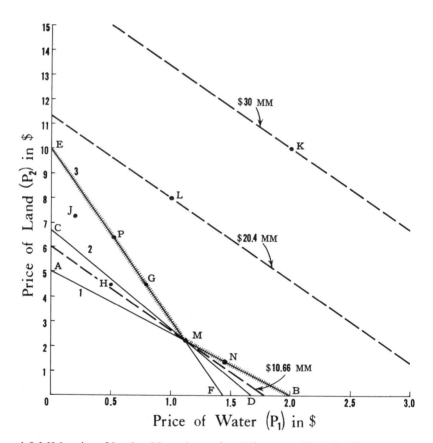

1.8 MM units of land. Note that point *K* lies on a $30 MM line, a locus of points representing all combinations of water and land prices which would yield $30 MM, provided 100 per cent of the stock of both water and land were utilized. But this total-returns figure is purely artificial. And henceforth we shall designate *W* as total *fictitious* returns. For if the price of water were $10.00 and that of land $2.00 (or if these prices were represented by any other point on the $30 MM line) unit-level costs in each of the three activities would well exceed unit-level income. Each activity would have to operate at a loss. There would, in fact, be no production and hence no employment of resources. Total *effective* returns to resource owners would be zero, and all resources would be idle. This situation is, of course, neither to the interest of the owners of the resources (whom we assume to be many in keeping with our framework of perfect competition) nor consistent with the objective of any regional planning authority interested in the wise use of resources.

We therefore seek a more desirable set of prices. Suppose we consider a set of lower prices, say $8.00 for land and $1.00 for water. (Such prices might be established by a regional planning authority or might result from competitive undercutting by the many owners of the resources.) These prices are represented by point L in Figure 2. Immediately it is seen that it would still not be profitable for any firm to engage in any activity. No resources would be employed. Total *effective* returns to resource owners would be zero, although total *fictitious* returns (i.e., the income W of equation 12 which would be realized if 100 per cent of the stock of water and land were sold at the ruling prices) would be $20.4 MM, having previously been $30.00 MM.

It is clear that the two prices must fall still more for production to occur. They must fall sufficiently so that they can be represented by some point on the segmented line EMB. (At any set of prices which can be represented by a point above and/or to the right of this segmented line, each activity operates at a loss.) Suppose we consider the set of prices, $6.50 for land and $0.50 for water, represented by point P, which set might have resulted from action by a regional planning authority or from the competitive process of price cutting. At this set of prices activity 3 can be carried on without loss, whereas activities 1 and 2 can be operated only at loss and hence will not be pursued. We may assume that activity 3 will be operated at the highest level permitted by the availability of resources. Since the stocks of water and land are 6 MM and 1.8 MM units respectively, and since 0.7 and 0.1 units of water and land are required per unit level of activity 3, activity 3 can be pursued at a level of 6 MM/0.7 or approximately 8.6 MM units. At this level all the stock of water and 0.86 MM units of the available 1.8 MM units of land are utilized. Income received by the owners of the water resources and of the land resources are $3 MM and $5.6 MM respectively, a total of $8.6 MM. Total *fictitious* returns (namely W) falls again, this time to the level of $14.7 MM.

This situation represents an improvement over the previous one from the standpoint of both the regional planning authority and owners of

resources.   Since not all the land is used, is there still a better situation ?
Certainly we could expect those owners of land who were unsuccessful in
selling their resource (and thus who receive no income) to explore another
situation.   Suppose, to decrease the amount of idle land, the regional
planning authority sets a lower price on land, say $4.4, or suppose this
price is reached as a result of competitive price cutting by land owners.
The corresponding price of water would be raised to $0.8, as given by
point G in Figure 2.[15]   Once again, only activity 3 would be pursued; and
if it were pursued at its maximum level, namely 8.6 MM units, all the stock
of water and 0.86 MM units of the available 1.8 MM units of land would
be utilized.   Income received by the owners of the land resource would
have fallen to $3.8 MM (because of lower land price), whereas income
received by water owners would have increased to $4.8 MM (because of
higher water price).   Total *effective* returns to resource owners would,
however, not have changed, being $8.6 MM, whereas total *fictitious* re-
turns (namely W) would have fallen to the level of $12.7 MM.

We conclude that, as a consequence of the price changes represented by
the shift from point P to point G on Figure 2, the pattern of resource use
does not change (the same amount of land being idle), total *effective*
returns to resource owners does not change (although land owners obtain
a smaller share), but total *fictitious* returns does continue to fall.   We
could examine other combinations of prices involving still lower prices for
land (reflecting the desire to encourage fuller resource use or the competitive process).   But all combinations represented by points lying between
points G and M, excluding point M, would not lead to any greater use of
land, or any increase in total *effective* returns to resource owners, although
the closer we approach M, the smaller the share of total *effective* returns
which goes to land owners and the smaller the total *fictitious* returns.   In
general it can be said that all combinations of prices represented by points
between E and M, excluding M, lead to the identical pattern of resource
use and yield the same *total effective* returns to resource owners.   The
closer the point is to M, the smaller (larger) the share of *effective* returns
received by land owners (water owners), and the smaller the total *fictitious*
returns.

The situation abruptly changes for a set of prices represented by point

If the price of water were not raised and were kept at $0.5 (with the price of land
set at $4.4), we would be selecting a set of prices, as represented by point H, which would
give rise to profits in both activities 2 and 3.   But this is inconsistent with our assumption of perfect competition (profitless production).   We are not permitted to select this
set of prices.   In contrast, if the price of water were raised still higher, that is, to a level
greater than $0.8, all activities could be carried on only at a loss.   There would be no
production and no use of resources, a definitely inferior situation.

M, where lines EF, CD, and AB intersect.   At such prices (namely $2.22 for land and $1.11 for water) it is possible to pursue more than one activity without loss; in fact it happens that in this particular situation it is possible to pursue all three activities without loss.   This provides much more flexibility in the use of resources (since each activity uses resources in different combinations—see Table 2) and does lead to full use of land and water resources.   Actually, each of an infinite number of combinations of levels of these three activities will lead to full use of resources. One such combination is 7.33 MM units of activity 1 and 3.33 MM units of activity 3; a second is 4 MM units of activity 1 and 6.66 MM units of activity 2; a third is 5.66 MM units of activity 1, 3.33 MM units of activity 2, and 1.66 MM units of activity 3, etc.[16]   Since each of these combinations fully utilize the resources, each yields to land owners *effective* returns of $4 MM, and to water owners $6.66 MM.   Total *effective* returns is thus $10.66 MM, a significant increase over the *effective* returns yielded by any other point on the line segment EM (or by any other point above and/ or to the right of it).   In contrast, total *fictitious* returns falls to the lowest level yet reached, namely to $10.66 MM, a level equal to total *effective* returns.

Is M the best point from the standpoint of both a regional planning authority and resource owners?   Clearly, none of the resource owners will have any incentive to shave prices since he can sell all his stock at the ruling prices.   (And if he should raise his price, no firm will purchase from him, since any firm doing so would operate at a loss.)   But a regional planning authority might not be convinced.   Suppose then we consider another set of prices, say $1.4 for water and $1.5 for land, as given by point N on stretch MB.   (Recall that stretch MB pertains to activity 1 and not to activity 3 as stretch EM does.)[17]   At these prices activities 2 and 3 are not pursued, since to do so would involve loss.   Activity 1 can be pursued without loss and may be presumed to be operated at the highest level permitted by the stock of resources.   Since 0.5 units of water and 0.2 units of land are required per unit level of activity 1 (see Table 2), activity 1 can be operated at a level of 1.8 MM/0.2 = 9 MM units, at

[16] The infinite number of combinations of activities 1, 2, and 3 which will fully utilize the available resources can be obtained (1) by starting with the combination of 7.33 MM units of activity 1 and 3.33 MM units of activity 3, and (2) by adding units of activity 2 (up to a maximum of 6.66 MM) and simultaneously subtracting units of activities 1 and 3 at a rate of one-half unit of both 1 and 3 for every unit of 2 added. This is consistent with the data of Table 5.

[17] Also, to select a set of prices represented by a point below stretch MB would imply profits in activity 1 and be inconsistent with the assumption of perfect competition among firms, whereas to select a set of prices represented by a point above stretch MB would involve loss in the operation of every activity.

which level the 1.8 MM units of available land are fully used and only 4.5 MM units of the available 6 MM units of water are employed. Returns to land owners are $2.7 MM and to water owners, $6.3 MM, which yields total *effective* returns of $9.0 MM. Total *fictitious* returns (namely W) is $11.1 MM. We therefore conclude that a shift from a set of prices given by M to a set given by N increases only total *fictitious* returns (the returns resource owners would receive provided they could sell all their stocks). Effective returns to both land owners and water owners falls, and thus total *effective* returns. Some of the stock of water is unutilized. Thus from the standpoint of both a regional planning authority and resource owners the set of prices defined by N is less desirable than that defined by M. And if there are many small competitive water resource owners, we would expect price cutting by those who were unsuccessful in selling their units, so that in effect an M set of prices would be realized if initially an N set were established.

In similar manner it can be shown that a set of prices represented by any other point along stretch MB is inferior to that represented by point M, both in terms of achieving full use of resources, and of maximizing total *effective* returns. Hence, M represents the desired set of prices. Here, full use of resources is achieved and total *effective* returns is maximized. Also, total *fictitious* returns is minimized at M. This is seen by studying the dashed lines of Figure 2. As already noted, each dashed line goes through all the points representing combinations of prices which yield the total *fictitious* returns associated with that line. As we approach the origin, the total *fictitious* returns associated with these parallel dashed lines declines. It would become zero at the origin where prices are zero; but we are not permitted to select such a set of prices. We are allowed to select only those combinations represented by points on, above, and/or to the right of segmented line EMB. Of all such points M clearly lies on the lowest dashed line. Thus total *fictitious* returns is minimized at M, given our constraints, which is the same point at which total *effective* returns to resource owners is maximized and full use of resources is achieved. Thus, in our problem, we have shown that to find the set of prices which will maximize total *effective* returns to resource owners and achieve full use of resources is *to find the set of prices that minimizes an artificial concept, namely, total fictitious returns to resource owners* [i.e., W where by equation 12: $W = R_1 P_1 + R_2 P_2$] subject to the condition that for nonnegative prices costs of activities 1, 2, and 3 (i.e., $a_{11}P_1 + a_{21}P_2$, $a_{12}P_1 + a_{22}P_2$, and $a_{13}P_1 + a_{23}P_2$) not be less than—or, put otherwise, be equal to or greater than—unit level income (c_1, c_2, and c_3) respectively. This is the dual of the original linear program.

E. The Linear Program and its Dual: Interrelationships

We now set down side by side the original linear program and its dual. [Recall the linear program was to select a set of nonnegative levels at which to operate each activity (i.e., X_1, X_2, and X_3) in order to maximize income (Y)[18] where the income from running each activity at unit level (i.e., c_1, c_2, and c_3 respectively) is \$1.00; subject to the constraints that the requirements of all three activities for land and water do not exceed the available stocks (R_1 and R_2).]

Linear Program	Dual
To maximize:	To minimize:
$Y = c_1X_1 + c_2X_2 + c_3X_3$	$W = R_1P_1 + R_2P_2$
subject to:	subject to:
$a_{11}X_1 + a_{12}X_2 + a_{13}X_3 \leq R_1$	$a_{11}P_1 + a_{21}P_2 \geq c_1$
$a_{21}X_1 + a_{22}X_2 + a_{23}X_3 \leq R_2$	$a_{12}P_1 + a_{22}P_2 \geq c_2$
$X_1 \geq 0;\ X_2 \geq 0;\ X_3 \geq 0$	$a_{13}P_1 + a_{23}P_2 \geq c_3$
	$P_1 \geq 0;\ P_2 \geq 0$

First, we note that the solutions to the two problems yield $Y = W = $ \$10.66 MM, that is, the maximum income achievable turns out to be equal to the minimum realizable total *fictitious* returns to resource owners (which is equal to maximum total *effective* returns to resource owners).[19]

Second, the constants c_1, c_2, and c_3, which respectively multiply the "choice" variables in the objective function of the linear program are each a limiting constant in a constraint of the dual. Therefore, there are as many constraints in the dual as there are choice variables in the linear program. At the same time, the limiting constants of the constraints of the linear program, namely R_1 and R_2, are the coefficients which multiply the choice variables of the dual. Hence, there are as many choice variables in the dual as there are constraints in the linear program.

Third, the coefficients of the set of constraints of the linear program, *when transposed,* are the set of coefficients of the constraints of the dual. Or, put otherwise, a *row* of coefficients in a single constraint of a linear program (such as a_{11}, a_{12}, and a_{13}) becomes a corresponding *column* which multiplies the single corresponding choice variable (such as P_1) in the dual and vice versa; and any *column* of coefficients in the linear program

[18] Also recall that $Y = $ \$1.00 $\times Z$ where $Z = X_1 + X_2 + X_3$; and that in equation 5 Y may also be viewed as the sum of the first three terms since by definition $c_4 = c_5 = 0$.

[19] Thus the linear program and its dual have a common solution here. It can be generally stated that a linear program and its dual have either a common solution or no solution at all.

(such as a_{12} and a_{22}) which multiply a single choice variable (here X_2) becomes the corresponding *row* in the set of constraints of the dual, and vice versa.

Fourth, the sense of the inequalities in the constraints of the linear program and dual are the reverse of each other. For example, where one is "less than" ($<$) as is the case for our linear program (and as must be the case for every maximum problem), the other is "greater than" ($>$) as is the case for our dual (and as must be the case for every minimum problem).[20] This rule holds except that the inequalities pertaining to nonnegative values for the choice variables in both the linear program (the X's) and dual (the P's) have the same sense.

Having presented the dual, its solution, and its relation to the linear program,[21] we can re-examine the usefulness of the dual. Clearly the magnitude to be minimized in our dual tends to be an artificial one, as is generally true of the magnitude to be minimized or maximized in the dual of any meaningful linear program.[22] Yet, posing and solving the dual permit deeper insight into the operation of the system and into the structure of the problem being examined. Useful, too, is the check on the formulation of the linear program which the formulation of the dual may afford, since certain corresponding relations must exist between a linear program and its dual. Perhaps the most important use of the dual, however, is to ease the computation task. In the previous section the simplex computation was developed for the linear program examined. Suppose we were to introduce a fourth possible activity into the linear program—an activity which yields an income of $1.10 per unit level of activity and which requires 0.40 units of water and 0.24 units of land per unit level of activity. The linear program becomes:

To maximize:

$$(13) \qquad Y = c_1X_1 + c_2X_2 + c_3X_3 + c_4X_4$$

subject to:

$$(14) \qquad \begin{aligned} a_{11}X_1 + a_{12}X_2 + a_{13}X_3 + a_{14}X_4 &\leq R_1 \\ a_{21}X_1 + a_{22}X_2 + a_{23}X_3 + a_{24}X_4 &\leq R_2 \\ X_1 \geq 0; \quad X_2 \geq 0; \quad X_3 \geq 0; \quad X_4 &\geq 0 \end{aligned}$$

[20] Thus, if the linear program is a minimum problem, the sense of the inequalities is "greater than", whereas the sense of the inequalities in the dual (which must be a maximum problem) is "less than."

[21] It is interesting to note here that the "dual" of the dual is the original linear program, as the reader may verify for the situation we have examined.

[22] For example, see R. G. D. Allen [1], pp. 539–541; and R. Dorfman, P. A. Samuelson, and R. M. Solow [7], chs. 3, 5, 7.

It is not possible to arrive quickly at the optimal solution to this new linear program via the simplex method. A set of computations would have to be made, as were performed in connection with Tables 3, 4, and 5. In contrast to this relatively time-consuming task we can convert the new linear program into its dual, which involves simply the addition to con-

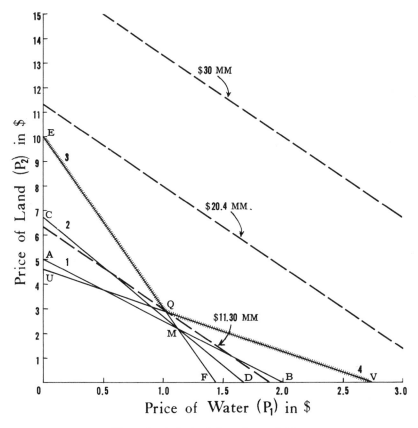

Figure 3. A dual solution: four activities.

straints (11) of one more constraint, namely, that for activity 4 unit-level cost be at least as great as unit-level income (i.e., $0.40P_1 + 0.24P_2 \geq \$1.10$). If we add to our graph this new constraint in its equality form, as designated by line UV in Figure 3,[23] we directly observe that total *fictitious* returns to resource owners is minimized at the combination of resource

[23] Figure 3 reproduces lines AB, CD, and EF of Figure 2, which indicate the first three constraints of the dual.

prices given by point Q. This immediately indicates that the optimal set of prices of water and land are, in round numbers, $1.02 and $2.89, respectively. Knowing prices, we calculate total *fictitious* returns to resource owners to be approximately $11.30 MM. This figure also represents the maximum total *effective* returns to resource owners and is also equal to the maximum of income achievable in the original linear program, that is, is equal to the total income which would be yielded by the optimal solution of the linear program. Also we note from Figure 3 that at the optimal prices (as given by point Q) the operation of both activities 1 and 2 would incur loss. Therefore, neither will be operated. In contrast, activities 3 and 4 can be operated without loss. We therefore let $X_1 = X_2 = 0$ in the two constraints 14, use the equality form of these constraints, and solve the resulting two equations in two unknowns for X_3 and X_4. We find that $X_3 = 5.63$ MM and $X_4 = 5.16$ MM, and that accordingly, by equation 13, $Y = \$11.30$ MM.

In this manner we quickly arrive at the solution of the new linear program by first solving its dual. This indeed makes the dual a useful device. But this case is a special case and is unlike the general situation. In the general situation where a linear program has more than two constraints, the graph of the dual will have more than two dimensions; and hence a quick graphic solution to the dual is not possible. Generally speaking we choose to solve the linear program or its dual, depending on which has the fewer constraints.[24]

The preceding problem, embracing four possible activities, also points up certain other relations between a linear program and its dual. When any choice variable of a linear program is at a positive level in the optimal solution, the corresponding constraint in the dual solution is binding (i.e., satisfied with exact equality). Thus we find that both X_3 and X_4 of this new linear program are positive in the optimal solution; concomitantly, constraints 3 and 4 are met with exact equality in the dual solution since point Q in Figure 3 lies on both lines EF and UV (i.e., unit-level cost equals unit-level income for both activities 3 and 4). In parallel fashion, when any choice variable of the dual is at a positive level in the optimal solution, the corresponding constraint in the linear program solution is binding (i.e., satisfied with exact equality). Thus we find that both P_1 and P_2 of the dual are positive; and correspondingly the two constraints of the linear program are met with exact equality, that is, the supplies of the two resources, water and land, are both fully utilized.

Furthermore, if a choice variable in the linear program takes the value zero in the optimal solution, the corresponding constraint in the dual

[24] This general rule, however, does not hold where a graphic solution is possible. In such a situation the dual may have the greater number of constraints.

solution will usually be satisfied with an inequality.[25] Thus X_1 and X_2, the levels of activities 1 and 2, are zero in the optimal solution of the new linear program; correspondingly, the constraints of the dual relating to activities 1 and 2 are not binding (i.e., satisfied with an inequality) in the solution to the dual. This latter relation is portrayed on Figure 3 where point Q, representing the optimal set of prices, lies above both lines AB and CD, which signifies that for both activities 1 and 2 unit-level cost exceeds unit-level income. In parallel fashion, if a choice variable in the optimal solution to the dual is zero, the corresponding constraint in an optimal solution to the linear program will usually be satisfied with an inequality.[26] For example, if we were to identify the optimal solution to the dual which corresponds to the linear program represented on Figure 1, we would find that the price of both labor and land is zero. Accordingly, the constraints on the use of labor and land can normally be expected to be satisfied with an inequality. This expectation is confirmed by the fact that on Figure 1 the optimal solution represented by point T lies below both RP, the labor limitation line, and LW, the land limitation line. This relationship indicates that the supply of labor and land are more than sufficient; therefore, some units of both land and labor must be idle, a situation consistent with the zero prices for land and labor.

These rules, which are extremely useful in proceeding from an optimal solution for a linear program to the optimal solution for its dual, and vice versa, can also be stated in converse fashion. When for an optimal linear program solution a constraint is found binding (met with an equality),

[25] The qualification "usually" must be made since in situations where more than one optimal solution to the linear program exists—as is true for the "three-activity" linear program which was first examined—a choice variable may be set at zero in one optimal solution, and yet the corresponding constraint in the dual will be satisfied with an equality. For example, in the linear program of three activities, to which Tables 3, 4, and 5 refer, and to whose dual Figure 2 pertains, one optimal solution is $X_1 = 7.33$ MM, $X_3 = 3.33$ MM, and $X_2 = 0$. Since $X_2 = 0$, we would normally expect the corresponding constraint in the dual to be satisfied with an inequality. Actually, it is satisfied with an equality as indicated in Figure 2 by the fact that line CD, which refers to activity 2, passes through point M, the point representing the optimal set of prices for the dual problem and therefore indicating for activity 2 that unit-level costs equal unit-level income. When such a situation obtains, it signifies that the activity run at zero level in the given optimal solution could be operated at a positive level in one or more other optimal solutions. (Recall that an infinite number of optimal solutions may be possible in the sense that all such solutions yield the identical, maximum income.) This is in line with the conclusion already reached that this combination of X_1 and X_3 is only one of an infinite number of optimal solutions for the three-activity problem considered. In each of these other solutions activity 2 would be run at a positive level.

[26] However, as observed in the previous footnote, the constraint will be satisfied with an equality, if there is more than one optimal solution to the dual, and if for these solutions the choice variable considered may be nonzero.

the corresponding choice variable in the optimal dual solution is usually positive.[27]   When for the optimal linear program solution a constraint is found nonbinding, the choice variable in the optimal dual solution is always zero.   Likewise, when a constraint in an optimal dual solution is binding, the choice variable in the optimal linear program solution will usually be positive.   When the constraint is nonbinding, the choice variable in the optimal linear program solution will be zero.

F. Intermediate Commodities

Before we can generalize the scheme thus far developed, we must consider intermediate commodities.   (The reader uninterested in further complication may skip directly to section K which treats certain simple applications of interregional linear programming.)   The nature and importance of such intermediate commodities have already been made explicit in the preceding chapters on input-output and industrial complex analyses.   In both these chapters matrices have been presented in which such commodities have been included.

To embrace intermediate commodities in the linear programming framework, it is convenient once again to formulate in a comprehensive manner the concept of an activity and to alter our notation accordingly.   We drop the assumption, hitherto implied, that the output from the operation of an activity at unit level was marketed at a fixed price and yielded to the region \$1.00 income (after allowance for other fixed unit costs).   As in the preceding chapter, in particular Table 1 of that chapter, we wish to make explicit this output.   We therefore associate with each activity, as is partly done in Table 1 of Chapter 9, a set of both inputs and outputs.   If we number commodities (including resources, services, etc.) from 1 to s (as we have done in Table 1 of Chapter 9 where $s = 76$), we can represent the inputs and outputs of an activity by a set of coefficients.   We may let the set $a_{11}, a_{21}, a_{31}, \cdots, a_{s1}$ denote the amounts of commodities 1, 2, 3, $\cdots$ and finally s associated with the operation of activity 1 at unit level.   (In Table 1 of Chapter 9, $a_{11} = -9.428$, $a_{21} = +2.074$, $\cdots$, and $a_{s1} = 0.000$. For a typical activity most of these coefficients will be zero.   For example, if activity 1 is wheat growing, and the fth commodity is iron ore, we would expect the coefficient a_{f1} to be zero, indicating that the input (or output) of iron ore per unit of the wheat-growing activity is zero.   When there are outputs associated with an activity, the relevant coefficients will be positive.   For example, if wheat and hay are products of the wheat-

[27] Thus, in the four-activity linear program just discussed, the constraints on the use of both water and land are binding; and as to be expected, the prices of both water and land are positive as indicated by point Q in Figure 3.

growing activity and if wheat is commodity 1 and hay commodity 8, both the coefficients a_{11} and a_{81} will be positive. When there are inputs associated with an activity, the relevant coefficients will be negative. For example, water, land, labor, and capital may all be required as inputs by the wheat-growing activity. If they are classified respectively as commodities g, h, k, and m, the coefficients a_{g1}, a_{h1}, a_{k1}, and a_{m1} are negative. (For concrete illustration of these points, see Table 1, Chapter 9.) *Note that by this convention we change the sign of the coefficient associated with an input. In the previous sections positive coefficients were used to denote inputs.* Such a convention was desirable in treating the simple situations involved. In the development of a more general statement on linear programming, it becomes highly desirable to change the previous convention and *treat inputs as negative items.*

If we now consider many possible activities, which number from 1 to n (in Table 1, Chapter 9, $n = 73$), we may say that associated with any activity, say activity j, there are a set of coefficients a_{1j}, a_{2j}, $\cdots$, a_{sj}, which indicate inputs and outputs per unit level of activity j. For each activity it becomes convenient to list these inputs and outputs in a column as follows:

$$\begin{bmatrix} a_{11}, & a_{12}, & \cdots, & a_{1j}, & \cdots, & a_{1n} \\ a_{21}, & a_{22}, & \cdots, & a_{2j}, & \cdots, & a_{2n} \\ a_{31}, & a_{32}, & \cdots, & a_{3j}, & \cdots, & a_{3n} \\ \cdot & \cdot & \cdot & \cdot & \cdot & \cdot \\ a_{s1}, & a_{s2}, & \cdots, & a_{sj}, & \cdots, & a_{sn} \end{bmatrix}$$

The first column refers to the set of inputs and outputs associated with the first activity, the second with the second activity, the jth with the jth activity, and finally the nth column with the nth activity. Such a listing of coefficients by columns according to the order of both the commodity and activity classification may be termed a matrix, an activity coefficient matrix (designated an interactivity matrix in Chapter 9). As already suggested, most of these coefficients will be zero. Also as we move across any one row, say the ith which refers to commodity i, we will note that for some activities the coefficient is negative, indicating that these activities use i as an input whereas for others the coefficient is positive, indicating that these latter produce i. If i is a good such as iron ore, most of the coefficients along this row will be zero. If i is a good such as power, most of the coefficients will be negative, although a few will be positive and some zero.

If we now restate the linear programming problem involving three activities and two resources—water, which we designate commodity

g, and land, which we designate commodity h—the constraints appear as

$$- a_{g1}X_1 - a_{g2}X_2 - a_{g3}X_3 \leq R_g$$
$$- a_{h1}X_1 - a_{h2}X_2 - a_{h3}X_3 \leq R_h$$

Note that all the coefficients $(a_{g1}, \cdots, a_{h3})$ are negative since they represent inputs; we thus multiply each by -1 to convert them into the positive numbers, $- a_{g1}, \cdots, - a_{h3}$. Multiplying X_1, X_2, and X_3 by the positive numbers, $- a_{g1}, \cdots, - a_{h3}$ permits us to state the constraints properly, that is, to state that the sum of the amounts (positive) of water and land required by each activity be equal to or less than the available supply of water and land, respectively.

Into this framework we can now introduce an intermediate commodity, say i. This commodity may be produced singly or jointly by one or several activities.[28] It may be a commodity, such as steel ingots, which is used solely in industrial production, or it may be a commodity, such as transportation, which is demanded as an intermediate by producers but also as a finished product by households. To simplify our exposition we examine a case where the intermediate commodity (1) is produced by a single activity only and is the only output of this activity, and (2) is consumed by only the three activities of our problem.[29] We designate the activity which produces this intermediate commodity i as activity 4.

The objective function of the linear program is not basically altered. For activity 4 income per unit level is zero, since it can be shown that the price of the intermediate i must exactly equal the cost of the required inputs to produce a unit of i.[30] Thus the term c_4X_4 is zero, and income realized still equals $c_1X_1 + c_2X_2 + c_3X_3$. However, the set of constraints changes. They become

$$- a_{g1}X_1 - a_{g2}X_2 - a_{g3}X_3 - a_{g4}X_4 \leq R_g$$
$$- a_{h1}X_1 - a_{h2}X_2 - a_{h3}X_3 - a_{h4}X_4 \leq R_h$$
$$- a_{i1}X_1 - a_{i2}X_2 - a_{i3}X_3 - a_{i4}X_4 \leq 0$$

To the first constraint has been added the term $-a_{g4}X_4$, which represents the water requirements of activity 4, the coefficient $-a_{g4}$ representing the

[28] When it is produced jointly, by the assumption of constant production coefficients it must be produced in fixed proportion with other outputs.

[29] As will be discussed below, a commodity which is consumed both by industry (as an intermediate) and by households (as a finished product) can best be treated as two commodities. In the list of commodities from 1 to s it appears once as an intermediate and a second time as a finished product. By this convention the structure of the activity coefficient matrix no longer corresponds exactly to that of Table 1, Chapter 9.

[30] See later. The reader is also referred to the general literature cited for discussion of this point.

amount of water required per unit level of activity 4, and X_4 representing the level at which this intermediate commodity-producing activity is operated. Thus the first constraint states that the requirements of water by the first three activities plus the requirement of water by the new activity 4 must not exceed the available supply.

To the second constraint has been added the term $-a_{h4}X_4$, which represents the land requirements of activity 4. The constraint now reads: The requirement of land by all four activities must not exceed the available supply of land.

Finally, we have added a third constraint which states: The sum of the requirements of the intermediate commodity i must not exceed the output of i; or, conversely, the output of i must be at least as great as the sum of the requirements of i by all activities. The first three terms of the constraint represent the consumption of i by activities 1, 2, and 3, respectively; since these are the only activities consuming i, the sum of the first three terms yields total requirements of i. The fourth term, $-a_{i4}X_4$, is the *negative* of the total output, since a_{i4} is a positive coefficient indicating the output of i per unit level of activity 4 and X_4 is the level at which activity 4 is operated. Thus the constraint reads that when total output $a_{i4}X_4$ is subtracted from total requirements, $-a_{i1}X_1 - a_{i2}X_2 - a_{i3}X_3$, (footnote 31) we obtain zero (in which case output would have equaled total requirements) or a negative number (in which case output would have exceeded total requirements).[32] This is essentially what the first sentence of this paragraph states.

G. A Generalized Single-Region Model

We now have presented the linear program in simple graphic and algebraic forms, developed the simplex method for a three-activity problem, formulated and solved the dual of this problem, sketched the more important relationships between the linear program and its dual, and

[31] Recall that a_{i1}, a_{i2}, and a_{i3} are negative coefficients representing inputs; hence $-a_{i1}$, $-a_{i2}$, and $-a_{i3}$ are positive numbers.

[32] In our simplified problem the third constraint could be written in the equality form only, that is,

$$-a_{i1}X_1 - a_{i2}X_2 - a_{i3}X_3 - a_{i4}X_4 = 0$$

We know that only activity 4 produces i and that this activity yields zero income per unit level and at the same time employs resources, some of which are scarce. Therefore excess production of i would be inconsistent with an optimal solution.

More generally, however, there could be an excess production of i if i were a joint product of one or several activities. In such a situation the inequality could hold (or, a zero-cost disposal activity could be introduced to dispose of the surplus i).

finally introduced intermediate commodities. All this was done for programs which involved from two to four activities, and from two to four resources in limited supply. At this point we may fruitfully generalize. (However, the materials in this section are more difficult. The reader may prefer to skip this section [33] and go on to the next section. The next section treats a simple interregional model and is easier to digest.)

Let there be for our hypothetical isolated region many, say n, possible activities for achieving new income. The region confronts many, say m, possible constraints which reflect fixed supplies of resources available for generating new income, limitations on the use of intermediate commodities, and other restrictions on commodity consumption.[34] Order the commodities associated with these constraints from 1 to m. Assume as given the prices of finished products, that is, of commodities $m + 1$ to s, where as before commodities run from 1 to s. (Clearly this assumption is most valid when the quantities of inputs and outputs to be associated with a linear program are very small relative to the inputs and outputs of the existing industrial structure. As these quantities increase in relative size, the reality of the assumption for a regional economy decreases.) The linear program and its dual become:

Linear Program

Max: $Y = c_1X_1 + \cdots + c_nX_n$
subject to:

$$-a_{11}X_1 - a_{12}X_2 - \cdots - a_{1n}X_n \leq R_1$$
$$-a_{21}X_1 - a_{22}X_2 - \cdots - a_{2n}X_n \leq R_2$$
$$\cdot \quad \cdot \quad \cdot \quad \cdot \quad \cdot \quad \cdot \quad \cdot \quad \cdot \quad \cdot \quad \cdot \quad \cdot \quad \cdot \quad \cdot$$
$$-a_{m1}X_1 - a_{m2}X_2 - \cdots - a_{mn}X_n \leq R_m$$
$$X_1 \geq 0; \quad X_2 \geq 0; \quad \cdots; X_n \geq 0$$

Dual

Min: $W = R_1P_1 + R_2P_2 + \cdots + R_mP_m$
subject to:

$$-a_{11}P_1 - a_{21}P_2 - \cdots - a_{m1}P_m \geq c_1$$
$$-a_{12}P_1 - a_{22}P_2 - \cdots - a_{m2}P_m \geq c_2$$
$$\cdot \quad \cdot \quad \cdot \quad \cdot \quad \cdot \quad \cdot \quad \cdot \quad \cdot \quad \cdot \quad \cdot \quad \cdot \quad \cdot \quad \cdot$$
$$-a_{1n}P_1 - a_{2n}P_2 - \cdots - a_{mn}P_m \geq c_n$$
$$P_1 \geq 0; P_2 \geq 0; \quad \cdots; P_m \geq 0$$

[33] This section might well be read after some later materials have been digested, particularly those in sections H and K.
[34] These latter restrictions will be discussed in a later section.

In this linear program and its dual each term on the left-hand side of each constraint has been multiplied by -1. As indicated in the previous section, this step is necessary in order to retain the meaning of each constraint since, except for coefficients representing intermediate outputs, each of the coefficients represents an input and consequently by our new definition is negative. Thus, for example, $-a_{12}X_2$ and $-a_{2n}P_2$ are each positive magnitudes, one representing a positive consumption, the other a positive cost. With coefficients indicating outputs of an intermediate, multiplying by -1 is appropriate since in the relevant constraint the output of an intermediate is to be subtracted from the total requirement for that intermediate.

In this statement R_i $(i = 1, \cdots, m)$[35] is the fixed available stock of resource i, or other limiting magnitude. In the case of an intermediate commodity, this limiting magnitude is zero. Also c_j $(j = 1, \cdots, n)$[36] represents the per-unit-level income of activity j. Where activity j uses as inputs one or more commodities numbered from 1 to m and produces only one commodity, say $m + 1$,

$$c_j = a_{m+1,\, j} \cdot \bar{P}_{m+1}$$

that is, is equal to the per-unit-level output of commodity $m + 1$ times its price which is already specified.[37] Where activity j uses as inputs commodities numbered from 1 to m and produces only two finished products, say goods $m + 1$ and $m + 2$,

$$c_j = a_{m+1,\, j} \cdot \bar{P}_{m+1} + a_{m+2,\, j} \cdot \bar{P}_{m+2}$$

that is, is equal to the sum of the per-unit-level output of $m + 1$ times the price of $m + 1$ plus the per-unit-level output of $m + 2$ times the price of $m + 2$.

Generally speaking, where many final products are associated with activity j, we have

$$(15) \qquad c_j = a_{m+1,\, j} \cdot \bar{P}_{m+1} + a_{m+2,\, j} \cdot \bar{P}_{m+2} + \cdots + a_{sj} \cdot \bar{P}_s = \sum_{q=m+1}^{s} a_{qj} \cdot \bar{P}_q$$

That is, the per-unit-level income of the jth activity, given the prices for commodities $m + 1$ to s, is equal to the sum of the products resulting from multiplying each per-unit-level output (positive) of a finished product by

[35] R_i $(i = 1, \cdots, m)$ represents the series of constants $R_1, R_2, \cdots, R_m$.

[36] c_j $(j = 1, \cdots, n)$ represents the series of constants $c_1, c_2, \cdots, c_n$.

[37] Since this price is given beforehand, we place a bar over its symbol to indicate this and to distinguish it from other prices which are not given beforehand and which are to be determined from the operation of the model. These latter are price variables and are unbarred.

its price.[38]   Per unit level of the jth activity this yields total sales values, that is, income.   Typically, all but a few of the a_{qj} will be zero, signifying that a single activity produces only a relatively few, if more than one, of the many possible final products.[39]

For activities which produce only intermediate commodities (which are commodities included in the group of commodities numbered from $1, \cdots, m$) income per unit level, namely c_j, is zero since all the coefficients, $a_{m+1, j}, \cdots, a_{sj}$ of equation 15 are zero.   For such an activity the corresponding constraint in the dual is

$$(16) \qquad -a_{1j}P_1 - a_{2j}P_2 - \cdots - a_{jj}P_j - \cdots - a_{mj}P_m \geq c_j$$

Take the term $a_{jj}P_j$ over to the right.   Also assume that the unit level of activity j has been defined so that $a_{jj} = 1$ and that activity j produces only one commodity.   We have, since $c_j = 0$:

$$(17) \qquad -a_{1j}P_1, \cdots, -a_{j-1, j}P_{j-1} - a_{j+1, j}P_{j+1}, \cdots, -a_{mj}P_m \geq P_j$$

That is, the per-unit-level cost of the first input $(-a_{1j}P_1)$ plus the per-unit-level cost of the second input $(-a_{2j}P_2)$ plus $, \cdots,$ plus finally the per-unit-level cost of the mth input $(-a_{mj}P_m)$ is greater than or equal to the price of intermediate commodity j.   We know that when activity j is actually operated, the equality holds for relation 17; and hence, when the intermediate commodity j is produced, its price must be exactly equal to the sum of all per-unit-level input costs.   Thus an optimal solution to a linear program and its dual yields not only prices (rents) for all resources (services) in limited supply but also prices for all intermediate commodities.[40]

[38] Recall that if an activity uses as input an item such as milk, which in reality is consumed by both industry (baking) and households, it is by convention using as input the commodity, *milk (as intermediate)*.   This commodity is listed among the first m commodities, whereas the commodity, *milk (as finished product)*, is listed among the commodities which run from $m + 1$ to s.   As a consequence, none of the coefficients $a_{m+1, j}, \cdots, a_{sj}$ can be negative.

[39] In addition, it may produce intermediate commodities, which production would be listed in the first m of the a coefficients associated with this activity.   (As will be observed later, an activity can produce an item only as an intermediate if that item is consumed by both industry and households.)

[40] Where activity j produces two or more strictly intermediate commodities—a case of joint production which we generally do not consider in this elementary statement—the two or more corresponding terms of relation 16 must be brought over to the right-hand side.   If the resulting supply of all but one of these intermediates is in excess (exceeds requirements), the price of all but the one not in excess supply will be zero, and the price of this latter intermediate can be derived from the equality form of relation 17. If the resulting supply of two or more of these intermediates is not in excess, additional relations of type 17 are required if a unique set of prices for the intermediates involved is to be derived.

In general, the discussion of the preceding sections concerning the interrelationships of a linear program and its dual and the derivation of an optimal solution may be taken to apply to this generalized regional model.

H. A Simple Interregional Model

At this point we are in a position to start the construction of interregional models. Our procedure will again be to develop a model for a very simple case, present and discuss the basic structure of interregional models by reference to this elementary model and certain extensions of it, and finally generalize.

Let there be a closed interregional system, consisting of two regions only, region A and region B. Each region may produce only three commodities: textiles (consumed by households only), coal (consumed by both industry and households), and transportation (consumed by industries only, each region being responsible for the delivery of its product to other regions). Available for production are resources, the only one in limited supply in any region being labor. We posit that R_1^A and R_1^B are the fixed supplies of labor available in regions A and B, respectively. Let the objective be to maximize the sum of the regional incomes.

It is convenient to set down systematically the list of commodities and set of activities. We bear in mind that any item in one region is a different commodity from the same item in a second region. Textiles in region A is a different commodity in our system from textiles in region B. This is reflected by the fact that the price of textiles in region A will usually be different from the price of textiles in region B; and this difference need not be equal to the cost of transporting one unit of textiles from one region to the other. Likewise, coal, transportation, and labor in region A are different commodities from their respective counterparts in region B. Consequently, there are eight different commodities in our simple case. However, two of these commodities, namely coal in region A and coal in region B, are used as both intermediates (by industry) and finished product (by households). In our case—and typically in interregional linear programming—each such commodity must be viewed as two commodities, that is, we must replace the commodity coal in region A by two commodities, namely, *coal (as intermediate)* in region A and *coal (as finished product)* in region A. Hence our model comprises ten commodities, as listed in the left-hand tab of Table 6.[41]

---

[41] Note that we have exactly the same items in each region. This convention is not at all necessary. We can have different types of resources in each region, different items produced in each region, as well as different numbers of commodities in each given

TABLE 6. ACTIVITY COEFFICIENT MATRIX OF A SIMPLE INTERREGIONAL SYSTEM

Activities (columns):

(1) 1,A. Textile production in A
(2) 2,A. Transportation production in A
(3) 3,A. Coal (intermediate) production in A
(4) 4,A. Coal in A: shift to finished-product status (dummy)
(5) 5,A. Shipment of transportation from A to B
(6) 6,A. Shipment of coal (as intermediate) from A to B
(7) 7,A. Shipment of textiles from A to B
(8) 1,B. Textile production in B
(9) 2,B. Transportation production in B
(10) 3,B. Coal (intermediate) production in B
(11) 4,B. Coal in B: shift to finished-product status (dummy)
(12) 5,B. Shipment of transportation from B to A
(13) 6,B. Shipment of coal (as intermediate) from B to A
(14) 7,B. Shipment of textiles from B to A

Commodities	(1)	(2)	(3)	(4)	(5)	(6)	(7)	(8)	(9)	(10)	(11)	(12)	(13)	(14)
1,A. Labor in A	a_{11}^A	a_{12}^A	a_{13}^A	0	0	0	0	0	0	0	0	0	0	0
2,A. Transportation in A	a_{21}^A	a_{22}^A	a_{23}^A	0	a_{25}^A	a_{26}^A	a_{27}^A	0	0	0	0	$a_{25}^{B\to A}$	0	0
3,A. Coal (as intermediate) in A	a_{31}^A	a_{32}^A	a_{33}^A	a_{34}^A	0	a_{36}^A	0	0	0	0	0	0	$a_{36}^{B\to A}$	0
4,A. Coal (as finished product) in A	0	0	0	a_{44}^A	0	0	0	0	0	0	0	0	0	0
5,A. Textiles in A	a_{51}^A	0	0	0	0	0	a_{57}^A	0	0	0	0	0	0	$a_{57}^{B\to A}$
1,B. Labor in B	0	0	0	0	$a_{25}^{A\to B}$	0	0	a_{11}^B	a_{12}^B	a_{13}^B	0	0	0	0
2,B. Transportation in B	0	0	0	0	0	0	0	a_{21}^B	a_{22}^B	a_{23}^B	0	a_{25}^B	a_{26}^B	a_{27}^B
3,B. Coal (as intermediate) in B	0	0	0	0	0	$a_{36}^{A\to B}$	0	a_{31}^B	a_{32}^B	a_{33}^B	a_{34}^B	0	a_{36}^B	0
4,B. Coal (as finished product) in B	0	0	0	0	0	0	0	0	0	0	a_{44}^B	0	0	0
5,B. Textiles in B	0	0	0	0	0	0	$a_{57}^{A\to B}$	a_{51}^B	0	0	0	0	0	a_{57}^B

Just as each commodity has a regional specification, so does each activity in our model. Thus, as recorded in Table 6, textile production in region A (the first activity in this region) is a different activity from textile production in region B (the first activity in region B); and likewise with transportation production and coal production, which are respectively the second and third activity in each region. In each of these production activities we encounter the usual input-output structure. Going down the first column of Table 6, which lists the relevant coefficients *per unit level* of activity 1 in region A, we note an input of labor in region A, as designated by a_{11}^A. The first subscript of this coefficient indicates the number of the commodity being used as input; the second subscript indicates the number of the activity using this input; and the superscript indicates the regional specification of both the commodity and the activity. [We shall examine later the case where the input (or output) and activity have different regional specifications.] The second coefficient in the first column, that is, a_{21}^A, indicates the input of the commodity 2,A (i.e., transportation in region A) into the activity 1,A (i.e., textile production in region A). The third coefficient a_{31}^A represents the input of coal in region A per unit level of activity of 1,A. The fourth coefficient is 0, indicating that coal (as finished product) in region A is neither an input nor an output of textile production in region A. The fifth coefficient in column 1 is a_{51}^A. This coefficient indicates the output of textiles in region A per unit level of textile production in region A. Usually, it is convenient to define a unit level of textile production in region A so that a_{51}^A is unity. Following our convention this coefficient, representing an output is positive, whereas the other nonzero coefficients in column 1, each representing an input, are negative. Observe, too, that coefficients associated with commodities of region B are zero. This follows since for any production activity of region A a commodity of region B cannot be used an an input until it is shipped to region A and thus, as will be seen below, becomes transformed by another activity (shipment) into the corresponding commodity in region A, the region of production. In similar fashion, any output of a production activity in region A cannot be considered an intermediate or finished product in region B until it is shipped to region B, that is, until another activity (shipment) takes place.

region. Yet we maintain regional symmetry in the model since doing so facilitates the exposition. Note, too, that we have constructed the model so that it embraces each type of commodity generally encountered in interregional linear programming. We have (*a*) a resource (labor) in each region which may or may not be mobile; (*b*) a pure intermediate (transportation) in each region; (*c*) an item (coal) which behaves both as an intermediate and a finished product; and (*d*) a commodity (textiles) which is strictly a finished product (i.e., for consumption by households only).

Columns 2 and 3 of Table 6, which refer to activities 2,A (transportation production in region A) and 3,A [coal (as intermediate) production in region A], do not introduce any new considerations. However, when we come to column 4, a new consideration is encountered. Whenever an item, such as coal in region A, can be used as both an intermediate and a finished product and hence must be represented in our commodity framework by two commodities, such as coal (as intermediate) and coal (as finished product), we also must introduce into our framework another activity in addition to the commodity production activities. We let the activities which produce the commodity produce the commodity *as intermediate*; the additional activity then refers to the shift of the status of the given commodity from that of an intermediate to that of a finished product, that is, to the transformation of the *intermediate* commodity into a *finished-product* commodity. Thus, in Table 6, activity 3,A refers to the production of coal as intermediate in region A; and activity 4,A, in a sense a dummy activity, refers to shift of coal (as intermediate) to a finished-product status, that is, to the transformation of coal (as intermediate) in region A into coal (as finished product) in region A. The corresponding coefficients are a_{34}^A (negative, representing an input) and a_{44}^A (positive, representing an output) where typically $-a_{34}^A = a_{44}^A = 1$.

Columns 5, 6, and 7 of Table 6 refer to shipment activities, that is, to shipment of commodities in region A to region B. As noted before, such shipment effects a transformation of the commodity of region A (which may be taken to represent an input) into the corresponding commodity of region B (which represents an output). Thus column 6 which refers to activity 6,A, that is, the shipment of coal (as intermediate) from A to B has as inputs the necessary transportation per unit level (i.e., a_{26}^A)[42] and the coal in region A to be shipped per unit level (i.e., a_{36}^A) and as output coal in region B (i.e., $a_{36}^{A \to B}$). Note that the coefficient representing output of a shipment has associated with it two regional superscripts, the first the region of origin and the second the region of termination. Such double superscripting is necessary in order to distinguish this output (i.e., $a_{36}^{A \to B}$) from the corresponding input a_{36}^A and from the input or output a_{36}^B associated with activity 6 of region B. The arrow between the two superscripts serves an obviously useful purpose.[43]

Columns 5 and 7 follow the pattern of column 6 and require no addi-

---

[42] Recall the convention that the transportation service required for an export is provided by the region of export.

[43] Since in this section double superscripts will be encountered only in connection with shipment activities, this notation facilitates the identification of shipment activities and corresponding exports and imports. In turn, the set of constraints is more easily constructed and the basic structure of a particular problem more easily perceived.

tional comment. Note, however, that in column 5, which refers to the shipment of transportation services from region A to region B, the coefficient a_{25}^A covers not only the transportation service which is shipped (exported) from region A to region B but also the transportation service which is required to effect that shipment (export).

In similar manner, the activities of region B are described by columns 8 through 14 of Table 6. The coefficients of these columns bear the same interpretation as those already discussed. Observe that all the coefficients relating to commodities of region A are zero, except where a commodity is an output of a shipment activity of region B and thus enters region A as an import.[44]

Given this activity coefficient matrix—from which consumption activities and activities producing joint products have been excluded[45]—we proceed to the statement of the objective function. Since we wish to maximize the sum of regional incomes, the objective function is

$$(18) \quad \begin{aligned} \text{Max } Y = {}& c_1^A X_1^A + c_2^A X_2^A + c_3^A X_3^A + c_4^A X_4^A + c_5^A X_5^A + c_6^A X_6^A + c_7^A X_7^A \\ & + c_1^B X_1^B + c_2^B X_2^B + c_3^B X_3^B + c_4^B X_4^B + c_5^B X_5^B + c_6^B X_6^B + c_7^B X_7^B \end{aligned}$$

The X's are the choice variables and the c's are the multiplying constants which represent income per unit level. As indicated earlier the c for any given activity is obtained by multiplying that activity's unit-level outputs of finished products by the *given* finished-product prices. The given prices in our model are the price of coal (as a final product) in region A $(\bar{P}_4^A)$, the price of textiles in region A $(\bar{P}_5^A)$, the price of coal (as finished product) in region B $(\bar{P}_4^B)$, and the price of textiles in region B $(\bar{P}_5^B)$. Note that as before we place a bar over each of these price symbols to indicate that each is a given constant. Thus for any c, say c_4^B, we have

$$c_4^B = a_{44}^{B \to A} \bar{P}_4^A + a_{54}^{B \to A} \bar{P}_5^A + a_{44}^B \bar{P}_4^B + a_{54}^B \bar{P}_5^B \quad \text{(footnote 46)}$$

[44] The activities of region B correspond in kind and number to those of region A. This symmetry is adopted to facilitate exposition. In the typical model such symmetry would not appear. Certainly, in situations where one region possesses a valuable deposit of an immobile resource not present in a second region, such symmetry could not exist (except in a formal mathematical sense, where the cost of extracting the resource in the second region might be taken as infinite). In general, sets of activities different in both kind and number would confront the several regions of any interregional system.

Note also that our model assumes that the resource of each region, namely labor, is immobile. This assumption is not required. When a resource is mobile, we need to introduce into each region one additional shipment activity, namely the shipment of the resource from the respective region.

[45] The incorporation into the matrix of such activities will be discussed later.

[46] Commodities 1 to 3 in each region are resources or intermediates, on the consumption of each of which a constraint will be imposed. Their prices are not *givens* of the problem and will be derived (as shadow prices) from the solution of the problem and its dual.

Since all the coefficients of this equation are zero save a_{44}^B (see column 11, Table 6), this equation reduces to

$$c_4^B = a_{44}^B \bar{P}_4^B$$

that is, income per unit level of the activity 4,B is equal to the unit level of output of the finished product coal in region B multiplied by its price. In this fashion we obtain[47]

(19)
$$\begin{aligned}
c_1^A &= a_{51}^A \bar{P}_5^A & c_1^B &= a_{51}^B \bar{P}_5^B \\
c_2^A &= 0 & c_2^B &= 0 \\
c_3^A &= 0 & c_3^B &= 0 \\
c_4^A &= a_{44}^A \bar{P}_4^A & c_4^B &= a_{44}^B \bar{P}_4^B \\
c_5^A &= 0 & c_5^B &= 0 \\
c_6^A &= 0 & c_6^B &= 0 \\
c_7^A &= a_{57}^A \bar{P}_5^A + a_{57}^{A\rightarrow B}\bar{P}_5^B & c_7^B &= a_{57}^{B\rightarrow A}\bar{P}_5^A + a_{57}^B \bar{P}_5^B
\end{aligned}$$

The particular significance of each of these constants will be discussed later in connection with the presentation of the corresponding constraint in the dual.

Since in our simple linear programming problem we have in each region one resource and two intermediate commodities, we have three constraints in each region. They are listed in the Part 1 of Table 7 under the objective function. The first constraint states that the total requirement of commodity 1,A (the labor resource in region A) by all activities must not exceed the available stock of this commodity. Similarly, the fourth constraint states that the requirement of commodity 1,B (the labor resource in region B) must not exceed the available stock of this commodity.

The second, third, fifth, and sixth constraints refer to intermediate commodities. They therefore read differently. For example, the second constraint reads horizontally, term by term: (1) the requirement of transportation by the textile production activity in region A $(-a_{21}^A X_1^A)$[48] *minus* (2) the output of transportation by the transportation production activity in region A $(a_{22}^A X_2^A)$ *plus* (3) the requirement of transportation by the coal production activity in region A $(-a_{23}^A X_3^A)$ *plus* (4) the exports of transportation from region A as well as the requirement of transportation to effect this export $(-a_{25}^A X_5^A)$,[49] that is, the transportation demand of the

[47] Activities 2, 3, 5, and 6 in both regions produce intermediates only. Hence, as is to be expected from the discussion of section 7, income per unit level of these activities is zero.

[48] Recall that the coefficient a_{21}^A is negative if not zero.

[49] Recall that $-a_{25}^A$ covers per unit level the transportation to be exported as well as the transportation input to effect this export.

transportation-shipping activity of region A *plus* (5) the requirement of transportation by the coal-shipping activity of region A $(-a_{26}^A X_6^A)$ *plus* (6) the requirement of transportation by the textile-shipping activity of region A *minus* (7) the import of transportation by region A $(a_{25}^{B \to A} X_5^B)$ which is the output of the transportation-shipping activity of region B—all these seven items must yield a result not greater than zero. Or, as stated previously, the demand for transportation by local activities plus exports must not exceed local output plus imports.

In a similar manner we may interpret the third, fifth, and sixth constraints. To complete the statement of our interregional linear program, we add the requirement that each activity level be nonnegative as indicated in the last row of Part I of Table 7.

The significance of our interregional linear program can be more clearly discerned if the dual is presented. This is done in Part II of Table 7. In the first row of Part II we state the objective function, which is to select nonnegative prices for the two resources, labor in region A and labor in region B, to minimize W, that is, fictitious returns to resource owners. Note that in the objective function there are six terms, each involving a variable price.[50] In each term a variable price (which is unbarred to indicate that it is a variable) multiplies the corresponding R (the limiting constant) in the constraints of the linear program. But four of these R's (specifically the R's that limit consumption of *intermediate* commodities) have a value of zero. Hence, whatever the level of the corresponding P's (which represent the prices of the corresponding intermediate commodities), the value of the objective function is unaffected.[51]

Since there are as many constraints in a dual as there are choice variables in the original linear program, we have fourteen constraints in our dual. They are listed in Part II of Table 7. The limiting constant (i.e., the c) for each constraint is the corresponding constant which multiplies the choice variable in the linear program. Its value, which is the income per unit level of the corresponding activity, has already been determined along lines discussed earlier. Observe, too, that the set of coefficients contained in the constraints of the dual is obtained by interchanging the rows and columns of the set of coefficients contained in the linear program. Thus the first column of a's in the constraints of the linear program becomes the first row of a's in the constraints of the dual, etc.

Each constraint of the dual states that for any given activity the value of

---

[50] Thus there are as many choice variables in the dual as constraints in the original linear program.

[51] Actually, however, for any feasible set of prices for labor in both regions, the prices of the intermediate commodities are determined by the constraints of the dual to be discussed later.

TABLE 7.   PART I: AN INTERREGIONAL LINEAR PROGRAM

Max:

$$Y = c_1^A X_1^A + c_2^A X_2^A + c_3^A X_3^A + c_4^A X_4^A + c_5^A X_5^A + c_6^A X_6^A + c_7^A X_7^A + c_1^B X_1^B + c_2^B X_2^B + c_3^B X_3^B + c_4^B X_4^B + c_5^B X_5^B + c_6^B X_6^B + c_7^B X_7^B$$

subject to:

1. $-a_{11}^A X_1^A - a_{12}^A X_2^A - a_{13}^A X_3^A \leq R_1^A$

2. $-a_{21}^A X_1^A - a_{22}^A X_2^A - a_{23}^A X_3^A - a_{25}^A X_5^A - a_{26}^A X_6^A - a_{27}^A X_7^A - a_{25}^{B\to A} X_5^B \leq R_2^A = 0$

3. $-a_{31}^A X_1^A - a_{32}^A X_2^A - a_{33}^A X_3^A - a_{34}^A X_4^A - a_{36}^A X_6^A - a_{36}^{B\to A} X_6^B \leq R_3^A = 0$

4. $-a_{11}^B X_1^B - a_{12}^B X_2^B - a_{13}^B X_3^B \leq R_1^B$

5. $-a_{25}^{A\to B} X_5^A - a_{21}^B X_1^B - a_{22}^B X_2^B - a_{23}^B X_3^B - a_{25}^B X_5^B - a_{26}^B X_6^B - a_{27}^B X_7^B \leq R_2^B = 0$

6. $-a_{36}^{A\to B} X_6^A - a_{31}^B X_1^B - a_{32}^B X_2^B - a_{33}^B X_3^B - a_{34}^B X_4^B - a_{36}^B X_6^B \leq R_3^B = 0$

$X_1^A \geq 0$; $X_2^A \geq 0$; $X_3^A \geq 0$; $X_4^A \geq 0$; $X_5^A \geq 0$; $X_6^A \geq 0$; $X_7^A \geq 0$; $X_1^B \geq 0$; $X_2^B \geq 0$; $X_3^B \geq 0$; $X_4^B \geq 0$; $X_5^B \geq 0$; $X_6^B \geq 0$; $X_7^B \geq 0$

TABLE 7.   PART II: THE DUAL

Min:

$$W = R_1^A P_1^A \; + 0 \cdot P_2^A \quad + 0 \cdot P_3^A \quad + R_1^B P_1^B + 0 \cdot P_2^B \quad + 0 \cdot P_3^B$$

subject to:

1.	$-a_{11}^A P_1^A - a_{21}^A P_2^A - a_{31}^A P_3^A$			$\geq c_1^A$
2.	$-a_{12}^A P_1^A - a_{22}^A P_2^A - a_{32}^A P_3^A$			$\geq c_2^A = 0$
3.	$-a_{13}^A P_1^A - a_{23}^A P_2^A - a_{33}^A P_3^A$			$\geq c_3^A = 0$
4.	$- a_{34}^A P_3^A$			$\geq c_4^A$
5.	$- a_{25}^A P_2^A$	$- a_{25}^{A \to B} P_2^B$		$\geq c_5^A = 0$
6.	$- a_{26}^A P_2^A - a_{36}^A P_3^A$		$- a_{36}^{A \to B} P_3^B$	$\geq c_6^A = 0$
7.	$- a_{27}^A P_2^A$			$\geq c_7^A$
8.		$- a_{11}^B P_1^B - a_{21}^B P_2^B$	$- a_{31}^B P_3^B$	$\geq c_1^B$
9.		$- a_{12}^B P_1^B - a_{22}^B P_2^B$	$- a_{32}^B P_3^B$	$\geq c_2^B = 0$
10.		$- a_{13}^B P_1^B - a_{23}^B P_2^B$	$- a_{33}^B P_3^B$	$\geq c_3^B = 0$
11.		$- a_{34}^B P_3^B$		$\geq c_4^B$
12.	$- a_{25}^{B \to A} P_2^A$	$- a_{25}^B P_2^B$		$\geq c_5^B = 0$
13.	$- a_{36}^{B \to A} P_3^A$	$- a_{26}^B P_2^B - a_{36}^B P_3^B$		$\geq c_6^B = 0$
14.		$- a_{27}^B P_2^B$		$\geq c_7^B$

$$P_1^A \geq 0; \quad P_2^A \geq 0; \quad P_3^A \geq 0; \quad P_1^B \geq 0; \; P_2^B \geq 0; \; P_3^B \geq 0$$

inputs of resources and intermediates less the value of the output of intermediates, if there is any such output, must not be less than the income per unit level of that activity. Thus, the first constraint states that per unit level of textile production in region A the cost of labor inputs $(-a_{11}^A P_1^A)$ plus the cost of transport inputs $(-a_{21}^A P_2^A)$ plus the cost of coal inputs $(-a_{31}^A P_3^A)$ must not be less than income per unit level (c_1^A), where, as earlier, this income per unit level is equal to sales value of the unit-level output of textiles $(a_{51}^A \bar{P}_5^A)$. Thus, too, the second constraint states that per unit-level production of the intermediate transportation the cost of labor inputs $(-a_{12}^A P_1^A)$ minus the value of transportation output $(a_{22}^A P_2^A)$ plus the cost of coal inputs $(-a_{32}^A P_3^A)$, must not be less than income (c_2^A) which is always zero since no finished product commodities are produced.[52]

Another type of constraint is the fourth. It simply states that per unit level of the dummy activity 4,A, which involves the shift of coal from an

[52] As already indicated, when the intermediate transportation is produced and when a unit level of the transportation-producing activity is defined so that a_{22}^A is unity, this relation implies that the price of transportation equals unit cost, that is, the cost of the required labor and coal per unit output.

intermediate to a finished-product status in region A, the cost of the intermediate coal $(-a_{34}^A P_{3!}^A)$ must not be less than the value of the output of coal as a finished product (c_4^A which equals $a_{44}^A \bar{P}_4^A$). If we set $-a_{34}^A = a_{44}^A = 1$, we have that in region A the price of the intermediate coal must not be less than the price of the finished product coal. When the dummy activity 4,A is operated at a positive level in an optimal solution of the linear program, this implies that the price of coal as an intermediate does not exceed and hence equals the given price of the finished product coal.

Still another type of constraint derives from the shipping activities of the linear program and interrelates prices among regions. For example, take the sixth constraint. It states that per unit level of activity 6,A, which ships coal (as intermediate) from region A to region B, the cost of transport $(-a_{26}^A P_2^A)$ plus the value of the coal to be exported $(-a_{36}^A P_3^A)$ less the value of coal imports (deliveries) in the region of import $(a_{36}^{A \to B} P_3^B)$ must not be less than zero ($c_6^A = 0$). Or, if we let $-a_{36}^A = a_{36}^{A \to B} = 1$, the price of coal (as intermediate) in the region of export (region A) plus the cost of transport must not be less than the price of coal (as intermediate) in the region of import (region B). When the operation of the coal-shipping activity is positive in the optimal solution to the linear program, such operation implies that the price of the intermediate coal in the region of import does equal the price of the intermediate coal in the region of export plus transport cost. This equality is the familiar equilibrium relation obtained when several regions trade under conditions of perfect competition.

The seventh constraint of the dual is a variant of the sixth. It states that per unit level of activity 7,A, which refers to the export of textiles from region A to region B, the transportation cost of the textiles to be exported $(-a_{27}^A P_2^A)$ must not be less than unit-level income c_7^A, where $c_7^A = a_{57}^A \bar{P}_5^A + a_{57}^{A \to B} \bar{P}_5^B$. In effect, this seventh constraint states that where $-a_{57}^A = a_{57}^{A \to B} = 1$ the price spread among the two regions must not exceed the cost of transport.[53] When the operation of this activity is positive in the optimal solution to the linear program, it is implied that the price spread just equals the transport cost. Such a result is once again consistent with equilibrium conditions for trade among regions under conditions of perfect competition.

I. The Choice of Finished-Product Prices

The last paragraphs of section H treat the several interpretations to be given to the fourteen constraints contained in the dual. However, in

---

[53] Recall that a_{57}^A is negative since it indicates an input. Hence if $-a_{57}^A = 1$, then $a_{57}^A = -1$ and $c_7^A = \bar{P}_5^B - \bar{P}_5^A$, that is, the price spread.

connection with the last constraint discussed, a major problem arises. As already indicated several times, the linear program requires that the set of final-product prices be predetermined, that is, given beforehand. More specifically in our problem, the prices of the finished products, textiles and coal, must be specified at the start. But this would seem to imply a previous knowledge of what the solution to the linear program is. To illustrate, consider the price of textiles in both regions. If beforehand we set a price for the finished product textiles in region B that is greater than the price of the finished product textiles in region A, we thereby have predetermined that the level of textile shipment from region B to region A, namely activity 7,B, be zero. Or if at the start we set the price of textiles in region A higher than in region B, this step precludes the shipment of textiles from region A to region B, that is, forces activity 7,A to run at zero level. Or if we set the two prices equal to each other, this step precludes any shipment in either direction, that is, specifies that activities 7,A and 7,B be run at zero level (unless the price of transport service reaches the extreme of zero).

This discussion clearly demonstrates that for our interregional linear programming model a consistent and meaningful set of final-product prices must be established at the start. The necessity for such a step is the more evident in an interregional system composed of many regions and many commodities, such as the generalized system to be presented later. The problem is simply this: If the technique is to determine among others the levels of shipping activities of an optimal program, we must not initially hypothesize finished-product prices which preclude such determination. Yet at the same time we cannot carry through the linear programming computation without setting these prices.

This dilemma is more apparent than real. In constructing any linear program, the researcher necessarily must have in the background certain hypotheses about feasible, likely, or desirable consumption levels. He will therefore set finished-product prices which are not inconsistent with these levels.[54] For example, if wheat is to be consumed both in Philadelphia and Pittsburgh and if the pattern of land resources dictates that wheat can be grown productively only to the west of these cities, he must not set the price of wheat higher at Pittsburgh than at Philadelphia. Nor may the analyst set the price of wheat at zero at Pittsburgh, or hypothesize an unreasonable spread of prices between those of Philadelphia and Pittsburgh. In general, he will select a set of prices which he judges will differ by an amount equal to the difference between transport costs on a unit of wheat to Philadelphia and to Pittsburgh. However, he bears in

---

[54] In certain cases such levels and prices will be related to levels and prices currently existing in an interregional economy.

mind that the price of transport service, and thus transport costs on wheat, is to be determined from the linear programming computation; hence he can at best make only a rough approximation of a meaningful spread of prices.

Despite all the ingenuity that the researcher may apply, he is most likely to find that an optimal program schedules the shipment of all wheat either to Pittsburgh, Philadelphia, or one or several other locations. This result will reflect the fact that his estimate of the difference in transport cost to these two locations, or other locations, was incorrect, even if by only a small amount. Thus in the problem such as we have posed, the analyst must *either* (1) introduce additional constraints which guarantee that the amount of each finished product available for household consumption in each region will achieve at least a certain level (although he must be careful not to stipulate amounts which cannot be met by the program), or (2) introduce another set of activities, namely consumption activities. The first of these alternatives is developed here.[55]

Consider the introduction of additional constraints in each region on the amounts of the two finished products, textiles and coal, to be made available for household consumption. Suppose we state that this amount of the finished product coal in region A shall be at least equal to the quantity R_4^A, of textiles in region A at least equal to R_5^A, of the finished product coal in region B at least equal to R_4^B, and of textiles in region B at least equal to R_5^B. We are therefore stating for region A that

1. The amount of the finished product coal yielded by activity 4,A $(a_{44}^A X_4^A)$ must be at least as great as the required amount of coal to be made available for household consumption in region A (R_4^A), that is,

$$a_{44}^A X_4^A \geq R_4^A$$

2. The amount of the finished product textile yielded by activity 1,A $(a_{51}^A X_1^A)$, less exports of textiles from region A to region B $(-a_{57}^A X_7^A$, which represent inputs of the textile-shipping activity of region A), plus imports of textiles into region A from region B $(a_{57}^{B \to A} X_7^B$, which represent outputs of the textile-shipping activity of region B) must be at least as great as the required amount of textiles to be made available for household consumption in region A (R_5^A), that is,

$$a_{51}^A X_1^A + a_{57}^A X_7^A + a_{57}^{B \to A} X_7^B \geq R_5^A$$

Similarly, for region B we have the two comparable constraints

$$a_{44}^B X_4^B \geq R_4^B \quad \text{and}$$
$$a_{57}^{A \to B} X_7^A + a_{51}^B X_1^B + a_{57}^B X_7^B \geq R_5^B$$

[55] For a fuller discussion of this alternative and for still another effective approach to this problem, see B. H. Stevens [28], chs. 4, 5.

These four new constraints, which we shall call *availability constraints*, are to be added to the six specified in Part I of Table 7 to form the set of constraints applicable to the new linear program. However, since the linear program is a maximum problem, the sense of the inequality of each constraint must be "less than" ($<$). Therefore, to conform to this requirement, both sides of these constraints are multiplied by -1, which then changes the sense of the inequality. In strict fashion the new constraints are

(20)
$$-a_{44}^A X_4^A \leq -R_4^A$$
$$-a_{51}^A X_1^A - a_{57}^A X_7^A - a_{57}^{B \to A} X_7^B \leq -R_5^A$$
$$-a_{44}^B X_4^B \leq -R_4^B$$
$$-a_{57}^{A \to B} X_7^A - a_{51}^B X_1^B - a_{57}^B X_7^B \leq -R_5^B$$

Despite these new constraints, the objective function remains unchanged in form. However, the optimal solution for this new linear program will most likely yield a lower value for Y, the sum of regional incomes, if any of the *availability* constraints is binding. For, if one or more availability constraints are binding, this usually signifies that the system is being forced to yield a solution which would not be optimal for a system unconstrained by minimum limits on the amounts of finished products to be made available for household consumption in the several regions.[56] That is, in order to fulfill the requirement that a certain amount of a commodity be available for household consumption in a region, the system is being forced to ship a commodity to a region or produce a commodity in a region or curtail a region's export of a commodity, or some combination of these activities, in a way that the system would otherwise not usually find efficient.

Once availability constraints are added to a linear program, both the objective function and the set of constraints of its dual are changed. Because four new constraints are added to the linear program, we must add four new choice variables to the objective function of the dual, more specifically $\breve{P}_4^A$, $\breve{P}_5^A$, $\breve{P}_4^B$, and $\breve{P}_5^B$.[57] These four variables, which can take only nonnegative values and which we shall find represent subsidy prices, multiply the corresponding new $-R$'s which are predetermined constants. Thus, to the objective function at the top of Part II of Table 7, we add the following four terms

$$+ (-R_4^A)\breve{P}_4^A + (-R_5^A)\breve{P}_5^A + (-R_4^B)\breve{P}_4^B + (-R_5^B)\breve{P}_5^B, \quad \text{or}$$
$$- R_4^A \breve{P}_4^A - R_5^A \breve{P}_5^A - R_4^B \breve{P}_4^B - R_5^B \breve{P}_5^B$$

[56] B. H. Stevens [28] has designated this type of solution as "semi-efficient."

[57] The " symbol above the P's indicates that these prices are *variables*. They contrast with the corresponding P's representing finished-product prices which are barred and are constants (fixed beforehand).

The number of constraints in the dual is not changed by the injection of availability constraints into the linear program. However, the statement of several of the constraints is changed by the addition to each of another term. Specifically constraints 1, 4, 7, 8, 11, and 14 become respectively

(1a) $\quad -a_{11}^A P_1^A - a_{21}^A P_2^A - a_{31}^A P_3^A \qquad\qquad - a_{51}^A \ddot{P}_5^A \qquad\qquad\qquad \geq c_1^A$

(4a) $\qquad\qquad\qquad\qquad\quad - a_{34}^A P_3^A - a_{44}^A \ddot{P}_4^A \qquad\qquad\qquad\qquad \geq c_4^A$

(7a) $\qquad\qquad\quad - a_{27}^A P_2^A \qquad\qquad\quad - a_{57}^A \ddot{P}_5^A - a_{57}^{A \to B} \ddot{P}_5^B \quad \geq c_7^A$

(8a) $\quad -a_{11}^B P_1^B - a_{21}^B P_2^B - a_{31}^B P_3^B \qquad\qquad - a_{51}^B \ddot{P}_5^B \qquad\qquad\qquad \geq c_1^B$

(11a) $\qquad\qquad\qquad\qquad\quad - a_{34}^B P_3^B - a_{44}^B \ddot{P}_4^B \qquad\qquad\qquad\qquad \geq c_4^B$

(14a) $\qquad\qquad\quad - a_{27}^B P_2^B \qquad\qquad\quad - a_{57}^B \ddot{P}_5^B - a_{57}^{B \to A} \ddot{P}_5^A \quad \geq c_7^B$

We now wish to interpret these altered constraints. Actually, we need to examine carefully only the first three of these constraints (which pertain to activities in region A), since the last three (which pertain to activities in region B) are identical to the first three, except that regional superscripts have been interchanged.

To begin, rearrange terms so that all $\ddot{P}$'s are on the right-hand side, and substitute for c_1^A, c_4^A, and c_7^A their definition in terms of finished product prices, as given in the set of equations 19. Assuming that we have defined activities 1,A, 4,A, and 7,A so that at unit level of operations each yields a unit of product, that is, that respectively $a_{51}^A = 1$, $a_{44}^A = 1$, and $a_{57}^{A \to B} = -a_{57}^A = 1$, we obtain for the first three of the altered constraints

(1b) $\qquad\qquad - a_{11}^A P_1^A - a_{21}^A P_2^A - a_{31}^A P_3^A \geq \bar{P}_5^A + \ddot{P}_5^A$

(4b) $\qquad\qquad\qquad\qquad\qquad\quad - a_{34}^A P_3^A \geq \bar{P}_4^A + \ddot{P}_4^A$

(7b) $\qquad\qquad\qquad\qquad - a_{27}^A P_2^A \qquad \geq (\bar{P}_5^B + \ddot{P}_5^B) - (\bar{P}_5^A + \ddot{P}_5^A)$

Constraint 1b states that per unit level of textile production in region A, the cost of labor $(-a_{11}^A P_1^A)$ plus the cost of transportation $(-a_{21}^A P_2^A)$ plus the cost of coal $(-a_{31}^A P_3^A)$ must not be less than the predetermined price of textiles in region A $(\bar{P}_5^A)$ plus the value attached to the availability (for household consumption) of a unit of textiles in region A $(\ddot{P}_5^A)$. This latter value, $\ddot{P}_5^A$, may be designated a subsidy price. In one sense it is the opposite of a rent. Rent on a resource is zero when the demand for a resource is less than the *fixed* available supply. When the demand would exceed the fixed supply if the resource were costless, rent becomes positive, thereby serving to curtail demand to a level equal to the fixed supply. In contrast, when the amount of textiles made available to region A exceeds the fixed availability requirement, that is, R_5^A (which some may wish to view as a minimum acceptable level of household consumption), $\overset{\smile}{P}{}^{A}_{5}$ is zero. However, when the amount of textiles made available to region A would be less than the constant R^{A}_{5} if $\overset{\smile}{P}{}^{A}_{5}$ were zero, then $\overset{\smile}{P}{}^{A}_{5}$ becomes positive. It represents a subsidy price[58] to be added to the specified market price in order to raise this amount (supply) to a level equal to R^{A}_{5}. Thus the variable $\overset{\smile}{P}{}^{A}_{5}$ serves to achieve equality of supply and demand by affecting the behavior of suppliers (producers and shippers); whereas a rent variable, say P^{A}_{3}, serves to achieve equality by affecting the behavior of demanders.

In similar fashion, constraint 4b states that per unit level of activity 3,A the cost of the input of coal as an intermediate (which is the price of coal as an intermediate since $-a^{A}_{34} = 1$) must not be less than the price of the finished product coal in region A plus its subsidy price. This subsidy price will be zero when the corresponding availability constraint is not binding; otherwise, it will usually be positive.

Finally, constraint 7b states that per unit level of activity 7,A the cost of inputs, which is the transport cost on a unit of textiles from region A to region B, must not be less than the difference between (1) the price of textiles plus subsidy price on textiles in region B and (2) the price on textiles plus subsidy price on textiles in region A. When the system furnishes to the respective region supplies of textiles which exceed R^{A}_{5} and R^{B}_{5}, both subsidy prices are zero. Where only one of the regions receives supplies of textiles in excess of its availability requirement, the corresponding subsidy price is zero, whereas the subsidy price of the second region is usually positive since the second region's availability constraint on textiles is binding. In still a third set of circumstances, the availability constraints of both regions are binding, and both subsidy prices are usually positive. In each case of this third set, the operation of the system, *if the system were free of availability constraints*, would furnish the respective regions with supplies of textiles short of R^{A}_{5} and R^{B}_{5}. Injecting availability constraints into the system forces, for these cases, the contraction of the output of coal as a finished product in one or both regions and diverts resources to the provision of additional textiles in both regions via the mechanism of subsidy prices on textiles.

In this manner we overcome the problem of setting finished-product prices which are required for the operation of the model and yet do not predetermine levels of activities. By the introduction of availability constraints, we bypass the dilemma just posed. At the same time we derive a set of subsidy prices which when added to the preassigned finished-product prices gives us a set of meaningful prices which we

[58] Alternatively, $\overset{\smile}{P}{}^{A}_{5}$ might be considered a location utility price, or a premium price, depending on the manner and situation in which a linear program is conceived.

designate *adjusted finished-product prices*. The adjusted finished-product prices are variables, since each is the sum of a constant (the preassigned finished product price) plus a variable adjustment (the variable subsidy price). They are meaningful because we can now operate the model without the availability constraints but with the adjusted finished-product prices as determined earlier substituted for the first set of preassigned finished-product prices (the $\bar{P}$'s); we can do this and yet be certain that in each region supplies of each finished product made available will at least equal the availability requirements (i.e., the desired levels). The adjusted finished-product prices are therefore a meaningful and consistent set of prices for an interregional system.

Another point is to be noted. Suppose an analyst operates a model not restricted by availability constraints with the adjusted finished-product prices as given data. Suppose he finds that the resulting regional distribution of finished product available for household consumption is not consistent with the system of *disposable* regional incomes (as perhaps estimated by procedures discussed in Chapter 4). He can then introduce once again availability constraints. On any finished product he can set an availability requirement in, let us say, a high-income region which exceeds the supply available for household consumption, whereas he sets an availability requirement in, let us say, a low-income region which falls short of supply available for household consumption. With such new availability constraints on one or more commodities for one or more regions, and with the derived adjusted finished-product prices as given data, he can operate the resulting new linear program. This new linear program will force shifts in the regional distribution of available supplies of finished products in accordance with the judgment of the analyst, as reflected in the new set of availability requirements. The dual of this new linear program will yield a set of subsidy prices which when added to the first set of derived adjusted finished-product prices yields a second set of adjusted finished-product prices which are meaningful and consistent in terms of the new availability requirements imposed. Again, the investigator may compare the resulting regional pattern of available supplies with the resulting new system of *disposable* regional incomes (however determined) and reach the decision to alter availability requirement by regions once again, etc., etc. By this iterative procedure, the investigator can work toward a final set of interregional prices consistent with his other research hypotheses, data, and findings, and toward a system which optimizes the sum of regional incomes within this latter framework.

J. The General Interregional Model

We are now in a position to generalize. Let there be U regions, any one region generally being designated by the superscript L ($L = 1, \cdots, U$).[59] Let there be in each region many resources. A resource may be either mobile or immobile; its initial supply (endowment) in any given region is fixed and specified beforehand. Also, let there be in each region many commodities, some of which are pure intermediates, some of which are pure finished products, and some of which can be consumed either as intermediates (by industry) or as finished products (by households). Moreover, let there be a commodity classification which, for ease of exposition alone, we take to be identical from region to region. In this classification commodities are designated from 1 to s. Resources and intermediate commodities run from 1 to m, commodity i being generally taken to represent a resource or intermediate. Finished products run from $m + 1$ to s, commodity q being generally taken to represent a finished product. As before, any item that is both an intermediate and a finished product is considered as two commodities; it is listed once as *intermediate* among the first m commodities; and it is listed a second time as *finished product* among commodities designated from $m + 1$ to s. Moreover, a resource, such as labor which is used as an input by industry but also may be consumed by households as *leisure*, may appear twice in the commodity classification, once among the first group of commodities as an *industrial resource* and again among the second group of commodities as *finished product*. For notational convenience, we order the finished products such that items which appear only as finished products run from $m + 1$ to r,

[59] In a pure theoretical model there is of course no restriction on the number of regions to be considered, provided the number is finite. Hence, in conceptually approximating reality, we can envisage as many one-point regions as desired. We can always expand the number of regions if we consider that the assumed number does not adequately represent the existing clusters of population, economic, and other units.

It is important to recognize that in practice the number of regions which is adopted depends on the existing interregional system to be analyzed. This dependence results from the structure of a linear programming model which requires that constant co-efficients characterize the operation of each activity, including shipping. Thus the transport inputs per unit level of any shipping activity must be constant. This in turn requires that each region be capable of being approximately represented by a single-point economy in which are concentrated all production and consumption activities of the region. Typically, too, as in this model, the assumption is made that intraregional requirements of transport inputs are zero. This last assumption is convenient, but not necessary, since we can incorporate into our scheme intraregional shipping activities. Each of these shipping activities, however, must require a constant amount of transport inputs per unit level; that is, the use of transport inputs in shipping any given commodity within a region must be approximately a constant, regardless of point of origin and point of destination within the region.

and items which appear both as finished product and as an intermediate (or resource) run in the finished-product classification from $r + 1$ to s.

In general we let R_i^L ($i = 1, \cdots, m; L = 1, \cdots, U$) represent the initial supply of resource or intermediate i in region L. This initial supply is fixed and specified beforehand. In the case of an intermediate, $R_i^L = 0$.

Associated with each region is a set of activities. Some of these are production activities; others are dummy activities which shift intermediates and resources to a finished-product status; and still others are shipping activities. Again, for ease of exposition alone, we assume that the set of activities is identical from region to region, although this will not be true for any given interregional system.

For each of the U regions we assume n production activities. As activities 1,A and 2,A in Table 6, each production activity employs as inputs resources and intermediate commodities. However, unlike the production activities of Table 6, each production activity may yield more than one output. It may yield more than one finished product, or more than one intermediate, or some combination of intermediates and finished products. Thus, more than one of the coefficients listed in the appropriate column of the coefficient matrix for this general interregional model may be positive.[60] (For example, see Table 1, Chapter 9.) Further, the same finished product, or intermediate, or combination of finished products and intermediates may be produced by more than one activity,

---

[60] Introduction of joint products for any production activity does not involve any complication. Of course, where more than one finished product is associated with a production activity, income per unit level of that activity will be the sum of more than one term, each term representing the product of price of a finished product and its output per unit level.

It is to be noted that when activities are defined such that an activity both produces the output and ships it to a specified region (i.e., requires as inputs the commodities normal to the production process as well as transport services for delivery), difficulty arises when more than one product is associated with a productive process. For suppose two finished products are yielded by a productive process. If both are delivered to region J, a defined amount of transport inputs are required per unit level of the activity embodying this productive process and entailing delivery of the two finished products to J. However, if one product is shipped to region J and a second to region L, another defined amount of transport inputs will be required per unit level, and a second activity will need to be recognized. Further, if one product is shipped to J, and the second to K, or if one is shipped to J and one-half the second shipped to both L and K, etc., then a third, fourth, etc., activity will need to be recognized, since each delivery pattern will require a different amount of transport inputs per unit level. Since an infinite number of delivery patterns is possible when more than one output is yielded by a productive process, an infinite number of shipping activities will need to be recognized. This will negate the usefulness of the model. Hence, if joint products are permitted in a production process, it becomes necessary to divorce production activity from shipping activity as we have done in our model.

that is, there can be in each region activities (processes) producing the same kind of output. (Again, refer to Table 1, Chapter 9.)

For each region, too, we have the same number of dummy activities, each one of which transforms an intermediate, or in some instances a resource, into a finished product. As with activities 4,A and 4,B in Table 6, each dummy activity has a single input and a single output, both of the same magnitude but opposite in sign. Since in each region there are m resources and intermediates, we may posit as many as m dummy activities in each region.[61]

Finally, for each region we have the same number of shipping activities. Any region L may ship any one commodity to $U - 1$ regions. Since region L is generally at a different distance from each of these $U - 1$ regions, its requirements of transport inputs to ship the commodity to each of these regions will be different. Hence, there must be $U - 1$ shipping activities in region L to allow for export of the given commodity to each region. But there are as many as r commodities in region L which may be shipped.[62] As a consequence there are $(U - 1)r$ shipping activities in region L. Each shipping activity has associated with it a single output, the commodity received as an import in the region of destination. Except for activities which export transportation, such as activities 5,A and 5,B in Table 6, each shipping activity requires at least two inputs, one being the commodity to be exported, the other being transportation. Generally speaking, each shipping activity is defined to require other inputs as well, such as management, insurance services, etc.

Altogether there are in region L, as well as every other region, $n + m + (U - 1)r$ possible activities. For notational convenience we let v represent the number of these activities, that is, $v = n + m + (U - 1)r$. We now number these activities from 1 to v, the first n being production activities, the next m being dummy activities, and the remaining $(U - 1)r$ being shipping activities. For any activity j in region L, we let X_j^L represent the level at which that activity is operated. Since there are v activities in each region (i.e., $j = 1, \cdots, v$) and since there are U regions (i.e., $L = 1, \cdots, U$), there are all told Uv activities in our interregional system.

Corresponding to every activity in every region there is an income per

---

[61] When a dummy activity converts a resource, say labor, into a finished product, say leisure, we have the single input, labor, and the single output, leisure.

[62] Finished products which run from $r + 1$ to s are not shipped since these items have as a counterpart an intermediate (or resource) and since we adopt the convention that any item which is both a finished product and an intermediate (resource) is shipped in its intermediate (resource) form. The use of another convention at this point would not basically alter the ensuing analysis.

unit level. That is, corresponding to any activity j in region L, there is a c_j^L. As in the discussion of sections 7 and 8, c_j^L is defined as the sum of the products obtained by multiplying each finished-product output of an activity by the given price of the finished product, that is, for all non-shipping activities

$$(21) \quad c_j^L = a_{m+1,j}^L \bar{P}_{m+1}^L + a_{m+2,j}^L \bar{P}_{m+2}^L + \cdots + a_{sj}\bar{P}_s^L = \sum_{q=m+1}^{s} a_{qj}^L \bar{P}_q^L$$

and for all shipping activities, each of which by definition ships only a single commodity,

$$(22) \quad c_j^L = 0 \quad \text{when an intermediate is shipped;} \quad \text{or}$$

$$(23) \quad c_j^L = a_{qj}^L \bar{P}_q^L + a_{qj}^{L \to J} \bar{P}_q^J \quad \text{when a finished product is shipped.}[63]$$

If the aim of the linear program is to maximize the sum of regional incomes, the objective function is

$$(24) \quad \begin{aligned} \text{Max } Z &= c_1^1 X_1^1 + \cdots + c_v^1 X_v^1 + c_1^2 X_1^2 + \cdots + c_j^L X_j^L + \cdots + c_v^U X_v^U \\ &= \sum_{L=1}^{U} \sum_{j=1}^{v} c_j^L X_j^L \end{aligned}$$

for nonnegative X_j^L. In this program there may be as many as Us constraints, which include (1) constraints on the use of resources,[64] immobile or mobile; (2) constraints on intermediates; and (3) availability constraints on finished products. There may be as many as Um of the first two types and as many as $U(s-m)$ of the third type. The general form of these constraints is

$$(25) \quad -\sum a_{kj}^L X_j^L - \sum_{\substack{J \\ J \neq L}} \sum_j a_{kj}^{J \to L} X_j^J \leq R_k^L \quad \begin{aligned} k &= 1, \cdots, s \\ L &= 1, \cdots, U \end{aligned}$$

[63] It is to be borne in mind that the c's change when the set of predetermined prices on finished products changes. Thus, if after a first run of the model the resulting regional distribution of finished product available for household consumption is not consistent with the system of disposable regional incomes, the investigator may try another set of finished-product prices—one that is adjusted in the light of the resulting set of subsidy prices. He may place new prices on such finished products as textiles and leisure and perhaps introduce new availability constraints relating to these finished products. In doing so, the c's change at the same time.

[64] Resources are defined very broadly so as to include not only specific types of natural resources, such as land of a certain soil type, ore of a certain quality, or coking coal of a certain grade, but also nonnatural resources such as industrial plant of a certain type, equipment of a defined specification, or labor of a certain skill, etc. Limited supplies (capacities) of the latter type of resources are of particular importance in short-run models such as some of the input-output schemes already discussed.

If k is an immobile resource in region L, the second term of this constraint is zero since all $a_{kj}^{J \to L}$ are zero (no shipment possible). Thus, only the first term remains which represents the sum of the requirements of this resource by all production activities in region L, by a possible dummy activity in region L which transforms this resource into a finished product, and by all shipping activities in region L where these shipping activities require the resource as local inputs and not for export. This sum must not be greater than R_k^L, the available supply in region L.

If k is a mobile resource, to this sum must be added the requirements of this resource by shipping activities for export to other regions. Also, the second term may no longer be zero. In this term, for all but one j in any other region, $a_{kj}^{J \to L} = 0$, since, as noted in section 8, no production, dummy, or shipping activity in region L can use as inputs commodities of other regions which have not first been shipped to region L and thus transformed into the corresponding local commodity in region L. The one activity in region J, however, for which $a_{kj}^{J \to L} \neq 0$ is that shipping activity which transports the resource from region J to region L.[65] Thus the absolute value of the second term of relation 25 represents region L's total imports of the resource from the rest of the system. Thus, for such a resource, relation 25 states that the requirements of this resource as local inputs by all activities plus requirements for export less total imports must not be greater than the given local supply.

If k in relation 25 represents an intermediate, the constraint reads: The requirements of k by all production activities in region L, plus the requirement of k by the dummy activity of region L which transforms k into a finished product, plus the requirement for both local use and export by region L's shipping activities, less the production of k by activities in region L, and less the imports of k from other regions [the absolute value of the second term of relation 25][66] must not be greater than zero, which is the value R_k^L takes when k is an intermediate. Or, in other words, the demand for the intermediate k must not exceed its supply.

Finally, if k is a finished product [i.e., runs from $m + 1$ to s], relation 25 states the following, *after we multiply both sides by* -1 *and change the sense of the inequality, which we may do without altering the relation*: The sum of the outputs of the finished product k by all production and dummy activities of region L less the amount taken by shipping activities for export to other regions plus imports of k from all other regions (i.e., the outputs of those shipping activities in the several regions that ship k

[65] Since the position of this resource shipping activity in the listing of activities will vary from region to region, we cannot designate by a specific subscript the activity in each region J ($J \neq L$) that ships this resource to region L.

[66] Note, again, that for all but one j in any region J, $a_{kj}^{J \to L} = 0$.

to region L) must not be less than $-R_k^L$ which is a positive amount fixing the quantity of the finished product k which must be available for household consumption in region L. Note a change in the definition of R_k^L. In the previous section R_k^L was defined as a nonnegative number. Here we define R_k^L as a non-positive number (but of the same absolute value) so that $-R_k^L$ is nonnegative.[67] We adopt this change in notation in order to embrace all constraints of the problem in a single statement of relations 25.

Observe that there is specified in this general model an R_k^L for every finished product in every region. However, let there be one or more finished products which are considered inessential and on which for other reasons we do not wish to place availability constraints. For those commodities in any or all regions we let $R_k^L = 0$. This procedure, in essence, erases the constraints.[68]

A still more general statement of our constraints as given by relation 25 is possible. Let the superscript symbol $L \to L$ represent L whenever the former occurs below, $L = 1, \cdots, U$;[69] then relation 25 becomes:

$$(26) \qquad -\sum_J \sum_j a_{kj}^{J \to L} X_j^J \le R_k^L \text{ (footnote 70)} \qquad \begin{array}{l} k = 1, \cdots, s \\ L = 1, \cdots, U \end{array}$$

The dual to the general linear program defined by relations 24 and 26 may now be stated. For notational convenience, we first let P_k^L replace $\ddot{P}_k^L$. Thus P_k^L becomes the relevant subsidy price which is a variable and is distinct from $\bar{P}_k^L$ which is a constant and is the predetermined finished-product price specified as a given for the model. Thus the dual is

$$(27) \qquad \text{Min } W = \sum_{L=1}^{U} \sum_{k=1}^{s} R_k^L P_k^L$$

subject to

$$(28) \qquad -\sum_J \sum_k a_{kj}^{L \to J} P_k^J \ge c_j^L \qquad \begin{array}{l} j = 1, \cdots, v \\ L = 1, \cdots, U \end{array}$$

The objective is, as in the previous section, to minimize fictitious returns

[67] By such a notational change we do not change the meaning of the relation. For when we define R_k^L as a nonnegative number, we at the same time multiply it by -1 so that we always use $-R_k^L$ in place of R_k^L when R_k^L was defined as a nonnegative number. For example, in the previous section if we were to redefine R_4^A as a nonpositive number, in the relations specified in that section we would always replace R_4^A by $-R_4^A$.

[68] It is to be noted that in a linear program outputs of finished products, *by definition*, can never be less than zero, and exports can never exceed supplies available for export. Hence, the left-hand side of relation 25 can never be greater than zero. Thus, when $R_k^L = 0$, the availability constraint on k can never be effectively binding.

[69] Thus $J \to J$ represents J, $U \to U$ represents U, etc.

[70] Recall that when in the summation $J \ne L$, $a_{kj}^{J \to L} = 0$ except for that j in J which ships k to L. When in the same summation $J = L$, $X_j^J = X_j^L$; and we have $a_{kj}^{J \to L} = a_{kj}^{L \to L} = a_{kj}^L$ which will be nonzero for some activities in L.

to resource owners after deduction of subsidy payments necessary to achieve the required availabilities on finished products.[71]   The constraints are also of the same order.   Where j is a production activity, all $a_{kj}^{L \to J} = 0$ when $J \neq L$, and the relation 28 states that per unit-level operation of j the costs of all local inputs less the value of intermediate goods produced less subsidy payments on all finished products produced must not be less than c_j^L, c_j^L being zero when j produces only intermediates.   Where j is a dummy activity, all $a_{kj}^{L \to J} = 0$ when $J \neq L$, and the relation 28 states that per unit-level operation of j the cost of the intermediate or resource having its status shifted less subsidy payment on the finished product must not be less than c_j^L; or, put otherwise, the price of the intermediate or resource less the subsidy price on the finished product must not be less than the predetermined price of the finished product.   Finally, when j is a shipping activity, all but one $a_{kj}^{L \to J} = 0$ when $J \neq L$, and relation 28 may be read in two different ways.   When an intermediate good i is shipped, such that $a_{ij}^{L \to J} \neq 0$, relation 28 states that per unit-level operation of j the costs of all local inputs, including the intermediate to be shipped less the value of the output (export) valued at the price prevailing in the region of destination (i.e., region J), must not be less than c_j^L which is zero.   When a final product good q is shipped, such that $a_{qj}^{L \to J} \neq 0$, relation 28 states that per unit-level operation of j the cost of all local inputs (excluding the finished product to be shipped) plus subsidy payment on the finished product in region L (the originating region) less subsidy payment on the finished product in region J (the terminating region) must not be less than c_j^L (which equals the spread between the finished-product prices in the two regions when the unit level is defined such that $a_{qj}^{L \to J} = -a_{qj}^{L \to L} = 1$).

At this point it may be helpful to present this linear program and its dual in the familiar matrix form.   Let

$A = [a_{kj}^{J \to L}]$, a matrix of technical coefficients of order $Us \times Uv$ $(k = 1, \cdots, s; \ j = 1, \cdots, v \quad$ where $\quad v = n + m + (U - 1)r;$ $J, L = 1, \cdots, U)$

$= \begin{bmatrix} A_i \\ A_q \end{bmatrix}$ where A_i is a $Um \times Uv$ matrix of technical coefficients pertaining to resources and intermediate commodities $(i = 1, \cdots, m)$; and where A_q is a $U(s - m) \times Uv$ matrix of technical coefficients pertaining to finished products $(q = m + 1, \cdots, s)$

---

[71] This deduction is effected in the objective function since R_k^L is negative when k runs from $m + 1$ to s.   At this point it should be recognized that the payment of subsidies tends to raise the returns to resource owners above what they would otherwise receive.   See Stevens [28].

$X = \{X_j^L\}$, a column vector of activity levels of order Uv

$\bar{P}' = [\bar{P}_q^L]$, a row vector of predetermined finished-product prices of order $U(s - m)$

$c' = [c_j^L]$, a row vector of per-unit-level incomes of order Uv

$\quad = \bar{P}'A_q$

$R = \{R_{k_j}^L\}$, a Us-order column vector of the limiting constants of the constraints pertaining to resource and intermediate commodity use and to availability of finished products; and

$P = \{P_k^L\}$, a Us-order column vector of resource and intermediate prices and of subsidy prices on finished products.

The linear program and its dual are

$$\text{Max } Z = c'X \qquad\qquad \text{Min } W = R'P$$

$$\text{subject to:} \qquad\qquad\qquad \text{subject to:}$$

$$-AX \leq R \qquad\qquad\qquad -A'P \geq c$$

$$\text{and} \qquad\qquad\qquad\qquad \text{and}$$

$$X \geq 0 \qquad\qquad\qquad\qquad P \geq 0$$

K. Some Simple Applications

Having developed step by step a rather full general interregional model, we may examine some recent applications. These applications employ rather simple models. For the most part these applications can be adequately understood by the reader who has covered only the materials of the early sections of this chapter.

The first application to be discussed refers to a study by Henderson of production and shipment in the coal industry. The problem is to identify for the short run the most efficient pattern of shipments from existing coal deposits in the regions of a system to consumers in the same system. First, the regions (districts) within the system must be specified. This specification, that is, the classification of states into a set of regions judged most useful from the standpoint of the entire study, appears in column 1 of Table 8.[72] The regions are lettered from A to N, and of these only the first K have capacity to produce coal.[73] Further, because underground

[72] See J. M. Henderson [13], p. 340, for discussion of considerations affecting the choice of a set of regions. As already indicated in previous chapters, the selection of an appropriate set of regions is largely related to the problem to be investigated. See also J. M. Henderson [11, 12].

[73] Capacities of districts L, M, and N are zero since capacity in any region is defined to be zero if the number of days the region's mines were active in 1947 is zero. For further details on capacity estimation see J. M. Henderson [13], p. 341.

TABLE 8.   UNIT EXTRACTION COSTS, MINING CAPACITIES, AND DEMAND, BY REGION, 1947

District (1)	States Included (1)	Unit Extraction Costs (per 10^{10} Btu) Underground Mines (2)	Surface Mines (3)	Estimated Mining Capacities (in 10^{10} Btu) Underground Mines (4)	Surface Mines (5)	Demand (in 10^{10} Btu) (6)
A	Pennsylvania, Maryland	$1,503	$ 828	225,598	142,982	221,400
B	West Virginia	1,329	893	381,733	97,282	66,276
C	Virginia, Kentucky, District of Columbia	1,391	655	270,831	40,506	139,708
D	Alabama, Tennessee, North and South Carolina, Georgia, Florida, Mississippi, Louisiana	1,891	1,308	49,918	7,613	107,089
E	Ohio	1,414	897	64,661	52,341	165,421
F	Illinois, Indiana, Michigan	1,238	934	165,348	74,997	283,305
G	Iowa, Missouri, Kansas, Arkansas, Oklahoma, Texas	2,471	1,088	12,828	27,682	62,773
H	North and South Dakota, Nebraska	1,659	1,185	690	3,365	15,763
I	Montana, Wyoming, Utah, Idaho	1,343	761	36,690	7,382	28,548
J	Colorado, New Mexico, Arizona, California, Nevada	1,704	1,220	20,424	927	18,108
K	Washington, Oregon	2,855	1,484	1,388	609	10,522
L	Maine, New Hampshire, Vermont, Massachusetts, Connecticut, Rhode Island	—	—	—	—	60,186
M	New York, New Jersey, Delaware	—	—	—	—	123,221
N	Minnesota, Wisconsin	—	—	—	—	47,005
	Totals			1,230,009	455,686	1,349,325

Source: J. M. Henderson [13], pp. 340–342.

and surface mining are quite different from a technical standpoint (as is reflected in the cost data to be presented later), an activity in a region, say region A, which extracts coal from underground mines and delivers to a second region, say region B, is different from an activity in region A which extracts coal from surface mines and delivers to region B.

In addition to regions, activities must be specified in a precise manner. In this study each activity is defined as combining both the extraction and delivery of coal. Since in any one of the eleven producing regions, say region J ($J = A, \cdots, K$), underground coal can be extracted and delivered to any one of the fourteen consuming regions, say region L ($L = A, \cdots, N$), for each region J there are fourteen possible activities associated with underground coal mining and delivery. Their levels may be designated by

$$X_u^{J \to A}, X_u^{J \to B}, X_u^{J \to C}, \cdots, X_u^{J \to N}$$

where the letter following the arrow in the superscript refers to the region to which the coal is delivered, and where the subscript u refers to underground coal. Similarly for each region J there are fourteen possible activities associated with surface coal mining and delivery. Their levels may be designated as

$$X_s^{J \to A}, X_s^{J \to B}, X_s^{J \to C}; \cdots, X_s^{J \to N}$$

Therefore the complete set of possible activity levels runs from

$$X_u^{A \to A}, X_u^{A \to B}, \cdots, X_u^{K \to N}, X_s^{A \to A}, X_s^{A \to B}, \cdots, X_s^{K \to N}$$

Next the objective function may be set down. Since the objective is to minimize the total cost of producing and delivering coal for the system, the objective function is

To minimize:

$$(29) \quad \tau = \pi_u^{A \to A} X_u^{A \to A} + \pi_u^{A \to B} X_u^{A \to B} + \cdots + \pi_u^{K \to N} X_u^{K \to N} +$$
$$\pi_s^{A \to A} X_s^{A \to A} + \pi_s^{A \to B} X_s^{A \to B} + \cdots + \pi_s^{K \to N} X_s^{K \to N}$$

where any $\pi_u^{J \to L}$ indicates the cost of both extracting and delivering a unit of coal from the *underground* mine in region J to the consumer in region L, and where any $\pi_s^{J \to L}$ indicates the same for coal from *surface* mines. Each $\pi_u^{J \to L}$, and each $\pi_s^{J \to L}$ is assumed to be a constant and given beforehand (on the assumption of constant unit extraction cost at each mine and constant transport rate). To obtain the values for these constant π's, it is first necessary to estimate unit extraction costs. These cost data for 1947 are listed in column 2 and 3 of Table 8, by region and type of mining.[74]

---

[74] Since quality of different types of coal varies, the tonnage unit is eschewed in favor of the more satisfactory heating value unit, the British thermal unit. (Because of its special properties, coking coal is not included in this study.) See J. M. Henderson [13], pp. 340–341.

Next, to such unit extraction costs must be added appropriate transport costs to obtain the full value for each π.[75] The resulting set of unit delivery (extraction plus transport) costs for year 1947 is listed in Table 9. [Where transport cost information was not available upon which to base particular estimates of region-to-region unit transport costs—primarily because such deliveries are not made and are not likely to be made under any reasonable circumstances—the unit transport costs are assumed to be so large as to preclude any shipment in any equilibrium (optimizing) model.   The corresponding cells in Table 9 contain the letter N.][76]   For example, according to Table 9

$$\pi_u^{A\to A} = \$2004$$
$$\pi_u^{A\to B} = \$2282$$
$$\pi_s^{A\to B} = \$1607$$
$$\vdots$$
$$\pi_s^{K\to N} = N$$

The objective function is subject to two sets of constraints.   The first relates to capacities.   For any producing region the sum of all underground coal shipments from that region must not exceed the capacity of that region to mine underground coal.   Likewise, the sum of all its surface coal shipments must not exceed its capacity to mine surface coal.   Thus, since a unit level of any activity requires as input one unit of coal (underground or surface), the first constraint appears as

$$X_u^{A\to A} + X_u^{A\to B} + \cdots + X_u^{A\to N} \le R_u^A$$

where R_u^A is total underground mining capacity (the underground coal resource) of region A.   (Actually, for computation purposes this constraint is restated so that the sense of the inequality is reversed.[77])   This set of constraints requires, therefore, that estimates of capacities be made. Such estimates for 1947 are listed in columns 4 and 5 of Table 8.   For example,

$$R_u^A = 225{,}598$$

75 The underground or surface capacity of each region is an aggregate of the capacities of many individual coal mines.   All the underground (or surface) mines of a region are assumed to have a single extraction cost.   Further, they are assumed to be located at one place in the region for calculation of relevant transport costs.   To the extent that such assumptions are not satisfactory, the investigator can establish a finer classification of regions, in the extreme case embracing each deposit as a separate region, or introduce a separate set of extraction and transport costs for each deposit as Henderson has theoretically done ([13], pp. 336–40).

76 For further details, see J. M. Henderson [13], p. 342.

77 See J. M. Henderson [13], p. 337.

TABLE 9. INTERREGIONAL UNIT DELIVERY (EXTRACTION PLUS TRANSPORT) COSTS, 1947

(In dollars per 10^10 Btu)

From Districts:		A	B	C	D	E	F	G	H	I	J	K	L	M	N
A	u^a	2004	2282	2546	2952	2170	2712	3529	3716	N	N	N	3037	2539	2453
	s	1329	1607	1871	2277	1495	2037	2854	3041	N	N	N	2362	1864	1778
B	u	2313	1456	2293	2556	2189	2575	2887	3687	6151	5123	N	2935	2469	2463
	s	1877	1020	1857	2120	1753	2139	2451	3251	5715	4687	N	2499	2033	2027
C	u	2607	1930	1895	2357	2266	2551	2945	2933	N	N	N	3146	2810	2548
	s	1963	1235	1197	1695	1597	1903	2327	2315	N	N	N	2544	2182	1900
D	u	3018	N	2620	2402	2747	3120	3563	N	N	N	N	N	N	3029
	s	2457	N	2051	1829	2180	2561	3013	N	N	N	N	N	N	2468
E	u	2198	1988	2252	N	1899	2317	3359	N	N	N	N	3264	2503	2191
	s	1678	1471	1735	N	1372	1800	2842	N	N	N	N	2747	1986	1674
F	u	N	N	1959	2621	2232	1804	2309	3009	N	N	N	N	N	2609
	s	N	N	1650	2308	1922	1497	1999	2694	N	N	N	N	N	2298
G	u	N	N	4390	3618	N	3874	3062	3793	5174	4687	7706	N	N	3903
	s	N	N	3044	2257	N	2518	1690	2435	3843	3347	6423	N	N	2548
H	u	N	N	N	N	N	5792	5299	2499	N	N	N	N	N	3378
	s	N	N	N	N	N	5318	4825	2025	N	N	N	N	N	2905
I	u	N	N	N	N	N	N	3802	3055	2200	3059	3506	N	N	3442
	s	N	N	N	N	N	N	3527	2686	1725	2691	3194	N	N	3121
J	u	N	N	N	N	N	N	3696	3820	3225	2073	4473	N	N	N
	s	N	N	N	N	N	N	3215	3339	2743	1590	3994	N	N	N
K	u	N	N	N	N	N	N	N	N	4300	N	3423	N	N	N
	s	N	N	N	N	N	N	N	N	2929	N	2052	N	N	N

The second set of constraints relates to consumption. For any consuming region, the sum (in terms of British thermal units) of all coal shipments received, whether underground- or surface-mined, must be at least as great as the fixed demand (in British thermal units) set for it.[78] Thus in symbols the last constraint appears as

$$X_u^{A \to N} + \cdots + X_u^{K \to N} + X_s^{A \to N} + \cdots + X_s^{K \to N} \geq D^N$$

where D^N is the fixed total demand set for region N. This set of constraints requires the predetermination of a spatial pattern of demand. For the problem under study, the (historical) spatial pattern of system demand in 1947, as recorded in column 6 of Table 8, was employed as the fixed pattern. In this pattern, for example, $D^N = 47,005$.

Given the regional demands which must be met, the regional capacities which cannot be exceeded, and unit extraction and transport costs, a computation was run to derive a solution that minimizes the over-all costs of production and transportation for the system.[79] One optimal solution is recorded in Table 10.[80] Twenty-nine shipping activities are run at positive levels. (For example, to region E region A ships 48,419 $\times 10^{10}$ Btu of underground-mined coal, that is, $X_u^{A \to E} = 48,419$.) Underground mining capacities of seven regions are not fully utilized.[81]

As an aside, this minimum-cost solution is consistent with conditions of both monopoly and perfect competition.[82] From this standpoint the

[78] In this study, demand is assumed price inelastic, an assumption which has meaning only for the short run (if at all), as do the assumptions of fixed production coefficients, fixed factor prices and transport rates, constant unit extraction costs, etc.

[79] In this static model the accumulation or depletion of inventories is not permitted. For details on the computation, which is different from the simplex procedure described in the text, see J. M. Henderson [12].

[80] Strictly speaking, there are an infinite number of minimum-cost solutions. For example, in Table 10 only underground mining operators in region A ship coal to region N. Yet, without causing total costs to rise, surface mining operators in region A could ship one, two, ..., up to 47,005 units of coal to region N and that much less to region A, provided underground mining operators in region A both decreased their shipments to region N and increased their shipments to region A by the same amount.

An infinite number of efficiency solutions of this sort are usually derived from a linear programming computation, although the indeterminacy thereby introduced typically does not raise serious problems in practice. Thus the solution is efficient in the sense that no possible rearrangement of delivery levels can reduce total cost.

[81] The surface capacities of all regions are fully utilized. This result is not unexpected since, as can be seen from Table 8, unit extraction costs for surface mining are lower than those for underground mining in every region.

[82] However, the dual of this problem, namely, the selection of a set of nonnegative delivered prices and unit royalties (one for each mining operation) which satisfies the condition that all possible shipments yield nonpositive profits and which maximizes total revenue net of royalty payments, is only meaningful for conditions of perfect

TABLE 10. AN OPTIMAL PATTERN OF INTERREGIONAL COAL SHIPMENTS, 1947
(In 10^{10} Btu)

Region From To	Type of Mining[a]	Level of Shipment	Region From To	Type of Mining	Level of Shipment
$A \rightarrow A$	u	78,418	$I \rightarrow K$	u	8,525
$A \rightarrow A$	s	142,982	$K \rightarrow K$	u	1,388
$B \rightarrow B$	s	66,276	$K \rightarrow K$	s	609
$C \rightarrow C$	u	99,202	$B \rightarrow L$	u	29,180
$C \rightarrow C$	s	40,506	$B \rightarrow L$	s	31,006
$C \rightarrow D$	u	99,476	$B \rightarrow M$	u	123,221
$D \rightarrow D$	s	7,613	$A \rightarrow N$	u	47,005
$A \rightarrow E$	u	48,419			
			Total demand		1,349,325
$E \rightarrow E$	u	64,661			
$E \rightarrow E$	s	52,341			
$C \rightarrow F$	u	42,960			
$F \rightarrow F$	u	165,348			

			Unused Capacities		
$F \rightarrow F$	s	74,997		Type of	
$B \rightarrow G$	u	35,091	Region	Mining	Level
$G \rightarrow G$	s	27,682			
$C \rightarrow H$	u	11,708	A	u	51,756
			B	u	194,241
$H \rightarrow H$	u	690	C	u	17,485
$H \rightarrow H$	s	3,365	D	u	49,918
$I \rightarrow I$	u	21,166	G	u	12,828
$I \rightarrow I$	s	7,382	I	u	6,999
			J	u	3,243
$J \rightarrow J$	u	17,181			
$J \rightarrow J$	s	927	Total		336,470

[a] Underground mines denoted by u, surface mines by s.
Source: J. M. Henderson [13], p. 344.

derivation of such a solution is useful. The solution describes a normative situation in that it suggests an efficient pattern under the assumptions of the model. A pattern of this sort is valuable for the social and physical planning of "new" regions. Further, through comparison with the actual pattern of shipments and outputs, the solution can point up certain inefficiences which exist. Moreover, as is demonstrated in the study, the

competition. (Under conditions of monopoly the price system is indeterminate.) Such a set of prices and unit royalties are derived by J. M. Henderson ([13], p. 344).

interregional model can be used to attack questions of comparative statics. Given specified changes in the data—in demand, capacities, and extraction and transport costs—it can indicate changes in the optimum values for outputs and shipments. In fact, the coal study does spell out in this way the implications of a 10,000-unit increase in the demand of region *I*. Obviously, the extent to which such results can be used to project changes in the existing pattern consequent to similar impulses depends on the extent to which the model approximates (or is believed to approximate) reality. Where the approximation is close, clearly this linear programming model and others can be employed to generate data on changing patterns of shipment and outputs which can be fruitfully used in conjunction with the combined locational-interregional input-output technique, the industrial complex approach, and other methods suggested in previous chapters.

This study presents concrete evidence of the potentialities of the linear programming technique for regional analysis. There are other applications which may be usefully noted at this point.

One such study, by the same author,[83] attempts to derive an optimal land utilization pattern for the production of field crops for each region of the United States, and thus in the given circumstances for the United States as a whole. The United States is divided into *n* regions. Within each, soil, climate, and methods of farming—and therefore per acre costs and yields—are assumed uniform. They differ among regions. Further, in each region there are identical farmers, so that land utilization for the production of field crops within any region may be related to the behavior of a *representative* farmer. The farmer desires to select a pattern of cultivation of field crops which will maximize his expected return. The crops are assumed to be produced independently. For each method of cultivating and harvesting a given field crop, there is posited for the given region a constant per acre cost, which is uninfluenced by the quantity of land devoted to the crop. Also, it is assumed that the farmer is unable to influence market prices, that he possesses a set of price expectations which does not vary with his land allocation pattern, that he makes decisions independently of the actions of other farmers, and that he anticipates yields based on "normal" weather. On the basis of these assumptions which determine a fixed profit per acre for each method of producing a field crop, the farmer's revenue can be expressed as a linear function of the quantities of land he devotes to the several methods of producing the several field crops. In maximizing his expected return, he is subject to certain outside and self-imposed restrictions. (1) The total of the quantities of land devoted to the production of the several field crops

[83] J. M. Henderson [14] and Harvard Economic Research Project [10].

must not exceed the amount of the cropland available to, or set aside by, the farmer. (2) For each crop receiving governmental price support, his planting must not exceed the governmentally imposed acreage allotment. (3) The farmer may impose certain limits on the land devoted to each of the crops that reflect both unwillingness to depart too much from an established production pattern and his estimate of the advantage of diversity. Since these restrictions can be expressed as linear inequalities, we have a linear programming problem whose solution yields for the farmer an optimal cropland pattern. Since this farmer is representative of all farmers in his region, his optimal pattern is optimal for the region (all farmers in the region confront an identical situation). Once the optimal pattern is established in this manner for each region of the nation—it will differ from region to region because of nonuniformities in soil, climate, position relative to market, etc.—we have a type of optimal cropland pattern for the nation. Further, the model can be employed to help determine the impact on regional patterns of certain changes in the given data, for example in price expectations, because of changes in governmental policy, and in this sense the model is useful for projection purposes.[84]

Still another application worthy of brief comment is one pertaining to regional production and processing and interregional flows in the dairy industry.[85] In many ways this study resembles the coal industry study. Regions are specified (with the assumption that all production, processing, and consumption of a region are concentrated at a central point).[86] In each region the demand for each of five dairy products— fluid milk, butter, cheese, evaporated milk, and nonfat dry milk solids— is set (i.e., posited to be price-inelastic) on the basis of historical materials, primarily 1953.[87] State production data by type product are tabulated. Differences among regions in processing costs and milk production costs are recognized and estimated from empirical materials.[88] Finally,

[84] For further applications, see J. M. Henderson [14]. One interesting extension concerns the derivation of a set of price expectations necessary to achieve specified national levels in the production of the several crops; another concerns the estimation of both individual and aggregate supply functions and curves.

[85] M. M. Snodgrass and C. E. French [21].

[86] For most programs examined in this study, each state is considered a region. However, in certain instances some aggregation of states was found necessary.

[87] All output of any one dairy product is treated as homogeneous, and consumers are indifferent about source of output. Also accumulation or depletion of inventories is not permitted.

For procedures in estimating 1953 consumption by product and by state, see M. M. Snodgrass and C. E. French [27], pp. 6–7.

[88] Differences in processing cost among states reduce essentially to differences in the labor cost component. Differences in milk production cost stem from differences in both the feed and labor cost components.

transport costs between every pair of regions for each of the several products are approximated.

With these empirical materials several kinds of programs can be erected. One is a simple minimum transport cost problem. For a given pattern of production by region, minimize total transport costs incurred to meet consumption requirements by region (differences among regions in processing costs and production costs being ignored). This problem is run for all dairy products when all dairy products are assumed to move as equivalent whole milk (the aggregate milk model). It is found that the minimum transportation cost bill for the production and consumption data of 1953 is $597,763,300, and that Minnesota, a large surplus state, acts as a balancing wheel, sending some milk in many directions.[89] In this problem various market restrictions—such as those imposed by state milk control agencies—may be introduced and their effects studied.[90]

A simple minimum transport cost problem of this same type is also run for each dairy product by itself—that is, for cheese, butter, fluid milk, evaporated milk, and nonfat dry milk solids. These are designated the individual product models.

A more relevant set of programs recognizes differences, within the system of regions, in the costs of processing fluid milk into the various dairy products. That is, the objective function becomes to minimize the combined costs of (1) processing milk from given production locations and (2) shipping both fluid milk and milk products to given consumption locations. (In operating this model the authors of the study were forced to aggregate the 48 states into 24 regions because of limitations of their

---

[89] Associated with an optimal solution are two sets of marginal-cost values. One set relates to the change in aggregate costs if a unit of production is shifted from one state to another. For example, it is found that a shift of a unit of production from Minnesota to California would involve a saving in costs of $3.96 per hundredweight and that a shift of one unit of production from Idaho to Arkansas would raise costs by $0.96 per hundredweight. The second set of marginal-cost values relates to the change in aggregate costs if a unit of consumption is shifted from one state to another. For example, a shift of a unit of consumption from Nevada to Wisconsin would involve a saving of $2.90 per hundredweight.

Also, associated with an optimal solution is an equilibrium set of prices, as developed in previous sections. If Minnesota is taken as base point, the equilibrium price of milk in North Carolina ($5.97) is the price of milk in Minnesota ($3.43) plus the cost of transporting the unit of milk from Minnesota to North Carolina ($2.54), etc.

[90] For example, if in each of the sixteen deficit states milk controls are postulated to have an effect equivalent to increasing cost of transportation of milk into these states by 5 per cent of the average price paid by dealers in each of these states, only minor shifts occur in the interregional pattern of milk flows, although the transportation bill rises by 9.5 per cent.

TABLE 11. OPTIMAL INTERREGIONAL MOVEMENTS REQUIRED TO MINIMIZE COSTS FOR THE MODEL PORTRAYING 1953 CONDITIONS WHICH INCLUDES PROCESSING AND TRANSPORTATION COSTS (1953)[a]

Exporting region	Importing region	Product	Amount of Milk Equivalents	Amount of Product[b]
			Pounds (000,000)	Pounds (000,000)
Mont., Idaho	Calif., Nev.	Cheese	837	83.7
Utah	Calif., Nev.	Cheese	40	4.0
	Ariz., N. M.	Fluid milk	114	114.0
Wyo., Colo.	Ariz., N. M.	Evap. milk	55	25.7
N. D., S. D.	Wash., Ore.	Butter	93	4.5
	Calif., Nev.	Cheese	133	13.3
	Calif., Nev.	Butter	1914	92.9
Neb., Kan., Okla.	Ariz., N. M.	Cheese	141	14.1
	Texas	Fluid milk	403	403.0
	Texas	Butter	962	46.7
	Texas	Cheese	927	92.7
Minnesota	Calif., Nev.	Butter	550	27.0
	Wyo., Colo.	Butter	245	11.9
	Ariz., N. M.	Butter	292	14.2
	Texas	Butter	971	47.1
	N. Y., Pa., N. J.	Butter	3826	185.7
Iowa	Ohio	Butter	1605	77.9
	Ala., Ga.	Butter	40	1.9
	Fla.	Butter	583	28.3
	S. Coastal States	Cheese	1296	129.6
	S. Coastal States	Butter	181	8.9
Mo.	Ark., Miss.	Butter	289	14.0
	Ala., Ga.	Butter	1044	50.7

Exporting Region	Importing Region	Product	Amount of Milk Equivalents	Amount of Product[b]
			Pounds (000,000)	Pounds (000,000)
Ark., Miss.	Texas	Evap. milk	367	171.5
Wis.	Ill.	Butter	1767	85.8
	Mich.	Butter	280	13.6
	Ky., Tenn.	Butter	84	4.1
	Fla.	Cheese	279	27.9
	S. Coastal States	Butter	2524	122.5
	N. Y., Pa., N. J.	Cheese	2695	269.5
	N. Y., Pa., N. J.	Butter	2203	106.9
	New England	Cheese	833	83.3
Mich.	New England	Butter	1830	88.8
	N. Y., Pa., N. J.	Evap. milk	111	51.9
Ind.	Ala., Ga.	Cheese	506	50.6
Ohio	S. Coastal States	Evap. milk	393	183.6
	New England	Evap. milk	342	159.8
	Ala., Ga.	Cheese	36	3.6
Ky., Tenn.	Ala., Ga.	Evap. milk	208	97.2
	Fla.	Fluid milk	568	568.0
Ala., Ga.	Fla.	Evap. milk	111	51.9
	Fla.	Fluid milk	99	99.0
N. Y., Pa., N. J.	New England	Fluid milk	80	80.0

[a] Intraregional movements not included.
[b] Milk equivalents divided by appropriate conversion factor: butter, 20.6; cheese, 10.0; and evaporated milk, 2.14.
Source: M. M. Snodgrass and C. E. French [27], p. 28.

computer.)[91]   The optimal pattern of shipments consistent with the model is presented in Table 11.   It is also depicted as a pattern of commodity flows on Map 1.[92]   Map 1 and similar maps of optimal patterns may be fruitfully compared and contrasted with maps of actual commodity flows such as those presented in Chapter 5.   (They may also effectively supplement estimates of balance of payments changes, interregional input-output studies, etc., in ways to be indicated in Chapter 12.)

Still more relevant is a model in which regional differences in milk production cost are also recognized and introduced.   The objective then becomes that of minimizing total over-all production, processing, and transportation costs, where the regional pattern of consumption is set as before.   This latter model is run in two forms.   In the first, the "ideal model," each region is assumed to have unlimited capacity to produce fluid milk at a fixed cost per unit.   When this model is solved it yields the results shown in the first three columns of Table 12.   The manufactured dairy products segment is almost exclusively served by Wisconsin and Minnesota, whereas in fluid-milk equivalents Wisconsin alone accounts for over one-third of the national total.[93]

Another form of this model, designated the "modified ideal model," recognizes that Wisconsin cannot in fact produce one-third of the system's milk supply.   For each state a capacity (resource) constraint based on total available cropland is injected, placing a ceiling on possible milk production in that state.[94]   The figures from the solution of this second form of the model are shown in the last three columns of Table 12.   The only states in which the production constraints turn out to be binding are Wisconsin and New York.   Most of the production lost by Wisconsin is

[91] See Map 1 for regional boundaries selected.

[92] Note also that the shipments portrayed on Map 1 are in fluid-milk equivalents but that the product (or products) making up each shipment are designated by letters. The over-all pattern shows that the longest flows consist of butter, with cheese and evaporated milk traveling shorter distances and fluid milk the shortest of all.   These results reflect the fact that, per whole-milk equivalent, transport costs are lowest on butter, higher on cheese and evaporated milk, and highest on fluid milk; these are precisely the results that would be expected from comparative cost-location theory.   See M. M. Snodgrass and C. E. French [27], p. 20. See also Chapter 7 of this book; W. Isard [17]; and E. M. Hoover [15].

[93] This model also suggests an increase of milk production in Iowa by over 50 per cent from 1953 levels.   The authors, however, point out that had the important factor of opportunity cost been incorporated into the analysis, such a large increase would not have been suggested.   This limitation of the model points up the need for a more general framework than linear programming itself can furnish.

[94] The model at this point closely resembles the coal model with capacity restraints on production in each region.   The dairy model is further complicated, however, by the existence of processing costs and alternative final products.

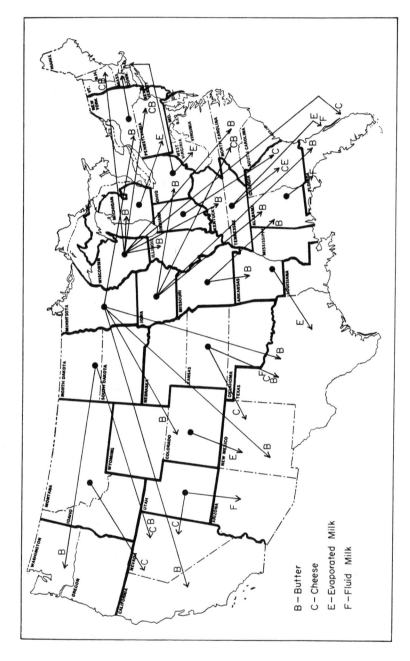

Map 1.   Optimal interregional flow pattern for fluid milk, butter, cheese, and evaporated milk to minimize processing and transportation costs, model portraying 1953 conditions.   Source: M. M. Snodgrass and C. E. French [27], p. 19.

B – Butter
C – Cheese
E – Evaporated Milk
F – Fluid Milk

TABLE 12. SUMMARY OF PRODUCTION NEEDS BY STATES AND PRODUCTS TO MEET REQUIREMENTS OF OPTIMAL SOLUTION—UNDER ASSUMED COST CONDITIONS (1953) FOR MODELS PORTRAYING IDEAL CONDITIONS

Model Portraying Ideal Conditions[a]			Modified Model Portraying Ideal Conditions[b]		
Producing State	Amount	Per Cent of Total	Producing State	Amount	Per Cent of Total
	MM lb.			MM lb.	
Fluid milk			Fluid milk		
N. Y.	15528	28.1	N. Y.	13899[c]	25.1
Iowa	8043	14.6	Iowa	8043	14.6
Calif.	4913	8.9	Calif.	4913	8.9
Ohio	4861	8.8	Ohio	4861	8.8
Ind.	3500	6.3	Ind.	3500	6.3
Ill.	3304	6.0	Ill.	3304	6.0
Ala.	3249	5.9	Ala.	3249	5.9
Mich.	2515	4.5	Mich.	2515	4.5
S. C.	2027	3.7	S. C.	2027	3.7
Miss.	1587	2.9	Pa.	1629	2.9
Wis.	1221	2.2	Miss.	1587	2.9
Minn.	1044	1.8	Wis.	1221[c]	2.2
Wash.	885	1.6	Minn.	1044	1.8
Idaho	759	1.4	Wash.	885	1.6
Utah	496	0.9	Idaho	759	1.4
Me.	303	0.5	Utah	496	0.9
Mont.	214	0.4	Maine	303	0.5
S. D.	214	0.4	Mont.	214	0.4
N. D.	197	0.4	S. D.	214	0.4
N. Y.	179	0.3	N. D.	197	0.4
Vt.	125	0.2	N. H.	179	0.3
Wyo.	106	0.2	Vt.	125	0.2
			Wyo.	106	0.2
Total	55270	100.0	Total	55270	100.0
Butter			Butter		
Wis.	1111	78.7	Wis.	883[c]	62.5
Minn.	301	21.3	Minn.	529	37.5
Total	1412	100.0	Total	1412	100.0
Cheese			Cheese		
Wis.	1060	78.8	Minn.	1293	96.2
Minn.	263	19.6	Wis.	30[c]	2.2
Iowa	22	1.6	Iowa	22	1.6
Total	1345	100.0	Total	1345	100.0
Evaporated milk			Evaporated milk		
Wis.	1839	72.0	Minn.	1623	63.5
Iowa	322	12.6	Iowa	661	25.9
Calif.	214	8.4	Calif.	214	8.4
Minn.	178	7.0	Wis.	56[c]	2.2
Total	2554	100.0	Total	2554	100.0

[a] Assumes no restrictions on producing areas.   [c] Restricted state.
[b] Assumes restrictions on producing areas.
Source: M. M. Snodgrass and C. E. French [27], p. 23.

shifted to Minnesota, and Pennsylvania increases production by the amount lost by New York.[95]

The authors indicate a number of ways in which the various models may be employed to study the effects of changes in data relating to one or more external or internal conditions. For example, in the processing–transport cost model, the authors posit a change in demand stemming from an expansion of exports of butter, cheese, and evaporated milk to four times the 1948–51 export level. Although the general pattern of product shipments is not greatly altered, the cost relations between the several products change significantly.[96]

In general any number of situations may be investigated through changing the parameters of the problem. We may estimate the impact of changing transport technology by appropriately altering transport rates, of changing consumer tastes by introducing new products and activities,[97] of innovation by modifying capacities and unit processing and production costs, of general population growth within the system and interregional shift by appropriately revising regional consumption estimates by product,[98] and of a number of other forces.[99]

L. SOME CONCLUDING, GENERAL REMARKS

A few concluding statements may now be made on the general inter-regional model developed in sections B through J of this chapter and the

[95] The restrictions on production also have the effect of raising the over-all production–processing–transport cost by 0.3 per cent.

[96] As the authors state, "... in face of such an export market expansion, the cheese and evaporated milk segments of the dairy industry should decentralize while the butter segment should remain the same" ([27], p. 23).

[97] For example, the authors add to the Modified Ideal Model a new product, fresh whole-milk concentrate. Under the processing and transport cost assumptions which are made, the study concludes that 44 per cent of the total fluid-milk market would be captured by the new concentrate if aggregate costs were minimized. See [27], p. 25.

[98] The authors estimate consumption by states in 1965 on the basis of a population forecast and procedures already cited. They rerun the minimum transport cost model with new production allotted to states in proportion to their 1953 production (each state's production was increased by 11.84 per cent). Except in absolute magnitude, the resulting optimal shipment pattern is changed only slightly by this allowance for population growth. Somewhat greater westward movements of milk toward the faster-growing regions of the country take place.

[99] For still another study of production and shipment patterns of a single commodity class, see A. R. Koch and M. M. Snodgrass [19]. In this study the authors follow generally the same procedures as in the dairy products study described in the text but modify the model in several respects to introduce certain aspects of imperfect competition in the tomato-processing industry. Among the aspects explicitly introduced in quantitative form are consumer preference, product differentiation, and price discrimination in spatially separated markets.

applications described in section K.   First, in selecting a set of levels at which to operate diverse activities, there can be many possible objectives. Maximizing the sum of regional incomes, as in the general interregional model, is only one of these.   Minimizing transport cost, and minimizing the *sum* of transport, processing, and production costs, as illustrated by the applications in the dairy and coal industries, are two more objectives. Maximizing firm profits, as involved in Henderson's agricultural study, is still a fourth.   Among many others which may be sought are maximizing growth rates of one or more regions,[100] maximizing per capita incomes, minimizing labor inputs,[101] maximizing new employment opportunities, and maximizing tax revenue from industrial development.   In each case, as is clear from study of the applications of the preceding section, it is necessary to restate the objective function, define the relevant constraints, identify the most meaningful classification of commodities and list of activities, etc.   However, the basic structural elements and procedures of an interregional model tend to remain the same.[102]

As already indicated, the general interregional model of this chapter has been developed in its purely formal aspects, primarily to serve as background against which specific, useful models might be developed.   An operational model would deviate from the general model in many respects. First, both the number and kind of production activities would vary from region to region.   (A coal-mining activity need not be listed for a region which completely lacks coal deposits.)   Further, the list of shipping activities would vary from region to region.   [A coal-shipping (export) activity need not be listed for a region which possesses no coal.   In fact, in Henderson's coal study three regions had no coal-shipping activities at

[100] See F. T. Moore [23].

[101] See L. N. Moses [24].

[102] For example, in the transport cost minimization problem (of which the minimum transport cost model of the dairy industry is a case in point), the objective function involves a summation of the transport inputs of all activities in all regions.   The constraints read "not less than" (that is ≥) some limiting constant.   Certain constraints require that deliveries of specific finished products in the several regions be at least as great as a set of prescribed constants.   Other constraints relate to the use of certain limited resources—such as the fixed capacity of a given rail line, the given endowment of arable land, the fixed industrial plant and equipment of a region, and the fixed capacity of a mine, etc.   The latter constraints, initially reading "not greater than," would be multiplied through by −1 in order to read "not less than."   The particular classification of commodities and set of activities selected would tend, for example, to give less attention to those commodities and activities directly and indirectly requiring little transport inputs, such as diamond processing, and emphasize those commodities and activities requiring directly and indirectly large amounts of transport inputs, such as steel and cement manufacture, etc.   Nonetheless, the basic framework of the model would not be altered.

all.] Moreover, the list of dummy activities would vary from region to region. [The dummy activity converting coal (as intermediate) into coal (as finished product) would not be listed in a tropical region where coal is not used for household purposes.] Additionally, the commodity classification would be different for different regions. (In a static model, iron ore would not appear in the commodity classification of a region which neither possesses deposits of iron ore nor has any steel capacity to consume iron ore.)

Aside from the differences among regions themselves, practical considerations of computation dictate major regional asymmetry. The general interregional linear programming model developed earlier is nonoperational as such. Many too many activities and commodities are envisaged. In any application, the model must be scaled down to a size which can yield numerical results. At the same time, the model must not be scaled down too much, so as to miss basic interrelations which can be incorporated. (For example, certain critics might consider Henderson's coal study too limited in scope and might contend that in the dairy study opportunity costs should and could have been explicitly included.)

In scaling down the general model, the investigator does not eliminate the same activities and commodities in each region, or even the same number of them. For certain regions which are off-center and produce specialized products, he may find it desirable to list a relatively small number of activities and commodities, whereas for a central diversified industrial region which tends to use, produce, and export many more commodities, he may tend to list a relatively large number of activities and commodities, *ceteris paribus.* Moreover, he tends to utilize other techniques and procedures to cut down an interregional linear program to a manageable size. He may use input-output techniques or comparative cost studies to derive certain magnitudes, or to eliminate certain activities as infeasible (as those which correspond to the cells of Table 9 containing the letter *N*); etc. Equally important, an investigator aiming at application must design the model in the light of existing data, possible new sources of data, and resources available for data collection and processing.[103] In this respect, interregional linear programming models confront many of the same problems as do interregional input-output models (see Chapter 8).

Finally, in this chapter no attempt is made to appraise the interregional linear programming technique as such. We have already made explicit some of its shortcomings—such as the assumption of linear production functions (as in the constant-unit-cost processing activities of the dairy study), price-inelastic demand (as in Henderson's coal study), and the

[103] For relevant discussion, see Harvard Economic Research Project [10].

need to specify beforehand finished-product prices or the equivalent (as in the general interregional model). In one sense it is too early to judge the promise of this technique. Several points are clear, however. The technique, at least for certain situations, can be of considerable use in establishing competitive norms, in pointing up inefficiencies in existing patterns of location, transport flows, and resource use, and more important in attacking the kind of resource scarcity problems in a region (or system of regions) sketched in the introduction to this chapter. Clear, too, is the fact that the technique is not a completely general one. It yields an efficiency system which is partial in a number of important respects. To the extent that it can be developed further— to embrace household behavior as approximated by consumption functions, agglomeration economies (including economies of scale, localization, and urbanization), etc.—that is, to the extent that it can more adequately depict a truly general interregional equilibrium system,[104] and at the same time remain operational, the more effective an optimizing technique it will be. Such progress of course must come via synthesis with the stronger elements of other techniques, such as input-output, industrial complex analysis, and gravity models, a topic to be explicitly discussed in Chapter 12.

REFERENCES

1. Allen, Roy G. D., *Mathematical Economics*, Macmillan, London, 1956.
2. Beckman, Martin, and Thomas Marschak, "An Activity Analysis Approach to Location Theory," *Kyklos*, Vol. 8 (1955).
3. Berman, Edward B., "A Model for Maximizing a Vector of Final Demand Deliveries under Regional Production and Transportation Network Constraints," *Papers and Proceedings of the Regional Science Association*, Vol. 5 (1959).
4. Charnes, Abraham, W. W. Cooper, and A. Henderson, *An Introduction to Linear Programming*, John Wiley, New York, 1953.
5. Chipman, John "Computational Problems in Linear Programming," *Review of Economics and Statistics*, Vol. 35 (Nov. 1953).
6. ———, "Linear Programming," *Review of Economics and Statistics*, Vol. 35 (May 1953).
7. Dorfman, Robert, Paul A. Samuelson, and Robert M. Solow, *Linear Programming and Economic Analysis*, McGraw-Hill, New York, 1958.
8. Garrison, William L., and Duane F. Marble, "The Analysis of Highway Networks: A Linear Programming Formulation," 1958, mimeographed.
9. Goldman, Thomas, A., "Efficient Transportation and Industrial Location," *Papers and Proceedings of the Regional Science Association*, Vol. 4 (1958).
10. Harvard Economic Research Project, *Report on Research for 1956–57*, Cambridge, Massachusetts, 1957.

[104] See W. Isard [16], W. Isard and D. Ostroff [18], L. Lefeber [21], and a forthcoming volume on regional theory.

11. Henderson, James M., "Efficiency and Pricing in the Coal Industry," *Review of Economics and Statistics*, Vol. 38 (Feb. 1956).
12. ———, *The Efficiency of the Coal Industry; An Application of Linear Programming*, Harvard University Press, Cambridge, Massachusetts, 1958.
13. ———, "A Short-Run Model for the Coal Industry," *Review of Economics and Statistics*, Vol. 37 (Nov. 1955).
14. ———, "The Utilization of Agricultural Land: A Regional Approach," *Papers and Proceedings of the Regional Science Association*, Vol. 3 (1957).
15. Hoover, Edgar M., *Location Theory and the Shoe and Leather Industries*, Harvard University Press, Cambridge, Massachusetts, 1937.
16. Isard, Walter, "General Interregional Equilibrium," *Papers and Proceedings of the Regional Science Association*, Vol. 3 (1957).
17. ———, *Location and Space-Economy*, John Wiley, New York, 1956.
18. ———, and David Ostroff, "The Existence of a Competitive Interregional Equilibrium," *Papers and Proceedings of the Regional Science Association*, Vol. 4 (1958).
19. Koch, A. R., and M. M. Snodgrass, "Linear Programming Applied to Location of and Product Flow Determination in the Tomato Processing Industry," *Papers and Proceedings of the Regional Science Association*, Vol. 5 (1959).
20. Koopmans, Tjalling C., ed., *Activity Analysis of Production and Allocation*, John Wiley, New York, 1950.
21. Lefeber, Louis, *Allocation in Space*, North-Holland Publishing Co., Amsterdam, 1959.
22. ———, "General Equilibrium Analysis of Production, Transportation, and the Choice of Industrial Location," *Papers and Proceedings of the Regional Science Association*, Vol. 4 (1958).
23. Moore, Frederick T., "Regional Economic Reaction Paths," *American Economic Review*, Vol. 45 (May 1955).
24. Moses, Leon N., "An Input-Output, Linear Programming Approach to Inter-regional Analysis," *Report, 1956–57*, Harvard Economic Research Project, Cambridge, Massachusetts, 1957.
25. Orr, Earle W., "A Synthesis of Theories of Location, of Transport Rates, and of Spatial Price Equilibrium," *Papers and Proceedings of the Regional Science Association*, Vol. 3 (1957).
26. Samuelson, Paul A., "Spatial Price Equilibrium and Linear Programming," *American Economic Review*, Vol. 42 (June 1952).
27. Snodgrass, Milton M., and Charles E. French, *Linear Programming Approach to Interregional Competition in Dairying*, Purdue University, Agricultural Experiment Station, Lafayette, Indiana, May 1958.
28. Stevens, Benjamin H., *Interregional Linear Programming*, doctoral dissertation, Massachusetts Institute of Technology, Cambridge, Massachusetts, February 1959.
29. ———, "An Interregional Linear Programming Model," *Journal of Regional Science*, Vol. 1 (Summer 1958).
30. Vietorisz, Thomas, *Regional Programming Models and the Case Study of a Refinery-Petrochemical-Synthetic Fiber Industrial Complex for Puerto Rico*, doctoral dissertation, Massachusetts Institute of Technology, Cambridge, Massachusetts, 1956.

Chapter 11

Gravity, Potential, and Spatial Interaction Models*

A. INTRODUCTION

A system of regions has an intricate structure. Only some of the fine strands which interconnect people, households, firms, social groups, governmental agencies, and a variety of other operating and decision-making units have been isolated and subjected to analysis. In time, with further developments of social science techniques, many more of these strands will be discovered and bared for study under the microscope of the regional scientist. Yet the balanced mind may still be uncomfortable, especially as it observes, perhaps at some distance in space, the geographic pattern in which human beings and their physical structures are massed in metropolises—metropolises which vary widely in size, configuration, and intensity of activity, such intensity tending to diminish in all directions from the core. True, the fine-stranded generalized interdependence schemes as crystallized in interregional input-output and linear programming are powerful analytical tools. Yet have they, even in a small way, been able to cope with spatial juxtaposition (or agglomeration) economies and diseconomies? Even the unsophisticated observer would judge that these economies and diseconomies must underly in a major way the important phenomena of human massing within any system of industrialized regions.

* This chapter was written with David F. Bramhall.

Viewed from another standpoint, is not society more than a matrix of intricately detailed connections among units, à la general equilibrium? Is not the structure of a system of regions more than the sum of the interactions of sets and patterns of units or sectors as conceived by interregional input-output and linear programming? Are there not over-all forces more akin to agglomerative factors which pervade society and confine the multitude of possible interactions among its innumerable units? This consideration motivates the analyst to explore fresh approaches, even though he attributes considerable significance to the more traditionally oriented approaches of input-output and linear programming. He may wish to pursue quite a different approach which has recently been developed. This is the approach associated with gravity, potential, and spatial interaction models.[1]

In the gravity, potential, and spatial interaction models—which for short we shall term gravity models whenever we speak generally of these models—the region is conceived as a mass. The mass is structured according to certain principles. These principles govern in an over-all fashion the range of behavior of the individual particles, both constraining and initiating their action. Interregional relations may be thought of as interactions among masses. Again general principles may be said to govern the frequency and intensity of such interactions; and by so doing they influence the behavior of individual units (particles) within each mass. As shall be observed later, this approach may be said to resemble an approach frequently used by physical scientists. For example, Boyle's classic studies of the effects of pressure and temperature on the volume of gases were essentially investigations into the behavior of masses of molecules; the movement of any individual molecule was not a matter of inquiry.

B. THE PROBABILITY POINT OF VIEW

To develop the concept of gravity models it is useful to adopt a rather simple probability point of view.[2] Suppose there is a metropolitan region with population P. Let the region be divided into many subareas. Let

[1] Development and applications of gravity models may be found in, among others, the references cited at the end of this chapter, especially G. A. P. Carrothers [12, 13]. In order to facilitate the understanding of the mathematical terms used in this chapter, we have followed traditional notation on gravity models and have refrained from using a strange (and to some extent more complicated) notation which would be consistent with that of the preceding chapters and with any mathematical formulation of the fused frameworks of the chapter to follow.

[2] In developing this point of view we draw heavily on J. D. Carroll and H. W. Bevis [11]. Also see S. C. Dodd [16] and F. C. Iklé [24].

there also be known the total number of internal trips taken by the inhabitants of this metropolitan region. We represent this number by the constant T. Further, let there be no significant differences among subareas in the tastes, incomes, age distributions, occupational structures, etc., of their populations.

Now, suppose we wish to determine the number of trips which originate in, let us say, subarea i, and terminate in, let us say, subarea j. Assume, for the moment, that no costs and no time are involved in undertaking a trip from one area to another, that is, that the friction of distance is zero. For this hypothetical situation we may expect that for a representative individual in subarea i the per cent of his journeys terminating in subarea j will, *ceteris paribus*, be equal to the ratio P_j/P, which is the population of subarea j divided by the total population of the metropolitan region. That is, if the total population of the metropolitan region is 1,000,000 and that of subarea j 100,000, we may expect the individual to make 10 per cent of the trips to j. Additionally, since a representative individual in subarea i is by our homogeneity assumptions identical with a representative individual in any other subarea, and since his transport time cost is zero, we may estimate the number of trips he undertakes as the average number of trips per capita for the entire metropolitan region. This average is equal to T/P. Designating this average by the letter k, we find that the absolute number of trips which a representative individual in subarea i makes to subarea j is $k(P_j/P)$. That is, if 10 per cent of the total population resides in subarea j, the individual in subarea i will tend to make 10 per cent of his trips to subarea j; if the average number of trips per individual is 20, the individual will make two trips to j.

This reasoning applies to one representative individual in i. But there are P_i individuals residing in subarea i. Therefore, the number of trips to subarea j which these P_i individuals will make will be P_i times the number of trips to subarea j which the representative individual in i makes. That is,

$$(1) \qquad T_{ij} = k \frac{P_i P_j}{P}$$

where T_{ij} designates the total number of trips taken by individuals in i (i.e., originating in i) which terminate in j. In like manner we can estimate the expected total number of trips for every possible combination of originating subarea and terminating subarea. Thus we obtain for the metropolitan region a set of expected or hypothetical trip volumes (total number of trips) between subareas.

Our next step is to determine the possible effect of the actual distance separating a pair of subareas on the number of trips occurring between them.   First, for a typical metropolitan region we obtain actual data on the number of trips between every pair of its subareas.   We let I_{ij} represent the *actual* trip volume between any originating subarea i and any terminating subarea j.   We divide this actual number by the expected or hypothetical trip volume T_{ij} to derive the ratio of actual to expected trip volume, that is, I_{ij}/T_{ij}.   We also note the distance d_{ij} which separates i

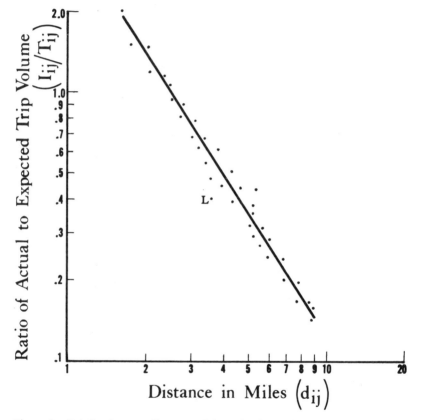

Figure 1.   Relation between distance and the ratio of actual to expected person trips (hypothetical data).

and j.   Finally, we plot on a graph with a logarithmic scale along each axis both the ratio I_{ij}/T_{ij} and distance d_{ij} for this particular pair of subareas.   For example, in Figure 1 where the vertical axis measures the ratio of actual to expected trips and where the horizontal axis measures distance, we may note point L.   Point L refers to a pair of subareas approximately 3.6 miles apart for which the ratio of actual to expected trips is approximately 0.4.

In similar manner, for every other combination of originating subarea and terminating subarea we plot the set of data on the ratio of actual to expected trips and intervening distance.   Suppose our data are as indicated in Figure 1.   They suggest a straight-line relationship between the log of the ratio of actual to expected trip volume on the one hand and distance on the other hand, a simple relationship which is not undesirable for analytical purposes.   A straight line may be fitted to the plotted data by least squares or by other methods.   Since our variables are the log of the ratio of actual to expected trip volume (the dependent variable) and the log of distance (the independent variable), the equation of the line is

$$(2) \qquad \log \frac{I_{ij}}{T_{ij}} = a - b \log d_{ij}$$

In this equation a is a constant which is the intercept of the straight line with the Y axis, and b is a constant defined by the slope of the line.[3] Removing logs from equation 2 and letting c equal the antilog of a, we have

$$\frac{I_{ij}}{T_{ij}} = \frac{c}{d_{ij}^b}$$

or

$$(3) \qquad I_{ij} = \frac{cT_{ij}}{d_{ij}^b}$$

Substituting in equation 3 the value of T_{ij} as given in equation 1, and letting the constant $G = ck/P$, where c, k, and P are constants as defined earlier, we obtain

$$(4) \qquad I_{ij} = G \frac{P_i P_j}{d_{ij}^b}$$

This simple relationship may then be taken to describe roughly the actual pattern of trip volumes within the metropolitan region, *ceteris paribus*. That is, it depicts the interaction of people within the metropolitan region as a function of the populations of subareas and the distance variable when this interaction is reflected in trips.

Suppose we study the relationship of actual to expected magnitude on the one hand, and distance on the other hand, for a number of other phenomena reflecting the interactions of people within the metropolitan mass and among metropolitan masses.   We might examine telephone calls, telegraph messages, railway express shipments, money flows, migration, etc.   Suppose that for all these phenomena we find, as in Figure 1,

[3] In Figure 1, $a = 3.9$ and $b = 1.5$.

a close linear association between the log of the ratio of actual to expected volume and the log of distance.[4] We might then conclude that the relationship

$$I_{ij} = G \frac{P_i P_j}{d_{ij}^b}$$

reflects a basic principle underlying the structure of metropolitan areas and systems of metropolitan areas. This relationship derived from a probability point of view is essentially the gravity model, although the gravity model did not evolve in this manner.[5]

Additionally, it is to be noted that equation 4 can be converted into another useful form. Suppose we are interested in the interaction between a single subarea i and *all* other subareas. We would therefore derive the interaction of i with the first subarea (i.e., I_{i1}) *plus* the interaction of i with the second subarea (i.e., I_{i2}) *plus* the interaction of i with the third subarea (i.e., I_{i3}), *plus* $\cdots$, and finally *plus* the interaction of i with the last of nth subarea (i.e., I_{in}). From equation 4 we find values for each of the interactions, $I_{i1}, I_{i2}, I_{i3}, \cdots, I_{in}$. By addition we obtain

$$I_{i1} + I_{i2} + I_{i3} + \cdots + I_{in} = G \frac{P_i P_1}{d_{i1}^b} + G \frac{P_i P_2}{d_{i2}^b} + G \frac{P_i P_3}{d_{i3}^b} + \cdots + G \frac{P_i P_n}{d_{in}^b}$$

or

$$\sum_{j=1}^{n} I_{ij} = G \sum_{j=1}^{n} \frac{P_i P_j}{d_{ij}^b}$$

Since P_i may be factored from the right-hand side of the equation, we derive, after dividing both sides by P_i,

(5)
$$\frac{\sum_{j=1}^{n} I_{ij}}{P_i} = G \sum_{j=1}^{n} \frac{P_j}{d_{ij}^b}$$

Note that the numerator of the left-hand side of equation 5 is the total interaction of i with all areas including itself,[6] which when divided by the

---

[4] Studies depicting such close association will be cited at later points in this chapter.

[5] Implicit in this model, as in all others to follow, is an appropriate unit of time, say a week, month, or year. Doubling the unit time, *ceteris paribus*, doubles the magnitude of expected interaction. If the reader so cares, he may explicitly introduce a time variable of this sort into the model. Cf. S. C. Dodd [16] for extensive treatment of this factor.

[6] For the moment we ignore a discussion of the interaction of subarea i with itself. This point is taken up later in connection with Stewart's concept of demographic potential.

population of i, namely P_i, yields interaction with all areas *on a per capita basis* or more strictly on a *per unit of mass basis*. Interaction on such a basis has been designated *potential at i*, for which we employ the symbol

$_iV$. By definition, then, $_iV = \dfrac{\displaystyle\sum_{j=1}^{n} I_{ij}}{P_i}$ and, from equation 5 we have

(6) $$_iV = G \sum_{j=1}^{n} \frac{P_j}{d_{ij}^b} \text{ (footnote 7)}$$

Equation 6 is the basis of potential models and as developed is a variation of equation 4, the basic gravity model.

C. THE STEWART-ZIPF HYPOTHESES

Further insight into the significance of the gravity model can be acquired by tracing its historical development. Although the gravity model may have been implied in the writings of Carey,[8] Ravenstein,[9] Young,[10] and Reilly,[11] the first major impetus in its development stems from the work of Stewart[12] and Zipf,[13] who simultaneously worked on this model from independent angles. Stewart formulated his hypothesis in terms of his concept of social physics. As already suggested, in the natural sciences there are laws such as those governing the density, pressure, and temperature of gases that were discovered only because matter was investigated as a mass. For example, if Boyle's investigation had dealt with the rapid and erratic movement of individual molecules as they bounced against each other, it is not likely that his laws would have evolved.

[7] It is to be noted that this equation can be derived directly from a simple probability approach as was equation 4.

[8] As early as the middle of the nineteenth century H. C. Carey [9] observed the presence of gravitational force in social phenomena, stating that the force was in direct ratio to mass and inverse to distance.

[9] See Chapter 3, pp. 67–69.

[10] See Chapter 3, p. 69.

[11] W. J. Reilly [35] proposed a law of retail gravitation which states that a city attracts retail trade from a customer in its hinterland in proportion to its size (population) and in inverse proportion to the square of the distance separating the customer from the center of the city. The boundary separating the market areas of two cities i and j competing for customers in a hinterland is thus defined as the locus of points for which $P_i/d_{xi}^2 = P_j/d_{xj}^2$ where d_{xi} and d_{xj} are the distances of cities i and j respectively from any point x on the boundary.

[12] See [36–40].

[13] See [50, 51].

Stewart reasoned that similar relations might underlie the interaction of social units, such as people, which relations could be discovered only by investigating large aggregates of such units. He presented three primary concepts based on Newtonian physics. Following the formula for *gravitational force*, Stewart defines *demographic force* as a constant times the product of two masses divided by the square of the distance separating the masses. Where the population of cities i and j, designated by P_i and P_j respectively, are taken as the relevant masses, demographic force F is

$$F = G \frac{P_i P_j}{d_{ij}^2}$$

where G is a constant corresponding to the gravitational constant.

Stewart develops a second concept corresponding to *gravitational energy*, namely *demographic energy*, where demographic energy E is defined as

$$E = G \frac{P_i P_j}{d_{ij}}$$

It is to be noted that the formula for demographic energy differs from that for demographic force only with respect to the exponent of the distance variable, d_{ij}. More important, both these concepts are derivable from equation 4. When the value of b in equation 4 is 2, the right-hand side of the equation defines gravitational force (i.e., $I_{ij} = F$). When the value of b in equation 4 is unity, the right-hand side of the equation defines gravitational energy (i.e., $I_{ij} = E$).

Stewart's third concept is that of *demographic potential* which corresponds to *gravitational potential*. The demographic potential produced at a point i by a mass at j, which may be designated $_iV_j$, is defined as a constant times the mass at j, say P_j, divided by the intervening distance, that is,

$$_iV_j = G \frac{P_j}{d_{ij}}$$

Thus, the potential created upon the center of Philadelphia by the New York City mass might be defined as a constant times the population of New York City divided by 90 miles. When, as in reality, more than one mass exists, the *total* potential at a point i, designated $_iV$, may be taken as the sum of the separate potentials produced by each mass. Thus, if the masses are numbered from 1 to n,

$$(7) \quad _iV = G \frac{P_1}{d_{i1}} + G \frac{P_2}{d_{i2}} + \cdots + G \frac{P_n}{d_{in}} = G \sum_{j=1}^{n} \frac{P_j}{d_{ij}} \quad \text{(footnote 14)}$$

14 It is to be noted that any mass at i creates potential upon itself. If the distance of this mass from i, that is, d_{ii}, is taken as zero, the value of $_iV$ becomes infinity. Hence,

Since it is possible to compute total potential for every point, or practically speaking for every relevant subarea of a nation or interregional system, we may construct a map of potentials. This Stewart has done with the use of equipotential contour lines. Map 1, which depicts "weighted" potentials of population for the United States in 1940[15] is an illustration. In the construction of this map the United States was divided into subareas, the population of each subarea being assumed to be concentrated at a control point. Any one contour line passes through those areas and control points having the same potential. For example, the equipotential contour line 30 (300,000 persons per mile) describes a wide arc which passes through central New England, upper New York, central Michigan, southern Wisconsin, etc., and swings around through Tennessee and North Carolina, all of which areas have approximately the same potential.

In general, the several equipotential maps constructed by Stewart and his associates depict New York City as the peak of demographic potential. East of the Sierras, every general contour line closes around New York City; all other cities are local peaks on the general downhill slope from New York in all directions. (As a consequence, a rural area in New Jersey comes to have a higher potential than the center of Omaha, Nebraska.) West of the Sierras, two separate humps appear. One centers around Seattle, Washington, the other around San Francisco and Los Angeles, the two major peaks of California.

The interpretation to be given to the concept of demographic potential is not yet entirely clear. Stewart speaks of population potential of a point as a measure of the proximity of people to that point, as a measure of aggregate accessibility, and more simply as a measure of influence of people at a distance. To point up the significance of this concept and the related concepts of demographic force and energy, Stewart and his associates have conducted a number of empirical studies. He reports high

as Stewart has clearly pointed out, it becomes necessary to conceive of any mass at i or concentrated around i as being located at some finite distance from i. For procedures used to compute this distance, see J. Q. Stewart [36], p. 48; [37], p. 477; J. Q. Stewart and W. Warntz [40], p. 121; G. A. P. Carrothers [13, 14]. An alternative formulation which avoids an infinite value for $_iV$ is to add a constant to d_{ij} in the denominator. See T. Anderson [3], p. 178, for a case where $1 + d_{ij}$ is a relevant denominator. Cf. F. C. Iklé [24], pp. 133–135.

Rigorously (but not practically) speaking, $_iV = G \int_s \dfrac{P}{d_i} ds$ where P is the surface density of the mass over the infinitesimal element of area ds and where d_i is the distance of that element from i.

[15] The concept of "weighted" potentials will be discussed later. For the moment the reader may ignore the term "weighted."

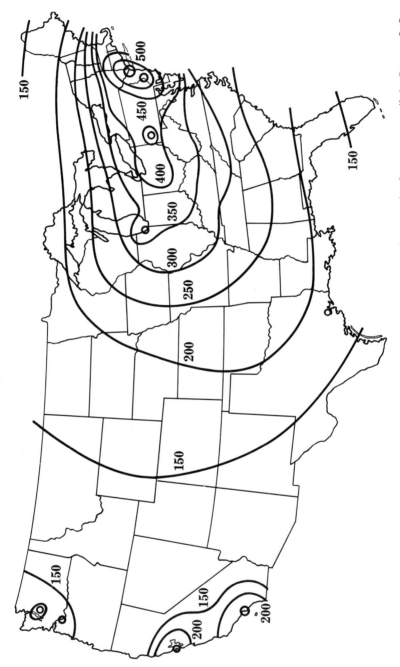

Map 1. Weighted population potentials, United States, 1940. (Potentials are in tens of thousands of persons per mile.) Source: J. Q. Stewart [38], p. 22, as modified in W. Isard [25], p. 67.

correlation within the United States of the spatial variation of population potential with spatial variation in a wide variety of sociological pheno-

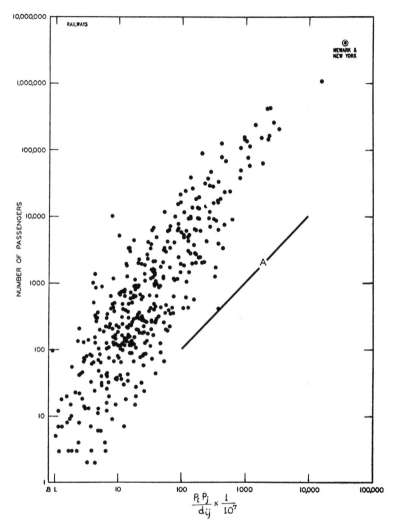

Figure 2. The number of passengers traveling by railways between 29 arbitrary cities during 1 month in each quarter of 1933. Source: G. K. Zipf, *Human Behavior and the Principle of Least Effort*, Addison-Wesley, Reading, Massachusetts, 1949, p. 396.

mena. Among others these phenomena include: rural population density, rural nonfarm population density, rural nonfarm rents, farmland values, miles of railroad track per square mile, miles of rural free delivery routes per square mile, density of rural wage earners in manufacturing, and rural death rates.[16]

In the historical development of the gravity model, the works of Zipf have also been influential. Zipf speaks variously of the P/D and P_1P_2/D factors which, using our symbols, are the P_j/d_{ij} and P_iP_j/d_{ij} factors, respectively.[17] These factors closely resemble Stewart's concepts of potential and demographic energy and have been interpreted as identical with these concepts on a number of occasions. However, in empirical analysis, Zipf's use of his relationships or factors differs from Stewart's use of his (Stewart's) demographic concepts. Essentially, Zipf examines for pairs of cities interaction phenomena and the P_iP_j/d_{ij} factor where the entire factor is raised to some power. For example, for each pair of a set of cities for which materials are available he plots on a double-log graph the number of railway passengers moving between them and their P_iP_j/d_{ij} factor. When the data for all the possible pairs of cities are plotted, as in Figure 2, Zipf finds a straight-line relationship.

Zipf also finds straight-line relationships between the P_iP_j/d_{ij} factor and other interaction phenomena between pairs of cities, such as bus passenger trips, airline passenger trips, telephone calls, and tonnage of railway express shipments. However, in each case the slope of the straight line refers to the exponent of the entire P_iP_j/d_{ij} factor and not to the exponent of d_{ij} as is true in equation 4 which embraces Stewart's concepts. Thus Zipf's findings do not directly test the validity of Stewart's concepts.[18]

D. Basic Issues of Gravity Models

Having presented both the probability point of view and some historical background on the gravity model, we must now discuss some general issues which arise particularly in the application of the model. One issue concerns the measurements of the two variables, mass and distance.[19]

[16] For full details, see J. Q. Stewart [36]. In a recent article J. Q. Stewart and W. Warntz [40] compare cities (in the United States and Great Britain) equal in population but located in areas of varying population potential. They find that cities in areas of low potential tend to have larger areas, lower taxes, and a greater excess of births over deaths than cities of equal population in areas of high potential.

[17] That is, Zipf's definition of P is the same as our definition of P_j, his of P_1 the same as ours of P_i, his of P_2 the same as ours of P_j, and his of D the same as ours of d_{ij}. See G. K. Zipf [50, 51].

[18] In the nontypical case, when the slope of Zipf's straight line is unity, Zipf's use of his so-called P_1P_2/D relationship becomes identical with Stewart's use of demographic energy.

[19] We do not discuss in this section problems connected with the use of existing data and the choice of an appropriate set of subareas or regions and control points. Excellent discussion of this latter problem is contained in G. A. P. Carrothers [14]. Carrothers investigates the degree to which a potential calculation actually represents

In empirical studies mass has been measured in a number of ways. This discussion has used population as a measure of mass. But if inter-metropolitan migration is to be studied, it is apparent that employment or income of regions or subareas tends to be a more significant index of mass than population.[20] Or, when the marketing problem for manufactured products is being examined, total dollar volume of retail and wholesale sales tends to be a more significant measure,[21] etc. Clearly, the measure of mass to be employed depends on the problem to be studied, available data, and related considerations. The array of possible measures of mass includes such magnitudes as total investment in facilities, number of families, car registrations, hospital beds, investment in tractors and farm equipment,[22] commodity output,[23] value added in manufacture, Gross

what it purports to represent when different sizes and shapes of regions are delineated and when different spatial distributions of relevant masses are hypothesized. He concludes that the best set of general-purpose regions tends to satisfy as closely as possible the following criteria: (1) absence of concentrations of mass on the peripheries of the region; (2) existence within each region of a definite nodal center of gravity of mass; (3) coincidence of the center of gravity of mass with the center of gravity of the physical area; (4) regular geometric shapes for the physical area of each region; (5) approximately equal areas of adjacent regions when density of mass is relatively uniform; (6) area of region varying in inverse proportion with density of mass. Since a gravity model implies for each region an intraregional distribution of *derived* interaction phenomena or mass proportional to the intraregional distribution of the generating mass (independent variable), these criteria are generally applicable. However, difficulty arises when an initial intraregional distribution of the independent mass, say income, does not conform to the initial intraregional distribution of an existing mass, say population, whose growth or change in interaction is to be derived. Then the initial intraregional distribution of the existing mass does influence the intraregional pattern of its growth or change in interaction; and it then becomes desirable to delineate regions by modifying these criteria to apply to this existing mass as well as the independent mass.

[20] Thus W. Isard and G. Freutel [28], pp. 434–439, use income as a measure of mass and develop the concept of income potential to parallel Stewart's concept of population potential. G. A. P. Carrothers [14] uses the income potential concept in his population and migration studies. W. Warntz [48] constructs an income potential map for the United States, 1950. J. Q. Stewart and W. Warntz [39] report for relevant sets of subareas high correlation between income potential and such magnitudes as road density, telephone wire density, average farm size, the size of wholesale dry goods market areas, number of vehicles registered per mile of highway and per dollar of income, number of auto fatalities per registered vehicle, ratio of individual taxes to all income, ratio of number of patents to dollars of income, and ratio of business failures to all businesses.

[21] Both C. D. Harris [22] and E. S. Dunn [17] have used retail sales as the relevant measure of mass in their studies.

[22] C. D. Harris [22] uses the number of tractors as a measure of mass in analyzing the location of agricultural equipment producers.

[23] In his study of the spatial variation in the prices of wheat, potatoes, and other agricultural commodities, W. Warntz [48] computes a commodity supply space potential with annual commodity output as mass.

Regional Product, economic opportunities, newspaper circulation, church attendance, and school enrollment.

Similarly, distance has been and can be measured in a number of ways. This discussion has measured distance physically along a straight line in terms of miles. However, if a metropolitan traffic study is being conducted, distance in terms of travel time is at least equally important.[24] Or, if industrial location is being analyzed, transport cost (or economic) distance is much more significant than physical distance.[25] Thus, as with the measurement of mass, the measurement of distance (many of whose forms are related to the state of transport technology) depends on the problem being attacked, the available data, and related considerations. Among other possible measures of distance are mileage along a specific transport route (waterway, highway, airline, railway, or pipeline), fuel (energy) consumption in transportation,[26] number of gear shifts or stops, and number of intervening opportunities and other forms of "social distance."[27]

Another basic issue relates to weights to be applied to the masses. In the specific models of equations 4 and 6, the weights of the masses are the same and are equal to unity. Should they be the same? According to Stewart[28] and Dodd,[29] different weights are valid. Just as the weights of molecules of different elements are unequal, so should the weights of different kinds of people be different. The average Chinese peasant does

[24] For example A. M. Voorhees [45] uses auto-driving time in studying the impact of distance on interaction.

[25] In studying the localization of manufacturing in general, Harris uses a generalized measure of transport cost rather than physical distance in computing his *market potential*. He estimates transport cost by different media according to the following table:

Method of Transportation	Terminal Cost Per Ton	Rate Per Ton-Mile	Delivery Charge at Destination
Truck	$6.00	4.0¢	
Railroad	$5.00	2.5¢	$6.00 (truck delivery)
Ship	$12.00 (including $6.00 truck delivery to port)	0.25¢	$6.00 (truck delivery)

Thus a 400-mile shipment by rail of 1 ton of products costs $5.00 (terminal cost) plus $10.00 (line-haul costs over 400 miles) plus $6.00 (truck delivery charge at destination), or altogether $21.00. According to the rates of this table, for all distances up to 333 miles it is cheapest to ship by truck. Beyond this distance up to mileages in excess of 3000 it is cheapest to ship by rail.

[26] See T. Anderson [3], pp. 177–178.

[27] Forms of "social distance" will be discussed later. See also E. H. Jurkat [30] and W. L. Garrison [19], pp. T4–6, which differentiates distance by trip purpose and road type.

[28] See [38], pp. 29–30.

[29] See [16].

not make the same contribution to "sociological" intensity as the United States urban dweller.[30]   But to justify the use of weights in a particular study does not require a physical analogy.   Suppose we are studying the volume of first-class or luxury travel.   It is reasonable to expect that, *ceteris paribus*, an area with high per capita income will generate a larger volume of such travel than an area of equal population but lower per capita income.   One way to correct for such a factor is to multiply the population of each subarea by its average per capita income.   Thus equation 4 becomes

$$(8) \qquad I_{ij} = G \frac{(w_i P_i)(w_j P_j)}{d_{ij}^b}$$

and equation 6 becomes

$$(9) \qquad V = G \sum \frac{w_j P_j}{d_{ij}^b}$$

where w_i and w_j represent per capita incomes in region i and j, respectively. But since Y_j the total income of region j equals $w_j P_j$, equation 9 becomes

$$(10) \qquad {}_iV = G \sum \frac{Y_j}{d_{ij}^b}$$

which is the equation for income potential.[31]

In a study of first-class travel it might be desirable to weight population by still another factor, say education level, or even by a third factor, say family size.   In such event w_i and w_j would represent composite weights, that is, averages reflecting the relative importance of the several weighting factors.[32]   Among other possible weights which might be employed are

[30] *Ibid*, pp. 247–248.   Dodd's discussion of this issue from a sociological standpoint is particularly enlightening.

[31] See W. Isard and G. Freutel [28], p. 436.

[32] When there are several weighting factors, it is convenient to use double subscripts. The term w_{1i} then represents the subarea i's weight according to the first factor, and the term w_{gi} represents subarea i's weight according to the gth factor.   Since it is necessary to derive the composite weight for subarea i, namely w_i, it is also necessary to assign a weight to each of the weighting factors.   Thus w_i is the sum of weighted weights, that is,

$$w_i = \sum_{g=1}^{g} c_g w_{gi}$$

where c_g is the weight of the gth weighting factor.   It also follows that

$$w_j = \sum_{g=1}^{g} c_g w_{gj}$$

occupational structure; sex or age composition; racial or ethnic composition; per cent of population receiving income above a certain level, attending church, or owning homes; urban-rural ratio; ratio of mail order to total retail sales; ratio of central business district sales to total metropolitan sales; ratio of capital investment to annual output; average capital investment per employee; etc.[33]   Actually, when we weight masses measured in certain ways, we may derive other measures of the same masses.   As already noted, when we weight population in subareas by per capita income, we derive total income as the measure of mass in subareas and thereby convert the population potential into an income potential measure.   Or, when we weight population in subareas by average number of years of school attendance, we derive total number of man-years of education as the measure of mass for each subarea.

More difficult than the selection of weights or of measures of mass and distance is the choice of exponents for variables in both the potential and demographic energy concepts. From a theoretical standpoint, Stewart maintains that the exponent of the distance variable d_{ij} should be either 1 or 2.[34]   However, numerous empirical studies do not support this contention (although the validity of these studies as tests of Stewart's hypothesis is yet to be established).   For example, in one study Carroll finds that the appropriate exponent tends to hover around the value of 3.[35]   Iklé finds considerable variation in the appropriate exponent of d_{ij}; his values range from 0.689 to 2.6.[36]   Carroll and Bevis find that for

[33] In many of his studies Stewart uses weights of 0.8 for population of the Deep South, 2.0 for population of the Far West, and 1.0 for all other population.   These weights were suggested by some of his initial empirical studies.

In studying interaction phenomena as reflected in number of telephone calls and airline trips between pairs of cities, C. Hammer and F. C. Iklé [21] use the gravity model of equation 8.   They determine weights for different cities which yield the best least-squares fit to actual interaction data.   The city weights range from 0.34 for Flint, Michigan, to 2.94 for Los Angeles in the analysis of telephone calls, October 1948. The weights range from 0.14 for Baltimore to 7.61 for Miami in the study of airline trips, March 1950.   Hammer and Iklé regard the derived city weights as indicating different "propensities to interact."   Using rank correlation, they find the weights to be positively associated with (1) the proportion of population who are managers, proprietors, and officials, (2) the average number of transient hotel rooms per capita, and (3) average per capita retail sales.   However, the city weights are negatively correlated with median income of families and unrelated persons.

Despite these correlations, the validity of any specific weight derived for a given city is to be questioned, especially for projection purposes.   This point will be discussed later.

[34] The exponent of 2 in Stewart's demographic force concept is consistent with W. J. Reilly's [35] early study on the law of retail gravitation.

[35] See [10].

[36] See [24].

intrametropolitan travel in the Detroit region the appropriate exponent for total person trips is 1.63.[37]   The exponent, however, varies for different types of trips.   Finally, Hammer and Iklé in their studies of telephone calls and airline trips find confidence limits of 1.3–1.8 for the exponent of distance and finally state that their data "fail to justify either the inverse linear or the inverse square 'law,' which previous investigators had suggested for the distance function."[38]

Although there is considerable evidence suggesting that the exponent of the d_{ij} variable need not be 1 or 2, depending on the concept employed, there has not been a definitive study of this question; and Stewart and Warntz cogently point to the inconclusiveness of existing studies and question the scientific basis of such studies.[39]   For the purposes of the ensuing discussion, the reader may consider b, which is the exponent of d_{ij} in equations 4, 6, 8, and 9 as either unity[40] or a variable taking positive values, as a number of investigators have proposed.[41]

A still more difficult issue concerns the exponent to be applied to the measures of mass.   (Since this issue and the remaining ones to be discussed in this section are rather nebulous, the reader interested in application may wish to proceed directly to the next section.)   In the basic equations 8 and 9 these exponents are unity.   But thoughtful researchers, such as Anderson and Carrothers, have suggested that the power to which mass is raised might be other than unity.   Carrothers notes that such factors as agglomeration (deglomeration) economies imply that the exponent to be applied to any mass is a function of the mass.[42]   In such a

[37] See [11].

[38] See [21], p. 314.   Also, W. Isard and M. J. Peck in studying tonnage of Class I railway shipments find such tonnage inversely related to distance raised to approximately the 1.7 power (see [25], pp. 71–73).   On the other hand, W. L. Garrison [18] finds little significant relation between trip volumes and distance in analyzing trips of rural residents in three counties of Washington State.

[39] See [40].

[40] Then the right-hand sides of equations 4 and 8 will correspond to Stewart's concept of demographic energy, and those of equations 6 and 9 to his concept of demographic potential.

[41] At this point it is instructive to consider the situation where transport cost is used as the measure of distance, and where graduated rate structures (rate increasing less than proportionally with distance) exist, as is true of most modern transport media in industrialized regions.   In this situation, if the exponent of "transport cost" distance is taken to be unity (as in C. D. Harris [22]), the exponent of equivalent physical distance (which can always be determined) not only will not be unity but will also become a parameter whose value changes with change in "transport cost" distance.

[42] Other factors such as degree of social integration and political stability may also be interpreted as justifying different exponents for the several masses involved.

situation the exponents of unequal masses will differ. Thus, equations 8 and 9 will become, respectively,

(11)
$$I_{ij} = G \frac{w_i(P_i)^\alpha \cdot w_j(P_j)^\beta}{d_{ij}^b}$$

(12)
$$_iV = G \sum_{j=1}^{n} \frac{w_j(P_j)^\beta}{d_{ij}^b} \quad \text{(footnote 43)}$$

As mentioned earlier, Zipf's empirical findings when graphed on double-log scale suggest straight-line relationships of the order of equation 11 where $\alpha = \beta = b$, but not necessarily unity, and where $w_i = w_j = 1$. Mylroie's study on intercity travel desire also casts light on the question of the appropriate exponent for mass.[44] Among several cases tested she finds best correlations in equation 11 when $\alpha = \beta = \frac{1}{2}$, $b = 2$, and $w_i = w_j = 1$, that is, where

$$I_{ij} = G \sqrt{\frac{P_i P_j}{d_{ij}^2}}$$

Until further systematic research is pursued on this question, it must remain unresolved.[45] The general equations 11 and 12 are still relevant, however. They embrace the simple models for which $\alpha = \beta = b = 1$ as well as the more complex models.

A final nebulous issue concerns the general form of the function to describe interaction, in particular the attenuating influence of distance. This issue can be neatly posed by reference to certain empirical materials collected by Carroll and Bevis in their pioneering studies. These materials relate to the effect of distance on the ratio of actual to expected total person trips within the Detroit metropolitan region. Fig. 3a is a reproduction of a figure which they have presented, except that the straight regression line through the plotted points has been omitted. (Figure 3a is constructed in the same manner as Figure 1.) For their purposes, it was appropriate to seek a straight-line relationship on double-log scale. Yet, as we observe the set of plotted points, we may be inclined to fit the points with a quadratic (as depicted in Figure 3c) rather than a linear function (as depicted in Figure 3b). In so doing, we will be abandoning the notion of a gravity model, at least as conceived by Stewart and many others.

[43] Here $_iV$ would be defined as $\sum_{j=1}^{n} I_{ij} \Big/ w_i(P_i)^\alpha$.

[44] See [32]. Data and procedures are extensively presented.

[45] For a set of statistical procedures suitable for general use, see G. A. P. Carrothers [14].

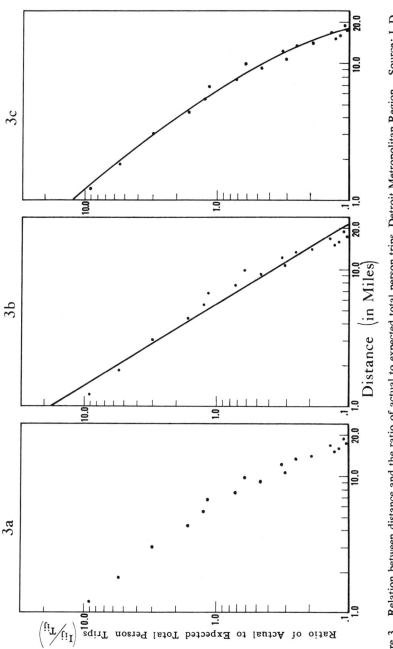

Figure 3. Relation between distance and the ratio of actual to expected total person trips, Detroit Metropolitan Region. Source: J. D. Carroll and H. W. Bevis [11], p. 193, except for curve of 3c.

Similarly, in many other empirical studies on the effect of distance, it is questionable whether the simple straight-line relationship on double-log scale as given by equations 11 and 12 is applicable. Although such studies may demonstrate that interaction falls off with increase of intervening distance, many types of function in addition to the ones described by equations 11 and 12 are consistent with this effect. For example, the attenuating influence of distance (or, as sometimes stated, the friction of distance) is embodied in the simple equations: $I_{ij} = k - bd_{ij}$; or $I_{ij} = aP_iP_j - bd_{ij}$ (footnote 46). Similarly, the attenuating influence of distance is implicit in more complex types of functions. One of these is similar to equation 11, except that the exponent of d_{ij} (namely b) is itself a function of the size of one or both masses[47]; the appropriateness of this type of function has been suggested by certain statistical tests performed by Anderson.[48] Another of these more complex functions is similar to equation 11, except that the exponents of P_i and P_j (namely α and β) are also variables, being different functions of P_i and P_j rather than constants; this type of function has been suggested by Carrothers.[49]

In short, the question of appropriate types of function must be at least theoretically faced. Although various sets of data which have been collected seem to be adequately described by equations such as 11 and 12, it is still an open question whether or not other types of functions (desirably simple) might not describe such data more satisfactorily, explain their underlying pattern to a greater degree, or both.

E. Some Problems in the Use of Simple Gravity Models

Although we have raised some basic questions regarding weights, exponents, and functional forms, we may examine some of the problems associated with the use of the gravity model in the relatively simple forms in which it has been formulated. It is to be borne in mind that gravity models, as input-output and other models, can be used for both descriptive and projective purposes. Hence, the type of problems we encounter is often influenced by the purpose to which the model is put.

One problem common to both types of use concerns the extent to which any whole, integral mass, population, or meaningful aggregate is cut into parts, categorized into sectors, or, in more technical terms, disaggregated. The notion of the gravity model, particularly as developed by Stewart and his associates, pertains to a relatively huge mass composed of a multitude

[46] Another simple function is $I_{ij} = a[(\log P_i + \log P_j)/d_{ij}^b]$.
[47] Or b may be a function of d_{ij} itself, or of both mass and distance.
[48] See [1].
[49] See [13].

of individual units. Within such a mass it is reasonable to assume that the irregularities, peculiarities, and idiosyncrasies of any individual unit or small subgroup of units are canceled or averaged out. In such a situation the *ceteris paribus* clause is valid to some extent at least. We can then justify a concentration on the two basic variables, distance and mass, and factors which can be encompassed in their weights and exponents, to the exclusion of other variables.

The significance of this point is illustrated by empirical materials on tonnage of commodity flows, as reported in studies cited in Chapter 5. When, for example, the data of the I.C.C. 1 per cent waybill sample of Class I railroad shipments for 1949 are examined, it is found that the volume of tonnage shipped any given distance falls off regularly with increase in distance. This "falling-off effect" is consistent with the gravity model. However, when the total of all shipments is disaggregated into the five major I.C.C. groups—(1) products of forests, (2) products of agriculture, (3) products of mines, (4) manufactures and miscellaneous, and (5) animals and animal products—it is found that the tonnage volume of the first four fall off somewhat regularly, although less regularly than the aggregate for all commodities, and that the shipment of the fifth group evidences no clear tendency to fall off with distance. When disaggregation is carried still further and individual commodities are examined, the set of individual commodity shipments does not reveal a systematic and pervasive influence of the distance variable.[50]

Similar conclusions seem to be implied by various traffic studies. When total volume of traffic is disaggregated by type of media, or trip purpose, by type of city, or other classification, the peculiarities of each category tend to become more manifest and dominant; and the extent to which the

---

[50] See W. Isard [25], ch. 3.   Also, see the works of Vining and others on commodity flows cited in Chapter 5.   This point is illustrated, *in reverse*, by some of Anderson's simple tests of the effect of population potential on densities. He estimated the hypothetical effect of a single mass, the population of New York City, on a random sample of one hundred United States counties. The population of New York was divided by the distance of each county from New York, and the resulting figure for each county was compared with its actual population density. A correlation coefficient of -0.606 was obtained, indicating that about 36 per cent of the variance in density among counties (1950) can be explained statistically by their distance from the mass at New York City. When he performed a similar calculation for the combined effect on each county of two masses, one at New York City and the other at Chicago, his statistical explanation of variance increased to about 46 per cent. A second test was made on all counties nearer to Birmingham, Alabama, than to any other metropolis. The correlation of the densities of these counties with the P_i/d_{ij} factor when just the influence of Birmingham was taken into account was only 0.012.   When the influence of twelve other masses (the twelve other closest metropolises) was computed and added to that of Birmingham, the correlation rose to 0.406.   See [3], p. 180.

gravity model describes or explains any regular "falling-off" effect tends
to decrease.   Thus, a basic problem is posed.   On the one hand it seems
desirable to disaggregate and stratify, in order to distinguish between
different exponents or weights which should be employed for describing

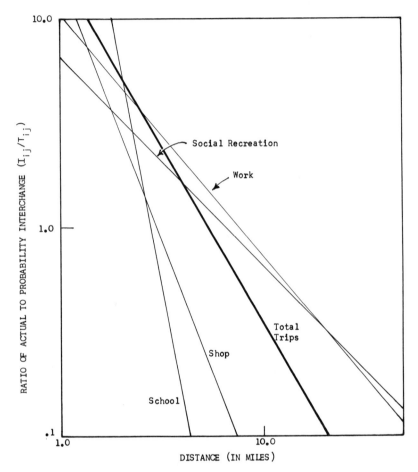

Figure 4.   Relation between distance and the ratio of actual to expected total person
trips for selected trip purposes, Detroit Metropolitan Region.   Source: J. D. Carroll
and H. W. Bevis [11], p. 194.

or projecting different categories.   [For example, in Figure 4 it is to be
noted that for the distance variable in the gravity model different exponents
(as measured by the slopes of the several straight lines) apply to different
trip purposes.   The exponent applicable to school trips has the greatest
absolute value, that to social and recreation trips the least absolute value.

Knowledge of the different exponents is desirable.] On the other hand, the gravity model as a tool to describe or explain volume of trips for a particular purpose tends to be less reliable for any particular stratum of a mass. And, if disaggregation is pursued too far, derived data such as the city weights computed by Hammer and Iklé (as noted earlier) may tend to have little significance, especially for projection purposes.

To restate the problem, disaggregation is desirable when additional information and precision is obtainable and when such disaggregation does not destroy to any great degree the inherent meaning and internal structural unity of the mass or population. Under these circumstances it will be fruitful to employ distinguishing exponents, weights, etc., such as ½, 3, and 2 as distinguishing exponents for the distance variable when work trips, social trips, and general shopping trips respectively are investigated. But if the inherent meaning and internal structural unity of the mass tend to be significantly destroyed, as perhaps we may argue in connection with the exponents suggested in a study by Voorhees,[51] disaggregation does not yield productive results.

When we seek to employ the gravity model as more than a descriptive tool, problems of a still more difficult character arise. A basic obstacle to its use for projection is the lack of any theory to explain values or functions which we assign to weights and exponents. Currently, the justification for the gravity model is simply that *everything else being equal* the interaction between any two populations can be expected to be directly related to their size; and since distance involves friction, inconvenience, and cost, such interaction can be expected to be inversely related to distance.

The lack of adequate theory is clearly perceived when we examine the pioneering attempts of Chauncy Harris and Edgar Dunn to advance practice in the application of the gravity model. Chauncy Harris[52] constructs a potential map of the United States which is here reproduced as Map 2. In doing so, Harris uses retail sales of a county as a measure of the mass of the county, transport cost over land as a measure of distance (along the lines discussed above in footnote 25), and unity for the exponents of distance and mass, for the weight of mass and for the gravitational constant.[53] His potential formula is therefore

$$_iV = \sum_{j=1}^{n} \frac{P_j}{d_{ij}}$$

[51] See [45].

[52] See [22].

[53] Harris' map was constructed from potentials computed for a set of selected cities. In his words, "In the actual computations concentric circles are drawn on tracing paper around each selected city representing transport costs of 6 (local county), 8, 10, 12, 14,

where P_j is the retail sales of county j. His potential map in many respects resembles Map 1.

Harris reasons that his potential map measures the accessibility of any county i to the entire market of the United States.   He justifiably maintains that such a map is significant for the analysis of the location of manufacturing in general, since such location is sensitive to the geographic distribution of the market.   But how significant?   This question he does

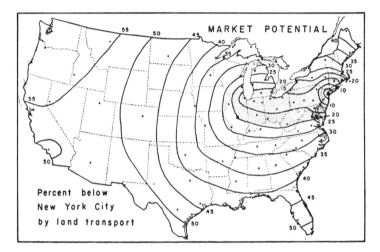

Map 2.   Market potential, United States, 1948.   Source: C. D. Harris [22], p. 320.

not attempt to answer.   He also bypasses the issue of the appropriate power to which d_{ij} should be raised, an important issue since different exponents of d_{ij} greatly influence the map of potential.[54]

18, 22, 30, 40, 50, 60, 70, and 80 dollars.   The retail sales of each concentric circle are calculated by simply adding the retail sales of all counties within the band included by that circle and not by a smaller circle.   (The county figures are recorded on a base map that can be used over and over again.)   The market potential of each band is then calculated by dividing the total sales of the band by the cost of reaching it from the city under consideration.   The total market potential for this city is then obtained by adding the market potential for all the bands or concentric circles" ([22] p. 323).

[54] When the exponent of d_{ij} is zero, the potential is everywhere the same, being equal to the total population of the United States.   As the exponent is gradually increased, the influence on any point of distant masses gradually decreases.   When the exponent is large, then effectively distant masses have no influence, and potential tends to measure the influence of local population only [provided reasonable values are established for $d_{ii}(i = 1, \cdots , n)$].

To be more specific, J. Q. Stewart and W. Warntz [39] find the weighted potentials of New York City and Chicago to be in the ratio of 72:51, an exponent of unity being

Harris also constructs a second map. He argues that transport cost on finished product to the market exerts, generally speaking, an important influence on the location of manufacturing. *Everything else being equal, a firm wishes to locate at the site that minimizes transport cost to the market.* Harris thus determines for each of his selected cities the transport cost of serving the entire United States market, where it is assumed that the size of the market in each county is equal to the retail sales of that county (each dollar of retail sales representing 1 ton of product)[55] and where the transport cost of reaching any market from a given location is equal to his d_{ij} as computed earlier. To illustrate the procedure, consider the transport cost of reaching the entire United States market from Chicago. The transport cost from a location in Chicago to the market in a first county, say Los Angeles County, is found by multiplying the market in Los Angeles by the distance (in terms of transport cost) between Chicago and Los Angeles. In turn, the transport cost to the market in each other county in the nation is computed. Finally, the resulting products are summed to yield a measure of the transport cost of reaching the entire United States market from Chicago. The formula for such a computation is

$$TC_i = \sum_{j=1}^{n} P_j d_{ij}$$

where TC_i is total transport cost for county i and P_j is the size of the market in county j. (Note that the transport cost computations require the same sets of data as the potential computations.) Harris' findings are summarized in Map 3, where all transport is assumed to be by land.

Compare Maps 2 and 3. Map 2 portrays New York City as the peak of potential; its contour lines connect areas (and points) where potentials are the same per cent below that of New York City. Map 3 portrays Fort Wayne, Indiana, as the trough of the total transport cost surface, that is, the point incurring least total transport cost in serving the entire United States market; the contour lines of this map connect areas (and points) whose total transport costs are the same per cent above that of Fort Wayne. As Harris notes, the differences between the peaks and contour lines of Maps 2 and 3 arise because in Map 2 the contribution of a given size market *declines* as the relevant distance increases, whereas in

applied to the distance variable. If, however, an exponent of 3 or 4 is used, the weighted potentials will be much closer to the ratio of 2:1 (approximately the ratio of their 1940 populations).

[55] This conversion is rather strange. However, the absolute value of the derived total transport cost figures is not employed. Only relative magnitudes are examined. Hence the conversion is justifiable.

Map 3 the contribution of the same market *increases* as the relevant distance increases.   More specifically, a large market at a great distance from a given point contributes little to the potential created on that point, whereas it contributes substantially to the total transport cost involved in serving the United States from that point.[56]

Maps 2 and 3 pose a dilemma.   The point which is the peak of market potential, that is, the point most accessible to the entire United States market, and which as a consequence promises to maximize sales, is New

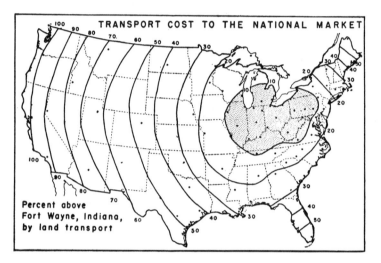

Map 3.   Transport cost to the national market, United States, 1948.   Source: C. D. Harris [22], p. 324.

York City.   The point that can reach the entire United States market with least transport cost is Fort Wayne.   Which is the more desirable location? Or is an intervening point still more desirable than either of these two?

After constructing a number of other relevant maps such as Map 4, Chauncy Harris brings his investigation to a close.[57]   But Dunn has

[56] To illustrate in Harris' words, "the retail sales of the Pacific Coast amount to 11.4 per cent of the total sales for the United States, yet because of their distance account for only 4.6 per cent of the market potential for Chicago, but for 22.0 per cent of the freight cost of serving a national market from Chicago" ([22], p. 328).

[57] In addition to the materials presented, Harris has investigated a number of interesting questions.   He constructs (1) both market potential and total transport cost maps when distance between any pair of subareas is measured in terms of transport cost by land or sea, whichever is the cheaper for the given pair; (2) a total transport cost map when the Pacific Coast is excluded from the national market; (3) both market potential and total transport cost maps for each of the following regions when each of these

attempted to go farther.   Cannot these two measures—market potential and total transport cost—be combined into a single over-all index to indicate the optimal location?   We shall outline, step by step, Dunn's attempt to attack this question and evaluate this attempt after it has been presented.

Dunn confines his investigation to a region comprising southern Georgia and all but the western part of Florida.   For each of the 103 counties in the region he computes (as the first step in his study) market potential à la Harris, interaction with all other counties of the United

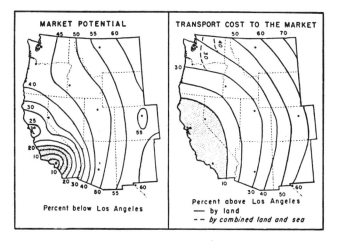

Map 4.   Market potential and transport cost to the market, the West, 1948.   Source: C. D. Harris [22], p. 330.

States being excluded.[58]   The market potential data for selected counties are presented in column 1 of Table 1, the data being expressed as percentages.   For each of these counties, too, Dunn computes (as the second step) total transport cost in reaching the market of the entire region (i.e., of the 103 counties).   Again, he follows Harris' procedure and expresses the resulting data in percentage form.   See column 2, Table 1.   A comparison of the data of columns 1 and 2 poses the dilemma already

regions is completely isolated (cut off) from the rest of the United States: the East, the Central states, the South and the West—the maps for the West are presented here as Map 4; and (4) both market potential and total transport cost maps when commodities to be marketed are commodities purchased by the mining segment of the United States economy, by the agricultural segment, and finally by the manufacturing segment.

[58] See [17].   He therefore treats these 103 counties as if they constitute a region isolated from the rest of the nation, a procedure he himself questions.

raised. Pinellas county is the county with highest market potential. Polk County is the county incurring least total transport cost in serving the entire market. Which is the better county for locating a general manufacturing establishment, especially when transport cost on finished

TABLE 1. COMPUTATION OF INDEX OF LOCATION, 1948
(Selected Florida and Georgia counties)

County	(1) Market Potential (Per cent of Pinellas)	(2) Transport Costs (Per cent of Polk)	(3) Weighted Transport Costs [(1) × (2)]	(4) Shift Base to Pinellas [(3)÷103]	(5) Net Differ- ential [(1) − (4)]	(6) Index of Location (Base Shifted to Polk)
1. Monroe	66.8	155.4	103.8	100.8	−34.0	−36.9
2. Dade	96.7	120.9	116.9	113.5	−16.8	−19.7
3. Lee	89.3	111.0	99.0	96.1	−6.8	−9.7
4. Hendry	92.2	108.6	100.1	97.2	−5.0	−7.9
5. Charlotte	89.8	109.2	98.1	95.2	−5.4	−8.3
6. Glades	93.5	107.0	100.0	97.1	−3.6	−6.5
7. DeSoto	93.7	105.3	98.7	95.8	−2.1	−5.0
8. Pinellas	100.0	103.0	103.0	100.0	0.0	−2.9
9. Hillsborough	99.3	102.5	101.7	98.7	+0.6	−2.3
10. Polk	99.2	100.0	99.2	96.3	+2.9	0.0
11. Osceola	97.1	100.6	97.7	94.9	+2.2	−0.7
12. Pasco	98.1	101.1	99.2	96.3	+1.8	−1.1
13. Citrus	94.6	103.7	98.1	95.2	−0.6	−3.5
14. Lake	97.4	101.0	98.4	95.5	+1.9	−1.0
15. Orange	97.9	100.5	98.4	95.5	+2.4	−0.5
16. Brevard	92.5	104.2	96.4	93.6	−1.1	−4.0
17. Marion	95.4	103.3	98.5	95.6	−0.2	−3.1
18. Dixie	86.8	113.4	98.4	95.5	−8.7	−11.6
19. Alachua	93.1	107.2	99.8	96.9	−3.8	−6.7
20. Duval	93.4	111.4	104.0	101.0	−7.6	−10.5
21. Madison	82.4	123.3	101.6	98.6	−16.2	−19.1
22. Leon	75.4	134.4	101.3	98.3	−22.9	−25.8
23. Colquit, Ga.	76.4	136.4	104.2	101.2	−24.8	−27.7
24. Chatham, Ga.	73.1	143.6	105.0	101.9	−28.8	−31.7

Source: E. S. Dunn [17], p. 188.

product is significant, when economies of scale dictate a single plant, and when other production costs tend to be the same from county to county?[59]

Dunn reasons that the total transport cost data must first be adjusted. Consider the alternative of a location in Monroe County (at the extreme

[59] Of course, if transport cost on finished product is negligible, or if the market for the establishment is invariant with its location, this dilemma does not exist.

southern tip of Florida) or in Pinellas County (in middle Florida). Being off-center from the standpoint of interaction, a manufacturer in Monroe County is not likely to sell as many units as he would if he were located at the center of interaction in Pinellas County. This is in fact what the market potential measure depicts. The measure specifically estimates that the market potential for a location in Monroe County is only 67 per cent of the market potential of a location in Pinellas (as recorded at the top of column 1). Hence if at a location in Monroe County the manufacturer is likely to sell only 67 per cent as many units as he would at a location in Pinellas County, his total transport costs at a Monroe location should be calculated on the basis of only 67 per cent of the total market in the 103 counties. Therefore, Dunn multiplies 155.4, the total transport cost percentage for Monroe County[60] (as recorded at the top of column 2), by 67 per cent to yield the percentage of 103.8 (as recorded at the top of column 3). In like manner, Dunn derives a *weighted transport cost* percentage figure for every other county. That is, he multiplies each figure of column 2 by the corresponding figure of column 1 to derive the respective figure of column 3. This adjustment constitutes his third step.

In order to facilitate the comparison by county of weighted total transport cost on a relative basis (column 3) with market potential on a relative basis (column 1), Dunn shifts the base of the weighted transport cost column. He does this so that Pinellas County comes to have a relative standing of 100 as it has for market potential in column 1. The procedure involved is to divide all the data of column 3 by 103 which is the percentage figure for Pinellas County in column 3. He derives the percentages of column 4.

If for the moment a simple postulate is permitted, Dunn's next step can be taken. This postulate is that a 1 per cent disadvantage in market potential exactly offsets a 1 per cent advantage in total transport costs, and vice versa. Thus, relative to Pinellas County, Polk County with a disadvantage of 0.8 per cent in market potential[61] offsets 0.8 of its 3.7 per cent advantage in transport costs[62] and has a *net* advantage of 2.9 (as recorded in column 5). To take another illustration, relative to Pinellas County, Monroe County has both a disadvantage of 33.2 per cent in market potential and a disadvantage of 0.8 in transport cost; its combined

[60] In the calculation of the figure of 155.4 per cent, it was assumed that 100 per cent of the market of the 103 counties would be served by a Monroe location.

[61] This disadvantage is measured by the number of percentage points the market potential for Polk County is below 100 (which is the market potential for Pinellas County).

[62] This advantage is measured by the number of percentage points by which the total transport cost figure for Polk County is below 100 (which is the total transport cost figure for Pinellas County).

disadvantage is 34.0 (as recorded at the top of column 5). By this procedure, which involves subtracting the percentages of column 4 from the
corresponding percentages of column 1, Dunn obtains the percentage
point differences of column 5.[63]   When the figure in column 5 is positive,
this implies, *relative to Pinellas County*, a net locational advantage for the
respective county; the county's advantage in transport cost more than
compensates for its disadvantage in market potential.   When the figure in
column 5 is negative, this implies a net locational disadvantage for the
respective county; the county's advantage in transport cost, if it has one,
does not offset its disadvantage in market potential.

   Column 5 presents the essential results of Dunn's procedure for combining the two variables, market potential and total transport cost on
finished products.   Although not necessary, a final step may be taken.
The figures of column 5 may be adjusted so that the county with greatest
net advantage, namely Polk, becomes the base for comparison, with a
corresponding figure of 0.0.   The adjustment is simple: from all the
percentage point differences of column 5, the quantity 2.9 is subtracted.
The resulting figures of column 6 are all negative, except for Polk County;
the figure for any county implies in percentage point terms the locational
disadvantage of that county relative to the best county (Polk).   Dunn
conceives the figures of column 6 as indicating the position of each county
along an *index of location*.   He maps the index values for all his counties.
As depicted on Map 5, he obtains a set of contour lines around Polk
County, the peak, each contour line passing through areas or points of the
same percentage point locational disadvantage.

   We now examine this procedure step by step and note its several
inadequacies, most of which have been recognized by Dunn.   First, there
is the question of appropriate market areas. So far as Polk County, the
central county, is concerned, the choice of market, that is, region, to be
investigated is not inappropriate.   Consider, however, the extreme county,
Chatham, Georgia.   By positing the defined region of 103 counties as
completely isolated, any possible sales from a location in Chatham to a
county just north of it is precluded.   It is clear that the defined region
is far from being a meaningful market region for any location in Chatham.   Thus, how can we justify the whole series of steps and subsequent
analysis?   This point raises a fundamental weakness of any market
potential map that has reference to a region which is not for practical purposes largely isolated (cut off) from other regions.   It suggests
that a market potential map for the United States and Canada is more
meaningful than a map for the United States alone, and the latter is

---

[63] The resulting figure for Pinellas County is 0.00, which is to be expected since
Pinellas County is the base for comparison.

much more meaningful than a map for any of the regions of the United States.

There is one means by which this inadequacy can be partially overcome.

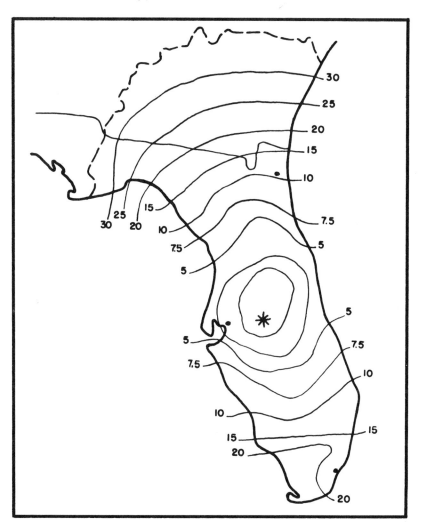

Map 5. Index of location, 1948. (Per cent below Polk County, Florida, with transport costs and market potential equally weighted.) Source: E. S. Dunn [17], p. 140.

It is true that the selection of a region which is not in actuality isolated tends to underestimate the accessible market of counties and subareas which are off-center, at least of those counties along the boundaries of the defined region.   On the other hand, it does not follow that a researcher should completely discard market potential computations and maps for the analysis of location within regions which cannot be conceived as isolated. The wise analyst tends to add to any region already identified as meaningful for his problem, one, two, or even more tiers of counties or subareas.   By this blowing-up step he corrects for underestimation of the market potential of counties and subareas along the boundaries of his meaningful region.   Thus, in Dunn's study we may consider the meaningful region for location analysis to include only counties in Florida and of these only counties east and to the south of the Suwannee River.   Counties like Leon, Florida, and Colquit, Georgia, may be excluded from serious location analysis, although they are to be included in all computations.   Still greater accuracy may be achieved by adding another tier of counties to the 103 counties already considered by Dunn.[64]

The second major inadequacy to note stems from the general dearth of knowledge and theory about the gravity model per se.   The previous discussion of appropriate weights, exponents, form of the function, etc., makes clear this inadequacy and does not need to be repeated at this point.

A third major inadequacy of Dunn's technique arises from weighting total transport costs by the percentage figure on market potential, that is, by multiplying each figure of column 2 by the corresponding figure of column 1.   It is to be reiterated that Dunn takes this step in order to account for the fact that a producer in a county with relatively low market potential will in effect not sell as many units as he would if he were located in a county with relatively high market potential; therefore he will not incur transport costs on units he does not sell.   For example, suppose he is located in Dade County.   Dade County's percentage figure on total transport cost is 120.9 (row 2, column 2), and its relative market potential is 96.7 (row 2, column 1).   When Dunn multiplies these two figures together, he is implying that the producer located in Dade County will sell only 96.7 per cent as many units as he would from a location in Pinellas County, and therefore that transport cost for the Dade County producer will be only 96.7 per cent of what transport cost would be if he were to serve the entire market.   But by this multiplication Dunn also implies that the producer located in Dade County will sell only 96.7 per cent as many units *in every county* as he would if he were located in Pinellas County.   That is, he will sell 96.7 per cent as much both in the neighboring county of Monroe and in distant Colquit County, Georgia.

[64] If the manufacturer seeking a location finds it feasible to ship his product by water, still other subareas—such as the Caribbean and the Gulf Coast districts—should be appended to form the "region of computation."

But, in fact, it is likely that the producer in Dade County will sell very little in a distant county; his sales there will be cut to less than 96.7 per cent of what sales would be from a location in Pinellas County. On the other hand, in Dade County itself and nearby counties such as Monroe, he is likely to sell much more than 96.7 per cent of what sales would be from a location in Pinellas County. Hence, it becomes necessary to pursue a more sophisticated type of market analysis than Dunn was in a position to conduct.[65] Such analysis should evolve a method of weighting transport cost which will differentiate between distant and nearby sections of the entire region's market.

A still more fundamental issue concerns the procedure by which a percentage point advantage (or disadvantage) in one measure (say market potential) is made comparable to a percentage point advantage (or disadvantage) in the second measure (say total transport cost). Why should a 1 per cent disadvantage in market potential exactly offset a 1 per cent advantage in transport cost? Or, to say the same thing, why should a 1 per cent disadvantage in transport cost exactly offset a 1 per cent advantage in market potential? Why should the former not offset a 2 per cent advantage in market potential, or a 0.67 per cent advantage in market potential, or any other per cent advantage in market potential? Dunn fully recognizes this issue. He thus treats his particular index of location as valid *only if we accept the assumption that a 1 per cent disadvantage in transport cost does exactly offset a 1 per cent advantage in market potential.*

One thing is clear. There is as yet no basis for such an assumption, or for any other reasonable assumption concerning the equivalence of different per cent advantages and disadvantages in the market potential and total transport cost measures. Dunn has brought into clearer focus the dilemma stemming from Harris' study. He has not resolved it. We know that *ceteris paribus* a location with a high market potential tends to be more favorable than a location with a low market potential. The former tends to be closer to the market *in general*. *Ceteris paribus*, the producer at the former may be able to gauge the size and composition of the market more accurately.[66] He may be able to establish better contact with customers,

[65] Such market analysis might follow more traditional lines (see W. Isard [25], ch. 7) and might estimate for a producer in a given county zero sales to a number of the 103 counties in the study, even though each county according to the market potential concept should provide some market for the producer in the given county. It would also take into account the share of the market in each county that might reasonably be expected to be won by existing or future competitors.

[66] For example, he may be able to conduct a sample survey at less cost and perhaps more knowingly. He may also be more sensitive to special conditions affecting his market, such as likely local tax changes, etc.

effect quicker delivery and servicing,[67] respond to changes in demand more rapidly,[68] and realize intangible administrative advantages from the juxtaposition of production and those sales and service activities which are market-oriented.[69]   He may be in a more effective position to undertake an advertising program and to maintain good public relations.[70]

But how compare these and other advantages of a rather *subjective* and *intangible* character with the *objective* cost advantage or disadvantage in transporting finished product? This is the unresolved question. It is important to recognize that if such a question were resolved, it would also be possible to treat more complicated location problems than the one presented by Dunn. For it would be possible, à la techniques discussed in Chapter 7, to use a comparative cost approach in its several forms. That is, if there were differences among counties not only in transport cost on finished product but also in labor cost, we should construct a *combined* (labor–transport) cost index for each county and express its index position as a percentage of the base county. (As with total transport cost alone, the resulting percentage values can be converted into *dollar differences*.) If a 1 per cent disadvantage in market potential could be made comparable to a 1 per cent advantage in total transport cost, and thus to the dollar amount represented by this 1 per cent advantage in total transport cost, it could then be made comparable to the dollar amount represented by a 1 per cent advantage in a combined (labor–transport) cost index, and thus directly to the 1 per cent advantage itself. Similarly, the problem could be broadened to encompass differences among counties in power costs, land costs, and other pertinent costs as well as in transport costs on raw materials.[71]   As a consequence, all the cost differentials

[67] For a rather large number of commodities a producer may find that speed of delivery is an important factor influencing his sales volume and that being on the spot or close by permits him to provide a more satisfactory service to his customers.

[68] For example, when a sudden drop in temperature increases demand for fuel oil, an oil refiner located at the market can rapidly adjust production operations and step up delivery of fuel oil. In contrast, an oil refiner far from the market can adjust production schedules as rapidly but requires time to effect a greater rate of delivery, especially if he transports his fuel oil by water tanker.

[69] He may, of course, face disadvantages as well as advantages from juxtaposition of activities. But very often a finer articulation and coordination of activities is possible, which in turn leads to *net* gains.

[70] For example, an attractive or impressive plant on a major passenger route may itself constitute extremely effective visual advertising. Information concerning plant operations may also appear in local newspapers and keep the name of the producer before a large part of the community. This factor has been cited by G. E. McLaughlin and S. Robock [31], pp. 23–24.

[71] Effectively, a set of isodapanes based on all cost differences and recognizing graduated transport rate structures and other special conditions expressible in cost

encountered in location analysis could be explicitly introduced into the problem were the fundamental question resolved.[72]

Although the fundamental question posed by Harris and sharpened by Dunn remains unresolved and may never be resolved, raising it does provide insight into and understanding of the nature of certain problems. Aside from the location and transportation problems previously discussed, there are other important social issues to which this question relates. One is the delineation of appropriate administrative areas, which it may be fruitful to discuss at this point.

A common criterion in the delineation of administrative areas has been efficiency in cost terms. A specific function such as police or fire protection is analyzed. Data on costs for a given quality and level of service are estimated. These costs are related to the size of the service area, where size may be measured in terms of population, land area, number of dwelling units, etc., or some combination of these. Costs per unit of service are computed for different-size administrative areas. These costs may be graphed as curve *EF* in Figure 5, where cost per unit (the dependent variable) is measured along the vertical axis and size of area (the independent variable) along the horizontal axis. The size involving least cost per unit may be, and frequently is, taken to be the most appropriate administrative area, at least from the efficiency standpoint. In Figure 5,

terms can be constructed. The base county would be the county at the center of these isodapanes, that is, the county of least total cost for all the items considered. Relative to this base county, any given county's cost disadvantage could be expressed in percentage terms and compared with its (the given county's) relative market potential position.

[72] A simple example may be instructive in understanding the fundamental question. Suppose that there are two areas of a metropolitan region suitable for residential housing construction. Both are equally desirable on an over-all basis and aside from land site cost incur the same cost for development. The first one, which is farther from the center of the metropolitan region and also from routes of heavy population movements, has associated with it lower land costs. At the same time, being more distant from the heavy routes of population movement and the metropolitan center, its market potential (i.e., its accessibility to the purchasing public as a whole) is smaller. A builder who considers the alternative of developing one or the other area must make a decision which involves the comparison of the difference in land costs with the difference in market potential. If the difference in land costs were to be gradually reduced to zero, he would clearly come to prefer to develop the second area *under our ceteris paribus assumptions*. On the other hand, if the difference in land costs were to become very large, he would clearly prefer to develop the first area. The fundamental question is: As the difference in land cost is gradually increased from zero, at what point and on what basis does the builder decide in favor of the first area?

It is evident that such decisions are constantly being made. But it is also evident that, given our analytical techniques, we have as yet been unable to weight objectively the several factors involved, one of which is market potential.

point P identifies the most efficient size of administrative area (which is OS) and the corresponding cost per unit level (which is PS). It can be seen that "economies of scale" are considerable and that insofar as cost is to be the criterion a relatively large area is desirable.

The concept of potential makes possible analysis along a second dimension. Consider the important role of community participation, especially in a democratic society such as the United States.[73]   We have

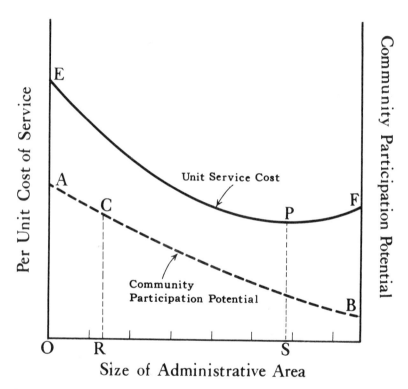

Figure 5.   Unit cost and community participation potential by size administrative area.

already noted the empirical investigations on population movement (whether such movement involves permanent migration or a journey to work; whether it is for the purpose of recreation, social visits, attending school or college, shopping, or courtship),[74] and on other forms of interaction (as reflected in telephone calls, telegram messages, newspaper

[73] The term community is defined broadly so as to refer not only to socially meaningful, local areas but also to other areas of larger size such as the metropolitan region, the state, and the nation.

[74] In addition to this discussion and to the literature cited, see J. H. S. Bossard [7].

circulation, advertisement, or spread of information and rumor).[75] These empirical investigations suggest that the participation of a representative individual in diverse affairs tends to fall off as the time, cost, and social distance to be traversed in such participation increases. Such behavior tends to characterize participation in at least certain community activities involving the political process, the utilization of community facilities, or both. Thus, if the area relevant for a particular service increases—say the area of a high school district—we can expect the level of community participation to decrease. For if a state is carved up into many small high school districts, people will on the average be close to the high school; and, on the basis of empirical gravity studies, individual participation will tend to be at a high level. In contrast, if a state is carved up into a relatively few large high school districts—say to achieve full economies of scale—people will on the average be relatively far from the high school; and individual participation will tend to be at a relatively low level.[76]

Suppose that for a specific function, such as high school education, we are able to conduct a sample survey and obtain relevant data on the behavior of typical individuals at different distances. On Figure 6 which measures level of participation[77] along the vertical axis and distance from the school (or other relevant points of participation) along the horizontal axis, we may construct curve UV which may be taken to summarize the findings for a representative individual. To proceed from curve UV, which estimates what the level of participation of a representative individual would be if he were located at different distances from the focal point of participation, to a community participation potential curve involves several steps.

First, establish the significant units of distance. Say they are in terms of quarter-miles. *Second*, for a typical administrative area of the given size set down the number of individuals at each quarter-mile distance from the focal point, where every individual is taken to be located at the quarter-

---

[75] In addition to this discussion and to the literature cited, see S. C. Dodd [15], pp. 393–396.

[76] It is recognized that individual participation varies with the homogeneity of a community (ethnic, political, and economic), with its historical tradition, with its rate of growth and cyclical stability, etc. In the analysis to follow all these factors are assumed to be averaged out. Of course, in the study of any particular community, such factors are basic for understanding the participation of its residents in the political process.

[77] Level of participation may be measured either in absolute or percentage terms and for the individual may refer to number of PTA or school board meetings attended, number of visits to teachers or amount of time spent at the school, etc., or some combination of these and other relevant measures.

mile mark closest to his residence.   *Third*, for the first quarter-mile mark, determine from Figure 6 the level of participation by a representative individual and multiply by the number of individuals at that quarter-mile mark.   This multiplication yields community participation by the population at the first quarter-mile.   *Fourth*, for the second quarter-mile, determine from Figure 6 the level of participation by a representative

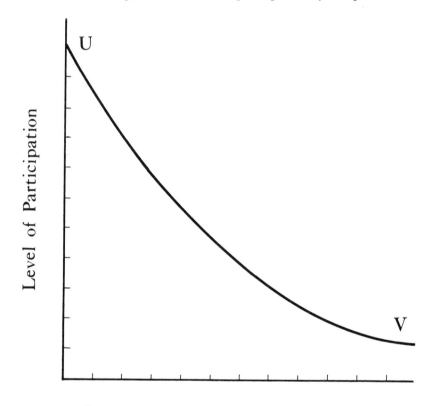

Distance from Point of Participation

Figure 6.   Variation of level of participation with distance for a representative individual.

individual and multiply by the population at the second quarter-mile mark to yield community participation by that population.   *Fifth*, do the same computation for all other quarter-mile marks on the defined radius of the given area.   *Sixth*, sum the amount of community participation at all quarter-mile marks and divide by the total population within the specific area.   This yields the community participation potential (on a per capita basis) for the typical administrative area of the given size.   *Seventh*, if it is desirable to base the estimate of community participation potential for a given size administrative area on more than one typical administrative area of that size, perform steps 2 through 6 for each such additional typical area to be considered. *Eighth*, average the community participation potentials of the several typical administrative areas considered to obtain the relevant community participation potential for a given size of administrative area.[78] *Ninth*, plot this community participation potential on a graph such as Figure 5, where the vertical axis measures community participation potential in appropriate units (as indicated on the right-hand side of Figure 5), and where the horizontal axis measures size of administrative area. (On Figure 5, for example, point C indicates a community participation potential of CR for administrative areas of size OR.) *Tenth*, for every other relevant size of administrative area, follow steps 2 through 9. *Eleventh*, connect the series of points so obtained to yield a curve, such as the dashed curve AB on Figure 5. We designate this curve the community participation potential curve. It refers to the average participation of population for different sizes of administrative areas for a given function and indicates how this participation declines as the size of administrative area increases.

To illustrate the use of the community participation potential curve, suppose curves EF and AB of Figure 5 relate to the function high school education. It has already been remarked that an administrative area the size of OS involves least cost per unit service.[79] But at the same time it involves a community participation potential which is significantly lower than the potential for smaller-size administrative areas. Since local debate and discussion is a highly valued activity in a democratic society, clearly the most desirable size of administrative area is not OS. For at least the sizes that are only somewhat smaller than OS, there is, according to the curves of Figure 5, little loss of efficiency (i.e., little increase in unit cost) but noticeable increase in community participation potential. Therefore, these sizes of administrative area are each more desirable than size OS. However, the specific size which is the most desirable cannot be determined. For as in the Dunn problem discussed earlier, we have no method of comparing gain in community participation potential with loss in efficiency as expressed in dollar terms.

---

[78] This averaging step is desirable since density of population, topography, land use patterns, and a host of other significant factors vary from one typical administrative area to another of the same size. Ideally, the community participation potential should be derived for each of the administrative areas (all of the same size) in a system and averaged. Such a procedure, however, would not be practical.

[79] Materials on economies of scale in high school education may be found in W. Isard and R. E. Coughlin [27], pp. 70–74.

Likewise, we may develop community participation potential and unit cost curves for elementary school education, university education (state-supported), and the host of other governmental functions. For elementary school education we might anticipate that the curve on per unit cost of service (for a given quality of education) will not fall off as sharply as the curve EF of Figure 5 and will reach a minimum point at a smaller size of administrative area.[80] Also, we might anticipate that up to the point where the unit cost curve reaches a minimum, the community participation potential will fall at least as rapidly as curve AB. Thus, we will reach a conclusion that the size of the elementary school district which we expect to be most desirable will be not only smaller than the size most efficient from a cost standpoint but also smaller than the most desirable high school district. But how much smaller than the most efficient size can be answered only after a considerable amount of further research is pursued on the "comparability" question.

In contrast, for university education supported by state funds it may be hypothesized that the community participation potential has only a slight slope.[81] If empirical studies were to substantiate this hypothesis, the case for operating a state university at the most efficient size would be a strong one.

The administrative area problem, of course, is not as simple as just depicted. Interaction between administrative units and citizens occur in at least two other forms. Many facilities provided by the government are intended to "promote the general welfare" and accomplish this purpose to the extent that the community as a whole utilizes them. Among services of this type are public health clinics, libraries, recreation facilities, etc. In decisions concerning the provision of such services consideration of lower unit costs with increase in size of a facility must frequently be weighed against the resulting decrease in the community use on a per capita basis.

Additionally, interactance may be in the form of information passing from citizens to government administrators who formulate policy. Again, a balance must be struck between the relatively low unit costs of a central office for a large administrative area (with an attendant low level of public contact) and the higher unit costs of small branch offices (with an attendant high level of contact).

Finally, the concept of community participation potential, especially if a scientific or quasi-scientific basis can be established for comparison with objective measures such as dollars, may be of value in studies relating to

[80] [27], pp. 70–74.

[81] The public, at least traditionally, participates little in the discussion and debate regarding this function, and average attendance on a per capita basis is small.

the allocation of diverse types of functions to the various levels of government of a society. Many factors are relevant in such an allocation, but clearly one of these is community participation potential. To illustrate very briefly: *ceteris paribus*, local government should tend to be assigned those functions with which are associated community participation potential curves that are high when the administrative area is small and fall off sharply when the size of area increases, with which little if any scale economies are associated, and for which local administration is not undesirable from other relevant standpoints. In contrast, federal governments should tend to be assigned those administrative functions for which community participation potential is at a low level for all size administrative areas, for which major-scale economies are achieved when the entire nation is taken as the administrative area, and for which other important elements suggest federal control rather than state or metropolitan control.

F. Other Hypotheses and Formulations

In addition to the important studies on the concept and formulation of the gravity model and on its use for transportation, location, and administrative area analysis, there are a number of other studies which concern related hypotheses and other significant formulations.[82]

One of these is the study by Warntz on the spatial pattern of prices. Warntz reasons that the supply and demand approach of traditional economics needs refinement. To study price variation over space—which variation for practical purposes may be considered as continuous—we must also treat demand and supply in a space continuum. That is, demand and supply should each be formulated as spatially continuous variables.

In accordance with the concept of potential as developed by Stewart, and as defined by equation (6) with $b = 1$, Warntz derives a *product supply space potential* for each of a set of commodities whose spatial variation he purports statistically to "explain." To derive a product supply space potential, say the *United States annual onion supply space potential*, Warntz sets $G = 1$ and simply uses as mass P_j in equation 6 the output of the product onions in subarea j. Thus, subarea j's contribution to the supply potential at subarea i is P_j/d_{ij} and the sum of the contributions of all subareas to the supply potential at subarea i is $\sum_{j=1}^{n} \dfrac{P_j}{d_{ij}}$.

---

[82] One group of studies not discussed in this chapter are those that attempt to use the gravity model for demarcating regional boundaries. For example, see W. J. Reilly [35], J. D. Carroll [10], and H. L. Green [20].

For every other subarea[83] Warntz computes its onion supply space potential. Following the standard procedures used in the construction of potential maps, Warntz develops a map of annual onion supply space potential. This map is reproduced as Map 6. It is to be interpreted in the same manner as Maps 1 and 2. In general, a map of product supply space potential designates the accessibility of an area to the diverse local productions of a commodity as they are geographically distributed.

Unfortunately, Warntz is not able to develop directly statistical materials on demand space potential. Local demand estimates by individual commodities are not readily available.[84] Therefore, Warntz utilizes income potential as a substitute,[85] maintaining that income potential measures accessibility to effective demand as a whole and that a map of income potential "serves to show the broad features of the geography of demand for a fairly wide variety of products."[86]

Warntz's hypothesis, advanced as a refinement of the law of supply and demand, is that in any local area the price of a commodity, say onions, varies inversely with the area's onion supply space potential and directly with the area's onion demand space potential for which he substitutes the area's income potential. But even more refinement is necessary. The price of onions in subarea i is also affected by the timing of onion supply potential in relation to onion demand (income) potential. That is, it is to be anticipated that if in a given subarea the peak of effective demand occurs in one month while the availability of supply reaches its peak six months later, the price will be higher than would be true if both peaks were to occur simultaneously, *ceteris paribus*. Because of formidable data problems, Warntz does not attempt at all to estimate the variation in the intensity of demand for onions (or any other commodity) over the year. He implicitly assumes a uniform intensity. On the other hand, with reference to the United States, Warntz is able to construct for each commodity a *product supply time potential*, and more specifically for onions, an *onion supply time*

---

[83] In his particular computations Warntz defines each of the 48 states as a subarea.

[84] However, as discussed in section B.2.d of Chapter 12, local consumption data can be estimated via input–output coefficients.

[85] As an alternative to the term income potential, Warntz frequently employs the term *gross economic population potential*, which emphasizes population as weighted by per capita income.

[86] W. Warntz [46], p. 122. As Warntz states, a more accurate concept of demand applied to a specific commodity would require that income "be modified by such things as income elasticity of demand, tastes, customs, prices of substitutes and the like" (*ibid.*, p. 120).

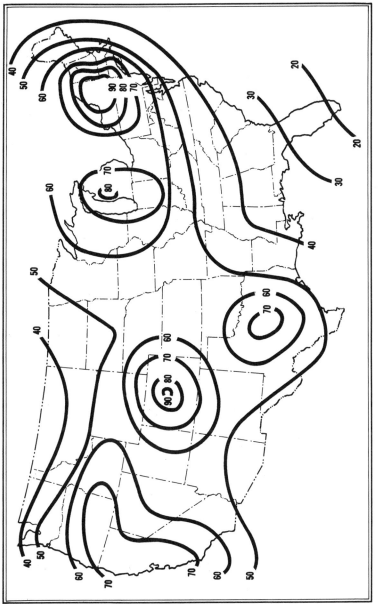

Map 6. United States annual onion supply potential. (In 100,000 sacks, 50 lb. each, per 100 miles, 1940–1949 average.)
Source: W. Warntz [46], p. 123.

potential.[87] His full hypothesis, which he subjects to statistical test, is that in any local area the price of a commodity not only varies inversely with the area's product supply space potential and directly with the area's income potential, but also varies inversely with the area's product supply time potential.[88]

By means of a standard multiple correlation technique Warntz carefully tests his hypothesis with data obtained for each of four commodities.   He obtains coefficients of multiple correlation ranging from 0.72 to 0.87 and finds all these to be significant beyond the 1 per cent level.   The specific terms of his hypothesis are borne out by the signs of the separate net regression coefficients; that is, for each commodity the net coefficient for income potential is positive, and the net coefficients for product supply space potential and product supply time potential are negative.[89]

---

[87] Warntz's procedure for the construction of a *product supply time potential* is as follows:

1. Production data for each subarea (state) are collected, and the entire production of that subarea is assumed to occur in one month only, namely the month of the greatest output.   (In certain cases widely separated seasons of production occur, and Warntz is compelled to make adjustments in this and later steps, about which we will not report.)

2. For the United States production by month is obtained by summing the derived data, that is, by summing for each month the total output of those subareas (states) whose harvest is concentrated in that month.   The output for any month is assumed to be concentrated at midmonth.

3. For the United States the *product time potential* for the middle of any month is computed by dividing output of each other month by each of two time intervals (backward and forward) which separates the given pair of months, and by summing the quotients.   For example, to compute the United States onion time potential for March, Warntz divides the United States output of onions in January by 2 (backward) and then again by 10 (forward), divides the United States output of onions in February by 1 (backward) and then again by 11 (forward), and so on.   If United States onion production (as indirectly derived by step 2) occurs in only six months, there will be twelve quotients which will be summed to yield United States onion time potential for March.

4. For any subarea its *product supply time potential* is found by identifying the month in which its production is concentrated (and thus to which its whole output is assigned). The United States product time potential at this month is the subarea's product supply time potential.

It is to be noted that many conceptual and other problems arise in connection with this procedure.   For further discussion see W. Warntz [48].

[88] If Warntz were able to construct a measure of *product demand time potential*, his hypothesis would be modified so that in any local area the price of a commodity varies directly with the area's product demand time potential.

[89] Warntz reports the results of his correlations including tests of significance, measures of the effects of individual variables, and standard errors of estimate in [48]. For example, the estimating equation for the price of wheat in any state is $X_1 = 203.9688 + 0.5074 X_2 - 0.1705 X_3 - 5.3095 X_4$ where for the given state X_1, X_2, X_3, and X_4 are its price of wheat, income potential, wheat supply space potential and wheat supply time

Aside from its use for statistical description, that is, for statistically explaining past and current patterns of prices over space, Warntz suggests the usefulness of his study for at least limited projection purposes. Suppose a major irrigation project opens up, for the production of a particular crop, hitherto infertile agricultural land. Suppose, too, the total harvest can be roughly estimated. What will be the impact of such a development on the spatial pattern of prices? The set of estimating equations developed by the Warntz technique does cast light on such impact. Since the output of the subarea in which the new project is developed changes, so will the product supply space potential for that and every other subarea.

Insertion in the estimating equation of the new values for product supply space potential for each subarea will lead to a new estimated product price for each subarea and thus to a new overall pattern of price variation over space. Nonetheless, such a procedure must be used with considerable caution in view of the various limitations of statistical explanation, let alone the uncertain validity of the potential concept.[90]

The extension of the potential concept to embrace supply (production) aspects and their synthesis with similar concepts relating to demand yield insight into the spatial characteristics of important economic and social phenomena. However, there are some basic questions to be investigated with respect to Warntz's approach, questions which are also basic to many

potential, respectively. As can be expected, the relative importance of the variables differ for the several commodities examined. For example, among the variables product supply time potential ranks first in importance for strawberries and last in importance for potatoes.

[90] The Warntz procedure promises to be of use in a number of other ways. For example, in section D.5 of Chapter 7 it is noted that a weakness of a number of measures of spatial association, such as the coefficient of localization, is that the results obtained are often significantly influenced by the number and size of subareas (regions) selected for study. Often the values obtained for the measure (coefficient) will change abruptly, with small changes in the particular areal subdivision used. In contrast, potential measures vary more continuously over space, since the potential at each point is a function of that point's position with respect to the entire mass. Consequently, the value of potential at any point is less dependent on spatial subdivision, although it is still affected to a significant degree by the number and location of control points used in computation. For fuller discussion see G. A. P. Carrothers [14]. As a result, too, for a change in the set of control points the change in spatial association between two potential measures is more continuous.

In this connection Warntz [47] proposes a measure of market orientation. For any commodity this measure is obtained for a given set of points (say state centers) by simple rank correlation of income potential and product supply space potential. However, the general validity of this measure is yet to be determined and is to be seriously questioned for a number of situations.

of the studies reported earlier. For example, what is the effect of intervening markets and demand? That is, what is the effect of the intervening New York metropolitan market on the price of Maine potatoes in Philadelphia? Suppose the New York metropolitan market were 90 miles southwest of Philadelphia instead of 90 miles northeast. According to Warntz's computations, Philadelphia would have the same income potential, the same product supply space potential, and the same product supply time potential. Hence, the estimated price of Maine potatoes in Philadelphia as derived from Warntz's equations would not change.[91]   Could we expect this to be true if this situation were reality?

This question can be posed still more sharply. Suppose we were to estimate traffic volume between Philadelphia and Boston by use of some form of the gravity model. Can the fact that the New York metropolis intervenes be ignored, as this fact seems to be by the model in its unmodified form? Or if we estimate migration from New England to Philadelphia, must not intervening New York City be explicitly recognized?

It is at this point that Stouffer's hypothesis on *intervening opportunities* may be appropriately introduced and evaluated. The hypothesis, formulated with reference to that type of spatial interaction reflected in migration, states

". . . there is no necessary relationship between mobility and distance . . . *the number of persons going a given distance is directly proportional to the number of opportunities at that distance and inversely proportional to the number of intervening opportunities. . . .* The relation between mobility and distance may be said to depend on an auxiliary relationship, which expresses the cumulated (intervening) opportunities as a function of distance."[92]

This hypothesis has been partially tested on several occasions. In examining data on residential migration between census tracts in Cleveland, 1933–1935, Stouffer finds encouraging agreement between actual migration and migration expected on the basis of the hypothesis. In their study of interstate migration in the United States based on 1930 population census data, Bright and Thomas conclude that such migration "has in general followed the pattern of opportunities and intervening opportunities very closely . . ." but ". . . only if we allow for the major disturbances in the pattern attributable to qualitative differences in the opportunities sought in California and elsewhere and if allowance is made for the directional factor in the movement from the Middle

[91] However, the set of constants derived from past and current data might be different.
[92] See [41], pp. 846–847.

West."[93]   Isbell performs a similar test of Stouffer's hypothesis on intercounty and intracounty migration in Sweden, 1921–1930, and again finds
that the empirical materials tend to substantiate the hypothesis.[94]

On two other occasions the Stouffer hypothesis has been not only
examined but also evaluated in the light of alternative hypotheses.
Strodtbeck[95] tests three alternative formulations of migration hypotheses
using 1930 census data for persons born in Kentucky and residing in cities
of 50,000 or more within 650 miles of the periphery of Kentucky.   In
processing the data he determines for each such city its distance from the
periphery of Kentucky by first-class, hard surface road.   Next he classifies
these cities by 25-mile intervals, the cities in any one 25-mile interval
forming a band.   He then examines the following hypotheses:

(i) $$M_{ij} = k_1 \frac{1}{d_{ij}}$$

(ii) $$M_{ij} = k_2 \frac{P_j}{d_{ij}}$$

(iii) $$M_{ij} = k_3 \frac{x_j}{\sum\limits_{h=1}^{j-1} x_h}$$

where M_{ij} is estimated migration from Kentucky (region i) to cities of
50,000 or more population in band j; d_{ij} is the distance from the periphery
of Kentucky to the center of band j; P_j is the sum of the population of
cities of 50,000 or more in band j; x_j is the number of opportunities in j,
which is taken to be proportional to the number of persons living in cities
of 50,000 or more in band j who were born outside the state of current
residence; $\sum\limits_{h=1}^{j-1} x_h$ is the number of intervening opportunities, that is, the
sum of opportunities in the several bands between the periphery of
Kentucky and band j:

$$\sum_{h=1}^{j-1} x_h = x_1 + x_2 + \cdots + x_{j-1}$$

and k_1, k_2, and k_3 are constants.   However, before we report on Strodtbeck's tests, it is desirable to reformulate these hypotheses so that their
relation to our previous discussion on gravity models is more apparent.

[93] See [8], p. 783.
[94] See [29].
[95] See [42, 43].

In Strodtbeck's hypotheses the source of migration, namely Kentucky (region i), is held constant. Hence P_i, which is the population of region i, is also constant, since i can refer to only one region, namely Kentucky. Therefore we can find a constant G_1 such that $k_1 = G_1 P_i$; and another constant G_2 such that $k_2 = G_2 P_i$; and still another constant G_3 such that $k_3 = G_3 P_i$. Substituting in hypotheses i, ii, and iii these respective values for k_1, k_2, and k_3, we obtain

(i alt.)
$$M_{ij} = G_1 \frac{P_i}{d_{ij}}$$

(ii alt.)
$$M_{ij} = G_2 \frac{P_i P_j}{d_{ij}}$$

(iii alt.)
$$M_{ij} = G_3 \frac{P_i x_j}{\sum\limits_{h=1}^{j-1} x_h}$$

which are simply alternative statements for hypotheses i, ii, and iii. Now it is clearly seen that the alternative form of hypothesis ii is identical with equation 4 when b in equation 4 is taken to be unity. Thus hypothesis ii is clearly Stewart's gravity model. Hypothesis iii is the Stouffer hypothesis, and when we write down its equivalent, namely hypothesis iii alt., we observe that the population of the source region may be viewed as a parameter of his hypothesis. Everything else being equal, the larger the value of this parameter (i.e., the population of the source region), the greater the amount of migration (M_{ij}) to be expected.

Strodtbeck finds rank correlation coefficients of 0.40, 0.87, and 0.91 for hypotheses i, ii, and iii, respectively. The fact that in all these hypotheses the estimation is a crude one is shown by the high values of chi-square.[96] He concludes that both hypotheses ii (the Stewart gravity model) and iii (the intervening opportunities hypothesis) are superior to the simple hypothesis i, but not to one another. Also, neither hypothesis ii nor hypothesis iii provides a truly acceptable fit.

Anderson reports on additional investigations. His basic data are numbers of migrants, 1935–1940, from each of 54 metropolitan subregions within the Northeast and North Central regions to each of the 30 nearest metropolitan subregions. One test which he performs compares hypothesis iii above (the Stouffer hypothesis) with the following hypothesis:

(iv)
$$M_{ij} = k_4 \frac{x_j}{d_{ij}}$$

[96] These values are, respectively, 5487, 1377, and 638. Values of less than 42 would be required in order not to reject the null hypothesis at the 0.05 level of significance.

Note that hypothesis iv is identical with hypothesis iii, except that highway mileage distance d_{ij} substitutes for intervening opportunities. His findings suggest that hypothesis iii is not superior to hypothesis iv, that is, that a denominator defined in terms of intervening opportunities is not superior to a denominator defined in terms of highway mileage. Or put otherwise, if the number of intervening opportunities is viewed as a measure of distance, a concept which will be developed later, the use of this measure of distance is not more accurate than the use of highway mileage. Although Anderson's findings do not deny the Stouffer hypothesis, they do cast doubt on the *superiority* of the Stouffer hypothesis and therefore on its utility.[97]

On net, it may be said that the several empirical investigations pursued tend to support the Stouffer hypothesis. Yet the tests performed do not constitute conclusive evidence of its validity. Rather they seem to emphasize the need for examining the theory with more homogeneous data than were available—data more homogeneous with respect to direction of migration,[98] type of opportunity (e.g. of employment opportunity or of residential vacancy), characteristics of migrants, etc. Equally important, these studies do not demonstrate that the Stouffer hypothesis is superior to an appropriately modified Stewart-Zipf hypothesis, although in certain cases the Stouffer hypothesis may prove to be more suitable in selection of factors relevant in specific types of interaction.

However, it should be noted that the Stouffer and Stewart-Zipf hypotheses are not as far apart as is suggested by a first reading of the original articles and later works. Comparison of hypotheses ii alt. and iii alt. indicates that in the latter x_j takes the place of P_j in the numerator. But frequently it is reasonable to expect x_j to vary proportionally with P_j, that is, for x_j (the opportunities at j) to equal a constant times P_j (the population of j).[99] Moreover, the denominators of hypotheses ii alt.

[97] In addition to this test Anderson compares formulations with the exponent of the distance variable taken as 1 and 2 and finds no more accuracy when an exponent of 2 is used (or in the case of intervening opportunities when an exponent of $\frac{2}{3}$ rather than 1 is used). However, as already reported, he performs certain tests which suggest that the exponent of the distance variable should be itself a variable inversely related to the size of the source subregion. He also notes some evidence to the effect that the measure of mass (population) should be raised to a constant power less than unity, and that there is a strong tendency for migrants to remain in the state of origin and to move toward areas of low employment. See [1].

For some interesting and relevant discussion on Anderson's statistical procedures, see F. J. Iklé [23] and T. Anderson [4].

[98] D. O. Price [33], M. Bright and D. S. Thomas [8], and E. C. Isbell [29] all emphasize this point. Also see E. L. Ullman [44], ch. 3, for comments on intervening opportunities and commodity movements.

[99] Then G_2 would equal that same constant times G_3.

and iii alt. namely d_{ij} and $\sum_{h=1}^{j-1} x_h$, may be viewed as alternative measures
of distance.   In fact, this is Anderson's view; and, as already noted, he
concludes from tests applied to the set of migration data he possessed
that intervening opportunities were not a more relevant (superior) index
of distance than highway mileage.   But Anderson examined only one set
of data.   It is possible that had he examined other sets of data—such as
data on migration within metropolitan regions, or on migration of particular income, occupational, or racial groups, or on the shipment of
Maine potatoes or other commodities, or on volume of diverse communication phenomena—he might have found the use of an appropriate
measure of intervening opportunities to yield more accurate results.

The use of the concept of intervening opportunities does raise the question of what is an appropriate measuring rod.   This in turn suggests the
concept of *social distance*, however vaguely and inadequately we can define
such distance.   In defining social distance the analyst must take into
account, among other factors, the level and type of information possessed
by interacting units, the binding force of cultural patterns, the linkage
among social and economic roles, etc.   For example, the analyst thinking
in terms of social distance recognizes that the Puerto Rican who migrates
to New York is, from a social distance standpoint, migrating to the
closest location of significance to him.   As a migrant he is traversing
little, if any, intervening social distance and is aware of few, if any, intervening economic opportunities.[100]   Also, this analyst recognizes that the
heavy volume of communications between Hollywood and New York
reflecting the complementary social roles among certain inhabitants of
these urban complexes covers a social distance much less than the actual
physical or economic distance, and passes over intervening opportunities
which are much fewer than suggested by magnitudes of actual physical or
economic distance.   Moreover, the same analyst interprets the unusually
heavy passenger movement between New York and Florida as movement
over a short social distance because of the complementary role of climate
and high income level.   And, to cite a final example, he regards the relatively light Negro migration to New England cities (compared to Great
Lake cities) as at least partly reflecting much greater social distance
resulting from the intervening opportunities in Washington, Baltimore,
Philadelphia, and New York.

It follows that in the use of the concept of social distance much of the

---

[100] In contrast, a boundary between two conflicting political units, such as that
between Israel and Egypt, may represent an immense social distance so far as migration
is concerned.

analysis that has been fruitfully developed with respect to the concept of physical distance and economic distance remains valid. For example, social distance is subject to change from institutional and cultural development just as physical and economic distance are subject to change from technological advance and transport development. Or we can even develop generalized gravity models based on social distance (or intervening opportunities). In such models the masses involved (i.e., the mass of the originating region, say population, and the mass of the terminating region, say available opportunities or population)[101] may be weighted. Additionally, the exponents of social distance and of the two masses may each be a constant other than unity or even a variable. Thus if we apply such generalization to hypothesis iii alt. when we assume that $x_j = KP_j$, with K a constant, we obtain

$$(13) \qquad M_{ij} = G \, \frac{w_i(P_i)^\alpha \cdot w_j(P_j)^\beta}{d_{ij}^b}$$

where d_{ij} is social distance and, if conceived as intervening opportunities, is equal to $\sum_{h=1}^{j-1} x_h$; where α, β, and b are the exponents to be applied to the masses P_i and P_j and social distance d_{ij}, respectively; where w_i and w_j are the weights to be applied to the adjusted masses; and where G is a constant equal to the product of K and G_3. But, not surprisingly, equation 13 is identical in form to equation 11, the basic equation for gravity models. Further, if we divide both sides of equation 13 by the weighted adjusted mass of the originating region, that is, by $w_i(P_i)^\alpha$, we obtain an equation identical in form with equation 12, the basic equation for potential models.[102]

Although it is tempting to generalize along the somewhat vague lines suggested, and even to expand the concept of social distance to embrace economic distance as a category, at this point we refrain from doing so. Until extensive and comprehensive empirical investigation makes possible a precise definition of social distance, it seems best to continue to view the gravity model as describing interaction over physical or economic distance, and to restrict the intervening opportunities hypothesis to the study of interaction within a sector, category, or selected portion of the whole integral mass. We prefer to maintain the point of view that the gravity model as defined by equation 11 applies to whole, integral masses; that is,

---

[101] Recall that in many situations opportunities may be reasonably assumed to vary proportionally with population.

[102] In the generalization of this paragraph the question of the most appropriate form of the function must also be squarely faced along lines developed in section D.

to migration of *all* income, occupational, and racial classes and not to migration of Puerto Ricans alone; to passenger trips of *all* classes by *all* media over *all* distances and not to airline trips between New York and Miami; to *all* shipment of *all* commodities over *all* distances via *all* types of media and not to the shipment of Maine potatoes alone. To reiterate, the incorporation of all cases in the analysis cancels out the peculiarities, irregularities, and idiosyncracies of interaction within a special sector or category of a population or along a selected channel. Just as the Brownian movements of any given microscopic particle are reduced to insignificance by the process of averaging over a multitude of particles, so are the capricious movements of any unit or small subgroup of units of population or other relevant social mass. On the other hand, many actual problems relate to sizable parts of the integral mass and to meaningful categories and sectors of the whole. Analysis of such problems may fruitfully employ intervening opportunities and related concepts as a flexible tool by which to describe or encompass or explain the special characteristics and patterns of the given category or sector of the mass.[103] This general over-all view of the respective roles of the gravity model and intervening opportunities hypothesis is not inconsistent with empirical studies already conducted.

G. Relative Income Potential Models[104]

Hitherto we have discussed concepts and models which are primarily static. They have been useful for descriptive purposes, although they have frequently been employed for projection with results of some value.[105] None, however, have proceeded beyond comparative static analysis. We now describe a concept and a series of models which are not only useful for comparative static analysis but also for generating and projecting a path of regional growth by key time points in the future.[106]

Suppose we wish to make projections of population by regions for a set of key time points in the future. We recognize that a sizable part of the population of a nation like the United States is economically immobile because of diverse cultural factors. Nonetheless, let us accept the

---

[103] In one sense, then, the intervening opportunities hypothesis may be considered a tool to explain statistically deviations from the expected values of actual observations on classes and categories of the mass (where the expected values may be given by the graph of the relevant equation or regression curve).

[104] This section develops difficult conceptual material and may be bypassed by the reader primarily concerned with immediate application.

[105] In this connection see E. H. Jurkat [30].

[106] In the development of these models the work of G. A. P. Carrothers [12] was particularly valuable.

judgment frequently expressed that the remaining part of the population does possess sufficient mobility such that both the regional pattern of economic opportunities and the force of climatic attraction as it differentially affects the several regions[107] will determine the regional pattern of population through migration of individuals within this latter, mobile part.[108]

The hypothesis may be advanced that a region develops because of three sets of factors. *One*, it develops because it possesses resources to which new plants in existing and new industries are attracted[109] and to which footloose population migrates, or because its market reaches a scale sufficiently large to justify new facilities, or both.[110] *Two*, it develops because the nation, of which it is a part, develops; this category of factors includes a multitude of political, financial, educational, and other institutional forces whose effects are not easily quantified, as well as the general growth of the market and productivity of the national economy. *Three*, it develops because *relative* to other regions its access to the several regional markets of the nation improves or deteriorates.

Given this hypothesis, several approaches may be followed in projection studies. If the magnitude to be projected is regional population, one fruitful approach would seem to involve (1) the use of such methods as comparative cost and industrial complex analysis, interregional input–output, interregional linear programming, and other relevant location and regional techniques discussed in the preceding chapters to encompass the first set of factors and a part of the second set; and (2) the use of a relative

[107] Rigorously speaking, sociological and attractive forces other than climate should be recognized. To do so, however, would complicate the model to be developed without adding to the results it is likely to yield.

[108] We recognize that different natural rates of increase characterize the several regions of a nation. But in the model to be developed we do not need to take such differentials into account. For a region with a high rate of natural increase, the tendency will be that many (if not all) of the new opportunities are filled by this natural increase and relatively few by migrants, *ceteris paribus*. For a region with a low rate of natural increase, the tendency will be that few (if any) of the new opportunities are filled by natural increase and relatively many by migrants, *ceteris paribus*. Migration, in essence, is the adjusting factor. But our model is designed to project changes only in total population based on employment opportunities, regardless of whether these opportunities are filled by new natives entering the labor force or migrants. Hence, the regional rate of natural increase is not a relevant variable for the model. On the other hand, if we construct a potential model to estimate migration alone, it becomes necessary to recognize explicitly the variation in regional rates of natural increase and to adjust the pull of regional employment opportunities accordingly.

[109] This factor should be taken to include relocation of facilities existing in other regions.

[110] Here, as well as later, development is considered to embrace situations of both growth and decline.

income potential model to be developed later to incorporate the third set of factors and the remaining part of the second.

It is not necessary to repeat here how the methods discussed in the preceding chapters can be used to quantify the direct regional impact of the first set of factors. However, it is desirable to comment on materials required for use of these methods in this approach and on the relative importance of this set of factors.

For the pursuit of this approach, it is necessary to have for the nation a total population projection for each key year. (Although the regional distribution of population which we seek to project may be justly claimed to affect the size of the national population, and therefore may tend to invalidate any national population projection which ignores this influence, the identification of the nature of this influence is as yet beyond the ken of social scientists; for practical purposes we must set it aside.) Needed also is an estimate of the required total national output of each industry. As discussed more fully in the following chapter, this estimate might be determined via input–output after a national bill of goods (final demand) associated with the total population is constructed, or by an alternative technique. (Once again for practical purposes we must set aside the regional distribution variable and its influence on total national outputs.)

Next, it is necessary to classify industries. There are certain activities which are resource-oriented—such as aluminum reduction (tied to cheap power), citrus fruit production (tied to favorable land conditions and climate), and each of a host of mining activities (tied to ore deposits). Any national expansion in each of these industries may be easily assigned to specific regions once the appropriate cost and other materials are assembled and analyzed. Such assignment recognizes that each industry's tendency to grow in each region at the same rate as in the nation (the proportionality effect) is modified by the relevant regional pattern of cost differentials (the differential effect).[111] Thus part of the second (as the nation grows) set of factors is involved in this analysis. In addition, there are many other economic activities for which the most efficient locations are determined by features specific to certain regions. Expansion in textile activities can be largely assigned to cheap-labor cost regions, the shifting pattern of labor cost differentials being duly considered. Because of major economies of urbanization, localization, and scale, a number of national administrative and financial-type functions may be assigned to specific metropolises. Expansion of other activities confronting major scale economies—such as farm equipment manufacture and synthetic rubber manufacture—are easily assigned to specific regions. Still more,

---

[111] We are indebted to Edgar S. Dunn for the suggestion of the terms "proportionality effect" and "differential effect."

other situations arise in which location of new plants may be projected with relative ease—such as automobile assembly operations for a region whose market at the beginning of the forecast period has reached a size which makes possible full economies of scale.

On the basis of analysis of such activities and others which are primarily cost-sensitive, that is, which seek the location that will involve least cost for serving a given or anticipated market, an investigator can estimate by region change in employment opportunities.[112] To the change in employment opportunities in these activities, which we shall henceforth designate *cost-sensitive* activities, there must be added an induced change in employment opportunities in certain local service and other market-oriented types of activity. This latter change reflects the round-by-round change in demand for diverse local products and services resulting from the change in input requirements of, and total income generated by, the cost-sensitive activities. The appropriate procedures for taking account of this local "multiplier" effect have been discussed at length in previous chapters.

[112] We speak of "change in" employment opportunities rather than new employment opportunities since it may develop that one or more regions are expected to suffer a decline in total employment opportunities afforded by these activities. Rigorously speaking, the change in employment opportunities thus obtained for any region is a first approximation, particularly for cost-sensitive activities which produce efficiently at several locations. For at each location the volume of output of such a cost-sensitive activity is largely geared to the size of that geographic market best served by that location. But the ultimate size of the market, which size is derived as one of the last steps in the model to be developed, depends in large measure on the first approximation of change in employment opportunities in cost-sensitive activities.

This circular dilemma, as it occurs in this model and either implicitly or explicitly in every operational model thus far developed in the social sciences, reflects general interdependence within a social, economic, or interregional system. Until a truly general equilibrium operational model can be developed, the investigator must be satisfied with first approximations as results and attempt by iteration to obtain better approximations if iteration is possible. Unfortunately, in the model to be developed, the investigator is limited in the use of iteration. (See footnote 129.) In other models, however, he can compare (1) the results (which a model obtains) on the regional market patterns of diverse products of cost-sensitive activities and (2) the crude regional patterns initially hypothesized. If he finds significant differences he can rerun the model with an initially hypothesized set of regional market patterns more closely resembling the derived set. In certain cases such iteration may yield significant changes in final projections. For example, in the first run of the model the size of a region's steel market may be underestimated, such that an integrated steelworks within the region is not justified. But on the basis of derived results on market size the region's steel market may be estimated to be sufficiently large to justify an integrated works. On a rerun of the model this latter possibility would be incorporated and could lead to significant differences in the final population projections. For further discussion of this iterative procedure, see section B.2.c of Chapter 12.

Also at this point the investigator must explicitly introduce the population which is footloose and whose regional pattern is determined by climatic factors.[113]   For this population as well as the employees and families of cost-sensitive activities, a local "multiplier" effect must be introduced.

On the assumption that this analysis can be performed on a rather complete and systematic basis, we would obtain by region change in population based on cost-sensitive activities and on the climatic attraction force.   In practice, however, such a thorough analysis is not likely to be realized; analysis is likely to be limited to those activities for which locational cost studies have already been conducted, or appropriate data exist, or both.[114]   Change in population based on those activities not encompassed may be accounted for either by an appropriate upward adjustment of change in employment opportunities in cost-sensitive activities for which analysis has been conducted, or, more desirably, by the procedure to be described later whereby we obtain estimates by region of change in employment opportunities (and thus associated population) in non-cost-sensitive activities.[115]

This analysis employing the techniques of previous chapters accounts for only one of two parts of each region's population which is to be projected.   As far as the analysis can, it encompasses for the cost-sensitive activities both the proportionality (as the nation grows) effect and the differential (cost-determined) effect.   We now develop a model to explain the second part of each region's population.   This part encompasses the population associated with (1) the non-cost-sensitive activities; (2) all cost-sensitive activities for which firm location analysis of the type

[113] Such footloose population includes retired and other individuals whose locations are independent of economic opportunity. It is assumed that demographic and sociological study will provide "best" estimates of net migration motivated by climatic considerations, although it is recognized that such estimates can only be crude because of the subjective nature of the forces at play.

[114] The lack of objective cost data is an obstacle to analysis, particularly of industries that are climate-oriented and for which other major cost differentials do not exist. For these industries the psychic cost savings or income realized is as yet beyond quantitative estimation.

[115] Although objective study has not been made of appropriate procedure at this point, the hypothesis may reasonably be advanced that the regional pattern of those cost-sensitive activities which cannot be locationally analyzed for reasons cited is more likely to conform with the regional pattern of non-cost-sensitive activities than with the regional pattern of cost-sensitive activities for which locational analysis is possible. The basis for such a hypothesis is found partly in the fact that the market factor which, as will be developed below, plays a significant role in the location of non-cost-sensitive industries is a location factor which is generally of significance to most cost-sensitive activities as well.

developed in the preceding chapters is not possible; and (3) that part of service and other market-oriented types of activity linked to the activities covered in 1 and 2. All these activities we shall henceforth designate "market-access-sensitive" activities or more briefly "market-access" activities.

The model to be developed consists of two elements or of two terms. The first expresses the proportionality (as the nation grows) effect on the market-access-sensitive activities. It involves for each region (1) multiplying the base year employment of any given activity not a local service and market-oriented type of activity by unity plus that activity's national rate of growth; (2) multiplying that fraction of base year employment of any local service or market-oriented type of activity which has been estimated not to be linked with cost-sensitive activities by unity plus that local activity's national rate of growth; and (3) summing over all activities to yield a total for each region.[116] This first term is

$$a \sum_{v=1}^{m} \frac{{}^{t+\theta}_{\text{US}}E_v}{{}^{t}_{\text{US}}E_v} ({}^{t}_{i}E_v)$$

where ${}^{t}_{\text{US}}E_v$ is United States employment in "market-access-sensitive" activity v ($v = 1, \cdots, m$) at base year t; ${}^{t+\theta}_{\text{US}}E_v$ is projected United States employment in activity v at year $t + \theta$, θ being the length of the forecast period and the ratio ${}^{t+\theta}_{\text{US}}E_v/{}^{t}_{\text{US}}E_v$ being equal to unity plus the national rate of growth of activity v; ${}^{t}_{i}E_v$ is employment in activity v in region i at base year t, or, if v is a local service or market-oriented type of activity, is employment not linked with cost-sensitive activities; and a is a constant which converts numbers of employees into numbers of population.[117]

---

[116] A simpler, but less satisfactory, alternative to account for the proportionality effect is to multiply the population of region i in year t that is based on market-access activities by unity plus the projected rate of growth of that same segment of national population. This procedure ignores the industrial composition variable among regions.

[117] A more precise determination of the proportionality effect formulates the first term as follows:

$$\sum_{v=1}^{m} a_{iv} \frac{{}^{t+\theta}_{\text{US}}E_v}{{}^{t}_{\text{US}}E_v} ({}^{t}_{i}E_v)$$

The coefficient a which is an average conversion factor over all industries and regions is in effect replaced by a series of a_{iv}. This step recognizes that differences among industries in the proportion of male to female workers, in average productivity per worker, in wages and salaries per worker, etc., lead to differences in the population supported per worker. Thus for any region i typically a_{ij} is not equal to a_{ik} ($j, k = 1, \cdots, m, j \neq k$). This step also recognizes that differences among regions in urbanization, age, sex, and racial composition, and diverse cultural factors, etc., lead to differences in

The second element or term of the model refers to a region's change in interregional position, that is, to an improvement or deterioration in a region's access to the markets of the several regions of a system. To motivate the argument, take a region, say New England. Suppose New York's income generated by the cost-sensitive activities already treated is expected to increase at a rate greater than the comparable segment of national income, that the corresponding part of California's income is expected to increase at a rate smaller than the nation's, and that the comparable income of all other regions is expected to increase at the same rate as that of the nation. *Ceteris paribus*, it can be reasoned that New England's interregional position will improve, since its access to new income (and thereby markets in general) is greater than its access to income in the base year. In contrast, if the same segment of New York's income is expected to increase at a rate slower than the nation, and that of California at a rate faster than the nation, *ceteris paribus* New England's interregional position will deteriorate, since its access to new income will be less than its access to base year income.

This reasoning implies that the "growth-inducing" effect on a given region of any dollar of new income varies inversely with distance. A dollar of new income in California can be expected to have less impact on New England than a dollar of new income in New York. Such an effect varying inversely with distance suggests the applicability of a potential model, at least until other forms of functions depicting the attenuating influence of distance are found to be equally or more desirable. Furthermore, since empirical studies have not demonstrated that the use of weights other than unity, or exponents other than unity, or both yield superior results, it seems most desirable to work with Stewart's simple, unweighted potential model.

At first thought, the concept of income potential seems relevant. The concept aims to catch the effect of income as it is spatially distributed. But on further thought, several major modifications are necessary. In its present form the income potential concept as defined by equation 10 uses total income as the relevant measure of mass. But we are interested in only a fraction of total income, namely, that income generated by cost-sensitive activities and the parts of local service and market-oriented

---

the population supported per worker in the same industry. Thus for any industry j typically

$$a_{ij} \neq a_{hj} \qquad (h, i = 1, \cdots, n; \, \text{h} \neq i)$$

Such refinement, however, may lead to some consistency difficulties since national projections are based on or infer cruder conversion factors. The implicit or explicit use of these cruder conversion factors ignores regional differences; that is, it assumes that $a_{ij} = a_{hj}$ $(h, i = 1, \cdots, n)$.

operations tied to these activities and to climate-oriented population. However, this modification of the concept is best made after we carry through a second major modification.

Generally speaking, income potential, as a measure, portrays a completely static picture. But in the model we wish to develop we are interested in how the regional pattern of income changes (for the moment, of total income changes) comes to influence total employment in market-access activities. Thus we wish to identify the effects of income *changes* as these *changes* are spatially distributed. To do this necessitates a comparison of the income potential of a region in a base year with that region's income potential at the end of the relevant time period, typically the year of projection. One method of comparison involves forming the ratio

$$\frac{^{t+\theta}_{i}V}{^{t}_{i}V}$$

where $^{t}_{i}V$ is income potential of region i at base year t and $^{t+\theta}_{i}V$ is income potential of region i at the end of the relevant time period.[118]

This simple ratio requires modification. If the income of the United States were to remain constant during a period, and if people and income were to shift to California during that period, then for a region like New England $^{t+\theta}_{i}V$ would be less than $^{t}_{i}V$ and the ratio would be less than unity.[119] And for a region like the state of Arizona, the ratio would be greater than unity. Such values for the ratio could reflect the influence we are attempting to measure. But if the income of the United States were to increase by 20 per cent during a period, and if only 5 per cent of its population and income were to shift to California, then for a region like New England $^{t+\theta}_{i}V$ would exceed $^{t}_{i}V$. This result would be obtained since the numerator of each of the terms which are added to yield $^{t+\theta}_{i}V$,

$$^{t+\theta}_{i}V = \frac{^{t+\theta}Y_1}{d_{i1}} + \frac{^{t+\theta}Y_2}{d_{i2}} + \cdots + \frac{^{t+\theta}Y_n}{d_{in}}$$

would tend to exceed the corresponding numerator in the terms which are added to yield $^{t}_{i}V$:

$$^{t}_{i}V = \frac{^{t}Y_1}{d_{i1}} + \frac{^{t}Y_2}{d_{i2}} + \cdots + \frac{^{t}Y_n}{d_{in}}$$

for the general rate of growth of 20 per cent would for most regions outweigh any outward shift. Thus we would obtain for New England a ratio

---

[118] A second meaningful method of comparison involves the computation of differences, that is, $^{t+\theta}_{i}V - ^{t}_{i}V$. For fuller discussion of this issue see G. A. P. Carrothers [12].

[119] Such a ratio would always be positive.

greater than unity. Such a ratio would imply an improvement in New England's relative interregional position when in fact its interregional position would have deteriorated.

It is clear that we must eliminate from this ratio of income potentials the general effects of national growth or decline of income. [The proportionality (as the nation grows) effects are already roughly encompassed elsewhere.] Such is easily done by multiplying the denominator of the ratio by ρ, which is defined as United States income in year $t + \theta$ divided by United States income in year t. The relevant ratio now becomes

$$\frac{{}^{t+\theta}_{\quad i}V}{\rho \, {}^{t}_{i}V}$$

This term has been designated relative income potential.[120]

Viewed from another standpoint, we have attempted to separate from one another two sets of forces acting on the market-access activities in each region. One set covers the forces that stimulate these activities in a region to grow as the nation grows. These are embraced by the first term of our model. The second set covers the forces that generate improvement or deterioration in a region's interregional position, such position being relative. If all regions were to grow at the same rate as the nation's, there would be neither improvement nor deterioration for any region. By our previous reasoning we would want the ratio of income potentials (${}^{t+\theta}_{\quad i}V$ and ${}^{t}_{i}V$) to be unity. But this will not be so unless the denominator of the ratio has been multiplied by the ρ factor.

Another major modification in the income potential concept which our framework requires is the substitution of a more relevant mass for the total income mass. This relevant mass is the sum of (1) the independent income of climate-oriented population and (2) that income generated by cost-sensitive activities and the part of local service and market-oriented operations tied to these activities and to climate-oriented population. We designate the sum of these incomes for region i in year t as ${}^{t}\overline{Y}_i$. We also designate the income potential measure for region i based on such income of regions as ${}^{t}_{i}\overline{V}$:

$$\overline{V}_i = \frac{{}^{t}\overline{Y}_1}{d_{i1}} + \frac{{}^{t}\overline{Y}_2}{d_{i2}} + \cdots + \frac{{}^{t}\overline{Y}_n}{d_{in}}$$

and unity plus the rate of growth of this income within the nation over the time period θ as $\bar{\rho}$. The relative income potential expression becomes

$$\frac{{}^{t+\theta}_{\quad i}\overline{V}}{\bar{\rho} \, {}^{t}_{i}\overline{V}}$$

[120] See W. Isard and G. Freutel [28], p. 437; and G. A. P. Carrothers [12, 14].

At this point a first model suggests itself.[121]   We consider the term

$$a \sum_{v=1}^{m} \frac{{}_{US}^{t+\theta}E_v}{{}_{US}^{t}E_v} ({}_{i}^{t}E_v)$$

which measures expected growth of that population of region i based on market-access activities *if employment in each of i's market-access activities grows at that activity's national rate.*   For convenience, we let

$$_{i}Z = \sum_{v=1}^{m} \frac{{}_{US}^{t+\theta}E_v}{{}_{US}^{t}E_v} ({}_{i}^{t}E_v)$$

The term is then simply stated as $a({}_{i}Z)$.   We then multiply this term by the relative income potential raised to the ϵ power to obtain an equation to estimate fully the population of region i to be accounted for by employment in market-access activities.   Representing this population by the symbol ${}^{t+\theta}_{i}P$, the equation is

(14) $$_{i}^{t+\theta}P = a({}_{i}Z)\left(\frac{{}_{i}^{t+\theta}V}{\bar{\rho}\,{}_{i}^{t}V}\right)^{\epsilon}$$

Equation 14 essentially depicts the proportionality (as the nation grows) effect, namely $a({}_{i}Z)$ as modified by a factor expressing change in interregional position.   The coefficient a essentially converts numbers of employees into numbers of population.   The exponent ϵ in effect determines the importance of the factor of change in interregional position relative to the factor of proportionality.   The greater this relative importance, the larger the value for ϵ.[122]

[121] The use of $\bar{Y}_j$ not only is more relevant as a mass but also avoids the difficulty of determining for the year of projection ($t + \theta$) the value to be assigned to mass when Y_j (all region j's income) is taken to represent mass of j ($j = 1, \cdots, n$). W. Isard and G. Freutel [28], pp. 436–438, found it necessary to determine ${}^{t+\theta}Y_j$ (and thus ${}^{t+\theta}_{i}V$) from a set of simultaneous equations. With the use of $\bar{Y}_j$ as the measure of mass of region j, we first determine ${}^{t+\theta}\bar{Y}_j$ on the basis of locational and other analyses already discussed. This value is then used directly in the model of equation 15. The solving of a set of simultaneous equations is eliminated. An internal inconsistency is also avoided by the use of $\bar{Y}_j$ as a measure of mass. In models using total income as a measure of mass, there is a tendency for population to continue to accumulate (that is, increasingly concentrate) in regions which initially experience improvement in interregional position. Were total income used as a measure of mass in equation 15, this tendency would be present, at least to some degree, in the framework being developed. (This framework will generate a series of population projections by region, that is, a path of growth for each region by key years in the future.)

[122] For a model designed to project interregional migration the right-hand side of equation 14 might also be multiplied by a second factor. This factor would be different from region to region and would be related to the amount by which the natural rate of growth for the nation algebraically exceeds that for a given region.

Although equation 14 represents a simple and yet reasonable model,[123] we choose to develop in detail a somewhat simpler model which is just as reasonable.   In this second model we view the proportionality effect and the factor of interregional position as additive and not multiplicative. We therefore obtain a model of two terms, as represented by equation 15:

$$(15) \qquad {}^{t+\theta}_{i}P = a(_iZ) + b\left(\frac{{}^{t+\theta}_{i}\overline{V}}{\bar{\rho}\,{}^{t}_{i}\overline{V}} - 1\right) {}_{US}{}^{t}P$$

where a and b are positive constants and where ${}_{US}{}^{t}P$ is the total population of the United States accounted for by market-access activities in year t. This model presents the factor of interregional position in a modified way. First, since the two terms are additive, each as a whole must be expressed in the same units, namely population numbers.   In the first term the coefficient a, as in equation 14, converts numbers of employees into population numbers.   In the second term the positive coefficient b and the relative income potential ${}^{t+\theta}_{i}\overline{V}/\bar{\rho}\,{}^{t}_{i}\overline{V}$ are both pure numbers; hence we must have in the second term a factor which is expressed in population numbers.   We have chosen ${}_{US}{}^{t}P$ to be that factor.[124]   At the same time we must also subtract unity from ${}^{t+\theta}_{i}\overline{V}/\bar{\rho}\,{}^{t}_{i}\overline{V}$.   This last step is required in order to state correctly the additive nature of the two effects.   For when

---

[123] When expressed in logarithms, equation 14 becomes

$$\log {}^{t+\theta}_{i}P = \log a + \log {}_{i}Z + \epsilon \log \left(\frac{{}^{t+\theta}_{i}\overline{V}}{\bar{\rho}\,{}^{t}_{i}\overline{V}}\right)$$

Since a is constant, and since $_iZ$, ${}^{t+\theta}_{i}\overline{V}$, $\bar{\rho}$, and ${}^{t}_{i}\overline{V}$ can each be determined from data already collected or developed, we need only determine an appropriate value for ϵ to predict ${}^{t+\theta}_{i}P$.   Such a value for ϵ can be derived from data for a relevant time period in the past.   For such a time period we could plot for each region a point representing the region's values for $\log {}^{t+\theta}_{i}P - \log a - \log {}_iZ$ and $\log ({}^{t+\theta}_{i}\overline{V}/\bar{\rho}\,{}^{t}_{i}\overline{V})$.   By regression procedure we could estimate a best value of ϵ, all regions being considered (ϵ would be the slope of the regression line of best fit).

Alternatively, for any given region i we could select a *series* of relevant time periods in the past.   For each time period we could plot a point representing the values for $\log {}^{t+\theta}_{i}P - \log a - \log {}_iZ$ and $\log ({}^{t+\theta}_{i}\overline{V}/\bar{\rho}\,{}^{t}_{i}\overline{V})$.   From the graph for region i we could determine a best value for $_i\epsilon$, either by regression procedure or in another judicious manner.   (Or the two values for each time period could be expressed in terms of a ratio; when the ratio is plotted chronologically for successive time periods, historical trend analysis could yield a value for $_i\epsilon$.)   This best value for $_i\epsilon$ would be substituted in equation 14 for ϵ in order to project region i's population in a future key year.   By this procedure we would obtain different values of $_i\epsilon$ for the several regions.   These different values would in part reflect the different sets of characteristics and influences impinging on the several regions which in turn cause the factor of interregional position to vary in significance from region to region.   Also compare with the later discussion concerning the determination of the value of b and $_ib$.

[124] The reader is referred to the later discussion on the rationale for the choice of this factor.   As will be indicated, any of a number of other factors can suffice.

all regions of the nation grow at the same rate that the nation does, the first term of equation 15 accounts fully for the entire growth of each region which is based on market-access activities.[125]   In such a case the value of the second term should be zero.   But from discussion in the preceding paragraphs we know that relative income potential $^{t+\theta}_i\overline{V}/\bar{\rho}\,^t_i\overline{V}$ will be unity when all regions grow at the same rate as the nation's.   Therefore we subtract unity from the relative income potential in order that the entire second term be zero in this standard theoretical case.   The resulting expression is $[(^{t+\theta}_i\overline{V}/\bar{\rho}\,^t_i\overline{V}) - 1]$, which we designate *modified* relative income potential.

Before discussing the coefficient b, the workings of the model may be examined.   When region i's *modified* relative income potential is negative, it means that the relative income potential $^{t+\theta}_i\overline{V}/\bar{\rho}\,^t_i\overline{V}$ must be less than unity.   When this relative income potential is less than unity, we know from previous discussion that region i's interregional position has deteriorated; region i's access to the *new* income generated by cost-sensitive activities and the parts of local service and market-oriented operations tied to these activities and to climate-oriented population is *less* than its access to the *base year* income generated by these activities.   Therefore, we cannot expect the population of region i which is based on market-access activities to grow at the same rate as the corresponding population segment of the nation.   But the first term of equation 15 does have this population of region i growing at the same rate.   This first term therefore overstates growth, and to it must be added a term which is negative.   This is exactly what takes place.   When modified relative income potential is negative, the second term of equation 15 is also negative, since by definition both b and $_{US}^t P$ are positive.

When region i's modified relative income potential is positive, it means that the relative income potential $^{t+\theta}_i\overline{V}/\bar{\rho}\,^t_i\overline{V}$ must be greater than unity. When this relative income potential is greater than unity, we know from previous discussion that region i's interregional position has improved; region i's access to the *new* income generated by cost-sensitive activities and the parts of local service and market-oriented operations tied to these activities and to climate-oriented population is *greater* than its access to the *base year* income generated by these activities.   Therefore we expect the population of region i which is based on market-access activities to grow at a greater rate than the corresponding population segment of the nation.   But the first term of equation 15 has this population of region

---

[125] Since regions are taken to differ in industrial composition, regions cannot grow at the same rate that the nation does unless each industrial activity tends to grow at the same national rate (except in the extreme case where in every region there are compensating effects that exactly balance each other).

i growing at only the same rate. The first term therefore underestimates growth, and to it must be added a positive term to effect the necessary adjustment. This is exactly what takes place. When modified relative income potential is positive, the second term of equation 15 is also positive.

From an examination of the workings of the model, it is evident that for the population for whose explanation it is designed the model does yield a pattern of regional growth relative to the nation's that is consistent in *direction* with our initial hypothesis. This hypothesis concerned the interplay of three sets of basic factors. The question now arises whether or not the model can do better than furnish the right direction of regional change relative to the nation's. Can it depict with approximate accuracy the absolute *magnitude* of growth of the relevent segment of regional population?

On the assumption that the potential concept as employed is valid, this question revolves around the determination of an appropriate value for the coefficient *b* if, indeed, a significant value for this coefficient can be obtained. One procedure which suggests itself is to estimate *b* on the basis of past relationships. We construct a graph. Along the vertical axis we measure $^{t+\theta}_{\ i}P - a(_iZ)$, namely, the discrepancy between actual size of the segment of population based on market-access activities and the size expected if region *i*'s market-access activities had grown at the national rate. Along the horizontal axis we measure the product of modified relative income potential and $_{US}^{t}P$. For each region we plot a point representing its respective values for these two variables. If the model is of significance, we expect the point to represent either positive values for both variables or negative values for both variables; ideally we do not expect any points to represent a positive value for one variable and a negative value for the other. By regression procedure, or other appropriate method, a straight line could be fitted to these data to determine a best value for *b* applicable for the projection of all regions.[126] Since the first term of equation 15 implies a weight of unity for the proportionality (as the nation grows) effect, the value of *b* may be viewed as the relative weight of the factor of interregional position.

[126] Where the data suggest a curvilinear relation, such a curve could be derived by regression or other technique. Then the value of *b* applicable to the several regions would be different. Therefore, the appropriate procedure for determining for any region its increase or decrease in population based on market-access activities due to change in interregional position would be to read off from the curve the population, as measured along the vertical axis, corresponding to the region's value for

$$\left(\frac{^{t+\theta}_{\ i}\overline{V}}{\bar{p} \ _i^t\overline{V}} - 1 \right) _{US}^{t}P$$

as measured along the horizontal axis.

An alternative procedure is to determine a specific $_ib$ for each region wherewith to replace the general b coefficient applicable to all regions. To do this we construct a figure. Along the horizontal axis we indicate at equal intervals successive time periods, say 1935–1940, 1940–1945, 1945–1950, etc. Along the vertical axis we measure the ratio

$$\left[\frac{{}^{t+\theta}_{i}P - a({}_iZ)}{\left(\dfrac{{}^{t+\theta}_{i}\overline{V}}{\bar{\rho}\,{}^t_i\overline{V}} - 1\right){}_{US}{}^tP} \right]$$

which by equation 15 is equivalent to b. For the given region i we compute this ratio, namely $_ib$, for each of the past time periods considered relevant and plot this value on the figure. By inspection or other means we determine a trend line through the points, if such a line is meaningful, and derive by extrapolation or on the basis of reasonable judgment a future value for this ratio, that is, a value for $_ib$ *for the period in the future for which a projection is to be made.*[127] Likewise, for every other region, we construct a figure and determine an appropriate $_ib$ for projection purposes.[128] By this procedure each $_ib$ derived for projection purposes tends to reflect the characteristics including position, size, resources, etc., which cause the factor of interregional position to be of different significance for the several regions.

Once an appropriate b or set of $_ib$'s is obtained, the model is ready for operation. For a key year of the future, say 1965 (base year 1960), it yields an estimate for each region of that population based on market-access activities. This population by region is to be added to the foot-loose population by region which is climate-oriented (initially given) and to the population (already estimated) which is based on cost-sensitive activities and that part of local service and market-oriented operations tied to these activities and climate-oriented population. This addition yields 1965 total population by region, as

[127] As G. A. P. Carrothers [14] has observed, for particular observations (time periods) this ratio may assume extreme values. Its value will be infinite when the modified relative income potential term is zero and the numerator is nonzero. Its value will be indeterminate in the "ideal" case when both numerator and denominator are zero. Its value will be zero when the numerator is zero and the denominator nonzero. Of course, note again that such a plot of the data may yield a meaningless value for $_ib$, such as a negative one.

[128] The independent determination for each region of $_ib$ raises the major question of consistency of regional and national projections, a question to be discussed later. Also involved is the difficulty of obtaining data on the segment of region i's population that is based on market-access activities, especially for the earlier years covered by a study.

accounted for by the full interplay of the three sets of basic factors initially hypothesized.[129]

Beyond this, it is possible to generate a series of population projections by region, that is, a path of growth for each region by key years in the future. From the projections of diverse types of industrial and service activity as well as population by region obtained from the model for 1965, we are able to estimate 1965 markets for various types of commodities. From this data plus 1970 data on *national* population[130] and *national* output by industry determined via input-output or other pertinent procedure, we can once again perform location analysis to determine 1970 regional projections of, *first*, that employment based on cost-sensitive activities and, *second*, that local employment tied to these activities and climate-oriented population. From these employment projections and the data already noted, estimates of that part of regional income defined previously by $\overline{Y}_i$ are made. These estimates are introduced into the second term of equation 15. Concomitantly relevant industry growth rates for the nation and 1965 employment levels (obtained from the first period projection) are introduced in the first term of equation 15. The model is operated to produce 1970 estimates by region of that population based on market-access activities. When such estimates are added to the climate-oriented population and the population associated with cost-sensitive activities, etc., we obtain 1970 total population by region.

In similar manner we may generate 1975 populations by region based on 1970 projections and the required national data; 1980 based on 1975; and so forth. Thus, a step-by-step set of regional projections, that is, a discrete path of growth for each region within the interregional system is yielded by the framework developed previously.

It is to be emphasized that we have sketched only one possible way to develop a simplified framework of general interdependence which when supplemented with appropriate national data yields regional growth patterns. We must emphasize again that there are a number of weak elements within this framework. Extensive empirical testing must be

[129] Note that the procedures for determining b and $_ib$ (and also ϵ and $_i\epsilon$) preclude reruns of the model in order to allow the initial determination of the regional pattern of cost-sensitive activities to be more consistent with results flowing from the operation of the model. Although for a future projection year we can modify the results of the model of equation 15 by a series of reruns aimed at greater consistency, we cannot operationally do likewise for past years and at the same time determine appropriate values for b and $_ib$. We cannot do so because we cannot for past years reverse the rerun process and unravel the associated interdependencies. Thus we cannot logically use both b's derived from historical and current data and the rerun process.

[130] Including estimates of footloose population whose migration will be induced by the climatic factor.

performed not only to evaluate the different ways in which the coefficients b or $_ib$ might be estimated,[131] but also to appraise the different types of potential or related concepts that can be evolved to accommodate the interplay of the factors supposedly encompassed by equation 15. Until such testing is performed, it is best to confine the remaining discussion to certain general issues which arise.

One general issue concerns the use of an appropriate factor against which to multiply modified relative income potential to yield population numbers accounted for by change in interregional position. In equation 15 we use $_{US}^{t}P$, namely the United States population in year t, which is based on market-access activities. We could have just as conveniently used $_{US}^{t}P$, the total population of the United States. Since $_{US}^{t}P = k_{US}^{t}P$, where k is a constant for the year t, the use of the factor $_{US}^{t}P$ requires that a coefficient c be substituted for the coefficient b in equation 15. But c would have to be estimated anew, since the relevant set of historical data for determining c would not be a k multiple of the data for determining b; however, c would be employed in an identical manner as b.[132]

Further consideration of this issue, however, suggests that the population factor to be used in the second term of equation 15 be a factor which varies from region to region. In fact, this factor may be that very population of each region itself which is based on market-access activities, namely $_i^tP$. The use of such a factor has one important advantage. It recognizes that, when a fixed value of b is applied to all regions, the same value of modified relative income potential for two regions of different size will tend to account for different numbers of population.[133] This

[131] As already indicated, $_ib$ is essentially a relative weight. It is applied to a potential measure in order to depict the importance of the factors represented by this potential measure relative to the importance of the factors represented in the proportionality effect. (The weight of the latter is taken as unity.) Hence, the problem of determining an appropriate $_ib$, that is, a relative weight for the potential factor, is not unlike the problem faced by Dunn in determining by how much to weight a 1 per cent advantage in market potential relative to a 1 per cent advantage in total transport cost. Nor is it unlike the problem in administrative area analysis of determining for a particular function the weight to apply to a 1 per cent advantage in community participation potential relative to a 1 per cent saving in total service cost. Such parallels suggest that it may be possible to develop somewhat analogous techniques for the estimation of relative weights in the diverse situations in which this problem arises.

[132] Or instead of $_{US}^{t}P$ we could use other population factors, even one of a previous period such as $_{US}^{t-\theta}P$. However, we would not be able to use in this specific (non-lagged) model a population factor of a future period since before the model is operated the magnitude of such a factor is not known.

[133] Introducing the regional population factor $_i^tP$ can be viewed as converting the numerator of the relative income potential expression into Stewart's energy concept since it involves multiplying one mass, namely $^{t+\theta}\bar{Y}_i (= K^{t+\theta}_iP$, K being a constant)

result seems logical. In contrast, for each region when the factor $_{US}^{\prime}P$ is used in equation 15, the same value of modified relative income potential will tend to account for the same numbers of population for each of two different size regions, a result which seems inferior.

On the other hand, if for each region an individual $_ib$ is computed à la historical trend procedure, there no longer exists a logical basis for substituting for the constant factor $_{US}^{\prime}P$ in equation 15 a regional population factor $_i^{\prime}P$ which varies from region to region. This point follows since, as indicated, the coefficient $_ib$ reflects the effects of size as well as other characteristics of region i.

Appraisal of the several alternatives discussed must cover the test of consistency. From this standpoint models based on the use of the same constant b factor for all regions are likely to be superior. They are likely to yield regional projections more consistent with national projections [134] than models based on the use of individual $_ib$ factors varying from region to region. This observation follows from the fact that in a regression estimation of b some averaging of regional factors occurs, whereas no such averaging is implicit in the derivation of an independent historical trend projection for each region.

Another issue revolves around the overlapping of the time period during which a set of generating or determining factors interplay and the time period during which the induced effects are realized. Thus far we have assumed that employment opportunities which come to exist during a given time period produce their effects on population growth wholly within the same period. More specifically, employment opportunities during the period 1960–1965 wholly determine population growth, 1960–1965; they do not affect whatsoever population growth during 1965–1970 or during later time periods, nor is population growth 1960–1965 affected at all by employment opportunities in 1955–1960, in earlier periods, or in periods after 1965.[135]

A more reasonable model than the one represented by equation 15 may

by a second mass $_i^{\prime}P$. Aside from the fact that the masses refer to two different points of time, it is to be recognized that such a step leaves the denominator of the relative income potential expression in potential form. Thus the model must still be viewed as a potential model.

[134] The reader is reminded again that national projections of the current type are not necessarily the most efficient ones. In time it may develop that regional projections, particularly when they encompass interregional effects, will provide a basis for more reliable national projections, in which case national projections could not serve here as a consistency benchmark.

[135] Prospects of growth in employment opportunities in future years can clearly influence current population via migration, as testified by historical material on the development of the United States railroad system and on the growth of California.

be constructed. For example, an analyst may wish to project regional population growth over the period 1960–1965 partly on the basis of regional employment opportunities (perhaps differentiated by industrial category) over the period 1955–1960. Or he may wish to project such growth partly on the basis of regional employment opportunities over the periods 1950–1955, 1955–1960, and 1960–1965, where different weights are assigned to the opportunities in each of these periods. He may even add as a relevant factor expected employment opportunities in certain industrial categories in the future period 1965–1970. Clearly, lag and lead models of this type and others which are more continuous and more complete (although less operational) become too unwieldy to sketch here.[136] But such models, in themselves or as an integral part of a framework which produces regional growth paths, must be duly considered in the selection of the most desirable approach for a regional study, although at the present time limited data and little experience in empirical implementation severely circumscribe the range of choice.

A final major issue relates to the possibility of disaggregating the relative income potential term. It may be contended that the term as defined is not in its most significant form and that more meaningful or accurate results can be obtained if this term is replaced by a series of relative potential terms. Each such term would be designed to express the impact of changing interregional position on a particular category of market-access activities and would be defined accordingly.[137] For example, it is clear that the relative potential term for various market-access activities which primarily produce goods and services for industrial consumers (such as the host of metallic and nonmetallic fabricators) should be different from the relative potential term for other market-access activities which primarily cater to the demands of households (such as jewelry, pharmaceutical, and toy manufacture). For the latter the use of income by region as the relevant mass is appropriate. For the former the use of some such measure as manufacturing output, employment, or value added by region

---

[136] The reader is referred to G. A. P. Carrothers [12] for the statement and testing of certain lagged models pertaining to migration. It is to be noted that in certain instances lagged models may make possible the use of actual data instead of estimated data. For example, if an investigator projects population in 1960 on the basis of employment opportunities during the period 1950–1955, and earlier periods, he may substitute actual 1955 data for estimates of $\bar{Y}_i$ based on locational investigations of cost-sensitive activities, on demographic studies of climate-oriented population, and on local multiplier analysis of effects induced by these activities and population; or, if he considers it still more desirable, he may substitute *actual* 1955 data on total income for estimates of Y_i.

[137] Thus, "across-the-board" adjustments for the impact of changing interregional position on all market-access activities are replaced by a set of adjustments, each adjustment being more suitable to the particular category of activities to which it is applied.

is much more appropriate than income by region. If just these two categories of market-access activities are recognized, the second term of equation 15 may be replaced by the following two terms:

$$f\left(\frac{{}^{t+\theta}_{i}\overline{V}}{\bar{\rho}\,{}^{t}_{i}\overline{V}} - 1\right){}_{\text{US}}{}^{t}P + g\left(\frac{{}^{t+\theta}_{i}\overline{\mathcal{V}}}{\ddot{\rho}\,{}^{t}_{i}\overline{\mathcal{V}}} - 1\right){}_{\text{US}}{}^{t}P$$

The first of these two terms is identical with the original second term of equation 15, except that it is multiplied by f rather than b, where f is a positive constant smaller than b. The constant f is less than b since with the term which f multiplies we are explaining the impact of changing interregional position on only a portion of market-access activities, namely that portion sensitive to income as a measure of mass.

The second of the two new terms explains the impact of changing interregional position on that portion of market-access activities sensitive to industrial demand as a measure of mass. In this term the symbol $\overline{\mathcal{V}}$ indicates a potential measure based on, say, manufacturing output as a mass, that is,

$$_{i}\overline{\mathcal{V}} = \frac{{}^{t}\overline{O}_1}{d_{i1}} + \frac{{}^{t}\overline{O}_2}{d_{i2}} + \cdots + \frac{{}^{t}\overline{O}_n}{d_{in}}$$

Here ${}^{t}\overline{O}_j$ represents for region j ($j = 1, \cdots, n$) in time t manufacturing output of cost-sensitive activities and that part of local market-oriented manufacturing tied to these activities and to climate-oriented population. The constant g of the second of the new terms is to be taken as positive; and $\ddot{\rho}$ represents unity plus the national rate of growth of the manufacturing output represented by $\overline{O}$.

In like manner, if the investigator deems it desirable to treat separately three, four, or even more categories of market-access activities, he can substitute for the second term of equation 15 three, four, or even more relevant terms. Or instead of differentiating market-access activities by relevant interacting mass the investigator may differentiate by sensitivity to distance. He may set up two categories of market-access activities. He may maintain that one category contains activities such as the production of nationally advertised household goods which are not transport-oriented, say toothpaste, pharmaceuticals, etc. These activities are less sensitive to distance than activities such as recreational services and the educational functions of national schools which are contained in the second category. He may therefore replace the second term of equation 15 by two potential terms. Both potential terms will be based on the same measure of mass. But the potential term representing the first category may be based on the square root of the distance factor, that is, use an exponent of one-half for d_{ij}, whereas the term representing the second category will use an exponent of unity for d_{ij}.

Even more, the investigator may differentiate by both relevant mass and sensitivity to distance and may have more than two categories by both classifications.[138] But it is clear that such differentiation or, put otherwise, such disaggregation of the relative income potential term of equation 15 confronts the analyst with still more complicated and questionable estimating procedures than those already discussed. The consistency problem is still more difficult to handle. And it becomes doubtful whether operational results can be obtained. Finally, it is to be borne in mind that, as we have cautioned earlier, such disaggregation, stratification, and division of the whole integral mass runs counter to the basic rationale of the gravity model.

H. Some Concluding Remarks

Although it is not possible to encompass in this chapter all the materials that have been developed in connection with the gravity model, it is hoped that the most important conceptual issues have been squarely faced and that the possibilities for application have been adequately presented. We have not taken the opportunity to speculate whether or not the spatial interaction describable by gravity models manifests an endeavor on the

[138] Differentiation by types of industry has been specifically examined to some degree in W. Isard and G. Freutel [28], pp. 449–454. In this study the classification of primary local, secondary local, tertiary local, primary interregional, secondary interregional, and tertiary interregional is advanced, the latter three categories being directly subject to a relative income potential effect. It is pointed out that the disaggregation can be pushed "still further by setting forth the industrial structure of region i in greater detail and by relating each industry in region i to industries in other regions via interregional flows. Such a procedure appears non-operational except where . . . a few major flows dominate the interregional trade of an area. However, with suitable modifications and restrictions, it leads toward an operational input-output model."

In this study, too, another criterion or principle by which to disaggregate is suggested. Instead of lumping all interregional relations of region i into one term—the second term of equation 15—the investigator may wish to keep separate the relations of region i to one or more particular regions with which i has both strong and atypical bonds. These bonds may exist because of complementarity of resources, physiography, cultural linkages, etc. Hence, he will introduce into equation 15 one or more terms which explicitly state the relationships of i to these one or more regions and use the second term of equation 15 to catch the changing interregional position effect with respect to all other regions. One form which the new terms might take is

$$b_{ij}\left(\frac{^{t+\theta}\overline{Y}_j}{_{\bar{\rho}}{}^t\overline{Y}_j} - 1\right)_{\mathrm{US}}{}^t P$$

where $\overline{Y}_j$ relates to the relevant portion of income of region j and where b_{ij} expresses the relative importance of region i's bonds with region j and implicitly embraces the effect of intervening distance (*ibid.*, pp. 438–439).

part of society to minimize some cost or effort or maximize some utility or output. Zipf strongly associates his empirical findings with a *principle of least effort* which pervades all human behavior. He and others either implicitly or explicitly link the gravity model to the rank-size rule which holds for cities[139] and diverse social phenomena and embraces Pareto's law of income distribution. Often implied in such linkage is an optimization process based on some crude probability reasoning.[140] If such an optimization process is in fact involved, as intuition strongly suggests, our understanding of the gravity model will be significantly advanced by an explicit statement of the process. Furthermore, the possibility of synthesizing gravity models and the analysis of conforming empirical materials with the interregional linear programming approach and other optimizing techniques discussed in the previous chapters will be greatly enhanced.

Also, in this chapter we have not explored the significance and applicability of concepts such as demographic cohesion and adhesion, the gradient of the potential,[141] and dynamical radius.[142] These concepts have been set forth by Stewart and Warntz, as further parallels of concepts in physics.[143] For example, Stewart maintains that over and above demographic energy there is an energy released when people come close together, in particular when they conglomerate in urban units. This additional energy is considered to be analogous to cohesion as it is defined in physics. Therefore this additional energy is termed demographic cohesion. This energy is taken to explain the fact that sociological activity *within urban areas*—as measured by local motor traffic and local telephone calls and as reflected in urban rents—increases by more than

---

[139] For some discussion of the rank-size rule see footnote 53, Chapter 2.

[140] W. Isard [25], ch. 3; S. C. Dodd [16]; J. Q. Stewart [37]. For example, it may be argued that the spatial pattern of people when classified by social role (broadly defined) tends to conform to a spatial pattern which minimizes effort involved in interaction subject to constraints imposed by nature and society. Per required social interaction the farmer must be alloted a relatively large land area; therefore the forces at play assign him a location at the periphery, a locus of points of low potential. Per required social interaction the administrator of a large enterprise is alloted a relatively small land area; therefore the forces at play assign him a location at a central node where potential is high. Such location assignment is consistent with the gravity model and at the same time reflects an optimization process which embraces most of if not all the economic optimization processes.

[141] At any point the gradient of the potential is defined as the slope of the potential surface at that point in a direction perpendicular to the equipotential contour line passing through the point. J. Q. Stewart and W. Warntz [39], pp. 177–178, find this concept useful in explaining deviations of locations from geographical centers.

[142] [39], p. 182.

[143] Also, see the interesting set of parallels suggested by S. C. Dodd [15, 16].

can be accounted for by change in demographic energy (potential) as the distance to the city center decreases.[144]

Still more, we have not investigated the interconnections between, on the one hand, agglomerative and deglomerative forces and, on the other hand, the forces purportedly encompassed in the gravity model, whether the latter reflect change in interregional position, change in capacity for community participation or sales generation, or some other relevant magnitude. Some may argue that these two sets of forces are as the two sides of the same coin. They may argue that in locating an attractively designed pharmaceutical plant the advantage of a high-market-potential site is essentially equivalent to an agglomeration advantage measured in terms of savings in advertising cost for a given output. Or they may contend that in locating a plant to manufacture a sensitive and complex calculating machine or similar equipment the advantage of a high-market-potential site is equivalent to an increase in revenue due to agglomeration, that is, due to a favorable shift of effective demand by customers sensitive to prompt service.

Others may maintain that the agglomerative and deglomerative forces are distinct and separate from the forces associated with the gravity model. They may assert that deglomerative forces—such as congestion, high urban land values, unwieldly management of large-scale enterprises—are not contained by, and in fact are contradictory to, the gravity model, at least as this model has thus far been developed. Further, such agglomerative forces as lower costs of power, of general urban facilities and services, of bulk commodity shipment, etc., are purely cost factors, fully capable of rather precise treatment by standard comparative cost procedures and industrial complex analysis; these need not, and in fact should not, be analyzed via a much less precise technique such as the gravity model.

Still more, they might insist that as such agglomerative and deglomerative forces are a category more significant for regional and locational study than the more nebulous forces supposedly encompassed by the gravity model. If research resources are limited, as is typical, they might demand that the interplay of agglomerative and deglomerative forces be given first priority, even to the exclusion of analysis via gravity models.

In spite of such cogent arguments, it must still be recognized that there are forces at play embracing spatial juxtaposition phenomena which

[144] Stewart's empirical study of residential rents suggests that demographic cohesion increases with city size but decreases with the potential in rural areas surrounding the city. In addition to demographic cohesion Stewart and Warntz propose still a third factor, namely adhesion. Adhesion would account for the attraction of people to sites (positive) or the repulsion of people from sites (negative). See J. Q. Stewart [36], p. 54, and [38], pp. 32–36; and J. Q. Stewart and W. Warntz [40], pp. 102–105.

standard comparative cost procedures, industrial complex, input-output, linear programming, and other methods discussed in preceding chapters do not embrace.[145] At the present time the regional and locational effects of these forces can best be depicted by the gravity model. Empirical studies have already demonstrated that these forces are significant. However, to attempt to evaluate exactly how significant they are in relation to other forces would be premature at this early stage in the development of the gravity model.

In closing, it is indicated that the gravity model constitutes a very promising technique for regional analysis. Yet our review of literature relating to this model demonstrates that much remains to be done in exploring its utility. Solutions to the problems of defining relevant mass and distance, assigning appropriate weights and exponents, establishing a basis of comparison with other research results, and broadening its probability framework, etc., require extensive systematic probing. Only with such research can we extend basic knowledge of the forces under-lying gravity models, construct more meaningful and useful descriptive and projective models, and desirably achieve a firm synthesis with other techniques of analysis and bodies of theory.

REFERENCES

1. Anderson, Theodore, "Intermetropolitan Migration: A Comparison of the Hypotheses of Zipf and Stouffer," *American Sociological Review*, Vol. 20 (June 1955).
2. ——, "Intermetropolitan Migration: A Correlation Analysis," *American Journal of Sociology*, Vol. 61 (March 1956).
3. ——, "Potential Models and Spatial Distribution of Population," *Papers and Proceedings of the Regional Science Association*, Vol. 2 (1956).
4. ——, "Reply to Iklé," *American Sociological Review*, Vol. 20 (Dec. 1955).
5. Bevis, Howard W., "Forecasting Zonal Traffic Volumes," *Traffic Quarterly*, Vol. 10 (April 1956).
6. Bogue, Donald J., *The Structure of the Metropolitan Community: A Study of Dominance and Subdominance*, University of Michigan Press, Ann Arbor, Michigan, 1949.
7. Bossard, James H. S., "Residential Propinquity as a Factor in Marriage Selection," *American Journal of Sociology*, Vol. 38 (Sept. 1932).
8. Bright, Margaret, and Dorothy S. Thomas, "Interstate Migration and Intervening Opportunities," *American Sociological Review*, Vol. 6 (Dec. 1941).

[145] Even where comparative cost study, input-output, industrial complex, or linear programming are conceptually superior methods, they may not be feasible in practice. They may require collection and processing of detailed data on a strict industry-by-industry basis which would incur costs well beyond resources available. Then recourse may be had to aggregation or to a conceptually inferior technique such as the gravity model which can yield a rough pattern on the basis of a generalized market force.

9. Carey, H. C., *Principles of Social Science*, J. Lippincott, Philadelphia, 1858–1859.

10. Carroll, J. Douglas, "Spatial Interaction and the Urban-Metropolitan Description," *Papers and Proceedings of the Regional Science Association*, Vol. 1 (1955).

11. ———, and Howard W. Bevis, "Predicting Local Travel in Urban Regions," *Papers and Proceedings of the Regional Science Association*, Vol. 3 (1957).

12. Carrothers, Gerald A. P., *Forecasting the Population of Open Areas*, doctoral dissertation, Massachusetts Institute of Technology, Cambridge, Massachusetts, 1959.

13. ———, "An Historical Review of the Gravity and Potential Concepts of Human Interaction," *Journal of the American Institute of Planners*, Vol. 22 (Spring 1956).

14. ———, "Regional Population Projection via Income Potential Models," *Papers and Proceedings of the Regional Science Association*, Vol. 4 (1958).

15. Dodd, Stuart C., "Diffusion is Predictable: Testing Probability Models for Laws of Interaction," *American Sociological Review*, Vol. 20 (Aug. 1955).

16. ———, "The Interactance Hypothesis: A Gravity Model Fitting Physical Masses and Human Groups," *American Sociological Review*, Vol. 15 (April 1950).

17. Dunn, Edgar S., "The Market Potential Concept and the Analysis of Location," *Papers and Proceedings of the Regional Science Association*, Vol. 2 (1956).

18. Garrison, William L., "Parameters of Spatial Interaction," *Papers and Proceedings of the Regional Science Association*, Vol. 2 (1956).

19. ———, "The Spatial Impact of Transport Media," *Papers and Proceedings of the Regional Science Association*, Vol. 1 (1955).

20. Green, Howard L., *The Reach of New York City and Boston into Southern New England*, doctoral dissertation, Harvard University, Cambridge, Massachusetts, 1952.

21. Hammer, Carl, and F. C. Iklé, "Intercity Telephone and Airline Traffic Related to Distance and the 'Propensity to Interact,'" *Sociometry*, Vol. 20 (Dec. 1957).

22. Harris, Chauncy, D., "The Market as a Factor in the Localization of Industry in the United States," *Annals of the Association of American Geographers*, Vol. 44 (Dec. 1954).

23. Iklé, F. C., "Comment on Theodore R. Anderson's 'Intermetropolitan Migration,'" *American Sociological Review*, Vol. 20 (Dec. 1955).

24. ———, "Sociological Relationship of Traffic to Population and Distance," *Traffic Quarterly*, Vol. 8 (April 1954).

25. Isard, Walter, *Location and Space-Economy*, John Wiley, New York, 1956.

26. ———, "Location Theory and Trade Theory: Short-Run Analysis," *Quarterly Journal of Economics*, Vol. 68 (May 1954).

27. ———, and Robert E. Coughlin, *Municipal Costs and Revenues Resulting from Community Growth*, Chandler-Davis Publishing Co., Wellesley, Massachusetts, 1957.

28. ———, and Guy Freutel, "Regional and National Product Projections and their Interrelations," in *Long-Range Economic Projection*, Studies in Income and Wealth, Vol. 16, National Bureau of Economic Research, Princeton University Press, Princeton, New Jersey, 1954.

29. Isbell, Eleanor C., "Internal Migration in Sweden and Intervening Opportunities," *American Sociological Review*, Vol. 9 (Dec. 1944).

30. Jurkat, Ernest H., "Land Use Analysis and Forecasting in Traffic Planning," *Traffic Quarterly*, Vol. 11 (April 1957).

31. McLaughlin, Glenn E., and Stefan Robock, *Why Industry Moves South*, National Planning Association, Washington, D.C., 1949.

32. Mylroie, Willa, "Evaluation of Intercity Travel Desire," in *Factors Influencing Travel Patterns*, Highway Research Board, Bulletin 119, Washington, D.C., 1956.
33. Price, Daniel O., "Distance and Direction as Vectors of Internal Migration, 1935 to 1940," *Social Forces*, Vol. 27 (Oct. 1948).
34. Ravenstein, E. G., "The Laws of Migration," *Journal of the Royal Statistical Society*, Vol. 48 (1885) and Vol 52 (1889).
35. Reilly, William J., "Methods for the Study of Retail Relationships," *University of Texas Bulletin*, No. 2944 (Nov. 1929).
36. Stewart, John Q., "Demographic Gravitation: Evidence and Applications," *Sociometry*, Vol. 11 (Feb. and May 1948).
37. ———, "Empirical Mathematical Rules Concerning the Distribution and Equilibrium of Population," *Geographical Review*, Vol. 37 (July 1947).
38. ———, "Potential of Population and Its Relationship to Marketing," in *Theory in Marketing*, ed. by R. Cox and W. Alderson, Richard D. Irwin, Inc., Homewood, Illinois, 1950.
39. ———, and William Warntz, "Macrogeography and Social Science," *Geographical Review*, Vol. 48 (April 1958).
40. ———, and ———, "Physics of Population Distribution," *Journal of Regional Science*, Vol. 1 (Summer 1958).
41. Stouffer, Samuel A., "Intervening Opportunities: A Theory Relating Mobility and Distance," *American Sociological Review*, Vol. 5 (Dec. 1940).
42. Strodtbeck, Fred, "Equal Opportunity Intervals: A Contribution to the Method of Intervening Opportunity Analysis," *American Sociological Review*, Vol. 14 (Aug. 1949).
43. ———, "Population, Distance and Migration from Kentucky," *Sociometry*, Vol. 13 (May 1950).
44. Ullman, Edward L., *American Commodity Flow*, University of Washington Press, Seattle, Washington, 1957.
45. Voorhees, A. M., "A General Theory of Traffic Movement," *Proceedings of the Institute of Traffic Engineers*, 1955.
46. Warntz, William, "Geography of Prices and Spatial Interaction," *Papers and Proceedings of the Regional Science Association*, Vol. 3 (1957).
47. ———, "Measuring Spatial Association with Special Consideration of the Case of Market Orientation of Production," *Journal of the American Statistical Association*, Vol. 51 (Dec. 1956).
48. ———, *Towards a Geography of Price*, University of Pennsylvania Press, Philadelphia, 1959.
49. Young, E. C., *The Movement of Farm Population*, Cornell Agricultural Experiment Station, Bulletin 426, Ithaca, New York, 1924.
50. Zipf, George K., *Human Behavior and the Principle of Least Effort*, Addison-Wesley Press, Reading, Massachusetts, 1949.
51. ———, "The P_1P_2/D Hypothesis on the Intercity Movement of Persons," *American Sociological Review*, Vol. 11 (Oct. 1946).

Chapter 12

Channels of Synthesis*

A. Aim and Procedure

We now confront the problem of synthesis.   In each of the previous chapters we deal with a specific tool or technique (or group of tools or techniques) which relates to a particular subsystem of the system of regions, or to the structure of a region as a system, or to both.   In some chapters a modest amount of synthesis is achieved.   (For example, in Chapter 8, input-output is synthesized to a noticeable extent with the comparative cost approach.)   But neither in these chapters nor others is there realized that kind of comprehensive synthesis whose desirability is constantly emphasized.   Can such synthesis be attained?

It is obvious that, within the confines of this last chapter, we cannot develop a full-blown empirical study which achieves the desired synthesis. Such would be well beyond the resources and time set aside for this book.   However, it is possible to set down in a systematic manner the types of synthesis that can be achieved with explicit differentiation between those that are both conceptual and operational and those that, in the light of available data, know-how, theory, and experience, are only conceptual. Put in another way, it is possible to identify the ways and procedures by which various systems and subsystems may be interrelated, again distinguishing between those relationships that can be grasped only conceptually and those that can be grasped both conceptually and in specific

* Sections A–F of this chapter were written with David F. Bramhall.

569

operational terms.   Put in still another light, we must now observe diverse phases of the spatial organization of society in a manner that points up the possibilities of their integration conceptually and, where possible, quantitatively and operationally.

Our procedure will be to sketch diagrammatically main channels along which synthesis of diverse techniques can be achieved.   Supplementary materials will be presented either diagrammatically or in table form.   We shall develop verbally the necessary discussion of the specific procedures to link techniques.

B. Channel I: A Fused Interregional Comparative Cost–Industrial Complex–Input-Output Framework

1. the central and early stages

We center the discussion of the first main channel around interregional and regional input-output.   This technique, certainly in its narrow regional form, has been demonstrated to be operational.   And in its interregional form sufficient investigation has been pursued to establish clearly that it is operational as well, provided it is supplemented by techniques such as comparative cost which eliminate certain of its basic shortcomings.

In Figure 1 the interregional input-output technique is noted in the heavy brackets in the center of the diagram.   As indicated in Chapter 8, this technique must be linked with meaningful comparative cost or other location-regional analysis if it is to assume significance.   Partial discussion of the manner in which this linkage can be effected is contained in Chapter 8.   Now that the industrial complex approach of Chapter 9 has been developed, it is possible to specify this linkage in greater scope.

One basic tie is achieved through the bill of goods (final demand) sectors by regions.   First those industries (say aluminum, steel, and aircraft) or parts of industries (say nonlocal agriculture) whose regional distribution can be fruitfully attacked via an industry-by-industry comparative cost approach (à la Chapter 7) are taken out of the structural matrix of an interregional input-output scheme.   Next the industries and parts of industries forming industrial complexes (say hydrocarbons and nucleonics) whose regional patterns can be meaningfully treated by a Weberian approach (à la Chapter 9) are also taken out.[1]   For each of these industrial

---

[1] If it is feasible or meaningful to treat only part of an industry by Weberian location analysis, the remaining part is left in the structural matrix to be regionally distributed in accord with the supposedly more meaningful spatial relations embodied in an interregional input-output scheme.   The justification for such a step is not unlike that for splitting the household sector of each region into two parts.   One part may be exogenously determined and represent, for example, minimum requirements for subsistence

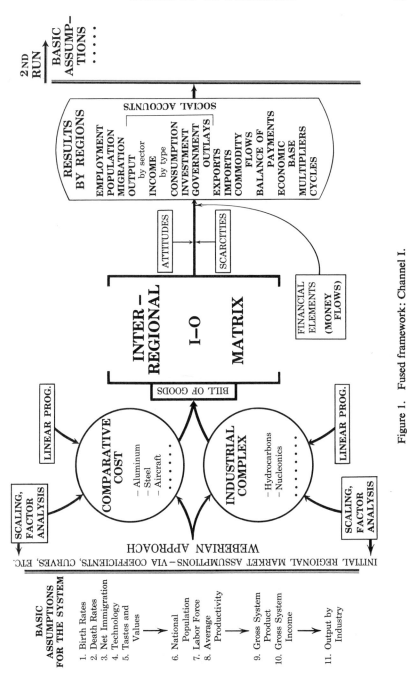

Figure 1.   Fused framework: Channel I.

complexes and industries the basic cost differential analysis is pursued, given a pattern of markets which will be discussed later. The regional distribution of each may be projected for a key year in the future. Then, as in the steel study reported in Chapter 8, for each region the input requirements of its share of these industrial complexes and industries may be added to its "customary" final demand requirements.

Specifically, we may consider a three-region model such as the one depicted by Table 2 of Chapter 8 and explicitly identify the final demand sectors for each region. We do this in Table 1 of this chapter. In the upper left quadrant is the customary interregional input-output flow (transactions) matrix, from which are deleted the industries and parts of industries that are to be attacked via comparative cost and industrial complex analysis.[2] (Thus, for example, for each region only *local* agriculture remains in the structural matrix.) In the upper right quadrant of Table 1 are listed both the *customary* and the *new* final demand sectors. Their input requirements from the various activities remaining in the structural matrix are noted in the cells in the upper right quadrant; and their accounting charges and input requirements from excluded (exogenous) sectors are recorded in the lower right quadrant. For example, in the first part of the upper right quadrant are listed the customary final demand sectors for the East: Government,[3] Capital Formation, Inventory Change, Foreign Trade, Households. Then Nonlocal Agriculture, Aluminum, Steel, ...,

or minimum welfare goals specified by a governmental unit or society in general. The other part may be endogenously determined and may refer, for example, to household consumption generated by regional income in excess of that required to purchase the exogenously determined part.

[2] Corresponding to the upper left quadrant of Table 1 is an interregional input-output coefficient table which in any column lists cents' worth of each commodity from each region required per dollar output of the activity listed at the head of the column.

[3] There are several ways of viewing and defining the Government sector. In this Chapter we shall not distinguish between the local, state, and Federal governments. Rather we slice the Federal government into several parts and allocate to each region a part proportionate to Federal government employment or expenditures in that region, or to some other appropriate *operational* measure of Federal government activity in that region. Likewise with the government of any state cutting any regional boundary. Thus, for example, the sector Government in the East comprises all local governments in the East, all state (and parts of state) governments in the East, and that part of Federal Government assigned to the East.

Since a number of government activities are in essence business operations (e.g. post office), and since the framework to be developed can explain in large part the levels of these business-type operations, the analyst may remove these activities from the final demand sectors, Government in the East, Government in the South, etc., and place them within the structural matrix, appropriately designating them as one or more endogenous producing sectors. To a large extent, this is done in an unpublished regional input-output study by W. Z. Hirsch [15].

Hydrocarbons, . . . , Nucleonics are listed. These latter are the new final demand sectors for the East whose levels are determined by comparative cost and industrial complex analysis.[4]

To illustrate even more concretely the linkage of techniques embraced by Table 1, suppose that analysis of hydrocarbon complexes indicates that only a Dacron A complex of the specific structure depicted in Figure 2 of Chapter 9 is feasible for the East. Then in the Final Demand quadrants of Table 1 there would be listed in the Hydrocarbons column of the East the set of input requirements of column 1 (Dacron A) of Table 2, Chapter 9,[5] disaggregated by region of origin.[6]

---

[4] In effect, when an entire industry is to be treated by comparative cost or industrial complex procedures, the columns representing that industry in the several regions are taken out of the structural matrix and set in appropriate places among the final demand sectors. Correspondingly, the rows representing that industry in the several regions are removed from the structural matrix and placed among the accounting rows under the structural matrix. When only part of an industry is to be treated by comparative cost or industrial complex procedures, that part is removed as before, the remaining part being treated as any other industry within the structural matrix.

[5] Recall that only the negative figures of column 1, Table 2, Chapter 9, are input requirements. The positive figures are outputs and are not recorded individually in the table. However, they are explicitly detailed on a worksheet to be later reconciled with system and regional requirements for these outputs and with the yield of these outputs by other sectors.

For example, suppose that the nucleonics complex of Table 1 were to produce only two outputs, say nuclear power and irradiated materials; or alternatively suppose, as we shall from here on, that this complex comprises two industries, one which produces nuclear power and the other irradiated materials. Also suppose no other sectors produce these two products. Then, when we make comparisons and reconciliations as will be necessary later on, we contrast the sum of the requirements of nuclear power and irradiated products from a given region, as will be recorded in the Total Gross Output column, with that region's level of the nucleonics complex which will be equivalent to the total figure (Total Gross Outlays) at the bottom of the relevant column of Table 1.

In more complicated situations, where more outputs are involved and where the outputs of a complex are also yielded by other sectors, comparison and reconciliation become more difficult and programming considerations enter when factors limit the yield of an output by any sector. However, the necessary steps to effect comparison and reconciliation in these situations will not be presented since such material is outside the scope of this volume.

[6] It is to be noted that any final demand sector may obtain its inputs from several regions. Thus, in the column listing the input requirements for the East hydrocarbons complex the cell corresponding to the Eastern power industry will contain a positive number, whereas the cell corresponding to the Southern power industry will be blank. In contrast, the cell corresponding to the East crude oil production will tend to contain a relatively small number, whereas the cell corresponding to the South crude oil production will contain a relatively large number.

In brief, in the interregional model all input requirements are disaggregated by region of origin, and thus any final demand column for a specific region implies input demands

TABLE 1.   AN INTERREGIONAL FLOW MATRIX FOR

SECTOR PRODUCING \ SECTOR PURCHASING	East			South		West		
	1. Local Agriculture	20. Drugs ...	44. Restaurants ...	1. Local Agriculture	44. Restaurants ...	1. Local Agriculture	44. Restaurants ...	
East 1. Local Agriculture								
.								
20. Drugs		...						
.								
44. Restaurants								
South 1. Local Agriculture								
.								
44. Restaurants								
West 1. Local Agriculture								
.		...						
44. Restaurants								
East GOVERNMENT								
CAPITAL FORMATION								
INVENTORY CHANGE								
FOREIGN TRADE								
HOUSEHOLDS								
NONLOCAL AGRICULTURE								
ALUMINUM								
STEEL								
.		...	...	...	...			
SYNTHETIC FIBER								
.								
NUCLEAR POWER								
South GOVERNMENT								
.		...						
HOUSEHOLDS								
NONLOCAL AGRICULTURE								
.								
NUCLEAR POWER								
West GOVERNMENT								
.		...						
NUCLEAR POWER								
TOTAL GROSS OUTLAYS		...	...	...	...			

COMPARATIVE COST–INDUSTRIAL COMPLEX–INPUT-OUTPUT ANALYSIS

Final-Demand Sectors

				East								South					West			Final Demand Totals	Total Gross Output
Government	Capital Formation	Inventory Change	Foreign Trade	Households	Nonlocal Agriculture	Aluminum	Steel	...	Hydrocarbons	...	Nucleonics	Government	...	Households	Nonlocal Agriculture	...	Nucleonics	Government	...	Nucleonics		
																						...
								...											...			...
																						...
								...											...			...
								...		...			...			...			...			...
																						...
								...											...			...
																						...
								...											...			...
								...		...			...			...			...			...

Once the new final demand sectors by regions are added to the inter-regional input-output framework (and the appropriate industries of the structural matrix deleted), the input-output model is set for use. That is, once the cells of the upper right quadrant of Table 1 are filled in (and simultaneously the cells in the lower right quadrant), the input-output model may be operated. Such operation yields for every region outputs for every industry (or part of industry) remaining in the structural matrix (i.e., for every endogenous sector).[7] Given these determined outputs, it becomes possible to fill in the cells of the upper left quadrant of Table 1. The desired figures are obtained by multiplying these outputs by the rele-vant interregional input-output coefficients.[8] In somewhat the same manner, the cells in the lower left quadrant of Table 1 can be filled in. The interregional input-output flow (transactions) table for a base year provides benchmark coefficients and ratios by which to estimate, per dollar output of the activity at the head of any given column, the set of accounting charges and input requirements from each exogenous sector listed in the lower half of the table.[9] Multiplying these benchmark coefficients and ratios by the determined output levels of the endogenous sectors yields the data for the cells in the lower left quadrant.

The steps of the previous paragraphs are graphically depicted in Figure 1. The two circles designated COMPARATIVE COST and INDUSTRIAL COMPLEX together with their detail and arrows briefly suggest these steps. (For the moment we ignore the rectangular blocks designated SCALING, FACTOR ANALYSIS, and LINEAR PROG.)

But to perform meaningful industry-by-industry comparative cost and industrial complex analysis à la modern Weberian dogma requires a set of

placed on all regions. Procedures for disaggregating input requirements among regions as sources, that is, for establishing supply channels, involve the use of current inter-regional flow data, market area analysis, etc.; these are discussed in Chapter 8 and the literature cited therein. Of course, in disaggregating input requirements for the "new" final demand sectors we can use as well the customary set of interregional input-output coefficients for a base year.

[7] This process involves the prior determination of an applicable set of interregional input-output coefficients for those industries and parts of industries remaining within the structural matrix (upper left quadrant of Table 1). Then, by premultiplying the upper half of the Final Demand Totals column of Table 1 by the inverse matrix, or by round-by-round iteration, we obtain the output of every endogenous sector for every region. It should be noted that those sectors remaining in the structural matrix refer not only to industries whose outputs in each region are geared primarily to local demands but also to those parts of industries partially removed as well as national-type industries (e.g. toothpaste and many other drug products) for which the cost differential approach of Weberian analysis is not particularly relevant.

[8] In this connection, see the discussion below on how the cells of Table 3 are filled in.

[9] Again, the reader is referred to Chapter 8 and the literature cited therein.

basic postulates for the system.   This is appreciated when we review the elements of Weberian analysis, which are listed in one of several possible ways in Figure 2.   The estimation of these elements requires a predetermination of the regional pattern of markets and raw material sources, transport rate structure, regional labor, power and water rates, production functions, etc.   In turn, such predetermination is related to a set of Basic Assumptions which is depicted by the column marked off at the extreme left of Figure 1.

As indicated by arrows in Figure 1, a type of basic information to be fed into comparative cost and industrial complex analysis must be derived from a set of assumptions on Initial Regional Markets, that is, on regional

A. Transport (Transfer) Cost Differentials
  1. On raw materials.
  2. On finished product.
     . . . .

B. Processing Cost Differentials (at Fixed Scales)
  1. On labor.
  2. On power.
  3. On water.
     . . . .

C. Market and Supply (Purchasing) Area Analysis.

D. Agglomeration—Deglomeration Economies
        (including spatial juxtaposition economies)
  1. Scale economies.
  2. Localization economies.
  3. Urbanization—regionalization economies.

Figure 2.   Modern Weberian framework.

population, income, and output by industry for the year of projection. This set may be related to a projection for the *system* of the level of each final demand sector and of the level (output) of each industry (listed as item 11 at the lower left corner of Figure 1), where such output is initially allocated among regions by some simple or complex device.   One simple and justifiable device is to allocate the level of any final demand sector or industry in the same proportion as it was distributed in a current base year (perhaps with some provision for the differential impact of climate upon regional population growth).   Another, somewhat more complex, allocation procedure might be built partly on the use of comprehensive sets of location quotients, coefficients of localization, or localization curves, etc., as listed in Figure 3, or some combination of these items.   For example, if for the current year and key years in the past coefficients of localization and localization curves for a given industry depict a clear trend of decreasing concentration, [10] and if the investigator attaches analytical significance to such a fact, he may wish to modify appropriately a simple allocation of this industry based on current distribution.[11]

A. Labor coefficients $\left.\right\}$ Weberian.
   Power coefficients
   . . . .

B. Location quotients.
   Coefficient of localization (of geographic association).
   Coefficient of concentration of population.
   Coefficient of deviation.
   Coefficient of redistribution.
   . . . .

C. Localization curve.
   Urbanization curve.
   . . . .

D. Shift-ratio.
   Relative growth chart.
   V:*P* and similar factors.
   . . . .

E. Coefficient of specialization.
   Index of industrial diversification.
   . . . .

F. Specialization (diversification) curve.
   . . . .

Figure 3.   Coefficients, curves, growth charts, and indices for preliminary use.

In turn, the national (system) output of each industry must be previously determined.   For this purpose a national input-output calculation may be pursued, based on estimates of final demand sectors directly related to Gross System Product or Income (items 9 and 10 in the column at the left of Figure 1) or some alternative social accounts.   For example, in their 1946 study, *Full Employment Patterns, 1950,* the U.S. Bureau of Labor

[10] Recall that localization curves α and γ of Figure 1, Chapter 7, portray a changing regional concentration of industry *i.*

[11] He may also check his hypothesis against a Relative Growth Chart, such as Figure 5, Chapter 7, and other tools discussed in Chapter 7, and in addition allow for such intangibles as climate.   Moreover, he may have already found these quotients, coefficients, and curves of considerable use in identifying sectors which may be profitably treated by comparative cost and industrial complex analyses.

Statistics projected to 1950 certain basic social accounts for the nation (system) which related to foreign exports, government expenditures, household expenditures, inventory change, and capital formation. In turn, each of these accounts were disaggregated (in large measure based on 1939 relations) into a set of final demands for the product of each industry contained in the structural matrix.[12] Then via a round-by-round application of an input-output matrix of coefficients the 1950 national (system) output of each industry was approximated.[13] In a similar manner, in connection with the interregional input-output study of Italy reported on in Chapter 8, a set of 1956 final demands for the product of each industry of the Italian economy was derived from a set of national accounts projected for 1956. From these detailed final demands national output by industry for 1956 was iteratively computed.[14]

It should be noted here that alternative derivations of national output by industry may be obtained from projected social accounts.[15] A direct translation of projected GNP and system income into national outputs by industry might, for example, be pursued. However, in view of the large magnitude of intermediate commodities consumed in a modern industrialized system such as the United States, an input-output-type computation, at least to a limited extent, is to be preferred.

The successive unfolding of layers of prerequisite data and information does not stop here. Basic aggregates such as Gross System Product, consumer income, governmental expenditures, and foreign exports require estimates of fundamental magnitudes as well as subjective appraisals of nonquantifiable social factors. As for the nonquantifiables—such as business confidence in the political regimes of other parts of the world,

[12] In their interindustry study for the United States economy of 1947, the Bureau of Labor Statistics presents fine detail on the derivation of final demands for the product of each industry, which are consistent with 1947 social accounts. (See W. D. Evans and M. Hoffenberg [6], and National Bureau of Economic Research [26].) More meaningful and accurate ways of proceeding from social accounts, especially consumer income, to detailed sets of demands and expenditures are currently being investigated at the Harvard Economic Research Project. Also, for an interesting suggestion of a framework for data collection which yields both national income accounts and interindustry accounts by industrial sector, see National Bureau of Economic Research [27], ch . 5, and Appendix X, Table A-6.

[13] The modern version, of course, involves the use of an inverse matrix.

[14] See U. S. Mutual Security Agency [35], ch. 4. Although here the set of 1956 final demands was not spatially disaggregated to yield 1956 final demands by region, this could have been rather easily performed. The application of these regional sets of final demands for 1956 could then have led to individual industry outputs by region.

[15] For an interesting application of this procedure *in reverse* see B. Brown and M. J. Hansen [2]. In this study GNP for 1975 is built up from separate projections of broad industrial categories.

which influences foreign exports, particularly of investment goods; or the state of international political affairs which largely determines military expenditures (included in the government sector); or social welfare, urban rehabilitation, and resource development policies which influence peace-time government expenditures—the best procedure is to introduce explicitly alternative possibilities.   For example, we may consider three alternatives for the state of international political affairs: one in which the maximum size of military program is undertaken, another in which current relative

A. Comparative Forecasting.

B. Projection by Extrapolation

    1. Graphic techniques.

    2. Extrapolation by mathematical function

        a. Polynomial curves.

        b. Exponential curves.

        c. Gompertz and logistic curves.

C. Ratio and Correlation Methods

    1. Ratio methods

        a. Ratio to total populations.

        b. Ratio to population components.

    2. Regression and covariance analysis

        a. Simple regression.

        b. Multiple regression.

        c. Covariance analysis.

D. Growth Composition Analysis

    1. Natural increase methods

        a. Crude birth and death rates.

        b. Cohort-survival.

    2. Inflow-outflow analysis

        a. Natural increase adjusted for migration (for migration estimates, see Figure 5).

Figure 4.   Population projection techniques.

levels of civilian and military expenditures by government are maintained, and a third in which only a minimum military establishment is supported.

In contrast, there are fundamental magnitudes whose projection can proceed at least partially on an objective basis and which underlie the sound projection of basic social accounts required for national input-output computations.   These include system population, system labor force, and average productivity (items, 6, 7, and 8 in the column at the extreme left of Figure 1).   Appropriate procedures for the projection of broad national social accounts based on these magnitudes have been well developed in the literature and need no detailed discussion here.   Typically, given a forecast of national population, a labor force is estimated based on projected rates of participation by the several age groups of each sex with allowance for a normal unemployment rate and an assumed size of the armed forces, etc.; an average work week is anticipated, considering such factors as number engaged in part-time employment and various pressures for a shortened work week; and finally, an average productivity (output) per man-hour is projected based primarily on past trends with an eye to foreseeable technological change and shift in the industrial composition of the national economy.   Multiplying forecast labor force, average work week, and output per man-hour by each other and adding to the result estimated government product (both in military and civilian activities) yields Gross National (System) Product.[16]

A. Estimation of Past Interregional Migration
   1. Gross and net migration totals
      a. Residual methods.
      b. Census population data.
      c. Population registers.
   2. Differential migration.
B. Estimation of Rural-Urban Migration.
C. Forecasting Future Migration
   1. Projection of historical trends
      a. Extrapolation.
      b. Ratio and similar methods.
      c. Subjective projection.
   2. Gravity, potential, and spatial interaction
      models (see section F, Chapter 11).

Figure 5.   Migration estimation and projection techniques.

Finally, the underlying forecast of national (system) population itself must be developed. Here, the demographic techniques discussed in Chapters 2 and 3, as they pertain to the system of regions as a whole, make fundamental contributions.   The population forecast for the system may be derived by one or a combination of techniques listed under subhead *D* of Figure 4 and subhead *C* of Figure 5.   Essentially, these techniques employ available materials on birth and death rates by age, sex, and ethnic groups *plus* materials on in- and out-migration for the system.   (See items 1, 2, and 3 in the column at the extreme left of Figure 1.)   As this demographic analysis is pursued, it must be recognized that changing tastes and cultural values, anticipated medical progress, the state of international

[16] For a succinct and lucid presentation of this standard method of estimating GNP, see G. Colm [4].

affairs, and a number of other factors have significance.   Here, too, alternative assumptions—for example, high, medium, and low fertility rates—
may be conveniently introduced.   [The assumptions made here must
obviously be the same as, or be consistent with, those required at various
stages, such as when transport, power, and labor rates are to be set in
connection with comparative cost and industrial complex analysis (see
Figure 2), or in the choice of relevant input-output coefficients.]

2. THE LATER STAGES AND RESULTS

Heretofore we have uncovered, layer by layer, sets of data and assumptions essential for the operation of the interregional input-output, comparative cost, and industrial complex techniques of Channel 1.   It is now
appropriate to consider the later stages of this channel and the set of results
which are attainable.

   a. Employment, population, and migration.   As has been indicated, the
operation of an interregional input-output framework yields as results for
each region a set of outputs by each industry and part of industry included
in the structural matrix.   These gross outputs appear in the upper half of
the last column (Total Gross Output) of Table 1.   Each of these outputs
may then be converted into an employment figure by the utilization of
information on base period wage rates adjusted for the general changes in
average productivity (output per man-hour) and average work week
assumed in connection with the estimate of Gross System Product (see
items 7, 8, and 9 in the column at the left of Figure 1).   The derived
employment figures may be summed for each region.

   But to derive an over-all employment estimate for a given region, there
must be added to the sum obtained in the preceding paragraph the employments in each final demand sector of the region.   Specifically, to the sum
for the East there must first be added employment in the government sector
of the East.   Such employment may be estimated from the dollar figure on
required government output in the East (= value of government services
required by sectors in the East), as recorded in the first cell of the lower half
of the Total Gross Output column in Table 1.[17]   Note that the total gross
outlay figure listed at the bottom of the first column in the final demand
section of Table 1, which refers to the Government sector in the East, is not
used at this point.   This figure is the one that is initially assumed.   The
relevant figure is the derived figure, reflecting the requirements of all sectors

---

[17] A procedure such as the one already discussed in connection with individual industries or some other standard method may be employed.   In any case, the procedure
must be consistent with the method employed in constructing the set of input (including
labor) requirements of the final demand sector, Government in the East.

in all regions, which is the sum of the figures in the cells in the row Government in the East, and which is contained in the Total Gross Output column.[18]

Further, to these employment figures for the East must be added employment in the capital formation, inventory change, foreign export, and households sectors in the East.[19] Finally, there must be added employment in nonlocal agriculture, aluminum, steel, synthetic fiber, and nuclear power industries and in other industries and parts of industries excluded from the structural matrix. As with government, at this point, the relevant output figure from which to derive an employment estimate is not the output of a sector in a region, as yielded by the initial comparative cost and industrial complex analysis. Rather it is the derived (required) output, which is the sum of the figures in the cells in the corresponding row below the structural matrix, and which is recorded in the Total Gross Output column in Table 1.[20]

In this manner the fused interregional comparative cost–industrial

[18] However, after the reconciliation process which is discussed in section B.2.c is effected, the total gross outlay figure for Government in the East will equal its total gross output figure. Thus, it will be immaterial, after reconciliation is effected, from which figure employment in Government in the East is estimated. It is to be recalled that the figure in each cell in the row, Government in the East, may be derived so that the total purchases of government services (from all regions) by any industry in a region, say restaurants in the East, are consistent with the national input figure indicating the cents' worth of government services purchased per dollar output of restaurants for the nation as a whole, as estimated for the year of projection.

[19] At best such employment estimates are crude and should be linked to national data as benchmarks. For excellent discussion of some of the technical and conceptual difficulties at this point, see National Bureau of Economic Research [26].

[20] Again, after the reconciliation process which is discussed in section B.2.c is effected, the total gross outlay figure for each sector of a region will equal its total gross output. [For an industrial complex, the gross outlay figure will equal the sum of the gross outputs of the several industries (activities) comprised by that complex.] It will then be immaterial from which figure employment in the sector is estimated.

Recall that the figures in the cells along any such row, say Nonlocal Agriculture in the South, may be derived on the basis of market area analysis (as part of the Weberian approach) and data based on national input coefficients. For example, in the year of projection it may be judged that per $1.00 restaurant sales of the nation, 5 cents' worth of agricultural commodities falling in the nonlocal categories (e.g., wheat, citrus fruits, etc.) will be required. This figure of 5 cents may then be taken to apply to restaurants in the East as well. When multiplied by the derived level of output of restaurants in the East, this figure yields projected purchases of nonlocal agricultural products by restaurants in the East. From previous Weberian analysis, the percentage shares of the market for nonlocal agricultural products in the East to be allocated to producers in each of the several regions has been determined. Thus the figure in the cell at the intersection of the column Restaurants in the East and the row Nonlocal Agriculture in the South is easily obtained.

complex–input–output framework yields for each region employment by sector and the aggregate of total employment. This result is noted as the first item in the RESULTS column at the right in Figure 1. But such a result, as others in the column, is only a first approximation at this point. Already we have noted that in each region the levels of the industries and parts of industries yielded by the initial Weberian analysis and placed in the final demand sectors may be inconsistent with the required levels as recorded in the Total Gross Output column at the extreme right of Table 1. Also, such inconsistency may be present for the customary final demand sectors. As one example, the assumed level of household expenditures in a region (based on an initially assumed level of regional income) may be inconsistent with realized income as recorded in the appropriate cell of the Total Gross Output column which sums payments for household services by sector of each region along the relevant Households row.[21] Finally, not only may the set of regional figures in the cells of the Total Gross Output column of Table 1 be inconsistent with the set of regional levels of those industries and parts of industries derived directly from comparative cost and industrial complex analysis, but also each one of these two sets may be at variance with the set of regional markets initially assumed (predetermined) for comparative cost and industrial complex analysis. However, before an improvement of employment estimates by region is attempted, it is pertinent to discuss other results of the fused techniques, since such discussion will facilitate the exposition of the reconciliation process.

The second and third items listed in the RESULTS column at the right of Figure 1 are, for each region, Population and Migration, respectively. At this stage first-run estimates of both these items are obtainable and are superior to the estimates either explicitly or implicitly projected prior to comparative cost and industrial complex analysis.[22] Given estimated employment by sector in a region, given relevant postulates on work week and labor force participation,[23] and given any other pertinent information such as occupational requirements, a total regional population number

[21] As another example, the initially assumed level of governmental expenditures in a region, which when disaggregated yields the government final demand column for that region, may be inconsistent with required governmental services as recorded in the appropriate cell of the Total Gross Output column.

[22] These items would have been *explicitly* projected had national population been derived as a sum of regional populations, each estimated by one of the growth composition techniques discussed in Chapter 2 using specific regional birth rates, death rates, etc. These items would have been *implicitly* projected as part of the assumptions on initial regional markets had national population been projected on the basis of national rates.

[23] These, of course, will be closely associated with the national postulates.

may be derived.[24] When this number is contrasted with a number obtained by the most relevant demographic techniques discussed in Chapter 2 (such as cohort-survival) based on natural rates of increase for either the nation or region, we can obtain regional net migration. Such migration is the difference between these two numbers and is at this stage an essentially crude reflection of the interplay of economic and social forces.[25] At a later stage, when the interplay of economic and social forces is more fully and accurately encompassed by a fully reconciled analytical framework, more refined estimates of regional population and net migration will be achievable. Such estimates may be said to be derived via *indirect* methods. These methods contrast with the direct methods discussed in Chapters 2 and 3 and outlined in Figures 4 and 5 of this chapter.

b. Basic social accounts. Beyond employment, population, and net migration by region, the fused interregional comparative cost–industrial complex–input-output framework yields estimates of basic social accounts. This outcome is clearly perceived when a triple-entry social accounting system is reproduced as in Table 2.

Table 2 of this chapter is constructed in much the same general manner as Tables 2, 3, and 4 in Chapter 4. (The specifics of this table, however, are different, reflecting a difference in specific conceptual framework.) We may begin its interpretation with the second column. This column measures Gross Regional Product in the East at the production stage. The data for this column are directly obtained from Table 1 and may be derived by two different procedures. One procedure measures the net output of each producing sector in the East, both endogenous and exogenous; the

---

[24] For example, in the study of the impact of steel development on the Greater New York–Philadelphia industrial region which is discussed in Chapter 8, new employment estimates are derived for various industrial and final demand sectors. The authors then divide the over-all new employment estimate of 180,228 by an estimated labor force participation ratio of 0.43. This yields a crude estimate of new population, namely 419,000, incident to the steel development (W. Isard and R. E. Kuenne [18], pp. 298–299).

It is to be noted that in the Isard–Kuenne study no sector as a whole is expected to contract, although *parts* of sectors are permitted to contract. Of any sector the contracting parts are at least equally balanced by the expanding parts. However decreases in certain sectors as a whole can be allowed. This will not unduly complicate the derivation of new population estimates, since decreases in employment opportunities will tend to be balanced by increases elsewhere provided there are no dominating occupational and other immobilities in the labor force.

[25] As in section G, Chapter 11, it is recognized that a sizable part of the population of a system like the United States is economically immobile because of diverse cultural factors. Yet, it is posited that there is sufficient mobility within the remaining population to allow both the regional pattern of economic opportunities and climatic and other social forces to determine the regional pattern of population through migration of individuals within the mobile sector of population.

TABLE 2.   GROSS REGIONAL PRODUCT IN THE EAST

Gross Regional Income	Gross Regional Output	Gross Regional Expenditure
1. Income of Households in the East *a.* Wages and Salaries *b.* Profits (incl. Dividends) *c.* Interest *d.* Rent 2. Receipts by Government in the East (excluding tax payments by Households in the East)	3. Value Added by *or* Net Output of : *a.* Endogenous sectors (1) Local Agriculture . . (44) Restaurants . *b.* Exogenous Producing sectors Nonlocal Agriculture Aluminum . . Nuclear Power (Nucleonics) 4. Adjustments for Excluded Transactions of Government, etc.	5. Consumption Expenditures by Households in the East 6. Expenditures by Government in the East 7. Net Investment in the East *a.* Capital Formation *b.* Inventory Change (Addition) 8. Rest of the World Commodity Account *a.* Outside System (Foreign Exports *less* Foreign Imports) *b.* Inside System (Exports to all other regions *less* Imports from these regions)
Totals		

other measures value added by each such sector. The net output figure for any producing sector in the East is obtained by summing its deliveries to the customary final demand sectors in the East (i.e., government, capital formation, inventory change, foreign trade and households), and all its deliveries to all sectors of other regions (all these deliveries are in effect exports), *less* all its purchases from all sectors of other regions and foreign countries (all these purchases are in effect imports), and *less* accounting charges for capital consumption and inventory depletion.[26] Summing the net output figure over all producing sectors in the East, as outlined in items 3*a* and 3*b* of Table 2 and adding certain adjustments for deliveries by customary final demand (nonproducing) sectors yield Gross Regional Product in the East.[27]

The alternative procedure to measuring Gross Regional Product in the East at the production stage (second column, Table 2) is to compute value added, instead of net output, by each producing sector in the East. The

[26] For example, in deriving net output for Local Agriculture in the East, we first go across row 1 of Table 1 and determine the sum of all deliveries to all the endogenous sectors in both the South and West (ranging from Local Agriculture to Restaurants) *plus* deliveries to the customary final demand sectors in the East (ranging from Government to Households) *plus* deliveries to all the final demand sectors in both the South, and West (ranging from Government to Nucleonics). Then we go down column 1 of Table 1 and subtract from the above resulting sum all purchases (imports) by Local Agriculture in the East from *all* sectors of both the South and West (ranging from Local Agriculture through Restaurants, Government, and to Nuclear Power), and imports from foreign nations (Foreign Trade in the East) as well as capital consumption and inventory depletion charges (noted in the rows on Capital Formation and Inventory Change in the East).

Alternatively, the net output figure for any sector in the East may be derived by subtracting from its total gross output (as noted in last column of Table 1) all sales to endogenous sectors of the East and also all sales to the exogenous producing sectors of the East (i.e., to Nonlocal Agriculture, Aluminum, Steel, etc.), as well as all purchases from the South, the West, and foreign countries, and charges for capital consumption and inventory depletion.

[27] These adjustments are required because, following standard social accounting practices, certain transactions of the customary final demand sectors are defined as contributing to Gross Product. For example, the deliveries of Households in the East to Government in the East (i.e., the labor services rendered by the former to the latter which correspond to wage and salary, interest, etc., payments of the Government in the East) are encompassed in Gross Product, as are deliveries of Households to other customary final demand sectors in the East. Likewise with any services of Households in the East and Government in the East furnished (exported) to sectors in other regions.

In theory, a net contribution must be derived for each customary final demand sector in the East (except Foreign Trade). In practice, a net contribution figure is significant for only Households and Government; and its exact determination is largely dependent on concepts and definitions in social accounting. (Discussion of these concepts and definitions is beyond the scope of this volume.)

value-added figure for any such sector is obtained by summing all its payments to the sectors Government and Households in the East, as listed in the two corresponding rows at the top of the lower half of Table 1.[28] When these payments are appropriately determined,[29] the measure of Gross Regional Product at the production stage in terms of value added is identical with that measure in terms of net output.[30]

As noted in the discussion of Tables 2, 3, 4, and 7 in Chapter 4, another point in the economic system at which Gross Regional Product can be measured is at the place where expenditures occur. This is demonstrated in column 3 of Table 2 of this chapter. Such expenditures are made by Households in the East for consumption purposes (item 5 in column 3), by Government in the East (item 6), and by all kinds of units for the purpose of Net Investment in the East (item 7). To the sum of these expenditures, the improvement (or deterioration) of the region's the Rest of the World Commodity account (item 8) is meaningfully added (or subtracted) to derive Gross Regional Product.[31] The four components of

[28] For example, value added in Local Agriculture in the East constitutes the sum of payments to Government in the East and Households in the East, as recorded in the first column of Table 1. Alternatively, the value-added figure for any producing sector in the East may be residually derived by subtracting from its Total Gross Output (as noted in the last column of Table 1) all its payments to endogenous producing sectors in all regions (ranging from Local Agriculture in the East to Restaurants in the West), all its payments for imports from foreign countries, all its charges for capital consumption and inventory depletion (noted in the rows Capital Formation in the East and Inventory Change in the East), all its payments to exogenous producing sectors in the East (ranging from Nonlocal Agriculture to Nuclear Power) and, finally, all its payments to all final demand sectors in other regions (ranging from Government in the South to Nuclear Power in the West).

[29] Payments to Households in the East at this stage is properly determined as a residual, as noted in the previous footnote. Hence, the predetermined payments to Households in the East by the exogenous producing sectors in the East do not apply. [For each producing sector these predetermined payments (outlays) are equal to its total gross outlays as listed in the last row of Table 1 less all its other outlays listed in its column.] It is to be noted that a discrepancy between predetermined and residual payments to Households in the East for any exogenous producing sector in the East is due to a discrepancy between an assumed level (= total gross outlays) based on initial comparative cost and industrial complex analysis and a required (realized) level (= total gross output) for the given sector. (For an industrial complex the required level is the sum of the required yields of all its outputs.) As already noted in the text, such discrepancy will be ironed out.

[30] Note that the *value-added* measure of Gross Regional Product is basically equivalent to that of Leven's, as described in Chapter 4 and in column 1 of Table 7 in that chapter; and that the *net output* measure is essentially the same as Leven's concept described in column 2 of Table 7 in Chapter 4.

[31] In one sense, the change in the Rest of the World Commodity account represents change in Net Investment in the Rest of the World.

column 3 of Table 2 can be derived directly from Table 1. Consumption Expenditures by Households in the East (item 5 of Table 2) is essentially equivalent to the total gross outlays recorded at the bottom of the Households in the East column less tax payments to Government in the East recorded in this same column. Expenditures by Government in the East (item 6 of Table 2) is essentially equivalent to the total gross outlays recorded at the bottom of the Government in the East column.[32] Net Investment in the East (item 7 of Table 2) is essentially the sum of the total gross outlays listed in Table 1 at the bottom of the two columns, Capital Formation in the East and Inventory Change (additions) in the East *less* the sum of total charges listed at the extreme right in the Total Gross Output column for the two rows representing Capital Formation (consumption) in the East and Inventory Change (depletion) in the East. Finally, the Rest of the World Commodity account (item 8, Table 2) is derived by adding together: (1) the total in Table 1 for the column Foreign Trade (exports) in the East *less* the total for the row Foreign Trade (imports) in the East; and (2) all deliveries (exports) from all sectors in the East to all sectors in other regions *less* all purchases (imports) by all sectors in the East from all sectors in other regions.[33]

Note that cell by cell in Table 1 the *expenditures* measure of Gross Regional Product in the East is identical with the *net output* measure of Gross Regional Product in the East.[34] That is, every cell which records a positive or negative contribution to Gross Regional Product from the *expenditures* standpoint also records the same identical contribution to Gross Regional Product from the *net output* standpoint.[35]

[32] As with all social accounting and input-output work, the precise definition of sectors is determined by the purposes of a study. The definitions relevant to both Table 1 and 2 are postulated to be conceptually consistent. Thus, the equivalence noted in the text is assured.

[33] The entire set of deliveries (exports) from the East to other regions are noted in the second, third, fifth, and sixth *major* blocks of cells in both the first and fourth *major* rows of Table 1. (Table 1 consists of six *major* columns and six *major* rows, as indicated by heavy lines, as well as two columns and one row containing totals.) The entire set of purchases (imports) by the East from other regions are noted in the second, third, fifth, and sixth *major* blocks of cells in both the first and fourth *major* columns of Table 1.

[34] Also, observe that in deriving the *expenditures* measure of Gross Regional Product, Personal Savings of Households in the East and Surplus (or Deficit) of Government in the East may substitute for items 7 and 8 in column 3 of Table 2. (As noted later, we assume for convenience that undistributed corporate profits do not exist.)

[35] For example, take expenditures by Government in the East (item 6, Table 2), as detailed in the first column in the right half of Table 1. Each nonzero figure in the top 44 cells of this column is a positive expenditure and corresponds to an identical contribution to net output by an endogenous producing sector in the East. In the next 88 cells (ranging from Local Agriculture in the South to Restaurants in the West) each figure, whether positive or zero, represents a transaction which contributes a zero amount to

Gross Regional Product in the East, since any positive government expenditure on a commodity represented in any of these cells is at the same time an import which is subtracted from Gross Regional Product in the East in the calculation of the Rest of the World Commodity account (item 8, Table 2). At the same time, these 88 cells record zero contributions to Gross Regional Product in the East from a *net output* standpoint, since they refer to producing sectors of other regions.

The next three cells in the Government in the East column may, according to the definitions employed, represent either nonzero or zero contribution to Gross Regional Product in the East from an *expenditures* standpoint. But, by such definition, they represent the same contribution to Gross Regional Product in the East from a *net output* standpoint. The figure in the Foreign Trade cell contributes zero amount to Gross Regional Product in the East for the same reason that government expenditures on products of other regions correspond to zero contribution. The following figure in the Households cell represents a government expenditure which is a contribution to Gross Regional Product in the East; but, as already noted in footnote 27, this expenditure is defined as an equal contribution of the sector Households in the East to Gross Regional Product in the East from a *net output* standpoint.

The next group of cells which refer to government expenditures on commodities supplied by exogenous producing sectors in the East contain figures which when nonzero represent positive contributions to Gross Regional Product in the East from an *expenditures* standpoint. Since these figures also represent deliveries to a final demand sector in the East by producing sectors in the East, they contribute identically to Gross Regional Product from a *net output* standpoint.

In the remaining cells of the Government in the East column, every positive figure is an expenditure on an imported commodity and, thus, represents, as noted above, a zero contribution to Gross Regional Product in the East. Every positive figure also represents an output of a sector in another region and hence, from a *net output* standpoint, makes a zero contribution to Gross Regional Product in the East.

In the same manner it can be demonstrated that a figure in any cell in any other column, which contributes either positively or negatively to Gross Regional Product in the East from an *expenditures* standpoint contributes identically to the same Product from a *net output* standpoint.

The converse also holds. A figure in any cell which contributes to Gross Regional Product in the East from a *net output* standpoint contributes identically to the same Product from an *expenditures* standpoint. For example, take the Local Agriculture sector in the East (first row, Table 1). The first 44 cells represent deliveries to endogenous producing sectors in the East, which by definition cannot count from either standpoint as contributions to Gross Regional Product in the East. The figures in the next 88 cells represent deliveries to sectors in other regions. These are exports and represent positive contributions to Gross Regional Product in the East from a *net output* standpoint. But these exports are recorded as positive amounts in the Rest of the World Commodity account (item 8, Table 2) and, thus, make identical positive contributions to Gross Regional Product in the East from an *expenditures* standpoint.

The next five cells represent deliveries to customary final demand sectors in the East. These deliveries, therefore, represent positive contributions to Gross Regional Product in the East from a *net output* standpoint. Since these represent successively a government expenditure, two investment expenditures, an export (which is recorded in the Rest of the World Commodity account) and a consumption expenditure, all in or from the East, they also contribute to Gross Regional Product in the East from an *expenditures* standpoint. The next group of cells refer to deliveries to exogenous producing sectors

Still another point at which Gross Regional Product may be measured is at the place where households receive wages and salaries, interest, rents, and profits as factor payments, and where government receives income (largely taxes) for its contribution to the productive process. As in Tables 2, 3, and 4 of Chapter 4, there is presented in column 1 of Table 2 this *income* measure of Gross Regional Product in the East.[36] Once again, each major item embraced by this income measure is directly derivable from Table 1. Income of Households in the East (item 1, Table 2) is simply the total of the figures[37] in the cells in the Households in the East row of Table 1, as recorded in the Total Gross Output column at the right.[38] Receipts by Government in the East, excluding tax payments by Households in the East (item 2 in Table 2), is directly obtainable from Table 1. It is simply the total of the figures in the cells in the Government in the East row of Table 1, as recorded in the Total Gross Output column at the right, *less* the figure in that cell intersecting the column headed Households in the East. As is immediately obvious by our definitions, the

in the East and contribute from neither standpoint to Gross Regional Product in the East. Lastly, any of the remaining cells containing a figure records an export and, by the same reasoning as before, represents an identical positive contribution to Gross Regional Product in the East from both standpoints.

But other cells contain figures relevant to the determination of the *net output* of Local Agriculture in the East. These cells appear in the first column of Table 1. These cells include those that record imports from other regions and are situated in the second, third, fifth, and sixth *major* rows of Table 1. Any figure in any one of these cells represents a negative contribution to Gross Regional Product in the East from a *net output* standpoint. Such a figure is also recorded as a negative item in the Rest of the World Commodity account (item 8, Table 2), and, hence, as a negative contribution to Gross Regional Product in the East from an *expenditures* standpoint.

Finally, figures in the cells registering Capital Consumption, Inventory Depletion, and Foreign Imports represent negative contributions to Gross Regional Product in the East from a *net output* standpoint. They also represent negative contributions from an *expenditures* standpoint since they represent negative items in either Net Investment in the East (item 7, Table 2) or Rest of the World Commodity account (item 8, Table 2).

[36] The contrast of the breakdowns in column 1 of Tables 2 and 3 of Chapter 4 brings to mind again the point that several itemizations are possible and that the most suitable one to employ depends largely on available data, objectives of a study, and the researcher's inclinations.

[37] For exogenous producing sectors, these payments are defined as residuals. See footnote 29.

[38] The breakdown of this income in terms of the several types of factor payments is not directly derivable from Table 1. Alternative tables which do disaggregate the Households row into two or more parts (for example, into wage and salary payments and all other income payments) of course provide additional detail for Table 2. Also, for exposition purposes, both here and later, undistributed profits are assumed not to exist. The Households row can of course be disaggregated to recognize this element, provided the requisite data are obtainable.

contribution which any figure in a cell makes to Gross Regional Product from an *income* standpoint is identical to the contribution which it makes from a *value-added* standpoint.[39]

[39] Since the contribution of any cell to both the *income* and *value-added* measures of Gross Regional Product in the East is identical, and since we have already established that any positive or negative contribution of any cell to both the *net output* and *expenditures* measures of the same product is identical, it remains to establish that the positive or negative contribution of any cell to both the *value-added* and *net output* measures is identical.

As defined, the contribution of any producing sector in the East to Gross Regional Product in the East in terms of *value added* (residually determined) requires, *first*, the recording of its Total Gross Output, which is the sum of the figures in all the cells in the relevant row of Table 1, and, *second*, from this sum the subtracting of all figures in all the cells of that sector's column, except those in the two rows, Government in the East and Households in the East. When this is done for all producing sectors in the East, it is seen that any figure in any of the cells in the first major block of the first major row of Table 1 makes on balance a zero contribution to Gross Regional Product from a *value-added* standpoint. (For example, any sales, say of Local Agriculture in the East, to any of the first 44 producing sectors, say Restaurants in the East, although entered positively in calculating value added by Local Agriculture in the East, is entered negatively to the same extent in calculating value added by Restaurants in the East, since such sales constitute input purchases by Restaurants in the East.) Likewise, any figure in any of the cells in that part of the fourth major block of the first major row, which refers to the deliveries to (and purchases by) exogenous producing sectors in the East, makes on balance a zero contribution, as does any figure in any of the cells in the first major block of the lower part of the fourth major row which refers to deliveries by (and purchases from) exogenous producing sectors in the East, and in only that part of the fourth major block of the fourth major row, which refers to transactions between exogenous producing sectors in the East.

Thus, if we consider any row and its corresponding column, say the first row and the first column which refer to Local Agriculture in the East, we find that for the East as a whole the figures in the first 44 cells of the first row contribute a zero amount to Gross Regional Product in the East, the figures in the next 88 cells contribute positively as do all other figures in the first row, except those that represent deliveries to exogenous producing sectors in the East. And going down the first column any figure in the first 44 cells involves no deduction from Gross Regional Product in the East, whereas figures in all cells in the second, third, fifth, and sixth major rows and in the cells on Capital Formation (consumption), Inventory Change (depletion), and Foreign Trade involve a full deduction. (As with the first 44 cells, those figures in the fourth major row representing purchases from exogenous producing sectors in the East involve no deduction.) But this corresponds exactly to the contributions and deductions made by the various cells along the first row and first column when the net contribution of Local Agriculture in the East to Gross Regional Product in the East is measured in terms of *net output*. See footnote 26.

Similarly, it can be shown that the cells along any row and its corresponding column involve identical contributions and deductions to the Gross Product of the corresponding region when *value added* is measured for the entire region, as do those contributions and deductions when the *net output* of the corresponding sector is measured. Hence, for the region as a whole the contributions (positive or negative) of each cell to Gross

Thus, as sketched in Figure 1, a fused interregional comparative cost–industrial complex–input-output framework yields by region estimates of basic social accounts which may be set down in multiple-entry form.[40] Strictly speaking, at this point the framework yields for each region new estimates of only Gross Regional Product, Net Output by sector, Household Income, Government Receipts, and Rest of the World Commodity account. New estimates of Consumption Expenditures by Households, Investment, and Government Outlays are not generated. However, if *realized* Household Income by regions is different than implicitly or explicitly estimated before comparative cost–industrial complex analysis, if Government Receipts by regions are different from anticipated receipts upon which the initially assumed Government Outlays were based, if the *realized* regional pattern of Employment, Gross Products, Sector Outputs, and Rest of the World Commodity accounts are different than initially anticipated, then it can be expected that a more realistic regional pattern of Consumption Expenditures, Investment Expenditures, and Government Outlays can be constructed. These more realistic expenditure patterns will then constitute the basis for a rerun of the model, to which we now turn. It will be seen that from successive runs of the model discrepancies can be expected to disappear, and a set of more accurate and consistent social accounts can be evolved.

c. Reruns and reconciliations. As is widely recognized among social scientists, and as has been implied at several points in this book, perfect projection and understanding of society would necessitate a complete general interdependence theory fully tested and set down explicitly in quantitative, operational form. No such theory currently exists or is likely ever to be attained. Far short of such a general theory and its operational framework, the analyst must have recourse to approximation. His methodology must involve the quantitative expression of as much interdependence as he can encompass, the testing of such expression against

Regional Product is the same whether such Product is measured in *value-added* terms or in *net output* terms; or in *income* or *expenditures* terms, already established as equivalent to *value added* and *net output*, respectively. (Of course, it does not follow for any given sector of a region that value added is identical to net output, as the reader can readily verify.) And after the reconciliation process discussed in the following section is effected, it will be seen that for exogenous producing sectors of a region household payments based on total gross outlays (which are related to levels determined via comparative cost and industrial complex analysis) are identical to those residually determined. Hence, it becomes immaterial how the investigator defines or determines household payments.

[40] This framework also yields the basic figures for the construction of a table similar to Table 8 in Chapter 4.

other logical constructs and empirical materials, and the successive reformulation and retesting of his initial quantitative expression.

This methodology must be pursued with regard to the fused framework hitherto developed. Not only must the entire framework be subject to successive refashioning, but also in each of its steps the quantitative materials, however derived, must in large part be subject to iteration. The latter process is the concern of this section.

To review succinctly the steps already covered:

1. Basic postulates on birth rates, death rates, technology, etc., are made for the system (assuming the framework is to be used for projection purposes).

2. System (national) population, its labor force, and average productivity are projected for the key future year.

3. Social accounts for the system (including levels of final demand sectors) are estimated.

4. System outputs by sector (industry) are derived via input-output or other techniques.

5. Initial assumptions are made on the regional levels of the customary final demand sectors by region and on the breakdown of these levels by type of expenditure (commodity). These levels and breakdowns are based on current data and estimates (such as those on regional populations, regional incomes, and rates of growth), on the use of the diverse coefficients, curves, relative growth charts, and indices noted on Figure 3, and on trend analyses and results of consumption function studies, government expenditure investigations, etc. Like assumptions are made on the regional levels of each producing sector.

6. Sectors and industries (whole or in part) to be subjected to comparative cost or industrial complex analysis are identified. The market of each region for the output(s) of each of these sectors and industries is crudely estimated on the basis of the assumptions of step 5, and with the use of input coefficients, commodity flow data, and other readily available materials.

7. By the pursuit of comparative cost and industrial complex analysis, the level of each exogenous producing sector in each region is estimated; further, by the use of such analysis and market area analysis of the type underlying the construction of the interregional input-output coefficient matrix, the inputs, by region of origin, into each exogenous producing sector are detailed.

8. An input-output computation is run based on final demands estimated by steps 5 and 7; from the derived outputs of endogenous sectors by region and interregional input-output coefficients, it becomes possible to fill in all cells of Table 1.

As already observed, these steps in all likelihood give rise to discrepancies. One set of discrepancies appears when step 7 is completed. From step 7 there is obtained for each region a pattern of output levels for its several exogenous producing sectors. This pattern, in all likelihood, will differ from the pattern of output levels for these same sectors initially assumed in step 5.[41] Further, the sum of payments to households generated by these sectors will, in all likelihood, differ from that sum of household payments by these same sectors which is implicit in the regional income (and household expenditure) levels assumed or estimated in step 5.[42] Still more, the sum of payments to government generated by these sectors will, in all likelihood, differ from that sum of government payments by these same sectors which is implicit in the regional government expenditure levels assumed in step 5.

Another set of discrepancies crops up after step 8 is performed. As already discussed, step 8 yields for any given sector (whether producing or customary final demand) the set of requirements for its outputs (and services), as listed along its row in Table 1. The sector's Total Gross Output (in terms of the requirements of the system) is recorded in the last column of Table 1. But this Total Gross Output may well differ from the level initially assumed in step 5. Thus, for any given region the pattern of sector outputs (and services) listed in the last column of Table 1 in all probability will differ from that assumed in step 5.

Moreover, a third set of discrepancies arises which relates to certain results of steps 7 and 8. The required level for any exogenous producing sector of a region, which is derived by summing the figures in its row of Table 1, and which is a result of step 8, is not likely to be the same as the level derived via comparative cost or industrial complex analysis. That is, omitting the customary final demand sectors of each region, the pattern of sector levels recorded in the lower half of the Total Gross Output column of Table 1 will in all probability be different from the pattern of sector levels recorded in the right half of the Total Gross Outlays row at the bottom of Table 1.[43]

It is clear that a chief cause of the appearance of discrepancies is the fact that the initial assumptions of step 5 on levels of final demand sectors and producing sectors by region are inconsistent with one another. The

---

[41] These discrepancies and others to be noted later arise only from different distributions (allocations) among the several regions of the system's level for a given sector. The regional levels of each distribution add to the same total which is the level of that sector for the system as a whole.

[42] Put otherwise, this implies a discrepancy between the required labor supply of a region and the available supply initially assumed.

[43] In view of the first two sets of discrepancies, the third set is to be expected.

identification and elimination of such inconsistency are facilitated by the use of an input-output general interdependence scheme as part of a fused framework. Also, as suggested in Chapters 7, 8, and 9, another cause of the appearance of discrepancies is the fact that the industry-by-industry comparative cost approach, and even the industrial complex–by–industrial complex approach, which are pursued in step 7, are likely to yield at least some inconsistent results on output and final demand levels. The identification and elimination of this inconsistency, too, call for the use of an input-output general interdependence scheme as part of a fused framework.[44]

These considerations suggest that the sector levels obtained in the Total Gross Output column of Table 1 have at least a partial internal consistency, a partial consistency greater than that consistency existing among the sector levels derived from step 5. Therefore, subject to certain constraints relating to the extent of change of each sector level, about which more will be said shortly, the levels of the Total Gross Output column obtained from the first run of the framework may be used to provide the basic information on *initial regional markets* for a second run of the framework. Household income for a region may be estimated by (1) summing payments to households over all endogenous producing sectors of all regions (as indicated in the appropriate Households row in the left half of Table 1) and (2) adding all payments to households by all customary final demand and exogenous producing sectors in all regions *based on the levels of these sectors recorded in the lower half of the Total Gross Output column*.[45] On such household income for a region, the households final demand sector for that region may be based, in line with procedures sketched in step 5.[46] Similarly, the other final demand sectors for a region may be re-estimated for second-run use, based on payments by endogenous sectors of all regions as recorded in the left half of Table 1, and on payments by customary final demand and exogenous producing sectors over all regions, these payments

---

[44] Recall that the exogenous producing sectors have been removed from the structural input-output matrix in order to gain a certain amount of precision in their locational analysis. The discrepancies noted represent one of the "costs" of such a step. This cost is, however, reduced when successive runs of the fused framework are performed.

[45] These payments are therefore not the payments which are recorded in the appropriate Households row in the right half of Table 1 and which are fractions of the levels of final demand and exogenous producing sectors recorded in the Total Gross Outlays column at the bottom of the right half of Table 1 (and derived from steps 5 and 7). Rather they are payments which correspond to roughly the same fractions of the levels of final demand and exogenous producing sectors recorded in the lower half of the Total Gross Output column (and derived from step 8).

[46] Note that at this point the investigator may dispense with the use of the diverse coefficients, curves, relative growth charts, and indices noted on Figure 3.

being related to the levels in the lower half of the Total Gross Output column.

In each region the levels of the customary final demand sectors may then be disaggregated by type of expenditure, as noted in step 5, and recorded on a worksheet. Also, input requirements consistent with the derived level of each exogenous producing sector in each region may be calculated and also recorded on the same worksheet. Lastly, input requirements consistent with the derived level of each endogenous producing sector, which requirements are recorded in the columns in the left half of Table 1, are listed on the same worksheet. When for each region the input requirements summed over all its producing sectors are added to the required deliveries to its customary final demand sectors, we obtain its set of initial markets to be employed in the second run.

Once the new sets of initial markets for all regions are obtained, steps 7 and 8 are repeated. That is, comparative cost and industrial complex analyses are conducted to establish a new (more logical) level for each exogenous producing sector in each region.[47] When these new levels are derived,[48] their input requirements may be recorded in a new Table 1. In this new Table 1 may also be recorded the list of required deliveries to each customary final demand sector in each region, which have already been recorded on the worksheet noted. These input requirements and deliveries, when summed along each row, constitute the new set of Final Demand Totals. In turn, these totals lead to required levels of endogenous producing sectors via standard input-output procedures. From these levels the figures for the cells in the left half of the new Table 1 may be obtained in a manner already outlined.

Presumably, the results of the second run (as recorded in the new Table 1) contain fewer and smaller discrepancies among themselves and

[47] In effecting such analyses, we should recognize that results of the first run of the model may also be inconsistent with certain initial postulates on transport rates, labor cost differentials, power cost differentials, etc. See Figure 2. For example, suppose that a power cost differential is postulated on the basis of a hydropower development in a region for which the derived demand of the first run turns out to be insufficient. Such hydropower development must not be assumed in the second run, and hence the power cost differential for comparative cost analysis must be revised. In similar manner, other postulates must be restated appropriately.

Despite such changes, it is to be expected that most of the basic materials and analysis performed in the initial comparative cost and industrial complex analyses will be relevant for the second and succeeding runs of the model. Rigorously speaking, the results of the first run may to some extent be inconsistent with birth and death rates, prices, and other elements assumed in steps 1 to 6. Adjustment for such inconsistencies is much less justifiable in terms of the effort required and the gains scored.

[48] The resulting set of new levels implies different interareal supply channels and thus suggests a new set of interareal input-output coefficients.

also differ less from the initial regional market assumptions than the results of the first run (as recorded in the original Table 1). Presumably, too, some of the remaining discrepancies can be ironed out by taking the results in the Total Gross Output column of the new Table 1 and conducting a third run of the framework. Presumably, this rerun process may be continued until any further elimination of discrepancies involves a refinement unwarranted in the light of inadequacies and errors of even the best available data.

Rigorously speaking, there is no proof that the rerun procedure will lead to smaller and smaller discrepancies, and, further, that the steps outlined lead to the best results. In particular, there is no proof that major geographic shifts of sizable portions of an industry sector will not ensue in proceeding from one run to the next because of scale economies. For example, in one run the initial regional market assumptions may not justify a sizable plant (say an integrated steelworks) for a particular region, whereas in the following run the new initial regional market assumptions may entail greater steel consumption for the given region and justify the location of such a plant within it.[49] In turn, major shifts of this sort may lead to major adjustments in later runs. In short, there is no proof that unrealistic geographic patterns will not evolve from the strict application of the fused framework, a framework which emphasizes the cost and engineering requirements approaches.

However, in practice the sophisticated analyst brings to bear on his research a number of realistic constraints, as hinted earlier. One set of these constraints relates to scarce resources. In each region an initial stock of each resource is either implicitly or explicitly assumed. The stocks of mobile-type resources may be augmented through interregional trade. The stocks of immobile-type resources, however, are subject to small increase, if any at all. Hence, for each of the latter resources requirements in a region must not exceed the region's available supply. The way this constraint operates has been fully described in Chapter 10 on interregional linear programming. It, therefore, is not necessary to repeat here how the investigator computes a region's requirements of an immobile resource and compares the resulting figure with the region's supply of that resource. Suffice it to say that the investigator must perform such an operation, and this step is indicated by the rectangle designated SCARCITIES in Figure 1.[50] From such operations realistic constraints emerge.

[49] Such a shift clearly involves a simultaneous contraction in one or more other regions.

[50] As pointed out in Chapter 10, for a pure interregional model the investigator must also bear in mind requirements and supply of mobile resources for the system as a whole when additional supplies are not available from outside the system. It is to be

Another set of realistic constraints pertains to cultural traits, patterns, and institutions of the peoples of the several regions of a system. These constraints disallow unreasonable shifts of population,[51] culturally infeasible rate of growth or decline of a region as a whole and of its major sectors,[52] unrealistic paces of industrial relocation[53] and capital formation,[54] and other excessive divergences from base year magnitudes. In brief, the analyst forces the results of successive runs to converge in a reasonable manner, broadly speaking. In all this, as is depicted on Figure 1 by the rectangle labeled ATTITUDES, he considers views and values of people, immobilities, institutional rigidities, and similar nonquantitative factors. He does so in a way that is generally similar to the manner in which all social science analysts, either implicitly or explicitly, must account for such factors in their applied operational studies. No more fundamental weakness is involved in imposing reasonable, subjective-type

noted that in a later section we discuss interregional linear programming as it may be synthesized into the fused framework of Figure 1. In such programming resource constraints explicitly appear.

[51] Suppose that a comparative cost study on textiles were to indicate, as successive runs were conducted, that all textile production should leave New England and that major shift of population should ensue in the short run. Because of occupational immobilities and various other factors, such a result would be recognized as unrealistic by the sophisticated analyst. He would also recognize that occupational immobilities and these other factors would lead effectively to a reduction in New England's labor cost disadvantage, so as to soften noticeably the projected decline. He would need to impose on the framework a reasonable constraint, in large part intuitive, limiting such decline in New England.

[52] For example, comparative cost study might indicate that all alumina production should be concentrated in Arkansas, using this state's deposits of bauxite. Aside from the resource constraint imposed by the limited deposits of bauxite in Arkansas, there is a more pressing cultural constraint which limits alumina output based on local bauxite to a level not inconsistent with the maintenance of sufficient bauxite reserves within the United States for emergency wartime use should foreign sources of bauxite be cut off. The sophisticated analyst works such a restriction in the various runs of his framework.

[53] Suppose that industrial complex analysis, on successive runs, suggests a steady or cumulative relocation of steel and steel-fabricating activities from the Pittsburgh region to other major market centers of the United States. Because of the heavy capital investment involved in these activities, let alone community forces within the Pittsburgh region, such relocation would be unrealistic. The sophisticated analyst would introduce appropriate constraints on relocation into the runs of his framework.

[54] For example, the successive runs of a framework may suggest a very high rate of growth of electrolytic processes in the Pacific Northwest based on the use of this region's hydropower resources. In view of the heavy capital requirements and extensive time involved in hydropower development, the analyst will impose a maximum time rate of growth of these processes in general for the Pacific Northwest, reflecting the planning perspective of a culture.

constraints in connection with reruns than in these latter studies.[55]   This points up once again the fundamental need to explore avenues relating to the measurement of attitudes, to the identification of behavioral patterns, and to the incorporation of resulting objective techniques into analytical frameworks such as the one hitherto developed.

Less satisfactory is the justification for the specific manner in which the derived results of one run on sector levels are employed in constructing the initial regional market assumptions for the next run.   Why not gear the initial regional market assumptions for a given run to some weighted average of the derived results and the initial regional market assumptions, both of the preceding run?   Or to some other seemingly reasonable amalgam of derived results and other information?   Admittedly, a better procedure than the specific one detailed may exist, but until it is identified by further research this specific procedure is suggested.   At the minimum, this specific procedure yields results clearly superior to the preliminary projections implied in the initial regional market assumptions of the first run, and to projections based solely on the derived results of the first run when they are associated with major discrepancies.

In this manner the investigator proceeds in an operational fashion to eliminate discrepancies.   After one or more runs, he attains a Table 1. In general in this table the required output of each exogenous producing sector is, except for minor discrepancy, the same as the sector's total gross outlays, where for the households sector in each region realized income (i.e., payments received from all sectors of all regions) is consistent with its expenditure level, and where like consistency holds for the other customary final demand sectors in each region.   Thus emerge his best, internally consistent, estimates by region of Employment, Population, Migration, Basic Social Accounts, and other magnitudes to be discussed subsequently.

d. Exports, imports, commodity flows, and balance of payments. Still another set of valuable results stemming from the framework of Figure 1 are the detail and totals relating to Exports and Imports by region, or, put in other terms, to Interregional Commodity Flows.   Most of these results have already been recognized in the previous paragraphs, but it is significant to obtain perspective on these results from a standpoint which emphasizes physical connections rather than social accounts.

Generally speaking, Table 1 (when fully reconciled) may be said to present a comprehensive picture of interregional commodity flows for a

---

[55] Because of this, it is reasonable to suppose that the use of the fused framework in the same setting but independently by several sophisticated analysts will not lead to substantially different results.

given year. Going across any single row yields the complete detail on exports of the corresponding sector of a region. Going across any pair of *major* rows which relate respectively to the endogenous and exogenous sectors of a given region yields the complete detail on the exports of the region.[56] Going down any single column yields the complete detail on the imports of the corresponding sector of a region. Going down any pair of *major* columns which relate respectively to the endogenous and exogenous sectors of a given region yields the complete detail on the imports of a region. In this sense the interregional flow matrix of Table 1, when constructed for a set of sufficiently small regions, may be said to substitute for many of the commodity flow studies mentioned in Chapter 5.

The last statement, however, fails to recognize the significant contribution which commodity flow studies make in the construction of an interregional flow matrix such as Table 1. As mentioned earlier, and as will become more apparent at a later point, three sets of data are required to derive the data in the cells. One set relates to *levels* of each sector in each region—the levels of the customary final demand sectors being initially assumed, the levels of the new final demand sectors being derived via comparative cost–industrial complex analysis, and the levels of the endogenous producing sectors being determined via an input-output computation. A second set relates to the cents' worth of each commodity input per dollar output or level of a sector of a region. The third set relates to the breakdown of each commodity input among the several regions as sources of supply.[57]

Commodity flow studies are significant for the derivation of both the first and third sets of data just listed. As indicated in Chapter 5, commodity flow studies in themselves are not explanatory. However, in both tonnage (weight) and dollar value terms, they can be extremely useful in generating and testing causal explanation. At the preliminary stage, by pointing up existing structure, they can help narrow down the range of sectors to be investigated and the critical factors to be examined in detail in comparative cost and industrial complex analysis.[58] And when each

---

[56] For example, going across major rows 1 and 4 yields the export detail for the East.

[57] In the purest form of the interregional model the second and third sets are combined into one set, since differences among regions in production practices, consumption behavior, etc., are recognized.

[58] For example, to an investigator having little acquaintance with a particular industry, short- and small-volume flows of its product suggest that this industry need not be attacked through comparative cost or industrial complex analysis. If, at the same time, its product is widely consumed, such flows suggest that the level of this industry in each region may best be determined by an input-output computation.

To cite a second example, if flows of the product of an industry are largely from a single region and are relatively heavy over both long and short distances, this suggests

commodity input is to be allocated among the several regions as sources of supply, current and past commodity flow studies can provide the initial benchmark data subject to modification to the extent justified by market area and other analysis.[59]

In this manner commodity flow studies can supplement the fused inter-regional comparative cost–industrial complex–input-output framework. For a current year this framework tends to reproduce the flows that provided initial material for the construction of a table such as Table 1. But this framework also yields data on interregional commodity flows which were not initially available and thus fills in gaps in current flow studies.[60] For a key year in the future this framework projects a comprehensive set of data on interregional commodity flows, data which tend to have more validity than simple trend projections of flows which are unable to encompass sector interdependence to the extent that this framework does.

Beyond the identification of flows for both current and future years, this framework permits the estimation of a basic account in balance of payments studies. This is the Rest of the World Commodity account which has already been discussed in the previous section. This account covers items A-1 and A-2 in Table 3 of Chapter 5. (The reader may recall from the discussion of Chapter 5 that these items are not easily estimated from the existing sources of data.) For any region this account is simply the

that scale economies, or other agglomeration (spatial juxtaposition) economies, are of moment, or that a weight-losing single-source raw material is being utilized, or that some significant production cost differential (such as labor or power) exists within the region, etc.

[59] For example, a historical study of interregional coal flows and flows of other fuels can be of basic value in establishing interregional coefficients, particularly when only limited cost analysis can be pursued. Additionally, where comprehensive and systematic commodity flow studies exist, we can derive from these in conjunction with regional production data commodity consumption estimates for regions (where regional consumption equals regional production plus net imports or less net exports). Working with these estimates and total outputs of diverse industrial sectors by regions, we can then move toward the construction of regional input coefficients to replace national input coefficients. These regional input coefficients will make it possible to move in the direction of a pure interregional input-output framework. For obvious reasons, the fewer the sectors in a region that consume a commodity, the easier it is to establish regional input coefficients for that commodity, *ceteris paribus.*

[60] Data may be inferred which relate not only to shipments via all transport media as a whole but also to shipments via a specific transport media. For suppose that fairly complete and reliable data are available with respect to a given commodity for all rail, water, and other forms of shipment except truck. Truck shipments may then be estimated as a residual, namely, as the difference between the net commodity balance, as established, for example, in Table 3, and the total of recorded shipments by all media but truck.

sum of its exports recorded in its corresponding pair of major rows in Table 1 *less* the sum of its imports recorded in its corresponding pair of major columns.

However, a comprehensive table such as Table 1 is not necessary for the determination of the magnitude of this account for a current year for a given region. A simpler procedure may be pursued, which may now be described in detail since comprehensive tables such as Table 1 are not yet available. Essentially, this procedure estimates indirectly the *net* export or import of a commodity by deriving a consumption estimate for that commodity and by postulating that the difference between production and consumption of that commodity in a region is equal to the region's net exports (when positive) or imports (when negative). To illustrate, we consider the derivation of the Rest of the World commodity balance for New England, 1947.

The initial step is to obtain and, where necessary, estimate the value of output for each industrial sector in each region.[61] Such data for New England are recorded in column 52 of Table 3. The second step is to multiply the total dollar output of each industrial sector in a given region by the set of input coefficients relating to each such sector. Ideally, these input coefficients should be those that would be contained in an inter-regional input-output coefficient table. Since such a table is not now available, in practice the procedure is to use the national input coefficients relating to each sector, where these coefficients are modified to reflect differences in production practice between the region and the nation as a whole.[62] These national coefficients indicate for the nation as a whole the average cents' worth of inputs from each industrial sector per dollar value of output of any given industrial sector. The multiplication yields for any given industrial sector of the region the estimated total input requirements from other sectors necessary to support the level of output of that sector in the region. Hence, in the case of New England, by multiplying $921,525,000 (which represents the level of agricultural and fishery output of New England in 1947—see row 1, column 52, Table 3) by the national coefficients indicating the cents' worth of inputs from every industrial sector per dollar's worth of agriculture and fisheries in 1947,[63] we obtain

[61] On procedure, see W. W. Leontief, et al. [19], pp. 123–128. Where an industrial complex is explicitly considered, the production of each commodity by this complex must be obtained directly from the worksheet on the industrial complex.

Much of the material and many of the statements of this and the following paragraphs are taken from W. Isard [16].

[62] See University of Maryland [37].

[63] Most of the national input coefficients used are listed in Table 5 of W. D. Evans and M. Hoffenberg [6]. We follow the 50-industry classification of this study.

TABLE 3. NEW ENGLAND : INPUT REQUIREMENTS AND COMMODITY

Industry (Sector) Producing	1. Agriculture and Fisheries	2. Food and Kindred Products	3. Tobacco Manufactures	4. Textile Mill Products	5. Apparel	6. Lumber and Wood Products	7. Furniture and Fixtures	8. Paper and Allied Products	9. Printing and Publishing	10. Chemicals
1. Agriculture and Fisheries	244.5	534.2	7.6	571.2	1.2	8.3	–	1.2	–	57.9
2. Food and Kindred Products	53.6	174.3	0.1	16.5	0.6	*	*	4.1	*	32.8
3. Tobacco Manufactures	–	–	8.1	–	–	–	–	–	–	†
4. Textile Mill Products	1.4	0.1	–	358.0	246.0	0.1	15.4	5.9	1.6	0.6
5. Apparel	1.0	7.2	–	–	124.2	–	0.3	2.8	–	1.4
6. Lumber and Wood Products	3.3	2.9	0.2	4.9	0.1	47.2	20.8	36.8	0.1	2.2
7. Furniture and Fixtures	–	–	–	–	3.3	–	0.4	0.7	–	–
8. Paper and Allied Products	†	16.1	0.6	21.4	1.6	0.2	0.8	358.0	70.3	15.8
9. Printing and Publishing	–	1.4	–	0.6	–	–	–	–	49.8	0.8
10. Chemicals	18.7	51.5	0.2	219.8	9.0	1.1	3.4	25.2	6.3	127.0
11. Products of Petroleum and Coal	10.3	2.1	*	8.2	0.3	3.2	0.1	8.7	0.2	15.5
12. Rubber Products	2.7	0.3	–	3.6	1.1	0.4	0.3	1.2	0.2	†
13. Leather and Leather Products	–	–	–	0.6	3.4	0.2	0.4	–	0.3	–
14. Stone, Clay and Glass Products	1.5	9.0	†	0.3	–	0.6	1.8	3.9	–	12.3
15. Iron and Steel	0.1	0.1	–	–	0.1	0.4	5.2	–	–	0.2
16. Nonferrous Metals	–	–	– .	–	–	0.1	0.9	–	0.9	9.0
17. Plumbing and Heating Supplies	–	–	–	–	–	–	–	–	–	–
18. Fabricated Structural Metal Products	–	–	–	–	–	–	0.3	–	–	–
19. Other Fabricated Metal Products	1.9	19.3	0.1	*	0.4	1.5	7.1	2.3	0.1	6.2
20. Agricultural, Mining and Construction Machinery	1.3	–	–	–	–	–	–	–	–	–
21. Metalworking Machinery	–	–	–	–	–	–	–	–	–	–
22. Other Machinery (except electric)	–	0.5	–	9.6	1.3	0.6	0.6	1.9	2.3	†
23. Motors and Generators	–	–	–	–	–	–	–	–	–	–
24. Radios	–	–	–	–	–	–	–	–	–	–
25. Other Electrical Machinery	–	–	–	–	–	–	–	–	–	–
26. Motor Vehicles	2.5	0.1	–	–	–	†	–	–	–	†
27. Other Transportation Equipment	0.2	–	–	–	–	–	–	*	–	†
28. Professional and Scientific Equipment	–	–	–	–	–	–	0.1	0.8	2.1	0.6
29. Miscellaneous Manufacturing	0.1	0.4	–	1.1	16.2	†	0.9	2.1	–	1.4
30. Coal, Gas, and Electric Power	1.4	6.9	†	28.8	2.3	1.0	1.0	17.0	1.9	9.0
31. Railroad Transportation	9.9	19.5	0.2	25.8	3.8	6.2	2.9	30.9	4.4	13.7
32. Ocean Transportation	1.6	4.5	†	3.6	0.7	0.4	*	2.2	*	2.1
33. Other Transportation	12.5	13.0	0.2	21.7	1.6	6.0	2.2	16.1	1.6	4.5
34. Trade	30.6	14.8	0.4	62.6	23.4	2.6	3.2	24.3	2.0	8.3
35. Communications	†	1.5	†	2.5	1.2	0.4	0.3	1.1	2.5	1.1
36. Finance and Insurance	5.4	5.1	†	5.5	1.5	3.3	1.0	2.5	1.5	0.9
37. Rental	53.9	3.2	–	6.9	6.1	0.8	0.9	3.6	4.0	1.6
38. Business Services	0.2	18.9	1.0	19.5	6.1	0.8	3.1	3.0	3.8	20.3
39. Personal and Repair Services	8.3	4.2	*	0.8	0.2	1.8	0.2	0.6	1.3	0.5
40. Medical, Educational and Nonprofit Organizations	–	–	–	–	–	–	–	–	–	–
41. Amusements	–	–	–	–	–	–	–	–	–	–
42. Scrap and Miscellaneous Industries	–	–	–	6.6	–	–	–	34.5	–	5.3
43. Undistributed	–	73.1	1.3	120.3	83.0	38.0	17.7	27.7	39.6	83.2
44. Eating and Drinking Places	–	–	–	–	–	–	–	–	0.1	–
45. New Construction and Maintenance	4.5	4.2	†	10.7	1.0	0.5	0.4	5.8	1.0	1.7
48. Government	18.3	40.3	1.0	175.6	23.8	14.6	6.0	68.5	21.8	36.5
50. Households[d]	431.7	222.3	3.8	902.8	254.3	110.6	57.3	297.9	197.2	164.1
Total Gross Outlays	921.5	1250.7	25.0	2612.9	814.6	251.1	154.9	991.4	416.8	636.9

BALANCES, 1947, ESTIMATED FROM NATIONAL COEFFICIENTS[a]

11. Products of Petroleum and Coal	12. Rubber Products	13. Leather and Leather Products	14. Stone, Clay, and Glass Products	15. Iron and Steel	16. Nonferrous Metals	17. Plumbing and Heating Supplies	18. Fabricated Structural Metal Products	19. Other Fabricated Metal Products	20. Agricultural, Mining and Construction Machinery	21. Metalworking Machinery	22. Other Machinery (except electric)	23. Motors and Generators	24. Radios	25. Other Electrical Machinery	26. Motor Vehicles
–	–	14.3	*	–	1.0	–	–	–	–	–	–	–	–	–	–
*	–	129.7	0.1	0.1	*	–	–	–	*	–	–	*	–	–	*
†	69.2	25.7	1.6	–	–	*	*	1.0	†	0.2	2.1	0.1	0.8	5.0	1.5
–	–	0.6	0.1	–	–	*	–	0.1	*	–	0.2	–	*	*	1.0
0.1	–	5.0	0.8	1.6	2.6	1.4	0.2	4.1	0.1	0.7	7.8	0.2	0.8	5.7	0.5
–	–	–	–	*	*	*	–	–	†	–	0.6	–	8.5	0.1	0.3
1.4	3.1	15.8	8.8	*	*	0.5	0.2	9.6	†	0.3	4.6	0.3	1.4	6.6	0.3
–	–	–	–	–	–	0.1	–	1.3	†	0.2	0.6	–	0.1	0.7	–
2.6	94.1	36.8	5.7	4.5	7.9	1.3	0.6	10.7	0.1	0.8	7.3	0.7	0.8	24.5	1.1
59.0	1.9	0.6	2.5	38.3	4.6	0.4	0.1	1.5	0.1	0.7	2.8	0.1	0.2	2.5	0.3
†	6.4	14.6	0.4	*	*	0.1	0.1	0.6	0.6	0.3	6.2	0.1	0.2	4.3	5.1
–	–	302.9	–	–	–	*	*	0.1	–	1.8	0.8	*	*	0.1	0.1
0.6	1.1	1.5	21.2	8.1	3.1	0.5	0.2	6.3	0.1	1.6	6.7	1.7	0.6	12.7	2.0
0.1	2.2	0.3	1.1	180.1	3.1	10.4	17.0	167.1	4.5	23.6	108.9	8.6	1.1	27.0	11.4
†	*	*	0.6	14.7	241.7	5.7	1.9	33.1	0.2	3.8	42.9	2.9	2.2	90.2	1.8
–	–	–	–	0.7	–	2.4	1.3	0.9	–	–	4.1	0.1	–	4.4	0.1
–	–	–	–	0.3	–	1.2	1.3	2.2	0.3	0.2	7.8	*	–	1.2	0.1
1.0	1.9	4.7	0.2	1.1	0.4	4.4	2.8	25.9	0.8	11.0	38.2	2.0	5.3	29.1	9.9
–	–	–	0.2	0.7	0.7	–	0.7	–	1.0	3.3	11.2	–	–	–	†
–	–	–	0.4	0.7	0.7	0.4	0.3	6.4	0.4	9.4	10.5	0.5	0.5	2.6	2.3
0.1	–	–	0.1	1.2	0.4	6.7	1.3	5.0	2.6	11.2	66.2	3.7	0.2	11.3	4.1
–	–	–	–	–	*	2.1	0.2	0.1	0.3	4.8	37.1	1.2	0.4	7.2	–
–	–	–	–	–	–	0.1	–	1.6	–	–	0.5	0.6	20.3	13.1	0.2
–	*	–	0.3	0.4	4.3	3.2	0.3	15.2	0.2	2.6	18.5	4.2	13.8	48.3	6.2
*	–	–	†	*	*	–	–	3.9	0.2	1.2	*	–	–	1.7	45.3
*	*	–	*	0.1	0.1	–	–	–	–	0.3	–	*	–	–	0.1
–	–	6.4	0.4	0.2	*	2.1	0.1	0.4	†	0.3	4.2	0.1	0.3	1.2	0.7
–	*	4.4	10.1	10.9	9.7	0.1	†	2.2	*	0.2	5.3	1.5	2.5	8.4	0.2
6.8	5.8	10.5	7.2	19.1	9.3	0.8	0.5	6.3	0.2	2.3	8.0	0.6	0.5	5.4	0.6
3.3	5.6	0.3	0.7	1.4	4.8	1.2	1.1	9.4	0.4	2.0	11.7	0.8	1.1	6.9	2.3
1.1	*	–	3.5	6.3	1.8	0.4	0.2	2.1	0.1	0.5	3.4	0.2	0.7	2.6	†
5.7	1.1	6.1	3.5	6.3	1.8	0.4	0.2	2.1	0.1	0.5	3.4	0.2	0.7	2.6	0.7
0.2	8.6	16.7	2.6	9.8	13.0	2.2	1.7	13.4	0.4	3.6	21.4	1.3	2.8	11.4	0.6
0.2	0.9	1.5	0.5	0.7	0.6	0.2	0.2	1.6	0.1	0.7	2.7	0.2	0.3	1.8	0.2
1.5	1.1	2.0	2.3	2.0	1.3	0.4	0.4	2.3	0.1	1.2	3.7	0.5	0.8	3.1	0.2
–	1.6	5.6	0.9	1.6	2.0	0.2	0.3	2.4	0.1	1.0	3.7	0.6	0.8	2.6	0.2
0.5	3.3	14.3	0.5	1.1	0.5	1.0	0.3	3.0	0.1	1.8	7.5	0.2	2.1	4.4	0.8
0.2	0.2	0.3	1.5	0.1	0.3	0.1	0.1	0.4	†	0.2	0.6	*	*	0.1	†
–	–	–	–	–	–	–	–	–	–	–	–	–	–	–	–
–	1.1	–	0.6	29.4	42.4	0.5	0.1	0.4	0.1	1.0	4.5	0.1	*	0.4	–
9.6	51.2	94.4	28.1	13.0	9.4	12.8	5.3	121.6	3.0	41.2	171.4	3.3	17.0	113.3	5.0
0.3	1.1	5.6	1.7	3.7	1.9	0.3	0.2	2.9	0.1	1.0	3.3	0.1	0.6	2.2	0.5
9.5	17.8	39.7	15.9	25.9	22.8	5.2	3.5	33.7	1.4	14.2	60.2	4.7	5.2	37.8	6.8
59.9	159.5	333.0	111.3	178.4	141.3	37.9	28.9	284.0	10.0	153.2	508.3	39.0	49.6	288.4	34.0
163.8	439.2	1093.1	231.8	555.9	531.2	106.0	71.0	782.9	27.7	301.8	1205.7	79.9	140.9	788.4	146.8

TABLE 3.—*Continued*

Industry (Sector) Producing	27. Other Transportation Equipment	28. Professional and Scientific Equipment	29. Miscellaneous Manufacturing	30. Coal, Gas, and Electric Power	31. Railroad Transportation	32. Ocean Transportation	33. Other Transportation	34. Trade	35. Communications	36. Finance and Insurance	37. Rental
1. Agriculture and Fisheries	–	0.6	0.7	–	0.2	†	0.5	–	0.2	–	–
2. Food and Kindred Products	–	0.7	3.8	†	3.1	0.2	2.0	4.2	0.7	–	–
3. Tobacco Manufactures	–	–	–	*	–	–	*	–	–	–	–
4. Textile Mill Products	0.8	6.9	13.9	0.4	–	0.2	0.5	1.6	*	–	–
5. Apparel	0.9	0.3	*	*	*	*	0.2	0.9	0.1	–	–
6. Lumber and Wood Products	3.0	0.7	11.9	2.7	–	0.1	0.1	1.7	*	–	9
7. Furniture and Fixtures	1.8	0.1	–	*	–	–	*	–	*	3.0	5
8. Paper and Allied Products	1.8	10.9	12.6	0.2	0.1	–	0.2	33.8	0.2	0.1	–
9. Printing and Publishing	–	0.3	–	–	1.4	0.1	1.2	5.8	2.6	15.6	–
10. Chemicals	2.0	8.0	30.5	2.5	1.2	0.1	1.2	4.3	0.2	*	–
11. Products of Petroleum and Coal	1.0	0.3	1.5	21.5	10.2	2.6	26.2	11.9	0.2	1.1	55
12. Rubber Products	1.1	0.7	6.8	†	†	–	7.6	3.7	0.1	0.5	*
13. Leather and Leather Products	0.3	1.2	1.8	*	–	–	0.1	0.1	–	–	–
14. Stone, Clay and Glass Products	0.5	3.8	10.8	0.8	0.5	†	0.1	2.2	*	–	–
15. Iron and Steel	33.3	2.3	6.4	2.0	5.8	–	0.4	–	0.1	–	–
16. Nonferrous Metals	5.6	8.0	31.1	0.3	1.7	–	0.1	–	*	–	–
17. Plumbing and Heating Supplies	0.5	–	–	*	–	–	–	–	–	–	–
18. Fabricated Structural Metal Products	2.8	0.1	–	*	0.3	–	0.1	–	–	–	–
19. Other Fabricated Metal Products	5.6	9.9	6.9	0.2	1.0	0.1	0.4	3.5	0.1	–	–
20. Agricultural, Mining and Construction Machinery	1.3	–	–	1.3	0.1	–	*	–	–	–	–
21. Metalworking Machinery	1.1	1.2	*	–	0.3	–	0.1	–	–	–	–
22. Other Machinery (except electric)	17.5	3.8	0.5	2.7	1.8	–	0.7	0.5	–	1.2	–
23. Motors and Generators	4.6	1.5	–	–	0.2	–	0.2	–	–	–	–
24. Radios	1.4	0.6	–	–	–	–	–	0.2	0.1	–	–
25. Other Electrical Machinery	4.8	3.1	3.3	0.8	1.1	–	0.5	0.4	3.9	–	–
26. Motor Vehicles	*	–	–	0.4	*	–	7.6	1.2	*	–	*
27. Other Transportation Equipment	26.5	–	–	*	1.4	2.3	7.7	–	–	–	–
28. Professional and Scientific Equipment	2.1	25.7	4.4	*	–	–	0.1	–	*	–	–
29. Miscellaneous Manufacturing	0.3	3.8	28.5	0.1	0.2	0.1	0.2	0.6	*	–	–
30. Coal, Gas, and Electric Power	2.5	1.5	4.6	58.2	16.7	0.1	5.3	29.3	0.8	4.6	216
31. Railroad Transportation	3.3	2.0	5.7	6.9	15.5	0.1	3.4	4.5	0.4	0.4	30
32. Ocean Transportation	*	0.3	1.8	*	–	6.5	–	–	–	–	–
33. Other Transportation	1.2	0.7	2.6	1.6	7.4	1.0	14.8	18.5	0.2	0.3	9
34. Trade	6.7	5.7	8.8	1.8	1.1	0.2	24.7	12.0	0.6	3.1	53
35. Communications	0.9	0.9	1.6	0.8	0.7	0.1	2.5	19.4	5.2	6.2	4
36. Finance and Insurance	1.9	0.9	3.3	2.2	0.9	3.6	17.4	59.6	0.4	135.4	39
37. Rental	1.8	1.6	6.4	2.1	0.9	0.2	8.6	116.7	4.1	15.4	14
38. Business Services	0.9	7.4	10.4	0.4	0.8	0.1	1.9	101.4	6.8	10.5	2
39. Personal and Repair Services	0.2	0.1	0.7	0.7	0.4	0.1	15.4	84.2	1.3	8.3	1
40. Medical, Educational and Nonprofit Organizations	–	–	–	–	–	*	*	–	–	1.2	–
41. Amusements	–	–	–	–	–	–	–	–	–	–	–
42. Scrap and Miscellaneous Industries	–	0.1	–	–	–	–	2.0	23.0	0.8	7.8	–
43. Undistributed	36.5	33.1	191.7	16.3	2.3	6.3	4.3	138.0	6.9	45.1	39
44. Eating and Drinking Places	–	–	–	–	–	–	0.6	–	–	–	–
45. New Construction and Maintenance	2.1	1.0	3.3	12.1	42.2	†	7.8	10.8	14.0	2.3	292
48. Government	10.8	19.5	34.9	52.2	40.6	7.6	44.8	223.1	27.1	81.2	286
50. Households[a]	169.2	124.8	363.4	231.7	214.4	27.1	362.7	1560.9	170.6	586.1	1003
Total Gross Outlays	358.3	294.3	814.5	420.7	374.4	59.0	574.1	2478.0	247.4	929.3	2067

* Denotes entry where corresponding entry in the national interindustry flow table is less than $0.5 million.
† Denotes entry of less than $50,000.
[a] All figures in millions of dollars. The data are preliminary and subject to rounding errors.
Source: W. Isard [16].

TABLE 3.—*Continued*

Final Demand spans columns 46. Inventory Change[b], 48. Government, 49. Gross Private Capital Formation, 50. Households.

38. Business Services	39. Personal and Repair Services	40. Medical, Educational and Non-profit Organizations	41. Amusements	42. Scrap and Miscellaneous Industries	43. Undistributed	44. Eating and Drinking Places	45. New Construction and Maintenance	46. Inventory Change[b]	48. Government	49. Gross Private Capital Formation	50. Households	51. Total Input Requirements	52. Total Gross Output	53. Commodity Balance[c]
–		7.4	–	–	15.9	54.7	4.8	-37.2	30.9	1.0	667.3	2188.5	921.5	-1267.0
–	0.1	15.9	*	0.6	8.5	219.3	0.1	+7.3	39.5	–	1510.0	2228.1	1250.7	-977.4
–	–	–	–	0.4	2.9	–	–	+0.7	0.2	–	101.3	113.7	25.0	-88.7
*	1.9	0.3	–	1.0	36.9	–	2.5	-16.2	5.5	1.0	100.2	893.4	2612.9	+1719.5
†	1.3	1.0	*	0.8	9.6	1.3	0.1	+1.8	10.5	†	681.1	849.0	814.6	-34.4
†	*	0.1	–	1.1	28.3	0.3	121.8	+7.5	0.8	1.7	4.6	346.0	251.1	-94.9
–	–	0.3	–	9.2	12.7	–	10.3	+3.5	2.8	26.9	99.5	189.6	154.9	-34.7
0.1	4.0	1.6	–	20.4	53.2	3.6	8.9	-5.9	3.2	–	23.5	710.4	991.4	+281.0
3.4	1.7	11.0	0.9	1.9	37.3	1.9	–	-1.7	8.5	4.2	101.7	343.2	416.8	+73.6
0.3	12.7	14.1	0.1	0.5	75.2	2.7	33.2	+7.9	10.1	–	133.9	1002.6	636.9	-365.7
*	3.7	3.6	0.1	0.3	22.7	0.9	32.2	+0.6	9.6	*	166.2	536.1	163.8	-372.3
–	4.6	0.3	–	0.9	29.8	0.3	2.9	+14.2	1.1	0.4	48.3	172.3	439.2	+266.9
–	2.2	0.4	–	0.2	18.0	–	0.1	+21.9	1.7	0.8	140.8	500.3	1093.1	+592.8
–	1.6	0.4	–	8.3	23.1	3.7	91.0	+4.8	0.9	0.7	23.3	273.7	231.8	-41.9
–	–	–	–	1.3	45.8	–	45.8	+2.4	0.7	–	–	718.9	555.9	-163.0
–	–	*	–	0.4	33.4	0.1	16.5	-0.4	0.3	–	1.3	551.0	531.2	-19.8
–	–	–	–	0.6	6.8	–	45.9	+3.9	0.4	2.8	27.1	101.7	106.0	+4.3
–	–	–	–	2.9	15.8	–	81.7	+0.5	0.2	6.9	0.9	127.0	71.0	-56.0
†	2.1	0.4	–	0.7	72.5	1.5	34.1	+15.1	2.1	3.5	36.6	373.7	782.9	+409.2
–	3.7	*	–	0.4	16.6	–	6.1	+0.9	4.5	77.7	4.5	136.1	27.7	-108.4
–	–	–	–	3.4	16.8	–	–	+2.8	0.6	34.8	2.1	97.5	301.8	+204.3
–	9.4	0.1	–	0.6	109.3	–	17.7	+33.3	4.6	163.4	73.7	569.1	1205.7	+636.6
–	0.2	–	–	0.1	16.4	–	0.2	+2.4	0.6	6.1	–	85.8	79.9	-5.9
*	1.5	–	–	1.6	4.7	–	–	+4.7	4.5	14.0	43.6	113.0	140.9	+27.9
0.2	4.0	0.3	–	4.5	38.7	–	37.4	+21.9	4.1	63.0	45.9	355.1	788.4	+433.3
–	67.7	*	–	0.9	42.7	0.1	1.9	+4.1	8.2	141.2	213.3	544.2	146.8	-397.4
–	0.1	–	–	0.4	29.0	–	0.1	+0.9	84.9	57.0	11.7	222.6	358.3	+135.7
0.3	3.3	11.2	–	7.1	14.6	–	1.2	-2.2	4.3	12.3	43.0	140.4	294.3	+153.9
6.2	10.5	2.9	3.7	–	40.6	1.3	1.7	-20.8	4.6	24.2	131.9	290.2	814.5	+524.3
0.2	19.7	10.3	3.7	0.6	1.5	13.8	1.6	+1.2	10.6	–	9.1	554.1	420.7	-133.4
1.1	1.9	3.3	0.1	0.3	50.8	16.0	36.9	+2.8	18.0	12.6	140.6	566.0	374.4	-191.6
–	–	–	–	0.4	0.1	–	–	–	6.8	–	7.0	46.3	59.0	+12.7
1.2	0.9	12.1	0.1	5.1	70.1	6.1	29.9	+2.2	10.1	4.9	263.3	577.9	574.1	-3.8
5.6	24.8	18.5	0.5	–	51.5	67.1	131.0	+8.9	2.4	110.6	1848.7	2669.6	2478.0	-191.6
17.9	7.9	4.2	0.8	–	5.3	0.7	2.3	–	8.0	–	86.5	199.2	247.4	+48.2
0.9	7.6	5.9	1.8	–	–	4.6	20.9	–	1.7	–	476.9	835.2	929.3	+94.1
2.4	45.6	25.5	12.4	–	–	24.4	4.4	–	12.1	38.1	1383.7	1825.4	2067.0	+241.6
2.7	7.8	1.1	6.6	1.9	26.8	3.5	7.0	–	2.1	–	12.2	333.1	213.0	-120.1
2.8	35.9	4.8	1.5	–	146.1	14.4	42.8	–	4.5	12.8	500.1	901.0	918.0	+17.0
–	–	5.4	–	–	22.2	–	–	–	294.8	–	535.8	859.4	849.0	-10.4
–	–	0.4	27.0	–	0.9	–	–	–	–	–	163.9	192.3	202.8	+10.5
0.8	0.1	0.1	0.9	–	0.8	–	0.1	-54.2	0.1	–	–	111.6	133.1	+21.5
24.0	83.6	60.9	18.5	–	–	33.9	–	–	–	–	–	1925.5	1572.7	-352.8
–	–	9.6	–	–	65.6	–	–	–	–	–	823.5	899.5	839.0	-60.5
0.1	3.6	21.7	1.7	54.2	–	4.6	0.4	–	306.0	743.9	10.5	1590.9	1500.0	-90.9
8.9	32.3	10.8	21.9	–	138.6	89.1	24.6	–	202.9	10.2	2135.2	4213.2	3170.9	-1042.3
43.6	510.4	583.5	100.4	–	114.7	269.0	600.5	–	2040.9	10.3	144.3	14289.4	12978.5	-1311.9
213.0	918.0	849.0	202.8	133.1	1572.7	839.0	1500.0	+39.5	3170.9	1587.1	12978.5			

[b] Minus sign represents inventory depletion, plus inventory accumulation.
[c] Minus sign represents deficit, plus surplus.
[d] Households row includes depreciation and other capital consumption allowances.

column 1 which represents estimates by industrial sector of input requirements into the New England agriculture and fisheries industry in 1947. Similarly, by multiplying $1,250,697,000 (the value of New England's output of food and kindred products) by the relevant national input coefficients we obtain column 2, namely, the estimated input requirements of New England's food and kindred products industry in 1947. In like manner, columns 3 to 45 are obtained, each indicating the estimated input requirements by industrial sector into the New England segment of the industry listed at the head of the column.[64]

The third step in deriving regional commodity balances is to determine the levels of the customary bill of goods (final demand) sectors in each region. More concretely, there must be specified for 1947 the change in the inventory of the product of each industrial sector which each region holds; the dollar value of each product which the government sector in each region requires; the amount of the product of each industrial sector absorbed in the process of building up the gross capital stock of each region; and the dollar value of each product which the households of each region consume.[65] For New England the bill of goods sectors were

[64] The reader is again reminded that these input requirements are crude estimates. For example, take the estimated input requirements of any region's agricultural sector. They deviate from the actual on at least two major counts. One, agricultural practices differ significantly from region to region. Farmers in one region may use more labor and less machinery than in another. As a consequence, their actual labor requirements will tend to be higher than the figure obtained by multiplying the value of their output by the coefficient indicating the cents' worth of labor per dollar value of agriculture for the nation as a whole. Two, the composition of agricultural output in the diverse regions differs. Regions tend to specialize along certain lines. We know that different lines of agricultural production tend to require different sets of inputs, at least to a limited extent. Hence, per dollar value of agricultural output, regional input requirements will differ from one another simply because of difference in composition of agricultural output. Thus, on this second score too, the input requirements of a region's agricultural sector computed above, which are based on the assumption that the character of agriculture is the same from one region to the next, will differ from the actual.

[65] A fifth bill of goods sector, namely Foreign Trade (exports) and the corresponding row, Foreign Trade (imports), which are included in Table 1 and in W. D. Evans and M. Hoffenberg [6], are omitted from Table 3. In the study for which Table 3 was constructed it was deemed appropriate to view foreign countries together as an additional region, and thus to subtract imports of a particular product from foreign countries into a given region from the given region's exports of the same product to foreign countries, when the exports and imports are competitive. Emphasis was on *net* exports or imports, much as in the Bureau of Labor statistics 192 interindustry flow tables. In contrast, when imports of a particular product into a given region are noncompetitive, that is, when the product is not produced at all in the given region (such as certain food products), there logically should be a Foreign Trade (imports) row in Table 3 where such imports could be recorded. Since competitive imports dominate noncompetitive

crudely approximated by assuming that its 1947 net accumulation or decumulation of inventories of the products of any given industrial sector bore the same ratio to national net accumulation or decumulation as its 1947 output of that sector bore to national[66]; that its governmental requirements of various products were for the most part related to the percentage of total United States Federal employees, the percentage of total state and local government payrolls of school and nonschool employees, the percentage of total United States new public construction, and the percentage of total national income occuring in New England in 1947; that, of the amounts of various products absorbed by the gross capital formation sector for the nation as a whole, gross capital formation in New England took a share of each equal to New England's share of national new construction[67]; and that the amount of any given product consumed by New England households was in the same proportion to national household consumption of this product as New England's income was to national. In this way the columns numbered 46, 48, 49, and 50 in Table 3 are filled in.

The last step is to sum the elements in each row up to and including the element listed in column 50. In Table 3 the resulting sums are recorded in column 51. Since each element represents the 1947 requirement of the New England segment of the industrial or bill of goods sector listed at the head of the column, the sum of the elements along any row represents total New England input requirements or consumption of the product of the industrial sector corresponding to the row. Hence, column 51 records New England's consumption of each of the products of the various industrial sectors. Subtracting New England's consumption of the product of any industrial sector from her own production of the product of that industrial sector (as recorded in column 52 in the corresponding row) yields for that industrial sector a net surplus or deficit, that is, a positive or negative commodity balance, for New England. Column 53 lists such derived commodity balances for New England by industrial sector.

In this manner, for the given region of study, net export or import

for the entire United States, and since not even a partially satisfactory technique was available to distribute noncompetitive imports (and also noncompetitive exports and net competitive imports or exports) for the United States by regions, the Foreign Trade row and column were omitted from Table 3. Hence, total gross outlays and total gross output are understated at least to the extent that New England does consume noncompetitive imports and does export noncompetitive items to foreign countries, respectively; both these totals are to be viewed as net of these items.

[66] This is in line with procedures adopted by W. D. Evans and M. Hoffenberg [6], p. 108.

[67] See W. W. Leontief et al. [19], pp. 129–133.

balances (in dollar values) can be obtained for each commodity.[68]   These balances can then substitute for any inferior direct estimates in a balance of payments table such as Table 3 of Chapter 5.   Also these balances by commodity may be added to yield for the region its Rest of the World commodity account.

In the case of New England (Table 3), a Rest of the World commodity account is not struck.   It was judged that the estimated final demand levels were not sufficiently firm to provide an accurate Rest of the World commodity account for New England in 1947, especially when national input coefficients are employed.   However, in another study for which more reliable figures on the levels of final demand sectors were available,

TABLE 4.   1947 GROSS PRODUCT: EIGHTH FEDERAL RESERVE DISTRICT

		Billions of Dollars
Consumer Expenditures		$8.911
Gross Private Capital Formation		1.432
Net District Exports		0.956
Government Expenditures		
Goods and Services	0.749	
Wage Payments	0.732	1.481
Gross Regional (District) Product		$12.780

Freutel has derived an estimate of the Rest of the World commodity account for the Eighth Federal Reserve District.[69]   The estimate for year 1947 is $956 million.[70]   With this figure Freutel then proceeds to derive a *Gross Product* for the region measured in terms of *Expenditures* (see column 3, Table 2).[71]   His figures are recorded in Table 4.   In this calculation procedures described in Chapter 4 for regional income estimation were used to estimate net household income and Consumer Expenditures.[72] Gross Private Capital Formation and Government Expenditures were

[68] For commodity balance studies of other regions, see, among others, G. J. Hile [13]; W. W. Leontief et al. [19], pp. 123–135; G. E. Freutel [11]; and University of Maryland [36].   Also see L. N. Moses [24] on implications of certain final demand changes for trade balances of each region with every other region in a system as well as with the system as a whole.

[69] G. E. Freutel [10, 11].

[70] However, commodity balances of trade were summed only for producing sectors. The balances of final demand sectors were excluded from this estimate.   For full details, see G. E. Freutel [10].

[71] It is to be noted that Freutel's estimate of Gross Product is gross of depreciation and other capital consumption allowances, whereas the measure in column 3 of Table 2 is net of these items.

[72] G. E. Freutel [10], p. 76.

derived via standard social accounting procedures, bearing in mind the fact that the Eighth Federal Reserve District is an open region.[73]

By means of the given procedure and steps, the analyst is able to construct a Rest of the World Commodity account for his region and in turn a Gross Regional Product estimate without the full detail of an interregional flow table such as Table 1. However, the analyst cannot proceed further to the construction of a balance of payments table for his region because, in a typical statement such as Table 5, the data required for the items Gifts and Unilateral Transfers, Gold and Currency Flows, and Long-Term and Short-Term Capital Movements are not furnished by the framework and methodology discussed thus far in this chapter.[74] Such items are essentially *money flows*. It thus becomes highly desirable to supplement and increase the reality of the fused interregional comparative cost–industrial complex–input-output framework (or any abridged form of this framework) with money flow studies and analyses. This step is graphically depicted by the box FINANCIAL ELEMENTS: MONEY FLOWS, and its corresponding arrow in the lower part of Figure 1 of this chapter.

e. Money flow studies and improvement of framework. Unfortunately, interregional money flow study and analysis has lagged far behind the types of analysis already treated. As noted in Chapter 5, not even a 36×36 grid of money flows representing clearings among the 36 Federal Reserve head offices and branches is available on a regular basis. Hence, we cannot add interregional money flow analysis to the fused interregional comparative cost–industrial complex–input-output framework which has thus far been derived and which is operational at least within an abridged

[73] If a Rest of the World Commodity account for New England had been struck in Table 3, its magnitude would have been + $726.3 million if commodity balances for producing sectors only had been considered. If to this figure are added the balances of the final demand sectors, Households and Government (which balances are negative), the magnitude of this account will be − $1627.9 million (subject to adjustment, however, for depreciation and capital consumption allowances which are inextricably included in the Households row of Table 3). If to the latter are added Consumer Expenditures of $12,978.5 million (column 50, Table 3), Government Expenditures of $3170.9 million (column 48), Net Inventory Change of $39.5 million (column 46), and Gross Private Capital Formation of $1587.1 million (column 49), a Gross Product for New England of $16,148.1 for year 1947 will be derived. Note that this figure tends to correspond to a Gross Regional Product from a *Residents* standpoint in contrast to a Gross Regional Product from a *Territorial* standpoint. The latter could be derived from striking a Rest of the World Commodity account for producing sectors only, that is, by the use of the above net export figure of + $726.3 million. See Tables 3 and 4 in Chapter 4.

[74] Or if we consider a table of the form of Table 3 in Chapter 5, data would be lacking for the items Gifts and Unilateral Transfers, Gold and Currency Movement, U.S. Treasury Transfers, and Private Savings.

TABLE 5. BALANCE OF PAYMENTS, 19XX

Dollar Inflows	Dollar Outflows	Net
A. On Current Account 　1. Exports of Goods 　　a. Wheat 　　. . . . . . 　2. Exports of Services 　　a. Freight and shipping 　　. . . . . . 　　y. (Receipts of) interest, dividends, rent, and profits 　　z. Labor and other household services 　3. Gifts and Unilateral Transfers B. Gold and Currency Outflow C. Capital Account 　1. Long-Term Capital Investment by Nonresidents 　2. Short-Term Capital Advances by Nonresidents D. Errors and Omissions	A. On Current Account 　1. Imports of Goods 　　a. Wheat 　　. . . . . . 　2. Imports of Services 　　a. Freight and shipping 　　. . . . . . 　　y. (Payments of) interest, dividends, rent, and profits 　　z. Labor and other household services 　3. Gifts and Unilateral Transfers B. Gold and Currency Inflow C. Capital Account 　1. Long-Term Capital Investment in Rest of the World 　2. Short-Term Capital Advances to Rest of the World D. Errors and Omissions	

form. Yet, because of the promise of interregional flow of funds study, it is instructive to review briefly the conceptual materials of section D of Chapter 5 and indicate points of linkage with the already developed framework.

A résumé of the conceptual materials of section D of Chapter 5 can be neatly made with Map 1 (p. 616) and Table 6. Map 1 relates to the three-region setup of Table 1 but can be easily extended to embrace as many regions as are appropriate for a study. Map 1 also lists the appropriate sectors in each region for which money receipts and payments are to be recorded. Specifically, the sectors are taken to range from Local Agriculture and Food Processing through Drugs and Banks and finally to Households. (These sectors are also listed at the top of Table 6 and are roughly equivalent to the sectors listed at the top of Table 1.) The number of sectors may be varied according to the needs and purposes of a study. At one extreme the number may reduce to one, the region itself.

The arrows of Map 1 depict money flows on a gross basis[75] between each sector of a given region and every sector of every other region. (For clarity of presentation the money flows between any pair of sectors in the same region are not depicted.) They can be viewed as illustrating all types of money flows. At one extreme they may refer to *total* money flows between any pair of sectors.[76] On a less aggregative basis they may refer to the money flows generated by a particular type of transaction, such as payrolls or mortgages, etc., as listed in the left-hand tab of Table 6 (or of Table 2 of Chapter 5). In this latter case it will be necessary to develop a map such as Map 1 for each type of transaction. And on a still more disaggregative basis the arrows may refer to the money flows associated with a finer classification of transactions, one which distinguishes, for example, between flows resulting from the extensions of new mortgages and flows stemming from payments on existing mortgages.[77]

A comprehensive set of maps provides one type of perspective of a system of interregional money flows. A table presentation of transactions of all types among diverse sectors of the several regions provides another valuable type of perspective. The latter also points up very clearly the interrelations of the interregional interindustry system, the interregional social accounting system, and the interregional money flow system. (In fact, the table corresponding to an interregional interindustry system, and

---

[75] If money flows were depicted on a net basis, each flow would be in only one direction.

[76] When the arrows refer to total money flows, and when the number of sectors is reduced to one (the region itself), Map 1 tends to be identical to Maps 17–20 in Chapter 5.

[77] Clearly many of the flows explicitly or implicitly depicted on Map 1 will be non-existent, the more so the finer the transactions category to which Map 1 may refer.

TABLE 6. AN INTERREGIONAL FLO⸱

		East											
SECTOR PAYING → SECTOR RECEIVING, BY CATEGORY OF TRANSACTION		1. Local Agriculture	2. Food Processing	···	20. Drugs	···	35. Banks	36. Investors	37. Other Investors	···	NONLOCAL AGRICULTURE	···	NUCLEONICS	GOVERNMENT	HOUSEHOLDS

East															
1. Local Agriculture	A. Commodity Exchange		···		···						···		···		
	B. Investment Account														
	C. Insurance											· · ·			
	·														
	K. Demand Deposits														
	L. Time Deposits											· · ·			
	·														
	Grand Total														
	· ·		· ··· ·		· ··· ·						· ··· ·		· ··· ·			
35. Banks	A. Commodity Exchange														
	·											· · ·			
	O. Corporate Securities														
	P. Mortgages														
	Q. Consumer Credit											· · ·			
	·														
	Grand Total														
	· ·											· · ·			
HOUSEHOLDS	A. Payroll														
	B. Investment Account											· · ·			
	·														
	Grand Total														
South	1. Local Agriculture A. Commodity Exchange														
	· ·		· ··· ·		· ··· ·						· ··· ·		· ··· ·			

OF FUNDS MATRIX

South				West			
1. Local Agriculture	...	35. Banks	HOUSEHOLDS	1. Local Agriculture	...	HOUSEHOLDS	TOTALS

thus to an interregional social accounting system, is directly obtainable from the more comprehensive table depicting interregional money flows in full detail. Thereby, at the minimum it facilitates data collection and estimation and provides highly useful cross checks.

There are several ways to construct an hypothetical table to depict interregional money flows in their full detail. (In practice, the limited availability of data will greatly restrict the breadth of the table and probably in a major way condition its form.) In Table 6 a form is chosen which will allow easy comparison with Table 1. At the top of Table 6 are listed the sectors and regions noted at the top of Table 1, except that these sectors are partially rearranged; and some of the sectors involved in financial transactions are explicitly noted. At the left the same regional classification—East, South, and West—is also retained. (Because of limited space there is not given in Table 6 the full row-by-row presentation of the regional classification of Table 1 which the reader should keep constantly in mind.) Likewise, in each region the same sectors are employed, again with more explicit identification of those sectors involved in financial transactions.

Unlike Table 1, Table 6 covers

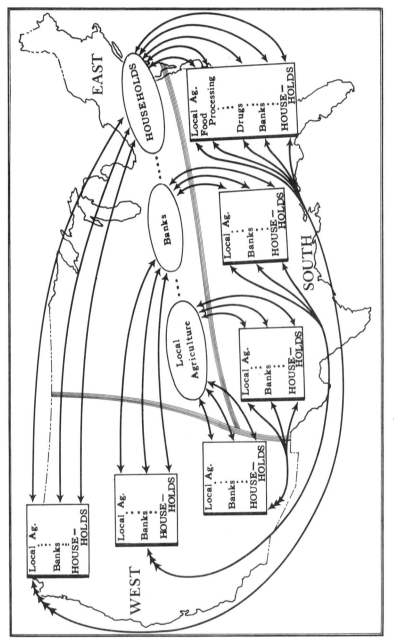

Map 1.   Hypothetical interregional money flows (intraregional flows omitted).

all kinds of transactions, financial and nonfinancial. This fact is evident from the diverse categories of transactions listed under each sector of each region at the left. These categories are largely those of Table 2, Chapter 5, categories that have been found to be useful for flow of funds analysis for the United States as a whole. However, money flows arising from commodity exchange (the interindustry transactions of Table 1, fully reconciled) are listed as category *A*, except for the Households sector for which Payrolls is the equivalent account. This change is obviously effected to lay bare the interrelations of the systems of Tables 1 (fully reconciled) and 6.[78]

The form of Table 6 contrasts rather sharply with the customary form of money flow tables, such as indicated by Table 2 of Chapter 5. Aside from introducing a disaggregation both by region and by producing sector, Table 6 deviates in the row and column presentation of data. In Table 2 of Chapter 5, each sector is listed at the top of the table. For each sector there are two columns, one listing its *sources* (receipts) of funds by type transaction, the second its *uses* (disposition or payments) of funds by the same classification of transactions. In Table 6 the sources (receipts) of funds of a particular sector of a given region are noted by going across the several rows pertaining to that sector. Its uses (payments) of funds are noted by going down the single column pertaining to that sector.

To illustrate, take Local Agriculture in the East. Its sources of funds from sales of its products are listed in the cells along the first row in Table 6; from investments, in the cells along the second row; from insurance, in the cells along the third row; from the use of time deposits, in the cells along the twelfth row, etc.[79] To illustrate further, take Food Processing in the East. Its uses of funds (payments or disposition) are recorded in the second column of Table 6. Its payments to Local Agriculture in the East

---

[78] Formally speaking, if Table 6 refers to *n* possible types of transactions and to *U* regions, each with *r* sectors, then exclusive of total rows and columns its body will contain *Urn* rows and *Ur* columns, provided no industrial complexes are involved. The presence of industrial complexes will cause the number of rows to exceed by still more the number of columns. In presenting the illustrative materials to follow, we shall discuss only single-industry sectors in order to avoid the cumbersome, technical exposition required by treatment of industrial complexes.

[79] Of course, most of the entries in the cells in these rows, except the first row, are zero. For example, Local Agriculture in the East is likely to receive insurance payments from only one sector, or at most a few sectors, in each region. Hence, along the Insurance row pertaining to Local Agriculture in the East, all entries will be zero except in those cells at the intersection of this row with the columns of these few sectors in each region. Likewise, in obtaining funds from reducing time deposits, Local Agriculture in the East is likely to receive funds from a single sector in each region, namely Banks. Hence, nonzero entries are likely to appear in only three cells of the row Time Deposits pertaining to Local Agriculture in the East.

for commodity (input) purchases are recorded in the first cell; and in other cells are recorded all its commodity purchases from all other sectors. Also, listed in the second column are its payments for all types of financial transactions with all sectors of all regions.[80]   For example, the cell at the intersection of the second column with the row designated Corporate Securities under the sector Banks in the East registers payments of Food Processing in the East to Banks in the East for purchases of all corporate securities (including retirement or repurchase of its own securities).   And the cell immediately below this cell records payments of Food Processing in the East to Banks in the East for mortgage retirement, etc.[81]

Now consider the first row of Table 6 corresponding to Commodity Exchange for the sector Local Agriculture in the East.   As noted, the entry in any cell records the money flow received by this sector from the sector at the head of the column for purchases on current account.[82]   But this money flow is obviously equal to the value of the commodity flow on current account from the sector Local Agriculture in the East to the sector at the head of the column, which is recorded in the corresponding cell of Table 1 representing an interindustry system.   Hence, after allowance for the changed order in which sectors are listed, the set of data in the first row of Table 6 is identical with the set of data in the first row of Table 1.

---

[80] Since Table 6 would be of order $Unr \times Ur$, when no industrial complexes are involved, each column is at least n times as long as each row and contains at least as many cells as n rows.   Hence, when we go down the single-payments column of a sector, we obtain at least as much detail as when we go across the n rows pertaining to receipts of that sector.

[81] Most of the cells of any column contain zero entries, as do most of the cells in the n rows pertaining to each sector.   For example, the group of cells in the second column immediately below the first cell are likely to record zeros.   Food Processing in the East is not likely to make any payments to Local Agriculture in the East representing interest, dividends, or other charges on account of investments which Local Agriculture in the East hold in the Food Processing sector in the East.   Nor is Food Processing in the East likely to make any payments to Local Agriculture in the East for Insurance services, or to make deposits with Local Agriculture in the East in order to increase its own Demand Deposits and Time Deposits.

[82] Unlike typical money flow tables, Table 6 distinguishes between purchases on current account and purchases on capital account.   (All purchases on capital account by sectors of a region are aggregated in two columns for each region, the Capital Formation and Inventory Change columns.)   Maintaining this distinction permits a more effective fusion of a money flow framework with the framework already developed in this chapter.   It is also consistent with the distinction effected in Chapter 8 between interregional interindustry flow tables which record transactions on current account and tables which record transactions on capital account.   Clearly, when intersectoral money flow data are available for only the total of these two accounts, the potential for synthesis of a money flow system with an interregional interindustry system is thereby weakened.

In like manner, in the first row of the set for the second sector, Food Processing in the East (which is not listed in Table 6), the set of data is identical to the set in the second row of Table 1. And so on for all sectors through Drugs in the East, Banks in the East, Drugs in the South, Drugs in the West, Nonlocal Agriculture in the West, and finally Households in the West. The first row of the set for each of these sectors in Table 6 is identical with the single row of each of these sectors in Table 1. And vice versa. Thus it can be said that Table 1 depicting an interindustry system is fully embraced by Table 6 depicting a money flow system.[83]

Seemingly, there are certain disparities between Table 1 and Table 6. Consider the sector Households in the East. In Table 6, toward the bottom, are the rows relating to Households in the East. As every other sector, it receives money on Payroll account (from sales of its commodity labor services), on Investment account (interest, dividends, etc.) and so on. That is, the income receipts of the households sector in each region appear in a more disaggregated form in Table 6 than in Table 1. But this is not a real disparity, for in the discussion of Table 1 it was indicated that if income data by household are available on a sufficiently disaggregated basis, the Households rows of Table 1 are to be split up accordingly.

There are other disparities between Tables 1 and 6, especially with regard to the final demand sectors and financial institutions. But these, too, are in essence definitional. We do not discuss them here, since such discussion is beyond the scope of this volume, and particularly since the interregional money flow data are so limited as to preclude the full presentation of such a detailed table as Table 6. However, it is instructive at this point to present a few more illustrations of entries in Table 6.

Suppose Local Agriculture in the East withdrew $1 million from savings accounts in local banks. Then the entry in the cell at the intersection of the row Time Deposits under Local Agriculture in the East and the column Banks in the East would go up by $1 million.[84] This represents a receipt by Local Agriculture in the East and a payment by Banks in the East. Or suppose Households in the East were to pay off $2 million in mortgages held by local banks. Then the entry in the cell at the intersection of the row Mortgages under the sector Banks in the East and the column Households in the East would go up by $2 million.

[83] Looked at columnwise, Table 1 of necessity must be reproducible from Table 6 by the appropriate deletion of nonrelevant rows.

[84] Behind an interregional money flow table is another comprehensive table, or set of tables, which lists for each sector its assets and liabilities. For example, as Local Agriculture in the East withdraws $1 million from time deposits in local banks, its assets of currency increase by $1 million and its assets of time deposits decreases by the same amount; at the same time holding of currency by Banks in the East falls by $1 million as well as its time deposit liabilities.

Because of the extremely limited quantity of interregional money flow data, interregional money flow analyses on the comprehensive scale outlined may be said to be currently nonoperational. We therefore do not discuss this approach any further in this chapter, since we wish to emphasize operational schemes.[85]   However, it is to be borne in mind that were such analysis conducted, it would be highly significant for the fused operational framework already derived. It would provide another source of vital information for estimating for each region basic social accounts such as Household Expenditures, Government Expenditures, Rest of the World Commodity account, Household Income, Government Receipts, Gross Regional Output, etc. All these are directly derivable from Table 6.[86]   It would also provide another source of vital information for estimating and providing checks on detailed intersectoral transactions.

On such a comprehensive scale, an interregional money flow study, too, would cast invaluable light on appropriate regional and thus national fiscal and monetary policy. It would clearly permit the sound construction of a balance of payments table for each region, such as Table 5 (or a suitable variation of this table). In this table items on Gifts and Unilateral Transfers, Gold and Currency Inflow, and Capital account (short term and long term) could be soundly estimated. Over a series of years such a table combined with regional elements study (see Chapter 5) and other information contained in Tables 1 and 6 could lead to better formulation of regional credit policy. An analyst could gain greater insight about capital availability over the years in order to judge better the influence of this factor on general industrial expansion within a region and thus project better the levels of a region's exogenous producing sectors. And if the system to which the interregional money flow study pertains is one comprising several nations, each nation being a region, the significance of such a study would be still greater. This point follows since the balance of payments position of a region and capital and credit availability are much more strategic as factors when that region is a nation. Within the existing international system the flow of capital is much more restricted than within a national system, and accordingly too great a deviation from a balance of payments position cannot be tolerated for any nation (region).

Lacking a comprehensive interregional money flow study, or even an abridged study of sufficient scope, we are not in a position *operationally*

---

[85] For further information on money flow studies, the reader is referred to, among others, M. A. Copeland [5], Federal Reserve Board [7], M. Mendelson [21], and S. J. Sigel [31]. This literature does not discuss an interregional system, whose details the reader must fill in for himself.

[86] This point follows since all these accounts are directly derivable from Table 1, which in turn is contained in a comprehensive table of the type of Table 6.

to fuse the money flow framework (except in certain balance of payments aspects) with the operational framework previously developed. Until such comprehensive or abridged study is performed, and the frameworks of relevant tables and sets of data are outlined, the investigator is compelled to use the limited money flow materials available in secondary ways only. (For example, he may use these materials along with others in reaching a subjective judgment on the extent to which, if at all, the general social-political milieu and economic atmosphere of a region may influence rates of growth objectively determined via comparative cost and industrial complex analysis.)   This conclusion on the restricted usefulness of current money flow materials pertains not only to the channel and framework depicted on Figure 1 and hitherto developed but also to all other channels and frameworks to be subsequently developed or suggested in this chapter.[87]

 f. Economic base, multipliers, cycles, and suggested revisions of framework. We now turn to another set of results stemming from the fused interregional comparative cost–industrial complex–input-output frame-work of Figure 1.   As noted at the right of the figure, these results pertain to economic base magnitudes and to measures of regional and interregional multipliers.   They also relate to the amplitude of regional cycles and some-what less explicitly to the duration and timing of these cycles.

This framework yields a direct and clear-cut picture of the economic base of each region of the system.   As already noted, employment by sector is easily obtained.   So also are gross output, net output, and value added by sector.   Table 1 (fully reconciled) also provides the data for determining both the export (basic) and nonexport (service) fractions for each sector. Hence, with the use of employment, household income, or value added as the unit of measure, the typical basic-service ratio for a region is quickly

---

[87] On the other hand, the empirical materials of the fused interregional comparative cost–industrial complex–input-output framework hitherto developed and to be refined later can be of great value for fiscal and monetary analysis which must be based on limited money flow studies.   This point follows since, as already indicated, many interregional money flows are the counterpart of interregional movements of goods and services.   (Recall that a table such as Table 1 is fully contained within a table such as Table 6.)   When the data on money flows are inadequate or available in a form which conceals many transactions, as is often the case, it may be highly desirable to estimate value of commodity movements between regions, or value of *net* exports or imports on commodity account, from a table such as Table 1, or by the short-cut input-output procedure already described.   These estimates will represent corresponding money flows opposite in direction.   Moreover, in many other ways this framework may be of assistance in money flow study.   For example, it may assist in understanding flows due to Treasury operations by casting light on regional requirements for diverse Federal government functions.

derived, for whatever descriptive value it may possess.[88]   Also, tables such as Table 1 of Chapter 6 which contain data for the calculation of basic-service ratios oriented to *change* in employment, household income, or value added are readily developed when tables such as Table 1 of this chapter are available for more than one year.

Ways in which this framework may be used to supersede the customary economic base–regional multiplier type of study have already been suggested in one connection or another at many points in this book.   When we discussed the impact of basic new industry on a regional economy (such as steel on the Greater New York–Philadelphia region)[89] or of a national investment program on the several regions constituting the nation (such as the *Cassa per il Mezzogiorno* program on North and South Italy),[90] or when we appraise the impact of foreign trade on a local economy (such as United States foreign trade upon Kalamazoo),[91] or of general growth of a region on the outputs of its diverse industries (such as the growth of Maryland on the output of its utilities and other services),[92] we deal with regional multipliers of one sort or another.[93]   However, none of these studies has attacked multiplier analysis per se in as comprehensive a manner as a study of the Utah economy by Moore and Peterson.[94]   In this study several types of multipliers are designed and computed, both in terms of income and employment.   For the most part standard procedures in constructing an input-output table for a regional economy are followed

---

[88] If the basic component of this ratio is to embrace activity linked productionwise to export activity, the computation is more difficult and involves an input-output calculation to be noted later.

[89] See Chapter 8 and W. Isard and R. E. Kuenne [18].

[90] See Chapter 8 and U.S. Mutual Security Agency [35].

[91] See National Planning Association [28].   In this study noteworthy progress is scored in developing a local interindustry (accounts) table which identifies each local sector's *sale to* and *purchase from* (1) each sector in the local economy, (2) each nonlocal sector in the national economy, and (3) foreign countries.   The development of such a table for Kalamazoo involved the considerable participation of local business in making available data, the wise selection of sampling procedures, and the extensive use of national interindustry data and of other diverse data published both for the nation and the local area.   Valuable comments relating to the feasibility of and desirable procedures in constructing such a table are contained in this study.   In addition, this study points up the difficulty of quantifying substitution effects and consequently the need for cautious and well-qualified use of the input-output technique.

[92] See University of Maryland [36].   Also see the unpublished regional input-output study by W. Z. Hirsch [15] for the Metropolitan St. Louis Survey (1958).

[93] For example, in the Isard-Kuenne study the impact of new steel–steel-fabricating activities employing 88,680 persons is estimated to lead to over-all new employment in the region of 180,228 persons; hence the multiplier is 2.03.   In the Chenery study a somewhat different type of multiplier is estimated at 2.53.

[94] F. T. Moore and J. W. Peterson [23].   Also see W. Z. Hirsch [14].

—such as utilizing national input-output coefficients at least as bench-marks when regional coefficients are not easily obtainable. Impacts of representative changes in the bill of goods are examined.

One effect that is investigated is the immediate *direct* effect of such changes. As an example, the demand for the exports of the iron and steel sector of the Utah economy is assumed to fall by $1 million. (Exports to other regions both in and outside the United States are treated as a bill of goods sector.) As an immediate consequence the income generated by this $1 million output (namely, one million times the cents' worth of house-hold inputs per dollar iron and steel output) is no longer realized. Utah income thereby decreases by $0.27 million (see row 4, column 2, of Table 7). Similarly, for a $1 million change in the demand for the exports of any other major producing sector of the Utah economy,[95] the direct income change can be computed. Such changes are listed in column 2 of Table 7.

Direct effects lead to a series of indirect effects. As noted, these latter can be approximated by a round-by-round computation, or by the use of an inverse which is equivalent to a calculation consisting of an infinite number of rounds. Excluding households from the structural matrix upon which the inverse is based,[96] the authors of the study compute the *direct plus indirect* effect of $1 million change in the exports of the Utah iron- and steel-producing sector. This is $0.68 million, as recorded in row 4, column 3 of Table 7. The direct plus indirect effects of similar changes, one at a time, in each of the six other major producing sectors of the Utah economy are also recorded in column 3.[97]

[95] The seven producing sectors are consolidations of 75 producing industries for which data were assembled.

[96] The structural matrix therefore pertains to the interrelations of the seven major producing sectors of the Utah economy.

[97] In the calculation of this multiplier the interregional feedback effect is assumed to be zero. Such an assumption does not seem inappropriate for this study. The Utah economy is a relatively small part of the United States economy. Utah's import re-quirements constitute a small fraction of total national demand; hence changes in these requirements lead to rather small, if not negligible, changes in the demand for Utah exports.

Less acceptable are other postulates. One is "that Utah-produced goods have a definite locational advantage, that input requirements will be met from locally-produced goods to the extent that local output is available" (F. T. Moore and J. W. Peterson [23], p. 372). This means that there are no exports of a commodity until all local needs are first met; and that there cannot be both imports and exports of a commodity such as iron and steel when in reality there are. A second is "that in those cases where Utah output is not sufficient to meet Utah needs each firm will distribute its input requirements proportionately between Utah production and imports of the particular commodity" (*ibid.*, p. 372). A third is that for reasonably small changes in the demand for Utah

TABLE 7. INCOME EFFECTS AND MULTIPLIERS, UTAH, 1947

Industry	Direct Income Change	Income Reactions to Changes in Demand		Income Reactions Including Induced via Homogeneous Consumption Functions		Income Reactions Including Induced via Nonhomogeneous Consumption Functions	
		Direct and Indirect	Multiplier	Direct, Indirect, and Induced	Multiplier	Direct, Indirect, and Induced	Multiplier
(1)	(2)	(3)	(4)	(5)	(6)	(7)	(8)
1. Agriculture and food products	$0.31	$0.74	2.39	$1.34	4.32	$1.12	3.61
2. Metallic and other mining	0.68	0.78	1.15	1.42	2.09	1.17	1.72
3. Coal and coke	0.56	0.79	1.41	1.44	2.57	1.19	2.12
4. Iron and steel	0.27	0.68	2.52	1.24	4.59	1.02	3.78
5. Nonferrous metals	0.09	0.73	8.11	1.32	14.67	1.09	12.11
6. Other manufacturing	0.36	0.52	1.44	0.94	2.61	0.77	2.14
7. Utilities, trade, services	0.59	0.74	1.25	1.34	2.27	1.13	1.92

Source: F. T. Moore and J. W. Peterson [23], p. 375.

At this point one type of income multiplier may be calculated,[98] namely the ratio of (1) direct plus indirect income effects to (2) direct income effect alone (i.e., the ratio of column 3 to column 2). This ratio is 2.52 for the iron and steel sector (as recorded in row 4, column 4 of Table 7); because of decline in export demand, for every unit decrease in income generated by the Utah iron and steel industry, Utah's total income falls by 2.52 units. The multipliers for other sectors are also recorded in column 4; the largest multiplier is associated with the nonferrous metals sector.[99]

This type of income multiplier, however, is incomplete. It does not encompass that part of the impact which stems from decreases in household demand incident to the initial and subsequent decreases in income generated. The households sector has been excluded from the structural matrix, and it becomes necessary to introduce it into the matrix at least in part. When the households sector is introduced *in whole* into the structural matrix and, further, when it is posited that household expenditures are directly proportionate to income (i.e., that the consumption function for each commodity is linear and homogeneous), the direct and indirect effects are obviously larger. The indirect effects now include not only first-round, second-round, third-round, . . . , nth-round changes in the outputs of the several sectors because of the initial change in export demand, but also second-round, third-round, fourth-round, . . . , nth-round changes in these same outputs because of round-by-round changes in household income and subsequently household expenditures and demand. Dollar estimates of direct effects and the more comprehensive indirect effects are recorded in column 5 of Table 7. For example, the estimate of such effects stemming from a reduction of $1 million in the export demand for Utah iron and steel is $1.24 million. Multipliers based on the ratio of (1) the direct plus indirect effects (with households sector as endogenous) to (2) the direct effect (i.e., on the ratio of column 5 to column 2) are recorded in column 6. Change in the export demand for Utah's nonferrous metals again

output the proportion between Utah-produced output and total requirements for any given particular commodity remains constant.

The authors fully appreciate the limitations introduced by these assumptions; on the other hand, the choice of Utah as a region for analysis is rather appropriate because the state is surrounded by a considerable space buffer which along with the simplicity of its economy contributes to the stability of the various relationships observed.

[98] Note that this type of income multiplier is not the Keynesian-type multiplier (discussed in section C of Chapter 6) which is essentially dependent on effects generated by change in local income itself. Although expressed in income units, the former catches only the interindustry linkage effect.

[99] It should be kept in mind that a unit decrease in income generated represents quite different changes in the gross outputs of the several sectors.

has the largest *income* multiplier effect, the relevant multiplier being 14.67.

When change in the bill of goods is accompanied by somewhat similar changes (relatively speaking) in population numbers and family units via in- or out-migration (as was largely assumed to be the case in the steel study of Chapter 8) the preceding treatment of the households sector is not too inappropriate. As a first approximation, it is not unreasonable to assume that when there is growth the new population will spend their (new) income much as the existing population. However, when change in population numbers and family units is not posited to accompany change in bill of goods sectors, such treatment of the households sector is not appropriate. The existing local population and family units for the most part experience the change in income and adjust their expenditure patterns. Such expenditure patterns are frequently derived from a linear and non-homogeneous consumption function, $C = a + bY$ where a and b are positive constants and where C and Y represent consumption and income, respectively. Change in income leads to a less than proportionate change in consumption of (household demand for) any given product or set of products; the smaller the value of b, the smaller the change in household demand for any given change in income.[100]

Such a linear and nonhomogeneous consumption function is also employed in the Utah study. (It can be argued that for an examination of the impact of relatively small changes in export demand for Utah's product, *numbers* of population and family units may be assumed to be unaffected, especially in the short run.) Utilizing consumption functions based on empirical studies, the authors adjust their first estimates of the direct and indirect effects (as recorded in column 3 in Table 7) derived by the complete exclusion of the household sector from the structural matrix. The decline in income associated with the direct and indirect effects of any impact (as recorded in column 3) is employed to derive the associated decline in household expenditures (via the consumption function). This latter decline then leads to a subsequent curtailment of production and thus household income, and hence to still another decline in household expenditures. This second decline leads to a further drop in production and household income and thus to a third decline in household expenditures, etc. By means of three round-by-round iterations of this sort,[101] the

---

[100] Different consumption functions may be employed to estimate expenditures for different commodities, if it is judged that such refinement leads to more accurate results. In the Utah study three different sets of values for a and b were used in the consumption function, $C = a + bY$—one for agriculture and food products, a second for manufactured products, and a third for utilities, trade, and service output ([23], p. 376).

[101] The authors justified three iterations on the grounds that the average annual

estimates of column 3 of Table 7 are revised to yield the magnitudes of column 7.[102] Taking the ratio of column 7 to column 2 gives the third set of multipliers which are recorded in column 8. The multiplier associated with the nonferrous metals sector still remains the largest, being 12.11, indicating that for every change of $1.00 in income generated by the nonferrous metals sector there is a change of $12.11 in Utah income. The third set of multipliers, as is to be anticipated, is larger than the first set but smaller than the second set.

Of the three sets of multipliers recorded in Table 7, probably the third set (column 8) is the most relevant. However, all three sets are *income-type* multipliers, whereas for certain studies and analyses *employment-type* multipliers might be more desirable. These latter can be fairly easily derived, once income-type multipliers have been computed. One typical procedure in input-output analysis is (1) to set down the change in output for each sector from all direct and indirect effects considered,[103] (2) through the use of an input-output coefficient which indicates the requirement of man-hours per unit of output to convert the change in output for each sector to change in employment, (3) to sum the change in employment over all sectors, and (4) to compute the ratio of this sum to the direct employment required to produce that amount of output corresponding to the change in export demand.[104] In the Utah study, a less standard procedure

income velocity of money is about three. They recognize, however, that money courses through different sectors of the economy at different speeds and therefore that the number of iterations might appropriately be varied from sector to sector.

There are, of course, other theoretical as well as practical objections to this procedure, into a discussion of which we cannot enter here. Some of these are presented by the authors. They also indicate other potential uses of the iterative approach (with or without the use of lead and lag times) in order to represent successive cycles of receipts and expenditure of income, together with associated production and employment levels, thereby to introduce a more realistic time dimension into the analysis.

[102] In essence, this procedure recognizes the importance (as suggested in the discussion in section E of Chapter 8 on final demand sectors) of retaining part of the households sector in final demand and placing the rest in the structural matrix. In the Utah study the "a" term of the consumption function $C = a + bY$ is that segment of the households sector (which of course may vary by type commodity consumed) retained in final demand. It is constant and therefore can be stipulated beforehand. The bY term of the consumption function is that segment of the households sector which is placed in the structural matrix. Its size varies with the magnitudes of other sectors and can be determined along with these other magnitudes by the use of an inverse.

[103] As already implied, this change will vary according to the definition of indirect effect (e.g., whether or not households are treated as an endogenous sector) and the extent to which such effect can be identified and measured.

[104] For example, if the change in export demand corresponds to $1 million in iron and steel products, and 0.12 man-hours are required per dollar of iron and steel products, the direct employment will be 120,000 man-hours.

is used to translate changes in output into changes in employment. Input-output coefficients are eschewed. Change in employment in each sector is related to change in output for that sector by a linear and nonhomogeneous function: $E_i = c + dX_i$ where E_i and X_i are respectively total employment (in man-hours) in and gross ouput of sector i, and where c and d are constants which vary from sector to sector and whose values are determined from empirical materials.[105] Aside from this different conversion procedure, the steps in calculating the employment multiplier are the same. Because of differences in type and amount of labor, capital, and other requirements, and of differences in dependence on imports, the relative magnitudes of income-type and employment-type multipliers by sectors do not correspond. For example, we find in the Utah study that employment multipliers for iron and steel and for nonferrous metals sectors are 2.18 and 5.40 respectively, being considerably smaller than the corresponding income multipliers in column 8 of Table 7. In contrast, the employment multipliers for the metallic and other mining sector and the coal and coke sector are 2.88 and 3.18 respectively, being considerably larger than the corresponding income multipliers in column 8 of Table 7.

This study effectively illustrates how a regional input-output framework replaces the customary economic base–regional multiplier type of study as outlined in item B of Figure 6. A still more desirable replacement is achieved when the superior interregional framework of Table 1 substitutes for the crude single-region input-output framework employed in the Utah study. This is so, whether the regional multiplier embraces the local income effect alone (i.e., the Keynesian-type multiplier of Chapter 6) or both the local income effect and the interindustry linkage effect.[106] Further, not only does the fused interregional comparative cost–industrial complex–input-output framework yield a greater amount of relevant detail, but also it avoids most of, if not all, the technical and conceptual difficulties of the customary economic base–regional multiplier study.[107]

[105] For example, the function for the iron and steel sector is $E_4 = 1561 + 52.53X_4$ which yields a change of employment of 52.53 persons for every change of $1 million in the gross output of the iron and steel sector.

[106] As in the Utah study, it is necessary to place the households sector of each region either in part or in whole within the structural matrix to determine both the local income effect and the interindustry linkage effect (the double multiplier of Chapter 6). At the same time it is also necessary to return most of, if not all, the exogenous producing sectors to the structural matrix. But, by the logic underlying the fused framework, this rearrangement leads to less valid analysis, which suggests once again the inferiority of an economic base type of regional multiplier as an analytical tool.

[107] For example, several units of measurement—employment, income, value added—are possible with the detail of Table 1, and hence the investigator need not be confined to a single unit. The formidable problem of identifying basic and service components of "mixed" industries disappears. Because several types of multipliers are derivable

As is implied, Table 1 depicts the basic economic structure of a system and its several regions.   When coupled with the fused framework, it permits impact studies possessing depth well beyond that achieved by the customary economic base–regional multiplier study.   Unfortunately, tables such as Table 1 can be constructed for only a relatively few regions and subregions of a system.   In most studies, particularly small area studies, the detail of Table 1 is not likely to be obtainable for the regions under investigation.   It is at this point that the customary economic base–regional multiplier, or some improved version of it, must be resorted to as

     A. Industrial Composition and Cyclical Behavior
          1. Durable versus nondurable commodity industries.
          2. Growth versus nongrowth industries.
          3. Secular rate of regional growth.
          4. Degree of regional diversification.
          5. Other regional factors.
     B. Regional Multipliers : The Economic Base Type
          1. Basic-service ratio as a descriptive tool.
          2. Multipliers for projection.
              a. Via interindustry linkage and local income effect.
              b. Via local income effect alone.
     C. Interregional Trade Multipliers
          1. Average and marginal.
          2. Measure of relative stability.
          3. Incorporation of autonomous local investment.
     D. Interrelations of Regional and National (System) Cycles
          1. Simultaneous empirical study of regional and national cycles
              a. Regional cycles as reflections of national cycles.
              b. National rate of change as weighted average of
                 regional rates of change.
          2. The historical approach.

       Figure 6.   Economic base, multiplier, and cyclical analysis.

an approximation.   From the previous discussion it is clearly seen that this multiplier is after all a shortcut device to depict structure and trace impact of basic variables in the way that Table 1 and the preceding framework do.   Therefore, when an investigator must of necessity employ this multiplier and the basic-service ratio as tools, he should do so as much as

from Table 1, the conceptual difficulty of selecting the most relevant type can be avoided ; and the use of benchmarks based on location quotients is rendered unnecessary.

Moreover, the fused framework explicitly and adequately treats many factors such as location shifts from scale economies and new technology which tend to invalidate the use for projection purposes of regional multiplier values based on current and past geographic distributions of industry.   The framework, too, avoids the use of an average over-all multiplier ; it specifically generates different multipliers for given changes in the several sectors, as the Utah study so neatly illustrates.   And so forth.

possible against the background of a table such as Table 1. Although such a table pertains to regions defined differently from those suitable for his study, he can at the minimum obtain useful benchmarks and gain insight into basic intersectoral connections within his regions.

Just as the economic base-regional multipliers for the regions of a system are superseded by the fused framework, so also are interregional trade multipliers pertaining to the long run. If such multipliers are constructed with reference to several customary economic base studies simultaneously pursued for the several interrelated regions of a system, they clearly cannot be based on the detail or be as valid as interregional trade multiplier effects directly obtainable from tables such as Table 1. Such tables are, in essence, designed to capture those very long-run interregional repercussions of diverse autonomous changes which the long-run interregional trade multiplier aims to approximate.

Not so, however, with the short-run Keynesian-type interregional trade multiplier. This latter multiplier is a "marginal" multiplier in contrast to the "average" long-run multiplier of the preceding paragraph. As with the industrial composition type of cycle analysis (if established as valid), the short-run interregional trade multiplier can uncover basic forces which escape the fused framework hitherto developed. Therefore, when the short-run interregional multiplier and industrial composition analysis (as outlined in items *A* and *C* of Figure 6) are combined with the fused framework, they can lead to better understanding of the historical process as well as to sounder projection.

This last point may now be expanded. As outlined under item *A* of Figure 6 and discussed in section *B* of Chapter 6, various hypotheses have been advanced describing how the industrial composition of a region conditions the amplitude, timing, and duration of its cyclical behavior. The percentage breakdown of a region's product among durables and nondurables; the distribution of a region's industries among those which are rapidly growing, slow growing, and declining; the long-run growth rate of a region; the extent to which the industry of a region is diversified; and the general character of the region itself have, among other factors, been highlighted by one hypothesis or another. The materials in Chapter 6 do not indicate that any firm hypotheses have yet been established. However, if an investigator does adhere to a hypothesis which attributes significance to industrial composition as a cyclical factor, he must condition his projections and modify his historical interpretations accordingly.

Consider projections. From Table 1 and the fused framework hitherto developed, projections are made on the assumption that cyclical phenomena have no influence whatsoever on the path of growth and contraction. Yet it is a recognized fact that cyclical phenomena do influence the path of development of a region of a system. They are part of the cultural pattern of an industrialized system and are constantly in process. Hence, any analysis of such a system, at least conceptually, should allow for the influence of cyclical phenomena upon long-run development. And if a hypothesis relating to industrial composition is propounded as significant, the detail of tables such as Table 1 when available for various key years will furnish the data required to specify the industrial composition variable for each region. (Further, if such tables were available annually for a relevant period of time, they could provide basic materials for testing any industrial composition hypothesis considered relevant.)

Unfortunately, to date the influence of cyclical phenomena on the path of development of a region of a system has not been firmly identified in an objective way. Further, even if it were, how proceed to appraise the cyclical impact of a specific industry mix? That is, if it were possible to develop for a system a somewhat valid reference cycle to be applied to a future set of years—a reference cycle perhaps along the order of those developed by the National Bureau of Economic Research—and if it were possible to modify the *system's* path of development appropriately, still how adjust a region's path in light of its industrial composition? Would a 50-50 mix of durables and nondurables retard, accelerate, or have no effect on a region's path relative to the system's? Would 100 per cent concentration in durables have, relatively speaking, an adverse effect on a region's path, and if so, to what extent? And so forth.[108] Furthermore, how reconcile the differential effects on the several regions with the consistency requirement of the fused framework hitherto developed? And would the degree of similarity (or dissimilarity) of patterns of industrial mixes among regions have any influence on the system's path of development?

All these questions can only be examined by an investigator at a conceptual level. Too, they must be viewed along with a host of other factors

[108] To the extent that the investigator can answer questions such as these in quantitative terms, he may incorporate his hypothesis in an operational way into the fused framework hitherto developed. As will be shown later in connection with the short-run interregional trade multiplier, quantitative materials which stem from an hypothesis and which relate to the levels of final demand sectors may be introduced into the framework in order to realize cyclical impact. For example, the analyst may estimate that because of their different industrial compositions, the East, South and West will experience declines in household incomes of 10, 15, and 5 per cent respectively for a given year. If he has at least rough estimates of income elasticities whereby to approximate differential reductions in the household demands for different commodities, he can develop new figures for the cells of the Households columns in the East, South, and West of Table 1. Introduction of these new figures into the fused framework will lead to a set of figures different from those recorded in Table 1. These differences will reflect the implications of the investigator's hypothesis, to the extent that it is valid.

which likewise can only be grasped at the conceptual level. In this way, he can proceed to effect subjective-type modifications of development paths yielded by an objective framework. Moreover, it should be recognized that no matter how firmly an industrial composition hypothesis may be established in an investigator's mind, there is always a general regional factor at play, a factor peculiar to each region. Because this factor embraces cultural attitudes, institutions, and anticipations of the people and social groups of a region—elements which thus far have not yielded much ground to scientific inquiry—whatever the objective framework developed to encompass the industrial composition variable, it must necessarily be imperfect.

In a somewhat more precise way, the relationships underlying the short-run interregional trade multiplier may be incorporated into the fused framework. As developed in section D of Chapter 6, this multiplier is defined in terms of basic social accounting magnitudes. Some of these magnitudes are:

1. Household and government expenditures on locally produced consumption goods.

2. Imports of consumption goods (covering not only household and government imports but also imports of intermediates by local producers of consumption goods).

3. Expenditures on locally produced investment goods.

4. Imports of investment goods (including imports of intermediates by local producers of investment goods).

5. Exports of consumption goods.

6. Exports of investment goods.[109]

However, the concept of the short-run interregional trade multiplier requires information in addition to the estimates which a table such as Table 1 can yield for the social accounts just listed.[110] This concept requires information relating to various marginal propensities, such as the marginal propensity to consume, the marginal propensity to import consumption goods, and the marginal propensity to import investment goods. Such information must be obtained from studies which are not discussed in this manuscript—studies, for example, on income elasticities for various consumption goods and on short-run investment behavior.

[109] Note also that these items conform to the social accounts listed in the right-hand column of Table 7 in Chapter 4.

Alternatively, the imports of intermediates by local producers of both consumption and investment goods may be taken out of items 2 and 4 and set up as a separate category.

[110] Or for any alternative set of social accounts.

To make this point in a more concrete fashion, suppose that an investigator postulates that the business community of a single region, say the East, will turn pessimistic, say two years hence. (Ideally, behavioral studies to be noted below might anticipate this development.) He would need to adjust downward the "average" data in Table 1 on the capital formation sector in the East projected as of two years hence. (These data are "average" in the sense that they smooth out short-run periods of pessimism and optimism, to the extent that such can be done.) Pursuing in reverse the approach of the steel study reported on in Chapter 8, the direct (first-round) impact can be ascertained. The direct reduction in the outputs of both local and nonlocal industries supplying this sector can be specified. The direct reduction in household income in each of the several regions can be established. And, of course, second-round, third-round, . . . , and finally nth-round intersectoral effects might be computed. But how encompass the psychological-anticipatory effects of the direct impact? How identify the adverse repercussion on business confidence and thus investment expenditure? How determine the curtailment of household expenditures because of changed outlook and expectations generated by this direct contraction? Still more, how appraise any spiraling, cumulative effects?

Clearly, Table 1 and the fused framework hitherto developed cannot embrace such behavioral aspects of the operation of a system and its regions. They can furnish useful direct impact data, which not only pertain to the initiating region but also to all other regions,[111] and hence to the spatial transmission of cyclical impulses.[112] And to this limited extent they can contribute some operational materials to short-run cyclical analysis of the Keynesian variety and help determine measures of cyclical stability as discussed in Chapter 6.[113] However, for all their comprehensive and quantitative character, Table 1 and the fused framework cannot proceed further. They fail to capture to any significant extent the several important behavioral factors at play.

As yet the interplay of these behavioral factors for a system of regions is to be reliably estimated. Until such is achieved, the short-run inter-

[111] That is, to the other defined regions of a system. For differently bounded regions, especially smaller regions, for which the detail of a table such as Table 1 is not available, resort must be had to benchmarks and other relations derivable from Table 1 as objective background materials for analysis.

[112] In particular, they permit easy identification of carrier industries and their respective weights in terms of their relative *direct* contribution to the spatial spread of cycles.

[113] In this way, too, they can help add an intraregional dimension to short-run interregional multiplier analysis which has been criticized for its relative neglect of forces internal to a region.

regional trade multiplier can be considered at a conceptual level only. We cannot in an operational manner synthesize this multiplier concept with the framework already developed.   If and when the interplay of the behavioral factors is determined, then at least partially it will be possible to attain a synthesis and to generate cycles à la Vining (see Figure 1 in Chapter 6).[114]

To illustrate one possible procedure whereby synthesis may be partially attained, suppose that from current and past empirical materials and his various multiplier studies an investigator anticipates a set of cycle patterns for his three-region system.   Suppose that the anticipated changes are recorded by basic final demand sector for the period 1965–1974 in a table such as Table 8.[115]   However, since such a pattern is yet to be developed and the relative magnitudes of changes are to be determined, there is recorded in Table 8 only a hypothetical pattern where the number of signs in any one cell depict the intensity of change in the indicated direction. (The zero mark in any cell denotes little or no change).[116]   Note that this table reflects the spatial transmission and spread of cycles, the years 1965 and 1974 being taken as "normal" years, for which key projections are made.   The initial cyclical impulse originates in the Investment sector in the West in 1966.   The expansionary effects of this impulse cumulate and the system attains a peak in 1969.   Contraction then ensues leading to a trough in 1972 and a return to normalcy in 1974.[117]   Also to help indicate the direction and relative changes of Gross Product in each region, Figure 7 is constructed.   This figure does not attempt to weight changes by sector.   Rather for any given year it measures for each region the number of positive signs less the number of negative signs over all the region's sectors, as recorded in Table 8.   Figure 7 is merely suggestive.

[114] Recall that in Figure 1, Chapter 6, the several regions of a system experience different intensities of cyclical fluctuation because of their different behavioral features. Regions I and III which are relatively unstable have a high marginal propensity to consume local products (i.e., a low income elasticity of expenditures on imports).   Also, the marginal propensities of other regions to import the commodities of Regions I and III are high.   In contrast, Regions II and IV whose cyclical ups and downs are relatively mild have a relatively low marginal propensity to consume local products and a high income elasticity of expenditures on imports.   Unlike Regions I and III, they possess no investment goods industry for export.

[115] Note that the two final demand sectors, Capital Formation and Inventory Change, are combined into one sector, namely Investment.   For each region the Export sector refers to sales to all sectors in all other regions.

[116] It must be reiterated that Table 8 is purely hypothetical.   It is constructed on the basis of hunch and imagination alone.

[117] Very loosely speaking, both years 1965 and 1974 may be considered to be on the secular trend line for each region, the data for the intervening years recording deviations from the long-run trend lines.

TABLE 8. HYPOTHETICAL PATTERNS OF REGIONAL CYCLES: POSITIVE AND NEGATIVE CHANGES BY SECTORS

1965

	Invest-ment	House-hold Expend.	Govern-ment Expend.	Ex-ports
East	0	0	0	0
South	0	0	0	0
West	+	0	0	0

1966

	Invest-ment	House-hold Expend.	Govern-ment Expend.	Ex-ports
East	0	0	0	0
South	0	0	0	0
West	+	0	0	0

1967

	Invest-ment	House-hold Expend.	Govern-ment Expend.	Ex-ports
East	+	o	o	+
South	o	o	o	+
West	+	+	o	o

1968

	Invest-ment	House-hold Expend.	Govern-ment Expend.	Ex-ports
East	+ +	+ +	+ +	+ +
South	+ +	+ +	o	+ +
West	+ + +	+ +	+	+

1969

	Invest-ment	House-hold Expend.	Govern-ment Expend.	Ex-ports
East	o	+ +	+ +	+ + +
South	o	+	+	+ + +
West	+	+ + +	+ +	+ + +

1970

	Invest-ment	House-hold Expend.	Govern-ment Expend.	Ex-ports
East	−	+ + +	+ + +	+
South	−	+ + +	+ + +	o
West				o

1971

	Invest-ment	House-hold Expend.	Govern-ment Expend.	Ex-ports
East	−	o o	o o o	−
South	−	o −		−
West	−			−

1972

	Invest-ment	House-hold Expend.	Govern-ment Expend.	Ex-ports
East	−	−	−	−
South	−	−	o	−
West	−	−	+	−

1973

	Invest-ment	House-hold Expend.	Govern-ment Expend.	Ex-ports
East	−	−	−	−
South	o	o	o	
West	−	−	−	−

1974

	Invest-ment	House-hold Expend.	Govern-ment Expend.	Ex-ports
East	o	o	o	o
South	o	o	o	o
West	o	o	o	o

The anticipated data of a table such as Table 8 may now be introduced into the fused framework, in particular into a model based on Table 1. The step is easily perceived when it is recognized that the 1965 data which Table 8 records for the several sectors of the three regions are simply changes in totals directly derivable from Table 1 for year 1965. For example, the data on Investment in the East in Table 8 for 1965 indicates zero change; this implies that the investigator assumes a level of Investment in the East which is the sum of Total Gross Outlays for the two sectors, Capital Formation in the East, and Inventory Change in the East (as

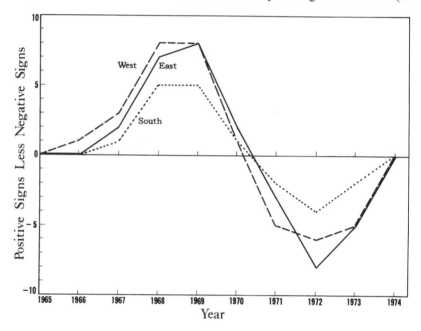

Figure 7. Hypothetical cycle patterns: a three-region system.

recorded in the Total Gross Outlays row of Table 1). Also, the data in Table 8 on Household Expenditures in the East and Government Expenditures in the East in 1965 are also zero, indicating levels for these two sectors corresponding identically to the relevant figures in the Total Gross Outlays row of Table 1. And the data in Table 8 on Exports of the East in 1965 likewise record zero change and signify that the level of exports is the sum of all the individual exports from all sectors in the East which are recorded in Table 1.[118]

[118] Recall that in Table 1 Exports of the East appear in (1) the second, third, fifth, and sixth *major* blocks of cells in both the first and fourth *major* rows and (2) the cells of the column Foreign Trade in the East which fall in the first and fourth *major* rows.

If the data on levels of final demand sectors for all regions implied by the set of changes noted on Table 8 for 1965 are introduced into the model framework associated with Table 1, Table 1 is reproduced. This is not surprising since these levels are entirely consistent with the levels recorded in Table 1. Not so, however, with year 1966. For this year the data of Table 8 do, it is true, indicate levels, except for Investment in the West, which are identical to those that would be recorded in a Table such as Table 1 for year 1966. (A Table 1 for 1966 would differ from a Table 1 for 1965 because of allowance for long-term growth—the secular trend factor.) But, as the plus sign of Table 8 indicates, the Investment in the West anticipated by the analyst is greater than is recorded in a Table 1 adjusted to year 1966 on the basis of long-term growth alone. Therefore, when the levels of the final demand sectors implied for year 1966 by Table 8 are introduced into the model framework associated with Table 1, a different set of results emerge than would be recorded in a Table 1 adjusted to year 1966. This difference reflects the cyclical impulse.

Similarly, for each subsequent year (except 1974) the levels for the various final demand sectors implied by the data of Table 8 differ from the levels that would be recorded in a Table 1 adjusted appropriately for long-term growth. Accordingly, when Table 8 levels are introduced into the model framework associated with Table 1, results are yielded which are different from those recorded in Table 1 adjusted for long-term growth. These differences reflect cyclical effects. Thus, these differences for each year portray the cyclical features of a region's path of development. In this manner, then, the interplay of behavioral factors encompassed in the short-run interregional trade multiplier concept may be *partially* synthesized in an operational manner with the fused interregional comparative cost–industrial complex–input-output framework hitherto developed.

It is to be reiterated that this procedure can effect only a partial synthesis. The procedure is based on an "additive" assumption. That is, it is assumed that a cycle pattern can be added on to a long-term growth pattern, and that these two patterns have no effect on one another. Such an assumption is invalid conceptually, as already indicated. Thus, although a more complete synthesis on an operational basis is not foreseeable at this time, yet conceptually a basic question may still be explored—namely, how do the cyclical behavior of a region and its long-run path of development impinge on each other?

This discussion has indicated the tremendous value that a table such as Table 1 and the fused framework coupled with quantitative short-run multiplier analysis would have for projection purposes. In practice, however, such interregional analysis is as yet unrealized. Therefore, as with any hypothesis based on industrial composition analysis, the investigator cannot be fully objective.   He can modify, in a subjective manner only, this long-run projections (à la fused framework) to take into account those short-run interregional multiplier effects he anticipates to be significant.

Moreover, it is to be realized that although it would be ideal to have a table such as Table 1 available on an annual basis, both in the past and future, such too is far from achievable.   It is clear that if such tables were available, in one sense they would provide the basic materials for, and thus supplant, that empirical multiregional–national cycle approach of Vining noted in item *D* of Figure 6 and discussed in section E of Chapter 6. (Recall that this study of national rates as well as regional rates of change of income aimed to uncover the interplay of cyclical forces from region to region, from region to nation, and from nation to region.)   These tables would illumine the diverse leads, lags, and sensitivities of the system, its several regions, and their various sectors.

Unfortunately, tables such as Table 1 do not exist for all years, or even for one year, in the past, or for years in the future.   Hence, as with economic base studies and diverse multipliers, the multiregion empirical approach, such as embodied in Vining's study, is extremely useful as a shortcut device.   It permits the approximation of certain basic information which could emanate from tables such as Table 1 over a series of years.   Especially does it become valuable to effect linkage between such an approach and the materials of a Table 1 for a base year.   On the basis of an anticipated national cycle, this linkage would permit projection of regional cycles, especially when the investigator can assume that the behavioral aspects, the industrial composition variable, and the regional factor specific to each region *will* operate in each region in the system much as they have in the past.   In effect, such a statistical projection implicitly, and only implicitly, contains a consistent explanation of regional cycles in terms of all factors thus far considered relevant.[119]

g. Interregional linear programming : inclusion in framework. The previous sections present the basic elements of Channel I.   However, certain refinements are possible.   These can easily be grafted on to the fused framework and are likely to be, as further progress is scored in the validation of certain relevant techniques.   One of these techniques is interregional linear programming, and in this section we shall examine its potential contribution to the fused framework hitherto developed.

As explicitly observed in Chapter 10, interregional linear programming

[119] For example, when Vining interprets the ups and downs by region recorded in Figure 2 of Chapter 6, he links industrial composition hypotheses with income elasticities and with various constructs associated with both the economic base multiplier and the short-run interregional trade multiplier.   His interpretation is thus a partial fusion of several theoretical ideas.

may relate to a number of objectives, for example, maximizing employment, or gains in per capita income, or output, and minimizing resource
inputs, or transportation costs, or delivery (including processing) costs.
Since Channel I employs a set of basic assumptions for the system which
tends to establish at the start a Gross Product, a total population, and an
average productivity factor for the system (see the column at the left of
Figure 1), and since the initial regional market assumptions tend to do
likewise for each region, the *minimizing* objectives of interregional linear
programming are typically the relevant ones for this channel. (In other
channels the *maximizing* objectives are typically the most relevant.) In
particular, since Channel I outlines a fused framework which emphasizes
the cost and engineering requirements approaches, the contribution of
interregional linear programming as it reflects an efficiency system is in the
identification of minimum cost patterns. (These patterns refer to production and transportation activities, either singly or in combination.)
Hence, as sketched in Figure 1, the rectangular blocks, LINEAR PROG.,
logically feed into and supplement comparative cost and industrial complex analysis.

The manner in which interregional linear programming can contribute
to Channel I can be specifically illustrated with the materials of section K,
Chapter 10. In that section, some details of an interregional coal study are
reported. A pattern of initial regional markets for coal is identified (see
column 6, Table 8, Chapter 10); this pattern of coal markets is not different
in form from the initial pattern which precedes comparative cost analysis
in the fused framework.[120] Further, in this coal study estimates of unit
extraction costs by mine are presented (see columns 2 and 3 in Table 8,
Chapter 10); cost differentials based on these estimates are in general no
different from the processing cost differentials required for and thus postulated in modern Weberian analysis (see item B in Figure 2 of this chapter).
Still more, in this coal study transport cost materials are assembled which
are the same as those essential for deriving the basic transport cost differentials required for and postulated by modern Weberian analysis (see item
A in Figure 2 of this chapter). Thus an interregional linear program
designed to minimize the total cost of producing and delivering coal for
a system requires and utilizes information which is, except in one respect,
required as well by comparative cost analysis.[121] The one respect in which

[120] In fact, for a year of projection, the successive runs of a fused framework provide
firmer estimates of a regional pattern of coal markets than a less general study, such as
this coal study, can obtain.

[121] Again, for a year of projection the successive runs of a fused framework coupled with
current information can provide a firmer basis for postulates on relevant cost differentials
and other factors than a less general study, such as this coal study, can furnish.

additional information and postulates are required pertains to the capacities of the various coal mines.   In the case of an interregional linear program these capacities must be specified beforehand; and the output of any mine must not exceed its *predetermined* capacity.   In the case of a comparative cost study these capacities are not explicitly recognized.   Their limiting effects on mine outputs are captured via a variable unit cost framework which allows for both diminishing returns and scale diseconomies; unit extraction cost rises sharply as the output of a mine approaches that level set as capacity output in a linear program.   Rigorously speaking, the comparative cost approach is superior since it does not necessitate the postulates of constant unit extraction cost and fixed capacities.[122]   But if these postulates are not too unrealistic for a given situation, and if the computation procedure of an interregional linear program involves important savings in research effort, then in a study of the coal industry for the fused framework the investigator foregoes the comparative cost approach for an interregional linear programming approach.

The materials of section K, Chapter 10, also illustrate how an interregional linear program may substitute for an industrial complex analysis. In this section the outlines and results of an interregional study on dairy production are presented.   This study may be viewed alternatively as relating to a dairy complex, such a complex being a rather simple one involving several processing and transportation activities oriented to a single intermediate product, namely, raw milk.   First, for each region in this study the market for each of the several final products—fluid milk, butter, cheese, evaporated milk, and nonfat dry milk solids—is specified;[123] this pattern of regional markets by type of final product is no different in form from that initial pattern which precedes industrial complex analysis in the fused framework.   Moreover, in this dairy study estimates for each region of unit cost of milk production and of each processing activity are made;[124] cost differentials based on these estimates are in general no different from the processing cost differentials required for and thus postulated in the Weberian approach to industrial complex analysis.   Finally, in this dairy study transport cost materials are developed[125] which are essentially the same as those basic to the calculation of transport cost differentials needed for industrial complex analysis.   Thus an interregional linear program designed to minimize the total cost for a system of producing and processing milk and delivering dairy products to specified regions requires and utilizes information which is, except in one respect,

[122] See the discussion of the coal study in section K of Chapter 10.
[123] M. M. Snodgrass and C. E. French [32], Table 1.
[124] [32], especially Tables 4 and A1.
[125] [32], Table 3.

required as well by industrial complex analysis. As when compared with comparative cost study, the one respect in which an interregional linear program requires additional information and postulates pertains to the production and processing capacities of the several regions and to their several resources in limited supply. In the case of an interregional linear program, capacities and resource limits must be specified beforehand; and the output of any activity or use of a resource must not exceed its *predetermined* capacity or *fixed* supply. In contrast, the industrial complex analysis to a major extent eschews the use of fixed capacities and fixed resource supplies and explicitly treats not only scale economies (inclusive of changes in factor proportions) but also other agglomeration–spatial juxtaposition economies (see item D, Figure 2 of this chapter). In this sense the industrial complex approach is a superior one. However, in situations in which the assumptions of fixed capacities and resource supplies and constant unit production and processing cost are not unrealistic, and when an interregional linear programming formulation can lead to important savings in research effort, such a formulation may justifiably replace an industrial complex approach.

To sum up, interregional linear programming may easily be synthesized into the fused framework hitherto developed along the lines described. From one angle the comparative cost, industrial complex, and interregional linear programming approaches are three variants of a general analytical approach which aims at the identification of efficient minimum-cost spatial patterns.[126] Each variant abstracts from certain relations in order to reach the goal of efficiency. Since the importance of these relations varies greatly from situation to situation, that is, from one partial study to another partial study, it therefore follows that for some situations one of these variants will be the most relevant and for others it will not be the most relevant.[127] Put otherwise, these three variants, synonomous in

[126] Thus it is not surprising that just as comparative cost and industrial complex analyses yield important information on market and supply areas (see item *C*, Figure 2 of this chapter) which assist in establishing interregional commodity flows and interregional input-output coefficients, so does interregional linear programming. The efficient pattern of interregional shipments which emanates from an interregional linear program can not only be checked against actual commodity flows for current and past years in order to test the relevance of such a program but can also help fill in gaps in commodity flow studies and perhaps point up inefficiencies in existing shipment patterns.

[127] Also, it is to be recognized that the objectives and desired results of a partial study may in an important way condition a decision on the most relevant variant. In studies where it is desired to try out different values for a few basic parameters—different levels of regional demand, prices, transport rates, each value being related to one of a set of rather similar hypotheses—the choice of a linear programming formulation may be indicated. Or when it is deemed appropriate to examine a large number of variables and relations at the expense of forcing these relations to be linear, the choice of a linear programming formulation may again be indicated.

certain respects, are effective supplements in the fused framework depicted in Figure 1—although historically the comparative cost approach has been most fully developed, tested, and recognized, whereas the interregional linear programming approach, the most recent on the scene, is yet to be fully evolved, tested, and extensively applied.

h. Factor analysis, scaling techniques, attitudes, and scarcities. In addition to interregional linear programming, there are other techniques which in an operational manner can be grafted onto the fused framework to permit its further refinement. In Appendices A and B to Chapter 7 we discuss scaling and latent structure techniques and factor analysis, respectively. These methods, especially the former, are of relatively recent origin and are yet to be fully evolved. They relate particularly to the quantification of attitudes and similar behavioral elements which are present in any society and which vitally affect the structure and functioning of that society.

In the appendices cited we have suggested how these methods may be linked with other techniques more specifically pertaining to regional analysis. We now wish to proceed further and indicate how, to at least some extent, these methods may be synthesized into the fused framework of Channel I.

First consider the problem common to all general regional and inter-regional analysis, namely, the choice of the most relevant set of regions for a study. Thus far it has been implicitly assumed that a set of regions was either predetermined or selected on some logical basis. Such basis, however, has not been identified, and it is in this connection that factor analysis can make a contribution.

As noted in Appendix B of Chapter 7, the problem of selecting for a study an appropriate set of regions exists not only because of different philosophical approaches and welfare values connected with regional studies but also because an analyst typically finds reasonable alternative interpretations of the same objective data for delineating regions. As a consequence, factor analysis may be resorted to. Some investigators may use this analysis in order to reduce data on a multitude of items to one or a relatively few basic dimensions, thereby diminishing the probability of error (or inconsistency) when some form of subjective judgment must be made. Others may use this analysis more boldly as the best form of an objective-type solution to the problem.

Whatever view the investigator sets forth on the validity of factor analysis, he may frequently find it of at least some utility in the delineation of regions. In the case of single-factor analysis he fully recognizes its many shortcomings: (1) the precise set of factor loadings computed depends

on the characteristics initially chosen as relevant and the method of calculation; (2) once a factor explaining variation in the many characteristics is
precisely identified, it can be designated as the regional factor only by
recourse to the analyst's conceptual framework; (3) variation not explained
by the single factor is ignored; and finally (4) a number of technical
assumptions are required which may be difficult to justify. In the case
of multifactor analysis, he is aware of the presence of some of these shortcomings and still others, especially: (1) the fact that an infinite number of
factor loadings can be obtained which thus permits multiple interpretations;
and (2) the difficulty of specifying which of the several derived factors is
the *regional factor*.

Nonetheless, factor analysis provides some objective basis for syntheti-
cally condensing measurements of a number of characteristics, the more so
because these characteristics are closely related. For single-factor analysis
it yields a single index in which similar values on such an index together
with fairly high correlations of "profiles" or patterns of characteristics
tend to identify subareas which logically form regions. In particular,
in connection with the fused framework hitherto developed, single-
factor analysis may be employed. In this framework widely differing
characteristics such as geological structure and ethnic composition are
not viewed as directly basic. Rather, a narrower range of characteristics
covering such items as income, employment, industrial structure, consumption patterns, and degree of urbanization is relevant. Hence, via factor
analysis the investigator may choose to combine subareas (e.g. counties,
states, etc.) to form the most appropriate regions for his system.[128] Such
use is suggested in Figure 1 by the boxes marked SCALING, FACTOR
ANALYSIS.

In addition to factor analysis, the scaling techniques discussed in
Appendix A of Chapter 7 can be synthesized in an operational way with
the fused framework thus far developed. In Appendix A we noted that,
generally speaking, the value of scaling techniques for measuring attitudes
and identifying dimensions of social structure lies in their ability to transform qualitative and noncomparable quantitative information into
numerical ranking (ordinal values). Specifically, we examined how a
Guttman scaling technique could be effectively utilized with an industry-by-
industry comparative cost approach. It was pointed out that for a set of
basic industrial projections for a region, say New England, to be in fact
realized, not only must attitude and behavioral patterns be generally
favorable or at least neutral in the region as a whole; they must also be

---

[128] It is to be recalled that even after index values have been established for subareas,
subjective judgment may enter extensively in the setting of cutoff points because of the
presence of peripheral (transitional) subareas.

generally favorable, or at least not too hostile, in the particular communities possessing the specific resources (such as a port facility) to which potential new industrial plants must be oriented.

It was illustrated how a scaling approach could be used to classify communities by attitude toward industrial development. Such classification needs to be based on a reasonable hypothesis such as "a community's resistance to industrial development varies directly with its socio-economic status." Based on responses to a set of questions or the presence of certain characteristics, an investigator may attempt to rank communities by socio-economic status. If he is able to rank them satisfactorily along such a single dimension, he proceeds specifically to identify scale types of communities likely to encourage the development of industry as well as scale types likely to resist new industry. Further, if current and past reactions of these communities toward industrial development are consistent to a fair degree with their classification by scale type, the investigator may then proceed to modify and refine the results of an industry-by-industry comparative cost study, if such alteration is appropriate.[129] For example, if the results of a scaling study indicate that the communities of a region which are logical sites for industrial development have intense and highly resistant attitudes toward new and additional industrial plant, the investigator must temper accordingly his projections for growth of the region, based on industry-by-industry comparative cost analysis alone.

In a very similar manner, scaling techniques may currently be operationally employed in the fused framework as indicated in Figure 1 depicting Channel I. (It is not necessary to present again the procedural materials of Appendix A, Chapter 7, which are directly applicable here in the same manner.) They may be used to condition initial market projections by region. They may be used to condition projections realized by both comparative cost study and industrial complex analysis. Too, they may be used to condition the results of a run of the framework, which in turn may provide the basis for estimating the initial regional markets for the following run. Of course, the technique possesses a number of shortcomings. One concerns the relevance of any reasonable hypothesis which may be employed by an investigator. Another concerns the subjective factor in the choice of items thought pertinent to the scale and further in the subsequent arrangement of both items and responses in the scalogram. And a third, among others, concerns the different possible interpretations of the findings and their significance when the coefficient of reproducibility is low. Yet, despite these limitations, the scaling technique may be judged

---

[129] Recall that such alteration is not required if there exists an abundance of communities which possess the relevant resources and whose attitudes favor industrial development.

by an investigator to have direct relevance to his study, especially for regions like New England where strongly influential community attitudes course from restrictive zoning ordinances at one extreme to subsidy-like financial encouragement at the other.

These paragraphs treat the synthesis of factor analysis and scaling techniques into the fused framework on an operational level. The analyst, however, may wish to look beyond what can be achieved today and think in terms of possible future investigations. On this conceptual level there are many other points at which factor analysis, scaling techniques, and latent structure analysis (currently nonoperational) may be grafted onto the fused framework hitherto developed.

For example, these procedures may perhaps be employed to furnish statistical and similar explanation of variation among regions in consumption patterns and behavior, capital formation activity, government expenditure patterns, birth, death, and migration rates, rate of innovation, pace of urban-metropolitan growth, and urban-rural shift. They may be useful in identifying one or a few basic dimensions of people's attitudes in a region, based perhaps on survey data, on data on voting patterns, or on intensity of participation in community affairs. Measurement along these dimensions of the attitudes of a region's people and groups of people can lead to firmer estimates of likely levels of Federal resource development programs, government participation in social welfare functions (e.g., urban redevelopment and educational, health, and social insurance programs), and of consumption expenditures and in turn consumers' savings. Such measurement can bear on business expectations, and in turn credit availability, interregional flows of funds, rates of investment as they are related to business confidence, and also acceptable tax structures and programs (in connection with both civilian and defense activities of the government).[130]

Generally speaking, when the data are quantitative—for example, on voting behavior, consumers' purchases, census materials—factor analysis may be the preferred approach. When the data are nonquantitative and may be ordered along a single dimension—for example, questionnaire data to determine business mood, attitude toward control, or readiness of a community for a soil conservation program—scaling techniques may be utilized. Finally, when data are nonquantitative and tend to be multi-dimensional—for example, in studying migration motives, or community attitude toward industrial development when the data exhibit

---

[130] In addition, measurement along one or several dimensions may cast light on the feasibility of focusing educational and other programs on particular groups, or it may facilitate the process of planning an effective chronological sequence of administrative steps.

no unidimensional tendency—the latent structure approach may be followed.

Needless to say, the investigator will need to select among the various possible studies and the several points at which they may be linked to the fused framework. His selection will be conditioned very much by the system he is studying, his objectives and data, and his inclinations. For example, if his system embraces Southeast Asia, he may judge that studies relating to attitudes toward birth control, labor force participation, and public health practices are critical (whereas he may reach an opposite judgment if his system is the United States). He will tend to synthesize the results of his study, as they pertain to the different regions (cultures) in his system, at several points of the fused framework of Channel I depicted in Figure 1. These results will be incorporated in any initial projection of a system population. They will be injected again into the initial regional market assumptions and synthesized, too, with the results of each run, thereby reconstructing on a firmer basis the initial regional market assumptions for each successive run.[131]

Or to take another example, if a system is unlike that of the United States and comprises several regions culturally heterogeneous, the investigator may study general cultural factors and patterns as they set limits to achievable rates of growth. Any enlightening materials which evolve might be relevant throughout Channel I of Figure 1. In particular, they are likely to be directly relevant at the point where results flow out of a run of the fused framework. (Hence, as already noted, we insert a rectangle labeled ATTITUDES at this point in Channel I of Figure 1.) These enlightening materials will provide a feasibility test, by region, for the results of a run and furnish certain relevant limits when results are partially infeasible. Observe that materials of this type which generally relate to feasible regional rates of growth may be claimed to include certain realistic constraints discussed in subsection B.2.c. Recall that these latter constraints are used by an investigator to disallow, among other phenomena, unreasonable shifts of population and unrealistic paces of industrial relocation and capital formation.

Although this section suggests many points at which factor analysis, scaling techniques, and latent structure methods may be grafted onto the fused framework, it has been indicated that linkage in an operational sense can be attained currently at only a relatively few points. It is fully recognized that many imposing obstacles beset the path toward more extensive operational synthesis. These obstacles will become still more evident later when we discuss Channel IV. In this channel, which con-

[131] In fact, as will be mentioned later, such reconstruction may force revision of an initial projection of system population.

cerns values and social goals, we more fully probe into certain points of synthesis, primarily because any increase in the objectivity with which attitudes and nonmaterial welfare considerations can be incorporated into the framework of a channel greatly enhances its fruitfulness.

With these remarks we conclude the discussion of Channel I, a channel which is centrally operational. It is certainly possible to add to it a number of other basic techniques, refinements, and results. We can introduce probability, gravity, and potential models to illustrate a basic technique. We can spell out more fully social goals as they set constraints and compel additional refinement. We can present further results, such as those bearing on urban-metropolitan structure. We choose not to do so at this point in order not to lose the emphasis of the channel. We prefer to move on to the discussion of several other channels, each placing central emphasis on other basic techniques, refinements, and results. At the end of this chapter we in a very general sense fuse all the channels, but by that time the fusion will also be obvious to the reader.

C. CHANNEL II: A FUSED FRAMEWORK WITH EMPHASIS ON URBAN–METROPOLITAN STRUCTURE

1. THE FUNDAMENTAL FEATURES AND RESULTS

As with Channel I, Channel II is designed to be operational and to produce results based on reasoning processes which are widely accepted as both valid and relevant. In contrast with Channel I, this channel emphasizes results pertaining to urban-metropolitan structure. This contrast explains the one major difference in the basic frameworks of Channels I and II.

As discussed in section G of Chapter 8, an alternative to a pure interregional input-output model is a balanced regional input-output model. The balanced regional model explicitly recognizes the hierarchy which exists among commodities in the size of their market areas and the average distance of their shipment. It thus explicitly recognizes and exploits the basic empirical materials underlying central place theories, as developed by Christaller, Lösch, and others. (See Appendix A, Chapter 6, which the reader may fruitfully review at this point.) For example, it hypothesizes that (1) in a given local neighborhood area the production of shoe repair and other similar services exactly equals the consumption of these services within this area, which *in fact* is approximately true; (2) in that district of a greater metropolitan region served by a major shopping center, the production of supermarket and similar retail services exactly equals the consumption of these services within the district, which *in fact* is approximately true; (3) in a greater metropolitan region as a whole, the production of newspapers, department store retail services, and similar commodities exactly equals the consumption of these commodities within the region, which *in fact* is approximately true; and so forth.[132]

Utilizing these highly realistic hypotheses, the investigator basically concerned with urban-metropolitan projection can fruitfully substitute a balanced regional input-output model for the interregional input-output model of the fused framework of Channel I. The structure of the resulting Channel II is depicted on Figure 8, when the rounded major block designated PROBABILITY, GRAVITY, POTENTIAL MODELS is deleted (a block which will be central to Channel III). As in Channel I, the investigator begins with a set of Basic Assumptions for the system. He proceeds through the same several steps to a set of Initial Regional Market Assumptions. In doing so he utilizes as preliminary tools the various coefficients, curves, growth charts, and indices indicated in Figure 3 of this chapter. Also involved in this process is the selection of a suitable classification of commodities and an appropriate delineation of regions and subregions of various orders. In particular, this selection is to be conditioned by the type and detail of urban-metropolitan results required.[133] To facilitate the ensuing discussion, suppose that the investigator decides on a fourfold classification of commodities and corresponding regions:

1. *National* (system) commodities (such as tractors) whose production and consumption balance only within the nation (system) as a whole.

2. *Regional* commodities (such as newspapers) whose production and consumption balance only within the nation and each metropolitan region as a whole.

3. *Subregional* commodities (such as supermarket retail services) whose production and consumption balance within each subregion of a metropolitan region but not within each local (neighborhood) area.

---

[132] Thus the balanced regional model recognizes, as central place theory does, that (1) because of scale economies and other factors some activities should be located at a major node or central point of a very large region, which as a consequence generates a large volume of commodity flows moving over a relatively long average distance; (2) because of high transport cost, travel time, perishability, and like factors, certain activities should be performed at a number of local sites, and as a consequence each such site generates a small volume of relatively short commodity flows; and so forth.

But in a major way the balanced regional input-output model goes beyond central place theory. The latter tends to ignore the existence of heavy resource and raw material-using activities, and tends to ignore the reality of heavy industrial concentrations at resource sites such as coal deposits. In contrast, the balanced regional input-output framework takes full cognizance of these actualities, as well as all the phenomena encompassed by central place theory.

[133] For full discussion of the difficulties and sources of error involved in this selection, see section G of Chapter 8 and literature cited therein.

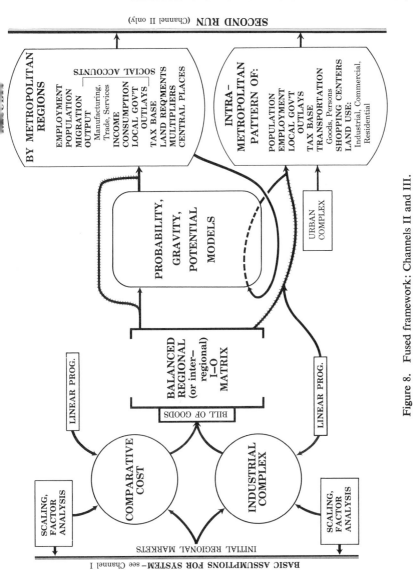

Figure 8. Fused framework: Channels II and III.

4. *Local* commodities (such as shoe repair services) whose production and consumption balance within each local area of each subregion, as well as within each subregion, each metropolitan region, and the system.

Given initial regional markets, the investigator then conducts COM-PARATIVE COST and INDUSTRIAL COMPLEX analyses, by a Weberian approach, as noted in Figure 8. Where feasible, he supplements these analyses with SCALING, FACTOR ANALYSIS, and INTERREGIONAL LINEAR PROGRAMMING in ways indicated in the discussion of the previous channel. He then has the basic materials for approximating the sets of constant allocating coefficients whereby the output of each national industry (activity) is distributed among the several regions and subregions (including the metropolitan regions and their subareas of various orders), and whereby the output of any regional industry (activity) is assigned to its several constituent subregions, etc. In such assignment industrial complexes as well as single industries are to be considered. However, in what follows we shall have reference only to single industries in order to keep the sketch of this channel as brief as possible. The reader can readily develop a full sketch inclusive of industrial complexes.

Following standard procedures as sketched in section G of Chapter 8, the investigator sets up the several BILLS OF GOODS required for the balanced regional input-output model and operates the model. He obtains results for (1) metropolitan regions as a whole, (2) constituent subregions of metropolitan regions, and (3) other regions and subregions which may be involved in his hierarchy. This link leading to results for urban-metropolitan regions as a whole and their constituent subregions is indicated in Figure 8 by the two hatched arrows which skirt around the rounded major block designated PROBABILITY, GRAVITY, POTENTIAL MODELS. The upper hatched arrow leads to results for metropolitan regions as a whole. The lower hatched arrow leads to results for the constituent regions of the several metropolitan regions, that is to results which pertain to *intrametropolitan* pattern and structure.

Before any further discussion of results per se, it is useful to indicate the discrepancies which are associated with the first run of the fused framework of Channel II. As in Channel I, a first discrepancy appears after the completion of the comparative cost and industrial complex analyses. Such analyses yield for any given region a pattern of national (system) industry outputs which may be inconsistent with the pattern implicit or explicit in the set of initial regional markets assumed for that region.[134]

---

[134] Because of the structure of the balanced regional input-output model, regional outputs of national industries which are recorded in the results column of Figure 8 are identical with the regional outputs derived from comparative cost and industrial complex analyses.

A second discrepancy emerges after the model is operated to yield for any given metropolitan region the levels of outputs of its regional industries. For the given region this pattern of outputs will in all likelihood differ from the pattern implicit or explicit in the set of initial regional markets assumed for that metropolitan region. Still a third discrepancy appears after the results of comparative cost and industrial complex analyses *for regional industries* are completed. These analyses are required to derive the set of allocating constants whereby to distribute the outputs of regional industries for a given metropolitan area among its constituent subregions. The results of these analyses will in all likelihood differ from the pattern of subregional levels for these same industries implicit or explicit in the set of initial regional markets assumed at the start of these analyses. Moreover, a fourth discrepancy appears after the model is operated to yield for any given subregion of a metropolitan area the levels of outputs of its subregional industries. For the given subregion this pattern of subregional industry outputs will in all likelihood differ from the pattern implicit or explicit in the set of initial regional markets assumed for that subregion. And so forth, there being two discrepancies for every other order of region considered.

The best procedure for ironing out the discrepancies at this point is not obvious. With Channel I discussed in section B.2 there is some basis for operating the entire model and utilizing the complete set of results for the establishment of a set of initial regional markets for a second run of the model. But with the balanced regional model such a presumption is to be questioned, since no discrepancies can arise between the results of a run of the model at any given level and order of regions and the bill of goods required for such a run. In any event, bearing in mind the considerations discussed in section B.2.c, the sophisticated analyst performs a series of runs, introduces realistic resource and cultural constraints, and disallows infeasible shifts, etc., so that discrepancies are reduced to insignificance and so that reasonable, internally consistent results emerge.

Many of the results which emerge from the fused framework of Channel II are not unlike those that derive from the framework of Channel I. The reader can note this parallel by examining the upper column of RESULTS in Figure 8. In addition, the reader finds in this column certain results which are typically of general interest to urban-metropolitan analysts and which are implicit in the previous presentation.

Since a full discussion of all the results of the framework of Channel II would to a large extent repeat what has been presented for Channel I, we comment primarily on the materials which thus far have not been examined and which pertain to metropolitan structure. In developing these comments, we do not present an elaborate, comprehensive table such as Table 1. The reader, however, should have such a table constantly in mind, about whose outlines a few remarks may now be made.

It is clear that a first table for Channel II may be constructed with reference only to the interrelations of the system with its metropolitan regions. Such a table would be comparable to Table 1 of Channel I, except that metropolitan regions would substitute for the regions of Channel I, and that endogenous producing sectors would consist of regional, subregional, and local industries (and industrial complexes) while exogenous producing sectors would comprise national industries (and industrial complexes). Hence, there would be a greater prevalence of zero items in such a table, reflecting the assumption that no exports are permitted for any regional, subregional, and local activity in any metropolitan region.[135]

As in Table 1 of Channel I, the Total Gross Output column of such a table yields the basic data from which Employment estimates and in turn Population and Migration can readily be derived, as discussed in section B.2.a. Next, a triple-entry social accounting system, such as depicted in Table 2, can be constructed from such a table. Gross Regional Product can be measured in terms of (1) Gross Regional Income; (2) Gross Regional Output (on either a Value Added, or Net Output basis); and (3) Gross Regional Expenditures, involving Consumption Expenditures, Government Expenditures, Net Investment, and the Rest of the World Commodity account. All these accounts can be determined in the same way that has been indicated in the discussion of Channel I. From such a table, too, Exports and Imports by region, and therefore Commodity Flows, are identifiable. Implications for, and interrelations with, Balance of Payments and Money Flow studies are also the same as those spelled out in conjunction with Table 1 of Channel I. Finally, the discussion in connection with Table 1 of Channel I which relates to the portrayal of a region's Economic Base, and which bears on Regional and Interregional Multipliers and Cyclical Analysis (as outlined in Figure 6) carries over basically unchanged to Channel II and its associated tables.[136] Hence, we shall not go over this ground again.

Aside from a breakdown of output which emphasizes trades and services, and a specific identification of Local Government Outlays, a result which is made explicit for the first time in the RESULTS column in Figure 8 is

---

[135] More specifically, if there were three metropolitan regions for the system corresponding to the East, South, and West regions of Table 1, there would be in the table for Channel II zero entries in all cells of the (1) second, third, fifth, and sixth *major* blocks of the first *major* row; (2) first, third, fourth, and sixth *major* blocks of the second *major* row; and (3) first, second, fourth, and fifth *major* blocks of the third *major* row.

[136] Thus far only one Channel II table has been discussed. Others will be mentioned later.

Tax Base.   The Tax Base is obviously a fundamental magnitude for comprehensive and systematic urban-metropolitan analysis.   Its determination is in one sense definitional, being dependent on the tax structure considered relevant, or projected, or both.   To the extent that a projected tax structure consists of a tax on retail sales, the base to which such a tax is to be applied is directly obtained for a region from appropriate cells in the relevant rows on retail activities and columns on household expenditures of a Channel II table.   To the extent that a projected tax structure embodies a personal income tax, or a property tax, the base to which the tax is to be applied is calculable with the aid of standard but crude rule-of-thumb ratios[137] from the data of a Channel II table.

Beyond Tax Base, Channel II points up Land Requirements, another fundamental magnitude for comprehensive and systematic urban-metropolitan analysis.   The base for the calculation of land requirements is directly obtainable from the data of a Channel II table.   This base may be subdivided in several different ways, in order to yield the requisite detail on land requirements for different types of uses.   One breakdown might distinguish between commercial, residential, industrial, and other uses on a gross basis.   Another might disaggregate each of these broad categories into a fine classification and even proceed to recombine certain classes by some meaningful criterion such as travel characteristics of employees or income generated per square foot.   For the grosser categories and most of the finer categories, the base to which relevant coefficients are to be applied is readily secured from a Channel II table, or from other magnitudes dependent on data of such a table.[138]

Finally, the upper RESULTS column of Figure 8 has reference to theoretical and empirical materials on Central Places.   As already implied, these materials can be of direct use in the construction of the balanced regional input-output model and thus of the framework of Channel II. For example, the maps presented in Appendix A of Chapter 6, the Löschian and Christaller conceptual designs,[139] and other materials of like nature are exceedingly helpful in coping with the difficult task of selecting an appropriate commodity classification and hierarchy of regions.   In

---

[137] For example, taxable property of an industrial establishment is typically calculated on the basis of a crude estimate of investment per employee in the industry to which the establishment belongs. (Sometimes this estimate is of necessity based on investment in industrial plant alone.) Since employment by industry is a result of the operation of the framework of Channel II, and since crude investment figures per employee are generally available by type of industry, the base for an industrial property tax in a given metropolitan region (and its subregions, as is to be noted later) is readily approximated. For example, see W. Isard and R. E. Coughlin [17], pp. 32–35, 109–111.

[138] For some interesting detail on land requirements, see D. A. Muncy [25].

[139] For relevant citations, see Appendix A, Chapter 6.

turn, Channel II can cast considerable light on central place analysis. The rigorous, consistency framework of a set of Channel II tables can compel a more fruitful and realistic formulation of central place hypotheses and a more productive organization of empirical materials relating to these hypotheses. Furthermore, the operation of the framework of Channel II through the various orders of regions can test the validity of central place theories and hypotheses, in the extreme case denying such hypotheses when the operation yields meaningless and contradictory results.

The interconnections between Channel II and central place analysis pertain not only to the interrelations of a system with its metropolitan regions but also to intrametropolitan patterns, that is, to the interdependence of a metropolitan region and its several constituent subregions. Recognition of this point leads to an examination of results listed in the lower RESULTS column of Figure 8. Channel II, as central place theory, yields knowledge (or implications and projections) pertaining to lower order (smaller area) regions, that is, subregions and local areas.[140] In line with the discussion in Chapter 8 of balanced regional input-output models, the operation of the framework of Channel II yields for each subregion outputs of subregional industries.[141] When an investigator sets these outputs for a subregion alongside its outputs of national and regional industries which are assigned to it as a consequence of comparative cost and industrial complex analyses,[142] he obtains a set of strategic economic magnitudes of that subregion. As with each metropolitan region, the basic economic structure of each subregion can be presented in table form. Such a table might be highly similar in structure to Table 1 of Channel I. Instead of refering to a system, the table would refer to a single metropolitan region (which in a sense can be regarded as a subsystem or a system of another order). Instead of referring to the East, South, and West, such a table might refer to subregion K, subregion L, and subregion M,

[140] And for other orders of regions which the investigator may wish to introduce explicitly into the framework.

[141] Once again the reader is reminded that this framework yields results on levels of industrial complexes but that such results are ignored in order to maintain a simple, brief exposition of Channel II.

[142] Ideally, such comparative cost and industrial complex analyses should be supplemented in an operational way with linear programming and scaling and factor analysis. In fact, we may propound the view that the smaller the region involved, the more relevant are scaling and factor analysis for the estimation of realistic allocating coefficients and the less relevant are cost differentials à la Weberian approach. Put otherwise, we may contend that as analysis proceeds to lower and lower-order regions (each of successively smaller area), reaching at one extreme the small neighborhood, attitude differences among regions of any given order become sharper and typical cost differentials tend to lessen. Hence, the greater relevance of techniques designed to measure attitudes and their intensities.

all of the given metropolitan region.   For each subregion the endogenous producing sectors would consist of subregional and local activities only, and the exogenous producing sectors would comprise national and regional industries.[143]

Alternatively, the basic economic structures of all subregions, and therefore of all metropolitan regions of a system, may be encompassed in one table constructed on a still more disaggregated level than Table 1 of Channel I.   Instead of having six major rows and six major columns for a system of three metropolitan regions, such a table would have at the minimum eighteen major rows and an equal number of major columns if each metropolitan region contains three subregions.[144]   The first three major rows and the first three major columns might refer to subregions K, L, and M of the first metropolitan region; the fourth, fifth, and sixth major rows and columns might refer to the three subregions of the second metropolitan region.   And so forth.   In short, such a table would be a simple tripartite disaggregation of Table 1 and would permit a single snapshot portrayal of the basic economic structures of all regions and subregions.[145]

However the investigator inclines to tabulate basic data which relate to economic structure of subregions, from such tabulation he can proceed to list directly the results of the operation of the framework of Channel II. Some of the more important of these results are noted in the lower RESULTS column of Figure 8.   From projected outputs of local, subregional, regional, and national industries in each subregion, he obtains Employment estimates for each subregion via the standard procedures discussed.   He also obtains estimates of Population, Gross Product, Income, Consumption Expenditures, Local Government Outlays, Imports and Exports, and other related Social Accounts.[146]   Further, Tax Base and

[143] As with the first table discussed in connection with Channel II, this second table will have a greater prevalence of zero items than Table I of Channel I, reflecting the assumption that exports are disallowed for subregional and local activities.   Also, it is to be noted that the levels of the exogenous producing (new final demand) sectors for any given subregion will be obtained by multiplying the national outputs of national industries and the metropolitan outputs of regional industries by the appropriate allocating constants previously determined.

[144] If it were desirable to retain in a separate block regional industries which are endogenous from the standpoint of a metropolitan region but exogenous from the standpoint of its constituent subregions, the number of both major rows and major columns would increase.

[145] Since such a table would be designed primarily to depict subregional structure, generally speaking, it would not portray as efficiently as other tables already discussed the economic interrelations of the several metropolitan regions of a system .

[146] In this connection, note the step which P. de Wolff and P. E. Venekamp [38] take in their attempt to construct a set of social accounts for a hierarchy of regions in the Netherlands.

Land Requirements by type and similar magnitudes are derivable. Moreover, the investigator may probe the implications of these results for, and their consistency with, Balance of Payments, Money Flow, Regional and Interregional Multiplier and Cyclical Analyses; he bears in mind that these results can be profitably supplemented by and re-examined in the light of such analyses.

However, at this point it is to be noted that the subregional results of the framework of Channel II are not on as firm a basis as the results for a metropolitan region as a whole. Generally speaking, it may be maintained that comparative cost and industrial complex analyses and the use of diverse coefficients, curves, charts, indices, and similar concepts as preliminary tools[147] are more valid when employed to allocate national industries among metropolitan regions of a system than when used to distribute both the national and regional industries of a metropolitan region among its constituent subregions. We may propound such a position with reference to both manufacturing activities and commerical and service activities. Such a point of view may be held, despite the lack of any supporting objective evidence and despite the fact that on occasion specific features of a metropolitan region, such as available industrial sites or zoning regulations, may furnish firmer grounds for industry distribution among subregions of a metropolitan area than for industry allocation among the metropolitan regions of a system. Such a point of view strongly suggests that the fused framework of Channel II as hitherto developed must be supplemented by other types of analysis, some of which will be explored later.

In a manner exactly analogous to the way in which the investigator proceeds from a metropolitan region tabulation of results to a subregional tabulation, he proceeds from a subregional tabulation to a local-area tabulation. For each subregion he may construct a table portraying the basic economic structure of each of its several local areas. Or he may still further disaggregate the first table of Channel II which refers to the several metropolitan regions to obtain a simultaneous picture of the economic structure of all metropolitan regions, all subregions, and all local areas. More specifically, if the system comprises three metropolitan regions, each of which has three subregions, each of which is classifiable into two local areas, such a highly disaggregated table would have at the minimum 36 major rows and 36 major columns.[148]

Analogously, such a table(s) would contain the basic data for presenting

[147] See Figure 3 of this chapter.

[148] The number of both major rows and major columns would be still greater if it were desired to keep in separate blocks the activities which for one order of regions are endogenous and for another order exogenous.

the results of the operation of the framework of Channel II, as they relate to all local areas. As with subregions, estimates of employment, population, Gross Product, income, consumption expenditures, local government outlays, imports and exports, tax base, and land requirements, among others, are obtainable. Also, the possibility of mutually beneficial linkage with multiplier and other similar analyses may be explored. But with local areas, even more than with subregions, the firmness of the results may be questioned. And we may even more strongly contest the validity of comparative cost and industrial complex techniques and the use of coefficients, curves, charts, indices, and similar concepts as preliminary tools for establishing coefficients by which to determine for each local area its share of national, regional, and subregional industries.

In this manner the investigator obtains from the operation of the fused framework of Channel II basic information, at least as a first approximation, for the projection of intrametropolitan structure and pattern— basic information on subregions, local areas, and other orders of regions which the investigator may deem relevant. The results are weak, especially for the lower-order, smaller types of regions. They need to be weighed and modified in terms of the materials that may be gleaned from the use of other analytical techniques, some of which we may now examine.

2. REFINEMENTS VIA SUPPLEMENTARY TECHNIQUES

One analytical technique which can be operationally fused into the framework of Channel II and which promises to upgrade its results is interregional linear programming. The basic features of this technique have already been discussed in Chapter 10. Also the manner in which it can be operationally synthesized into a fused framework, in many ways similar to that of Channel II, has already been presented in section B.2.g of this chapter. Hence, we can be brief.

We have already indicated that interregional linear programming resembles in many ways both comparative cost and industrial complex techniques.[149] In one sense these three techniques are three variants of a general analytical approach which aims at the identification of efficient minimum-cost spatial patterns. As already noted, the decision to use one rather than another rests on the purpose of a particular partial study, the number of parametric values for variables to be tried out, the types of assumptions which are realistic, the available data, and, last but not least, the inclinations of the researcher.

Although interregional linear programs have not been run for the subregions of a metropolitan area, or for the local areas of a subregion, the

---

[149] See section B.2.g of this chapter.

design of a typical program can readily be sketched. For example, suppose the problem is to allocate among the local areas of a subregion the total retail and wholesale services associated with lumber and building supplies. (This total is obtained directly from the Total Gross Output column of the Channel II table relating to this subregion and its corresponding metropolitan region.) Should there be one large yard for the entire subregion, or a group of smaller yards, one in each local area, or some other spatial pattern? To answer this question by the use of an interregional linear program, the required deliveries to households and other users in each local area must be specified. (These serve as constraints and are part of the set of initial regional market assumptions on the local area level.) For each yard considered relevant in any spatial pattern, the unit processing or production cost of its service operation must be specified, where such cost includes the transport cost on supplies from rail heads and other transportation termini to the yard. Because of major economies of scale in yard operation, each yard must be defined in terms of both location and size. Accordingly, the operation of each size yard at a given location must be considered a separate activity and may be viewed as a production activity, such as those listed in Table 6 of Chapter 10. Additionally, numerous shipping activities need to be introduced. Each shipping activity refers to the transport inputs required to ship the supplies corresponding to a unit service operation of a yard in one location to an average consumer in a given local area.[150] Subject to other internal constraints, the problem may be solved to minimize the over-all total cost involved in operating yards and in getting the required goods to the establishments of the consumers (the predetermined market). The solution yields the desired distribution, by size and location, of services of lumber and building supply yards among the local areas of a metropolitan subregion. This new information may then substitute in Channel II for estimated data on lumber and building supply yards derived less efficiently and reliably by some other technique or tool.

In similar fashion, other partial problems can be attacked via interregional linear programming.[151] But it is to be reiterated that each pro-

---

[150] See Chapter 10 for a full discussion of shipping activities and their number in a program. In the problem given, the cost of such shipping activities takes account of the transport cost to and from the yard incurred by consumers who purchase supplies directly at the yard. This transport cost is admittedly difficult to estimate but must be explicitly considered in any sound urban analysis.

[151] Another type of linear program may be associated with a maximization problem. For example, an industrial real estate corporation may hold certain land in a local area for development as an industrial district. The set of industrial plants, by size, which maximizes total (discounted) returns over a period of years, subject to the constraints

gram requires certain types of predetermined data, such as the size of local area markets in the problem just given. These data are initially approximated by the framework of Channel II and are constantly revised as results of successive runs are achieved. Obviously, the weaker the initial assumptions, especially on markets of local areas, the less valid the results of an interregional linear program and the greater the need for its subsequent recomputation.

Thus, interregional linear programming can contribute to and be operationally synthesized into the framework of Channel II. This fact is noted in Figure 8 by the arrow which courses from the lower LINEAR PROG. rectangle and connects with the lower hatched arrow leading from the BALANCED REGIONAL I-O MATRIX.

Other refinements which may be operationally welded to the fused framework of Channel II emerge from the use, particularly on the subregional and local level, of a variety of statistical techniques. Many of these have already been discussed in Chapters 2 and 3, as they relate to population and migration estimates. (See Figures 4 and 5 of this chapter.) These techniques range widely in degree of sophistication.

At one extreme are simple trend projections of the distribution among subregions and their constituent local areas of population, employment, Gross Product, income, consumption expenditures, and government outlays. These trend projections may be based on free-hand or more formal graphic extrapolations, or precise (but presumably no more reliable) mathematical equations, and may utilize data on spatial distributions for one or more metropolitan regions over the last several decades. From these projections additional materials such as on tax base and on industrial, commercial, and residential land requirements can be obtained.

Alternatively, a simple form of comparative analysis may be pursued. Because of similarity of key characteristics, the growth of one or more local areas of one or more subregions may be assumed to follow the pattern of another older area whose growth is substantially completed. This form of projection has been particularly pursued in population studies and is discussed in section B of Chapter 2. Or, simple ratio methods may be employed which project, for example, the population, employment, or Gross Product, etc., of a local area as a ratio of the projected population, employment, or Gross Product, etc., of its metropolitan region or

of the problem, represents for the given local area relevant information which should be utilized in Channel II.

As noted in Chapter 10, relevant objectives for other partial problems might be to maximize tax base, new employment opportunities, or increase in per capita income, or to minimize traffic volume, average journey to work, required outlays by local government, etc.

subregion.[152]   Such a ratio may be constant or, more desirably, it may be allowed to change regularly over time.   By such procedure magnitudes for local areas of a metropolitan region are developed independently; but as a next step these magnitudes must be adjusted to sum to the projected total for the region.

Additionally, these simple techniques may be used in conjunction with location quotients, coefficients of localization and geographic association, coefficients of concentration and of redistribution relating to population and other magnitudes, localization curves, urbanization curves, shift ratios, relative growth charts, and other related indices and concepts. For example, trend projections of total employment (or a number of other magnitudes) may be directly geared to a set of localization curves, one for each past census year.   In the construction of these curves employment is cumulated percentagewise along the vertical axis; and the area of the metropolitan region contained in its diverse local areas[153] is cumulated percentagewise along the horizontal axis.   Consequently, as mentioned in Chapter 7, the slope of any curve over a stretch corresponding to a given local area measures the location quotient for that local area—that is, that local area's percentage share of metropolitan employment as a ratio to its percentage share of metropolitan acreage.   By being able to study these slopes as they change for each local area from census year to census year, and by being able by means of the set of localization curves to view these changes for all local areas in one single diagram, the investigator can much more intelligently construct a trend extrapolation of employment by local area.

In similar manner, other tools listed in Figure 3 of this chapter can be linked to the simple methods of projection just discussed and detailed to some degree in Chapters 2 and 3.   But it is to be constantly borne in mind that the use of these tools and methods, linked as they may be to achieve greater strength, is not a real substitute for analysis, such as comparative cost analysis, which bares basic relations motivating decisions by individuals and groups.   Recourse to such tools and methods is had only when fundamental analysis cannot be pursued.

Recognition of the desirability of uncovering those basic relations which influence and condition consumer, business, and government decisions and behavior has led to the development of a set of more sophisticated statistical techniques (although in their application to the explanation of metropolitan structure, these techniques have not always directly employed

[152] And in turn, other basic magnitudes of the subregion may be related by ratios to corresponding basic magnitudes of the metropolitan region.   Again, for further discussion, see Chapter 2.

[153] Or in successive one-mile concentric zones.

variables with behavioral implications). Such techniques cover the regression, multiple regression, and covariance analyses discussed in Chapter 2 and the scaling, latent structure, and factor analyses discussed in Appendices A and B in Chapter 7.

Simple regression is much like ratio analysis; and multiple regression is in many ways compound ratio analysis. Covariance analysis, embracing both multiple regression and variance analyses, is still more ambitious. In the pure statistical sense it attempts to uncover, with greater accuracy in relative emphasis, more deeply underlying relations. As discussed in section D.2.c of Chapter 2, such analysis has been aimed at explaining statistically variations in the rates of growth of metropolitan regions and of their constituent parts. For example, Bogue and Harris[154] have applied multiple regression and covariance analyses to explain statistically the population growth of central cities (one type of subregion), of the urban fraction of the suburban ring, and of the rural fraction of the suburban ring. The influence of such variables as degree of industrialization of metropolitan region, growth rate of metropolitan region, past growth rate of the subregion, relative size of subregion, etc., are explored when metropolitan regions are grouped in terms of census-type regions of the United States.

Somewhat analogously, factor and scaling analyses may be attempted. We have already discussed how such analyses aid comparative cost and industrial complex techniques, especially in reaching industrial projections consistent with community attitudes.[155] Such analyses may be applicable at this stage as well. For example, Price employs factor analysis in an attempt to uncover fundamental dimensions of metropolitan centers.[156] He identifies four factors which may be considered significant: (1) degree of maturity of city, (2) the extent to which a city is a service center, (3) the level of living within a city, and (4) the per capita trade volume of a city. If indeed such are fundamental dimensions, they cast light on significant variables for statistical "explanatory" equations.[157] Further, such analysis may be performed for other parts of metropolitan regions and compared with the results for metropolitan centers. And to the extent that the factor approach has been employed to delineate subregions and local areas, some significant factors will already have been identified; they may

[154] D. J. Bogue and D. L. Harris [1], chs. 4 and 5.

[155] Recall that such attitudes in effect place constraints (limits) upon possible spatial distributions of industry.

[156] D. O. Price [30].

[157] To be particularly noted is the promise of scaling and factor analysis for uncovering expectational, attitude-type variables for use in an ordinal form in estimating equations.

be claimed to have a direct bearing on extrapolation of population distribution, density of retail sales, patterns of land use, and other internal aspects of metropolitan regions.

In this manner one or more of the given set of statistical techniques, ranging from simple trend projection at one extreme to covariance and factor analysis at the other, may be employed. As a whole, each method of this set represents an approximative estimation technique. Its use may be justified when it yields firmer results than those techniques which have greater causal significance but which fail in a given situation to grasp adequately the interplay of forces at the local level. These firmer results may then be substituted in the fused framework of Channel II for the inferior results derived by the latter techniques. In this fashion the fused framework of Channel II, already expanded to embrace interregional linear programming at the intrametropolitan level,[158] may be further extended.

Even with the incorporation of these refinements, the fused framework of Channel II is confronted by a number of shortcomings. In addition to those associated with the fused framework of Channel I, there are limitations stemming from the difficulties of classifying commodities and of selecting a hierarchy of regions. Others concern the assumptions of identical production practices and consumption patterns, region by region, and the need to use national input-output coefficients. Still others relate to the required use of constant allocating coefficients and to the inadequacy of such coefficients at the small region level. Finally, to mention one other critical shortcoming, the fused framework of Channel II, as well as that of Channel I, fails to achieve a full perspective on agglomeration (spatial juxtaposition) forces and on the behavior of social masses. Such forces and behavior have not as yet been successfully dissected by the efficiency approach of the comparative cost, industrial complex, and linear programming techniques or by the requirements approach of input-output and other linear systems. The very size of the industrial agglomerations, urban-metropolitan masses, and social populations involved suggest exploration of the applicability of probability-type gravity models, to which we now turn.

D. CHANNEL III: A FUSED FRAMEWORK INCORPORATING THE GRAVITY MODEL

As covered in Chapter 11, the probability-type gravity model (defined to embrace potential and similar interaction models) seeks to identify

---

[158] And, of course, appropriately designed to take cognizance of scarcity and attitude restraints, and of financial elements and materials emanating from money flow studies.

stable structural relationships governing the behavior and structure of masses, at the neglect of individual motivation and peculiarities of specific situations. It thus holds up a promise of effectively supplementing techniques hitherto discussed, which on net have been deficient in capturing social and economic behavior in the aggregate. The framework for such supplementation, and hopefully operational synthesis, constitutes Channel III. This Channel is outlined in Figure 8 when the results flowing from the BALANCED REGIONAL I-O MATRIX are fed into the rounded major block designated PROBABILITY, GRAVITY, POTENTIAL MODELS which in turn yields RESULTS, by Metropolitan Regions, and when the latter results are fed back into PROBABILITY, GRAVITY, POTENTIAL MODELS to be joined with input-output and linear programming techniques to yield RESULTS on Intrametropolitan Patterns. This sequence of steps is depicted by the arrows of Figure 8.

Briefly put, the central concept of the probability-type gravity model may be summarized by the following expression:

$$G \frac{w_i(P_i)^\alpha \cdot w_j(P_j)^\beta}{d_{ij}^b}$$

where P_i and P_j are basic masses involved; w_i and w_j are their respective weights (single or composite); α and β are the respective powers (variable) by which these masses are appropriately revaluated; d_{ij} is intervening distance appropriately revaluated by the exponent b (variable or constant); and G is an ordinary constant. Full discussion of this concept, its variants, and all its parts is presented in the preceding chapter. In very simple terms this concept states that pervading the aggregate behavior of society as a mass is a basic proclivity for interaction and interchange which varies directly with the product of the masses involved, however measured, revaluated, and weighted, and inversely with their spatial spread as indicated by intervening distances, however defined and revaluated.

Chapter 11 presents the various forms in which the gravity model has been conceptualized and employed. In this chapter we are interested in examining how these various forms may be operationally fused with the frameworks already attained. We therefore begin with the form closest to these frameworks, namely, the form involving the use of relative income potential terms, either in an additive or multiplicative manner.

1. FUNDAMENTAL DIMENSIONS FOR MAJOR REGION ANALYSIS

Suppose, à la Channel I, an initial set of basic assumptions is established, initial regional markets are identified, comparative cost, industrial complex, linear programming, and scaling and factor analyses are conducted, an interregional input-output computation is run, and its results are modified in the light of attitudes, scarcities, and any available materials on money flows and financial elements.[159]   The results by regions may then be listed as is done in Channel I.   But, what about spatial juxtaposition economies?   Or agglomeration forces?   Since gravity models generally purport to capture these economies and forces, the investigator may be inclined to explore a fused framework which on the one hand presumably may be less rigorous and consistent than that of Channel I, but on the other hand may be more realistic.

Before depicting the specifics of the fused framework of Channel III, it is instructive to compare the probability-type gravity model of section G of Chapter 11 based on a relative income potential concept and the fused framework of Channel I.   The fused framework of Channel I achieves a high degree of consistency.   The data for the base year for at least a first projection period are actual and thus necessarily internally consistent. The estimates for the year of projection undergo a series of adjustments in the successive reruns in order to achieve internal consistency.   By the end of the projection period it is implicitly assumed that all forces for change have had their full impact.   Further, some investigators may implicitly conceive the successive reruns as a procedure for partially tracing the sequence of repercussions.

In contrast, the gravity model of section G of Chapter 11 fails to achieve such consistency.   Although the data for a base year for a first projection period are actual and internally consistent, the results for the year of projection implicitly contain within themselves basic discrepancies and disequilibria which set in motion forces leading to change during the following period.   The rerun procedure is dispensed with, the basic notion being that there is a time path of regional growth during which successive decisions are made on cumulating outcomes, tending to eliminate discrepancies and disequilibria.   But such decisions generate new discrepancies and disequilibria; and in this manner a nonending series of regional adaptations must take place.

In spite of these contrasts, the fused framework of Channel I and the gravity model are not incompatible.   As hitherto developed, the fused framework applies to a long time span between base year and year of projection, during which it is legitimate and in fact necessary to require that most of the discrepancies generated throughout the period be eliminated by the end; hence the need for reruns.   On the other hand, the gravity model applies to a relatively brief time span, at the most a five-year period and perhaps most logically to a one- or two-year period.   In such

[159] Recall that when conditions so warrant, an alternative, impure interregional input-output model may be substituted for the pure model of Channel I. See the discussion in section H, Chapter 8, in connection with Chenery's impure model.

a model, then, disequilibria among the results and discrepancies between the results for the year of projection and the initial assumptions on which business decisions were based are to be expected and provide the basic motivation for change.

When these points are appreciated, it is easily seen how a gravity model may be linked to the diverse techniques synthesized into the fused framework of Channel I. First, the time span of any projection period must be reduced to one for which a gravity model is valid. Second, the procedure of reruns must be abandoned, a procedure which is rather anemic once the time span of projection has been appropriately reduced. Third, in line with the form of the gravity model of section G of Chapter 11, for example, that of equation (15),[160] division of endogenous producing sectors into *non-cost-sensitive industries* and *local service and other market-oriented industries* must be pursued. Once these preliminaries are undertaken, the investigator is ready to develop the fused framework of Channel III.

Suppose that successive two-year projection periods are deemed relevant, that is, periods running from year $t - 2$ to t; t to $t + 2$; $t + 2$ to $t + 4$; etc. Suppose, too, that the fused framework of Channel I when coupled with the gravity model is judged to represent the proper mix of research techniques. Then, as in Channel I, all steps are taken through the computation of the Total Gross Output column of Table 1 for year $t + 2$. At this point a relative income potential model is introduced. There are listed for each region (1) the non-cost-sensitive activities (as defined in section G of Chapter 11); (2) all cost-sensitive activities for which it has not been feasible to pursue a comparative cost, industrial complex, or linear programming analysis; and (3) local service and other market-oriented industries. For each activity in the first two categories output in year t in the given region is set down; for each activity in the third category only that output delivered in year t to activities in the first two categories is recorded.[161] Each of these outputs is multiplied by unity plus the projected rate of growth of the respective industry within the nation during the period t to $t + 2$. This yields for each such activity (or fraction of activity) *expected* output for year $t + 2$ if the activity grows within the given region at the same rate as within the nation (the proportionality effect). When such output is summed over all these activities, the investigator obtains for the given region the corresponding (unadjusted) contribution of these activities to Gross Product of the given region. The magnitude of this contribution represents the first term of the gravity model being designed.

---

[160] Bear in mind that this is only one of many possible variants.

[161] Recall that this is the output which is directly dependent on the levels of activities in categories 1 and 2.

This step, however, ignores the sensitivity of these activities to changing interregional position.   One way of taking account of such sensitivity is by means of a modified relative income potential term applicable to the given region.   As discussed in section G of Chapter 11, this term may be computed in a number of different ways.   One significant way, which is also easily pursued, is to assume that expectations and locational decisions pertaining to the activities in the three categories of the preceding paragraph are at a given point of time oriented to the pattern of regional income changes during the preceding two-year period.[162]   Accordingly, the modified relative income potential is calculated for each region in the manner outlined in Chapter 11.   This potential is the second term of the gravity model of this section.[163]   For each region its magnitude may be taken as a percentage of the first term.   If positive for a given region, it indicates for each of that region's activities in the three given categories the per cent by which its expected output for year $t + 2$ (calculated on an "as the nation grows" basis) must be adjusted upward.   If negative, it indicates the per cent by which the expected output for each such activity must be adjusted downward.   The resulting adjusted outputs for these activities (and parts of activities) are then to be considered final outputs for year $t + 2$.   When over all regions these outputs are listed along with the outputs (already projected to year $t + 2$) of cost-sensitive activities for which comparative cost and related analysis have been conducted, and listed along with the projected accounting charges for customary final demand sectors, and when they are consolidated with the outputs (already projected to year $t + 2$) of those parts of local service and other market-oriented activities linked to these cost-sensitive activities, the investigator obtains a final adjusted Total Gross Output column to replace the Total Gross Output column of Table 1.[164]

Once the final adjusted Total Gross Output column is obtained, year $t + 2$ estimates by regions of employment, population, migration, basic social accounts, exports, imports, commodity flows, etc., may be derived in practically the same manner as discussed in connection with Channel I.

[162] Note that this assumption differs from that underlying the version of the modified relative income potential model explicitly detailed in Chapter 11.   In that model decisions were postulated to be based on income changes during the current period, and, in order for the model to be operational, on only those regional income changes generated by activities for which comparative cost and similar techniques could reliably project regional patterns.

[163] Roughly speaking, it corresponds to the second term of equation 15 of Chapter 11, where output magnitudes substitute for population magnitudes.

[164] Outputs in these two columns differ only for those activities contained in the three categories of the preceding paragraphs, that is, to the activities sensitive to change in interregional position.

Supplementary forms of analysis may also be pursued and incorporated into the framework in much the same fashion as discussed in connection with Channel I.

Given the final adjusted results for year $t + 2$, projections for year $t + 4$ may be undertaken. The results for year $t + 2$ provide the essential empirical materials on structure relevant in the determination of initial regional market assumptions.[165] On the basis of such assumptions, which provide the fundamental motivation for new locational decisions and changes, the fused framework of Channel III, which includes the gravity model, may be run to yield results for year $t + 4$; and then successively in like fashion to yield results for years $t + 6$, $t + 8$, $t + 10$, etc. In this manner, for each region of the system a step-by-step, discrete path of growth is projected.

The fused framework thus far sketched involves one variant of the gravity model. It involves a basic postulate on locational decisions pertaining to (1) the non-cost-sensitive activities; (2) all cost-sensitive activities for which it has not been feasible to pursue locational cost analysis; and (3) those parts of local service and other market-oriented activities serving activities in categories 1 and 2. The postulate is that such decisions are based on regional income changes during the immediately preceding period. But the analyst might consider as still more realistic or reasonable the postulate that such decisions are based on regional income changes generated by basic cost-sensitive industries (exclusive of those of category 2) during the current period, as is spelled out in Chapter 11. Or he may wish to postulate that such decisions are related to regional income changes during the current period and one or more preceding periods, appropriately weighted. Thus, as noted in Chapter 11, a number of reasonable variants of the gravity model involving different degrees of lagged effects may be designed.[166] Correspondingly, a number of reasonable variants of the fused framework of Channel III may be designed.

[165] They also furnish basic materials for the adjustment of interareal input-output coefficients, which adjustment is necessary for internal consistency. For example, suppose that Channel I *sans* gravity model yields an output of $1 billion for non-cost-sensitive activity X in the West. Suppose, too, that when modification is made for the West's improvement in interregional position the final adjusted output for X is $1.1 billion. The investigator must then adjust the interareal coefficients indicating inputs from X in the West and other regions into all sectors of all regions in order that total requirements (including final demand) for the product of X in the West be $1.1 billion.

[166] In all these variants it may be reasonably assumed that decisions in cost-sensitive activities for which locational cost analysis is pursued are based on all available information up to and including the year at the beginning of a projection period. Those parts of local service and market-oriented activities linked to these cost-sensitive activities are assumed to expand and contract in each region as their products are demanded.

2. FUNDAMENTAL DIMENSIONS FOR SUBREGIONAL AND LOCAL-AREA
ANALYSIS

Beyond projecting estimates of Gross Regional Product, population, basic social accounts, and other critical magnitudes for major regions of a system for a series of future key years, probability-type gravity models can approximate like magnitudes for subregions of each major region. Also they are particularly valuable for anticipating distribution patterns within metropolitan regions. This latter utility is explicitly indicated on Figure 8 by the arrow which flows from the upper RESULTS column to the rounded major block designated PROBABILITY, GRAVITY, POTENTIAL MODELS and thence leads, in combination with LINEAR PROG. and INPUT-OUTPUT techniques, to the lower RESULTS column.

In proceeding to the analysis of lower-order (smaller-area) regions, several types of interregional and regional input-output schema may be designed. Because the balanced regional input-output scheme has been previously discussed in connection with intrametropolitan patterns, it is convenient to refer to its use at this stage of the exposition.

Suppose that up to this stage the fused framework of Channel III thus far sketched has involved an interregional input-output scheme of the type consistent with Table 1. Further, suppose that the regions employed are metropolitan-oriented regions. That is, suppose the investigator has already exhaustively carved the United States into three or five or eleven major regions, each region à la central place theory being dominated by a central metropolitan node.[167] A balanced regional input-output design may then be employed to allocate the diverse outputs of each given metropolitan-oriented region among its several subregions. (Some of these subregions may be wholly rural; others may be wholly urban, such as a central city; and still others may be both urban and rural, such as a town and its surrounding hinterland.)[168]

In such an allocation the gravity model may conceivably play a role. However, assume that the investigator chooses instead to pursue the procedures discussed in Channel II to derive relevant magnitudes for each subregion.

When the investigator considers still lower-order (smaller-area) regions,

[167] For further materials on this concept of region refer to the writings of McKenzie, Hawley, Bogue, Philbrick, and other literature cited in the Appendix to Chapter 6 and to materials and maps contained therein.

[168] For example, if the reader refers to Map A-1 in the Appendix to Chapter 6, he may, following Philbrick, conceive a metropolitan-oriented region in the South as centering around Atlanta, Georgia. Atlanta in itself may constitute a wholly urban subregion; certain areas coursing through southern Georgia and northern Florida may constitute a primarily rural subregion; Charleston, South Carolina, and its immediate hinterland may be considered an urban-rural subregion.

for example the local areas of subregions and in turn sublocal areas of local areas, the relative utility of the gravity model increases. This increase is due partly to the decreasing validity of other techniques noted in the discussion of Channel II and partly to the fact that a relatively large quantity of empirical materials has been amassed on the small-area level to help assess the validity and basic parameters of the gravity model.

There are several specific ways in which the gravity model may be utilized for projecting intrametropolitan patterns. Typically they involve the use of the model in conjunction with (1) some form of trend analysis or comparative-growth analysis; or (2) a set of ratios, location quotients, coefficients of localization, or data based on some other measure;[169] or (3) a regression, multiple regression, covariance, factor, scaling analysis, or some other form of statistical explanation; or (4) some combination of these methods and data. We may now illustrate one such way.

We begin with the magnitudes for a subregion, say a small standard metropolitan area (census definition) which is part of a region dominated by a central metropolitan node.[170] For this subregion the determined expansion of industry by type is noted. To the extent that this industry is heavy or is of a general nuisance type, and to the extent that location of available sites for such industry is geographically circumscribed and rigid zoning restrictions are in force, to that extent the local-area allocation of this industry's new output is both easily and firmly estimated. The remaining fraction of industry expansion may be distributed among local areas in accordance with careful examination of past trends. Concomitantly, population of the subregion may be distributed among its local areas by a similar examination of trends relating to internal structure. In this distribution occupational, income, ethnic, racial, and other characteristics of the population are duly considered.

At this point a probability-type gravity model may be introduced. The location of industrial expansion together with existing plant establishes a spatial pattern of jobs, by type. The spread of population establishes the spatial pattern of labor force, by occupation. Are these two patterns consistent in terms of known journey-to-work behavior as revealed by empirical gravity model investigations?[171] If not, the investigator

169 See Figure 3 of this chapter for a partial listing of some of these measures.

170 For example, the Trenton metropolitan area would be such a subregion of the major region dominated by New York City, or the South Bend area of the major region of which Chicago is the node.

171 For example, see studies by Carroll, Carroll and Bevis, Bevis, Mylroie, Garrison, Reilly, Voorhees, and others cited in Chapter 11. Note that the type of gravity model used here is of the interaction type involving pairs of masses and generated flows, whereas the type employed in the early paragraphs of this section is of the potential type involving the simultaneous influence of all masses on a single point (region).

accordingly modifies his distributions of both industry whose location is flexible and labor force whose location is flexible.[172]   He conducts such modification, bearing in mind the probability basis on which projections of journey-to-work patterns rest.   This basis allows at least some degree of divergence from precisely defined relations and "best" estimates of constants and parametric values for variables.[173]

Once the investigator establishes spatial patterns of industry and population based on trend analysis and consistent with the empirical findings of gravity models, he may proceed to an allocation of commercial activities.   He may perform trend analyses of central business district sales, shifts of commercial establishments to and from business thoroughfares, neighborhood centers, and satellite shopping centers of diverse size.   But he must also consider the spatial pattern of population already outlined, the changing scale economies and market areas of various commercial operations, and shopping trip behavior again evidenced in empirical data processed in gravity model form.   A pattern of shopping centers and other commercial locations may then be projected.[174]   The person trips and commodity movements generated by this pattern together with those generated by the spatial patterns of population, jobs, plants, warehouses, terminals, public and community facilities, recreational and cultural sites, etc., must be consistent with projections of likely or feasible transportation capacities.   If not, appropriate adjustments must be made, again consistent with empirical findings of the probability-type gravity model.[175]

[172] It must be borne in mind that attitudes and other cultural factors frequently impose informal, if not formal, restrictions on the location of diverse segments of the labor force.

[173] For example, in Figure 4 of Chapter 11 the slope of the line representing work trips is approximately 1.2.   This represents a "best" estimate for the variable exponent to which distance is raised in the gravity model.   Clearly, from the discussion in Chapter 11 of other empirical materials and diverse hypotheses, this value of the exponent is subject to considerable leeway.   On the other hand, the friction of distance is clearly established in the study from which Figure 4 is taken, and the investigator cannot, without good and strong reasons, allow the exponent of distance to assume an unduly small value.

[174] If the investigator judges that a rank-size distribution of shopping centers is both logically consistent and characteristic of reality, he may force the resulting pattern of shopping centers to conform to such a distribution.   See footnote 53, Chapter 2.

[175] The analyst must fully recognize not only the restrictive influence of a transportation net, both existing and projected, but also the significant impact which new transportation routes and facilities may have on the mass of a subregion (i.e., its population numbers and industrial output) as well as on its spatial structure.   Hence, in making projections of such mass, he must bear in mind likely transport developments and allow in later stages for possible modification of such mass in those situations where unanticipated transport volumes are estimated by his methods.   For a more explicit statement of this interdependence, see J. D. Carroll and H. W. Bevis [3].

It is realized that this procedure involving a round-by-round succession of estimates, checks, and adjustments is arbitrary in many respects. Moreover, we fully recognize that the use of the gravity model involves problems (already indicated) in determining (1) the appropriate measure of mass, and the weights and exponents to be applied to this mass; (2) the appropriate measure of distance and the exponent to be applied to it; (3) the specific form of function and derivation of appropriate constants; (4) the extent to which disaggregation by type trip or other interaction is permissible, the extent to which intervening opportunities are to be considered (or perhaps even substituted for the distance variable); and so forth. (The reader is referred to Chapter 11 for the full discussion of all these problems.) Nonetheless the gravity model does provide at this local level a useful consistency check which in conjunction with trend analysis provides the investigator with firmer results than trend analysis alone. This statement is valid even when limited resources for research confine the investigator to a simple operational use of the gravity model.

We have illustrated only one way in which the gravity model can be synthesized into the analytical framework. Another way might involve the imposition of the consistency framework of the gravity model upon spatial patterns of population and jobs, or of land uses of diverse types derived from multiple regression, covariance, factor, and scaling techniques. Or, the gravity model may be used to adjust spatial patterns derived simply by comparison with other similar subregions or by ratio computations. In fact, if the investigator's resources permit, he may achieve on the small region level still further synthesis of gravity models with existing techniques. He may conduct a number of partial linear programs to derive, for example, spatial patterns of certain industries which minimize transport cost, maximize local tax base, etc. Such spatial patterns together with other patterns derived by the more standard procedures may then be subjected to the consistency check of the gravity model.[176] This linkage with INTERREGIONAL LINEAR PROGRAMMING and with those results of a BALANCED REGIONAL INPUT-OUTPUT model judged to be valid on a local level is indicated by the arrow leading to the lower RESULTS column of Figure 8.[177]

[176] Note that the gravity model catches the social behavior that is nonanalyzable in terms of approaches emphasizing efficiency in cost terms. Most notably it encompasses the movement of people that is inconsistent with the least dollar and time cost pattern, as is the case, for example, with many journey-to-work trips via automobile.

[177] The discussion of this and the preceding paragraphs has centered around a subregion which is primarily urban. But, as pointed out, subregions of a metropolitan-oriented region may also be urban-rural and wholly rural. For such subregions, methods of analysis would tend to be somewhat different but could profitably employ

With the operational use of the gravity model in one of the ways suggested, the analyst directly derives for each local area of a subregion (and
going still further, for each sublocal area of a local area) certain magnitudes
listed in the lower RESULTS column of Figure 8.   These magnitudes relate
to (1) Transportation of goods and persons, Shopping Centers, and Land
Use, by type—items not directly obtained via Channel II—and (2) Population, Employment, Local Government Outlays, and Tax Base—items
that can be alternatively estimated via Channel II.

As in Channel II, the investigator may proceed from the lower RESULTS
column of Figure 8 to important social accounts beyond Local Government
Outlays.   Given population estimates and labor force composition, he may
proceed to crude estimates by local area of (1) income (on a *resident* basis)
using some rule of thumb procedure to catch property income; (2) Gross
Output based on the pattern of industry by type; (3) consumption; (4)
exports, imports, and commodity flows.   In fact, the sophisticated analyst
would have already crudely estimated and utilized such social accounts in
his projection of the spatial pattern of shopping centers and his subsequent
rectifications.   He would have estimated local area income since, among
other items, both the amount of retail sales by type and shopping trip and
other trip frequencies (i.e., travel desires) are directly related to both the
level of disposable local income and the manner in which it is distributed
among the family units in the local area.   (Such consumption function
study for local residents would need to be supplemented by similar analysis
pertaining to nonresident commuters.)   He would have estimated exports,
imports, and commodity flows and analyzed industrial outputs in checking the adequacy of transportation capacities projected as either likely or
feasible.   And so forth.[178]

the gravity model. It is beyond the scope of this chapter to develop a second illustration
on the local area of the fused framework of Channel III. Some of the directions along
which the gravity model may be adapted are indicated by the various findings of Stewart
and Warntz on rural areas, as reported in Chapter 11.

[178] Ideally, if complete and detailed balanced regional input-output studies could be
conducted as well as fine-grained commodity flow analyses, money flow, and balance
of payments studies and sound Weberian cost analysis where applicable, all for a
significant hierarchy of regions, the investigator could develop a set of social accounts
which would be subject to multiple checks and balances. In this situation gaps in diverse
sets of data could be bridged and the description of the system associated with each
approach improved. Here, the friction of distance would be evident not only in the
flows of commodities and in person trips of all types, but also in money flows of all
kinds. These latter flows would reflect the increase of transportation and communication costs with distance as well as the fact that the flow of information and frequency of
contact in all cultural spheres tends to decrease with distance. For example, see the
materials on financial flows in J. Q. Stewart [34].

3. URBAN COMPLEX ANALYSIS: A POTENTIAL REFINEMENT

The preceding paragraphs refer for the most part to *operational* fusion of gravity models with other techniques. Before concluding the discussion of this channel, which of all channels considers urban-metropolitan structure in greatest detail, it is instructive to consider one more approach. This approach—the urban complex approach—is as yet nonoperational. It closely resembles the industrial complex approach fully presented in Chapter 9. When fully conceived and implemented, it offers the possibility of effective synthesis with the gravity model and other operational techniques of the fused framework of Channel III. This is so indicated at the lower right of Figure 8. Consequently, it promises to add to our understanding of the structure and functioning of urban-metropolitan regions and to projection of their basic features.

As in industrial complex analysis, it is first recognized that many activities within metropolitan areas tend to be bound by strong technical (production), marketing, and other interrelations. Oftentimes these are so pronounced and exert such an integrating effect that an adequate locational or other economic analysis must consider the activities together as an urban complex rather than separately.

Thus far, no urban complex analysis has been attempted. The approach is purely conceptual. Hence there is no empirical study to guide the selection of one out of the several possible ways in which this approach may be developed. However, in order to keep the length of the presentation to a minimum, we shall set forth this approach in a way parallel to the development of the industrial complex approach in Chapter 9.

An obvious first step in the urban complex approach is to identify general groups of urban-metropolitan activities, where the activities within each group have strong links affecting their costs and revenues. One such group might comprise the several retail activities of major department stores, women's ready-to-wear shops, specialty stores of all types, drugstores, variety stores, etc., as well as services of restaurants, theaters, hotels, lawyers, doctors, dentists, diverse repair shops, and in fact the whole host of activities characteristic of a central business district. At the other extreme, another group might consist of retail services of a local corner grocery store plus the services of one or a few other highly local establishments such as a shoe repair shop or a drugstore. Between these two extremes might be a group consisting of branch department stores, supermarkets, women's ready-to-wear shops, drugstores, variety stores, music shops, sporting goods stores, etc., as well as services of restaurants, bowling alleys, filling stations, partly specialized professional personnel, and other activities characteristic of regional shopping centers. Still a fourth group, of a lower order and smaller scale, may embrace the activities of a supermarket, a drugstore with lunch counter, a shoe repair shop, a radio and television repair shop, a dry cleaner, a tailor, a bakery, and a delicatessen, establishments typical of smaller community shopping centers.

In the delineation of general groups such as those of the preceding paragraph, a considerable amount of subjective decision is involved. Many activities can be and are involved in several of these groups. Yet there are those that preliminary analysis excludes from some—such as funeral parlors in central business districts and in regional shopping centers, or auto repair shops in central business districts, or high-grade specialty stores in local neighborhoods in general, or hotels in smaller community shopping centers.[179] Clearly, when detailed empirical analysis of the sort to be described is in fact conducted, the selection process in the delineation of groups can be pursued further with a greater degree of precision.

Once general groups of activities are identified in a systematic manner, a set of basic questions must be faced. It is immediately evident that an over-all pattern of commercial establishments for a metropolitan area which consists of urban complexes of two orders only—say the order corresponding to central business districts and the order corresponding to local neighborhood areas—is economically unwarranted, given the travel desires and shopping habits of consumers of a modern urban-industrial society. It is also evident that a pattern which excludes either of these two orders of urban complexes is also unrealistic. But exactly how many orders of urban complexes should there be? How dominant should be the central business district? What shares of total metropolitan activity should be allocated to the several other orders of urban complexes? How should the centers of each order be spatially distributed, and what should be their number and size? All these questions are interdependent. To a major extent, answers can only be found simultaneously.

Urban complex analysis, in essence, attempts to cope with the requirement that these interrelated questions be answered simultaneously. As in industrial complex analysis, the basic input-output data are to be tabulated for each activity. Following Table 1 of Chapter 9, the entire set of relevant urban activities may be listed horizontally, each activity being at the head of a column. Along the left tab of the table, all commodities (including services) may be set down, one for each row, whether they are inputs or outputs (or both) of the urban activities to be explicitly considered. In each column the requirement of each input (or the yield of each output) per unit level of the activity at the head of the column is noted, provided

---

[179] In contrast, there are some activities, such as parking area services, which are required intermediates of all complexes. In any one complex their required levels are determined à la input-output procedures.

such input (output) varies approximately in direct proportion to the level of that activity (i.e., varies linearly with scale). As in Table 1 of Chapter 9, inputs may be designated by negative signs and outputs by positive signs. In a second table of roughly the same form, the requirement of each other input (or yield of each other output) per unit level of the activity at the head of each column is noted. These inputs (and outputs) are nonlinear. Desirably their variation with the level of the activity should be approximated in a simple form, for example by an engineering-type factor such as noted in Chapter 9. But whatever the form approximating their variation with level, the relevant parameters (factors) must also be recorded.[180]

The next logical step would seem to involve computation of total inputs and outputs for each urban complex of each given order. To do so, however, requires that the investigator make a prior determination of the set of metropolitan patterns which he considers economically feasible and from which he desires to select the best.[181] (A metropolitan pattern consists of an hierarchical set of urban complexes, where the number of urban complexes in each order and their sizes, activity mix, and locations are specified.) Then for each such pattern he can compute total inputs and outputs for each urban complex of each given order.[182]

After the preceding computation for each pattern is completed, the investigator must cost the inputs and value the outputs. This step requires that he be given or postulate a set of approximate prices of each good and service at the location of each urban complex. With these prices he derives the total of both revenues and costs for each urban complex of each order

[180] For example, within the range of feasible economic scales of operation, labor inputs of an activity may vary directly with scale raised to the 0.2 power. (Scale is measured in terms of multiples of unit-level operation. See section 3 of Chapter 9.) Or, yield of an output (good or service) may vary directly with scale raised to the 1.1 power, unit level of operation being defined in terms other than output.

[181] Although a great variety of patterns are conceivable, in practice the number which realistically need to be investigated can be greatly reduced. For example, an investigator would not conceive of a pattern with a supermarket at each local neighborhood area, or a variety store at each neighborhood corner, or a department store in each smaller community center, or a dozen local grocery stores (as a substitute for a supermarket) in each regional shopping center. Further, the number of feasible patterns is greatly restricted by available land and existing physical structures and transportation networks.

[182] The actual steps of the computation are very similar to those taken in the computation of total inputs and outputs for the industrial complexes examined in Chapter 9.

Note, however, that the procedure of this paragraph is more locationally complicated than in the Puerto Rico case study of Chapter 9. In that case study the problem was limited to the feasibility of locating a complex in a given region, Puerto Rico, rather than on the Mainland with all activities but the fiber concentrated in the Gulf Coast, and with the fiber activity concentrated in the South. By previous cost analysis, this Mainland pattern had been estimated as having, in general, overwhelming cost advantages and had been projected as the dominant one.

in each pattern. When he sums all the costs for the various urban complexes of a given pattern, he obtains the total costs associated with that pattern. Total costs as derived in this manner can be compared for all patterns. The pattern having the least total costs may be judged to be the most efficient.[183]

This computation yields differences in total costs for each pattern, which may be explained in terms of Weberian categories. (See Chapter 9 and Figure 2 of this chapter.) Take transportation costs. Such costs are incurred by each urban complex in connection with shopping trips of consumers, that is, the transport inputs required by consumers to journey to urban complex locations and back home.[184] These transport inputs are priced at the appropriate transport rate which takes due account of time spent, media used, and inconvenience (congestion) in travel.[185] Thus, transportation costs on this account will significantly vary from urban complex to urban complex depending on both average distance to the appropriate groups of consumers and the ease with which the site of an urban complex is reached. Thus, too, such costs will differ significantly from metropolitan pattern to metropolitan pattern.

Transportation costs are also incurred by each urban complex in connection with the delivery of goods to its location from warehouses, terminals, and other distribution points. Again, the transport inputs associated with this delivery of goods are priced at appropriate transport rates, due account being taken not only of bulk, weight, perishability, fragility, etc., of the goods but also of congestion and other related factors. Among urban

---

[183] Observe that total revenues associated with each pattern—which revenues are derived for any given pattern by summing the revenues of the various urban complexes of that pattern—are not significant in comparing the desirability of different patterns. This point stems from the fact that the total gross output (sales valued at delivered prices) has already been determined for the given metropolitan area (subregion) as a result of the application of the balanced regional input-output framework on the subregional level and thus is identical for each metropolitan pattern the investigator considers economically feasible. Rigorously speaking, such a predetermination is to be somewhat questioned. In practice, it makes the operation manageable.

However, from the standpoint of a private real estate developer or local municipality, the revenue figure associated with a specific urban complex is a very significant magnitude. Hence, decisions by private developers and local municipalities frequently run counter to what is best for the metropolitan area as a whole. In a complete analysis the impact of such decisions should be included. We do not do so in the fused framework of Channel III.

[184] Deliveries of merchandise from stores to their homes are to be included in these transport inputs.

[185] It is fully recognized that acceptable procedures for estimation of such rates, as well as transport inputs involved in shopping trips, are yet to be developed.

complexes, and hence metropolitan patterns, major differences in transportation costs on this account arise.[186]

A second important Weberian category refers to labor costs. Such may or may not differ among urban complexes of the same size and order but differently located. This point follows since wage rates may or may not differ at these locations.[187] But labor costs will in general vary from urban complexes of one order to urban complexes of another order because of their different activity mix and consequent need for labor. On this account labor costs will also differ among metropolitan patterns. Likewise with power costs, water costs, taxes,[188] and a number of other costs.

A more interesting and widely studied Weberian category refers to land costs. The price of land varies greatly among the locations of a metropolitan area. Major cost differences among urban complexes are to be expected because of different effective distances from the metropolitan core. Thus, identical urban complexes will incur different land costs because of different locations alone. When variations in their size and activity mix are recognized as well, differences may be expected to be even greater. However, it must be observed at this point that such differences are tempered by the substitution effect. When a factor such as land is relatively cheap at a given location, more will be used per unit output of a given activity than at a location where the factor is relatively dear. The working of such a substitution effect is obvious when the horizontal spread and vertical dimension of an outlying regional shopping center are compared with the same features of a central business district.

Still another Weberian category which must be given major attention is scale economies. Scale economies are frequently inextricably bound with varying factor proportions and process substitution, a point which the reader will find discussed in Chapter 9. Such economies are already captured in the procedure for calculating input requirements and output yields when certain inputs and outputs are nonlinear with level of activity. In our previous computations such economies are counted, for example, when engineering-type factors other than unity are applied to diverse unit-level inputs and outputs. More specifically, when a labor factor is set at

[186] For example, delivery of a consignment of goods to a department store in a central business district will, in general, generate much greater transportation costs than delivery of such a consignment to a regional shopping center located at the same road distance from the given warehouse.

[187] Journey-to-work costs of employees of urban complexes may be accounted for either in wage rates or as part of transportation costs on goods and services flowing to the locations of urban complexes.

[188] If locations are in different political jurisdictions, major tax cost differentials may arise from contrasting tax structures.

0.22,[189] major economies of scale arise in the use of labor, for when the level of a relevant activity increases by 100 per cent, labor inputs rise by only 17 per cent. Or, when a land factor is set at 1.30, diseconomies of scale are involved in the use of land since when the level of a relevant activity increases by 100 per cent, land inputs rise by 146 per cent.

Finally, one more Weberian category which pertains to urbanization and spatial juxtaposition economies (as defined in Chapter 9) is to be noted. Many of these economies have already been embraced. They are counted in, for example, in the estimates for each urban complex of requirements for parking areas, trucking terminals, loading and unloading facilities, and power and utility systems. They are also accounted for in the estimates of numbers of shopping trips by consumers, and in estimates of both transport inputs on commodities and relevant transport rates. They may also be allowed for in estimates of advertising and general promotional expenses where one activity benefits from the customer pulling power of another.[190]

Yet such urbanization and spatial juxtaposition economies are not *fully* encompassed. As in the case study for Puerto Rico (in Chapter 9), there are noneconomic costs and gains involved which bear on the general welfare of a metropolitan area and of its constituent communities and neighborhoods. These costs and gains may be associated with change in the amount of congestion, with change in the extent to which citizens participate in community affairs and use community facilities, with change in other factors bearing on the general social health of the metropolitan area and its parts. These urbanization and spatial juxtaposition economies (diseconomies) can only be subjectively assessed, if at all, in terms of the ultimate values of the citizenry concerned. They thus preclude a full and complete objective analysis and hence restrict the general validity of results of the fused framework of Channel III.

In summary, the operational development of the urban complex approach can considerably upgrade intrametropolitan analysis. By extending the virtues of the industrial complex technique to urban study, this approach when operationally grafted onto the fused framework of Channel III promises to add to it considerable strength and to enhance substantially our understanding of urban-metropolitan structure and

[189] As is the case for many activities in the Puerto Rico study of Chapter 9.

[190] Localization economies do not appear to be extensively involved in urban complex analysis. Although the presence in a single urban complex of several establishments performing like services may lead to economies, say in transportation costs and advertising costs, it is exceedingly difficult to unravel such economies from urbanization economies. It seems best not to attempt a separate treatment of localization economies and to proceed on the basis that when significant they are caught as part of urbanization economies.

function. Once again, in reciprocal fashion the urban complex approach contributes to the validity of the gravity model and other techniques as well as to the fused framework as a whole and simultaneously relies on these techniques and the entire framework for basic information and parametric values. For example, the urban complex approach adds a desirable cost–revenue dimension to the income-expenditures dimension of the social accounts approach to the gain of the fused framework, and provides a spatial pattern of shopping centers for use in testing adequacy of transportation capacities. At the same time it requires from the framework basic magnitudes on population and output, and specifically from the gravity model the spatial distribution of consumers and from local social accounting expected levels of local consumer expenditures.

In bringing the discussion of Channel III to a close, it is pertinent to hark back to the objective motivating the development of this channel. It was recognized at the conclusion of section C on Channel II that the fused frameworks of both Channels I and II fail to achieve a full perspective on both agglomeration (spatial juxtaposition) forces and the behavior of social masses. These forces and behavior have as yet not been successfully dissected by the efficiency and requirements approaches of interregional comparative cost, industral complex, input-output, and linear programming techniques. Do the probability-type gravity models, and, on the purely conceptual level, urban complex analysis permit the investigator to incorporate such forces and behavior into his study?

First, let us critically appraise the application of a relative income potential concept to the problem of understanding and projecting systems of population, interregional migration, industrial location patterns, interregional commodity flows, interregional money flows, income and social accounts, and other items. In this application projection is attempted for only (1) non-cost-sensitive activities, and (2) those cost-sensitive activities for which comparative cost and industrial complex analysis is not undertaken for one reason or another.[191] Such projection by regions is based on improvement or deterioration in interregional position, as measured by relative change in income potential during a preceding period.[192] We may strongly contend that such a procedure is justified because relative change in income potential does catch, more fully than any alternative factor, the interplay of the host of both identifiable and unidentifiable forces associated

[191] Although that part of local service and other market-oriented industries tied to the activities of these two categories is also projected through the use of a relative income potential concept, the justification for this procedure is the simple hypothesis that in any given region the output of this part of local service and other market-oriented industries will expand or contract in direct proportion to the change in the over-all output in the given region of activities in the two categories listed above in the text.

[192] Or some combination of preceding and current periods.

with urbanization and spatial juxtaposition economies. Following loose probability reasoning it can be argued that as a whole firms engaged in the activities of these two categories may be expected to shift their operations among regions in accordance with relative income potential changes. Such shifting enables these firms to be closer to the market in general and thus to be able to gauge the size and composition of the demands of their customers more accurately, to establish better contact with these customers and be more sensitive to their changing needs, to maintain a higher quality service and better public relations, and to advertise more effectively, and gain other intangible advantages.[193] At the same time such shifting does not entail, in general, any major new disadvantages comparable in magnitude. Note that this kind of argument does not require that each firm reconsider its location at the beginning of each projection period.[194] It requires only that there are among the numerous firms many which are in a position to, and do, reconsider location; and that in terms of their aggregate output, in line with their self interest,[195] there are many which do shift to a sufficient extent.

The preceding argument with reference to major regions is not inconsistent with the existence of urbanization (and spatial juxtaposition) *diseconomies* such as increase in agricultural commodity prices as a major region expands, or rising land prices throughout the region. These diseconomies (frequently designated deglomeration economies) are, in the traditional Weberian fashion, netted from urbanization (and spatial juxtaposition) *economies*. These latter economies are and can be expected to be dominant for major regions as a whole.[196]

In sum then, it can be claimed that the impact of urbanization and spatial juxtaposition economies is at least to some extent grasped by a relative income potential model for major regions.

[193] For concrete illustrations of these points, see pp. 525–526, Chapter 11.

[194] The projection period may involve a time span of two years, as in the design sketched for Channel III or some other appropriate length.

[195] Recall that the investigator may choose to disaggregate to some extent the relative income potential term in order to fit better his conception of forces governing decisions of firms. For example, as noted in section G of Chapter 11, he may distinguish between firms producing intermediates for later use in the industrial process and firms producing final consumer goods. For the former, he might construct and use a relative potential term based on the changing distribution among regions of manufacturing output or employment. For the latter, he might use a relative potential term based on the changing distribution of disposable personal income.

[196] If in fact it should develop that deglomeration economies come to outweigh agglomeration economies for major regions as a whole, especially were land to become generally scarce, such a phenomenon would be reflected in the values of the ϵ and b coefficients of equations 14 and 15, respectively, in Chapter 11. The value of ϵ would tend to become less than unity, and of b negative.

Turning to the internal structure of metropolitan regions, we observe that the relative income potential form of the gravity model is not proposed for use. Moreover, the suggested use of the gravity model in "interaction" form is not as a scheme which catches the interplay of urbanization and spatial juxtaposition economies and diseconomies. Its proposed use is to provide a check on projected spatial distributions of industry and population based on comparative cost, industrial complex, linear programming, and other techniques including statistical "estimation" procedures. (These techniques to some extent take account of scale, localization, and urbanization economies.) The gravity model tests whether or not such distributions are consistent with empirical findings relating to the behavior of social masses, particularly in their travel habits. On the other hand, the urban complex approach, still in the conceptual stage, is put forth as a technique which when fully developed and implemented can catch to a much greater extent the interplay of urbanization and spatial juxtaposition economies and bring them to bear on urban-metropolitan analysis and projection.

Thus we conclude that Channel III, more than Channel I or II, does capture the net interaction of agglomeration and deglomeration forces, as generated by the industrial and urban concentrations of reality. Also, for this reason and because it utilizes empirical regularities on mass behavior and interactions, Channel III promises to be most relevant for the study of intrametropolitan structure within a system. Moreover, through the use of a relative income potential concept in a lagged or nonlagged form, Channel III does permit the projection of a time path of development (growth) for each region of a system. Yet it must be constantly kept in mind that Channel III has numerous shortcomings—not only many of those noted in the discussion of Channels I and II but also others (already enumerated) associated with the use of the gravity model.

E. Channel IV: A Values–Social Goals Framework

1. values (culture) as the central theme

A careful cutting into social processes with a fine-edged analytical scalpel exposes a primary stratum of premises underlying each of the three channels already discussed. These fundamental premises make clear that the three channels are each a special case of a more general system. These premises make clear that the three channels attack only problems which are primarily economic and for the most part postulate optimizing behavior of an economic type.[197] Viewed from a broad social welfare

[197] This statement is valid for the techniques central to these channels. Exceptions are involved, for example, in the introduction of gravity models for describing patterns

standpoint, such channels, therefore, are at best suboptimizing. This point is evident when we review the central techniques employed by each channel.

Channel I begins with a spatial pattern of population and societal behavior, which is then translated into a set of consumer wants (inclusive of governmental services). These wants set markets, by region—to be later revised to achieve economic consistency. Comparative cost and industrial complex procedures (supplemented by interregional linear programming) are applied. They reflect the businessman attempting to minimize cost given his market, that is, to maximize profits.[198] Interregional input-output is next injected, a technique which essentially establishes requirements and in the process generates income and employment—but on the premise that inputs are in accord with best engineering practice and are supplied from least-cost sources. A set of purely descriptive social accounts for a system of regions results. Reconciliation is effected to eliminate inconsistencies with a maximum-profit spatial pattern.

Channel II begins similarly, utilizes comparative cost and industrial complex techniques (supplemented by interregional linear programming) to identify maximum profit behavior, and injects a balanced region variation of the input-output model. This variation, more operational than the pure interregional model, establishes requirements, generates income, etc., and does so by approximating those inputs that are in accord with best engineering practice and are supplied from least-cost sources. Another set (presumably somewhat less precise) of purely descriptive social accounts for an hierarchical system of regions results which is to be revised to be consistent with maximum profits.

Channel III extends Channel II. It attempts to capture more of the spatial juxtaposition economies of reality. It is recognized that non-cost-sensitive industries are not adequately analyzed by Channels I and II. In Channel III changes in the spatial pattern of such non-cost-sensitive activities are linked to relative income potential changes—on the basic premise that such a relationship best reflects a maximum-profit motivation. Further, growth paths of the regions of the system are governed by decisions of businessmen seeking to maximize profits in the light of information which is both available and relevant. However, in the analysis of intra-metropolitan structure, a first major exception to the fundamental premise of profit-maximizing behavior is made. The gravity model, reflecting empirical information on travel desires and habits, is introduced to provide

of travel desire, and of scaling and related techniques for measuring local attitudes as a qualifying factor.

[198] This motivation is assumed to govern the behavior of businessmen individually and in groups.

a consistency check. Subsequent treatment of the urban complex approach returns to purely economic behavior—economic efficiency via cost minimization.

Society transcends the economic. Hence, Channel IV. Central to Channel IV are *values*. This is not to deny that a value system does underlie Channels I–III. One does. Implicit in the postulate of profit-maximizing behavior unconstrained by social institutions and legal restrictions is a value system that places high, if not highest, priority on *Liberty*, if we may speak in terms of the Great Values of the political scientist.[199] By failing to impose restrictions which assure minimum educational opportunities for all, minimum standards for food and drug products, minimum housing levels, minimum wage payments, equal opportunity to engage in business and enter trades, and so forth, Channels I–III place a relatively low priority on the basic values of *Equality* and *Welfare*. Thus, Channels I–III do rest on an underlying value system—one that may be said to be in many ways consistent with the system in the United States during the nineteenth century, or at least during parts of that century. Yet many other value systems are possible and do in fact exist. Hence, it is relevant, perhaps even imperative, that we examine the interrelations of value systems with the fused framework and with the numerous subsystems relating to a system of regions. In so doing we shall in Channel IV depart to a major extent from the frameworks hitherto developed. [But later, in Channel V, we shall return to these frameworks and extend their syntheses to embrace some of the results of the fundamental decision-making processes which at the margin equate political, social, and other values with economic (efficiency) values.] Thus in Figure 9 VALUES and GOALS enter the limelight of regional analysis and science.

A cursory overview of the wide range of conditions and achievements of the diverse cultures and subcultures of the world is instructive at this point. The analyst may conceive the social system as subject to, among others, resource constraints, technological-production constraints, and institutional-legal constraints reflective of culture. Or he may view the evolutionary pattern of any society as determined by the complex interaction of its cultural-attitudinal-institutional structure with its technological level (measured by know-how both available and embedded in practice) and its resource base. Attitudes and culture germinate motivating forces and stimuli and largely govern the pace of development as they, through know-how and inherited structure, actively impinge on the less active, but no less important, resource base (including access to resources of other societies). The resource base itself, together with its cost patterns, is relative, being highly conditioned and constantly revalued by the state of technology

[199] See A. A. Maass [20], pp. 9–10, and Chapter 2.

which in turn reflects accumulated means of communication and dissemination of knowledge, previous investment in the education of a populace,
builtup stock of industrial plant and equipment, current levels and composition of industrial output, population, labor force, consumption and
savings, governmental expenditures, and past and current resource use
patterns. This intricate general interdependence framework, as it changes
over time, in line with both equilibrating and disequilibrating forces, can
be pointed up and illustrated in a partial way from many different angles.
For example, where social and political attitudes preclude dissemination of
technological know-how, or discourage saving and investment in productive equipment, or stifle the development of entrepreneurial ability in the
education process, or overlay the spirit of enterprise with rigid custom,
taboo, and the like, etc., little progress, if any, is scored as measured by
GNP (total or per capitawise). India and Libya are cases in point; so is
the Belgian Congo with its relative wealth of resources. Or, where the
resource base is niggardly, however positive and growth-inducing the
attitudes and general cultural environment of a society, limits bind the
rate of development. Japan, before World War II, is an example, especially when contrasted with the United States and Germany.

Numerous other partial, concrete illustrations can be cited and are
common in the literature on economic development. In each, however,
the central place of values, attitudes, and social goals is clear, although
not always explicitly discussed.

2. THE GOAL-SETTING PROCESS OF SOCIETY

In Figure 9, the central theme is indicated by VALUES (CULTURE) at the
extreme left. They lead to GOALS: SYSTEM AND SUBSYSTEM, both formally
and informally established. However, the *process* by which goals are
established by a social system is not well understood, even in broad subjective outlines. And, accordingly, their quantitative identification rests
on a very shaky foundation.

As the box and arrow at the lower left of Figure 9 indicate, HISTORICAL
STUDY, SOCIOLOGICAL–POLITICAL THEORY, and in fact all types of contributions from all social sciences are required to increase our knowledge of
the goal-setting process. For example, we need to know much more about
the structure of social groups, ranging from household (family) through
neighborhood, community, town, metropolis, major region, national
community, world region, and world community. What are their roles,
both competitive and complementary? How do they function? How do
ideas and information flow among these groups, both vertically and horizontally? What additional knowledge is acquired by the classification of
the population of these groups by type religion, race, age, sex, educational

attainment, occupation, or socio-economic status in a broad sense? How is the individual's behavior conditioned by his relevant reference groups? Can the hypothesis be advanced that the spatial distribution of population conforms to a pattern which minimizes effort involved in all types of inter-action involving individuals and groups of all orders, bearing in mind (1) the diverse structure, roles, and functions of these individuals and groups, and (2) constraints which nature and society impose?[200]

Answers to these and many more fundamental questions are required for sound analysis of the goal-setting process. And beyond this, such answers are desired in connection with a number of other steps and procedures of Channel IV. For example, a system of meaningful regions whose delineation is required by the Channel is in fact a system of peoples, each with its own internal group and social organization. Clearly, the geographic delineation of these peoples must be closely related to their attitudes and values, their activities and roles, etc., as well as to such physical features as mountains, rivers, soil, climate which differentially impinge on human interaction.

Although our social science theories and methods are extremely inade-quate to answer these questions, nonetheless there are theories and tools which are and promise to be valid on a limited basis. Among these are factor, scaling, and latent structure techniques discussed in the Appendices to Chapter 7. As indicated in Figure 9, these techniques have at least some validity at this point of the channel. It has been noted several times that factor analysis can serve to reduce a mass of undifferentiated data to a limited number of variables consistent with the investigator's hypotheses. Thereby it can suggest useful typologies and classification schemes and identify workable social groups, workable regions, and workable aggre-gates of units of various sorts. Scaling techniques furnish a means to transform qualitative and noncomparable quantitative information into numerical ranking, for example, (1) to measure in an ordinal way such variables as the intensity of an attitude held by different groups, and the intensities with which an individual identifies himself with diverse reference groups; or (2) to rank diverse subregions by key social and political dimen-sions; or even (3) to explore the existence of "social regions." Latent

---

[200] See the discussion in footnote 140, Chapter 11. Further, is there justification for introducing a broad concept of social distance, along lines suggested by certain sociolo-gists and touched upon in Chapter 11? Can a matrix of social interaction among groups (and even individuals) be constructed in a fashion roughly comparable to an interregional interindustry matrix, where the interaction between any two groups varies directly with the degree to which they perform complementary roles and inversely with intervening social distance? Does such interaction resemble those economic flows (interaction) between two regions which are largely determined by the broad comple-mentarity of these regions and intervening economic distance?

structure analysis promises to yield insight on the presence and characteristics of social groups when they are not unidimensional, and thus to permit much more comprehensive and systematic approaches to the study of interaction and to our understanding of the goal-setting process.[201] Recall, however, that these techniques offer statistical explanation only; and as with other statistical techniques they can only test and generate hypotheses, not establish them.

A brief glance at the contents of the rounded major box of Figure 9 headed GOALS: SYSTEM AND SUBSYSTEM suggests the basic need for not only greatly improved sociological, psychological, and anthropological theory and methods but also considerable advance in political theory and administrative analysis.   It is recognized that the path from VALUES (CULTURE) to GOALS is composed of a host of decisions made by individuals acting in diverse political roles, formal and informal.   Citizens vote.   Grass roots decisions are made, but not independently of other decisions.   For current wishes and desires of citizens represent the accumulated impacts and repercussions of previous decisions over the course of history.   They may also reflect anticipated decisions.   Similarly, decisions are made by leaders at all levels above the grass roots in the hierarchy of power structure (frequently viewed as a pyramid).   This power structure is both formal and informal, and is precisely defined at certain levels and extremely nebulous and undefinable at others.   Once again, decisions made at any level are not independent ones, since the relative influence and leverage of a political leader at any level reflect previous and even anticipated decisions all along the pyramid over the course of time.   Furthermore, partly overlapping and partly superimposed upon the power structures of the system and its regions are administrative structures.   These latter perform services; but as implied they also condition and introduce policy-setting decisions.

[201] Suppose that improved latent structure methods prove useful for the development of a meaningful classification of people by groups.   Such a classification might be viewed as analogous to the grouping of economic units (firms) by type of output, number of employees, investment per employee, or research and development expenditures, etc. Much as such classifications of economic units are chosen according to the purpose of a study, so might a valid classification of social units be selected from those consistent with the empirical data.   The identification of the different groups associated with a selected classification might be in terms of voting behavior, local community participation, church activity, expenditure and savings patterns, reproduction behavior, etc.

In line with the previous footnote, the social groups corresponding to a meaningful classification may be appropriately interrelated by interaction matrices or other schemes. Such interrelation furnishes not only a partial view of social structure at a given point of time but also a means by which social behavior can be in part anticipated.   This behavior may relate, for example, to migration phenomena, birth rates, degree of labor unionization, pressures applied by labor organizations, occupational and similar immobilities, etc.

At present, our theory and techniques pertaining to power and administrative structures and decision-making processes are subject to major improvement and advance. Of possible new approaches to a better understanding of why and how goals are set for a society, the concept of community participation potential merits extensive exploration. As noted in section E of Chapter 11, this concept attempts to uncover basic relations (functions) which describe community participation (behavior) on the local level by a spatially distributed population. For each given governmental function it thereby permits the specification of a magnitude of community participation to be associated with each relevant size of administrative area. With each such area is also associated an efficiency (unit cost) measure in dollar terms. If by scaling or other similar attitude measurement technique it becomes possible roughly to equate for representative individuals and thus for their community a unit gain in level of community participation potential with a unit loss in efficiency (in dollar terms), a major step forward will have been achieved. It will then be possible to compare considerations of both efficiency and participation, perhaps à la indifference curves and surfaces. It will be possible to attack with some objectivity the major problem of Chapter 11 concerned with the proper allocation of diverse types of functions to the various levels of government (Federal, regional, state, metropolitan, . . . , local) in a system.[202]

Speaking even more broadly, if considerations of welfare (efficiency) and equality (as reflected to some extent in local community participation) can be linked together even in a very partial manner, further advance is to be anticipated. That is, if via the community participation potential concept and attitude measurement techniques a net figure or index can be obtained, after appropriate weighting, to summarize all relevant gains and losses in both welfare and equality considerations associated with the simple problem of appropriate administrative area for a given function, then it seems possible that further development along the same lines will yield considerable fruit in attacking problems involving social values on a still broader scale. (Some of these values are listed in the rounded major box to the left of Figure 9 and will be discussed later.) For example, it should be possible to evaluate in broad benefit-cost terms alternative major

---

[202] As a by-product, it might also be possible to obtain a net value incorporating change in both market potential and total transportation (and even production) costs to resolve the dilemma confronted by both Chauncy D. Harris and Edgar S. Dunn, as discussed in section E of Chapter 11. This step in turn would permit more effective operational synthesis of the market potential concept with the techniques of comparative cost, industrial complex, interregional input-output, and interregional linear programming, and with the fused frameworks of Channels I–III.

resource development proposals and to formulate more desirable policy. Likewise with capital budgeting and many other major problems with which many social scientists are concerned and constantly grappling.

The preceding paragraphs pertain to a stage in Channel IV which is non-operational at the present time. The integration of political, social, and economic values which are involved, and which must be ultimately confronted by all general social science theory, is still far distant. Yet despite the purely conceptual nature of this stage of Channel IV, it is fruitful to proceed to other stages and to see its interrelations with these later stages. By so doing the investigator obtains greater insight into some of the internal logic which must be met by each set of specific social accounts embodying system goals.

3. SYSTEM AND SUBSYSTEM GOALS AND SOCIAL ACCOUNTS

The next stage of Channel IV pertains to the statement of specific goals which are implicit or explicit in the general values of a culture and which emerge from its kaleidoscopic pattern of decisions. There are numerous ways in which such specific goals can be verbalized and listed, let alone the infinite number of sets of specific goals conceptually possible. The particular set partially listed in the rounded major box to the left of Figure 9 is thus one of many. Roughly speaking, it is intended to have some relevance for the current culture of the United States (the system) and its constituent regions. These goals are both formal (as freedom of speech embodied in the Constitution) and informal (as freedom of the consumer to select from a diversity of goods). They exist not only for the SYSTEM but also with different emphases for its constituent regions (SUBSYSTEM); for example, the goal of preservation of historic tradition is a system goal given greater than average weight in New England and less than average weight in Southern California.[203]

In Figure 9 GOALS are arbitrarily subdivided into three classes, Political, Social, and Economic. A typical trinity of political goals is Liberty, Equality, and Welfare.[204] The goal of Liberty may be defined in terms of "Constitutionalism with a goodly admixture of laissez-faire."[205] The goal of Equality may be defined in terms of wide-scale participation on the grass roots level of citizens in political policy formation, equal opportunity of all (supposedly guaranteed by law) to enter trade and business of all sorts, etc. The goal of Welfare may be alternatively interpreted as constituting the sets of Social and Economic goals. Social goals may pertain to

[203] In fact, there may be system goals which have no counterpart in the set of subsystem goals (e.g. that constituent regions should be allowed considerable diversity in their goals), and vice versa.

[204] For example, see A. A. Maass [20].

[205] [20], p. 32.

the full development and education of the individual and to the attainment of healthy community morale and a high level of individual and group stability and responsiveness.   Economic goals may embrace a high level of productivity and efficiency as well as equitable income distribution and vigorous and stable rates of system and subsystem growth.

Having in mind a set of specific goals such as these, an investigator (or regional planning authority or society itself) proceeds to translate them into a quantitative, consistent, and appropriately weighted set of social accounts. To him the full development and education of the individual may imply:

1. A minimum acceptable diet for each individual.   This requirement suggests a level of welfare and social security expenditures by government as well as minimum-wage and similar legislation[206] and adequate agricultural output.[207]

2. Minimum housing standards.   This requirement may suggest government expenditures for public housing construction and urban redevelopment (as well as private investment).

3. At least twelve years of schooling of a given quality.   This requirement implies certain government and private expenditures.

4. Minimum medical-hospital services, minimum access to recreational and cultural facilities, etc.

In a competitive market system each of these items tends to be duly weighted by existing or expected prices.

To an investigator, a healthy community morale and a high level of individual and group stability and responsiveness may mean:

1. A minimum standard of police protection and thus levels of local government expenditures for this function.

2. A minimum of social service activity to combat juvenile delinquency, family disruption, mental illness, etc.

3. A minimum civic activity program, etc.[208]

The political goal of Liberty (constitutionalism, laissez-faire, etc.) may imply to the investigator:

1. Certain governmental expenditures to maintain courts and judiciary structure.

2. Certain governmental expenditures for the legislature, for conducting elections, and for the support of the activities of the executive office.

[206] It will be seen that such legislation serves as a constraint limiting production to only those firms that can pay, say, a minimum wage.

[207] Whether or not adequate agricultural output can be produced will later be seen to be a test of the feasibility of the goals embodied in social accounts.

[208] This requirement is clearly related to the previous requirement of minimum recreational and cultural facilities and to others to be specified.

3. Certain governmental expenditures for defense and military purposes, etc.[209]

4. A maximum limit to governmental activity and control (including that activity involving the setting and enforcement of minimum standards) so that the consumer may choose among a reasonable diversity of goods and services and the worker among a range of occupations and trades.

To the investigator the goal of Equality as fostered by wide-scale participation in local community activities, local debate and discussion, antitrust legislation, small business assistance, etc., may imply:

1. Presence of a town hall or similar public facility in each local area.

2. A free local press and other facilities for disseminating information and opinion.

3. Administrative expenditures to enforce anticoncentration measures, fair employment practice laws, regulations to prevent discrimination in housing, etc.

Among Economic goals, a high level of productivity and efficiency and vigorous rates of growth for the system and its regions may imply:

1. Educational standards, as already listed.

2. Minimum amounts of investment in new plant and equipment by private as well as government sectors.

3. Minimum amount of expenditures on research and development.

4. Tariff policy which allows importation of items which can be produced at a significantly lower cost outside the system.

5. Adequate credit and banking facilities, etc.

Equitable distribution of income (disposable) implies not only minimum wage legislation but also inheritance taxes, steeply graduated income taxes, and other forms of progressive taxation. The goal of cyclical stability and sustained rates of growth for the system and its constituent regions may imply:

1. Expenditures for a central banking (Federal Reserve) system to exercise monetary controls, for an agency to regulate issues of securities, and the like.

2. Expenditures on public works, area redevelopment, and other resource utilization and conservation programs, and on research and other activity of a Council of Economic Advisers, etc.

3. Restrictions on the growth of industries in the several regions in

[209] And perhaps even a certain level of support of private educational institutions by business and citizens, and certain levels of contribution to nongovernmental group activity, to political party activity, etc., as is consistent with the structure of checks and balances underlying constitutionalism.

order to insure an industrial mix (composition) for each region which is not too sensitive to cyclical forces.[210]

In this manner the investigator generally proceeds from system and subsystem goals to system and subsystem social accounts. In practice he tends to develop system accounts first and then, by allocation and other procedures, subsystem (regional) accounts. But when there are significant differences in values among subsystems, and thus in their goals, it may be strongly contended that we should derive system social accounts from *subsystem* accounts based on subsystem goals. For example, because of differences among regions in cultural practices, religious affiliations, and family aspirations (these items may well have been employed by factor analysis to delineate regions), there may exist important regional differences in birth rates, death rates, age-sex composition, etc. When these rates and characteristics are used to project population for each region of a system, the system population as a sum of these regional populations may well differ significantly from a system population figure derived directly from average system rates. Since the former projection of system population reflects the interplay of more variables, it is to be preferred, *ceteris paribus*. And accordingly consumption accounts based on the former projection are also to be preferred.

Or, among regions there may exist differences in investment propensities. These reflect differences in a variety of factors such as age structure of industry, the degree of conservatism among business leaders and their willingness to assume risk, the relative emphasis given to efficiency as a goal, historical traditions, labor productivity, and union restrictions, as well as resource endowments, factor prices, and markets. When against a background of existing capacities these factors are used to project the capital formation sector (investment account) for each region, the resulting system account as a sum of the regional capital formation sectors may well differ from that directly derived from average system-wide characteristics.

Or, differences among regions in production practices, in consumer expenditure patterns, in pension and insurance funds supported by its businesses and institutions, in climate, and in other socio-economic characteristics may be recognized in developing other types of regional social accounts. When these accounts are summed appropriately, they yield corresponding system accounts which differ from those traditionally derived from average factors for the system.

Again, since system accounts derived as sums of the corresponding regional accounts presumably capture the interplay of a greater number of significant variables, they are to be preferred to accounts based on average

[210] This may involve for the several regions planned industrial expansions over time, somewhat along the lines of the study by F. T. Moore [22], to be discussed later.

system characteristics alone, *ceteris paribus.* Going even further, it may be claimed that a still more rigorous procedure will involve the simultaneous determination of both system and subsystem social accounts. But clearly this last procedure is nonoperational. And for practical purposes, even the derivation of system accounts as sums of independently derived subsystem accounts is likely to be too costly of research time and resources. Hence, Channel IV as all previous channels largely derives national (system) magnitudes directly and then allocates these among the constituent regions (subsystems).[211] And, in practice, except when differences in subsystem goals are critical, the investigator tends to allocate among constituent regions national (system) accounts derived directly.

2. DETAILING OF SOCIAL ACCOUNTS AND CONSTRUCTION OF INTERREGIONAL LINEAR PROGRAM

The preceding discussion points up clearly direct links between goals and certain social accounts. Governmental expenditures on all levels represent social accounts which are very directly related to goals. Other social accounts, such as consumption expenditures, net investment (private capital formation), Rest of the World commodity account, etc., are less directly related. Yet, they too must be explicitly detailed (and in a way which is ultimately consistent with goals). This detailing constitutes the next stage in Channel IV. It is represented by the BASIC SOCIAL ACCOUNTS box in Figure 9. The arrow which feeds into this box indicates the fundamental bond of SOCIAL ACCOUNTS with GOALS.

At this point it is to be noted that not all types of social accounts need be constructed. Certain social accounts will emerge as results at the final stage of the channel (such as Gross Regional Product and Gross System Product measured in terms of value added or net output by sector).[212] Moreover, the specific accounts to be detailed at this stage vary not only with the manner in which goals are framed but also with the set of techniques to be subsequently employed.

For example, were the central emphasis to be placed on input-output

[211] Strictly speaking, Channels I–III, as Channel IV, should have arrived at national and regional magnitudes simultaneously. In the derivation of Initial Regional Markets (noted at the left of Figure 1), regional birth and death rates, regional tastes, regional labor force participation rates and productivity, etc., should have been employed. Fine adjustments should have been made—such as those to take account of birth and death rates of expected migrants into a region (see section E.2, Chapter 2), or those to take into account the effect of the regional factor on average productivity in a given industry whose spatial pattern of output is projected to change, or those to take into account the effect of the regional factor via the changing spatial pattern of income on the national level and composition of consumption expenditures. At the present time such adjustments are generally too costly for most operational use.

[212] The reader may wish to refer to Table 2 at this point.

with major supplementation by comparative cost and industrial complex techniques (as in Channel I), the investigator would need to specify the *customary* final demand sectors for both the nation and region. [Recall that these cover Government Expenditures, Capital Formation, Inventory Change (additions), Foreign Trade (exports), and Household Expenditures.] Also, he would need to set down the *new* final demand sectors corresponding to those industries and parts of industries treated by comparative cost and industrial complex analysis. (See Table 1.) Additionally, he would need to specify still more new final demand sectors, each of which stems from a specific goal. One goal might be that private enterprise should support $1 billion of educational services by private colleges, to be allocated among the several regions. The new final demand sector in each region corresponding to this goal might be designated *Private College* (*Business Supported*), and the expenditures listed in the corresponding columns of a table such as Table 1 would add to $1 billion.[213]

A second goal might aim at a certain level of nongovernment welfare activities to be supported by local citizenry and business. This goal may be an outgrowth of a widely held view that a minimum of active, direct community support contributes to high morale and integration. The target might be $3 billion for each region. Then in a Table 1 there would be three more new final demand sectors, one for each region,[214] whose lists of expenditures would each sum to $3 billion.[215]

In this manner goals which are not already embodied in the final demand columns of a Table 1 may be incorporated into a channel such as Channel I. But the pursuit of this approach is the domain of Channel V which will be discussed in section F of this chapter. In this Channel IV, we wish to follow another direction and to detail the effective fusion of goals and social accounts with interregional linear programming rather than input-output

[213] In the lower part of a Table 1 there would be a corresponding new row for each region, listing contributions by industry (sector) to the private colleges of each region. These, too, would sum to $1 billion. Note that these contributions are to be considered as transfer payments. Any one contribution is not necessarily related to the level of operations of the contributing sector, although that sector may follow an informal practice of contributing say one mill for every dollar of sales.

[214] Once again, there would be three new rows in the lower half of a Table 1. In contrast with the first goal, the sources of funds to meet this second goal might include not only private enterprise but also households and government sectors.

[215] To illustrate a third goal, suppose society (its citizens, business, and other units and groups) judges that the political process basic to constitutionalism, operating as it must under day-to-day pressures, is incapable of long-run basic research. Suppose that such research is considered vital for the maintenance and orderly adjustment of the political, social, and economic system, and that a nongovernmental, central authority organized much like a university (but independent of any university) is supported by contributions. Then, as above, new columns and rows must be added to a Table 1 with appropriate breakdowns and totals.

as the central operator.[216] Interregional linear programming has considerable promise; and, although it is nonoperational at the moment, its use at this point does not detract from the strength of Channel IV. For we have already made clear that this channel must be conceptual since the process of translating VALUES (CULTURE) into GOALS is only conceptual at the present stage in the development of the social sciences.

Once the choice of the central operator is made, the investigator may start the process of detailing social accounts. When interregional linear programming is the central operator, those accounts associated with constraining magnitudes must be detailed. But what will the constraining magnitudes be? The answer to this question depends on the objective of the program. But since practically each goal may be either established as a constraint to be met or embodied in an objective function, many linear programs are possible. It therefore becomes necessary to treat simultaneously the detailing of social accounts and the construction of a relevant interregional linear program. Hence, in the following paragraphs we shall discuss concomitantly the BASIC SOCIAL ACCOUNTS box and the INTERREGIONAL LINEAR PROGRAM matrix.

a. The objective function. At this juncture fundamental decisions must be made regarding (1) the specific goal(s) to be embodied in an objective function and (2) the specific goals to be contained in the full set of constraints. The objective function may be to maximize Gross System Product, outputs of the several sectors of the several regions being weighted by the appropriate regional prices. Or the objective function may be to maximize labor income under a schedule of money wage rates which is uniform for all regions of the system—an objective which might be characteristic of a society dominated by labor unions. Or the objective may be to maximize recreational and cultural services (including green, open spaces in urbanized areas). Or the objective function may be to maximize a combination of items such as (1) recreational and cultural services and (2) long-run research and development expenditures (where these items are to be realized in some fixed proportion consistent with the investigator's or society's values).[217] Or the objective function may be to maximize a

---

[216] Still a third approach might project several basic social accounts on a very gross basis against the background of a few broad goals (e.g. full employment). From these accounts the investigator might proceed directly to outputs by industry for the nation, and in turn to outputs by industry for each region. This approach might perhaps employ some Keynesian analysis peppered with location quotients, coefficients of localization, and the like.

[217] This latter condition actually involves a constraint which forces the system to produce these items in fixed proportion, say $1.00 of recreational and cultural services for every $2.00 of research and development expenditures. For the interregional linear program to be feasible, the yield of each of these two items must exceed some absolute minimum which in the extreme may be zero.

combination including these two items as well as community welfare services and local community participation, these four items to be weighted in accord with relevant values and yielded in fixed proportions.[218]   Or the objective function may be to minimize the average work week; or to minimize a combination of work week and use of a strategic resource; or to minimize a combination of work week, use of a strategic resource, and degree of industrial specialization by region, where appropriate measures are constructed and relevant fixed proportions established.

Corresponding to each of these objective functions is, of course, a set of constraints.   To illustrate how a set of meaningful constraints may be developed, suppose that the objective function is to maximize Gross System Product (GSP).   Let this function pertain to the GSP of a key projection year, say 1965.[219]   An immediate problem concerns the choice of appropriate weights (constants).   These weights are required to multiply the several industrial outputs in the several regions in order to obtain a measure of Gross System Product consistent with the values of an investigator or society.   This step is indicated in Figure 9 by the arrow which links the box WEIGHTS (PRICES) to the Objective Function of the INTERREGIONAL LINEAR PROGRAM.   One set of weights which might be selected comprises the ruling or perhaps projected market prices in each region. But such a set might be inconsistent with certain values.   The market price of opium may be high (and positive).   Yet society may place a negative price on it reflecting the undesirability of its consumption.   Or the market place may set only a low price on a unit of cultural activity, whereas society may place a relatively high price on such a unit.   In short, the precise formulation of the objective function is intimately associated with the values and goals of a system.   This close bond is indicated by the arrow which proceeds from the block GOALS: SYSTEM AND SUBSYSTEM to the box WEIGHTS (PRICES).

Although ruling prices are convenient to apply, such application is not legitimate if prices deviate significantly from social values and goals.   At the same time, it is fully recognized that precise quantitative weights reflective of social values and goals are not easily established, and that therefore ruling (historic) prices can be extremely useful, if only as benchmarks.[220]

[218] Helpful in the derivation of relative weights to be applied to these several items are scaling and similar techniques.

[219] Alternatively, it may pertain to a current year.   Then the program might be employed to establish norms for that year, against which to compare actual performance.

[220] In connection with the determination of relevant prices, see the simultaneous equations approach of K. A. Fox and R. C. Taeuber [9] briefly outlined in footnote 263 below.

b. Minimum standards constraints. Given the objective function—in this illustration, to maximize Gross System Product (GSP) for 1965[221]—the full set of constraints must be stated. Again many sets are possible, depending on the investigator's or society's values. These sets may range from those characteristic of a cradle-to-grave welfare state to those typifying a rugged individualistic laissez-faire society. Nonetheless, there are certain constraints which must be common to all existing societies which have the objective of maximizing GSP. The system must produce enough food for subsistence of its projected populace; and enough housing and clothing to afford that populace protection from the elements to the extent necessary for life itself.[222] Beyond these and other minimum standards it would seem reasonable that the system for the most part deliver to consumers in the year of projection the set of final products they have received in the current or relevant base year. (Or, in recognition of likely increases in average productivity reflecting technological and educational advance and accumulating capital stock, such required deliveries may be increased to allow for, say, at least a 2 per cent increase in per capita disposable income and shifts in consumption patterns which such increase implies.) Of course, certain changes in this pattern of consumer deliveries may be imposed, for example, delivery of radios may be curtailed 50 per cent and of family aircraft increased by 75 per cent to allow for changing tastes.[223]

In addition to setting constraints requiring a minimum (customary) pattern of deliveries to consumers of the entire system, the investigator must establish for each region of a system a pattern of deliveries which also must be met.[224] Recognizing immobilities and other characteristics of a

[221] As previously intimated in Chapter 4 and at other places in this book, if GSP is defined as GNP is typically defined for a nation, then GSP is not the sum of GRP's (Gross Regional Products). This point follows since GNP nets out interregional trade within a nation while Gross Regional Product for a region of the nation does (or at least should) not. (Net regional exports for a region of a nation are as significant a part of Gross Regional Product as net foreign exports for a nation are of GNP. This point can be better appreciated when it is recognized that if Gross Product for the World were computed as Gross National Product is for a nation, all international trade would be netted out; and hence, Gross Product for the World would not be a sum of Gross National Products.)

[222] In a dictatorial society, for example, planned output of such products need not exceed these minima. In practice, however, there would be a tendency for some additional product to be set aside for consumption by political leaders.

[223] Additionally, differences among consumption patterns of diverse income groups may be explicitly recognized. The implications of these differences for the required pattern of consumer deliveries may be based on expected distribution of income among income groups, or on a constrained distribution imposed as a goal, or both.

[224] This step is necessary to insure that the entire system output of any single consumer

population, about which more will be said later, the investigator may require that for the year of projection deliveries to any given *region* roughly correspond to 90 per cent of that region's current or base year deliveries.[225] Here, too, some changes in regional consumption patterns may be effected to recognize changing tastes and characteristics of likely migrant population, as well as legal and other restrictions precluding consumption of certain items. In making such changes the investigator may be guided by changes in location quotients, coefficients of localization and population redistribution, and other similar measures as noted on Figure 3 of this chapter. The preliminary use of these measures as guides is indicated on Figure 9 by the arrows leading from the box designated COEFFICIENTS, CURVES, RATIOS.

Moreover, the required pattern of final product deliveries to consumers in each region may be still more realistically modified to recognize many other more general, but equally relevant, forces, whether they pertain to a totalitarian system, a rugged individualistic laissez-faire economy, or a welfare state. To discuss such modification in a lucid manner (as well as many other points to be glossed over in subsequent paragraphs) requires the construction of a comprehensive and elaborate interregional table. Such a table, however, would necessitate extensive explanation and is beyond the scope of this volume which places primary emphasis on operational schemes.

The specific identification of the preceding limiting magnitudes on deliveries to household consumers represents a setting up of detailed minimum accounts on Consumption Expenditures for each region as well as the nation. In each account, the listed expenditure on each commodity item represents a minimum permissible level.[226] The system of course may deliver beyond this level. Hence, the full statement of each Consumption Expenditures account is only possible after the framework of Channel IV is run.

In establishing minimum levels for system and regional Government Expenditures accounts, the investigator may pursue procedures parallel to those relating to consumption expenditures. Expenditures to meet the goal of minimum police protection must be either implicitly or explicitly included somewhere in the several regional and system government

product is not delivered to one and only one region, namely the region with the most favorable price situation. See Chapter 10 and B. H. Stevens [33] for further discussion of this point.

[225] This may be taken to reflect approximately a maximum permissible decline in the population of a region.

[226] In some cases, an expenditure on a commodity item is to be interpreted as a maximum permissible level.

accounts.   Such expenditures may range from zero in a communal-type society to an exorbitant amount in a Fascist state.   Expenditures to meet the goals of minimum fire protection and public health programs, and to preserve Liberty and Equality all, too, must be either implicitly or explicitly covered in these same government accounts.   Capital expenditures, particularly by local governments, to develop parks, transportation facilities, and other urban capacity must be included, etc.   In practice, again the investigator may find it convenient to work with current or base year patterns as benchmarks.   He may recognize a mounting public insistence on more effective measures to combat juvenile delinquency, to upgrade urban services especially those relating to transit and recreation, to protect civil liberties subject to more frequent encroachment in an increasingly complex society—in general a need to maintain and raise standards of government services of diverse sorts.   Accordingly, he may adjust current or base year governmental accounts, not only for the system as a whole but for each region of every order.[227]   Again, a full presentation of the process of setting up these government accounts, in terms of minimum permissible levels for each expenditure item, is beyond the scope of this volume.   These levels serve as limiting constants in the sense that at least the quantities of goods and services (including labor and capital) which correspond to these levels of government expenditures must be delivered and rendered to the government sectors by the system.[228]

Still another set of constraints which are simultaneously minimum level social accounts relates to Net Investment including Capital Formation and Net Inventory Change.   (See Table 2 of this chapter.)   These constraints spring from the desirability of maintaining at the minimum a specific rate of growth for the system and each of its regions, that is, of achieving a goal of continuing increments in average productivity.   Again for each region as well as the entire system, base year (or period) data on capital formation (including inventory change) may be employed as benchmarks.[229]   For any given region the minimum permissible level of capital formation (including inventory change) may be taken as not less than say 50 per cent of the base year (period) rate.   For the system as a whole the minimum permissible level of capital formation may be taken to be not less than say 80 per cent of base year (period) level of capital formation.   These levels

[227] Also, appropriate modifications of these benchmarks may be undertaken in the light of changes in the diverse coefficients, curves, and ratios listed in Figure 3.

[228] Once again, among societies there will be great variation in the levels and patterns of governmental expenditures reflecting differences in basic values attributed to (needs for) governmental functions and services of diverse types.   Also for certain cases these levels are to be interpreted as maximum permissible levels.

[229] Again, these benchmarks may be suitably modified in the light of changes in any of the coefficients, curves, and ratios listed in Figure 3.

yield another set of minimum permissible social accounts, whose breakdown by specific commodities yields deliveries to the several capital formation sectors which must not be undermet.[230] The constraints discussed in the preceding paragraphs may be appropriately designated *minimum standards* constraints and are so noted under *constraints* in the INTERREGIONAL LINEAR PROGRAM matrix of Figure 9. It is to be noted that the three classes of minimum standards constraints given cover only four of the five customary final demand sectors. Foreign Trade (exports) is not included. To be complete at this point, we can set minimum levels of delivery to the Foreign Trade sector in order to insure the wherewithal to pay for necessary imports. Such levels might be considered another class of minimum standards constraint. However, it is more convenient to classify these constraints as balance of payments restrictions, to be discussed later.

c. Resource constraints. A second major category of constraints pertain to *resources.* The significance of resource restrictions as such and the manner in which they bind the system and each of its constituent regions has been fully discussed in Chapter 10. At this point, therefore, it becomes necessary only broadly to identify resources.

For the purposes of Channel IV resources may be defined to include the common minerals such as iron ore in the ground; water, soil, climate, and other characteristics associated with land as a resource; plant, equipment, inventory on hand, and other forms of capital; and finally management and the labor force with all their education, skill, and technological know-how. The stock of each resource expected to exist in the year of projection becomes a limiting magnitude. After allowance for imports and exports, the system must not require more of any resource than is available for current use. This general rule applies to all resources, mobile or immobile. In the case of immobile resources other potentially more binding restrictions obtain. At any one place (region) the requirement of any resource must not exceed the amount locally available for current consumption. Observe that the values and goals of a system and its regions can be critical in establishing the effective supply of a resource for any given year of projection. For example, considerations of conservation, preservation of amenities and recreational features of a landscape, as well as of defense and of the increasing noneconomic value attached to leisure per se, may significantly reduce the limiting magnitude on the supply of a resource below that physically available.

[230] Although positive levels of capital formation preclude net capital consumption for any given region, the system may permit capital consumption (insufficient replacement of plant and equipment) in one or more industries or locations which are supposedly "obsolete."

The explicit statement of resource constraints clearly points up the integral relationship between interregional input-output analysis and interregional linear programming. It points up the need for an input-output type computation, whether or not we consider this computation as part of a linear program computation. An input-output type computation is appropriate since a linear programming framework necessitates the use of constant production coefficients for each activity—that is, a set of constant inputs and outputs per unit level regardless of the scale of an activity. This computation yields the total required use (or demand for, or deliveries) of each resource, intermediate, and finished product. (See the discussion in Chapters 8 and 10.) These totals are, of course, to be compared with the relevant limiting magnitudes in the major category of *resource* constraints as well as in other categories. In Figure 9, the box at the extreme right designated I-O MATRIX (TECHNOLOGICAL REQUIREMENTS) with an arrow leading to *constraints* indicates the general use of an input-output-type computation.

d. Stability constraints. Still another major category of constraints relates to the goal of *stability* for both the system and its regions. As noted in the discussion of Channel I (in particular, section B.2.f), it is highly desirable for most projections to link both secular and cyclical factors. It is clear that wastes generated by depression periods are undesirable in themselves. It is equally clear that depression periods can have a major retarding effect on long-run growth, even if only because labor, plant, equipment, and other resources that can build up production potential remain idle. Hence a wise society generally places some value on a reduction of severe cyclical swings to which it is subject. It does so recognizing that in a dynamic, capitalistic system and many others such swings may be in part unavoidable and even in part desirable if only to eliminate vested interests, deadwood, and spur invention.

With a goal of partial stability in mind, a planning model for policy purposes may set one or more *stability* constraints as noted in Figure 9. To set relevant constraints, however, is not a simple task. In Chapter 6 and in section B.2.f of this chapter we have indicated that cyclical and secular effects are not simply additive. Rather, they are multiplicative. And at this point of time we know little about how cyclical and secular forces interplay. We do not know how to appraise the cyclical implications of a particular industrial mix, or the significance of variation among regions in industrial mix, or to anticipate investment and consumer behavior and psychology, or to evaluate the interrelation between rate of growth and such behavior, or to identify the nature and significance of the general regional factor in each region. And so forth. Yet, there have accumulated some knowledge and partially validated hypotheses on regional and system cycles; and society, or the investigator, may judge it worthwhile to set some constraints based on such knowledge and hypotheses rather than none at all.

Suppose that industrial composition hypotheses are considered relevant.[231] The investigator may accordingly set constraints. For each region he may set a very simple constraint. The sum of the gross outputs of all industries classified as durable must not exceed say 50 per cent of total gross output. This constraint reflects the simple hypothesis that undue relative concentration of durables in one region tends to generate severe cycles and foster their spread throughout the system. Observe that, when binding, this constraint, as all constraints in general, interferes with the search for pure economic efficiency per se. Generally speaking, society must be satisfied with a lower total gross output (GSP) in order to attain a certain amount of stability.

For each region, the investigator may choose to add to, or substitute for, the previous simple constraint a second simple constraint. The sum of the gross output of all industries classified as slow-growing or declining must not exceed say 70 per cent of total gross output. (This reflects the view that too great a concentration on slow-growing or declining industries is undesirable.)[232] Or the output of any single industry must not exceed say 40 per cent of total gross output. (This reflects the view that a one-industry region is unhealthy.) Or for each region the investigator may choose to set a more complex, but not necessarily better, constraint. He may require that the coefficient of industrial specialization not exceed 0.60.[233]

Or the cyclical analysis associated with the Keynesian short-run interregional trade multiplier may be considered relevant rather than that oriented to industrial composition. The investigator then sets other kinds of stability constraints. For the nation total level of private capital formation (including inventory change) plus government expenditures on public works and similar investment projects must not be less than $\$K$ billion; and for each region the same total must not be less than $\$K_i$ billion. Note, however, that this constraint has significance only if the level of the private capital formation sector (covering investment in steel plant plus all other private plant and equipment) which is required by the constraints on minimum standards is less than $\$K$ billion for the system,

[231] See section B of Chapter 6 for full details on these hypotheses.

[232] Or, if the investigator accepts the hypothesis that system and regional cycles tend to be less severe when regions do not develop at greatly divergent rates, he may impose for each region both a minimum and maximum level for its rate of growth. Or he may impose a maximum spread between the rates of growth of any two regions, or some equivalent condition.

[233] See Chapter 7, section E, for definition of this coefficient.

or $\$K_i$ billion for each region, or both.[234]   This constraint insures in the Keynesian sense sufficient driving force for the system and each region, that is, a public works program supposedly adequate to offset the effects of pessimistic business behavior in the system and its constituent regions.[235]

Aside from the difficulty of determining the most relevant hypotheses to which to orient stability constraints, the investigator confronts the technical problem of setting limiting parameters.   Helpful in this regard are comprehensive empirical studies of past cyclical behavior of a system and its regions, such as conducted by Vining (see section E, Chapter 6). Helpful, too, are data on changes in coefficients of localization, location quotients, and corresponding localization and specialization curves, relative growth charts, shift ratios, etc.[236]

   e. Financial constraints and money flow study.   Closely related to some of the constraints bearing on stability are constraints embedded in financial institutions and practices.   This close association is particularly apparent in government policy—credit, tax, public works, monetary, and more broadly fiscal—which can be instrumental in setting both types of constraints.   Such government policy may be conceived as an attempt to equate at the margin anticipated gains from greater stability and the like and anticipated sacrifice of social values from increased regulation of the economic system and the like.   But *financial* constraints embody much more than government policy; and to their discussion we now turn.

   As has been developed in previous chapters, a system and its regions represent a host of underlying subsystems.   In this chapter we have placed emphasis on the industrial location system (comparative cost and industrial and urban complex techniques), on the commodity flow and interregional interindustry systems (linear programming, input-output, and gravity techniques), and on an interregional social accounts system.   But as important as any of these is the interregional money flow system via which financial constraints are imposed.   Unfortunately in practice we cannot harvest the potential fruit of this system because of inadequate data and the dearth of past studies.   However, since Channel IV is purely

---

[234] Also bear in mind that a projection in the future for one key year only is being considered here.   At a later point, the possibility of a growth model over time will be briefly, and of course only conceptually, examined.

[235] Or the investigator may have constraints which automatically require government welfare payments to maintain certain levels of disposable income and hopefully consumption expenditures.

[236] These materials may suggest the desirability of having different values for the limiting parameters of the several regions.   They also may permit the construction of less complex constraints.   For example, the outputs of completely market-oriented activities (such as a number of services), as evidenced by low values for the coefficient of localization, need not enter into output constraints mentioned in the above paragraphs.

conceptual anyway, it is not inappropriate to investigate here certain facets of the interregional money flow system. Moreover, the monetary and banking institutions of a culture impose both formally and informally major constraints on the operation of an economy and thus on the performance of a society. These constraints are associated with such phenomena as discount and interest rate policy, open-market operations, deficit financing, tax structures, Treasury policy, and even moral suasion as may be exercised by Federal Reserve banks. Hence it is highly desirable to probe as deeply as possible into money flows and their associated financial constraints. This step is further justified when the investigator recognizes that however firm his comparative cost, industrial complex, input-output, and linear programming analyses per se, his system is engulfed in a culture. The values and attitudes of such a culture undergo constant change and exert a shifting and major influence on the structure of the system via the constraints of its financial institutions. These constraints cannot be ignored, no matter how anemic our analysis of money flows and of values, attitudes, and decisions governing such flows.

Before a specific examination of how financial procedures and rules, again both formal and informal, can be made explicit in terms of constraints, it is well to recall an important relationship. In its most general form an interregional money flow system has close and intimate links with both an interregional system of social accounts and an interregional interindustry system. Each of these three systems may be viewed as affording comprehensive statistical descriptions.[237] As already noted, the interregional interindustry system emphasizes technical linkages with due consideration for efficient supply channels. For the most part it reflects

[237] Obviously, in practice the investigator is severely limited in developing comprehensive statistical descriptions. Too often he must compromise; he cannot have all three systems for every set of regions considered relevant when attacking social problems. He generally must set a priority on one of the three systems (if he is able to develop even one) and accordingly choose the most appropriate set of regions. Where money flow data are to be extensively employed, in the United States he tends to use Federal Reserve regions and districts. He adapts his interregional interindustry matrix and interregional social accounts as best he can. Or, when data are required in order to evaluate the performance of a system and its regions in terms of predetermined goals, another set of regions appropriate for social accounting is selected; and the investigator orders his money and commodity flow data as best he can.

Although in theory the three systems mentioned above can contribute to each other in filling gaps in the several sets of data, in affording cross checks, and in forcing consistent reconciliations and the like—all in ways already mentioned several times in this and preceding chapters—in practice such reciprocal contribution may be severely circumscribed. This point follows since as already noted the set of regions appropriate for one of the three systems need not, and typically will not, be appropriate for the other two systems. Hence, the gaps in the data of the first system usually are not easily filled by the available data of the other systems which pertain to different sets of regions.

business, consumer, and government decisions on commodity purchases and sales. Each commodity purchase and sale generates a money flow—a flow which, from the discussion of Table 6 in section B.2.e, is also an item in an interregional money flow system. Thus the interregional inter-industry system is completely contained in the interregional money flow system.

Similarly, the interregional system of social accounts is fully embodied in an interregional money flow system. Each item in a social account, it may be recalled, is either a receipt on income account (household and government), a payment on production account or a receipt on output account, or an expenditure on consumption or investment account. Every such item must by definition be also an item in an interregional money flow table; and decisions underlying any such item must also pertain to money flow analysis.

Thus, to reiterate, the interregional money flow system stands as the most comprehensive of the three. It reflects (1) the technical explanations of an interindustry system, for example, the need to consume approxi-mately 9 kw-hr per pound of aluminum produced; (2) the efficiency con-siderations of the system of industrial locations (including retail and other commercial locations) to the extent that this system is already con-tained in an interregional interindustry system; (3) the economic oppor-tunities factor underlying an interregional system of population (to the extent that such is implied by the interregional interindustry system);[238] and (4) the value- and goal-oriented elements of an interregional system of social accounts (e.g., local government purchase of fire equipment). But beyond these the interregional money flow system reflects a host of other financial-type decisions relating to money flows (frequently invisible), which decisions are not readily explainable via orthodox frameworks and are oftentimes regarded as capricious. Altogether, then, the intricate interregional money flow system of reality may, on a conceptual level, be claimed to contain a number of other systems and in fact to be the most general of all capable of objective portrayal.

Added support for the previous statement stems from the fact that the interregional money flow system can reflect much more comprehensively than any other system the entire set of decisions made by individuals and diverse groups of all sorts, as they function in their kaleidoscopic roles of reality. Take a corporation's decision to consummate a major purchase of equipment for a plant in Arkansas. In the interregional interindustry

---

[238] Since interregional input-output coefficients may be established to reflect diverse labor inputs required per unit output of a given industry, the interregional interindustry system implies an occupational structure for each region, and hence to a major extent an interregional system of population.

system this decision is manifest as expenditures in one or more cells in the capital formation sector of the region including Arkansas. In the inter-regional money flow system this decision is manifest as payment items of corresponding magnitude in one or more cells of an interregional money flow table; these items represent money flows from the corporation to the equipment-supplying industries. Influential to this decision, however, may be a prior decision by a local, national, or even international banking house to advance the necessary funds as a loan. This latter decision is nowhere manifest in an interindustry system and table; it is manifest in the money flow system and table, in terms of both region and sector of origin and region and sector of termination. Affecting this latter decision are, of course, values and attitudes of all sorts, local, national, and international, as well as current business anticipations and psychology. None of these, however, can be explicitly inferred from a money flow table, let alone an interindustry table.

Still other considerations bear upon this decision to invest in Arkansas. The favorable sale of an obsolete plant and its site in Ohio provides additional liquid capital. The earlier decisions behind such sale are manifest in a money flow from a purchaser in San Francisco to the corporation (legally existing in Delaware), but not in any flow of an interindustry matrix. Moreover, the decision to invest may have been prompted by a previous decision to call a special meeting of a board of directors, growing out of an informal discussion on a golf course in Connecticut. This latter decision is manifest in neither a money flow nor a commodity flow. It reflects an aspect of societal structure which is outside the framework of the systems discussed in Channel IV, as are aspects pertaining to the choice of, say, Pittsburgh as the location for the meeting of the board whose members may reside in New York, Rhode Island, Florida, and Texas, and who act as proxies for stockholders scattered over all states and the world. Furthermore, the decision to invest may be significantly influenced by a court decision in Missouri, which is based on an interpretation of a clause of an antitrust law made in Washington, D.C., subsequent to pressure by a senator from Montana, etc. Behind these facets of social and political power structure, and behind the decisions emanating therefrom, are a still more intricate maze of formal and informal communication lines through which ideas and information flow.[239]

Admittedly, an interregional money flow system falls far short of depicting this maze, let alone simpler facets of social structure. Nonetheless,

[239] For example, important consumer decisions influenced by Hollywood films in turn importing ideas from a London show costumed by a Polish designer copying an idiosyncratic notion of a Parisian artist illustrates well this maze in which not physical or economic but social distance is primary.

this system still represents the most comprehensive one for which at the present time the necessary statistical materials can be potentially gathered. Yet, as already noted, even these materials are largely unassembled, so that currently this system must remain for the most part conceptual.

The one area of money flow study, however, where operational constraints can be clearly and forcefully established concerns the balance of payments, whose statement does summarize basic aspects of a money flow system. It is recognized that a balance of payments constraint is not of significance for all systems of regions. For example, consider the United States, a system wherein there is considerable mobility of population as well as of capital. An imposition of a balance of payments constraint upon any of its regions does not fulfill a basic goal of that region and, concomitantly, sacrifices an important degree of freedom. Should a region such as New England import considerably more than it exports (after allowing for both receipts and payments on interest, rent, dividend, profit, gift, and similar accounts), the difference can be bridged by a capital movement. (This capital movement may embody transfer of wealth and titles to wealth to outsiders, credit extension by outsiders, investment by outsiders, etc.) Or if such capital movement develops to be insufficient, and if the New England population as a whole is not productive enough at its specific locations to match imports with exports, part of such population can and is motivated to move to other locations at which greater productivity obtains. Hence, given current and likely values and social structure in the United States, a balance of payments restriction by region is to be considered an undesirable infringement on this culture's remaining principles of laissez faire.

In contrast, a balance of payments constraint by region can be firmly justified for an international system of regions, where each region is a nation. Here major cultural differences may exist among the populations of the several regions and, because of different historical development paths, may be associated with major differences in productivity. These cultural differences in many cases tend to induce (cause) a region to place a top priority on the preservation of its own particular culture, which may be revealed not only in major obstacles placed on in-migration but also informally in a deep-seated reluctance of population to migrate across national boundaries. It may also be revealed in specific restrictions which a culture (region) may judge it imperative to impose upon gold outflows, certain classes of imports, investment by foreign companies, etc. Although such restrictions may tend to depress per capita real income in the long run, it can be argued that they contribute to financial stability and to the maintenance of cultural identity, political autonomy, etc.

In short, then, the inclusion of a balance of payments constraint is often justifiable. This constraint, listed in Figure 9 under *financial* constraints, may take various forms. A simple one may state that in equivalent dollar terms imports must not exceed exports by more than $1 billion, or 10 per cent. A more complex one may state that imports of certain items must not exceed specified quotas, others imports being unrestricted.[240] Or the balance of payments constraint may state that the export of gold must not exceed 5 per cent of gold reserves. Or, on a finer level, that investment by outsiders must not account for more than 49 per cent of the equity in any industry of the region. Or, as a final illustration, a balance of payments constraint may be set, especially in a planned economy, in terms of a minimum level of foreign exports to be attained by the system in order to insure the wherewithal to purchase a predetermined set of imports deemed essential. [This is in essence setting a minimum level for the Foreign Trade (export) final demand sector.][241]

Whatever the form of the balance of payments constraint, when regions are nations this constraint can clearly add significance to Channel IV without detracting from any operational potential this channel may attain in time. The imposition of this type of constraint does achieve an effective fusion of certain basic aspects of the interregional money flow system with the industrial location system, the interregional interindustry system, and the interregional system of social accounts. It does permit to an important extent the effective fusion on an operational level of corresponding techniques of analysis, as previously developed in the discussion of Channel I.

The construction of other specific financial constraints is not easily

[240] The price of foreign exchange as established on the market may be relied on to determine the quantities of each unrestricted item imported. Or the constraint may state that imports from a *group* of regions—say the sterling bloc—must not exceed exports by more than a certain per cent.

[241] Balance of payments restrictions tend to be operational on an international level. Requisite data have been and currently are accumulated in order to construct necessary statements. Such data are much more abundant than comparable data for the regions of a nation. This situation obviously reflects the fact that regions which are nations have a greater need for balance of payments statements.

On the other hand, other types of money flow data tend to be more copious for the regions of a nation. These regions tend to have greater cultural homogeneity and greater similarity of political goals and monetary institutions. Hence, internally generated data tend to be more comparable and thereby permit closer examination of more facets of a money flow system.

Obvious, too, is the fact that the quality of data for a system of regions in an advanced industrialized nation is generally superior to that for regions (nations) in an international system. For an international system is likely to contain some underdeveloped regions whose data are sparse and very questionable.

As a corollary, it is to be noted that money flow data become less abundant, and hence money flow analyses becomes less relevant, as smaller and smaller regions are considered.

performed.   Not only are relevant data unavailable, but also these constraints frequently have effect through influence on behavior of the
financial or other community of society.   For example, rediscount rate
setting, open-market operations, moral suasion, and other activities of
the Federal Reserve System all impinge upon the behavior of the financial
and business communities.   But we do not really know precisely how they
impinge.   Hence the investigator cannot quantify the implications of such
policy, and hence he cannot set meaningful limiting parameters.   Or the
financial constraint presumably embodied in a severe and regressive government tax program designed to curtail consumption expenditures impinges
directly upon consumer behavior.   But again we know not how and to
what extent consumer purchases are affected in different circumstances of
time and space, and how and to what extent consumers may respond with
counteracting changes in behavior.   Hence, the investigator cannot construct a corresponding constraint in quantitative form.   And hence for
the most part financial constraints of Channel IV (with the exception of
balance of payments restrictions) must remain conceptual at this stage of
development of the social sciences.

   f. Mass behavior—attitude constraints. No more operational are another
set of constraints subtly embedded in social structure.   These may be
conveniently listed in Figure 9 as *mass behavior, attitudes* constraints.
Even though they may be less identifiable, they are as critical as any others
to the values–social goals framework of Channel IV.

   One type of mass behavior constraint which some investigators may be
inclined to impose at this point is conformity of metropolitan regions to the
rank-size rule.   (See footnote 53, Chapter 2, for a discussion of how this
rule applies to urban and metropolitan populations.)   The tantalizing
stability of this rule over United States census history (extending back to
1790) may lead the investigator to the position that metropolitan population
projections for a key year in the future which are in accord with this simple
rule have more validity than projections stemming alone from regional
demographic analysis and other regional methods.   Although the rank-
size rule establishes a rather precise relationship among the populations of
ranked cities and metropolitan regions, it leaves undetermined the actual
rank of a given city or metropolitan region which presumably is to be
established by other analytical techniques.[242]

   [242] However, there are problems in the sophisticated use of this rule. An investigator
recognizes that in a dynamic industrial society shifting among cities in their rank order
must occur. Therefore, a certain amount of deviation from the rule must be permissible
for at least some years for at least some cities. For example, at some point in the past
Chicago's population was equal to Philadelphia's, a situation contradictory to the rule.
The investigator may nonetheless place greater stock on projection in accord with this

Another constraint, in general more acceptable, may be based on the application of both a probability-type gravity model and scaling analysis to interregional migration. As already implied by earlier constraints limiting regional decline, there are in practice basic geographical immobilities in a system's population. Various techniques such as scaling may be employed to uncover the extent and intensity of such immobility.[243] With these results a constraint upon total out-migration from any given region may be established. Once this *total* constraint is established, additional constraints may be imposed to set both minimum and maximum limits on the proportion of a region's out-migration terminating in any other region.[244] These limits may be determined via a probability-type gravity model. It is recognized, of course, that the probability-type gravity model requires considerable development before a firm application should be attempted.[245]

Still other attitudinal constraints may be introduced. Community resistance to industrial development—for example, the resistance of the residents of Jamestown Island, Rhode Island to an oil refinery, the hostility of a high-class suburb to a meat-packing plant, zoning restrictions on size of lot to control population densities, or formal and informal discriminatory practices to control racial composition, income level, and other characteristics of local communities, which in turn affect the spatial spread of a metropolitan population, may all be represented conceptually. Moreover, workers' desire to commute by automobile, society's regard for a high level of community participation potential which implies that at least a certain magnitude of local debate and discussion will be guaranteed, a community's assumed obligation to provide at least a minimum amount of certain

rule than on other analyses alone. He, therefore, may impose it, perhaps with some modification, as a constraint, especially in the first run of Channel IV.

[243] Such techniques would hopefully illuminate the changing significance of climate, educational level, communications channels, and other factors as well as occupational immobility. Occupational immobility enters in as a factor since industrial mixes of some regions are quite different, and migration between them must often entail occupational shift. For example, in the analysis of out-migration from New England, where potential migrants are heavily weighted with textile workers, substantial occupational shift must be presumed which in turn may significantly reduce any projection of out-migration.

[244] See Chapter 11. Also in this connection compare with P. Nelson [29], whose supporting materials appeared after Chapter 11 was written.

[245] One of the major problems, it is to be recalled, is the determination of an appropriate measure of distance. In the case of migration, distance is to be conceived not only as economic distance (as measured by transportation cost) but also as social distance which influences and in turn is influenced by the flow of ideas and information via relatives, friends, institutional and similar channels, and in addition by the similarity of occupational structure between originating and terminal regions.

health and cultural facilities—all these and many others lead to constraints which may interfere with the attainment of a maximum of economic efficiency per se. They lead to spatial juxtaposition diseconomies, diseconomies which, however, are more than matched by subjective gains in social and political welfare.

Additional attitudinal constraints appear on the system level as well. The extent of a nation's military program, its participation in foreign aid, its support of an urban redevelopment and renewal effort and of internal resource development are goals that reflect voting behavior of a citizenry and become explicit as constraints through the political process. Even the structural interindustry coefficient matrix is sensitive to attitudes. The set of interareal input-output coefficients for any given process reflects the degree to which firms are willing to abandon old practices and accept new technology. It also reflects firms' attitudes toward shifting allegiance among suppliers of inputs from the several regions as cost conditions change.

Briefly put, attitudes and goals of various sorts—many only nebulous and many already incorporated in part—may be injected at this point. In one sense, these attitudes and goals, together with those already explicitly treated, centrally govern the values–social goals framework of Channel IV. To reiterate, they are extremely difficult to state in quantitative form and await further development in the social sciences for clearer identification.[246]

---

[246] It is tempting to view social and political values and attitudes as the central force contributing regularity to society's spatial configuration, much as transport optimization contributes regularity to the industrial location structure of modern Weberian theory. See *Location and Space-Economy*, p. 138. In the latter case, cheap-labor points, excellent hydropower sites, scale economies, and low tax rates are among the several forces which may, and in reality do to a major extent, deviate production from that spatial pattern which is optimal from a transportation standpoint. In the former case locations which allow major scale, localization, urbanization (spatial juxtaposition), and other economies deviate a system's population from a spatial pattern which is optimal from the standpoint of social and political values alone. To be specific, it may be claimed that despite the cosmopolitan attraction of world metropolitan centers such as New York and Chicago, a pattern of small towns, each with a goodly, if not complete, diversity of cultural functions, will tend to optimize a "social and political values" function. But in reality the forces of economic efficiency (both beneficent and ugly) creep in. An integrated steel works operates best, say, when six to seven million tons of capacity concentrate at a single site (scale economies), and when a diversity of market-oriented and service activities locate within commuting distance (urbanization and transport cost economies); and a host of steel-fabricating operations works best when it crowds in around an integrated works and its ancillaries (localization and spatial juxtaposition economies). As a consequence, a city of major size must emerge, deviating population from the optimum social and political value pattern.

g. Locational efficiency constraints. A final set of constraints relating to the interregional linear program of Channel IV must now be introduced. In one sense these constraints represent a basic addition to Channel IV. These constraints bear upon *locational efficiency.* They tend to capture for Channel IV a good part of, if not all, the firm results which can be yielded by COMPARATIVE COST, INDUSTRIAL COMPLEX, URBAN COMPLEX techniques. Their addition, which is indicated in the lower right and central part of Figure 9, upgrades the efficiency character of Channel IV. More comprehensively than interregional linear programming, these techniques can consider existing and anticipated cost differentials among alternative locations. On the other hand, their use must be restricted since they treat individual industries or complexes and, as already noted, cannot capture interdependence relations as comprehensively as can an interregional interindustry (activity) matrix, whether it be associated with input-output or linear programming.

An effective synthesis into Channel IV of comparative cost and industrial complex (and when operational urban complex) may repeat a number of steps already covered in Channel I. Specifically, the first seven steps of this channel, as succinctly summarized in section B.2.c of this chapter, may be pursued. However, in pursuing these steps the investigator must make certain adjustments in the light of values and goals and minimum social and other accounts already established in Channel IV. For example, if he has set as a basic goal a major expansion and upgrading of educational services, he must accordingly alter the estimated government expenditure account for the system (covered in the third of the seven steps of Channel I). Or if he has already incorporated in Channel IV goals which bear on consumer expenditure patterns, he may need to make certain adjustments in the magnitudes of several of the seven steps.

Because Channel IV is primarily conceptual and because its development is already lengthy we shall not enter into a discussion of the diverse adjustments that would be required. Suffice it to state that these steps would yield outputs by regions for those sectors and industries subject to comparative cost and industrial complex analyses. (Recall that these sectors were designated exogenous producing sectors.) Such analysis would fully consider labor, power, tax, and other cost differentials, and scale and other economies—which differentials and economies are critical but not easily embodied, if at all, in a linear programming formulation. The investigator may then proceed to detail the set of inputs required by each of these exogenous producing sectors in each region. He may establish these inputs as deliveries to be met in the very same sense in which consumer expenditures and government expenditures in each region are set as deliveries to be met.   (See the previous discussion of minimum standards constraints.)[247]

For example, comparative cost analysis may establish that 40 per cent of the system's aluminum output in year 1965 should be located in the West.   Multiplying down the Aluminum in the West column of an inter-regional input-output coefficient table by the dollar value of the estimated aluminum output in the West will yield a set of deliveries to the aluminum industry in the West which the system must meet.[248]   But the investigator recognizes that inconsistencies are embedded in the seven steps of the first run of Channel I.[249]   He also recognizes that it is inappropriate to allocate among regions 100 per cent of the system output of each exogenous producing sector.   Such a complete allocation contradicts the validity of that general over-all system efficiency which in essence is being sought by the central framework of Channel IV.   Accordingly, the investigator may choose to apportion among regions, say only 90 per cent of the system's projected output of exogenous producing sector Z, 85 per cent of sector Y, etc.   For each sector the exact amount to be apportioned may vary according to the investigator's judgement.   The inputs required by the output of each sector assigned to any given region are to be treated as minimum deliveries to be met (another set of minimum standards con-straints).   For each exogenous producing sector, the inputs required by unassigned system output also constitute deliveries to be met by the system, but deliveries unrestricted in terms of region of destination.   The alloca-tion by region of this unassigned output and its set of required inputs is the task of the interregional linear program itself.

By this procedure, which because of space limitations can only be very crudely sketched here, the analyst is able to fuse on the conceptual level comparative cost, industrial complex, and urban complex techniques with interregional linear programming, the central technique of Channel IV. Thereby he achieves a framework incorporating more of the efficiency motives and behavior of reality.   The reader may note at this point that this fusion can be approached in an alternative manner.   We can begin with the first seven steps of Channel I and then add an interregional linear programming framework (inclusive of basic goals) as a substitute

[247] Note that output of such exogenous producing sectors breaks down into deliveries to either producing sectors (in which case such output represent "intermediates" and is not counted in GSP) or the final demand sectors already described above (in which case such output has already been counted in GSP).   Also, all input deliveries to such exogenous producing sectors do not enter into GSP (here viewed as final product deliveries to the final demand sectors described above).

[248] Once again, bear in mind that this is a crude oversimplification of appropriate procedure.

[249] For full discussion of some of these inconsistencies, see section B.2.c.

for the interregional input-output framework of Channel I. This operational alternative will be discussed later in connection with Channel V.

The reader may also note that at least conceptually a relative income potential model may be added and fused into the framework at this point. This step is indicated at the lower center of Figure 9 by the arrow leading from the box POTENTIAL MODEL to the interregional linear program matrix. Such a step may be well justified, especially if regions are metropolitan regions. For it may be claimed that a relative income potential model more than any other analytical technique captures the net interaction of agglomeration and deglomeration forces, particularly as they influence the locational patterns of *non-cost-sensitive* industries. (See section D of this chapter.) Such a model will yield outputs by region for a number of these industries.[250] As before, the set of inputs required for the production of each of these outputs would then be listed as deliveries to be met by the interregional linear program.

5. PROGRAM FEASIBILITY AND REFORMULATION

We have now covered the basic framework of the values–social goals Channel IV. Conceptually, the highly constrained interregional linear program is run to maximize the objective function, which in our illustration is GSP. One possible outcome is that a solution cannot be reached. The basic set of goals as reflected in the minimum social accounts and diverse constraints may not be achievable. (For example, agricultural output may fall short of the appropriate minimum standards constraint.) The program is thus infeasible. It is then necessary to reformulate goals— in essence to lower sights. Eventually a feasible program, one that can realize the specified goals, is attained.

The identification of a feasible program, however, does not terminate the analysis for Channel IV. The achievement of a feasible program is, after all, much like a first run of Channels I or II. In many ways it may yield results that are inconsistent with and contradictory to certain underlying values and goals. This is clearly seen when the program itself furnishes more than the constraints require, that is, provides a "surplus" viewed from the standpoint of the constraints alone. For example, all the "surplus" may be embodied in a single final product, that is, all final product deliveries and other constraints may be fully met, but only met,

---

[250] Refer to section G of Chapter 11 and section D of this chapter for procedures in determining regional outputs of these industries by means of the potential model. Also, as with industries subject to comparative cost analysis, it is not necessary to assign 100 per cent of system output of these industries to regions. A smaller per cent can be assigned, the remaining to be allocated through the efficiency drive of the interregional linear program.

except for the single final product whose output exceeds required deliveries. Or, all the "surplus" may be concentrated in shipments to a single region, deliveries to all other regions just meeting the levels required by the constraints. Or some combination of these and other unrealistic as well as undesirable outcomes may develop.

In examples given, it clearly becomes necessary to refine goals and the constraints and objective function reflecting them. The binding constants of the constraints may be simply increased (or lowered) proportionately or selectively—that is, sights may be raised. Or the weights of the objective function may be changed to effect a more desirable distribution of "surplus" both among final products and regions. Or new constraints reflecting additional values and goals may be introduced. A discussion of appropriate procedures at this point is beyond the scope of the chapter. However, such procedures have much in common with the problem of the choice of finished product prices and the setting of *availability* constraints examined in section I of Chapter 10, to which the reader is referred.

Additionally, there are many other places at which the investigator needs to adjust the basic framework of Channel IV after a first set of results is obtained, or to re-examine his assumptions, or to iron out discrepancies and logical inconsistencies. Identification of these places cannot be undertaken in this chapter and must be left to future work.

After Channel IV is refined, refashioned, and rerun so that its results are of sufficiently high quality, or are not subject to much improvement, the investigator may then establish the traditional basic social accounts. (He follows the procedures of Channel I.) Examples of such accounts are presented in Table 2 of this chapter. It is to be noted that these accounts will typically exceed the minimum social accounts which enter into the minimum standards constraints. For example, in the GSP problem given, consumption expenditures in a given region will usually exceed the set of minimum final product deliveries to the household sector in the same region.

In addition to estimates of Consumption, Investment, Government Outlays, Income and Output, all by region, the framework of Channel IV yields projections of Employment, Population, Migration, Exports, Imports, Commodity Flows, all again by regions. These results correspond to RESULTS of Channel I listed in Figure 1. Moreover, the framework of Channel IV casts light upon the Economic Base of each region, regional and interregional Multipliers, regional Balance of Payments statements, regional Money Flows, and perhaps regional Cycles as will be indicated later. Moreover, when regions are metropolitan regions and parts of metropolitan regions, the framework of Channel IV helps to estimate

Tax Base, Land Use, and Transportation structure, results also stemming from Channels II and III (see Figure 8).

6. TWO CONCEPTUAL EXTENSIONS AND CONCLUDING NOTES

Before concluding this channel, two further extensions may be conceived. One extension concerns the problem of how a system and its regions proceed (noncyclically) from a base year structure to the structure projected for a key year in the future. This problem of dynamics is clearly beyond the ken of social scientists, except when grossly oversimplified. This problem incorporates basic capital budgeting in the planning sense (public and private). It also incorporates the growth process in the economic development sense.

One greatly oversimplified version of such an extension is to develop a step-by-step model of the sort discussed in Chapter 11 and in connection with Channel III. However, the specifics of the version to be developed are very different. In this latter version there must be a complete statement of relevant constraints (such as those listed in Figure 9) for not only a key year in the future, say 1965, but also every year from the base year up to that year. Moreover, there must be an explicit and much more careful comparison for each year of (1) capacity (plant and equipment) requirements and (2) capacity in existence. Via a capital budgeting and programming process, the system must have available each year in each of the diverse sectors that plant and equipment needed to produce the total output required of a sector. (This output is required by both producing sectors and the minimum standards and other constraints.) After allowance for imports and depletion of inventory,[251] this condition necessitates the delivery, in a prior year, of diverse inputs to the capital formation sector in order that necessary expansions in plant and equipment be realized.[252]

Of course, if there already exists in the base year the capacity required to produce a 1965 level of a commodity output, there is usually no need to program capacity expansion in the sector producing that output. (Failure to replace used-up capacity may even be tolerated for some time.)

Of relevance in this connection is a partial model developed by Moore.[253] The model deals with a single region only, namely California, for the period 1954–1960. The problem is not to optimize Gross Regional

---

[251] Recall that imports necessitate in turn a program of exports, and depletion of inventory implies an inventory management program which provided for prior stockpiling.

[252] In this connection see the discussion of the capital flow table and capital coefficients in section B.2 of Chapter 8.

[253] F. T. Moore [22].

Product or some variant of this magnitude. Rather it is to test the feasibility of different annual growth rates in final demand (in California) over a period of years and to approximate an "optimal" pattern of growth rates by sectors. The model is based on certain assumptions regarding permissible imports and the amount of autonomous investment and exports expected (based on factors external to the model). Involved are a set of constant production coefficients (à la input-output) which are taken to characterize production for current account, although these coefficients may differ from year to year. Involved also are a set of capital coefficients (à la input-output) which are taken as the basis for calculating necessary inputs for building during the intervening years the new capacity to produce that the system requires; these coefficients, too, may differ from year to year.

On the assumptions of unchanging population and import-export pattern, zero autonomous investment, zero lead times, a one-year lag in the availability of new capacity and other simplified relations, the model (designed in the block triangular form of Table 9) indicates a feasible over-all annual growth rate of almost 5 per cent for the final demand sector of the California economy, 1954–1960.[254]   But, as the author fully

[254] From communication with the author.   In formal terms Moore's model is:

(1) $$Y_\tau = X_\tau - aX_\tau - bM_\tau - S_\tau$$

(2) $$C_t = X_\tau + U_\tau - \sum_{g=t}^{\tau-1} M_g \qquad \tau = t, \ldots, t + \theta$$

where t represents initial year of projection period;
   $t + \theta$ represents terminal year of projection period;
      τ is a subscript referring to any year of the projection period, t to $t + \theta$;
      Y_τ represents for year τ a column vector of final demands, exclusive of capital formation and inventory change (see Appendix to chapter 8);
      X_τ represents a column vector of industry (sector) outputs in year τ (see Appendix to Chapter 8);
      a represents the input-output matrix of production coefficients (see Appendix to Chapter 8);
      b represents the input-output matrix of capital coefficients (see section B.2 of Chapter 8);
      M_τ represents a column vector listing in order for year τ the *induced* expansions in capacities by industry (sector);
      S_τ represents a column vector listing in order for year τ the additions to (depletions of) inventory stocks by commodity (each commodity corresponding to an industry output);
      C_t represents a column vector listing in order for year t capacities by industry;
      U_τ represents a column vector listing in order for year τ *unused* capacities by industry;

TABLE 9. ACTIVITIES OVER TIME[a]

	X_t	M_t	S_t	U_t	X_{t+1}	M_{t+1}	S_{t+1}	U_{t+1}	$\cdots$	$X_{t+\theta}$	$M_{t+\theta}$	$S_{t+\theta}$	$U_{t+\theta}$
Y_t	$(I-a)$	$-b$	$-I$										
C_t	I			I									
Y_{t+1}					$(I-a)$	$-b$	$-I$						
C_t		$-I$			I			I					
$\cdot$	$\cdot$	$\cdot$			$\cdot$			$\cdot$					
$\cdot$	$\cdot$	$\cdot$			$\cdot$			$\cdot$					
$\cdot$	$\cdot$	$\cdot$			$\cdot$			$\cdot$					
$Y_{t+\theta}$										$(I-a)$	$-b$	$-I$	
C_t		$-I$				$-I$			$\cdot$	I			I

[a] Based upon a single region (California) model by F. T. Moore [22].

and where $\sum_{g=1}^{\tau-1} M_g$ represents a column vector listing in order by industry the total of expansions in capacities, from year t up to but not including year τ.

Equations 1 of the model state that for year τ (where τ may be any year of the projection period, $t, \ldots, t + \theta$) deliveries to final demand sectors by any given industry i ($Y_{i\tau}$) equal its total output ($X_{i\tau}$) *less* its deliveries to all producing sectors on current account $\left(\sum_{j=1}^{n} a_{ij} X_{j\tau} \right)$ *less* its deliveries to all producing sectors for capacity expansion $\left(\sum_{j=1}^{n} b_{ij} M_{j\tau} \right)$ *less* its deliveries to (or *plus* withdrawals from) the inventory stock of the commodity which it produces ($S_{i\tau}$). Equations 2 of the model state that for the initial year t capacity of industry i (C_{it}) equals output of i in any year τ ($X_{i\tau}$) *plus* unused capacity of industry i in year τ ($U_{i\tau}$) *less* the total of capacity expansions of industry i from year t up to but not including year τ $\left(\sum_{g=t}^{\tau-1} M_{ig} \right)$.

For computational purposes, the above input-output type equations may be conveniently cast into the linear programming form of Table 9. In Table 9, I represents the identity matrix. For any given year equations 1 and 2 are obtained by identifying the two corresponding (major) rows at the extreme left of the table, and by setting each of the magnitudes at the extreme left in these two (major) rows equal to the sum of the products obtained by multiplying every element along its row by the magnitude at the top of the element's column.

recognizes, there are many problems in the use of this model—such as those relating to production lag times,[255] lead and lag times on capital and the availability of new capacity,[256] reasonable or likely levels of imports[257] and exports,[258] of autonomous investment,[259] and of relevant mixes of growth rates for the several final demand items, which items obviously cannot be expected to increase by the same rates.[260]   Nonetheless, this model does forcefully illustrate an important aspect of realistic programming[261] and is suggestive of how this extension to the conceptual framework of Channel IV may be undertaken.

The investigator may desire to conceive still another extension, one which goes even beyond the one just given.   He may be impelled to attempt to add on a feature to recognize the reality of cyclical experience.

Already we have noted how the investigator may set constraints to temper cyclical effects, constraints which control industrial composition, regional growth rates, levels of total public and private investment, etc.[262] If such constraints do not completely eliminate the cycle for the system—

[255] Such lag times would allow the investigator to specify explicitly that the realization of an output from the use of an input is not instantaneous.   Where the unit period of time employed in a model is considerably shorter than a year, it might be especially desirable in a number of processes to schedule the use of several inputs at one or several different periods of time to yield outputs at one or more later periods.

[256] As with outputs, new capacity becomes available at times different from those at which inputs are required.   Thus, where possible, it is desirable to introduce a timing pattern into the model and in addition to adjust the timing pattern to allow for depreciation of existing capacity.

[257] A reasonable projection relative to imports is essential since an increase of imports can substitute for locally produced output from new capacity.

[258] A reasonable projection relative to exports is essential since the amount of new capacity to be programmed depends on level of exports as well as the magnitude of local consumption of output.

[259] As with exports, autonomous investment affects the amount of various outputs from current production which must be scheduled for capital formation.

[260] Clearly, in the California economy, final demand for output of services can be expected to increase by more than for agricultural output.   The problem is to select a most appropriate set of rates, with the use of consumption functions and other theoretical and empirical materials.

[261] In addition to identifying an "optimal" pattern of growth rates, Moore's model can be designed to answer other questions such as what are achievable investment levels or gross regional outputs, or how is it possible to economize on the use of a particular commodity or resource subject to the achievement of certain levels of consumption, exports, and Gross Regional Product.

In closing his study, Moore emphasizes that his noninterregional model holds greater promise for closed regional economies (such as nations) than for open regional economies.   In dealing with closed regions it is less difficult to select reasonable levels of exports and imports, of autonomous investment, of population, etc.

[262] See section E.4.d.

as is likely when the system is both dynamic and capitalistic—the investigator may build qualified cyclical experience into his framework. He may conceive for the system a standard reference cycle—in many respects similar to a National Bureau reference cycle, but one which is modified by the stability constraints which he has already introduced. Also, for each region he may conceive a particular cycle. This latter cycle might reflect to a major degree the system cycle. It might also reflect the region's particular industrial composition, secular rate of growth, or social-political-cultural institutions, according to the relevance which the investigator attaches to these factors. Or it might reflect the region's particular structure of basic social accounts, thus attributing significance to the short-run Keynesian-type of interregional trade multiplier. (Recall that in this multiplier framework, social accounts have explanatory value.) In fact, the characteristics of each region's particular cycle may be approximated and roughly sketched, desirably in more precise terms than those of Table 8 and Figure 7.

However, it is clear that any attempt at such an extension encounters both thereotical and empirical obstacles of major magnitude, and like Channel IV as a whole must dwell primarily in the conceptual realm.[263]

[263] Still a third extension might involve the use on a partial basis of a simultaneous equations approach to estimate by region relevant price and quantity variables for one or two sectors at a time. For example, Fox and Taeuber have used such an approach in their spatial equilibrium models of the livestock-feed economy (K. A. Fox [8] and K. A. Fox and R. C. Taeuber [9]). In this particular study, for each region there is predetermined:

1. A demand function for feed (which relates the variable, price of feed, to the three variables : consumption of feed, production of livestock, and price of livestock).

2. The supply of feed (given as a constant).

3. A demand function for livestock (which relates the variable, price of livestock, to the variable, consumption of livestock, and to the two exogenously determined magnitudes, human population and disposable personal income per capita).

4. A supply function of livestock (which relates the variable, production of livestock, to the variables, the price of livestock and the price of feed).

Subject to the gross equilibrium conditions that system consumption of feed equal system production of feed, and that system consumption of livestock equal system production of livestock, the model is operated under usual spatial equilibrium conditions : (1) price of a commodity in any region must not exceed the price of that commodity in a second region by more than the transport cost ; and (2) demand and supply must be equated on each regional market. In their study Fox and Taeuber use a ten-region model of the United States and determine regional prices, consumption, and trading patterns for feed and livestock under approximate 1949–1950 conditions.

It is clear that a partial approach such as the above can be useful, especially when comparative cost and industrial complex techniques are difficult to apply to a given sector (perhaps because of limited data), and when variation in market and production conditions significantly influence supply channels for this sector. It can furnish more

In bringing the discussion of Channel IV to a close, it is appropriate to reiterate the purpose of Channel IV. As already noted, Channels I–III develop fused frameworks which place emphasis upon economics—upon the attainment of efficiency and profit maximization. Although these frameworks have implicit within themselves a set of values and goals characteristic of a system and its regions, they obscure the fundamental role of values and goals. Channel IV is designed to correct this imbalance. Its central emphasis is on values and goals. But by insisting on this emphasis, the fused framework of Channel IV loses the operationality which Channels I–III can claim.

Channel IV is primarily conceptual, and no hope is proferred that it will ever evolve beyond this realm. The process whereby goals are established in a cultural system is little understood. Tremendous advances in social science theory and techniques are necessary before we can objectively translate values into specific system and subsystem goals, and in turn identify social goals with specific sets of social accounts. Closely allied to this need are required procedures for equating at the margin the diverse gains and losses associated with alternative programs, policies, and actions when some of these gains and losses in values can be couched in subjective terms only. More specifically, useful implementation of Channel IV calls for a deeper understanding of decision-making processes, of the role and behavior of the individual and group in a constantly changing social structure, of the nature and operation of political organizations and administrative networks, of communication channels through which ideas flow and power is exercised, etc. The conceptual nature of Channel IV is most evident when attempts are made to set limiting constants for attitude constraints, and for a number of financial, stability, and minimum standards constraints which are primarily oriented to attitudes and behavior. Limiting constants for economic-type constraints—such as locational efficiency, resource, and certain stability and minimum standards constraints—are more easily established.

Because of the conceptual character of Channel IV, no attempt is made to tabulate it and spell out in rigorous logical terms a detailed structure. For the same reason it is not profitable at this point to enumerate the various specific and technical limitations of this channel. To repeat, its prime value is to develop a proper perspective on the role of values and goals in an interregional system and thereby to provoke appropriate extensions of Channels I–III.

meaningful estimates of prices and consumption levels than can be obtained by other methods. On the other hand, this approach involves estimation of diverse functions and is subject to a number of shortcomings. Moreover, in order to be operational, this approach like comparative cost encompasses little of the interdependence of reality.

However, it is noteworthy that Channel IV achieves on the conceptual level a fused framework which is still more general than those of Channels I–III and which contains these frameworks as special cases. All the techniques and methods of Channels I–III contribute to the fused framework of Channel IV at one place or another. Put otherwise, when certain features of Channel IV are suppressed, each of the other three channels emerge. That is, if we suppress values and goals as a variable and prescribe the cultural system of the United States and its regions with goals fully identified in terms of traditional GNP accounts, the entire left part of Figure 9 disappears. Also, the objective function of the interregional linear program becomes trivial, the WEIGHTS box disappears, BASIC SOCIAL ACCOUNTS essentially reduce to Bill of Goods sectors, and the various constraints of the interregional linear programs are either set aside as too subjective or else are incorporated in the bill of goods via the setting of reasonable levels for national and regional final demand sectors. All that remains, then, is an emaciated interregional linear program format which is in essence an interregional input-output matrix. Into this matrix are fed materials from comparative cost, industrial complex, and urban complex analyses (supplemented by scaling and factor analyses, and linear programming on a single-industry or industrial complex basis); and the matrix yields results which may be modified by the operation of a relative income potential model or by subsequent reruns, etc.

Thus, the investigator may conclude that on a conceptual basis Channel IV is more comprehensive than Channels I–III and includes these channels as special cases. From such a conclusion he is logically led to a basic research question. If Channel IV is conceptually more comprehensive than Channels I–III, and if Channels I–III are operational and Channel IV is not, is it possible to broaden the frameworks of Channels I–III via fruitful synthesis with elements of Channel IV without losing operationality? To this question we turn briefly.

F. CHANNEL V: OPERATIONAL FUSED FRAMEWORKS INCORPORATING VALUES AND GOALS

Channel V is presented as an operational channel. Its framework is designed to extend beyond those of Channels I–III. It views values and goals as significant variables and attempts to incorporate into a fused framework the values and goals that are subject to approximate quantitative representation. In this manner it aims to correct some of the imbalance of Channels I–III.

Already the structure and operation of the fused framework of Channel V have been anticipated. The discussion in section E.4 of this chapter comments on how the set of techniques to be employed in Channel IV conditions the detailing of specific social accounts.   It was indicated that the set of techniques constituting the framework of Channel I could be employed at the start.   Then several illustrations were presented to show how goals translated into detailed social accounts could be introduced into the framework of Channel I as new final demand sectors, etc.   In essence, Channel V follows this line, but in a more systematic fashion.

Channel V may be diagrammatically represented by a figure very similar to Figure 1 (or Figure 8).   However, there would be one major difference. Instead of two large circles (designated COMPARATIVE COST and INDUSTRIAL COMPLEX) feeding into the Bill of Goods of the interregional input-output matrix, there would be three.   The new circle would be designated GOALS: SYSTEM AND SUBSYSTEM and would in essence be a condensation of the rounded major box to the left of Figure 9.   It would, at least theoretically, carry the same weight as the other two and would contribute basic social accounts (as translated from goals) to the Bill of Goods.

In fact, in Figure 10 such a representation is made.   If for the moment the matrix headed INTERREGIONAL LINEAR PROGRAM is suppressed, if the rounded major box PROBABILITY, GRAVITY, POTENTIAL MODELS is set aside, and if the lower column of RESULTS is dropped, there remains that extension of Channel I outlined in the previous paragraph.   Such an extension is viewed as the first variant of Channel V.[264]

As is to be expected, Channel V begins with the initial steps of Channels I–III.   Basic Assumptions for the system are made on birth rates, death rates, net immigration, technology, tastes and values—the first five items at the extreme left of Figure 10.   However, the goals and values of a channel such as Channel IV may have explicit bearing on these assumptions.   For example, a goal that aims at the attainment for each individual of a high educational level—to be explicitly introduced later as a social account—may condition postulates on birth rates, tastes, and later postulates on work week, average productivity, etc.   This influence is depicted by the arrow connecting the circle designated GOALS: SYSTEM AND SUBSYSTEM with Basic Assumptions for the system.

Once the investigator sets the first five items at the extreme left of Figure 10, he proceeds to a national population projection.[265]   The traditional

---

[264] As with Figures 1, 8, and 9, light arrows stemming from a box indicate contributions which for the most part are not realizable at this time.   This statement holds particularly for contributions from Urban Complex analysis, Financial Elements (Money Flow) studies, and Historical Study and Sociological and Political Theory.

[265] Since we wish Channel V to be operational, we forgo the procedures which would estimate system population and other system magnitudes as sums of (or simultaneously with) corresponding subsystem magnitudes.

way in which this step is taken is fully described in the discussion of Channel I. So also are ways in which the investigator moves on to estimates of labor force, average productivity and in turn to Gross System Product and income and to system output by industry.

With judicious application of Coefficients, Curves, Relative Growth Charts and the like to current and past data, and with whatever use of SCALING and FACTOR ANALYSIS that is appropriate, the investigator determines Initial Regional Market assumptions (see Figure 10), tempered perhaps by certain predetermined goals. He then follows the Weberian approach and conducts COMPARATIVE COST and INDUSTRIAL COMPLEX investigations (with refinements from SCALING, FACTOR ANALYSIS, and INTERREGIONAL LINEAR PROGRAMMING on an industry or an industrial complex basis). The outcome of these investigations establishes the levels by region of the exogenous producing sectors which become new Bill of Goods (final demand) sectors.[266]

But at this point too in Channel V the major contributions of GOALS: SYSTEM AND SUBSYSTEM in the form of social accounts must be put in place in the Bill of Goods sectors. This is indicated in Figure 10 by the arrow leading from the circle GOALS: SYSTEM AND SUBSYSTEM which joins arrows leading from the circles COMPARATIVE COST and INDUSTRIAL COMPLEX, all coursing to the Bill of Goods of the INTERREGIONAL I–O MATRIX.[267]

To illustrate concretely, suppose that, as in section E.4 of this chapter, one goal for the year of projection is $1 billion of private college support by business. In the final demand sectors of each region (see Table 1) there would be introduced a column Private College (Business Supported). The cells of these columns would list projected expenditures which over all regions would sum to $1 billion.[268] Or if the goal of $3 billion support of nongovernment community welfare activities is established, a corresponding column would be introduced into the final demand sectors of each region.[269]

System and subsystem goals typically have a deeper involvement in social and system planning and policy and are associated with a much wider range of effects. For example, suppose that coupled with the aim

[266] See Table 1 and its discussion.

[267] At this point we could even determine for one or two sectors relevant delivery levels (and corresponding prices) with the use of the simultaneous equations, spatial equilibrium model of Fox and Taeuber. (See footnote 263.)

[268] Corresponding rows would also be added to the lower half of a flow (transactions) table.

[269] Again, corresponding rows would be introduced.

In like manner the goal pertaining to the establishment of a nongovernmental central authority to pursue long-run basic research may be translated into regional social accounts and put in place as regional bill of goods sectors.

of armaments reduction is a goal to increase by the same dollar amount the extent of nonmilitary foreign aid. An armaments reduction program implies that in each region government expenditures (that is, deliveries to the government sector) are curtailed. The extent of curtailment varies by item of expenditure in each region, as well as by region. At the same time an increase in foreign aid implies increases in foreign trade (exports) sectors of the several regions—directly to the country receiving aid or indirectly to other countries engaged in multilateral world trade. Again regions and items of export are differentially affected. Also, it is clear that the differential effects associated with armaments reduction are not the same and may sharply contrast with the differential effects of increased foreign aid. That is, contractions and expansions by item in the final demand sectors of a given region will not be exactly offsetting and may show great differences. And viewing any given region as a whole, there may be a wide gap between total dollar contractions and total dollar expansions. Further, via the interregional input-output matrix and subsequent reruns, these differences and gaps lead to differential impacts on sector outputs of a given region and among regions on total income, employment, population, etc.

Or instead of an increase in foreign aid which for the system matches (dollarwise) armaments reduction, a less ambitious increase in foreign aid may be combined with a tax reduction program. This combination will imply increases in the foreign trade (export) sectors of the several regions, but not as large as in the previous paragraph. It will also imply for each region both increases in the level of expenditures of its households sector (since a curtailed tax program would in all likelihood leave households with more disposable income), and increases in the level of its capital formation sector (since in a full-employment economy business may be presumed to increase its investment expenditures when its tax burden is reduced).

Or the reduction in expenditures on armaments program may be matched instead by an increase in capital expenditures by government in order to achieve a high rate of increase in productive potential. (Such might characterize an aim of a totalitarian society or an underdeveloped region seeking rapid industrialization.) This goal might be translated into a set of social accounts which explicitly treats the government capital formation sector in each region, and which requires the system to deliver to this sector major quantities of commodities, while at the same time significantly curtailing deliveries to the government military sector of each region. This goal may even infer adjustments in still other social accounts. For example, deliveries to the households of luxury items—say yachts, motel services, swimming pools, Cadillacs—may be set at zero, reflecting prohibitive legislation. Even household income and savings may be forced to higher levels through the legal imposition of a longer work-week, thus leading to increased outputs of the diverse sectors of the several regions for purposes of capital formation.

Or stemming from the circle designated GOALS: SYSTEM AND SUBSYSTEM in Figure 10 may be a still more complex set of programs for the year of projection. Such a situation will reflect the fact that in reality an intricate pattern of goals typifies a modern, industrialized society. Not only may there be programs to uplift the educational status of a citizenry, to foster welfare on a community level, to reduce the threat of war and wasteful expenditures on armaments, to make a positive contribution to world development through foreign aid, to lighten tax burdens on households and business, and to step up the rate of capital formation, but also there may be programs to conserve resources, to rehabilitate urban areas, to combat forces of crime and instability, to aid small business, to afford greater leisure through reduction of the work week, to foster freer trade, etc. In fact, such a complex diversity of programs, often impossible to unravel, may well be said to characterize the platforms put forward by political parties in the United States and other interregional systems. Actual voting by citizens represents one effective channel of communications whereby the values of a culture become crystallized into a set of specific programs.

In this manner, goals translated into social accounts may be put in place in the final demand (Bill of Goods) sectors of the several regions. The interregional input-output computation is then run. The magnitudes of the upper RESULTS column of Figure 10 are obtained, as indicated by the upper hatched arrow. (Again the rounded major box PROBABILITY, GRAVITY, POTENTIAL MODELS and the lower RESULTS column are to be ignored, as well as all arrows leading to and from this box and column.) In line with the procedures of Channel I, the framework is rerun in order to eliminate discrepancies and inconsistencies and to reach significant and noncontradictory results. Constantly, however, values and goals enter in as the framework is rerun. For example, if a set of programs has a greatly differing impact on the several regions, one being forced to contract sharply and another being overstimulated, the investigator may inject into the fused framework restrictions or compensations, or a combination of both. He may do this in recognition of the social goal that no region be unduly harmed by a set of programs.

Thus by a careful classification of industries and sectors, by an adroit manipulation and treatment of final demand accounts, by selective decomposition of endogenous sectors and careful shifting of parts of these sectors from the structural matrix to the bill of goods, and by skillful rerun operations, the investigator can effectively bring to bear upon projected magnitudes values and goals of a system and its regions. In brief, the investigator refashions final demand sectors and matrix structure—often ignoring sectoring which is convenient to use and is in keeping with traditional economic thinking—in order to achieve, subject to data availability, a more sophisticated level of analysis.

The preceding paragraphs sketch the development of the fused framework of Channel V as an extension of Channel I.[270] In like manner, another version of Channel V may be evolved from Channel II. This version substitutes a BALANCED REGIONAL I–O MATRIX for the INTERREGIONAL I–O MATRIX and adds to the framework the lower RESULTS column of Figure 10 and the lower hatched arrow leading to it. Still a third version of Channel V can be constructed around Channel III. This version adds to Figure 8 the circle designated GOALS: SYSTEM AND SUBSYSTEM and is essentially depicted in Figure 10 when the INTERREGIONAL LINEAR PROGRAM matrix and all arrows leading to and from it are suppressed. It is to be recalled that Channel III does not involve rerun procedures but develops a step-by-step, discrete path of growth for the system and its regions. Hence, in this third version of Channel V goals are to be attained, in general, in step-by-step fashion; and procedures must be developed so that the social accounts introduced into the bill of goods in successive periods represent the cumulative attainment of goals.[271] The formulation of such procedures is left to the reader.

Finally, we proceed to what certain investigators may consider a still more efficient, operational Channel V. In this fourth variant the optimizing process of a general interregional linear program is reintroduced into the picture. It is once again recognized that comparative cost and industrial complex techniques treat individual industries or somewhat larger but still relatively small parts of an economy. They therefore fail to capture that general over-all system efficiency which an interregional

[270] To the sketch of this variant of Channel V the investigator may be inclined to add a Moore-type scheme (see section E.6 of this chapter) to insure the availability, at the beginning of the key year of projection, of sufficient capital stock (plant and equipment) for turning out and delivering the projected outputs. Doing so would involve a year-by-year statement of all final demand sectors, including those reflecting social goals. Also, the capital formation sector of each region would tend to be disaggregated so as to permit the programming of the specific types of capital expansions by sectors to be achieved by the key year of projection. Clearly, the addition of such a scheme alters the need for rerun procedures and the types of consistency checks to be applied. These matters require extended discussion which is not possible here.

[271] Of course, certain specific goals can be realized only upon the complete development of a facility, although resources flowing into the construction of such a facility may be programmed over several periods of time.

linear program purports to. Thus, to some extent the role of comparative cost and industrial complex analysis may be justifiably diminished
and interregional linear programming on a systemwide basis may be
brought into the framework and assigned some weight.

Immediately it is appreciated that an extensive computational problem
develops as a result of this step. The channel becomes nonoperational
unless the investigator is willing to posit that it will be possible successfully
to feed such a problem into a high-speed computer of sufficient capacity
and obtain a solution.

On the assumption that the fourth variant of Channel V remains
operational, the simplest way to elucidate the step whereby linear programming is introduced is first to posit that the first variant of Channel V
is developed as previously outlined. Then the investigator reconceives
the items of the final demand sectors *as deliveries to be met*, that is, as a
set of limiting constants. However, he effects certain important adjustments. For example, take in each region the aluminum-producing sector.
This is an exogenous producing sector, for comparative cost analysis can
efficiently allocate to regions the system's level of aluminum production.
But it is to be recognized that some of the market for aluminum cannot be
firmly predetermined and logically must be eked out of a general interdependence scheme. Thus the investigator may judge that say only 90
per cent of the system's level of aluminum production should be distributed among its regions on the basis of comparative cost analysis, and that
the remaining 10 per cent should be allocated via interregional linear
programming. Hence the investigator will reduce deliveries to the
aluminum-producing sectors of the several regions so that they correspond
to only 90 per cent of the system level of aluminum production. Likewise
for other sectors and parts of sectors treated by comparative cost and
industrial complex techniques.[272]

Given adjustments of this sort, an objective function is set up, say to
maximize GSP. Weights and prices are selected from the best available
information and in certain cases reflect values and goals. Other logical
constraints are introduced, such as those relating to labor inputs, use of
capital equipment, and balance of payments. The framework is run.

---

[272] It is to be noted that in this particular case the investigator does not tamper with
the deliveries to customary final demand sectors (Government, Capital Formation,
Inventory Change, Foreign Trade, and Households) and to those sectors (accounts)
representing translations of social goals. Hence the interindustry relationships will
force the system to produce at least that quantity of aluminum which is yielded by the
first variant of Channel V. However, it may produce more aluminum output since the
fourth variant of Channel V yields a more efficient structure for the system and its
regions.

In general, it is to be expected that a Gross System Product will develop which will exceed the Gross System Product associated with the first (input-output) variant of Channel V. This expectation is in keeping with the hypothesis that the introduction into the framework of an interregional linear program, as a partial substitute for comparative cost and industrial complex techniques, will lead to greater system efficiency. The resources of the system will be more productively utilized; hence, their full utilization (within limits imposed by resource constraints) will result in greater GSP for the fourth variant of Channel V. Since the GSP implied by the results of the first variant of Channel V is exactly identical with the initially assumed GSP, it follows that the GSP of the fourth variant exceeds the initially assumed GSP. This suggests that the fourth variant of Channel V requires goal refinement and reformulation. Such refinement and reformulation proceeds simultaneously with the required examination of how the linear program allocates the "surplus" both in terms of final products and regions. The latter is performed in order to avoid a meaningless and even a contradictory pattern of results.[273]

These statements touch on just one of several ways in which interregional linear programming can be introduced into a Channel V framework. The full presentation of these ways must be left to future research. Diagrammatically, the introduction of interregional linear programming can be depicted via Figure 10. If in Figure 10 the BALANCED REGIONAL or INTERREGIONAL INPUT-OUTPUT MATRIX and all arrows leading to and from it are suppressed, if the arrows leading from COMPARATIVE COST and INDUSTRIAL COMPLEX are construed to define *locational efficiency* constraints, if the arrow from the major rounded box PROBABILITY, GRAVITY, POTENTIAL MODELS to the INTERREGIONAL LINEAR PROGRAM matrix is construed as helping to define *locational efficiency* constraints, and if the arrow leading from PROBABILITY, GRAVITY, POTENTIAL MODELS to the upper RESULTS column is suppressed, then a sketch of the framework of the fourth variant of Channel V remains. To this framework there may or may not be added the arrow stemming from the upper RESULTS column and leading to PROBABILITY, GRAVITY, POTENTIAL MODELS and thence to the lower RESULTS column.

It is also helpful at this point succinctly to summarize in mathematical terms the fourth variant of Channel V. Bearing in mind that the definition of sectors in this chapter differs greatly from that in Chapter 10, that commodities and resources are conceived somewhat differently, that process substitution and the possibility of joint production are given different play, etc., we can nonetheless use the symbols of Chapter 10. The fourth variant of Channel V may be broadly stated:

[273] See the discussion in section E.5 of this chapter.

To maximize $$Z = c'X$$

subject to

$$-AX \leq R$$

and $$X \geq 0$$

where $Z = $ Gross System Product;

$X = $ the column vector of activity (sector) levels, covering activities of all regions;

$c' = $ a row vector of weights and/or unit-level incomes (prices) to be applied to these activity levels;[274]

$A = $ an activity coefficient matrix, largely resembling an interregional input-output coefficient matrix;

and $R = $ a column vector of the limiting constants of the constraints pertaining to deliveries to final demand sectors and resource supplies.[275]

With this symbolic statement[276] which the reader should detail in a

---

[274] Recall from sections F, G, and H of Chapter 10 that $c_j^L = 0$ when activity j in region L produces intermediates only. Also recall that when an activity produces a commodity which is used both as intermediate in production and as final product by households, it too is treated as producing intermediates only and is assigned a weight of zero. However, there is simultaneously introduced a dummy activity which converts the intermediate into final product for households and which is assigned a positive weight, typically a ruling price.

[275] R_k^L is a negative number when k is a commodity delivered to final demand sectors, being the negative of total required deliveries. R_k^L is a positive number when k refers to a resource used in production. For helpful details see sections H, I and J of Chapter 10. It is clear that the fourth variant of Channel V requires a redefinition of an intermediate commodity.

[276] Because the dual of the interregional linear program of Channel V does not have significance, it is not set down. Also note that the fourth variant of Channel V can be extended into time á la Moore. We may set positive weights (i.e., per-unit-level incomes or prices) to sectors producing and delivering final goods in the terminal year of the projection period (say 1965). Per standard definition, all activities producing intermediates are assigned zero weights. But also all activities producing and delivering final products in all nonterminal years may be assigned zero weights, such activities being viewed as producing intermediates from the standpoint of GSP in 1965, the terminal year. Accordingly, in each nonterminal year there must be set constraints which insure (1) deliveries of final goods to households, government, and foreign trade, perhaps consistent with rising incomes, and (2) deliveries of items to the capital formation (including inventory) sectors in order to realize capital expansions required by the goals established for the terminal year.

For the above extension, the mathematical statement in the text still pertains. Z refers to GSP in the terminal year (1965). The column vector X refers to activity levels in all regions in all years (a process in a given region in one year being defined as a different activity from the same process in the same region in a different year). The

manner which generally parallels the exposition of Chapter 10, we bring to an end our brief discussion of Channel V. Although only sketchily presented, this channel is put forth as the most advanced of all, operationally speaking. Numerous versions of this channel are possible, which combine the several techniques in both simple and more complex ways and which the reader may explore. We have touched on four variants. The first of these has most of the virtues and limitations of Channel I but is superior in the sense that it forces the investigator to consider basic values and goals of a society and to introduce them as social accounts into the framework at least to some extent. Similarly, the second and third versions of Channel V, as extensions respectively of Channels II and III, retain most of the virtues and limitations of these respective channels but are superior for the reasons just noted. Finally, the fourth variant of Channel V incurs both major advantages and disadvantages when compared with Channel IV. Channel IV represents the most complete conceptual synthesis, a synthesis well beyond that attained by the fourth variant of Channel V. On the other hand, the fourth variant of Channel V is operational which is its *raison d'être*. In a sense it is Channel IV reduced to a manageable size.[277]

row vector c' refers to weights, weights being zero for all activities in any nonterminal year. A is a greatly expanded activity coefficient matrix, wherein each coefficient pertains to one year only, and wherein there are as many coefficients linking one activity in a region to any second activity of the same or any other region as there are years. R is a column vector of limiting constants of all constraints over all regions for all years.

[277] For the most part, the fused frameworks of Channels I–V have been developed primarily with the purpose of projection in mind. These frameworks, however, also hold considerable promise for the realization of more penetrating historical studies. This promise exists, despite major imperfections in historical data.

Speaking first of all in somewhat ideal terms, construction for key years of the past of tables such as Table 1, however reduced and limited they would be because of the lack of data, could permit and provide basic empirical background for systematic analyses. They would point up the changing industrial composition and interindustry linkage of the nation and of each of its regions, the changing regional structure of the system (especially as frontiers and other new areas are developed and new regions and interregional bonds are added to the system), the changing spatial pattern of its population and of migration, the changing rural-urban structure of the system and its regions, the changing spatial distribution of income and gross output, of governmental expenditures, of private investment, of commodity and perhaps money flows, of resource utilization, etc. In fact, such tables would greatly facilitate the historical study of a nation such as the United States as a system of regions, wherein regions as well as industries, social groups, political organizations, decision-making units, etc., are constantly being redefined and re-evaluated over time. Such a study could make major contributions to our understanding of the social and economic history of the United States.

On a less ambitious scale, but yet with more probing into causal relationships, the frameworks of Channels I–V are valid for historical analysis. Suppose that it is desired

G. SUMMARY

It is now appropriate to summarize the ground covered in this lengthy chapter. We shall briefly review the channels, whose purpose has been synthesis; synthesis on a comprehensive scale, both conceptual and operational; synthesis which necessarily involves the effective linkage of the systems and subsystems that each technique analytically attacks.

1. Channel I centers around an interregional input-output framework basically enlarged to include comparative cost and industrial complex techniques in their full dress. Figure 1 illustrates this channel. Table 1 outlines much of its detail. A fundamental step involves the lifting out of the structural matrix the industries and parts of industries that are subject to meaningful comparative cost and industrial complex analyses. The

to appraise the national and regional impacts of one or more major developments in United States history—say the construction of the Erie canal and other important links of the canal network of the nineteenth century, or of the construction of the net of railroads, or of the discovery of Lake Superior ore, or of tariff policies, or of the annexation of Texas. The investigator may start with a relevant base year, whose choice is largely influenced by available data. He may estimate direct impact, say of the opening of the Erie Canal, on industrial location employing comparative cost, industrial complex, and other techniques. Then by means of an interindustry matrix such as Table 1, however abridged, and with the judicious use of the appropriate lags and perhaps of relative growth charts, coefficients, etc., he may project total direct and indirect impacts, by both region and industrial sector, for a subsequent year. He then compares his projections with the actual data for this subsequent year. Discrepancies may be attributed to the operation of other forces affecting efficiency and cost minimization (or profit maximization), to irrationalities in industry behavior, to the operation of social forces (say sectionalism) which reflect values and goals other than efficiency and cost minimization. Even if no discrepancies appear, irrationalities and other social forces, etc., may be actively at play, but in a compensatory manner.

Whatever the set of historical interpretations reached, clearly such a framework adds depth to the analysis. It may provide some basis for inferring the set of values and goals held by a society in the past and the relative weights attached to them. This basis is widened when other quantifiable forces are added to the framework of the study—such as immigration from foreign countries, shifts of household expenditure patterns, growth of manufacturing and service trades, tariff policy—and when the cyclical effects of, say, canal construction and foreign immigration on building activity, urban growth, and industrial investment are grafted on, with due allowance for intensification by a prevalent speculative fever.

Moreover, not only does the partial use in this fashion of one of the frameworks of Channels I–V illuminate for a past period attitudes and the interaction of social groups, and the relative importance attached to such goals as Liberty and Equality and Welfare; it also yields greater understanding of development processes, of the changing mix of primary, secondary, and tertiary activities for a system and its regions, of the significance of industrial composition as a cyclical factor and of specific industries as carrier industries, etc., and finally insight on values for basic parameters to be used in fused frameworks designed to project magnitudes for future years.

results of such analyses indicate how these industries and parts of industries are to be put in place in the final demand (bill of goods) sectors. This step represents the chief innovation of Channel I.

Other steps of Channel I are more conventional. For projection purposes, basic assumptions on birth rates, death rates, technology, tastes, etc., are made for the system. System population, its labor force, and average productivity are anticipated for the key future year. Social accounts for the system are estimated. These are expressed in terms of levels of final demand sectors, such as government expenditures and capital formation. System outputs by sector (industry) are derived via input-output or other techniques. Initial regional markets are then established on the basis of current data and by the use of diverse coefficients, curves, relative growth charts, trend analyses, and consumption expenditures and other studies. These market magnitudes then permit the pursuit of comparative cost and industrial complex analyses which establish by region levels of new final demand sectors. When these levels are coupled with the levels of customary final demand sectors by region, it becomes possible to run a standard interregional input-output computation to achieve the desired results. However, because of discrepancies between estimates of initial regional markets and the set of regional markets consistent with the results of this computation, it may be necessary to re-estimate initial regional markets and rerun the framework. The rerun process is continued until in fact results are obtained which are in harmony with the initial regional market assumptions underlying these results and with resource scarcities and community attitudes of reality.

In the discussion of Channel I considerable time is spent in detailing procedures for the operation of a fused framework and in describing the structure of a table, specifically Table 1, which is useful for recording the relevant empirical materials of a fused framework. This detailing and description is not developed for the fused frameworks of subsequent channels since such would involve considerable repetition. Also, in connection with Channel I a close examination of results is undertaken, an examination which is not repeated for subsequent channels except when strikingly new types of results are obtained.

Sector outputs, sector employments, total employment, population, and net migration estimates by region are among the results stemming from the operation of the fused framework of Channel I. Gross Product of each region is also obtainable whether measured (1) at the production stage (in terms of either net output or value added of producing sectors); or (2) at the places where household consumption, government, and investment expenditures occur; or (3) at the places where households receive income, and government, revenue. It is demonstrated how the detail for the measurement of Gross Regional Product from each of these three standpoints and for the determination of other basic social accounts is contained in a table such as Table 1 which records the data for the fused framework of Channel I. Hence, regional social accounts are an integral part of the results of Channel I.

Other results pertain to the detail and totals on exports and imports by region and on interregional commodity flows. These results supplement and to some extent supplant existing interregional commodity flow studies, whose materials can fruitfully be utilized early in the operation of the framework in developing an appropriate classification of sectors, in indicating sectors subject to comparative cost and industrial complex analyses, in establishing initial regional markets, and in estimating interregional input-output coefficients. A closely related result is the magnitude of the Rest of the World commodity account, a basic account of any balance of payments study; but this magnitude may also be crudely estimated from national input-output coefficients, without the full detail of an interregional flow table such as Table 1.

Ideally, the fused framework of Channel I should embrace the dimension pertaining to financial elements and money flows. Doing so would enable it to yield much more complete balance of payments statements. More important, doing so would tremendously upgrade its validity and usefulness for monetary and fiscal policy. This latter point is appreciated when it is recognized that a complete interregional money flow system embraces or reflects in full the interregional interindustry system and in turn the interregional social accounting system. More specifically, a detailed interregional money flow table, such as Table 6, contains (1) all the empirical materials (and considerably more) of an interregional interindustry flow table such as Table 1, and (2) the magnitudes for all the items listed in a regional social accounts table such as Table 2. Unfortunately, interregional money flow studies are extremely scarce, and relevant data are not readily available. Until such comprehensive interregional money flow studies are developed, the operational use of the fused framework of Channel I must eschew this conceptual extension and must be restricted to the use of the limited money flow materials available in secondary ways only.

Still other results of Channel I have reference to economic base, multiplier, and cycle analysis. In a real sense the derived framework and a table such as Table 1 yield a direct and clearcut, multiphase picture of the economic base of each region of a system. The use of this framework supersedes the customary economic base–regional multiplier type of study oriented to basic-service ratios and other oversimplified concepts. It permits a much superior calculation of diverse types of multipliers (impact effects), encompassing both local income variation and interindustry linkage. However, the framework and a table such as Table 1 can be developed for a relatively small number of regions only, in particular for those regions considered relevant for the one or few specific designs of the framework which it is feasible to implement. Hence for other regions, especially small areas, the data of a Table 1 of Channel I are to be used as background against which customary economic base–regional multiplier study is to be conducted.

Beyond the identification of structural effects (generally speaking of a long-run nature) based on assumptions of unchanging behavior by consumer, business, and government units, the framework of Channel I cannot operationally proceed in the analysis of multiplier and cyclical effects. Even conceptually, the industrial composition variable (if it is judged relevant) or the short-run Keynesian-type interregional trade multiplier can be added to the framework of Channel I in an oversimplified, partial manner only—because of the regional factor at play, the nonadditive nature of cyclical and secular effects, etc.

Lastly, a number of refinements of the framework of Channel I are possible. On a single-industry or industrial complex basis, interregional linear programming, the comparative cost method, and the industrial complex technique may be viewed as three variants of a general analytical approach which aims at the identification of efficient minimum-cost spatial patterns. Consequently, in the framework of Channel I, interregional linear programming may substitute for the comparative cost or industrial complex techniques in the limited number of situations when such a step leads to more valid and effective locational analysis for a particular sector or industrial complex. Also, where meaningful quantification of attitudes and similar behavioral elements can be achieved by scaling techniques and factor analyses—for example, in gauging the impact of community attitudes on industrial location or in delineating the most relevant set of regions—these techniques too are to be operationally synthesized into the fused framework of Channel I.

2. Channel II, like Channel I, is designed to be fully operational. Its emphasis, however, is on urban-metropolitan structure. It substitutes the balanced regional input-output model (incorporating the valid aspects of central place theory) for the interregional input-output scheme. It is illustrated by Figure 8 when the rounded major block designated PROBABILITY, GRAVITY, POTENTIAL MODELS is deleted.

As with Channel I, Channel II begins with a set of basic assumptions for the system, proceeds through several steps to initial regional market estimates, and then employs comparative cost and industrial complex techniques supplemented by interregional linear programming and scaling and factor analysis to develop the final demand (bill of goods) sectors by regions. In the process, however, the balanced regional input-output scheme requires the establishment of a meaningful hierarchy of regions of several orders [say a nation (system) which is subdivided into major metropolitan regions, each of which consists of a set of subregions, each of which is composed of a set of local areas, etc.] and a suitable classification of commodities [say national, regional, subregional, local, etc.]. As a consequence, the framework of Channel II requires that comparative cost and industrial complex techniques supplemented by other methods and coefficients, curves, etc., establish constants not only for allocating output of national industries among metropolitan regions, subregions, local areas, etc., but also for distributing regional outputs of regional industries among subregions, local areas, etc., and subregional outputs of subregional industries among local areas, etc. As a consequence, too, the detail of Channel II can be presented only in a single table of many times the size of Table 1 of Channel I or in a hierarchical set of tables.

Typically, the first run of the framework of Channel II will generate inconsistencies which must be largely ironed out by reruns, as is the case in Channel I. For metropolitan regions, Channel II yields results that parallel the results yielded by Channel I for its regions. Among these are sector outputs, sector employments, total employment, population, net migration, Gross Product (measured in each of three ways), income, governmental outlays, net investment, exports, imports, commodity balance of trade, and economic base. Additionally, other types of results such as tax base and commercial, industrial, and residential land requirements are explicitly noted because of their strategic importance for the analysis of metropolitan problems.

The framework of Channel II also yields these results for each subregion of a greater metropolitan region and for each local area of a subregion, etc. Hence, it basically outlines intrametropolitan structure and pattern (as noted in the lower RESULTS column of Figure 8). However, the results on intrametropolitan pattern (and in turn on the internal pattern of each subregion) are not likely to be as firm as those pertaining to the metropolitan region as a whole. They are to be supplemented and reconciled with results on spatial patterns which may emerge from interregional linear programming studies for particular sectors and from the use of a variety of statistical and graphic techniques, which range from simple trend projection of local populations, ratios, etc., through relative growth charts, and finally to multiple regression and covariance methods and factor analysis. As with Channel I, the fused framework of Channel II may be conceptually extended to embrace cycle and multiplier concepts and techniques and a financial elements–money flow dimension.

3. Channel III is motivated by the failure of Channels I and II to achieve an adequate perspective on both agglomeration (spatial juxta-position) forces and the behavior of social masses. It attempts to over-come such deficiency by fusing into the frameworks of Channels I and II certain gravity, potential, and other probability-type concepts. Hence, Channel III is depicted on Figure 8 when the rounded major block designated PROBABILITY, GRAVITY, POTENTIAL MODELS and the arrows leading to and from it are considered fully relevant.

One fruitful direction is to introduce into the framework of Channel I a relative income potential concept. First, endogenous producing sectors (those not subject to comparative cost, industrial complex, and inter-regional linear programming analysis) are to be subdivided into (1) non-cost-sensitive industries and (2) local service and other market-oriented industries. Second, the time stretch between the base year and the key future year must be considered as a series of successive short time periods, for each one of which a projection is to be made. Third, the framework of Channel I is run to project at the end of the first time period regional levels of (a) those sectors subject to comparative cost, industrial complex, and interregional linear programming analysis, and (b) those parts of local service and other market-oriented activities tied to these sectors. (Reruns are eliminated; discrepancies and inconsistencies motivate various units to adjust and change their location, production, and consumption levels, etc., in the following time period.) Fourth, levels of non-cost-sensitive sectors and those parts of local service and other market-oriented activities tied to these sectors are projected for each region on an "as the nation grows" basis, adjusted by a modified relative income potential term reflect-ing changing interregional position of a region. Fifth, the regional pro-jections for the terminal year of the first period are used as base year materials for regional projections for the terminal year of the second period. And so forth until regional projections are attained for the key future year. As a consequence, a step-by-step discrete path of growth obtains for each major region and the system, involving for the terminal year of each time period estimates by region of outputs by sector, employ-ment, population, Gross Product and diverse social accounts, tax base, and other critical magnitudes. In somewhat similar fashion, projections by subregions are obtainable as well when there is introduced into the frame-work of Channel II a relative income potential concept—a concept which, some may claim, catches more fully than any other concept the effects of the interplay of the host of agglomeration and spatial juxtaposition forces which are so closely associated with markets and accessibility to markets.

Another fruitful direction in the use of the probability-type gravity model is in testing the consistency of projections of spatial patterns of several phenomena within metropolitan regions and their subregions. Based on diverse procedures, an industrial location (job) pattern, a population (residential) pattern, a shopping center pattern, etc., may each be independently projected for the same metropolitan region or subregion. Together, they imply patterns of journey-to-work trips, shopping trips, commodity shipments, etc. Such patterns may be compared with the patterns generated by a probability-type gravity model, where the parameters of such a model are derived from extensive empirical data on trip behavior and commodity shipments. If the former patterns deviate markedly from gravity model expectations of trip behavior and commodity shipments, re-examination of the industrial location, population, shopping center, and each of the other independently derived patterns is suggested. Such re-examination may be undertaken in order to effect rearrangement of these patterns without jeopardizing the validity of any one and in order to achieve (if necessary, by iteration) greater consistency with gravity model expectations based on current and past transportation data. This direction in the use of the gravity model is of particular significance because of the relative abundance of transportation data on the one hand and the limited applicability of other analytical techniques to small area and subregional study on the other hand.

Conceptually speaking (and hopefully operationally in the near future) Channel III can be extended further to embrace urban complex analysis. This analysis parallels industrial complex analysis. It purports to attack directly scale and spatial juxtaposition economies as they affect metropolitan structure and function. It may first involve identification of meaningful complexes of urban activities of different orders, ranging from the central business district type down to the small neighborhood cluster. Next, reasonable metropolitan patterns (hierarchical sets of urban complexes) are noted. With input-output type data and local price data or estimates, costs and revenues for each urban complex of each order in each metropolitan pattern are then computed. These lead to total cost estimates for each metropolitan pattern, where total cost differences among the metropolitan patterns may be due to differences in cost of transportation (persons and commodities), labor, taxes, land, etc., and in scale economies. (Differences in certain non-quantifiable social costs cannot, of course, be embraced.) The total cost computations in turn lead to the isolation of the most efficient metropolitan pattern.

Briefly put, Channel III does operationally attack and at least to some extent does encompass spatial juxtaposition economies on the major region and subregion level, and does bring to bear upon projections of intrametropolitan structure behavior phenomena of social masses, especially with regard to travel and transportation. Channel III adds the probability-type gravity model to the fused framework of Channels I and II, using it to supplement the techniques already synthesized into these frameworks. Thus Channel III can achieve all the basic results of Channels I and II, presumably with greater validity. Such validity will be even further enhanced when urban complex analysis can be operationally fused into the framework.

4. Channel IV places central emphasis upon values (culture) and social goals. It is thus broader in scope than Channels I–III which emphasize economic efficiency, just one of several basic goals. In fact, on the conceptual level Channel IV contains Channels I–III as special cases. Yet Channel IV is nonoperational, as is clear when we study its portrayal on Figure 9. Accumulated historical study and political, sociological, and other social science theory and empirical investigations offer insufficient understanding of the goal-setting process—that is, how to proceed from values and culture through the decision framework to system and subsystem goals. Thus the quantification of goals rests on a very shaky foundation and is likely to for quite some time, despite the promise of new techniques and concepts such as scaling, latent structure, and community participation potential.

Once a set of specific goals is crudely developed for a system (culture) and its regions (subsystems) such as the one denoted in Figure 9, the next step in Channel IV requires the translation of these goals into specific, detailed social accounts. Here, too, inadequate social science knowledge plagues the investigator. The quantitative implications of certain goals are clear-cut, such as the implications of the goal of at least twelve years of schooling for governmental expenditures. But how translate the goal of economic stability (let alone social and political stability) into specific social accounts?

The detailing of social accounts in Channel IV is conditioned significantly by the operational techniques to be subsequently employed. In the version presented in this chapter, general interregional linear programming is taken as the central operator. This necessitates both (1) the embodiment of one or more goals in an objective function and (2) the translation of other goals into social account magnitudes which serve as limiting constants of constraints.

Many objective functions are possible. A common one is to maximize Gross System Product. Whatever the function, typically difficulties are encountered in the choice of weights, since weights supposedly reflect the values of a society which, as already noted, too frequently defy quantification. Even market prices are poor indicators of values.

If the objective is to maximize Gross System Product, one group of constraints may relate to minimum standards. For each region these constraints insure the delivery to its households of that food and clothing, the provision of that housing, medical services, education, etc., and the supply of that new plant and equipment consistent with the minimum standards implied by system and subsystem goals. (Goals relating to household consumption and governmental services may frequently be governed by levels and patterns of consumption and services already attained.) A second group of constraints may relate to resources and insure that resource requirements do not exceed available supply. At this point, as well as at others, the interregional input-output matrix of coefficients is of considerable utility in calculating requirements.

Other groups of constraints may relate to stability, financial elements (and money flows), and mass behavior and attitudes. These constraints largely involve relations which can be treated at the conceptual level only. However, industrial composition hypotheses and Keynesian short-run interregional trade multiplier analyses may contribute to the specification of stability constraints. Balance of payments considerations may lead to a precise financial constraint, other financial constraints being difficult to quantify, even though the interregional money flow system is the most comprehensive of all examined in this book and reflects more thoroughly than any other the structure and pattern of decisions in a society. The rank-size rule, voting records, and scaling analysis may contribute to the quantitative statement of a mass behavior-attitude constraint. Finally, another set of constraints may relate to locational efficiency, whose specification ensues from analysis by comparative cost, industrial complex, and eventually urban complex techniques. Through these locational efficiency constraints, the latter techniques become effectively fused into the framework of Channel IV. Also, even a relative income potential model may be fused into the framework of Channel IV at this point through locational pattern constraints on non-cost-sensitive industries.

Once the objective function and constraints of the interregional linear program of the values–social goals Channel IV are set down, a solution may be sought. If no solution is possible, the program is infeasible, and the basic set of goals as reflected in the minimum social accounts and diverse constraints must be reset; sights must be lowered. If a solution is possible, and in addition a "surplus" is yielded, it may be necessary to reset constraints and refashion the program if the program's allocation of this surplus among commodities, units, and regions is inconsistent with underlying values and goals. When a satisfactory solution is attained, practically all, if not all, the basic social accounts and other magnitudes are obtainable in the same manner as in the previous channels—even when

Channel IV is conceptually extended to encompass the growth (capital formation and capacity expansion) process and cyclical features of reality.

5. Channel V is an operational channel. It is designed to incorporate significant values and goals which are at least approximately quantifiable into the fused frameworks of Channels I–III, thereby correcting some of their imbalance. Channel V is represented on Figure 10.

One variant of Channel V systematically injects in a major way values and social goals into Channel I. It does so by (1) translating social goals into specific accounts, whether the statement of such goals is relatively simple as in an armaments reduction program or exceedingly complex as in a political platform, and (2) putting these accounts in place in the final demand (bill of goods) sectors of the several regions. In general, this first variant of Channel V follows the steps of Channel I, but, in the light of values and social goals, constantly requires modification of these steps all the way from the establishment of initial basic assumptions through the reruns.

In similar fashion, second and third versions of Channel V may be constructed around Channels II and III, respectively.

A fourth variant of Channel V reintroduces interregional linear programming into the framework. It does so by substituting this technique in part for comparative cost and industrial complex techniques, and thereby purports to throw light on more efficient spatial patterns. The regional allocation of at least some of the national output of industries which are cost-sensitive and thus subject to comparative cost or industrial complex analysis becomes a duty of the interregional linear program. Moreover, additional values and social goals can be explicitly treated in the objective function and constraints of the program.

Of all channels, Channel V is the most advanced, operationally speaking. It achieves the highest level of synthesis of analytical techniques. Thus, its fused framework is the most effective in attacking the interrelations which pervade an interregional system and its diverse subsystems, both interregional and intraregional. Of the variants of Channel V, the fourth one looms as the most promising one, provided the investigator judges that high-speed electronic computation capacity and practice will be able to cope with the general interregional linear program involved.

References

1. Bogue, Donald J., and D. L. Harris, *Comparative Population and Urban Research Via Multiple Regression and Covariance Analysis*, Miami University, Scripps Foundation, Oxford, Ohio, 1954.
2. Brown, Bonnar, and M. Janet Hansen, *Production Trends in the United States through 1975*, Stanford Research Institute, Menlo Park, California, 1957.

3. Carroll, J. Douglas, and Howard W. Bevis, "Predicting Local Travel in Urban Regions," *Papers and Proceedings of the Regional Science Association*, Vol. 3 (1957).
4. Colm, Gerhard, *The American Economy in 1960*, National Planning Association, Washington, D.C., 1952.
5. Copeland, Morris A., *A Study of Moneyflows in the United States*, National Bureau of Economic Research, New York, 1952.
6. Evans, W. Duane, and Marvin Hoffenberg, "The Interindustry Relations Study for 1947," *Review of Economics and Statistics*, Vol. 34 (May 1952).
7. Federal Reserve Board, "Summary Flow-of-Funds Accounts, 1950–55," *Federal Reserve Bulletin*, Vol. 43 (April 1957).
8. Fox, Karl A., "A Spatial Equilibrium Model of the Livestock-Feed Economy in the United States," *Econometrica*, Vol. 21 (Oct. 1953).
9. ———, and Richard C. Taeuber, "Spatial Equilibrium Models of the Livestock-Feed Economy," *American Economic Review*, Vol. 45 (Sept. 1955).
10. Freutel, Guy E., "The Eighth District Balance of Trade," *Monthly Review*, The Federal Reserve Bank of St. Louis, Vol. 34 (June 1952).
11. ———, "Regional Interdependence and District Development," *Monthly Review*, Federal Reserve Bank of St. Louis, Vol. 33 (Aug. 1951).
12. Harvard Economic Research Project, *Report on Research*, Cambridge, Massachusetts, annual.
13. Hile, Gloria J., *The Balance of Payments of the Southeast in 1950*, doctoral dissertation, University of Michigan, Ann Arbor, Michigan, 1954.
14. Hirsch, Werner Z., "An Application of Area Input-Output Analysis," *Papers and Proceedings of the Regional Science Association*, Vol. 5 (1959).
15. ———, *Projecting Economic Activity and Population of the St. Louis Metropolitan Area*, Metropolitan St. Louis Survey, 1958, mimeographed.
16. Isard, Walter, "Regional Commodity Balances and Interregional Commodity Flows," *American Economic Review*, Vol. 43 (May 1953).
17. ———, and Robert E. Coughlin, *Municipal Costs and Revenues Resulting from Community Growth*, Chandler-Davis, Wellesley, Massachusetts, 1957.
18. ———, and Robert E. Kuenne, "The Impact of Steel Upon the Greater New York–Philadelphia Industrial Region: A Study in Agglomeration Projection," *Review of Economics and Statistics*, Vol. 35 (Nov. 1953).
19. Leontief, Wassily W., et al, *Studies in the Structure of the American Economy*, Oxford University Press, New York, 1953.
20. Maass, Arthur A., ed., *Area and Power: A Theory of Local Government*, Free Press, Glencoe, Illinois, 1958.
21. Mendelson, M., "A Structure of Moneyflows," *Journal of the American Statistical Association*, Vol. 50 (March 1955).
22. Moore, Frederick T., "Regional Economic Reaction Paths," *American Economic Review*, Vol. 45 (May 1955).
23. ———, and James W. Peterson, "Regional Analysis: An Interindustry Model of Utah," *Review of Economics and Statistics*, Vol. 37 (Nov. 1955).
24. Moses, Leon N., "The Stability of Interregional Trading Patterns and Input-Output Analysis," *American Economic Review*, Vol. 45 (Dec. 1955).
25. Muncy, Dorothy A., "Land for Industry—A Neglected Problem," *Harvard Business Review*, Vol. 32 (March–April 1954).
26. National Bureau of Economic Research, *Input-Output Analysis: An Appraisal*, Studies in Income and Wealth, Vol. 18, Princeton University Press, Princeton, New Jersey, 1955 (including a Technical Supplement).

27. National Bureau of Economic Research, *The National Economic Accounts of the United States*, General Series, No. 64, U. S. Government Printing Office, Washington, D.C., 1958.

28. National Planning Association, *Local Impact of Foreign Trade*, Washington, D.C. 1959.

29. Nelson, Philip, "Migration Flows and Population Distribution," *Journal of Regional Science*, Vol. 1 (Spring 1959).

30. Price, Daniel O., "Factor Analysis in the Study of Metropolitan Centers," *Social Forces*, Vol. 20 (May 1942).

31. Sigel, S. J., "A Comparison of the Structures of Three Social Accounting Systems," in *Input-Output Analysis: An Appraisal*, National Bureau of Economic Research, Studies in Income and Wealth, Vol. 18, Princeton University Press, Princeton, New Jersey, 1955.

32. Snodgrass, Milton M., and Charles E. French, *Linear Programming Approach to Interregional Competition in Dairying*, Purdue University, Agricultural Experiment Station, Lafayette, Indiana, May 1958.

33. Stevens, Benjamin H., *Interregional Linear Programming*, doctoral dissertation, Massachusetts Institute of Technology, Cambridge, Massachusetts, 1959.

34. Stewart, John Q., "Potential of Population and Its Relationship to Marketing," in Reavis Cox and Wroe Alderson, eds., *Theory in Marketing*, Richard D. Irwin, Inc., Homewood, Illinois, 1950.

35. U. S. Mutual Security Agency, *The Structure and Growth of the Italian Economy*, Rome, 1953.

36. University of Maryland, Bureau of Business and Economic Research, *Estimating Maryland Government and Business Potentials*, College Park, Maryland, March 1955.

37. ———, *A Regional Interindustry Study of Maryland*, College Park, Maryland, Sept. 1954.

38. Wolff, P. de, and P. E. Venekamp, "On a System of Regional Social Accounts for the City of Amsterdam," *International Statistical Institute Bulletin*, Vol. 35, Part 4 (1957).

Chapter 13

Retrospect and Prospect

To the best of our knowledge, we have presented systematically the significant existing methods and techniques for regional analysis. We have tried to evaluate these techniques and methods in a general fashion. Although it would be presumptious to claim that the appraisal is fully objective and balanced, nonetheless we trust we have accomplished one of the objectives of this book.

Whether or not we have substantially achieved a second objective is questionable. As is crystal-clear, sound regional analysis is interdependence analysis. This fact has motivated the attempt to synthesize the strong elements of existing techniques—to develop new, broadened frameworks for analysis. Hopefully these frameworks are markedly superior to the existing partial techniques for the understanding and projection of population numbers, migration, industrial location, economic base, regional income and other social accounts, commodity and money flows, balance of payments position, multiplier effects, cyclical sensitivities, etc., which have been discussed in Chapters 2 through 7 and parts of Chapter 11. Hopefully, too, these frameworks are superior to the more general interdependence techniques of regional and interregional input-output, industrial complex, and interregional linear programming presented in Chapters 8 through 10, and to the probability-type gravity formulations of Chapter 11.

Although Chapters 8 through 11 do attempt some fusion with partial techniques, the real effort at synthesis is the domain of Chapter 12. In this chapter five channels of synthesis and a number of variants are developed. Although different analysts would undoubtedly develop these channels and their variants with different emphasis on techniques and with different detail, it seems at this point that by and large the major channels of both operational and conceptual synthesis have been covered.

In a real sense, the frameworks of the several channels of Chapter 12 may be said to supplant all the techniques discussed in Chapters 2 through 11. To repeat, this situation obtains not because these frameworks discard the materials of Chapters 2 through 11. Rather these frameworks do utilize and find valuable the materials of Chapters 2 through 11 and in fact build upon these materials. For example, in Chapters 2 and 3 direct techniques of population projection and migration estimates are discussed. These techniques are employed, to the extent that they are valid, in several of the channels of Chapter 12. At the outset, these techniques are fundamental to the construction of the basic assumptions, system social accounts, and initial regional markets of these channels. In turn through fusion with comparative cost, industrial complex, interregional input-output, interregional linear programming, etc., as is effected by these channels, these techniques lead to superior population projections and migration estimates—superior in the sense that the fusion brings to bear upon the problem economic optimizing motives, technological relations, social standards and goals, etc., as they come to influence, often very indirectly, the location and size of families. It is in this sense then that at least one of the frameworks of Chapter 12 can be said to substitute for the techniques of Chapters 2 and 3.

Similarly, the detailed discussion of the framework of Channel I makes clear the following points:

1. The techniques of regional income estimation and regional social accounting of Chapter 4 are fully utilized in Channel I as well as extensively supplemented by interindustry and technological materials, comparative cost, and demographic data, etc.; and hence in their Channel I dress yield without question superior regional income and other social accounts.

2. Superior commodity and money flow analyses and balance of payments statements are possible, via Channel I, even if, only at the minimum, a crude comparative cost–input–output framework is added to the concepts, tools, and methods discussed in Chapter 5.

3. Industrial composition hypotheses and short-run interregional trade multiplier considerations presented in Chapter 6 are encompassed in

Channel I, to the extent that they are considered valid by the investigator; and superior regional cycle and business outlook analyses result when via Channel I there are added to such hypotheses and considerations projections by region of changes in industrial mix and in the structure of basic social accounts.

4. Regional economic base and the associated regional multiplier analysis as discussed in Chapter 6 are significantly advanced by the much greater detail of Channel I, however crude the interindustry table of this channel.

5. Multiregion empirical and historical studies (as noted in Chapter 6) and the diverse coefficients, indices, curves, etc. (as presented in Chapter 7) are exploited to the fullest extent by the sophisticated analyst, and in turn interpretation in such studies and of such coefficients, etc., which emphasize the *what* of systems can be immensely advanced through fusion with the explanatory (the *why*, the motive-identifying) techniques of comparative cost, industrial complex, etc., together with the consistency framework of input-output.

Additionally, the discussion of Chapters 7 through 10 and 12 makes clear that the techniques of comparative cost (Chapter 7), regional and interregional input-output (Chapter 8), industrial complex (Chapter 9), and interregional linear programming (Chapter 10) each suffer major limitations when employed singly. Each gains significantly from fusion with one or more other techniques via a channel (however abridged) of Chapter 12. Finally Channel III of Chapter 12 carefully details how all the valid materials of Chapter 11 may be fused to some extent with other regional techniques, ranging from free-hand graphic extrapolation of population numbers to interregional linear programming; necessarily, the results of a well-designed, abridged Channel III must yield results superior to those obtainable from Chapter 11 procedures alone.

Thus, to recapitulate, all that is valuable in the concepts, tools, techniques, and methods of Chapters 2 through 11 are encompassed by one or more of the channels of Chapter 12. In this sense one or more of the Chapter 12 frameworks, or variants or abridgements, supplant the frameworks of any one of the preceding chapters. Hence the tasks of evaluation, of painting the prospect, and of pointing up fruitful areas for basic research can best proceed against the background of the Chapter 12 designs.

As has already been intimated, Channel I is the most operational of the channels discussed in Chapter 12, and perhaps the most valid in terms of orthodox doctrine. It is most operational because it centers around techniques already designed to utilize traditional sources of data, or for whose implementation data have been assembled and processed. That is, Channel I is least restricted by the data inadequacies (both quantitative and qualitative) that plague the full empirical implementation of all the channels of Chapter 12, and for that matter all comprehensive social science frameworks aimed at general interdependence analysis.

In an extremely narrow sense it may be claimed that Channel I has had a try. In Chapter 8 we reported a study of the impact of steel development on the Greater New York–Philadelphia region. In this study a simple regional input-output model is fused with a single-industry (steel) comparative cost investigation—crude coefficients, ratios, etc., being used to establish firm minimum levels of new steel fabrication and other partly exogenous variables. But this study cannot really be claimed to represent a Channel I framework; it lacks even a simple interregional structure. Hence it appears that one very fruitful investigation would be to attack a clear-cut regional or interregional problem via an empirically implemented abridgement of a Channel I framework (or variant)—an abridgement which embraces at the minimum (1) an interregional input-output dimension, and (2) some comparative cost analysis, and which is designed to yield (3) an interregional system of social accounts. (This investigation, for example, might relate to a critical resource problem, involving a relatively few, but large, resource regions.) Of course a still more complete study is preferable, such as the one outlined at the close of section 4 of Chapter 8 which encompasses a full set of industry-by-industry comparative cost studies within a simple interregional input-output structure. Yet another fruitful project would introduce some industrial complex analysis into this structure—especially when such analysis fruitfully extends (supplants) the comparative cost approach in attacking nonlinear interdependencies among certain activities, as, for example, is frequently the case in the study of economically depressed areas. Still more depth is of course achievable in a project when a fuller complement of industrial complex analyses is undertaken; or when interregional linear programming is utilized on an industry or industrial complex level to expose efficient spatial patterns for certain activities. An even more advanced project would involve the use of comparative cost, industrial complex, and interregional linear programming in "correct" proportions for the construction of the bill of goods for an interregional input-output framework; at the same time this project should yield a significant interregional system of social accounts.

Pursued concomitantly with one or more projects of the set just described may be one or more projects aimed at an adequate resolution of the problem of ironing out discrepancies which arise between the results of a first run of an abridged or full Channel I framework and initial basic and regional market assumptions. Such a set of projects would necessarily first attempt the resolution for one of the simpler interregional frameworks, such as the first one mentioned in the preceding paragraph. In orderly step-by-step fashion, resolution might next be attempted for the more comprehensive abridgements of the Channel I framework and finally for the full Channel I framework itself.

Still a third set of research projects might place central emphasis on the development of a full-scale interregional system of social accounts. Such a set of projects would rely on an interregional interindustry framework for sets of basic data, but would also develop anew GRP and other concepts and would include the full use of commodity balance of trade accounts with the Rest of the World. In such a study national accounts might be used, but only as background material. Embraced by this set of projects would be a study centering around regional balances of payments, and utilizing in full available commodity flow data via all transport media. This study would scrupulously exploit the detail of at least a simple interregional input-output structure based on the use of national input-output coefficients modified as much as possible to take into account regional differences in production practices and consumption habits. Such a study would not only lead to more incisive balance of payments accounts for each region of a system, but would generate, as a result of consistency requirements, valuable information on regional input-output coefficients.

A still bigger bite would assuredly be involved in a study of interregional money flows. This relatively unexplored area is subject to fruitful research, expecially if it can be attacked with a Channel I framework in mind. Such a framework would facilitate and expedite the use of all forms of commodity flow, regional production and consumption, and interregional interindustry coefficient data. As a consequence, many money flows could be estimated and control totals established. Obviously a first study would not (and probably could not) have the fine detail of Table 6 of Chapter 12, but it certainly could proceed much farther than the study reported in Chapter 5.

A number of other important research projects can be designed around Channel I. For example, it would be extremely valuable if scaling studies, along lines suggested in Appendix A of Chapter 7, or similar attitude studies could be performed in order to qualify appropriately results of comparative cost, input-output, and other calculations and analyses embraced in the Channel I framework. An initial study would not only indicate feasible and infeasible projections and rates of change in a given regional situation, and perhaps even estimate the intensity with which community resistance may be expected to mount and receptiveness to diminish as industrial development proceeds; it would also break ground in the establishment of methodology and appropriate procedures for the modification of quantitative economic projections in the light of subjective-type attitudinal and behavior factors.

Or another set of studies might attempt to link, more successfully than hitherto, cyclical analysis with the long-run trend type of projection attainable by a Channel I framework or one of its variants or abridgements. A careful attempt to work cyclical features into a Channel I framework to yield a projection path—either through the industrial composition variable of a tested hypothesis, or a short-run, Keynesian-type interregional trade multiplier of a tested model, or at a later stage both—can possibly throw new light on the socio-economic process. This possibility exists even if at first such study postulates, as does the discussion associated with Figure 7 and Table 8 of Chapter 12, that cyclical and secular effects are simply additive (and not multiplicative) and that no regional factor is at play.

Or, from a different angle, a research project might attempt to work into the first simple interregional model of the first set of research projects mentioned a Moore-type growth model. From year to year this type of model would provide for not only production on current account but also production on capital account, in order that there exist in the key year of projection as well as each previous year the capacity necessary to produce the required output. Once such a capacity-building framework were successfully woven into a simple interregional structure, other research projects might attempt the introduction of this framework into some of the more advanced studies already suggested.

Or, with extensive application in mind, a study may investigate how the relatively fine detail on the economic base and structure of the set of regions covered by a Channel I investigation may be utilized as benchmarks and in other ways to make possible, given limited research resources, relatively sound economic base and structure analysis for any of the numerous regions and areas which are not involved in such a Channel I investigation.

Finally, an extremely valuable research project would broadly follow the lines suggested in footnote 277 of Chapter 12. It would (1) look at some historic period of the past, (2) attempt to foresee developments with an abridged Channel I framework, due consideration being given to expectations and other relevant factors, (3) observe the discrepancies between magnitudes projected by the model and actual, (4) endeavor to explain these discrepancies, and (5) accordingly modify the model or suggest reinterpretations of history, or both, and even obtain insight into relevant parameters for models designed to project future magnitudes.

Or, if the historic period were a recent one and relatively short, and if an abridged Channel I framework for one or more base years were developed to complement an empirical multiregion–national cycle investigation à la Vining (see section E, Chapter 6), greater depth could be achieved in the interpretation of regional experiences during this past period, and presumably greater knowledge for anticipating the interplay of cyclical and secular forces when projections for future years are to be constructed.

The previous sets of research projects represent only a partial list of studies which can fruitfully unfold around a Channel I framework—a framework which is particularly strong for investigations of large resource regions, both developed and underdeveloped. Many of these projects can also be conducted around a Channel II framework. This point logically follows since, as indicated in section G of Chapter 8, the balanced regional input-output model essentially short-cuts the data and computation requirements of a pure interregional input-output model. It does so by utilizing materials on balances of production and consumption of commodities within different-size regions. At the same time the balanced regional model is forced to employ national input-output coefficients; it cannot allow regional differentiation among production functions for any endogenous sector, or among patterns of consumption expenditures associated with that part of the household's sector which may be placed in the structural matrix. As a consequence, the balanced regional input-output model is less valid theoretically speaking than the pure interregional model. However, in urban-metropolitan analysis where the loss of validity is least—since for this analysis the postulate of balance of production and consumption most closely obtains—such loss of validity is more than compensated, presumably, by the reduced data and computation requirements.

As with the Channel I framework, it would be highly desirable at first to attack a metropolitan problem or intermetropolitan problem via an abridgement of the Channel II framework—an abridgement which embraces at the minimum some comparative cost analysis and a multiregion input-output structure, and which is designed to yield a rather simple interregional system of metropolitan accounts. Another highly desirable study would explore in detailed empirical terms how one or a few partial intrametropolitan linear programs of the type discussed in section C.2 of Chapter 12 might be incorporated into this abridgement. Again, studies still more complete than these two are to be desired. They might cover a full set of industry-by-industry comparative cost analyses, or some industrial complex analysis together with some comparative cost analysis, or a full complement of industrial complex analyses, or some combination of comparative cost, industrial complex, and interregional linear programming analyses. Or, at a still more advanced level, a study might concentrate on criteria for the determination of "correct" proportions in the use of these analyses.

Another set of studies would be of a more technical nature. One might be concerned with ironing out discrepancies arising between the results and the initial assumptions of the first run and of later runs of a Channel II framework. A second might carefully consider the various factors governing the selection and identification of hierarchies of regions and classifications of commodities for diverse situations, and aim to establish general criteria. Such a study would of necessity both utilize and advance central place theory. A third study might appraise the different sets of tables whereby organization of the data for the several orders of regions is possible; consideration would be given to efficiency as well as to facility in the use of the tables for economic base and other analyses.

Still another major study would place central emphasis on the development within the Channel II framework of a full-fledged interregional system of social accounts for metropolitan areas and parts of metropolitan areas. This study would be highly desirable in view of the difficult problems faced by metropolitan regions and parts of metropolitan regions in planning capital expenditures and in evaluating the benefits and costs to be associated with various capital outlays on roads, schools, recreational and cultural facilities, redevelopment and slum clearance, etc. A still more advanced study would involve the addition of a Moore-type growth model in order to point up the need for (and program better over time) capital expenditures for building up physical plant and capacity. Closely allied with these studies might be land use, transportation and other analyses as well as fiscal studies requiring estimates of community and metropolitan revenues (tax yields) and costs.

Yet another project might develop procedures and methodology whereby the economic base detail for major metropolitan regions and subregions of a Channel II study may be put to use as benchmarks, control totals, etc., for economic base and structure analyses for the many regions, especially smaller towns and cities, not covered by such a study.

Finally, because the projections of a Channel II framework are weakest for higher-order regions (the smaller local areas), a comprehensive survey may be made on how diverse analytical techniques may be employed to strengthen results on the local-area level and on intrametropolitan patterns. These techniques would include among others those which are noted in section C.2 of Chapter 12 and which range from simple trend projection to covariance and factor analysis. At the same time intensive scaling, latent structure, and other attitudinal studies and multiple regression, covariance, and factor analyses may each be pursued within a simple or advanced Channel II framework to develop better "forecasts."

In passing on to the prospects for Channel III, the regional scientist encounters a host of new promising investigations. Many of these are associated with the two new approaches introduced for the first time into the fused frameworks, that is, the gravity model and urban complex analysis—approaches interjected in order to secure more valid results, especially on urban-metropolitan structure and subsystems. Because these new approaches are as yet relatively unexplored, we cannot suggest, as we can with respect to Channels I and II, that a simple abridged framework of Channel III be set up and tried out as a first promising project. Such an abridged framework should await further research on both the gravity model and the urban complex approach.

Fruitful research on the probability-type gravity model can be pursued in several directions. We have already fully indicated in Chapter 11 that several studies are urgently required to consider carefully (1) appropriate measures of mass and distance, (2) suitable weights and exponents to be employed to qualify the significance of the masses and distance, and (3) form of function to be utilized. Another study might probe into the degree of disaggregation permissible in any given situation, it being recognized that (a) on the one hand disaggregation and stratification are desirable in order to distinguish between different exponents, weights, functions, and even measures of mass and distance which should be employed for describing or projecting different categories of magnitudes, and (b) on the other hand the validity of the gravity model as a descriptive or projective tool decreases when it is applied with reference to sectors of an integral mass rather than to the integral mass itself. Yet another research project might inquire into the proper delineation of regions for use in the gravity model, the choice and number of control points, and similar technical considerations. And other studies might explore the usefulness and validity of such concepts as demographic adhesion, cohesion, gradient of the potential, dynamical radius, product supply time potential, and product supply space potential.

Central to all these studies and others would be an imaginative and yet rigorous inquiry into the theoretical foundations of the gravity model. This inquiry would certainly explore thoroughly the probability basis for the gravity model. It would necessarily investigate whether or not an optimization process is involved, and the relations of the gravity model to the rank-size rule and to agglomeration and spatial-juxtaposition economies. This inquiry would be closely linked to, if not inclusive of, parts of other extensive studies. Of these we might attempt to establish a basis for the comparison of a given percentage change in say market potential with the same percentage change in say unit costs. A second might examine the ability of the concept of intervening opportunities to represent various forms of social distance, and hence to be of basic significance for gravity model investigations into the behavior of social masses. And a third might be concerned with the full exploration and development of the concept of community participation potential and its relevance to administrative theory and to the allocation of functions among diverse levels of government.

Turning to the urban complex approach as a potential major component of a comprehensive Channel III framework, the regional scientist confronts another group of promising studies. One study might be concerned with ways to identify meaningful groups of activities, that is, activities with strong links of various sorts. Closely allied with this study would be an inquiry into criteria for establishing meaningful metropolitan patterns and orders of urban complexes. Yet others might be concerned with procedures and steps for determining the best of the meaningful metropolitan patterns, methods for estimating transport inputs, applicable transport rates, nonlinear relationships, etc. In addition to these, the full development of the urban complex approach would require an empirical study, involving the use of techniques such as scaling and covariance analysis and concepts such as community participation potential whereby to obtain crude evaluation of noneconomic costs and gains.

Once the validity of the gravity model is more firmly established and, desirably, an empirical implementation of the urban complex approach consummated, it becomes relevant to pursue a study aimed at the operational (empirical) development of a simple, abridged Channel III framework. At the minimum such a framework would embrace some comparative cost analysis, a simple balanced regional input-output model, and a simple gravity (perhaps relative income potential) model, and would be designed to yield an interregional-metropolitan system of social accounts. As with Channels I and II, more advanced projects may then be successively undertaken which involve the adequate and proper use of comparative cost, industrial complex, input-output, linear programming, scaling, latent structure, multiple regression, covariance, and the Moore-type capacity building frameworks; these would yield more satisfactory and complete results on an interregional-metropolitan system of social accounts, and regional balances of payments and money flows, and permit more penetrating historical, cyclical, fiscal, land use, transportation, and economic base analyses. We do not outline these more advanced projects here, since to do so would only repeat what has been said in the preceding paragraphs. And when the urban complex approach is proved, a still more comprehensive framework can be developed in a research project and utilized to yield still more satisfactory results.

However, in addition to these sets of more advanced projects which may in an orderly way be executed in connection with a Channel III framework are other sets of new exploratory studies which should be concomitantly pursued. One study would inquire whether the relative income potential or some variant of it, or some quite different concept, is the most relevant for use in a fused framework. Further, this study might examine whether the relative income potential (or other concept) should form the basis for projection of all non-cost-sensitive activities or only for some, and a parallel concept, based on say manufacturing output as it is spatially distributed, would be more relevant for others. Another study might look into the question of whether the model should be multiplicative (as equation 14 of Chapter 11) or additive (as equation 15 of the same chapter); this project might also be concerned with procedures for estimating values for ϵ, $_i\epsilon$, b, and $_ib$. Still another project would revolve around the determination of a proper time period for successive projection in models that abandon the rerun procedure. This time period question concerns not only the length of the time period but also the degree of lead and lag in locational decision making in the non-cost-sensitive industries. A fourth project might explore criteria for differentiating between cost-sensitive and non-cost-sensitive industries and for determining in a given situation how many of the cost-sensitive industries it is worthwhile to handle in a detailed comparative cost fashion. A fifth project, which may or may not be pursued independently of the others, would investigate the extent to which a balanced regional input-output model or a pure interregional input-output model or a combination of both should be employed; and if a combination, it should establish criteria for a determination of the proper mix.

On the local level new exploratory studies should examine how the gravity model may be used in conjunction with various techniques, some of which are listed in section D.2 of Chapter 12. In providing a consistency check, what are appropriate procedures for carrying through the successive rounds of estimates, comparisons, adjustments, etc? Certainly a simple investigation should be conducted here and extended as experience and knowledge accumulate. One of the questions involved would concern the leeway permissible in values of exponents, constants, functional form, etc. At the same time it would be very fruitful to conduct a number of spatial interaction studies within a metropolitan region involving the joint and intensive use of the gravity model and the scaling technique, or a latent structure model, or a multiple regression or covariance analysis, or an interareal linear program—and in time combinations of these and others.

We now turn to the prospects for promising projects which center around Channel IV. As already noted, Channel IV is conceptual. Its operational development is contingent on extensive, path-breaking research in the social sciences. In order to proceed from values to the setting of goals, studies are needed to throw much more light on (1) the interrelated and constantly changing roles and functions of individuals, groups, and communities in a society constrained by resource limitations; (2) the processes of communication, interaction, attitude formation, and decision making; (3) the power structure of a culture, its relation to political organization and administrative practices and diverse institutional features; and other basic questions raised in section E of Chapter 12. These questions are, of course, fundamental to the social sciences in general and are largely outside the realm of regional science per se. However, significant contributory studies can be made on the local and regional level which probe, for example, into local and regional attitude formation with an improved version of scaling techniques, or into the multidimensional character of group organization within a region with factor and latent structure analyses and with other more advanced methods. In particular, a very promising project would develop the concept of community participation potential and fully explore with the use of diverse attitude measurement techniques the possibility of roughly equating gains in community participation with dollar losses in efficiency. A successful attack here could in turn lead to significant studies on the proper allocation of functions among diverse levels of government, the development of more satisfactory benefit-cost procedures, the advancement of capital-budgeting practices, and various basic social problems, as well as greatly facilitate the required restatement of values as system and subsystem goals, especially when these values are conflicting.

Closely associated with these studies would be a project designed to develop procedures for translating different sets of goals into a quantitative, consistent, and appropriately weighted set of social accounts. This project might cover as well the full detailing of social accounts into, for example, demands and requirements by type of commodity and would fully utilize whatever procedures and information were developed by studies just noted. Another type might investigate the possibility for the development of superior system accounts as the sum of corresponding subsystem (regional) accounts, or still more desirably the simultaneous determination of system and subsystem accounts, in order to eschew the inferior practice of allocating a system's totals among its regions. Or this research problem might be conceived as involving several projects, one concerned with general methodology and each of the others with the full development for the system and its regions of a major social account, such as capital formation, government expenditures, or consumption expenditures.

A third set of fruitful projects revolves around the use of interregional linear programming as the central operator in Channel IV. As yet the development and testing of interregional linear programming has been on a narrow, industry-type basis—such as in the coal mining and dairy industry studies noted in Chapter 10. Hence, an early, important project would involve the constructing and solving of a simple interregional multi-industry (or multi-industrial complex) linear program. (This project, for example, might have reference to a major resource problem—say river valley development—for a few large regions.) This study in turn could lead to other, more penetrating, specialized projects. One might be concerned with the problem of appropriate weighting (pricing), and the considerations governing the construction of an objective function, although this project could not be conducted successfully without some attention being given to the problems of appropriate constraints and reconciliation. Each of a number of other projects might delve deeply into the construction of one of the sets of Channel IV constraints—minimum standards, resource, stability, financial, mass behavior (attitudes), and locational efficiency—in ways suggested in sections E.4.b to E.4.g of Chapter 12. Or more than one project might be required for an adequate treatment and formulation of each of these sets of constraints, or other sets that may be deemed more relevant. Each such project could profitably draw heavily on any of these studies which might be completed and would need to give some general consideration to the problems of reconciliation and construction of the objective function. Finally, the very problem of reconciliation—of refinement of goals and restatement of assumptions in order to eliminate inconsistencies—is itself a point at which an important research project can be launched, although again not without reference to the problems of objective function and constraint formulation.

Although there are other research projects which might be conducted in connection with Channel IV—projects which would resemble many of those associated with other channels—it would seem advisable not to pursue these until Channel IV promises to be more operational. This point has validity, particularly since the fourth variant of Channel V purports to cover a good deal of the ground of Channel IV, without sacrificing operationality.

Lastly, in connection with Channel V there are a number of research projects which should be conducted. This is especially the case since

Channel V has been designed to be the most valid of the operational channels. Its first three variants introduce into Channels I–III respectively those values and goals subject to approximate quantitative statement, without sacrifice of operationality. Its fourth variant reduces Channel IV to a manageable, operational framework by the purposeful neglect of important values, goals, and relationships which cannot be approximately quantified.

A first set of important research projects might center around the first variant of Channel V. One project might explore the ways in which diverse system and subsystem values and goals condition the initial basic assumptions of Channel I and in turn initial regional markets. Another might develop procedures for putting in place in the several regional bills of goods the set of social accounts which best reflects system and subsystem goals; in essence, it would involve an appropriate refashioning of the final demand sectors and the structural matrix of Channel I. Still another might carefully investigate how values and goals influence rerun operations and the ironing out of discrepancies. Moreover, practically all, if not all, the host of projects sketched in connection with Channel I— to which the reader should refer—contribute to the development of the first variant of Channel V and are worthy of pursuit if they have not already been conducted.

A second and third set of important research studies might center, respectively, around the second and third variant of Channel V. Each set might parallel the set of the preceding paragraph and involve the reformulation and re-examination of initial basic assumptions, initial regional markets, final demand and endogenous producing sectors, and rerun operations. However, there would be one exception, namely, that if the rerun procedure is eschewed in a framework of the third variant of Channel V, a research project should be conducted to develop procedures whereby social accounts may be appropriately introduced into the regional bills of goods in successive periods so as to represent the cumulative attainment of goals. This project would substitute for the project on the influence of goals on rerun operations. And again the host of projects noted previously in connection with Channels II and III contribute respectively to the development of the second and third variant of Channel V. Practically all, if not all, these are worthy of pursuit if they have not already been undertaken.

A fourth set of important Channel V research projects is associated with the fourth variant of Channel V—a variant which may be judged to be the best, provided a manageable framework can be realized which involves an interregional linear program that is not too large and complicated for solution by high-speed computers. A major research project here would be to set up criteria to determine what per cent of the system output of a producing sector is to be regionally allocated by comparative cost, industrial complex, and other procedures (and thus to be treated for the most part as deliveries to be met) and what per cent by the interregional linear program. These per cents will, of course, vary from sector to sector. Many other significant projects would duplicate those already listed in these paragraphs in connection with all channels. Of immediate note are those associated with Channel IV—projects concerned with establishing system and subsystem goals, with translating goals into social accounts, with detailing social accounts, with demonstrating the validity and gaining experience with the operation of multi-industry interregional linear programs, with formulating appropriate objective functions, with constructing each of the meaningful sets of constraints, and with effecting reconciliation and refining goals. Of later significance would be other projects to be linked to the fourth variant of Channel V. They might be concerned with the proper mix of techniques, the establishment of a superior interregional system of social accounts, the inception of more comprehensive money flow study, and the pursuit of much more penetrating commodity flow study, the linkage with regional cycle hypotheses, the use of results on economic structure of regions embraced by a fourth variant study for economic base analyses pertaining to other regions, the use of a set of simultaneous equations to estimate for a given sector relevant magnitudes, the addition of a Moore-type framework to insure the realization of required expansions in productive capacity, the identification in conjunction with the use of gravity models of efficient intrametropolitan patterns consistent with mass behavior, and so forth.

A final Channel V project would carefully examine the features and interrelations of the four variants already noted and seek the development of a new and superior set of variants.

With these remarks we bring this book to a close. We cannot claim that we have presented an exhaustive list of research projects; we hope, however, to have noted the more important ones. Nor can we claim that we have exhaustively spelled out the various techniques for regional analysis and developed their potential in full. What can be said is that we have introduced the reader to the complexities involved in the proper development of methods of regional analysis which aim to lay bare the intricate network of bonds interlacing the diverse systems and subsystems of a spatial order. Bluntly put, what we have accomplished is an introduction to regional science, and at that only a partial introduction. For the vast field of regional science—it does seem vast to the author at this point—must go beyond methods, even when complemented by an abundance of well-conceived and well-organized empirical studies by geographers and other scientists. It must probe the area of theory—theory which has regional and interregional structure and function at its core; theory which cuts into and generalizes the system and subsystem interdependencies sketched in Chapter 1; theory which cuts across the orthodox social science disciplines and emphasizes basic interactions of political, social, and economic forces that have been traditionally neglected; but theory which like all social science theory must be concerned with not only general equilibrium constructs and frameworks but also dynamic schema for understanding the impact of disequilibrium forces and the processes of growth and change. We hope to take a stab at this theory in a future volume.

Author Index

Subject Index